READER'S DIGEST

TREASURES IN
YOUR HOME

TREASURES IN DISGUISE *Despite its battered state, the boulle desk is the highlight here, although the tarnished silver basket and oil painting are also collectable; all are 19thC. The desk – entirely unrestored – would make £3000-£4000, the basket or picture up to £800. (Previous page) Just a glimpse is enough to identify a bold Clarice Cliff 'Bizarre' design jug and plate; c. 1928; value: £250-£350 each. In the foreground are a set of silver-plated fish knives and forks with Art Nouveau decoration. Made c. 1910, they would go for £40-£80.*

READER'S DIGEST

TREASURES IN YOUR HOME

Published by The Reader's Digest Association Limited

LONDON · NEW YORK · SYDNEY · CAPE TOWN · MONTREAL

Contributors

Editor Michael Wright

Art Editor Judy White

TREASURES IN YOUR HOME
was edited and designed by
The Reader's Digest Association Limited, London
First Edition Copyright © 1993
The Reader's Digest Association Limited,
Berkeley Square House, Berkeley Square,
London W1X 6AB
Copyright © 1993 Reader's Digest
Association Far East Limited
Philippines Copyright © 1993 Reader's Digest
Association Far East Limited

Printed in France
ISBN 0 276 42038 1
The text in this book is set in Goudy Old Style.

WORLDS APART *Collectables come in all shapes and
sizes. For around £40 you could buy either this much-
repaired 1960s toy robot or a single cup and saucer
from the graceful Rockingham tea service, c.1835.*

CONSULTANT EDITOR

David A. Battie
*Director of Sotheby's; former head of Sotheby's
Belgravia, and head of its Ceramics and Oriental
departments*

SPECIALIST CONSULTANTS

PRE-1870 INTERIOR STYLES
Peter Thornton, FSA
Curator, Sir John Soane's Museum, London

LATE 19TH AND 20TH-CENTURY STYLE
Eric Knowles
Director of Ceramics department, Bonhams

FURNITURE
John Bly
Antique dealer in London and Tring, Hertfordshire

POTTERY AND PORCELAIN
Lars Tharp, MA
*Director of Sotheby's; former head of European and
Oriental Ceramics departments, Sotheby's Sussex*

GLASSWARE
Charles Hajdamach
*Director of Broadfield House Glass Museum,
Kingswinford, West Midlands*

SILVER, GOLD AND JEWELLERY
Jim Collingridge, FGA
*Deputy chairman and former head of Jewellery and
Silver departments, Christie's South Kensington*

CLOCKS AND WATCHES
Richard Garnier, BA
*Head of Antique Clock department, Garrards;
former head of Clock and Watch department,
Christie's London*

OTHER COLLECTABLES
Hilary Kay
*Director of Sotheby's; founder and former head
of its Collector's department*

CARPETS
Ian Bennett

WRITERS

THE STORY OF STYLE
Antony Mason, MA

COLLECTOR'S GUIDE
*Various articles were written by the consultants,
and also by the following contributors*

Paul Atterbury, BA, FRSA

John Baddeley
Head of Collector's department, Sotheby's

Keith R. Baker
*Director of Art Nouveau and Decorative Arts
department, Phillips Auctioneers*

Sarah Battie
Former head of Glass department, Sotheby's

Mark L. Bowis, BA, FGA
Jewellery specialist, Christie's South Kensington

Robert Bowman
*Sculpture dealer in London; former head of Sculpture
department, Sotheby's*

John Brooks
Dealer in antique glassware in Rothley, Leicestershire

Bunny Campione
*Consultant on automata, dolls, teddy bears, soft toys
and dolls' houses to Sotheby's*

Richard Charlton-Jones
*Deputy director of Old Master Paintings department,
Sotheby's*

Roger Dodsworth, BA, AMA
*Keeper of glass, Broadfield House Glass Museum,
Kingswinford, West Midlands*

Edward S. Dolman, BA
*Director and head of Furniture department, Christie's
South Kensington*

Philip A. Duckworth
*Associate director and furniture specialist, Phillips
Auctioneers*

Sally A. Everitt
Jewellery specialist, Christie's South Kensington

Alexandra Fennell, BA
*Specialist in Portrait Miniature department, Christie's
South Kensington*

Diana Fowle, MA
Textiles department, Christie's South Kensington

Melvyn A. Gallagher, FSVA
*Associate director and head of Valuations department,
Christie's South Kensington*

Roger Griffiths
Director of Sotheby's; specialist in Books department

Elizabeth Harvey-Lee, BA, member IFPDA
Print dealer in London

Stephen J. Helliwell, BA
*Director and head of Silver and Objects departments,
Christie's South Kensington*

Peter Hornsby, MSc
Metalware specialist

Sally Kevill-Davies
Former porcelain expert at Sotheby's

Alison Kurke, BA, MPhil
Formerly of Collector's department, Sotheby's

WRITERS *continued*

David J. Lancaster, FGA
Director and head of Jewellery department, Christie's South Kensington

Jeffrey Lovell
Cataloguer in Silver department, Christie's South Kensington

James A. Mackay, MA
Formerly keeper of philatelic collections, British Library

Susan Morris, BA
Deputy editor, 'The Antique Collector'

Martin Mortimer
Managing director of Delomosne & Son, antique dealers in Chippenham, Wiltshire

James Morton
Deputy director of Coins department, Sotheby's

Sabine Dauwe Naghdi, PhD, MD
Expert in Tribal Art department, Sotheby's

Mark A. Newstead, BSc
Deputy director of European Ceramics and Glass department, Sotheby's

Raymond Notley
Tutor in 19th and 20th-century decorative arts, Sotheby's Educational Studies

Robert Opie
Director of the Museum of Advertising and Packaging, Gloucester

Christopher Payne
Director of Sotheby's; specialist in 19th-century furniture

Christine Potter, BA
Former assistant curator, Haworth Art Gallery, Accrington

James Rylands, BA
Director of Garden Statuary department, Sotheby's

John Sandon, SOFAA Dipl
Director of Ceramics, Phillips Auctioneers

William J. D. Strafford, BA
Furniture specialist, Christie's South Kensington

Kerry Taylor
Consultant on European costume and textiles to Sotheby's

Alexandra Walker, DA, AMA
Harris Museum and Art Gallery, Preston

Graham Wells
Director of Musical Instruments department, Sotheby's

Alex Werner
Museum of London

Patrick Whitehouse, OBE, ARPS
Chairman, Millbrook House Ltd

Peter Williams
Former director of Sotheby's

ILLUSTRATORS

Richard Bonson
Nicholas Hall
Malcolm McGregor
Bill Prosser
Tony Richards
Gill Tomblin
Ann Winterbotham

CALLIGRAPHER

Mike Pratley

COMMISSIONED PHOTOGRAPHERS

Ken Adlard *Sotheby's*
Theo Bergstrom
Martin Cameron
Glynn Clarkson
Stuart Chorley
Michael Crockett
Laurie Evans
Ian O'Leary
Vernon Morgan
Clive Streeter

HISTORICAL PICTURE RESEARCH

Anne-Marie Ehrlich

SPECIAL THANKS

The publishers also wish to thank the following for their assistance in the preparation of this book:

Christine Bloxham
The British Museum
Christie's Press Offices, London and
   South Kensington
David Coombs *editor, 'The Antique Collector'*
Margarita Crutchley
Christie's Colour Library
Christina Donaldson *Sotheby's Sussex*
Gloria Harris *Christie's New York*
Paula Hunt *Mallett's*
Jessamy Johnson *Miller's Publications*
Katie Klitgaard *Sotheby's Marketing department*
Nick Lumley
Nicole Murray *Phillips photographic library*
Murray Cards (International) Ltd
Royal Doulton Crystal, Stourbridge
Charles Rudd *LAPADA*
Sotheby's Press Office
Victoria and Albert Museum (in particular,
   Ceramics, Glass and Furniture departments)

The following (together with those credited individually at the end of the book) kindly lent objects and/or provided facilities for photography:

Alvin Ross, London NW8
Annie's Antique Clothes, London N1
Atlantic Antique Centres, London SW3
The Badger, London W5
Beverley, London NW8
N. Bloom & Son, London W1
John Bly, London SW1
Bushwood Antiques, London N1
S. Fairbrass, London SW17
D. J. Ferrant, London, N1
M.S.M. The Furniture Cave, London SW10
Ben Maurice-Jones, London, W11
The Old Cinema Antique Store, London W4
Plowden and Smith, London SW18
Risky Business, London NW8
M. & D. Seligman, London W8

TRINKETS OR TREASURES? *It would be a lucky spring-cleaning that turned up an 1880s cameo glass vase (value £1500-£2500) or 1920s bronze figurine (£600-£800). The 1920s sequinned jacket lacks a famous label but is worth about £250.*

Contents

The Story of Style

Collector's Guide

FURNITURE

RICHES FROM THE EAST *Blue and white porcelain and a telltale bulbous shape give away the treasure here: a Chinese drinking vessel or 'kendi' from c. 1700, valued at £800-£1200. Also collectable are the Hornby train set and the Victorian papier-mâché chair. And at £20-£30 each, the 'La Parisienne' plates could be a good investment.*

POTTERY AND PORCELAIN

GLASSWARE

SILVER, GOLD AND JEWELLERY

Collector's Guide

Reference Section

A FINE CATCH *By a miracle, the 16 ft (4.9 m) rosewood and greenheart fishing rod lying by the creel has been unused since it was made c. 1875. Still perfect, it would fetch over £300, the other items £5-£100 each.*

An Expert Examines

A Georgian dining chair 97
Two Windsor chairs 100
A drop-leaf dining table 109
Three 18th-century tripod tables 114
An early Georgian bureau 130
A blue and white porcelain bowl 164
Three kraak dishes 188
Two porcelain figures 195
Two cut-glass jugs 211
Three wine glasses 215
Silver and plate 238
An 18th-century dress 314
A flapper dress 317
A tin-plate toy car 343
A bisque doll 353
A musical box 394

The Pleasure of Collecting

WHAT DRIVES SOMEONE to spend more than $80 million – the current world record price – on one painting? Is it ostentation, a desire for publicity, investment potential, acquisitiveness or a real love of the object? Sadly, in most cases at this level of buying, this last factor is the least important, if it figures at all. What pleasure can such collectors get from filling a bank vault with racks of purchases which they rarely see? In truth they are not collectors at all, they are accumulators. True collectors have a real love of their objects, getting a surge of euphoria every time they pass them on the wall or in the cabinet. They spend an enormous amount of time trawling antique shops, markets and auctions, occasionally pouncing and not infrequently finding a bargain.

Curiously, the idea of an object having value simply because of its age is only about a hundred years old – by coincidence corresponding to the legal definition of an antique. Before that, except in the case of Greek and Roman antiquities, items were judged purely on their artistic merit or how fashionable they were; age meant little. Very often furniture and other important works of art filtered down through the social strata as the landed gentry refurnished their houses. This frequently involved a complete updating, replacing not only the decorations and all the contents, but occasionally remodelling the fabric of the building as well. Some outdated or unfashionable furniture and other items were banished to the attic or the servants' quarters, but many were given away or simply dumped, to be recycled by estate workers. Passed on down the centuries (and often altered on the way), these objects eventually find their way onto the market – sometimes without the current owner appreciating their value. The anticipation that an undiscovered treasure may be lurking in the next shop is part of the thrill of collecting.

The majority of the new band of collectors who have appeared over the past 25 years have no training in the history of art or in craft techniques. Nor do they begin with much awareness of fine craftsmanship. They buy what they like and derive great pleasure from it. A few will be spurred on by curiosity to find out more about the objects acquired and their background. Such buyers are likely to become more and more absorbed, their eye will mature, and they will become true collectors. *Treasures in Your Home* will be a valuable aid in this process. For others, almost anything will satisfy the collecting urge. As the bug has spread, so has the number of objects that have become 'collectable' – as the swaying heaps of secondhand dinner plates in any 'antiques' market testify. It is impossible to predict how the future will judge these mass-produced, apparently meritless castoffs. But it is worth remembering that the pottery of Clarice Cliff (see p. 179) was counted among the damned only a decade ago, and look what has happened to that!

Another driving force in the market is a growing realisation that standards of craftsmanship are not what they were. Paying £300 or so for a modern reproduction chair is unlikely to be money well spent: the following day it will be worth £60, if you can get anyone to buy it. The antique will hold its value and over time appreciate. Then there is the effect of the BBC's *Antiques Roadshow*. Without doubt the appearance of ordinary people winning the jackpot with their often disregarded works of art has been a powerful stimulus to car boot sales, fairs, markets and auctions all around the country. In my 25 years at Sotheby's I have seen greater change than there was in any other period of its 250-year history. When I joined, the vast majority of lots were sold to the trade – to antique dealers – of this country; now private buyers from around the world predominate.

With this growing interest from the general public has come a demand for knowledge and books to supply it. There are numerous price guides to almost everything and academic books which enable readers to identify and date an object. Both types of book assume that readers can already, for example, distinguish pottery from porcelain from bone china from stone china. *Treasures in Your Home* starts from first principles and makes no such assumptions. It also, uniquely for this type of book, gives prices.

What of the future? Recessions will come and go, as they always have. Typically the antiques business continues to thrive long after the financial or industrial markets feel the bite. On the other hand antiques pick up long after other trades are booming. It takes a brave buyer to buck the trend and buy when markets are flat, but those who do invariably enrich their collection at bargain prices. Losers spend too much on second-rate objects in a flourishing market. To the true collector, these financial considerations are of secondary importance – it is the objects that matter. Nevertheless, a good buy means more money left to spend on something else. And *Treasures in Your Home* guides you through the intricacies of the market, how and where to buy, what points of quality to look for and what the pitfalls are. It also helps you to judge the value of your own possessions; and it can be a great source of satisfaction to find that something that has lain around the house or in an attic for years may be worth much more than you thought.

Almost all collections start with one or a very few items, whether bought, inherited or found. Some people leave it at that, but many others go on to acquire more and more. People seem to have an innate desire to collect – perhaps a hangover from the hunting instinct of primitive forebears leading to the urge to track down another scalp to add to the collection. Having identified the prey and with the adrenalin pumping, however, the sensible collector stands very still and takes stock. The temptation is to hand over the cheque as fast as possible in case the quarry should escape. Instead you should calmly and rigorously question the object as to its pedigree, condition and necessity to your collection. Delve into this book for comparable pieces or general price guidance. Buy only if it fills a gap in your collection or improves on an existing piece – and if the price is right. Follow this and other guidelines in *Treasures in Your Home* and your collection will never grow stale, remaining a source of constant pleasure.

David Battie

The Story of Style

Tracing the strands that mesh to give each
age its distinctive look – from the skills
and materials available to the changes in lifestyle
and income, from buyers' zest for the new
to designers' visions of beauty

REGENCY CHOICE *This elegantly Classical rosewood window stool of 1815 was given a fashionably yellow cushion with a hint of military stripes. But the Napoleonic wars had just ended and a Regency gentleman could again make travel plans as he used his silver-framed spectacles to pore over the pocket globe and William Bradford's 'Sketches in Portugal and Spain'. His French watch's chimes would tell him when to slip on the plum-coloured wool coat with cut-steel buttons and step out with ebony cane to an assembly.*

MEDIEVAL AND EARLY TUDOR 1066-1550

On the Move with Prized Possessions

Easy to move on or to move aside, the possessions of wealthy medieval households included little furniture but sumptuous hangings and clothes, and silver and gold to show status.

GRAND HOUSEHOLDS were frequently on the move in medieval Britain, and they made impressive sights, Mounted soldiers in livery went at the head of the procession, bearing arms and banners. Then came the lord and his family and officials, some on horseback, some in covered wagons. Behind them followed an enormous baggage train carrying coffers and furniture, kitchen equipment and provisions.

When the journey ended, at one of the lord's castles, out came wall coverings, bedding, cushions, musical instruments, dishes and utensils, and silver and gold plate. The sparse furniture was assembled to make one or two chairs, many more stools, trestle tables and the lord's fine but knockdown bed.

It was the Norman Conquest in 1066 that brought this mobile life to Britain. The few favoured Norman nobles who were granted vast domains by the king built castles to keep control over their lands, then spent much of the year circulating among their strongholds to check on taxpaying and the accounts, to deal with grievances, and to sweeten key lower lords whose support they needed. For most of the year the nobles' castles were bare shells; they came to life only with the arrival of the lord with his household and the baggage.

Beneath the nobles, descending ranks of more local lords held estates in return for loyalty and military support to their immediate superior in the hierarchy. They lived with their retainers in lesser strongholds – often fortified manor

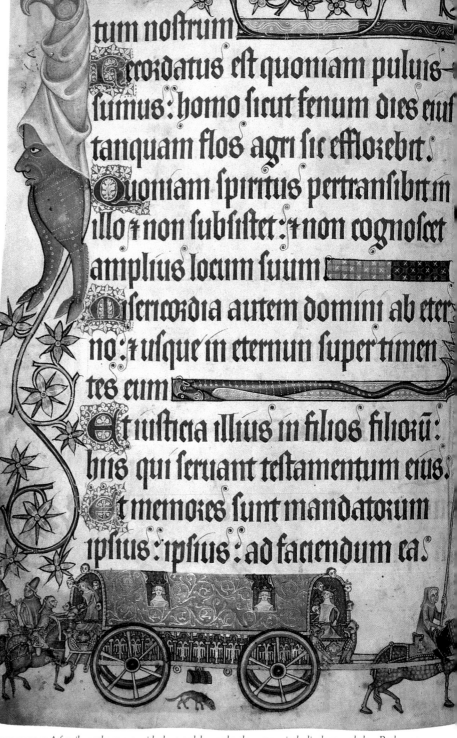

SHORT STAY *A family on the move, with chest and dog under the wagon, is the lively scene below Psalm 103 in the early 14th-century Luttrell Psalter – telling that man's life is brief as a flower of the field.*

STANDARD TRAVEL *With a pole through its side rings, a travelling chest, or standard, like the Bishop of Durham's, made c. 1340, was slung under a wagon.*

houses with a great hall and a straggle of outbuildings around a courtyard. Whether in large castle or small manor, the great hall was the principal – sometimes the only – room and the setting for a communal life. Most of the baggage carted behind a nobleman's procession was destined for the hall.

At one end was the high table of wide boards on trestles with the lord's heavy-framed, box-seated wooden armchair behind it and the large silver salt cellar, another

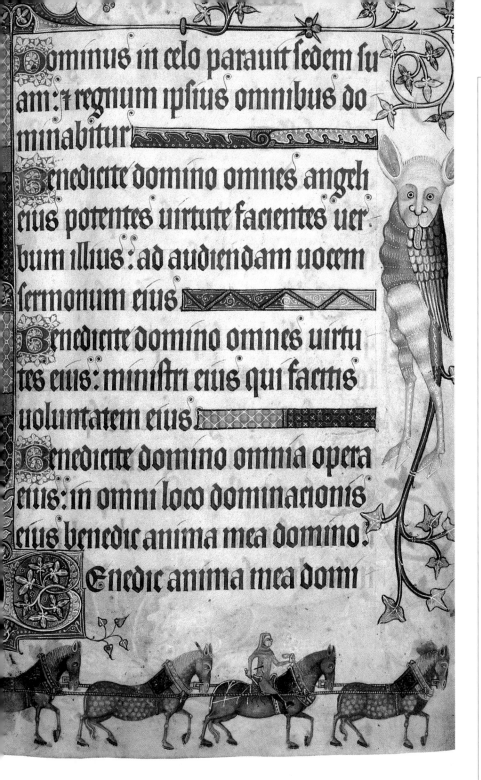

Dominus in celo parauit sedem su
am : z regnum ipsius omnibus do
minabitur

Benedicite domino omnes angeli
eius potentes uirtute facientes uer
bum illius : ad audiendam uocem
sermonum eius

Benedicite domino omnes uirtu
tes eius : ministri eius qui facitis
uoluntatem eius

Benedicite domino omnia opera
eius : in omni loco dominacionis
eius benedic anima mea domino.

Benedic anima mea domi

THE DARK AGES
Life before the Norman Conquest

STATELY PUBLIC BUILDINGS and elegant villas decorated with mosaic floors, painted walls and sculpture were part of the legacy the Romans left behind when they quit their colony of Britain in the 5th century AD to defend their homeland from the Visigoths and Vandals. They took with them their silverware and glass – and a sophisticated style of life that Britain would not know again for a thousand years. Britain

Among the Sutton Hoo grave treasures was this skilfully worked gold buckle of c.625.

disintegrated into warring tribal regions while invaders and raiders – Angles, Saxons and Jutes, Norsemen and Danes – made order and prosperity rare.

Most of the objects made in these Dark Ages (AD 500-1000) were crudely useful, not prized and kept but discarded as they wore out. Nor did buildings last; poor people lived in round wooden huts with thatched or turfed roofs while officials and nobles had larger, but still wooden, halls. Only a few churches and monasteries were of stone.

Yet from excavated sites – at Sutton Hoo, Suffolk, and elsewhere – have come decorated armour and intricate brooches, jewellery and buckles. Some Church plate and beautiful illuminated manuscripts such as the 7th century Lindisfarne Gospels have also survived. These rare articles suggest that there were creative talents and deft craftsmen at work in the supposedly unlearned and unenlightened Dark Ages.

symbol of high status, marking his place at table. Nearby was another trestle table – called a cup-board – where the lord's gold and silver (usually silver-gilt) cups, bowls and other plate were shown off during meals. Later cup-boards had a shelf or two above the main board. There might also be a serving table with a front-opening hutch or aumbry – a cupboard in the modern sense – fitted under it.

Trestle tables for the lesser members of the household were set up in the body of the hall near benches against the walls. Stools made up the rest of the seating. Three-legged stools with their legs splayed were the most stable on an uneven floor, but there were also boarded stools like miniature benches, with end supports and stretchers held in with wedges.

Even in households that stayed put, having no other estates to keep an eye on, early furniture was scanty and simple – no great loss in case of attack and easily stacked away to make space for dancing or entertainers.

Gradually, as means allowed, there was more permanent furniture – a table and chair too solid to cart about, and built-in benches, shelves and aumbries. But textiles, clothes and silver were more prized than furniture.

Most English furniture was oak but other woods were used if they grew locally. Much furniture was painted rather than polished and it might have rather crude geometric patterning called 'chip-carving', done with a chisel and gouge. Turners made a different

EMPTY STAGE *Plain and bare under its lofty hammerbeam roof, the 13th-century great hall of Stokesay Castle, Shropshire, still has the atmosphere of medieval days, as if it awaits the bustle of a lord's household.*

style of furniture, such as stools with turned legs, and chairs (called 'thrown' chairs) with turned back supports topped by a turned rail.

LIFE IN THE GREAT HALL

Gathered in the dim and smoky hall to do business, dine, sleep and make merry, there could well be a crowd of dozens, even 100 or more, made up of family, officials and servants – and the crowd was often swelled by guests and their retainers. After dusk, light would come from candles on the table, fixed to the wall, or grouped on a hanging metal ring or wooden candlebeam which was lowered for snuffing and refilling. There would be light also from the fire – in the centre of the earliest halls but later against a wall and given a chimney. In humbler homes there was no separate kitchen and the fire was set about with spits, hooks, cauldrons, ladles, cleavers and other necessities for cooking.

Meals were conducted with some ceremony in a grand household, with courses brought from the kitchen by a procession heralded by trumpets, and served to the diners in order of rank. Fingers and silver or pewter spoons were used for eating – there were no forks – and people at the high table might be given a knife, or guests might bring their own knives. Basins and ewers of scented water were there for rinsing greasy hands during the meal.

The very richest folk might dine off silver, but more often trenchers (platters), dishes and drinking vessels were of pewter, which was replacing treen – wooden platters and utensils. Where masers – turned wooden bowls – were still used, they might be given silver mounts and rims. Earthenware, especially jugs, would be used by the cooks but rarely appeared on the table.

After a meal came entertainment, perhaps dancing, or some music and foolery from minstrels and jesters. Gambling with dice or on chess, draughts and backgammon was a more costly amusement. Most expensive of all was to lay on a tournament at which contesting knights displayed the skills they learned for battle. Spectators revelled in the colour

SELF IMAGE *The carpenter at work among an array of tools was carved by a 15th-century craftsman under a church seat at King's Lynn, Norfolk.*

THE RENAISSANCE

THE RENAISSANCE
Ancient Learning and Beauty Reborn

THE MEDIEVAL STYLE of life was shaken in Italy during the 13th and 14th centuries by scholars seized by an urge to investigate everything, including the pagan past which the powerful Church viewed as sinful. There was a rebirth – a renaissance – of the poetry, philosophy, science, art and architecture of ancient Greece and Rome. The Renaissance ideal was to have a range of knowledge and talents. Leonardo da Vinci, for example, was scientist and inventor as well as artist and architect.

From studying surviving Roman buildings and the writings of Vitruvius, an architect of the 1st century BC, Renaissance architects developed strict mathematical ratios for all aspects of a building, including the size and position of every wall, window, arch and column – inside and out.

Renaissance ideas spread slowly to Britain – in philosophical writings, by Erasmus, for example, then in decorative arts and finally in buildings. By Henry VIII's reign (1509-47), there was already an awareness of Classical form and decoration; it was reinforced by the work of continental craftsmen and artists, for whom Henry's court was a magnet. Renaissance decorative motifs caught on fast, and swags and urns, cupids and caryatids, vines and mythological characters became part of the designer's visual vocabulary.

The writings of the Dutch scholar Erasmus opened minds in Britain to the Renaissance.

and excitement, and had a chance to show off their own fine clothes of velvet and silk, richly embroidered and adorned with jewelled silver and gold clasps and girdles.

THE RETREAT UPSTAIRS

By the 14th century many lords and their families had withdrawn from the communal life of the hall to the privacy of the solar, or great chamber, up a flight of stairs from the hall. This retreat was made increasingly comfortable. After 1400 it was hung with decorative, draught-defying tapestries – some imported French or Flemish work, others poor local equivalents – or 'stayned cloth' painted to look like tapestry. Oak or fir wainscoting (panelling) was an alternative draught excluder and might be painted or carved. In the late 15th century panelling began to be carved with the gentle vertical grooving aptly called linenfold.

The most important piece of furniture in the great chamber was the curtained bed, a symbol of status. Its fine hangings of wool or silk velvet screened it from view, light and draughts. Other furniture might include settles, chests softened with cushions to serve as seats; and trestle tables, which after about 1500 might be covered with Turkish rugs.

POSSESSIONS TO LAST

By the late 15th century many lords and their families found even the great chamber too public, and so a suite of more private rooms developed. Other changes too ended the medieval style of life. The Wars of the Roses (1455-85) had weakened the rival nobles, and the new, powerful Tudor king, Henry VII, imposed order. The landed classes settled in homes that no longer had to be fortresses, and gave more thought to permanent comforts.

Wool and cloth were making Britain an export power, and trade and travel grew. As the decades unrolled and newly discovered sea routes to the East were exploited, silks and ceramics, carpets and glass, new woods and

TOP TABLE *The silver is on show, tapestries hung and fanfare sounding for Richard II and his dinner guests. Everything is ready – bread, meat and trenchers, knives and beakers, and the ship with salt is carried round.*

new foods made their way back to Britain. Prized curiosities such as coconuts and ostrich eggs were set in silver mounts for display.

As Britain prospered, the demand grew for well-made goods. Wills and inventories show that small merchants, and even craftsmen, often had a silver bowl or cup and silver spoons. Richer houses also had a silver salt cellar and goblets. For the first time, fine goods were not just for rulers and the Church.

Throughout the medieval period, creative minds had been preoccupied with glorifying the church. Craftsmanship was focused on gold and silver croziers, censers and other church treasures in styles that secular art copied. Skills were also lavished on misericords – the humbler, lively carvings under church seats – on the gargoyles, animals,

angels and saints carved on doors and arches, and on beautifully decorated manuscripts.

When Henry VIII split with Rome and declared himself head of the Church in England (1536), he also ended the Church's hold over patronage. Craftsmen who turned to secular work to survive found their new patrons had developed an eager appetite for possessions. When native craftsmen could not supply them, the patrons imported Italian maiolica, Venetian glass and Oriental carpets – and workmen. The king himself employed the German Hans Holbein as court painter.

Filtering in with continental scholars, craftsmen and goods came the first glimmerings in Britain of the Renaissance ideals (see box, p.14) that had taken over Italy and France and were to pervade Elizabethan life.

MEDIEVAL STYLE

Oak or local woods made simple, sturdy furniture of boards fitted on trestles or pegged and wedged in place. Linenfold panels, chip-carving and paint decorated it. Pewter tableware was ousting wood and the well-off had some silver. Earthenware, leather jugs and ironware were used by cooks. Costly textiles were the chief delight – many imported along with glass, porcelain and maiolica.

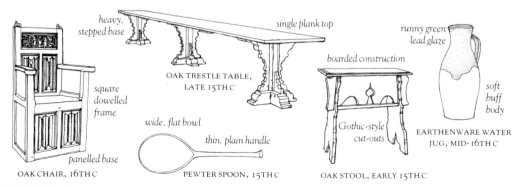

heavy, stepped base · *single plank top* · *runny green lead glaze*

square dowelled frame

OAK TRESTLE TABLE, LATE 15TH C

boarded construction

wide, flat bowl

thin, plain handle

soft buff body

Gothic-style cut-outs

EARTHENWARE WATER JUG, MID-16TH C

panelled base

OAK CHAIR, 16TH C

PEWTER SPOON, 15TH C

OAK STOOL, EARLY 15TH C

ELIZABETHAN AND JACOBEAN 1550-1660

Age of Oak and Ornament

Country-house life with the family was the ideal of Elizabethan and Jacobean gentlefolk. They could set themselves up with fine silver, rich textiles, lavish clothes and coveted goods from abroad.

A NEW KIND OF HOUSEHOLD had been established for people of power and influence by the mid-16th century. No longer did they share a communal life with a motley assembly of officials, military supporters and other retainers. Now they lived in families in substantial homes on their country estates, some on lands that were previously owned by the Church, until they were seized after the Dissolution of the Monasteries in 1536 and bestowed on supporters of the monarch as rewards for their loyalty. Some families had more than one estate.

It was the ownership of estates that shaped the style of life. Rents and produce from their lands enabled even the minor aristocracy and gentlefolk to live well. Many landowners enlarged their houses or built one or more lavish new ones. When they visited London, perhaps to consult their lawyers or occasionally to attend court or parliament (for landowners were entitled to a seat in parliament), they saw the fashion and furnishings of Elizabeth I's courtiers, cosmopolitan visitors and other rich folk, and ordered new clothes and goods for themselves.

Some landowners were quick to take the latest style back to their homes. For a generation or two, rich Elizabethan men decked themselves in extravagant clothes made from the finest embroidered fabrics which were slashed to reveal exquisite linings;

they wore feathered caps, high, pleated ruffs around the neck, dainty rosetted shoes and jewelled clasps, chains, miniatures and pins.

The family group at home could be large, including perhaps a widowed mother, and unmarried sisters and daughters. There might be the heir too – if there was not a second estate for him to occupy – and younger sons who had not sought wealth by marrying into a merchant's family.

PLANNED FOR THE FAMILY

To accommodate the family comfortably, bedchambers and living rooms proliferated. Many of them were walk-through rooms in the wide-fronted but shallow houses with an E, H or half-H ground plan. The most ambitious country houses had a 'long gallery' where the family and guests could walk in poor weather, admire the portraits and other paintings displayed there, amuse themselves with games, and play or hear the harpsichord.

Outside, the houses presented a symmetrical array of tall gables or turrets, clusters of chimneys and huge bay windows soaring through all the storeys. Some were veritable lantern houses – glittering acres of glass supported in delicate stonework.

After 1600, in Jacobean times, the windows may have shrunk and the roof been given smaller, curved gables, but the basic style was slow to change; property owners did not readily take up the Classical lines favoured by Inigo Jones (see box, p.20).

IMPROVING THE FURNITURE

Elizabethan furniture was still massive, mainly of oak and scanty, far outstripped in quantity by hangings, rugs and cushions. Defter joinery – chiefly the mortise-and-tenon joint pinned by dowels – was used in making the furniture, but its appearance was changed most by profuse decoration. This was where the Renaissance at last began to impinge on the way things looked in Britain.

Everywhere there was fluting and gadrooning, columns and caryatids, cartouches and lion masks, acanthus leaves and strapwork, and grotesques – fanciful people and beasts copied from the unearthed ancient Roman ruins known as *grotte*. The decoration was

QUEEN'S MOVE *Shaded by an embroidered canopy, Elizabeth I goes to a June wedding at Blackfriars in London in 1660. She and her courtiers are decked out in the exquisite clothes they loved so much.*

deeply carved on the frame-and-panel chests, over the court cupboards used as dressers, and on the press cupboards used as wardrobes.

If there is one decorative emblem of the age, it is the bulbous 'cup-and-cover' on bedposts, table legs and court cupboards. Long, solid, six-legged or eight-legged dining tables were made with cup-and-cover legs and an elaborately carved frieze below the table

NEEDLEWOMAN'S SKILL *Silk, silver gilt and sequins create the flowing pattern on a linen nightcap made for a mid-17th century gentleman.*

top. There were also draw tables with leaves below the main surface which pulled out to double the table's length. Small bedside-cum-breakfast tables were made too.

Stools, still more numerous than chairs, were now 'joint stools', their parts held together by pegged mortise-and-tenon joints instead of by crude wedges. The sturdy box chair was still made for the master but it was slightly less hefty and less likely to be panelled in below the seat. Legs were not carved or fluted but turned balusters or shaped like columns. Seats were narrower, the open arms were sloped forward and the panel back had side ears and might be inlaid with pale holly or fruitwood. There were still rather clumsy 'turned' chairs, with supports that were shaped by a foot-operated pole lathe.

By about 1600, upholstering was coming in, but upholstered chairs were usually kept out of the public rooms to reduce wear on them. Early upholsterers often simply glued fabric, carpet or leather onto the wood. Fortunately for the ladies, the type of back-stool often called a farthingale chair was devised. Low-backed, armless and high-seated, the thinly upholstered chair offered a practical perch for ladies who until about 1620 wore dresses that made sitting difficult. The stiff bodice dipped at the front to a sharp point over the stomach, and the heavy skirt spread out wide over a whalebone, wire or cane frame called a farthingale.

A LIGHTER STYLE

Jacobean furniture continued the Elizabethan style but was less heavy and less extravagantly decorated. Cup-and-cover supports became more slender, and geometric patterns, often

AT EASE *A padded seat with no arms and a backrest pleased ladies in skirts held wide by a farthingale frame.*

with diamond and semicircle shapes, were used. Decoration was less deeply carved – and perhaps not carving at all but glued-on mouldings or turned pieces split lengthways.

As the 17th century progressed, most chairs still had a flat wooden seat with a needlework cushion on it, but homes were likely to have a few thinly upholstered chairs to bring out for important guests. The X-chair (whose seat was cradled in the upper part of two X-shaped supports) increasingly had a permanently padded seat instead of just a squab cushion resting on webbing, and many more stools were given back rests.

Ladies could sit in more comfort by then; their gowns were high-waisted with the full skirts falling in soft folds. Men too, by the less-flamboyant reign of James I, wore sagging bucket-topped boots and sober woollen suits proper to country gentlemen.

Among the new pieces of furniture was a compact games table whose double-layer top folded out to rest on a swivel 'gate'. Similar gate legs were fitted to narrow tables which had hinged flaps to lift and rest on the gates. The chest sprouted drawers with iron handles and became a chest of drawers – which by about 1650 had doors over the drawers.

DECORATING THE WALLS AND CEILING

Panelling and plasterwork gave Elizabethan and Jacobean craftsmen ample scope for embellishment with exuberant Renaissance motifs. Once the technique was developed of sawing timber across the grain and neat joins could be made, large panels were fitted in grander rooms and carved with arcading, strapwork and geometric patterns. The walls of lesser rooms were generally wainscoted – covered with small, plain panels.

A plaster frieze above the panelling was moulded with arabesques and flowers, beasts and family crests. Similar (continued p. 20)

AN ELIZABETHAN BEDCHAMBER

ALTHOUGH A PRIVATE ROOM in the main, and a retreat from the bustle of the great chamber, this bedchamber of about 1600 still had a public to impress. A lady might work at her embroidery here, pursue religious studies, learn to play a musical instrument and talk with her closest friends. A gentleman would take guests to his bedchamber to talk business, play chess or backgammon, or have a meal.

This bedchamber is comfortable and yet grand, with an elaborate plasterwork ceiling and an ornate frieze above the panelled walls. A striking tapestry also enriches the room. The imposing bed is heavily carved on the oak headboard and on the posts that carry the tester or canopy. Ropes hold the mattress filled with rushes, wool, or feather and down.

Bed-hangings, some of the most expensive fabrics in the house, could be woollen worsteds, as here, or silk damask or velvet. They hang from iron (or bone) rings which slide along an iron rod hidden by the tester. The hangings stop draughts and keep out light from the stone-mullioned, large bay window, which has no curtains or shutters. Curtains also give privacy, for this is a typical walk-through room, one of several in a string.

HEAVY CARVING IN LIGHT OAK

The sparse oak furniture includes a chest, a small table and a stool. Sometimes upholstered chairs would be kept in the bedroom to protect their covers from wear. The court cupboard is not just open shelves but has a section with doors to hold refreshments. The honey-coloured oak bed, court cupboard and panelling by this time show Renaissance influence in the decoration of Classical-style pilasters, capitals and caryatids (female figures as columns), arched arcading, bulbous cup-and-cover supports carved with acanthus leaves, and twining strapwork.

The tapestries over the panelling help to reduce the chill in winter, but might be taken down in summer. Bedchambers were now upstairs, so had a floor of suspended oak boards. These might be left bare or, as here, be covered with rush matting, perhaps with a rug or two on them. It was becoming increasingly fashionable to coordinate the designs and colours of hangings, cushions, carpets and table covers, in the French manner.

Deep warming pans of brass with long iron handles were first made in Elizabethan times – to hold embers, not water. A servant would

take one from room to room to slide between the sheets and take off the chill before the room's occupant climbed into bed. Small candlesticks (chambersticks) with a curved side handle were made to light the way to the bedroom. In the main rooms of a rich household the candles would be wax, which was expensive; tallow candles were cheaper but gave off an unpleasant smell. Small oil lamps were also used, but whatever the source of light, the bedchamber would be a dark and shadowy place after nightfall.

A personal servant, who slept on a pallet or folding bed in an adjoining closet or ante-chamber, would bring a basin and ewer of water for the morning wash and a chamber pot for the night. The servant also saw to the small room among the string of bedchambers and closets that was known as the *garderobe* – the French word for 'wardrobe' and one of many

euphemisms
to precede 'toilet'
or 'lavatory'. It was
equipped with a close-
stool – a lidded box holding a basin
which the servant had the task of emptying.

There is no one opinion about how often or
how thoroughly people washed in Elizabethan
times. The queen herself is said to have
bathed once a month; others expressed the
view that a bath was not very necessary if
clothes were changed sufficiently often. Some
houses had a room set aside for baths in the
basement, where water could be carried
without too much effort. But it was more
common to take a wooden tub up to the bedroom or an adjoining closet to be filled with
water carried up laboriously by the servants.
How frequently this was done appears to have
been entirely a matter of personal preference.

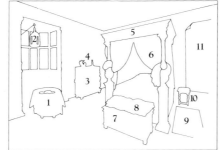

1 Octagonal table with fringed carpet
2 Brass birdcage containing a linnet
3 Court cupboard with enclosed part for food
4 Tigerware jug, wooden goblet and latten
   candlestick on linen runner
5 Heavily carved full-tester bed
6 Fine worsted-wool hangings and valance
7 Chest with carved arcading and caryatids
8 Tasselled silk-velvet cushions
9 Turkish rug with typical geometric design
10 Oak joint-stool with squab cushion
11 Flemish 'verdure' (plant design) tapestry

INDOOR PROMENADE *Arcaded panels, moulded ceiling and French tapestries show Jacobean taste in the long gallery – 136 ft (41 m) of it – at Aston Hall, Warwickshire (built 1618-35).*

mouldings on the ceiling were divided by ornamental ribs that were elaborated with bosses and pendants where they crossed.

Jacobean ceilings were more restrained, often having simple geometric designs around a central circle or oval. But Jacobean fireplaces grew to a massive size and became riots of carved female torsos, mythological beasts, grapes, flowers and interlaced patterns.

Similar Renaissance motifs also appeared in the many hangings and soft furnishings. Tapestries for the walls were usually from Flanders, but some were home-produced from Elizabethan times at the Warwickshire and Worcestershire estates of William Sheldon. In Charles I's reign a tapestry factory was set up near the Thames at Mortlake. Richly gilded embossed leather hangings from Spain were sometimes used instead of tapestry.

SOFT TOUCHES

Carpets on the floor and curtains at the windows were rare through Elizabethan and Jacobean times – but carpeting and curtaining were profusely used for other purposes. Fine woollen fabrics, or silks and velvets from China and Italy were hung around the bed, while cushions and table coverings were often of harder-wearing turkeywork – wool knotted into a backing like Turkish rugs.

Many soft furnishings were made by the ladies of the house who worked pillowcases and bed coverlets, cushions and book covers, purses and bodices. Trellises set with flowers and animals wound across their fabrics. The needlewomen could use pattern books of motifs, pricking along the lines, then pressing powder through the holes onto the fabric.

EVERYDAY METALWARE

Pattern books of designs were used also by silversmiths keen to copy the fashionable work of craftsmen from Germany and the Low Countries. The wealthiest folk – merchants and professional men as well as landowners – could afford cupboards full of silver, not just to display but to use. The status-conscious became almost indifferent to it and instead coveted glass as the most prized possession. Salt cellars were still made as status symbols and in many styles, Classical columns and bells being popular. Other pieces included covered cups, serving dishes, plates, goblets, beakers, tankards, toiletry pots, jewel caskets and candlesticks.

During Elizabethan times silverware was smothered with columns, mythical heroes and beasts, urns, swags of foliage and strapwork. Finials on lids were large, some in the

INIGO JONES
Gifted Designer Far Ahead of his Time

A MAN OF GREAT LEARNING, a talented draughtsman, and a connoisseur of art, Inigo Jones (1573-1652) was the son of a Smithfield clothmaker and trained as a joiner. Through working at the Danish court he got work at the English court, at first designing sets and costumes for masques. Jones drew on what he had learned during travels in Italy, where he had admired especially the architecture of Andrea Palladio, based on the styles of ancient Rome. When he became chief architect to the Crown, Jones used this style, for example in the Queen's House, Greenwich, and the Banqueting House in Whitehall.

Classically inspired façades are now familiar to us from stately homes and public buildings, but then the style was startlingly novel. Instead of an upward emphasis of turrets and gables, horizontal lines were stressed in box-like buildings. Inside and out, cube rooms, ranks of windows and columns obeyed mathematical rules of proportion. The result was a harmonious elegance that was not to flower fully until the 18th century.

The Queen's House, designed c.1616 and completed for James I's widow in the 1630s, introduced Classical architecture to Britain.

ELIZABETHAN STYLE

Most furniture was still heavy and oak, but better made with joints and panelled frames. It had copious decoration of fluting, strapwork, leaves and figures, cup-and-cover supports and some inlay. People still preferred silver, jewellery, clothes and hangings. They prized Venetian glasses although rather bubbly British copies were made. Some ceramics were precious enough to set in silver mounts.

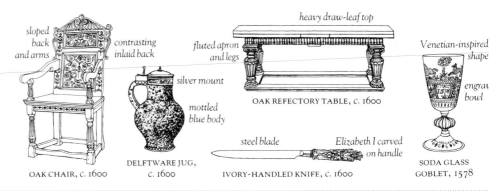

sloped back and arms

contrasting inlaid back

OAK CHAIR, c.1600

silver mount

mottled blue body

DELFTWARE JUG, c.1600

heavy draw-leaf top

fluted apron and legs

OAK REFECTORY TABLE, c.1600

steel blade

Elizabeth I carved on handle

IVORY-HANDLED KNIFE, c.1600

Venetian-inspired shape

engraved bowl

SODA GLASS GOBLET, 1578

PURITAN STYLE

Designed to be Purely Useful

Only its scrolled handle breaks the plain lines of this wide-skirted 1653 silver tankard.

MOST FASHIONS have been set by people with power and money, but in the Commonwealth years (1649-60) style in Britain matched the notions of the commoners who had become the rulers. The Parliamentary Party that ousted King Charles I was supported by many Puritans, whose movement started in Elizabeth I's reign to 'purify' the Church. Hardworking and austere, they abhorred aristocrats' high living.

Under Puritan influence, royal and Church treasures were destroyed or converted into money. Simplicity and usefulness prevailed. Furniture was usually oak, its decoration limited to turned legs and shallow carving. Such austerity could produce a pleasing elegance, seen especially in the rare silverware. It was thinner than Elizabethan silver, lightly decorated, and sometimes had openwork to save metal.

After the Restoration, Puritans had no influence in Britain, but those who had gone to America on the *Mayflower* in 1620 inspired the simple style of early American furniture and textiles – and Shaker style 200 years later.

form of warriors, many like steeples. Jacobean silver had less flamboyant ornament.

Spoon-bowls were rounder, less fig-shaped. The few forks were for serving, so ewers and basins for rinsing hands were still put on the table. Queen Elizabeth avoided both hand-washing and greasy fingers by wearing gloves – a fresh pair for each course.

There was still plenty of pewter on most tables. Each diner had food served on a pewter plate and then lifted anything that needed cutting onto a rectangular trencher of harder pewter. Servants would later buff out the knife marks from the trenchers. Pewter was also used for broth bowls, meat platters and ale tankards. There were brass and iron pieces, too, at the fireplaces and in the kitchen.

IMPORTED FINERY

The making of glass was still dominated by Venice. English craftsmen were able to produce only inferior imitations, but Italian immigrants to England started making Venetian-style glass in the 1570s. However, fears that wood, the main fuel, was becoming scarce led parliament in 1615 to restrict its use to industries important in defence, such as shipbuilding and iron-smelting. Glass-makers had to use coal, and many furnaces that had no coal locally closed.

Glass had additional glamour when it came from abroad, as had rock crystal, large shells, ostrich eggs and tobacco. Tankards in German tigerware – mottled brown stoneware – were sufficiently valued to be given silver mounts and lids, until people were enchanted by goods from farther afield.

The East India Company, set up in 1600, brought in Japanese lacquered chests and the brightly patterned Indian cotton fabrics known as 'chintzes' – and also increased the availability of Oriental carpets and Chinese porcelain. The main porcelain wares were vases, plates and bowls, and prized pieces were mounted in silver for display. New imports arriving from China after the mid-century

were to serve the new habit of tea-drinking.

Much English pottery was comparatively crude, decorated with trails and pads of slip (runny or soft clay). There was also earthenware with a tin glaze that gave a smooth, white surface to paint on. This painted earthenware competed with Italian maiolica and imports from elsewhere. As the craze grew for blue on white Oriental porcelain, English potters decorated their wares to imitate it from the 1590s on. In Holland, too, it was imitated soon after 1600, and the Delft production centre was soon to give its name to the ware.

A BRIEF FLAVOUR OF FRANCE

The refinement and excellence slowly infiltrating all the arts and crafts were given added impetus when Charles I became king in 1625. His taste for French style – and his French wife, Henrietta Maria – favoured increasingly ornate and luxurious rooms in the French manner, with gilded panelling and plasterwork and richly painted ceilings. Charles had a passionate interest in the arts, encouraged artists such as Van Dyck and Rubens to work in England, and built up a collection of superb paintings.

But Charles I's views of the monarch's rights and his refusal to bend to the wishes of parliament finally proved unacceptable to the nation. The Civil War and the ensuing Commonwealth (1649-60) led by Oliver Cromwell were a sobering and destructive interlude for royalty and gentry. The costs of war made heavy taxes inevitable and there was little money left to spend on fine goods. Like earlier rulers who were short of funds, Charles I and Oliver Cromwell had precious plate melted down and minted.

Even when the fighting was over, many of the former leaders of fashion were dead or destitute, or in exile on the Continent. High fashion stood still and a more austere tone prevailed – for a time. Exuberance and indulgence were to be embraced even more enthusiastically at the Restoration.

JACOBEAN STYLE

More types of furniture were made – folding tables, cupboards, chests of drawers, backstools. They were plainer, lighter and polished, with more slender supports, including fancy spindles. More seats were upholstered. Silver had lighter decoration, and glass was delicately engraved. In ceramics blue and white wares were popular. Rugs, chintz, lacquerwork and porcelain were imported from the East.

armorial engraving

long bowl

SODA GLASS CIDER FLUTE, c. 1650

narrow cup-and-cover supports

panelled doors

OAK PRESS CUPBOARD, 1610

scroll handle

helmet shape

tall pedestal foot

SILVER EWER, 1637

fluted baluster legs

mortise-and-tenon jointed frame

OAK JOINT STOOL, c. 1625

tall, tapering shape

blue flowers, birds and inscription

DELFTWARE MUG, 1629

HAPPY AS A KING *With an expression to match his nickname and wearing the last word in fashionable clothes, the Merry Monarch, Charles II, gazes from a delftware charger that has a typical blue-dash rim.*

RESTORATION AND QUEEN ANNE 1660-1720

Extravagance gives way to Elegance

Returning to post-Puritan Britain from exile on the sophisticated Continent, aristocrats indulged a taste for finery and pleasure which many other well-to-do people were glad to copy. Delighting in dramatic impact in their homes, clothes and entertainments, designers and patrons worked through a passion for curves and Chinoiserie.

WHEN THE MONARCHY was restored in Britain in 1660, and Charles II became king, he and his courtiers brought back a desire for the luxurious style of life they had briefly shared during their exile in the royal households of Europe, especially at the French court. Released from the pious austerity of the Commonwealth, Britain's upper classes indulged in lavish comforts in the home, sensuous clothing, enjoyment of the arts, and robust entertainments at the theatre, at horseraces and at the gaming table.

With parliament and monarch in accord, a standing army established to back up their authority, and new banking, investment and insurance organisations growing to fund commerce, the nation prospered. Overseas trade grew and London was rapidly becoming the greatest port in the world, bringing in spices, tea, coffee, chocolate, pineapples, Oriental porcelain and lacquerwork, cane, tortoiseshell, ivory, rugs and Indian chintzes.

The basic order and prosperity lasted through the Restoration years and, in 1688, proved sound enough to survive the turmoil of ousting Charles II's Roman Catholic successor, James II. It continued through the reigns of James's two daughters – Mary, who ruled jointly with her Dutch husband William of Orange, and Queen Anne – and was ruffled only briefly when the succession of George I, a prince of Hanover, outraged the Jacobites who wanted a Stuart to be king.

During such affluent times, the band of people who could afford luxuries widened. They wanted not only more goods but skilled craftsmanship and sophisticated French style – and, by chance, the demand coincided with a massive immigration of French Huguenots. They were fleeing from persecution after the Edict of Nantes, which had given them freedom of worship, was revoked in 1685. Some 50,000 Huguenots came to Britain, among them skilled workers of all kinds, but in particular silk weavers and silversmiths.

BAROQUE DRAMA

The most striking development of style, in buildings as well as furnishings, during the Restoration period was the dramatic use of curvaceous ornament – the look known as Baroque. Arising from Italian, Spanish and German influences, and abundantly displayed in the grandeur surrounding King Louis XIV of France (see box, p.28), the Baroque used Classical motifs such as floral swags, cornucopias, fruit, helmets, nymphs, *amorini* (winged cupids) and scallops. These were now very boldly executed and tended to be overpowering in their profusion and flamboyance. On furniture, the wood was often deeply carved, covered with gesso – a mixture of plaster of Paris and glue – and gilded.

In Britain, the taste for Baroque that seized the court was slower to reach the rest of the country, where many still preferred austere marble floors, oak chests and high-backed chairs. The principal decorations of such furniture were carved panelling and turned supports. Bobbins, barley-sugar twists and inverted cups were a feature of legs, backrests and arm supports through the later 17th century. High-backed chairs were also given a

carved, bow-shaped rail under the seat front, a crest along the back, and a woven cane back and seat. Such chairs were not exactly comfortable, even with a quilted pad on the seat, yet they were hugely successful as both dining chairs and withdrawing-room chairs, and they were exported widely in Europe.

But Baroque curves were to prove irresistible and were reflected in a new look in furniture. Walnut, mostly imported from France, now began to replace oak, and walnut veneer (on a deal carcass) made decoration possible without carving. Patterns found in

cabriole leg's flowing lines frequently stood free. Light, yet strong enough for tables and tallboys as well as chairs and footstools, it heralded an era of shapeliness and delicacy.

With comfort now a major consideration, loose pads and cushions were more and more replaced by fixed upholstery. Padding was held in place by a lining and covered with increasingly lavish fabrics (imported or made by immigrants) such as brocades, silks, velvet and embroidery work. The upholstered armless chair progressed to one with full back and arms and by the 1690s to the wing chair in

STRONG BREW *With unerring aim, a servant pours a stream of coffee into a bowl. More pots stand ready in this simply furnished coffee-house, the 18th-century meeting place for plotting and gossip.*

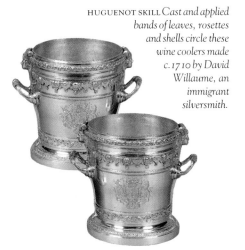

HUGUENOT SKILL *Cast and applied bands of leaves, rosettes and shells circle these wine coolers made c.1710 by David Willaume, an immigrant silversmith.*

burrs, root wood and 'oysters' (cross-sections of small branches, often of laburnum) were used to advantage. Strips cut across the grain were used for crossbanding along edges, and marquetry created floral designs from the differing colours of walnut, rosewood, sandalwood, box and sycamore. Intricate 'seaweed' or 'endive' marquetry constructed a web of arabesques from two contrasting woods.

CABRIOLE LEGS AND CURVES

The taste for curves embraced the leg, too. It was transformed, first with a scroll or hoof foot (the Braganza leg), then with a projecting 'knee'. Eventually, this crooked form was simplified into the cabriole – a leg with a gentle S curve, wide and carved at the knee, tapering to a rounded pad. The first cabriole legs were still linked by stretchers but the finer grain of walnut and greater skill in jointing made stretchers unnecessary, and by 1710 the

which only the cabriole legs showed wood.

A greater diversity of furniture pieces was designed for particular needs – oval and round gate-legged and drop-flap tables, card tables, kneehole desks and escritoires, glass-fronted display cases, corner cupboards and dropfronted writing desks. There were kneehole dressing tables too, and some had matching swing toilet mirrors on stands fitted with drawers. These elegant pieces of furniture had handles and hinges in brass, not iron.

By the early 18th century, the robust chests of drawers of 50 years earlier had yielded to walnut-veneered tallboys raised on stands, some with cabriole legs, many with barleysugar twist legs, flattened-globe 'bun' feet and curving X-shaped stretchers. Despite the greater variety of furniture available, however, rooms were still comparatively empty.

The great bed remained a house's most important item, now taller than ever with its posts often topped by ornate finials and plumes and an increasingly lavish treatment of the tester (canopy) and valance.

COORDINATED DECOR

One feature of the bed, its curtaining, was put to new use – at the windows. Used at first to keep out sunlight, curtains were soon recognised as valuable pieces of decoration.

Increasingly, designers tried to harmonise the elements in a room, especially the textiles. The growing awareness of overall room decoration was stimulated by the French-born designer (and later architect) Daniel Marot, who worked for William of Orange in Holland and came to work for him in England (1694-8). Published collections of Marot's designs (*Oeuvres*) appeared in 1702 and 1712, and enabled the middle and upper classes to apply his coordinated French-style schemes for furniture and hangings in their homes.

People were quick to glean furnishing ideas from publications. When John Stalker and George Parker produced a *Treatise on Japanning and Varnishing* in 1688, for example, they started a vogue that had amateurs up and down the country – especially the ladies of the house – japanning pieces of furniture. They, and manufacturers too, produced some passable imitations with paint and varnish of the coveted Oriental lacquerware, without either the gum of the lac tree or the great cost of the real thing.

TWO STYLES FOR HOUSES

Patrons who bought the increasingly elegant and comfortable furniture put it in houses that were now Classical in inspiration as the seed sown by Inigo Jones (see p.20) germinated. The most celebrated architects of the day were Sir Christopher Wren, Nicholas Hawksmoor and Sir John Vanbrugh. All worked in the Baroque style, which bent the Classical conventions to create dramatic effects. Their buildings combined massive stonework, giant double columns, bold juttings and deep

ELOQUENT PINE *Grinling Gibbons showed the most minute detail in his dramatic carvings of game, berries and pods, fruit and wheat ears.*

recesses, curved walls, oval windows, and a skyline punctuated by domed lanterns, campaniles, balustrades, urns and statues. It was a style chiefly for public buildings and palatial ceremonial houses – for St Paul's Cathedral, Blenheim Palace and Castle Howard.

Inside these lavish buildings, the rooms were often ornately decorated. Plasterers created ceilings divided into sections by high-relief mouldings that often served as frames for ceiling paintings in rich colours. In some houses, such paintings spread down the walls. Generally, though, walls were panelled, but now the panels were often painted with plain colours or with marbled effects. Expensive cloth was also stretched on panels, trimmed with braids and fitted on the walls.

Block-printed wallpaper was used occasionally; tapestry, however, was still widely

RESTORATION STYLE

Upright oak furniture with barley-sugar legs yielded to figured woods, especially walnut, and a style less hefty but showily carved, inlaid and gilded. Ornate silver was made by skilled Huguenot smiths and forks were used for eating. Sturdy drinking glasses were made in new, sparkling lead crystal and mirrors were avidly bought. Delftware and the imported Oriental porcelain it imitated were ever more popular.

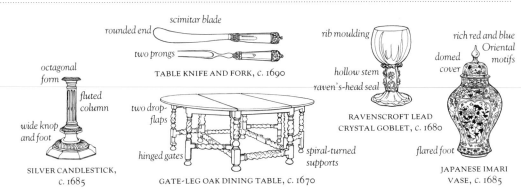

scimitar blade
rounded end
two prongs
TABLE KNIFE AND FORK, *c.* 1690

octagonal form
fluted column
wide knop and foot
SILVER CANDLESTICK, *c.* 1685

two drop-flaps
hinged gates
spiral-turned supports
GATE-LEG OAK DINING TABLE, *c.* 1670

rib moulding
hollow stem
raven's-head seal
RAVENSCROFT LEAD CRYSTAL GOBLET, *c.* 1680

rich red and blue Oriental motifs
domed cover
flared foot
JAPANESE IMARI VASE, *c.* 1685

used – and the workshop established in 1691 in Soho, London, produced hangings to compete with French and Flemish imports. Wooden bands carved with fine detail in high relief also decorated the walls. Most in tune with Baroque taste were the carvings of Grinling Gibbons – extravaganzas of flowers, fruit, birds, fish, musical instruments and quivers of arrows.

For less grand, but still substantial, homes a simpler style of architecture had developed by 1680 and continued in the early 18th century – the style known as Queen Anne. Its compact box shape had a symmetrical red-brick façade with stone dressings, a central pediment, sash windows, a pediment or shell canopy over the door, and an emphatic cornice or eaves under a steep roof broken by dormer windows and thick chimneys.

PERSONAL IMAGES IN TUNE WITH THE TIMES

The appearance of society folk had its own Baroque extravagance. Restoration men and women alike needed to spend an age at the cheval glass applying their personal veneer. The most favoured visitors would be received while the lady or gentleman of the house was

TEA CEREMONY *Shapely but comfortable clothes, gentle curves in the furniture, a silver kettle and an imported porcelain tea set all contribute to the restrained elegance that was in fashion by 1720.*

MADE TO LAST *Wing chairs with carved cabriole legs and full upholstery have been made since the 1690s.*

being arrayed for public view. Men wore coats that flared out into full skirts over their breeches but fitted closely above the waist. Ruffled shirts peeped out and the tying of the lacy cravat showed fine degrees of taste. Only a tricorn hat could sit amid the massive curled and powdered wig rising from a central parting. The face was a white and red contrast of powder and rouge, set off by a little patch or two that imitated beauty spots but were often hiding scars left by smallpox.

The ladies too were rouged, powdered and patched. Masses of ringlets framed faces plumped with cheek pads. Paint enhanced the eyebrows, lips and fingernails. Curves made ample by a tight-laced bodice spilled over the low neckline, and off-the-shoulder sleeves ended in ruffles. A full skirt was open at the front to show a trimmed underskirt. Gradually a less extrovert style began to curb

Restoration excesses and by Queen Anne's day a decent, flowing elegance was in vogue. Such stylish dressers were not the people to be tearing food apart with their hands.

ADVANCES IN SILVER AND SCIENCE

From the late 17th century, diners in polite society had forks to match their silver spoons and silver-handled knives. Other new silver tableware included centrepieces, sauceboats and soup tureens, breadbaskets, teapots, coffee pots and chocolate pots, kettles and stands for the tea table, and little trays for spoons. Many pieces bore embossed and repoussé work or engraved floral decoration.

Aristocrats whose possessions had been sold during the Civil War or seized during the Commonwealth needed to set themselves up in style, as did loyal men (continued p. 28)

QUEEN ANNE STYLE

Line rather than detail was supreme. The cabriole leg typified the new shapely elegance of furniture. Japanning imitated the coveted Oriental lacquerwork. All things Chinese were in vogue – and the blue and white porcelain was still much copied in delftware. Flowing line overrode ornament in silver and glass with the graceful baluster shape being used for drinking vessels, stems and feet.

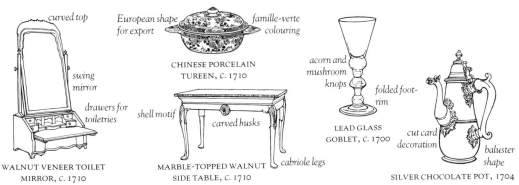

curved top

swing mirror

drawers for toiletries

WALNUT VENEER TOILET MIRROR, C. 1710

European shape for export　*famille-verte colouring*

CHINESE PORCELAIN TUREEN, C. 1710

shell motif　*carved husks*

cabriole legs

MARBLE-TOPPED WALNUT SIDE TABLE, C. 1710

acorn and mushroom knops

folded foot-rim

LEAD GLASS GOBLET, C. 1700

cut card decoration　*baluster shape*

SILVER CHOCOLATE POT, 1704

A RESTORATION WITHDRAWING ROOM

WHILE THEIR HOMELAND was Oliver Cromwell's Commonwealth, Royalists who had taken refuge in France experienced the French style of life. One of its features, which they copied on returning home after 1660, was the arrangement of rooms. The public, formal core of a house was the hall or vestibule and the main reception room, often called the *salon* (saloon) or great parlour. The private suite of rooms had its own slightly less formal reception room – the withdrawing room – which was an antechamber to the bedrooms.

The largest houses had separate private suites for the master and the mistress of the house, and for other family members or for guests; each suite had a withdrawing room. In smaller houses just one room served as public reception room and family living room. This withdrawing room of about 1680 was not yet a comfortable room. It declared the owner's status to visitors and provided a setting for conversing with due etiquette.

UPRIGHT FORMALITY

Furniture was still placed against the wall and much of it still had an upright, rectangular quality. The tall, caned chairs, for example, were not made for relaxing in, although a touch of comfort was given by cushions on the seats. Upholstered armchairs and other comfortable furnishings were still kept mainly in the bedroom or the closet (see p.29). There was often an addition of more up-to-date and exotic pieces such as imported lacquer cabinets resting on gilded Baroque stands, and walnut-veneered pieces in a lighter style.

The basis of the room was generally Classical, the dado and cornice of the walls echoing

1 Triad of table, mirror and candlestands, with floral marquetry
2 Light silk curtains with tie-backs
3 Garniture of Japanese Imari porcelain
4 Chinese Kangxi jar with tree pattern
5 Turkish carpet with geometric pattern
6 Blue velvet hangings with silk damask
   panels and blue and yellow silk fringes
7 Walnut and cane Charles II crown-
   back chairs with Braganza legs
8 Japanned cabinet on carved, gilt base
9 Walnut and gilt brass bracket clock
10 Velvet cushions with silk tassels

the plinth and capital of a Classical column. The space between was enhanced perhaps by carving, by specially commissioned paintings, by lacquerwork or, as here, by panels of fine cloth. Towards 1700, ceilings were increasingly painted with dramatic trompe l'oeil domes or cloudy skies.

Windows, spaced regularly along the walls, were usually of the sliding sash type, held open by weights hidden inside the frame. The triad, or triolet, was developed to fill the space between windows. It consisted of a table with a looking glass above it and flanked by a pair of tall candlestands. Lighting continued to be by candles, which were often numerous. They were in chandeliers of gilded wood or of glass hung just above wig height, in silver and brass

sconces fixed to the wall, and in candlesticks and candelabra on the furniture.

The floor was usually of scrubbed oak or deal boards and covered with rush matting. Although it was becoming more common to place Turkish and Oriental carpets on the floor, the practice of laying valuable carpets on tables persisted until the 1720s. Parquet flooring in the French manner was expensive and it tended to break apart; if it was used at all, it was most often in the bedroom or the

closet, where fewer people would walk on it.

Touches of more casual decoration began to enter the withdrawing room. On the mantel shelf there might be English pottery figures or a garniture – a set of vases, usually three large and two smaller, in Chinese or Japanese porcelain or in delftware. Jardinières and vases of flowers or plants (real or of silk or paper) stood about the room. And later on there was often a hint of fun given by a dummy board – a realistic cut-out wooden figure.

BY DESIGN *Daniel Marot's schemes harmonised rooms – for example with complementary fabrics and trimmings on stools, chairs and curtains.*

newly ennobled by Charles II and merchants now growing rich from booming trade. They wanted plates and dishes, tankards and mugs – and toilet sets including glue pots, patch and powder boxes, bowls for lotions and ointments, and candlesticks. They even bought solid-silver furniture and fire 'irons'. Elaborate silver wall sconces for candles became status symbols.

Huguenot silversmiths such as Pierre Harache and David Willaume benefited from the demand. They excelled at exuberant Baroque ornament, and the new, purer silver that became the legal standard in 1697 was heavier, softer and thus better for their method of casting ornament to apply separately to an item. The Huguenots also brought the technique of cut-card work, in which scrolls, medallions, leaves and other motifs were cut from thin sheets of silver and soldered flat onto a plain surface. The technique gave a much sharper outline than embossing.

Gradually elegance of line rather than fussy ornament was appreciated. The swelling baluster shape especially was used for drinking vessels, candleholders, the feet of dishes and all manner of objects.

Beneath the surface show, keen minds were engaged in scientific study, and enterprising manufacturers were eager to turn new techniques into profits. This was the age when Sir Isaac Newton discovered the natural laws of gravity and motion, Robert Boyle defined chemical elements and established how gases behave, and Thomas Newcomen invented a steam engine. Amateur scientists toyed with

microscopes and orreries and absorbed the reports published in the new scientific periodicals. Thomas Tompion worked with scientists to develop accurate watches, travelling clocks, and bracket and longcase clocks. He and others also made barometers.

HOMEMADE GLASS AND EXOTIC PORCELAIN

By 1676 George Ravenscroft had found a method of making clear lead-oxide glass free of fine cracks, a breakthrough that allowed a British glass industry to compete with imported Venetian glass. The new glass was not as runny in its liquid state as Venetian glass and it could not be blown as thin, so styles were adapted to suit it. Wine-glass stems, for example, were sturdy but graceful balusters at first, then a variety of shapes including mushroom, globular and multiring. A bubble of air in the stem was a popular decoration. Soon sweetmeat dishes, cream jugs, candlesticks, toilet pots and other items were made, some with applied ornament.

Particularly coveted were products of the workshop that George Villiers, 2nd Duke of Buckingham, had opened in 1663. It made silvered glass and created a huge market for mirrors. Only the larger output that was made possible by the development of cast glass about 1700 could begin to satisfy the demand.

In pottery too, more home-produced wares were available. There was earthenware covered with cream and coloured slips, or with the tin glaze that fired to a white background for the brightly painted decoration of delftware. None of it equalled the translucent but tough and cheap white Chinese porcelain painted with dragons, birds and flowers in blue or polychrome. Demand for this was part of the taste for Chinoiserie that also encouraged Chinese motifs in furniture, textiles and silverware.

Imitation of Oriental blue and white ware (see p. 161) was the seed of the boom in the delftware industry in both England and Holland during the 17th and 18th centuries. William of Orange brought with him from Holland a taste for delftware (as well as for bulbs, see p. 24).

William's wife, Queen Mary, was a keen collector of Chinese and Japanese porcelain – one of many who collected not just blue and white but the more colourful and more expensive famille-verte, which the Chinese made for export from the late 17th century. Pieces of furniture, and even whole rooms, were designed for displaying the precious porcelain; other specialised items, too, were collected (see p. 29). This gathering of objects of antiquity, curiosity and beauty was to grow even more during Georgian times.

LOUIS XIV STYLE

Extravagant Symbols of Majesty

APTLY KNOWN as the Sun King, Louis XIV of France (reigned 1643-1715) was the centre of a glittering, immensely wealthy court from which all power radiated. The court lived in the utmost luxury at the Louvre and Versailles, royal palaces that Louis furnished in the height of current French fashion. With

his patronage, craftsmen and manufacturers – of glass and silks, for example – thrived. The old Gobelins weaving workshop in Paris made tapestries, furniture, and gold and silverware, and the Saint-Gobain glassworks developed new processes to make the large plate-glass mirrors for Versailles.

The Louis XIV style of furniture was imported by the fashionable in Britain and elsewhere in Europe. It is massive, rather sombre and heavily carved and gilded, or intricately patterned with veneers of costly tortoiseshell and foreign woods, and inlays of ivory and brass. Legs on chairs and console tables in particular bear profuse floral garlands, acanthus leaves, scrolls, scallop shells and cupids. Symbols of the king appear in the form of the sun god Apollo and L monograms. Exceptionally fine is the exquisite marquetry finish given by André Charles Boulle to furniture and clocks – now known as Boulle, or Buhl, work.

Marquetry of ebony, ivory, tortoiseshell and brass enriches a 1700 Boulle dressing table.

A QUEEN ANNE CLOSET

As the pattern of rooms in later 17th-century England drew closer to the French model, a typical private suite developed in fashionable houses. It consisted of the with-drawing room (see p.26), the bedroom, and the closet. The bedroom had a role as a reception room where privileged guests were received, usually in the morning when the host was getting up and being dressed. For completely private relaxation another room developed – the closet – after the fashion of the French *cabinet*.

The closet lay beyond the bedroom and was the most intimate of the private rooms. Being invited to it was a mark of the visitor's closeness to the host – or sometimes of the host's desire to flatter a visitor of high social standing. But principally the closet was a place to entertain close family and friends, to read and write, and to take tea – or chocolate.

It was usually small, but richly decorated with the most comfortable furniture in the house, such as upholstered armchairs or, as in this lady's closet, a daybed. It was a snug retreat when the portière curtain was drawn over the door and the fire in the marble corner fireplace shone on the delft-tiled surround and the wrought-iron and brass fire irons.

PRIVATE COLLECTIONS

A general interest in science in the late 17th century, as well as experience of travel, sparked off an enthusiasm for collecting. Large objects could be displayed in the long gallery, but smaller ones would be kept in the closet – perhaps in a purpose-made glass-fronted case. A gentleman might collect paintings, Classical sculpture, coins, curios from abroad or minerals and shells. A lady might fancy birds' eggs, butterflies or Oriental porcelain. Oriental lacquer panels, screens or cabinets might also be treasured in the closet.

If a house had several private suites, they were arranged along the sides of the upper storey. The closet was put at the very corner with a staircase beside it – partly for servants to get about without passing through more public rooms. But such stairways also allowed political plotters, moneylenders, lovers and mistresses to reach the closet unseen.

1 Red and gold japanned cabinet on stand
2 Chinese porcelain and delftware collection
3 Lacquer panels taken from a Chinese screen
4 Walnut stool with silver chocolate pot and blue and white cup and saucer
5 Geometric-design Turkish rug on parquet
6 Giltwood daybed with damask upholstery
7 Small writing bureau with octagonal silver candlestick, silver inkpot and quill pen
8 Brass wall sconces
9 Japanned chair on early hoofed cabriole legs

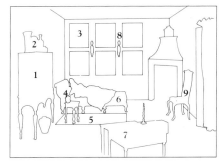

EARLY GEORGIAN 1720-1760

A Taste for Light-hearted Curves

Willing to accept the newly rich as well as new designs, the gentry in early Georgian Britain swelled in numbers and indulged their spending urge – often to excess. This led many to ruin, but it also allowed craftsmen, designers and artists to make great reputations for themselves.

MERIT, GOOD FORTUNE, education and patronage, corruption and service to the nation were among the varied means of advancement in mid-18th century Britain. The band of people deemed to belong to polite society broadened to receive many from comparatively humble backgrounds. Artists and architects, bankers and businessmen, as well as those born into the nobility and the landed gentry could join the fashionable upper set in the reigns of George I (1714-27) and George II (1727-60).

There was little to hinder the quickening pace of prosperity apart from the Jacobite Rebellions of 1715 and 1745 supporting the Stuart claimants to the throne, and the bursting of the South Sea Bubble in 1720 – when over-ambitious investors in a company trading with the South Sea islands suffered financial collapse. Many more investors, and merchants, grew rich, however, through the success of the East India Company.

THE SOCIAL ROUND AT HOME AND ABROAD

In this prosperous age, the well-to-do enjoyed a constant, extravagant round of dinners, balls, gambling and horseracing. Spending money – and being seen to spend it – was in vogue. No shame was attached to going bankrupt if it was done with style. For all its acceptance of the lowly who rose to join it, polite society liked to show itself a cut above the rest. Its absurd clothing, for example, used expensive imported fabrics beyond the means of social inferiors, and in excessive quantities. Women's oblong hooped skirts measured some 6 ft (1.8 m) across and men's coat cuffs doubled back to their elbows.

Style demanded that the autumn and winter should be spent in London. Social life, business interests, attending parliament and the inconvenience of travel all made it desirable to have a house in London. A summer trip must be made to a spa town, where a leader of fashion would act as master of ceremonies, as 'Beau' Nash did at Bath. And style decreed that each year, those of polite society's sons who had finished their formal education should go to the Continent for the Grand Tour. Learning and culture were increasingly the marks of a gentleman.

The Grand Tour lasted anything up to five years and took the young men, in the company of tutors, to visit the great houses, palaces and cities of France and Italy, to admire the ruins of antiquity and to collect trophies – imitations as well as genuine pieces of Classical sculpture, and paintings not just by masters of the past but by the very latest successful artists – Canaletto, for example.

A TASTE FOR CLASSICAL TEMPLES

One influential young man, the Earl of Burlington, returned from his travels in Italy inspired especially by the work of the 16th-century architect Andrea Palladio. Lord Burlington studied the work of Palladio's only previous British champion, Inigo Jones (see p.20), before he designed Chiswick House and built it between 1725 and 1729 to hold his collection of art and sculpture.

Its restrained, Classical-temple style was taken up for many of the town houses that now sprang up in London and in fashionable spa towns such as Bath, Tunbridge Wells and Scarborough. Terraces lining the streets and built around squares had the façades and proportions of Palladian villas.

The buildings were Classical inside as well as outside. The proportions of the rooms were based on the cube, and the measurements of columns and pilasters agreed with Classical rules – the height of a Corinthian column, for instance, is ten times its diameter. Doorways were framed with columns and pediments.

Classical restraint did not yet extend to the furniture, however. William Kent, a protégé of Burlington and one of the first architects to involve himself with every detail of exterior and interior design, had no qualms about ornate furniture. He developed his own line of heavy, richly carved pieces, typified by marble-topped tables on gilded pedestals of birds or female or animal figures. Kent's furniture, essentially Baroque, set the pattern for many other designers until about 1740.

THE LIGHTER TOUCH OF ROCOCO AND CHINESE STYLE

On the Continent, the ponderous and florid Baroque had, about 1730, suddenly lightened into the more delicate style known as Rococo. The name is derived from the French *rocaille*, 'rockwork', and *coquillage*, 'shell'. The style evokes rocky grottoes, and makes liberal use of scallops, garlands, and 'S' and 'C' curves. It is often asymmetric and suggests swirling movement and playfulness.

When the Rococo reached Britain after 1740, it rarely featured in exterior design as it did in France. It tended to appear in graceful details – on mirror frames, girandoles (wall-fixed candleholders), chimney pieces, furniture, wallpaper, textiles and ceilings.

Similarly light-hearted was the use of Chinese motifs. The excitingly foreign style of porcelain, lacquerwork, embroidered textiles and hand-painted wallpaper imported from the Far East was the inspiration for decorating whole rooms, especially ladies' bedrooms, with Chinoiserie. Chinese figures, pagodas and the long-necked 'ho-ho' birds similar to cranes found their way onto mirror frames and European porcelain. Thomas Chippendale (see box, p.33), applied this style so emphatically to a range of his furniture that it is called Chinese Chippendale.

Just as ideas from distant places were used in Chinoiserie, ideas from distant times were

SILVER UNSURPASSED *Paul de Lamerie's technique and artistry shaped the high-relief dolphin, cherubs, clouds and scrolling on this 1736 sideboard salver.*

CULTURED SET *Although a musical tea party is a sedate enough occasion, there is more than a hint of Baroque drama in the boldly carved table, chair and stool and in the dominating paintings.*

PLAYFUL CURVES *Its focus is a coy glance, but Hogarth's 1759 painting also shows swirling motifs on the wallpaper and clock, a curving card table and – popular touch of the day – a tripod pedestal on the pole screen.*

adapted to give a Gothic touch. The pointed arches and tracery seen in Medieval churches appeared on furniture – in chair-backs and the glazing bars of bookcases, for example – and in sham ruins built on country estates.

All these styles – Palladian, Rococo, Chinoiserie, Gothic – could be used in one house, even in one room. A variety of tasteful effects was the aim of the fashion-conscious.

ADAPTING TO MAHOGANY

Nature forced changes on furniture, in which solid walnut and walnut veneer had reigned supreme for some 50 years. In 1709 France suffered severe weather that killed off many of its walnut trees. In 1720 France stopped exporting walnut, and furniture-makers in

Britain lost their major timber source. The Caribbean solved the problem and mahogany was imported from Jamaica, Hispaniola, Puerto Rico and Cuba from about 1730.

It was appreciated for its colour and the close grain that made it suitable for precise joinery and for carving. Many shapely pieces were made in solid mahogany, among them the typical Georgian armchair with wide, upholstered seat, pierced splat of interlacing bands, gently curving arms, and cabriole legs with carved knees and – the emblem of early Georgian furniture – ball-and-claw feet.

Another typical early Georgian item is the three-footed pedestal table with a round top, often with a 'piecrust' border and hinged to swing up for the table to stand flat against a

wall when not in use. The tripod pedestal was also used on kettle stands, candlestands, dumb waiters – and pole screens to shield heavy face make-up from the heat of a fire.

Tallboys and bureau-bookcases, incorporating architectural forms, were topped by a pediment. Whereas in 1700 such pieces were generally given cabriole legs, now they tended to have bracket feet – low, straight feet curved at the inner edge. The Rococo influence was seen in the lines and ornament of armchairs and the serpentine or bombé shapes of commodes (elaborate chests of drawers).

SILVER, CERAMICS AND GLASS

The Palladian, Rococo, Chinoiserie and Gothic styles inspired other craftsmen besides furniture-makers. The best silversmiths of the age, such as Paul de Lamerie, worked in all these styles. A salver might have restrained, Classical-style borders and a candlestick might represent a Classical column, while a basin and ewer might bear the shells and garlands of the Rococo. One dish might be engraved with Oriental figures and another be heavily chased with Gothic traceries.

Ceramics, and particularly the new ranges of European porcelain from Meissen and Sèvres, also showed varying styles. After many abortive attempts, Johann Friedrich Böttger, an alchemist working in Meissen near Dresden, Germany, for the Elector of Saxony, devised a hard-paste porcelain to equal the translucent porcelain of China and Japan. A factory was set up which by 1719 was making excellent pieces, among them vases, plates and tea services with superbly painted and gilded scenes. From about 1730, Meissen made figures of people, animals and pastoral scenes that embodied the Rococo vision.

Meanwhile, France had managed to develop only a soft-paste porcelain. In 1740 a factory was set up at Vincennes, moving to nearby Sèvres in 1756; it produced very fine work, usually vases, plates and other such wares – rarely figures, except the renowned

EARLY GEORGIAN STYLE

Baroque boldness in line and ornament was followed by lighter swirling and scrolling Rococo. It was used for silver and for the new European porcelain as well as for furniture. Mahogany was the main wood, piecrust table rims and ball-and-claw feet the typical details. Chinese, Gothic and Classical styles were adopted as well. Glass tended to be thinner and was skilfully engraved.

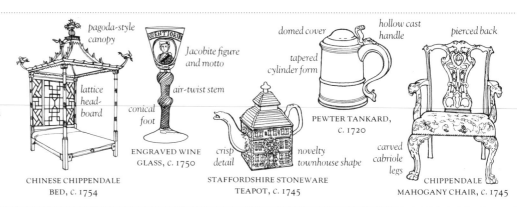

pagoda-style canopy

lattice head-board

CHINESE CHIPPENDALE BED, C. 1754

Jacobite figure and motto

air-twist stem

conical foot

ENGRAVED WINE GLASS, C. 1750

crisp detail

novelty townhouse shape

STAFFORDSHIRE STONEWARE TEAPOT, C. 1745

domed cover

tapered cylinder form

hollow cast handle

PEWTER TANKARD, C. 1720

pierced back

carved cabriole legs

CHIPPENDALE MAHOGANY CHAIR, C. 1745

biscuit figures. British craftsmen were starting to make soft-paste porcelain but were far behind the skills of the German and French. The great English porcelain factories were soon established – set up by and for the merchant and middle classes. The Chelsea factory (1745-69) was noted particularly for its delightful figures and other factories were producing at Bow (1746-76), Derby (from 1750) and Worcester (from 1751).

Britain's glass industry had now developed its own style – which European countries were copying. The tax by weight on English glass from 1745 encouraged makers to produce thinner glass, more suitable for engraving, which was in any case the most frequent method of decoration.

Drinking glasses tended to have conical or trumpet bowls, skilfully engraved and set on plain or baluster stems. The stems often contained either air bubbles or opaque glass rods formed into spring-like twists. A wide selection of other pieces were made, including little glasses for sweetmeats, jellies and custards, bowls and salvers, decanters and jugs. There was some shallow cutting – of faceted diamonds, for example – on glass chandeliers.

DRESSING THE FLOORS, WINDOWS AND WALLS

There were well-made knotted carpets from Axminster, Kidderminster and Wilton, but they were more expensive than imported Oriental carpets. Many rooms had fitted carpets made of broad strips and a border sewn together; or floors might be painted or spread with 'floorcloths' of canvas painted with a design or simply with black and white squares.

In curtains, now more elaborate, the festoon (see p.34) was the most popular form, but pairs of curtains drawn to the centre were becoming commoner. Popular fabrics were lightweight, with delicate Rococo designs printed by a new copperplate process.

Rich fabrics were still used to decorate walls. They were not broken up into panels as

before but stretched across the whole wall, or at least down to the dado. Wooden panelling painted white, stone-colour or, sometimes, olive-green was also used.

Block-printed wallpapers were now much cheaper than textile hangings. Flock paper imitating Italian silk velvet was considered highly desirable. Papers with *chiaro-oscuro* (light and shade) effects imitated Classical niches with statues, and Rococo designs included medallions enclosing landscapes. Some designs with sprays of flowers on plain grounds were of a kind that is still popular.

PICTURES OF THE AGE

Paintings in gilded frames were increasingly a part of the decor, some of them collected on the Grand Tour. Family portraits were much in vogue, too, keeping popular artists such as

Sir Joshua Reynolds busy. During a long career, Reynolds was eventually to paint some 2000 portraits, characteristically showing the sitters in their best light.

Quite a different style of painting came from William Hogarth – no flattery from him. He portrayed mercilessly the ills and absurdities of a London where crime, drunkenness, debauchery and disease were rife. This was an age in which many a lord made himself a beggar by his extravagance. Sir Robert Walpole (Prime Minister 1721-42) could spend more than £1200 on the trimmings for a state bedroom while the annual wage of a farm labourer was £30.

Early Georgian society was shot through with excesses for all its efforts at refinement. But refinement was coming, and was to be the hallmark of the late Georgian period.

THOMAS CHIPPENDALE

A Reputation Larger than Life

A JOINER'S SON from Otley in Yorkshire, Thomas Chippendale (1718-79) went at the age of about 20 to London, where he set up a workshop near Covent Garden market. Chippendale was never as celebrated in his day as his reputation suggests now, when he is one of only three or four British furniture-makers whose names are widely known. His fame comes chiefly from his influence – indeed little so-called Chippendale furniture was actually made in his workshops.

Chippendale's influence was established largely by *The Gentleman and Cabinet Maker's Director*, published in 1754. This was the first catalogue by a cabinet-maker dealing exclusively with furniture. It contained some 160 designs and in effect summarised current tastes, including Chinese, Rococo and Gothic styles. Just as important for cabinet-makers was that the book showed in a practical way how they could apply fashionable detail to their work. No one style

encapsulates Chippendale, but a common thread in his designs is their understanding of the wood – usually mahogany – and their union of elegance and inventiveness.

Further editions of the *Director* kept Chippendale in vogue. He produced some of his finest work for the designer Robert Adam (see p.36), and his work was known as far away as the USA, where it dominated furniture of about 1760-85.

The 'Director' gave varied finishes for basic shapes.

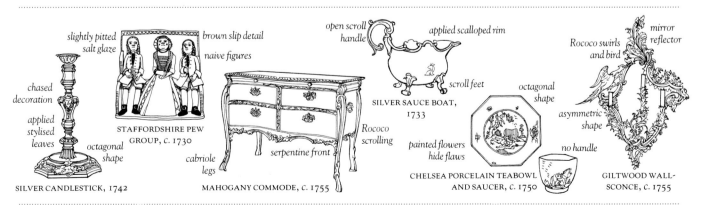

chased decoration

applied stylised leaves

SILVER CANDLESTICK, 1742

slightly pitted salt glaze

octagonal shape

brown slip detail

naive figures

STAFFORDSHIRE PEW GROUP, C. 1730

serpentine front

cabriole legs

MAHOGANY COMMODE, C. 1755

open scroll handle

applied scalloped rim

scroll feet

SILVER SAUCE BOAT, 1733

Rococo scrolling

painted flowers hide flaws

octagonal shape

no handle

CHELSEA PORCELAIN TEABOWL AND SAUCER, C. 1750

Rococo swirls and bird

mirror reflector

asymmetric shape

GILTWOOD WALL-SCONCE, C. 1755

AN EARLY GEORGIAN DRAWING ROOM

ROCOCO STYLE was the height of fashion in the 1740s and 50s, but few purely Rococo rooms have survived in Britain. Perhaps it was too difficult to make a pleasing scheme of such profuse ornament with its swirling flowers and scrolls, asymmetric forms and figures caught in the instant of movement. Nevertheless, householders – especially in London – eager to be in tune with the latest trends, included Rococo features in some of their rooms.

This was the era of the assembly, when polite society would gossip and show themselves off, listen to music, play cards, dine and sometimes dance in the Assembly Rooms built in fashionable towns up and down the country. Pleasure grounds such as London's Vauxhall Gardens served a similar function. Assemblies were also held in private homes and usually centred on dinner and dancing, or musical entertainment.

ROOMS FOR ENTERTAINING

The bedchamber and closet at the end of a suite of rooms were now less public and the drawing room, which was reached before the bedchamber, became a focus for entertaining. Even better was a suite of rooms for entertaining in the centre of the house – a saloon, a drawing room and a dining room.

Dinner was eaten in the early afternoon, in the saloon if there was no separate dining room. Afterwards the ladies went to the drawing room and took tea, ceremonially prepared by the lady of the house herself. The gentlemen joined them later, and they all went to the saloon for dancing.

Tea was an increasing passion in the 18th century, creating a need for tea tables, kettle stands, teapots, teacups and – because tea was expensive – caddies with locks. Tea was drunk at breakfast as well as after dinner and, as the dinner hour slipped to early evening, after-noon tea was taken to stave off hunger.

This drawing room of about 1755 has plenty of Rococo ornament but it is not over-powering. The scheme is calmed and unified by the use of the same cool blue silk damask on the walls and for the curtains and upholstery; its scrolling pattern is discreet but Rococo in feel. The curtains, made in the current festoon style, are drawn up by tasselled cords which are secured on cloak pins at the side. The tacks pinning the damask to the walls are

concealed at the dado and the top by scrolling fillets moulded from papier-mâché. The cornice and ceiling decoration here are also papier-mâché, but many houses had mould-ings in plaster or in the much closer-textured stucco which could be carved with fine detail.

The mirror frames have typically profuse ornament incorporating plants, birds, 'S' and 'C' curves, and extravagantly swirling candle branches. Mirror frames were probably the most popular expression of Rococo, perhaps the only Rococo element in many houses.

1 Carved mahogany Chippendale chair
2 Sofa with curved back, high, scroll arms and mahogany cabriole legs
3 Mirror-backed Rococo girandole
4 Mirror in carved, painted wood frame
5 Petit point and mahogany firescreen
6 English needlework rug on oak floor
7 Side chair with walnut cabriole legs; cover fixed with brass studs
8 Tilt-top mahogany tripod table
9 Liverpool porcelain teabowls and pot
10 Silver spoon plate and tea caddy
11 Carved tripod table with piecrust rim
12 Cane-handled silver kettle engraved with crest, on lamp-heated stand

LATE GEORGIAN 1760-1800

Graceful Lines from Rome

Adam, Wedgwood and Sheraton are names that conjure up the delicate Neoclassical style of the late 18th century. It was a style ideal for the factory methods that were starting to nudge at the craftsman's pre-eminence.

LOUIS XV AND LOUIS XVI
French Tastes and Follies

UNDER THE SWAY of his favourites and mistresses, notably Madame de Pompadour, Louis XV (reigned 1710-74) was a spendthrift patron of craftsmen. They worked in the Rococo style and produced exceptionally well-finished and ornate furniture, mirrors, ormolu clocks, Aubusson tapestries and Sèvres porcelain. Included in the furniture were marquetry-work bombé chests, delicate writing tables and bedroom suites. There were also settees and chairs set on cabriole legs and upholstered in silk or tapestry.

The self-indulgent extravagance and neglect of political reform were continued by Louis XVI (reigned 1774-92), whose folly was to take him to the guillotine after the French Revolution. While he ruled, luxurious richness prevailed in style. Even when Neoclassical straight lines ousted the Rococo curves and scrolls, lavish ornament gave a sumptuous effect.

French influence in late Georgian Britain was less than usual. Indeed the keynote of restraint in Britain contrasted with opulent French design. However, French styles were picked up by Hepplewhite, Sheraton and Robert Adam when a rich effect was desired, and by Henry Holland in his work for the Prince of Wales (later the Regent).

Simple lines but rich detail mark the Louis XVI Neoclassical style.

A MARKED CHANGE in decorative style coincided with the start of George III's reign in 1760 – not that the devout, industrious 22-year-old king had much to do with the change. He became a cultured and devoted family man with an interest in science, but he was no society leader.

Fashion and style were still set by people of consequence living in quite grand houses, usually in the country. Some of these people were not born to titles or land but gained wealth and position through trade and manufacturing, or marriage – for sons of the gentry readily married merchants' daughters.

The style that now appealed to the fashion setters was still inspired by the Classical world, but new windows had been opened on that world. Excavations at Herculaneum (from 1748) and Pompeii (from 1758) – two Roman cities near Naples engulfed by the eruption of Vesuvius in AD 79 – revealed rich interiors, and designers were entranced by the delicate, symmetrical decorative motifs.

ADAM'S NEOCLASSICAL STYLE

Chief creator of the style – the Neoclassical – in Britain was the architect and designer Robert Adam, ambitious son of a leading Scottish architect. He had studied the major known Classical sites during his Grand Tour (1750-4), and came back with his own distinctive vision of Classical decoration.

His most characteristic design element was chains of Classical motifs such as garlands of flowers and husks, palmettes (palm leaves), anthemions (honeysuckle flowers), round and oval paterae (plaques), urns and cameos. These were painted on pale pastel walls and ceilings or applied as low-relief plaster or papier-mâché. Frequently they were inset with medallions painted in intense colours and depicting landscapes or Classical figures.

In partnership with his younger brother James, Adam employed teams of skilled craftsmen. Some were famous names in their own right, such as the painters Angelica Kauffmann and her husband Antonio Zucchi, and the plasterer Joseph Rose.

The Adam brothers transformed many houses in London, Edinburgh and elsewhere with new façades and coordinated designs for entire rooms or suites. Robert Adam designed

CAPITAL CHIC *Symmetrically placed mirrors and pictures and a Sheraton satinwood pier table are in latest style in this 1782 London drawing room. The wide-shouldered chairs are 1760s Chippendale.*

furniture, carpets to echo the ceiling decoration, and even upholstery materials.

Inspiration for furniture came from contemporary French design (see box, left) as well as from Classical sources. Typical Adam furniture was decorated with paint, marquetry and mouldings. Pieces generally had a rectangular look – but many chests of drawers after 1775 were given a curved front.

Leading London furniture-makers eagerly followed Adam style, and Chippendale (see box, p.33) did some of his best designs for Adam rooms. When *The Works in Architecture of Robert and James Adam, Esquires,* was published in several volumes from 1773 on, architects and craftsmen throughout the

country were able to copy the style. However, a great deal of the imitation was inferior.

Silverware, pottery, glass and jewellery as well as furniture took up the theme and Adam style was dominant from about 1760 to 1785. It was ideal for smaller houses, where the Rococo could be overpowering and had been confined mostly to details such as mirrors.

FROM DECORATION TO FORM

During the 1780s, a more serious scrutiny of Classical design made the later Adam style seem fussy and superficial. Gothic style and Chinoiserie were also reappraised and the Romantic movement was burgeoning, but the strongest change was away from decoration towards refinement of form.

The change was most eloquently expressed in the furniture designs of George Hepplewhite and Thomas Sheraton (see box, p. 39).

Their most successful pieces of furniture depended on clear, elegant lines and on the effective use of the colours and patterning of the woods for veneers, stringing and crossbanding. Timbers came from all over the world, among them tulipwood, rosewood and zebrawood from Brazil, thuya from Africa, calamander from Ceylon and blond satinwood from the West Indies.

The fragile look of the typical designs – notably in chairs and the proliferating tables such as Pembroke tables, breakfast tables and card tables – belies a robust structure based on extremely skilful craftsmanship.

TAXING TIMES FOR GLASS

Throughout the period, craftsmen continued to make furniture by hand – with help from machinery coming in the 1790s. Glass too was still handmade. The major changes of this

TRUE FAME *Still instantly recognised over 200 years on, Josiah Wedgwood's jasperware embodies Neoclassical style, here with sculpted maidens as well as the typical motifs in the detailed relief.*

LOOK OF THE DAY *Swagged husks, garlands and paterae, repeated on walls, ceilings, furniture and carpets, created the airy and delicate Adam style.*

period were to make the most of the sparkle of British lead crystal, and to create a new style of chandelier. The ungainly curving glass branches imitating older wooden chandeliers were transformed by the addition of twinkling festoons of cut-glass drops.

After glass was taxed by weight in 1745, cut glass became more expensive and a greater amount of thinner glassware was made to engrave rather than cut. Clear glass, opaque

white glass, and blue, green, and purple glass were also enamelled with flowers, birds and figures and highlighted with gilding. Vases, fingerbowls and scent bottles were among the items made in this fashion in Bristol, London, Newcastle, Warrington and Staffordshire.

Cutting was still admired as decoration, however, and drinking glasses, decanters and cruets were deep-cut with triangles and diamonds. When the tax by weight on glass was increased in 1777, cut-glass prices rose again. A flatter style of cutting, producing broad fluting, was used more and deep cutting was used less. Many skilled cutters went to Ireland where glass was not taxed.

CRAFT VERSUS INDUSTRY IN PORCELAIN AND POTTERY

Although hand skills continued, science and technology were advancing on all fronts. Pottery and porcelain were soon to prove a field for industrialisation. While British factories could not yet match Meissen and Sèvres, attractive and popular pieces were made. Highly decorated soft-paste porcelain figures were still made by Chelsea (for tables, mantelshelves and cabinets), now with coloured and gilded scrolls instead of the earlier mounds forming the base. Tiny figures known as 'toys' were made to hold scent, needles and bonbons. Earthenware figures and Toby jugs were made in the Staffordshire potteries to appeal to a mass market.

Chelsea also made vases and teawares with painted panels on richly coloured grounds.

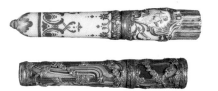

TO TEMPT THE LADIES *Patience and skill were lavished on these gold-trimmed bodkin cases, one in Chelsea porcelain, the other in carved agate.*

SENSUAL DELIGHTS *A pleasure to both eye and nose, these scent bottles are cut, enamelled and gilded. The caps are brass and the case shagreen.*

Derby Porcelain Company was making fine figures and tablewares, and around the late 1760s it absorbed the ailing Chelsea and Bow factories. The Worcester company excelled in porcelain vases and tableware, using every fashionable style and becoming noted especially for blue fish-scale-patterned grounds. Worcester also made numerous wares with transfer-printed pastoral and Classical scenes in black, red, purple, blue or sepia.

It was with tableware that Josiah Wedgwood made his first impact (see *The Wedgwood revolution*, p. 168). Born into a Staffordshire family of potters, Wedgwood had practical experience, but he also had a pioneering spirit and a keen nose for business. Tea had become the regular drink of all classes and Wedgwood's Queen's Ware exploited the huge market for inexpensive teawares.

Next Wedgwood developed a fine, hard, black stoneware – basaltes – and then the Classically inspired jasperware that is most readily associated with his name. He used it for a wide variety of objects, practical and decorative – urns, dishes, pots for the dressing table, buttons, bracelets, furniture plaques, and even souvenir portrait cameos.

Wedgwood adopted industrial methods to produce more goods at lower prices, but he also pursued customers among the rich and powerful (including Queen Charlotte and the

LATE GEORGIAN STYLE

Furniture became slender and clean-lined, and carving gave way to delicate inlaid and painted Adam-style motifs. Silver used the same motifs. Glass was engraved, cut, coloured and gilded. Derby and Worcester porcelain and Wedgwood creamware and jasperware were big successes. Sheffield-plate silver and transfer-printed pottery became available. Superb craftsmanship marked the age.

shield-shaped back

tapering legs

HEPPLEWHITE MAHOGANY CHAIR, C. 1775

cream-coloured earthenware

restrained border

WEDGWOOD QUEEN'S WARE TUREEN, C. 1775

fluted tapering stem

circular form

SILVER CANDLESTICK, C. 1780

bold flower painting

Classical urn form

DERBY PORCELAIN ICE PAIL, C. 1795

half-moon shape

restrained decoration

tapering legs

spade feet

MAHOGANY SIDEBOARD, C. 1790

Empress of Russia) to gain prestige for his products. By the end of his life, his pottery was being exported worldwide.

HARD TIMES FOR SOLID SILVER

Matthew Boulton was a man with inventive zest to match Wedgwood's. He started out in Birmingham with a workshop-based company making metal buttons, buckles and the like and, by exploiting new techniques and inventions, ended up with a huge industry.

Boulton developed an industrial process for making ormolu objects and high-quality mounts that the best cabinet-makers used. He also used factory methods to increase the production of Sheffield plate. This had been invented in 1742 by Thomas Bolsover, who fused a thin layer of silver on top of a copper ingot before rolling. Its use grew greatly after 1758 when Joseph Hancock developed a lapped edge, which hid the copper. Many items were made in the plate, those for food being tinned inside until the 1760s when the copper was coated with silver on both sides.

Suddenly a huge range of items previously made from solid silver – such as tankards, teapots, coffee pots, snuffboxes, inkwells, candlesticks and cake baskets – could be made in fashionable style and sold at a third of the price of silver. Many silversmiths fell upon hard times, although the best craftsmen still found a market for beautifully produced work.

The style of the day particularly lent itself to factory-production methods. Shapes were symmetrical, based on the circle, oval (often angled into a hexagon or octagon) and square. Teapots were in these shapes, with C-scroll handles and straight spouts. Sugar bowls, tureens and salt cellars were of shallow urn shape, with domed lids and graceful upward sweeps towards the handles. Decoration was regular Classical motifs, mostly in relief but sometimes in the shallow faceted bright-cut engraving that sparkles more than deep cuts.

In cutlery, the fork now had four prongs. Fork and spoon handles, previously curved up at the end, now curved down – the style known as Old English – and the pieces were laid on the table with prongs and bowls face up (not down as before); crests were engraved on the new upper side. Handles were edged with a feathering, bead or thread pattern and decorated with bright-cut engraving.

CHEAPER HARDWARE AND FABRIC

There were other metal goods that were much cheaper than silver. In 1770 James Emerson made a more golden-looking brass that was easy to work and widely used for candlesticks and desk furniture, and for the glass-chimneyed oil lamps that gave a light much brighter than candles could give.

Copper was mainly for kitchenware and for warming pans, which from the 1770s held water, not embers. Iron canisters, trays and other small items were japanned to look like Oriental lacquerwork. From about 1790, pewter was used for britannia metal wares. Thinly rolled sheets shaped by being spun (pressed against turning wooden moulds), produced cheaper pewter articles than casting

---

HEPPLEWHITE AND SHERATON
Synonyms for Elegance

LITTLE IS KNOWN of George Hepplewhite except that he trained in Lancaster, worked in London from about 1760 and died in 1786. Two years later his widow published his *Cabinet-Maker and Upholsterer's Guide*, whose 300 illustrations show how fashionable lines and Adam-style motifs can be adapted for all kinds of uses. Some of the more elaborate, French-influenced styles are known as French Hepplewhite, but more typical is simple and light furniture.

Hepplewhite is best known for elegant chairs with straight, tapering legs and oval, heart-shaped or, especially, shield-shaped backs. Furniture-makers all over the country used the guide, and continued to use it long after its designs were out of vogue in London.

When the highly decorative Adam style waned in the 1780s, the man who encapsulated the new taste was Thomas Sheraton (1751-1806). This leading light of British furniture design, who also wrote philosophical tracts and was a Baptist preacher, died in poverty. He was clearly a trained cabinet-maker, but no piece of furniture is known for certain to have been made by him, and it is possible that he never actually made one.

Sheraton's three-part *Cabinet-Maker and Upholsterer's Drawing-Book* (pub. 1791-4), includes echoes of contemporary Louis XVI design and Chinoiserie, but its core is designs of elegant Neoclassical taste. What distinguishes Sheraton-style furniture is its delicate appearance, displayed particularly in tables with tall, slender legs tapering down to spade feet. All superficial ornament has been stripped away to emphasise the essentially straight lines, which are given interest by skilful veneering and stringing, rather than by ornate marquetry or carving.

Decorative stretchers with a central ornament are features of Sheraton's curved pier tables, as are japanned borders on the top and frieze.

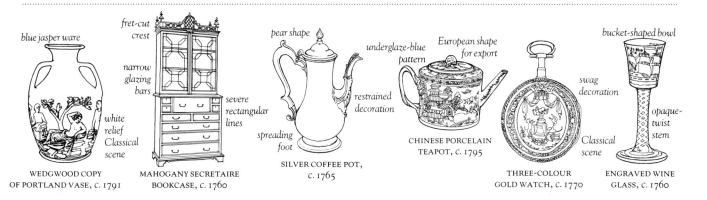

blue jasper ware

white relief Classical scene

WEDGWOOD COPY OF PORTLAND VASE, c. 1791

fret-cut crest

narrow glazing bars

severe rectangular lines

MAHOGANY SECRETAIRE BOOKCASE, c. 1760

pear shape

spreading foot

SILVER COFFEE POT, c. 1765

underglaze-blue pattern

restrained decoration

European shape for export

CHINESE PORCELAIN TEAPOT, c. 1795

swag decoration

Classical scene

THREE-COLOUR GOLD WATCH, c. 1770

bucket-shaped bowl

opaque-twist stem

ENGRAVED WINE GLASS, c. 1760

and hand-finishing, and allowed pewter to compete with mass-produced ceramics.

As the century neared its end, lower-cost factory production was dominating textiles, including those for curtains, bedhangings and upholstery. The taste was for plain satin, watered silk, subdued velvet, damask, cotton, and small all-over patterns. Eye-catching designs were out of keeping with the light and delicate style of the walls and furniture. Carpets were more boldly coloured and heavily patterned than fabrics but still harmonised with the room decoration.

FUN AND FASHION

With plenty of money to be made in manufacturing, in the colonies or in trading abroad, people were extravagant spenders on amusements. They gambled wildly, not just with cards, dice and gaming but on horses, fighting cocks and prizefighting men. Nor did they stint on clothing.

The lighter look could be said to have spread to clothing with both men's and women's fashions narrowing and fitting closer to the body. Men's coats, woollen for day, rich velvets or silks for evening, were narrow and had a cutaway front below the waist. After 1780 they were usually double-breasted and had a high, fold-over collar. They were worn over tight breeches, buckled at the knee.

Men wore powdered wigs, puffed high at the front with sausage-like curls at the ears or hanging in a bunch at the back. Women's hair styles grew immense with the hair raised over pads to give great height and curled into fat rolls at the back and sides.

Women liked to wear French silks and French styles. Their skirts slimmed down and had a bustle effect at the back, while puffy bodices exaggerated the bust. When the war with France (after the French Revolution of 1789) made imported silks harder to get and dearer, the ladies took to Indian cottons.

The fashionable clothes for men and women looked best on a youthful figure – and high society now had a young set making the pace. Increasingly the limelight fell on the stylish Prince of Wales and his circle, whose tastes were to pervade the Regency period.

IDEAL TO COPY *Its symmetrical decoration, oval form and straight sides and spout made the late Georgian teapot well suited to factory production.*

A LATE GEORGIAN LIBRARY

SETTING ASIDE A ROOM of one's house for books was an idea that developed slowly from the later 17th century onward. Before that, people had few books and these were usually kept in the closet or cabinet. There were outstanding exceptions, however, such as the celebrated diarist Samuel Pepys, who had a library lined with bookcases built especially to hold his collection of books.

Books became markedly cheaper during the 18th century and the fashion for book collections grew. Bookcases, both open and glass-fronted, were developed to house them. The drawing room had taken over the social role of the closet (see p. 29), and the small paintings, sculptures, scientific instruments and curios a man would once have kept there were now kept in the library. This room remained a retreat for the man of the house, where he could read and write away from the hubbub of the public rooms.

This country gentleman's library of about 1770 has a suitably serious and masculine atmosphere with its green-painted walls and the architectural style – with plinth, frieze and cornice – of the tall bookcases. These are of pine and painted white, with brass-grilled doors at the base over the shelves for larger books; steps are needed to reach the upper shelves. Leather strips hang from the shelves to keep dust off the line of books beneath. A decorative touch, as well as evidence of the interest in the distant past, is given by Classical-style busts (of plaster simulating marble) and the amphora, no doubt collected during the owner's Grand Tour.

GENTLEMEN'S TASTE

The furniture is mahogany with chairs upholstered in leather – a style still favoured in gentlemen's clubs today – and the matching window stools are of Classical form. Tufting, not buttoning, holds the upholstery in place and brass-headed nails fix it to the frame. The paterae on the arm supports and the ornament on the desk are further Neoclassical touches.

The décor is softened by the folds of the reefed curtains, hung in pairs here but still drawn up rather than to the sides. As the drawstrings gather them towards the corners, the decorative centre tassel is revealed.

The Smyrna rug is a reminder that Oriental carpets were still cheaper than the fine English hand-knotted carpets produced at Axminster or the Moorfields factory in

London, but even cheaper would have been the new moquette or Brussels loop-pile carpets from Kidderminster or Wilton, made from narrow strips stitched together. The rug lies on polished boards – still oak and not yet of a standard width. They could vary from 7 in (17.8 cm) to 11 in (28 cm) in one room.

The leather-topped pedestal desk represents a new, large style of desk, designed for use in the spacious library. The snuffbox, candlestick and inkstand would be made of brass, silver or Sheffield plate. The inkstand included a pounce pot (used to sprinkle a powder called pounce over writing to absorb surplus ink). Although several forms of oil lamp were now available, candles were still the main form of lighting.

The library was soon to become a room for all the family and guests to use. To the books on religion, philosophy and science would be added novels, plays, travel books and newspapers. This library's scientific instruments – the globe with latitude and longitude marks on the brass mounts, and the barometer that incorporates thermometer, hygrometer and timepiece – would be joined by board games and even a billiard table, making the room a place for amusement as much as for study.

1 Side chair with intricately carved back
2 Wheel barometer in mahogany case
3 Fully adjustable reading stand
4 Line of Classical-style ornaments
5 Library steps with handrail/bookrest
6 Globe in plaster-coated papier-mâché
7 Desk with Neoclassical decoration
8 Corinthian column candlestick
9 Inkwell, pounce pot and penholder
10 Window stool with scrolled ends
11 Silk curtains with fringed edges
12 Leather armchair with leather castors
13 Rug with stylised palmette pattern

Sharing a Prince's Passions

With a feverish desire to be in tune with high society, the well-to-do aped the taste of the Prince Regent's court. The result was a Classical elegance with exotic flourishes.

No STYLE IS MORE APTLY NAMED than Regency, for unlike most styles that bear the name of a current ruler, Regency has at its heart the tastes of the Prince Regent himself. The architects he employed set the style in buildings, and the furnishings in his homes were copied by the fashionable set. Even his critics fed off him by lampooning and caricaturing his scandalous private life and outrageous cronies.

In historical terms, the Regency began in 1811, with George, Prince of Wales (1762-1830), taking the place of his ailing father, King George III who, after prolonged bouts of illness, had been declared insane. It ended when the Prince became George IV on his father's death in 1820. However, the term Regency is applied more liberally to cover styles and fashions from about the end of the 18th century until George IV died in 1830.

PALACE OF HIGH FASHION

Regency style at its most sumptuous was embodied in Carlton House, in London's Pall Mall, which was given to the feckless, headstrong Prince of Wales when he came of age in 1783. Delighted to escape his father's staid court at Buckingham House (only later renamed Buckingham Palace), George chose the architect and designer Henry Holland to make Carlton House into a palace where he could shine among his chosen friends, a coterie of high-living dandies.

Holland used French craftsmen to create magnificent state rooms shimmering with ornate gilding and mirror-glass. They made a fittingly grand setting for the dazzling collection of opulent pre-Revolutionary French furniture. The furniture that Holland himself designed or commissioned had restrained Classical lines but its decoration was lavish.

Until it was found unsafe and demolished in 1827, Carlton House was a showpiece of

Regency high society's taste. When it was thrown open for public viewing for three days in 1811, so many people crowded in to see it that visitors collapsed in the crush.

KEEPING UP WITH THE NEW

Staying abreast of high society's fashions was an obsession of the wealthy. They grew rich in a booming wartime economy while Britain fought Napoleon on and off from 1793 to 1815. For most of that time the war penned them in their own country, although they were quick to swarm across the Channel again during the brief spells of peace. Apart from

this, they devoted themselves to the good life in London, in genteel spas, at seaside resorts, and at their country houses. They eagerly studied the trends shown in journals and publications such as Rudolph Ackermann's *Repository of Fine Art* (published 1809-29) and Thomas Hope's *Household Furniture and Interior Decoration* (published 1807).

Hope was a collector, antiquarian and designer who travelled widely in Greece. He copied the furnishings depicted on Greek vases and decorated them first with typical Classical motifs such as lion's masks, Ionic scrolls and acanthus leaves, and later with the

FASHION FOR ALL *The latest styles of Grecian gowns for ladies, sabre-legged chairs and sofa tables were adopted in the homes of modest gentlefolk as well as by people in the social swim.*

Egyptian motifs that were to become a distinctive Regency feature – winged discs, sphinxes and lotus leaves, for example.

Hope's furniture designs were widely copied, in particular by George Smith, the owner of a London cabinet-making firm, but Smith was less interested than Hope in Classical accuracy and more intent on making furniture that was usable and comfortable. His designs sold well and popularised the style.

The new look in furniture veered from the spindly ultra-delicacy of the later 18th century towards a more robust, opulent style, still Classical in inspiration but exuberant in ornament. Shapes were simple and solid with rather low horizontal lines, broad unbroken surfaces, gentle curves and some discreet reeding and fluting. Legs were splayed with sabre curves; later, legs swelled out greatly at the knee and tapered to a tiny ankle.

Many tables were supported by one or more pedestals which spread at the base into three or four feet and these often ended in scrolls or carved paws. Round tables were in vogue. As it was now fashionable to recline rather than sit upright, chaises longues, ottomans and sofas became increasingly popular.

MORE SHOW AND MORE SHINE

In the buoyant mood of Britain after the final defeat of Napoleon in 1815, a richer style came into favour, adding gadrooning, ormolu mounts and Boulle-style inlay, for example, to the more restrained earlier fashion. Decoration was sometimes in brass but often in gilded or wood-grained cast iron. Knobs that would once have been made of brass might now be of glass, china or wood. The favourite woods were dark rosewood, mahogany and amboyna, showy striped calamander, zebra-wood and kingwood, and maple veneers.

New machines helped to produce the volume of pieces demanded by the swelling number of people who were becoming prosperous through trade and industry. Mechanical planes, saws and veneer knives were in use in the furniture factories. Rebates and grooves, dovetails and mouldings could also be machine made, so the work of individual craftsmen diminished. Polishing too was changing from the laborious applications of oil, dust and elbow grease to the cheaper and shinier gloss of French polish.

REARRANGING THE FURNITURE

The style books that fashion-conscious people pored over so avidly displayed room settings as well as furnishings. Now the furniture was no longer ranged against the walls. Instead it was set out in informal groups across the room, perhaps around circular pedestal tables or in front of the fire, and left there. At first it was so startling to see furniture standing in the middle of a room that uninitiated visitors believed all the servants must have been dismissed or fallen ill.

House guests were encouraged to come and go and do as they pleased – reading, writing, playing cards, or conversing in informal groups as took their fancy. New pieces of furniture designed to suit their pursuits were

nests of tables (quartetto tables), ladies' work tables, sofa tables, card tables, small bookcases and canterburies.

Only the dining room remained formal, the setting for quantities of glass, silverware and porcelain. Grandiose tablepieces and vases were made and bone china, perfected by Spode in the 1790s, was produced to increasingly sophisticated standards by the factories of Worcester, Minton and Derby. The decoration ranged from flowers, animals and country scenes to dragons and coats of arms.

Silver, and especially ceremonial plate, received new impetus with the patronage of

AT HOME ABROAD *Britons took their own lifestyle to the colonies. In his 1824 watercolour Charles D'Oyly shows his house in India with typical Regency carpet, chandeliers, and furniture informally scattered and suiting many activities. People could stroll through the rooms, including a billiard room, and out to the garden.*

the Prince of Wales, which brought great silversmiths such as Paul Storr and Benjamin Smith to the fore. Dishes and candelabra, heavier and more ornate than the late Georgian silver of the previous century, were raised on plinths and decorated with Classical maidens, elaborate borders, swags of flowers and foliage, or Egyptian motifs. Cutlery was weightier in the hand and the handles were heavily patterned on both sides.

Manufacturing methods were changing, as in furniture. Following Matthew Boulton's development of factory-based techniques (see p.39), more high-quality tableware and candlesticks, inkstands and snuffboxes were available in Sheffield plate as well as solid

silver. Boulton also pioneered the manufacture of the English ormolu that was now in fashion for embellishing the furniture.

MAKING THE MOST OF WALLS AND WINDOWS

Fashionable rooms now had their wooden floors carpeted, often wall to wall. Draperies were lavish, with fabric not just festooned across rods above the windows and hanging as curtains crossing over at the centre, but sometimes covering the walls as well. Other wall treatments included wallpaper and painted decorative effects such as marbling, graining and stencilling. Walls, furniture coverings and curtains might have the same

pattern, frequently of flowers or of country scenes, sometimes of stripes (evoked by the military mood). Pale colours, with yellows and lime-greens among the most popular, gave rooms an airy look.

The architect Sir John Soane, a pupil of Henry Holland, was particularly skilled at creating rooms in an uncompromising Neoclassical style, with their rather cool austerity softened by the play of light from lantern windows and domes in arched recesses.

Rapid developments in British cotton manufacture made roller-printed chintzes and other fashionable materials available in larger quantities. Block and roller-printed wallpapers provided replicas of textile hangings

REGENCY STYLE

Simple Classical-inspired furniture shapes, heavily built and with ample decoration, appealed to Regency taste. Woods were dark or patterned, sometimes ebonised, gilded or painted. Ancient Greece and Rome were the source for many decorative motifs, Egypt and the Far East for others. Silver was heavy and ornate, ceramics drew on local or exotic nature, and glass was deep cut or shallow fluted.

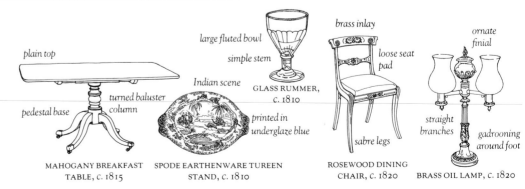

plain top

pedestal base

turned baluster column

MAHOGANY BREAKFAST TABLE, c. 1815

large fluted bowl

simple stem

Indian scene

GLASS RUMMER, c. 1810

printed in underglaze blue

SPODE EARTHENWARE TUREEN STAND, c. 1810

brass inlay

loose seat pad

sabre legs

ROSEWOOD DINING CHAIR, c. 1820

ornate finial

straight branches

gadrooning around foot

BRASS OIL LAMP, c. 1820

and painted decoration. Tastes might change with whimsical speed and the fashionable set could now change their printed wallpaper and fabrics within months.

Mirror glass, much used on the walls, gave a feeling of greater space and also improved the light – as did large windows and, at night, cascading cut-glass chandeliers. A few people might have portraits by Thomas Lawrence on their walls, but this favourite artist of the Regent was much in demand and his fees high. Sporting pictures by Ben Marshall and scenes by J.M.W. Turner were also in great demand. Old Masters were in favour, too, and might be picked up in one of the London auction houses, for London had become the centre of the European art market.

Family and guests would wander around informally through a suite of several rooms – the library (now used as a general living

CAST-IRON TOUCH *Delicate 'umbrella' canopies and balconies grace the otherwise plain fronts of terraces, as here in Cheltenham's Priory Parade.*

EMPIRE STYLE
A Grandeur befitting Napoleon

FRANCE HAD ALWAYS BEEN the single most powerful influence on British style. Even during lulls in the Napoleonic wars, British visitors flocked to Paris. Traffic the other way brought Britain skilled French craftsmen fleeing the Revolution. Style in France and Britain continued to develop in parallel.

In France, the Neoclassical style of Louis XVI lost its extravagant flourishes for a time in the austere Directoire style (1795-9). This was soon enriched into Empire style which prevailed until about 1830.

Empire style was above all solid and stately. Furniture of rather sombre wood such as mahogany, ebony and rosewood was mostly uncarved, but generously ornamented with brass inlay and ormolu mounts in such forms as burning torches, urns, lions' masks, eagles and swans. Later, papyrus leaves, crocodiles, sphinxes and other Egyptian motifs were also used on all manner of furnishings and fittings. Distinctive motifs were the Emperor's initial N and the close-fitting brimless Phrygian cap that was a symbol of the Revolution.

Empire style spread across continental Europe and beyond. In the USA it was adapted to include local motifs such as fruit, flowers and the American eagle. In Britain its impact was less – partly because Henry Holland, Thomas Hope and others had anticipated it, but also because Gothic Revival was taking hold.

Heavily built and encrusted with gilt ornament, this Empire-style fire screen bears the Imperial symbol, an eagle.

room), the drawing room, and the breakfast room. The rooms were filled with light pouring in at the carefully placed long windows, and often opened onto a conservatory.

With houseplants in the rooms, views through the large windows and, for the first time, French windows opening directly onto the garden, inside and outside formed a harmonious whole. This was, after all, the age of the Romantic movement in literature and art, which rated instinct and emotion highly and revelled in nature and landscape.

The linking of indoors and outdoors was fostered particularly by the landscape gardener Humphrey Repton, who was for several years in partnership with John Nash, the architect who is most readily associated with the Regency period. Nash was the Prince Regent's most favoured architect after 1812. He was responsible for developing the area of London that stretches north from Pall Mall as far as Regent's Park.

BUILDINGS FOR A GENTEEL LIFE

Prime examples of Nash's grandest style are the magnificent buildings around Regent's Park – massive villas and terraces whose brilliant ivory-white stucco façades, with columns, pediments and side pavilions, draw heavily on styles that were used in Greek, Palladian and Tuscan architecture.

Their less grand counterparts are seen in the terraces, crescents, squares and villas designed by Nash, Decimus Burton, Joseph Kay and others, which sprang up in several other cities, spa towns and (continued p. 48)

Classical urn form

painted rural scene

WORCESTER PORCELAIN VASE, c. 1820

ormolu lion's mask

lion's-paw feet

MAHOGANY SIDE TABLE, c. 1810

intricate branches

Greek maidens

shell and dolphin motifs

SILVER-GILT PAUL STORR CENTREPIECE, c. 1814

pattern both sides

shell and fish-scale motifs

SILVER CUTLERY, c. 1815

gilt beechwood frame

lion's head

scrolled end

lion's-paw feet

GRECIAN-STYLE COUCH, c. 1805

ornate handle and spout

flattened shape

decorative bands

SILVER-GILT TEAPOT, c. 1809

A REGENCY
DINING ROOM

'DINNER CONSISTED of a soup, fish, fricassée of chicken, cutlets, veal, hare, vegetables of all kinds, tart, melon, pineapple, grapes, peaches, nectarines with wine in proportion. Six servants wait upon us, a gentleman-in-waiting and a fat old housekeeper hovering round the door. Four hours later the door opens and in is pushed a supper of the same proportions.' So the Countess of Granville recorded in 1810 a meal served just to her husband and herself. Food and drink were central to luxurious living and the wealthy offered guests dozens of dishes at dinner.

At a house party the company would eat an enormous late breakfast at 10 or 11 o'clock, and an informal light luncheon would ensure their survival until dinner. In some houses, buffet meals called breakfasts were laid out at any time for guests to help themselves and wander the house and garden with plate in hand. But by 6.30 or 7 pm family and guests, now in formal dress, gathered in the drawing room to form up in order of social standing and go in procession to the dining room.

AT THE TABLE

In this dining room of about 1810, the long windows to the garden are standing open to let in the summer evening sun. At other seasons the firelight would heighten the warm gleam of the furniture – mostly mahogany – and with the candles already lit, the strands of the chandelier would sparkle, and be doubled by the large overmantel mirror in its black marble and ormolu frame.

The side tables are ready with glasses, wines, plates, ice, and port, Madeira and little rout cakes for later. The dining table itself glitters with arrays of ornately cut glass, heavy silverware and, as the meal progresses, richly decorated porcelain; plain white plates would be used for the earlier courses. Standardised dinner and dessert services were now being made with 12 place settings, or often in sets of 24 or 36, some sets amounting to over 500 pieces. Among them were pieces designed by potters for specific foods, for example custard cups and asparagus trays.

Sectional tables, introduced in the late 18th century, were clamped together to extend the table seemingly without limit. Since ordinary table legs made seating awkward, pedestal legs now replaced them and became a badge of the Regency era. Cellarets held bottles of red wine and lead-lined wine coolers filled with ice held the white wine. Most country estates now had an ice house to store ice cut during the winter. The sideboard often had urns standing on it, some of them knife boxes, some to hold water in which the servants could rinse glasses and cutlery during the meal. Often, as here, all the diners had a glass rinser set before them, holding water in which to swish the used drinking glass before the next wine was served.

For the dinner to run smoothly, at least one servant was needed for every diner, but conversation would be censored since many topics were thought unfit for servants' ears. A way round this was for the servants to place the desserts on a side table, then leave, letting guests serve themselves. Another solution was the 'dumbwaiter' (tiered shelves) on castors introduced in the mid-18th century. It held the desserts and the diners pushed it from one to another.

At the end of the meal the ladies would retire to the withdrawing room, leaving the gentlemen at table. Each group was free to gossip about special interests without censure, before the men joined the ladies.

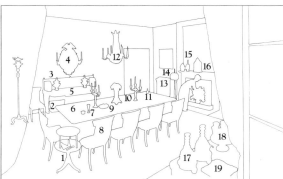

1 Dumbwaiter and Coburg-pattern silver
2 Locked cellaret for wine from the cellar
3 Velvet-lined mahogany cutlery case and Old Sheffield plate wine cooler
4 Convex mirror in eagle-crested gilt beechwood with serpent candle-arms
5 Sideboard with green splashback curtains
6 Pedestal-leg extending dining table
7 Champagne flute and glass rinser
8 Chair with cane seat and squab cushion
9 Old Sheffield plate vegetable dish
10 Brass copies of Paul Storr silver-gilt centrepiece and candelabra
11 Green Nailsea glass table bell
12 Cut-glass and brass chandelier
13 Marble-topped rosewood and ormolu chiffonier with silk back panel
14 Black and gold lacquer pole screen
15 Worcester porcelain potpourri beside clear cut-glass lustre
16 Brass-inlaid mahogany clock
17 Hobnail-pattern, cut-glass decanters in Old Sheffield plate wagon
18 Glass goblets cut with broad fluting and diamond patterns
19 Imari-pattern Coalport porcelain plate

Sharp Views of the Times

WIDER DISTRIBUTION of newspapers had, by the end of the 18th century, created a thirst for news – and gossip – about politics and people. Newspapers rarely carried illustrations until the late 1830s, but one way to see what public figures and events looked like was through prints, and the most popular prints were by satirical cartoonists. Such was the power of their irreverent imagination, that it is impossible not to see the Regency through their distorting prism.

The greatest cartoonists of the time were Thomas Rowlandson (1756-1827), James Gillray (1757-1815) and George Cruikshank (1792-1878). Rowlandson is best remembered for his jolly lampoons laying bare the frailties of refined society. Gillray produced some of the sharpest cartoons of all time, savaging the royal family and politicians. Cruikshank was at first equally vituperative. Cartoons softened from 1820 and Cruikshank turned to book illustration, leading to rumours that he had been paid to stop portraying the misbehaviour of the newly crowned King George IV.

Fallen from favour, the Regent was mocked in prints by Cruikshank (below) and others.

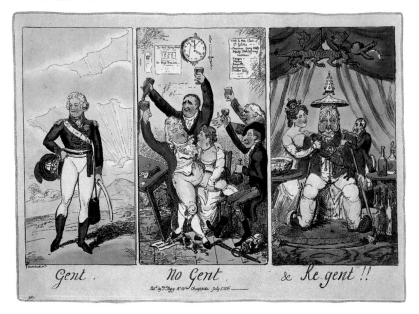

seaside resorts such as Tunbridge Wells and Hove, as one of the most memorable manifestations of Regency taste.

Under low-pitched roofs and wide eaves, the walls are of brick, or smoothed over with painted stucco, and pierced by tall windows with thin glazing bars and no surround. There is little decoration, but the façades may be gracefully dressed with bow-fronts, umbrella-roofed cast-iron balconies and verandahs, and curved or angled bay windows. The houses were increasingly built with convenience in mind, and architects finally abandoned the symmetry first taken up in Elizabethan times.

In such elegant surroundings, the genteel gatherings of the social season at spas and resorts were generally presided over by a master of ceremonies. Foremost among these was 'Beau' (George) Brummel, a close friend of the Prince Regent and a leader of society. Beau Brummel was notoriously fastidious in all matters of taste, and high society lived in fear of attracting his criticism – until he gambled his way into debt and in 1816 fled penniless to France. There he finally died in a madhouse. While Beau Brummel ruled, he was the arbiter of what gentlemen wore – dark, simply-cut coats, trousers rather than breeches, and fussy neckwear. Their ladies could have stepped straight off Grecian urns, with their hair dressed high in Grecian topknots and wearing what was virtually a uniform for the first two decades of the century – long dresses of muslin, with short sleeves, low neckline and a waistline raised almost to the armpits.

ROMANTIC THEMES TAKE OVER

Among the Romantics, fervour for the picturesque embraced not just nature but far-off countries and times. It encouraged a last great flowering of Chinoiserie during this period, as well as the introduction of some attractively novel Indian features in architecture.

No single building demonstrates this breadth of Regency taste better than the Royal Pavilion at Brighton, a small house enlarged for the Prince Regent first as a severely Classical domed temple by Henry Holland, and then redesigned by John Nash as an elegant, gleaming confection of Mogul domes, minarets, pierced stonework and crenellations. Inside, too, its imaginative and palatial rooms, some rich with gilding and drapery, some bright and airy, were a medley of delicate Classical restraint, Egyptian splendour and Eastern fantasy.

TOWARDS VICTORIAN VALUES

Nash was also one of the growing number of architects who were enthused by the Gothic Revival, which first surfaced in the 1750s and was now seizing the imagination of architects' patrons, as it was writers and their readers. Old houses that had grown piecemeal, receiving asymmetrical additions over the centuries, fitted perfectly into the Romantics' concept of beauty. If a genuine Medieval house was not available, then an imitation could be built and tricked out as a baronial fortress or a more modest *cottage orné*, or 'ornamented cottage'.

As the decades of the mid-19th century unfolded, style was to shift more and more towards the Gothic. And accompanying this move came a more sombre and ponderous mood, the decline of informality and the reassertion of dignified ceremony.

Meanwhile in the larger world, where matters of fashion were remote, the Industrial Revolution was well under way, mechanisation was drawing production into factories and the factories were pulling in thousands to work exhaustingly long hours. The new methods made possible the great age of mass production that brought objects of fashion and style within easy reach of the middle classes of the Victorian age.

LADY'S AID *When a lady opened this fan to hide her stares, its pleats showed a scene commemorating a military victory and its blades Egyptian motifs.*

PRIVATE DEVOTION *Robust Neoclassical furniture remains in fashion – no lighthearted Rococo here – and the mantel shelf is only sparsely decorated with hyacinth glasses. The plain suit and demure dresses and caps aptly express sober Victorian ideals, as does the morning lesson read by the master to his household.*

WILLIAM IV AND EARLY VICTORIAN 1830-1850

New Money in Pursuit of a Style

Piety, propriety and domestic comfort were the aims of early Victorian households. They expected sober family life to ensure the first two and industry gave them goods and money enough for the third. Moral certainty was not equalled by aesthetic certainty, however, and buyers turned to the past to prove their own good taste.

SPENDING COMFORTABLE INCOMES on comfortable goods, the fast-expanding middle classes began to influence style in Britain after the Regency. Although the rather stately, Classically-inspired tastes of Regency days lingered, even in William IV's brief reign (1830-7) there were hints of the more romantic designs to come. The boom in prosperity, generated by factories, mines, banks and world trade, filtered down to a growing middle class and these newly well-off people created a huge demand for goods. Lacking confidence in their judgment on matters of taste, and wary of revealing themselves as upstarts, they chose existing styles.

Fortunately mechanisation could satisfy the increased demand. The furniture industry went into mass production, assisted after 1845 by steam-powered carving machines; by the 1840s wallpaper was printed from engraved cylinders onto rolls of paper on steam-driven machines; and one-colour or two-colour printed cotton cloth was produced cheaply enough to be available to almost everyone.

Mass production changed retailing. In the past, craftsmen had made items specifically ordered by customers. Factories, however, produced a line of virtually identical goods which were advertised through illustrated catalogues or sold in the growing numbers of

49

TOP CHOICE *Victoria and Albert were among the people and places depicted in multicolour transfers, introduced in the 1840s on Prattware pot lids.*

high-street shops. For the first time the public could visit a store, such as Heals or Maples, and make their choice from stock.

Catalogues and pattern books had been consulted by craftsmen, manufacturers and buyers for over a century. Now the new well-to-do seized on publications developed to advise them – not only about furnishing but also on niceties of etiquette.

One of the most influential authors was John Claudius Loudon, whose *Encyclopaedia of Cottage, Farm and Villa Architecture and Furniture* (1833) and *The Suburban Gardener and Villa Companion* (1838), covered every aspect of taste. In the 1840s people also saw current styles at exhibitions of design and technology run by the Royal Society of Arts in cities such as Manchester and Birmingham.

Manufacturers and buyers found more than one style that had already proved acceptable. As a result, the Neoclassical taste of the Regency persisted in furniture shapes and in the decoration of silverware for example. A revival of opulent 'Old French' styles was seen in marquetry furniture and in richly curvaceous and gilded Rococo-style chairs.

Patriots spurned the 'Old French' and sought 'Olde England' in the romanticised Gothic style described in the novels of Sir Walter Scott. Gothic building style was fast becoming the predominant one in railway stations, libraries, schools and, notably, in the new Palace of Westminster (see box, p.54). Trefoil, quatrefoil and lancet window shapes, and the crockets on spires were borrowed for furniture and silverware.

THE COMFORTS OF HOME

Early Victorian society liked to see itself as moral and pious, and looked back with distaste on Georgian and Regency excesses. However, the excesses of poverty (described in Charles Dickens's novels), and the squalor in factories, it seemed quite able to stomach.

The middle classes concentrated on self-improvement, and on the family circle, taking Queen Victoria's family as the model.

The home – be it a manufacturer's Gothic mansion, a city banker's apartment in a Neoclassical mansion block, or a shopowner's red-brick villa with stucco semicircles over windows and doors – was chiefly a private and comfortable setting for close-knit family life, not a place for entertaining on a grand scale.

Seating was particularly comfortable, designed with upholstery as a priority, not an afterthought. Plenty of affordable and serviceable upholstery fabric was coming from the Yorkshire woollen mills. Sofas, easy chairs and ottomans were all fully sprung and padded, with buttoning often holding the upholstery in place, and with scarcely any wood showing. Sofas and easy chairs had rounded backs curving to continue as arms.

The balloon-back chair, with its padded seat and elegant curving woodwork, was one

---

THE BIEDERMEIER PERIOD

Solid Charm for the Continental Bourgeoisie

IN GERMANY AND AUSTRIA after the Napoleonic wars, an unpretentious, clean-lined style of furniture and furnishings was developed – later known as Biedermeier.

Typical Biedermeier furniture is light-coloured, in pale figured maple, cherry or apple veneer with sparing ebony inlay and perhaps some restrained gilding. Essentially Classical in its form, the furniture echoes Empire style (see box, p.45), but the shapes are simplified, with little ornament.

To modern eyes the best Biedermeier furniture has a pleasing elegance, and yet the term Biedermeier was originally derogatory. It refers to a fictional character, Gottlieb Biedermeier, invented about 1855 by Ludwig Eichrodt; the character embodied all the cosy and conformist attitudes of the bourgeoisie. The style was indeed a middle-class one, perhaps adopted because the middle classes had failed to wrest political power from the aristocracy in the wars and were compensating by furnishing their homes with solid status symbols.

With time, the Biedermeier style became more curvaceous and absorbed other influences, such as the Gothic. It had a wide influence in other countries, especially in Scandinavia and Central Europe. Wherever the style became prevalent, the years from about 1815 to about 1860 are broadly referred to as the Biedermeier period.

Simple but solid forms in light wood such as maple typify the Biedermeier style in furniture.

EARLY VICTORIAN STYLE

The well-made furniture was in Neoclassical, Rococo and Gothic styles, often in mahogany. Upholstery was thick and buttoned. Silverware was in swirling Rococo and upright Gothic styles, and became available in electroplate as well as solid silver. All-over engraving and mass-produced press moulding were new in glass. Pottery had multicolour transfers, while most porcelain was Rococo.

balloon back

turned front legs

MAHOGANY DINING CHAIR, c. 1845

wood mosaic imitating Berlin woolwork

TUNBRIDGE WARE JEWEL BOX, c. 1840

doll-like face

deep underglaze-blue robe

STAFFORDSHIRE FIGURE OF QUEEN VICTORIA, c. 1838

heavy Rococo decoration

scroll feet

SILVER COFFEE POT, c. 1845

Rococo outline

thin bone china

TEACUP AND SAUCER, c. 1845

of the happier manifestations of early Victorian Rococo; it usually had straight legs until about 1850. A different style of chair was the prie-dieu, with low seat and high back. It was generally fully upholstered, covered with Berlin woolwork in bright colours.

Much furniture followed the lines of the upholstered pieces. It had smooth, rounded, continuously flowing lines with every edge and angle bevelled and no interruption by contrasting decoration. Mahogany was the typical wood for a piece such as a round pedestal table whose thick stem flowed into a flat trefoil or quatrefoil base. An early Victorian favourite was the whatnot, not invented by the Victorians but taken up by them enthusiastically from about 1840. It was freestanding with three or four square or rectangular shelves for ornaments.

Most of the furniture was extremely well made. Furniture-makers were regularly using powered circular and band saws and planes, and they prepared mortise joints by machine, but carving and fretwork would still be done by hand on expensive pieces.

The new semi-industrial craft of papier-mâché was developed by the Birmingham company of Jennens & Bettridge, using a process patented by Henry Clay in 1772. Layers of glued paper were pressed onto a mould and then heat-dried in an oven until rigid. The surfaces were hand finished with japanning, painted flowers, gilding and inlaid mother-of-pearl. At first, papier-mâché items were small – trays and picture frames, for example – but as the material was made more robust, it was used for desks and chairs.

PATTERNS AND STYLES GALORE

Since Jacquard looms were now generally used in the Yorkshire woollen mills and the silk mills of Macclesfield and Manchester, elaborate woven patterns in furnishing damasks and brocades were plentiful. Among roller-printed cottons there were some Audubon flower and bird prints and many showy designs

LIGHT AND AIRY *This bedroom of 1848, with the approved open windows and open space, shows a lady's taste in its flowery chintz, lace-trimmed dressing table, scrolled Rococo mirrors and graceful flounced chairs.*

of roses and hydrangeas. The light, bright yellows, greens and scarlet of Regency times continued to be favourites for a time, but by about 1840 bottle-green, crimson and other darker colours were preferred.

In carpets, too, patterns became available from the power looms of carpet-weaving centres such as Kidderminster, Wilton, Axminster, Halifax, Edinburgh and Kilmarnock. Most in tune with the times were the tapestry carpets made from 1832 and especially the multicoloured, profusely patterned Axminsters available from 1839.

Decoration within one house was as varied and piecemeal as style generally. Sober Neoclassical and Gothic or Tudor styles were thought apt for 'masculine' rooms, notably dining rooms and libraries, while a lighter touch suited the 'feminine' drawing-rooms

and boudoirs. Here the Rococo Revival came into its own (see p. 52).

Many people remained unaffected by fashion. Their rooms were simply furnished, and papered with reticent floral prints, perhaps with a stencilled border. This was a style also for lesser bedrooms and servants' rooms – and any house of some substance had at least one live-in servant. A range of cheap furniture was made for these rooms, including caned bedroom chairs, painted pine chests-of-drawers, and cast-iron bedsteads.

SCIENCE HAS A SAY ON STYLE

For fashionable principal rooms, however, schemes were more daring. Many designers heeded theories on the colour spectrum, and believed science could help them in choosing successful colour combinations. Science also

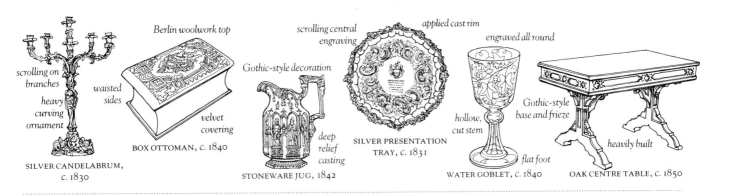

SILVER CANDELABRUM, c. 1830
scrolling on branches
heavy curving ornament

Berlin woolwork top
waisted sides
velvet covering
BOX OTTOMAN, c. 1840

Gothic-style decoration
deep relief casting
STONEWARE JUG, 1842

scrolling central engraving
applied cast rim
SILVER PRESENTATION TRAY, c. 1831

engraved all round
hollow, cut stem
flat foot
WATER GOBLET, c. 1840

Gothic-style base and frieze
heavily built
OAK CENTRE TABLE, c. 1850

had its say on curtains. Fringes, tassels and braids abounded, but swags above the curtains were declared by medical wisdom to harbour dust, even vermin. Stiffened pelmets called lambrequins were used, or curtains were hung on rings from poles left unconcealed. Roller blinds – some of them painted to look like stained glass – were also used.

In the bedroom, where floral-patterned chintzes were popular, drapes around the bed were reduced in the cause of hygiene. Instead, a canopy was suspended from the wall or ceiling to hang curtains at the bedhead only.

Medical wisdom had nothing to say of ladies' corsets, an indispensable means to the fashionable tiny waist, which could hamper breathing until the wearer swooned. Ever more voluminous ankle-length dresses were

IMPROVING TASK *A Victorian girl struggled with perspiring hands at many a grubby piece of stitching before she worked a sampler that was fit to frame.*

pushed outwards by up to nine petticoats. Sleeves were a great puffed leg-of-lamb shape until the 1840s when a sloping shoulder came in, emphasised by flat folds around the shoulders and down to the waist.

Gentlemen, however, were comfortably dressed. Their light-coloured trousers were narrowly cut while their dark frock-coats, full-skirted to near knee length, were left unbuttoned at the waist and fastened high on the chest. High collars were lowered and had a narrow cravat tied in a wide bow.

CHEAPER WAYS TO HIGH FASHION IN SILVER AND GLASS

The variety of styles of the early Victorian period also permeated the crafts. Fine silverware was made in Gothic style, complete with pointed arches and tracery, but the freer, swirling style of the Rococo Revival was more popular. The Neoclassical acanthus leaves and vines of Regency days (*continued p. 54*)

AN EARLY VICTORIAN DRAWING ROOM

THE LADY OF THE HOUSE in the 1840s carried out her more formal duties in the drawing room. In larger houses she would relax and receive close friends in the more private 'morning room' among the main reception rooms, or her boudoir close to her bedroom.

During the morning the drawing room was the setting for a string of brief calls, which etiquette imposed on the hostesses of the locality, and in the afternoon it was where the lady presided over the serving of tea and cakes. Before dinner in the evening, guests gathered in the drawing room and at the end of the meal the ladies returned there, leaving the men to linger over port and cigars.

The Rococo style, which first flourished in France (and then Britain) in the early 18th century, was considered a suitably feminine style for the drawing room. It was revived in the 1830s as part of a vogue for 'Old French' styles and remained popular for much of the century. The revival did not aim for historical accuracy, but freely borrowed the lively, flowing, curvaceous feeling of the Rococo.

STRAIGHT LINES BANISHED

In this late 1840s drawing room, the mirror frames, chandelier and wall-sconces, the marble fireplace and its ormolu and bone china candlesticks, the draped pelmets and the furniture have scarcely a straight line among them. But despite the abundant scrolls and the deep-buttoned upholstery, the overall effect is light, airy and pretty.

The cornice and the wall panel borders (and the tray and several pieces of furniture) are made of papier-mâché. The panels have a luxurious watered-silk covering and nails are driven through them to hold the paintings.

The daylight is softened by muslin subcurtains, while at night the velvet curtains give the privacy Victorians valued. Although oil lamps were in wide use, and gas lighting was common in town houses by 1840, this room is lit by candles, in keeping with its 18th-century model. The soft light of candles was kinder to ladies in make-up, and to a delicate colour scheme. The pastel shades and floral pattern of the carpet are authentically French. It is an Aubusson carpet, but the style was copied by British and other carpet firms.

The ottoman, the upholstered sofa and chairs, and the prie-dieu are comfortable but

practical: they are not constricting for ladies in wide skirts. Other practical touches are the covers on the ottoman and on what is clearly a much used chair since one of the set of quartetto tables has been placed beside it. Covers were not always removed when guests came. The frigger, a glass confection of birds and branches, has a dome to keep off the dust that was something of a pre-occupation in well-ordered Victorian homes.

The goldfish in their bowl in a wooden stand by the window may not like the light but it would benefit the palms, the favourites among the many exotic plants now being brought home from the Empire and beyond by collectors and enthusiasts. The plants were raised in glasshouses to fill the decorative jardinières and pots of proud householders.

1 Papier-mâché/mother-of-pearl tray
2 Rococo Revival Rockingham tea set
3 Papier-mâché chair with mother-of-pearl inlay and cross-stitch seat
4 Lacquered quartetto tables
5 Floral-pattern Aubusson carpet
6 Glass frigger on papier-mâché table
7 Tripod-pedestal mahogany palm stand
8 Stiffened and swagged pelmets
9 Prie-dieu covered in Berlin woolwork
10 Rococo gilt mirror over marble-topped gilt Rococo pier table
11 Ottoman with flounced chintz cover
12 Scrolled and carved cabriole-leg chair
13 Footstool with curved gilt frame
14 Scroll-backed, cabriole-leg sofa
15 Marquetry games and work table
16 Clock in floral porcelain case
17 Rosewood and papier-mâché pole screen with scrolling tripod
18 Cotton loose cover over buttoned velvet and mahogany chair
19 Marble-topped japanned side cabinet
20 Flowered Coalport porcelain vase

AUGUSTUS PUGIN

A Passionate Architect Making a Point

THE MOST INFLUENTIAL DESIGNER in early Victorian Britain was the architect Augustus Welby Northmore Pugin (1812-52), who first showed his precocious talent when, aged 24, he assisted Sir Charles Barry with the designs for the new Gothic Revival Houses of Parliament. It was Pugin who created many features of the interior.

Pugin was passionate about Gothic style, claiming it was not only beautiful, but the only truly Christian style, while Classical architecture was pagan and unacceptable. A Catholic convert when Catholicism was legal but still not respectable, he hammered home his beliefs in several books, including *True Principles of the Pointed or Christian Architecture* (1841). Pugin's abrasive and moralistic fervour intensified the Gothic versus Classical slanging match known as the Battle of the Styles.

Using a bold, rather heavy Gothic look, Pugin designed many churches and houses, and furniture, wallpaper, stained glass, ceramics and silver for them. Just before he died he said, 'I have done the work of a hundred years in forty, and it has worn me out.'

Pugin used pointed-arch niches, canopies and ceiling vaults for a soaring Medieval look.

An X-chair variant by Pugin has carved Gothic arches at the sides.

HOMELY DISPLAY *Although its rug, stone flags and bare chairs are spartan, this Wiltshire cottage in 1849 has rows of mass-produced crockery, ornaments and japanned trays over the fire, and an imposing clock.*

In Sheffield plate, the silver was fused onto a copper ingot before it was rolled. There was a limit to the decorative work that could be done without revealing the copper core. The process was superseded by electroplating, in which unlimited decoration could be done before the piece was plated. In theory, the very best design could be offered at a low price, but in fact there was a slight loss of detail in electroplate and design standards fell.

Mass production techniques reached glass during this period. Moulded glass, mostly made in Birmingham and Stourbridge, was the new technique of the 1830s and 40s. Press-moulding – in which molten glass was forced into shapes to resemble cut glass – could be carried out by semi-skilled labour and sold at prices that a wide public could afford.

There was still handmade lead crystal glassware for the better-off, typically patterned with horizontal bands of diamonds, but broad fluting was also in vogue and shapes were modified from bow-sided to straight-sided cylinders to take the fluting. Engraved flowers were also popular and there was a flurry of popularity for coloured glass, including the continental style of cased glass cut through to show differently coloured layers.

COLOUR FROM THE POTTERIES

Porcelain was in love with the Rococo during the 1830s, Coalport in particular using its asymmetric forms and scrollwork. In the 1840s there was a taste for relief flowers and sprays artfully applied to suit the shape of the object – often a jug. Most of the big names produced Sèvres-style porcelain in the 1840s, Coalport again being in the forefront.

The Gothic idiom also appeared, in stoneware jugs for example, and Neoclassicism took over porcelain figures, which Minton and Copeland made in hard parian to resemble marble statues.

The mass market preferred the colourful, cheap, naive figures of the Staffordshire potteries. The enamelled figures of animals and famous or infamous characters from life or fiction were produced in huge quantities, especially as 'flatbacks' after 1840, which reduced effort and cost. These were flat at the back to stand on a shelf, not on a table.

Popular wares were still made in slipware, salt-glazed stoneware, lustreware and ironstone. Transfer-printed earthenware reached its height of appeal and all the big Staffordshire potteries made it in quantity – much of it for export. Many pieces bore real or imaginary scenes, Copeland gave their wares Rococo borders of scrollwork and leaves, and Wedgwood specialised in all-over flower patterns. Blue, black, red, purple, yellow, brown or green were now the colours for underglaze transfers until F. and R. Pratt of Fenton introduced multicolour transfers in the 1840s, to use mainly on decorative and commemorative lids for jars – known as Prattware.

Commemorative items, new production techniques and designers' zeal were to have a glorious union in the show that launched the mid-Victorian age.

were used more naturalistically, and were not just decorations but influenced the whole form of the object.

The artistry of the silversmith was already under pressure from mass-produced items in Sheffield plate (see p.39), and the pressure was increased by the new electroplating process patented by Elkington & Co in 1840.

LADY'S CHOICE *The lighter boudoir style has small patterns, bare curtain rod and rings, and delicate openwork on the chairs and display shelves. Fringed wall brackets, tablecloths and billowing net curtains give a hint of the wealth of draperies used elsewhere in the house.*

MID·VICTORIAN 1850·1870

The Celebration of Industry

Seizing on mass production's promise of giving them all they wanted, the swelling ranks of the mid-Victorian middle classes enthusiastically set about filling their houses with massive pieces of furniture, then smothering them with covers, trimmings and a thickening mass of knick-knacks.

THE ENDURING IMAGE of mid-Victorian style is a sombre drawing room with red flock wallpaper, heavy curtains and tablecovers trimmed with braids and fringes, thickly upholstered seating, and ornaments and knick-knacks jostling on the mantelpiece, on tables and on display shelves. In fact the clutter gathered gradually after 1850, but it was well established by the 1860s.

Mid-Victorian style is often dismissed as lack of style. Certainly it had no single vision, but embraced many visions with eclectic enthusiasm. Yet the numerous unrelated elements making up its cluttered effect were deliberately put together and the result was a recognisable look. It expressed what the newly rich chose to buy, and was the first style to reflect the taste of the broad middle band of society, not its small upper set.

These consumers could find out about the latest available goods from retail shops, from

STYLE BOOKS AND CATALOGUES

Advising and Tempting the Public

REGENCY TIMES saw the birth of books that advised on all aspects of current furnishing taste, from furniture to carpets and paint schemes (see p.42). Improvements in printing presses and typesetting methods, and the repeal of the tax on paper in 1860, made it possible to produce far more books – and there was an eager market for them.

A special field was advice on running households. The *Shilling Cookery for the People* (1854), by the master chef Alexis Soyer, sold more than 250,000 copies. Mrs Isabella Beeton's *Book of Household Management* (1861) sold 20,000 copies in its first year. Cassell's *Household Guide* (early 1860s) and *The Gentleman's House* (1864) by Robert Kerr were other bestsellers.

Extensive catalogues of their wares were issued by furniture-makers, wallpaper manufacturers, dress-makers, hatters, iron founders, potters, nurserymen and all manner of tradesmen. The new retail stores also advertised their stock in catalogues, soliciting orders from all over the country and even

In a brief life, Mrs Beeton (1836-65) learned all the arts of running a home – cooking skills, prudent economics and managing the servants. Her book made her a byword for domestic know-how.

from the colonies. Through these publications, the public could be well informed about new products and changing fashions.

The beautiful engravings of products, methodically arranged by category, speak of the Victorian love of order. But the bewildering diversity of goods also helps to account for the period's crammed rooms with no coherent style.

even further towards excess in an attempt to go beyond what mass production could achieve. For example, the Warwick firms of furniture-makers William Cookes and James Morris Willcox made for the exhibition massive sideboards that dripped with deeply carved, naturalistic sculptures of dead game, allegorical figures and scrollwork.

There were also some imaginative attempts to press new materials to old uses. Shellac (secreted by Asian beetles) and gutta-percha (a rubbery resin from South-east Asia) were moulded into inkstands and picture frames to compete with carved wood and papier-mâché. The new materials had great appeal to the Victorians, but would not come into their own until there were telephones and gramophone records to make use of them.

The Great Exhibition was not universally acclaimed as a triumph: 'tons upon tons of unutterable rubbish' was the verdict given by William Morris – who was soon to succeed with his own concept of design (see p.62). Mid-Victorian design was at a crossroads. Thrust into a new era by technology, it was not yet bold enough to develop new forms to suit the technology. For the time being it fumbled in the basket of styles that had been recycled for the last 500 years.

HEAVY-HANDED DECOR

Cosy family life remained the aim of mid-Victorians. This still demanded comfortable furnishings such as deep-buttoned chairs, ottomans and chesterfield sofas, but now everything had a heavier look, showed more wood – along the top of seat backs, for example – and bore fancy carving or fretwork. The front legs of the graceful balloon-back chairs were elaborated into carved cabrioles.

numerous catalogues, and from the series of trade fairs held in British cities in the late 1840s. None of these fairs neared the scope of The Great Exhibition of 1851, which opened the mid-Victorian years on a high note of excitement about design and production.

A DESIGN SPECTACULAR

The grandly named 'The Great Exhibition of the Works of Industry of All Nations' was the brainchild of Queen Victoria's husband, Prince Albert, and Henry Cole, President of the Royal Society of Arts. Its aim was no less grand: 'To present a true test and living picture of the point of development at which the whole of mankind has arrived.'

And so it did. All that technical skill and inventiveness could produce was gathered into a massive display in London's Hyde Park, housed in a specially built glass and metal giant designed by Joseph Paxton and named by the magazine *Punch* the Crystal Palace. There were 14,000 exhibitors, half from foreign countries and half from Britain and its colonies. The exhibits ranged from agricultural implements to toys, printing presses to textiles, and sculpture to the glass fountain in the centre of the 1500 ft (457 m) long building. There were fire engines and coffee services, furniture and cast-iron fireplaces, clocks and church vessels. Ingenuity knew no bounds: an extravagant forerunner of the Swiss army

knife had more than 80 blades and instruments, and a rubberised cape could be inflated by pocket-sized bellows to become a canoe.

The main focus of the exhibition was manufacturing – and Britain was clearly seen to be at the forefront. Between May 1 and October 11, 6 million visitors saw the exhibition, many of them Britons revelling in the confident view it gave of their country.

NOVELTY ABOVE ALL

The exhibits were endlessly talked about and discussed in print, and in the long term were to influence design, manufacture and fashion throughout the nation. And yet the great show did not capture the style of its age. The closest it came was in its zest for novelty.

There were some novelties that were ingenious without being gimmicks, for example the screw mechanism on adjustable piano stools and extendible tables. Many contributors, however, anxious for their exhibits to be noticed, took design to startling lengths. Manufacturers keen to show that industrial techniques could equal, even outdo, the traditional skills of craftsmen, piled ornament onto everything – cutlery, furniture, glassware, carpets – with little attention to proportion. Such exhibits were not typical of the goods generally on sale.

Paradoxically, craftsmen working against the tide of industrialisation pushed ornament

NATIONAL EMBLEM *The plump velvet seat scarcely gets a glance in this sturdy accumulation of curves and scrolls, carving and piercing which frames Prince Albert on a porcelain plaque – but the British lion comes out on top.*

Pieces such as cabinets and sideboards were massive and ornately decorated.

Precisely detailed images from nature were popular in all design fields. Fabrics, carpets and wallpaper bore huge tropical flowers, ferns or large-leaved plants, or realistic scenes with people in them, even royal portraits. Although impressively executed, the patterns were overwhelming in a room.

Drawing rooms were crammed with easy chairs, ottomans, sofas, settees, pouffes, footstools and confidantes or 'conversation settees' on which three or four people sat around a central backrest. The parlour suite was introduced – a matching suite of settee, two armchairs and up to ten 'parlour chairs' (similar to dining chairs but with less upright backs). There would be screens too: cheval screens in the 1850s and multi-panel folding screens in the 1860s.

Drawing-room furniture might also include japanned and gilded papier-mâché chairs, set with mother-of-pearl and perhaps with a romantic landscape painted on the backsplat. Corner whatnots were introduced in this period and often fitted with fretwork rims, mirrors at the back and plush covers on the shelves. House plants were popular – palms, for example, and increasing numbers of aspidistras which also went by the name of 'cast-iron plants' for their tolerance of dingy rooms and the fumes of gas lamps. Plants were set on wooden, majolica or terracotta stands or on marble-topped console tables. When ferns became the rage in the 1860s, they were displayed on pedestals trimmed with ormolu and circled by a brass gallery.

SETTING THE SCENE FOR FAMILY MEALS

In the dining room, heavy furniture was practical as well as popular. The sturdy table was large to accommodate the numerous family members for meals of five or more courses, and the chairs were robust to survive their lengthy use. The sideboard was a showpiece of current taste, curving in and out at the front, fussy with mouldings, glossily varnished, and with a large back mirror whose curved top frame was intricately carved.

Bone china, usually Sèvres-style or flowery Minton, Copeland or Royal Worcester, was needed in abundance – as were drinking glasses. Cut glass went briefly out of style as coloured and engraved glass became the fashion. Ferns were the most popular engraved motifs of the 1860s, but the Greek key pattern was also common after John Northwood invented a machine to engrave it in 1865. On the table also were glass dessert dishes, candleholders, fruit baskets and little blue or red salt dishes cased in pierced silver or electroplate. Showy glass or silver centrepieces dangled dishes of nuts and dragées.

The way of serving meals changed in the 1850s. Instead of dishes being carved and served on the dining table, carving was done at a side table before servants went around serving the diners. As a result the damask tablecloth, which previously became spattered and was removed before the dessert, now remained clean enough to stay in place throughout the meal. The table offered a new field for dressing up – for example with menu and place cards in china or silver holders, posy pots at each place, and finger bowls set upon fancy doilies on dessert plates.

ON THE FRINGES

The generous use of textiles played a large part in the cluttered style. Apart from the amply swathed curtains, the cloths on tables and pianos, and the braiding, fringing and tassels everywhere, there were pelmet-like hangings on the mantel shelf. Some chimneypieces were dressed like windows with curtains that were opened when the fire was lit. Even the chain of the chandelier and the picture cords might have a fabric cover. All the textiles matched or were coordinated in colour – frequently a wine red or deep green – creating a sumptuous but dark effect. Fireplaces were most often of white marble but mottled green and red marble were also common.

The walls would be dark, probably papered, and covered with a mass of gilt-framed pictures and mirrors above the dado rail. Below the dado the wall might be covered in a tough paper to withstand knocks from furniture, and painted a dark colour such as brown. This paper was often embossed to look like Spanish leather wall hangings and was later sold under various names including Lincrusta and Anaglypta. The ceiling was coloured, as white was thought harsh, and in any case would have been discoloured by gas lighting or by the new forms of petroleum lamp. The doors might be painted a deep reddish-brown and grained to imitate mahogany.

MACHINE-MADE AND HOMEMADE TREASURES

Ornaments and knick-knacks crowded on every surface. Some were homemade, the result of the family's female members keeping themselves busy – idleness was regarded as close to moral turpitude. The ladies made arrangements of wax flowers and fruits to sit under protective glass domes. They created pictures from feathers or shells, painted vases, decorated wooden plaques with poker work, embroidered Berlin-woolwork covers for

DAY OUT *Frock-coated family men and their poke-bonneted ladies manoeuvring in hooped crinolines throng the exhibition hall. And after viewing all the ingenious marvels of technology, their chosen souvenir might be the Crystal Palace itself on a japanned tray.*

footstools and workboxes, diligently stitched together patchwork for cushion covers, and crocheted antimacassars.

Ready-made ornaments were chosen for a variety of reasons. There was an immense choice of machine-made ornaments. Some were exact replicas of valuable objects of the past – such as ancient Classical statues in cast bronze or parian porcelain. Some were admired items that were comparatively new, or at least newly affordable by the mass market, such as electroplated inkstands, transfer-printed pots, millefiori paperweights and Tunbridge-ware boxes.

Among the truly new arrivals were portrait photographs in velvet-lined cases and *cartes de visite* (see box, p.61). Photography was to have a profound effect on fashion and on the Victorians' self-image.

Another photographic novelty was the stereocard, introduced in the 1850s. When two mounted photographs taken at a slight distance from each other were looked at through a special viewer, a (continued p.60)

A MID·VICTORIAN ENTRANCE HALL

THE DISTANT ANCESTOR of the entrance hall was the great hall of medieval times. By the 17th century the hall had lost its role as living room and place for entertaining, but it made the vital first impression on visitors. It was still used in the Victorian age to declare the owner's status – in suburban villas as well as in the grand mansions of manufacturers.

In the mid-Victorian period the Gothic Revival style remained popular but, in tune with the age, it was increasingly dressed up with ornate Tudor and Jacobean touches while keeping its rather sombre and masculine air. Stained-glass windows, linenfold oak panelling and dark-patterned, gilded wallpaper added to the rich gloom. Often the style was not applied to the structure but confined to furnishing details. In this hall of the 1860s, however, the building itself sets the tone. The marble columns are topped by pointed arches, and pointed arches and tracery are features of the door, the huge fireplace and the carved oak banister of the staircase.

The style of a hall was partly dictated by the heavy use it took as the crossroads between outside and inside, between rooms and between floors. Here the floor is of hardwearing encaustic tiles in a typical, busy mosaic.

BARONIAL IN SPIRIT

A less-than-medieval touch is given by the tiger skin (rimmed by its black-felt backing). The hunting trophies include kob and impala heads, giving further hints of forebears who governed the colonies. Dutch landscape tiles in the fireplace and the exotic plants are out of period, too. But medieval flavour was the aim, not authenticity, so there is no qualm about displaying papier-mâché pikes and armour.

The elaborate, polished brass lanterns may have an ancient look but they are gas lamps, and mass-produced in British foundries, as are the decorative fire irons and the brass ember pan beside the suit of armour. The pan could be used for holding coals and logs rather than for taking away the embers.

As few houses had separate cloakrooms a new piece of furniture, the hall stand, was introduced in the Regency period and just about every Victorian house acquired one. In smaller houses a flattened form would be fixed to the wall. But this hall has ample space for a large, well-fitted stand as well as for other hefty furniture and a flourishing palm, its pot swathed to prevent the roots from chilling.

1 Oak chair with Gothic tracery and mouldings
2 Lever bell-pull in polished brass
3 Oak candlesticks and clock with pointed face
4 Hall stand with coat hooks, branches for hats,
    mirror, drawer, umbrella rack and seat
5 Oak board-stool pierced with Gothic arches
6 Table with stepped oak base and marble top
7 Brass jardinière, walnut box for outgoing
    letters, tin candle-lantern, silver card tray
8 Brass gong in black oak frame
9 Hanging brass lantern (gas fuelled)
10 Oak chair with tall 'church-window' back
11 Oak stool and chair with Gothic tracery

stereoscopic effect was created. By 1858, the London Stereoscopic Company offered for edification and amusement of all the family a choice of 100,000 images, from landscapes to scenes of knockabout comedy.

The newly introduced smoking room, to which men could retire with their cigars after dinner, contained as much clutter as the drawing room, but with an emphasis on hunting trophies and sporting and military memorabilia. The library or writing room was a retreat for the gentlemen, too. Its large, pedestal desk arrayed with glass, electroplate or brass inkpot, pen tray, blotter, stationery holder and paperweights was indispensable. The heavy, round, pedestal table sometimes called a loo table was often kept there – although not necessarily used for loo or other card games. The 1850s loo table had a pedestal flowing uninterrupted into the curves of the legs. In the 1860s the pedestal was often divided into several separate columns and the round top was stretched to an oval.

The fussy look also edged into the ladies' domains – the morning room or parlour, and the boudoir, though here the colour scheme was altogether lighter, with cream or pastel shades in the wallpaper, upholstery and

NEW TRICKS *While the ladies chat in the boudoir, the men enjoy a few hands of cards in the heavily draped and cluttered comfort of the drawing room – and hold their pose for the photograph.*

GARDENER'S PRIDE *Lions' heads and paws add to the impact of coloured glazes on this majolica jardinière. It would hold a sober foliage plant.*

curtains. The tables and writing desk, perhaps with painted panels or with insets of flowery imitation Sèvres, held many trinkets.

HYGIENE IN THE BEDROOM

The bedroom, like the boudoir, had a lighter feel and tended to be more simply and sparsely furnished. Apart from the bed, there would be a bedside table, dressing table, perhaps an easy chair or two, and some lighter chairs. From about 1860 these often included the new bentwood chairs with slender, rounded frames, outcurved legs and cane seats. There

was also a washstand; even well-to-do families would have only one bathroom, if that, and many people still washed and bathed in the bedroom using basins and hip-baths filled with jugs of water brought by a servant.

Current theories of hygiene approved of the free circulation of air in the bedroom – and since this was where the sick convalesced and where the numerous babies were born, it was a reasonable view to take. Accordingly, draperies were reduced and thinner fabrics, such as floral chintz, were used for the curtains. Half-tester beds were still made, but

---

MID-VICTORIAN STYLE

Furniture was heavier, fancier, carved and inlaid; Gothic and ornate French styles were revived. Balloon-back chairs had carved cabriole front legs. Flowers and colours smothered porcelain and textiles. Glass was coloured and copiously engraved, often with ferns. Swirling Rococo was the main style for silver and electroplate. Mother-of-pearl and papier-mâché made pretty knick-knacks.

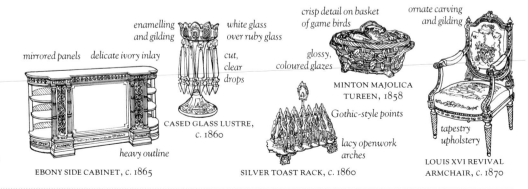

mirrored panels   *delicate ivory inlay*

enamelling and gilding   *white glass over ruby glass*

cut, clear drops

crisp detail on basket of game birds

ornate carving and gilding

glossy, coloured glazes

CASED GLASS LUSTRE, c. 1860

MINTON MAJOLICA TUREEN, 1858

Gothic-style points

tapestry upholstery

heavy outline

lacy openwork arches

EBONY SIDE CABINET, c. 1865

SILVER TOAST RACK, c. 1860

LOUIS XVI REVIVAL ARMCHAIR, c. 1870

generally there was a move to uncurtained iron and brass bedsteads.

Knick-knacks could not be resisted entirely, despite the care for hygiene, so there would be a sprinkling of toilet accessories, ringstand, glove box, hatpin cushion, fans, and boxes for powder, brooches and ribbons. They were made of glass or flowery china, or of wood covered with ivory or mother-of-pearl, which became very popular in the 1850s.

FRENCH DELICACIES AND MEDIEVAL FANTASIES

Two mid-Victorian fashions rejected the smothering cosiness. One was inspired by France, where nostalgia for the furniture of Louis XVI (see box, p.36) had produced a mishmash of pre-Revolutionary styles with a sprinkling of the brass or ormolu used in the Empire style (see box, p.45).

In Britain this vogue was imitated, and rooms decorated with white and gold paper held delicate French-style furniture decked with veneers and marquetry of woods such as satinwood, amboyna and purpleheart. Pottery manufacturers, notably Minton and Coalport, produced close copies of Sèvres, while the Worcester Royal Porcelain Company produced high-quality 'Limoges ware'.

The Gothic Revivalists also rejected cosiness. They still carried the torch of native British design and their creations speak of mid-Victorian style as loudly as assorted clutter does. The pointed arches, pinnacles and crocketed spires of London's St Pancras Hotel (completed 1871) and Albert Memorial (completed 1872), both designed by Gilbert Scott, exemplify the distinctive style as it was applied to buildings.

The Gothic style was taken up not just for other public buildings but for houses – and for their contents as well as their architecture, especially in the hall (see p.58) and the library. Newly rich magnates chose the Gothic style for their country mansions because it suggested an ancestry steeped in

PORTRAIT PHOTOGRAPHS
Captivated by the Camera

PHOTOGRAPHERS COULD OFFER the Victorians cheap portraits of themselves, some one-off prints, many printed in sets and then cut into separate *cartes de visite*, the size of visiting cards. Never before had people been able to see such realistic and readily made likenesses of themselves. Portraits of families and friends were collected in albums, copies were sent to friends and the delightful novelty quickly became a craze.

The royal family, celebrated poets, engineers, generals and politicians all found their way into albums, along with more sensational subjects such as the survivors of disasters, Siamese twins, and trick shots of ghosts.

These black-and-white (or sepia-and-white) photographs have given us an image of the Victorians as sombre and stuffy. But this may be because the long exposure times required the sitters to hold a pose for ten seconds or more – too long to wear a spontaneous smile.

By the 1860s every small town had its professional photographer, and 400 million cartes de visite a year were produced.

history. Stained-glass windows with heraldic emblems, and suits of armour were part of the illusion of medievalism. The ancient look in furnishing widened to embrace 'Jacobethan' (Elizabethan and Jacobean) features – both in genuine Tudor panelling and furniture and in newly produced imitations.

In art, the medieval period was evoked by the Pre-Raphaelites Holman Hunt, John Everett Millais and Dante Gabriel Rossetti. Imitating early Italian painters, they used heightened colour and painstaking detail to create distinctive, romantic work.

Buildings in Gothic style had luminous interiors, with richly dark, gilded wallpaper, and decor based on a vivid main colour backed by two or three contrasting but complementary colours. Colour combinations were a distinctive feature of mid-Victorian buildings. Many of the new suburban terraces had designs on outside walls of red, yellow and blue or purple bricks. The hall floor was laid with encaustic tiles in which the colour was applied as a clay slip and fused to the tile body in a second firing; these were used to make complex geometric patterns.

A studious approach to colour was taken by Owen Jones, an architect and designer who became one of the most influential of the period through his publications. In his encyclopedic *The Grammar of Ornament* (1856), Jones set out his theory of decoration, citing 37 'General Principles in the Arrangement of Form and Colour'. Principle number six asserts that: 'Beauty of form is produced by lines growing out one from the other in gradual undulations: there are no excrescences; nothing could be removed and leave the design equally good or better.'

This concept of beauty went right to the heart of what was wrong with mid-Victorian design, where a good deal could be removed without loss. The opinions of Jones and others who disliked current style led the revolt that stirred up radically new ideas about design in the late Victorian period.

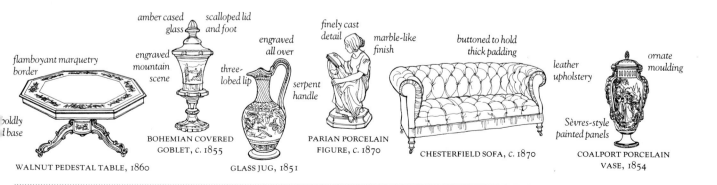

flamboyant marquetry border

boldly ...d base

WALNUT PEDESTAL TABLE, 1860

amber cased glass *scalloped lid and foot*

engraved mountain scene

BOHEMIAN COVERED GOBLET, C. 1855

engraved all over

three-lobed lip

serpent handle

GLASS JUG, 1851

finely cast detail

marble-like finish

PARIAN PORCELAIN FIGURE, C. 1870

buttoned to hold thick padding

leather upholstery

CHESTERFIELD SOFA, C. 1870

ornate moulding

Sèvres-style painted panels

COALPORT PORCELAIN VASE, 1854

DOMESTIC DRAMA *Victorian admiration for artists made many people create rooms to echo a casually furnished studio. Objects chosen for their striking effect and to declare the owner's aesthetic sense might include skins, rug-covered divans, exotic plants, antique chairs, ornaments and, here, a magnificent stuffed peacock.*

LATE VICTORIAN AND EDWARDIAN 1870-1914

The Style Rebellion

While Victorian householders were still revelling in the comforts and novelties that mass production offered, designers pined for the individual craftsmanship of earlier centuries. Oddly, their yearning for the past led to progressive styles that gave a foretaste of today.

OSILY CLUTTERED ROOMS with red flock wallpaper, heavy curtains and ample deep-buttoned seats draped with antimacassars were still at the height of their popularity during the 1870s. The love of curtaining had found yet another outlet in the massive *portières* that now hung at the large, open arch between two rooms. To the majority of Victorians, this was the kind of living

room to aspire to. The spoils of conspicuous consumption were laid out on tables, shelves and display cabinets to be admired by those who could find a path through the furniture. This required fine judgment from ladies dressed in the fashionable heavy bustles of the time. Added to the pottery figures, photographs, plants and products of homemade handcrafts, there would soon be numerous

souvenirs of the beloved Queen's golden jubilee in 1887 (and diamond jubilee mementos were to come in 1897).

But the trend-setters of the time were already declaring passionately their dislike of the ever-thickening clutter. Foremost among them was William Morris, undoubtedly the most influential designer of the late Victorian period. Son of a wealthy Essex businessman, he had the financial security to devote himself entirely to art and was at the centre of a like-minded group of friends.

Between them the group designed and decorated a home for Morris and his bride in 1859. The Red House at Bexleyheath in Kent was one of the era's most innovative houses, for Morris abhorred the mainstream style of the late Victorian middle classes.

His objections to it were not simply to do with the spurious ornament of manufactured goods but with their effect on society. Manufacturing techniques involved repetitive tasks in which the worker simply contributed one small part to the final product. This worker made no individual imprint on the finished article, and so could have little pride in it. Such industrial products, argued Morris, had neither soul nor beauty, and impoverished the lives of people who made them and lived among them. With a moral reformer's zeal, he was looking for a new style that would restore the maker's creative role and avoid the ugly drudgery of industry.

Like the earlier Victorian Gothic Revivalists, Morris looked to the Medieval style for inspiration – but not to preserve native design or to promote Christian architecture. For him, Medieval products had a simple beauty which came from the craftsman's fulfilment of his own ideas with his own hands. This belief was forcefully expressed by the art historian and critic John Ruskin, but it was William Morris who put the beliefs into practice.

MORRIS & COMPANY

Morris's guild of associates went on from the Red House to work together again. The group included the Pre-Raphaelite painters Dante Gabriel Rossetti, Ford Maddox Brown, and Edward Burne-Jones, and the architect and designer Philip Webb. The group designed and made furniture, stained glass, tapestries, wallpaper, paintings, ceramics and sculptures for the homes of individual customers, producing a range of elegantly simple pieces.

Morris was the group's leader, and was the moving spirit of the later Morris & Company (formed 1875). He mainly designed textiles and wallpapers with intricate, symmetrical floral patterns, but he also designed furniture, stained glass, metalwork, jewellery and carpets. He claimed there were two categories of furniture – 'workaday' and 'state'. Workaday items such as dining chairs and tables should simply serve their function, have a minimum of ornament, and openly show the marks of their making by hand. Rush-seated chairs and unpolished oak settles were of this type.

State furniture, on the other hand, he said, was to be elegant and elaborate, decorated

KEEPSAKES *The 78-year-old Queen Victoria was high in public affection by her diamond jubilee year, and souvenirs of the occasion were hoarded. Few people had the chance to go to the Lord Mayor of London's ball. Many more could have a photograph brooch with the Queen encircled by braid, ribbon and spangled lace.*

with carving, inlays or painting. Sideboards and cabinets accordingly had simple straight lines but incorporated sections painted in glowing, jewel-like Pre-Raphaelite style and incorporating flowers and gilding. The combination gave a refreshingly new look.

Morris rooms, in which nothing was left to chance, were dignified and rather sombre, with densely detailed wallpaper, painted panels and gilding, and bold features such as bare oak beams. The dado was usually set high, with the wall above intensely coloured, and topped by a strongly contrasting frieze.

MAKING A MODERN LOOK FROM OLD THEMES

Others whose admiration of the Medieval equalled Morris's included the architect and interior designer William Burges. He was not, however, inspired by the vision of social reform that drove Morris. Burges's chief work was the reconstruction, for the Marquess of Bute, of Cardiff Castle, where he cleverly wove Moorish elements into the Medieval.

Charles Eastlake echoed Gothic and Tudor styles more distantly in his designs. He concentrated on suiting his style to his materials and produced a range of ruggedly simple furniture. It was made from large panels of unpolished wood, jointed conspicuously with pegs and sparingly carved. Eastlake's *Hints on Household Taste in Furniture, Upholstery and other Details* (published 1868 and into its fourth edition by 1878), savaged the heavy naturalistic ornament and plumply stuffed furniture so beloved by his contemporaries. He promoted a more severe look – simply hung curtains, iron bedsteads and a box-like, Jacobean style of drop-end sofa called the Knole sofa, which has been a favourite in reproduction furniture ever since.

A far more distant source of style was Japan, now emerging from two centuries of self-imposed isolation. Enticing glimpses of this hidden world reached the West through the accounts of travellers, and through a growing flow of goods. These, traditional in their own design culture, had to European eyes a modern, free-flowing style that entranced the buying public (see box, p.66).

LOVE OF THE ARTISTIC LIFE

The late 19th century was a time when people were fascinated by the lives and lifestyles of artists. Many modelled their own homes on an artist's studio and the relaxed atmosphere of an artist's house with its comfortable chairs, collections of paintings and etchings hung in tiers from a picture rail or perhaps standing on an easel, a scattering of rugs and furs, potted plants and dried flowers, collections of interesting objects, including Oriental ceramics and furniture, and antiques.

A more contrived version of this came to be called the 'Aesthetic movement'. The Aesthetic room had a background of patterned wallpapers of the Morris kind and displayed a mass of items suggesting the owner's connoisseur tastes. Bold figurative wallpaper, or rows of ceramics, around the frieze of the room added to the rather restless impression.

Furniture for such rooms was broadly based on Morris and Eastlake designs, but tended to be given their design features simply for effect. Display cabinets would incorporate panels of tiles, and curtains would disguise the shelves. Comfortable upholstered seat furniture might be decorated with rows of turned balusters – often stained black – beneath the arms.

Robert Edis, who wrote *Decoration and Furniture of Town Houses* (1881), was an important influence in the Aesthetic style. The so-called progressive furniture designed by Edis and his imitators was generally advertised as 'Art furniture'. At first this meant handmade furniture but later manufacturers used it of any furniture, even if machine made, that was intended to appeal to buyers who claimed to have progressive tastes.

FOLLOWING THE CLASSICAL THREAD TO A DEAD END

Today the Aesthetic house seems unbearably fussy and claustrophobic. By comparison, even the plush, cluttered look of mainstream Victorian taste seems relatively calm. To the unstylish middle-class majority, progressive taste, as represented by Morris and the Aesthetes, smacked of reform and socialism, and they wanted to have (continued p.66)

FAIR AND SQUARE *Leading Arts and Crafts designer in ceramics was William de Morgan, a member of Morris's group from the 1860s. Tiles were one of his specialities and typically bore stylised but lush motifs of animals and plants.*

A PROGRESSIVE LATE VICTORIAN LIVING ROOM

BEAUTY WITH USEFULNESS was the aim of the Arts and Crafts movement's followers, and their homes made a striking contrast with the crowded rooms of the same time furnished in mainstream taste (see p.68). Although seen as progressive in its day, the Arts and Crafts style, developed largely by William Morris, showed a nostalgic yearning for the simple pre-industrial cottage. This living room combines dining and sitting room, echoing cottage life. Progressive people were furnishing their rooms like this as early as the 1870s but, as more designers worked in Arts and Crafts style, similar rooms were more common in the 1880s and 90s, and the momentum continued into Edwardian days.

The room, down one step and with a beamed ceiling, has as its focus the vast fireplace. The stained floorboards are softened with a rug at the hearth and saved from spartan severity by the warm colours of the hand-knotted carpet. An oak settle at the fireside, blocking draughts from the door, was a popular feature of Arts and Crafts and 'Queen Anne' (see p.66) living rooms. The furniture is in plain, upright style with a pleasing light, unfussy look. The dining table is handmade of oak. The flared, square shape of its feet is a typical feature, seen also at the top of the dresser, games table and armchair.

The handmade theme continues in the hammer marks left showing as a design feature on the metalware, including the long hinges on the dresser and overmantel cupboards.

A variety of rush-seated chairs were among the most popular Arts and Crafts designs. There is no plump upholstery. Serviceable leather is used on the armchair and thin pads on the dining chairs. At the small casement window there are thin, plain curtains.

Among the colourful highlights in the room are the striking pottery, the glass and silver cruet displayed on the sideboard along with the muffin dish, and a silver mustard pot set with amethysts. There is also glowing beaten copper – the jugs and wall mirror, the charger on the mantelshelf and the candle sconces beside the mantel. Candlelight was deemed appropriate lighting to eat by, although this room also has electric lighting.

Despite the pared-down simplicity (which entered the spirit of much 20th-century Modernist design), this room must have been a snug spot to spend a winter afternoon. Friends could sit near a blazing fire to play cards, and swiftly empty a dish of hot muffins.

1 Turned ash ladder-back chair with rush seat
2 Oak sideboard with brass-hinged cupboards
3 Electroplate muffin dish with hammered finish and mother-of-pearl lid finial
4 Oak settle with hinged seat and ebonised wood and pewter inlay
5 Oak mantel clock with pewter face
6 Two Eltonware slipware vases with lustre highlights, flanking a Minton ewer
7 Oak games table inlaid with copper motifs of the four suits of cards
8 Stained oak 'Thebes' stool with D-shaped seat
9 Brass-studded leather-upholstered oak chair
10 Oak extending dining table, and chairs with characteristic heart-shaped piercing

11 Ruskin flambé-glaze stoneware vase
12 Electric lamp with brass base and beaten copper shade
13 Floral-patterned Della Robbia pottery plaque

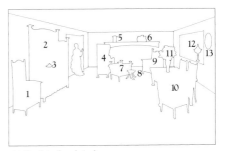

PERFECTLY SIMPLE *Clear handles and a crimped collar give an unusually restrained trim to this bowl in the cranberry glass so beloved by Victorians.*

nothing to do with it. If they wanted a new style, they could choose from many acceptable Classical revivals. Renaissance, various French Louis styles, Grecian and Empire all reappeared – as did a version of Adam style combined somewhat incongruously with Louis XV and Louis XVI.

Not all revivals were pastiche, however. Publications such as *Country Life* and *Architectural Review*, both founded in the 1890s, encouraged a greater respect and understanding for historical styles. Manufacturers made some high-quality responses to this interest. Royal Worcester, for example, produced beautiful urns and vases of Classical form. Minton executed Classical-style scenes precisely and laboriously in pâte-sur-pâte, painting layer upon layer of slip to give a cameo effect. The Stourbridge glass-makers also produced some exquisite Oriental and Classically inspired wares using techniques such as acid etching and cameo cutting.

PICTURESQUE BUT PROGRESSIVE SIMPLICITY

For all its popularity, mainstream taste was in a cul-de-sac, and it was through progressive taste that 20th-century styles were to develop.

It was William Morris's own Red House that anticipated a design of house that was to become popular in the 1880s. Its steep roof,

asymmetrical arrangement of windows, and warm red brick gave it the antique charm of a small 17th-century manor house. Architects of the 1880s, notably Norman Shaw, evolved from it the 'Queen Anne style' – a misnomer coined after Philip Webb designed such houses in Chelsea to fit in with surrounding Queen Anne architecture.

The picturesque, friendly style, a rejection of the Victorian, became the model for comparatively modest villas all over the country, especially in the new suburbs. The red-brick walls were dotted with varied white-painted windows – sashes, oriels and casements – and the steep roof was broken up by gables and dormer windows.

Inside, the house seemed to have been added onto over the centuries, with rooms of varying size, low ceilings, deep bays with window seats, inglenook fireplaces and other snug little corners, all combining to give a feeling of intimacy and relaxed comfort. The rooms were light and airy, with white or cream walls, or sometimes apple-greens and lemon-yellows, and plainly hung pale curtains. There was simple furniture of scrubbed oak, or old pieces with a comfortable used look, such as armchairs and sofas with fading upholstery.

A thriving antiques trade and reproduction industry developed around the Queen Anne style, and extended to reproduction furniture drawing upon Elizabethan, Queen Anne, Chippendale and Sheraton styles – and even to outright forgeries. Cretonne was the favourite upholstery and curtain material. This mixture of cotton and other fibres came into its own when cotton supplies faltered following the American Civil War (1861-5). Patterns printed onto its comparatively rough finish had the desired look of faded tapestry.

BIRTH OF ARTS AND CRAFTS

Furniture designers looking to supply this market found ways of adapting the simpler styles of William Morris and Charles Eastlake. C.F.A.Voysey was a leader in the field. He

Seeing the World with Different Eyes

WHEN JAPAN SENT AN EXHIBIT to the London International Exhibition of 1862, its display caused a sensation. Japan began to send a flood of goods westward and by 1870 the whole of Europe was gripped by a craze for japonaiserie, which did not begin to let go until the end of the century.

The American painter James Mac-Neill Whistler, who came to live in London in 1859, had been captivated by things Japanese while working in Paris and now fired London's artistic elite with his enthusiasm. He had his own house decorated in Japanese style – as did his neighbour Dante Gabriel Rossetti. Oscar Wilde was one of the many who followed their lead. Japanese prints and screens, fans and kimonos, bamboo furniture, pottery, carvings in ivory and weapons appeared in British homes. Many of the items were specially produced to fulfil European images of Japan and to display them, devotees had their rooms painted in a pale yellow, rose or grey, and hung with light curtains.

Thousands of elegant Japanese vases, such as this in cloisonné enamel, were bought.

Japanese design, immensely varied and free, represented a different way of seeing the world. It might be symmetrical and geometric, asymmetric and abstract, muted or strident, but it was almost invariably pleasing.

LATE VICTORIAN STYLE

Heavily ornamented furniture styles continued in numerous revivals, but new, more spare styles came in – some of nostalgic simplicity and handmade, others of remarkably modern lines. Art Nouveau was used mainly for small items, and there was a craze for all things Japanese. In glass, silver and ceramics, plain Arts and Crafts and sinuous Art Nouveau were the new looks.

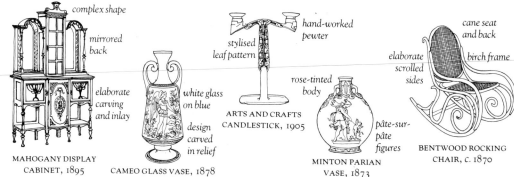

complex shape

mirrored back

elaborate carving and inlay

MAHOGANY DISPLAY CABINET, 1895

white glass on blue

design carved in relief

CAMEO GLASS VASE, 1878

stylised leaf pattern

hand-worked pewter

ARTS AND CRAFTS CANDLESTICK, 1905

rose-tinted body

pâte-sur-pâte figures

MINTON PARIAN VASE, 1873

cane seat and back

elaborate scrolled sides

birch frame

BENTWOOD ROCKING CHAIR, c. 1870

created a beautifully crafted, if austere, look that reduced ornament utterly, concentrated on pure function and emphasised strong horizontal lines. Ernest Gimson also produced cabinets with simple straight lines but decorated with skilfully crafted veneers.

Many other pieces of this type were produced by guild-like groups such as Morris advocated. Use and beauty were their themes. The term 'Arts and Crafts movement' was applied to the groups after the Arts and Crafts Exhibition Society was formed in 1888.

All the crafts, from pottery, metalwork and glass-making to jewellery and bookbinding, were influenced by the Arts and Crafts movement. It spread to the United States, where the furniture designer Gustav Stickley was a principal advocate of its style.

MARK OF THE CRAFTSMAN

The style was essentially nostalgic, much of its detail and ornament inspired by the Medieval – for example, the large metal hinges fitted on the outside of cabinet doors. The products looked handmade: wood was often left unpolished; beaten metal showed hammer marks; dowels were often left conspicuously visible. Glass was simply blown – cutting was disparaged as an industrial technique – so that the natural beauty of the material itself could be seen, unobscured by ornament.

Ceramics went through a particularly fruitful period as craftsman-based production allowed labour-intensive techniques such as applied relief decoration and experiments with glazes. Distinctive lustre-glazed earthenware, decorated with Renaissance or Persian motifs such as putti, scrolling foliage and ships, or with raised and intertwining floral patterns, was made by craftsmen such as William de Morgan in London and the Della Robbia Pottery in Birkenhead (founded 1894). Complex and colourful glazes were exploited in the mottled, spattered flambé wares for which the Ruskin Pottery in Birmingham (founded 1898) is noted. William

COUNTRY BEDROOM *A clean, spare look was given to this room at Standen, Sussex, a house designed in the 1890s by Philip Webb. The wallpaper, chair covers and curtains are typical Morris & Company designs.*

Moorcroft added his own particular style, decorating generously shaped vases with bold, loose designs based on mushrooms, poppies and trees set in landscapes. Some of these patterns remained popular into the 1930s.

The most distinctive metalwork of the period is decorated with repoussé work. Typical pieces bear stylised, spade-like flowers on long stalks. Silverwork came to life with novel designs, for example by Christopher Dresser. His books on the principles of design and his own designs for carpets, furniture, glass, ceramics and metalware showed that he understood that industrial methods could

work with, not against, good design. He was particularly attracted by the economy of line of Japanese design. In his own work, his silver (and electroplate) jugs and teapots, for example, were strikingly geometric and angular, anticipating Modernist work by 40 years.

From the various fresh approaches to design, two distinct tendencies emerged. The potential of free, swirling lines was exploited by the architect and designer Arthur Heygate Mackmurdo. Undulating, seaweed-like tendrils appear in the pierced chair splats and panels of his furniture. It was a development that would soon evolve into (*continued p. 70*)

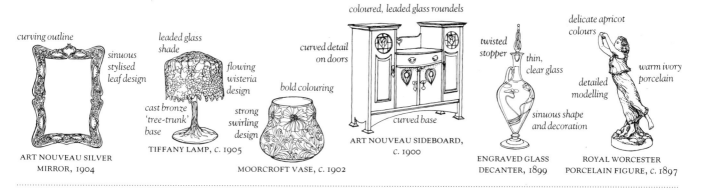

curving outline

sinuous stylised leaf design

ART NOUVEAU SILVER MIRROR, 1904

leaded glass shade

flowing wisteria design

cast bronze 'tree-trunk' base

strong swirling design

TIFFANY LAMP, C. 1905

bold colouring

MOORCROFT VASE, C. 1902

coloured, leaded glass roundels

curved detail on doors

curved base

ART NOUVEAU SIDEBOARD, C. 1900

twisted stopper

thin, clear glass

sinuous shape and decoration

ENGRAVED GLASS DECANTER, 1899

delicate apricot colours

warm ivory porcelain

detailed modelling

ROYAL WORCESTER PORCELAIN FIGURE, C. 1897

A TRADITIONAL LATE VICTORIAN SITTING ROOM

Few people in any era have the will or the means to refurnish their home in totally contemporary style. Most make do with hand-me-downs and inherited pieces, adding some special purchases which may be chosen to complement what is already there.

The distinctive flavour of this 1890s room is the result of long accumulation. Yet among its traditional furniture is a display cabinet in the style of the forward-looking designer Robert Edis, made in the 1880s and looking somewhat out of place here. This is a middle-class home – comfortable and manageable. A grander home would have separate rooms for different social and domestic functions but in this one the same room is used for writing letters, doing needlework, playing music and entertaining guests to afternoon tea.

UNLIMITED DELIGHTS

This home would have at least one servant, perhaps a general maid, to keep it dusted and in good order. And there is plenty to clean and polish and dust, for the room holds a welter of decorative objects on the walls and on every surface. The architectural white marble fireplace has an ornately carved cheval screen and a banner pole screen (both with Berlin woolwork panels) at hand for when the fire is lit, and its mantelshelf is crammed.

Pairs of vases flank the gilt, architectural bracket clock, and matched candelabra with gilt cherubs on Neoclassical pedestals stand at the ends, one almost concealing the pot of peacock feathers. All these are set on a fringed velvet mantel cloth which matches the fringed seat of the balloon-back chair and the braid-trimmed cloth on the heavy-based Jacobethan tea table. Leather-topped oak is used for the Gothic-influenced writing table but the round pedestal table is more elegant in walnut with a brass and cross-banded edge.

NEW GOODS FOR NEW MONEY

Comfort is the keynote of Victorian style. Industry and empire had created a well-off middle class with money to spare. They spent it on an unprecedented array of luxury goods. Using new techniques in printing, manufacturers created the much admired richly coloured wallpapers, while power looms permitted the mass production of patterned carpets, curtains and upholstery fabrics that in previous eras only the most well-to-do householders could have the chance of buying.

World trade brought new tropical woods to the furniture manufacturers, coveted ceramics from Japan, occasional furniture from North Africa, and exotic plants. Photography, widely available after 1860, had become a passion and family portrait photographs stand in silver frames on the writing table while others are displayed alongside the collection of painted portraits, silhouettes, still lifes and landscapes on the walls.

In the later part of the 19th century, a younger generation of designers such as William Morris and C.F.A. Voysey sent a fresh breeze rustling through the overstuffed muddle of the Victorian drawing room. Their progressive taste demanded more space and simplicity. But many people remained quite unmoved. Up and down the country, sitting rooms like this passed through the twilight years of the Victorian age in the dim glow of the oil lamp and overhead gasolier, and a few have survived to this day barely changed.

1 Chesterfield sofa draped with shawl
2 Screen with black japanned frame and panels painted in Japanese style
3 Giltwood and tapestry Rococo Revival chair and footstool decorated to match
4 Oak platform (fixed-base) rocking chair
5 Brass-inlaid wooden tea caddy and electro-plate silver teapot in Rococo style
6 Wax fruits under a glass dome
7 Ebonised Arts and Crafts movement display cabinet with inset tiles and painted panels
8 Majolica jardinière and stand
9 Oil lamp with base in Chinoiserie style
10 Tunbridge ware wood-mosaic trinket box
11 Enamelled glass posy vases
12 Prie-dieu chair with Berlin woolwork cover
13 Mahogany and velvet button-back chair
14 John Broadwood semi-grand piano
15 Painted papier-mâché spoonback chair
16 Mother-of-pearl inlaid N. African table
17 William IV balloon-back fringed chair
18 Papier-mâché writing case and leather-bound stationery box
19 Late Regency rosewood bergère chair
20 Walnut-veneered octagonal sewing table
21 Marble-topped giltwood console table

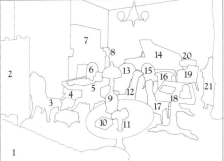

NEXT TO GODLINESS *Cleanliness was attained with pleasure in this Edwardian bathroom, well fitted with concealed lavatory cistern, bidet, and a bath whose shower has side as well as overhead sprays.*

Art Nouveau (see box, right). By contrast, the Glaswegian architect and designer Charles Rennie Mackintosh used angular, geometric forms in which function dominated. His furniture, with a strong vertical quality, was startlingly original. Mackintosh was also one of the first designers of stained glass to break free of ecclesiastical models.

Mackintosh's vision was admired in Europe more than in Britain, where more backward-looking Victorian tastes continued as the mainstream of the Edwardian age. And yet while people liked the nostalgic 'olde worlde' charm of their new Queen Anne style houses, they also wanted modern technology. Houses

DREAM SEMI *The picturesque appeal of a timbered gable, steep roof and tall chimneys drew businessmen to semidetached villas, out in the leafy suburbs yet with swift transport laid on.*

could have electric lighting from the 1890s, although usually they had gas lighting as well. When a piped pressurised water supply reached houses in towns during the 1870s, bathrooms became a must. Initially dressing rooms and minor bedrooms were sacrificed to take the bath, but new houses had purpose-built bathrooms. A washbasin was plumbed in and the great enamelled cast-iron bath with roll top and ball-and-claw feet was installed. Bath water was heated nearby in a gas geyser.

Piped water also put paid to the system of levers and valves by which the old water closets operated. While many poorer homes and rural houses still had an outside earth closet, the well-to-do in towns from about 1875 could have an efficient flush lavatory with an overhead cistern. Manufacturers developed elegant vitreous china lavatory pans, often patterned with blue-and-white transfers or with raised scrollwork.

ACCEPTING THE NEEDS OF THE TWENTIETH CENTURY

Ironically, the progressive styles of the late Victorian and Edwardian period were inspired by reaction against the progressive methods of industry. But industry's contributions were essential to the modern world. Before the end of Queen Victoria's reign in 1901 it was possible to telephone from London to Paris, to ride in an electric underground railway, to produce a letter on a typewriter and to take photographs with a Kodak camera. During Edward VII's reign (1901-10) Blériot crossed the channel in an aeroplane, and Ford produced the first popular motor car.

The Arts and Crafts and Aesthetic movements saw the drawbacks of industrialisation but failed to take account of its benefits. By the end of the century, however, it was clear even to craft-centred designers that the machine was here to stay, and that it was futile to ignore it. Whatever a craftsman came up with, manufacturers could copy for the mass market at a fraction of the price.

In the reconciliation between designers and the mass market a crucial role was played by high-street shops – above all Liberty's of London. As manager of the Oriental department of the London store Farmer & Rogers, Arthur Lasenby Liberty encouraged the firm to buy all the stock left from the Japanese exhibit at the 1862 International Exhibition. When Farmer & Rogers ceased trading in 1874, Liberty bought their Oriental stock and set up on his own in Regent Street. The shop succeeded with fashionable modern furniture and a range of popular textile prints.

Much of Liberty's stock was produced on a factory basis – for example the silver Cymric

ART NOUVEAU

Flowing Forms for the New Century

As DESIGNERS EXPERIMENTED with freer, more sinuous lines, a distinctive new style began to emerge during the 1890s. It used long flowing curves, twisting shapes and wavy, swirling decoration based on such natural subjects as trees, waterlilies and peacock tails. When a shop in Paris, *La Maison de l'Art Nouveau*, opened in 1895 to sell objects by new designers, the style became known as Art Nouveau. By the 1900 Paris Exhibition, Art Nouveau was all the rage; it remained popular across Europe for some 20 years.

Art Nouveau was eagerly adopted by architects, interior designers, potters, glass-makers, metalworkers, graphic designers and furniture-makers. Some of the most striking work was in jewellery design, especially by Lalique.

At its most intense, Art Nouveau had a restless, dizzying feel to it, and many designers in Britain and the USA considered it too overwhelming, but they used its motifs on smaller items. The interlacing floral designs typical of Art Nouveau style are most often seen on book covers, tankards and photograph frames, and also in the tiles and cast-iron surrounds of many a bedroom fireplace.

A table lamp by the Bohemian firm Loetz has an iridescent glass shade and milky glass insets in the gilt base.

ware and the pewter Tudric ware, both decorated with Arts and Crafts motifs and with traditional Celtic patterns adapted to Art Nouveau style by Archibald Knox. But Liberty also used factory methods to make furniture in cruder versions of Arts and Crafts and Art Nouveau styles.

Such work intensified the heated debate about appropriate ways of making designer objects. Designers would soon have to face up to worldwide industrial production and develop styles to work within it. But before it could address the issues, Europe had to endure a war that ended for ever the assumptions in which the Edwardian style of life was rooted.

HIGH IDEAL *A glossy, brittle jazz-age romance was played out on this set for the 1928 silent film 'Our Dancing Daughters', starring Joan Crawford as a flapper. It represents the high style of the time – shiny surfaces, simple furniture shapes and boldly geometric architectural features dramatised by oblique lighting.*

BETWEEN THE WARS 1914-1940

Seeing Beauty in Function and Geometry

The racy, geometric shapes and highly finished surfaces of Art Deco and the spare functionalism of the Modern movement were celebrated in high society and watered down for suburbia, where these styles were applied to three-piece suites and cocktail cabinets, electric fires and wireless sets, and front-room ornaments.

IN THE SHOCK WAVES that rippled through Europe from the First World War, no aspect of life was left unshaken – and this included the style of buildings, furnishings and fashions. Some people looked back nostalgically to Edwardian values and tastes, and for them the Arts and Crafts movement kept its appeal; but others still admired much older styles and revived the Neoclassical lines of late Georgian and Regency times.

Progressive designers, however, sought to wipe the slate clean. They wanted a new look to reflect the new world. The progressives developed two distinct strands, Art Deco and

the Modern movement, which were pursued particularly enthusiastically in France and Germany, and later in the United States.

British designers were left out. Only dress designers showed enthusiasm for radical change. Women's legs were in public view for the first time as 'flappers' took to shift-like knee-length dresses. Flat chests, dropped waistlines and hair styled into neat caps banished traditional signs of femininity, but shapely legs, hip-hugging waistlines and swaying fringes on dresses had a new allure.

By the 1930s, however, both Art Deco and Modernism began to influence style in

Britain, and not just among the smart set. Ordinary homes too had some Art Deco and Modernist objects because industry produced masses of them and shops promoted them.

PARIS DRAWS THE CROWDS WITH ART DECO

Modern design's first public impact was made by the *Exposition des Arts Décoratifs et Indus-triels Modernes*, held in Paris in 1925. Britain's mainly Arts-and-Crafts exhibit drew little interest. People had tired of the hand-crafted look and Medieval imitation. The hit of the show was France's exhibit (continued p. 74)

THE BAUHAUS
Pure Form Unsullied by Ornament

THE MODERN MOVEMENT found a powerful voice for its ideals in the Bauhaus design school founded in 1919 in Weimar, Germany, by Walter Gropius. His aim was to coordinate all training in art, architecture and design.

Bauhaus architecture used boxlike forms broken up by bold vertical or horizontal strips of metal-framed windows. Large windows gave wide views over the landscape, in keeping with the contemporary enthusiasm for sunlight, nature and outdoor activities. White was the preferred colour and ornament was regarded as almost a sin.

Traditional fittings such as skirting boards and picture rails were abandoned to leave walls smooth and blank. Doors were not panelled but faced entirely with sheets of painted plywood. Plain door handles were fitted instead of less efficient knobs. Built-in furniture such as cupboards, bookcases and kitchen cabinets helped to produce the desired impression of modernity and hygienic efficiency.

The Bauhaus attracted a lively – but quarrelsome – miscellany of talents, including Marcel Breuer, Mart Stam and Ludwig Mies van der Rohe. There was prolonged discussion and model-making to pare down designs before prototypes were made of everyday objects – coffee sets, light fixtures, curtain fabrics, for example – which industry could then produce en masse.

Of the few prototypes that progressed to production before the Nazis closed the Bauhaus in 1933, the tubular-steel-framed chairs, including Breuer's Wassily chair, are by far the best known. After 1933, many leading Bauhaus designers moved to the USA and remained influential in postwar style.

Despite its austere lines, the Wassily chair cradles the body comfortably.

A HIGH-FASHION BEDROOM

GLAMOUR WAS THE KEYNOTE of Art Deco, and it was the kind of glamour where money counted, not titled ancestry. It spoke of the social mobility that whisked away Edwardian Britain's stuffy rules. A potent symbol of the time was the transatlantic liner, where the wealthy international set danced, played and ate among glittering Art Deco design before retiring to opulent Art Deco bedrooms. Private bedrooms too evoked the world of liners, grand hotels and film sets. They were smart and luxurious, if a little impersonal.

The plinth for the beds and the striking bedheads indicate that this bedroom of the late 1920s has been designed with the same glamorous style in mind. The overall look is spacious with a soft glow from the frosted uplight and bedside lamps. The geometric pattern on the brocade chairs harmonises with the design on the thick bedside rugs, while the zebra skin adds drama.

DESIGNED FOR WOMEN

This is a shared room, but the woman's needs have come first. Her silk nightdress lies on the silver satin bedspread and a silk kimono is near the simple but bold lady's wardrobes that take up a considerable wall space. A gentleman's wardrobe is no doubt against another wall. The 1920s and 30s were a time for assertive women. More women played sports, drove cars, and had successful careers – among them designers such as Syrie Maugham, Betty Joel, Marion Dorn, Clarice Cliff and Susie Cooper.

The clothes of the day suited free, confident women. Paris couturiers such as Coco Chanel and Paul Poiret were quick to exploit fashion accessories such as their own perfumes in distinctive bottles. On the dressing table here there is a Chanel bottle that became a classic and another stylish black-dashed French bottle among a tray of others by René Lalique – although none of the master glassmaker's most expensive ones; the white-flowered red powder box too is by Lalique. Less well-known makers also produced many pretty containers for the eager market.

Both furnishings and clothes were easy for industry to adapt for the mass market, so that any girl sitting in her shiny rayon dressing-gown at a boldly geometric dressing table could wield her Bakelite hairbrush with its sunrise motif – and see reflected in her step-cornered mirror something of the glamour of a Hollywood star.

1 Frosted glass uplight in sunray shape
2 Macassar ebony wardrobe with walnut trim
3 Silvered bronze female archer on ebony base
4 Lamp with frosted glass shade
5 Rayed-panel bedheads in peach mirror glass
6 Bedside rug with bold geometric design
7 Lalique milky glass clock with frosted birds
8 Modern carved wooden-bead necklace and red Bakelite powder compact
9 Green Celluloid bowl for loose powder
10 Glass tray with scent bottles and powder box
11 Sunray motif blue enamel mirror and brushes
12 Coty powder box and Max Factor lipstick
13 Glass scent-spray with silk-covered bulb

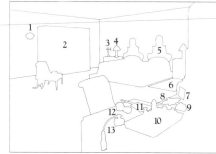

in the brash new *Style Moderne* – soon called Art Deco, from the title of the Exposition.

Designers had seen the folly of ignoring modern materials and machinery, for these offered the chance to express the carefree and racy fashionable mood. Society people were blotting out horrid memories of the war with a giddy round of parties, dances and cocktails, with the syncopated rhythms of jazz and of frantic new dances such as the Charleston. Art Deco – modern, glamorous and fun – provided a suitable backdrop for this life.

Art Deco, like Art Nouveau, centred on a bold, progressive style and aimed to give a visual surprise. But instead of the sinuous lines of Art Nouveau, Art Deco favoured flat surfaces and angular, geometric shapes. It was closely related to the fragmented, multi-faceted view of Cubism and Futurism then dominating art. There is also an echo of Aztec style in Art Deco's stepped and sunray motifs – as seen in jewellery, clocks and door frames.

A fascination with speed, movement and mechanics shows in Art Deco's treatment of the human form, for example in the angular profile of a face with streaming hair raked back with machine-like precision. The wild splashes of colour in Art Deco – vermilion, emerald-green, cornflower-blue and a vivid orange called tango – can be traced to the exotic costumes designed by Léon Bakst for Diaghilev's ballets staged in prewar Paris.

STILL NOT MODERN ENOUGH

There were plenty of critics of Art Deco who protested that it continued to look back to old, if exotic, styles. Apart from Aztec inspiration, there was a flavour of things Egyptian in the use of motifs such as papyrus leaves and eagle's wings after the tomb of Tutankhamun was found in 1922. There was even a hint of Classical, especially Biedermeier, elegance in the furniture of Jacques-Emile Ruhlmann.

Art Deco was also criticised for aiming at a narrow band of wealthy clients. Despite its claim of celebrating the machine age, many of its most famous products were made by craftsmen. Furniture by Louis Süe and André Mare, for example, was beautifully crafted in exotic woods such as amboyna and ebony, decorated with repoussé leatherwork and inlaid with ivory, mother-of-pearl and sharkskin. The outstanding silversmith of the era, the Frenchman Jean Puiforcat, produced cube-shaped tea sets with glass handles, pieces that were simple and innovative, but certainly not factory made.

Some critics complained about Art Deco's hint of decadence, found in the figures of scantily clad, athletic young women in provocative poses. Exquisite Art Deco figures were made in gilt bronze, or in chryselephantine (a combination of bronze and ivory), by such skilful modellers as Dimitri Chiparus, Ferdinand Preiss and Bruno Zach; many cheaper figures were made in spelter.

THE MODERN MOVEMENT STRIPS OFF FRIVOLITY

Art Deco had a frivolity that was at odds with serious social attitudes. A greater concern for the needs of industrial society drove some designers to seek a truly new international style. They developed a severe look, pared of ornament, which became known as the Modern movement or Modernism.

Function was its main criterion. What does a cupboard look like if it is designed simply as

FACTORY FASHION *Chairs, laundry baskets and other pieces woven by Lloyd Loom in paper-covered wire had echoes of the pared-down Modernist look.*

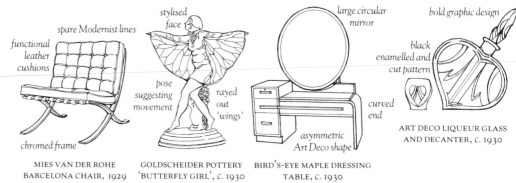

AID FOR MAIDS *Kitchen toil eased with mains water and gas, linoleum, and tiled walls, here in smart 1925 cream and green. But it was still a time for sweeping clean. Few homes heard the purr of the labour-saving vacuum cleaner.*

STYLE BETWEEN THE WARS

Revivals persisted in 1920s Britain but new looks took hold of smart society by the 30s. Shiny surfaces, geometric shapes, stepped and sunray motifs, lines suggesting swift movement, and vivid colours were used. Furniture, ceramics, glass and metalware took up the style. Designers in the Modern movement used new materials and factory methods for a severely functional style bare of ornament.

functional leather cushions

spare Modernist lines

chromed frame

MIES VAN DER ROHE
BARCELONA CHAIR, 1929

stylised face

pose suggesting movement

rayed out 'wings'

GOLDSCHEIDER POTTERY
'BUTTERFLY GIRL', c. 1930

large circular mirror

asymmetric Art Deco shape

curved end

BIRD'S-EYE MAPLE DRESSING
TABLE, c. 1930

bold graphic design

black enamelled and cut pattern

ART DECO LIQUEUR GLASS
AND DECANTER, c. 1930

an efficient unit to put things in? What does a chair look like if it is built simply to support the human form? Such questions produced a daringly fresh approach to architecture, furniture, lamps, glassware – to all fields of design.

Any material could be used if it was suitable to serve the function. The design potential of steel, laminated wood, plate glass, Bakelite plastic, and other industrial materials was explored. The Bauhaus designer Marcel Breuer produced the first chair made of tubular steel – his Wassily chair (see box, p. 72) – as early as 1925. Another Bauhaus designer, Ludwig Mies van der Rohe, made chairs exploiting the tensile strength of steel, notably his 'Barcelona Chair' (1929).

Many Modernist architects liked to carry their vision into the furniture and fittings for their buildings. A cold, austere result was all that some achieved; but others, notably the American Frank Lloyd Wright, composed shapes with a new geometric elegance that has been influential ever since.

Although the Modern movement claimed to design for the masses, like Art Deco it depended on a wealthy clientele, for many of its products were hand-finished and costly. Modernist rooms – simple, efficient and hygienic – were conceived as ideal for workers' families in apartment blocks. In practice they appealed only to a fashionable elite willing to take a stylistic leap. The rest of society clung doggedly to homely comfort.

MODERNISM MARRIES ART DECO

The fun-loving tone of the 1920s was already fizzling out before the economic depression and massive unemployment of the 1930s. The straitened circumstances favoured a sober tone in design yet the Modern movement, which seemed to suit such a mood, still held little appeal for the general public.

Art Deco, on the other hand, was too frivolous – but it adapted, swallowed some features of Modernism and became Modernist

Art Deco. This simpler and more geometric version lost the richly inlaid surfaces of the original and relied more on hard-edged shiny effects from chrome, plate glass and mirrors.

Manufacturers played a key role in this development. Art Deco was a style that lent itself to industrial methods at lower costs. And designers were looking to industry as an employer now that the flow of private commissions for individual pieces of furniture, jewellery and metalwork had ended.

TRANSATLANTIC INGREDIENTS

The United States had a strong influence on international style by the 1930s, although it had not exhibited at the 1925 Exposition in Paris. Streamlining, developed in the United States, was a feature of 1930s Art Deco. Speed was still smart, and it was evoked in design by such devices as closely set, parallel, horizontal lines and fluid, rounded corners. Vacuum

cleaners, refrigerators and buildings were streamlined as readily as cars, trains and ships. The United States was also the source of another powerful modern symbol: the skyscraper. Its tapering, staged silhouette was used in decorations on buildings, lighting equipment and company badges.

In the United States itself, Modernist Art Deco flourished in lavish interiors for wealthy clients despite the Depression. Hollywood sets reflected the styles commissioned for real rooms and of course Hollywood films spread the vogue across the world.

The films of Fred Astaire and Ginger Rogers show rooms where Modernist severity is offset by deep upholstery on armchairs with rounded lines; by carefully planned lighting effects from globe-shaped milk-glass lamps and uplights on the walls; and by deep-pile, geometric-patterned rugs. Films of the thirties also show the wide-shouldered, tailored suits

SUPREME MODERNIST *Architect Serge Chermayeff designed his Sussex home in 1938. This restful room has a wooden wall, a glass wall facing the terrace, a plain floor and low, elegant furniture free of ornament.*

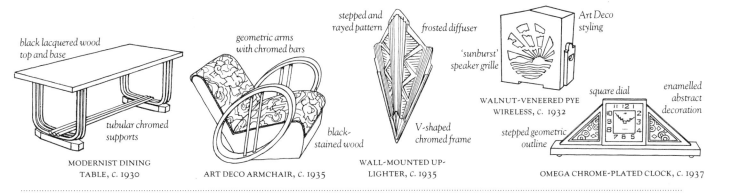

black lacquered wood top and base

tubular chromed supports

MODERNIST DINING TABLE, C. 1930

geometric arms with chromed bars

black-stained wood

ART DECO ARMCHAIR, C. 1935

stepped and rayed pattern

frosted diffuser

V-shaped chromed frame

WALL-MOUNTED UP-LIGHTER, C. 1935

'sunburst' speaker grille

Art Deco styling

WALNUT-VENEERED PYE WIRELESS, C. 1932

square dial

stepped geometric outline

enamelled abstract decoration

OMEGA CHROME-PLATED CLOCK, C. 1937

the women wore by day and their figure-skimming, bias-cut evening frocks held up by shoe-string straps. The men meanwhile wore easy-fitting, wide-cut suits.

SUBURBAN PEOPLE'S TASTE

The 1920s and 30s witnessed a massive boom in building and home ownership in Britain, mainly through the work of speculative builders who put up some four million homes on new estates around the cities and towns. Most builders tended to opt for safe revivalist styles (see p.66). Modernist buildings with their blank façades and metal-framed corner windows generally provoked public outcry.

The new generation of householders in their suburbs were able to make choices about decoration and furnishing that only a much narrower and wealthier band of citizens had previously had the luxury of making. Industry, waking up to the spending power of suburbia, created a vast range of furniture, crockery and tableware, paints, wallpapers and ornaments to fill the shelves of shops. Suburbia also offered a large market for those designers who could tap it successfully.

Many of the most collectable pieces from the period were produced on a factory basis. The ubiquitous Lloyd Loom products, for example, were factory made; they appealed to both popular and high-fashion tastes.

It was a similar story with pottery. Susie Cooper added bright, abstract designs to pottery made for her in the Staffordshire potteries. Clarice Cliff designed for the Newport Pottery Company series with such names as 'Bizarre' and 'Fantasque'; the pieces had bold and colourful hand-painted decoration but were none the less produced in bulk.

Through industrial design, therefore, Art Deco and some traces of the Modern movement reached the furnishings of a very broad band of homes in Britain, though often in a watered-down version. In their purer forms, however, especially in architecture, these international styles were not much liked, except possibly in a few extravagantly Art Deco cinemas – and time has not made the British public feel any fonder of them.

SIMPLE VIGOUR *Bold geometric and stylised motifs hand painted in vibrant colours give this vase the rather primitive appearance that is typical of Clarice Cliff's work.*

A SUBURBAN FRONT ROOM

BETWEEN THE WARS the Metropolitan Railway, whose line ran north-west out of London through Wembley, Pinner and Chorleywood to Amersham, created the concept of Metroland as an ideal place for city workers to live, outside the spread of London but conveniently linked to it by train. Given the vogue for fresh air and sunlight, outdoor sports and hiking, it was an inviting prospect which speculative builders helped to fulfil with a rash of tidy suburban homes in the revived 'Queen Anne' style (see p.66).

The house buyer had the choice of a miscellany of fixtures and fittings displayed in builders' catalogues. In this 1936 room, the picture rail could be from an Aesthetic house of the Late Victorian period, and the fireplace with its simple lines and stepped top pays lip-service to Art Deco and the Modern movement, as does the mirror above it. The sunray pattern in the stained glass of the bay window, and the Egyptian-influenced motif in the pelmet, are also inspired by Art Deco.

MASS-PRODUCED MEDLEY

Householders in Metroland bought factory-made furniture, ornaments and fittings from the major retail outlets, again in a hotchpotch of styles to suit their own tastes. Here the display cabinet has the spare, functional shape of Modernist furniture. It contains both sentimental Royal Doulton bone china figures and brightly coloured abstract Art Deco pottery by Susie Cooper. The factory-made flying ducks were extremely popular ornaments in the 1930s. They echo the Art Deco taste for representing movement, but loosely. The windowsill ornament too is an adaptation of the favourite Art Deco woman holding back a greyhound. The dancing figure is more authentically Art Deco; semi-nude females in athletic poses were typical subjects.

The brown and beige colour scheme, dowdy to modern eyes, was fashionable in the 1930s. The three-piece suite, with a solid but simple shape that seemed innovative at the time, has upholstery in a geometric pattern favoured by contemporary designers. Such comfortable and practical suites have held a place in the living room ever since.

Geometric patterns appear again in the carpet, which has linoleum around it. Fashionable designer-made rugs of the time were usually small and sat on stained or bare boards, wooden parquet or lino. The curtains

have a striking geometric pattern, but they are hung in the uncomplicated way made popular by the Arts and Crafts movement. Net curtains hang over the plain glass.

Electrical gadgets were taken for granted in 1930s suburbia. The wireless increased in popularity and was designed as a piece of furniture with a fashionably bold geometric shape. Electric light comes from the central pendant lamp and from the standard lamp with its tasselled parchment shade. The telephone, in Bakelite, is a Siemens Neophone No. 162 – the first successful model with a combined handset.

The style of this lounge – imitating, but missing, both the pure Art Deco and the pure Modernism of fashionable society – has a character that is quite its own. It makes a comfortable spot where family and friends can relax once their commuter train has brought them home from work in the city.

1 Chrome-topped ashtray stand
2 Susie Cooper teacup in 'Kestrel' pattern
3 Bronze-painted plaster figurine of woman
   with German Shepherd dog
4 Sunray-shape bowl in peach pressed glass
5 Doulton bone-china 'Umbrella Girl'
6 Walnut-veneered display cabinet
7 Step-cornered mirror on chain
8 Statuette of dancing girl, in spelter
9 Chrome companion set of fire irons
10 Free-standing electric fire
11 Set of pottery flying ducks
12 Ekco wireless in walnut-veneer case
13 Glass-topped walnut-veneer side table

THE POSTWAR YEARS
1940-1970

High Styles for Everyone

Unadorned simplicity still inspired serious designers but the ever-younger mass of consumers with the spending power imposed their own taste for ease and, above all, fun.

VICTORIOUS AND WEALTHY, the United States emerged from the Second World War in 1945 as the most powerful nation, and its influence spread quickly across much of the globe. The USA was the world leader in industrial technology, and was also the main maker of films, whose images of style and manners fed the dreams and aims of the Western world's cinema-going millions.

With industry in optimistic mood, US designers continued to explore new materials and production techniques. They were joined by several of the most original European designers, who had been driven from their homes by Fascism in the 1930s.

NEW SHAPES TO FIT THE BODY

The American furniture designer Charles Eames took a particular interest in chairs to fit the human body. His new concept in seating has simple, moulded plywood shells on steel-rod stands. More luxurious versions such as his 'Chair 670' have buttoned leather upholstery cradled in rosewood-veneered plywood on a base of cast aluminium. Experiments with form led Eames to his 'Lounging Shape' chair – a hollowed blob on a spindly base.

Like all Modernist designs, such chairs focused on function and shunned decoration,

FREEDOM OF FORM *Steel mesh and skins slung on tubular metal look spartan but are deftly shaped for comfort by Organic Modernist designers. Irregular tables and curvy blobs of sofas follow the organic theme.*

but they are more rounded than the severe early Modernist furniture. Because their shapes echoed those of waves, eggs, plants and other natural forms, their style was called 'Organic Modernism'. Its rounded lines were seen in a range of design fields from strikingly curvaceous buildings to free-form glassware.

Eames worked with a number of like-minded designers including Finnish-born Eero Saarinen and German immigrant Hans Knoll and his Swiss-born wife Florence. The Knolls went on to found an international furniture manufacturing company which in 1950 produced Harry Bertoia's startlingly

ECONOMY SUITE *Scarcity of labour and materials led to wartime controls on making furniture. Serviceable, no-frills 'Utility' goods were the result.*

novel 'Chickenwire' chair, a diamond-shaped moulded shell of coated steel mesh resting on a spindly frame. In 1957 the Knolls manufactured Saarinen's 'Tulip' chair, whose white, bucket-like, glass-fibre seat rises from an aluminium stalk with a flared circular base.

Mass production ensured that such pieces had a much wider influence than previous Modernist furniture. They also had a clean-cut, efficient look which made them popular for offices and public buildings – and the style is still recognisable in today's office furniture.

While progressive designers pursued functionalism, American industry pursued a mass market that was eager to spend and more interested in fun than form. The age of consumerism had arrived, fostered by advertising, particularly through television. The

consumers relished a postwar style that was all their own, owing little to elitist imports of the past. The style often focused on novelty – as in the lavish Wurlitzer jukeboxes and the fanciful tail-fins of outsize automobiles.

During the 1950s, manufacturers, retailers and advertisers recognised a huge new consumer group – teenagers, whose easy-going culture embraced rock-and-roll music and simple, workaday clothing. Their blue jeans, T-shirts, and big 'sloppy joe' jumpers were to become a fashionable style that has long been an acceptable classless uniform.

THE FESTIVAL OF BRITAIN

Meanwhile Europe had to tackle wartime damage while stricken by postwar poverty. Britain was grimly determined to 'win the peace' in the face of continued rationing and the need to rehouse some 200,000 people. 'Utility' production of necessities, with controlled use of materials, had begun in 1941 and still continued. Utility furniture, made from 1943, was basic and well designed with an Arts and Crafts air, but for the public it was an unloved reminder of wartime austerity.

One bright point in these years was the six-month Festival of Britain, held beside the Thames in 1951, 100 years after the Great Exhibition (see p.56). The Royal Festival Hall is a survivor of the exhibition's concrete, glass and steel buildings. Seen by some 8 million people, the exhibition's modern designs had a wide impact on style.

The bead-and-rod models of molecular structure in the 'Dome of Discovery' inspired the steel-rod base and ball feet of chairs and coffee-tables. The image was popularised into the 'cocktail-cherry' style of black plastic-coated rods tipped with bright plastic beads,

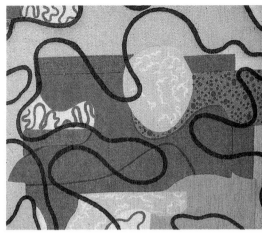

ABSTRACT PRINTS *Many 1950s fabrics bore irregular motifs connected by spidery black lines. Muddy greens, mustards and dusky reds abounded.*

used for magazine and record racks, rows of coat hooks and wall decorations.

The Festival's show buildings were decorated with flat panels of faded red, pastel blue and milky green, all further muted by the presence of black. These colours appeared together in abstract shapes on textiles and singly, overlaid with small, black markings, in curtains, upholstery and Formica panels. The same colours are found in pottery, for example in Poole pottery designed by A.B. Rhead.

EUROPE'S NEW LOOK

When austerity eased in Britain and manufacturing picked up in the mid-1950s, the American influence was strong. Furniture designers adapted the ideas of Charles Eames and others for the mass market, and also wedded metals, plastics and laminated woods to familiar shapes. Ernest Race, for instance, used bent steel and moulded plywood to echo Queen Anne winged chairs. Such designs, although modern, had not the dramatic impact of Chickenwire and Tulip chairs.

More progressive ideas came from Italy, where designers worked not for the mass market but for a wealthy, pace-setting clientele. Designers such as Carlo Mollino created tables, chairs and lamps with smooth, sculptural silhouettes. The delicately poised lamps have become classics of modern design.

The Scandinavian style of furnishing (see box, p.80), considered avant-garde at the beginning of the 1950s, had by the end of

SELF-HELP *When the austerity years ended, home improvement boomed and the DIY culture began. Buyers were assailed by advertisements for home appliances and furnishings, offers of easy terms and detailed advice on every task from bricklaying to paperhanging.*

SCANDINAVIAN DESIGN
Warm Wood and Oatmeal Tweed

A DISTINCTIVE, MORE FRIENDLY strand contributed to the 1920s and 30s style by Scandinavian designers contrasted with the highly functional work of other Modernists, and really caught on in the 1950s and 60s through designers such as Alvar Aalto, Arne Jacobsen and Tapio Wirkkala. Rooms across Europe were given curved beechwood or oiled teak furniture, shelving and light fittings, and textured fabrics in neutral colours such as oatmeal.

These furnishings were set in a background of box-like neatness – polished, narrow tongue-and-groove flooring, white walls and picture windows; the overall effect was of clean-cut efficiency. Decoration was spare, but softened by warm-toned wood, woollen rugs on the floor, and tweedy or pliant leather upholstery. Glassware was plain and heavy-based, sometimes coloured a smoky grey or green, and unadorned cutlery and serving dishes were made in stainless steel, which in many households took on the role at the table previously played by silver.

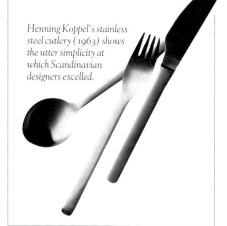

Henning Koppel's stainless steel cutlery (1963) shows the utter simplicity at which Scandinavian designers excelled.

them been merged with some US features to make the mainstream 'Contemporary' style.

In clothes, Paris had the strongest say. After wearing the fabric-saving skimpy skirts and mannish tops of the war years, women revelled in Christian Dior's 1947 New Look. Full, flaring skirts, hemlines at the calf, softly draped bodices and rounded shoulderlines reached every small town. Men too wore a fuller cut of suit with double-breasted jackets.

BRITAIN SWINGS AHEAD

In the mass market London led by the 1960s. Newspaper colour supplements, introduced in 1962, helped to spread awareness of contemporary design. 'Swinging Sixties' people – whose taste in clothes included shift dresses, miniskirts and flared trousers – admired furnishings with a compact look spiced with novelty. British manufacturers were generally keen to explore plastics, glass fibre, fibreboard, PVC, smoked glass and spun aluminium. Robin Day's moulded polypropylene stacking chair on a steel-rod base was first seen in 1963 and still has not dated.

While the first ventures into space triggered by-products of bizarre futuristic design – in clothing, furniture and toys – there was a contrary interest in traditional skills. Studio pottery gained in status as Bernard Leach, Lucie Rie and others made pottery into an art form. Studio glass-makers benefited from 1960s research which devised new formulas for glass with lower melting temperatures. This enabled small studios to operate their own furnaces. Glass-makers created sculptural pieces with flowing forms that showed off the beauty of the glass itself.

CONSUMERISM VERSUS FLOWER POWER

A close link grew between design and the art world. Pop Art, entwined with consumerism, touched clothing, furniture, posters and the sleeves of records with its brash colours and forms. Consumer-objects became fit subjects

BRASH NOVELTY *Bold images created dazzling 1960s fabrics. Easy informality was dictated by the wicker chair – which made sprawling unavoidable.*

for art, as in Andy Warhol's soup-tin paintings – which as prints and posters themselves became popular consumer objects.

Mass production created, and to a degree depended on, obsolescence – a short life for goods creating a need for more. Designers in all fields, in furniture, clothes, tableware as well as industrial goods, experimented with disposable goods, such as furniture made of corrugated cardboard or cheap plywood, giant beanbag seats and inflatable plastic chairs.

Modernism failed to win over the public as far as buildings were concerned. Grand urban redevelopments, with tower blocks, multistorey car parks and flyovers, were not comfortable to live in or among. Thoroughgoing Modernism was being spurned in all design fields by the late 1960s. Indeed, the views of experts and authorities generally were being spurned, especially by young people.

Gentler ways and less conformist lifestyles appealed to the 'hippies' and 'flower people' anxious for an 'alternative society'. Some

POSTWAR STYLE

Mass production and consumer spending power spread a rapid succession of international styles. Functionalism persisted but was rounder. Plywoods, plastics, metals and man-made fabrics were used more and young buyers opted for eye-catching novelty and fun. But there were countercurrents: potters and glass-makers created handmade pieces and spriggy Victorian country styles were revived.

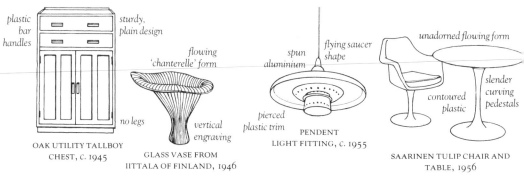

plastic bar handles

sturdy, plain design

OAK UTILITY TALLBOY CHEST, c. 1945

flowing 'chanterelle' form

no legs

vertical engraving

GLASS VASE FROM IITTALA OF FINLAND, 1946

spun aluminium

flying saucer shape

pierced plastic trim

PENDENT LIGHT FITTING, c. 1955

unadorned flowing form

contoured plastic

slender curving pedestals

SAARINEN TULIP CHAIR AND TABLE, 1956

sought a more human scale of values in the unmodernised regions of India, Africa and South America. One result of this was a vogue for ethnic clothing, ornaments, hand-woven rugs, big floor cushions and wall-hangings. Others took a rosy backward look at rural life in Britain and chose a Victorian country style in clothes and furnishings. Yet others tried to express the drug culture of the late 1960s in frantic 'psychedelic' designs that often used Day-Glo luminescent colours.

HIGH STREET STYLE

As in all periods, many people in the 1950s and 60s remained largely unaffected by fashion's whims. In their homes the well-to-do tried to combine historic styles with modern comfort and convenience. Interest grew in genuine antiques and in furnishing old houses in historically appropriate styles. Country-house style was especially popular and was applied even to small urban homes – through wallpapers and fabrics, for example.

In the high street the wilder manifestations of 1960s design were squeezed out towards the end of the decade by a greater appreciation of good industrial design and of high quality. Inventiveness alone was no longer enough. As more and more people sought well-made goods, high-street retail chains proved powerful channels for mainstream taste.

Some of the chains were long established: Waring and Gillow had originated in an 18th-century Lancaster firm of cabinet-makers, and Marks & Spencer had been founded in 1903, for example. One of the most influential retail chains in the postwar period has been a newcomer, Habitat, founded by the designer Terence Conran in 1964 to bring 'good taste' to a mass market.

Habitat's success has lain in a careful selection of good modern industrial design, more homely, craft-based goods and a sprinkling of self-assembly furniture for young home-makers. Modernist furniture, stainless steel cutlery, 'high-tech' lighting and plastic

WITHOUT WALLS *Central heating and double glazing made the 1960s open-plan house feasible. Unbroken areas of tweedy carpet, plenty of golden-brown wood and shelf-unit dividers were all part of the smart look.*

furnishings and fittings, well-designed and in bold primary colours, are offered alongside more traditional enamelled cast-iron cooking utensils, Indian scatter rugs, hand-made glassware and terracotta pots.

Another chain that has satisfied a broad-based but identifiable band of customers is Laura Ashley. It played a large part in the 1970s revival of Victorian and Edwardian country styles in flower-sprigged, subtly-coloured clothing, furnishings and wallpaper.

TOMORROW'S ANTIQUES

A curious mixture of styles has existed in every era; only with hindsight can the style that gives an era its distinctive tone be detected. It is too early to say what will encapsulate the flavour of the 1970s and 80s, but it is clear that greater manufacturing output and greater purchasing power for most people have generated more objects for collecting. Furthermore, the time lag before any new object becomes collectable is shortening: articles

from the 1940s and 50s, and even some from the 60s, are already collectable.

Beautiful objects made by skilled craftsmen will always be cherished, but these may be joined by industrial products such as hair-dryers, calculators and compact-disc players. Any object, no matter how humble, may one day be prized if it embodies the spirit of its time or fits a very particular slot in the story of style.

DESIRABLE MODERNISM *Gleaming US kitchens with sleek, built-in units and bulky 'iceboxes' were the envy of 1950s Britain – and copied by the 60s.*

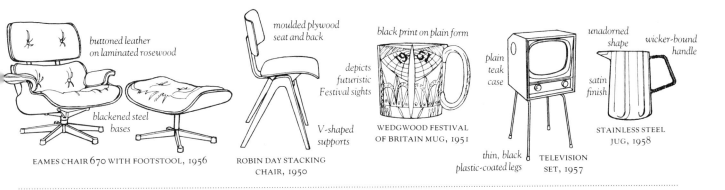

buttoned leather on laminated rosewood

blackened steel bases

EAMES CHAIR 670 WITH FOOTSTOOL, 1956

moulded plywood seat and back

depicts futuristic Festival sights

V-shaped supports

ROBIN DAY STACKING CHAIR, 1950

black print on plain form

WEDGWOOD FESTIVAL OF BRITAIN MUG, 1951

plain teak case

thin, black plastic-coated legs

TELEVISION SET, 1957

unadorned shape

wicker-bound handle

satin finish

STAINLESS STEEL JUG, 1958

A POSTWAR BEDSIT

YOUNG PEOPLE in the 1950s and 60s were generally more mobile and independent than any earlier generation, often leaving home in their teens to go to university, to start work or to train. Increasing numbers of them were benefiting from grants for education and changed attitudes towards careers.

These young people wanted cheap accommodation – preferably free of the restrictions in lodgings ruled by a resident landlady. At the same time many city homes originally built for extended Victorian families and their servants were sold off as they proved too big and too expensive to run. Divided and fitted out as self-contained units, they made bed-sitting rooms or 'bedsits' to rent out, each one serving as bedroom, living room and kitchen.

Bedsits needed space-saving innovations in furniture. Here a divan doubles as sofa and single bed; the desk has drawers only at one end so they can be wide enough to serve as a chest of drawers; a wall-hung shelf-unit saves floor space; and over the end of the kitchen worktop are shelves that act as a larder.

EASY-CARE EFFICIENCY

This room is furnished in the comfortable 'Contemporary' style of the late 1950s. The decor is simple and rather stark, with wipe-clean emulsioned walls to tone with the one feature wall hung with a washable paper. There is no picture rail. The curtains are hung in the simplest style and backed by a venetian blind, considered to give a look of office-like efficiency. Although used since Victorian times, venetian blinds now had washable painted aluminium slats instead of wooden ones. The reeded hardboard pelmet is simple, and inexpensive to fit and maintain.

Austerity is softened by the comfortable and welcoming furniture. The fashionably unmatched chairs have shapes that hint at traditional wing chairs, but with foam filling, soft tweedy upholstery, moulded laminated beechwood frames and the splayed tapering legs common at the time. The natural colours of the wood, and the emphasis on strong horizontal lines in the furniture and shelving, are in keeping with the 'Contemporary' style.

The magazine rack and the wall-clock show the continuing popularity of 'cocktail-cherry' design, based on models of molecular structure, and a common design feature after the Festival of Britain in 1951. There is a similar spindly look in the steel-rod base of the desk

chair and the coffee table. The chair has a one-piece laminated wood shell fixed to the separate base, a concept used much more after the development of plastic shells in the 1960s.

Coffee tables suited the informal style of bedsit living. They also helped to bring down the eye-level in the room. A low eye-level was part of a general trend during the postwar decades, leading eventually to floor seating on cushions and giant beanbags in the late 1960s. The record player on tapering beech-wood legs stands in a prominent position beside the armchair, as befits its major role as entertainer in bedsit life.

The streamlined kettle and toaster, and the metal desk lamp, perhaps house-warming presents, indicate up-to-the-minute taste, which is confirmed by the porcelain coffee pot by Rosenthal, a German company noted for factory-produced goods commissioned from distinguished designer-artists. Another sign of modern taste is an English copy of the 'handkerchief' vase by the Italian glass-maker Venini. It stands on the windowsill along with two typical pieces of smooth, heavy-based Swedish glass. Above the desk there is a Poole pottery vase of the kind designed by A.B. Rhead. It may be more commonplace than the handkerchief vase, but its spindly-line decoration and quiet colours were much more typical of contemporary popular taste.

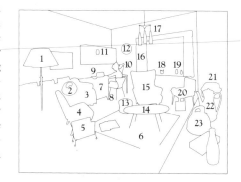

1 Plastic and brass lamp with heavy card shade
2 Melon-shaped wicker basket
3 Divan with candlewick cover
4 Chair with splayed legs and woollen-covered
   foam rubber upholstery
5 Magazine rack in 'cocktail-cherry' style
6 Fringed woollen rug with abstract design
7 Beech-veneered desk on metal frame
8 Laminated wood chair on spindly metal base
9 Transistor radio and Finnish glass ashtray
10 Anodised metal desklamp with flexible stem
11 Poole pottery vase
12 'Atom' clock based on molecular models

13 Vinyl-covered pouffe
14 Melamine coffee table on spindly metal legs
15 Wing-back armchair with laminated beech
   frame and bouclé cover
16 Neat geometric-print cotton curtains
17 Teak pendant light with milky glass shades
18 Copy of Venini handkerchief vase
19 Finnish glass vase and pear paperweight
20 Portable record player with leather-cloth
   covering and screw-in legs
21 Streamlined chrome-finished toaster
22 Hessian-pattern coffee pot of waisted form
23 Steel whistling kettle with Bakelite handle

Collector's Guide

A world of antiques and collectables,
ranging from medieval oak stools to 20th-century
enamelled advertising signs, and everything else in
between: how to identify and date them, how to spot
forgeries and copies – and what they may
fetch at auction

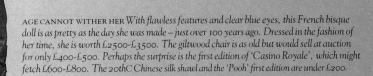

AGE CANNOT WITHER HER *With flawless features and clear blue eyes, this French bisque doll is as pretty as the day she was made – just over 100 years ago. Dressed in the fashion of her time, she is worth £2500-£3500. The giltwood chair is as old but would sell at auction for only £400-£500. Perhaps the surprise is the first edition of 'Casino Royale', which might fetch £600-£800. The 20thC Chinese silk shawl and the 'Pooh' first edition are under £200.*

A QUESTION OF VALUE

THROUGHOUT THE COLLECTOR'S GUIDE, prices or values of items are frequently mentioned. These generally represent what our experts estimate the object illustrated – or class of objects described – would fetch at a London auction at the time of going to press. They are usually given as a range rather than a single price, and refer to the 'hammer' price, without the buyer's premium being added or expenses such as the seller's commission deducted (see pp. 421 and 423). So buyers should expect to pay somewhat more and sellers to pocket somewhat less.

Like all estimates, they are subject to variation. Presale publicity or two or more people keenly bidding for a lot may force the price up, while lack of interest may keep it down. London auctions tend to give more predictable results, because they are usually well attended by knowledgeable trade and private buyers; in the provinces prices often show more variation, both down and up.

Most prices can be expected to go up over time, but movements in particular categories of antique cannot be predicted accurately. A certain style or period may move in or out of fashion; or one type of object – whether walnut bureaux, Chinese blue and white porcelain or golfing memorabilia – may arouse abnormal demand or disdain in buyers.

If you buy from an antique dealer, you may pay more or less than you would for the same piece at auction. But, on average, dealers' prices tend to be roughly 1 ½ to 2 ½ times auction prices – perhaps less in times of recession, more when demand is high. A notable exception is jewellery, for which four or even five times the auction price is not uncommon. Jewellers point out that they must offer a wide range of high-value stock.

When you insure an item, cover it for the replacement value – what you would have to pay to replace it with an identical piece. Since you could not be sure of finding a replacement at auction, you should insure for the full dealer's price – or at least double the auction estimate, and more for jewellery. If in doubt, get an expert valuation; see also page 423.

Some items fall outside the usual scope of auctions. For cheap collectables (priced at a few pounds or less), estimates have been based on going rates at specialised collectors' fairs or 'swap meets'. At the other end of the scale are a few extremely rare items; these are labelled 'museum piece' and the actual price they fetched at auction is given.

Furniture

Marquetry on Napoleon III secrétaire à abattant; c.1860

Collecting furniture

Antique furniture is to be used and enjoyed as well as admired. Generations of owners leave their mark, adding to the character of pieces great and small.

ONE OF THE JOYS of antique furniture, as with all practical antiques, is that it is a tangible link with the past. Sitting at an 18th-century desk, it is easy to imagine an earlier owner leaning on the same surface, struggling with an important letter. An ink stain or a well-rubbed drawer edge adds to this sense of continuity.

The way antique furniture carries the mantle of age is one of its most appealing characteristics. While porcelain and glass are little altered over the centuries, a piece of furniture changes in subtle ways. Its timbers gradually shrink and mellow through handling, polishing and exposure. This slow maturing gives it a unique patina that cannot be matched – or reproduced – by the finest new pieces.

Fashion in furniture tends to follow price rather than vice-versa. When early Georgian furniture became too expensive for the ordinary buyer, people began to look seriously at late Georgian and Regency pieces. As these too began to get out of reach, Victorian furniture found favour. Such a price spiral helps to broaden taste and open people's eyes to good design and craftsmanship, of whatever period.

Prices – and investment potential – are always affected by the amount of restoration a piece has seen. A big anxiety for buyers is how much damage or restoration is acceptable. Broadly speaking, the rarer the piece, the less the effect of minor damage or restoration. The value of a £20,000 dining table will not be much affected by a small candle burn, for example, while a table that cost £500 might lose much more in proportion – just because many unmarked pieces of the same standard exist. Genuine old domestic furniture always shows the wear and tear of age, and it is quite likely to have been mended or renovated at some time. True restoration should be unobtrusive but not pretend to be something it is not; it is a fine line. Replacing a chair leg and colouring it to match the other three is quite different from converting a wardrobe into a bookcase, for example.

Alterations enter the realm of faking in the case of a 'marriage' – where two separate pieces of furniture have been combined to make, say, a table (with a different top and base) – or where a piece has been cut about to alter its proportions. Arm yourself with a mental checklist before buying, to help authenticate a piece. Is the timber correct for the period? Does the form of the piece jell with its purpose and with the fashions of the day when it was supposedly made? Look at it carefully, both close up and from a distance, where proportion becomes more apparent.

Nothing can replace the knowledge and feel that comes from years of studying antique furniture, but a reputable dealer who belongs to a recognised trade body should advise you honestly and stand by his word – though you may well pay more than the auction price. What really matters is the enjoyment you derive from the piece – how happily you can live with it. But nothing is forever; no true collector will hesitate to sell an item so as to buy something better.

Understanding furniture

Furniture-makers have always followed the demands of their customers in terms of fashion and function, but the materials and techniques they used can help to reveal whether a piece is a genuine period item or a later copy.

THE DESIGN of a piece of furniture is influenced mainly by fashion and purpose, but also by the timber and other materials used in it, and by the tools and techniques available when it was made.

Identifying the wood can often give a first clue as to date. Although local joiners always made full use of native timbers such as ash, beech, elm, yew and fruitwoods (apple, pear, cherry and so on) for everyday furniture, finer items tended to be made of certain woods at certain times. Most surviving furniture of the 16th and much of the 17th centuries, for instance, is made of oak, and this 'Age of Oak'

was followed by ages of walnut, mahogany and then of satinwood (along with other exotic timbers such as rosewood).

You can therefore assume that an English satinwood table cannot predate 1760 because the wood was not in general use until after that. So versatile was mahogany that it never went out of use after the 1720s, but in the late 18th century it was overshadowed for the finest furniture by satinwood. On the other hand, a walnut table purporting to date from the mid-17th century must either be a top-quality piece (because only the wealthy could then have afforded walnut) or a later copy.

CUTTING AND JOINING *Modern machinery may have ousted the two-man saw, but many 18thC cabinet-making techniques are still used today.*

Oak and country furniture

English oak was in plentiful supply when the demand for home furnishings began to grow in the 16th and 17th centuries. This hard and durable wood was not easy to work finely with the tools of the time, and was mostly made into heavy, solid furniture. The logs were usually cut or split vertically into quarters and then each quarter riven radially – like ever-thinner, elongated slices of cake. Straight-sawn planks would tend to warp across the grain. This quartering process also produced a better grain pattern, or figure, than straight cutting. Adze marks are often seen on early oak furniture, where the wedge-shaped planks were roughly hewn with a trimming tool.

Boarded construction – planks, sometimes slotted together, then simply joined with iron nails or wooden dowels – was common in the Middle Ages for items such as trestle tables, chests and stools. The 16th-century frame-and-panel construction was both lighter and more versatile. The corner pieces were joined by mortise-and-tenon joints, without glue; the tenon was secured by a peg or dowel made of split willow. In cupboards and chests particularly, the panels may be coffered (thinner than the framework) or fielded (as thick or thicker but with chamfered edges) and set into rebates (grooves) in the frame.

Rounded parts, such as bedposts and chair legs, were shaped with a pole-lathe, whose shaft was turned by a treadle and wound back by a springy pole. By using a lathe with a sliding rest for the cutting tool, the 'barley-sugar twist' legs for tables and chairs that came into fashion about 1660 could be made.

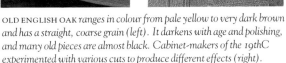

OLD ENGLISH OAK *ranges in colour from pale yellow to very dark brown and has a straight, coarse grain (left). It darkens with age and polishing, and many old pieces are almost black. Cabinet-makers of the 19thC experimented with various cuts to produce different effects (right).*

FRUITWOOD *It may be impossible to distinguish individual fruitwoods. This c.1740 games table is a typically unsophisticated country piece without elaborate decoration.*

FRAMES AND PANELS *This cradle has carved panels set into rebates in the framework. The surrounding wood will have shrunk with age across the grain, so the dowels securing the mortise-and-tenon joints should protrude very slightly.*

NAILED CONSTRUCTION *This chest is held together by handmade iron nails. Such early pieces often still show the marks made by the adze used in hewing the planks to shape.*

TURNED LEGS *A foot-operated lathe could produce complex turnings such as this barley-sugar twist form. The bulbous legs seen on Elizabethan refectory tables were made by 'cheeking' – gluing 'thicknessing' pieces onto the sides of the leg before it was turned.*

DECORATIVE EFFECTS

After painting in the Tudor period, the main method of decoration on early oak and other solid timbers was various types of relief carving, sometimes heightened with basic colours. Some fine carving was done from the 16th century onwards, including the cut-out, interlacing patterns of strapwork, and linenfold, which resembles flat folds of cloth.

Scratch carving was incised on the surface with a gouge, while fluted vertical lines, made with the curved edge of a gouging tool, are known as gouge carving. In sunk carving the background was removed to leave a relief pattern and then stippled with a punch or pointed tool. Chip carving – in which the design was chipped out with a chisel – often

forms a roundel enclosing a geometric pattern drawn with compasses and set square.

The fretsaw, introduced in the late 16th century, enabled slivers of wood to be intricately shaped and sunk in grooves and recesses in solid timber. This inlay was laid in patterns or strips with other materials such as bone or mother-of-pearl. Holly, boiled to preserve its whiteness or stained to various colours, poplar (white with a pink or brown tint) or box (yellow) could be contrasted with red-brown yew, stained sycamore, black ebony or bog oak. Inlaid decoration was popular for the borders of cabinets and tables in the 16th and 17th centuries, and was revived by the Arts and Crafts movement.

INLAID BORDER *A channel was cut into the wood surface with a gouge or chisel, then small slivers of a different-coloured wood were fitted in to form a pattern on this oak chest, which is also carved.*

EARLY CARVED OAK *This Elizabethan four-poster bed displays a wealth of decorative carving, including strapwork and foliage on the frieze and a carved figure.*

Walnut and other fine timbers

Until the second half of the 17th century, solid-walnut furniture was the province only of the very rich. But by the 1670s it had become the fashionable timber for much high-quality furniture. A growing demand for a wider range of furniture – especially cabinet or case furniture of various kinds – coincided with the revival of veneering techniques in the Netherlands and the recognition of the attractive grain patterns of walnut as suitable for veneers (see right). From the 1660s, oak was relegated more and more to provincial and country furniture until the great revivals of the 19th century.

The light golden-brown European walnut, mainly from France, was Britain's most common veneer timber from the 1680s, until widespread storm damage in France in 1709 was followed by an embargo on exports in 1720 and a shortage even of stocks being seasoned from about 1730. By then the

purplish American black walnut and reddish, mahogany-like Virginian walnut ('red walnut') were being imported, and all along some English walnut had been used. But the new fashion was to be for mahogany.

Walnut's close grain meant that it could be more finely cut, carved, turned and polished than oak, and this led to a host of innovative construction and decorative techniques in the late 17th and early 18th centuries. The elegantly curving cabriole leg became fashionable, and joints could be cut far more precisely, so the stretchers used to give chair legs rigidity could be dispensed with (although many chairs of this period do have them). Dovetail joints had been used in fine oak furniture since the mid-17th century, but now they really came into their own (see opposite). And screws were first introduced in about 1720.

WALNUT CHAIR LEG *First widely used in the late 17thC, walnut polished to a rich golden-brown that has faded attractively over the centuries. It could be carved crisply, and its advent coincided with the fashion for cabriole legs.*

BURR WALNUT *Cut from burrs (irregularities in the growth of the wood), burr walnut was a prized veneer for early case furniture such as this bureau. The numerous knots create a complex curly pattern.*

MAHOGANY

Fable has it that trading ships returning from the West Indies used mahogany as a ballast cargo, and cabinet-makers soon found that it was ideal for solid and veneered furniture alike. It proved strong and durable, polished to a deep reddish-brown and could be carved with minute detail. It came from huge trees, and wide planks could be cut which would not shrink or warp to any great degree.

The first mahogany reached Britain from Jamaica early in the 18th century, but soon so-called Spanish mahogany was arriving from Cuba and other Spanish Caribbean colonies. Later in the century much Honduras mahogany – lighter in weight and colour, and

CARVED MAHOGANY *Even more than walnut, close-grained mahogany could be crisply carved with superb decoration, as on the knee of this Chippendale chair from the wood's peak period.*

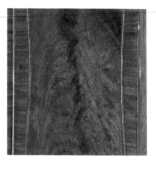

FLAME MAHOGANY *Some pieces showed rich reddish streaks, as on the door panel of this mid-18thC clothes press. Wood with such markings was aptly called flame mahogany.*

more open in grain – was imported and used for middle-quality furniture. In the 19th century came the much lighter and paler, only distantly related, African mahogany.

Mahogany furniture was a British speciality by the mid-18th century, its heyday being the period 1740-80. It reached France with the turn of the century Empire style, and then caught on in the rest of Europe.

BIG TREE *Mahogany, whether Spanish or (as here) Honduras, could be cut in planks wide enough to make complete leaves for a dining table.*

SATINWOOD AND OTHER TIMBERS

Mahogany continued to be widely used, but it was not long before a whole host of other exotic tropical woods began to rival it as a veneer. First, from the West Indies and in complete colour contrast to mahogany, came golden-yellow satinwood, the foremost timber for high-quality furniture from the 1780s. It was an ideal 'canvas' for painted decoration, for which there was a vogue at the end of the 18th century – the Sheraton period. A paler yellow variety came from the East Indies after 1800, then others.

Rosewood, a dark timber with red-brown streaks, was named for its rose-like fragrance when cut. It was used mainly for contrasting small panels and decorative banding from the late 18th century, and rarely, until the early 19th, to veneer the main body of a piece. Other streaky timbers used for contrast were kingwood (pale and dark golden-brown, sometimes with purplish tones), tulipwood (deep red and yellowish, fading to resemble rosewood), coromandel (black and yellow) and zebra wood (a pronounced dark brown and light yellow). The late 18th and early 19th centuries were the great era of decorative timbers, which also included the curly-grained amboyna (light brown), bird's-eye maple (very pale) and thuya (darker), and the plain but richly coloured ebony (black) and harewood (silver-grey).

PAINTED SATINWOOD *The even grain and pale yellowish colour made satinwood ideal for painted decoration, as on this top of a c.1790 side table in the manner of leading cabinet-maker George Seddon.*

CALAMANDER *Striking, streaky calamander wood was often used in the Regency period for prominent pieces such as this sofa table, c.1810.*

MULTITUDE OF TIMBERS *This Victorian specimen table from Ceylon (Sri Lanka), c.1840, incorporates a number of exotic timbers inlaid into ebony.*

ROSEWOOD *Much used for inlaid details, rosewood also appeared as an overall veneer and later in the solid. If protected by polish it fades attractively, but if the polish is stripped the wood is liable to turn black.*

HAREWOOD *The silvery-grey of harewood resulted from treating sycamore or maple with iron oxide.*

Veneered furniture

Walnut and other close-grained timbers could be cut into thin slices of richly figured wood that could then be glued onto a carcass made of cheaper timber. There was far less wastage, and the softwood used in Britain to make the carcass was far easier to work than the more decorative hardwoods. The new skills were the province of the cabinet-maker.

THE CARCASS AND DRAWERS

Oak was favoured for carcass work on the Continent, but British cabinet-makers preferred the softer Baltic pine. Particularly smooth, close-fitting joints were required

DOVETAIL JOINT *Through dovetails (right) are made with interlocking wedge-shaped teeth that remain visible when the joint is assembled (below right).*

STOPPED DOVETAIL *Here the dovetails are not cut right through the thickness of one of the panels (above left). The resulting joint (left) is neater.*

where two panels met at right angles, since any movement would crack the veneer. The dovetail joint, with fan-shaped interlocking projections (see previous page), was ideal – particularly in the lapped or stopped form, which concealed the dovetails.

Dovetail joints were also used to make drawers. Early drawers have one or two large dovetails at each corner, sometimes reinforced with a nail, but by the late 18th century there were four or more neater dovetails to a side (see pp. 130-1). Machine-cut dovetails came in the 19th century. Veneered drawer fronts were almost always pine, but the sides (or linings) on better pieces were of oak. An oak strip might be added along the top front edge to improve the appearance of an open drawer. The drawers on oak furniture of the 17th century were hung on grooves midway up the drawer depth. Once veneering became common, the drawer sides were made thinner and simply slid over the dustboard beneath. From the early 18th century a pair of bottom runners was usual.

The finish on the interior and back of the carcass was often quite rough. On early furniture designed to stand against a wall the back boards were invariably fixed with uneven, hand-forged clout nails. Carcass wood should match – any abrupt change of thickness or colour may betray alterations. But hidden parts will tend to be paler.

BOMBÉ COMMODE *The curved front of fashionable late 17th and early 18th-century bow, serpentine and bombé pieces, such as this Louis XV kingwood commode, was usually built up with blocks of wood fitted together like courses of bricks, then veneered.*

VENEERS

Until the early 19th century, veneers were cut with a multi-blade, two-man handsaw, and after planing were at least one-sixteenth of an inch (1.6 mm) thick. The introduction of the circular saw about 1830 made possible veneers about half as thick, and from the end of the 19th century they were sliced even thinner with a machine-operated blade, producing a noticeably smoother surface.

The sheets of veneer used for any one piece of furniture usually came from the same log, so that the colour and grain patterns would match. Depending on the angle of cut and the part of the log, the pattern varied from a straight grain – often used on the sides or less noticeable parts – to the strongly figured cuts (produced by crosscuts and especially by knots, burrs and forks) reserved for the showpiece top and front surfaces.

The more elaborate decorative veneering effects included pieces paired like a butterfly's wings, or cut in quarters or reversed to give an even more striking effect. Oyster veneer, popular around the end of the 17th century, was cut straight or diagonally across the grain of small branches, particularly of laburnum, to produce whorls with a central 'eye', like the shell of an oyster. The diagonal cuts created oval slices, the straight cuts roundels.

Various methods were used to enhance further the appearance of veneered furniture, the simplest of which was stringing. This consisted of strips of a contrasting timber, often pale boxwood or black ebony, cut about ⅛ in (3 mm) wide and set into the veneer a short distance in from the edges of the top, of drawer fronts and so on. Or wider strips of wood known as banding were often used, the grain of which formed a contrast with the main veneer; depending on the direction of the grain, it is described as straight, cross or herringbone (feather or chevron) banding.

BUTTERFLY VENEER *By arranging two adjacent slices of veneer like the wings of a butterfly or the pages of a book, an arresting mirror-image effect was created, as on this French kingwood secrétaire à abattant, c.1880.*

QUARTERED VENEER *By slicing veneers from a log previously cut in quarters, and then arranging adjacent slices like a fan, the cabinet-maker could create a fourfold symmetrical effect, as on this 18thC Louis XVI secretaire.*

OYSTER VENEERING *This William and Mary chest of drawers, c.1690, is a good example of oyster veneering using laburnum cut from branches of varying thickness.*

STRINGING *Narrow lines of veneer cut from boxwood or a dark timber such as ebony – or from another material altogether, such as brass, ivory or mother-of-pearl – were used as an edging contrast and for general decoration.*

CURL OR FAN VENEER *The veneer in the centre of this drawer from a c.1725 walnut tallboy was cut from the fork of the trunk and a branch of the tree, giving the interesting spreading pattern.*

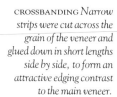

CROSSBANDING *Narrow strips were cut across the grain of the veneer and glued down in short lengths side by side, to form an attractive edging contrast to the main veneer.*

HERRINGBONE BANDING *Also known as feather or chevron banding, this was made from diagonally cut strips paired to create a small-scale version of butterfly veneering.*

PARQUETRY AND MARQUETRY

The most complex forms of veneering are parquetry and marquetry, both of which use veneer to decorate large areas. In parquetry the veneers form a geometric or symmetrical pattern, whereas marquetry is freer in form.

Marquetry was brought to Britain by Dutch craftsmen in the 1690s. Sheets of the various coloured veneers would be temporarily glued and clamped together between rough timbers and the pattern cut right through with a very fine-toothed saw. When the sheets were separated, the different colours could be fitted together like a jigsaw puzzle and glued down.

There were two main styles: floral marquetry used a great variety of woods to create leaf scrolls, vines, flowers and sometimes birds, while seaweed or arabesque marquetry depended on just two colours laid with great skill in symmetrical scrolls. Marquetry fell from favour during the Queen Anne period, but was revived in the second half of the 18th century and again in the mid-19th – when it was produced by machine.

A similar form of decoration using brass and tortoiseshell rather than contrasting woods appeared in the late 17th century. Boulle (or buhl) work, named after André Boulle, failed to catch on in Britain then but was revived during the Regency period.

PARQUETRY *By laying diamonds of contrasting colour and grain in the manner of parquet flooring, the cabinet-maker could create a trompe l'oeil three-dimensional effect.*

VICTORIAN MARQUETRY *Now machines could cut the intricate patterns for decorative panels quickly and cheaply.*

FLORAL MARQUETRY *Panels of floral marquetry decorated countless pieces of 17th and 18thC furniture. This octagonal example is taken from a late 17thC Franco-Flemish cabinet.*

SEAWEED MARQUETRY *This inlaid panel from a William and Mary chest of drawers shows the swirling pattern in walnut contrasted with a lighter wood.*

LATE 18TH-CENTURY MARQUETRY *The top of this c.1775 card table (left) is decorated with a rococo shell motif, floral swags and arabesques.*

BOULLE WORK *Created in the same way as traditional marquetry, Boulle work used interlocking brass and tortoiseshell veneers, as on this Louis XIV bureau mazarin (right) of c.1700.*

The finish

A wood's colour varies with the type of wax, polish or other finish used on it, how much it has faded and the patina of age. Polishing was introduced after 1600 (earlier pieces were often painted) and solid or veneered timber would be treated with nut or linseed oil, which darkened it, or with a beeswax and turpentine paste, which did not. Mahogany's colour might be enhanced with brick dust.

From the late 17th century, most veneered furniture was varnished with an oil or spirit-based resin or lacquer varnish, while French polishing, which gave a glass-like surface, was introduced about 1820. Unfortunately, much early furniture has been stripped and French polished during the last 170 years, destroying the softer sheen of the original patina.

The hard gloss finish of Chinese lacquer (see p.401) had a great impact when lacquered chests and cupboards were imported in the late 17th century. European craftsmen copied the process with japanning, applying a shellac-based varnish in numerous thin coats, each of which was dried and polished before applying the next. Other finishes included staining (often on a fruitwood base) and gilding.

GILDING AND EBONISING *This crowned female mask is from the frame of a Regency mirror of c.1810. The carved face and wreath of leaves were stained to resemble ebony, while the rest was gilded. Before gilding, the wood was coated with gesso, a form of plaster which could be finely carved; it shows where the gilding on the frame has worn.*

JAPANNING *This early 19thC Pontypool side cabinet is decorated to imitate Chinese lacquer, and includes Chinese motifs and figures. Fine japanning dates back to the 17thC, and many 'Oriental' pieces were in fact japanned here.*

ORMOLU MOUNTS *This swagged decoration from a mid-18thC Chippendale urn-topped pedestal is made of ormolu, or gilt bronze. The mounts were cast and then mercury-gilded to give a brilliant, non-tarnishing pure gold finish.*

Stools

Probably the oldest type of seat furniture, stools have existed for thousands of years. Elegant late Victorian examples were inspired by finds in ancient Egyptian tombs.

MOST STOOLS have no back or arms, and seat just one person. There are stools for more than one – usually called forms or benches – and so-called backstools in which a leg is extended as a backrest or a separate backrest is added. But in general stools are the simplest of seats, and three-legged examples have been used in Britain for at least a thousand years. Indeed, their construction is so basic and unchanging that they can be very difficult to date.

EARLY TYPES

'Fald-stools' or folding stools of 'X' frame construction are shown in illuminated manuscripts from the mid-12th century. Later versions did not fold, but those made for the nobility often had a squab cushion of rich silk or damask with fine embroidery. The lower orders had to make do with bare wood.

By the mid-16th century, joiners were making robust stools from oak, elm, walnut or ash. Only stools from the latter years of the century survive in any numbers. Called 'joined' or 'joint' stools, they have turned legs held together below the seat by a deep apron

Gothic slab-ended oak stool; c.1480; 18 in (45.7 cm) high. The carving and piercing make this piece a rarity.
£3000-£5000
Victorian copy: £400-£500

Oak joint stool with ring-turned columnar legs; 17thC; 18 in (45.7 cm) wide. Signs of a genuine period example are pegs securing the joints that stand proud of the surface, due to greater shrinkage across the grain.
£1500-£2000

George II walnut stool; c.1750; 19½ in (49.5 cm) high. The graceful cabriole legs and ball-and-claw feet epitomise mid-18thC cabinet-making, but the modern upholstery does not show them at their best.
£1500-£2000

Pair of Victorian giltwood footstools in Louis XV style; c.1850; 12 in (30.5 cm) wide. The gilding is original but the upholstery modern.
Pair: £1000-£1500; single: £300-£400

FALLING BETWEEN TWO STOOLS *This detail from a Pieter Bruegel painting illustrates the proverb and also shows a pair of rustic three-legged stools; a leg of the stool on the right extends as a backrest.*

that is often decoratively carved. Normally stretchers are added for extra strength.

Because of their rarity, joint stools sell at auction for £1000-£8000 or even more, and inevitably there are forgeries. Sometimes old oak is used, making dating very difficult. The constructional details need examining to ensure a stool is not a marriage of old parts. 'Honest' copies made from old wood about 100 years ago sell for around £300.

UPHOLSTERED STOOLS

The stool with fixed padding rather than a squab cushion was introduced at Knole, in Kent, about 1610, but did not become common until the end of the 17th century. The use of walnut encouraged carvers to decorate all four sides of these pieces.

By about 1700, the introduction of the cabriole leg gave an elegant line. Cabinet-makers now had the skill to construct joints in the upper frame strong enough to do away with stretchers. Intimate double stools appeared, and by the 1760s these were made

William IV rectangular rosewood stool with lotus-carved legs; c.1830; 30 in (76 cm) wide. The bobbin-turned apron reflects a revival of interest in Jacobean style.
£1200-£1800

with upholstered scrolled sides – a design that later evolved into the window seat.

From the second half of the 18th century, stools followed the styles of the period, matching most designs of upright chair (see opposite). Although stools still remained popular as informal pieces, chairs now took pride of place in all but the meanest homes.

A good, generous stool will realise more than a 'mean' chair, especially a two-seater stool or one that can serve as a coffee or magazine table. In recent years, stools have gained in popularity. A good pair of Queen Anne stools can realise more than £20,000. Even a pair of copies from around 1910 can change hands for between £3000 and £4000.

Victorian parcel-gilt walnut music stool; c.1870; 18½ in (47 cm) high. The circular top swivels and rises on a metal thread. The style is a revival of the Louis XVI Neoclassical.
£200-£300

'Thebes' stool by Liberty & Co; c.1885; 15 in (38.1 cm) high. This rosewood, ebonised mahogany and ivory-inlaid stool copies an Egyptian original.
£2500-£3500; poor condition: £1200-£1800

It is also possible to find good copies of both 18th-century and Regency stools made during the late Victorian period. These can make acceptable substitutes, selling at auction for only about half the price of the originals.

VICTORIAN INNOVATION

The Victorians were stool enthusiasts and, apart from reviving earlier styles, introduced novelties such as footstools with built-in ceramic or pewter hot-water bottles. They also made box ottomans – updates of 17th-century designs but with lids that opened so the ottomans could be used for storage. Many Victorian stools were richly upholstered in embroidery, Berlin woolwork or beadwork.

The style revolution begun by the Aesthetic movement impinged on stools, however. One of the most famous examples is the 'Thebes' stool sold by the London firm of Liberty & Co from 1884. Inspired by archaeological discoveries, it used a square, ancient Egyptian design to bring new elegance to mankind's oldest form of seating.

Upright chairs

Dining and other upright chairs are among the most abundant of antiques and range in price from a few pounds to many thousands. Persistent hunting may enable you to assemble a set, one or two at a time, for a bargain price.

CHAIRS FOR HEIRS As Philip Hussey's painting of an Irish family makes plain, by the 1750s the upright side chair had already taken on the form we know today. It was usual to arrange the chairs along the walls rather than around a table.

AMONG CHAIRS with an upright back, comfort varies a good deal. Dining chairs generally have an upholstered or caned seat and a wooden back, and may have arms – in which case they are known as arm or elbow chairs, or carvers. Upright dining chairs without any arms are also known as side chairs because they were placed around the sides of the room when not in use. Virtually identical chairs were also used as occasional chairs in the drawing room.

Hall chairs were designed to range along the walls in the hallways of great houses and generally have a solid seat and rather narrow back, perhaps painted with the family crest. They are not usually very comfortable, or popular with collectors, and pairs can often be bought for under £500. Grand mid-Georgian examples and those with a decorative feature such as Regency sabre legs fetch more.

BUYING SETS OF CHAIRS

A chair's age is not necessarily an indication of its value. Style, shape and practicality, combined with quality of workmanship, determine a chair's price. No matter what the style, however, a fairly simple series of rules can be followed to value a set of chairs.

Most 18th and some 19th-century chairs were made in sets of 14 (twelve side chairs and two carvers), but these sets were often later split into two smaller groups, one consisting of six side chairs and two carvers, and the other of six side chairs. Of these, the 'six and two' combination is far more valuable: a good-quality set of six and two from around 1900 is likely to cost £4000 or more, whereas six equivalent side chairs might sell for only

Mahogany hall chair with inlaid armorial; c.1740. The waisted back and shaped supports (derived from 16thC Italian models) are typical in hall chairs of this date.
Pair: £1500-£2000

One of a pair of early Victorian mahogany hall chairs; c.1850. Such chairs are still fairly cheap today, despite their ornate carved decoration.
Pair: £300-£400

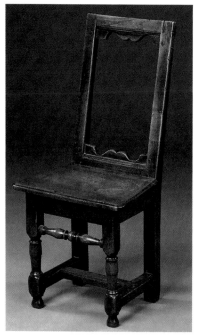

Oak backstool; c.1680. For reasons of comfort, collectors will pay more for examples with a deeper top rail or solid back.
£300-£500
Four: £1500-£2500

Queen Anne walnut side chair with seaweed marquetry on splat; early 18thC. The tall back influenced early 20thC designs.
Pair: £2000-£4000

George II mahogany dining chair with pierced vase splat; 1740-50. Though plain compared with later Chippendale-style chairs, a set of eight would fetch more than twice as much as this.
Six: £5000-£8000

Queen Anne walnut dining chair; early 18thC. Although this example is quite crudely carved, it is in a much sought-after form.
£3000-£5000

£1500. 'Long sets' of ten chairs or more are valuable and should always be sold as a whole.

A cheaper way of putting a dining set together is to buy pairs of chairs, each pair as similar as possible to the others. Pairs can be found for far less than the equivalent cost in a longer set. Hepplewhite-style chairs are often good candidates for collecting in this way, as they have been much copied and can regularly be found in pairs – or singly.

EARLY UPRIGHT CHAIRS

The forerunner of the upright dining chair was the 17th-century backstool, in which the back legs of a stool are extended up to form a backrest. A Cromwellian backstool – with a rectangular back and seat, in some cases upholstered in leather or woolwork – and the more elaborate Derbyshire backstool, whose back is pierced and arched, may fetch £1000 for a pair. Chairs from the later part of the 17th century have a taller

Derbyshire oak backstool; c.1680. This distinctive style of chair back has been much copied since the 19thC.
Set: £4000-£6000

back, sometimes with caned back and seat panels, and elaborate carved Baroque scrolls.

Curved-back chairs on elegant cabriole front legs and plain rear legs appeared during the reign of Queen Anne and show the influence of the current French Louis XIV style. They typically have a tall waisted back with a single vase-shaped splat (back piece) and a bowed seat with either an overstuffed or a drop-in padded seat. Although still continuous, the back legs and back are now quite distinct and for the first time cross-stretchers may be dispensed with. This form became the prototype for dining chairs for the next 200 years. Walnut examples are particularly popular today and well-carved pairs can cost £10,000. These chairs were widely copied in the 1920s and 30s, and a good reproduction set of eight can fetch £3000-£5000 today.

Early Georgian chairs dating from the 1720s to 1740s are often squatter and more substantial than Queen Anne pieces; the legs are sturdier and the splat may have simple piercing. Provincial sets (continued p.98)

CORNER CHAIRS
A Georgian Oddity

Early Georgian walnut corner chair; c.1730. This is a particularly fine example.
£4000-£6000

DESIGNED FOR THE CORNER of a room, corner chairs are built on the diagonal, with one leg at the front and back and one at each side. The top rail is usually a deep bar and the arms have broad, flattened ends. The most valuable examples are rare early Georgian pieces in walnut with a cabriole front leg. These can fetch as much as £6000. Mid-Georgian mahogany corner chairs are more plentiful, and sell for around £1000, while provincial versions in oak or elm can be found for under £500.

The style was revived by the Edwardians. Spindly plain or inlaid mahogany examples go for £400 or less.

Sets are of eight (two carvers and six side chairs) unless stated otherwise.

An Expert Examines

JOHN BLY MEETS 'A GRAND
OLD GEORGIAN GENTLEMAN'
OF A CHAIR

'THE STURDY, *no-nonsense look of this chair certainly suggests that it is Georgian, though it has to be remembered that this design was also a favourite with late Victorian furniture-makers. Fortunately, there are ways of telling if it was made around 1750, as it should have been, or if it's an 1895 copy.*

To set my mind at rest, I would first look at where the chair was handled most – like the top rail. You see, in the mid-18th century, they used to apply a grain filler made of red brick dust and wax, which gave a deep bronze hue. Here, where thousands of hands have grasped the rail, the bronze has rubbed and mellowed to a rich, shiny red. A similar patina can also be seen by the arm support.

The rich patina on the top rail

Now let's turn the chair up and look at that wonderful cabriole leg. A nice, full curve to the knee; a good, sturdy ankle. Later, in the 19th century, they tended to over-refine the ankle. Then there's that Oriental-inspired foot of a dragon's claw grasping the sacred pearl of wisdom. The English were besotted by Chinoiserie in the 18th century, and this was a favourite motif. It's also beautifully carved. Generally, the finer the ball, and the more talon-like the claw, the more desirable the piece of furniture.

The cabriole leg with ball-and-claw foot

Next, let's see the way the chair was made. Few 18th-century craftsmen, carving by hand, would bother too much about the bits that weren't normally seen. Even though the

front is handsomely carved, the back of this leg is fairly rough. Then too, at that time, when they made a seat like this, it was given strength by two little angle braces dropped in from the top – and there's one of them, with the single saw cut they always made for the rebate.

Saw marks and brace

Again, the back of the frame, which would seldom be seen by the chair's owner, is quite roughly finished. If you look closely, you can see some of the old hand-saw marks, and there are the heads of the hand-made clout nails that pin this moulding onto the frame.

Handmade clout nail

JOHN BLY SUMS UP

Style and craftsmanship both tell me that this chair is the real thing. During the first 70 years of the 18th century, furniture design was much influenced by the Baroque and Rococo movements. The back rail of this chair is Rococo in the way it curves out towards the wings. Earlier versions were much more curvilinear, so this chair has to be after 1735. On the other hand, that touch of flamboyance says it can't be later than the 1770s move to Classicism. All told, 1745-55 seems right. As for craftsmanship, it's all handmade in a chunky, positive way, that's the joy of it. The saw and adze marks underneath, those hefty nails, and the patina on the places where the chair has been handled for 200 years and more – no forger would imitate those things. So, being all of a piece genuine, I'd say the chair would fetch a good £5500 at auction.'

may be made of elm, walnut or a grainy mahogany. A good set of eight will fetch £8000-£12,000, although heavily restored or 'improved' sets start at £2000.

THE LEADING DESIGNERS

The shape of chairs from the mid-18th century was largely dominated by the work of Thomas Chippendale. Sets that are close to his original designs can change hands for six-figure sums, and even later copies sell well. For example, a set of eight late Victorian chairs in Chippendale's early loop-back design can fetch as much as £7000-£10,000. Most of his designs were more obviously Rococo in style, and 18th-century provincial examples of designs from his pattern book, *The Gentleman and Cabinet-Maker's Director* (1754), made in elm or oak, can sometimes be found for under £3000 a set. Well-carved Victorian copies of his most imitated style, which has an undulating top rail and a pierced, vase-shaped splat, now fetch up to £3000 a set.

Late 18th-century chairs generally show signs of the prevailing Neoclassical style which Robert Adam made popular. Chairs with these uncluttered lines have become synonymous with the name of designer George Hepplewhite. Instantly recognisable among such chairs is the shield-back variety, its pierced splat often carved with delicate husks, bellflowers or Prince of Wales feathers.

The quality of 18th-century chairs in Hepplewhite style varies enormously and prices range accordingly. A well-carved mahogany set of eight or more is rare, and could cost over £10,000, but humbler sets can be found for under £5000. Good late 19th-century sets fetch £2000-£3000 but early 20th-century reproductions fetch less. As this was such a widely imitated style, singles or pairs can quite easily be built up into a 'harlequin' set.

Lighter chairs in the Sheraton style also date from the end of the 18th century. They have a delicate, pierced trellis back and are carved and decoratively painted. Long sets of these are among the most sought after of all late Georgian chairs today, and a set of eight will fetch £10,000 or more.

REGENCY ONWARDS

More affordable for most collectors are plain, bar-backed chairs of the Regency period. Sets of six and two with turned legs can usually be found for upwards of £2000-£3000. Features

Mahogany carver; c.1890. This good Victorian chair closely follows a Georgian design.
Set: £7000-£10,000

Mahogany dining chair; 1750-60. This is a country-made chair with Chippendale-style Gothic details.
Six: £3000-£4000

Mahogany ribbon-back chair and carver; c.1885. These copy one of Chippendale's most complex Rococo forms.
Four and two: £6000-£8000

Mahogany carver; c.1780. The shield back is a favourite Hepplewhite form.
£1000-£1500
Set: £5000-£8000

Mahogany dining chair; c.1780. The restrained design, Neoclassical motifs on the splat and square legs are typical of Hepplewhite-style pieces.
Six: £3000-£5000

Mahogany carver; 1750-60. 18thC Chinoiserie chairs like this, with asymmetric lattice back and pagoda cresting, are rare.
£4000-£6000
Four and two: £20,000-plus

such as decorative carving, brass inlay or sabre legs will generally push the price up into the £3000-£5000 range. Particularly desirable are Greek Revival pieces based on designs by Thomas Hope, embellished with sabre legs and ebony inlay or applied gilt metal mounts; these can change hands at over £10,000 a set.

William IV dining chairs – with reeded or baluster-turned legs, often with lotus-leaf mouldings – can generally be found for £1500-£2000 for a set of eight, although sets well carved along the top rails and including carvers often exceed £2500.

Sets of Victorian chairs rarely include carvers and seldom consist of more than six pieces. Mid-Victorian balloon-back chairs

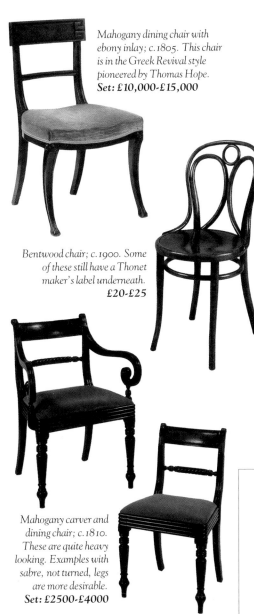

Mahogany dining chair with ebony inlay; c.1805. This chair is in the Greek Revival style pioneered by Thomas Hope.
Set: £10,000-£15,000

Bentwood chair; c.1900. Some of these still have a Thonet maker's label underneath.
£20-£25

Mahogany carver and dining chair; c.1810. These are quite heavy looking. Examples with sabre, not turned, legs are more desirable.
Set: £2500-£4000

Oak dining chair; 1876. This design by architect Norman Shaw combines an Arts and Crafts approach, seen in the turned legs, with a tall Queen Anne-inspired back.
Six: £2000-£3000

Mahogany balloon-back chair; c.1840. This is a typically sturdy early Victorian piece. Those with deep top rails fetch more.
Set: £1500-£2000

Bar-back rosewood dining chair; c.1830. The spindly form indicates that this chair is William IV or Victorian rather than Regency.
Set: £1500-£2500

are often pierced with delicate scroll-carved ornament. Although many were made in mahogany (as well as oak and beech), the best are usually in rosewood or finely figured burr walnut and can fetch more than £1000 for six.

Vast numbers of chairs imitating all styles since the 17th century have been produced in the past 150 years. These include designs inspired by the Aesthetic, Arts and Crafts and Art Deco movements, but among the most affordable and practical are bentwood chairs, developed in Germany and later Vienna from the 1840s by Michael Thonet. Made of steamed and bent birch, some 50 million of the standard, hooped-back Thonet chair were produced and they can still be picked up for around £20 each. Stylish Art Deco dining chairs with clean lines and striking veneers of bird's-eye maple and burr walnut are much collected, and sets of six can cost over £1000.

DINING CHAIR SETS
What Can You Get for Your Money?

SETS OF DINING CHAIRS are a staple commodity in the salerooms. So what can you expect for your money? Unless otherwise stated, sets are of eight chairs, including two carvers; long sets will be worth much more.

Up to £500
- Long set bentwood chairs
- Set poor 20thC Georgian-style chairs
- Six late-Victorian oak chairs, no carvers
- Six 20thC Regency-style chairs, no carvers

£500-£1000
- Set good early 20thC reproduction Regency-style chairs
- Set average early 20thC reproduction Hepplewhite-style shield-back chairs
- Set average Victorian/Edwardian reproduction 17thC chairs
- Six average Victorian balloon-back chairs, mahogany or beech, turned legs, no carvers

£1000-£2000
- Set good Victorian/Edwardian reproduction mid-18thC-style pierced vase splat or Hepplewhite-style shield-back chairs
- Six good Victorian balloon-back chairs, rosewood or walnut, cabriole legs, no carvers
- Six plain Regency bar-back chairs with turned legs, no carvers

£2000-£5000
- Six plainish 17thC chairs, possibly restored
- Set average Regency bar-backs, turned legs
- Six average or set poor 18thC Chippendale or Hepplewhite-style chairs
- Set good 19thC reproduction Chippendale or Hepplewhite-style chairs
- Set good 20thC reproduction Queen Anne walnut chairs

£5000-£10,000
- Set best late 19thC reproduction Chippendale-style ribbon or loop-back chairs
- Set good 18thC Chippendale interlaced vase splat or Hepplewhite shield-back chairs
- Set good Regency chairs, sabre legs or inlay
- Set 18thC Sheraton-style painted chairs
- Long set 'desirable' Victorian chairs such as Gothic Revival or ones made by Gillows

Over £10,000
- Set good mid-18thC Chippendale period ribbon or loop-back, or Chinoiserie chairs
- Set exceptional Queen Anne or early Georgian walnut chairs

Country chairs

Originally found in taverns, country kitchens, gardens and poorer homes, these basic but attractive chairs are now snapped up by collectors.

AMID FICKLE FASHIONS, country chairs remained largely unchanged for some 300 years. Best known and loved are hoop-backed Windsor chairs, which first emerged in the 18th century and were made in various regions. Other familiar styles include Mendlesham chairs, ladder-backs (or Lancashire chairs), stick-back chairs with a shaped top rail, and the equivalents on rockers.

Windsor chairs are very simple in construction. The legs (joined by stretchers) slot into an elm seat, and stick uprights (in ash, beech, yew or various fruitwoods) form the back – all joined without glue. There is often a pierced, vase-shaped splat, sometimes with a central star or wheel device, Prince of Wales plumes (especially on Regency examples) or a distinctive lobed surround (usually indicating a north of England origin). The top rail and arms are made of continuous hoops. Most single armchairs sell for £250-£500, or more if of rich colour or with original painted decoration. Examples in yew fetch far more.

Sets of Windsor chairs are rare, but spindle or ladder-back sets are not difficult to find. However, many are harlequin (mixed) sets, betrayed by slight differences in detail and colour. Individual chairs without arms can be picked up for under £100 and a good harlequin set of eight (including two carvers) for £1500-£2500. A genuine matching set, however, can fetch £4000-£5000.

Other 19th-century country-style chairs include captain's or smoker's chairs (also known as smoker's bows). These tub-shaped chairs with slatted or pierced uprights and a deep, bowed top rail make good desk chairs. They are usually made of mahogany, but some are of oak, beech or walnut, and usually sell for under £200.

Wavy ladder-back rocking chair; c.1800. The rush seat is in the familiar diagonal weave. Rockers are not so sought after and tend to fetch less.
£300-£500

Windsor armchair in yew; c.1750. This piece is of the type often called 'Strawberry Hill Gothic' after the house refurbished in Gothic Revival style for Horace Walpole.
£2000-£4000

Mendlesham armchair; c.1800. This chair has a ball-decorated top rail, and a good colour raises its price.
£600-£800

Smoker's bow armchair; mid-19thC. The elaborately turned bobbin uprights as well as the rich colour of this attractive piece increase its price considerably.
£300-£500

Open armchairs

Midway between the dining chair with arms and the comfortable easy chair are practical but elegant padded armchairs, best known as library chairs.

Oak 'wainscot' open armchair; c.1660. The distinctively carved back of this chair suggests a north-country origin. A lack of decorative cresting and slightly squat porportions limit its value.
£1000-£1500

Walnut armchair; c.1680. The exuberant carving shows continental influence but is typically Charles II.
£1000-£1500
Copy: £300-£500

Walnut open armchair with shepherd's-crook arms; c.1720. Although rather inelegant, this chair has an appealing colour.
£1500-£2500

Victorian walnut shepherd's-crook armchair; c.1880. This George I-style chair illustrates how convincing many Victorian reproductions are.
£2000-£3000
Early 18thC:
£8000-£12,000

Mahogany Gainsborough open armchair; c.1760. This early George III chair is well proportioned and quite plain, apart from the restrained foliate carving on the arm terminals.
£3000-£5000

THE DISTINCTION between the armchair and the upright, armless dining chair stems from the Middle Ages, when authority was symbolised by the lord's more elaborate, armed seat of office. But although most early armchairs are an extension of dining-room furniture, specialist armchairs first introduced in the early 18th century are distinctly different in form and use.

COLLECTABLE EARLY CHAIRS

The oldest British armchairs still in circulation date from the mid-17th century, and are sometimes called 'wainscot' chairs. These simple chairs are basically an extended back-stool with arms and a panelled back, and a broad, often tapering seat. The tapering seat is most pronounced in a narrow-backed version popular in the West Country and Scotland, which was based on French 16th-century *caqueteuse* (chattering) chairs. These are rare and can fetch £3000 or more.

The more conventional joined armchair of the mid-17th century is almost always made in oak and is sometimes carved with elaborate cresting. A well-carved original piece of good colour will usually fetch £2000-£4000.

Impressive, Baroque-influenced walnut or oak chairs from the late 17th century, with downswept scroll arms, often have also a carved back surrounded by stylised leaves. Individual examples sell for around £1000-£2000 while a pair can realise £3000-£5000.

GEORGIAN DISTINCTION

Queen Anne and early Georgian armchairs tend to be squatter, with a lower back and broader seat, than their dining-room counterparts. The 'shepherd's-crook' chair, so named because of its distinctively shaped arms, is a typical example. It is almost always veneered in walnut, with a solid, vase-shaped splat. The seat rail and perhaps the cabriole legs may have finely carved Rococo shells, and these chairs can exceed £20,000 at auction.

Variations include chairs with a fully upholstered back and seat. These and the shepherd's-crook versions were reproduced a great deal in the 1920s and 30s, and can fetch up to £1000-£2000. Examples that date from 1720-40 often have an eagle's head as the terminal to outscrolled arms. Many heavily carved Victorian 'Chippendale' dining-room armchairs reproduce this.

The typical mid-Georgian library armchair has a rectangular padded back, downswept arms with padded armrests, an upholstered seat and often an arched top rail. The quality and price of these 'Gainsborough' chairs – so called from their appearance in paintings by Thomas Gainsborough – vary enormously; the plainest sell for £1000-£2000, more decorative examples for £4000 or more.

Cabriole legs add a lot to the value, and a chair that also has its original needlework or tapestry upholstery can fetch as much as £10,000-£20,000. Pairs go for much more. Many fine Victorian copies were made, and a

English Neoclassical-style giltwood armchair; c.1770.
£2000-£4000

One of a pair of French Louis XV walnut open armchairs, or 'fauteuils à la reine'; c.1750;
£20,000-£40,000 the pair
19thC copies: £2000-£3000

Victorian gentlemen's open armchair; c.1860. A plainer piece would fetch a lower price.
£700-£1000

Louis XVI giltwood fauteuil; c.1770. The precise value of such Neoclassical chairs generally depends on the maker.
£3000-£5000

OPEN COMFORT *The open armchair became closely associated with the gentleman's library and the formal luxury of the salon.*

well-carved example may fetch over £2000.

Neoclassical armchairs, dating from the late 18th century, have an oval or cartouche-shaped padded back surrounded by mahogany or giltwood, and padded arms often with scroll terminals. A fine example will exceed £3000, but can fetch considerably more if attributed to an important maker such as John Linnell.

STYLE AND COMFORT

The library open armchair shows off distinctive features of Regency style. Designer Henry Holland's model – with an outswept back, scroll arms and stylish Grecian legs – was used in some of his most important commissions. A good period example with painted and parcel gilt decoration will generally fetch over £10,000, although modern copies occasionally appear on the market for far less.

Comfort became more important than style as the 19th century wore on, and later

Regency examples tend to be more tub-shaped, often with an upholstered top rail. Others are robust versions of the dining-room armchair, and fetch £1000-£2000.

Ladies' and gentlemen's armchairs of the Victorian era – often matching companions in two different sizes – made in walnut or rosewood have a waisted 'spoon' back with buttoned upholstery, scroll arms with padded crests and cabriole legs. Well-carved individual chairs can exceed £1000, although lesser examples can be picked up for £500-£800. A pair of companion chairs, however, will generally sell for £2000-£5000.

Over the years, British open armchairs have often borrowed from contemporary French designs. Chippendale, for example, loosely based some of his library chairs on Louis XIV originals, and called them 'French' chairs. Also highly influential were the Rococo Louis XV and the Neoclassical Louis XVI styles. Louis XV armchairs (or *fauteuils*) have an undulating, cartouche-shaped back, serpentine seat and cabriole legs, while Louis XVI examples have an oval or rectangular back, bowed seat and turned legs.

Many salon suites were made in the 19th century in Louis XV and Louis XVI styles, the most valuable of which retain their contemporary Aubusson tapestry upholstery. A standard French-made, three-piece sofa suite with a pair of armchairs in either style will usually sell for £800-£1500, but with fine upholstery and crisply carved, gilded detail a suite can fetch more than £2000.

READING CHAIRS
Back to Front in the Library

EVEN MORE SPECIALISED chairs would be found in the Georgian and Regency library than the ubiquitous library armchair. There were clever 'metamorphic' chairs that converted into library steps (see p. 127) and reading chairs designed to be used back-to-front.

These are usually of close-grained mahogany or walnut and have a distinctive bowed, padded seat. These chairs – sometimes called cockfighting chairs – date from the early Georgian period and are now rare. Good examples fetch well over £5000. A rather similar type of Regency library chair will fetch £1000-£2000.

Early Georgian mahogany reading chair; c.1730. The bookrest, designed for reading and note-taking, hinges up at the back.
£1500-£2500

Easy chairs

The creation of the easy chair was an inevitable development in the search for comfortable seating. Today, the upholstery can be just as important as the frame in determining the value of these chairs.

IT WAS A NATURAL PROGRESSION from the simple padded chair to one with arms and an upholstered back, and then to the fully upholstered easy armchair: This was first seen towards the end of the 17th century, and has remained popular ever since.

Most 20th-century easy chairs are mass-produced and consequently of little or no interest to collectors. However, there are some exceptions, including chairs by the Modernist architect-designers of the 1920s and 30s, such as Marcel Breuer and Mies van der Rohe, and by the new generation of 1950s and 60s designers such as Ernest Race and Charles Eames, whose tubular steel and leather chairs already fetch £800-£1500.

The earliest type of armchair designed with an extra degree of comfort was the wing armchair; the wings sheltered the sitter from draughts, or shielded the face from the fire. Among the earliest types inspired by French designs are the elegant tub-shaped bergères (deep armchairs) of the Hepplewhite period.

WING CHAIRS

The oldest and rarest wing chairs date from the late 17th and early 18th centuries, and have exaggerated out-scrolled arms and back. They are usually tall, their turned legs and ball feet joined by flattened stretchers. Examples that still have their original, tasselled velvet cushions can fetch over £5000 today. Queen Anne and early Georgian versions, dating from slightly later, are more decorative and fetch even more. Most are of walnut and have cabriole legs that end in pad feet, some with elegant, shell-carved knees. Those with original tapestry or needlework upholstery are the most valuable, selling for up to £20,000 or more, but many heavily restored examples go for £1000-£3000.

Copies from the 1920s and 30s, can also make substantial sums. Decoratively upholstered examples regularly reach £1000, and more if one of an attractive pair, but run-of-the-mill reproductions go for under £500.

BERGERES

The value of a late Georgian bergère largely depends on the style of leg, which may be cabriole (the most desirable), turned, or square and tapering. Individual examples can fetch as much as £3000-£5000, or £1000-£2000 for more mundane models. Regency bergères typically have a rectangular seat and back, and turned arm terminals. The most desirable Regency examples have reeded or sabre legs; they sell for over £2000 while those with plain turned legs will make under £1500.

Rarer, and sometimes slightly smaller, are the tub-shaped, caned library chairs, sometimes called curricle bergères. These have a more severely Grecian form than other

George III wing armchair (above); c.1770; 42 in (1.06 cm) wide. The price is boosted by the generous proportions and good-quality, studded leather upholstery.
£1500-£2500

Regency mahogany library bergère (right); c.1810. Note the outswept top rail carved with Grecian-style scrolls and the elegant sabre legs.
£2000-£4000

Bergère chair; early 20thC. Bergère suites had a run of popularity in the late 1980s.
£200-£300
Suite £600-£1000

Queen Anne walnut wing chair; 1705-10; 42 in (1.06 m) wide. The fine cabriole legs have scroll headings and ball-and-claw feet.
£7000-£10,000; more with original upholstery

Regency rosewood library armchair; c.1815. The richly carved acanthus scroll terminals make this generous-sized chair a very grand piece.
£3000-£5000

Regency bergères, and can realise more than £2000 at auction, especially if they have sabre legs; plainer ones generally fetch £800–£1500. Beware of late 19th-century imitations of Regency bergères, which can be difficult to distinguish from originals. Most are very plain and fetch less than £500.

The William IV bergère armchair of the 1830s is less stiff, and has a top rail that scrolls outwards, foliate scroll arms and reeded baluster legs. It combines comfort with elegance, and can fetch up to £2000.

Bergères continued to be made into this century, in the form of low-slung caned armchairs with voluminous loose cushions. Most Edwardian examples came as part of a suite consisting of two matching armchairs and a sofa. Double-caned versions (with two layers of cane) with a richly carved frame, and in good order, are the most popular. Bergère suites change hands for £800–£1500.

VICTORIAN EASY CHAIRS

The second half of the 19th century was a golden age for the easy chair, as a passion for stuffed, upholstered furniture raged in both Britain and France. As a result, well-made, affordable and comfortable furniture became more widely available than ever before.

It was the Victorians who started to deep-button upholstered chairs. Many are thickly padded and they are very expensive to re-upholster, which lowers their purchase price. A typical mid-Victorian easy chair with buttoned upholstery is made in walnut, rosewood or mahogany with a distinct waisted (or 'spoon') back above a serpentine seat and cabriole legs. The arms may be padded or open, and they usually have scroll terminals. Most of these chairs originally formed part of a 'parlour suite' (consisting of a matching sofa and side chairs, and ladies' and gentlemen's armchairs; see p.102), but they are usually found on their own today.

The value of a Victorian easy chair depends on the crispness of the carving and to some extent on the quality of the timber. The very best examples sell for over £1500 apiece, while more ordinary examples can be bought for £600–£1000. Lower-slung versions without

One of a pair of spoon-back gentlemen's armchairs with buttoned upholstery; c. 1860.
Pair: £2000–£3000
Single: £800–£1200

Mid-Victorian nursing chair; c. 1860; 35¾ in (90 cm) high. The top and the cabriole legs are carved.
£300–£500

Oak reclining armchair; c. 1860. It was designed with Gothic features by Charles Bevan.
£800–£1200

Walnut and leather button-back tub chair; c. 1860. A matched pair fetches far more than double the price of a single chair.
Pair: £2000–£3000
Average single: £500 or less

Lloyd Loom tub chair; c. 1930. This rather unusual and dumpy example bears the makers' label (below).
£50 or less

LLOYD LOOM
FURNITURE
PAT. NOS. 118606, 117908

Armchair by Howard & Sons, c. 1890. The chairs are usually stamped and have a distinctive raked back. The original fabric (detail above) included the firm's initials.
£300–£500

Chairs from Art Deco leather 'Cloud' suite; 1930s. Suites in this style are currently very popular with collectors.
3 pieces: £2500–£3500

arms are known as nursing chairs, and these often sell for less than £500 each.

Tub-shaped easy chairs of this date are also low to the ground, and have fully upholstered back and arms. Most have cabriole legs, but examples from the 1870s and 80s are often turned and fluted, and some ebonised and parcel gilt. Later examples have square legs. Chairs of this type fetch up to £500, although they can be found for as little as £200-£300.

Distinctive chairs by Art Nouveau and Arts and Crafts designers range from extravagantly carved examples to chairs of simple lines from firms such as Morris & Co. Many have original upholstery and are relatively affordable – at £300-£400 – but rarer pieces made in limited numbers fetch more.

Other variations on the easy chair that were popular during the Victorian era range from steamer and colonial planter's chairs – designed for relaxing on board ship or on the verandah – to the rocking chair and recliner. Both of the most familiar versions of the rocking chair – bentwood and spindle-turned – can be bought for under £150 at auction.

Reclining armchairs, often called invalid or gouty chairs, usually have a complicated ratchet mechanism to allow the back to recline as a sliding footrest appears. Many are stamped with a maker's mark or have a plate or label, and the majority change hands for between £800 and £1000, with the exception of pieces of high quality or rarity.

PRIE-DIEU CHAIRS
Not for Easy Sitting

PIOUS VICTORIANS introduced praying, or prie-dieu, chairs from France. The fully upholstered seat was for kneeling on and the top rail – a support for the arms – was also upholstered. Although too low to sit on in comfort, these chairs can be attractive, with needlework on the seat, a tall, narrow back, and a pierced carved surround. Bought mainly as decorative items, prie-dieus may fetch as much as £500.

Mid-Victorian, fairly plain prie-dieu; c.1860; seat 12 in (30.5 cm) high.
£200-£300

Settles, settees and sofas

Space-saving, multi-seat furniture fetches surprisingly low prices and plays a highly practical role in these days of cramped living accommodation.

THE TERMS sofa and settee are virtually interchangeable today, although they originated from very different sources. 'Sofa' comes from the Arabic word *suffah* or the Turkish *sopha* (the dais on which the Grand Vizier received guests) but came to refer to any movable seat on which it was possible to recline. 'Settee', on the other hand, probably comes from the earlier English 'settle', and described a seat with back and arms for two or more people.

All three terms were in use by the end of the 17th century, and at that time there were already three distinct varieties of multi-seat furniture: the oak settle, the chair-back settee and the fully upholstered sofa. Their usefulness meant that variations of one sort or another have been seen in most communal areas ever since. Among them have been upholstered sofas in the drawing-room, long buttoned benches in snooker halls and circular-seated 'bornes' or ottomans in Victorian hotel foyers.

Examples with their original upholstery are always the most valuable. If they have to be re-covered, it should be with a material in keeping with the original style, as unsympathetic upholstery can bring down the value a great deal. Finely woven tapestries and silk damasks are most often found on 18th-century sofas, while velvets and brocades are seen on 19th-century pieces.

SETTLES

The oldest settles, from the 15th century, are of panelled construction with mortise-and-tenon joints, and are effectively chests with a back and armrests. Church pews of the same date are very similar, decorated with Gothic

Oak settle with raised-panel back; c.1700; 48 in (1.22 m) wide. It is very rare to find one of these rather spartan pieces in original condition.
£3000-£5000

Edwardian Sheraton-style triple-chair-back settee; c.1910; 66 in (1.68 m) wide. This satinwood example has painted decoration.
£2500-£3500
George III: £7000-£15,000

Burr-walnut twin-chair-back settee; c.1720; 57 in (1.45 m) wide. The decorative motifs – shells, bearded masks and eagle heads – are typical of the early Georgian period.
£30,000-£40,000

PERFECT LINE 'An Elegant Figure', by French artist Edouard Gelhay (b.1856), draws the eye more to its elegant Louis XVI style of furniture than to its sitter.

Louis XV-style canapé; c.1860; 45 in (1.14 m) wide. Such 19thC Louis XV Revival pieces are often mistaken for period 18thC originals.
£3000-£5000

tracery and linenfold panels. Both of these are extremely rare, but similar examples from the late 17th century can still be found for £3000-£5000 for a settle, or £800-£1200 for a lightly decorated pew.

Oak settles that date from the mid-18th century, with a panelled back, open arms, solid seat and cabriole legs, can be bought relatively cheaply. Even good examples make as little as £500-£800 at auction, while plain, 18th-century church pews and long refectory benches can occasionally be found for only £200-£300. More popular are French refectory benches of the same date, which consist of no more than a long plank on legs yet can still fetch £400-£600 apiece.

Numerous copies of late 17th-century settles were made by the Victorians. These are usually of very high quality but are easily distinguished from originals by their over-exuberant machine carving and a lack of ageing in the wood. A good Victorian settle can be bought for as little as £250-£400, while one that is put together from older fragments of timber can often fetch a price in the region of £1500.

Pine seat furniture from the 18th century is rare and usually in poor condition. Better 19th-century pieces exist in larger numbers – the most common being the bowed-back settle of slightly curved form with a high planked back and solid winged ends. A good example will fetch around £3000-£5000.

SETTEES

The caned panel settee has been much reproduced since its introduction in the first half of the 17th century. Originals are rare and valuable, worth perhaps between £6000 and £8000, while a good copy from the 1880s can go at auction for as little as £500-£800.

By the late 17th century, the chair-back settee was in common use, and clearly different in form from the oak settle of the same date. Twin-chair-back, or two-seater, settees

George III mahogany sofa; c.1775; 83½ in (2.12 m) wide. This example with its flowing lines and feminine feel is clearly influenced by the Louis XV style of the canapé design.
£20,000-£30,000

Early George III mahogany 'hump-back' sofa; mid-18thC; 80 in (2.03 m) wide. This example has been re-upholstered in green silk damask.
£20,000-£30,000

George IV scroll-end sofa (left); 1820s; 91 in (2.31 m) wide. The style of this piece reflects Egyptian influence.
£8000-£12,000

Victorian chaise longue; c.1890; 72 in (1.83 m) wide. This late example is of medium quality with weak, turned legs.
£700-£900

consist of two individual chair frames 'fused' together and sharing the same central upright. The settee that has been most widely copied, however, is the early 18th-century Queen Anne walnut model, with its plain, cabriole legs, 'shepherd's-crook' arms and padded back and seat upholstered in tapestry. Whereas originals can cost between £8000 and £12,000, a copy from the 1920s can be bought for only one-tenth as much.

EARLY SOFAS

During the late 18th century, both Thomas Chippendale and Robert Adam produced gilded sofas that were strongly influenced by the contemporary French Neoclassical-style

'canapé'. These masterpieces have a padded oval back, padded arms and seat in contemporary Aubusson tapestry, and can be worth tens of thousands of pounds. Good 19th and 20th-century copies themselves fetch £1500-£2500, while lesser examples may change hands for £300-£500. The canapé proved an enduring design in Britain, and was produced throughout the 19th century.

Following on from delicate Regency designs came heavy scroll-end sofas during the reign of William IV (1830-37). These also show continental influence, this time of the Biedermeier style from central Europe. However, both Regency and William IV scroll-end sofas are relatively unpopular, the former

Empire-style mahogany and ormolu-mounted settee; c.1800; 50 in (1.27 m) wide. By the end of the 19thC, seat furniture was being produced in a wide range of styles.
£1500-£2500

Mid-Victorian button-back sociable; 68 in (1.73 m) wide. This swivelling sociable allows its occupants to turn to address one another face to face or at a rather more distant angle.
£2500-£3500

Chesterfield sofa; c.1880; 72 in (1.83 m) wide. It has been re-upholstered; examples with original buttoned leather upholstery in good condition, are very rare and very valuable.
£2500-£3000

Knole sofa with cord-supported ends (left); 19thC; 91 in (2.31 m) wide. Such pieces are usually of high quality.
£1200-£1800

Art Deco maple sofa; 1925-35; 72 in (1.83 m) wide. Sofas and suites of strong Art Deco style, even by unknown designers, are now becoming valuable.
£5000-£8000

because, although elegant, they are not practical, and the latter because they are uncomfortable and too large. Plain examples can change hands for as little as £400-£600.

VICTORIAN INNOVATIONS

The chaise longue was first seen during the Regency period, but was particularly popular with the Victorians. It developed from the scroll-end sofa, and is in fact a scroll-end day bed with a fixed back. In its most typical form it has a carved frame in walnut or mahogany decorated with flowers and foliage, but there is great variation in quality of construction and design. Chaises longues are currently out of fashion, and only outstanding examples

make as much as £800-£1200; more ordinary pieces will usually go for about £400-£600.

Over the past few years, interest has increased in the bergère suites of the 1920s. Sofas from these distinctive suites have a low seat fully enclosed by a twin-panelled back and outscrolled arms, and six short legs. They are more valuable with their accompanying armchairs, but a well decorated, parcel gilt black lacquer example can make £1500-£2000, and a plain version £250-£400.

One of the most elaborate and valuable Victorian sofa designs is the ottoman or borne – a circular, upholstered sofa with a central backrest. The base is generally divided into three, four or more seats. Bornes were

designed primarily for hotel foyers, and later examples often have a jardinière (plant pot) at the top of the central rest. Many were designed as an eyecatching centrepiece and have tasselled velvet upholstery or an ornately carved frame made of walnut or mahogany. Depending on its design, a small borne with its original upholstery can make £2000-£3000, a large example considerably more.

The 'confidante' or conversation seat is a sofa with an S-shaped top rail, allowing two people to sit together but facing in opposite directions. A good Victorian or Edwardian example sells for £600-£900. A mechanical variant, the 'sociable', has swivelling seats, allowing the occupants to face in any direction they choose. These are quite rare, and a good example could fetch up to £3500.

DROP-ARM DESIGNS

During the 19th century numerous patents were taken out on many pieces of adjustable and convertible furniture. Among the best known and most desirable is the Knole sofa. It is named after the earliest surviving example, found at Knole in Kent. Such sofas were first made in the early 17th century and have an upright back and high, hinged arms which can be reclined by means of a ratchet mechanism. Some later examples are hinged and supported by braided cords. It is one of the most collectable fully upholstered sofas. Good Victorian copies fetch as much as £2000-£3000, while examples from the 1930s and 50s go for sums in the region of £250-£700.

A very elaborate, cast-iron ratchet mechanism was also fitted onto one of the most popular Victorian designs, the Chesterfield. In many ways, the Chesterfield epitomises Victorian furniture design as it incorporates another important 19th-century innovation, spring upholstery, which afforded new levels of comfort, but not necessarily elegance.

A fine Victorian example with drop ends and good, original leather upholstery fetches £3000-£5000, and a plain, re-upholstered example £500-£800. One needing to be completely re-upholstered (a very expensive job) will fetch only £100-£200. Chesterfields with fixed arms generally cost around ten per cent less than drop-end equivalents.

The Victorian adjustable day bed, or couch, often has its seat divided into three fully adjustable cushions, with a movable headrest and arm supports. Made by various manufacturers, and often patented, these are modestly priced, fetching £500-£800.

Dining and breakfast tables

It is colour and size that generally count most in pricing a dining table, and these considerations are as important today as two hundred years ago.

Antique dining tables available to a buyer today vary enormously in style, quality and price. A 17th-century refectory table in original condition is very hard to come by, for example, and may cost many thousands of pounds, whereas a Victorian reproduction can be bought for a few hundred. Small, foldaway breakfast tables, which first appeared in the early 19th century as one answer to the space restrictions of small town houses, are still extremely popular, and for similar reasons.

Before buying any antique table, you should check it carefully for alterations, as marrying a table top to a different undercarriage is fairly common (see box, opposite).

DINING TABLES

The simplest form of dining table, its plank top supported by movable trestles, dates from medieval times, when food and feasting were a major pleasure in life. After meals, tables would be moved or dismantled to make room in the great hall for dancing or other activities.

Dining in large groups was also the norm in 16th-century monasteries, where monks ate in the refectory, seated on either side of long tables. By the 17th and 18th centuries, these more permanent tables were found in lay households. The basic refectory table consists of a plank top above a frieze, sitting on four or more supports which are joined by stretchers at the bottom. The shape of the uprights can be used to date a table. They range from plain columns to cup-and-cover and vase forms, some influenced by styles introduced by 17th-century Dutch Huguenot craftsmen.

Refectory tables are most commonly of oak, but also of yew, walnut or various fruitwoods. Impressive examples in original condition are

AT A LORD'S TABLE *A 15thC trestle table may seem primitive but fine linen and sumptuous fare make it fit to bear feasts for the wealthiest guests.*

Restoration oak refectory table; 1660-80; 108 in (2.74 m) long. Few examples have survived without repair.
£8000-£12,000
Restored: £3000-£5000
19thC copy: £2000-£3000

French cherrywood draw-leaf table; c.1820; 168 in (4.27 m) fully extended. Tables of this type are favoured by interior decorators for rustic schemes. This example has a particularly good colour.
£1000-£1500

Victorian copy of an early 17thC refectory table in oak; c.1850; 215 in (5.46 m) long. The contrast between the bulbous baluster uprights and the shallow frieze gives it away as a Victorian reproduction.
£2000-£4000
Original: £12,000 or more

Walnut Art Deco dining table; c.1930; 66 in (1.68 m) long. The U-shaped support and the veneers of this dining table make it eye-catching.
£600-£1000

Oak Arts and Crafts-style refectory table (left) by Philip Webb; c.1880; 125 in (3.17 m) long. Original examples such as this are keenly sought by collectors.
£10,000 or more

now avidly sought after, and change hands at auction for £5000-£10,000 or even more, but humbler examples fetch £1000-£3000.

A variation was the earliest extending dining table, the draw-leaf table, introduced in the mid-16th century, and popular in the early 17th. The top lifts up to allow an extra leaf to slide out on runners at each end. The original top settles back between the leaves.

Although quality refectory tables were rarely made after the early 18th century, cruder 'farmhouse' examples, made of oak and elm, appeared well into the Victorian era. The Victorians also made reproductions of 17th-century refectory tables, which are generally more ornately carved than originals. Since the wood had not yet darkened with age, many were stained to appear more authentic. A number of 19th-century reproductions have a single lengthwise stretcher down the centre of the table, forming an 'H' pattern (as opposed to stretchers joining each leg to the next). These can fetch around £1000-£2000 today, but check that an old top has not been married with a later support.

SWING-ACTION TABLES

Small gate-leg tables combine flexibility of size with ease of storage. The round gate-leg table, together with the later drop-leaf table, is increased in size by flaps raised on each side to rest on legs that swing out from the frame. In the true gate-leg, the swinging leg is joined top and bottom by stretchers to another upright which pivots on the frame, forming a structure very much like a gate.

Considerable numbers of gate-leg tables of varying quality have survived, most made of oak with others of walnut and fruitwoods. The majority have a central drawer, while some larger tables have two, with a double gate-leg

Oak gate-leg dining table; c.1700; 49 in (1.25 m) long. The slender, turned uprights on this table point to a fairly early date.
£2000-£4000
In poor condition: £800-£1500

An Expert Examines

JOHN BLY TURNS UP A DROP-LEAF TABLE

'THE FIRST THING TO DO *with an antique drop-leaf table is turn it upside down and take a good long look. The underside should be dry and rather dusty; any sign of treatment with stain raises suspicions of restoration. There's almost always a carpenter's look to it, quite rough and ready. The parts that usually show are mahogany, but the underframing is made of selected cheaper timbers: oak for the frame itself, split-resistant beech for the rails and resilient pine for the fixing blocks. It's all fastened together with handmade nails; screws were only used to fix the hinges and attach the frame to the top. Deep slots were hand-gouged into the rails for those screws.*

Gouged slot for screw   Saw cuts for hinge bed

I always go straight to the hinges, to see if they're original, as these are. They're held by lovely dome-headed, early screws. You can see the saw cuts the craftsman who fitted the hinges made before he chiselled out the bed for the hinge. And, as you'd expect, the hinge fits the bed exactly.

The key part of a drop-leaf table is the knuckle joint. It is the hinge on which the strut and leg swing out to support the leaf when it is in the raised position. It is the design feature that

Knuckle joint

distinguishes the drop-leaf from the earlier gate-leg table, enabling the designer to do away with all the paraphernalia of stretchers and rails underneath. The knuckle joint was hand-cut in the timber of the rail and strut, and swings on a flat-topped iron pin that was dropped into place before the frame was attached to the table top – very simple and tidy.

JOHN BLY SUMS UP

*The good, no-nonsense carpentry alone tells me that this piece dates from the 18th century – probably about 1745. But for confirmation, look at the patina on the struts where for 200 years people have pulled out the leg that supports the leaf. No one could fake that – nor indeed the swing track on the underside of the leaf that precisely matches the top of the leg. It is such a simple piece of furniture, but it's beautiful and clean; all original.'

No sign of alterations to underframe and its angled stiffening strut; wear on underside of leaf exactly matching leg action

action on each side. These larger tables are few and far between and in original condition fetch very high prices. Small gate-legs are more affordable, ranging from about £500 to £5000, while 19th and 20th-century copies generally fetch less than £500.

The drop-leaf dining table developed along the lines of the gate-leg, and has a similar swing-leg action. Round, oval and, later, rectangular side flaps made from a single piece of mahogany are supported by elegant cabriole legs and pivot on knuckle joints (see box, p.109). Early mahogany drop-leaf tables are never veneered or crossbanded, and any decoration of this sort would have been added later. Most sell for between £400 and £2000.

MULTI-SECTION TABLES

The development of the formal dining room in the late 18th century created a need for dining tables that were permanent but flexible in size. The result, in its basic form, was the rectangular drop-leaf table extended with additional, free-standing, D-shaped or rectangular tables added to each end. When not needed, they could be simply placed against the wall as a pair of side tables or put together to form a smaller serving or dining table.

Many such tables are on the market today, and remain popular because of their obvious suitability to the modern, compact home. Prices vary between about £1500 and £3000 depending on the colour of the top and the table's overall size. These tables should be checked for signs of marrying.

The extended drop-flap table has the drawback of numerous legs, however. The pedestal dining table avoids this by supporting the table top with two, three or four central pedestals, usually with splay legs. It can also be extended where necessary with D-shaped

end tables or an extending leaf. Two and three-pedestal tables are topped with two table leaves, while the larger four-pedestal tables have an extra leaf in the centre.

Three and four-pedestal tables are far more expensive than two-pedestal ones, and should always be checked for alterations. As well as the normal marriages of top and base, the central leaf is sometimes from another table.

Many Regency-style reproductions of D-ended pedestal tables were produced in the 1920s and sold through the larger department stores, but a genuine Georgian or Regency twin-pedestal example in reasonably original condition is worth at least £2500-£3000.

Some of the largest dining tables date from the early years of the 19th century and are

extended mechanically, reflecting the age of the patentee. In 1800 Gillows of Lancaster took out a patent for an extending dining table that was to become a Victorian classic. It retained stability and strength even though it had only four legs. Such tables are usually made of mahogany, sometimes of oak or walnut, and several mechanisms are used.

BREAKFAST TABLES

Single pedestal tables with a tip-up top, first seen around 1770, have become known as breakfast tables, after the informal daytime meal of the 18th and 19th centuries. The compact size of such tables – they are generally about 4 ft (1.2 m) across – and the fact that

Late Georgian elm drop-leaf table; c.1770; 48 in (1.22 m) long. This table would fetch less than its oval counterpart, and less still if it was made of oak.
£400-£800

George IV D-ended extending dining table; c.1825; 170½ in (4.33 m) long. These tables are popular today because of their versatility. The ends can be taken off and placed against a wall when not needed for dining.
£5000-£7000; smaller example: £3000-£5000

Late George III mahogany twin-pedestal dining table; c.1790; 142 in (3.6 m) long when fully extended. Two leaves are replacements; an early replacement that has mellowed is preferable to recent work.
£7000-£10,000
Without extra leaves:
£3000-£5000

Early Victorian mahogany dining table in extending design by Jupe; c.1850; 112 in (2.84 m) across fully extended. The top can be formed of eight large or eight small leaves.
£20,000-£30,000

they can conveniently be stored flat against a wall when not in use has meant that they have remained popular since they first appeared.

Most early breakfast tables have a rectangular top of mahogany, although this was sometimes later cut down to an oval or circular shape. Examples from the Sheraton period are occasionally found in rosewood. The table top is supported on a simple turned

Regency mahogany five-leaf concertina dining table; c.1810; 102 in (2.59 m) long fully extended. This example in well-figured wood is easy to extend and would fetch even more with reeded legs.
£5000-£8000

Reproduction 'Chippendale'-style mahogany extending dining table; c.1910; 48 in (1.22 m) wide. This practical and sturdy table is designed for flexible seating, but it was certainly not designed by Chippendale.
£1000-£1500

Regency rosewood breakfast table with brass inlay; c.1810; 48 in (1.22 m) across. Legs splayed from a small platform are characteristic of Regency tables.
£4000-£6000

Through the Green Baize Door

THE PLAIN KITCHEN TABLE, doubling as a chopping board and below-stairs dining table, has remained largely unchanged since the early part of the 18th century.

It has become beloved of interior designers and young homemakers alike in recent decades. Most examples are in pine which has survived frequent scrubbing and mellowed through age to a rich, warm tone, but

they can also be found in elm and various fruitwoods. These tables are hard to date accurately as the style has been so constant. Only wear, colour and patina offer any real clues to their history.

French provincial tables produced in the last two hundred years are also fairly common in Britain. They were made from various fruitwoods and often have a distinctive small, hinged drop-flap at each end, sometimes on cabriole rather than square legs.

Plain pine kitchen table; c.1770-90; 48 in (1.22 m) long. This typical late 18thC piece is desirable because of its rich colour. A larger example would fetch more, but one of poor colour would sell for less.
£600-£900

George III mahogany breakfast table; c.1790; 54 in (1.37 m) across. The restrained decoration is typical of the period.
£5000-£7000

Burr walnut breakfast table; 1850-60; 48 in (1.22 m) across. Larger tables or those with elaborate inlay decoration command higher prices.
£1200-£1500

---

shaft and splayed legs, and is embellished at most with crossbanding in an exotic wood such as harewood or rosewood.

The colour of the top often decides a table's value. Prized examples are termed 'faded' when the right degree of natural ageing is present, and can fetch £5000-£6000 or more. More ordinary tables sell for £1500-£3000.

The splay legs of such tables take considerable strain, and the design was modified in Regency breakfast tables of the early 19th century. These have an elaborate base, where the legs extend from a platform connected to the shaft, helping to spread downward pressure on the pedestal. Ornate examples – with a baluster-turned or carved shaft, a striking top of zebrawood or rosewood, and decorated with borders of brass inlay – can fetch £4000-£6000. But plainer tables with minimal decoration such as hipped legs or a reeded shaft sell for about £1500-£3000.

Some of the most lavish breakfast tables available today are Victorian exhibition pieces made to demonstrate the maker's artistry and skill. Some display superb floral marquetry on a plain background, while others use ormolu and linear inlay. Tables such as these can sell for more than £10,000.

Good quality Victorian burr walnut breakfast tables can be identified by a moulded edge around the top, sometimes with shallow relief carving, and scroll-carved legs issuing straight from a heavy baluster shaft. They usually sell for £1000-£2000, or more for well carved examples. Cruder versions in mahogany can be found for under £1000.

Occasional tables

Portable, practical and decorative, occasional tables can be useful for many purposes: serving tea or wine, playing cards or just holding lamps.

Nest of four Regency mahogany quartetto tables; c.1800; 18 in (45.7 cm) wide. These delicate tables are rarely found in completely original condition. Any replacement will severely reduce their value.
£5000-£8000 the set
Edwardian copy: £1500-£2000

Pair of adjustable Victorian papier-mâché music stands that double as small tables; c.1860; 20 in (51 cm) high. The value is enhanced if they bear the maker's stamp.
£1000-£1500

Early Georgian mahogany wine table; c.1740; 13 in (33 cm) wide. Early examples are rare and keenly sought after.
£4000-£6000
Good Edwardian copy: £600-£900

Regency pietra dura table; early 19thC; 34 in (86.5 cm) wide. Pietra dura was always highly prized and is here on a gilded Egyptian-Revival base.
£5000-£8000

Georgian mahogany piecrust tripod table; c.1755; 33 in (84 cm) wide. This is a particularly ornate example.
£8000-£12,000
Plainer style: £3000-£5000

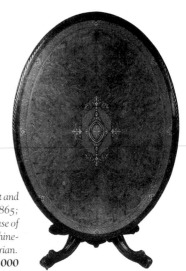

Victorian burr walnut and marquetry loo table; c.1865; 36 in (91 cm) wide. The use of figured veneers and machine-made marquetry is typically Victorian.
£2000-£3000

THE VERSATILE occasional table – made to be brought out as the occasion demanded – has proved so indispensable since it was introduced in the 18th century that it is still being manufactured in considerable numbers today.

NESTS OF TABLES

Nesting tables of different sizes – sometimes known as 'quartetto' tables because there were usually four of them in a set – first appeared around the end of the 18th century. Their design, a rectangular top supported by four turned uprights joined by a single, bowed rear stretcher and raised on splayed feet, has remained much the same ever since.

Although relatively small, good nests of tables are generally expensive. A plain mahogany Georgian nest in fair original condition will fetch £2000-£3000 at auction, a satinwood nest – much rarer – up to £6000. Nests with complementary veneers or inlaid designs on each of the four tops (some have inlaid chessboards) are often even more expensive, fetching upwards of five figures.

Papier-mâché nest tables decorated with painted floral designs, mother-of-pearl and gilding are typically Victorian, as are tables painted in oils with romantic scenes evoking the style of the 18th-century French artist Antoine Watteau. Prices range from £800-£1200 for a papier-mâché nest, but may be only £300-£500 for a set of painted tables.

Late Georgian Neoclassical designs were revived by the Edwardians, and some of these are extremely valuable. Satinwood examples painted in the style of the Adams decorator Angelica Kauffmann or of her 18th-century contemporaries Giambattista Cipriani or Francesco Bartolozzi can fetch £3000-£4500.

Few quartetto tables were made outside

Britain, although some makers brought out designs in the French Louis XV and Louis XVI styles. Oriental rosewood tables were made in late 19th-century China for export to Britain, and now sell for several thousand pounds.

TRIPOD TABLES

Since the days of George II, there has been a demand for small tripod tables, most of which have a tilting top up to 40 in (1 m) across, a pedestal support and three splayed legs. Some have a revolving top on a 'birdcage'.

The first tripod tables, produced in the early 18th century, were designed for serving tea or supper. The high standard of workmanship – with features such as a raised 'piecrust' border or brass line inlay – commands a high price. A piece by cabinet-maker John Channon will fetch £30,000-£40,000 and even a later imitation can go for as much as £10,000-£15,000.

Plainer, cheaper tripod tables were made in almost every type of wood. Completely unrestored examples are rare and sell for about £2000, but even a small amount of repair or restoration can halve the figure.

Victorian tripod tables are often made in highly figured walnut with arabesque line inlay. The top is usually fixed rather than tilting. Auction prices range from £500 to £800. In the 1920s numerous copies were made of mid-18th-century tables in the Chippendale style. Auction prices for these are in the region of £1000-£1500.

Some tripod tables were made specifically for wine-drinking and have a special place for a decanter and a notched rim to hold glasses. Late 18th-century examples are extremely rare, but much plainer, 19th-century wine tables – simply small tripod tables to stand beside sofas and chairs – can be found for £400-£600. Pieces from the 1920s or 30s sell for £100-£200. Many plain tripod tables have been embellished or 'improved' and should be checked for signs of restoration (see p. 114).

LOO TABLES

The card game of lanterloo (commonly 'loo') was popular throughout the 19th century. By the 1850s and 60s, special loo tables were being made in large numbers. Most have an oval top, which tilts to save space, and seat eight people. Many are decorated with lavish machine-made marquetry, burr walnut being the primary veneer on better-quality tables.

Among the most sought-after loo tables today are those produced by various cabinet-makers to the designs of a London dealer, E.H. Baldock. Veneered in highly figured walnut and decorated with rich bands of floral marquetry on an ebonised ground, Baldock's tables have an ornate pedestal support – on the grandest examples, a flared trefoil shape on scrolling feet. They range in price today from £3000 to £10,000, depending on size. Slightly less ornate but far more common are tables made by the Gillows firm. These fetch nearly as much as Baldock's designs, particularly if they bear their maker's stamp.

OTHER SMALL TABLES

At about the end of the last century a vogue developed for display tables with lined interior compartments and glazed top and sides; they are also called vitrine tables. Most are small – about 36 in (91 cm) wide and 29-30 in (73-76 cm) high – and they come in a variety of styles, for example Louis XV, Chinese Chippendale, giltwood George II and Edwardian marquetry. Prices range from £800 to £1200 for plainer versions and up to £5000 for a satinwood or gilt example.

Some fine occasional tables were made in France, many marble-topped, or with drawers or writing slides. Most popular was the guéridon – a term originally given to small, 18th-century French tables. The many 19th-century variants often show outstanding workmanship and are in highly figured wood. They sell for thousands of pounds.

French Napoleon III mahogany display table with gilt-bronze mounts; Paris, c.1870; 25½ in (65 cm) wide.
£4000-£5000

High-quality French marquetry side table in kingwood, ebony and snakewood with ormolu mounts; early 19thC; 28 in (71 cm) high.
£10,000-£15,000

Louis XVI marble-topped guéridon; c.1785; 14 in (35.6 cm) across. The height of the top adjusts using the brass peg in the shaft. This is an unusual example of an item made in large numbers.
£1500-£2500

END OF THE GOOD LIFE *This scene of an intimate supper at the court of French King Louis XVI – engraved just a decade before heads began to roll – clearly illustrates the usefulness of the small occasional table.*

An Expert Examines

JOHN BLY CHECKS OUT THE ORIGINALITY OF THREE 18TH-CENTURY TRIPOD TABLES

The best way to detect any signs of skullduggery is to tip up the top and take a good look at the various bruises it has sustained over the years. Now, as you can see, at some time someone has put a couple of screws in the top of the birdcage to stop it turning. They've gone now, but while they were there, the heads made indentations in the underside of the table top. The point is, the marks match exactly. That would be very difficult to fake, and strongly indicates that the base and top have always been together.

Bruising by screws

A similar point is made by this simpler table, which lacks a birdcage and tips up but doesn't turn. It has a protuberance in the base, too – the end of the column, which was cut to form a through-tenon to join it to this little platform where it tilts. Over a long period, the tenon has made a matching indentation: again, a sign of authenticity.

The tenon mark

'**T**RIPOD TEA TABLES like this were so useful. They could be set up for a light meal, or a card game by the fire. And when they weren't in use, they could be tipped up against a wall.

Looking at the base of this table, I can see that the legs were dovetailed into the column. This to me suggests a date after 1745, as does the bit of decoration above the join. Before that they were plainer, with column and legs emerging from a central wooden block.

'birdcage' device that enables them to swivel as well. The gadget also conceals a peg that, when pulled out, enables the top to be lifted off entirely. Altogether a plus for a table of this type when it comes to valuation, but the most important thing we've got to do is to make sure that the bottom belongs to the top, because it's all too easy to add a top to the cut-down stand of a pole-screen, say.

Another variant is this elegant little wine table. No birdcage here, or even a tilt-top: the top is smaller than a tea table's, and takes up less room, so there's no need for it to tip up.

Small, fixed top

JOHN BLY SUMS UP

All three tables belong to the 18th century, but are from different periods of it – early, middle and late. The birdcage table is probably the most typical. Although it is a country piece, it has a well-proportioned stem with a wrythen-turned vase at the bottom – and, of course, the birdcage. At auction, I'd say it would fetch around £2500-£3500, while the one without the birdcage might make about half that. The smaller, later wine table would probably go for somewhere between £850 and £1500.'

Before 1745   *After 1745*

Most tripod tables of 24 in (60 cm) or more in diameter were made to tip up, and some, like the de luxe model we're looking at, have this

Checking the underside and the birdcage

Folding, games and work tables

From the time of their invention in the late 17th century, small tables for special purposes have been produced in considerable quantities, many of them extendible and many decorated with beautiful inlay, marquetry and veneer.

SMALL TABLES for use when sewing, playing board or card games, reading or writing were popular from the early 18th century. Some have a double top which folds over to increase the table's size, while others have small drop flaps at the sides. Folding tea and card tables were generally made in a small rectangular or half-moon shape, the top opening out to reveal a polished wood or baize surface. Most were fitted with drawers or a storage well in the middle to hold games pieces, a lady's sewing equipment or other small possessions.

Easily movable tables such as these were found in almost all upper and middle-class Georgian and Victorian living rooms. As with all popular types of furniture made in large quantities, the value of a piece depends on the quality of the table's design and construction, its rarity, and how original it has remained.

GAMES AND WORK TABLES

Games tables, like card tables, were first introduced in the late 17th century, and by the early 18th had settled into their standard form: a folding top on a frieze, sitting on cabriole legs (which evolved into a number of different shapes as fashions changed). Some of the finest tables, made at the beginning of the 19th century, have a sliding panel in the top, inlaid underneath with a board for chess or draughts and enclosing a backgammon board and counters. Such Regency games tables are usually of extremely high quality and incorporate expensive veneers. A good example will sell at auction today for between £4000 and £6000.

The Victorians produced more affordable, machine-made tables, for the growing middle classes. In place of the sliding panel, they have a fixed, inlaid chessboard, and some have compartments at either side of the board to hold the chessmen. Victorian games tables can be bought at auction for £800-£1200.

The work table, or sewing table, was designed exclusively for women – though

some dual-purpose games/work tables were also made. Most work tables have small frieze drawers beneath the folding top, under which is a deep, sliding, upholstered drawer, or well. The most refined, late 18th century mahogany and satinwood examples can cost £2000-£3000, but more common are 19th-century walnut or mahogany pieces which sell for around £400-£600.

CARD AND TEA TABLES

In the 18th and 19th centuries more small folding tables were made for playing cards than for anything else. Like the very similar tea tables of the same date, they usually have a

Regency brass inlaid rosewood work table; 1825; 36 in (91 cm) wide. Similar tables for games are often topped by a reversible sliding panel inlaid with a chessboard and covering a backgammon board.
£4000-£5000

Victorian octagonal sewing table; c.1870; 20 in (51 cm) wide. This example is typical of those produced from about 1860, although it is unusual in being made of rosewood rather than walnut.
£400-£600

Pair of Sheraton-period work tables in rosewood, satinwood and marquetry; c.1790; 16¾ in (42.5 cm) wide. The high level of decoration and expensive veneers make this pair far more valuable than plainer examples.
£6000-£9000 the pair
Single: £2000-£3000

Victorian walnut card table (open); c.1870; 40 in (1.01 m) wide. The supports are richly carved with foliage.
£1000-£1500

Late Regency mahogany work table; c.1825; 32 in (81 cm) wide (open). This table would be more valuable if its well were in better condition.
£800-£1200

George III demilune (half-moon) card table (closed); c.1785; 42⅛ in (1.07 m) wide. The finest card tables tend to be in satinwood like the example above.
£4000-£6000

George I walnut card table (open and closed); c.1720; 36 in (91 cm) wide. Very few of these tables exist in their original form. They were also much copied during the 19th and early 20thC.
£4000-£6000
Copy: £1200-£1800

ON THE CARDS *In 'Hearts are trumps', Sir John E. Millais's oil painting of 1872, Victorian ladies at their ornate card table take a game seriously.*

Rosewood envelope card table (open); c.1895; 24 in (61 cm) wide (closed). A more ornate example with high-quality marquetry and inlay would fetch more.
£250-£400

Arts and Crafts blond oak card table; c.1900; 24 in (61 cm) wide (closed). This useful table is very collectable due to its style and neat proportions.
£600-£900

rectangular or semicircular ('demilune') fold-over top surface. The open top is generally covered with baize and may have wells for counters. The table's frieze usually has a small drawer for holding gaming cards and pieces. The legs may hinge out (in the manner of the larger drop-leaf table; see p.109) to support the opened top, or they may move out on a concertina mechanism.

These tables vary hugely in quality and value. Early walnut examples from around 1730 with carved cabriole legs and a top fitted with counter wells can fetch as much as £4000-£6000, while a good-quality, late 19th or early 20th-century reproduction (of which there are many) might cost £400-£600.

Early 19th-century George III mahogany examples are generally far less ornate, with a rectangular top and square, tapered legs. So many of these come up for sale at auction that they rarely reach prices above £500-£800. The value is increased if the top is semicircular or if there is any painted or inlaid decoration.

Victorian card tables vary greatly, from impressive ormolu-mounted walnut examples to plain mahogany or walnut tables; prices start as low as £200 and rise to £4000. One of the period's more interesting variations, the

'envelope' card table, appeared in the late 19th century. It has a square top with four triangular flaps that fold to the centre (like the back of an envelope) or open out to form a larger baize-covered playing surface with counter wells. The top rotates into position over the legs. Envelope tables are often of very high quality, with marquetry decoration, and sell for as much as £1000-£1500.

PEMBROKE AND OTHER TABLES

Legend has it that an 18th-century Countess of Pembroke first devised the wonderfully useful small drop-flap table now known as the Pembroke table. These round, oval or

rectangular tables can be extended as required with side flaps that are generally small in relation to the central part of the table. The table became extremely popular because of its practical size, and has been produced in a variety of styles, following contemporary fashions, up to the present day.

Early examples – such as those designed by Thomas Chippendale as breakfast tables for Nostell Priory, near Leeds, in 1760 – were decorated with ornate carving, but by the end of the century this was generally replaced by magnificent marquetry, epitomised by work in the style of Thomas Sheraton.

Prices for Pembroke tables can vary widely,

Late Georgian burr-wood and satinwood Pembroke table; c.1780; 40 in (1.01 m) wide (open). The serpentine shape to the flaps adds value, as do the figured veneers.
£4000-£6000

George III mahogany and satinwood-banded sofa table; c.1800; 45 in (1.14 m) wide (closed). A great number of very good copies (valuable in their own right) exist. This table is of 'medium' quality.
£5000-£8000
With slight damage: £2500-£3500

Early Victorian mahogany pedestal card table; c.1830; 36 in (91 cm) wide. Generally, pedestal card tables do not fetch as much at auction as their four-legged counterparts.
£300-£500

Victorian mahogany Sutherland table; c.1845; 41¾ in (1.06 m) long (open). The value of these tables is enhanced by rarer or highly figured woods.
£500-£800

George III satinwood Pembroke table; c.1790; 42 in (1.07 m) diameter. The exotic veneers, oval form and intricate marquetry make this an expensive piece. An example with less decoration could fetch as little as a quarter of this price.
£25,000-£35,000

Victorian Pembroke table; c.1840; 72 in (1.83 m) wide (open). It would fetch less if converted from the centre part of a dining table.
£400-£600

As sofa tables often formed the centrepiece of a room, especially the drawing room, many are veneered in very decorative, rare woods, have flamboyantly designed supports, and in some cases are extensively inlaid.

Since they were designed to be worked on from a sofa, such tables generally have a central pedestal or end standards rather than legs at the corners. Unusually they extend lengthways to create a narrow surface 4-5 ft (1.2-1.5 m) long; this was achieved by having the flaps on the short sides. Most also have a set of drawers in one side of the frieze and false drawer-fronts on the other.

A good, 18th century mahogany sofa table of Sheraton design will fetch £3000-£8000, with more extravagant examples making up to three times as much. Even 19th and 20th-century copies sell for £500-£2000.

Other 19th-century forms of sofa table are much less popular, and less elegant, than their 18th-century counterparts. Heavy mahogany pedestal versions can sell for as little as £300-£500, although fine rosewood examples with brass inlay can make up to £2500. Some pedestal sofa tables have been converted into the more popular type with end standards, as a careful examination should reveal.

from £100-£200 for a plain Victorian mahogany example to £500-£800 for a good Regency piece with line inlay, and right up to £6000-£9000 for a fine George III table in the rare and much sought-after satinwood. Most expensive of all are the beautifully inlaid Sheraton Pembroke tables of the late 18th century, which can fetch over £20,000.

The Sutherland table first appeared in a design catalogue of 1849, its very narrow central section flanked by two wide side flaps. This form meant that while it could be stored neatly against a wall, it opened out into a good-sized table. The finest examples date from around 1870 and are made in burr

walnut, decorated with turned uprights sometimes joined by intricately carved fretwork panels. These sell for £700-£900. Satinwood or marquetry examples fetch £400-£600 and a small, plain mahogany Sutherland from around 1900 will generally sell for about £100.

SOFA TABLES

One of the finest variants on the drop-flap theme is the sofa table, introduced at the end of the 18th century. This was originally designed to stand in front of a sofa to provide a surface for reading, writing or drawing. Today, however, sofa tables are often positioned behind a sofa rather than in front of it.

Serving tables, sideboards and dressers

Whether made to display the family china and silver or just to provide storage, the best pieces of dining room or kitchen furniture, from aristocratic Adam sideboards to humble dressers, are now worth thousands of pounds.

THE SIDEBOARD can be traced back to the side table, originally used for serving food. The dresser, on the other hand, probably developed from the 17th-century court cupboard used to display plate.

SERVING TABLES AND SIDEBOARDS

Serving tables were important items of furniture and therefore followed the fashions of the day. They are stylistically similar to pier and console tables but longer, and at one time were often flanked by urns on pedestals.

Gothic-style serving tables of the mid-18th century are more sober than the contemporary Rococo console table, and are notable for their clean lines. Refined pieces in mahogany sell for £10,000-£15,000 today, or more if they are close to a design from Chippendale's

Director. Cruder examples fetch £2000-£4000 and Victorian copies under £1500.

Also noteworthy are elegant Adam-style serving tables from the 1760s to 80s, often with matching pedestals to hold plates, topped by urns to hold cutlery or cold drinks. The tables often have a fluted frieze and fluted legs decorated with Classical motifs. Giltwood or painted versions are rare, but mahogany examples can be found at prices of up to £6000. Edwardian Adam-style copies are common at £1000-£1500.

The sideboard, which combines counter, cupboards, cutlery drawer and cellaret, evolved from the serving table with pedestals. A late 18th-century Hepplewhite or Sheraton sideboard is characterised by a bowed or serpentine outline, satinwood bands or box-

wood inlay in a mahogany base, and a central frieze drawer with an arched apron below, which may conceal a deep drawer and cupboard. Although still quite numerous, good 18th-century examples regularly make more than £5000. They can be distinguished from later copies by their construction. With 18th-century pieces, look for a pine back panel and a visible joint between drawer sides and back; 19th-century pieces have a mahogany back panel and are clumsier, often with elaborate inlay. George III and Regency examples fetch £1500-£3000, while Victorian and plainer Georgian ones (often 'improved' later with inlay) go for £1000-£2000.

The pedestal sideboard was introduced in the early 19th century. The first ones were fairly plain; those from the 1830s are always

NEOCLASSICAL REFINEMENT *This serving table designed by Thomas Chippendale is still in its original place at Harewood House in Yorkshire. It is accompanied by a matching pedestal and urn for plates, cutlery and drinks.*

Early George III mahogany serving table; c.1760; 81 in (2.06 m) wide. This piece is closely related to a design in Chippendale's 'Director'. Originally, it may have had a marble top.
£30,000-£50,000

Hepplewhite-style mahogany sideboard; c.1790; 81 in (2.06 m) wide. Note the inlay and the 'flame' veneers.
£4000-£6000; restored: £2000-£3000

Side cabinet in burr walnut, marquetry and parquetry; c.1870; 53½ in (1.36 m) high. This piece was made by Gillows to a design by Bruce Talbert.
£4000-£6000

Mahogany pedestal sideboard; c.1850; 60 in (1.52 m) wide. Such pieces do not fetch much, but this benefits from good colour and relatively small size.
£700-£1000

made of mahogany, and sometimes have carving on the back and spandrels below the frieze. Later versions in oak or walnut tend to be massive, with a vast, mirrored back.

In general, pedestal sideboards sell for under £1000. Even less popular is the centre-sunk sideboard of the late Victorian era. Often described as 'Chippendale style', they are of overpowering size, with heavily gadrooned edges and ball-and-claw feet, and can be picked up for less than £200 despite their high-quality timber and construction.

COURT CUPBOARDS AND DRESSERS

The early 17th-century 'cup-board' or 'buffet' consists of two or more open shelves supported on turned uprights similar to those of contemporary dining tables. They are now rare and fetch £5000-£8000 or more.

Much more common is the closed 'court cupboard', introduced by the mid-17th century. (Some early examples, also known as 'livery cupboards', were partly enclosed with an open base.) Most have some restoration and some were entirely reconstructed in the 19th century from old pieces, which makes them hard to spot. Their awkward bulk means that even well carved, 17th-century examples rarely exceed £5000 at auction.

The oak dresser was a feature of farmhouse kitchens for almost three centuries. By the last quarter of the 17th century it had rows of slim open shelves in place of the upper section of the court cupboard. Such pieces are often called 'Welsh dressers', as they are common in Wales, but they were made throughout the British Isles well into the 19th century.

Before long, the upper rack of shelves and the base became separate components. Many dressers are now made up of a base with a later rack. This is so common that it only slightly reduces the value, as long as the two are a reasonable match. Beware of 1920s reproduction oak dressers, worth less than £1000.

Some dressers had no upper rack – a form known as a low dresser or dresser base. Early low dressers are best dated from their style: geometrically moulded drawers and turned or block feet indicate 17th-century origin; cabriole or columnar legs, sometimes joined by an undertier, are found on plainer, Queen Anne and early Georgian dressers. Exceptional examples may sell for £10,000 or more, as their low height is suited to modern homes, but most go for under £5000.

Also popular, and generally less expensive, are mid-Georgian enclosed dressers. These have two or more frieze drawers, usually on top of cupboards, and are sometimes embellished with mahogany crossbanding. An example in good condition with a rack will fetch £2500-£5000, but beware of late 19th-century copies with poor patina.

Pine dressers have been made up to today and unless outstanding cost less than £1000.

Oak court cupboard dated 1629; 78 in (1.98 m) wide. It is in fine original condition. More run-of-the-mill and restored examples are worth much less.
£7000-£8000
Average example; £3000-£6000

Aesthetic movement ebonised and painted sideboard; c.1880; 78 in (1.98 m) wide. The curious mix of medieval figures, Grecian motifs and the 'Oriental' japanned finish typifies Aesthetic taste.
£1500-£2000

Late 17thC oak low dresser; 1670-90; 69½ in (1.76 m) wide. Geometrically panelled drawers such as these were also used on chests of the same period. This piece has a good colour and patina.
£4000-£6000

George III enclosed oak dresser, with contemporary rack, from north Wales; 1750-70; 78 in (1.98 m) high. The arrangement of narrow drawers and cupboards is unusual. Victorian or heavily restored pieces would be half the price.
£7000-£10,000

Console and pier tables

Intended for grand houses, console tables are mostly for show, displaying superb craftsmanship and speaking eloquently of the style of their time.

George II giltwood and ebonised console table with later marble top; c.1730; 36 in (91.5 cm) wide. This very grand example epitomises the Baroque style of William Kent. The eagle on a rockwork base symbolises Imperial Roman might.
£30,000-£40,000
Later copy: £2000-£4000

Adam-style giltwood pier table with marble top; c.1780; 60 in (1.52 m) wide. This table shows an effectively restrained use of Neoclassical motifs in the anthemion frieze and uprights copied from Roman originals.
£20,000-£30,000 (more if famous source)
19thC copy: £4000-£6000

George IV mahogany console table; c.1825; 52 in (1.32 m) wide. This example is typical of the period with its elaborately carved supports and brackets, but the marble top is probably later.
£2000-£3000

Early Victorian rosewood console side table; 1835-45; 57 in (1.44 m) wide. The finely carved scroll supports are decorated with acanthus and headed by bold paterae.
£1500-£2500

Edwardian satinwood pier table; 1900-10; 56½ in (1.43 m) wide. The Sheraton-style painted top is combined with an Adam-style gilt painted base.
£3000-£5000
George III example: £15,000-£20,000

THE CONSOLE TABLE is essentially a floor-standing bracket, usually with one or two supports, and in most cases it is fixed to a wall. It was introduced into Britain at the beginning of the 18th century following the lead of the French court of Louis XIV, where a combination of console tables and tall, narrow mirrors was fashionable.

The pier table also dates from the early 18th century. Unlike consoles, pier tables have four legs and are freestanding.

CONSOLE TABLES

Two main styles are found in 18th-century console tables – the rather architectural Neoclassical style and the Rococo. Both have been widely reproduced since.

One of the best-known designs is William Kent's eagle console, whose marble top is supported by the spread wings of a large bird perched on a rocky base. There is often a spiral or S-shaped scroll frieze. A pair of genuine Kent consoles is worth hundreds of thousands of pounds. Regency pieces also command high prices: a pair of Regency dolphin consoles recently sold at auction for £340,000.

French late 18th-century Louis XVI giltwood consoles are hard to find. Most in this style on the market are 19th-century reproductions, often accompanied by rectangular pier glasses. Genuine examples can fetch as much as £20,000-£30,000 at auction, or sometimes much more if they are from an important maker or commission, whereas a

19th-century reproduction table and glass will sell for around £2000-£3000.

British consoles of the Adam period contemporary with Louis XVI are in more restrained Neoclassical style. These can reach prices of around £20,000-£30,000, sometimes more if from an important maker.

The exuberant Rococo style found a natural outlet in the console table, both in Britain and in France. Many British consoles, by 18th-century makers such as Thomas Chippendale and John Linnell, were inspired by French Louis XV designs. They became the prototypes for numerous 19th and early 20th-century copies.

Single 19th-century examples in Louis XV style can usually be found for under £1000, whereas a single 18th-century piece will fetch

£3000-£5000 and upwards, and a pair considerably more. English 18th-century Rococo console tables are not common and may fetch £10,000-£15,000. Rococo Revival console tables of the 1830s occasionally come up for sale, generally for under £3000.

PIER TABLES

Marquetry in Neoclassical style is often incorporated in pier tables, using such exotic woods as satinwood and harewood. Many satinwood pier tables date from the late 19th century. Although keenly sought after, they are at the low end of the price range: a good Victorian or Edwardian pair will fetch £7000-£10,000, whereas even a moderate pair of painted or marquetry Georgian pier tables will top £20,000.

Desks and writing tables

*Once a world away from the computer and the fax machine,
antique desks are coveted for modern homes and offices.*

FROM THE HUMBLE farmer's son at a village
school to the young gentry with their
private tutors, there have been literate
people at all levels of British society for
centuries. The writing furniture they used
varies just as widely: from cramped, utilitarian
designs to priceless pieces specially commissioned for great country houses.

KNEEHOLE AND PEDESTAL DESKS AND LIBRARY TABLES

Introduced in the late 17th century, the
kneehole desk is the oldest form of flat-topped
writing table. It is essentially a small chest
with one or two long drawers at the top, a
recessed cupboard below and short drawers on
each side. Early Queen Anne walnut versions
of fine colour and patina can fetch £8000 or
more (£2500-£5000 otherwise), but mid-Georgian mahogany pieces under £3000.

By the middle of the 18th century, kneehole designs had given way to pedestal desks

with separate top and side
sections. Prices generally
increase with size. For
example, a partners' desk
(which has an extra-large
top, and drawers at 'back'
and 'front', allowing two
people to work face to
face) will always cost more
than a standard model of
similar quality. Georgian
partners' desks with good
colour can sell at auction
for £20,000 to £40,000,
while some 19th-century
desks of cruder construction fetch less than £1500.

The library table emerged at about the same
time as the pedestal desk. It was a writing table
with a leg at each corner and a row of drawers
in the frieze (sometimes both sides). The
earliest versions date from the 1760s and have

PIECE WITH A HISTORY *John Forster, shown at his writing table c.1850,
was a historian and a biographer – most notably of Charles Dickens.*

a plain top and square tapering legs. By the
1780s, the legs were slender and turned, and
not long after, reeded decoration was added.
Georgian examples, especially of the partners'
type with drawers either side, are highly

*Walnut-veneered pedestal desk; c.1930;
75 in (1.9 m) wide. Had this Art Deco desk
been the work of a well-known furniture
designer, it would have sold for twice as much.*
£800-£1500

*Queen Anne walnut-veneered kneehole desk;
c.1710; 30½ in (77.5 cm) wide. Rich original
colour and a firmly moulded edge increase the value
of such a piece, but beware converted chests.*
£5000-£8000
Converted piece: £2000-£4000

*Walnut-veneered pedestal desk; c.1850; 60 in
(1.52 m) wide. Victorian examples are common, but
this desk's superb colour increases its value.*
£4000-£6000

*George III mahogany and satinwood tambour
desk (above); c.1790; 50⅜ in (1.28 m)
wide. The style was based on French Louis
XVI period pieces. Early Victorian mahogany
pedestal cylinder desk (left); c.1840; 47¼ in
(1.2 m) wide. This was a forerunner of the
ubiquitous roll-top desk.*
Above: £5000-£8000
Edwardian copy: £2000-£3000
Left: £1000-£1500

George III mahogany library table; c.1770; 50 in (1.27 m) wide. One of the simplest library tables of this period, such a piece is easy to fake, but discrepancies between old and new timbers show.
£6000-£8000
Reconstructed: £2000-£4000

Regency calamander-veneered writing table; c.1810; 75 in (1.9 m) wide. Exotic veneer and gilt embellishment make this a particularly costly piece.
£20,000-£40,000

Mahogany
*library rent table; c.1760;
44 in (1.12 m) diameter. Such
tables were used for the safekeeping of tenants' rent.
Original examples are rare and extremely expensive.*
£30,000 or more

sought after and commonly fetch over £10,000 – or up into six figures for the grandest Neoclassical or Egyptian Revival designs. Even the more heavily proportioned late Regency and William IV versions often exceed £5000. Victorian library tables with solid baluster turned legs and deep drawers sell for about £2000-£4000, although you may find a plain example for under £1000.

DRUM AND RENT TABLES

A form of library table popular with makers of reproduction furniture is the drum table. This has a circular or sometimes polygonal revolving top above a frieze fitted with true and false drawers. Drum tables were made in the late 18th century and all through the 19th.

Rent tables – so called because landlords used them for the safekeeping of tenants' rent records or even money – are an interesting and rarer variant. They are generally quite large, and have frieze drawers inscribed with letters, numbers or even the days of the week. The heavy square-section centre support may hide a secret compartment.

Many drum and rent tables seen in salerooms and antique shops today are mixtures of old and new components, and those that are not can be prohibitively expensive: a George III mahogany drum table, for example, is likely to fetch as much as £15,000 at auction, and Regency versions are scarcely more affordable – although some can be found for under £5000. Good rent tables can now fetch more than £20,000, whereas a later Victorian

table – either of a heavy 19th-century design or a copy of an 18th-century one – usually sells for between £3000 and £5000.

DAVENPORTS

The first reference to the davenport comes in the late 18th-century records of the Lancaster-based firm of Gillows, where one entry records: 'Captain Davenport, a desk.' Essentially it is a narrow upright cabinet with a sloping leather-lined top that slides forward, and often a galleried superstructure. Underneath a bank of drawers opens to one side with false drawer-fronts on the other, and sometimes a narrow hinged drawer for ink.

The earliest davenports, dating from 1800, are usually in mahogany or rosewood. Particularly fine examples can fetch over £5000, although £2500-£5000 is more usual. William IV davenports – sometimes with a spindle-turned gallery and reeded bun feet – generally go for £1500-£2500.

The most sought-after Victorian versions are in burr walnut, with carved scroll uprights supporting the slope. Particularly valuable is the 'piano-top' style with a rising pulley-driven superstructure and hinged fall – like the lid of an upright piano. These can sell for over £2000, but £1000-£1500 is more usual for other mid-Victorian styles.

FRENCH INSPIRATION

The bonheur-du-jour is a distinctive style of writing furniture introduced in France in the 1760s and produced in England soon afterwards. Often referred to at the time as a 'lady's cabinet', it is basically a rectangular side table

Regency mahogany drum table (right); 1805-10; 45 in (1.14 m) diameter. This piece is original, but beware of those reconstructed from odd parts.
£4000-£6000

George III mahogany architect's table (left); c.1750; 36¼ in (92 cm) wide. Its front legs pull out to reveal compartments, and the writing surface is held up by ratcheted supports.
£3000-£5000

with single frieze drawer and a shallow superstructure of drawers and pigeonholes, sometimes with doors over them.

English versions – by Hepplewhite and by Gillows – are usually in satinwood, sometimes decorated with painted Neoclassical designs. Eighteenth-century examples fetch £7000-£10,000, or even more if little restored. Even Edwardian Sheraton Revival versions, usually larger and more decorated, can go for £5000.

The French bonheur-du-jour is most familiar in its 19th-century versions, which were closely imitated in Victorian Britain. Two of the most common versions were in Louis XIV style. One has tortoiseshell and cut-brass inlay on an ebonised ground in the manner of the French cabinet-maker André Boulle. The other uses elaborate floral marquetry combined with decorative veneers such as burr walnut, tulipwood and kingwood. Prices vary between £2000 and £5000.

It is sometimes difficult to tell whether a French-style bonheur-du-jour was made in France or in England. However, most English versions have mahogany-lined drawers – the French tended to use oak – and finer dovetails. They are also without the double-throw mechanism unique to French locks.

OTHER TYPES OF DESK

One of the most ingenious pieces of writing furniture was the architect's table, first made in the early 18th century in the time of Queen Anne. Basically a rectangular table, it has front legs that pull out to reveal compartments and a ratcheted writing surface, while the top hinges up to form a reading slope. Smaller versions were made for lady watercolourists, and in the 19th century a folio cabinet was often incorporated below.

Early 18th-century architect's tables in walnut, often with candleholders either side, are now scarce and can change hands for over £10,000. Plain mid-Georgian mahogany versions can be found for £2000-£4000, or rather more with Gothic-style blind fret decoration, which was thought suitable at the time for the monastic library atmosphere.

In more lavish style is the Carlton House desk – named after a U-shaped desk, now at Buckingham Palace, but originally located in the Prince Regent's bedroom at Carlton House. Similar desks appear in design books of the period such as Hepplewhite's *Cabinet Maker's Book of Prices* (1793) and Sheraton's *Drawing Book* (1791-4). Carlton House desks dating from the Regency period are now rare and fetch more than £15,000 at auction. Even late 19th-century examples and modern copies can exceed £5000.

Among the Victorians, one of the most sought-after pieces of library furniture was a kidney-shaped pedestal desk, and today such desks are highly collectable. They were often veneered in burr walnut and commonly had open shelves on the front. Prices of such desks have increased rapidly in recent years, and figures above £30,000 are not uncommon.

The mid-19th century also saw a revival of Louis XV opulence, particularly in the form of *bureaux plats* (flat-topped writing tables), both French and British versions. A good example will fetch about £3000-£5000 and a modern copy £1000-£1500.

Regency rosewood and satinwood lady's writing table; c.1805; 20 in (51 cm) wide. This piece's lyre uprights are typical of the period.
£6000-£8000

Victorian walnut bonheur-du-jour; c.1860; 48½ in (1.23 m) wide. French and English examples can be difficult to distinguish.
£2000-£4000

Regency mahogany davenport; c.1820; 20½ in (52 cm) wide. It has a brass gallery, beaded edge, turned feet, and its original finely turned brass handles.
£2000-£3000

Regency mahogany Carlton House desk; c.1820; 60 in (1.52 m) wide. This fine example is in flame-veneered mahogany with ebony stringing.
£20,000-£40,000
Edwardian copy: up to £5000

Victorian walnut-veneered davenport; c.1860; 23 in (58.5 cm) wide. This example has finely figured veneer and well-carved cabriole uprights characteristic of the period.
£1500-£2500

Victorian walnut kidney-shaped desk; c.1850; 51 in (1.3 m) wide. These most luxurious of Victorian desks have rocketed in value.
£20,000-£30,000
20thC reproduction: £6000-£10,000

Racks and shelves

Glass perches, delft racks, whatnots and canterburies are just a few of the strangely named solutions to our ancestors' storage and display needs.

Pine 'delft' or dresser rack; late 18thC; c.72 in (1.8 m) wide. Regional styles varied but the basic form hardly altered over time.
£600-£900
Victorian example: £100-£200

Victorian pine plate rack; 1850-80; 36 in (91 cm) wide. This simple rack has acquired a patina from years of use and has not suffered from painting and subsequent stripping.
£30-£50

Regency whatnot; c.1825; 55½ in (1.41 m) high. This attractive rosewood whatnot is unusual because it has a folding music stand. It would be less valuable in poor-quality mahogany or without the stand.
£2000-£3000

Victorian rosewood canterbury; c.1850; 19 in (48.2 cm) wide. This ornate piece displays an eclectic mix of Rococo, Baroque and Louis XVI influences.
£400-£600

Regency mahogany canterbury; c.1815; 20 in (51cm) wide. Concave dividers are also found on late 18thC pieces, but the turned legs are typically Regency.
£2000-£3000

CHAUCER, IN THE MILLER'S TALE, written in the 14th century, refers to 'shelves couched at his beddes head' – probably for books – but shelving for more general uses was rare before the 16th century. By the 19th century, however, a whole variety of other storage and display solutions had appeared.

WALL RACKS AND SHELVES

In the 16th century 'glass perches' usually in the form of open shelves, occasionally with doors, were used to store fragile drinking vessels. By the 17th century the more substantial 'dresser' or 'delft rack' had evolved for showing off plate and ceramic wares; fixed to a base this became the high dresser (see p.119). Delft racks of the 17th and 18th centuries are the earliest items of this type you are likely to find today; most of these pieces have been repaired or altered in size. Made of oak, the largest are some 6 ft (1.8 m) wide with four or five shelves, indicating a wealthy owner with many objects to display. Early racks often have elaborate inlay, carving and mouldings, befitting the treasures they held.

From the early 18th century, shelving was widely used in large houses. Some rooms had fitted shelves to display Chinese porcelain, but these cannot be removed from listed interiors and appear only very occasionally on

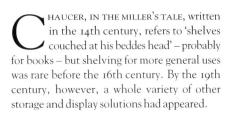

PIANO LESSONS *Playing the piano was a required accomplishment for young ladies in the 19th century. This modish group painted by George Leslie Dunlop store their music in a canterbury. In the background is a dwarf bookcase in painted wood.*

the market as part of an entire 18th-century panelled room. More common today are hanging shelves, themselves often ornamented with chinoiserie – a vogue that continued into the second half of the century, as several designs in Thomas Chippendale's *Director* of 1754 show; others are decorated with Gothic motifs. Many hanging shelves have decorative fretwork sides in three-piece mahogany, an early form of plywood. Fine examples sell for as much as £8000-£12,000 today.

More severe Neoclassical shelves date from the late Georgian and Regency periods; ones based on designs by George Hepplewhite or Thomas Sheraton can fetch £3000-£6000.

From the early 19th century, brass tubing was often used to support two to four wooden shelves, while the Victorians also used cast iron and papier mâché. Many simple late 19th-century units, often originally for home assembly, can still be found for about £20 each. So-called 'Victorian' pine shelves are very common and have usually been made up by dealers from old pine boards. As they are so useful, they may nonetheless fetch £500.

WHATNOTS AND CANTERBURIES

The whatnot (known in France as an *étagère*) first appeared in the late 18th century and consists of three or more open tiers of shelves on corner supports, usually on castors. Most are mahogany, although rosewood, bird's-eye maple and other timbers were also used. Later examples often have walnut or rosewood veneer on a mahogany base. Prices depend as much upon elegance and condition as on age. For example, an elegant Regency rosewood whatnot might sell for £2500-£3500, whereas one of the same date with mahogany veneer and beading would fetch only £800-£1500.

The canterbury also appeared in the late 18th century; it originally stored sheet music but today is often used for magazines. Early pieces are simple and elegant, consisting of three or four vertical compartments above a fitted drawer on straight legs. Regency examples often have turned tapered legs, and late Victorian canterburies tend to be heavily carved. Late designs may have X-framed dividers and a removable tray or table-top.

Almost all early canterburies are mahogany or sometimes satinwood. From 1810 rosewood was popular, although other woods were also used. Georgian examples can fetch £5000 today, Victorian ones £500-£1500. A fitted drawer increases the value, as do good colour, condition and construction, but elegance is again the main criterion. The canterbury was superseded in the Edwardian era by music cabinets in mahogany veneer with a glazed door; these are good value at £100-£300.

Bookcases

Despite encompassing some of the most expensive items of furniture ever made, many bookcases are still to be found at affordable prices.

STYLE-SETTING DIARIST *This is one of the 12 original oak bookcases made for Samuel Pepys in the 1660s and now in the Pepys Library at Magdalene College, Cambridge. Its style is architectural. Good late Victorian or Edwardian copies fetch £4000-£6000 today.*

George IV mahogany bookcase of inverted breakfront form; c.1825; 90 in (2.29 m) wide. It mingles Neoclassical and Gothic elements, echoing designs of 50-70 years earlier.
£8000-£12,000

IN THE 1660s, the English diarist Samuel Pepys had a set of 12 oak cases made to house his collection of books. These are among the first recorded specialised bookcases made for a private individual. Previously, books were considered so precious that small cabinets were constructed to transport them safely from place to place. From the late 17th century, books were increasingly housed in large glazed and fitted bookcases, but it was more than a century before smaller bookcases became commonplace items.

Special care needs to be taken when buying a bookcase, as many pieces have been altered in one way or another. Marriages between a differing top and bottom are quite frequent, styles of glazing have sometimes been altered to give an added appearance of age and, most commonly, large bookcases have often been cut down in size. Worst of all, a bookcase may have started life as an entirely different piece of furniture (see box, p.126).

LARGE BOOKCASES

Queen Anne bookcases – the earliest large examples still commonly found – are generally simple in style and veneered in walnut. By the 1740s, bookcases followed grander architectural styles and were often breakfronted, with Gothic, Rococo or Classical motifs according to current fashion; some had a pull-out secretaire drawer for writing on (see p.131). Most are made of mahogany with glazed doors, although painted pine and, in the Regency period, satinwood and rosewood are also found. Today, very large, unwieldy pieces – perhaps as tall as 9 ft (2.8 m) – are often worth much less than smaller ones, but even so the best can fetch well over £50,000.

One of the best ways to date a bookcase is by the glazing bars. Until the 1730s, bars were solid and the glass panes rectangular. Bookcases with astragal glazing bars, dividing

Victorian pine bookcase (above); c.1870; 90 in (2.29 m) wide. This would originally have been painted but has been stripped to suit modern taste.
£1500-£2500
Made up from old wood: £800-£1200

Mahogany revolving bookstand; c.1810; 32½ in (82.5 cm) in diameter. The leather bookspines – from real books – form clever dividers to hold the books in place.
£4000-£6000

Oak book cabinet; c.1875; 68 in (1.73 m) high. Pieces such as this in Arts and Crafts style are very practical; those by noted designers cost more.
£600-£800

hexagonal or shaped panes, are almost always (reproductions aside) from 1730-1800.

From the 1820s on, wire grilles became popular for the doors as they allowed the books to 'breathe'. Some examples have glazed doors in the centre and wired ones at the sides, and probably doubled as display cabinets. In rosewood, these realise £5000 up to £25,000 depending on grandeur, but painted pine examples are usually cheaper.

SMALLER BOOKCASES

In the 1780s, small, open bookcases became popular – to fit against the pier walls between windows. Most have four or five shelves, and many incorporate a drawer. In some cases, the

One of a pair of late Regency mahogany open bookcases; c.1820; 42 in (1.06 m) wide. They are in plain style with adjustable shelves.
£6000-£8000 the pair
Single: £2500-£3500

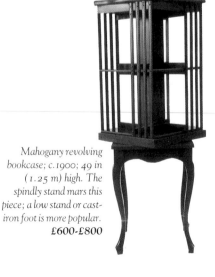

Mahogany revolving bookcase; c.1900; 49 in (1.25 m) high. The spindly stand mars this piece; a low stand or cast-iron foot is more popular.
£600-£800

shelves sit above a small cupboard and the books are held in place by S-shaped supports. Late Georgian examples sell today for £2500-£10,000, but there are many less expensive copies dating from the 1880s onwards.

Another late 18th-century invention is the cylindrical revolving bookcase. In most examples, the tiers decrease in size towards the top – like a wedding cake. Some have false book spines at the shelf ends to keep the books in place. Georgian drum bookcases sell today for about £5000; 1920s copies start at £800.

Square revolving bookcases appeared in the late 1890s, made of satinwood, mahogany, beech and, most commonly, oak. Many are severely functional and were probably intended for public libraries or schools, but others are attractive, useful and affordable for modern homes. Plain oak examples with cast-iron feet cost £200-£300 and fancier versions in mahogany or satinwood up to £1250.

When it became fashionable in the late 18th and early 19th centuries to dedicate large amounts of wall space to picture collections, 'dwarf' bookcases were introduced. These are generally half the height of earlier designs – at about 4 ft (1.2 m) high – but may be as much as 8 ft (2.4 m) wide. Better quality Victorian pieces were often topped with leather – now usually replaced by veneer – but other plain mahogany or oak examples can be found for a few hundred pounds.

WARDROBE CONVERSIONS
Is it What it Seems?

BOOKCASES are always expensive, but only a genuine example can be expected to be a really good investment. Fakes are common, and late Georgian or Victorian breakfront wardrobes are particularly prone to conversion, as they can be bought cheaply, were made of fine materials, and their size and form are already close to that of a bookcase.

To convert the wardrobe, it is cut at 'waist' height, and smaller panel doors are made to fit the lower section. The upper section is reduced in depth, the remaining parts of the panel doors are glazed, and shelves are fitted inside.

Most conversions are performed for maximum profit, and dubious origins are often given away by short cuts. Looking at the back and inside, you may see obviously new pieces of wood. Glazing bars and new glass can also give the game away. Most genuine bookcases have some original, thin and uneven glass left. Conversions may have glazing bars glued to the frame, rather than inset, or even glazing bars stuck over a single pane of glass.

Other questions to ask include: Are there signs of old catches or hinges? Are there strange holes left by hooks or even scuff marks? And is the overall colour and grain of the mahogany consistent? New veneers often have to be used in certain places.

George III mahogany-veneered breakfront bookcase; c.1770; 111 in (2.82 m) wide. This is the real thing, but is the sort of piece that is frequently imitated by cutting down a wardrobe.
£10,000-£15,000
Adapted wardrobe: £3000-£5000

Other library furniture

Few modern homes have a library, but many people are keen to acquire examples of ingenious 18th and 19th-century library furniture.

BY THE MIDDLE of the 18th century, not only were books housed in bookcases in special rooms but imaginative cabinet-makers had begun to create other specialised pieces of furniture for use in libraries

STEPS AND LADDERS

The metamorphic library chair is one of the most collectable items, transforming itself in a number of ways from a comfortable chair into a low set of steps 'for the use of raising a person so as to reach any book', in the words of Thomas Sheraton's 1803 design book.

The earliest known version of such a chair dates from the mid-18th century and is made of padouk, a heavy, reddish wood. Apparently an armchair, its back hinges forward until the top rail rests on the floor, and four stair treads are revealed. Folding library steps are also disguised as stools and, more rarely, as Pembroke tables. However, the folding arm-chair proved the most popular design and was revived by the firm of Morgan & Sanders and other cabinet-makers in the Regency period. Regency library chairs sell for £3000-£5000, Georgian examples for £4000-£6000. Simpler small Victorian folding library chairs in pine, without arms, can be found for about £150 and were probably made for schools.

Folding library pole ladders, usually in pine but sometimes in mahogany, were made in the late 18th and early 19th centuries. When closed they look like a simple cylindrical pole, some 6 in (15.2 cm) in diameter; the pole opens into two halves revealing an iron ladder within. Pole ladders are rare and sell for about £2000 today, as do similar pieces by British architect and designer Sir Edwin Lutyens, who reinvented the design in the 1920s, probably unaware of its previous existence.

OTHER LIBRARY FURNISHINGS

Large globes with magnificent wooden stands were housed in libraries from the mid-18th century on, and normally came in pairs – one for the earth (terrestrial), the other for the heavens (celestial) – each with a built-in compass. Dating is difficult as the stands rarely kept pace with furniture styles, and the maps were often replaced by new ones showing the latest discoveries. Globes rarely fetch less than £2000, and a pair in good Regency stands may sell for over £30,000 (see also p.297).

Folio stands were made in large numbers in the Regency and Victorian periods. They are now in great demand and even the plainest beech examples can realise £2000.

Small table-top bookrests resembling piano music stands appeared in the late 17th century; 18th-century examples start at £500 but may reach £3000 if inlaid or carved. Book carriers, which hold two rows of small books, were used in late 18th century and Regency households, as were 'cheverets', in which a book tray with handle stands on a small table with tapering legs. Usually in satinwood, the two parts may fetch £1000 separately but £4000-£6000 or more together.

Pair of George III library globes with compasses on mahogany stands; c.1800; 48 in (1.22 m) high. In the case of single globes, the terrestrial globe is more popular than the celestial.
Pair £15,000-£20,000
Single globe: £4000-£5000

Regency rosewood folio stand (above); c.1820; 28 in (71 cm) wide. Folio stands are keenly sought by picture dealers. This stand is similar to ones made by Gillows. Its ratchet-prop folio rest opens flat for viewing prints.
£3000-£5000
Victorian beech: £2000-£3000

Mahogany metamorphic library chair (below); c.1820. This Regency armchair made (and name-stamped) by Weeks of London opens to make library steps 36 in (91 cm) high.
£3000-£5000

Fold-away library steps from a design by Thomas Sheraton; c.1820; 34¼ in (87 cm) wide when closed. These rosewood steps with brass inlay close to make a long low stool. Satinwood examples cost even more, but oak or painted 'faux bois' would go for less.
£4000-£6000

Bureaux and secretaires

The bureau neatly combines the function of a writing table with that of a decorative filing cabinet – features which make it doubly sought after.

Queen Anne walnut bureau-on-stand (left); c.1705; 25½ in (65 cm) wide. The style was faithfully reproduced in many 1920s and 30s copies.
£10,000-£15,000
Copy: £800-£1500

Plain mahogany Georgian bureau; c.1760; 45 in (1.14 m) wide. This example is raised in value by its good colour, quarter column uprights and well-shaped ogee bracket feet.
£1500-£2500

Queen Anne walnut bureau; c.1710; 37 in (94 cm) wide. The mouldings around the drawers later developed into Georgian cockbeading.
£4000-£6000
If restored: £2000-£3000

William and Mary walnut-veneered bureau; c.1700; 39 in (99 cm) wide. Such a bureau would be worth far less if it were re-veneered, of poor colour or of a slightly later date.
£5000-£8000

Queen Anne lacquer bureau cabinet; c.1710; 40½ in (1.03 m) wide. Black and gilt lacquer cabinets such as this are worth much less than similar red-japanned pieces.
£30,000-£50,000
19th or 20thC copy: £3000-£5000

THE BUREAU'S DISTANT ANCESTORS were the medieval lectern and its more portable version the lapdesk, which had a hinged flap like the top of a bureau. By the late 17th century, the lapdesk was given a stand so the user could sit at it – and thus the bureau-on-stand was born. The need for extra storage space led to the bureau proper, with a bank of drawers under the writing slope, which appeared in the William and Mary period (1689-1702). Since that time these pieces have been made in a variety of forms.

BUREAUX

The earliest bureaux come in two sections, with a writing box sitting on a chest of drawers. The top section, which can be lifted off, commonly hangs over the drawers slightly at each side. In superficially similar early 18th-century examples the join between the two sections is hidden by a strip of heavy continuous moulding, even though by then most bureaux were made as a single piece.

William and Mary bureaux are almost invariably veneered in walnut and are usually wider and squatter than later pieces. They are rare, and in original condition will comfortably top £5000 at auction.

Still rarer is a form of bureau-on-stand which was made well into Queen Anne's reign (1702-14). It was given gently curved cabriole legs and ball-and-claw or hairy paw feet. An original Queen Anne bureau-on-stand will fetch £7000-£25,000 and upwards, particularly if the legs have fine carving.

Bureaux-on-stands were much imitated in the 1920s and 30s, and a good 1930s example could change hands for £500-£800.

By George I's reign (1714-27), the bureau form was fully developed, and remained largely unchanged for the rest of the century. The earliest type had a secret 'well' compartment over three tiers of drawers. Later the well was replaced by another tier of drawers with one long or two short drawers.

Bureaux of the first quarter of the 18th century are the most sought after, and they were generally veneered in walnut, which is notoriously fragile. Many have therefore been repaired or even totally re-veneered, lowering the value significantly. A restored George I

WRITING STYLE *A medieval clerk, pictured in a 1485 manuscript, works at his prototype bureau.*

Queen Anne walnut-veneered bureau bookcase; c.1705; 77 in (1.96 m) high. This classic double-domed bureau on bun feet seems to have its original mirror panels.
£15,000-£20,000
19thC copy: £3000-£5000

George III mahogany secretaire bookcase; c.1800; 87 in (2.21 m) high. A standard example such as this will fetch no more than a good Victorian example. Drawers instead of cupboards in the base would increase the value.
£1500-2500

George III mahogany bureau bookcase; c.1760; 37 in (94 cm) wide. This bureau's value is increased by its convenient narrow width, Gothic-style ogee arches in the interior, and finely carved Greek key cornice.
£4000-£6000

Sheraton period mahogany secretaire chest; c.1790; 48 in (1.22 m) wide. Such chests are relatively cheap at present. This example has a good colour and a nicely detailed interior.
£800-£1200

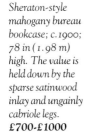

Sheraton-style mahogany bureau bookcase; c.1900; 78 in (1.98 m) high. The value is held down by the sparse satinwood inlay and ungainly cabriole legs.
£700-£1000

walnut bureau of the standard width of about 42-48 in (1.05-1.2 m) will usually sell at auction for £2000-£4000, whereas a small Queen Anne example in original condition could fetch £6000-£8000. It may make even more if the veneer is the particularly rich, deep colour beloved by collectors (see p. 130).

In early 18th-century Britain, walnut was veneered onto a pine carcass (pine being much cheaper than either oak or walnut), and, therefore, an English walnut bureau with an oak carcass is unlikely to be an original. However, an 18th-century oak bureau that has not undergone such veneering can be good value at less than £1200 in most cases.

The bureaux that come up most often at auction today are mahogany. Their colour is the most important single factor after size and originality in determining the price of pieces. Mid-18th-century examples made with richly figured mahogany tend to be the most keenly sought after. Prices vary comparatively little, however, and most sell at auction for between about £1000 and £2000.

Bureaux remained popular pieces of furniture throughout the 19th century, especially in their cylinder and roll-top forms. These do not open with a hinged fall front. Instead, the cylinder bureau has a sliding drum front – a solid piece of curved wood; the roll-top type has a series of hinged slats that can be pushed up and pulled down (see p. 121).

BUREAU CABINETS AND BOOKCASES

From the start of the 18th century, cabinets and bookcases were added to the top of bureaux and were produced in a range of contemporary styles. The rarest and most sought after today are the japanned versions from the beginning of the 1700s. Auction prices of £100,000 are not uncommon for these. Even 19th or 20th-century copies, especially if in red lacquer, will fetch as much as £3000-£5000 and sometimes even more.

Queen Anne period walnut bureau bookcases and cabinets with an ornate double-domed cornice are also highly prized, often selling for £20,000-£40,000. Even fully refurbished versions, or 19th and early 20th-century copies, will fetch over £5000. Less spectacular versions with a simple cornice, with or without mirrored doors, sell for £5000-£10,000 – but in every case it is vital to check the amount of restoration.

Early Georgian bureau cabinets, made in mahogany during the William Kent period, can fetch in excess of £10,000-£15,000. These are often topped with Neoclassical features such as a pediment in the form of a broken triangle or a scroll. Most Georgian bureau cabinets and bookcases are fairly plain and relatively inexpensive. A straightforward example in reasonable condition will rarely exceed £3000. But buyers should inspect these pieces for signs of a 'marriage' between a separate base and top, which lowers the value.

Over the last few years, early 20th-century Edwardian bureau bookcases have come to cost nearly as much as their original Georgian counterparts. They are generally more decoratively inlaid and less (continued p. 131)

An Expert Examines

JOHN BLY CHECKS THE CREDENTIALS OF AN EARLY GEORGIAN BUREAU

'IN THIS WICKED WORLD, a small, 18th-century, walnut-veneered bureau like the one we have here must prove itself beyond any doubt. Few were made, so there has always been the temptation to add thousands to the value of a similar piece in oak by giving it a walnut veneer. Equally, someone might have cut down a larger bureau to make a more desirable small one.

Straight-grained, thickish veneer suggests the 1730s

On the edge of the slope you can see that the veneer is little less than a sixteenth of an inch (1.5 mm) thick. This suggests a date in the early 18th century, since thinner, machine-cut veneers didn't come in for another 100 years.

The inside is plain – I would be suspicious if I saw anything too fancy in such a functional piece of furniture – and the overall colour is good. The straightish graining of the veneer suggests 1720-35, when English cabinet-makers were running out of walnut; the French had embargoed its export in 1720, after a hurricane in 1709.

The plain interior of small drawers and pigeonholes

Let's take out one of the drawers and look at it as a whole. The handles are original, and none of the tiny bolts shows any sign of newness or scratching. The locks, too, are steel and original, and the nails are hand-made clout nails – another good, 18th-century sign. Now, you see that the inside of the drawer-front, which doesn't normally show, is made of pine? That's because English cabinet-makers, if they were making something that was to be veneered, as a rule – and with some exceptions – constructed the carcass with pine, or some other cheap, soft wood. Partly this was for economy's sake, and partly because of available supplies of timber. And of course, had a faker tried to improve an oak piece with walnut veneer, the drawer's inside would have been of oak too.

Checking that the locks are original, and that marks on the drawers match gaps in the back of the carcass

Other telling points are those three darkened patches on the back of the drawer. They correspond exactly to the position and size of those three gaps in the back of the bureau that must have been there since the wood shrank, soon after it was made. Most likely the patches were caused by dust filtering through the gaps, to stain the wood over many years.

Here's something to gladden the heart of a furniture detective. That crack, in the base of the drawer: that's a shrinkage crack, too. You can tell by the way that splinter has gradually been pulled away by the strain. You wouldn't get that with a fake crack – wood will never split where you want it to. If the drawer had been made with that gap, then you wouldn't have the splinter. So that indicates that the drawer was made before the wood shrank.

All these things are very encouraging, but for me the real clincher so far as the age of the piece is concerned is the fact that there are only two dovetails where the sides of the drawer meet the back and the front. The importance of this is that, after the early 18th century, the method of construction changed from the two basic dovetails – usually one big *and one slightly smaller below – to a regular pattern of two equal-sized dovetails. By about 1730, you start to see the development of more dovetails until, by the end of the 18th century, you get four or five or more.*

Two dovetails, characteristic of early construction

The continuing trend in dovetail construction is shown by these other two drawers. The one with four dovetails belongs to a mahogany chest of about 1810, while the other, with seven, comes from a Sheraton Revival desk made around 1900.

Four dovetails: post-1750s *Seven dovetails: later 19th century*

But has it been cut down from a larger, less valuable bureau? This would be done by bringing the sides into the middle, so if you suspect skullduggery look at the proportions. Here, the top drawer is quite shallow. You can't imagine a bureau that was once 18 in (46 cm) wider having a drawer as shallow as that. The proportion of the mouldings would be different, too. So, all in all, it seems OK.

JOHN BLY SUMS UP

Small, early 18th-century bureaux like this can fetch anywhere between £1500 and £15,000 at auction. Condition is what counts. Even if it is broken, provided all the bits are there and the patina is intact, it would fetch more than if it had been stripped down to make it look clean, with new locks and regilded handles. But this one is complete, and the patina is centuries old. I'm sure it would make top-dollar at auction – at least £15,000. '

bulky, and now fetch upwards of £1500. A similar inlaid Edwardian bureau without a bookcase top will go for around £500.

SECRETAIRES

A variation on the bureau, developed in the second half of the 18th century, was the secretaire, not to be confused with the French secrétaire à abattant (see below). In the British secretaire, it is the top (false) drawer-front of the chest, as opposed to the sloping front of the bureau, that lowers to form the desk surface. Secretaire chests were made throughout the late 18th and 19th centuries. Most will sell for between £800 and £1500.

As with bureaux, however, the extended type with a bookcase or cabinet on top was also made (as was the altogether larger-scale breakfront bookcase with a secretaire drawer; see p.125). A Georgian secretaire bookcase of good proportions will fetch upwards of £3000–£4000, although most go for between £1500 and £3000. Many heavy Victorian examples can be found for £1500 or less.

The French secrétaire à abattant is an upright cabinet standing about 60 in (1.5 m) high with a hinged flap halfway down for the writing surface and drawers below. Early examples are rather severely Neoclassical in style, with a marble top surrounded by a brass gallery. Empire and mid-19th-century examples are chunkier and are often made of deeply figured mahogany enriched with ormolu mounts. The style was never very popular in this country, probably because it was rather awkward to work at. Even now, prices are comparatively low: about £2000–£5000 for all but the very best pieces or signed examples by famous makers.

Echoes of French-style secretaires can be seen in two 18th-century British designs. The first, the escritoire, appeared late in the William and Mary period. In essence it is a broader version of the secrétaire à abattant, but in two sections and usually made of walnut. Well-figured or attractively inlaid examples usually fetch £3000–£6000.

About 50 years later, another French-inspired form of secretaire was made by such designers as Thomas Chippendale and Vile & Cobb. It consists of a narrow upright chest with a secretaire section. The distinctive feature is a Chinoiserie or Gothic fretwork gallery of one or more shelves. Now rare and keenly sought after, good examples may change hands for more than £10,000.

Napoleon III secretaire; c.1860; 26¾ in (68 cm) wide. The French secrétaire à abattant owes its form to the Louis XVI period, although in this fine example the marquetry in thuya wood on an ebonised background is typical of Louis XIV.
£2000–£4000

George III mahogany secretaire; c.1760; 28⅓ in (72 cm) wide. An elaborately pierced, fret-carved gallery in the then fashionable Chinese/Gothic manner is an addition to the basic chest section of this Chippendale period piece.
£5000–£8000

William and Mary walnut-veneered escritoire; c.1700; 42 in (1.06 m) wide. In comparison with other furniture of the period, escritoires are undervalued, but this example has fine veneer.
£4000–£6000

Cabinets

Cabinets have been prized possessions since the 17th century, and are among the most visually arresting and impressive forms of furniture.

THE EARLIEST CABINETS made in Britain, in the mid-17th century, were used to store precious belongings and papers. By the end of the 17th century, however, they had become objects of distinction and elegance in their own right, and were often highly decorated. Some of the most luxurious cabinets were made on the Continent. Early cabinets-on-stands were prestige items and were often presented as gifts to visiting dignitaries at the great courts.

However, many cabinets are the result of a 'marriage' of separate items: a cabinet and a stand or a cabinet and chest. Pointers to such a marriage include a top and base that are not decorated with the same quality of veneer; or a top that differs slightly in size from the base.

CABINETS-ON-STANDS

Generally the cabinet-on-stand has a pair of solid doors concealing a set of small drawers; the whole thing – as its name suggests – is supported on a stand. Two basic types were produced during the 17th and early 18th centuries: the lacquered or japanned cabinet on a giltwood stand, and the marquetry cabinet on a veneered stand. The solid surface of the doors, and sometimes the whole piece, provided a backdrop for a dazzling array of decorative effects. Numerous examples of both types have survived, although many are marriages or have been extensively altered.

Lacquer cabinets were imported from the Far East in the late 17th century and throughout the 18th century, and are generally mounted on expensive, European-made giltwood stands. The stand might be in dramatic Baroque form, with carved leaves and figures, or in the simpler Queen Anne style with cabriole legs and perhaps a shell motif. Good-quality period examples are rare – and cost upwards of £15,000-£20,000 – but a lacquered cabinet-on-stand of average condition on a plain stand will fetch £4000-£6000.

Although the finest pieces have original Japanese lacquer, the majority of 'lacquered' cabinets-on-stands were made in Europe and japanned in imitation of Eastern lacquerwork. Some incorporate panels taken from Chinese incised lacquer screens. Giltwood stands in both Baroque and Queen Anne style were also copied in the 19th and early 20th centuries. Such copies, and associated or restored examples, often sell at auction for around £800-£2000.

All forms of inlaid decoration were used on cabinets which had veneered stands, notably 'oyster' veneers and the 'seaweed' and floral marquetry introduced into Britain by Dutch and French craftsmen in the late 17th century. The luxury pieces made by continental workshops, especially in Holland and Italy, are often rather wide and inset with semiprecious gemstones, or mounted with bronze figures on an ebony background.

Such fine pieces have always been out of reach of all but the wealthy, and

Charles II cabinet-on-stand; c.1670; 45 in (1.14 m) wide. This walnut, oyster-veneered and marquetry cabinet displays a range of decorative techniques; the marquetry shows Dutch influence.
£7000-£10,000
19thC or re-veneered: £3000-£5000

Charles II japanned cabinet-on-stand; c.1670; 76 in (1.93 m) high. This intricately carved giltwood stand has rare and original cresting.
£10,000-£15,000
20thC copy: £2000-£4000

Dutch marquetry display cabinet-on-stand; c.1780; c.60 in (1.5 m) wide. The Neoclassical escutcheons and tapering supports indicate the date of this piece.
18thC: £10,000-£15,000
19thC: £5000-£8000

The Badminton cabinet; 1725; 91½ in (2.32 m) wide. This cabinet of pietra dura, ebony, ormolu and semiprecious stones was made in Florence, Italy, for the 3rd Duke of Beaufort. It sold in 1990 for £8.58 million – a world record for furniture or any other field of applied arts.
Museum piece

Sheraton-style display cabinet; c.1900; 40 in (1 m) wide. The satinwood inlay boosts the value of this typically refined item from the Edwardian age.
£2000-£4000

Louis XV-style vitrine; c.1900; 45¼ in (1.15 m) wide. High quality gilt metal mounts and vernis martin panels enhance this French rosewood piece.
£3000-£5000
Without mounts: £2000-£3000

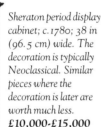

Sheraton period display cabinet; c.1780; 38 in (96.5 cm) wide. The decoration is typically Neoclassical. Similar pieces where the decoration is later are worth much less.
£10,000-£15,000

Mid-Victorian walnut credenza; c.1860; 75 in (1.9 m) wide. Naturalistic floral inlay as seen on this fine, serpentine-fronted credenza was influenced by early 18thC French and Dutch work, and is particularly popular at the moment.
£3000-£5000

Arts and Crafts oak cabinet; c.1900; 61 in (1.55 m) wide. The design of this cabinet is enlivened by the pierced tulips and stained-glass stylised foliage.
£1500-£2000

Regency chiffonier; c.1810; 45 in (1.14 m) high. A typically useful and decorative Regency piece, with the added attractions of a brass gallery, cut brass inlay and upholstered doors.
£2500-£4000

today even a more down-to-earth British marquetry cabinet, if in fine original condition, fetches more than £10,000. Restored and adapted, but nevertheless presentable versions, can be found for less than £5000.

DISPLAY CABINETS

Designers working in the Palladian style of the 1730s and 40s incorporated glazed doors or compartments into their designs. These early display cabinets are extremely rare, as are the Chippendale and Sheraton versions seen in 18th-century design books. However, numerous 19th-century reproductions (some very loosely based on 18th-century designs) have survived. Chippendale-style plain mahogany pieces are the most common, their legs and frieze decorated with blind-fret carving and the cabinet topped with moulding.

The Edwardian display cabinet is typically based on the late 18th-century Sheraton style. Examples in satinwood are fairly common and keenly sought after, often changing hands for £3000-£4000 or more. Mahogany Sheraton and Chippendale-style pieces will usually fetch £800-£1500, although sometimes as much as £2000-£3000. The lacquered display cabinet, in blue, red, green or black and loosely based on late 18th-century prototypes, was especially popular in the 1920s. Such a piece generally sells for less than £1000.

Between the mid-18th and mid-19th centuries, Dutch cabinets changed remarkably little, with an arched, glazed upper section – its moulded cornice often with a central carved motif – and a lower bombé section fitted with drawers. Relatively common, they fetch £5000-£10,000 or sometimes more.

Original 18th-century, glazed French display cabinets – vitrines – are rare, although 19th-century reproductions abound. The originals are seen in two distinct styles. Ornate Louis XV vitrines often come in kingwood or tulipwood, with concave glass panels topped by an arched moulding and asymmetrical ormolu mounts. Louis XVI versions are squarer and altogether more restrained, usually made of mahogany with turned and fluted legs. Prices range from £5000 up to £10,000 for a large 19th-century example, especially for one stamped with the mark of a quality maker such as Sormani or Linke.

SIDE CABINETS

The small side cabinet, or chiffonier, originated in Regency times as a dwarf side cabinet with open shelves, curved at either end. With time, it evolved into the more familiar form of a small cupboard raised on legs with a ledge, or shelf, at the back of its flat, sideboard-like top. Victorian examples often

Late Victorian display cabinet; c.1880; 44 in (1.12 m) wide. This rosewood, bone-inlaid and marquetry cabinet is typical of its date, with mirrored backs, assorted shelves and fine Neoclassical marquetry.
£1200-£1800

sport elaborate, carved scrolls on the ledged back. Regency pieces fetch £3000-£4000 or more, especially if they are decorated with brass inlay or are in fine, original condition.

The credenza, based on French and Italian models, was back in vogue in the 1840s and 50s. Most examples have a flat back, serpentine front and central door (often flanked by columns), with glazed display compartments on either side. A variation of the credenza is a rectangular cabinet in two sections supported by four legs, the upper section with shelves and compartments. Such pieces are often veneered in rosewood or mahogany.

Many later credenzas are in ebony with parcel gilt or ivory inlay. However, a good-quality piece rarely exceeds £1500-£2000, unless by an outstanding maker such as Jackson & Graham. Walnut credenzas regularly sell for over £3000, although humbler examples fetch less than £1500.

A distinctive form of late 19th-century side cabinet shows the influence of the Aesthetic movement. It often includes mirrored panels between the cabinet top and the shelf above and may be decorated with painted panels, usually on a gold background. These can be

Art Deco black lacquer cabinet; c.1930; 45 in (1.14 m) wide. The clean lines of this typically futuristic piece are accentuated by the mirror back. Such cabinets are often veneered in walnut or maple, but sometimes strikingly in calamander.
£1000-£2000; more in calamander

found for under £1000, although exceptional examples can fetch amounts up to £10,000.

Large display or side cabinets introduced towards the end of the 19th century have two sections. The lower part is similar in shape to a dresser base, with drawers and a cupboard on short legs joined by an undertier; and the upper section has an array of shelves, cupboards and mirrored panels. The whole thing is topped by a triangular, gable-like pediment. Good-quality examples are generally in rosewood, often combining marquetry with ivory inlay, but because of their bulk they rarely exceed £1500 at auction.

Art Nouveau designers produced distinctive display cabinets at the turn of the century, and stylish examples can be found for £500-£1000. Art Deco display and cocktail cabinets are even cheaper, most selling at auction for under £500, although pieces in luxurious materials can command high prices.

CORNER CUPBOARDS

Showy Space-Savers

CORNER CUPBOARDS have over the centuries been made either to hang in a corner or to stand on the floor, combining useful storage space with an attractive exterior.

One of the earliest types to come up for sale regularly is the early Georgian hanging corner cupboard in lacquerwork. Some are flat-fronted, but most are bowed, the door hiding a set of graduated shelves. Although few of these lacquer cupboards were actually made in the Orient, most were japanned to mimic the Chinese lacquerwork fashionable at the time. A run-of-the-mill example can fetch as little as £200-£400, but one in red or green lacquer can command £1000.

More common are veneered hanging cupboards of the mid to late 18th century. Most are plain and fetch under £500. Those with extra decoration go for more, but few exceed

£750. Floor-standing corner cupboards tend to be more expensive, and interesting examples of the later 18th century often seem more severely architectural in style than hanging cupboards, incorporating Neoclassical features such as an open-arched upper section. Many such cupboards are of pine and generally fetch between £1000 and £2000.

Many high-quality Georgian-style corner cupboards, both hanging and standing, were made in the Edwardian era. Despite being relatively modern, such cupboards, particularly floor-standing examples, may exceed £1000 when attractively inlaid.

Edwardian standing corner cupboard; c.1910; 37 in (94 cm) wide. This mahogany cupboard is decorated with marquetry inlay, and is in mint condition.
£1500-£2000

Bow-fronted mahogany hanging corner cupboard; c.1770; 27½ in (70 cm) wide. Such plain, functional mid-Georgian pieces are fairly inexpensive, despite an attractive colour.
£800-£1200

Chests and chests of drawers

*Some magnificent pieces of furniture developed out of the humble chest.
Today, collectors can choose from many styles and forms.*

NO MATTER how luxurious or humble, a chest of drawers can trace its ancestry back to the simple top-opening chest (also called a coffer) – one of the oldest items of furniture. Other descendants include the chest-on-stand, tallboy (chest-on-chest) and bow-fronted and serpentine chests.

The simplicity and usefulness of the chest has meant almost constant production since its introduction, and the same is true of all types of chests of drawers since they first appeared in the mid-17th century. As a result, the range available – in both style and quality – is huge. But the temptation for a dealer to 'improve' a run-of-the-mill piece to get a better price means that buyers should check for signs of adaptation (see box, p.137).

CHESTS

Most chests are made from oak, although examples in walnut, chestnut, elm and ash are not unusual. Chests can often be dated by their method of construction: surviving 13th-century examples, for instance, are made of planks often simply nailed together and bound with iron. They are sometimes called boarded chests and are very rare.

Those from the 15th century onwards have panels of wood held in a frame of upright stiles and cross members, with mortise-and-tenon joints held by pegs. Chests such as these were made in huge numbers throughout the 16th and 17th centuries, and can be distinguished from more modern imitations by the pegs used. Early chests have sharp-angled pegs; reproductions usually have circular ones.

Most Victorian Gothic and Elizabethan Revival pieces have the correct, panelled mortise-and-tenon construction but are generally over-carved; they sell for as little as £300-£500, while original 16th and 17th-century examples can cost £1500-£2500.

CHESTS OF DRAWERS

As antique chests of drawers still exist in large numbers, only the most unusual, or those of the highest quality, command high prices at auction. The best are well proportioned, made of quality timber, and still in original condition. Generally, smaller good-quality pieces tend to fetch more than large pieces, and those with a serpentine or bombé front more than plain examples. The most common

exotic wood veneers – found only on the best pieces – are satinwood and to a lesser degree partridge wood, calamander and tulipwood.

Many chests of drawers have been adapted from their original form to increase their value, and 18th and early 19th-century pieces are particularly prone to this. They may be cut down to a more desirable size, and it is not unusual to find a tallboy converted into two chests of drawers, or a chest-on-stand into a chest of drawers and a lowboy (see p.141).

Pine was used for the construction of chests of drawers from the earliest examples, but it was rarely used in an unfinished state. Pine chests dating from the 18th-century are usually veneered in walnut, while 19th-century examples were often painted. From the mid-18th century onwards, unfinished pine was used only for cheaper pieces which were bought and used by the poorer sections of society. Although they are rare, painted Regency examples can be worth as much as

George III tulipwood and kingwood marquetry bombé commode with ormolu mounts and marble top; c.1770; 32½ in (82.5 cm) high. This fine commode attributed to Pierre Langlois is heavily influenced by French design of the same date.
£75,000

Jacobean carved oak chest with fruitwood inlay; c.1620; 48 in (1.22 m) wide. This type of stylised carving was much imitated in the 19thC but copies tend to be over-elaborate.
£1500-£2000
Victorian copy: £300-£500

William and Mary oak chest in two parts; c.1690; 52 in (1.32 m) wide. The geometric, moulded decoration is typical of the period but the chest would originally have had bun, not bracket, feet. The panels of cedarwood veneer enhance its value.
£4000-£6000
Victorian copy: £600-£900

TREASURE CHEST *German chests often have attractive walnut veneer. The one in Rudolf Epp's painting is clearly for display as well as storage.*

Classic George III tallboy; c.1765; 44 in (1.12 m) wide. The blind-fret ornament, ogee bracket feet, brushing slide and fine 'plum-pudding' mahogany veneer signify high quality. **£3000-£5000**

Queen Anne chest of drawers; c.1700; 31½ in (80 cm) wide. Most pieces found today are copies or reconstructions using period veneer. **£4000-£6000**
Good reconstruction: £1000-£1500

George II walnut bachelor's chest with folding top; c.1740; 30 in (76 cm) wide. Originals are rare but copies made in the 1920s fetch £800-£1200. **£5000-£8000**

Queen Anne-style mahogany tallboy; 1930s; 54 in (1.37 m) high. 'Queen Anne' tallboys with cabriole legs were popular in the 1920s and 30s. **£400-£600**

George III serpentine chest of drawers in satinwood; c.1790; 36¼ in (92 cm) wide. **£6000-£9000**
1920s copy: £800-£1200

£800-£1200 today, while 'stripped' 19th-century chests (found in abundance) usually change hands at auction for less than £300.

EARLY STYLES

Fully enclosed chests of drawers were already being made by the mid-17th century, their drawer fronts generally decorated with geometric panels, and sometimes veneered in walnut or fruitwood. Rare examples in original condition fetch £1500-£2500, while one with some repair or restoration, but still essentially period, would make only £700-£1000. Victorian copies from the end of the 19th century can fetch as little as £150-£250.

Late 17th-century chests of drawers, especially those from Holland, are noted for their surface decoration. The best are inlaid with 'seaweed' and foliate marquetry, or veneered in strongly figured walnut. Walnut veneer is also a feature of early 18th-century Queen Anne chests of drawers, tallboys and chests-on-stands. Good 19th and 20th-century copies are still desirable.

GEORGIAN TO VICTORIAN

The shape of a chest of drawers became more important than its surface decoration in the mid-18th century. The creations of leading British cabinet-makers such as Thomas Chippendale, Mayhew & Ince and Vile & Cobb are among the very finest ever made, way beyond the pocket of most collectors at prices in six figures. Even good, late 19th-century copies of these beautiful pieces are very expensive, as few were made.

Among the best-value reproduction pieces are those from the 19th-century firms of Maples, Edwards & Roberts, Howard & Son and Hamptons, who produced fine chests in a variety of revival styles – including Jacobean, Georgian, Louis XV, Louis XVI, Regency, Empire, Biedermeier, and Arts and Crafts. These are excellent value today, as a plain example in pine may sell for as little as £100-£200 and a fancier piece for £600-£900. A maker's stamp increases the price, especially that of Gillows, who made some of the finest reproduction chests of drawers.

BOMBÉ AND SERPENTINE FRONTS

Some of the most elaborate bombé chests of drawers seen today, known as commodes, were made in France during the reigns of Louis XV and XVI (1715-93). The magnificent, bulbous pieces produced by the royal cabinet-makers are now extremely valuable and have been repeatedly copied, mainly in the 19th century. Commodes often have a marble top, inlaid decoration and ormolu mounts.

The ormolu mounts are the most obvious guide to a piece's quality. Good mounts are very bold, deep and heavy, and are finely chased with sharp details. Cheaper mounts tend to be flatter, more lightweight, blurred and imprecise. Some late 19th-century bombé commodes are themselves valuable, making £6000-£9000 at auction, while lesser examples fetch only £1000-£2000.

The majority of 19th-century bombé chests were made in France, Italy, Spain or Holland. Dutch examples are invariably of solid oak construction, with good-quality figured mahogany or walnut veneers, but many have had over-elaborate marquetry decoration added later. Such marquetry examples are

Gillows mahogany chest of drawers; c.1830; 42 in (1.06 m) wide. Pieces that were stamped, like this, fetch more than unstamped examples. **£1200-£1800**

Victorian pine chest of drawers painted to simulate bamboo; c.1840; 48 in (1.22 m) wide. Most pine chests have been stripped of their original decoration. **£800-£1200**

Continental ormolu and marquetry commode (above); late 18thC; 60 in (1.52 m) wide. This style of commode has been widely copied. **£40,000-£60,000** **19thC copy: £6000-£8000**

Mahogany Wellington chest; c.1845; 20 in (51 cm) wide. Such chests were first made by Gillows, loosely based on the French 18thC semainier. **£1200-£1800**

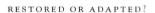

Teak campaign chest with secretaire drawer; early 19thC; 48 in (1.22 m). **£1200-£1800**

Regency mahogany bowfront chest (left); c.1820; 43¼ in (1.1 m) wide. The colour and grain of the wood are good. **£1000-£1500**

very popular, however, and a good 19th-century marquetry piece can fetch £1500-£2500 today. An 18th-century chest with later marquetry can fetch even more.

Some of the most popular serpentine chests of drawers, which have a double-curved outline, are German walnut pieces dating from the late 18th century. These distinctive chests, often raised on bun feet, usually have a pine carcass covered with highly figured walnut veneer, further enhanced by banding that is often ebonised. They were imported into Britain in large numbers, and a good example will fetch £6000-£9000 today.

OTHER FORMS

The Wellington chest – tall and narrow, with drawers that could be locked – first appeared at the start of the 19th century. Such chests were very popular in the mid-19th century and today a good one will fetch £2000-£3000.

Portable campaign chests emerged around the same time, split into upper and lower sections. The distinctive handles are made of either brass or turned wood, and are inset to allow the chest to be stowed away neatly. Good campaign chests, some fitted with a secretaire drawer, will fetch anything up to £3000, although the many modern reproductions have very little resale value.

RESTORED OR ADAPTED?
What to Look out For

MANY 18TH-CENTURY CHESTS have been 'adapted' from plain examples into highly desirable ones by re-veneering or reducing in size. Small chests, 34 in (86.5 cm) or less across, are always more valuable than larger equivalents. Adapted pieces are worth far less than similar original examples. However, genuine restoration work – such as new feet or replacement handles – will not greatly alter the value of a chest of drawers.

● **Carcass** Early 18th-century English veneered chests were usually of pine, including the drawer fronts – only the drawer linings were of oak. If you find a chest with oak drawer fronts or carcass, it is not necessarily adapted, but it needs close examination.

● **Veneers** On most 18th-century chests of drawers the veneers show some shrinkage, splitting and lifting. Beware of a walnut chest with a perfectly flat veneer.

● **Handles** Where replaced, signs of previous handles show inside and outside the drawer. If not, the front has probably been re-veneered.

● **Drawers** These can be a good guide as to whether the piece has been cut down. The dovetails at either side of the drawer front may not match. Older dovetails are hard to imitate and machine-made ones are usually smaller.

● **Discoloration** Check for rust staining around the nails fixing the drawer backs and discoloration where the drawers do not quite reach the back panel. If it is too clean the depth may have been reduced.

● **Proportion** The top drawer of a cut-down piece will look too deep. A chest with very small top drawers, particularly if there are three, is probably the top half of a tallboy.

● **Serpentine chests** Beware a serpentine chest of drawers with more than two pieces of mahogany veneer on each drawer front. It may be a 20th-century conversion.

'Chest-on-stand' – in fact, a cut down early Georgian walnut tallboy of c.1720 on a 1920s stand; 43 in (1.09 m) wide. The origin is given away by the three short top drawers and unveneered top. **£800-£1200**

Beds and cradles

Modern beds may win on comfort, but their forerunners were often status symbols of much grander proportions.

Oak tester bed; early 17thC; 90 in (2.29 m) long. The impressive carved and inlaid decoration includes figures and fluted balusters on the front uprights. The value will depend on how much of the bed is genuine.
£10,000-£20,000
19thC copy:
£4000-£6000

LINEN AND LACE *Sumptuous drapery, favourite pieces of furniture and cherished ornaments characterise this bedroom at Langton Hall, Leicestershire, c.1835.*

Louis XVI giltwood bed; late 18thC; 79½ in (2.02 m) long. Original carved and gilded beds like this are rare, but 19thC copies can be found. The canopy is probably a 19thC addition.
£3000-£5000

I N ONE OF THE MOST FAMOUS WILLS of all time, Shakespeare bequeathed to his wife his second-best bed. There was nothing particularly unusual about the mention of a bed. In many households, from the Middle Ages to the 18th century, the bed was the most valuable possession, and was frequently listed in wills and inventories. As well as being at the centre of family life, bedrooms served as reception rooms and meeting places. The importance of the bed was reflected in its high cost and lavish construction, which often included carved details and expensive silk and velvet drapery.

THE FOUR-POSTER

The four-poster (or tester) bed developed from the medieval canopied bed, with wood substituted for some of the original fabric at the head to cut down the cost. Curtaining was still used at the front and sides, however, to keep out the cold and the light.

Four-poster beds were popular throughout the 16th and 17th centuries, and continued to be made in the 18th century to the same basic design, but with a distinctive Neoclassical lightness and elegance. The four-poster was

George III mahogany four-poster; c.1780; 74½ in (1.89 m) long. Value depends on decoration, how much of the original remains, and its history.
£4000-£6000
19thC or reconstructed: £2000-£3000

Victorian brass and iron bed; 1860-80; 75 in (1.9 m) long. This typical late Victorian style is still being produced today.
£300-£400
Reproduction:
£100-£200

Brass hanging cradle; c.1860; 48 in (1.22 m) long. This is a typically extravagant Victorian piece. A canopy would have hung from the overhead pole.
£1000-£1500

Oak cradle; c.1750; 36 in (91 cm) long. Similar ark-like cradles were made in the 17thC. Carved pieces are worth more than plain ones.
£500-£800

revived yet again in the late Victorian period. Seventeenth-century four-posters are the earliest beds to appear on the market in largely original condition, but are scarce and may cost £15,000-£20,000. Late Georgian four-posters, although more common than early 18th-century pieces, are seldom sold complete, but may then fetch over £20,000. Bed-posts are more affordable: a well carved 18th-century pair will cost £2000-£3000.

Four-posters dating from the 19th century are more stiffly carved than 18th-century examples. Well carved 19th-century oak beds fetch between £3000 and £5000, and less than £2000 if more clumsily carved.

OTHER STYLES

The most magnificent of all antique beds are 'state' beds of the 18th century, finely upholstered Baroque constructions specially made for royal visits. Most of these are now museum pieces, and seldom come up for sale.

More easily collectable are bedroom suites produced by furniture-makers such as the Frenchman Linke in the 19th century. These Louis XV and XVI-style pieces, often richly gilded and upholstered, or in fine marquetry, now sell for up to £10,000, or £2000-£5000 for less elaborate examples.

The Victorians loved brass beds, which were made in large numbers throughout the 19th century and are not difficult to find now. A plain design should cost under £500, a more elaborate one rather more.

The French boat-style lit-en-bateau of the early 19th century re-created the bed as a throne as well as a sleeping place. Elaborate specimens with tent-like canopy and lavish ormolu mounts can fetch £10,000 or more, less ornate ones about £3000-£4000.

CRADLES

Three main styles of cradle are of interest to collectors. The earliest are made of oak in the shape of a miniature ark, with a canopy at one end and vase-shaped finials. The sides are sometimes carved, and the whole cradle is mounted on solid rockers. Such examples fetch £400-£800. This style continued with only slight modification from the Middle Ages to the end of the 18th century.

Around that time, mahogany cots hung from a frame became fashionable. Most examples available today date from the Regency and late Georgian periods, and usually have slatted sides and little decoration. They usually sell for £400-£800.

Victorian cradles keep the suspended 18th-century design, but are usually of brass or iron, painted white, rather than wood, and generally sell for less than £500.

Other bedroom furniture

Although antique bedside tables are increasingly popular today, a preference for fitted bedrooms has made much bedroom furniture – especially English wardrobes, linen presses and dressing tables – seriously undervalued.

IN THESE DAYS of fully fitted bedrooms with *en suite* bathrooms, there seems to be little place for an elaborate Georgian dressing table or a sturdy Victorian washstand, and even less for a freestanding wardrobe or press. But these almost obsolete pieces of bedroom furniture are in many cases beautifully made, practical articles which often change hands today at prices far below the cost of making them new or of modern equivalents.

The bedroom suite was at its most popular during the second half of the 19th century, when no bedroom was complete without its matching bed, wardrobe, dressing table, bedside cupboards and, of course, marble-topped washstand. Pieces from that period are found in varied styles, including Gothic and Rococo Revival, Arts and Crafts, Art Nouveau, Louis XV, Empire and Biedermeier.

PRESSES AND WARDROBES

One of the earliest forms of bedroom cupboard is the linen press, so named because its double doors enclose large sliding trays which held folded linen. The earliest presses date from the 17th century. Some of the finest examples were produced a century later by Thomas Chippendale. His pattern books show presses with shelves above a combination of long and short drawers. Later Georgian and Victorian

Sheraton period mahogany linen press; 1790; 48 in (1.22 m) wide. By the end of the 18thC figured veneers replaced carved ornament.
£1500-£3000

Victorian linen press; c.1870; 40 in (1.01 m) wide. This burr walnut linen press on a mahogany carcass is of high quality but something of an acquired taste.
£800-£1200
Plain mahogany: £400-£600

Fine Dutch walnut and floral marquetry bombé armoire; mid-18thC; 78 in (1.98 m) wide. Most early examples were originally plain, with marquetry decoration being added in the 19thC.
£10,000-£15,000; less ornate: £5000-£8000

presses are generally less grand, displaying restrained banded decoration. A good late George III mahogany press can be bought at auction for as little as £800, while a Victorian copy will go for half that amount.

CONTINENTAL ARMOIRES

The form of the linen press was clearly influenced by Dutch armoires of the same period. These are generally large, usually combining a swelling bombé form with an arched cornice, and have linen trays enclosed by doors above drawers. During the 19th century, floral marquetry was applied to many earlier pieces. These decorated examples fetch the highest prices – usually around £6000–£9000 – while the original, plainer versions go for as little as £3000–£5000.

The curving Rococo influence is also clearly seen in French provincial armoires of the late 18th and early 19th centuries. These usually have a pegged construction and are made of oak, chestnut or fruitwood, with varying degrees of carved decoration. Most are fitted with two doors enclosing a hanging space, and some examples also have a drawer in the base. Fruitwood examples invariably make the most at auction, selling for between £1500 and £2000 for a good example.

WARDROBES

Breakfront wardrobes first appeared around 1800, adapting the form of the linen press by adding hanging cupboards on either side. The centre section generally has two small doors which enclose linen trays, above a combination of short and long drawers, and a tall door hangs at either side. Later Georgian and Victorian reproductions tend to enclose the drawers and linen trays with tall, matching doors and often include mirrored interiors. A late Georgian example of this type will make £1500–£2000. A Victorian piece in mahogany or walnut may fetch only £500–£800.

Victorian wardrobes are solidly made and often huge. The smaller examples, under 40 in (1 m) wide, are more practical but rarer and more expensive. Many late Victorian pieces are very ornate – as was the fashion at the end of the 19th century – and are commonly decorated (and in many cases over-decorated) with arabesque marquetry and Adam Revival motifs. Large numbers of such wardrobes were produced, and they are well worth picking up at auction today,

French provincial mahogany armoire; late 18thC; 66 in (1.68 m) wide. These pieces are often found in oak or fruitwoods such as cherry or chestnut.
Mahogany or chestnut: £2000–£3000
Poorer oak example: £800–£1200

Victorian breakfront mirrored wardrobe; c.1880; 84 in (2.13 m) wide. These wardrobes often bear the maker's stamp which increases their value. Similar, smaller wardrobes fetch more.
£600–£800

Chippendale mahogany linen press; c.1760; 54 in (1.37 m) wide. This superior example, probably one of the first of its type, has superbly figured veneers, restrained carving and a Rococo bombé base as seen in Dutch presses of the same period.
£50,000–£80,000; 19thC copy: up to £8000

Biedermeier wardrobe; c.1820; 54 in (1.37 m) wide. Strongly influenced by the Prussian Neoclassical Revival of the early 19thC, this wardrobe typifies the style.
£2000–£3000
Modern copy: £400–£600

Austrian painted pine armoire; late 18thC; 60 in (1.52 m) wide. The stylised leaf and marbleised decoration are typical of its place and period, but few such pieces retain their original paintwork.
£2000–£3000
Redecorated or over-restored: £800–£1200

often costing as little as £400-£600. Examples made of pine can be bought for £100-£200, while late Victorian bamboo and wickerwork pieces go for £200-£300.

An interesting Edwardian derivative of the wardrobe is the 'gentleman's compendium', fitted with compartments for shoes and socks and hanging bars for braces and ties. Examples are generally quite small and often bear a maker's mark; they fetch £500-£800.

DRESSING TABLES

For most people, the most familiar form of dressing table is the Victorian one. Its most basic form has a swing mirror above two small jewellery drawers, one on either side, and a flat table top raised on legs and fitted with frieze drawers. Dressing tables such as these vary greatly in quality, fetching perhaps £100 for a late Victorian example and up to £2000 for the best mid-Victorian pieces. These grand examples, influenced by the Rococo Revival of the mid-19th century, are usually veneered in mahogany, walnut or satinwood.

They are often of complicated serpentine form with ledge backs carved with flowers, fruit and urns. By Edwardian times, however, restrained Neoclassical lines were in vogue.

Some of the most intricate and fanciful designs were illustrated in the *Cabinet-maker and Upholsterer's Drawing Book*, published in 1791-4 by English furniture-maker Thomas Sheraton. These tables were generally made of satinwood, mahogany or fruitwoods, and were often decorated with inlay or marquetry. They were extremely expensive in their own day, but can fetch as little as £1500-£2000 at auction, being sold mostly as novelty pieces.

LOWBOYS

The forerunner of the Georgian dressing table was the early 18th-century lowboy, used both as a dressing table and for writing. The form of the lowboy is very like that of stands made for chests-on-stands of the same period (see p.137), their rectangular top set above a selection of long and short frieze drawers. Very few early 18th-century lowboys are in their original state. Many survivals started life as the lower section of a chest-on-stand.

An early 18th-century walnut lowboy in original condition will fetch in the region of £4000-£5000, whereas one with considerable

restoration and repair might make some £1000-£1500. Mahogany lowboys from the mid-18th century were invariably plain but of superb quality, and they too will fetch around £1000-£1500. The lowboy form was revived in the 1920s and 30s, producing some good examples in walnut which were often fitted with mirrors. Today, these can be picked up for as little as £200-£300.

BEDSIDE TABLES

In terms of craftsmanship and quality of materials, the night tables of the mid to late 18th century are the finest examples of bedside tables. They are generally larger than their 19th-century counterparts, and are fitted with a rectangular tray top which sits above cupboard doors and a drawer. A good example will fetch £1200-£1800, although rare pieces in satinwood may reach £6500 at auction. Bedside tables of the late 18th and early 19th centuries may fetch £400-£600 for a single table, but £2000-£3000 for a pair.

The fashion for the bedroom suite took hold worldwide, so it is not surprising that examples of Continental and American bedside tables are often found. The most common are marble-topped with painted decoration,

Victorian 'duchesse' dressing table veneered in burr walnut; c.1870; 48 in (1.22 m) wide. Despite fine carving, such pieces fetch low prices at auction because of their bulk.
£400-£600; less in mahogany or oak

George III mahogany bedside cupboard; c.1765; 30 in (76 cm) wide. More valuable examples are usually in a highly figured mahogany.
**£1500-£2500
Satinwood: £6000-£9000**

George III mahogany dressing table (left); c.1790; 26 in (66 cm) wide. This elegant example with delicate lines has a hinged top enclosing a compartmented interior. Heavier examples are cheaper.
£4000-£6000

George II walnut lowboy with fine pierced scroll apron; c.1730; 32¼ in (82 cm) wide. Any restoration or reveneering would lower the value considerably.
£3000-£4000

Louis XV/XVI kingwood and tulipwood top-opening dressing table; late 18thC; 32 in (81 cm) wide. It bears the maker's name: N. Petit.
**£6000-£9000
Late 19thC copy: £1200-£1800**

George IV bedside cabinet to a Gillows design (unstamped); c.1820; 16 in (40.5 cm) wide.
**Single: £500-£800
Pair: £2500-£3000**

or in mahogany, pine or walnut. A good pair in the ornate Louis XV or more restrained Louis XVI style will fetch £1500-£2000. Bedroom furniture in the heavy Biedermeier style has become increasingly popular lately, and a good pair of mid-19th-century cupboards will fetch perhaps £2500-£3500.

WASHSTANDS

A feature common to all Victorian bedroom suites was the marble-topped washstand. Most were in mahogany, walnut or pine, often inlaid with boxwood and ebony lines and arabesque decoration. Highly figured walnut examples are most in demand today, with a good piece fetching £800-£1200. But even pine washstands from the lower end of the range are becoming popular. Many of these have a decorative tiled ledge back to the marble top, incorporating Art Nouveau or Arts and Crafts movement designs, and were

often originally painted; these can be bought for as little as £200-£300.

Washstands marked with the maker's name, either embossed on top of the drawer front or stuck to the drawer bottom on a paper label, fetch more than unidentified pieces. But bedroom suites commissioned directly from the Maples or Gillows workshops were generally not stamped, and even unstamped pieces of good quality can fetch large sums: an extremely fine, unstamped Victorian washstand fetched £1450 at auction in 1990.

The recent trend for stripping Victorian pine furniture can detract from the value of most washstands. The original painted decoration of trailing flowers and foliage on a plain coloured ground often disguises the rudimentary nature of the construction as well as the poor quality of the timber. Pine washstands in their original painted livery and in good condition are sought after and can make as much as £4000-£6000 at auction.

Swedish birchwood bedside cabinet in Biedermeier style; c.1830; 16½ in (42 cm) wide. A stylish 'interior decorator's' item.
£400-£600

Victorian marble-topped mahogany washstand and mirror; c.1895; 60 in (1.52 m) wide. The value of these washstands is affected by the tiles. Strong designs fetch higher prices.
£500-£800

Gordon Russell washstand; c.1927; 28½ in (72 cm) wide. Early pieces by this maker are becoming increasingly collectable, fetching high prices at auction.
£600-£1200

VICTORIAN CABINET-MAKERS
The Quality Firms

No VICTORIAN BEDROOM belonging to the middle classes was complete without its bedroom suite. By the late 19th century all the major furniture manufacturers were producing matching bedroom furniture, usually bearing the maker's stamp or label.

Notable names include Gillows of Lancaster, most of whose pieces after 1820 were stamped 'Gillow & Co', or 'Gillows', and numbered; after 1900 items were stamped 'Waring & Gillow'. Also well known were Johnstone & Jeanes (stamped 'Johnstone & Jeanes'), Shoolbred & Co ('Jas. Shoolbred & Co'), Howard & Sons, and Maples.

All produced suites in a vast range of styles and prices, as trade catalogues of the period show. Bedroom suites could be ordered in 17th-century Jacobean style, or in Empire style, Arts and Crafts style, lacquered Chinese Export style or, of course, in the daring Art Nouveau style of the 1890s and 1900s.

STAMP OF QUALITY *The Gillows label is as desirable today as in the 19thC; even unlabelled Gillows pieces fetch good sums.*

Victorian marble-topped pine washstand; c.1890; 30 in (76 cm) wide. These pieces were made for servants' quarters and are not of high quality. Those with original painted decoration fetch much more.
£100-£200

Mirrors and screens

Since they became an integral part of interior decoration in the 18th century, these items have been made in a diverse range of materials and styles.

BOTH MIRRORS AND SCREENS were originally designed for a practical function, beyond mere vanity or decoration: wall mirrors to reflect the dim light of candles at night, and screens to protect sitters from draughts or from heat. However, they quickly became decorative objects in their own right. Production declined only with the arrival of electricity and central heating.

WALL MIRRORS

The majority of today's collectable mirrors were made between the earliest appearance of plate mirror glass in the late 17th century and the introduction of electric light around 1900. Most are wall mirrors, and examples with ornate candle sconces, or girandoles, are generally more valuable than those without. Many have lost their sconces or had them removed when electricity was introduced.

Large wall mirrors from the early and mid-18th century often have two or more pieces of glass; mirror glass was expensive and could only be made in small plates. Mirrors from this period generally have elaborately carved and gilded frames. Huge pier glasses date from this same era, many with girandoles for candles.

Wall mirrors were framed in all prevailing fashions in the 18th century, and designers created highly elaborate and attractive forms that are much sought after. Thomas Chippendale designed mirror frames decorated with Rococo foliage and Chinese ho-ho birds, with delicate Gothic tracery, or sometimes with Chinoiserie figures in a style influenced by imported ceramics. Good single examples can realise £20,000, and a pair will fetch about three times this figure.

Overmantel mirrors were made to go above imposing fireplaces, and the frame of these broad, 'landscape' mirrors is often decorated with ball pendants and a female figure reclining in a chariot. An original late 18th or early 19th-century example may fetch as little as £1500-£2000, and copies dating from the end of the 19th century will sell for around £300-£500. Regency overmantel mirrors tend to be shallower than their predecessors.

Small convex wall mirrors about 18 in (46 cm) across became popular around 1800, and were fashionable throughout Victorian times. It is worth checking these carefully, however, as reproductions of Regency designs appeared at the end of the 19th century,

and usually have a narrower frame. Original examples often have an eagle cresting to symbolise British military power. The more elaborate the cresting, the more a mirror will fetch at auction, and if it has candle-arms these increase the price even more. Few sell for under £2000, although late 19th-century reproductions fetch in the region of £500.

Many 19th-century mirror frames appear

William and Mary mirror; 1695; 30¾ in (78 cm) high. The 'seaweed' marquetry frame is typical of the high-quality cabinet work of the period.
£2000-£3000

MIRROR IMAGE *Mirrors were an ostentatious sign of wealth, as depicted in this painting by Charles Robert Leslie (1794-1859).*

George III giltwood mirror; c.1765; 46 in (1.17 m) high. This style returned to fashion in the 1830s – and such later examples are cheaper.
£6000-£10,000

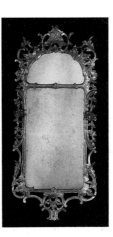

One of a pair of Regency giltwood and plaster mirrors; c.1805; 45 in (1.14 m) high.
£4000-£5000
Single: £1800-£2500

George III giltwood pier mirror; 1775; 92 in (2.34 m) high. Its original glass raises the value.
£8000-£10,000

Victorian D-shaped overmantel mirror; c.1870; 48 in (1.22 m) wide. Many mirrors of this type were made, so prices are not high.
£200-£300

to be made of carved wood but are in fact composition or plaster. These materials often break, so plaster-frame mirrors – even gilt or highly decorated ones – are far less expensive than earlier wooden examples. It is worth examining any breaks to see whether there is wood or a smooth plaster underneath.

MIRRORS ON STANDS

Among freestanding mirrors, the most desirable to modern collectors are cheval mirrors, introduced to Britain by Thomas Sheraton in the late 18th century. These large, adjustable toilet mirrors in a frame stand on the floor, and are also known as 'horse dressing glasses' and 'psyches'. Georgian and Regency cheval mirrors are hard to find and change hands for between £1500 and £4000. Victorian examples can be found for about £300-£500.

Adaptations of the idea introduced in the 19th century include the shaving stand (see p.145), which combines an adjustable mirror with a ledge for storing shaving equipment. These are relatively cheap, as are toilet, or dressing-table, mirrors, even of the Georgian and Regency periods. An 18th-century toilet glass can

be bought for £150 upwards, and will usually have small drawers under the swing mirror. The cheapest Victorian examples do not have drawers and start from just £10.

SCREENS

The Victorians produced a variety of screens using many different materials, including solid wood, embroidered silks, plain and stained glass, mirrors and ceramic tiles. Some examples were embroidered with Berlin wool-work (see p.310). These range in price from £50 to £500, depending on quality.

Small decorative fire-screens were imported in large numbers from the Orient from the 1880s up until the First World War. These are still cheap but can be in poor condition. A good example fetches around £500.

Sliding pole screens have been used since medieval times and have survived in fair numbers. Examples fetch £200 up to £2000.

Large folding screens from the early 18th century are often covered with embossed leather wall panelling. These fetch up to £10,000.

A fashionable 19th-century pastime for young women was to cover large screens with a collage of specially made 'scraps' of paper. These appealing pieces fetch only £300-£500.

Much rarer and more valuable are Chinese lacquered screens, which first reached Europe about 1700 (see pp.167 and 401). Some Japanese examples were cut up and made into cabinets. Such screens may have as many as 12 panels, and sell at auction for £5000-£10,000.

Victorian mahogany toilet mirror; c.1835; 33 in (84 cm) high overall. Most toilet mirrors of this time have drawers.
£150-£250

Regency mahogany cheval mirror; c.1820; 69 in (1.75 m) high. The turned supports indicate that this mirror was made some time after 1800.
£1000-£1200

Regency giltwood convex mirror; c.1810; 49½ in (1.26 m) high. A plainer example, without the eagle cresting or apron, would fetch far less.
£2500-£4000

Early Victorian cheval fire screen; c.1840; 36 in (91 cm) high. The embroidered panel is in the style of contemporary paintings.
£300-£400

Mirrored screen with mahogany frame (above); 1900; c.6 ft (1.8 m) high. The elaborate cresting is in flowing Art Nouveau style.
£2000-£3000

Early Victorian embroidered pole screen; c.1840; 64 in (1.62 m) high. Pole screens were often made in pairs to stand at either side of the fireplace.
£180-£220; Georgian: £800-£1200

Stands

Stands of all kinds often find uses quite different from their original purpose. A butler's tray, for example, makes a good drinks table.

GUERIDONS were among the first stands. Made in various styles, they were used from the 17th century for supporting candlesticks or lamps. One popular design has a black human figure holding a circular tray. Candlestands became less common with the spread of gas lighting in Victorian times.

Low stands for tea urns or kettles are the right height for modern sofas and are often used as wine tables. Many have a piecrust edge and tripod legs. Good Georgian examples fetch up to £20,000 at auction, and made-up pieces around £1000. From the 1760s, taller stands on four tapered legs became popular.

Hat stands and hall stands were 19th-century inventions and were usually made of wood or cast iron. They were the first pieces of furniture a visitor noticed and so were highly decorative. Many hall stands are large, incorporating cupboards and a mirror, coat hooks and a tray at the bottom to catch the drips from wet coats and umbrellas.

FOR FOOD AND DRINKS

Dumbwaiters – with two or three circular tiers around a central column – were left in the dining room for diners to serve themselves after the servants were dismissed. Most 18th-century examples are mahogany, but late ones may have brass supports. Dumbwaiters will fetch between £1500 and £5000; check that two-tier examples have not lost a third tier.

Voiders were the earliest form of tray and, from the early 18th century, often had a separate folding stand. Early voiders and some rare Victorian ones made of papier-mâché are kidney-shaped. Butler's trays make good drinks tables so demand has pushed up prices, to £500-£1500 for a tray and its original stand.

FOR SHAVING AND MUSIC

The Georgian period saw the introduction of shaving stands, with foldaway mirror and concealed basin; some doubled as writing tables. Fine examples designed by Thomas Sheraton fetch £10,000 or more. Simple Victorian shaving stands fetch £500 or less.

From the late 18th century, music stands became common in middle-class homes. They are typically of walnut or mahogany with ornate lyre-shaped lattice work. Today 19th-century examples fetch £500-£2500.

Arts and Crafts oak hall stand; c.1900; 79 in (2.01 m) high. This piece cleverly unites practical elements such as coat hooks and mirror with a decorative design.
£400-£600

Regency mahogany plant stand; c.1825; 18 in (45.7 cm) across. The legs are a 19thC adaptation of popular mid-18thC cabriole legs.
£1200-£1800

George III mahogany dumbwaiter; c.1750; 45¼ in (1.15 m) high. The tiers are galleried and the feet well carved, boosting the value significantly.
£5000-£8000

Regency mahogany coat stand; c.1825; 78 in (1.98 m) high. It is unusual, but turned uprights are common features of 19thC chairs and tables.
£1500-£2000

Victorian walnut and brass music stand (right); c.1850; 48 in (1.22 m) high, extending. The ornate fretwork is typical.
£700-£1000

Victorian mahogany and brass shaving stand; c.1850; 48 in (1.22 m) high, extending. It is the kind of practical item the Victorians loved.
£600-£800

Mahogany butler's tray (left); 19thC; 26 in (66 cm) high. The top lifts off to carry items between sitting room and kitchen.
£400-£600

Boxes and buckets

From the most utilitarian boxes to elaborately embellished caskets, the field of container collecting is inexhaustible.

Pair of mahogany knife boxes; c.1770; 15 in (38.1 cm) high. The architectural pilasters and ogee fronts make them desirable.
£1200-£1800
Single: £300-£400

Regency rosewood teapoy; c.1815; 16 in (40.5 cm) wide. This Neoclassical piece is worth more than one on a plain turned support.
£1500-£2000

Late Georgian mahogany wine cistern; c.1780; 21 in (53.5 cm) wide. This cistern is on its original stand with brass castors and could be wheeled around. Cracking at the front reduces the value.
£1500-£2000

Late Georgian plate pail; c.1780; 16 in (40.5 cm) high. The slot allows plates to be removed.
£1200-£1800

Regency boulle-work fitted dressing box; c.1830; 9½ in (24.1 cm) wide. This piece would fetch much more if it contained hallmarked silver fittings.
£1500-£2000

CONTAINERS MADE in every conceivable shape and size and of myriad materials were an indispensable part of Georgian and Victorian life, and were used to hold everything from cutlery to cosmetics.

Tea was prepared by the lady of the house and served with some ceremony. The teapoys and caddies that held the precious leaves are popular collectables today. They usually contained two lidded boxes – for black and green teas – and perhaps a glass bowl in which the teas could be blended or sugar could be kept.

Caddies range in value from thousands of pounds for 18th-century silver examples to just a few pounds for 20th-century tinware caddies. Those from before about 1850 usually have a brass or silver lock to guard against pilferers. Tortoiseshell caddies of this period fetch around £150-£650, wooden caddies inlaid with mother-of-pearl about £150, and less ornate wooden examples under £100.

Women's workboxes for sewing, writing or travelling equipment reached a peak of craftsmanship in the late 18th and early 19th centuries. They were decorated in similar ways to tea caddies and lined with luxurious materials. Plain mahogany examples now fetch £200-£300, ornate inlaid pieces £2500.

Cutlery boxes have suffered the ravages of dealers and changing fashions, the great majority having been altered – frequently by replacing the cutlery divisions with divisions for stationery. Open rectangular boxes are common and even Georgian examples fetch only £100 or so. More elaborate George II

TUNBRIDGE WARE

Marquetry for the Masses

WOODEN ARTICLES decorated in a distinctive style that mimics marquetry were made in enormous numbers at Tunbridge Wells, Kent, in the 19th century and known as Tunbridge ware. The technique used dates back to the late 17th century. Strips of different-coloured woods were carefully arranged and glued in a bundle so that the ends formed a mosaic-like pattern. Thin layers were then cut across the pattern and glued onto the object, like veneer.

Produced more quickly and cheaply than marquetry, the range of Tunbridge ware included anything from Yo-yos to tables, but above all boxes – until competition from the Far East proved too much. Quality and condition are crucial to the value of Tunbridge ware, but many pieces are well within the reach of most collectors, with prices starting at just a few pounds.

Fine Tunbridge-ware ladies' workbox; c.1840; 10½ in (26.7 cm) wide. Typical of the period, this box features a view of The Pantiles in Tunbridge Wells.
£1000-£1500

lidded upright boxes were made in pairs, although few matched pairs now survive.

Small wine coolers are generally silver (see p.249), but larger floor-standing versions, also called cisterns, are usually of mahogany lined with lead or zinc, and are often coopered like a barrel. Most such pieces sell today for £2000-£5000, but fine Georgian or Regency examples may top £10,000 (see p.88).

Plate pails were used by servants to carry plates to and from the dining room. They have a vertical slot on one side for handling the plates, but these have often been closed to convert the pails into wastepaper baskets. Log and peat buckets are much rarer and more expensive, fetching up to £10,000, but late Victorian oak coal scuttles, or 'purdoniums', are quite easy to find for about £100, as are copper or brass 'helmet' scuttles (see p.368).

Pottery & Porcelain

Detail of Staffordshire leaf-moulded earthenware plate; c.1840

Collecting pottery and porcelain

No area of collecting can offer a wider range of objects, originating from a wider range of cultures and historical periods, than articles fashioned from clay.

IN A TYPICAL HOME there are likely to be more objects made of ceramics – earthenware, stoneware and porcelain – than any other single category of material. Most will be of the 20th century, a fair proportion will be late Victorian, and perhaps a few pieces will be earlier.

Oriental ceramics have a far richer history than those in the West. Fine porcelain was made in China from at least the 8th century, and started to reach Europe from about 1600. Despite their inherent fragility, many early Chinese pieces survive and are keenly collected – as are rare ancient Greek and Roman items. But ceramics need not be as old as that to attract collectors. Some people amass 19th-century Staffordshire pottery figures, lured by the colourful characters they depict. Others love French soft-paste porcelain from 18th-century factories such as Chantilly. Or early slipware or delftware may appeal.

Ceramic objects do not have to be in perfect condition to be enjoyed. You can build up an extensive collection at reasonable cost if you are prepared to accept imperfect pieces – and can learn a great deal in the process. Any

FORGERY *This looks like early Ming (c.1400) porcelain, but it is not. It could be an 18thC copy worth £50,000 but is actually a brand-new forgery worth only about £40.*

damaged or restored object will be worth less than it would be if perfect, but the difference depends on the type of object and degree of damage. A tiny chip or hairline crack might reduce the value of a Chinese dish from the reign of the Emperor Qianlong (1736-95) to one-tenth. But an English delftware bowl with a chipped edge or flaking foot will be worth very little less than a perfect one, since it is delftware's nature to chip. Of course, a great rarity, even damaged, will always be valuable if no better example exists.

If buying for investment rather than for enjoyment and education, it is vital to get expert advice on the cost of any necessary restoration, and its effect on value. Restoration never restores the full value of a piece – indeed, you may not even cover the cost of restoration. Any reputable dealer or auction house should give advice without charge. If the restoration is purely for sentimental or aesthetic reasons, then the cost may be irrelevant.

The detective work involved in identifying a ceramic object's origins is part and parcel of collecting. Even when buying from a major auction house or dealer whose descriptions you feel you can trust, you need to learn as much as you can about your chosen field so that you can recognise the materials and method of manufacture, the style and means of decoration, and so on. Only then will you be able to identify the object and distinguish it from copies and forgeries. Eventually, you will probably know more than many of the people from whom you buy – and then you should be able to cash in on your knowledge.

PRIZE ITEM *This exceptional Tang funerary horse (8th-9thC) in glazed earthenware fetched £3.4 million in 1990, a record auction price for Oriental art.*

LUCKY FINDS *Bought at a car boot sale for £1.50 by a quickwitted art student, the Hans Coper stoneware dish (left) was sold at auction in 1989 for £20,900. The rare 1939 Royal Doulton 'Bunnikins' figures (below) were similarly bought for £4.60 but resold in 1992 for £3960.*

COLLECTOR'S TIP *Printed tablewares are mass-produced and so take time to acquire value, but certain designs stand out. This bold early 1960s range of pottery, 'La Parisienne', could be a collectable of the future.*

Understanding pottery and porcelain

The detective work involved in identifying a ceramic object's nature and origins is part of the fun of collecting. Shape, decoration and glaze all help to place a piece once the material and technique used have been established.

CHINESE POTTERS AT WORK *In the centre of this 19thC Chinese watercolour a vase is being thrown by a centuries-old method on a hand-driven wheel.*

THE TERM 'CERAMICS' – from the Greek *keramos* (clay) – covers anything that was shaped from wet clay and then fired in a kiln to make it hard and give it a permanent shape. Clays of different colours and consistencies, mixed with a variety of other ingredients, produce different types of finished ceramic body, from coarse-grained, porous earthenware to the finest porcelain.

How and where ceramics developed depended largely on the availability of local materials. Britain lagged behind other European producers of true porcelain, for example, partly because no convenient deposits of china clay and china stone – the main ingredients – had been identified here. Yet Staffordshire was the focus of many other important developments in ceramics because of its rich local clay deposits. China, on the other hand, learned early on to make use of its vast resources of china stone (or petuntse) and china clay, and over 1000 years ago was producing high-quality porcelain – at least seven centuries before any European factory.

The body

There are three fundamental types of ceramic material or body: more or less coarse-grained earthenware and its harder cousin stoneware, which are together referred to as pottery, and the finer-grained porcelain. (Though widely used, mostly to denote porcelain, the term 'china' is best reserved for a British sub-group of porcelain known as bone china; see p.150.) The differences in texture of different bodies can best be seen or felt on the surface of a chip or fracture, which exposes a cross-section where the grain has not been worn by use or disguised by a glaze. However, other factors such as weight, translucency and 'ring', or resonance, can also be useful clues to identity.

EARTHENWARE

Where unglazed earthenware is exposed, it is rough and gritty to the touch. It was first made from coarse sedimentary clays containing many impurities and could be fired only to about 800°C (just under 1500°F). At this temperature, the grains of clay would stick firmly together to form a hardened structure, but it still had minute air spaces, so liquid could seep through. Earthenware therefore had to be coated with a glaze to be waterproof.

Earthenware clays come in many colours, but these can often be seen only if the glaze is transparent or the article chipped. The colour can give a clue as to the earthenware's origins – Torquay and Watcombe earthenwares, for example, reflect the rusty orange of iron-rich Devon clays. However, it may also have been affected by conditions in the kiln during firing. Unglazed Chinese funerary wares clearly illustrate this. Figures from the Han dynasty (206 BC-AD 221), which were fired in an airless or smoky kiln with little oxygen, are usually grey-black; Tang dynasty (AD 618-906) figures – fired in an airy environment – are generally chalky with a pink or yellow tinge.

Not all earthenware is coloured, however. Creamware, basically a form of earthenware made with a good-quality, white Devon clay, was developed in Staffordshire in the mid-18th century as a cheap, home-grown alternative to porcelain that was at the same time much stronger than delftware (tin-glazed earthenware; see p.151). Creamware could be fired at a higher temperature than other earthenwares, so while not as tough as hard-paste porcelain, and still porous if unglazed, it has been consistently used for everyday crockery ever since.

GREY EARTHENWARE HOUSE *The typical grey-black colour of this Han dynasty model farm excavated from a tomb in Guangzhou (Canton) is the result of firing in an airless or smoky kiln.*

CREAMWARE TEAPOT *Commercially one of the most important developments of the Staffordshire potteries, creamware – so-called because of the colour of its glaze – was cheap and durable. This pot is in Josiah Wedgwood's version, 'Queen's Ware'.*

AFRICAN TERRACOTTA BOWL *Terracotta (literally, 'baked earth') is a very soft, porous, low-fired – or even sun-dried – form of unglazed earthenware.*

STONEWARE

As its name implies, stoneware is harder than earthenware, but it is also finer-textured and non-porous even if unglazed. The clays used could be fired to higher temperatures of around 1300°C (almost 2400°F), at which point the grains of clay fused together.

Most stoneware clays are grey, and so-called 'brown' stoneware tankards, flasks and so on often have only a wash of colour on the outside: a chipped edge will show that the brown colour is skin-deep. However, the fine red Chinese stoneware of Yixing, near Nanking, is coloured all through. Strong and able to be polished to a high shine without being glazed, it was copied by German, Staffordshire and other European potters in the 18th century (and was sometimes glazed).

Fine white stoneware was developed by Staffordshire potters in the first half of the

18th century to compete with imported Chinese porcelain. The white, strong clay could be potted very thinly and produced a creamy-coloured body. Other fine stonewares include black basaltes and jasperware, made by Wedgwood from the 1760s (see p. 168).

RED STONEWARE VASE BY BÖTTGER *Chinese red stoneware was imported, mainly as teapots, from the 17thC. Johann Friedrich Böttger at Meissen reproduced it in the early 18thC, hoping to discover the secret of porcelain.*

WHITE STONEWARE BEAR JUG *Staffordshire and Nottinghamshire 18thC potters used a fine-grained white clay to make white stoneware. This bear jug has 'shredded' fur and black slip details.*

BROWN STONEWARE JUG *The colour on this mid-19thC puzzle jug comes from natural iron in the clay which fires brown at the surface only. Darker areas are from a wash of iron oxide added before firing.*

PORCELAIN

First developed in China during the late Tang dynasty period, well over 1000 years ago, porcelain can be white, greyish or creamy. Porcelain articles are strong yet delicate and generally translucent, and hollow pieces usually resonate when struck.

There are two types of porcelain. The hard-paste, or true, porcelain which originated in China is watertight even if unglazed. Its ingredients – a mixture of china clay (kaolin) and a ground feldspar mineral called china stone or petuntse – allowed it to be fired at over 1400°C (2550°F). (The higher the firing temperature, the more effectively a ceramic paste would vitrify, or change into an impermeable glassy body.) The resulting shiny surface and very compact body of true porcelain is hard to scratch.

A true porcelain similar to the Chinese product but creamier was finally made at Meissen in Germany by Johann Friedrich Böttger in about 1708. It was first produced in Britain at Plymouth in 1768, using china clay

and china stone from Cornwall. Before that, however, soft-paste porcelain was made in Europe from the 16th century onwards. This slightly coarser imitation of true porcelain was fired at 1100-1200°C (about 2000-2200°F) – rather lower than hard-paste porcelain. Its development resulted from experiments in adding various materials (such as ground glass, flint, quartz and bones) to the clay base.

MEISSEN HARD-PASTE PORCELAIN JUG *The white, impermeable, translucent body first discovered in China was reproduced in early 18thC Europe at the Meissen factory. This jug mimics unpainted 'blanc-de-Chine'. It has the hard, brittle look of true porcelain, the glaze merging with the body.*

CHELSEA SOFT-PASTE PORCELAIN GROUP *Often slightly porous, soft-paste porcelain may stain where it is cracked or unglazed. Creamy and softer in appearance than true porcelain, its surface is more easily marked and the glaze forms a more superficial coating on the body.*

BONE CHINA *A durable late 18thC British derivative of hard-paste porcelain which was attractive and cheap, this used ground burned animal bones as a flux. It is still widely produced.*

Shaping the piece

Various potting methods have been used to shape lumps of wet clay. Among the oldest and most basic ways of hand-shaping hollow-wares are pinching and coiling. In the first, a ball of clay was pinched between thumb and forefinger to make small objects. Coiled vessels – such as large terracotta oil pots – were made by rolling out a long clay sausage and then winding it in a spiral to form a pot. Equally primitive is making a vessel from flat

THUMB, OR PINCHED, POT *Pinched pieces, such as this 17thC Japanese Raku bowl, tend to be irregular, and may show fingerprints where the clay was squeezed.*

SLAB POT *Square-sided vessels such as this modern vase by Bernard Leach were created by rolling the clay flat – like pastry – before assembling the sides.*

slabs of clay. Throwing – shaping clay on a rotating wheel – is the best-known method of making more regularly shaped hollow articles. Clues to a piece's origin and date can lie in the way a piece was finished, including how it was cut from the wheel at the base (see p. 189), and the techniques used to clean the base afterwards. Larger pieces could be built up from several thrown sections that were then luted – joined together with slip (liquid clay).

THROWN IN PARTS *This 17thC Korean porcelain vase was thrown in two halves, which were then luted (joined) at the edges. The join is clear to see.*

THROWING CLAY *This 1883 self-portrait plaque by Edwin, one of the Martin Brothers, shows how a ball of clay on a wheel was opened up in the middle before being squeezed at both sides to raise the walls.*

MOULDING AND CASTING

Some ceramic figures were sculpted directly, but most were reproduced in quantities ranging from tens to thousands using moulds made from an original model. Clay pressed into the mould was left to harden before the figure was freed and fired. For more complex forms with bold or undercut detail, parts of the figure or vessel would be made in separate moulds and then stuck together – or 'repaired' – with slip. This produced heavy, almost solid pieces such as those made at Meissen.

From about 1720, many factories used moulds made from plaster of Paris, into which liquid clay was poured and left to stand. As the plaster absorbed the water it left a layer of

clay to harden on the mould's inner surface. Excess slip was poured off, and after drying the hardened clay could be removed. Called slip-casting, this method allowed finer detail.

STAFFORDSHIRE PORTRAIT FIGURE *This late 19thC study of General Lord Napier standing beside his horse was made by slip-casting in a number of sections which were then joined with more slip.*

SOLID-MOULDED FIGURES *The original model of this Meissen group, sculpted by J. J. Kändler, would have been fired and then cut up to make master moulds. A group such as this might have been assembled from up to 20 separate pieces.*

The glaze

Glaze is a glassy film fused onto the ceramic body during firing, usually formed from powdered minerals mixed with water and washed over the body. Its characteristics – such as how closely it adheres to the body, whether it has an even or a bubbly surface or is cracked, its precise colour tone and other features – can help with identification and may also betray a forgery.

Glazes can be shiny or matt, hard or soft. Transparent or translucent glazes can be colourless – as on porcelain – or coloured, as on Chinese green celadon wares. Opaque glazes may form a white background for other decoration, as on delftware (see p. 165), or a glutinous monochrome as on pieces from Song (Sung) dynasty China (960-1279).

Earthenware glazes were commonly based on either lead or tin. Powdered lead or lead oxide made a transparent glaze on its own but gave an opaque white finish when tin oxide was added. The glaze on Chinese hard-paste porcelain was made of a material chemically close to the body itself, while European hard-paste porcelain used glazes based on ground feldspar. Early soft-paste porcelain had a colourless lead glaze, but later a mixture of ingredients known as frit, consisting of crushed flint and/or glass, was used.

GREEN-GLAZED TRIPOD VESSEL *Lead glazes were widely used until the 19thC, when less dangerous materials were found. On this Han dynasty food bowl, copper was added for a bronze-like tint.*

TIN-GLAZED CHARGER *Tin glaze chips easily but provided a white ground which could be left plain, as here, but was more often decorated with colours.*

SALT-GLAZED STONEWARE *Surfaces of salt-glazed wares like this German jug show the typical 'orange-peel' effect caused by throwing salt into the kiln.*

CRACKLURE OR CRAZING *This occurred when the body and glaze shrank at different rates as they cooled. On this Song dynasty tripod vessel a stain emphasised the crazing.*

CELADON CUP AND STAND *Iron oxide colours the thick greenish 'celadon' glaze on these Yuan dynasty (14thC) stoneware articles. Millions of bubbles make it opaque.*

FAULTY GLAZE *Hairline cracks caused by different rates of shrinkage in the body and glaze are considered a fault in most pieces.*

Decoration

Pottery and porcelain could be decorated before or after glazing, or the glaze itself might form the decoration – as, for example, with the splashed greens, yellows and browns of English Astbury-Whieldon pottery of the 18th century. Three-dimensional, relief or incised designs were always done before applying the glaze, while coloured designs could be added to the piece before glazing (in the case of underglaze colours) or after (overglaze colours, or enamels, and gilding).

RETICULATION *Reticulated wares such as this 1914 vase by George Owen were made by piercing the still soft clay with various tools, to create the intricate latticework pattern, before firing the piece.*

ENCRUSTED FLOWERS *Handmade flowers with petals pressed between fingertips – as here on the lid of a 19thC German porcelain vase – were applied after the rest of the piece was made.*

SPRIGGING *Decorative shapes – often sprigs of flowers or leaves – were moulded or stamped from clay and then stuck onto the vessel (here a 14thC Chinese celadon vase) with thin slip before firing.*

SGRAFFITO OR SGRAFFIATO *The red earthenware body of this signed and dated 1767 dish was immersed in a cream-coloured slip (liquid clay). The design was then carved and incised in the slip layer to allow the contrasting colour of the body to show through.*

TRAILED SLIP DECORATION *The effect on this 17thC Staffordshire slipware dish was created by dipping the piece in pale slip, then trailing slip of various colours onto it. Here, the dark slip lines are picked out with slip dots. A yellow honey glaze brings out the colours.*

PÂTE-SUR-PÂTE *Porcelain paste was built up in layers on a contrasting ground to look like cameo glass (see p. 183).*

UNDERGLAZE COLOURS

After an initial firing – but before the glaze was applied – a design could be painted or printed onto the ceramic body with a solution containing a metal oxide, such as cobalt, chromium, manganese or iron. When these were fired at high temperature, the oxide matured to produce a colour that appears to come from within the body. Cobalt, for example, would mature from black to blue. The shade of colour produced depended on the firing temperature and other conditions as well as on the metal oxide used. Copper, for example, produced green or red depending on the amount of oxygen in the kiln, and brown and black came from iron and manganese.

Underglaze colours were restricted to those pigments that could withstand the high temperature of the kiln. Cobalt blue has long been the most widely used in both Oriental and Western ceramics (see p.161). The others are iron red, manganese purple, chromium yellow, and copper green or red.

BLUE AND RED *This Japanese porcelain teapot of c.1890 shows the use of two of the commonest underglaze colours: cobalt blue for the background and copper red to highlight the fishes' scales.*

UNDERGLAZE COLOUR *Holding the piece so that a highlight falls across the pattern shows that this Worcester porcelain tankard is decorated under the glaze.*

OVERGLAZE DECORATION *The highlight on this Worcester tankard clearly shows the lines of the pattern, which must be on (or 'over') the glaze. It can also be felt with the fingers.*

OVERGLAZE COLOURS AND GILDING

When a design was applied on top of the glaze the colour borders can often be seen or felt with the fingertips. On porcelain, colours were applied with enamel paints, of which a far wider range was available than of underglaze colours, since they did not have to withstand such high temperatures. Different coloured enamels harden at different temperatures, so those fired at the highest temperatures were applied first, followed by those needing the next lowest temperature and so on. Gilding almost always came last.

The colours used on a piece can help point to its place and date of origin. For example, pink enamel – from a mixture of gold chloride and tin chloride – first appeared on Chinese export porcelain after 1720. It varied with firing temperature from pale pink to purple.

OVERGLAZE COLOURS *Against a highlight it is usually possible to see clearly how the glassy enamels sit on top of the glaze, as on this early 18thC Chinese wine cup. They fire in the 700-900°C (1300-1650°F) range.*

GILDING *This fires at the lowest temperature, so was almost invariably the last to be added. Various techniques were used; this early 19thC British plate shows the deep, rich tone of honey gilding.*

UNDERGLAZE WITH OVERGLAZE *The phoenix design on this late 18thC Chinese wine cup was first painted in underglaze cobalt blue. After firing and glazing, the other colours were added as overglaze enamels. The combination is called doucai ('contrasting colours').*

PAINTING OR PRINTING?

Ceramic designs could be either hand-painted or transfer-printed onto the body, or sometimes a combination of the two. An outline or cartouche, for example, might be transfer-printed but the details then painted in by hand. Transfer-printing, developed in the 1750s, speeded production and enabled British manufacturers to compete with cheap Oriental imports; at first, only one colour could be printed on at a time, but multi-colour transfer-printing was developed in the 1840s. Transfer-prints could be applied either under or over the glaze.

It may sometimes be difficult to distinguish between transfer-printing and painting. But there are clues, usually best picked up by close examination with an eyeglass. Shaded areas, for example, will be crosshatched on a transfer-print taken from a copperplate engraving. In a painting they will be colour-washed (although Chinese porcelain with a design copied from a European engraving may show crosshatching done by hand).

On a printed image the vertical lines, particularly, are consistently straight and even because its perspective is related to the flat surface on which it was drawn. It gives a different impression from a painting, where the artist turned the vessel as he worked. In some cases it is possible to recognise the 'hand' of an individual artist. Very few pieces are signed, but some factories added a code to the factory mark to indicate who painted the decoration. The signature of a renowned artist such as François Boucher or Angelica Kauffman invariably indicates a transfer print as these artists never directly painted commercial porcelain.

FAMILLE-ROSE COLOUR PALETTE *This Chinese plate of the Yongzheng period (c.1725) represents perhaps the peak of achievement in enamel painting by hand onto porcelain. The wide range of colours, including the distinctive rose-pink, had to be fired at different temperatures. The gilding was added last.*

TRANSFER-PRINT *The break in the pattern shows where the print had to be cut to fit as it was wrapped around this English pearlware jug. There may also be an overlap visible where the two edges of the transfer meet, or parts of the image may not join properly. These faults are not seen on hand-painting, which was applied direct to the surface.*

HAND-PAINTING *The blotchiness in the shaded areas on this Chinese porcelain mug was caused by a brush discharging its load of cobalt blue. There is no sign of cross-hatching. Irregularities in repeated patterns and uneven colouring may also indicate hand-painting, though underglaze blue fired at too high a temperature starts to trickle, which can make a printed line look like a painted one.*

COMBINED METHODS *On this Vienna vase of c.1900, the transfer-printed design was touched up by hand with white enamel, and the gilding emphasised, to give an impression that the whole piece was hand-painted.*

Dinner services and tablewares

Since Chinese porcelain led the field three centuries ago, a vast range of wares have been produced for the dining table. And as food fashions have changed, so too have table accessories, giving collectors enormous scope.

THE FIRST CERAMIC TABLEWARES to be manufactured were individual dishes or series of dishes, not full dinner services. The idea of a full service – consisting of side plates, soup bowls, dinner plates, meat dishes in various sizes, vegetable dishes, soup tureens and sauceboats – was introduced only in the 18th century. One of these services would fetch a huge price now, but individual pieces can be found relatively cheaply.

Specialised dishes such as supper sets or sardine dishes were made to fill gaps in the tableware market as culinary fads changed from one generation to another. Some are still in use today while others have disappeared into obscurity, but all are fascinating to collectors on a modest budget.

EARLY FLATWARES

As early as the 14th century, Chinese potters were making sophisticated blue and white bowls and dishes. By the 16th century, wares were reasonably thinly potted and painted in inky underglaze blue with boldly drawn birds, animals, flowers, grapes and dragons, surrounded by radiating panels which formed the border. These early dishes did not filter through to Europe until the reign of the late Ming Emperor Wanli (1573-1619). They are still known as *kraak* porcelain after the Dutch

word for the Portuguese carracks, or galleons, that brought them to Europe. Compared with other examples of Ming porcelain, they remain surprisingly inexpensive, fetching between £150 and £3000 apiece (see p. 188).

TIN-GLAZED EARTHENWARE

In southern Spain, lustreware dishes and chargers influenced by Moorish potters were made from the end of the 14th to the 18th centuries, with bold copper or gold designs on a buff background. Rare, early, armorial pieces might reach £20,000, but more modest examples fetch £400-£800.

Tin-glazed earthenware was also made in Holland and Britain from the 17th century onwards – the former known as Delft, the latter as English delftware. Throughout the 18th century, the major centres of production in London (principally Southwark and Lambeth), the West Country (Bristol, Brislington and Wincanton), Liverpool, Glasgow and Dublin made English delftware dishes and plates in their thousands.

These are virtually never marked and even experts find it hard to identify the place of production, but this does not really affect their price. Plain plates sell for £50-£300, although some West Country pieces with powdered manganese-purple or 'bianco-sopra-bianco' (white enamel over the white

Covered Meissen sugar bowl; c.1740; 7 in (17.8 cm) high. Taken from the famous Swan Service – one of the greatest services of all time – this sugar bowl bears the coat of arms of the service's owner, Count Brühl. The sculptured knop is typical of important Meissen services of this date.
£20,000-£30,000

background) borders fetch more. Inscribed or dated plates can make £150-£2000 each. Most Dutch Delft plates are cheaper than English delftware, and are often marked on the base with initials or a sketchy drawing representing the factory's name.

STONEWARE AND CREAMWARE

Delftware was not ideal for table use as its glaze chipped easily, exposing the soft porous earthenware underneath. This made it both imperfect and unhygienic. Much more satisfactory was the fine, white, salt-glazed stoneware developed in Staffordshire from the 1720s. This could be thinly potted, and so was more elegant than the thicker earthenwares.

Large oval meat dishes, as well as plates of all sizes, were made in large quantities, both

DINING LIKE KINGS *Even a relatively informal 18th-century dinner was an impressive occasion, as this painting by Michel Olivier of 'Dinner at the Temple of the Prince Conti' shows. The tableware used here would have been of the highest quality, as would the silver and glass.*

Chinese Canton porcelain coffee, tea, dinner and dessert service; c.1825-30. This service is painted in authentic Chinese famille-rose style, but the shapes of the dishes are typically British, and are copied from contemporary Spode porcelain.
£15,000

Earthenware meat dish; c.1810; 13½ in (34.3 cm) across. Dishes such as this Regency transfer-printed example by Job Ridgway are keenly sought after by collectors today.
£400

Spode earthenware hot-water plate; c.1825; 9½ in (24.1 cm) across. These practical plates, which kept the food warm, are less decorative – and therefore less valuable – than ordinary plates, despite being quite rare.
£180-£220

Composite ironstone dinner service; c.1815-20. 'Composite' services are made up from several different periods or firms. This service includes pieces from Davenport, Hicks Meigh & Johnson, and Mason's.
Full service: £2500

Vincennes écuelle (soup bowl) and cover; 1753; stand 8 in (20.3 cm) across. Vincennes wares are sought by serious porcelain collectors, as the factory was only in operation from 1740 to 1756. Vincennes decoration is always restrained, and birds in gilding – as here – are a particular favourite.
£20,000

plain and with coloured painted decoration. Although white stoneware is rarely marked, a porridge-like colour and the 'orange-peel' texture of the glaze are telltale characteristics. Undecorated plates and dishes are among the cheapest of 18th-century tablewares still found: large dishes sell for £150-£300, 9 in (22.9 cm) plates for £40-£80.

Even more suitable for the table was creamware – cream-coloured earthenware with a transparent lead glaze. The version developed by Josiah Wedgwood around 1763 was named Queen's Ware, as a shrewd compliment to Wedgwood's patron Queen Charlotte. It was light and thin, and could be produced at remarkably low cost, although enamelling added considerably to the expense. Many pieces, especially those for export, had pierced borders of decoratively shaped holes giving a lacy effect, and huge quantities were exported to Holland and elsewhere. Unpainted plates fetch £30-£50 today, pierced examples £50-£150, and most printed or enamelled pieces £100-£1000.

DINNER SERVICES

During the 18th century, a continuous stream of porcelain dinner services arrived from China while others were manufactured in Europe. They originally copied shapes that had been made in contemporary European pewter or silver.

CHINESE EXPORT PORCELAIN

At first, Chinese porcelain was unrivalled as it was both fashionable and cheap. Throughout the 18th century, services by the ton packed the holds of the East India companies' ships. Many were meticulously painted to order with the armorials of aristocratic British families in 'famille-rose' enamels (see p.167), but sometimes amusing mistakes occurred – as when a family motto 'Unite' appeared on hundreds of pieces as 'Untie'. A service such as this, or with unusual associations, will fetch far more than ordinary services. Other designs included delicately painted Chinese flowers, birds and family scenes, and an exotic pattern of overlapping coloured leaves known as the 'Tobacco Leaf' design.

Cheaper and more utilitarian services abounded, painted with Chinese landscapes and river scenes in underglaze blue. These plates originally cost as little as 2d (less than 1p) each but now change hands for £20-£40 apiece. Although such wares virtually never carry a mark, they can be recognised by the hardness of the porcelain, the unglazed edge of the footrim, and the blue-grey appearance and pitting – small black (continued p. 157)

Plates

Individual painted or transfer-printed plates can be built up into a diverse and decorative collection for a relatively modest investment.

Wedgwood printed plate; mid-late 19thC; 9 in (22.9 cm) across. This earthenware plate is transfer-printed with the Ferrara pattern.
£20-£40

Doulton earthenware plate; 1932; 9 in (22.9 cm) across. This good example of mass-produced art is loosely based on Eastern motifs. The design's outline was transfer-printed, then hand coloured in Persian style.
£30-£60

Chinese export porcelain plate; c.1770; c.9 in (23 cm) across. Blue and white plates with added colour fetch less than those with all-over decoration.
£30-£50

Staffordshire leaf-moulded plate; c.1840-80; c.9 in (23 cm) across. Most green-glazed earthenware dessert plates found today are from the late 19thC. The design is 18thC.
£20-£30

English dessert service plate; c.1835; c.9 in (23 cm) across. This unmarked plate from Staffordshire is painted in 'botanical' style, copied from books of botanical prints.
£100-£150

Middlesbrough Pottery child's plate; mid-19thC; c.6½ in (16.5 cm) across. A maker's mark, which is rare on such pieces, boosts the value.
£30-£50

Rare Worcester porcelain plate; c.1865; 9⅜ in (23.8 cm) across. This plate was decorated in Canton style by the Chinese artist Po Hing, working in England.
£300-£500

Samson of Paris copy of 18thC Chinese armorial plate; c.1880; 9¼ in (23.5 cm) across.
£50-£120

Ridgway Homemaker plate; 1950s; 10 in (25.4 cm) across. This plate in postwar collage style was designed for Woolworths.
£5-£10

Transfer-printed and hand-coloured plate; c.1930; 8 in (20.3 cm) across. Designed by Clarice Cliff and Laura Knight.
£150-£200

Worcester Barr, Flight & Barr porcelain plate; c.1804-13; c.8 in (20.3 cm) across. This superbly painted plate is typical of the firm.
£1000-£1500

Russian plate; c.1920; 8½ in (21.6 cm) across. The curiosity value of this well-painted plate makes it very collectable today.
£1000-£2000

indentations like pinpricks – of the glaze. A 100-piece service will make £4000-£7000, although the equivalent in famille-rose enamels will cost three to five times as much.

FRENCH AND GERMAN SERVICES

The factories of Meissen in Germany and Sèvres in France were the leading European manufacturers of porcelain tablewares and dinner services, and were widely patronised by royalty and the nobility. From the 1730s, Meissen created services finely painted with birds, landscapes, hunting scenes, flowers and figures, and with moulded flower, scroll or basketwork borders. Coloured borders became more fashionable from the 1760s, remaining so throughout the 19th century. Meissen's crossed swords mark is nearly always to be found on the base, although this was much copied (see box). Whole services from the 18th century are rare, and single plates are well worth collecting, especially if in good condition. A modest deutsche Blumen ('German flowers') design sells for around £150, while a desirable Kakiemon or Swan Service plate can reach up to £3000-£5000.

The French Sèvres factory also made large, magnificently painted services, but in soft paste rather than the hard-paste porcelain used by Meissen. The 18th-century Sèvres porcelain has a creamy, soft look, and pieces of this date give an impression of lightness and delicacy. Entwined monograms formed of flower garlands are more common than coats of arms, and the colours tend to be pinks, greens, blues and turquoise instead of the stronger reds, blues and yellows of Meissen. Rims are often decorated with rich but graceful gilding, the surface tooled or engraved with flowers and leaves. Pieces range from £300 to several thousands for those from known services and are often marked with a date letter (starting with A in 1753) and a painter's mark. But many copies exist.

Sèvres later introduced services in the Empire style, made popular in France by Napoleon around 1800; the style influenced the porcelain factories of Berlin, Vienna and St Petersburg. It is distinguished by its 'Imperial' colours, such as dark blue and dark red, with deep bands of burnished gilding and superb paintings of battle scenes, great buildings and copies of contemporary paintings. Such plates cost £2000-£5000 today.

While these and a few lesser manufacturers were making fine porcelain, numerous services in tin-glazed earthenware were being produced in rural France and Germany (where it is known as faience) and Italy (maiolica) throughout the 18th and 19th centuries. These were generally painted with

Part of a 32-piece Derby botanical dessert service; c.1795. Services with a yellow border and well-painted flowers always fetch a high price as yellow is so difficult to fire. Named artists also push up the price.
£5000-£8000 as shown
Complete service: £12,000-£18,000

Minton porcelain dessert service; c.1878. Painted by Desiré Leroy, this turquoise blue is typical of Minton (as is brilliant pink) and was copied from Sèvres.
£2000-£2500

Spode set of tulip cups and stand; c.1810-20; stand 11¾ in (29.8 cm) across. This unusual set of dessert cups, used for custards or ices, is marked SPODE in red. Such sets are rarely found complete, as they were so prone to damage.
£12,000

Bow sauceboat; c.1750; c.5½ in (14 cm) long. This good example of early British porcelain uses a contemporary silver shape and Chinese famille-rose style decoration.
£800

Minton majolica oyster dish; c.1880; c.11 in (28 cm) wide. Although Minton's majolica was unwanted up until the 1970s, it is widely collected today. Bright turquoise was a favourite colour.
£300

simple sprays of flowers and landscapes. Much used, and often much chipped, such plates are attractive and inexpensive at £50-£500 each.

BRITISH TABLEWARES

British factories were hard put to match the continental makers' versatility. The secret of how to make hard-paste porcelain was not discovered in England until 1768, and the soft, unstable paste developed at Chelsea, Bow, Derby and Longton Hall in the 1740s and 50s was better suited to small, precious pieces. Chelsea produced a series of plates decorated with botanical flowers, copied from engravings of plants in the Chelsea Physic Garden. Now known as 'Hans Sloane plates' – after the garden's patron – these highly desirable items change hands for £1000-£3000 apiece today.

Few large-scale dinner services were made in Britain at that time because of the instability, cost and vulnerability to heat of English porcelain. Not until the end of the 18th and the early 19th centuries were porcelain factories such as Worcester and Derby regularly making large services.

The technological advances of the Industrial Revolution had a big impact on British potteries, speeding up production and bringing down the price of many wares to levels affordable by the new middle classes. One of the most notable inventions was that of transfer-printing, first used on any scale on porcelain at Worcester during the 1760s and 70s. During the first quarter of the 19th century it became the standard method of decoration for cheaper wares.

Continuing the creamware and pearlware tradition, quantities of fine earthenware dinner services were printed in underglaze blue with romantic ruins and landscapes by Spode and other potters. Their large tureens and meat dishes, especially if complete with drainers, are much sought after by collectors today and fetch £300-£2000, depending on the decoration. Such patterns as Spode's 'Caramanian' and 'Italian' are particularly popular, as are Indian sporting scenes and American views. Large dishes can fetch up to £1000, while a rare plate with an American view might reach £1500.

Stone china, such as the ironstone china patented by Charles James Mason in 1813, was stronger than ordinary earthenware. Mason produced impressive dinner services with large tureens on separate stands, decorated with fantastic, oriental-style patterns. The outlines of the designs were printed but these were then filled in by hand, a technique also employed by many other Staffordshire

Derby porcelain asparagus server; c.1775-80; 3 in (76 mm) wide. Fan-shaped asparagus servers were made both in earthenware and in porcelain.
£250-£350

Chinese porcelain blue and white trencher salts; c.1770-90; 3 in (76 mm) wide. The shape of such salts was taken from contemporary British silver equivalents.
£400 the pair

Copeland & Garrett Argyle; c.1840; 6½ in (16.5 cm) high. Hot water in the base keeps the gravy warm, and the low-set spout draws it off without the fat, which floats to the surface.
£500

Chinese famille-rose goose tureen; c.1770; 13 in (33 cm) high. These spectacular pieces were made for export to Europe, as much for table decoration as for soup. Beware 20thC copies.
£50,000-£80,000

English blue and white pickle dish; c.1760-70; 3½ in (89 mm) long. Most 18thC English porcelain factories produced large numbers of these, mainly in leaf or shell shapes.
£250

potters. Single Mason ironstone plates fetch from £60, soup tureens around £1000, and a typical famille-rose or Japanese-style service of 100 pieces, £5000-£10,000.

DESSERT SERVICES

During the later Georgian period, it became fashionable to finish a meal with a dessert course – consisting of pies, ices, tarts, fruits, nuts, syllabubs and custards – in place of the earlier 'banquets' of spiced sweetmeats and biscuits. Dessert was laid out at a separate table or on a three-tier dumb waiter.

Dessert wares were part of Chinese export dinner services from the 1760s onwards, and

included sauce tureens and covers, pierced baskets, low, circular, oval or boat-shaped fruit stands (or *tazzas*) and dessert plates, which are a little smaller than dinner plates. But since dessert was served cold, wares did not need to be heat-resistant to be suitable, and as a result, British soft-paste porcelain was able to compete with imported Chinese and continental dessert services.

EARLY ENGLISH AND WELSH

During the 1760s and 70s, the Worcester factory produced some magnificent dessert services, consisting of plates, dishes in four shapes, and small sauce tureens with covers and stands. These are painted with birds,

Wedgwood two-colour jasperware biscuit barrel; early 20thC; 6¾ in (17.1 cm) high. Biscuit barrels date from the second half of the 19thC. Two-colour examples are more desirable than the numerous blue and white pieces, which sell for £40-£60 apiece.
£100

Chinese porcelain hors d'oeuvres set; c.1830; 12½ in (31.7 cm) across. Single dishes are worth very little, but a complete set of nine dishes with their hardwood or lacquer tray, as here, is very collectable.
£800

Lowestoft blue and white soft-paste porcelain patty pan; c.1768-75; 3½ in (89 mm) wide. Patty pans were rarely marked, so can be hard to attribute.
£200

Wedgwood jasperware cheese dish; late 19thC; 11 in (28 cm) high. Designed to hold a whole Stilton, these were also made in olive-green and beige 'drab' ware.
£180

Knife and fork with white, soft-paste Chelsea porcelain handles; c.1750-2; 4 in (10.1 cm) long. These unmarked handles are inspired by Chinese 'blanc de Chine' porcelain, and are quite rare.
£200-£500 the pair

landscapes and flowers against a spectrum of blue-scale, apple-green, claret, turquoise and yellow grounds inspired by Meissen and Sèvres. Among many other patterns, the 'Catherine Wheel' and 'Royal Lily' designs remained popular for decades, and are now very collectable. A 24-piece setting for 12 people (including tureens, dishes, and so on) will sell for £3000-£6000.

Fine Welsh porcelain dessert services from Nantgarw and Swansea – with shaped rectangular fruit dishes on low stands, delicate gilding and unsurpassed flower painting – were popular at the beginning of the 19th century for the translucency and whiteness of their porcelain. Even single plates are highly

prized nowadays, changing hands for around £500-£2000. Derby botanical flower plates, many of which have the plants named on the reverse, are also prized. They formed part of dessert services from the 1790s, and now fetch £200-£500 per plate, and as much as £8000-£15,000 for a 24-piece service.

The 'Regency' porcelain dessert services produced by the Worcester Flight & Barr factory between 1783 and 1840 are among the most flamboyant ever made. The dishes and plates, with gadrooned and shaped rims imitating their silver equivalents, are painted with armorials, flowers, shells, birds, feathers, landscapes and views of Worcester or country houses on backgrounds of pale pink, deep

claret, salmon and marbling, or all-over gilt patterns. Single plates from these services are worth £200-£4000 today.

NINETEENTH CENTURY

During the first part of the 19th century, Wedgwood made a series of imaginative creamware dessert services while some very decorative porcelain services were made by Ridgway, Coalport, Davenport and others. Decoration not seen on dinner plates was lavished on the more luxurious dessert services, some combining moulded and painted borders. Minton was the leading producer of these later in the century, and pierced fruit baskets on tall stands copied from Sèvres,

Wedgwood caneware game pie dish; c.1860; c.12 in (30 cm) wide. Pottery pie dishes were first made to cook pies without pastry during the Napoleonic Wars, when flour was scarce.
£150-£500 depending on condition

Wedgwood creamware jelly mould and core; c.1780-90; c.8½ in (21 cm) high. Rare core moulds are much more valuable than traditional earthenware moulds and are seldom found complete. The decorative core showed through the jelly at the table.
£2000-£2500

German porcelain comport, or centrepiece from a dessert service, 13 in (33 cm) high. Such pieces were particularly popular during the second half of the 19thC, but until recently they have been considered 'too Victorian' to be collectable.
£500-£800

Derby porcelain chestnut bowl with pierced cover; c.1760; 6 in (15.2 cm) high. Early Derby is rarely marked but can be identified by three patch marks (like thumbprints) on the base.
£2000

French faience porringer; 1870-1900; 5 in (12.7 cm) across. This might be from Quimper, in Brittany, where a faience industry still flourishes – even 20thC pieces are collectable.
£280

One of a pair of English (probably Worcester) ice pails, covers and liners; c.1820; 13 in (33 cm) high. Superbly painted by Priscilla Bradley, these central pieces of a dessert service held fruit or ice cream, which was kept cool by iced water in the base.
£8000-£12,000 the pair

some supported by putti – cherubs or cupids – are typical of its wares.

From about 1850, Minton also introduced dessert services, tall fruit stands and other tablewares in high-quality earthenware covered with brightly coloured glazes – vivid pink, turquoise, green, ochre, brown and others. This majolica ware is much collected for its fine quality, bright colours and imaginative design, fetching up to £2500 for a service, or £200-£400 for a fruit stand.

TABLE ACCESSORIES

Many specialised items of ceramic tableware originally appeared as part of comprehensive dinner services, while others were sold as additions to the fashionable table. Some firms made ranges of such wares – Minton's moulded oyster plates, breadboards, asparagus dishes, fish tureens and butter dishes in majolica are one example – but most manufacturers produced at least a few pieces, varying from the mundane to the spectacular.

Early collectable salts were often part of a larger service, and include flat-bottomed trencher salts made from the late 17th century onwards and circular footed salts from Liverpool, Bow and other 18th-century porcelain factories, copied from George II silver. Occasionally, 18th-century cruet sets for oil and vinegar are found in Leeds creamware, Italian maiolica, French faience or Sèvres porcelain, as are salad bowls and mustard pots. Pots with their original small porcelain spoons are rare and fetch £500-£1500 today.

Soup tureens, with cover and stand, have always been a central feature of dinner services. Highly decorative table centrepieces were moulded in animal shapes at the Chelsea porcelain factory, and today fetch £15,000-£20,000; smaller tureens modelled as fruit and vegetables fetch £1000-£3000.

Other collectable table decorations include small sweetmeat dishes in shell or leaf shapes. Most have stands which are either pyramid shaped or which take the form of figures, such as Turks or Chinamen, holding small baskets or shell dishes. These range from £300 to £1200 a pair. Even more unusual are creamware 'core' jelly moulds made by Wedgwood in the 1770s, which were intended to be covered in a translucent jelly light enough to allow the floral decoration to be seen.

A vast array of everyday table accessories include patty pans, sauceboats, pickle trays, asparagus shells, game pie dishes, butter tubs and cheese dishes. Most were made in both porcelain and earthenware, and are a good introduction to ceramic tablewares for the collector on a budget.

The blue and white tradition

Unexpected finds of early Chinese porcelain do still occur – when a lamp base, for example, or a dog's bowl turns out to be a valuable early Ming piece. But there is also plenty of later blue and white to attract the collector.

THE ORIGINS OF UNDERGLAZE-BLUE decoration are debatable, but certainly it was in use in China by the second quarter of the 14th century. Cobalt oxide, a black pigment which turns blue on firing, had been imported from Persia in Tang times (AD 618-906) and used to colour glazes. But it was the idea of painting it onto a white porcelain body before glazing and final firing that produced the blue and white style of decoration that is still in wide use today.

IN THE FAR EAST

Ming dynasty potters (1368-1644) quickly achieved a high level of expertise. Their main problem was to control the amount of pigment they painted onto the unfired body. Too much led to small black spots breaking through the glaze, an effect known as 'heaping and piling' which is much admired today.

Major mid-14th-century pieces now fetch hundreds of thousands of pounds, but less important examples start at about £5000. Fairly common items, particularly provincial boxes made for the Filipino market, can go for £60. A 15th or 16th-century bowl from a minor kiln may fetch £60-£100.

The first reign mark appeared under the Emperor Yongle (1403-24) on pieces from the potteries at Jingdezhen. Unmarked pieces can be dated because throughout the Ming period styles, the nature of the porcelain, potting, glaze and colour changed – but dated or genuine reign-marked pieces (see p.508) are worth ten times as much as unmarked ones.

Towards the end of the Ming dynasty, large quantities of blue and white were made for export to Europe. The predominant *kraak* style, named after the carracks then used to carry the cargo (see p.188), lasted from the mid-16th to the mid-17th century. The most common forms are dishes and bowls painted with panels of flowers and animals. A cracked 16 in (40.5 cm) kraak dish – most are cracked – sells for between £300 and £800; undamaged ones start at £800. Bowls are less expensive as they are difficult to display.

AFTER THE MING DOWNFALL

The 50-odd years surrounding the end of the Ming dynasty in 1644 are referred to as the Transitional period. Transitional porcelain is

Chinese blue and white Ming vase; early 15thC; 14⅜ in (36.5 cm) high. The separation of the design into bands is typical of wares of this date.
£400,000-£600,000

Chinese blue and white Ming bowl with lotus and dragon design; 16thC; 6 in (15.2 cm) across. Provincial centres made similar bowls, most for export to south-east Asia.
£300-£400

Garniture of vases; Kangxi period (1662-1722); 20¾ in (52.5 cm) high. Sets of three covered vases and two of trumpet form were for display on a mantel or cabinet. They were also made in Japan.
£20,000-£25,000 the set
Single vase: £1500-£2500

A HOUSEHOLD'S PRIDE AND JOY *Chinese blue and white porcelain has been collected and displayed since travellers first brought it to medieval Europe.*

Chinese 'sleeve' vase, or 'rolwagen'; Transitional period, mid-17thC; 17⅛ in (43.5 cm) high. The decoration on this vase has features typical of the period, including figures – one holding a banner – V-shaped grasses and a cloud.
£4500-£5500

Teabowls and saucers from the 'Nanking Cargo'; c.1750; saucers c.4¾ in (12.1 cm) across. The Dutch ship 'Geldermalsen' left Canton in 1751 with porcelain, gold and tea but sank in the South China Sea. A salvage operation in 1985 brought up some 190,000 pieces of porcelain. Most were unremarkable blue and white, but in amazingly good condition.
£70-£300 each piece

distinctive, being much heavier, better potted and more refined than the preceding kraak. It is now beginning to attract considerable attention. A vase that a few years ago could be bought at auction for £400 is today worth nearer £1500 – and rising.

From the end of the 17th century the vast output from Chinese kilns consisted mainly of blue and white garnitures – sets of five large vases – and tablewares, all made for export to Europe. There were also a limited number of polychrome porcelain pieces made; these were more expensive.

The bulk of the tablewares were dinner and tea services (see pp. 154 and 173), the remnants of which provide remarkable bargains for collectors: a teabowl costs about £15, or with its saucer £30. Plates will fetch about £80, or under £40 if they are damaged. Eighteenth-century teapots sell for around £80, or £25 if damaged. The pieces are thinly potted and plates are prone to chip at the rim, but a small amount of chipping is acceptable.

A distinguishing feature of much Chinese porcelain of this date is the orange tint of the body where the glaze has been removed (on foot rims and teapot rims, for example).

This orange tint is not seen on European porcelain of any date.

Chinese copies of Ming blue and white – including 'heaping and piling' – were made during the 18th century, and are much sought after, particularly by Hong Kong Chinese collectors. Prices start at about £800, but can soar to over £200,000 if a piece bears the *nien hao*, the reign mark of the emperor.

Large dishes were made as part of a service or for display, and these vary enormously in quality. An undamaged 16 in (40.5 cm) circular dish from the mid-18th century may cost £200-£800, but most fall at the lower end of the scale. A hairline crack can reduce the price to as little as £30-£50.

JAPANESE WARES

Very little Japanese blue and white porcelain was imported into Europe; the few imports were copies of kraak dishes. These can be distinguished from their Chinese counterparts by heavier potting, the finely bubbled

glaze and the presence of 'spur' marks on the base (see p. 189). They fetch £1500-£5000 – more than the Chinese originals. Small dishes, teabowls and saucers made for the Dutch market, and influenced by Delft ware, fetch £300-£1000.

The blue and white pieces made by the Kakiemon kilns at Arita can rarely be bought for under £1000. Eighteenth-century blue and white from Nabeshima is highly prized by Japanese collectors, and starts at £1000 a piece. However, 19th-century Nabeshima – which is in exactly the same style – is worth considerably less, selling for about £200, and distinguishing between the two is difficult.

From the mid-19th century onwards, the kilns at Hirado made very fine wares in blue and white; examples sell in the £150-£3000 range and are perhaps underpriced. Later in the century, Makuzu Kozan rescued Japanese porcelain from the poor state into which it had fallen. His work is much sought after, fetching from £800 up to £20,000 today.

IN EUROPE

Cobalt-blue was first used in Europe on 15th-century Italian maiolica. Porcelain made by the Medici factory in Florence included copies of Chinese and Persian wares in blue and white, but by the early 17th century the French factories of Rouen, St Cloud and Chantilly were all making soft-paste blue and white porcelain simply decorated and with scrolling borders known as lambrequins. A St Cloud cup and saucer now costs about £300 – but more than twice this if it bears the sun face factory mark. A piece of Rouen will fetch perhaps up to £10,000.

Meissen produced very little blue and white during the 18th century, with the exception of a few dinner and tea services. Its 'Onion' pattern, which is still in production, is the most collected of these, and plates start at about £80. Copies of the 'Onion' pattern range were made in Thuringia, in Bohemia and at Copenhagen. Such pieces are

Chinese vase and cover; c. 1880; 14 in (35.6 cm) high. Wares with prunus blossom on a 'cracked ice' ground were extremely popular in the late 19thC.
£120-£150
Pair: £400-£600

Chinese plate (left); c. 1780; 9 in (22.9 cm) across. This well-painted landscape uses many design elements that inspired the hugely popular Staffordshire 'Willow' pattern.
£70-£100

Japanese vase by Makuzo Kozan; late 19thC; 24 in (61 cm) high. Kozan's work is always signed and fetches large sums.
£5000-£7000

Japanese Arita apothecary's bottle; late 17thC; 15⅛ in (38.4 cm) high. This bottle was made for the Dutch market and bears the initials 'IC' on its base, possibly standing for Johannes Campys, a director of the Dutch East India Company.
£15,000-£18,000

generally bought for use rather than investment, and are found from around £20 each.

It was Britain that made a virtue out of the monochrome palette, specialising in blue and white from the mid-18th century. The Bow factory made more than any other, and exported much to North America. Its potting was heavy, enabling it to make large dishes when other factories failed, but its wares have a tendency to brown discoloration where chipped or cracked. Pieces start at £80.

The Worcester factory made large numbers of blue and white services, mostly for tea. Its soapstone porcelain body withstood boiling water better than others, and today Worcester teapots sell for £150 or more. See also p. 164.

BRITISH MASS PRODUCTION

The great contribution to ceramics made by the British was the development of transfer printing (see p. 153). The method of off-setting a printed image from tissue onto the ceramic body was first used in Liverpool for applying overglaze prints to tin-glazed tiles. It was soon adapted to decorate wares in underglaze blue and was employed by most of the 18th-century factories.

From late in the 18th century the Staffordshire potters began to produce enormous quantities of blue and white transfer-printed wares. Making a wide variety of pearlware, earthenware and stone china at low cost and to high standards, they cornered the international market. Most of these dishes sell today for between £80 and £300, although more sought-after patterns, such as Spode's 'Sporting' series, fetch double that, and a 'Prize Bull' print more than £1000.

The technique is still being used, and many willow, ruin and Italianate landscape patterns are being produced from the original copper plates. Always bear in mind that the words 'England' or 'Made in England' stamped on the base indicate that the piece is less than 100 years old.

Bridging of Styles

THE BEST-KNOWN 'CHINESE' PATTERN printed onto blue and white ceramics did not in fact originate in China at all. 'Willow' pattern was designed for Caughley in Shropshire by Thomas Minton about 1780, probably to cash in on public enthusiasm for all things Chinese. Many other factories copied the pattern, including Wedgwood, Spode and Davenport in Staffordshire, and it was even adopted by the Chinese (although hand-painted) and then exported back to Europe.

The design varies, but it always includes a willow tree, a temple, figures crossing a bridge, and a distant island – all beneath two birds representing a pair of lovers. As the pattern evolved during the 19th century, it became increasingly crowded.

Despite the fact that 'Willow' pattern is the most common and least expensive of printed decorations, early wares are now very popular with collectors. A pearlware plate can fetch £50 and a meat dish £150, while marked items fetch double this.

Swansea pearlware meat dish, c.1810 (left); and a more fully patterned late 19thC Staffordshire one, 22 in (56 cm) across.
Left: £100-£200
Right: £50-£80

Wedgwood pearlware jug; c.1815; 8 in (20.3 cm) high. It is printed with stylised flowers below Classical buildings.
£300-£400

Spode earthenware plate; c.1815; 9⅞ in (25 cm). The transfer-printed 'Indian Sporting Scene' is now one of the most sought-after patterns on blue and white Staffordshire wares.
£100-£150

Bow dish; c.1755-60; 7⅞ in (20 cm) across. The painted 'Golfer and Caddy' design is adapted from a Chinese design in which the servant carried paper scrolls.
£1500-£1800

Meissen cream jug and stand; c.1730; stand 7 in (17.8 cm) across. The painting in Chinese style has fishermen inside. The outside imitates Chinese Batavian ware, made for the Dutch to trade in Batavia (Java).
£1000-£1500

Worcester mug; c.1770-80; 3½ in (89 mm) high. Printed with two common designs, a fisherman and a strolling Oriental figure, the mugs were much imitated at Caughley.
£200-£300

Derby tureen and stand; 1760; stand 9½ in (24 cm) wide. The attractive tureen has pierced decoration on the lid, is sprigged with flowers and has crabstock handles.
£2000-£3000

An Expert Examines

DAVID BATTIE RUNS A CHECKLIST ON A BLUE AND WHITE PORCELAIN BOWL

'AN ATTRACTIVE BOWL in Rococo style with a scalloped edge and moulded shells: a nice piece. But I need to run through a mental checklist: where did it come from, and is it damaged?

The bowl – 9¼ in (23.5 cm) across

The character of the glaze suggests soft-paste, rather than hard-paste, porcelain, while the underglaze blue is reminiscent of Chinese. But although they made a little soft paste, the moulding rules out China, as does the soft tone of the blue, which is more characteristic of Japan. But the Japanese

Blue crescent mark and missing line of glaze

didn't use soft paste, nor did they make bowls in this form. So – soft paste, underglaze blue: most likely England. Now the crescent mark on the underside suggests Worcester, though other factories used it too. But there's also that line of scraped-off glaze just inside the foot-rim; Worcester did that to prevent pieces sticking to the kiln floor, and the design is altogether characteristic of a Worcester junket bowl of the mid to late 18th century.

Blue-green translucency   Cell diaper pattern

Another clue is the strong, blue-green translucency of the porcelain when you hold it up to the light. That's typical of 1760s Worcester; by the 80s, it was brownish-yellow. Then, there's the way the painter has drawn the flowers and the border of small rectangles – it's called the cell diaper pattern, very much in tune with the 1760s. Having got that far, I would clinch the matter by checking the Worcester pattern books to see if this design is recorded. And indeed it is.

Now to assess its condition. Whenever I pick up a piece of porcelain, it's second nature to give it a knock with a knuckle. It's not infallible, but generally speaking, a clear note is a good sign, a nasty buzz probably indicates a crack, while a dull thud says it may have been restored. And there's a distinctly muffled note with this one.

The tooth-tapping test for restoration

If you suspect restoration, tap the piece on your teeth. Glaze yields a sharp click, while the softer paint of restoration gives a dull thud. Or run a blade or pin lightly over the surface; it glides over glaze, but sticks as it comes to the restored part. Now, with doubts aroused, I can see a difference in colour in one of the flower sprays. The blue is purplish, quite unlike the original inky blue, and there's an orange-peel texture that suggests paint rather than glaze. I think there's been a major filling-in job where a piece was lost.

Testing by touch   Restored flower spray

DAVID BATTIE SUMS UP

The difference in value between a restored and a perfect piece can be large. The problem is that no one can tell how far the damage went on an article that's been restored and painted over. Did it have a one-inch crack, or a whole chunk missing? A knowledgeable buyer will assume the worst, and will pay accordingly. This bowl, undamaged, would be worth £300-£400. Damaged but unrestored it could fetch between £80 and £250, depending on the injury. But as it is, it would make no more than £100 – more or less what the restoration must have cost.'

Maiolica, faience or delft?

These are the names used for stylistically distinct types of European pottery that are all covered in an opaque glaze made white by ashes of tin.

BRIGHT COLOURS ARE LOST if they are painted onto earthenware with a clear lead glaze – the earliest type widely used – since the glaze deepens the underlying clay colour. However, a primary coat of white or cream tin glaze creates a pristine surface on which other colours stand out brilliantly.

The various names for tin-glazed wares from different countries reflect the historical sequence in which the technique passed from one to another. It probably originated in the Middle East some 1100 years ago. The Moors in Spain introduced it to Europe and, in the 13th century, started producing what we now call Hispano-Moresque wares. In Italy, tin-glazed pottery was known as 'maiolica' (after the island of Majorca, from which Hispano-Moresque wares were exported). The French, German and Scandinavian versions are called 'faience' or 'fayence' (after the Italian pottery centre of Faenza), the Dutch 'Delft' (a major Dutch centre), and the English 'delftware' (derived from the Dutch name).

QUESTIONS OF IDENTITY

Tin-glazed earthenware can be spotted by the way its brittle glaze tends to chip or splinter on edges and corners. Unlike a porcelain body, the clay beneath is grainy and quite different in colour from the glaze. Few tin-glazed earthenwares more than 100 years old are unchipped, so this is easy to check. While you may confuse Dutch decoration with Chinese or Japanese, checking the actual material will soon tell you which is which (see p.188).

The decoration, form and rarity of tin-glazed earthenware vary greatly. Hispano-Moresque chargers made for Florentine nobles in the 15th century may sell at auction for well into five figures. A mid-18th-century English delftware blue and white plate may fetch £30-£100. Fine Italian maiolica from Urbino with Classical decoration sells for between £5000 and £50,000, even if it has been broken and stuck or riveted together.

In the middle and late 18th century, competition from Chinese imports and new porcelain products seriously damaged the market for north European tin-glazes. But in Mediterranean countries the tradition continues today. For £10-£100 you can buy a souvenir that is unlikely ever to have collector's value. For £5000-£20,000 you can acquire a dish or jug by Picasso (see p.185), as accomplished as the best of his paintings.

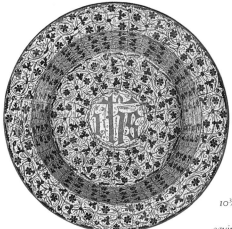

Hispano-Moresque lustreware charger from Manises near Valencia; mid-15thC; 19 in (48.2 cm) across. In the centre is the sacred monogram IHS (standing for Jesus).
£30,000-£40,000

Italian maiolica armorial flask; Faenza, late 16thC; 12¼ in (31.1 cm) high. The potter mimicked a well-known metalware form.
£1200-£1500

Dutch Delft doré (gilded) plate decorated in Chinese Kangxi style; c.1700; 9 in (22.9 cm) across. Gilded Delft is rare and much sought after, and some wear is acceptable.
£2500-£3500

German faience jardinière; c.1725; 10¾ in (27.3 cm) high. English and Dutch equivalents cost far more.
£600-£800

French faience plate (left); Marseilles, c.1765; 9¾ in (24.7 cm) across. This piece, attributed to J.G. Robert's factory, is decorated with naturalistic flowers and a fish in coloured enamels.
£1500-£2500

Delftware fireplace tiles; Liverpool, c.1760-5; each 5 in (12.7 cm) square. Prices start around £20-£30 each for 18thC blue and white tiles, and rise according to subject, colour and condition.
£150-£200 each

MAJOLICA
Colourful Victoriana

AS A FOOTNOTE to the story of tin-glazed pottery, 'majolica' was a name coined in the late 19th century for relief-moulded pottery decorated with coloured translucent (non-tin) glazes. It was made mainly in Britain and North America, and some in France. The style recalled the colourful, three-dimensional creations of the della Robbia family of sculptors in 15th and 16th-century Italy. For examples of majolica wares, see pages 200-1.

The China and Japan trades

Out of the East came the finest ceramics Europeans had ever seen. Their impact was unforeseen and immeasurable, and revolutionised Western techniques and design.

'BEAUTIFUL VESSELS and plates of porcellana, large and small . . . for one Venetian groat you could actually have three bowls so beautiful that no one would know how to devise them better. . . .' So wrote the young Venetian Marco Polo about the *yingqing* ('misty blue') porcelain he saw on his journeys through China in about 1271-5.

Until this time, China was virtually unknown to Europeans except as 'Seres', the land of silk, although as early as the Tang dynasty of AD 618-906, jewels, horses, medicines, wild animals and literature were flowing into the country from India, Arabia and Japan.

Then, towards the end of the Ming dynasty (1368-1644), Jesuit missionaries to China spread knowledge of science and technology, and opened the way for trade with the West. Initially, the main trade was in silks and spices, mostly in exchange for silver bullion, but in the late 16th and early 17th centuries, large kraak

CHINA CRAZE *Chinese blue and white wares and painted fans in this late 19thC painting by J. A. Grimshaw reveal the enthusiasm for all things Oriental.*

dishes (see p.188) and vases were imported by Portuguese and Dutch traders. A very few rare, commissioned examples with inscriptions and coats of arms were the precursors of a huge trade in made-to-order Chinese porcelain which developed in the late 17th century.

TEA AND CHINA

But it was tea that caused the real explosion of trade between East and West. The first tea arrived in Europe from China in the middle of the 17th century and was an immediate success despite its huge cost – around £300 a pound at today's prices. Chests of tea soon included a teapot, usually in either the red stoneware of Yixing, which was widely imitated in Europe, or in 'blanc-de-Chine' porcelain from Fujian province. These white wares were also much copied, and a lot of early European porcelain

Yingqing chrysanthemum dish; c.11thC; 7⅝ in (19.4 cm) wide. Such dishes are very thinly potted and can fetch high prices.
£4000-£6000

Celadon dish; 14thC; 17⅜ in (44.1 cm) wide. The shape derives from Arab metalwork.
£30,000-£35,000

Chinese blanc-de-Chine group of a Dutch family; c.1700; 6¼ in (15.9 cm) high. Dutch family groups were made for export and many were originally painted and gilded.
£1500-£2000

Famille-verte jar; c.1680; 9⅛ in (23 cm) high. Such jars were copied in both China and France.
£600-£900
19thC copy: £80-£120

Famille-rose vase (lid missing); 1770; 5 in (12.7cm) high. This vase, with figures of the Daoist deities, is typical of the lowest-quality wares coming from China at that time.
£300-£400
With lid:
£400-£600

Chinese blue and white porcelain tankard; mid-18thC; 5¼ in (13.3 cm) high. This tankard was 'clobbered' (had enamels and gilding added) in Holland, reducing its value.
£100-£350

of the 18th century, including that by Meissen, Chelsea and Bow, was in this style.

Before long, tea sets and dinner services of all sorts were being sent by the shipload to Europe. Many of these were thinly potted, white porcelain services painted in underglaze blue (see p. 161), of much higher quality than contemporary European earthenware and yet fantastically cheap.

Other wares were painted in enamel colours in Canton (Guangzhou). The style of enamel painting known in Europe as 'famille-verte' was fully developed by the Kangxi period (1662-1722) and was revived late in the 19th century. The enamels are transparent and are dominated by a distinctive green along with red, yellow and blue. Variations on famille-verte – famille-jaune and famille-noire – have the same design against a yellow or black background respectively. These were much copied by the Chinese in the late 19th and early 20th centuries.

The famille-rose colour scheme, based on pink, was introduced in the 1720s and was immediately successful both in China and in Europe. It remained the most popular of the Chinese colour families throughout

the 18th and 19th centuries. Huge numbers of dinner and tea services, tureens, vases, wall dishes and figures were decorated in this way.

OUT OF ISOLATION

Trade between the West and Japan was much more limited than that with China, especially after the Shogun Ieyasu Tokugawa closed the doors to Western influence in the 1630s. By 1640, the Dutch and Chinese were Japan's only trading partners, and even they were restricted to an island in Nagasaki Harbour.

Japanese porcelain was always much more expensive than Chinese wares, and in addition to plain blue and white, arrived in Europe in two distinct enamel styles: Imari and

Kakiemon. Imari wares are mostly in the form of large wall dishes or garnitures of vases, and were popular from the last quarter of the 17th century onwards. But Kakiemon porcelain, with its distinctive colours, was more sought after – and copied – in Europe, and remains the most prized Japanese porcelain today.

The isolation of Japan was broken by the Americans in 1853, and a craze for all things Japanese dominated the Aesthetic movement of the 1870s. High-quality porcelain, pottery (particularly 'Satsuma' ware – a finely-crackled earthenware with enamelled and gilt decoration), bronzes, ironwork, ivory carvings, cloisonné enamels, prints and lacquer all poured into Europe and the USA.

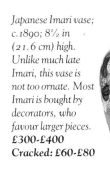

Japanese Imari vase; c. 1890; 8½ in (21.6 cm) high. Unlike much late Imari, this vase is not too ornate. Most Imari is bought by decorators, who favour larger pieces.
£300-£400
Cracked: £60-£80

Japanese Kakiemon bowl (left); c. 1700; 4⅝ in (11.7 cm) wide. The boys on this damaged bowl were copied by Meissen.
£600-£800; perfect: £2000-£3000

Fine Japanese porcelain vase (right); c. 1890; 23 in (58 cm) high. It is enamelled and gilded with flowers against a basket-weave ground.
£3000-£4000

Large Japanese Imari vase; c. 1880; 52 in (1.32 m) high.
£1600-£2300
Pair: £5000-£7000

Japanese Satsuma vase; c. 1920; 5 in (12.7 cm) high. Poorly painted Satsuma ware is very common, and this has lost most of its gilding.
£20-£30

THE EAST INDIA COMPANIES
Ships from the East

SILKS, TEA AND SPICES were the main interests of the various East India companies – chiefly the British and Dutch companies – as these offered the greatest profits. By the 18th century, other luxury articles had been added. Black and gold lacquered screens used to partition off a room – and even to provide a discreet area where diners could relieve themselves during long meals – and other pieces of lacquered furniture, especially chests, had a great influence on 17th- and 18th-century European design.

A mid-18th-century vogue for all things Chinese brought in a vast array of items, including hand-painted wall-papers, gouache paintings, furniture and incense burners. Also among them were carved figures, mirror frames and other wares of ivory, soapstone, jade and tortoiseshell (see p. 397).

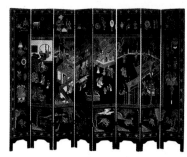

Eight-fold coromandel lacquer screen; late 18thC; 86 in (2.18 m) high. Many screens were imported, but they vary in quality.
£4000-£6000

The Wedgwood revolution

Josiah Wedgwood (1730-95) combined artistic and technical skill with a large measure of entrepreneurial flair. His innovations revolutionised British ceramics.

AT THE AGE OF JUST 29, in 1759, Josiah Wedgwood founded his own pottery business at Burslem, in Staffordshire, after five years in partnership with the master potter Thomas Whieldon. Spurred by criticisms of Staffordshire potting standards, Wedgwood began to experiment with ceramic bodies and their firing.

His first big success came in the early 1760s, when he introduced a superior clear-glazed cream-coloured earthenware containing pipe clay and ground calcined flint. This 'creamware' proved cheap to produce and became a rival to tin-glazed earthenware. George III's wife, Queen Charlotte, was so delighted with her creamware services that she allowed him to advertise as 'Potter to Her Majesty'. He, in turn, marketed his product as 'Queen's Ware'.

Other potters produced versions of creamware, but Wedgwood's technical and selling skills gave him the edge. His most challenging order was for a service of almost 1000 pieces for Empress Catherine the Great of Russia in 1773. It was known as the 'Frog Service' – a reference to her palace at La Grenouillière (*grenouille* is French for 'frog').

The commercial success of Queen's Ware

PORTRAIT OF A PIONEER *This painting of Josiah Wedgwood by George Stubbs in 1780 is in enamels on a Wedgwood biscuit Queen's Ware disc. Stubbs did only about 37 paintings on Wedgwood blanks.*

enabled Wedgwood to experiment with other ceramic bodies, especially 'black basaltes' – an extremely hard, unglazed black stoneware – and a fine red stoneware called 'rosso antico', inspired by the ancient pottery of Italy.

Further experiments led to the development, in 1774, of 'jasperware' – Wedgwood's best-known product. Jasper is a high-fired, dense white stoneware which is easily tinted,

holds very sharp detail and can be decorated with bas-relief work of contrasting colour. It was ideal for the imitations of Greek and Roman seals and cameos then in fashion. The practice of using 'jasper-dip' backgrounds was introduced in 1777. This coated a white base with a thin layer of base colour rather than dying the clay. Various combinations were tried, of which blue and white remained the most popular, the colours perfectly suited to the fashionable Classical motifs and interior style introduced by Robert Adam (see p. 36).

Wedgwood's replica of the Portland Vase (see p. 182) is his most striking achievement in jasperware. More affordable jasper and basaltes wares, from both the 18th and 19th centuries, are much sought after today. These start from around £100, although prices of up to £50,000 are paid for the rarest, most beautiful work. But beware: pieces are difficult to date, and are easier to restore than glazed earthenware, so examine any potential purchases carefully. Pieces later than the 18th century are generally coarser to the touch.

Wedgwood, a social reformer as well as a successful businessman, campaigned for the abolition of slavery. He made a jasperware medallion showing a slave with the words: 'Am I not a man and a brother?'

Wedgwood & Bentley imitation hardstone vase with applied medallion depicting the Three Graces; c.1775; 11½ in (29.2 cm) high. Josiah Wedgwood was in partnership with Thomas Bentley 1769-80.
£1000-£1500 (restored handles, no cover)
In perfect condition: £4500

Wedgwood black basaltes potpourri vase, or bough pot; c.1800; 11½ in (29.2 cm) wide. This design is inspired by a Graeco-Roman 'krater', a vase for mixing wine and water.
£700-£1000

Wedgwood blue and white jasper-dip oil lamp (right); 19thC; 9 in (22.9 cm) high; and lilac and white jasper-dip potpourri vase with pierced cover; 19thC; 8¼ in (21 cm) high.
Oil lamp: £400-£500 (missing cover)
Vase: £800-£1000

Wedgwood Queen's Ware plate painted with a view of West Cowes Castle; c.1774; 8⅞ in (22.5 cm) diameter. This is based on Catherine the Great's 'Frog Service' and was probably made for publicity after the originals were shipped to Russia.
£8000-£18,000, depending on condition

Ceramics for drinking

From crude earthenware spirit barrels to exquisite Ming dynasty Chinese porcelain wine cups, pottery and porcelain items used for the enjoyment of wine and other alcoholic drinks span a vast range of styles and prices.

CERAMIC VESSELS have been used for storing and serving alcoholic beverages for thousands of years, as numerous Greek wine vases (or kraters) and amphorae dating from around 600-300 BC confirm. These are seldom found outside museums today, but their Classical shapes and decoration have influenced the design of countless European vessels produced since.

Even though drink-related items inevitably run the risk of careless handling, buyers have a wide and interesting selection of Oriental and European objects to look out for, most dating from the last 300 years.

ORIENTAL CONTAINERS

Long before the Chinese developed the first porcelain wine vessels, glazed earthenware ewers and cups were being made during the Han (206 BC-AD 220) and Tang (AD 618-906) dynasties. By the time of the Ming dynasty (1368-1644), the Chinese were making hard-paste porcelain. Ewers and stem cups of this period are among the finest porcelain ever made, and collectors pay £200,000-£400,000 for a blue and white ewer and twice as much for one in copper-red. Even 18th-century Chinese copies are highly sought after.

Later Chinese exports include wine pots, which resemble small teapots. These usually have an overhead handle and are decorated

with enamels in the 'famille-verte' colour range (see p.167). They date from the Kangxi period (1662-1722), and today change hands for £200-£2000, depending on condition.

Also highly collectable, and equally rare, are 17th-century Japanese square bottles for saké, or rice wine, copied from those carried by European merchants and sea captains. If painted with asymmetrical Kakiemon-style enamel decoration – long-tailed birds amid flowering shrubs in blue, green, yellow and red – they can fetch £10,000-£40,000.

EARLY EUROPEAN VESSELS

In the later Middle Ages, the valley of the Rhine became an important wine-producing area, and countless flagons, bottles, ewers and

Chinese blue and white wine jar; c.1600; 15 in (38.1 cm) high. Wine was very much associated with the scholar/gentry class of Ming China, so this design of a scholar and his servants is particularly apt. Figures are more desirable than floral motifs.
£10,000-£15,000

Chinese famille-verte wine or teapot; c.1700; 5¾ in (14.6 cm) high. This hexagonal pot has reticulated, or cut out, panels; the double wall which is created insulates the liquid.
£1000-£2000

Greek Attic amphora; 5thC BC; 16½ in (42 cm) high. Amphorae are more often seen than kraters, but rare and early pieces such as this – with an integral foot in place of the more usual pointed end – are seldom found outside museums today.
Museum piece

Japanese Imari porcelain saké bottle; c.1700-20; 12 in (30.5 cm) high. This square-shaped bottle is typical of Japanese porcelain of this date, but the ormolu mounts are probably later, and French. The Imari palette of iron-red, underglaze blue and gilding was much copied on later British porcelain.
£1500-£2500

GRACIOUS LIVING 'A Portrait of a Gentleman Smoking', attributed to Stephen Slaughter, c.1740-50, clearly shows in the foreground an Oriental porcelain punchbowl very much in use.

tankards were made by local potteries. From the 16th century on, the Cologne area produced large numbers of the heavy brown stoneware jugs, bearing the face of a bearded man, that are known as bellarmines. Original German examples with silver-gilt mounts might fetch £5000-£10,000, but later 19th-century copies without mounts sell for as little as £40-£60. Large, brown, baluster-shaped stoneware bottles similar to bellarmines (but lacking the mask) were made in Britain from the 17th century onwards, and can be found at country auctions for as little as £20-£80.

Small wine bottles also of the same shape as bellarmines were produced in London delftware in the mid-17th century and finished with an opaque, milky-white tin glaze. Some bottles have the name of their contents – Sack, Claret or Whit (for Rhenish white wine) – painted on the side in blue, with a date below. They are usually from 1640 to 1660. Such lettered and dated examples may be worth £3000-£6000, the commoner plain ones £500-£1000. But beware of forgeries: originals have a soft, pinkish body under the glaze which is hard to imitate.

POSSET POTS AND PUNCHBOWLS

A mainly British peculiarity of the 17th century was the drink of posset, made with spiced milk and egg beaten up with ale or wine. It was drunk by everyone – from Oliver Cromwell to Samuel Pepys – when under the weather. To avoid the curdled head of froth, posset pots were made with an integral 'straw', or spout, which allowed the liquid to be sucked from the bottom of the pot. Delftware examples with domed lids were made in London and the West Country, and are generally decorated in blue.

Towards the end of the 17th century, cylindrical posset pots, with two or more loop handles but no built-in straw or spout, were made in Staffordshire slipware. They are decorated in trailed and dotted slip with names, initials and dates, and simple inscriptions such as 'the best is not too good for you'. Slipware 'tygs', or many-handled drinking vessels, were also made at Wrotham in Kent throughout the 17th century. They fetch up to £10,000, compared to about £5000 for similar delftware posset pots. Inscriptions and dates always increase the price.

By about 1700, the fashion for drinking posset had been largely overtaken by a vogue for punch. This was a brew of some force, made with brandy or rum, water, sugar, citrus juice and spices – ingredients newly arrived from the West Indies – mixed in a bowl and

German bellarmine jug; mid-late 17thC; 9 in (22.9 cm) high. Thousands of these jugs bearing the mask of Cardinal Roberto Bellarmine were imported into Britain and copied by London potters, notably John Dwight of Fulham.
£300-£500

London delftware wine bottle; 1676; 7½ in (19 cm) high. The crown and royal cipher honour Charles II, but inscriptions usually refer to the contents.
£6000-£8000

Staffordshire slipware posset pot; 1704; c.13 in (33 cm) wide. This piece is unusual as it retains the original small spout attached to an integral straw. Chips and cracks on the soft earthenware body of such a piece are almost inevitable.
£20,000-£30,000

Lambeth delftware punchbowl; 1752; 10½ in (26.7 cm) wide. It was made for a christening, and is therefore a rarity. Although it has been considerably restored, its value is enhanced by being dated and initialled.
£20,000-£25,000

Chinese porcelain famille-rose punch-bowl; c.1770-5; 13 in (33 cm) across. This bowl may look British, but its origins are clear from the riders' Oriental features and its unglazed footrim.
£3500-£4500

Staffordshire earthenware punch pot; c.1760-5; 8¼ in (21 cm) high. This 'tortoiseshell' lead glaze was favoured by the much-collected potter Thomas Whieldon.
£3000-£5000

served with a ladle. Punch-drinking was almost exclusively a male habit, and punch-bowl decoration includes pithy political comments, patriotic slogans and boisterous verses urging the company to drink: In Bristol and Liverpool, many English delftware bowls were made for ships' owners or captains, and decorated with a likeness of the boat inside. Good, mid-18th-century examples in pristine condition can fetch £6000-£10,000, ones with longer inscriptions and dates even more.

Far finer than these delftware bowls – though often fetching lower prices today – are those in Chinese porcelain. They are meticulously painted in blue and white or in one of the 'families' of enamel colours – most are in the pink-based famille-rose, some in the earlier, green-based famille-verte – with flowers, birds and landscapes, or figures. The most sought-after are those painted with European subjects: Masonic emblems, views of the 'hongs' (European trading stations) in Canton or copies of European engravings.

The Chinese origins of these pieces are given away by supposedly European figures with Oriental-looking eyes or hairstyles or curious, but precisely drawn, animals. The best punchbowls with European subjects fetch up to £20,000, but lesser blue and white pieces can be found for £250-£500.

In politer company, punch was served from pots resembling outsize teapots, some with an overhead handle. Such punch pots, made in Staffordshire during the late 18th century in unglazed red stoneware, creamware or with coloured glazes in the manner of Thomas Whieldon, are also very collectable. Those with their original pierced brazier stands can fetch up to £10,000, but even without a stand, punch pots make £500-£5000.

WINE ACCESSORIES

Foreign wines flooded into Britain during the 18th century, and a wide range of accessories were produced in response. Among the rarer items found today are porcelain funnels for straining wine and small wine-tasters, or tastevins, both made at the Worcester factory, founded in 1751. Unlike their silver counterparts, few of these have survived, and those that have can fetch up to £3000 for a wine-taster and £2000 or more for a funnel.

Much more affordable are rectangular ceramic bin labels, which make an interesting collecting field for those with limited space. Some of these bear the names of a fascinating range of long-discontinued wines, neatly painted in bold lettering. The earliest by a few years are in English delftware, but from about the 1790s they were made in considerable numbers at the Wedgwood factory in Queen's Ware and pearlware. Prices, even for delftware examples, rarely exceed £400, and common Wedgwood labels cost £50-£100.

Many of the new wines that arrived in Britain, and particularly the white ones, were best served chilled. Circular or oval basins known as monteiths were designed as glass coolers. Notches in the rim held wine glasses, bowl downwards, in iced water. Monteiths were first made in silver (see p.249), but these were copied both in delftware and in Chinese and French porcelain. Prices vary depending on the subject matter, date and manufacturer, and range between £2000 for a poor delftware example up to £20,000 or more for the finest pieces in Sèvres porcelain.

JUGS

As urban populations grew with industrialisation after the 1770s or so, pubs sprang up to serve them. Most water was unfit to drink, so everybody – including children – drank beer. Large jugs were needed to collect the beverage from the inns, and many styles were produced, including porcelain cabbage-leaf moulded jugs from Worcester, Caughley and Lowestoft, and creamware jugs from Leeds and Liverpool.

Earthenware harvest jugs made in the West Country, at centres such as Barnstaple in Devon and Donyatt in Somerset, are now regarded as desirable examples of folk art, identified by their striking, incised sgraffito decoration. Collectors are drawn by their handmade appearance and misspelt rhymes or inscriptions such as 'God speed the plough', and may pay up to £3000 for a good example.

Lustreware jugs were popular from the first years of the 19th century, and were made in Staffordshire, Leeds and Sunderland. Most pieces are unmarked, and the most sought after are the 'silver' lustre jugs (in reality made with platinum) decorated in the resist technique, popular between 1810 and 1830, which leaves a pattern in a background colour surrounded by lustre. Those with a yellow

One of a pair of Sèvres porcelain wine coolers; 1771; 7 in (17.8 cm) high. From a service made for Madame du Barry, Louis XV's mistress. Early Sèvres pieces often have a small hole in the footrim.
£18,000-£22,000 (pair)

Chinese porcelain monteith; early 18thC; 12⅝ in (32 cm) wide. This wine-glass cooler, based on a European silver shape, is decorated in famille-verte enamels; the dominant green is clearly seen in the bowl's crocodile feet.
£30,000-£50,000

Spode earthenware bin label; c.1820; 5⅛ in (13 cm) wide. Bin labels for the cellar were made in various types of ceramic materials, but rarely in porcelain.
£80-£120

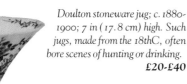

Doulton stoneware jug; c.1880-1900; 7 in (17.8 cm) high. Such jugs, made from the 18thC, often bore scenes of hunting or drinking.
£20-£40

Worcester wine funnel; c.1754-6; 4 in (10.1 cm) high. This is extremely valuable due to its fine condition and rarity.
£6000 upwards

Bristol blue and white porcelain tankard; c.1750-2; 4½ in (11.4 cm) high. This early piece from the Lund's factory is very valuable, despite its plain decoration. The shape derives from contemporary silver patterns.
£7000-£10,000

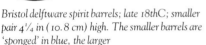

Bristol delftware spirit barrels; late 18thC; smaller pair 4¼ in (10.8 cm) high. The smaller barrels are 'sponged' in blue, the larger one in manganese-purple.
£500-£700

Stoneware spirit flask; c.1840; 8½ in (21.6 cm) high. Such pieces, in the shape of a flintlock pistol, were made by Stephen Green of Lambeth. The slightly dappled 'orange peel' appearance of the glaze is typical of salt glaze.
£120-£150

('canary') background fetch the highest prices, with collectors paying up to £500-£700 or even more for a commemorative piece.

Silver lustre jugs were also made with blue-printed decoration, while pink lustre jugs are most commonly decorated with a black transfer print of Sunderland's New Iron Bridge over the River Wear, opened in 1796. Most of these were made by Dixon Austin of Sunderland between about 1800 and 1850, and can now fetch £400-£600.

Traditional brown stoneware jugs were made at centres in London and Bristol throughout the 19th century. Many have a two-tone brown glaze and are decorated with moulded scenes of hunters or drinkers enjoying themselves outside an inn. They are close copies of similarly decorated, large, 18th-century tankards and loving cups.

TANKARDS, FLASKS AND BARRELS

Cylindrical and bell-shaped ceramic tankards have been made in every type of ware over the centuries. Examples from 18th-century porcelain factories such as Worcester, Bow, Lowestoft, Derby and Liverpool, and those in delftware and white Staffordshire salt-glazed stoneware, are the most desirable and can be found for £400-£2000. Many are decorated with Chinese themes in blue and white or coloured enamels.

Also easily found are cheap, printed earthenware beer mugs made during the Victorian era, when it was customary for regular drinkers to leave their own mug at the pub. They stopped being made after glass beer mugs came into production earlier this century. Such mugs can be found with a wide range of decoration, and can cost as little as £5-£50.

The earliest earthenware spirit flasks, dating from the late 18th century, are a flattened oval or circular shape and can be found for £300-£600; later examples from the 1830s and 40s fetch £50-£300. Many carry commemorative slogans and pictures, and some are shaped as fishes, pistols or jolly drinkers. Stoneware flasks from the 19th century are more popular than brown-glazed earthenware examples of the same date.

Large, buff-coloured stoneware barrels from the second half of the 19th century are also much collected, selling for up to £400 apiece. They may bear a royal coat of arms in paler relief and a darker coloured band around the body. Also desirable are Edwardian vinegar bottles, made in plain, buff stoneware, many of which are impressed with the name of the brewery or retailer. They are still very cheap, selling for £30-£60 apiece, although those stamped with a local name will generally fetch more.

TOBY JUGS
A Personal Drinking Companion

THESE EARTHENWARE JUGS, usually shaped like a stout, seated man in a three-cornered hat, first appeared during the late 18th century. They are particularly associated with Staffordshire potter Ralph Wood and other members of his family, and are based on Harry Elwes, a noted toper who was also known by the nickname of Toby Philpot.

Early jugs are finely modelled and are covered in translucent lead glazes in grey, ochre, brown, green, manganese-purple and blue. Ralph Wood examples generally sell for about £1000-£3000. Yorkshire-made Tobies from the late 18th century are sponged or spotted in brown, ochre, green and blue, while 19th-century Staffordshire pieces are painted in enamel colours. Unfortunately, these tend to flake and blister and so fetch as little as £200-£500.

Several different versions of the figure were made by Ralph Wood and his contemporaries, including the Thin Man, the Squire, Admiral Lord Howe and Rodney's Sailor. Among the many poor-quality copies are crude, late 19th-century pieces from France.

Royal Staffordshire Toby jug; c.1916; 12 in (30.5 cm) high: 'Hellfire Jack' – Lord Jellicoe.
£250-£400

Ralph Wood Toby jug; c.1775; 10 in (25.4 cm) high. The translucent glazes confirm its early date.
£1500-£2000

Tea, coffee and chocolate wares

Although the finest complete services are out of reach for most collectors, it is possible to find beautiful single pieces such as teabowls, coffee cups and saucers, teapots, jugs and chocolate beakers at reasonable prices.

Chinese porcelain spoon tray; c.1750-60; 5¾ in (14.6 cm) long. This example depicts a family group of high-born or Mandarin Chinese, and dates from the Qianlong period (1736-95). The decoration is painted in famille-rose enamels.
£100-£150

TEA, COFFEE AND CHOCOLATE have been firm favourites with the British ever since a 'drink called by the Chineans tcha' was introduced in the 1630s, the first coffee house was opened in London in 1650, and chocolate was first advertised for sale as a drink in 1657. The three beverages were to have a profound influence on the ceramics industries of Britain and the rest of Europe.

The high cost of tea when it first arrived in Europe was responsible for keeping early wares small, so that such a luxury item would not be wasted. By the 1750s, tea drinking had essentially become the domain of women of the leisured classes, and this had a distinct effect on the teawares of the time. Until the end of the 18th century, coffee and chocolate were breakfast drinks for the gentry, although chocolate fell from favour during the 19th century. The Edwardian 'smart set' drank coffee as a post-prandial digestif, to settle the stomach and stimulate the food-fogged brain.

Since boiling water is the key requisite for tea-making, it was essential to produce vessels that could withstand heat. The Chinese overcame the problem as early as the Song (Sung) dynasty (960-1279). Black-glazed teawares were developed in Fujian province and some found their way to monasteries in Japan.

EARLY EUROPEAN TEAWARES

In addition to rare tin-glazed teawares from Delft, European imitations of Chinese wares were produced at Meissen in Saxony around 1710, in a hard red stoneware invented by Johann Friedrich Böttger. Teapots, teabowls and saucers, and beakers for coffee or chocolate were all made subsequently in a Baroque style, and white hard-paste porcelain teawares followed. By the 1730s, copies of Chinese blue and white porcelain were in production, as were services with chinoiserie decoration. Most notable are those decorated by J.G. Höroldt, appointed patron founder of the Meissen factory in 1723. Today a complete service is out of reach of most collectors at £40,000 and upwards; even a single cup and saucer will fetch £2000-£3000.

From the 1730s on, Höroldt introduced coloured grounds, including yellow, puce, lilac, gold, red and sea-green. The decoration

found on Japanese Kakiemon porcelain was also copied at Meissen, and Japanese-inspired wares can change hands for £2000 and more.

THE ROCOCO INFLUENCE

As the lively Rococo style took hold in Europe in the 1740s, especially in France, potters began to produce ranges of delicate, soft-coloured wares decorated with scrolls, shells and other natural forms. From the 1750s the Sèvres porcelain factory, renowned for this lighter type of teaware, used coloured grounds that included shades such as turquoise blue, green and pink, and services were painted with garden scenes, birds, flowers and a wide variety of more formal decorative motifs.

Great skill was displayed in the gilded teawares of Sèvres, which captured the market during the Seven Years' War (1756-63). Teacups, rather than handleless teabowls, were made at Sèvres, and after the introduction of hard-paste porcelain at the factory in 1769, the coffee can, or cylindrical coffee cup, appeared during the 1780s and 1790s. Its straight sides provided an excellent 'canvas' for the miniature painting

Meissen red stoneware coffee pot and cover with broken handle; c.1712-15; 6⅔ in (16.9 cm) high. This great rarity by J.F. Böttger might have been intended for the Turkish market; the 'onion'-shaped cover shows an Islamic influence.
£20,000-£25,000
If perfect:
£40,000

TEA FOR THREE *By the mid-18thC tea drinking was a fashionable habit among the upper and middle classes. This painting of c.1740 shows a family group taking the still-expensive beverage from Chinese porcelain.*

Meissen porcelain tea and coffee service; c.1745. A variety of shapes common at this date can be seen here, including an oval, lidded sugar box and a tall, rectangular tea caddy. The low, handle-less bowls are for tea, the taller, handled cups for coffee.
£15,000-£20,000

Staffordshire agate ware chocolate pot made to resemble the stone; c.1750; 9⅞ in (25 cm) high. Hexagonal pots with spout and handle at right angles, not opposite, are usually for chocolate.
£7000-£9000

Paris (Nast factory) part tea and coffee service; c.1815. It is in Empire style, popular during the reign of Napoleon I. Its straight-sided coffee cans and deep saucers are typical, as is the burnished gilding.
£4000-£6000; complete: £15,000

COW CREAMERS
Jugs with a Difference

SMALL EARTHENWARE JUGS modelled as cows were first produced in the mid-18th century, particularly in the north of England. Today, cow creamers by Staffordshire potters John Astbury and Thomas Whieldon are most sought after, fetching £800 up to £5000. Those made at the St Anthony pottery at Newcastle-upon-Tyne (1780-1804) are easily identifiable by their blue-ringed eyes and fetch £800-£1500. Less refined and cheaper are black-glazed 'Jackfield' creamers (after the 18th-century Staffordshire Jackfield pottery), ones in the blue and white 'willow pattern' and 19th-century silver lustre examples.

Chelsea porcelain cream jug; 1745; 4¼ in (10.8 cm) high. Known as a 'goat and bee' jug, the shape is formed by two goats with a bee perched above them. Coloured examples are the most sought after.
£8000-£12,000

Lowestoft soft-paste porcelain coffee pot; c.1765-70; 9 in (22.9 cm) high. The pear-shaped body, curved spout and S-scroll handle are typical of English coffee pots of this date, as is the painted chinoiserie decoration.
£700-£1000

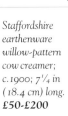

Staffordshire earthenware willow-pattern cow creamer; c.1900; 7¼ in (18.4 cm) long.
£50-£200

Staffordshire salt-glazed tea caddy; c.1760-70; 4 in (10.1 cm) high. Although this caddy is a typical mid-18thC shape, the unusual chinoiserie painting increases the price.
£10,000

Worcester chocolate cup and saucer, c.1770; cup 4 in (10.1 cm) across, saucer 6 in (15.2 cm). Yellow is the most sought-after ground colour.
£3000-£4000

Chelsea porcelain beaker; c.1750-55; 2¾ in (70 mm) high. This Kakiemon-style beaker bears a rare 'raised anchor' mark on its base.
£6000-£9000

Worcester sugar bowl with cover; c.1770-5; 5 in (12.7 cm) high. The hop-trellis pattern was exclusive to Worcester: it is one of the classic, and today most expensive, of the factory's early designs.
£1500

Prattware tea caddy and cover; c.1790-1800; 6¼ in (15.9 cm) high. This caddy depicts the day's fashionably eccentric 'Macaronis'.
£300-£500

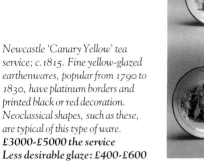

Newcastle 'Canary Yellow' tea service; c.1815. Fine yellow-glazed earthenwares, popular from 1790 to 1830, have platinum borders and printed black or red decoration. Neoclassical shapes, such as these, are typical of this type of ware.
£3000-£5000 the service
Less desirable glaze: £400-£600

of Classical and mythological scenes that was fashionable at the time. Similar cups were produced at Vienna, and single examples with saucers fetch £600-£2000 at auction.

BRITISH WARES

In the early years of British tea and coffee consumption, imported Chinese blue and white porcelain was most commonly used. English delftware, which was in everyday use at the time, was not suitable for teawares as it chipped easily and was thickly potted.

Staffordshire salt-glazed stoneware was more successful. Pieces are recognisable by their porridge-grey colour and 'orange-peel' texture. Collectors pay between £600 and £10,000 for such mid-18th-century coffee and teapots. Pieces crisply moulded into houses, ships, shells and animals are also desirable, fetching about £2000.

Staffordshire potters Thomas Whieldon and John Astbury are connected with the very collectable 'agate' teawares made of marbled, coloured clays. Tea and coffee pots in agate ware may sell at auction for £1000-£5000.

As the Industrial Revolution got under way during the 1760s, Josiah Wedgwood introduced Queen's Ware, his version of creamware (see p.168). This smooth-glazed, light cream earthenware was well suited to tea and coffee services, as was his black basaltes ware. Creamware pieces are relatively easy to find today and sell for £40 and upwards.

EARLY ENGLISH PORCELAIN

The Chelsea factory in London was among the first British producers of soft-paste porcelain, from about 1745. Its teawares were aimed at the luxury market, and decoration included the iron-red, blue, yellow and turquoise enamels seen on Kakiemon porcelain, mythological scenes and Classical landscapes in puce, Meissen-style flower decoration and Rococo Sèvres-style wares. Most Chelsea

'Sèvres' wares were produced during the 'gold anchor' period, from 1758 to 1769 (named after the gold anchor mark; see p.195), with rich-coloured backgrounds decorated with figures and birds in panels with gilded edging. Such services are rare, and even a single cup and saucer may fetch as much as £400.

Imitations of Japanese Kakiemon patterns were also made at the Bow soft-paste factory, established in 1748. Bow's porcelain bodies were more durable, but the decoration less attractive, than pieces made in Chelsea paste. As a result, more have survived. A single Kakiemon-style coffee cup or teabowl and saucer can be found for £800-£1200, a plain blue and white example for about £300.

However, the British factory that made the greatest impact on tea and coffee-drinking wares was Worcester, founded in 1751, whose porcelain was more durable than earlier types. Transfer printing was one of their greatest innovations. From the 1760s, designs printed in underglaze-blue were particularly popular, and are now keenly collected, although painted patterns generally fetch more.

MASS PRODUCTION

During the last quarter of the 18th century the centre of the British porcelain industry was in the heartlands of the Staffordshire potteries. The New Hall factory of Shelton was just one of those producing large numbers of tea and coffee services for the rising urban middle classes in hard-paste porcelain, copying the clean shapes of late Georgian silver. Typical helmet-shaped cream jugs (£60-£100) and oval teapots decorated with small gilt or monochrome floral sprigs (£200-£500) can be identified by their pattern number.

Similarly decorated wares with straight or spiral flutes were produced at the Worcester factories of Chamberlain and Flight, and also by Miles Mason, Caughley and Coalport. Covered sugar bowls were fashionable at the time, as were the commonly found saucer-shaped bread and butter dishes; sugar bowls now fetch as much as £80-£200.

19TH-CENTURY TEAWARES

As tea prices dropped at the start of the 19th century, porcelain tea caddies and teabowls went out of production, although earthenware teabowls were made until the 1820s.

The search for finer porcelain for teawares resulted in Josiah Spode's formula for bone china, in which large amounts of bone-ash had been added to the paste. Bone china was instantly in demand. The white, translucent, high-quality tea and coffee services were

finely painted with romantic landscapes, flowers or figures, or bat-printed with designs taken from the engravings of Francesco Bartolozzi and Adam Buck. They were produced in large numbers; a cup and saucer can often be found at auction today for £50-£200 and a teapot for £300-£500.

Transfer-printing was also used on Spode's earthenwares, and a wide range of exotic scenes in underglaze-blue appeared, the scene covering the entire surface. The 'Blue Italian' pattern is still made today.

AGE OF REVIVALS

Indian tea was introduced to Britain in the 1840s, and was served from teapots with moulded, scrolled rims and knops like ice-cream swirls. These were made during the 1830s, 40s and 50s in a Rococo Revival style.

Early Rococo Revival pieces generally have rich background colours, such as royal blue or claret, but these were soon replaced by restrained buffs and greys. Minton, Coalport, Davenport and Ridgway are just some of the factories that produced such services; prices range from £10 to £60 for a cup and saucer.

A multitude of borrowed styles appeared in the second half of the century, including japonaiserie designs. The Royal Crown Derby factory produced a number of services using the Imari palette of iron-red, underglaze-blue and gilding, pattern numbers 383 and 1128 being the most keenly collected.

Some of the finest services from the end of the 19th century are those made at Copeland and Royal Worcester, decorated with drops of enamel backed with foil to resemble jewels. Worcester also produced a range of boxed sets of coffee cups with gilded interiors and scenes of Highland cattle, game birds or hunting painted on the exteriors. A complete boxed set will fetch £1000-£5000 and single cups and saucers £100-£200.

Moustache cups are pieces of the period, designed to accommodate the extravagant moustaches fashionable around the turn of the century. These held back the moustache by means of a guard, and sell for £20-£60.

JAPANESE TEAWARES

The Japanese have been enthusiastic tea drinkers since the 8th century. The very first bowls used for tea were imported Chinese Song (Sung) stoneware, and later indigenous *raku* pottery was produced.

Limited quantities of porcelain teawares were made in Japan from the 17th century, mainly for export. Most are in the typical Oriental blue and white style, and a teabowl and saucer today fetches £150 or more at auction – or as much as £700 if painted with a European subject. Rich Imari colours of dark blue, iron-red and gold were also used, and odd teabowls sell for £30 upwards.

European demand for Japanese wares grew in the late 19th century, and increasing quantities of pottery and porcelain of varying quality were produced, including Satsuma wares from such factories as Kinkozan at Kyoto. Most date from the 1890s and sell for £20-£30 for a cup and saucer. Later Kinkozan output is better painted and more valuable.

Boxed sets were issued by other, inferior makers, most of which fetch around £300 a set. Banko ware was revived in the 19th century, made of grey stoneware and often in the form of a lotus or flowers. Cups and saucers sell for £10-£20, teapots for £30-£60.

The Kutani region issued many distinctive teawares using iron-red, black and gilding. But these pieces are often of poor quality, with odd cups and saucers often fetching only £1-£15. A flood of eggshell porcelain appeared from the end of the 19th century until the 1930s. Most is badly painted and can be picked up for as little as £1 an item.

Staffordshire bone china tea service; c.1830-40. Services in this style are often wrongly attributed to the Yorkshire Rockingham pottery, whose few services are generally marked on the saucers. Such florid services have only recently become popular. **£400-£600 the service**

Japanese black raku chawan (teabowl); 19thC; 4 in (10.1 cm) across. The crane on this late raku piece is a symbol of longevity. **£600-£800**

Royal Worcester coffee set; c.1920-30. Such presentation sets are often in very good condition, and sometimes include matching enamelled spoons. Pheasants, fruit and hunting scenes were all popular subjects. **£4000-£6000**

Royal Crown Derby part tea service; early 20thC. Royal Crown Derby is very collectable, but this set loses value because its teapot and sugar basin are missing. It is decorated in imitation Japanese Imari style. **£100-£200**

Kutani eggshell plate and milk jug; c.1920; plate 5½ in (14 cm) across. These fragile Japanese wares came to the West by the shipload. On many, the basic design is transfer or stencil printed; here, the sky has been sprayed on with an airbrush. **£1-£2 a piece**

Teapots

Bizarrely shaped teapots have been made since the mid-18th century, some of the earliest moulded into houses, ships, shells or animals. Both these and more traditional shapes are collected avidly, with items to be found that suit almost every pocket.

Creamware teapot; mid-18thC; 5 in (12.7 cm) high. Black polychrome ('en grisaille') decoration is most unusual. £3000-£5000

Wedgwood rosso antico teapot; early 19thC; 3⅛ in (80 mm) high. Note this pot's squat Egyptian style. £150-£250

Japanese Kakiemon teapot; c.1710; 6 in (15.2 cm) long. The replacement silver spout reduces the value eightfold. £500-£800

Royal Worcester teapot; 1882; 6 in (15.2 cm) high. This rare teapot pokes fun at Oscar Wilde and the Aesthetic Movement. £2500-£3500

Staffordshire salt-glazed teapot; c.1760; 4¾ in (12.1 cm) high. A pink ground is more desirable than blue. £1000-£1500

Royal Crown Derby teapot; c.1890-1900; 4¾ in (12.1 cm) high. 'Royal Crown Derby', post 1890, is better quality than the earlier 'Derby Crown'. £150-£200

White Chelsea teapot; 1745-9; 6⅞ in (17.5 cm) high. A rare piece of early English porcelain. £3000-£5000

Worcester teapot; c.1775; 4¾ in (12.1 cm) high. Barrel shapes first appeared in the 1760s. £600-£1000

Staffordshire teapot; c.1880; 5½ in (14 cm) high. This originally had a matching stand. £40-£70

Staffordshire red stoneware teapot; c.1760-70; 4½ in (11.4 cm) high. It imitates 17thC Chinese stoneware. £200-£400

Staffordshire creamware teapot; c.1760; 5⅛ in (13 cm) high. Green, ochre and brown glazes are hallmarks of potter Thomas Whieldon. £4000-£6000

Chinese blue and white teapot; c.1775; 9½ in (24.1 cm) high. Solitary figures in vast landscapes suited the meditative act of Chinese tea drinking. £1200-£1800

Belleek teapot; c.1875-80; 9½ in (24.1 cm) wide. Belleek's pearly porcelain suited marine shapes. £200-£400

Moorcroft 'Spanish' pattern teapot; c.1910; 7½ in (19 cm) high. It is decorated in typical Art Nouveau style. £500-£800

Pair of Meissen teapots; c.1740-50; cockerel 8 in (20.3 cm) long. Such pairs in good condition are rare indeed. £4000-£6000 the pair

Twentieth-century teawares

Although not yet officially antiques, many collectable items are already emerging from the bewildering range of 20th-century designs.

THE DEMAND for attractive yet mass-producible articles in the 20th century led to radical changes in the design of teawares, as in other products. Traditional services continued to be produced, and to sell well, but the wares that stand out today were experiments in new shapes, colours and decorative styles. At the moment, collector interest is centred on teawares of the 1920s, 30s and 50s, all rapidly increasing in value.

THE EARLY YEARS

As the century dawned, the catalogues of leading British tableware manufacturers such as Wedgwood and Minton were full of enduringly popular blue and white transfer-prints (such as 'Willow Pattern'), more colourful Orientally inspired wares and traditional floral and Neoclassical designs.

Art Nouveau never really caught on in Britain for teawares, but there were several echoes of its flowing lines in items for the popular market after 1910. Before that, some adventurous services were made by smaller firms; a good example now fetches £50-£100.

Faced by indifference from customers at home, many British manufacturers produced tablewares specifically for the French market. Wedgwood's range included designs by leading Parisian designers Paul Follot and Marcel Goupy shortly before the First World War. Moorcroft's 'Powder Blue' range, with a speckled blue glaze, dates from 1913. One of the most successful modern British designs, it sold well abroad; today a coffee pot or toast rack will fetch £20-£40.

INTO THE JAZZ AGE

The 1920s brought a new, more decorative approach in teawares, with an emphasis on bright colours, reflective lustres and hand-painted patterns. Many popular designs still featured landscapes, country cottages and other stereotypes of rural romanticism, but Modernism made its influence felt in two

FLYING COLOURS *Synonymous with the Jazz Age, Clarice Cliff began her ceramics career at the age of 13, painting pottery at a local Staffordshire factory.*

Plate from the former Russian Imperial porcelain factory, c.1923, painted by 'Suprematist' Kasimir Malevich. Such designs expressed the spirit of the Revolution, and influenced the development of Art Deco.
£30,000-£40,000

Clarice Cliff 'Sunray' tea set; 1932; teapot 4½ in (11.4 cm) high. Clarice Cliff designs were hand-painted by teams working quickly in a vibrant, crude style to satisfy market demand.
Set: £2000

Noritake porcelain table setting; c.1968. The work of American architect Frank Lloyd Wright, the design was originally created for the Imperial Hotel, Tokyo, in the 1920s.
Six-piece individual setting: £1500

Susie Cooper earthenware 'Kestrel' teapot (below); c.1932; 5 in (12.7 cm) high. This Modernist shape, with its subtle graduated banding in soft colours, is typical of the period.
£50-£80

Carlton Ware teapot by Wiltshaw & Robinson of Stoke-on-Trent; c.1930; 6½ in (16.5 cm) high. With its applied anenome ornaments, this teapot typifies the 1930s enthusiasm for decorative naturalism.
£60-£85

Shelley teawares; c.1926. The popularity of children's book illustrator Mabel Lucie Attwell in the 1920s led to her characters being used for pottery and porcelain. The pixie tea set is most unusual.
Three-piece set: £300-£350
Napkin rings: £50-£70 a pair

Shelley bone-china tea set from 'Regent' range; c.1933. Shelley was devoted to the promotion of modern shapes and motifs, and this design represents the practical Modernism fashionable at the time. The polka-dot pattern was available in various colours.
Set: £250-£300

Items from the Midwinter 'Stylecraft' range designed by Sir Terence Conran (left) and Sir Hugh Casson (right); 1950s. Quite avant-garde but highly successful at the time, the range is keenly collected today.
Service: £80-£150

Portmeirion 'Botanic Garden' teacup and plate; 1992. Introduced in 1972, this design has become a best seller and may become a collectable of the future.

Royal Worcester tea set designed by Scottie Wilson; c.1965. The range, issued in two colourings – black on terracotta and black and grey on white – proved unpopular with the public and was discontinued.
Set: £450

ways. First, the exuberance of the Jazz Age was reflected in garish teawares with simplified shapes, patterns and styles, epitomised by the work of Clarice Cliff. Her designs – colourful and contemporary, decorated with dynamic but crudely painted patterns – are still vastly popular. 'Bizarre', the trade name for her most successful range, accurately describes the teawares of this period of extremes, when square plates and cups with triangular handles went side by side with teapots in the shape of cars and trains. Cliff's designs had many imitators, but genuine pieces are invariably marked and so can be identified. A tea service for six might sell today for £1000 or more, but a service in the quite common 'Crocus' design may fetch no more than £300.

The other face of Modernism in 1920s and 30s teawares was far more elegant and restrained, with flowing, streamlined shapes under a matt glaze. Such teawares capture the essence of the Art Deco movement which became so fashionable internationally.

One of the pioneers of this style was Wedgwood, which commissioned ranges of vases and tablewares in the early 1930s from Keith Murray, a New Zealand-born architect.

Murray's monochrome wares are in great demand today, fetching £25 for a mug, £300-£400 for a vase. They were imitated by a number of manufacturers including Poole, Carlton Ware, Grays, Spode and Minton, all of whose pieces go for around £20-£30.

Stylish Art Deco teawares were produced in large numbers in the early 1930s, particularly by Shelley and Royal Doulton. A key figure was Susie Cooper, who has emerged as the most important ceramic designer of her generation, and who from around 1930 became known for her clean-cut Modernism and simple patterns in soft colours. Her designs are now as widely collected as those of Clarice Cliff; an earthenware service from 1935 could sell today for £400-£500.

The outbreak of the Second World War brought this inventive period to an abrupt end. From the early 1940s, the production of all decorative or colourful pottery and porcelain was forbidden, except for export. The Utility scheme, introduced in 1941, compelled manufacturers to stick to simple, modern tablewares in plain white or cream, and sell them for a fixed price.

FUTURE COLLECTABLES

Full-scale production of decorated wares was resumed in 1952. Teawares of the 1950s are cheerful and decoratively modern, with overall patterns both hand-painted and printed by new techniques, for example lithography. Common decorations include French scenes, yachts, abstract florals and modern interiors. Typical are the flowing, rounded shapes in ranges by Carlton Ware, Beswick, Ridgway (whose 'Homemaker' range was designed in 1955 by Enid Seeney) and above all Midwinter, whose distinctly modern 'Stylecraft' range includes patterns by Sir Hugh Casson, Sir Terence Conran and Jessie Tait.

The postwar classics of British tableware are now keenly collected. A Midwinter tea service with a Casson or Conran design can fetch £100 at auction. At the same time, a similar service can still be found at a car boot sale for just a few pounds. Postwar pieces by Susie Cooper, Copeland, Hornsea, Poole, Derby and other leading makers are all likely to increase in collectability – and value.

Vases

Apart from imported Oriental pieces, vases were virtually unknown in Europe before the 17th century. Then they evolved an astonishing range of decorative forms.

MANY A FLOWER ARRANGER has been frustrated at the seemingly unsuitable shapes of vases for holding cut flowers. In fact, in the world of antiques and ceramics, that is not their main purpose. A vase is seen as an ornament designed to be complete in itself or to balance as a pair.

Vases were luxury items right up until the mid-19th century, and most were made of porcelain. But pieces dating from that time on vary enormously in quality. In the late Victorian era, many of the finest porcelain vases were copied and mass-produced (with printed decoration) in cheaper bodies.

Ming fish jar; c.1522-66; 13½ in (34.3 cm) high. This jar was dug up in pieces in an English farmyard. Glued together, it was seen to be a rare kuan jar. In spite of the damage, it sold at auction in 1979 for £17,000; values have risen a great deal since then.
£60,000-£120,000 (as damaged)

GRECIAN URN *The decoration suggests that this 6thC BC Greek amphora, a much copied vase form, was for a presentation. Many held oil or wine.*

Canton 'Rose Medallion' pattern vase; c.1870-80; 12½ in (31.7 cm) high. Pairs of such vases were made in many different sizes, and their value is determined by size and the care given to the painting of the figures.
Pair: £300-£500

One of a pair of Japanese Imari vases; c.1890; 29½ in (75 cm) high. This large piece is a later example of the typical Imari style first imported into Europe some 200 years earlier.
Pair: £2000-£3000

ORIENTAL VASES

In China, vases were respected as objects of beauty as long ago as the Song (Sung) dynasty (960-1279). Although they are rare today, these elegant stoneware pieces – carved beneath a celadon glaze or with hand-painted decoration – have been a major influence on modern studio potters (see p.184).

Among the finest vases still found are those in porcelain from the Ming dynasty (1368-1644). These can command up to seven-figure sums, and many people dream of finding such vases. But many are crudely made and worth little. This is especially true of 16th-century provincial pieces from what is now Vietnam, which may fetch £100-£400.

Chinese and Japanese vases made specifically for export to Europe are among the most keenly collected today. The Chinese potters concentrated on shapes that were popular in the West, and early European collectors even had entire rooms redesigned to house their

Japanese Satsuma vase, probably by Kinkosan; late 19thC; 8¼ in (21.6 cm) high. This earthenware vase represents the peak of the Satsuma artists' skill, unlike the more commercial pieces of the same period.
£4000-£6000

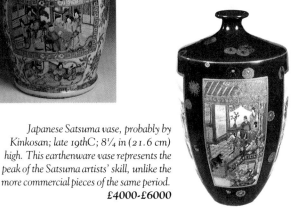

Garniture of Chinese famille-rose vases; c.1750; 13-14 in (33-35.5 cm) high. The three covered jars and two beaker-shaped vases were made for export and had ormolu bases added in Europe.
£10,000-£15,000 the set

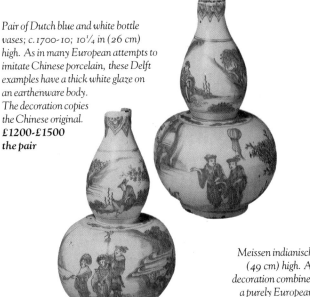

Pair of Dutch blue and white bottle vases; c.1700-10; 10¼ in (26 cm) high. As in many European attempts to imitate Chinese porcelain, these Delft examples have a thick white glaze on an earthenware body. The decoration copies the Chinese original.
£1200-£1500 the pair

Meissen indianische Blumen vase; c.1730; 19¼ in (49 cm) high. Although the shape is Chinese, the decoration combines Japanese and Chinese design in a purely European way, typical of 1730s Meissen.
£13,000-£18,000

Pair of Chelsea vases; c.1765; 12½ in (31.7 cm) high. These Chelsea vase shapes are in fanciful Rococo style. The deep 'mazarine' blue ground was a speciality of Chelsea and is combined here with painting in the style of the French artist Antoine Watteau.
£5000-£7000 the pair

Modern Meissen copy of an 18thC indianische Blumen vase; c.1960; 9⅞ in (25 cm) high. This piece lacks the spirit of the original painting, and its shape is rather more clumsy.
£200-£250

Pair of Wedgwood creamware vases; c.1775; 8⅝ in (22 cm) high. Wedgwood embraced the Classical revival in the 1770s and produced many vases simulating stone to adorn marble fireplaces.
£10,000-£13,000 the pair

European market via Holland about that time, and are recognised by their distinctive colours of iron red, underglaze blue and gold.

Distinguishing between Imari of around 1700 – now worth £800 up to £10,000 for a vase – and 19th-century versions can be hard. However, early Japanese glazes have millions of small bubbles, which soften the edges of the decoration, while most later designs use a brighter blue and are more crowded. A typical 19th-century Imari vase will fetch £60-£500. European trade with Japan ceased again in the 1740s, but continuing imports of Chinese imitation Imari ware meant that the style remained popular in the West.

Japanese art was reintroduced to Europe in the 1860s, and carved ivory and cloisonné enamelled metalwork again became fashionable. They were imitated in porcelain, especially at the Worcester factory, whose copies of Chinese and Japanese vases were themselves very influential. As a result, substantial numbers of wares were again imported from Japan. Prices for these today range from just a few pounds right up to £10,000 or more.

EUROPEAN VASES

European potters had little experience of making ornamental vases before the 17th century. (Most earlier 'vases' are in fact decorative medical jars; see p.202.) The earliest European true vases found today are reproductions in tin-glazed earthenware of Oriental shapes and designs. Some are such close copies that they can deceive the unwary. Gradually European potters modified the Chinese patterns to create their own Oriental style or 'Chinoiserie', epitomised by German faience of the 17th century and then by Meissen porcelain of the 1730s and 1740s. Meissen's *indianische Blumen* ('Indian Flowers') pattern combined elements of both Chinese and Japanese design and decoration, but used much brighter colours than the originals and showed European figures dressed in fanciful Chinese clothes. These early Meissen vases are eagerly sought after by collectors, who pay up to £20,000 or more for a good example.

In the 1750s, pieces in Meissen or 'Dresden' style (from both Meissen and other German factories) competed with the French soft-paste porcelain vases from Sèvres. The more colourful and softer-looking Sèvres pieces were designed to complement Rococo interiors. Some were decorated with scroll work

substantial collections of blue and white Chinese porcelain. Vases were arranged in patterns on mantelpieces and on top of cabinets (see pp.26, 29), a practice that led the Chinese to make matching sets – known as garnitures – of three or five vases.

Decoration was adapted to European tastes, and included richer, more complex patterns – particularly panels incorporating Chinese figures. Such a set is likely to fetch between £1500 and £10,000, or even more,

today. Examples from the mid-19th century onwards often have a background of bright green enamel scrolls embellished with gilding, a pattern known in the United States as 'Rose Medallion'. Vases range in height up to 78 in (2 m), and current prices range from £100 to as much as £20,000.

There was little European trade with Japan until the chaos after the fall of the Ming dynasty in 1644 disrupted production in China. Japanese Imari wares reached the

French swan-handled vases; c.1815; 14⅜ in (36.5 cm) high. These sumptuously decorated Paris porcelain vases were designed to be the focal point on a mantelpiece in an Empire style room.
£3500-£4500 the pair

Pair of Viennese vases; c.1900; 38½ in (98 cm) high. Vienna was a centre for fine porcelain painting from the late 18thC, mainly of historical figures on strongly coloured backgrounds.
£8000-£10,000 the pair

and applied with flowers, others painted with flowers and pastoral scenes. Such vases were luxury items in their own time and today fetch sums ranging from £10,000 to £50,000.

British vases from the mid-18th century are usually of porcelain. After China and Japan, Meissen was the main inspiration until about 1760 for major factories such as Worcester, Chelsea, Bow and Derby. A pair of richly decorated English vases from 1760 to 1780 can fetch between £2000 and £15,000.

CLASSICAL REVIVAL

Because vases were so prominently displayed in rooms, it was vital for manufacturers to keep abreast of the latest developments in architecture and style. In Britain from the 1760s that meant following the Neoclassical style of Robert Adam and his contemporaries.

It was the potter Josiah Wedgwood (see p.168) who was to transform and dominate the market for English vases. Through his influential London shop, Wedgwood came to dictate public taste. By clever use of coloured clays and mottling he copied expensive, imported marble urns, modelling many on ancient Greek or Roman originals.

Wedgwood's vases of 1770 onwards remain in demand today, with pieces in 'black basaltes' and red 'rosso antico' fetching about £4000-£6000 a pair. But he is best known for his jasperware, with its white relief decoration on a coloured (especially blue or black) body, and for his copies of the Roman cameo glass Portland Vase (see box, right).

Despite the fact that European factories were still unable to compete with the low prices of Chinese export wares, many vases of an original European shape were finished with Oriental-style decoration. Among these are vases in Classical campana, or bell-shaped, form decorated in the Japanese Imari style.

Known at the time as 'Japan' pattern, the colourful all-over Imari decoration had the advantage of disguising any blemish on a

Rockingham Imari-style vases; c.1825; largest 16¾ in (42.5 cm) high. Many makers worked in this style, often richer than the Japanese original.
£4000-£5000 (lid missing)
If complete: £6000-£7000

Potpourri vases; largest 14½ in (36.8 cm) high. The Royal Worcester vase (centre; c.1900) has an inner cover for the potpourri; the square vase is French, c.1840; the vase with applied flowers is by Minton, c.1835.
Royal Worcester: £280-£350
French: £300-£350
Minton: £600-£1000

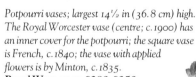

porcelain body. However, a piece such as this fetches less than a perfect example: £400 as opposed to £1000.

Pairs of vases in Empire style – a French variant of the Neoclassical – were made in every European country around the turn of the 18th century. Examples from the major porcelain factories, including Berlin, Meissen and the Paris firms, can be found with finely painted panels on grounds of burnished gold, often with matt borders. Most English examples do not match the quality of their hard-paste European rivals, although pieces from the Worcester Flight & Barr partnership are the exception. These can command prices of £10,000-£20,000 a pair.

VICTORIAN VARIETY

Richly decorated porcelain vases were still luxuries in the 19th century and their expense could be justified more easily if they were useful in some way. By the early Victorian era, two vase types had become standard in many British homes: spill vases and potpourri vases.

Small cylindrical spill vases, designed to hold rolled-up paper spills for lighting the fire, today fetch £100-£2000. Equally collectable are the vases with a pierced, crown-like lid which held potpourri, a strongly scented mixture of flower petals used to disguise the smells of poor sanitation.

Some potpourri vases have modelled porcelain flowers applied – those produced at the Minton factory in the 1830s, for example – and such a vase will sell at auction today for between £400 and £1000.

While the wealthy continued to patronise the great European porcelain houses in the mid to late 19th century, the less well-off, too, were acquiring a taste for decorative vases – and were generally buying the same styles. The difference was in the quality of workmanship. New methods of mass production enabled competitive copies of fine pieces to be made in cheap porcelain and earthenware.

Nineteenth-century pottery manufacturers were also copying Chinese Cantonese vases, including Mason's with its 'Ironstone' stone china. But despite using the transfer-printing technique to apply decoration, few British factories could even then compete on price with Chinese imports. English copies today fetch the same price as Cantonese originals, £500-£10,000 a pair, depending on size.

THE TWENTIETH CENTURY

Most collectable vases of the 20th century are from the art and studio pottery movement (see p.184), and are individually decorated and usually signed. Among the most widely sought after are vases by Doulton with multiple glaze effects. Some of the most interesting are those developed by the chemist and designer C.J. Noke in the 1920s. Given Chinese names such as 'Chang' and 'Sung', they change hands at auction today for £300-£1000, in contrast to more run-of-the-mill items of Doulton stoneware which sell for £60 and upwards. Individual, one-off pieces were also produced by Staffordshire potters William Moorcroft and Wedgwood.

One popular group of strikingly designed vases, which were in fact commercially manufactured, are those of Clarice Cliff. The lively, brightly coloured patterns of perhaps the most famous British designer of her time show the geometric leanings of the 1930s Art Deco movement. As with Cliff's teawares (see p.179), these can change hands for high prices, vases fetching £100 up to £5000.

Garniture of Vienna-style vases made in Czechoslovakia; c.1930; 15¾ in (40 cm) high. The panels and gilding are printed, making them far cheaper than hand-painted Vienna porcelain.
£250-£350 the set

Royal Crown Derby vase by Desiré Leroy; 1902; 6¾ in (17.1 cm) high. The quality of the gilding and painting on this piece would have made it very expensive when new, and it was intended for display in a cabinet.
£4000-£5000

Carlton Ware Coptic jar; 1925-30; 16 in (40.5 cm) high. This style was popular in the late 1920s after Tutankhamun's tomb was discovered.
£1500-£2000

Pair of Minton vases in Sèvres style; c.1870; 15 in (38.1 cm) high. Sèvres of the 18thC was keenly collected in the Victorian era, and vases were copied by several makers. This Minton pair reproduce an original French shape, but the style of painting has been updated.
£1500-£1800 the pair

Minton pâte-sur-pâte vase by Marc Louis Solon; c.1872; 13 in (33 cm) high. Pâte-sur-pâte involved building up a design in white clay on a coloured background, and Solon was the greatest exponent of the technique.
£6000-£8000

Art and studio pottery

Over the last century, individual potters and decorators have produced unique, sculptural ceramics that stand apart from mass-produced pieces.

Bird figures by the Martin brothers; late 19th or early 20thC; largest 15⅜ in (39 cm) high. The four Martin brothers – Robert Wallace, Charles, Walter and Edwin – produced imaginative, 'humanised' animal statues at their Fulham and Southall workshops; each piece was unique.
Small: £3000-£5000
Medium: £4000-£6000
Large: £8000-£12,000

Vase by William Moorcroft; c.1905-10; 7½ in (19 cm) high. Inspired by an ancient Classical shape, this vase is decorated with the naturalistic 'Claremont' pattern.
£800-£1200

Double-moon vase by Christopher Dresser (right); c.1880; 16⅝ in (42.2 cm) high. The vase is testimony to the designer's Japanese inspiration.
£3000-£4000

Doulton stoneware vase; c.1895; 36¼ in (92 cm) high. Plain shapes and strong design were suited to Doulton's late 19thC glazed stoneware.
£600-£800

THE TERM 'ART POTTERY' has been used since the second half of the 19th century, often interchangeably with the similar 'studio pottery'. Both refer to one-off, individually designed and decorated pieces produced in a workshop run by a craftsman or craft group. The term also encompasses the work of artists who finished individually signed pieces in studios set up by firms such as Doulton and Minton.

THE FIRST STUDIOS

By the mid-19th century, almost all Britain's pottery and porcelain was industrially produced. In an effort to counter this, a number of small pottery workshops sprang up under the umbrella of the Art Pottery movement. They were inspired by John Ruskin's call for a return to the crafts tradition of workers being allowed to express their creativity freely.

The first products of these new potteries came in the 1860s when Doulton began a collaboration with students of the Lambeth School of Art in south London to produce salt-glazed stonewares. Some of the hand-thrown pieces produced at their Lambeth studio were decorated by leading artists of the day such as Hannah Barlow or George Tinworth, and at auction today these sell for several hundred pounds or more apiece.

Individually signed articles were also produced by the four Martin brothers, whose imaginative animal forms were influenced both by natural history and by ancient grotesques. No two pieces produced at their Fulham and Southall workshops between 1873 and 1915 were the same. These too are highly collectable today; their vases fetch between £100 and £3000 and their distinctive bird tobacco jars from £400 to £40,000.

The influence of Japanese design on studio potters has been considerable, and can be seen in the work of the 19th-century makers associated with the Aesthetic and Arts and Crafts movements. Their work was designed as 'art pottery' and intended to be beautiful rather than practical.

William de Morgan, who was closely associated with the Arts and Crafts movement, is best known for his blue-green so-called 'Persian' wares, based on Turkish Isnik designs of the 16th century. They range from large plaques (see p. 186) to a variety of vases, and command very high prices today. Such was the success of these striking one-off pieces that other potters turned to studio work. Staffordshire potter William Moorcroft was responsible from 1898 for the art pottery department at J. Macintyre & Co, where he developed a range of art pottery vases and teawares known as Florian ware.

Other pieces much sought after today came from Pilkington's Royal Lancastrian Pottery, and from the Della Robbia Pottery established at Birkenhead in the 1890s.

LATER DEVELOPMENTS

In the 20th century new names came to be associated with art pottery. Bernard Leach, probably the best-known British potter of the century, established his own works at St Ives, in Cornwall, in 1919, and led a group known as the Craftsman Potters. Working with him were potters such as Shoji Hamada, Michael Cardew and Katherine Pleydell-Bouverie.

Vase by Hans Coper; c. 1960; 7½ in (19 cm) high. Scratched decoration revealing a white body under a brown-black coating characterises Coper's work.
£8000-£10,000

Vase by Elizabeth Fritsch; 1989; 12½ in (31.7 cm) high. Fritsch's work is noted for its precise geometrical designs which produce optical effects, and for its matt textures.
£5000-£7000

Bowl by Lucie Rie; 1965; 8¼ in (21 cm) wide. Rie developed several distinctive forms and designs, including sgraffito bands and inlaid lines, as here.
£3000-£4000

Vase by Bernard Leach; 1958; 11¼ in (28.5 cm) high. Leach's designs were greatly influenced by Chinese, Korean and Japanese work, and he aimed to produce simply decorated functional forms.
£3000-£4000

Vase by Shoji Hamada; c. 1964; 9 in (22.9 cm) high. Hamada's use of angular moulded or slab-built forms such as this inspired many other potters. He is the best known Japanese potter of the 20thC.
£4000-£6000

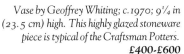

Vase by Geoffrey Whiting; c. 1970; 9¼ in (23.5 cm) high. This highly glazed stoneware piece is typical of the Craftsman Potters.
£400-£600

STAR GAZING *Actor Gary Cooper (left) and the Aga Khan – two favourite visitors – mesmerised by their host Picasso in 1956 and caught by American photographer Lee Miller.*

Lucie Rie's work is noted for its simple, flowing lines, and is much in demand today. She was born in Austria and her early work in earthenware was inspired by the simple forms of metalworker Josef Hoffmann (co-founder of the Wiener Werkstätte in Vienna in 1903). After her move to London in 1938, she favoured porcelain and stoneware.

From 1947 to 1958, Rie shared a studio with Hans Coper, now widely regarded as the most influential European (if not world) potter of this century. They made domestic wares together, as well as producing pieces of their own. Coper worked within a limited range of dramatic forms using subtle textures.

ARTIST POTTERS

When, about 1907, potter André Metthey opened his Asnières studio, near Paris, to painters he had met through a dealer, Ambroise Vollard, he started a trend that continued throughout this century. Many distinguished painters of the time, including Edouard Vuillard, Maurice de Vlaminck, André Derain and Henri Matisse, experimented with ceramics under Metthey's technical guidance. A similar collaboration existed from 1922 between Raoul Dufy, Joan Miró and Georges Braque and the Catalan potter Joseph Llorens Artigas.

But perhaps the most innovative ceramics to be produced by an artist this century are those by Pablo Picasso. In 1947 he started to work with Georges and Suzanne Ramié, who ran the Madoura pottery at Vallauris in the south of France, and set up a studio, where he worked regularly until 1966.

Prices for Picasso's pottery are very high because he is regarded as one of the greatest artists of the 20th century. As with the work of all great ceramicists, Picasso's pottery designs fuse three-dimensional form with linear ornament and colour to create a coherent whole. He often left the clay unglazed in areas to accentuate details. In this way, he transformed a plate, pot or vase into a work of art without losing sight of the original object.

Chargers and plaques

Tiles, sideboard dishes, furniture plaques – few items reveal the teamwork and artistry of potter and ceramic decorator better than these showy objects.

SINCE POTTERS first began to decorate their work, there has been a market for display pieces as well as useful items. Outstanding show objects include large shallow dishes, or chargers – normally hung on a wall or placed on a table or sideboard – and flat plaques for ornamenting anything from furniture to jewellery or for hanging like pictures. Decorative wall tiles are in the same category.

CHARGERS

The technique of tin-glazing earthenware came to Europe with the Moorish invasions of Spain in the 8th to 12th centuries, and 15th-century Hispano-Moresque armorial lustreware chargers are considered among the finest examples of the potter's art (see p.165). Tin glaze soon spread to Italy where it was called 'maiolica'. From the late 15th century, potters in Italy produced maiolica dishes decorated in blue, green, ochre and manganese. Many, notably from Urbino, are lavishly painted in the *istoriato*, or story-telling, style with rim-to-rim scenes from mythology or the Bible, often based on works by the great Renaissance artists. Although usually damaged, istoriato wares sell for £5000 up to £60,000 today.

Meanwhile, in mid-16th-century France, Bernard Palissy and his followers were working with coloured lead glazes to produce relief-moulded dishes applied with fruit, reptiles and insects (often moulded directly from specimens). Such pieces are very rare.

However, a number of Portuguese factories copied the style in the late 19th century and these decorative Palissy-style pieces can be bought for a few hundred pounds.

By the 17th century, tin-glazed chargers had become popular right across Europe, mainly through the Dutch potters of Delft. The Dutch used both European and Oriental designs, and it is not unusual to find a Madonna and Child within a Chinese-style floral border. Some purely Oriental designs come so close to Chinese 'kraak' chargers (see p.188) that they could almost be mistaken for genuine late Ming imports if they were not made of earthenware rather than porcelain.

British 17th-century tin-glazed 'delftware' chargers were displayed alongside pewter. Their subjects – often humorously depicted – range from Adam and Eve to royal commemoratives. Tulip designs were also popular and may have been influenced by Turkish dishes from Isnik. So-called 'blue-dash' chargers have a border of blue brush strokes around the

London delftware Adam and Eve charger; c.1660; 16½ in (42 cm) across. This design was popular from the 1630s to the 1740s.
£8000-£12,000
18thC piece with damage: £750-£1500

Staffordshire slipware charger; 1777; 16⅝ in (42.2 cm) across. This piece bears a bold bird design used since c.1700. The notched rim reveals the brown earthenware base.
£6000-£8000

Damascus tin-glazed pottery tiles; 17thC; 25¼ in (64 cm) high. The Arabic reads 'Glory to God'; similar panels are in shrines in Damascus.
£4000-£6000

The 'Apollo' charger by William de Morgan; 1901; 19½ in (49.5 cm) across. This is an exceptional piece; de Morgan typically fetches £2000-£5000.
£30,000-£50,000

Pearlware plaque; c.1820-30; 7½ in (19 cm) across. Such pious plaques were made cheaply throughout northern England.
£50-£200

Japanese Imari porcelain charger (left); late 19thC; 22 in (56 cm) across. This is a typical 19thC revival of the original 17thC Imari style.
£300-£400

rim. As tin was expensive, chargers often have a cheaper, clear lead glaze on the back.

In the second half of the 17th century, English slipware potters such as Thomas and Ralph Toft, William Talor and Ralph Simpson began to create striking chargers with freehand designs in slip (semi-liquid clay) of birds, animals and royalty. Prices start at around £3000, but royal commemoratives rarely fetch less than £20,000. Soon after 1700, the process was speeded up by using press-moulded designs filled in with slip.

A TRADITION RENEWED

The late 19th century saw a revival of handmade pottery in Britain as a result of the Arts and Crafts movement. Craftsmen such as William de Morgan produced decorative dishes, plaques and tiles in a variety of historic styles. Prices for his wares have doubled recently – his Renaissance-style maiolica 'Apollo' charger sold for over £40,000 in 1991, but items inspired by Islamic and Hispano-Moresque designs typically fetch £2000-£5000. At this time also, Minton and Doulton set up 'art pottery' studios in London to make chargers and other decorative wares, and in this century studio potters have continued the charger tradition (see p.184).

ORIENTAL PORCELAIN CHARGERS

The Chinese art of porcelain manufacture reached Japan via Korea at the end of the 16th century. By the late 17th century, Japan was producing vast amounts of porcelain – including chargers – for export through the port of Imari. 'Imari' wares are typically decorated in underglaze blue and iron-red with gilding, becoming more elaborate in the 19th century.

TILES AND PLAQUES

As early as the Middle Ages, decorative flooring was being created in Britain by stamping designs into partially dried coarse brown clay tiles and filling in the impression with cream slip prior to firing and glazing. Glazed wall tiles have an even longer history in Moorish and Turkish palaces and mosques, where their use dates back to the 9th century.

In northern Europe, wall tiles reached a high point in 17th and 18th-century Holland. Dutch interiors of this period – particularly kitchens – were often covered from floor to ceiling in hand-painted blue and white Delft tiles. Today, these tiles sell for £10-£50 each and rarer polychrome tiles for £40-£400 depending on their design and date. But beware: there are many later copies of blue and white tiles from Holland and elsewhere.

Some outstanding individual plaques were produced by the Dutch painter Frederick van Frijtom who specialised in intricately stippled landscapes. They fetch £4000-£10,000 each.

In Italy, Antonio Carlo Grue and his sons at the Castelli factory maintained the Renaissance tradition of pictorial maiolica into the 18th century. Their plaques were massproduced using the technique of 'pouncing' – stencilling the outline of the design onto unpainted plaques as a guide for the painter.

Britain also produced considerable quantities of delftware tiles during the 18th century, mostly for mundane ends such as fireplace and washbasin surrounds. The Dutch influence was strong, but so was the spirit of innovation. In 1756, John Sadler and Guy Green began transfer printing onto tiles from wooden blocks, and were soon using even finer copper engravings. These 6 in (15.2 cm) tiles now fetch £200 up to £1000.

Around 1760, Staffordshire potteries made relief-moulded tiles both in white salt-glazed stoneware and in earthenware decorated with coloured lead glazes – typically olive-green, grey-brown and slate-blue – in the style of Thomas Whieldon. These are now rare, selling at auction for up to £4000. You are much more likely to come across brightly coloured moulded plaques in Prattware (a form of creamware or pearlware) from the late 18th and early 19th centuries, with subjects as varied as famous people and Classical figures, battle commemoratives and rural scenes. Prices range from £150 for a common subject in reasonable condition up to £3000 for a good commemorative pair.

Of all the potters operating in the second half of the 18th century, Josiah Wedgwood was the undoubted leader in the field of

Wedgwood 'Fairyland' lustre plaque (right); c.1925; 10¾ in (27.3 cm) high. This plaque by Daisy Makeig-Jones is in complete contrast to normal Wedgwood tradition. The brilliant colours and glazes make her wares very collectable.
£2000-£2500

Castelli tin-glazed earthenware plaque; c.1725; 12 in (30.5 cm) wide. Prices of plaques from this Italian factory depend on the subject matter; landscapes may fetch up to £7500.
£2000-£2500

Dutch Delft polychrome plaque; c.1750; 13¼ in (33.6 cm) high. The mix of chinoiserie and Rococo moulding is common on Dutch pieces.
£1500-£2000

Pair of Herculaneum Pottery miniature George IV Coronation plaques; c.1821; 3 in (76 mm) across. The transfer-printed decoration suggests that large numbers were made, but this is the only known pair.
£2000-£3000

Set of three flying duck pottery wall plaques; 1930s; largest 7 in (17.8 cm) long. Such sets, made in England in ceramic or plaster, were very popular.
£30-£40

Poole Art Pottery earthenware charger; c.1925; 10 in (25.4 cm) across. This decorative dish from the Poole Art Pottery, established in 1921, was painted by Rene Hayes.
£100-£150

Berlin porcelain plaque; c.1870-80; 12¾ in (32.3 cm) high. The voluptuous subject, high degree of skill and opulent frame are typical of 19thC Berlin plaques.
£10,000-£15,000

Royal Worcester porcelain plaque; 1918; 8⅞ in (22.5 cm) wide. This landscape plaque is signed by John Stinton.
£1500-£4000

Victor Vasarely zebra plaque; 1977; 13¾ in (35 cm) high. This was commissioned by the Rosenthal factory for its 'Year Sculpture' series.
£300-£500

plaques and cameos (see p.168). Technical innovations in the 1770s allowed him to mass-produce the Classical bas reliefs that are still a distinctive Wedgwood style today.

PORCELAIN REFINEMENT

The start of porcelain manufacture in Europe in the 18th century allowed the production of fine ceramic plaques. Sèvres made a name for itself with pieces in brilliant enamel colours mounted in ormolu for setting in furniture, clocks, inkstands and even snuff boxes. Sèvres also made larger plaques – known as tableaux – intended to be hung as paintings. Some were sold ready-framed in carved and gilded wood, others had the framework moulded and gilded in the porcelain itself. Most Sèvres plaques now cost £2000-£5000, but a good figure tableau may fetch £30,000. There are also numerous 19th-century Sèvres-style plaques – often depicting Louis XVI, his queen and mistresses – worth £400-£800.

In Britain, few porcelain plaques were produced before the end of the 18th century, although the Worcester factory had made a porcelain plaque as early as 1757 – a transfer-printed portrait of Frederick the Great of Prussia. High-quality landscape and still-life plaques painted for Worcester by artists such as Samuel Astles and Thomas Baxter in the early 19th century now fetch £1000-£7000.

By the second half of the 19th century several British factories, including Derby, Coalport and Davenport, were manufacturing decorative plaques, often painted as a sideline to the artist's factory duties. Few are signed and most sell for £300-£3000.

By the late 19th century, decorating studios throughout Germany were being supplied with blank porcelain plaques from Berlin. Many carry the desirable 'KPM' mark and are decorated with copies of famous paintings. The more risqué the subject the higher its price is likely to be today.

INTO THE TWENTIETH CENTURY

Some 20th-century plaques are also sought after. Royal portraits by the Royal Crown Derby painters Reuben and Douglas Hague now fetch £600-£2000, and Royal Worcester plaques – usually mountain scenes – by painters such as Harry Davis and John, James and Harry Stinton about £1500-£4000.

Art Deco human profiles by the Viennese Goldscheider factory and skeins of flying ducks are both 20th-century versions of the plaque. And since the Second World War, the Rosenthal factory in Germany has commissioned notable modern artists to design striking plaques that it produces in limited editions, and which are already collectable.

*I*N THE EARLY 17TH CENTURY, *the Portuguese were shipping blue and white porcelain dishes from China by the ton in armed merchant ships, or carracks. Having hijacked one of these vessels and its cargo, the Dutch auctioned the wares, calling them 'kraak porselein' after the ships. The style soon became popular. When the Ming dynasty collapsed in the 1640s, and Chinese exports dried up for 50 years, the Dutch got the Japanese to produce copies. Meanwhile, European potters were getting in on the act.*

And that's what we have here: three blue and white dishes about 12-14 in (30-35 cm) across, each decorated with a rather similar pattern of a bird on a rock framed by almost identical motifs. All, in short, are fairly typical kraak-style dishes of the 17th century. One is in fact Chinese, one Japanese and one European. The question is, which is which?

First dish: Chinese porcelain

Second dish: Japanese porcelain

Third dish: European tin-glazed earthenware

The temptation for the beginner is to focus on the decoration. It's the most obvious feature, but it's superficial and can mislead. It is far more important to concentrate on materials and glazes. For example, when I look at these three rims, I can see straight away that two of them are more or less translucent porcelain, but the third shows all the signs of European tin-glazed earthenware. It's more thickly potted, and where the glaze has splintered on the rim – it's always weakest there – you can glimpse the digestive-biscuit colour of the earthenware body.

Earthenware shows on rim

An Expert Examines

LARS THARP PRESENTS THREE KRAAK DISHES

Chinese: broad foot-rim; chatter marks

Japanese: small foot-rim; central spur marks

European: spur marks on rim; crack in glaze

By contrast, the Chinese dish has all the panache of an already well-established tradition: The foot-rim is broad, but there are no spur marks – they didn't need spurs to stop sagging. But see those lines – chatter marks – radiating from the centre? They were made by the potter's knife, planing away the unfired paste on the upturned dish as his wheel turned. Friction made his knife judder, or chatter. That is typical of Chinese pieces, as is the abrasiveness you can feel on the foot-rim itself. It's due to sand scattered on the kiln floor to stop the pieces sticking.

Sand gives Chinese foot-rim an abrasive feel

Finally the tin-glazed European dish is much less subtle. This potter too needed spurs, in this case to stop the outer rim flopping. So he used flanges that left straight marks an inch (25 mm) or so long, by the rim. And the clay or firing was imperfect, causing this long firing fault, like a crack in the glaze, running almost halfway round. The whole piece nearly exploded in the kiln.

LARS THARP SUMS UP

If you had concentrated on the pattern, you would have said that the European tin-glazed dish is the closest to the Chinese original. But under the skin the Chinese and Japanese are the closest cousins. As for prices, fashion dictates that the Japanese piece would fetch £1000-£1500, the Chinese about half that, the European copy only £300-£400. That's partly because the shiny glaze and darkish body show it to be continental, not English. An English dish would be worth much more, especially if it had an inscription and date.'

This makes a striking contrast to the bright glaze and brittle edge of the first dish, and the velvety appearance and soft feel of the second. Peering closely at this second one, I can see that the glaze has a soft orange-peel look. This is caused by millions of tiny trapped air bubbles, which also give the pattern an out-of-focus air. It's typical of Japanese porcelain of the 1650s, when it was not yet as good as the Chinese.

Misty appearance of glaze

Inspecting the velvety texture of Japanese glaze

Now to go back to the first porcelain dish – which you'll have deduced by now is the Chinese one. The rim is hard and brittle. The effect of the glaze is very hard too, but sparkling. There's no trace of mistiness here, and the colours are clear and bright. In fact, in a few places there is some spitting of the cobalt blue where it's broken through the thin glaze. The effect is absolutely typical of Chinese blue and white porcelain of the first decade or two of the 17th century, when those Portuguese carracks were first shipping dishes like this to Europe.

Bright and brittle glaze

But now let's turn the dishes over. The most obvious thing is that the foot-rim of the Japanese dish is much smaller, while inside it are four small scars. These are the marks left by ceramic spurs used to prevent the centre sagging when it was fired – remember, the Japanese were still learning about porcelain in the mid-17th century.

Figures and groups

Modelled ceramic figures of all periods reflect something of their creator's, and collector's, view of the world – whether colourful, plain, romantic, statuesque, sentimental, serious or comic.

I N MOST BRITISH HOMES there is a fireplace. Above most fireplaces there is a mantelpiece. And on most mantelpieces there are ornaments, often including a pair or several porcelain or earthenware figures.

Since man first discovered that clay could be formed with his hands, he has made figures and models of people, of animals, of situations and of mythical or contemporary personalities in the world about him. Such figures continue to give glimpses of the human situation in which they were created.

IN CHINA

Nowhere is this clearer than in the figures taken from the tombs of ancient China. As in most early cultures, it was customary to slaughter a large part of the household retinue upon the death of a prince or emperor: wives, servants, stewards and other retainers, pets, horses and even livestock were expected to accompany the deceased into the afterlife. This custom was understandably as unpopular as it was wasteful, and by the time of the Qin (Ch'in) dynasty (221-206 BC) life-size clay effigies had been substituted for humans.

But even this was very labour-intensive, and during the Han dynasty (206 BC-AD 221), the burial of much smaller pottery figures became more usual. These funerary ceramics were generally made of a dark grey earthenware which was either left unglazed, covered in a thin white slip and coloured, or covered in a green glaze. Their subject matter is often informal and domestic: a pigsty complete with pigs (which would sell at auction today for some £2000-£4000), a miniature oven (£500-£1000) or a cart and driver (£5000 or more) – all relatively inexpensive considering their age. Collectors pay more for those with a

Pottery horse and rider; Han dynasty; 17¼ in (43.8 cm) long. The sockets in the haunches of this unusual and attractive funerary horse were originally for wooden legs.
£7000-£10,000

Chinese blanc-de-Chine figure of Guanyin, goddess of mercy; 17thC; 9⅞ in (25 cm) high. This ware inspired some of the white 'magot' figures produced by early European porcelain factories.
£6000-£12,000

Sicilian terracotta figure of a goddess; c.480 BC; 10⅛ in (25.7 cm) high. Such figures were used for domestic ornament but also as sacrifices at wells where favours were asked of gods.
£2200-£3500

Celadon glazed stoneware figure; Ming dynasty; 9½ in (24.1 cm) high. Coating with wax before glazing gives face, hands and feet a different colour and texture.
£2000-£3000

Set of famille-rose figures of the Eight Immortals; Qianlong (1736-95); 9½ in (24.1 cm) high. Each is dressed in colourful robes and carries his respective attribute. The Immortals were popular as deities in China, and as export items to Europe.
£6000-£8000 the set

green glaze, although prices at the lower end of the funerary antiques market have dropped.

The same applies to the Tang dynasty tomb sculptures of AD 618-906, which were prepared on a production-line basis: arms, legs, trunks, heads and bases were made in separate moulds, the parts then assembled, smoothed, individually detailed and fired.

Some animal and human figures were left unglazed, others painted or covered in a monochrome or a splashed 'egg-and-spinach' glaze. An unglazed Tang figure of a groom will fetch as little as £300-£500; straw-glazed, the same figure might reach £400-£600; and covered in splashed yellow and greens, £1000-£5000. The addition of the rarely seen blue to the same figure will boost the price further. Take care with the cheaper, unglazed

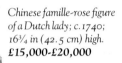

Chinese famille-rose figure of a Dutch lady; c.1740; 16¾ in (42.5 cm) high.
£15,000-£20,000

Satsuma figure for export of Fukurokuju, Japanese god of good fortune; c.1890; 12¾ in (32.4 cm) high.
£1200-£2500

pottery figures, though. They can easily be forged using moulds taken from a genuine piece and then 'distressed' to make them look older. The commonest methods of ageing include snapping off the head, arms and legs and then gluing them back on, and encrusting the figure with yellow tomb earth saved from the bellies of genuine Tang horses. Glazed figures are less easy to forge.

The later Ming (1368-1644) tomb figures, including human beings, chairs, tables and domestic altars, frequently appear at auction decorated with glazes of yellow, green, purple and turquoise-blue. These attractive models give a vivid insight into the furnishings of the time, and individual pieces may be bought for between £200 and £2000.

RELIGIOUS SUBJECTS

Human and animal figures for purposes other than funerary offerings, and dating from the same period, include Buddhist statues made in celadon ware. Their often unglazed terracotta

hands and faces are in vivid contrast to the rich green celadon glaze on the rest of the body. The price of a single piece depends on the quality of the glaze and complexity of modelling, but ranges from £500 to £20,000.

Exquisite figures of the Bodhisattvas (Buddhist deities) – in particular of Guanyin, the goddess of mercy – were produced in 'blanc-de-Chine' porcelain in the late 17th century. The figures were made of a paste which, at its best, has the density and appearance of ivory. Some of these blanc-de-Chine figures also have a potter's mark impressed on the back. A few were painted upon arrival in Europe. Prices for blanc-de-Chine figures vary tremendously, depending upon factors such as quality, size, condition and date. Collectors may pay as much as £20,000 for a superbly sculpted Bodhisattva, but only £200-£800 for an unexceptional 18th-century figure of Guanyin, 9-12 in (23-30 cm) high. Figures

Canton elephant; c.1840; 5¾ in (14.6 cm) high. The saddle cloth bears the designs and colours often seen on table wares exported to Europe in the 19thC.
£600-£900

from the late 17th and 18th centuries tend to be more solid than 19th-century pieces, while examples made during the 20th century show less delicate modelling and less subtle glazing.

ON THE CONTINENT

It was probably Buddhist figures such as these that inspired the earliest European porcelain figures – 'magots' or models of humorous little Chinese Buddhas produced on the Continent – at Meissen, Saint-Cloud, Chantilly and Mennecy – from the 1720s to 40s, and in Britain from about 1780.

THE MEISSEN CONTRIBUTION

The European porcelain figure as we know it today, however, developed not from burial goods or religious models but as centrepieces for the banqueting tables of the aristocracy. Soon after its founding in 1710, the porcelain factory at Meissen was commissioned to produce both monumental, life-size porcelain sculptures of animals and birds for Augustus the Strong's Japanese Palace at Dresden (rarities which may fetch £50,000-£200,000 today), and small porcelain figures intended as table ornaments. These are generally 5-8 in (12.5-20 cm) high, and were modelled by two supremely skilful sculptors: Johann Joachim Kändler and Johann Gottlob Kirchner.

Early porcelain figures of human subjects were intended to be seen from all sides and were given the illusion of movement through a vertical twist or flourish, a pose known as 'contraposta'. Commedia dell'arte characters (such as Harlequin and Columbine), birds and animals, risqué groups of pastoral couples, and recognisable court figures were all made, as were humorous studies of monkeys dressed as humans. Among the best known of these is the Affenkapelle (see p.204).

Meissen figures of 1730-70 usually stand on a solid base which, in a few of the surviving pieces, is scratched with a 'KHC' (*Königlich Hofconditorei*, or royal pantry) inventory number. These figures and groups can fetch up to £25,000 – far more than the less lively, later 18th-century figures designed to be kept in cabinets and viewed from one side only, which sell for £2000-£10,000.

Meissen figures from the 19th century are generally conservative, and hark back to the previous century. Large groups of 18th-century children and allegorical figures relating to industry ('Trade', 'Exploration', and so on) stand 12-18 in (30-46 cm) high and can fetch £1500-£4000. A smaller Meissen piece in the 18th-century manner can cost £250-£400, and a pair three times as much. These 19th-century Meissen figures and groups

Two Meissen figures; c.1735-45; taller 5½ in (14 cm) high. Such figures replaced traditional marzipan and sugar table centrepieces.
Left: £8500; right (restored): £3500

Meissen group of Fröhlich and Schmiedel (court jester and postmaster) by J.J. Kändler; c.1741; 9⅔ in (24.5 cm) high. Many Kändler figures have flat bases encrusted with flowers.
£15,000-£25,000

Meissen group of children at play; 1850-70; 10 in (25.4 cm) high. The subject matter is based on an 18thC work by Acier, but the brighter colours show this to be a 19thC piece.
£1500-£2500

Nymphenburg porcelain commedia dell'arte figure of Capitano Spavento by F. A. Bustelli; 1763-7; 7½ in (19.1 cm) high. Many Bustelli figures have a spiral pose.
£15,000-£20,000

were much imitated, but original pieces are much heavier than copies (being press-moulded rather than slip-cast); the modelling is crisper and more finely detailed; the enamelling is superior and seems to be almost part of the glaze, especially the face painting; the gilding is a deeper tone of gold; and the marks are different, with the underglaze-blue crossed swords painted in a very particular way. Nonetheless, a good imitation can still fetch £300-£1500 at auction, while smaller Meissen-style figures sell for £30-£100.

French biscuit porcelain figures, Vice and Virtue; c.1880; 27 in (68.5 cm) high. The crisp modelling is heightened by colouring straight onto the unglazed porcelain.
£2500-£3500 the pair

FROM OTHER FACTORIES

Franz Anton Bustelli at Nymphenburg and Johann Peter Melchior at the Höchst factory were among the figure sculptors working elsewhere in Germany in the 18th century. Bustelli's delicately featured figures often have their head and arms at angles, giving a powerful zigzag line, while the rustic, plump-faced children by Melchior have intense, dark brown eyes. A porcelain original will fetch £3000-£20,000, a Höchst-Damm revival figure £400-£1000.

Soft-paste figures made at the French factories of Vincennes and Sèvres include work by the master

Höchst group of 'The Fencing Lesson'; c.1765; 6⅞ in (17.5 cm) high. Flat Rococo bases and delicate colouring distinguish many Höchst pieces.
£15,000-£25,000

Lenci group of a girl on a hippo; c.1930; 12¼ in (31.1 cm) long. Lenci's skilful use of a fine spray achieves these soft colour tones under a glassy glaze.
£2000-£3500

Biscuit figure of 'The Bather'; 18thC; 14 in (35.5 cm) high. This piece is by Etienne-Maurice Falconet, director of the Sèvres modelling division 1757-66.
£4000-£6000

Pair of Nymphenburg figures of
18thC gentlemen by Josef Wackerle;
1930s; 22 in (56 cm) high.
£3000-£4000 the pair

Staffordshire salt-glazed white stoneware pew
group; 1745; 7½ in (19.1 cm) high. The back
prevented a group from collapsing during firing.
£50,000-£80,000

Staffordshire earthenware
flatback group of
Napoleon III and Prince
Albert; c.1854; 14 in
(35.5 cm) high.
£200-£300

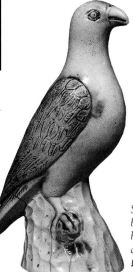

Staffordshire salt-glazed stoneware
bird; c.1750; 9¼ in (23.5 cm)
high. It is press-moulded, incised
and washed with cobalt.
£15,000-£20,000

Staffordshire lead-glazed
white earthenware
Whieldon model of a
dovecote; c.1755; 7¾ in
(19.7 cm) high.
£20,000-£30,000

Ridgway & Robey
porcelain figure; 1839;
9½ in (24.1 cm) high.
£300-£500

18th-century sculptor Etienne-Maurice Falconet. His three-dimensional interpretations of groups from paintings by François Boucher were often left 'in the biscuit' – unglazed – and were produced from the same moulds over a number of years. Prices vary greatly, but groups can fetch £5000-£10,000. Coloured models and groups are more popular today than those in biscuit or 'in the white'.

In the late 19th century, large coloured biscuit figures and busts were made in Germany and France, again in the 18th-century style. Prices range from £1000 to £3000 for a pair, although mass-produced figures 4-10 in (10-25 cm) high, often made as fairground merchandise, sell for around £20-£80. Most 'fairings' proper, depicting couples in ambiguous situations, fetch £20-£100 (see p.204).

Elaborate Art Nouveau pieces made at the Bohemian factory of Royal Dux and standing 20-25 in (50-64 cm) high, are usually matt-finished and muted in colour. They sell for £600-£2000. In the 1930s white porcelain figures and groups with bold Art Deco lines and forms were modelled in southern Germany and Austria. These can be very stylish indeed and can sometimes be bought for as little as £300-£1000.

IN BRITAIN

Very few earthenware figures were produced in Britain – or elsewhere in Europe – before about 1700, but early to mid-18th-century white, salt-glazed stoneware pieces are now among the most sought-after items of ceramic

Prattware pottery watch stand; 1790s; 9½ in (24.1 cm) high; it is in a popular colour combination of the time. (Right) Pearlware group of St George and the Dragon; late 18thC; colours suggest north-country origin.
Left: £1000-£1500; right: £1500-£2500

Staffordshire pearlware
figure of the actor John
Liston in the role of Sam
Swipes; c.1825; 5⅞ in
(15 cm) high.
£400-£600

art. Some are freestanding and single, while others are grouped on a pew. Pew-groups in good condition rarely fetch less than £60,000.

Staffordshire potter John Astbury worked in lead-glazed earthenware in the early 18th century. His figures of Scottish bagpipers, mounted dragoons or a party taking tea generally change hands for between £5000 and £30,000. Astbury-type productions from

the mid-18th century are covered in splashed green, yellow and manganese-purple glazes: a Chinese boy on a buffalo or an English dovecote may fetch up to £25,000.

In the same tradition are the often superb creamware figures and groups made during the late 18th and early 19th centuries and attributed to the Wood family. They include music-makers, shepherdesses and rustic swains,

English porcelain candlestick figures; c.1750; tallest 8¼ in (21 cm) high. They were made by the Chelsea 'girl-in-a-swing' factory, named after one of its groups.
£50,000-£80,000

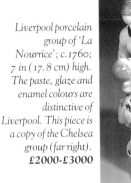

Liverpool porcelain group of 'La Nourrice'; c.1760; 7 in (17.8 cm) high. The paste, glaze and enamel colours are distinctive of Liverpool. This piece is a copy of the Chelsea group (far right).
£2000-£3000

Chelsea group of 'La Nourrice' (The Nurse); c.1756; 7½ in (19.1 cm) high. This is a copy of a 17thC French group.
£7000-£10,000

Shelley slip-cast pottery figures of children, c.1937, 6 in (15.2 cm) high; and 'The Shelley Girl' (centre), c.1925, 12 in (30.5 cm) high. The girl was made to advertise Shelley ware.
Girl: £1500-£2500; others: £400-£600

Staffordshire Parian figure of a bather; mid-19thC; 13½ in (34.3 cm) high. This piece is reminiscent of earlier Sèvres biscuit figures by Falconet. Parian figures resemble marble and were cast in large numbers.
£220-£280

Pair of Royal Worcester candlestick figures; c.1890; 10¼ in (26 cm) high. These slip-cast figures are decorated in soft enamels.
£700-£1000

Falstaffs, Neptunes and other gods and goddesses, and can be recognised by the splashed and transparent colours that leave large parts of the figure glazed but uncoloured. These items can fetch £800-£5000, while later creamware pieces of 1790-1810 are cheaper. These were produced to a lower standard, since the British porcelain factories were now catering for the top end of the market. They feature more enamel colour, with less emphasis on good modelling. Some deal with subjects relating to the Napoleonic wars: they fetch £200-£2000.

Highly coloured Staffordshire pearlware figures and groups of the 1820s feature pairs of small children, fashionable dandies or naively modelled animals, most standing before a flattened tree. Prices range from £100 to £4000 a pair – or, if the subject matter is highly amusing, £5000 up to £25,000.

By the mid-19th century, this tradition had evolved into Staffordshire 'flatbacks'. These are one-sided models, figures or groups slip-cast in a very small number of parts, then assembled, coloured by a team of children and sold for just a few pence each. Victorian celebrities, from murderers to royalty, are identified by an embossed or script title on the oval base. Depending on the subject's rarity, popularity and quality of colouring, they sell for £100-£2000 apiece. Other untitled pastoral figures, groups and animals range from £50 to £1000.

PORCELAIN, PARIAN AND CHINA

The early British porcelain factories at Bow, Chelsea, Longton Hall and Derby were established between 1745 and 1755, and produced up-market pieces in the temperamental soft-paste porcelain. Figures from the 1750s and 60s are desirable for their charm and artistic appeal rather than their technical excellence, and many were copied directly from Meissen and Sèvres pieces.

'Home-made' designs include Bow figures of Thames watermen, which can cost up to £6000 today, and portraits of actresses or celebrities which fetch £2000-£12,000. A pair of late Rococo Chelsea figures, each standing before a leafy tree on a gilt-trimmed base, fetches £800-£2000. Each piece may have one or two candlesticks incorporated.

Statues, groups and busts were made in Parian porcelain (similar in texture to marble) by Copeland, Worcester, Minton and others from the 1840s onwards. These are much larger than earlier porcelain figures – generally 12-18 in (30-46 cm) high – and are marble-white and unglazed. The modelling is often superb. Depending on a piece's size, subject and crispness of cast, Parian figures fetch between £200 and £2000.

Porcelain figures produced at the Royal Worcester factory from the late 1860s onwards include pairs of figures, figure groups and especially children dressed in contemporary and fashionable 'Aesthetic' attire. They were cast in a dense, ivory-coloured body characteristic of Worcester and delicately coloured and gilded. They now change hands for £400-£2000. Worcester's larger figures of the same period – some in Classical style, others Oriental – are enamelled in flushed pale peach and ivory tones with gilt line borders and can make £2000-£4000.

More recently, early 20th-century bone china figures were made by the Staffordshire branch of the Doulton factory. These figures – of theatrical performers, of prim bathing beauties and of Cockney characters, among others – are usually very well enamelled and currently fetch £150-£2500 for examples dating from before the Second World War.

Other figures from this century use many of the subjects and styles of earlier potters, with the addition of striking Art Deco designs and such well-known 20th-century phenomena as Walt Disney's cartoon characters.

'Age of Jazz' group by Clarice Cliff; c.1930; 5½ in (14 cm) high. This dramatic Art Deco piece, decorated on both sides, has echoes of cubism.
£4000-£4500

An Expert Examines

LARS THARP QUIZZES TWO PORCELAIN FIGURES

'HERE WE HAVE *two decorative figurines, one of a boy playing a recorder and the other of a parrot, both neatly coloured and both collectable. Now, the first thing that strikes me is the difference in materials. The parrot is made of hard-paste porcelain, which has a hard, brittle quality about it. When it's painted with enamels, they tend to sit on the top of the glaze, without interacting much with the glaze. The boy, on the other hand, is made of soft-paste porcelain, a physically softer material. Colours here tend to fuse with the glaze, giving a somewhat warmer, gentler appearance.*

The two figurines

Taking a closer look, you can see that both pieces are marked on the back with a gold anchor. That was the trademark of the great Chelsea porcelain factory from 1758 to 1769. But are they genuine? Note that the boy's anchor is small and discreet, while that on the parrot is larger and more obvious. Also, while the base of the parrot is cleanly finished, in the boy's case the glaze ran down over the foot-rim during firing and was smoothed off on a

The gold anchor marks (parrot on left)

grinding wheel afterwards. But the most noticeable difference, of course, is the hole in the base of the boy figurine. That was made to enable gas from the paste to escape during firing. All hollow ceramic figures must have such a hole; otherwise they'd explode in the kiln.

Comparing the bases

Vent holes in stump and wing of the parrot

The parrot in fact has two vent holes, one under its wing and another in the tree stump. Very small vent holes in the upper, visible part of the figure suggest 19th or 20th-century manufacture. Earlier they were more hidden.

LARS THARP SUMS UP

In the 1760s, hard-paste porcelain was rarely made in England, and never at Chelsea. But they had been making soft paste for at least 15 years, and Chelsea did have trouble with its glazes – hence that rough foot-rim. So I think the boy is genuine gold-anchor Chelsea, and would fetch about £800 at auction. But the parrot has the mass-produced look of a 19th-century copy – perhaps by Samson or another continental maker. That great big anchor is a giveaway, too. So it's only worth about £60.'

Commemorative wares

Royal weddings, military campaigns, the sinking of the Titanic and the exploits of the Beatles are just some of the events commemorated by potters.

ITEMS MADE AS SOUVENIRS of events have an immediate appeal that sets them apart from other fields of antiques. Pieces as varied as storage jars and complete dinner services have been decorated with pictures, mottoes and dates, and many can still be picked up cheaply. It is a collecting area where the subject matter is of greatest importance.

ROYAL SOUVENIRS

The monarchy and royal occasions are ever-popular subjects, and Britain has produced more royal commemorative souvenirs than any other country in Europe. Among the oldest are the blue and white delftware chargers made at Lambeth and Bristol from the 17th and early 18th centuries and decorated with naive portraits of Charles II, Queen Anne, George I and other monarchs (see p.22). The pieces were hand-painted and made in small numbers, and are rare today. They sell at auction for several thousand pounds. But with the Industrial Revolution came transfer printing, and souvenirs could be produced cheaply and quickly by the million.

Pieces made to celebrate Victoria's accession to the throne in 1837, and her coronation a year later, are now quite rare, but objects made for her jubilees of 1887 and 1897 are common. When Edward VII was crowned in 1902, Royal Doulton alone made a million commemorative beakers, and thousands must still survive. Even items made for the coronation of Edward VIII (which never took place) are far more common than most people realise, because hundreds of thousands had already been made when he abdicated.

The cost of each item will vary according to rarity. An 1838 coronation mug can fetch £500, while one made to celebrate Victoria's golden jubilee is worth only about £30 because there are so many.

All the major manufacturers, including Royal Doulton, Wedgwood, Crown Derby, Minton, Spode, Coalport and Royal Worcester, have produced royal souvenirs, but the majority were made by lesser-known potters, and may be unmarked. Even so, the simple flatback royal figures and groups produced in the Staffordshire potteries during the 1850s and 60s are very collectable today, and may fetch prices of around £250.

The quality of royal souvenirs can vary greatly, as can their value. Many cheaply produced Victorian mugs are decorated with appalling representations of the queen – bad enough to earn them the nickname 'uglies' – and these are worth little. But there are also well-designed rarities, including busts and figures of Queen

Brislington delftware dish; c.1690; 9½ in (24.1 cm) across. This blue and white dish portrays Queen Mary, joint sovereign with William of Orange.
£6000-£8000

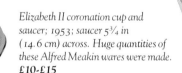

Elizabeth II coronation cup and saucer; 1953; saucer 5¾ in (14.6 cm) across. Huge quantities of these Alfred Meakin wares were made.
£10-£15

George III jug; c.1790; 6½ in (16.5 cm) high. The Worcester Flight and Barr factory, one of the most illustrious names in porcelain, produced a number of wares depicting George III, including this jug.
£1200-£1800

George VI coronation mug; 1937; 3¼ in (82 mm) high. The circus motifs identify this mug as the work of Dame Laura Knight.
£40-£50

Crown Devon jug made for Edward VIII's coronation; 1936; 8 in (20.3 cm) high. An addition just below the lip records his abdication.
£200-£300

Royal Doulton Queen Mother figurine; 1990; 8¼ in (21 cm) high. It is one of a limited edition of 2500 bone china figures issued at £250 each.
£350-£400

Victoria's many children, and the 20th-century coronation mugs designed by Dame Laura Knight and Eric Ravilious. These pieces are keenly sought after by collectors.

MILITARY AND POLITICAL ITEMS

Military commemoratives concentrate to a large extent on great leaders such as Admiral Lord Nelson and the Duke of Wellington and their campaigns. Political commemoratives usually mark elections, key events and ultimately the death of leading political figures such as Sir Robert Peel, Benjamin Disraeli and William Gladstone.

Lord Grey's Reform Bill of 1832 was the first political event to be marked by potters on a national scale, but less well-known events and personalities have also been remembered, including the Chartist reform movement of the 1830s and 40s. Wares made to commemorate strikes are now very collectable. The tradition was kept alive by potters recording the 1984 miners' strike, and these could well become popular with collectors in the future.

Some of the earliest military souvenirs relate to the Napoleonic Wars of 1792-1815, although most of the objects were actually made in the 1830s or later. More contemporary pieces were produced during the Crimean War (1853-6), mainly because it was the first to be reported in detail at the time, and the 1880-1 and 1899-1902 South African campaigns. Many items were made during and after the First World War, but the 1939-45 war saw far fewer, mainly because of restrictions imposed on the manufacture of decorative pottery.

Rarer pieces commemorate the lesser campaigns of the 19th century, figures including the Russian Communist leader Joseph Stalin, and events such as the Berlin Airlift of 1948-9. Items like these can fetch up to £500, although it is worth remembering that wares actually made at the time of an event will always be worth more than those made afterwards, or for anniversaries.

CELEBRATING DISCOVERIES

Advances in science and engineering during the 19th century were regularly commemorated in pottery. Souvenir pieces with transfer designs of Rowland Burdon's iron bridge at Sunderland, Brunel's Thames tunnel at Wapping and his Clifton suspension bridge at Bristol, the Manchester Ship Canal and other important achievements of the Victorian era can still be found for around £100.

Railways and shipping also were the subjects of commemorative wares, and the most desirable of these are decorated with specific

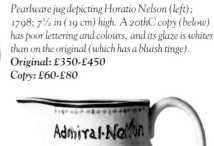

Pearlware jug depicting Horatio Nelson (left); 1798; 7½ in (19 cm) high. A 20thC copy (below) has poor lettering and colours, and its glaze is whiter than on the original (which has a bluish tinge).
Original: £350-£450
Copy: £60-£80

Staffordshire plate; c.1831; 9 in (22.9 cm) across. This transfer-printed plate satirises the tumultuous scenes in Parliament during the debate on the great Reform Bill.
£400-£500

Margaret Thatcher character jug; c.1990; 9 in (22.9 cm) high. Political fortunes are subject to change, so modern commemoratives should be picked for pleasure rather than investment.
£100-£125

Copeland tyg; c.1900; 5¼ in (13.3 cm) high. Queen Victoria is depicted as liberator of the oppressed on this Boer War three-handled loving cup.
£700-£800

Staffordshire model of Sir Robert Peel; c.1840; 12 in (30.5 cm) high. The crude decoration and casual lack of proportion are characteristic of Staffordshire portrait figures.
£600-£800

locations or identifiable locomotives or liners. Those celebrating the opening of a particular railway or the launching or maiden voyage of a great liner, such as the Titanic, are always sought after, and can fetch up to £750.

Important events and personalities in the worlds of travel (including space travel), exploration, medicine and the social sciences have all been celebrated, as was the 1851 Great Exhibition at the Crystal Palace.

MISCELLANEOUS ITEMS

Other collectable pieces commemorate the opening of public buildings such as churches, town halls, shops and hotels; eminent figures in the worlds of theatre, literature and popular entertainment; and religious leaders. Notable collectables include busts and statues of the Nonconformist preachers of the Victorian era, such as the Americans Dwight Lyman Moody and Ira David Sankey, or the founder of Primitive Methodism, William Clowes. Another good area of collecting is pop memorabilia – the Beatles and Elvis Presley being the most in demand.

Important sporting events have also been widely commemorated, in cricket especially but also in football, racing, golf and boxing (see p.379). Anything relating to the early years of motor sport and aviation is much in demand and will sell for upwards of £100 at auction (see p.415).

A final category is personal commemoratives. A large range of one-off wares was made to celebrate marriages, births, christenings and anniversaries. Potters in Britain have produced these highly individual pieces since the 17th century or earlier, and where they can be traced back to their original owners, they are especially valuable.

Royal Doulton Beatles jugs; 1990; 12½ in (31.7 cm) high. These jugs, continuing a long tradition of Doulton character jugs, are still in production (1992) and will not increase in value until withdrawn.
£32 each

Titanic commemorative miniature urn; 1912; 1½ in (38 mm) wide. Items rescued from the Titanic fetch the highest prices, but cheap commemorative wares, like this urn issued soon after the disaster, remain popular.
£50-£100

Prattware Great Exhibition pot lid; 1851; 3 in (76 mm) across. Cheap multicolour transfer-printing onto pottery was perfected by Felix Pratt, of Stoke-on-Trent, who produced millions of pictorial pot lids.
£80-£120

Buyer Beware

LIMITED EDITION CERAMICS first appeared in the 1930s, when a number of leading companies, including Doulton, Minton, Coalport and Copeland, began to issue special commemorative wares in small, numbered editions to celebrate royal and historic events. These issues were invariably of high quality and were limited to production runs of 500 or less. The buyer could rest assured that his purchase was one of a fixed number and was therefore likely to increase in value.

Such editions were halted during the Second World War, but the market started up again after the war finished and became increasingly lucrative. Although most companies kept their editions small and their quality high, the 1960s and 70s saw a massive expansion of the limited edition concept, especially in the United States.

Decorative wall plates printed with transfer designs were easily and cheaply produced, either singly or in a related series, and were then marketed through advertising in magazines and newspapers. Although the advertisements stress controlled production runs, the number of pieces produced in these 'limited editions' may be high or 'limited' to the number of replies to the advertisement.

Robert Burns sash window rests; c.1860; 3½ in (89 mm) wide. Among the many extraordinary items produced by 19thC potters are these hand-painted depictions of Scotland's national poet.
£80-£120

Cottages and crested souvenirs

Ceramic souvenirs celebrating places and buildings reached a peak with the booming Victorian tourist trade. Today, they can still be picked up cheaply.

Cottage teawares; c.1955; biscuit barrel (centre) 4¾ in (12.1 cm) high. The fashion for such teawares began in the early 20thC; beware of new pieces made from original moulds.
Butter dish: £30-£40; biscuit barrel: £50-£80; jug: £15-£25

Crested-ware cup and saucer; c.1910; saucer 5 in (12.7 cm) across. Tableware bearing local coats of arms was launched with great success in the 1880s, primarily as souvenirs for the tourist trade.
£15-£30

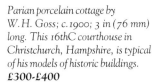

Cottage pastille burner; c.1825; 4½ in (11.4 cm) high. Such burners are highly collectable today – and have been much copied. Look for marks contemporary with the piece beneath the glaze.
£300-£500

Parian porcelain cottage by W.H. Goss; c.1900; 3 in (76 mm) long. This 16thC courthouse in Christchurch, Hampshire, is typical of his models of historic buildings.
£300-£400

Staffordshire watch stand (far right), c.1850, 10½ in (26.7 cm) high; and pastille burner, c.1860, 6 in (15.2 cm). Not all were cottages. Other designs included castles, lighthouses and follies.
**Watch stand: £400-£500
Pastille burner: £200-£300**

THERE IS A LONG HISTORY, dating back to the 18th century, of British potters making small, decorative objects to commemorate places and buildings. The ceramic cottage had as its forerunner the architectural teapot, shaped like a formal Queen Anne-style house and produced by a number of Staffordshire potteries around the 1750s, either in salt-glazed stoneware or in earthenware. Similar buildings, and many that were less grand, were the models for brown earthenware money boxes produced by Derbyshire, Nottingham and Lambeth potteries in the early 19th century.

COTTAGES

The ceramic cottage really came into its own during the golden age of bone china, between 1820 and 1850. It was primarily for ornament, but some examples also served as inkwells, nightlight holders or pastille burners (to burn pastilles of sweet-smelling gums).

Unnamed potters and the large porcelain factories all produced ceramic cottages. After the 1840s, cheaper, cruder versions appeared in earthenware, and production of these continued well into the 20th century. Early pieces in bone-china are the most sought after today and may sell at auction for £500 or more. Later earthenware models usually fetch around £100.

The architectural teapot reappeared in the 1930s in the form of rustic, timber-framed cottages, and since then cottage wares, including jugs and biscuit barrels, have been made by companies such as Carlton Ware and Wade; all are sought after.

CRESTED SOUVENIRS

Crested china was a phenomenon of the late 19th and early 20th centuries. Pieces were decorated with local landscapes or amusing mottoes, designed to attract the tourist trade.

Among the first big sellers of tourist wares was the Staffordshire potter W.H. Goss. In the 1880s, he made glazed parian articles bearing the crest or badge of a particular place, to which he later added small-scale models of local objects: Roman pots with the crest of York or Chester, or Robert Burns's cottage stamped with the crest of Ayr. Today these pieces fetch up to £2000, compared with £10-£25 for a simpler early Goss crested piece.

Crested souvenirs boomed during the First World War, when ships, aircraft and buses were reproduced. War models are always in demand and can sell for up to £80.

Garden and conservatory items

From Wedgwood hedgehogs to towering jardinières, collectable plant pots abound, but ceramic statues and furniture for outside use are much harder to find and often much newer than they look.

POTS AND OTHER CONTAINERS for growing and displaying plants existed as early as Song (Sung) dynasty China (AD 960-1279). In Europe, potters were making such containers from at least the 17th century, spurred by the import of exotic plants and the breeding of new varieties which the wealthy displayed in their homes. It was a field that eventually included majolica statues and seats and other objects that today attract both collector and gardener – though some are too valuable to be used for their original purpose.

POTS FOR DISPLAY

Vases made especially for displaying tulips, sometimes individually, were first made in 17th-century Holland. Rare blue and white Delft tulip pyramids with a separate nozzle for every bloom (see p.24) change hands at auction today for up to £30,000.

Flower bricks – literally brick-shaped delftware flower holders dating from the 1750s – could also have been used for small bulbs. They were the forerunners of the semicircular 'bough pots' produced by most English and French porcelain factories in the late 18th and early 19th centuries. These had a loose metal liner and separate pierced cover. In some cases the holes in the cover are small, for flower stems, but in others they are large so that bulbs could sit on top. Today, bough pots fetch anything from £300 to £3000.

JARDINIERES

Decorative plant pots for use inside the home or conservatory are known as jardinières, from the French word *jardin* (garden). The term applies to a wide range of containers, from small bucket-shaped pots on saucer-like stands to massive bowls on tall pedestals. (Strictly speaking, jardinières have drainage holes; those without holes, to hold potted plants, are called *cache-pots* – 'pot-hiders'.)

Jardinières of the 18th century held artificial trees blossoming with lifelike porcelain or paper flowers, but these are rarely found at auction today for less than £5000. The most costly – Sèvres square tubs of fine porcelain dating from the 1750s and 60s – are hardly ever seen today, but late 19th-century copies by Minton fetch £800-£1000.

It was in the Victorian era that jardinières proliferated. Large, heavily glazed examples

Sèvres porcelain watering can; 1753; 7¾ in (20 cm) high. It was probably made for Madame de Pompadour and used for sprinkling scented water on porcelain flowers at the palace of Versailles.
£50,000-£65,000

Wedgwood black basaltes bulb holder; c.1780; 6½ in (16.5 cm) long. This appealing hedgehog was designed for snowdrop bulbs.
£800-£1200

French majolica jardinière and stand by Jérôme Massier; c.1890; 50 in (1.27 m) high. Giant pottery butterflies are poised on this eccentric piece by the son of esteemed potter Clément Massier.
£1500-£2000

Chinese porcelain fish bowl; Kangxi period (c.1700); 23 in (58.5 cm) diameter. The Chinese kept ornamental carp in such bowls, and often decorated them with fish; in Europe they were used as jardinières.
£5000-£7000

Pair of Doulton jardinières and pedestals; c.1890; 48 in (1.22 m) high. Doulton were used to working on a massive scale and able to control their coloured glazes remarkably well. These pieces are typical of the company's architectural style.
£1500-£2000 the pair

Minton majolica plant trough; c.1870; 14 in (35.5 cm) high. A brilliant turquoise glaze was one of Minton's specialities. This piece – heavily decorated with Classical-style motifs – added vibrant colour to the greenery of the conservatory.
£6000-£8000

Garden seats: (left) in Minton majolica, c.1880; (right) in Chinese export porcelain, c.1850-80; both 18½ in (47 cm) high. Minton made large quantities of garden wares, but few of those actually used outside have survived. Chinese pieces in underglaze blue weather better than those with enamel colours.
Minton: £2000-£3000; Chinese: £360-£450

Minton majolica peacock, modelled by Paul Comolera; 1876; 59½ in (1.51 m) high. Comolera created many animals for Minton. Pieces as tall as this were a problem to fire.
£25,000-£35,000

Scottish stoneware rustic furniture and Czechoslovakian terracotta gnome; furniture c.1850-80, gnome 1920s; larger chair 43 in (1.1 m) high. All are highly collectable.
Chair: £400-£600; planter: £150-£250; gnome: £250-£400

Doulton's 'The Lily Maid', modelled by Gilbert Bayes; c.1930; 24 in (61 cm) high. It was made of Doulton's durable architectural stoneware, and was designed to be used as a fountain head.
£1500-£2500

were made in most countries, but especially in Britain, where many middle-class families had aspidistras and ferns standing in the drawing room or conservatory. Many colourful Minton majolica pieces were made from about 1850. Other makers followed suit, particularly in Germany and France, where Clément Massier and Théodore Deck combined majolica glazes with painted decoration. Today, Victorian jardinières range in price from £300 up to £10,000 for the most eccentric designs by the best-known makers.

Far more restrained are the 'drawing room flowerpots' patented by Grainger's porcelain factory of Worcester in 1840. The decorated outer cache-pot was sold with several porous clay liners in which flowers were raised in the greenhouse to provide a continuous display.

GARDEN SEATS AND ORNAMENTS

Stools, statues and life-size modelled animals, as well as jardinières, can all be found in colourful majolica. A Minton novelty seat may fetch up to £4000, a large animal up to £30,000. Barrel-shaped seats were also made in 19th-century blue and white earthenware, copying Chinese porcelain originals, but they could not withstand harsh weather. Survivors are mostly those kept indoors.

One ceramic material that has proved as weather-resistant as cast iron is salt-glazed stoneware, and it was used to make rustic furniture from the 1850s to the 1870s in Germany and particularly in Scotland. This simulated tree trunks and gnarled branches, often on a massive scale. Today, objects such as small planters, troughs, seats, benches – even tiered fountains – fetch anything from £100 up to £2000 for the largest items.

Ceramic sculptures and ornaments were produced as cheap alternatives to stone and bronze, but again most were not hard wearing and often look older than they really are. A terracotta statue, for example, may appear ancient but is very unlikely to be so – and if 'Czechoslovakia' is stamped on the back it could not have been made before 1918.

Far more durable are garden statues in Coade stone, a form of highly fired stoneware of the late 18th century that was marketed as artificial stone (see p.362), or in the architectural stoneware of a century later. These latter were mainly made by Doulton, manufacturers of hard-wearing sanitary ware; they are sometimes finished with strongly coloured glazes that have retained their brilliance.

Just when the ceramics industry devised weatherproof materials, however, new forms of concrete were developed to cast figures, especially gnomes, much more cheaply. As a result, ceramic statues are surprisingly rare.

Medicinal and toilet wares

Bedpans, drug jars, eye baths and shaving bowls are just a few of the mundane household ceramics that have survived the centuries.

RELATIVELY FEW everyday ceramic items for personal use – ranging from pap-boats for feeding the sick to discreetly shaped chamber pots for women to use in church or when travelling – have survived to become today's collectors' items. Those that have lasted in significant numbers are generally decorative as well as functional.

FOR MEDICAL CARE

Feeding cups were made in most countries, but especially in Britain, for use by children and the infirm. The most basic type, shaped like a slipper, are known as 'pap-boats'. They were made in large numbers in the Staffordshire potteries between 1830 and 1860 and decorated with blue transfer designs, often in willow pattern. These can be bought for as little as £15-£60 today. Late 19th and early 20th-century examples bearing the Red Cross badge are also regularly found. Rare 18th-century designs – with an enclosed circular bowl, a long spout and in some cases a handle – sell at auction for as much as £1000.

Many medicinal objects were made in fine pottery or porcelain, and among the most valuable are early eye baths. Rare 18th-century examples can be worth up to £2000, despite appearing very simple and unimportant. Indeed, many such eye baths have been found in junk shops or markets for just a few pounds.

Among the most common medical items found today, however, are drug or apothecary's jars, used for storing and dispensing medications in pharmacies. Sets of decorative pottery jars were first made in the Middle East in the 13th century and were exported to hospital and monastic pharmacies across Europe. By the 16th century, sets of hundreds of jars – often decorated with coats of arms – were commissioned at considerable expense by leading Italian families for private use. As their dazzling colours have remained bright up to the present day it can be difficult to distinguish an original 16th-century jar

worth many thousands from a 19th-century reproduction worth less than £100. Later Italian drug jars were not so well made, but from the 17th century fine porcelain examples were imported from China and Japan.

The earliest English drug jars date from the 17th century. Distinctive sets were made in London in blue and white delftware, and massive jars made for display rather than use began a tradition that lasted well into the 20th century. Sets decorated with matching bands of plain colour were made in Staffordshire and France, but most have now been split up. Single covered jars of this type can usually be bought today for between £40 and £200, the main exception being large jars marked 'Leeches'. These sell for £500 or more.

Ointment-dispensing pots are also very collectable, as they were produced in their thousands only to be thrown away once the ointment inside was finished. An amusing

APOTHECARY'S SHOP *In Pietro Longhi's mid-18thC painting, fine maiolica jars labelled with their contents stand on the shelves in the background.*

Victorian printed example – or just the pot lid – can be bought for as little as 50p upwards. English or Dutch 18th-century delftware versions can be worth as much as £400 if inscribed with the name of the apothecary or of a

Italian maiolica syrup jar; 1501; 10⅝ in (27 cm) high. The elaborate decoration includes the emblem of a pharmacy; other examples bear the coat of arms of the aristocratic owner.
£40,000-£50,000

London delftware drug jar; late 17thC; 16 in (40.5 cm) high. The name on the jar is Diascordium, a popular herbal remedy for the plague – a continuing threat to health 300 years ago.
£2500-£3000 (damaged)
Undamaged: £5000-£7000

London delftware pill slab; 1664; 9½ in (24 cm) high. Apothecaries used such plaques to roll pills and for display. Many bear the arms of the Apothecaries' Company, but the royal arms and date make this example rare and very valuable.
£80,000-£120,000

Staffordshire pottery pharmacy jars with gilded labels; c.1870-80; 5-8½ in (12.7-21.6 cm) high. Jars like these were used in chemists' shops until the 1950s. The strong colours and shapes make them popular decorative objects.
£50-£80 each

popular remedy such as Singleton's Eye Ointment. The very earliest ointment pots, dating from the 17th century and painted with coloured stripes, can fetch even more.

CHAMBER POTS

Chamber pots from the 16th to 18th centuries are remarkably rare. Very few of the surviving pieces are decorated, although 17th-century examples inscribed with puritanical mottoes have been found at Harlow, Essex. Wealthy 18th-century families used chamber pots of Chinese porcelain, some bearing the owner's coat of arms and some with matching lids. As these were expensive, they were cared for better than cheap English pottery ones, and many more of them have survived. They sell at auction for £600-£1000.

Most Victorian and Edwardian chamber pots formed part of a complete wash set and vary little in shape. But they are decorated with every conceivable type of design, from flowers to irreverent satire, some even printed with a comical face looking up from inside. The most famous and valuable are Irish pots from the Belleek factory containing a portrait of the English Liberal Prime Minister William Gladstone (1809-98). British wartime propaganda potties with the face of Kaiser Bill or Adolf Hitler are also highly collectable.

Narrow pots for women to use under their skirts in church or when travelling were made from the 1730s up to the early years of the 20th century. These bourdaloues (supposedly named after a French priest renowned for his long sermons) are sometimes mistaken for sauceboats but lack a spout. They are very desirable and fetch from £60 to over £1000.

SHAVING EQUIPMENT

Shaving bowls, or barbers' bowls, were made from the 16th century onwards, and shaving mugs from the 19th. As a result, a huge variety of such pieces are available to collectors.

Shaving bowls were produced in France and Spain, mainly in tin-glazed earthenware, and large numbers of porcelain examples were also imported from China and Japan early in the 18th century. All shaving bowls have a cut-out section to fit around the customer's neck as he was being shaved, most have holes to hang by, and some have an indentation in the rim to hold the soap.

Most shaving mugs found today are of cheap English pottery or imported German porcelain and were made around the turn of this century. The American barber-shop vogue for displaying mugs inscribed with their customers' names or illustrating their professions has led to a keen collectors' market, with rare examples fetching over US$1000 (£580).

English chamber pot in Metropolitan slipware; c.1660; 6¼ in (15.9 cm) high. The motto reads 'Fast and pray and pitty the poor Amend thy life and senne [sin] no mor'.
£1400-£1700

Chinese porcelain spittoons recovered in 1985 from the cargo of the wrecked Dutch ship Geldermalsen, which sank in the South China Sea in 1752; 4¾ in (12.1 cm) across. The ship's inventory calls them 'spuijg potjes' ('spit pots'); until this was found, such objects were thought to be children's chamber pots.
£600-£1200 each

Caughley porcelain eye bath with scroll moulding and blue painted sprigs; c.1790; 2⅛ in (54 mm) high. All porcelain eye baths are keenly collected and expensive.
£900-£1200

Scottish pottery bourdalou made by Bell of Glasgow; c.1840; 9¼ in (23.5 cm) long. A romantic Swiss alpine scene decorates this chamber pot for women travellers.
£130-£150

English ointment pots; 18thC; 1⅛-2½ in (30-63 mm) high. Pots such as these were used for dispensing medicines in apothecary shops, and large numbers of them have been dug up where they were discarded.
Inscribed delftware: £200-£400
Plain: £20-£40

Minton earthenware wash set decorated in 'Secessionist' style; c.1905; jug 15 in (38 cm) tall. It lacks only its soap dish. Earlier sets fitted into the wooden top of a washstand, but by the late 19th century most washstands had a marble top on which all the washing paraphernalia stood.
£600-£800

Spanish barbers' bowls in tin-glazed earthenware; mid-18thC; 11-11⅜ in (28-29 cm) across. The cut-out part fitted around the client's neck.
£150-£200 each

Blue-printed earthenware pap-boat of typical shape; mid-19thC; 5 in (12.7 cm) long.
£35-£50

Comic and curious items

Pottery is a good medium for subversive humour, and those who enjoy a joke have plenty of wares to choose from.

Staffordshire Prattware stirrup cup; c.1800; 5½ in (14 cm) high. One way up the face is a frowning Pope, the other a smiling Devil. 'Gin and Water' figures are similarly reversible.
£300-£500

English delftware puzzle jug; mid-18thC; 7 in (17.8 cm) high. The hollow rim and handle act as a drinking straw. You suck one nozzle while covering the others.
£600-£800

North Italian maiolica bust of a toothless beauty; c.1550; 8¼ in (21 cm) high. This 'beauty' is an amusing antidote to the flattering portraits of young women on many contemporary dishes.
Museum piece

Figures from a Meissen monkey band; 19thC; 4½-6½ in (11.4-16.5 cm) high. Original examples from the mid-18thC would fetch four times more than these.
£400-£600 each figure

Fairing; c.1900; c.3½ in (90 mm) high. Such pieces, often with titles containing social comment, were made in Germany or Austria as fairground gifts or prizes.
£40-£60

JOKE JUGS AND MUGS, trompe l'oeil plates and satirical figures date back to the 16th century in Europe, although as early as the Song (Sung) dynasty in China (960-1279) potters were making wittily modelled pillows in the form of recumbent tigers or concubines. However, the mass of comic wares found today date from the late 18th and, particularly, the 19th centuries. They range from biting satire to erotica, simple mistakes (as in Chinese export porcelain plates showing Jesus with female disciples) to the deliberate bawdiness of many decorated chamber pots.

Mocking figures by the Martin Brothers, often in the form of birds with sly, self-satisfied or arrogant expressions (see p.184), are highly collectable, fetching anything from £800 to £30,000 depending on size and outrageousness. Far more affordable are the many transfer-printed earthenware plates made in France and Staffordshire in the 19th and 20th centuries. These carry satirical prints of contemporary events, such as life in the trenches, unflattering portraits of politicians or royalty, or the social adventures of an

Edwardian heroine. They can be bought for £5-£40 apiece. From an earlier era, pottery decorated with anti-Napoleon prints by Thomas Cruikshank fetches £200-£1000.

Among the earliest practical joke pieces to survive are English delftware fuddling cups and puzzle jugs, designed to spill on the inexperienced drinker. These can fetch £500-£5000. Much later were Staffordshire pottery jugs which leaked water down the unsuspecting user. Often decorated with Cashmore, Everybody's Clown, they were made in some quantity in the late 19th century and can be found today for around £40-£60.

FIGURES OF FUN

Humorous pieces were produced in fine porcelain at Meissen in the mid-18th century. The most famous are the *Affenkappelle*, or monkey band – a group of monkeys dressed as an orchestra. Commedia dell'Arte figures and

satirical figures aping members of the court of Augustus the Strong are among the most desirable items modelled by Johann Kändler, and originals sell at auction in the £2000-£5000 range. They were much copied, however, both at Meissen itself (19th-century copies fetch £500-£900) and elsewhere.

Many 18th and 19th-century Staffordshire groups were perhaps not intended to be comic but seem amusing today. Among the best are those by Obadiah Sherrat titled 'Now Captin Lad', 'The Death of Munrow', 'Teetotal' and 'Polito's Menagerie' – the eccentric spellings adding to their value. They fetch between £2000 and £20,000 today.

The humour is intentional in many fairings (small 19th-century fairground prizes) showing scenes of married life with suggestive titles – as it is in Chelsea porcelain teapots in the form of a Chinaman with a serpent or parrot emerging from his robes for a spout (see p.177).

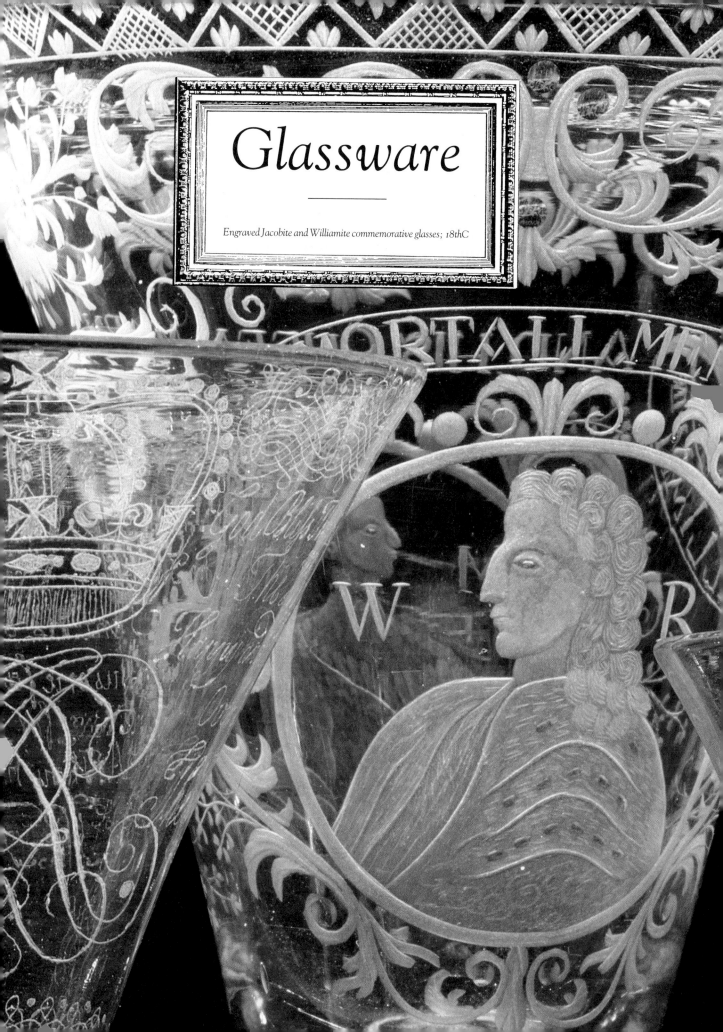

Glassware

Engraved Jacobite and Williamite commemorative glasses; 18thC

Collecting glassware

Although not as plentiful in the salerooms as other classes of antiques and with few specialist auctions, glass has a unique appeal and offers surprising scope at modest prices.

GLASS HAS A MAGICAL QUALITY born of its transition during manufacture from sand and other minerals to vessels of transparent delicacy. Barring breakage, scouring pads or dishwashers, it is wonderfully resistant to age, neither warping like furniture nor tarnishing like metal. It can look much the same after 200 years as it did when it was new, its shape and style reflecting the customs or habits of its time – the 18th-century cordial glass, for instance, was designed specifically for after-tea tippling, and the ale glass for small amounts of potent brew.

Considering its fragility, an extraordinary amount of beautiful glass survives from the 18th century and even earlier. There is an enticing choice for collectors of every financial level, from exquisite early and mid-Georgian pieces to Victorian jelly glasses, knife rests or lampworked figures that can often be picked up for just a few pounds. Even ancient glass can be surprisingly affordable. The discovery of blowing techniques in the Middle East some 2000 years ago prompted the Romans to make glass in vast quantities. Much was preserved in burial mounds, and Roman scent bottles can still be bought for £150-£200.

You are unlikely to see dramatic short-term rises in the value of glass (other than in certain rarified areas). But if paying £300-£700 for a late 19th-century, silver-mounted engraved claret jug seems excessive, bear in mind that a modern reproduction without the silver would take four days to decorate, and would cost about £1000. As glass gets broken, there is a more flexible attitude to the value of what remains. Few complete sets of 18th-century drinking glasses survive, and most collectors are happy to buy singles – there is no huge differential between the value of one and its cost as part of a set. Sets or singles of good-quality Victorian wine glasses (often only £10-£20 each) are particularly worth looking out for.

Glass of the early 20th century can also be a good investment, although pieces produced by the big French names such as Daum, Gallé and Lalique can be hugely expensive. Look instead for between-the-wars British art glass, ranges with a period character from big companies such as Stuart Crystal, or the pressed glass mass-produced by Bagleys. If you are buying today's art glass for tomorrow's gain, go for special, one-off pieces by individual craftsmen; they may well be pricey to begin with, but they are much more likely to appreciate in value in the long term.

Glass objects are mainly dated by their shape, form and colour, as they are far less often marked or signed than, say, ceramics. Much glassware made between the late 19th century and the 1930s reproduced earlier styles – most (but not all) in response to market demand rather than with any deliberate intention to deceive. Sometimes, these copies become collectable in their own right, but it is important to know the difference. Examine any prospective purchase in good light, looking out for the signs of wear that give a seal of authenticity to genuine old glass (see p. 215).

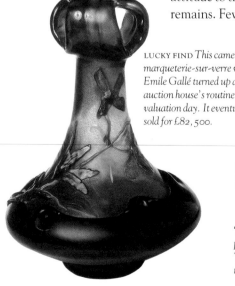

LUCKY FIND *This cameo and marqueterie-sur-verre vase by Emile Gallé turned up at an auction house's routine valuation day. It eventually sold for £82,500.*

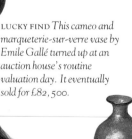

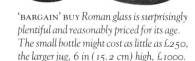

'BARGAIN' BUY *Roman glass is surprisingly plentiful and reasonably priced for its age. The small bottle might cost as little as £250, the larger jug, 6 in (15.2 cm) high, £1000.*

FORGERY *Engraved commemoratives are favourites with forgers. This 'Williamite' glass ostensibly dating from c.1690 was in fact made c.1890, possibly in Ireland. Plain stems with two knops, as here, were unknown on late 17thC glasses. More difficult to detect is later engraving added to an original period glass.*

Understanding glassware

Glassware rarely carries any marks of identification and changes very little with age, so what you can deduce about its composition and the way it was made may be the only clues you have as to its origins, quality and maker.

ARTICLES OF GLASS all started life as an unpromising sand-like mix, or batch, of dry ingredients. When heated to around 1100°C (about 2000°F), this mixture fuses and vitrifies (literally, becomes glass-like) into a molten mass known as the 'metal'. While molten the glass can be cast, moulded or blown into shape, but on cooling it hardens into the stable waterproof substance we know.

The basic characteristics of glass – its clarity and strength and the rate at which it solidifies – depend on the mix of ingredients. The main ones are the vitrifying ingredient silica – usually sand, but sometimes quartz or flint – and an alkaline flux such as soda or potash, which causes the silica to vitrify far below its normal melting temperature.

Soda glass, mainstay of the ancient Roman and Venetian glass industries, was made with washing soda (sodium carbonate) originally extracted from seaweed. It is thin and fragile, sometimes with a pale yellow or greenish tinge. The Venetians later improved standard soda glass by adding manganese oxide, which produced the clearer cristallo.

Much old glass, including medieval Bohemian glass, was made with potash from burned wood and bracken. The toughness of potash glass made it ideal for engraved decoration. In 17th-century Britain, George Ravenscroft experimented with potash and ground flints to make the first flint glass. Later red lead (lead oxide) was substituted for some of the potash to create lead glass – the staple product of British and continental glasshouses.

GLASS-MAKERS AT WORK *Hollow blowing irons, blocks for shaping the 'gather' and iron moulds were all in use in this mid-18thC glasshouse.*

SODA GLASS *Although it has to be constantly reheated while working, soda glass can make thin forms and fantastic shapes, such as the serpentine stems of these 17thC Venetian cristallo wine glasses. Small air bubbles in the bowls are typical.*

POTASH GLASS *This 15th/16thC south German vessel is made of the early hard, greenish potash glass. The Bohemians later discovered that adding chalk made a colourless glass good for engraving. Its strength also makes it ideal for modern everyday glassware.*

LEAD GLASS *This tough, heavy glass with great clarity and light refraction is viscous when molten but makes thick pieces able to be cut in glittering faceted patterns, as on this late 19thC covered bowl.*

FLINT GLASS *George Ravenscroft used ground flint in the batch of dry ingredients in an attempt to achieve the clarity of Venetian cristallo. The resulting flint glass was prone to crizzling, as in this jug (left) of c.1674, probably made by Ravenscroft.*

Hot processes

The final appearance of a piece of glass depends both on processes carried out in its hot, fluid state and in many cases also on the decorative effects added once it had cooled. Whatever the method of forming the vessel, a vital stage is annealing – slow cooling in an oven – without which internal tensions may cause the piece to shatter easily.

SHAPING GLASS

Much of the earliest glass was cast, either by pouring molten glass into a mould or by firing crushed glass in a mould in a kiln. The solid chunks of cast glass produced were then hollowed out and ground into shape using a rotating wheel. Pâte de verre is a 19th-century version of the kiln firing method, while glass has been cast for basic or solid shapes up to the present day, using iron moulds in two or more parts for complex pieces. A related method is press-moulding, which was developed in the 1820s and uses a mechanical press to squeeze the molten glass between dies (see p. 226).

Other ancient hollow glass vessels were formed around a core shape of dried mud and animal dung fixed to a metal rod. This was dipped into molten glass or had glass wound around it. Alternatively, crushed glass was

CAST PIECE *The ancient art of casting glass produced this fragment of an Egyptian cosmetic palette in the shape of a bound oryx, c.1500 BC. Pieces were cast in an open mould and when cooled laboriously ground into shape with drills.*

applied to the core and fused by heat. The mud core was chipped out after cooling.

Another technique used in the Middle East in ancient times was glass mosaic, later perfected in millefiori (see p.494). But it was the introduction of glass-blowing – probably about 2000 years ago and also in the Middle East – that transformed the scope of glass-making. The glass-maker could scoop a small blob or 'gather' of molten glass onto the end of a long, hollow blowing iron. He might shape it in a curved block or on a flat surface (for a straight-sided piece) and then either blow it into a clay or cast-iron mould (for standard sizes), or free-blow it without a mould.

The basic methods have evolved only a little ever since. The blown bubble could be shaped or drawn out with tools such as pincers and tongs – to make the drawn stem of a wine glass, for example. Separate gathers were shaped and attached to form feet or handles. To shape the rim, the piece would be transferred to a carrying iron called the pontil rod, or punty, attached to the foot. When the glass was finally snapped off the rod, it left a scar known as the pontil mark (see p.215) which could be ground off or left on.

COLOURED GLASS

Metallic oxides in the batch or the molten metal produce coloured glass. Green glass contains iron oxide, and yellowish 'Vaseline' glass uranium oxide. Other common colours are cobalt (blue), manganese (purple) and ruby glass, first made in 17th-century Germany by adding copper and gold dust. (Cranberry glass is a more dilute form.)

Articles with two or more layers of different-coloured glass have been made since Roman times. The easiest method was flashing – dipping a molten blown bubble of one colour into molten glass of another. This gave a very thin top layer, but it was not always of uniform thickness. Flashed glass may be difficult to distinguish from cased glass, made the other way round. A gather of coloured glass would be inserted into a cup-shaped hot 'blank' of the second colour, and the two then blown as one.

MOSAIC GLASS *This Venetian bowl made in 1876 imitates ancient bowls of the Roman Empire. Here, sliced coloured glass canes were arranged in a decorative pattern in a concave mould and then heated until they fused together to make the solid piece. Ancient glass-makers may have fused the canes into a solid flat disc before shaping it over or within a curved mould.*

CORE-FORMED *Dating from c.1000-1500 BC in the Middle East, this flask is decorated with trails of glass in contrasting colours, blue and yellow being a favourite combination. After completion, the core was chipped out.*

MOULD-BLOWN *The pattern on this 1930s Thomas Webb & Sons vase was formed by blowing the gather of glass into a dip mould, an iron mould cut with a reverse pattern on the inside. A 'ghost' impression of the mould can be felt on the inside.*

COLOURED AND CASED GLASS *Advances in the control of impurities in the 18th century enabled glass-makers to experiment with colour. By fusing together different-coloured layers and cutting away areas of the outer to expose the contrasting inner layer, they created decorative effects as in the 19thC scent bottle (far right) and cameo glass (see p.222).*

TRAILING, PRUNTING AND LAMPWORK

Other 'hot' processes of decoration include trailing (applying threads of molten glass), and adding blobs of glass known as prunts, stamped into shapes such as flowers with a metal stamp. For centuries trailing was done by hand, as on Nailsea glass, but in the 1870s a glass-threading machine was invented.

Related techniques include latticino (see right) and making the spiral opaque or coloured glass twist of some 18th-century wine-glass stems. Lampwork, in which glass rods are heated over a single small flame such as a Bunsen burner, was used to make tiny novelties and ornaments (see p.230).

PRUNTING *The hollow stem of this 18thC goblet is decorated with applied raspberry prunts, stamped out as small blobs of molten glass with a metal die. Lion-mask and portrait prunts are also common.*

LATTICINO *Any Venetian glass decorated with white stripes is known as latticino, although certain patterns have specific names. The filigree-like effect comes from fusing separate rods of coloured or opaque glass together. They are then fused onto a sheet of clear glass, formed into a closed cylinder and then blown into shape.*

Cold processes

For many pieces, shaping the hot glass was only the start of the manufacturing process. Decoration could then be applied by cutting, engraving, etching, enamelling, gilding – or by a combination of these.

CUTTING AND ENGRAVING

Since ancient times, glass-makers have decorated suitably heavy glass with incised geometric designs (see p. 216). This was done by holding the glass body against a grinding wheel, with a wooden wheel lined with brushes or felt used for final polishing. Early this century, acid polishing was introduced.

Engraving was scratched or 'drawn' on glass with a diamond point as early as the 16th century. In the Netherlands in the 18th century, Frans Greenwood introduced stipple engraving, in which dots were chipped into the surface with a diamond engraver. It was often combined with line work.

Copper-wheel engraving, introduced to Britain by German engravers in the early 18th century, permitted greater detail – often like a drawing. It developed in the late 19th into 'rock-crystal' (to resemble hardstone carving) and intaglio work. Intaglio used small stone cutting wheels to create curvaceous, asymmetric cuts, one edge of which is at right angles to the surface, the other shallow.

Acid etching was faster, and followed the discovery of hydrofluoric acid (which dissolves glass). By scratching through an acid-resistant coating (by hand or machine) the acid could be allowed to eat away only the areas required for the design. This method was ideal for mass production, and became widespread from the 1860s. Acid-etched designs are more uniform than those of wheel engraving and less grainy than sandblasting.

ENAMELLING AND GILDING

All-over colour effects could be produced by spraying hot glass with metal oxide solutions, as for so-called carnival glass (see p. 228). For more conventional decoration, coloured enamels similar to those used for pottery and porcelain were painted on the cold glass and fused in a low-temperature muffle kiln. Cheaper cold-enamelling involved no firing, but the decoration was liable to wear off.

Gold decoration was applied by oil, honey or mercury gilding (see p. 475), or powdered gold mixed with borax was fired like enamel. Gold or silver leaf could also be sandwiched between layers of glass. In the late 19th century, electrogilding and silvering (versions of electroplating) came into use.

DIAMOND-POINT ENGRAVING *The decoration on this mid-18thC English Jacobite 'Amen' wine glass was made by scratching the surface with a diamond point. A similar tool was used on stipple-engraved Dutch glass.*

ROCK CRYSTAL *Heavy rock-crystal glass like this 1884 decanter was deeply cut to imitate Oriental hardstone carving, the fine detail added by copper-wheel engraving, and then highly polished.*

ENAMELLING *This 1762 goblet is the work of renowned glass enamellers William and Mary Beilby of Newcastle upon Tyne. Little British enamelled glass dates from before the mid-18thC.*

COPPER-WHEEL ENGRAVING *Engravers operated a foot-treadle lathe, holding the glass against a revolving copper wheel fed with abrasives to create the pattern, as on this 18thC Dutch wine glass. The copper wheel could be as small as a pinpoint – allowing very fine drawing on thin glass – or up to c.6 in (15 cm) across.*

SANDBLASTING *A mass-production technique invented in the United States in 1870, sandblasting worked by firing abrasive powders through a stencil applied to the glass. It was used mainly on cheap commemorative glass, as here, and for excise marks; today it has replaced acid etching for inscriptions on presentation goblets and decanters.*

INTAGLIO *This decorative technique used small stone wheels to create mostly curved cuts – such as for flowers and leaves – on the glass. It was introduced in Stourbridge c.1891, where it has now superseded copper-wheel engraving.*

ZWISCHENGOLDGLAS *This 1788 German beaker had gold leaf wrapped around the glass; it was needle-engraved and then covered with a tight-fitting outer cylinder of glass.*

ELECTROGILDING *For gilt decoration on mass-produced glassware, an extremely thin layer of gold, silver or copper was deposited by a method akin to the electroplating of metalwares.*

Bottles, decanters and jugs

Drinking bygones of the last two centuries encompass both fascinating early, handblown bottles and beautiful cut-glass decanters and claret jugs.

DARK GREEN AND BROWN bottle glass was introduced into Britain in the early 17th century, and was adopted as the best available material for storing wine. The more elegant decanter came into common usage for serving wine and spirits early in the 18th century, and was particularly popular during the Victorian era. Bottles were also used for drugs, medicines, poisons, ink and food relishes from the 19th century onwards.

BOTTLES

Most bottle collections today date from the 17th to the mid-19th century. Many early English glass bottles show irregularities because they were handblown, but this will not necessarily diminish their value.

One of the easiest ways to date old wine bottles is by their shape. Between their introduction around 1630 and a century later, bottle shapes changed radically from a round, bulbous-bodied form with a long neck to a cylindrical shape close to the one we know today. Spherical 'shaft and globe' bottles, as the earliest examples are known, are rare and can fetch up to £3000 when sold at auction.

The retail sale of wine was not permitted in Britain until around the end of the 17th century, so bottles were sent to specialist wine merchants for filling. Wealthy people had bottles specially made with a personal seal impressed on the side, and these often have a date as well. Bottles with seals were made until the mid-19th century, and examples in good condition sell for £1500-£2000. Any peculiarities such as a deformed seal make these bottles even more desirable and expensive.

The earliest moulded bottles date from the last years of the 18th century, although the shoulder and neck were still formed by hand. Bottles of this type can fetch up to £300.

DECANTERS AND JUGS

The glass decanter was introduced during the early 18th century. Many decanters from the second half of the 18th century – including some in 'Bristol' blue glass – are engraved or gilded with a name label, and these and later decanters are now coming back into fashion.

Magnum cognac bottle with comet seal; mid-19thC; 13 in (33 cm) high. It was made for cognac of the fine 1811 vintage, when a comet was sighted.
£250-£350

Diamond-engraved wine bottle; 1687; 9½ in (24.1 cm) high. The Dutch inscription means 'the world's fortunes ebb and flow', and celebrates an important marriage in Leiden.
£6000-£10,000

'Old Hock' decanter; c. 1770; 11¼ in (28.5 cm) high. The gilt lettering imitates labels that were sometimes hung on decanters.
£6000-£8000

Wine bottle sealed with the name John Weller; 1735; 8⅓ in (21.1 cm) high. Seals on old bottles such as this are those of the owner.
£1500-£2000

Gilt 'flask' decanters for sherry and port, designed by the artist Richard Redgrave; c. 1848; 13¼ in (33.6 cm) high. There would originally have been a decanter for brandy too.
£3000-£4000 the pair

MISHAPS IN THE BOTTLE WORKS Nineteenth-century glass-blowers demonstrate their craft – and its pitfalls – to an appreciative audience. Finished bottles line the shelves.

DR SYNTAX IN THE GLASS-HOUSE.

A pair of matching early Georgian wine decanters, for example, may fetch from £200 up to £1000, depending on their size, decoration, whether the glass is clear or coloured and whether the stoppers are original or replacements. Individual examples, pairs and sets of all dates are sought after today.

Large matching wine services, which include glasses as well as jugs and decanters, first appeared in the 1840s. Original services would have as many as five or six different decanters and either six or 12 of each type of drinking glass, including tumblers. Glasses are usually found singly, but some have also survived in sets. Green glass items used for white wine and made in the fashionable, broad-fluted cut-glass style can fetch as much as £350 for a decanter, although single green glasses can still be found for £20-£40 each.

Late 19th-century decanters from such sets are generally one of three types – pint, quart or the distinctive claret decanter with a handle. These claret jugs often have elaborate engraved, etched or cut decoration on the sides, a silver engraved collar and a silver or glass handle. A typical example may fetch £300-£700. A tantalus (cased set of decanters) from this period sells for about £500 up. A Victorian water set consisting of a jug and two goblets can be had for about £500, depending on its condition. But complete sets are rare and it is more common to find a jug alone for £200-£300.

Claret decanter; c.1897; 13²⁄₃ in (34.7 cm) high. This decanter is engraved with the Indian 'cone' motif in the rock crystal style inspired by hardstone carving. **£3000-£5000**

Jug with separate, corked central cylinder to hold ice without diluting the drink; c.1900; 9²⁄₃ in (24.5 cm) high. The pink-tinted glass cased with green is cut with scrollwork. **£250-£500**

An Expert Examines

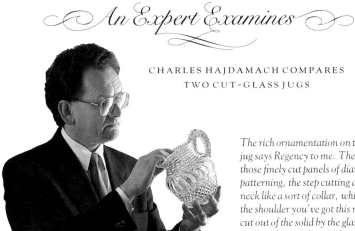

CHARLES HAJDAMACH COMPARES TWO CUT-GLASS JUGS

'TAKE TWO JUGS, both decoratively cut. To discover when they were made you must pick them up – by the body, not the handle – for a close look. This first one has virtually the entire surface, including the handle, ornamented by the regular, deep incisions that were made by the steam-driven

Regency jug of about 1820

cutting lathes that came in around 1800. Then there's the way the handle was applied. It's thicker at the top than the bottom, showing that the upper end was stuck on first and the glass pulled down, getting thinner as it went. After about 1860, this was usually reversed, and the thinner part was at the top.

Pre-1860 handle

Post-1860 handle

The rich ornamentation on this first jug says Regency to me. There are those finely cut panels of diamond patterning, the step cutting around the neck like a sort of collar, while around the shoulder you've got this ribbing, cut out of the solid by the glass-cutter, working by eye alone. Then on the base, the pontil mark has been ground off and replaced by a 32-point star. All these features, taken together, add up to a date of about 1820. For a clincher, jugs of this time were polished with a slurry of putty powder, applied by a stiff brush mounted on a wheel. This was quite gentle and did nothing to blur the edges of the cutting. If you run your fingers over them you'll feel the edges, as crisp as ever.

The 32-point star

The second jug is much the same shape, even to the drawn-down handle, but it's a lazier piece altogether. A lot of the cutting is irregular, and some areas of glass have simply been left blank – no Regency craftsman would have done that. I'd say it's a copy from about 1920. Again, confirmation lies in the polishing, which in this case has been done in an acid bath, leaving rounded edges to the cuts.

Jug of 1920

CHARLES HAJDAMACH SUMS UP

A final pointer is that glass made in 1920 is much whiter and more brilliant than that of 100 years earlier. But it's the craftsmanship that counts: the painstaking Regency cutting and polishing versus the mass-produced air of the other. And that is reflected in values. The 1820s jug, of a type that's getting scarce now, would make about £400 at auction, but the other would be lucky to reach £60. '

Scent bottles

Collecting these small bottles is a natural choice for all who appreciate form, colour and decoration in glass.

UNTIL THIS CENTURY, most perfume was bought in plain containers and decanted into something more decorative. Only some 100 years ago did perfumers begin to have bottles specially designed – some by the greatest glass-makers. René Lalique (see p.227) designed bottles for the French perfume houses of Coty, Worth, Guerlain and others – but far more affordable today are classic bottles introduced early this century by Guerlain and Chanel, at £15-£25.

EARLY TYPES

The heavy use of scent and cosmetics became fashionable in the 18th century, and it was from that time that scent bottles of delightful and frivolous design, mostly in glass, became widely available. Some have compartments to hold patches, rouge, or even a few little bonbons. Often fluted or facet-cut, their shapes include tubes, flattened lozenges or ovals and, by the 1820s, squat, heavily cut bottles with domed stoppers. Prices today generally range from £80 to £350, but very decorative bottles can fetch up to £5000.

In the 1830s, Apsley Pellatt began making sulphides (also called cameo encrustations), which incorporated ceramic medallions in the glass by a process which he had patented in England in 1819. Pellatt's cut-glass sulphides are much sought after today, those incorporating intaglio profiles of famous personalities fetching up to £2000. Cased glass was also used for bottles from the 1840s, sometimes combined with latticino glass, gilding or painting. Bottles of this type range in price today from £80 to £800.

Particularly attractive cameo glass bottles made in the late 19th century are flattened globe and tear shapes with flowers cut to show off the coloured layers. Unusual examples, for which collectors will pay up to £1500, were made by the Stourbridge firm of Thomas Webb & Sons in the form of finely moulded and carved birds' heads in various colours.

FOR SMELLING SALTS

Closely related to scent bottles, and equally varied and attractive, are vinaigrettes (see p.260) and smelling-salt bottles. While most scent bottles have a narrow mouth to prevent evaporation, those for smelling salts are wide-mouthed to make it easy to sniff the vapours. They are generally cheaper than perfume bottles of equivalent quality.

Some of the most sought-after bottles are double-ended; one end is for scent, the other for smelling salts. These were popular from the 1840s to the early years of this century. Most are fastened at the scent end with a silver screw top over a ground-glass stopper, while the smelling salts are covered by a hinged lid, usually silver, that snaps open when a button is pressed. The most desirable double-ended bottles are those in coloured glass with silver or silver-gilt mounts dating from the third quarter of the 19th century.

Miniature scent bottles; c.1760; 1½ in (38 mm) high. Facet-cut and gilded, and with gilt tops, they still have their sharkskin case.
£1200-£1500

Apsley Pellatt sulphide scent bottle; c.1830; 4½ in (11.4 cm) high. It has a moulded ceramic medallion embedded in the glass.
£500-£750

Cameo glass scent bottle; 1883; 5½ in (14 cm) high. This bottle, with a fuchsia pattern and hinged silver cover, is the work of Thomas Webb & Sons.
£400-£600

'Bouchon Eucalyptus' bottle by René Lalique (above); 1929; 5½ in (14 cm) high. Bottles with such 'tiara' stoppers are rare and highly coveted by collectors.
£3000-£4000

Double-ended scent bottle; 1873; 4 in (10.1 cm) long. The silver lids of this bottle are inset with turquoise and have London hallmarks.
£150-£300

Pair of opaline scent bottles with stoppers; c.1860; 7 in (17.8 cm) high. Portrait pieces were made in large numbers, the enamelled and gilded decoration being added later.
£200-£300 (pair)

Edwardian scent bottles; early 20thC; 4½ in (11.4 cm) high. Their attraction lies in their printed paper labels and original silk ribbons.
£30-£50 each

Drinking glasses

Drinking glasses from the 18th and 19th centuries are enormously varied and survive in surprisingly large numbers, making them affordable and attractive items for collectors.

German Humpen; 1662; 8 in (20.3 cm) high. It is enamelled with the Reichsadler, the crowned Imperial Eagle.
£4000-£6000

PAST SPIRITS *In 'The smoke room of the Dudley Arms Hotel' (1829), W.J. Pringle painted a surprisingly stolid assembly of Regency worthies taking hot punch from bucket-shaped and cup-shaped rummers, which are typical of the time.*

A̱ᴛ ᴛʜᴇ ᴇɴᴅ of the 2nd century ʙᴄ the Romans were making cups and beakers in pale green or blue-tinted glass in large numbers. Glass was a material of every-day use in a way that was not to be seen after the fall of Rome until the 19th century.

It was only at the start of the 15th century, when the Venetians introduced their revolutionary clear soda-lime glass or *cristallo*, that the drinking glass came into existence once again. However, drinking glasses were an expensive luxury and remained so even after the mid-16th century, when Venetian and other northern Italian glass-makers took their skills to central and northern Europe.

Venetian technical expertise brought a new sophistication to local European glass-making traditions. German shapes such as the *Humpen* (beaker) now had decoration that used Venetian techniques such as enamelling and diamond-point engraving, while the Belgian serpent-stemmed goblets made in Antwerp and Liège are very hard to distinguish from the original Venetian models.

During the late 17th century, glass-makers in Bohemia and in some of the German states developed a new, thick, hard type of lustrous glass that lent itself well to the techniques of engraving and cutting. During

the 18th century a steady stream of richly decorated ceremonial goblets and wine glasses poured out from the central European glass factories, with Saxony, Silesia, Bohemia and southern Germany becoming important centres. Many of these survive today – simple examples fetch £1000 upwards for a single glass while the rarer, more elaborate examples command in excess of £100,000 each.

BRITISH MAKERS

The development of lead glass by George Ravenscroft and his followers in the 1670s and 80s laid the ground for a British glass industry. British 18th-century wine glasses are usually classified by the style of their stems, which changed as the century progressed. The first distinctive types had a baluster stem. Balusters were succeeded in the middle of the

English Rummer; c.1820; 5 in (12.7 cm) high. A monogram and a forge are engraved on it.
£300-£500

One of a pair of fine Beilby enamelled wine glasses (left), c.1765, 7 in (17.8 cm) high; and (right) a colour-twist wine glass, c.1770, 6 in (15.2 cm) high.
Left: £800-£1200 (pair)
Right: £1500-£2000

Tall engraved ale glass and dwarf ale glass with 'wrythen' bowl; English, late 18th and early 19thC; tall glass 6¾ in (17.1 cm).
Left: £120-£150
Right: £40-£50

Ruby glass goblet; Saxony, c.1740; 10¼ in (26 cm) high. This example has a faceted base and Baroque-style scroll engraving on the bowl.
£1500-£2000

century by the air twist and the opaque twist. In some cases coloured canes were used instead of opaque white to give a colour-twist stem, and air and opaque twists were combined to make mixed-twist stems. In the last quarter of the 18th century cut-glass stems became fashionable. Continental copies of British wine glasses exist, and telling them apart from the originals can be difficult.

Eighteenth-century drinking glasses are sought after by collectors, and more unusual examples are not cheap. Beilby enamelled glasses can fetch anything from £1000 to £50,000 depending on the decoration. Jacobite glasses engraved with motifs celebrating the Jacobite cause also command high prices, with £63,000 having been paid recently for a rare 'Amen' glass. Standard opaque-twist and air-twist wine glasses can still be purchased for around £150-£200. Watch out for the addition of later engraving to some plain wine glasses – a trick that was carried out to enhance the value of the glass.

VARIETY OF FORM

In Britain the same small wine glass holding some 2-3 fl oz (about 50-90 ml) seems to have been used for all the different wines that were available. However, special glasses were made for other drinks. Cordial, for example – a brandy-based drink infused with herbs, spices and fruit – was served in exceptionally small long-stemmed glasses. Thick, squat glasses known as drams were made for gin and rum, which were consumed in large quantities. Ale, a very strong drink in the 18th century, was drunk from a small glass with a tall narrow bowl. The same general flute shape was also used for champagne. Current prices of glasses for cordials, ale and champagne are similar to those of wine glasses; small glasses such as drams go for under £100.

Mugs and tumblers were made throughout 18th-century Europe for beer and punch. In Britain towards the end of the century the rummer – with its large cup or bucket-shaped bowl set on a short stem and foot – was used for serving such drinks as the watered-down rum called grog. Plain

Georgian rummers fetch prices in the region of £40-£80 each, but engraved examples are much more expensive.

By the late 19th century the wine service had reached the peak of its development. In Britain it would usually consist of a dozen each of six kinds of stemmed glass – for sherry, hock, claret, port, champagne and liqueur. A complete set, with decanters, jugs, tumblers, plates and finger bowls could number over 100 pieces. Grand wine services existed throughout Europe; most have long since been split but pieces are worth collecting as the standard was high. It is still possible to buy etched or engraved Victorian wine glasses for £10-£20, though prices are beginning to rise.

TWENTIETH-CENTURY GLASS

Sherry sets consisting of a decanter and six glasses began to appear in the 1920s, and at the same time a fashion emerged from the Continent for tall coloured hock glasses. However, unless they are associated with a famous designer, their prices are low.

The cocktail fashion, which spread to Europe from the United States in the 1920s, led to the manufacture of shakers and brightly painted cocktail glasses, mainly of continental origin. The majority of examples on the market are Czechoslovakian and the quality is not always very high. Only a small number of cocktail sets were made in Britain, where the leading manufacturer was undoubtedly Stuart & Sons of Stourbridge. The company produced some attractive enamelled designs, often in a humorous vein, including devils, spiders and cobwebs, and lucky symbols.

Wine goblets; Venice, late 19thC; taller 6⅞ in (17.5 cm) high. These handmade glasses demonstrate the revival of shapes and decorative techniques that originated in Venice during its golden age of Renaissance glass-making. **£100-£150 each**

Cut and frosted water jug and goblet; English, mid-19thC; jug 12½ in (31.7 cm) high. Sets of a jug and two goblets did not match other glasses because they were used only at the end of dinner. **£200-£300 (complete set)**

Lemonade set; English, 1930s; jug 7⅛ in (18.1 cm) high. In amber and clear glass with intaglio decoration, the set would also be used for water or other soft drinks. **£100-£150**

WIDE CHOICE *Late Victorian catalogues offered dozens of different sets of table glass. This one echoes the Gothic style with its tall, intricately cut panels and pointed motifs. Jugs and finger bowls match the glasses.*

Bohemian hock glass; c.1900; 8⅓ in (21.1 cm) high. This tall glass has colourful enamelled petals and leaf sprays carried out in the flowing Art Nouveau style. **£80-£120**

No. 5013 Liqueur

No. 5013 Sherry

No. 5013 Port

No. 5013 Tumbler

No. 5013 Custard

No. 5013 Claret

No. 5013 Jelly

No. 5013 Champagne

No. 5013 Finger Basin

An Expert Examines

CHARLES HAJDAMACH TASTES THREE WINE GLASSES

Now run your finger around the rim and foot. It should be nicely rounded – hand-finished – but in fact there is a very slight bevel on the edge of the air-bubble glass. A tiny chip must have been ground out. And there's a chip on the foot, but grinding that out would spoil its proportions. The air-twist glass, on the other hand, is perfect.

Testing the rim for chips or regrinding

Finally, hold them up to the light – you need good daylight – and look at the colour. Compare them with this third glass, which was made in 1911, as the inscription shows. All three are of lead glass – they ring nicely when you flick them – but this late one is far clearer than the others. They are grey by comparison, like all 18th-century glass.

N O MAKER'S MARKS *or other easy clues help in dating wine glasses, and glass-making techniques stayed much the same down the years. But changes in style, fashion and composition of the glass can help if you know what to look for – as I'll try to show with these wine glasses.*

This first glass is typical of the period 1720-40. It's called a drawn trumpet glass from the shape and because the bowl and stem were blown and drawn from a single lump of molten glass; you can see there's no join. It has an air bubble in the stem made by pushing a sharp point into the molten glass, then squeezing it to seal the bubble in. The foot – applied afterwards – is also typical: slightly domed on top and with a pontil or

Air twist

all round. He pushed them into the lump of molten glass to admit air, then pulled the glass out to form the stem, twisting as he went. They did that after about 1740; then, from 1760, you get a white opaque twist. Of course, those are the earliest dates such glasses were made.

Looking underneath, there's the pontil mark again – but the foot is folded over at the edge to make a more durable, double thickness. That's a feature of glasses from the 1720s into the 1740s and beyond. And while you are looking at the foot, check it for wear. Old glasses should have a fine network of grey abrasions in random directions – and that's what we have on both of these. Wear that's too sharp and uniform may have been made by sandpaper in an effort to deceive.

Colour difference of 20th and 18th-century glasses

CHARLES HAJDAMACH SUMS UP

The fact that the air-twist glass is perfect, the folded foot and the intricate workmanship in the stem mean an auction price of around £150. The damaged, single-bubble one would struggle to make £50, but if perfect it would fetch £100-£120.

Air bubble   Pontil mark on domed foot

punty mark beneath. That's where the pontil rod was sheared off after the glass-maker had completed his final shaping of the bowl.

The next glass is also a drawn trumpet, but it shows a slightly later style: a series of air twists instead of the bubble. The glass-maker used something like a cork with pins stuck in

Pontil mark and folded foot

Cut glass

The diamond-like brilliance of cut crystal glass exudes wealth and even opulence. While it is still costly new, there are antique bargains to be had.

THE LONDON GAZETTE of October 1, 1709, noted the arrival of a set of German cut and carved glasses, the like of which had 'not been exposed to public sale before'. The newly developed lead glass was ideally suited to this technique, and within 20 years several London manufacturers were producing a variety of cut-glass cruets, casters, salts, punchbowls and dishes.

The basic technique has not changed since then. After cutting by revolving wheels, until the mid-19th century each line or groove was buffed with rotating brushes and progressively finer abrasives to produce a clear, smooth and regular surface. Late 19th and 20th-century pieces were acid polished instead by dipping into hydrofluoric acid, giving a glossier surface but very slightly rounding the cut edges.

There are subtle colour differences, too. Comparing a collection of 'clear' cut glass in daylight reveals a range of shades, including grey, purple, black, yellow and blue. The colours come from impurities in the raw materials. The best English cut lead crystal and also the finest Irish Waterford glass have hardly any colouring impurities, and modern glass in particular is sparkling white.

Eighteenth-century glass was often flat or diamond cut (see illustration, p.461). Facets, or shallow diamond-shaped cuts, triangles,

flutes and arches were incised into wine-glass and candlestick stems, and in the bodies of ewers and decanters. Cruets with similar forms of cutting, with or without their silver mounts, are quite common and collectable. They can be found for between £50 and £200. Small items such as jelly, sweetmeat and syllabub glasses can be picked up for under £100.

Mitre cutting was particularly popular between 1800 and 1830. A field of diamonds was often made by cutting a series of grooves and then another series at a 90-degree angle. Thickly cut horizontal grooves became another common form of decoration. One of the most popular styles of the period is known as 'strawberry diamonds'. It has a cut field of diamonds, with each diamond further cut with tiny crisscross lines. An amazing variety of cut patterns and motifs exists on 19th-century decanters, and these and other items can be found for around £60 to £150.

A broader style of cutting was introduced from the 1820s, with vertical cut flutes. At first the intention was to give the glass a lighter, more extended feel, but

mitre cutting was soon added, as well as other deeply cut, Gothic-style patterns that emphasised the weight of the body.

New heights of cutting skill were reached in the 1880s. Glass-makers working in Scotland and the Midlands, such as Stevens & Williams and Thomas Webb & Sons, experimented with complex prismatic and geometrical patterns. Pieces from this period sell at auction for between £40 and £120.

Many patterns were revived in the late 19th and early 20th centuries, and it can be difficult to tell when a piece of cut glass was made except by subtle colour differences. Modern pressed glass (see p.226), made in imitation of cut glass, may look very similar. But it can be distinguished by the slight blurring of lines and the lack of really sharp edges. In cut glass the lines are cut, dissected and polished extremely finely and the edges are crisp.

Heavy cut-glass bowl; c.1910; 8 in (20.3 cm) across. The thickly scalloped rim contrasts with the more delicate, star-like patterns. This type of glass was popular in the Edwardian period.
£80-£100

Cut-glass ewer (left); c.1765; 9¾ in (24.7 cm) high. It has a scalloped rim and foot, notched handle and shallow-cut diamond panels on the body.
£2500-£3000

Cut-glass decanter and bowl; c.1820; decanter 12¼ in (31.1 cm) high. Engraved portraits and large diamond facets decorate the decanter. The bowl is cut with strawberry diamonds and ovals. Engraved details can be later additions, but cutting is rarely faked, except to hide damage.
£700-£900 (pair)

Wine glass; c.1760-70; 8¾ in (22.2 cm) high. The foot, stem and lower bowl are flat-cut glass and the upper bowl is decorated with a wheel-engraved scene. Flat cutting is found especially on 18thC glass.
£2000-£2500

Large bowl and cover (right); c.1815; 12½ in (31.7 cm) high. Made in the shape of a pineapple, this piece is lavishly mitre cut. The glass of this period is very heavy.
£2000-£2500

Candleholders and lamps

Few modern homes have room for a large chandelier, but a fine set of candlesticks or a graceful lamp can add a touch of elegance – at a price.

DYING LIGHT *The chandelier, alluring combination of twinkling glass and flickering candlelight, meant work for the servants, as hinted in this painting by François-Auguste Biard (1799-1882).*

T HE EARLIEST GLASS light fittings from the mid-17th century were designed to hold candles – either singly or in groups – and some designs were extremely elaborate, particularly in France. As technology brought new ways of creating light, styles of fittings evolved to accommodate first oil, then gas and eventually electricity.

CHANDELIERS

The design of chandelier components was largely dictated by the need to capture the wax dripping from burning candles. Most early glass chandeliers are relatively plain, although some Baroque designs were made in the 17th century, with a gilded brass frame and hanging ornaments cut from natural rock crystal. Nowadays these are seen only in great continental palaces such as Versailles.

By the middle of the 18th century, glass-cutting techniques had become more sophisticated and British makers started to add ornamental glass pendants or drops to most designs. Soon the drops were linked to form festoons and loops, and by the end of the century so many chains and ornaments had

been added that the structure beneath was often hardly visible. Such chandeliers sell for anything from £5000 to £50,000 today, depending on size and design.

In the 19th century, manufacturers started to produce chandeliers with hollow glass arms through which to pipe gas. Most were plainer in style than late 18th-century chandeliers. Quality fell towards the end of the century with the increasing use of cheaper, acid-polished glass drops imported from Bohemia.

Chandelier designs changed again at the turn of the 19th century with the advent of electricity. Some chandeliers were adapted to the new power source, others sold with false 'candles' and flame-shaped electric lamps. These go at auction for £1000 up to £10,000.

The demand from interior decorators means that buyers rarely find bargains even among 19th-century chandeliers, as most sell for £5000-£10,000. French Baroque chandeliers have been copied in various sizes and qualities since they were first made in the 17th century, and small mid-19th-century versions can be found for just a few hundred

Cut glass eight-light Regency chandelier; c.1810-20; 36 in (91 cm) high. The drops, which formed a minor element of 18thC chandeliers, became the dominant feature in the early 19thC.
£7000-£9000

Cut glass six-light, three-tier chandelier; c.1770; 50 in (1.27 m) high. It was a common practice to reassemble the components of chandeliers, perhaps adding extra pieces as fashions changed.
£8000-£10,000

Set of four white glass taper sticks; 1755-60; 7⅛ in (18.1 cm) high. These taper sticks were made in imitation of enamelled porcelain.
£6000-£8000 the four
Pair: £2000-£3000; single: £400-£500

Pair of candelabra with long drops, c.1830; and (centre) a composite candelabrum, late 19thC, 31 in (79 cm) high. This was made up of a base of c.1790, and later elements; a pair could fetch about eight times as much.
Centre: £300-£350; outer pair: £3500-£4500

Pair of ruby-red glass lustres; late 19thC; 11 in (28 cm) high. Although the clear drops help to reflect light, lustres were used more for decoration, perhaps sitting on a mantelpiece, than for holding candles.
£300-£500

Edwardian cut crystal lamp; c.1910; 12 in (30.5 cm) high. The shade of this mushroom-shaped lamp rests on three arms fixed to the central support. This type of lamp is enjoying a revival.
£100-£150

French oil lamp with central draught burner; late 19thC; 18 in (45.7 cm) high. The glass reservoir is hand-painted and gilded, and sits on an elaborate silver-plated base.
£200-£300

Victorian lampshade; c.1890; c.8 in (20 cm) across. This shade was blown into a mould to achieve the honeycomb pattern. The frilly rim was produced by a crimping machine and its darker colour was created by re-heating.
£25-£50

Daum electric table lamp; 1920s-30s; 20½ in (52 cm) high. This lamp is deeply acid etched with an Art Deco geometric pattern. It would have a low-wattage bulb to give a soft light.
£4000-£8000

pounds. Determining the age of glass can be difficult but, in general, genuine 18th-century pieces have a darker tint, with uncut surfaces showing a slight swirling texture. Acid polishing from the late 19th century onwards, by contrast, leaves a granular surface texture.

SMALLER CANDLEHOLDERS

Glass candlesticks from both the 18th and 19th centuries are relatively common and can be bought either singly or in sets. Early 18th-century examples usually have a baluster stem, sometimes incorporating beads of air, and sell for £750-£1500 apiece. Later designs are usually more complex, with twists of air or of opaque white glass; and these commonly fetch £2000 each. Plainer candlesticks with cut facets sell for about £2000 or more a pair.

Candlesticks hung with drops are known as lustres, and were popular until the late 19th century. Regency candlesticks adorned with long drops can sell in pairs for less than £1000, as can late Victorian decorative pairs.

Branched holders – or candelabra – are rarer than single candlesticks. Various designs were produced, some quite simple, some in the ornate Rococo style of the early Georgian period; prices range between £5000 and £35,000. Even rarer are fixed wall brackets (sconces) with glass arms for two or more candles. These first appeared in the mid-18th century in similar designs to contemporary chandeliers. A pair will fetch up to £30,000. Even copies of good, late 18th-century pairs can realise £1500-£3500 at auction.

LAMPS

Many ingenious and elaborate oil burners were produced in the 19th century, often with a heavy base of coloured or moulded glass. Some of the simplest were in the style of a Classical column as much as 24 in (61 cm) high, with brass or silver-plated Corinthian capitals. These can sell for upwards of £1000 each, but smaller versions were made around 1900 by Clarkes and sell for £400-£500 each, and £1000-£1400 for a pair.

After the arrival of electric lighting, huge numbers of small fittings were made to hold one or more bulbs. Some were made up from 19th-century chandelier drops and others were entirely new. They sell for a few hundred pounds. Electric lamps from the early 20th century can be highly collectable, especially those made by Art Nouveau masters such as Tiffany, Gallé and Lalique (see opposite, and pp.223 and 227), and wall and table lamps made in Art Deco style.

In the United States genuine Tiffany lamps start at $100,000 and can reach up to $250,000, or even more for rarities such as the Wisteria lamp. Gallé and Lalique examples begin at around £8000 but can fetch £60,000 for a rare or limited-edition piece. There are, however, many imitations on the market.

In the 18th century lanterns were used to illuminate halls and entrances. These are usually found in furniture sales and can fetch £2000 or more. Lanterns from the Arts and Crafts movement sell for £300-£400.

Glass in imitation of nature

American Art Nouveau designer Louis Comfort Tiffany (1848-1933) is renowned for his fluid designs. His 'art', mosaic and stained glass is collected for its great beauty.

A LASTING PASSION for the forms and colours of Art Nouveau fired Louis C. Tiffany's lifelong interest in glass. The son of Charles Louis Tiffany, the founder of the jewellers Tiffany & Co, he studied to be an artist and was inspired by both English designer William Morris and, later, French glass-maker Emile Gallé (see p.223). Tiffany's success is a tribute to both his own talent and the technical skill of his English associates, Arthur J.Nash and Joseph Briggs.

DESIGNER AND EXPERIMENTER

In 1879 Tiffany established an interior decorating firm in New York, which later became Tiffany Studios. He also began to experiment with glass, trying to reproduce the effects seen in medieval stained glass, and in Roman glass. In 1880, he patented a type of iridescent glass under the trademark Favrile (meaning 'handmade'), although stained glass and mosaics were to form the bulk of his business over the next 20 years. At first, his glass was made to specification by an independent firm, but in 1892 he set up a glass factory – later named Tiffany Furnaces – at Corona, Long Island.

His hand-blown vases and bowls were immediately popular when first marketed in

NATURAL TALENT *Prosperous, confident Tiffany faces the camera c.1900 at the peak of his career.*

1896, and the first lamps with leaded-glass shades appeared in 1899. These, too, were instantly successful, and Tiffany soon set up a workshop to make them. Floor lamps, hanging lamps, table lamps and others were made,

reflecting Tiffany's passion for all natural forms. Despite being a virtual production line, scope for variation in colour and form meant that no two pieces were ever identical.

Totally confident of its lasting value, Tiffany had most of his work signed. His lampshades carry a small copper tab with the words 'TIFFANY STUDIOS NEW YORK', sometimes with a number. The bronze bases were similarly stamped, and these date the pieces quite precisely. Favrile glass carries the signature 'LC Tiffany' or 'LCT', and items with a numbered prefix or suffix can be dated. Copies have always abounded but few can compare with the carefully crafted originals.

Tiffany diversified into gift items, boxes, inkstands and the like; these were made in such quantities that they became known as 'wedding present' Tiffany. Jewellery, enamel wares, pottery and silver were all produced. Today his products are keenly sought, particularly Tiffany lamps and Favrile vases, and they fetch high prices. Among the items that fetch more affordable sums are some examples of his metalwork and his glass tableware.

Sulphur crested cockatoos; c.1895; 31½ in (80 cm) high. This glass mosaic exhibition piece is attributed to Joseph Briggs. **Museum piece**

Iridescent glass vase; 1902; 5½ in (14 cm) high. The pale yellow glass is decorated with trails and delicately shading lily pads. **£1200-£1800**

Wisteria table lamp; c.1902; 27 in (68.5 cm) high. The shade contains more than 1000 pieces of glass. **Over £100,000**

Seven-light lily lamp; c.1920; 20 in (51 cm) high. The flower-form shades are washed with gold lustre. **£6000-£10,000**

Favrile 'Jack-in-the-Pulpit' vase; c.1900; 15⅞ in (40.2 cm) high. The flower-form vase is made of iridescent glass. **£4000-£6000**

Vases and bowls

The variety and decorative nature of vases and bowls, combined with their practical uses, make them doubly appealing objects to collect.

IT IS OVER 2000 YEARS since the first glass vases and bowls were made, but most older items are so rare and expensive that they are virtually all museum pieces. Collectable pieces date from the last 300 years or so, and most of them follow the fashions seen in other glass of their time.

COLOURLESS GLASS

By the 18th century Bohemian and British glass-makers could at last equal – even surpass – the clear, colourless glass of the Venetians. Thick enough for deep cutting, heavy finger bowls and punch bowls were elaborately cut with diamond and triangle patterns. Such pieces can sell at auction for as much as £1000.

Thinner pieces, more suitable for engraving, were produced in Britain from 1745, and Jacobite emblems such as roses and oak leaves are typical. Bohemian glass-makers, whose products were less sparkling, always favoured engraving, and flowers, mythical figures and coats of arms are frequent subjects.

Flowers, leaves and especially ferns are also common on vases from the 1860s onward, with the Holyrood glassworks of Edinburgh a big producer. These fetch about £100-£700. Another style much in vogue at the end of the 19th century was deep engraving extended all over bowls and vases to give a carved effect. The articles were then polished all over, which gave a brilliant 'rock crystal' look. The British firms Thomas Webb and Stevens & Williams and the American firm of T.G. Hawkes excelled in these 'carved' pieces, which can change hands for £500 or more.

COLOURED GLASS

The opaque-white glass made in the 1760s to rival the very popular imported Chinese porcelain was produced in Bristol and Staffordshire, as well as in Italy, France and Bohemia. Lidded, pear-shaped vases and wide bowls enamelled and gilded with chinoiserie motifs sell today for more than £400.

Coloured glass known as 'Bristol' blue, but also made in London and Staffordshire, appeared from the mid-18th century. Early straight-sided finger bowls, perhaps with gilded decoration, sell for as little as £150.

The Victorians loved rich colour and showy decoration, and glass amply provided both. A particularly popular colour was ruby (and the paler variant known as cranberry) and this was made in Britain at Stourbridge

and elsewhere in the Midlands, and also in France. Frilly topped vases set on stands of looped clear glass are often seen in pairs or garniture sets of three or more – a single vase may cost £100 – and cased and flashed bowls and vases cut to show clear glass below a layer of red can often fetch £150. Large, similar, Edwardian bowls with stands were made as impressive centrepieces for tables. By this time, deep blue and red were both popular, with cutting showing the clear glass beneath.

Irish cut glass bowls and sweetmeat dishes; c.1800; largest 11¾ in (29.8 cm) high. The oval bowls are typical of the date, and their pressed glass feet are an early example of the technique that burgeoned in the 1820s.
Bowls: £800-£1200 each
Sweetmeats: £300-£500 the pair

Lead glass punchbowl with diamond-point engraving; c.1720; 7⅛ in (18.1 cm) high. Punchbowls were often seen on the 18thC table, especially in gentlemen's drinking clubs or at hunt breakfasts.
£3000-£5000

Many strikingly coloured 'art' glass bowls and vases in milky opaline glass date from the late 19th century. Mixtures of colours gave marble, onyx and agate effects, to which painting, gilding, cameo carving and clear glass trails were added. Thomas Webb of Stourbridge and James Powell of London were among the British makers, and the American Mount Washington Glass Works and New England Glass Company, both of Massachusetts, were also notable producers. A small vase of this kind can sell for as little as £40.

PRESSED GLASS

The American development of pressure moulding in the 1820s, quickly taken up in Britain, produced all manner of glassware in

Bohemian enamelled vases; c.1850; taller 15⅜ in (39 cm). Bohemian glass, exported to Europe and America in the 1840s, was often cold-painted by women at home.
Larger: £1800-£2500
Smaller: £800-£1200

French opaline vases; c.1850; largest 17¾ in (45 cm) high. Continental glass of this type tends to be more ornate than English examples.
Larger pair: £1500-£2000
Smaller pair: £800-£1200

intricately patterned iron moulds. These include many bowls, some decorated all over, others more discreetly, with fluting, basketwork, and dots and stippling that give a lacy look. Commemorative pieces – such as those marking Queen Victoria's various jubilees – can be picked up at markets and car boot sales for around £15, while coloured, marbled and opalescent pressed bowls and vases also go cheaply, fetching as little as £40.

Pressed glass from the 1920s and 30s, used for Art Deco designs, was radically different. British bowls, and to a lesser extent vases, were usually produced in the fashionable colours of amber, green and blue, while on the Continent, Czechoslovakian factories (in what used to be Bohemia) capitalised on the fashion for geometric shapes and cool colours, such as ice-blue and light emerald green. Prices of such British and Czechoslovakian pieces can start as low as £10.

DESIGNER GLASS

Work by named designers is generally more expensive than anonymous pieces. Among the most expensive of all are iridescent 'Favrile' vases designed in the late 19th century by Louis Tiffany (see p.219). Although these are beyond the reach of most collectors, similar pieces by other producers, such as Loetz, can be found at £200-£500.

Vases by the great French masters Lalique, Gallé and Daum (see pp.223 and 227), fetch huge prices at auction – sometimes into six figures. Glassware designed by Philip Webb in the 1860s for Whitefriars of London is the forerunner of British Art Nouveau glass, and one of his vases may go for £500-£800. The Spaniard Salvador Ysart designed for the Moncrieff Glassworks in Perth, Scotland, in the 1920s. In the 1930s, Keith Murray designed pieces for Stevens & Williams, and Graham Sutherland, Paul Nash and Dame Laura Knight for Stuart & Sons. Prices range widely from about £200 to £3000.

Modern studio glass – made by single artists or groups of two or three in their own workshops since the 1960s – is an area where collectors can acquire one-off bowls and vases at reasonable prices: perhaps £200 for a dolphin bowl by Malcolm Sutcliffe.

Cameo glass vase; c.1880; 3⅜ in (86 mm) high. Probably by Thomas Webb, this run-of-the-mill vase would have cost £2-£5 in its day, as opposed to £150-£250 for a unique, signed Webb piece by George or Thomas Woodall.
£1000-£1500

Davidson's 'Cloud' glass bowl (left); 1934; 12 in (30.5 cm) across. Orange was the last 'Cloud' colour introduced by the factory and is rare.
£100-£150

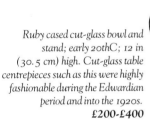

Ruby cased cut-glass bowl and stand; early 20thC; 12 in (30.5 cm) high. Cut-glass table centrepieces such as this were highly fashionable during the Edwardian period and into the 1920s.
£200-£400

Monart vase; c.1920; 10 in (25.4 cm) high. Characterised by swirling coloured enamels, Monart glass was the creation of the Spanish family of glass-makers, the Ysarts.
£1300-£1800

British 'Art' glass vase; c.1930; 10½ in (26.7 cm) high. James Powell & Sons were the makers of some of Britain's best 'art' glass, such as this piece.
£150-£200

Moulded glass celery vase; c.1935; 7¾ in (19.7 cm). Produced by Joblings of Sunderland, this vase is one of many items of coloured pressed glass fashionable at the time.
£20-£30

Vase with applied clear glass acanthus leaves by John Northwood for Stevens & Williams; c.1880; 4 in (10.1 cm) high. The satin finish was achieved by dipping the vase in acid.
£80-£100

Cameo glass

Examples of signed, handmade cameo glass command high prices, but less expensive mass-produced pieces are still very collectable.

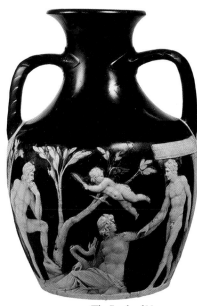

ROMAN MASTERPIECE *The Portland Vase, probably made in Rome between 25 BC and AD 25, is the most famous example of cameo glass. It was eventually brought to England and acquired by the Duchess of Portland. Josiah Wedgwood's 18thC copy in jasperware (see p. 182) was so accurate that when the real vase was smashed by a madman in 1845, the copy was used to help restore the original.*

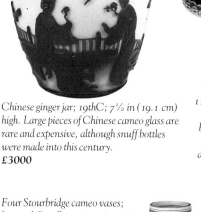

Chinese ginger jar; 19thC; 7½ in (19.1 cm) high. Large pieces of Chinese cameo glass are rare and expensive, although snuff bottles were made into this century.
£3000

George Woodall's 'Origin of Painting'; late 19thC; 9½ in (24.1 cm) high. The artist's skill is demonstrated in this scene where he even captures a shadow on a marble column.
£35,000-£45,000

Baccarat vase; mid-1860s; 11¾ in (29.8 cm) high. The thin layer of blue glass has been acid etched to leave the figurative scene, which has also been modelled with acid rather than by hand.
£800-£1000

Four Stourbridge cameo vases; late 19thC; tallest 7⅞ in (20 cm) high. The top layer of glass has been carved, revealing the colour below.
£500-£2000

Back and front of Webb & Sons three-layer bowl; c. 1890; 3½ in (89 mm) high. The middle (red) layer adds colour and depth to the leaves and flowers.
£300-£400

UNTIL ABOUT 1880 cameo glass, made with different coloured layers, was carved on a wheel and with hand tools to reveal shades of the lower layer. After that acid etching was often used, and today sandblasting may be employed.

The first cameo glass was made by the Romans. After the fall of Rome, cameo skills re-emerged in 9th and 10th-century Persia. The Chinese made cameo glass in the 18th and 19th centuries – in particular, beautiful snuff bottles that now sell for £400-£600. It was only after the Portland Vase – the most famous piece of cameo glass – was deliberately smashed in 1845 that English glass-makers began to imitate the technique.

John Northwood of Wordsley, near Stourbridge, was the first to copy the Portland Vase accurately, in 1876, establishing a fashion for cameo glass. The major Stourbridge glass-makers quickly geared up to produce it on a commercial scale, using copper-wheel carving and hydrofluoric acid etching for speed. Thomas Webb & Sons and Stevens & Williams became the leading British makers,

eventually producing pieces involving up to seven different-coloured layers of glass.

George and Thomas Woodall were Webb's most respected artists from the 1880s until 1911, and their work is much sought after. Signed pieces are extremely expensive, and a Thomas Webb vase of three colours by the Woodall brothers sells for £30,000-£40,000. However, later examples of unsigned Webb cameo glass can go at auction for some £800-£2000. Even mass-produced pieces are highly collectable – and are much more affordable than handmade, signed examples. A two-colour acid-etched Webb vase, for example, is likely to change hands for £800-£1500.

Baccarat and St Louis were the leading

French factories to produce cameo glass, but probably the most renowned were Emile Gallé and the Daum brothers (see opposite), whose pieces often fetch well into five figures. British 19th-century designs were usually Classically inspired, whereas French artists preferred a less restrained, freeform approach typical of the Art Nouveau style.

In 1916 the Orrefors factory in Sweden pioneered 'Graal' glass, in which cameo glass was reheated, covered with clear glass and blown out to create a soft, watery quality. Such pieces sell for £1000-£2000. Thomas Webb & Sons also revived cameo glass-making in the 1930s, and the technique is still being used by contemporary craftsmen.

Masters of cameo glass

Art Nouveau glass-makers Emile Gallé (1846-1901) and Antonin Daum (1864-1930) created superb art glass, and today signed examples of their work are valued very highly indeed.

PROBABLY THE MOST CREATIVE and influential glass-maker of the late 19th century, Emile Gallé was the son of a successful ceramics and glass decorator and designer. After an apprenticeship at the Meisenthal glass-works, he opened a glass workshop at his parents' home in Nancy, eastern France, and took over the family business in 1874.

The firm of Daum, also in Nancy, was established when Jean Daum, a lawyer, took over an existing glassworks in 1875. But it only began producing art glass in 1887 – after Gallé's initial success – by which time Jean's son Antonin was its creative force.

Early pieces produced by each factory were generally made of clear glass, enamelled in colours with traditional or patriotic motifs such as the cross of Lorraine or the region's emblem, the thistle. Gallé was a far more innovative craftsman, and although the Daum factory developed its own style, their work was perhaps never as refined as that of Gallé. Many of Daum's pieces have a characteristic mottled appearance, which was created by mixing powdered glass and various additives into the glass before it was smelted.

FERTILE SOURCE *Emile Gallé, pictured in 1892 by his friend Victor Prouvé, found inspiration in the world of nature.*

A keen botanist and strongly influenced by Japanese art, Gallé favoured naturalistic subjects such as flowers, insects and landscapes.

He is best known for his carved and etched cameo glass (see opposite). It was acid-etched to varying levels to create a relief image. A piece was often finished off by wheel-carving to give soft, fine detail to foliage or flower petals.

One of the most beautiful techniques used by both factories was *marqueterie-sur-verre*, in which preformed glass motifs were pressed into the piece while it was still hot. After cooling, the piece was enhanced by wheel-carving.

Major Gallé and Daum pieces are out of reach of most collectors, fetching well into five figures, but 'industrial' (mass-produced) items are much cheaper, starting at a few hundred pounds. Elegant shapes, strong colours and Art Nouveau motifs will, however, increase the value of a piece, as will applied decoration.

Gallé almost always signed his work; pieces produced by the factory between his death in 1904 and its closure in 1914 have a star next to the name. Daum's pieces are also marked and his signature always incorporates the cross of Lorraine. But good forgeries of both makers do exist, although many are the wrong weight and lack the fluidity of design of originals.

Gallé enamelled glass cup and cover (right); c.1890; 11 in (28 cm) high. The acid-etched sunflowers have applied cabochon centres.
£2000-£2500

Daum vase; 1900; 21 in (53.5 cm) high. Overlaid with green, brown and red, and then acid-etched, this vase is a fine example of mass-produced Daum.
£4000-£6000

Imitation Daum vase (above); 1980s; 11 in (28 cm) high. Although a forgery, it would fetch a fair price for its interest value and workmanship.
£500-£600

Gallé cameo glass landscape vase (left); c.1900; 18½ in (47 cm) high. This acid-etched vase has little or no hand finishing and so, despite being attractive, is not particularly valuable.
£3000-£4000

Daum glass vase (left); c.1900; 10½ in (26.7 cm) high. The body of this vase has been given a multicoloured glass 'skin', acid-etched and decorated with vines and a pair of applied snails.
£7000-£8000

Table glass

Useful, decorative, easy to store and not prohibitively expensive, small pieces of table glass are an ideal field for the new collector.

FORMAL MEALS were important social occasions in the life of well-to-do families of the 18th and 19th centuries, and every well-equipped household had many decorative yet functional items of glassware to adorn the table. From glass salvers and sweetmeat dishes to celery glasses and epergnes, most are now highly collectable.

SALVERS AND SWEETMEAT DISHES

The first raised glass platters for displaying food at the table were the work of 17th-century Venetian glass makers. By the early 18th century, glass salvers had become popular in Britain and they remained in vogue for some 200 years. Eighteenth-century British salvers have a raised border made by folding the glass down at the edge and then turning it up again. This procedure leaves a small lip below the surface as well as above, whereas most 19th-century examples have only a turned-up edge.

Salvers were made in a range of sizes – from 3 to 13 in (7.5-33 cm) in diameter – so that they could be stacked in a grand pyramid-shaped display. Various stem designs were made, the commonest being an eight-sided style known as the Silesian stem. Some, however, followed changing wine-glass styles with baluster, opaque twist or air twist stems. Salvers are relatively inexpensive today: £150-£350 should buy an early hand-made example, just £2-£35 a later mass-produced piece (often called a comport or cake stand).

Sweetmeat glasses were stemmed vessels used for the small sweet items that accompanied the dessert, such as sugared almonds and candied peel. The double-ogee bowl was most popular – usually with moulded or cut decoration and a Silesian stem; it now goes for £350-£550. Bowls with stems in contemporary wine-glass styles tend to be worth more. One distinctive type of bowl has a toothed edge – known as a 'dentil' rim – often combined with a short, plain or opaque twist, stem and a foot with radiating grooves.

A system of glass taxes meant that glass thick enough for deep cutting was particularly expensive. Eighteenth-century cutting therefore tends to be rather flat and shallow on thinner glass. In the Regency period, decorative cutting was made deeper and more detailed, with the use of flat panels, bands of diamonds and fine, close lines.

JELLY AND CUSTARD GLASSES

Special serving glasses for creams, custards, jellies and other set desserts have been made since the 17th century. Most 17th and 18th-century jelly glasses are funnel or narrow-bell shaped, and 3½-5 in (9-13 cm) high. A variation intended for syllabub has a wider top section, or 'pantop', to hold a layer of whipped cream. Jelly and syllabub glasses vary widely in value from around £30 up to £500, but most

Glass salver; c.1760; 11 in (28 cm) across. Used to display food, this raised salver, or tazza, has a wide flat top with characteristic 18thC turned gallery or rim and a hollow stem.
£180-£280

Sweetmeat dish; mid-18thC; 7 in (17.8 cm) high. This has a typical double-ogee bowl with domed foot to match, and elaborate cut decoration on bowl, stem and foot.
£300-£450

Syllabub glass with 'pantop' bowl (left), c.1750, 4 in (10.1 cm) high; and ribbed bell-shaped jelly glass (right); c.1800. Jelly glasses offer a range of styles to collect; the bell shape first appeared c.1710.
Left: £60-£90; right: £35-£55

Cut-glass custard glasses; early 19thC; top 2¾ in (70 mm) high. These early glasses tend to be more solid than later Victorian and Edwardian glasses. Always check for cracks at the handle base.
Top: £15-£20
Bottom: £25-£45

JUST DESSERTS *Sweet puddings served in small 'jelly' glasses tempt the senses in Philippe Mercier's early 18th-century painting. At this time, glass was a luxury affordable only by the well-off.*

Cruet set; mounts hallmarked 1849-50; c.6 in (15 cm) high. This set is a marriage; the simple papier-mâché and brass stand is earlier than the silver-mounted cut-glass cruets.
£250-£300

Celery glass; c.1850; 10 in (25.4 cm) high. As the name implies, this was used for serving sticks of celery. Although 19thC celery glasses can be found in cut glass, as here, and in engraved and etched glass, most are in pressed glass.
£150-£200

Sugar sifter in cranberry glass with silver-plated top; c. 1900; 5 in (12.7 cm) high. The cranberry colour was extremely popular between 1880 and 1920, and was used for every type of table glass.
£30-£40

Lidded jam pot with enamelled decoration; marked Stuart England; c. 1930; 4 in (10.1 cm) high. Until the mid-19thC jam pots were usually of cut glass and found only in wealthy homes; a Regency pot in this style would fetch almost ten times as much.
£20-£30

'Vaseline' glass epergne; c.1890; 21 in (53.5 cm) high. This is a simple epergne for holding flowers. The branches are easily broken, so check that all the parts match.
£250-£350

Knife rest with intaglio decoration; probably French; c.1930; 2¾ in (70 mm) wide. Knife rests went out of fashion in Britain after the First World War, but are used in France.
£2-£3; pair: £6-£10

pieces are moderately priced and the range of styles gives ample scope for the collector.

The 1830s saw the introduction of shorter cups, usually maintaining Regency cutting styles, and with a single handle. Initially for punch, by the 1880s they were being sold as custard glasses. Regency examples now fetch £30-£45, Edwardian ones £8-£12. Jelly and custard glasses from the 1880s on tend to be more thinly blown, with fern-leaf engraving or acid-etched decoration.

A particular type of dish was developed for serving posset (a hot spicy milk drink curdled with wine or ale). Posset cups from the 17th and early 18th centuries generally have a spout and two handles, occasionally in a double-loop or 'B' handle design, and are worth £500-£1000. If you find one with a single 'B' handle, check carefully to make sure it did not originally have two.

During the 18th century, first spouts and then handles were gradually left off. At the same time, the variety of styles of bowl and decoration increased. As with sweetmeat glasses, flat, shallow cutting is usually a sign of an 18th-century piece, while moulded vertical ribs, with or without finely cut notches, indicates a 19th-century date.

OTHER TABLEWARES

Among the variety of table glass that can be found from the early 19th century are Regency cut-glass decanters, celery vases and water jugs – which can be bought for £80-£250 – and cut-glass salt cellars which go for £40-£80. Coloured glass became popular for cream jugs, sugar bowls and decanters and is now very collectable. A small, plain blue decanter may cost £80, a matching set of decanters with gilt labels for Brandy, Rum and Hollands (gin) £800-£900, while a large elaborate coloured decanter may make £1500.

In the late 19th century, new manufacturing techniques made glassware available to a much wider market. With press moulding all these items could be made more cheaply – sometimes to imitate cut glass. Prices start at £1-£2 for simple objects such as knife rests, rising to £100 or more for moulded and coloured bowls by particular makers.

The Victorians also introduced decorative table items such as epergnes and posy troughs for holding flowers. Prices today range from about £120 for a simple clear-glass epergne to around £500 for an elaborate coloured one with as many as six branches. Press-moulded posy troughs often came in a mixture of curved and straight sections so that they could be assembled in different patterns. Plain single sections can be found for £5-£10 each, but a patterned four-section set could cost £250.

Pressed glass

With the advent of mass production, decorative glassware could be seen on almost every table – and it now provides striking items for modern collectors on a budget.

Opaque yellow bowl;
c.1880; 6½ in (16.5 cm) diameter. This is one of the rare 'aesthetic' colours, named after the Aesthetic movement in vogue in the 1880s. The shape was later issued in carnival glass.
£500; in carnival glass: £30-£100

Opalescent
swan bowl; 1885;
5¼ in (13.3 cm) high.
This piece was made in Manchester, but similar swans were made by other factories in Britain and the United States. Examples in pink-grey glass command a premium price.
£30-£150

Opaque blue posy vase; c. 1885-1910; 3¼ (82 mm) high. Nursery designs – including Little Bo-Peep – were a common feature of such wares made by Sowerby at Gateshead.
£35-£200

Locomotive
candy container;
c. 1890-1914; 4 in (10.1 cm) long. Novelty packaging objects were an American speciality. Other candy containers include six-shooters and kitchen stove shapes.
£35-£60

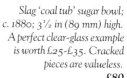

'Grape and Cable' pattern ivory glass bonbon dish; c.1910; 7½ in (19 cm) across. The mark of the Northwood Glass Company, West Virginia, raises the value of this dish.
£40

Slag 'coal tub' sugar bowl; c. 1880; 3½ in (89 mm) high. A perfect clear-glass example is worth £25-£35. Cracked pieces are valueless.
£80

T HE MACHINE AGE affected the glass industry, as it did almost every other; the invention of mechanical press-moulding changed glass-making from an ancient handcraft to a cheap, fast, factory process. The technique of pressing soft, hot glass into patterned iron moulds was developed in the United States during the 1820s.

The first pressed-glass objects were simple shapes, such as open salts and small cup plates for the tea table. They were often in clear glass, but opaque milk glass and solid pale blue were also used. Pieces often featured an elaborate pattern set against a stippled background that camouflaged imperfections. As demand grew, so did the range of shapes.

EARLY PIECES IN EUROPE

The technology reached Europe in the 1830s. Early European pieces tend to be heavy with deep, crisp patterning and strong vertical lines typical of the Gothic Revival. Jugs, goblets and caskets were made in black or opaque red glass and fetch about £50, or up to £500 for elaborate caskets. The style was superseded in the 1840s by the curvaceous scrolling of the Rococo Revival. Cream jugs and sugar dishes in such a style fetch around £30, while large vases can cost up to £100.

The main early producers in Europe were France and Bohemia. Pressed glass was not widely made in Britain until the repeal of the glass tax based on weight, in 1845.

Technical advances in mould-making later in the century made it possible to create more complicated shapes. A bewildering variety of domestic and novelty wares were produced by companies throughout Britain, Europe and the United States. Most colour recipes were used, to make marbled slag, 'porcelain' and 'creamware'. Other finishes include milky opalescent edges and highlighting. Such pieces, particularly those made in England at the Sowerby factory in Gateshead, today sell for hundreds of pounds.

Fancy pieces in unusual colours and shapes are keenly collected, and can fetch as little as £5 or as much as £1500. Examples bearing factory marks – or those that can be identified from company catalogues – are more valuable than unidentifiable pieces.

As the 19th century ended, the industry was in crisis. Tastes were changing and makers could not afford the new moulds that would have maintained the momentum of the market. American factories survived by amalgamating. They offered technically advanced, thin glass with detailed 'cut' designs, often embellished with 'gold' and 'silver' trim and ruby or amber staining. Today such pieces are generally affordable, fetching £10-£30. Unable to compete with the American companies, many European factories closed and their moulds were destroyed.

During the 1920s, totally mechanised continuous production of pressed glass became possible. Ruby and pale acid-pink pressed glass came to the fore, and innovative French designer René Lalique produced opalescent and coloured pressed glassware (see opposite).

Dressing-table sets of the 1920s and 30s, decorated with sunray patterns or nymph-like figures, are very popular with collectors. Odd items cost around £5, and a whole dressing-table set up to £100. An attractive flower bowl of the same period will fetch up to £50.

A sculptor in glass

Darling of the rich and stylish even in his student days, celebrated French jewellery designer René Lalique (1860-1945) brought a new appreciation of form to glass-making.

FATHER-FIGURE *This portrait of the jeweller and glass artist René Lalique was painted in 1931 by his daughter Suzanne Lalique.*

AROUND 1907, the Paris perfumier François Coty commissioned the leading Art Nouveau jeweller of the day to design a series of paper labels for his glass perfume bottles. Excited by the challenge, the jeweller – René Lalique – presented Coty not only with labels, but with brand new bottle and stopper designs too. Thus began one of the most illustrious careers in the history of glass.

By 1910, Lalique had turned his attention exclusively to glass design and bought his own glassworks at Combs-la-Ville, just outside Paris. Eight years later he acquired a second, larger factory at Wingen-sur-Moder, in Alsace, to cope with the increasing demand. For the next 31 years Lalique designed and produced a huge variety of frosted, opalescent and clear-glass objects, including bottles, clocks, vases and tablewares, and it is these pieces that most interest collectors.

Lalique's initial venture into glass – the perfume bottle – remained an important part of his business. All his styles are now highly collectable, and the rarest sell for over £20,000. However, the original Coty bottles, quite simply designed in panel form but with decorative stoppers, are worth around £100.

Most other pieces of pre-1945 Lalique can be found for under about £800, although scarcer items such as car mascots, figurines and coloured vases fetch very much higher prices. Rare pieces, such as one-off *cire perdue* (lost wax) moulded vases, can fetch around £50,000.

After Lalique's death in 1945, his factories continued to produce fine glassware, but using different techniques. In particular, the pale blue milky effect, or opalescence, which became almost synonymous with Lalique glass before 1945, was discontinued. Postwar Lalique glass is also much 'whiter' than earlier pieces, which have a greyish hue by comparison. Items from 1945-50 are beginning to be collected, but later pieces are not considered desirable.

Identifying Lalique glass can be confusing, as at least 16 different marks were used even during René Lalique's own lifetime. Some were engraved or etched, others moulded and stencilled. Pre-1945 glass almost always has an 'R' before the Lalique signature; the 'R' was dropped after his death.

Always examine any piece carefully for repairs. These can be difficult to detect, but reduce the value enormously. Some modern Czechoslovakian vases have a forged Lalique signature engraved on the base.

Worth display bottle; 1952; 11½ in (29.2 cm) high. This version of the original 1930s 'Je Reviens' scent bottle has a cap by Lalique's son Marc.
£120-£180

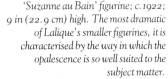

'Suzanne au Bain' figurine; c.1922; 9 in (22.9 cm) high. The most dramatic of Lalique's smaller figurines, it is characterised by the way in which the opalescence is so well suited to the subject matter.
£7000-£9000

Cire perdue vase; c.1920; 6¼ in (15.9 cm) high. A rare Lalique example of lost-wax moulding.
£25,000-£35,000

Serpent vase; c.1924; 10¼ in (26 cm) high. This sculptural dark amber glass vase illustrates Lalique's genius at combining form with function.
£6000-£7000

Grey-coloured clock; c.1925; 14¾ in (37.5 cm) high. The figures represent Night and Day. The clock was also produced in several other colours.
c.£30,000

Carnival glass

Once mistakenly regarded as funfair kitsch, carnival glass – charged with brilliant colour and a rich lustre – is now a worthy collectable.

BY 1905 ART NOUVEAU was all the rage. Expensive 'art' glass was in vogue, and American factories were soon mass producing affordable substitutes sold under exotic names such as Etruscan and Venetian. By spraying metallic salt solutions onto still hot moulded pieces, they could imitate the brilliant peacock-tail sheen and rich lustre of handmade Tiffany 'Favrile' glass (see p. 219).

It was said that once the maid could afford to buy iridescent glass the mistress promptly lost interest in it, and the glass of Tiffany and his followers fell out of fashion in the 1920s. In the 50s a re-evaluation of the style began. Collectors and dealers were puzzled by the existence of so many moulded items with an iridescent finish. Their true history forgotten,

the mass-produced pieces were incorrectly labelled 'carnival glass' as they were assumed to have been used as prizes in funfairs. They are now collected worldwide and there is an active collectors' society in London.

The earliest pieces, sold by the Dugan Glass Co (renamed Diamond in 1913) in 1905, are opalescent, milky-edged forms with a simple golden lustre. Their curvaceous vase shapes hint at the soft organic lines of Art Nouveau. Pressed dishes with distinctive patterns and a rich iridescent finish were also mass-produced by the Fenton Art Glass Co from 1908. The main producers were all based in the Ohio valley and also included Northwood Glass Co (the only one to mark all its glass, usually with an underlined 'N' in a circle) and Imperial Glass Co. Today only Fenton survives.

The prime period of production lasted until 1918. The factories often used one another's designs. Naturalistic leaf, fruit, flower and peacock motifs are typical, as are mythical

creatures such as dragons; the most popula[r] glass colours are clear, blue, purple and green. Dark colours generally fetch higher price[s] than light ones, with the colour known a[s] 'golden marigold' being much the cheapest, and there is a premium on items with [a] particularly fine lustre. Condition is als[o] important, and cracked pieces are valueless.

OUTSIDE NORTH AMERICA

Carnival glass was exported from 1909, but b[y] 1925 production had slumped in the Unite[d] States. Factories in Europe, Australia an[d] South America produced their own iridescen[t] pressed glassware from the 1920s until 1939. In Britain, Sowerby's of Gateshead used ol[d] moulds and plagiarised patterns to produce [a] variety of pieces with dark or golden lustres. I[n] Germany, Brockwitz specialised in extensiv[e] matching suites of tableware in geometric intaglio (incised) designs.

A revival of carnival glass productio[n] began in the United States in the late 1960s, often using old moulds. A factory in Portuga[l] has recently reproduced some Northwoo[d] dishes, but these are relatively easy to distin[-] guish as they have a harsh mirror-like lustr[e] and a crudely forged Northwood mark.

'Peacocks' dish; c. 1912; 9 in (22.9 cm) wide. This piece was made by Northwood, but beware of Portuguese fakes with a harder, glossier finish.
£80-£100

'Persian Medallion' plate; c. 1911; 10⅝ in (27 cm) across. This richly textured design was also used on comports, bowls and bonbon dishes. Any damage reduces the value considerably.
£100-£200
Bowl: £15-£50

Sweet-pea vases; c. 1915; taller 10½ in (26.7 cm) high. The fine rib vase is in Fenton's sought-after 'Celeste Blue', the 'Ripple' vase by Imperial Glass Co.
Left: £140-£160; right: £20-£30

Hatpin holder; 1910-15; 6¾ in (17.1 cm) high. This is in the popular 'Grape and Cable' pattern and was once part of a dressing-table set. Lighter colours are cheaper.
£75-£200

Moulded pitcher and tumbler (below); c. 1912; pitcher 8¾ in (22.2 cm) high. These are in Fenton's popular 'Orange Tree' design.
Tumbler: £25-£50; jug: £100-£400

Covered 'Hen' butterdish; 1920s; 7½ in (19 cm) long. This Sowerby piece used moulds from France. Golden lustre, plain pink or green versions fetch less.
£85-£100

Paperweights

Where a stone or an inkwell once sufficed, paperweights in the 19th century became glass works of art.

DECORATIVE PAPERWEIGHTS were first made of semiprecious stones, silver, bronze or ormolu. The use of glass began in the 19th century and reached a high point in France, although other countries also produced some fine work, as France, Britain and the United States still do.

Many of the most decorative paperweights incorporate a 'millefiori' design of coloured glass canes (see p.450), such as 'crown' (with radiating twisted ribbons), 'mushroom', 'swirl' or 'scrambled' (a random pattern). The most sought after and expensive weights today use animal or plant motifs. The design is covered in clear glass to enclose and magnify the pattern, and sometimes overlaid again in one or more colours. Windows might be cut in the overlay to reveal the pattern, or a star may be cut into the base.

Most paperweights measure between 2½ and 3⅛ in (63 and 80 mm) across, but there are miniatures less than 2 in (51 mm) across. Chips and scratches occur very easily. Such marks can be removed by grinding and polishing, but this greatly reduces the value.

The golden era of French paperweight making was from about 1845 to 1880. The very best came from the Baccarat, St Louis and Clichy factories. Identifying the maker is not usually difficult. Some millefiori weights include canes with the manufacturer's initials, so others can be attributed by comparison. Some are signed and dated, and fetch comparatively higher prices.

Many maker's pieces include characteristic canes – for example, the pink and green 'Clichy rose', and the fine arrowheads and silhouetted human and animal figures of Baccarat and St Louis. Clichy specialised in mushroom weights, overlays and swirls. Baccarat produced flower, fruit and vegetable weights, while St Louis made a cross pattern and used a salmon-pink colour. Most mid-19th-century weights from these factories sell at auction for anything from £200 to £1000.

Paperweights were also made in other French centres, in Bohemia (later part of Czechoslovakia) and in Venice, but none matched the standard of the 'top three'. George Bacchus of Birmingham and Whitefriars of London made weights, but their canes are large and crude by comparison. Prices for these makers are usually in the low hundreds.

Clichy dark blue overlay weight (below); c.1850; 3⅛ in (80 mm). Windows reveal a concentric millefiori mushroom.
£2500-£3000

Pantin miniature pear weight; c.1850; 1⅝ in (41 mm). Its clear glass holds a russet pear.
£600-£800

St Louis crown weight (above); c.1850; 2 in (51 mm). The design is of twisted latticino canes.
£600-£900

Baccarat snake weight (above); c.1850; 3⅛ in (80 mm). The decoration in 'lampwork' weights like this was moulded with a blowlamp.
£4000-£5000

Clichy weight (below); c.1850; 2⅛ in (54 mm). It has a concentric millefiori design.
£600-£800

Bohemian weight (above); late 19thC; 3⅛ in (80 mm). It holds five stylised windmills on a speckled ground.
£100-£150

Clichy swirl weight; c.1850; 3⅛ in (80 mm). The blue and white spirals centre on a large turquoise and white cane.
£800-£1200

St Louis pompom and pansy weight; c.1850; 2¾ in (70 mm). The flowers rest on a double spiral latticino ground.
£2000-£2500

St Louis miniature scrambled weight; c.1850; 1¾ in (44 mm). One of the most frequently found weights, this example incorporates a random pattern of millefiori canes.
£100-£150

Friggers

Humour, variety and joy in his skill show in the glassmaker's novelty pieces, made to please only himself.

TRUE FRIGGERS, with the occasional exception, have no useful purpose. They are one-off curiosities, made by glass-makers in their spare time to relieve the humdrum work of producing standard commercial articles over and over again.

They were made in Britain from the 18th century, but most of those found today date from the 19th and early 20th centuries. The commonest shapes are walking sticks, rolling pins, trumpets and hats. But almost anything may be depicted, including bellows, balls and animals – most often pigs and swans.

Friggers are often described as products of the Nailsea glassworks near Bristol, and no doubt many were made there. But in fact they were made everywhere, and since few bear any mark it is difficult to attribute them to a source. They are also difficult to date: swans and pigs are still occasionally made by glass-makers in the Stourbridge district and are virtually identical to older items.

Some friggers were blown as gifts and some as souvenirs for exhibitions. Others were made as proof of the glassmaker's skill, and would be carried in one of the processions that occurred in all Britain's glassmaking districts in the 18th and 19th centuries.

Although most friggers were blown and shaped from the furnace, others were created by lampwork – shaping glass rods over a flame. Major glassworks had a resident lampworker for small pieces, and he might produce friggers, but it was more often travelling craftsmen who used the lamp. Sailing ships were the most popular subject, followed closely by birds of paradise in fountain settings; such pieces sell today for £150-£600.

By the late 19th and early 20th centuries, sweets for children were being sold in pressed glass friggers; collectors can pick these up for as little as £20-£50. Various unusual objects, such as smoothers, flycatchers, cucumber straighteners and grape ripeners, are sometimes bracketed with friggers. But although obsolete, these were once for use and are therefore disqualified as true friggers.

Friggers make good collectors' items, as they are both varied and attractive. You can begin a collection quite cheaply: simple items sell for as little as £5-£20. More unusual or complicated pieces range from £75 to £150, while specialists will pay up to £600 for an intricate scene such as a rigged ship with crew or a foxhunting scene with hounds.

Stag hunt; early 19thC; 7¼ in (18.4 cm) wide. The mirror panels inside the case enhance the impression of distance. This piece is valuable because it is signed.
£300-£450

Glass ashtray; c. 1930; 8 in (20.3 cm) high. Although this piece could be used, the exuberant palm tree places it in the category of a frigger.
£100-£150

Assorted glass canes; 19thC; longest 38 in (96.5 cm). Glass walking sticks and crooks were said to be good luck charms.
£60-£200

Stourbridge glass Jacob's ladder; late 19thC; 11½ in (29.2 cm) high. The spiral ladders were made by winding a thread of glass along the pincers used by the glassmaker.
£80-£100

Stourbridge bellows; late 19thC; 13 in (33 cm) long. Skills perfected on friggers, such as this trailed and pincered decoration, found use in mainstream production.
£150-£200

Spun glass birds of paradise; late 19thC; 9 in (22.9 cm) high. These ornamental pieces were made by lampworkers. The tails of the birds are formed of spun glass filaments.
£100-£200

Glass pig; c. 1908; 2 in (51 mm) long. This example, with its original box, was made by Thomas Webb & Sons for the Franco-British Exhibition held in London.
£10-£80

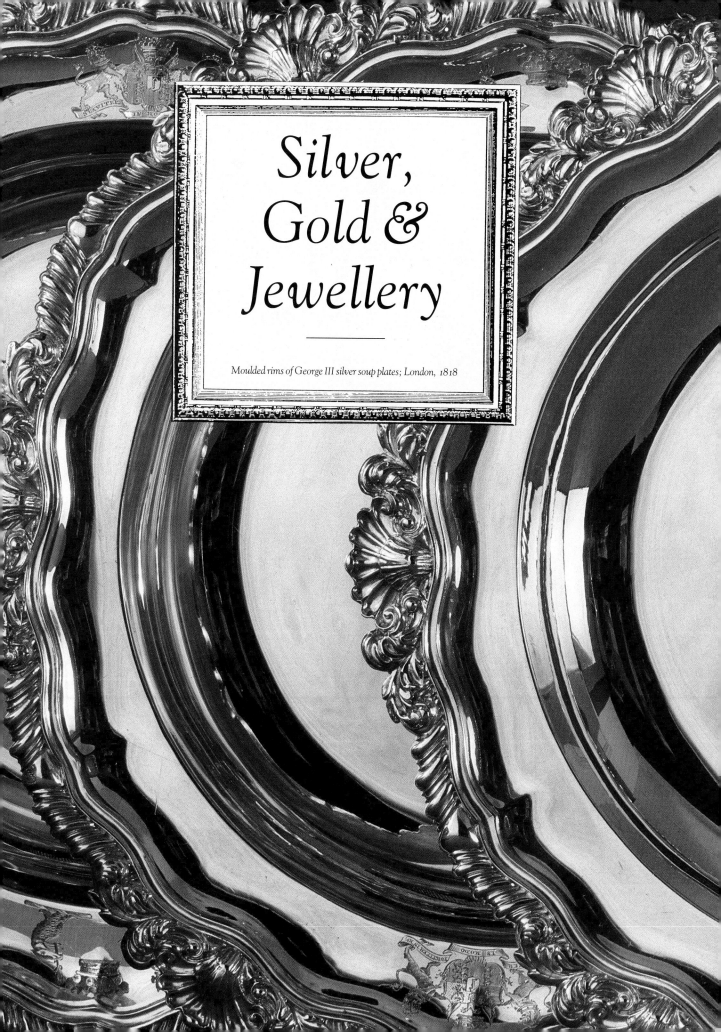

Silver,
Gold &
Jewellery

Moulded rims of George III silver soup plates; London, 1818

Collecting silver

Always glamorous, silverware can offer superb craftsmanship at what many consider to be a historically bargain price.

EVER SINCE IT WAS DISCOVERED, silver – like gold – has been converted into gleaming artefacts of great opulence and beauty. Such symbols of power and wealth are collected for their superb craftsmanship, but smaller, less ornate pieces also have a unique attraction. This is in part because silver has long been a precious metal. Today silver bullion is cheaper than ever in real terms, but nobody knows whether or for how long this will continue.

The intrinsic value of the metal has had one unfortunate result: silver objects have long been regarded as recyclable, and thousands of pieces have been lost over the centuries, melted down to finance wars, to cover up thefts or simply to make something more fashionable. The tradition of valuing items for their weight of metal is brought vividly to life by many old items, which have scratched figures underneath. These were often added by pawnbrokers as an article was used to raise money time and again. Even today, auction catalogues quote the weight of pieces, and the value of silver objects is often expressed in such terms – £30-£40 per ounce at auction for late 18th-century coffee pots, for example – although such prices do also reflect desirability. (Weights always refer to Troy measure; see p.523.)

Silver has long been alloyed with small amounts of base metal – usually copper – to make it tougher and more malleable (see opposite), but its value was also a temptation to defraud the consumer. Philip Stubbes, in 1408, complained of the widespread use of 'drossie rubbage and refuse metall' by unscrupulous silversmiths. Early attempts to protect consumers led to a system of testing and stamping items with a set of marks – hallmarks – as early as the 14th century. The system is still in use, and every silver article over ½ oz (15.5 g) must be submitted for assay and marking (see p.479). But hallmarks can be forged or transposed, and it may take considerable detective work to establish a piece's authenticity (see p.238).

Silver's ability to withstand day-to-day use means that collectors can still enjoy an enormous range of

PRIZE ITEM *One of a pair of George IV silver-gilt wine coolers, 9¼ in (23.5 cm) high, made in 1825 by Paul Storr. He is widely regarded as the greatest silversmith of his era, and the pair would fetch £35,000-£45,000.*

objects. Hand-worked items from the early 18th century on are plentiful, although Victorian silversmiths 'improved' many of these – especially the plainer ones – with chased decoration. The market is overflowing with Victorian silver, when the expanding middle classes took to showing off their new-found wealth. This fashion was fuelled by the introduction of cheaper lookalikes made of Old Sheffield plate and later electroplate, and at the same time the cost and quality of even solid silver fell dramatically with the introduction of mass-production techniques such as die-stamping and minimal hand-finishing.

It is almost impossible to predict which markets or objects will prove to be good investments for the future. Prices for most 18th and 19th-century silver have at best kept pace with inflation over the past 20 years, and Georgian silver is cheaper now in real terms than in the 1940s and 50s. At the same time, pieces by the great masters such as Paul de Lamerie and Paul Storr have continued to set records. Some see good-quality middle-range silver as a good area to collect, but remember that scrap now fetches only about £2 per ounce as against £20 15 years ago, so bullion value counts for less than it used to.

LUCKY FIND *The 1987 gales turned up three 17thC German tankards (two shown) in the roots of a fallen tree, wrapped in a leather bag. Two years later, they sold at auction for a total of £21,153.*

BUDGET BUY *Individual spoons make a good starting point for an inexpensive collection. The fiddle and thread pattern tablespoon of 1832 would cost £20-£30, the 'berry' spoons £80-£100 a pair.*

FORGERY *This clumsy 'cheese scoop' was originally an 1805 soup ladle. The silversmith who reshaped it took care not to harm the hallmarks, but it is illegal to sell a silver item such as this whose function has been altered.*

Understanding silver and plate

The most versatile and widely available of precious metals, silver combines brilliance with strength and the ability to be intricately worked by a variety of techniques to create objects of great beauty.

PURE SILVER is too soft to be made into articles that must withstand daily wear and tear, so it is alloyed (blended) with a base metal – usually copper – to make it tougher and more malleable. Most antique and modern silver in Britain is of sterling standard, which contains 92.5 per cent pure silver to 7.5 per cent base metal. From 1697 to 1720, a higher proportion of silver – 95.8 per cent – had to be used. This is now known as Britannia standard silver because the standard mark on such pieces – one of the hallmarks (see p.479) – is the figure of Britannia. The purity of Britannia silver means that it is slightly whiter and softer than sterling silver, usually showing more wear. After 1720, Britannia standard became optional and the slightly less pure sterling silver was once again

the legal minimum that silversmiths could use. (Alloys with less silver may only be called 'white metal' or 'silver-coloured metal'.)

There was always a demand for articles with the appearance of real silver but at lower cost. The answer was to make the silver only skin-deep – a thin coating on an article made mainly of base metal. The earliest successful solution was fused or Old Sheffield plate – copper sheet coated on one or both sides by sterling silver – which could be worked and decorated by most methods used for solid sheet silver (see below).

In the mid-19th century, fused plate was eclipsed by electroplating – the use of an electric current to deposit a thin coating of pure silver on an article prefabricated from base metal. This was much easier and more versatile than working with Old Sheffield plate – it could encompass casting as well as sheet-metal working – and the silver could be even thinner and therefore cheaper.

TRADITIONAL CRAFTS *This engraving of a mid-18thC silversmith's workshop shows craftsmen using processes still employed today. The ingots being made in the foreground were then hammered into sheet metal and shaped around a wooden form.*

Forming silver articles

Refined and molten sterling silver could either be cast directly into the required shape or cast into ingots which were hammered or rolled to make sheets of uniform thickness. These were then shaped or fabricated. (Much sheet silver was made by hammering well into the 19th century, in spite of the first rolling mills being built in the late 17th.)

CASTING

The most common use of casting has been for small parts, such as handles, feet, spouts and decorative swags, which were then soldered onto the body of an article made from sheet silver. But entirely cast pieces include some candlesticks, cups, salt cellars, and large, elaborate objects such as epergnes and sculptural candelabra. Larger pieces may have been cast in two or more parts which were then soldered together.

Casting could produce multiple copies from a single master or model of wood, plaster or metal. The usual method was sand-casting using a two-part mould, but for some complex objects the lost-wax process might be used.

CAST CANDELABRUM *This elaborate piece is extremely heavy, like most cast items. The purity and temperature of the molten metal had to be just right or the result might be brittle or full of bubbles.*

CAST COPY *Casting could easily be used to produce exact copies of existing pieces – as with this mid-18thC candlestick. Faint traces of the original's hallmarks can be seen on the underside of the*

candlestick (above; at the base of the shell motifs), while the copy's own hallmark – the crisp harp mark of Dublin – is on the outside of the base (left).

RAISING AND FABRICATING; FINISHING TOUCHES

Many silver vessels were 'raised' into shape from a sheet of flat metal by hammering. The metal was held over a 'raising stake' – which could vary from a simple wooden post to an anvil-like support with variously shaped heads – and the sides gradually hammered to the desired form. This prolonged hammering would make the metal brittle, however, and the silver had to be annealed from time to time as it was worked – heated to dull red heat, then quenched in cold water – to make it malleable again.

For simple, tall shapes such as a conical or octagonal teapot, the silver might be bent and soldered to form a cylinder before final shaping, or soldered together from precut pieces of silver. A quicker process for circular vessels, introduced in the late 18th century, is known as spinning. The sheet silver was forced gradually into the required shape against a wooden form, called a chuck, while the two rotated slowly in a lathe.

After the shaping process, some finishing stages were needed to remove blemishes and produce a gleaming surface. The silver might be 'pickled' in acid to remove any dark 'fire' marks caused by traces of copper oxidising just beneath the surface. Dents and scratches might be removed by filing and buffing, or on a plain piece ironed out with a smooth-headed 'planishing' hammer. Finally the metal would be burnished, often with a mixture of ground pumice stone, soft red sand and oil, or sometimes with jeweller's rouge – a form of polishing powder.

RAISED VESSELS *These two late 17thC cups were shaped by hammering sheet silver by hand around a wooden stake – in two parts, later joined, for the left-hand stem cup. The process needed great care to prevent the silver splitting.*

FABRICATED COFFEE POTS *These mid-18thC pots were constructed by cutting and shaping flat sheet silver around a wooden stake and then joining the edges with solder. It may be possible to detect the seam – usually in line with the handle.*

Decorating silver

A silver article may rely for its appeal on elegance of form and light-reflecting angles, or any of a wide range of techniques may have been used to create surface decoration. This may have been applied in the form of cast motifs soldered on, it may rely on designs impressed upon the surface by various techniques, or may simply alter the colour or texture of the surface.

SURFACE DECORATION

Pure surface techniques include acid-etching to create a matt effect, and gilding (coating with a thin layer of gold). Not only is gilding decorative, but it also gives a non-tarnishing finish that is unaffected by salt, acid, sulphur or other chemicals that occur in food and drink. When just part of an article has been gilded – the inside of a cream jug or spoon, for example, or raised parts of a decorative design – it is said to be 'parcel' gilt.

The original gilding method was mercury or fire gilding; an amalgam (soft alloy) of mercury and gold was applied to the piece, which was then heated in a furnace. This produced a mellow, 'old gold' colour, but the mercury fumes created during firing were poisonous, and the process was replaced by electrogilding – a form of electroplating – in the late 1850s. Electrogilt articles tend to look brassier than mercury-gilt pieces.

SILVER-GILT *Many articles for the table, such as this naturalistic sugar bowl, cream jug and cream ladle (left), were gilded – either all over, as here, or partially – to prevent tarnishing by fruit acids and other chemicals in food, as well as to enhance the appearance.*

ACID ETCHING *The action of hydrofluoric acid was responsible for the pattern on the rim of this c. 1890 Tiffany basket (below). Other parts were protected from the acid's corrosive action by a wax coating.*

PARCEL GILDING *The rather brassy appearance of this parcel-gilt dish is the product of electrogilding; mercury gilding would give a warmer tone. The parts not to be gilded were coated with wax before the piece was put in the electrogilding bath.*

CHASING

The highly skilled and time-consuming techniques of chasing are found on both sheet and cast silver. On sheet metal, the design was impressed onto the surface and so shows in reverse on the back or inner surface. Cast silver was chased with fine details. Chasing embraced several related techniques, including embossing and repoussé work, but in each case no metal was removed. Instead the silver was 'chased' or moved around.

The article was held on a bed of pitch which was yielding enough to work on, but firm enough to hold the piece steady. The chasing was carried out by tapping various sizes and shapes of punching tools with a hammer. The simplest form is flat-chasing – shallow working to produce a design in low relief by punching back the background. It is often found on Old Sheffield plate because, unlike engraving (see below), it did not cut through the silver to the copper core. Punching the inner surface of a piece to produce a raised design on the outside against a flattened background is called embossing. The silversmith used a snarling iron – a long, angled punch with a domed end – to reach inside a hollow vessel such as a jug. Embossing produced a much stronger relief effect than flat-chasing, but for the highest, sharpest relief the background was then further punched in from the front. This is known as repoussé, from the French for 'pushed back'.

FLAT-CHASING *Fine flat-chased work in low relief can superficially resemble engraving, as on this 18thC salver, but the punched edges are softer than engraved lines. The applied cast rim of this piece has also been chased to enhance and crispen the pattern.*

REPOUSSÉ WORK *Chasing at its most intricate can involve working from both sides with dozens of different-shaped punches. The pattern on this rose bowl has been embossed from behind, with the background chased from the front.*

DIE-STAMPING

Die-stamping with a mechanised drop hammer was developed in Sheffield in the mid-18th century, but became widespread only in the 19th. It was much cheaper than chasing. Thin-gauge sheet silver could be stamped into a patterned block with a patterned steel die, shaping the piece and impressing a design at the same time. It was ideal for mass-producing comparatively low-cost silver, often with high-relief decoration. To give items such as candlesticks and knife handles solidity, the thin silver skin was loaded (filled with molten pitch, which then hardened). The same process was used to make decorative strips – lengths of metal stamped with patterns such as gadrooning – to be soldered onto hollow-ware such as teapots.

DIE-STAMPED PEDESTAL BOWL *Mass-produced lightweight silver for the new middle classes was a feature of the Victorian era. High-relief designs that appear to be chased were in fact stamped by a drop hammer, as was the pierced work on this 1901 piece.*

ENGRAVING

In engraving, tiny slivers of metal were gouged out of the metal surface with a sharply pointed tool called a scriber or burin. On Old Sheffield plate, the engraver could easily cut right through the silver to the copper layer beneath. The problem was overcome by letting in a cartouche or band of thicker silver where the engraved decoration was to appear.

Early silverwares, of the 17th century and before, are often scratch-engraved with a simple floral design, the initials of the original owner, and date. This primitive engraving has a spontaneity that few forgers can reproduce. By the first quarter of the 18th century, a more sophisticated range of effects became possible using burins with various head shapes; some cut two or more lines at once, others made either broad or fine lines. Many engravers copied published designs, but

ENGRAVED SALVER *By varying the depth of their cuts, skilled engravers could create the effect of light and shade – a technique best seen on 18thC work such as this fine silver-gilt tray, which was enhanced with an engraved coat of arms.*

BRIGHT-CUT ENGRAVING *The burnished edges of the engraved lines on this tea caddy give the design a distinctive sparkle as light reflects from the small facets.*

the greatest work was by specialists such as William Hogarth (better known for his printed engravings), who never signed his pieces. Twentieth-century engraving rarely achieves the fine lines of 18th-century work.

Bright-cut engraving – fashionable about 1780-1800 – was done with a special burin that burnished the edges of the line to form reflective facets as the metal was gouged. But this effect, like all engraved work, softens and dulls with age, use and cleaning, and it is rare to find a piece in mint condition. Another way to emphasise an engraved pattern was to fill the grooves with a black alloy of lead, copper, silver and sulphur, a technique known as niello. Most niello tends to wear.

Just as with chasing, a mechanised version of engraving was developed in the mid-18th century in the quest for mass production at low cost. Known as engine turning, it used a lathe to rotate the object being worked while a cutting point was held against it. The pattern is usually more or less regular, but quite complex decoration could be produced by using an attachment that made the scriber move eccentrically.

PIERCED AND APPLIED DESIGNS

Pierced decoration cut right through the metal. At first it was done with a hammer and very sharp chisel, but more elaborate designs created from the mid-18th century were cut with a fine-toothed handsaw. Die-pierced silver, an extension of die-stamping in which a shaped mechanical punch cut through the metal, was introduced in the late 18th century. It lacks the spontaneity of hand-sawn work, but was cheaper to make.

In some cases, sheet ornament was cut from a plate of metal and then soldered flat onto an article. This is known as cut-card work, and was introduced to Britain about 1660 by Huguenot craftsmen. It was often used around handle and spout joints on tea and coffee pots to strengthen them, and in the late 17th century became fashionable for decorative friezes. In the early 18th century it was often combined with applied cast decoration and chasing, but by 1730 was out of fashion. Revival pieces using cut-card work appeared in the 19th century.

Apart from cast ornament, silver wire was used decoratively for applied mouldings such as rim mounts and bodywork bands, and also for filigree – openwork decoration. The wire was made by drawing the silver through holes of decreasing size and various shapes in a steel drawplate. By chasing the wire or hammering it over a die, a skilled smith could create designs such as beading or gadrooning.

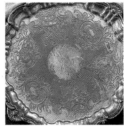

ENGRAVED OLD SHEFFIELD PLATE *To avoid cutting through the thin silver layer to the copper beneath, Old Sheffield plate articles were decorated mainly with flat-chasing. For an engraved armorial, as in the centre of the salver (far left), a thicker disc of silver would be 'rubbed in'. This shows up very clearly on the badly worn salver (left), whose surface (also with a chased design) has worn almost entirely away to copper. Note the borders of thin die-stamped silver filled with lead solder.*

NIELLO SNUFFBOX *The black and white design was created by filling engraved lines with a powdered alloy of lead, copper, silver and sulphur. When heated, this melted to form a solid black material that was then polished flush with the surface.*

ENGINE TURNING *The regular pattern of engraved lines was produced by a cutting head as the piece rotated in a lathe. Various types of guide were used to create rosettes and other complex patterns.*

PIERCED BASKET *A fine-toothed saw would have been used to cut the design on this 18thC piece (left). Close examination with a strong magnifying glass could well reveal the minute jagged edges left by the saw's teeth.*

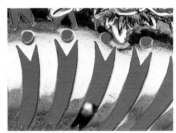

MACHINE PIERCING *The smooth and regular edges of the pierced work of this basket give away the fact that it was produced by machine.*

CUT-CARD WORK *Cut-card decoration – sawn from thin-gauge silver – was often based on leaf and flower motifs. Here, it is combined with cast beading.*

APPLIED CAST DECORATION *The decorative rim and spout on this teapot were cast and then soldered on.*

FILIGREE WORK *Silver wires of varying widths were soldered together to make free-standing objects, or could be mounted on a flat sheet of silver for decoration.*

Silver plate

Thomas Bolsover of Sheffield developed the process of making fused or Old Sheffield plate in the early 1740s. The silver thickness varied, but was generally about one-tenth of the thickness of the copper core. At first the copper had silver on one side only, and the unsilvered side was coated with tin. In the 1760s, plate was successfully produced with silver on both sides. But to save money many manufacturers continued to make articles such as tea trays and meat-dish covers with the underside – not normally visible – tinned.

Wear and polishing mean that much Old Sheffield plate has the rosy glow of copper showing through. Copper edges were often exposed when a piece was shaped. At first they were concealed with fine pure or plated silver wire – which can still be felt with a fingernail. By the 1780s, raw edges were given a border of stamped-out thin-gauge sheet silver, which was filled with tin and lead solder and bent over and soldered to the back of the piece. The ridge can be seen or felt (see p.239); on a piece worn by cleaning, the dull colour of the solder may show through. From 1824, edges indistinguishable from solid silver were possible with a method patented by Samuel Roberts; this used silver thread which was soldered into place and then hammered flat and burnished until it merged with the silver skin.

Reproductions of Old Sheffield plate are common. They were made from electroplated copper, and when worn they have a red glow. But reproductions can be spotted by their border mounts, feet and handles, which are cast in copper or brass before plating. Cast components were never used on genuine heat-fused plate, with the exception of border mounts which were cast in solid silver.

ELECTROPLATING

Vast quantities of fused plate were made in Sheffield and Birmingham, especially in the first half of the 19th century, but the industry had all but died by 1860. The reason was the industrial development of electroplating by the Elkington brothers, George and Frederick. The public loved the naturalistic designs it made possible at low cost.

Any base metal could be used for the new process, and the article was assembled before plating. Easily worked materials such as britannia metal (a form of pewter) or brass could be used for shaping a piece, with harder alloys to cast fragile parts such as hinges, handles and spouts. These could be soldered together before plating, with no need to disguise the joints as they would be covered by

silver. Later the ideal base material was found to be nickel silver – a white alloy of copper, zinc and nickel – resulting in EPNS (electroplated nickel silver).

The longer the piece was dipped in the electroplating bath, the thicker the layer of silver deposited. Better-quality goods were dipped for several hours, and may be marked 'double' or 'triple'. Othes were sectionally plated, with thicker coatings given to parts prone to wear, such as handles and feet.

Until quite recently, electroplate was scorned by most collectors, but this attitude is changing. Indeed, the avant-garde designs of Dr Christopher Dresser from the 1880s – but looking 50 years ahead of their time – now fetch thousands of pounds apiece.

PATCHED ELECTROPLATE *Electroplating was ideal for creating the ornate, deeply embossed forms beloved of the Victorians. This teapot has been clumsily patched with a plain silver disc soldered over an earlier engraved cartouche. Its edge can easily be felt.*

STEPPED JOINT *For seamed objects such as coffee pots, a clue to authentic Old Sheffield plate is the seam itself (under the handle). The soldered 'dentil' (toothed) joint was usual, which was stronger than a straight line. The solder makes the seam visible.*

ELECTROTYPING *This sideboard dish (see also p.234) was made by electrotyping or electroforming, a development of electroplating. A wax or other pattern was thickly electroplated with copper to form a very precise duplicate of the original design. The piece was then electroplated with silver and parcel gilded.*

FREE FORM *The fluid, naturalistic forms of Art Nouveau, such as this lamp, could never have been made from Old Sheffield plate. With electroplating, the various components could be cast and soldered together, then silver-plated.*

An Expert Examines

Then feel the body of the pot, to see how much meat there is left in the silver. Do this with care, with your hand on the inside as well, in case you indent it. And straightaway you can see how the side yields to the pressure of my thumb. There's certainly a weak place there, probably caused by overpolishing.

Testing the thickness of the silver

As we check the pot, you can see that it's been repaired around the bottom of the spout with greyish soft solder. That's bad. It should have been filled in with silver solder, which at least would be the same colour. It could be rectified if the worth of the pot justified the expense.

Greyish soft solder

'HALLMARKS can be a trap for the unwary. They are widely thought of as an easy way of dating a silver or gold article, but they are as open to forgery as any other aspect of a piece.

Before checking the hallmark on any piece of silver, I like to stand back and get some idea of its date by the style. Most silver follows fashion, and plain, unadorned silver like this teapot was very popular towards the end of the 18th century. But this cast rim and the acanthus leaf under the spout are a bit ornate for the 18th century and more like the 19th. So probably we're looking at a mixture of the two: late Georgian or Regency.

Checking the hallmarks against reference book

Oval-shaped teapot typical of the early 19thC

Only then do I look at the hallmark, which should be on the base or, as here, on the side, level with the top of the handle. It's very worn, thanks to years of polishing, so I'll look inside the lid to see if it's repeated. And it is. Secondary marks like this are often no

Main marks on body of pot

Marks on lid

more than the lion passant of sterling silver, but here we have a small letter 'm' as well. A hallmark reference book shows this to be the London mark for 1827 (see p. 479), which neatly fits in with my original impression.

It may sound silly, but you need to check whether the piece is still capable of doing its job. It's by no means unusual for an antique teapot like this to leak, for instance. So open the lid and look at it against the light, especially around the base of the spout and any deep embossing. Small holes are quite easy to fill, but repairs will add to the cost.

The handle seems OK. It's the original ebony, and the rivets are firm. If it were silver, you'd have to check the insulators. The hinge is nice, tight-fitting and flush, and the finial on the lid matches the main handle, as it should. That ebony ring is the insulator. Most lid handles unscrew with a wing nut for cleaning, and an awful lot of insulators get lost, leaving people to burn their fingers.

JIM COLLINGRIDGE SUMS UP

It's a nice, decorative George IV teapot, but it won't stand much more use. In two words, it's clapped out. If it were sturdier and in better order it would be quite desirable. It's a good, simple design, and it has acquired a nice patina over the years. But a collector wouldn't touch it. In an auction, it wouldn't fetch more than £150, whereas in good condition, with a nice crisp hallmark, it would be worth three or four times that.

WHEN THE MARKS DON'T MATCH

At first glance, this little helmet cream jug might be taken for George III. Indeed, that's what the hallmarks on the plinth say. But the plinth looks wrong to me; it's ugly and out of scale. Anyhow, normally the marks would be on the lip of the spout. And why are they in such a neat, straight line – suspiciously like the marks on the back of a spoon. In fact, that's what the plinth is – the handle of a George III spoon. I think the thing was put together in the last century, and I'm not at all sure that the body is silver anyway. It could well be electroplate.

Plinth with George III hallmarks

A similar kind of alteration went on to evade tax. From 1784 to 1890, the sovereign's head was added to the hallmark to show that silver duty had been paid. Here, a watch back bearing George III marks, and on which duty was paid, has been let into the base of a large silver sugar basket – on which it was not. There's no fraud in the usual sense of swindling the customer, as they're both of a period, but no doubt the tax office would have seen it differently! And this method has been used to give a date to forgeries. It's fairly easy to spot. If you breathe on the metal, the edges of the disc usually show up, at least on a plain surface.

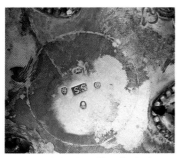

Watch back clearly visible in basket base

SPOTTING ALTERATIONS

Silver is easily refashioned to suit current tastes. Legally, no harm is done so long as the piece has not been changed radically – a christening mug turned into a cream jug, say. Then it should be re-assayed, especially if any silver has been added. Take this jug, for example. The body shape and the thumbpiece

to flick the lid back both suggest to me a tankard. The base has a set of George III hallmarks, but the Victorian look of the spout is at odds with the rest. So is the handle, which has insulators that you'd never see on a tankard – they must

Jug or tankard?

have been inserted. Frankly, if this came in for sale at auction with an unhallmarked spout, we'd have to submit it to Goldsmith's Hall for re-assay – it would be illegal to sell it, knowing in our bones that the spout was added long after the tankard was made. And that's what has happened. Although I'd say that the spout was added in the 19th century, it has a small 1991 hallmark under the lip.

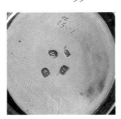

George III marks on base   *1991 mark on spout*

SILVER PLATE

Just because something was created as a piece of dining-table one-upmanship doesn't necessarily imply shoddy craftsmanship. In fact, this early 19th-century cake basket is rather attractive, with its 1830s-style gadrooned edge. But it's not solid silver; it's made of Old Sheffield, or fused, plate – copper sandwiched between thin sheets of

Regency-style cake basket with gadrooned edge

silver. In this case it's easily distinguished from silver by the base metal visible on the underside. The diners wouldn't normally see

that bit, so the silversmith could economise by making it out of one-sided plate. The idea was to make the article look like an expensive piece of silver but save money – including silver duty.

Base metal visible beneath

The sheet of Old Sheffield plate was worked just like solid silver. At the edges, it was rolled over to hide the copper, and there's often an applied rim as well to disguise the rolled edge. You always need to look for joint marks. In this case, you can see them down the side – those fine lines, where the two edges have been sweated together, then very carefully hammered and rolled in. On a tea or coffee pot, the joint mark is often below the handle. In solid silver or electroplate any joins would have been burnished smooth.

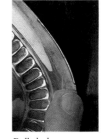

Rolled edge

Fine line shows where edges of plate were joined

HALLMARK THAT NEVER WAS

Electroplate was also intended to mimic real silver, and sometimes the makers' marks were made to look like hallmarks. On the base of this Victorian electroplated teapot, the maker's initials – 'W & Co' – are scattered at random, much as hallmarks are. Their Gothic lettering might also help to mislead a casual inspection. '

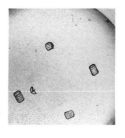

Cutlery and servers

Complete canteens of silver are very hard to come by, but assembling your own set from odd finds in junk shops and markets is quite feasible.

Part of a set of 12 tablespoons and 12 forks; London, 1735-6. Odd Hanoverian spoons of this date are quite common, but it is rare to find a full set.
Set of 24: £10,000-£15,000
Single spoon: £40-£60: single fork: £150-£200

THE USE OF FORKS is taken for granted today, but a mere 350 years ago it was considered an eccentric whim. Knives and spoons were far more important, spoons often being given as christening or betrothal gifts. They were topped with finials modelled as apostles or baluster-shaped vases and often engraved with the owner's initials. Hosts were not expected to provide cutlery and wealthy guests carried their own in a leather case.

The earliest sets of silver flatware followed the development of rolled sheet metal in the 17th century – hence the term 'flatware'. A fashion for decorated matching sets of cutlery, die-stamped from sheet metal and including forks, sprang up in France during the mid-17th century, and was brought to Britain by Charles II at his restoration in 1660.

Three spoons (left to right): London, c.1652; Exeter, 1635; London, 1688; c.7 in (17.8 cm) long. The centre spoon ends in a variation of an apostle terminal, a cast 'lion séjant'. The plain example on the left is typical of the Commonwealth period, when decoration was discouraged; that on the right has a trefid end and is stamped with 'lacework', or scrolling foliage.
£400-£1000

CANTEENS

Full sets of cutlery dating from before about 1800 are very rare, indeed they are almost impossible to find today. However, complete silver sets from the 19th century do sometimes come up for sale. A 12-place setting, for example, will sell at auction for between £2000 and £5000. However, a collector who is not too concerned about owning cutlery of varying sizes can create a canteen of matching cutlery by buying single pieces at perhaps only £10-£20 per piece. It is best to choose one of the commoner patterns, such as Hanoverian, Old English, Fiddle or King's – first seen about 1710, 1760, 1770 and 1810 respectively (see p.461).

It is more difficult, but more valuable in the long run, to build up a collection of pieces by the same maker, preferably hallmarked in the same year. This is not quite as hard as it sounds, as most cutlery was made by a handful of firms – the Eley, Fearn, Chawner and Smith families in the late 18th and early 19th centuries, and Francis Higgins and George Adams in the later 19th.

Antique and secondhand electroplated canteens of cutlery are also still an excellent buy at £200-£500. Even those produced as late as the 1930s are often of better quality than their modern, expensive counterparts.

A typical early British canteen generally consisted of tablespoons, dinner knives and

George I style walnut canteen of silver rat-tail pattern cutlery; Sheffield, c.1934-42. The canteen includes items with mother-of-pearl as well as bone handles.
£5500-£7500.

Silver fiddle-pattern flatware; 19th and 20thC. This single place setting is taken from a large, composite canteen of 12 place settings, although the knives are in fact modern replacements.
Canteen: £1500-£2000
EPNS: £300-£500

Turn-of-the-century fish eaters and matching servers in their original oak box. They have mother-of-pearl handles and engraved blades and prongs in electroplate.
£200-£250

forks, dessert spoons and forks, teaspoons and serving utensils. Many American and Continental canteens might contain additional items ranging from spaghetti and pea forks to spoons for both hot and cold soup. These pieces are generally inexpensive in Britain: around £5-£15 per ounce compared to British flatware at around £12-£20 per ounce.

British-made canteens were expanded in the late 19th century. Fish eaters and soup spoons were introduced for the first time, and were made to match existing canteens.

Dessert sets have often survived intact. Until the 1820s, most such sets consisted of knives and forks only, sometimes gilded and with carved mother-of-pearl or ivory handles. A 12-place setting in a case will sell for £350-£600, whereas the electroplated equivalent will sell for only £120-£200. Later sets include spoons, often ornately engraved. Many of the plain Georgian tablespoons were adapted for dessert sets with added decoration and gilding, and surprisingly these altered 'berry spoons' (see p. 232) often fetch up to

Electroplated dessert canteen set; Sheffield, late 19th/early 20thC. Impressive sets of plate such as this always sell well, even though loose oddments of plated cutlery fetch only a pound or two.
£400-£600; in silver: £1200-£1500

Bacchanalian-patterned parcel-gilt fruit set in its original satin-lined leather case; London, 1870-80; spoons 6¾ in (17.1 cm) long. The set is of excellent quality, struck with well-defined Classical figures, but is not by one maker, thus the value is reduced by about 50 per cent.
£250-£350

George III silver marrow scoop; London, 1775; 7¾ in (19.7 cm) long. Marrow scoops are comparatively inexpensive as they are no longer used
£70-£120

£70-£100 a pair, whereas their plain, original counterparts may sell for only £30-£40 a pair.

More extensive dessert sets come with grape shears, sugar sifting spoons, nutcrackers and picks. Folding fruit knives, forks and apple corers were also made for travellers.

SETS OF TEASPOONS

Teaspoons were usually part of a large canteen of flatware, but many sets were also sold separately. Attractive odd spoons can still be found for a few pounds each. Among the most

Tea (bottom), coffee and condiment spoons of various styles, showing comparative sizes; teaspoon 5¾ in (14.6 cm) long.
Tea and coffee spoons: £5-£8 each (set of six: £50-£80); condiment spoon: £8-£12

Pair of toasting forks; Birmingham, 1866; 22 in (56 cm) long. The handles are of blackbuck antelope horn.
£400-£600

charming are the tiny Hanoverian-pattern spoons made in the mid-18th century, especially those known as 'picture backs' or 'fancy backs'. These were made from thin sheet silver, with die-stamped decoration under the bowl, and sell for £150-£200 per half dozen.

More unusual are historical commemorative spoons, including political and coronation examples, and those decorated with symbols of rural plenty, such as sheaves of corn, milkmaids and hens with chicks. These sell at £250-£350 per half dozen. Souvenir spoons date from the mid-19th century on. You can find them at flea markets and junk shops for as little as £5-£15 each.

For caddy spoons, see page 253.

SERVING UTENSILS

Serving implements, originally supplied as part of a canteen, are usually found separately.

Sugar tongs, widely used from the 1780s and made in a variety of styles, sell for around £15-£30 each today. Their earlier equivalent, scissor-action sugar nips, are more difficult to find, although Victorian copies can be found quite easily at about £120-£180. Asparagus tongs were also first made with a scissor action, but by the late 18th century the U-shape had become standard.

In the mid-19th century, fish slices were fashioned from sheet metal to match popular flatware designs of the day, and fish-serving forks also appeared. Slices and forks were often paired and boxed in leather cases. Solid-silver sets now fetch £150-£400 and electroplated sets £30-£100, depending on how decorative they are.

Butter spades of the 18th century closely resemble slices, but often have green-stained ivory baluster handles. Good examples are rare and expensive, for they were replaced by butter knives towards the end of the century.

Marrow scoops (for eating bone marrow) were made in large numbers in the 18th and 19th centuries. They are usually one piece of silver with a flat, elongated bowl at each end. Most sell at auction for about £70-£120, but early examples, or those whose bowls face in opposite directions, may fetch up to £200. Early 18th-century marrow spoons – which have a scoop at one end and a tablespoon-sized bowl at the other – are rarer still, and fetch up to £150-£250. Beware of fakes made by converting or reshaping early tablespoons.

Ivory-handled silver cheese scoops of the 18th and early 19th centuries – some fitted with a slide to push the cheese onto the plate – are usually in poor condition. But by the 1830s they were entirely of heavy-gauge silver and much sturdier. They can be found in popular canteen styles for about £120-£160.

Silver for the table

Silver articles in great variety have been made for the dining table, some to impress guests but most for family meals that once ran to many courses. People collect this silver for its beauty and for the pleasure of using it.

Silver serving platters with cast and applied gadrooned rims, engraved with the royal arms; London, 1744; smaller 15½ in (39.4 cm) long. Heavy scratching bears witness to years of use.
£1500-£3000 the pair

DISHES, PLATTERS AND PLATES were made in silver for use and display from the earliest times, although few have survived from before the early 17th century. Added to this group is a huge variety of objects created for specific uses on the dining table.

FOR EATING AND SERVING

The oldest silver serving dishes designed for use rather than display are simple, with moulded or gadrooned rims. Display pieces are often silver gilt, with elaborate chased and applied strapwork and lobing. Most date from the 17th century, although similar ones continued to be made until the early 19th century, mainly for ceremonial services.

Sets of silver plates and platters are very expensive, even if Victorian, but single specimens can be found quite easily at about £250 for a typical 10 in (25 cm) plate. Rarer items include strawberry dishes, venison dishes, and mazarines – dish liners pierced with hand-sawn arabesques to allow cooking liquids to drain away. Large domed covers for meat platters were first made in the early 19th century. Most are in Old Sheffield plate or in electroplate, and are fairly cheap at £100-£300 for a single cover. Sets of three or more, ranging in size from around 12 to 25 in (30-64 cm), are now often bought to hang as wall decorations and are more expensive.

Tureens evolved from deep serving bowls with covers, and followed current stylistic fashions in design and decoration. The first were circular and quite plain, but by the early 18th century they were oval and more ornate with elaborate cast handles. Tureens are expensive, ranging in price from £1000-£1500 for a lightweight Edwardian copy to many thousands for a good 18th-century piece.

Entrée dishes date from the reign of George III. Most were made with a detachable handle, so that the lid could be used for serving cold foods. Silver examples are quite scarce, fetching £600-£800 apiece, but Old Sheffield plate specimens are still easily found for £250-£450 a pair in good condition. They often come with a detachable hot-water

Set of Regency silver soup and sauce tureens; London, 1815-17; largest tureen 18½ in (47 cm) long. This excellent quality set is made from heavy gauge sheet silver with cast legs and handles. Complete sets are rare, hence the high price.
£30,000-£50,000 the set

Set of Regency silver dinner plates (half shown); London, 1815; 10 in (25.4 cm) across. This unusually large set of 24 was probably once part of a huge service.
£15,000-£20,000 the set
Single plate: £250-£350

OYSTERS AND WINE *There are matching silver plates and platters aplenty for the young men seen dining so lavishly in Jean François de Troy's early 18thC painting. Note also the silver salts and flatware.*

Silver salver; London, 1733; 15½ in (39.4 cm) across. This shape was used for both salvers and waiters. This has a moulded border; more elaborate pieces have applied shell borders.
£4000-£6000

George I octafoil silver salver; London, 1719; 13¼ in (33.6 cm) across. The bold shape is typical of the early 18thC.
£15,000-£20,000

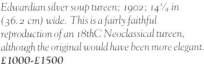

Edwardian silver soup tureen; 1902; 14¼ in (36.2 cm) wide. This is a fairly faithful reproduction of an 18thC Neoclassical tureen, although the original would have been more elegant.
£1000-£1500
18thC original: £8000-£12,000

Electroplated entrée dish on warming stand; Sheffield, c.1885; 14¼ in (36.2 cm) long. More flamboyant electroplate would fetch much more.
£100-£150

Late Victorian silver strawberry set; 1897 and 1899; 13½ in (34.3 cm) long. Sets are much rarer in silver than electroplate – but this is a composite: the stand is later than the cream jug and sugar bowl.
£600-£800
Electroplate: £100-£150

Set of silver entrée dishes by John Bridge; London, 1826; 14¾ in (35.8 cm) long. They have warming stands to hold hot water in Old Sheffield plate – these by Matthew Boulton of Birmingham.
£18,000-£24,000 (for set of four)

Pair of Regency silver-gilt two-handled trays on feet; London, 1823; 23 in (58.4 cm) long overall. Massively heavy, these superb trays by Philip Rundell also benefit from a ducal provenance.
£50,000-£70,000

stand. Electroplate is even cheaper, at £100-£200 a pair. Single specimens are less popular and therefore cheaper – often under £50.

SALVERS AND TRAYS

Early salvers are circular on a trumpet-shaped base. By about 1715 this was replaced by three or more smaller feet on the underside of the rim, a type that has persisted to the present day. While most of the earliest salvers were undecorated, silversmiths soon realised that the flat surface was ideal for display pieces with chased or engraved decoration. In the Regency period, rounded oblong salvers appeared, on paw feet and with gadroon and shell borders. After the mid-19th century, silversmiths merely reproduced earlier styles, often with increasingly elaborate decoration.

Early salvers currently sell for £4000-£8000, or more if particularly large and fine. Mid-18th-century examples cost £1500-£2500. George III and Regency specimens are only slightly cheaper at between £1000 and

£1500. Victorian salvers can be found for £500-£800. Single waiters – small salvers less than 9 in (23 cm) across – are easily found and cost £400-£600 for a good 18th-century example, but sets of salvers and matching waiters are scarce and very expensive.

The term 'tray' originally referred to large, heavy, oval or oblong salvers, on feet so they were easy to pick up. Trays with handles appeared in the 1750s, and lighter trays with pierced galleries around 1760. They were too flimsy to carry substantial weights, so were

strengthened with wooden inserts. By the 1770s the tray as we know it today had evolved. Trays became increasingly elaborate up to about 1840, but from the mid-19th century most are lightweight adaptations of earlier styles. Trays with inscriptions are hard to sell and cost less than blank trays.

OTHER SERVING DISHES

With the Victorian age came a host of dishes for specific purposes. These included ovoid revolving-top breakfast dishes, muffineers, biscuit barrels and biscuit warmers, asparagus dishes and strawberry sets. Prices for most of these start at around £100 in electroplate; silver examples are rarer and more expensive. Egg boilers fitted with a tiny spirit lamp range widely in price from ovoid electroplated examples with bird finials for £100-£150 to rarer silver ones with an egg timer for £1500.

The first butter dishes were made in the early 18th century in the form of a shell. Good cast pairs can fetch £1000-£2000, but by the

1750s most were of sheet metal. Victorian and later pairs sell for £150-£300. Covered butter dishes with a cow finial appeared in the late 18th century and sell for £300-£500.

The earliest cake and bread baskets and bonbon dishes also date from the early 18th century and can fetch as much as £40,000. These are usually oval or round with a central cast handle, or in the form of shells on dolphin bases. Baskets from the mid-century are much lighter in construction; both chased and wirework examples sell for £2000-£4000, if in good condition. Solid oblong baskets from the Regency period and slightly later circular baskets on domed pedestal bases sell for £1000-£2000. After about 1890 all baskets became increasingly flimsy, except for a few heavy-gauge reproductions of earlier styles.

Toast racks made from drawn wire date from the 1770s, but most early examples are in poor condition. Folding and telescopic specimens, usually in Old Sheffield plate, are quite scarce today. By the early 19th century sturdier examples in silver were fashionable, with gadrooned rims and cast feet. Late Victorian novelty toast racks formed from crossed tennis racquets, cricket bats or golf clubs are sought after by sports enthusiasts.

Silver sauceboats appeared in the early 18th century. The earliest have a lip at either end and two cast scroll handles to the sides; they can cost £2000-£4000 a pair, or more. Single-lipped sauceboats date from about 1740. Despite being prone to damage, they now sell for £1500-£2500 a pair, although singles are much cheaper. Most modern sauceboats reproduce earlier styles. However, Viners of Sheffield made a good number in Art Deco style, which now sell for £200-£250 per pair with matching ladles and original case.

A late 18th-century invention was the lidded gravy jug, or Argyle, with a hot-water compartment to keep the gravy warm. Many have a spout that rises from the bottom, so that the fat at the top does not pour off.

TABLE ACCESSORIES

Among the stands designed to keep hot dishes off polished tables are dish rings – waisted rings with pierced decoration – often wrongly described as 'potato rings'. Most 18th-century examples were made in Ireland and have typical Irish chasing of farmyard scenes, exotic birds or flowers and foliage. Originals cost £1200-£1600, Edwardian reproductions

£400-£600. But beware: on some copies the marks have been defaced to imply greater age.

Wirework dish rings, which appeared in the 1770s, and dish crosses – stands with revolving arms and adjustable supports – both carry bowls of differing sizes and shapes and usually have a spirit lamp to keep the dishes hot. Silver examples sell for £400-£600, Old Sheffield plate for £200-£300.

SALTS, CASTERS AND CRUETS

In the past, salt was valuable and kept in elaborate containers. Beautiful medieval salts rarely appear on the market, but early 18th-century trencher salts are still quite common. These are small oval, circular or oblong salt cellars with a dished centre. However, most are now in poor condition as they were generally made from thin sheet silver; a

Silver strawberry dish; London, 1729; 7½ in (19 cm) across. With its fluted upcurved rim, this is a typical strawberry dish of the sort first made in the late 17thC. Many have been repaired along the flutes.
£2000-£3000

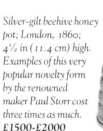

Silver-gilt beehive honey pot; London, 1860; 4½ in (11.4 cm) high. Examples of this very popular novelty form by the renowned maker Paul Storr cost three times as much.
£1500-£2000

perfect pair could fetch £700-£1000. By the 1740s most salt cellars were shaped like round cauldrons, with three shell-and-hoof feet and a moulded or gadrooned rim. These are readily available for £400-£600 a pair, or £600-£800 for the rarer oval type with four feet. Victorian cauldron salts with chased or applied decoration make £200-£300 a pair.

In the late 18th century, oval salts on pedestal feet became fashionable. They now sell for £400-£600 a pair. Most have bright-cut friezes and simple bead or reed rims. This form was soon superseded by pierced and bright-cut oval salts with 'Bristol' blue glass liners and shell or ball-and-claw feet. Many are now in poor condition, but a perfect pair might fetch £400-£500.

As with most silver tableware, the Regency period saw the introduction of much heavier

Electroplated britannia metal egg cruet; 1890; 10¾ in (27.3 cm) high. The revolving handle opens the doors to reveal the egg cups; closed, they keep the eggs warm. Such pieces are rare and popular, especially with American buyers.
£200-£250

Irish silver dish ring; c.1765 (unmarked); 8¼ in (21 cm) in diameter. Unmistakably Irish, with exuberant Rococo piercing and chasing, the ring has no hallmarks, so the auction value is quite low.
£800-£1200

George III silver bread basket; London, 1769; 13¼ in (33.6 cm) long. This typical drawn wire basket has a cast handle appropriately decorated with ears of corn.
£2000-£2500

pieces. Such salts, often in silver-gilt with cut-glass liners and applied cast masks, rims and feet of great quality, are justifiably popular today, often costing even more than their earlier counterparts. The same applies to Victorian copies of earlier styles. However, numerous small, machine-stamped and rolled salts were also produced in the 19th century, including shell designs on dolphin bases. These are light and easily damaged, so they sell for as little as £60-£80 a pair.

Pepper and spice casters sell very well today. The early 'lighthouse' form with straight sides and domed top originated in France and was made in Britain from about 1670. Today they sell for about £1500-£2500, but later types are cheaper at £200-£300. By the early 18th century, they were usually baluster shaped, with a lid that simply slides into place and a cast circular base. Octagonal casters that catch the light were also popular. After 1750 casters were made from lighter, machine-rolled silver. Most were decorated with beading or reeding, and had spiral-fluted or acorn-shaped finials. Most Victorian and later casters copy earlier pieces, but some novelty examples were produced, including a suffragette holding bakelite placards.

By the mid-18th century, mustard was served ready-mixed, usually in drum-shaped pots with glass liners. These pots are still made, although many later examples suffer from a wealth of stamped decoration. In the late Georgian period, vase-shaped mustard pots on a domed base became popular, replaced in about 1810 by clumsy oblong examples on ball feet. Antique mustard pots fetch £300-£500 or more, depending on age,

style and condition. Victorian anthropomorphic specimens are particularly popular. Those by the Hennell family of London, modelled as owls, monkeys, pigs and even kangaroos, can make £1000-£1500.

Cruet sets with bottles and casters fitting into a frame date from the reign of Queen Anne. Today, they are relatively inexpensive. Although 'Warwick' cruets may reach £2500-£3000, later examples can still be found for £400-£800. Warwick cruets have a cinquefoil base and scroll feet, and generally hold two silver-topped glass bottles for oil and vinegar and three casters. Similar, but smaller

Silver sauceboat and ladle; London, 1737 and 1750; sauceboat 7½ in (19 cm) long. Although both are by Paul de Lamerie, they were not made as a pair.
£10,000-£15,000 the two

Set of silver casters; London, 1719; 5¾ and 7½ in (14.6 and 19 cm) high. Early sets are quite rare; later copies are generally more flimsy.
£5000-£8000 the set
Later copies: £100-£150 each

Silver cauldron salts; London, 1826; 4 in (10.1 cm) wide. Ornate examples are much rarer than plain ones. Unusually, the liners are silver gilt, not glass.
Pair: £1200-£1500
Set of four: £3800-£4200

Silver novelty pepperettes; London, 1875 and 1877, parrot 3¼ in (82 mm) high. Well-modelled novelty pieces like these are much sought after.
£300-£800 each

Silver and glass cinquefoil Warwick cruet; London, 1745; 9 in (22.9 cm) high. This fine set still has its original Rococo-style casters and bottles.
£2500-£3000

Set of silver-gilt salts by Paul Storr; London, 1811 and 1813; 4½ in (11.4 cm) long. These cellars, of the highest quality, were 'discovered' on a BBC 'Antiques Roadshow' programme. Storr is highly collectable, and they fetched £60,000 at auction in 1991.
Auction estimate £35,000-£45,000

cruets hold only two bottles. Most have openwork frames, but others have tall sides hand-pierced with arabesques.

Much lighter cruets appeared in the late 18th century. Boat-shaped examples, with eight or ten bottles, were also quite common. Victorian cruets are large and flamboyant, with applied decoration of flowers and foliage. After about 1850 most were oblong or square.

NAPKIN RINGS AND PLACE MARKERS

The Victorians were the first to fold napkins for table decoration, and used silver rings originally sold in sets engraved with numbers or initials. But by the mid-19th century these had become popular christening presents and were sold singly. Although plated American novelty pieces – for example, rings modelled as children, chariots or tiny vases – may fetch £100-£200 in the United States, plainer silver rings are cheaper at £15-£20. There is little

demand for napkin clips – tiny hooks designed to hold a napkin firmly in place – and they can be found for a few pounds.

Prices have soared recently for sets of Victorian and later silver place markers (which can double as menu holders). Most popular are those cast as birds or animals, or with enamelled discs showing sporting or nautical vignettes. These can bring as much as £400-£600 for a set of four – although quality and styles vary enormously. You may find singles for as little as £30-£50.

MAINLY FOR SHOW

Table centrepieces, or epergnes, were used from the mid-18th century to display crystallised fruit, sugared almonds and other sweetmeats. Early versions are enormously heavy, with cast scroll legs and branches supporting dishes and candle sockets. By about 1760 the bowls were usually pierced with arabesques,

and many epergnes also show the influence of Chippendale's Chinese designs in pagoda tops with tiny bells. By the 1780s, epergnes were much lighter and Neoclassical in style. Heavy centrepieces, often gilt to match dessert flatware, reappeared in the Regency period. Most had cut-glass bowls, now usually missing or broken. From about 1830, naturalistic epergnes modelled with trees, rocks and figures were the fashion, and at the end of the century Neoclassical reproductions.

Despite their size, centrepieces are popular with serious collectors. George II examples may sell for over £50,000, and Neoclassical for £15,000-£25,000. Regency and Victorian specimens sell for £6000-£10,000, or more if they have a stand or plateau with inset mirrored base. Even readily available plated versions can sell for £1000-£2000.

Vases and rose bowls were popular from the late 19th century. Many are in lightweight silver with machine-stamped decoration.

Silver owl menu holders; Chester, 1904; 1¼ in (32 mm) high. The Victorians and Edwardians loved novelty pieces; the original case adds to the value.
£400-£600 set
Individual: £30-£50

Edwardian silver rose bowl; Birmingham, 1903; 14¼ in (36.2 cm) high. Rose bowls of high quality such as this are extremely popular.
£2500-£3500

Silver and cut-glass Regency vine-and-shell centrepiece; London, 1814; 12¼ in (31.1 cm) high. This adaptable piece, made by Benjamin Smith, can be fitted with either cut-glass bonbon dishes to match the fruit bowl or candle sconces. The matching mirror plateau was made by Philip Rundell in 1823.
£8000-£12,000

One of a pair of continental silver and ivory table figures; Chester import mark, 1904; 19¾ in (50.2 cm) high. Model knights have always been among the most popular of the silverwares imported since the end of the 19thC, and most are well made and detailed.
£4000-£6000 (pair)

Parcel-gilt electroplate and glass centrepiece by Elkingtons; 1884; 35 in (88.9 cm) long. This is part of a larger set including small oval dishes and four circular bonbon dishes. Individual dishes are far cheaper.
£10,000-£15,000 the set
£400-£600 per dish

Silver for drinking

The enjoyment of alcohol has long been thought worthy of the attention of fine silversmiths. Their creations are sought out by both silver collectors and wine connoisseurs, and are available at a wide range of prices.

OUR ANCESTORS CONSUMED enormous quantities of alcohol in many different forms, some simple everyday thirst-quenchers, others only for entertaining or for ceremonial occasions. Vessels and accessories were needed for serving ale, cider, 'small beer' (a weak homebrew drunk as tea and coffee are today), wine, spirits and mixed drinks. Tankards (with handle and lid), mugs (with handle but no lid), beakers (with neither) and stemmed goblets are all collected today, as are accessories as diverse as punchbowls, corkscrews and bottle labels.

FLAGONS AND JUGS

Flagons are tall jugs with a hinged lid and cast handle, usually scroll or harp-shaped. Original 17th-century flagons sell for £7000–£10,000, but many reproductions were made in the 19th century and are much cheaper.

Lightweight claret jugs made at the end of the 18th century, in machine-spun metal with bright-cut Neoclassical decoration, are well worth looking out for, although many are flimsy and have had repairs. In good condition, they fetch £700–£1000, as can the later, heavier, more ornate 'Cellini' jugs, made in a Victorian adaptation of Renaissance styles. Silver-mounted cut-glass jugs from the mid-19th century can be found for £400–£1000. From the end of the century there are novelty jugs shaped as ducks and walruses, and 'chota pegs' – miniatures to hold a dram of whisky.

TANKARDS, BEAKERS AND GOBLETS

British tankards from the late 16th to early 18th centuries have straight, tapering sides and a flat or domed lid; they are quite rare. Elaborate northern European tankards, often with chasing, inset coins or caryatid handles, are more common and fetch £2500–£4000.

From the mid-18th century, mugs were mainly baluster-shaped. Many have survived and, in good condition, now fetch £350–£500 in silver or £70–£100 in Old Sheffield plate. Smaller mugs made for women and children cost less. Mugs from the end of the 18th century are usually tapered or barrel-shaped, and the best – decorated with hoops, staves and a wood-effect texture – can fetch £500.

All styles of mugs and tankards were widely reproduced in the late 19th century, in both silver and electroplate; in many the shape is lost beneath a wealth of chasing. Check hallmarks with care, as reproductions (now usually plainer) are still being made.

Beakers made in Britain in the 17th and 18th centuries are quite plain and sturdy, while continental ones are lighter and often have a chased frieze of foliage. Collectable variations include the tumbler cup, which has curved sides so it rolls upright if put down awkwardly, and the Scottish quaich – a shallow, uncovered drinking cup generally made in silver and wood or horn.

Silver wine goblets were widely used until they were ousted by wine glasses in the mid-18th century. Originals are now very

Silver beer jug; London, 1733; 10½ in (26.7 cm) high. An engraved armorial and scroll handle enliven the basic pear shape.
**£2500–£3500
Pair: £10,000–£15,000**

Claret jug in silver and glass with ebony handle, designed by Christopher Dresser; London, 1897; 8½ in (21.6 cm) high.
**£600–£800
If signed by Dresser:
£5000–£10,000**

Late 19th-century silver/silver-gilt and glass claret jugs; tallest 14¾ in (37.5 cm) high. A leading Paris firm of silversmiths, Odiot, made the centre jug.
**Jug by Odiot: £2000–£4000
Others: £800–£1200 each**

Silver tankard; London, 1714; 6¾ in (17.1 cm) high. Tankards were sturdy, for heavy use, so most are in good condition.
£2200–£2600

Early Georgian mugs, both made in London: (left) 1749, 4¾ in (12.1 cm) high; (above) 1758, 5 in (12.7 cm) high. The baluster shape is typical of the period, but the mug on the left has been 'Victorianised' with Rococo-style chasing. Most collectors prefer the original, but there is a demand for florid decoration, largely from Italy.
**Plain and original: £400–£600
With later chasing: £300–£400**

Silver tankard with inset gold and silver medals; London; 1814; 7 in (17.8 cm) high. The winner of the medals, from Irish agricultural shows, probably commissioned this highly individual piece.
£2000-£3000

Rare Charles I silver wine goblet; 1626; 8¼ in (21 cm) high. Most early silver was melted down in the Civil War. Hallmarks are often randomly struck on originals and copies.
£10,000-£15,000
Modern copy: £100-£150

Restoration silver wager cup; 1665; 7¼ in (18.4 cm) high. The wager was to drain both the pivoting top cup and that formed by the skirt – with no spills. English wager cups were much copied on the Continent from the late 19thC.
£20,000-£25,000
Modern copy: £200-£400

Left to right: Flamboyant Victorian silver-gilt cup; London, 1875. Silver wine funnel with original stand; Dublin, 1838; 7 in (17.8 cm) high. Silver cup of Classical 'campana' shape with gadrooning and applied vines in typical Regency style; London, 1819.
Cups: £500-£700 each
Funnel: £800-£1200

Russian stirrup cups in silver with sapphire eyes; St Petersburg, 1863; 3⅛ in (80 mm) high. These finely modelled cups are unusual – most stirrup cups depict foxes.
£1200-£1600 each

hard to find, but they have been much copied since Victorian times. Victorian goblets with prize inscriptions are not in demand and sell cheaply, but pieces depicting farming, military or sporting scenes sell for £200-£400.

WINE COOLERS AND COASTERS

Large numbers of wine coolers, designed to hold a single bottle in ice, survive today, especially in Old Sheffield plate and electroplate. Most have an urn or inverted bell (campana) shape, applied vine or floral decoration and applied scroll handles. Many imitate the campana shape of the Warwick vase – a Greek marble vase from the 2nd century AD. Pairs of such coolers fetch £1500-£2500 in Sheffield plate and £1000-£1500 in electroplate, but beware of poor-quality modern electroplated copies.

From the 1760s onwards, quantities of wine coasters were produced to protect the table and linen from spillages. Pairs of Georgian coasters cost about £1000-£1500 in silver and £150-£500 in the much more common Old

Sheffield plate; Victorian pairs cost slightly less and singles much less. Early coasters were shallow and quite plain, but the form gradually became taller and more decorative, especially in the elaborate pieces of the 1830s.

Wine trolleys are two coasters mounted on wheels. Some, in boat form and known as 'jolly boat' trolleys, fetch £2500-£4000 in silver, or £800-£1500 in Sheffield plate.

CORKSCREWS, FUNNELS AND LABELS

The majority of silver corkscrews found today were made in Birmingham from the late 18th century. Most were for travellers and have the iron 'worm' concealed inside a silver sheath; the handle is generally mother-of-pearl or green-stained ivory. Prices for these and for unusual Dutch and French corkscrews (with animal or scroll handles) start at around £250.

Champagne taps, similar in shape and size to corkscrews, were made from the late 19th century, usually in electroplate. A tiny tap allows small amounts of champagne to be

poured out without losing the fizziness in the rest of the bottle. Taps are easy to find and reasonably priced at £50-£150.

Wine funnels incorporating a sieve were used for straining wine to remove any sediment. Georgian funnels are quite small and simple; those from the 1820s on are larger and more elaborate. Funnels fetch £350-£600, so long as the spout has not been shortened.

Silver labels to hang around the neck of a decanter first appeared in the 1730s, and were then known as 'bottle tickets'. The oldest are cartouche-shaped and usually plain. Before 1784 most labels had only a maker's stamp, as

Pair of Old Sheffield plate wine coolers; c. 1775; 9 in (22.8 cm) high. Old Sheffield plate was much used for large pieces such as wine coolers. This pair are in typical late 18thC Classical style.
£3000-£4000 the pair
Single cooler: £600-£800

Silver wine trolley; London, 1839; 20 in (50.8 cm) long. Silver trolleys are now scarce – most are Sheffield plate or electroplate.
£2500-£4000
Old Sheffield plate: £800-£1200

Pair of silver-gilt 'Warwick vase' wine coolers by Paul Storr; London, 1814; 10 in (25.4 cm) high. These luxury examples of the many copies of the 2ndC marble vase weigh 412 oz (12.8 kg) in all.
£50,000-£70,000 the pair
Victorian copy: £20-£30 per oz

Assorted silver wine labels, the earliest – 'Lisbon' (for port) – by Sandilands Drinkwater; c. 1755; 1½ in (38 mm) wide.
£30-£100 each

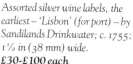

Set of four silver-gilt wine coasters with die-stamped and pierced decoration; 1812, regilded later; 5¾ in (14.6 cm) across.
£7000-£10,000 the set
Pair: £1500-£2000

Silver punchbowls, both from London: (left) 1734, 8¾ in (22.2 cm) wide; (above) 1701, 7 in (17.8 cm) wide and lighter in construction.
Left: £8000-£12,000
Above: £4000-£6000
19thC copy: £800-£1200

---

they weighed too little to require a hallmark. The unaptly named Sandilands Drinkwater was the most prolific early maker. His labels, marked with a crown over the letters SD, are very popular, and change hands for as much as £80-£120. The die-stamped vine-leaf label, introduced in 1824, is also still quite common but double and triple leaf labels are rarer.

Initial labels – 'S' for sherry, 'P' for port, and so on – from the 1830s, and novelty labels made from mounted tigers' claws, can be found for £40-£80. Some collectors search out unusual names. Cream of the Valley and Nig, for example, are euphemisms for gin, once seen as a working-class drink and therefore disguised in snobbish households.

ACCESSORIES FOR SPIRITS, PUNCH AND TODDY

Few 18th-century hunting or travelling flasks survive. However, there are plenty of late 19th and early 20th-century flasks, in both silver (see p.258) and silver-mounted glass. They are often curved to fit against the chest

and accompanied by a gilt-lined cup. They fetch £150-£400, but less if inscribed. There are also stirrup cups made to drink from when on horseback, just before a journey or hunt.

Brandy bowls are shallow, two-handled vessels originally designed for both drinking and testing brandy. They are often heavily chased with floral and fruit motifs. Original bowls fetch £800-£1200 today, 19th-century continental reproductions £150-£250.

Brandy saucepans, used to warm brandy, were first made in the late 17th century. Early examples are small with flaring sides. By the 18th century narrower, baluster-shaped bowls with a lip and turned wooden handle were more common. Some later pans have a lid and a stand with a tiny spirit burner. Early pans fetch £500-£800, Edwardian copies – usually identifiable by an ivory handle and scrolling wirework stand – £200-£500.

Punch became very fashionable during the second half of the 17th century, as did its stronger equivalent, toddy, in the late 18th century. The serving of punch required

special equipment, including punch bowls, ladles, sugar and spice boxes, nutmeg graters and juice strainers. Toddy was served in smaller vessels suited to a stronger drink.

Early punchbowls were decorated with chased Chinese motifs or vertical fluting, and had applied scroll handles and rim. Larger 'monteiths' were dual-purpose: used either for serving punch, or to cool wine goblets suspended from a detachable rim – which was scalloped to hold them. Most punchbowls found today are Victorian copies of earlier designs and were made as presentation pieces.

Punch ladles generally have a handle made from a material that does not conduct heat, such as wood or whalebone. After the mid-18th century, most ladles were inset with old silver coins and few were hallmarked. They fetch up to £150 today. Punch strainers were introduced in the early 18th century to remove the pips from fruit juice. Most have a finely pierced circular bowl and a single side handle, but some later ones have two wirework handles. A full set of marks is rare.

Tea, coffee and chocolate wares

Tea, coffee and chocolate were all being imported to Europe by the middle of the 17th century, and a demand arose for the vessels for making, serving and drinking them – in silver as well as porcelain.

George I octagonal silver teapot; 1723; 4¼ in (10.8 cm) high. The broad panels provide an ideal surface for the contemporary engraved armorial, which adds to the value of the piece.
£5000-£8000

Old Sheffield plate teapot; 1760-80; 4¼ in (10.8 cm) high. This example is in good condition and has very little copper appearing through the silver skin.
£150-£200

Chinese export teapot; 1680; 5 in (12.7 cm) high. This great rarity, cast and chased with village scenes, is struck with London hallmarks. This seems to be the earliest-known example of imported Chinese silver and is now in an American museum.
£50,000 or more

Reproduction 18thC silver teapot, stand and warmer; London, 1913; 8½ in (21.6 cm) high. This reproduction Huguenot teapot has an ebony handle and is typical of Victorian and Edwardian copies of early pieces.
£500-£700
Original: £10,000-£15,000

Victorian silver teapot; 1839; 7¾ in (19.7 cm) high. The exuberant style of this piece is typical of the Rococo Revival throughout the mid-19thC.
£700-£1000

George II tea kettle with stand and burner; London, 1740; c.13 in (33 cm) high. This silver kettle with wooden handle is chased with a frieze of Rococo flowers, scrolls and bulrushes, the decoration echoed on its legs and mounts.
£5000-£7000

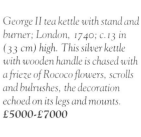

Old Sheffield plate and copper tea urn; 1803; 12¼ in (31.1 cm) high. Although Old Sheffield plate was often used in making large items such as tea urns, this example is unusual because it has Old Sheffield plate mounts attached to a copper body and base.
£300-£400

TEA FOR THREE *Wealthy families of the early 18thC built up silver tea services bit by bit – and they often included a tray for teaspoons.*

TEA WAS A LUXURY when it first reached the West, its precious leaves kept under lock and key, so a finely chased silver teapot and caddy seemed quite appropriate for it. All manner of teapots, coffee pots, cream jugs and sugar bowls have been produced since the mid-17th century, most following contemporary silver styles.

TEAPOTS, KETTLES AND URNS

The earliest teapots, dating from the 1670s, were small and had tapering straight sides and a conical cover. Pear-shaped and globular teapots were being made by the early 18th century. Both types were made for a long time and are still easily found today, but they are invariably expensive if in good condition. A London example could cost £4000-£6000, a provincial one even more.

Tea was much cheaper by the mid-18th century so could be used more freely. Teapots became larger, holding four or more cups. Many drum-shaped and oval George III teapots are very light, as they were made from thin machine-rolled silver, and few are found in good condition. Despite this, Neoclassical pots of this period sell for £600-£1000.

Novelty shapes and decoration are typical of the mid-19th century. Indian-style pots chased with dancing figures, 'Aesthetic' pieces with Japanese-influenced designs, and even pots modelled as fruit and vegetables were made. Prices vary enormously: £300-£1000 for silver examples and £70 upwards for good-quality electroplate. Silver tewares of the 20th century generally fetch £10-£15 per ounce, but Art Nouveau and Art Deco pieces change hands for about £15-£25 per ounce.

Early teapots were often supplied with a separate stand, some of which had an inset wooden base while others had applied tiny feet. Teapot stands are still relatively cheap, at £200-£400, although a particularly early example could cost more.

Tea kettles had a stand and also a lamp or burner. These appeared around 1690 but went out of favour in the 1770s when tea urns were introduced, returning in the mid-19th century. Early kettles change hands at auction for £4000-£8000; examples from the mid-19th century normally fetch £800-£1500. Always check that the marks on the stand and lamp match those on the kettle itself. If components have been replaced, the value is likely to be halved.

By 1790 most tea urns were fitted with a spirit lamp. Small urns were used for coffee, larger ones for water with which the hostess would brew tea. Silver urns are quite scarce today, selling for £1500-£4000, but many can be found in both Old Sheffield plate and electroplate, including some splendid 'tea machines' with one large and two smaller urns standing on a shaped tray; these were probably for use at breakfast in large country houses. Electroplated tea urns may fetch £250-£500 at auction, while Old Sheffield plate tea machines now sell for £4000-£6000.

COFFEE AND CHOCOLATE POTS

Like early teapots, the first coffee pots have plain tapering sides. They date from the end of the 17th century, and many have a handle set at right angles to the spout – some in a scroll form, others turned into a baluster shape. It is a myth that a handle at such an angle distinguishes a chocolate pot. Octagonal pots are somewhat rarer than plain ones, but both types now fetch £4000-£7000.

By the early years of the 18th century, the base of a coffee pot was made to curve inwards, gradually evolving into the baluster or pear shape by about 1740, although straight-sided coffee biggins – pots with a built-in filter – appeared in the late 18th century. These were sold with a warming stand and burner and are usually smaller than other pots of the period.

All types of mid to late 18th-century coffee pots can be found for £1500-£2500, although a particularly fine example might well fetch more. In the 19th century they were made to correspond with the styles of tea sets, and followed a similar evolution in design. Single coffee pots fetch a better price than single teapots, however, and will go for about £15-£25 per ounce.

Chocolate pots and hot water and milk jugs are similar to contemporary coffee pots. Chocolate pots can be distinguished by a finial that either lifts off or swivels on a pin, revealing a hole in the lid. A stirring stick, or molinet, was inserted through this hole to stir the chocolate up from the bottom.

Genuine chocolate pots are much sought after, changing hands for £4000-£8000. Specimens with their original silver-mounted molinet are very scarce, and would fetch at least double this price. Always inspect a chocolate pot carefully, since coffee pots were often converted by having the finial removed to create the opening for the molinet.

CREAM JUGS

Cream jugs first appeared during the reign of Queen Anne. Early examples follow teapot designs, but by the 1720s plain, pear-shaped jugs raised on shell-and-hoof feet had become fashionable. By the mid-18th century most were chased with arabesques. These traditionally shaped cream jugs may fetch several

Silver and wood tea set; London, 1884; teapot 4½ in (11.4 cm) high. This ornately decorated bachelor set is in exceptionally good condition.
£600-£800
Plainer version: £250-£350

Tea set and tray; 1911 and 1908; tray 27½ in (70 cm) long. This heavily engraved example is typical of the many tea sets produced in the early 20thC; sets with a coffee pot instead of a hot-water jug are the most desirable. A monogram reduces a piece's value by a third.
Tray: £1000-£1500
Tea set: £600-£800

George II provincial chocolate pot; Exeter, 1741; 9¼ in (23.5 cm) high. This pot is identical to a contemporary coffee pot in shape but has a detachable finial to allow a stirring stick to be used.
£2500-£3500

Silver tea-caddy set; London, 1752; 5¼ in (13.3 cm) high. It is rare to find a set of caddies with their matching sugar box, especially if their original wooden box has been lost, as here. This set is chased with Chinese and Rococo motifs.
Set: £7000-£10,000

Silver-gilt cream jug; London, 1738 5 in (12.7 cm) high. Typical of its period, this well-made piece is cast and chased with Rococo ornamentation. Poorer-quality examples are still readily available for a few hundred pounds
£2500-£3500

Old Sheffield plate coffee pot; 1760-80; 11½ in (29.2 cm) high. Sheffield plate is a collecting area in its own right. It is always cheaper than silver, but can still fetch high prices if in good condition.
£200-£250

George II boxed tea-making set; London, 1752; 5½ in (14 cm) high. This rare and complete set includes a sugar box, teaspoons and sugar tongs.
£6000-£8000

thousand pounds, although George III and IV specimens can be found for £180-£300. Later examples may cost as little as £80-£200.

A host of novelty cream jugs were manufactured throughout the 18th and 19th centuries, including cast shell jugs raised on a dolphin or dragon base, cow creamers (jugs modelled as cows), and jugs in the form of goats, geese, cockerels and even pug dogs. All types are popular today, and a genuine mid-18th-century cow creamer might fetch £4000-£8000. Later examples sell for £300-£600, depending on the quality and rarity of design.

Cream pails with a swing handle first appeared in the 1730s, although most survivors date from about 1755-1805, in late Georgian times, when they were made in sets with pedestal sugar basins. Most are decorated with machine piercing and are fitted with a 'Bristol' blue glass liner. These change hands at auction today for £300-£600 each.

TEA CADDIES

Tea caddies were made in silver almost as soon as teapots themselves. During the 1760s, matching tea-making sets first appeared in large numbers, although it is difficult to find a complete set today. When they do come up for sale, such sets are very expensive. A complete 18th-century tea set with two caddies, a sugar bowl, spoons and other pieces can easily sell for £10,000 or more.

Early square or oblong silver tea caddies dating from the end of the 17th century are now very scarce. Much easier to find today are mid-18th-century caddies of bombé shape with Rococo or chinoiserie chasing, or vase-shaped caddies applied with cast scrolls. These were made in sets of three – the larger box meant for holding sugar – and fitted snugly into a wooden box veneered with exotic woods, tortoiseshell or mother-of-pearl, or covered with shagreen.

Later caddies from the 1770s are larger fluted ovals, many divided to hold two types of tea, and with a lock to prevent pilfering by the servants. Few silver caddies date from after 1820, although some small, inexpensive pieces were made, mainly in Birmingham and Chester, around the end of the 19th century. These are generally of poor quality, with die-stamped decoration.

Caddies are popular with collectors: early 18th-century examples sell for £2000-£3000

English coffee pots of the 18thC. A good plain coffee pot, like the earliest example (9¾ in, 24.7 cm high), will fetch more than most chased examples as it can be difficult to confirm that the chasing is contemporary. The two in the middle have had chased and engraved decoration added later, and therefore their value has been reduced by about a third. Vase-shaped bodies are typical of the late 18thC.

1745 **£2000**   1775 **£1600**   1775 **£1200**   1792 **£1200**

Silver sugar box; London, 1716; 4¾ in (12.1 cm) long. Most early 18thC pieces, like this one which weighs 20 oz (622 g), are sturdy and well constructed. Below the angled facets, which reflect the light, there is space for engraving.
£10,000-£15,000

Silver sugar bowls (right); Dublin, 1717 (without lid), and London, 1728; c.3½ in (89 mm) high. Plain and sturdy 18thC silver is in great demand, especially if engraved in period with an armorial.
Complete: £1500-£2000
Without lid: £1000-£1500

Cow creamer (left); London, 1758; 6 in (15.2 cm) long. Produced in great quantities, these creamers have been much copied, especially by late 19th and early 20thC Dutch silversmiths.
£4000-£8000
19th/20thC copy: £300-£600

each, while later specimens are somewhat cheaper. Edwardian silver tea caddies may change hands at auction for £150-£300.

OTHER ACCESSORIES

The style of sugar bowls has always closely mirrored that of contemporary teapots, and silver examples were made from the time tea was first introduced. Sugar boxes for storage were also produced both in Britain and on the Continent, and can be confused with tea caddies, although by the 18th century caddies were usually fitted with a lock. Buyers should be wary of German and Dutch examples, as many were later engraved with Hebrew inscriptions to suggest they were originally used as *Ethrog* boxes – containers to hold a citrus fruit in Sabbath ceremonies. Items

connected with Judaism are now widely collected, hence the deceptive conversions.

Smaller tea accessories include mid-19th-century silver and plated cups with saucers, most designed for show rather than use. Moustache cups in electroplate are not uncommon, fetching £100-£150. Small, silver mounts for clipping onto the rim of porcelain cups to protect the splendid waxed moustaches worn by many gentlemen in the 19th century can be found for £20-£30.

Thin silver holders for porcelain coffee cups were produced in sets from the late 19th century onwards, sometimes with spoons and tongs. Highly decorative sets complete with porcelain cups sell for £300-£400 or even more if the porcelain was made by Royal Worcester or another popular maker.

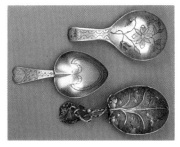

English coffee pots. These pots show a development in 19th and early 20thC styles. The 1837 pot (11¼ in, 28.5 cm high), is bright cut, a decorative technique more typical of the late 18thC, while the 1904 example is die-stamped – a cheaper technique – and less valuable than the earlier pieces. The Victorian coffee pot of 1837 is hand-chased.

1806 **£1200**   1837 **£800**   1903 **£800**   1904 **£450**

Candleholders and lamps

Antique silver candlesticks are unashamedly luxurious, but are unmatched in their ability to create 'mood' lighting and a romantic atmosphere.

AT ONE TIME, the dim, flickering light and smoky fumes of candles and oil lamps were accepted as a necessity, but now their glow is appreciated for the ambience it creates. Prices have risen in recent years, but a good variety of 18th and 19th-century candlesticks and other pieces can be found.

CANDLESTICKS AND CANDELABRA

The earliest domestic silver candlesticks you are likely to see are from the 1660s. Most were made from sheet silver, usually with an octagonal or square base and a fluted stem, and some are decorated with gadrooning.

By about 1675 candlesticks were usually shorter, up to about 7½ in (19 cm) high, and cast in three sections – base, stem and sconce. Early cast candlesticks had an octagonal or hexagonal base – often faceted to catch the light – and a knopped stem. By the 1720s, most had a square, dished base with angled corners. A little later, shell motifs became popular on the cast base and shoulders. From the late 17th century onwards, some figural candlesticks were also made, with cast human figures holding the sconce aloft; Oriental figures were popular in the 1750s, Classical caryatids in the 1770s.

After about 1740 table candlesticks were again slightly taller – about 9 in (23 cm) high – and had detachable nozzles, still cast with shells. The nozzles often have no hallmark, although some are stamped with a lion passant or with the maker's initials. Cast candlesticks, often with flamboyant Rococo decoration, continued to be popular into the 1760s. Pairs of cast candlesticks are now very pricey: a mid-18th century pair may fetch £1800-£2500 at auction, and anything earlier £7000-£12,000. But a single candlestick may make only a quarter the price of a pair.

From the 1770s candlesticks were again made from sheet silver, but with the stem strengthened by an iron rod and the base filled with pitch or plaster and covered with baize. Quality fell off after this time, pieces from Sheffield especially being flimsy. Inspect them carefully, as many have small holes from over cleaning. Be wary of buying crooked candlesticks, as they are hard to straighten.

Many late 18th-century candlesticks have a stem in the form of a Corinthian or Doric column. Other Neoclassical features, such as rams' heads, urns and paterae, are also common. These styles are still popular and have been endlessly reproduced right up to today. Most recent copies are stamped from very thin metal with poor-quality dies, and so lack the sharpness even of Edwardian copies. You might pay around £1200-£1600 for a pair of Georgian filled candlesticks in fair condition, or £400-£600 for a pair of Victorian or Edwardian copies; smaller copies suitable for dressing tables fetch £300-£450 a pair.

Cast candlesticks appeared again during the Regency period, many copying earlier designs. They are often gilded and finely decorated with crisp chasing. They are now very expensive, fetching £3000-£6000 per pair. Plainer Regency candlesticks with a gadrooned frieze, and invariably filled, are much less popular, selling for £800-£1200 a pair. This style was widely produced in Old Sheffield plate, and pairs in good condition cost £200-£300. Telescopic candlesticks also date from the Regency period and sell for half as much again as their static counterparts. A patented action extends the stem as the candle burns down, so they throw a constant light. They are usually in Sheffield plate.

Candelabra closely followed the design of candlesticks. It is rare, however, to find one made before 1760. Most early candelabra have two sconces and branches, but three-light examples became common after 1770. If you find an earlier specimen with unmarked branches, these may have been added later.

Candelabra of the 18th century are much in demand, and pairs sell for £5000-£10,000. By the Regency period, huge candelabra with five or more branches were fashionable. Old Sheffield plate specimens are the easiest to find today, selling at auction for £800-£1500 a pair. Silver examples could fetch £6000-£10,000, while candelabra with a solid silver base and Sheffield plate branches sell for somewhere between the two.

CHAMBERSTICKS

Chamber candlesticks, or chambersticks, have a broad, stable base – usually dished – and a carrying handle, and were designed for the bedroom. On mid-17th century examples the handle is long and flat, but by the early 18th century it was a rising scroll or loop, often with a socket to hold a conical extinguisher. Although decoration varied enormously, the basic shape changed little even into late Victorian times. Some later chambersticks have a hole through the stem for holding a

IN THE BOUDOIR *Dressing for dinner by candlelight was part of Victorian life, the candlesticks placed in front of a mirror to throw more light.*

Pair of Restoration candlesticks engraved with the Mercer family arms; 1667; 9¼ in (23.5 cm) high. They may have been part of a christening gift from King Charles II.
£80,000-£100,000 (pair); no royal link: £40,000-£60,000 (pair)

William III silver candlesticks, each one of a pair: (left) 1700, 5¼ in (13.3 cm) high; (right) by Benjamin Pyne, 1699, 6½ in (16.5 cm) high. Fine decoration and clear marks add to the latter's value.
Left: £4000-£6000 (pair)
Right: £8000-£12,000 (pair)
19th or early 20thC copies: £300-£400 (pair)

Set of four Regency cast silver candlesticks; 1819; 13½ in (34.3 cm) high. Also (centre) smaller pair; 1823; 12¼ in (31.1 cm) high. The early 19thC saw superb quality cast silver.
Set of four: £20,000-£30,000; pair: £7000-£10,000
If loaded: £1200-£1600 (pair)

George IV silver-gilt taperstick with conical extinguisher; 1823; 3¾ in (95 mm) wide. This stick, once part of an inkstand, held a thin taper for melting sealing wax. The small size makes it desirable.
£250-£300
Old Sheffield plate: £40-£70

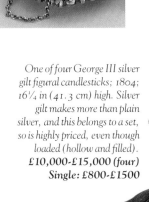

One of four George III silver gilt figural candlesticks; 1804; 16¼ in (41.3 cm) high. Silver gilt makes more than plain silver, and this belongs to a set, so is highly priced, even though loaded (hollow and filled).
£10,000-£15,000 (four)
Single: £800-£1500

One of a pair of electroplated candelabra in Neoclassical style; mid-19thC; 17¾ in (45.1 cm) high. This desirable Victorian piece, unlike many, is small enough for modern homes.
£600-£800 (pair)

One of a pair of William III wall lights; London; 1701; 10½ in (26.7 cm) high. A candle sat in front of the silver backplate, originally held by an iron spike that was later replaced by a detachable sconce (not shown).
£30,000-£40,000 (pair)

Pair of silver telescopic candlesticks; 1800; 10¼ in (26 cm) high. Also one of a pair of silver chambersticks with extinguisher but no wick-trimmers; 1839; 6½ in (16.5 cm) wide.
Each pair: £800-£1200
Old Sheffield plate: £180-£220

wick-trimmer. 'Storm' chambersticks from the Regency period have the sconce surrounded by a pierced gallery; this originally held a tall glass shade which shielded the flame from draughts.

Single 17th and early 18th-century silver chambersticks are expensive, selling at auction for £2000-£3000. Later specimens can be found for £300-£400. Huge numbers of Old Sheffield plate chambersticks were produced in the first half of the 19th century, and today fetch £50-£150 each, or £180-£220 for a pair.

WALL SCONCES AND LAMPS

Early wall sconces have a plain base and small candle socket, and some have a back plate of heavily chased sheet silver or of mirror glass to reflect light back into the room. A pair may sell for £30,000-£40,000. Sconces with two branches, some in the form of human arms, are rare, and can fetch very many thousands.

Oil lamps with a silver Corinthian column stem and cut-glass reservoir date from the mid-19th century. Most are over 20in (50cm) tall, and fetch £1000-£1500 in silver, or £400-£600 in electroplate. Small lanterns for use in carriages fetch £700-£1200.

Silver smalls and objects of vertu

Small, beautifully crafted personal possessions – some quite plain, others ornate – make a fascinating collecting field, combining fine workmanship and rich materials with an intimate look at lives of the past.

OVER THE YEARS, both silversmiths and jewellers have produced countless small objects for everyday use. Those made of silver are known as silver smalls or smallware, while others are luxury articles using silver, gold and other precious materials, sometimes combined with porcelain or tortoiseshell, or decorated with enamels or gemstones. This second group is referred to as objects of vertu, an 18th-century term loosely translated as 'precious objects'; most were made between the 17th and 19th centuries. Although many pieces were designed to be carried on the person, others were obviously made specifically for household use.

Silver smalls in particular represent a good point to start a collection as they often come up for sale in both antique markets and junk shops. More adventurous collectors can bid for mixed lots – literally a cardboard box containing ten or more assorted items – at a provincial or downmarket London saleroom. Selling off the pieces singly may leave the one you really wanted costing nothing.

Decorative and unusual objects of vertu are also a fascinating collecting field, and many of these are available at well under £100, although jewel-encrusted rarities can fetch thousands of pounds at auction.

HOUSEHOLD ITEMS

Small household items range from desk equipment and dressing-table accessories to a wide variety of random objects which pop up just about anywhere, such as photograph frames and bells for calling the servants.

LIBRARY EQUIPMENT

From the late 17th century, permanent desks were increasingly used in many well-to-do homes, the more so when the library became a part of a gentleman's house. Among the silver smalls that consequently appeared were inkstands, equipment for sealing letters and (from the 1840s) stamp boxes.

Open inkstands were used from the 18th century onwards. These usually rectangular or

Novelty inkstand in the form of a child's cot; Birmingham, 1936; 6½ in (16.5 cm) long. Although presentation inscriptions generally detract from a piece's value, very unusual inscriptions can boost the price.
£600-£800

Gold and hardstone seals: (left) c.1830-45, 3 in (76 mm) long; (right) c.1880, 5⅛ in (13 cm) long. Both desk seals have gold mounts, and that on the right has a 'tiger's eye' quartz handle.
Left: £800-£1200
Right: £2000-£2500

GLEAMING FINISH *The importance the wealthy 19thC lady placed on elaborate personal grooming was reflected in the silver toilet aids on her dressing table – a setting caught in this portrait of Elisa Hofer by Austrian artist Ferdinand Georg Waldmuller (1793-1865).*

Silver carriage clock; Birmingham, 1901; 5 in (12.7 cm) high. This ornate example was designed to grace a desk rather than for travelling use. Such pieces can fetch £1000, especially those with stamped decoration or with hardstone or tortoiseshell plaques.
£500-£700

oval stands hold various pots and pens, and some even have a receptacle for a small bell or a taperstick. A complete George III inkstand or a later Victorian novelty example will fetch £2000-£2500, but even the smaller items that have become separated from the main stand can command very high prices: silver bells, for example, have been known to change hands for anything up to £1000.

Before the mid-19th century, letters were always closed with sealing wax before sending. Good-quality silver wax jacks, used from the mid-18th century to hold a coiled taper for melting wax, fetch about £800-£1000, especially if they have retained their tiny conical snuffer, originally attached by a fine chain. Tiny silver stamp cases in the form of an envelope, made to hold perhaps half-a-dozen

stamps, can be found for only a few pounds. Also still quite common are small stamp troughs, no more than a few inches long, that were placed on a desk.

DRESSING-TABLE ITEMS

Silver dressing-table pieces first appeared in the late 1660s, although small pots and jars survive from even earlier periods. Complete sets of the earliest objects – with a mirror, comb, brushes, toilet jars and more unusual accessories such as button hooks and glove stretchers – are very rare, and prices are high.

Simple 19th-century dressing-table sets including a silver-backed mirror, a comb and perhaps two or three silver-backed brushes sell for £50-£100, although few are in good condition. Sold individually, a mirror will fetch £60-£80, a comb £30-£40, a clothes brush £30-£50, and a hair brush £10-£15.

The Victorian silversmithing firm of William Comyns, still in business today, made

many silver lids and pierced mounts for glass toilet jars and bottles. A Comyns cologne bottle from the turn of the century with stamped silver mounts will probably sell for about £200-£300; a pair will make more than double that figure. Bottles with more run-of-the-mill silver mounts fetch £80-£120.

Circular powder boxes, often set on small feet, are still quite common and therefore inexpensive. They can be found at fairs and auctions for as little as £50-£60, although more ornate examples will cost a little more.

AROUND THE HOUSE

Table bells, used for calling servants, originated in the early 18th century and are mostly hand-held. Early bells are rare and sell for many hundreds of pounds, but even Victorian and Edwardian reproductions can be quite expensive, fetching £200-£250.

In the late 19th century, novelty bells were introduced, and one of the most appealing is

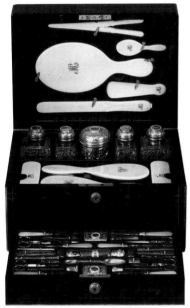

Veneered and inlaid fitted dressing case; London, 1873; 20 in (51 cm) wide. It contains toilet jars, grooming accessories and sewing equipment.
£7000-£10,000

Silver and glass-cased necessaire; mid-19thC; c.3½ in (90 mm) long. This rectangular necessaire may well be continental.
£600-£800

Continental singing bird boxes; c.1880; each 4 in (10.1 cm) wide. The left-hand box is cast in relief with putti, while that on the right is silver-gilt and enamelled, with pastoral scenes.
Left: £1500-£1800
Right: £3000-£3500

Table bells (left to right): Elkington electroplate, late 19thC; Birmingham, 1907; London, 1881; tortoise 5¼ in (13.3 cm) long. Table bells – particularly novelty items – are highly collectable.
Left: £200-£300
Centre: £500-£600
Right: £150-£250

Christening mug by George Angell; London, 1855; 4 in (10.1 cm) high. The chasing depicts a hurdy-gurdy man and performing dog.
£400-£500

SEWING ACCESSORIES
Small Is Beautiful

MANY OF THE TOOLS found in needlework cases or étuis are made at least in part from silver. Among the most collectable of these items are thimbles, which were produced in their thousands. Many are decorated and may be marked with a number to indicate the size, or with a trade name – 'Dorcas' is one of the best known. A few makers produced thimbles in limited editions, and these are usually marked and identifiable. Some of them are beautiful and can fetch up to £100.

Late Victorian silver thimble in its original case; 1890; ¾ in (19 mm) long.
£20-£30

in the form of a tortoise. When the tail is depressed a buzzing noise sounds and the animal's head nods up and down. If hall-marked and in working order, these sell for around £500; a pair will change hands for more than double this price.

Towards the end of the 19th century, when photographic portraits were all the rage, silver-mounted photograph frames were made in profusion. William Comyns manufactured many thousands, and his original, turn-of-the-century frames can cost £200-£300, depending on size and wear; modern reproductions can be bought for a quarter of this price, but Art Nouveau frames are expensive.

Although most snuffboxes were for carrying on the person (see p.260), larger examples were also made, probably to pass around the table at the end of an evening. By the 19th century they were anything up to 5 in (12.5 cm) across. These are generally sold as 'table snuffboxes', and fetch around £800-£1200, depending

on their workmanship. Snuff mulls – large containers of horn or bone mounted in silver – were made in Scotland in the late Georgian and Victorian periods. Good examples sell for as little as £120-£150.

Georgian and Victorian needlework accessories, such as scissors, needles, needle cases and thimbles were made from silver (see p.257). Rare Georgian examples fetch £100-£150, while more plentiful Victorian items sell for £10-£20. Decorative needle cases were also made in enamel and gold, and even set with pearls. The most luxurious needle cases sell for as much as £1000-£1500.

CHRISTENING PRESENTS

Apostle spoons were a favourite christening gift from the 16th century onwards, although complete sets of 13 spoons from then are very rare indeed. Today, 19th-century

copies fetch around £300-£400 for a complete set and £20-£30 for a single piece. Christening sets made up of a knife, fork and spoon were also popular in the 19th century and are relatively cheap today, at £80-£120. These pieces were often engraved with the child's initials; this does reduce their value, but inscriptions can be professionally erased.

Christening mugs were manufactured in large quantities from 1850 to 1900, and range from the totally plain to the extremely ornate. There is often a presentation inscription featuring the child's initials or name and birth date. Prices can vary enormously, ranging from £150 for dull or heavily inscribed mugs to £500 for more elegant or unusual examples. A rattle has long been a traditional gift at

Game-bird menu or name-card holder; London, 1912; 3 in (76 mm) across.
£70-£100
Set of six: £500-£700

Hip flask (left); London, 1922; 5¼ in (13.3 cm) high. An inscription would reduce the value.
£200-£300

Stamped silver photo frame on velvet base; Birmingham, 1913; 4½ in (11.4 cm) high. Modern reproductions abound, so check the hallmarks.
£80-£100

Silver-lidded glass rouge pot (right) for the dressing table; Birmingham, 1900; 1⅜ in (35 mm) across.
£30-£40

Silver pillbox; Birmingham, 1908; 1¼ in (32 mm) across. Very similar handbag compacts were also produced at this time.
£40-£60

Fiddle-pattern silver salt spoon; London, 1860; 4½ in (11.4 cm) long. It was for use with a large trencher salt; later examples are smaller.
£10-£40

Silver-handled paper knife or letter opener with mother-of-pearl blade; late 19thC; 6¾ in (17.1 cm) long. The handle is die-stamped. Other examples have an ivory blade; both types are fashionable with collectors today.
£70-£120

christenings. Most rattles have a coral handle or teether – a throwback to the days when coral was believed to protect the owner from the Evil Eye – and many have bells and a whistle mouthpiece. Good examples with their bells can fetch £500 or more.

PERSONAL ITEMS

Small personal possessions have always been carried by both men and women. Some double almost as jewellery, combining beauty with practicality. Whereas men might wear a seal or stamp box attached to a watch chain, women often carried étuis.

Étuis were designed to hold a selection of personal items and were popular from the early 17th century onwards. Some were attached to the chatelaine worn at the waist. Most étuis are around 3 in (76 mm) long, and they can be highly decorative, with painted or enamelled scenes. Early pieces can fetch as much as £1000, while later 19th-century examples can be found for around £100.

The chatelaine – an arrangement of chains and clips fastened to a belt hook on which many household objects were carried – was introduced in the 17th century, but then went out of fashion. Chatelaines made a comeback in the 19th century, when the lady of the house or her housekeeper would rarely be seen without one. An example with good clips and a wide variety of attachments – which might range from stamp carriers and scissors to mirrors and seals – can fetch £600-£800, but even small accessories that have become detached (identifiable by a small loop or hook) are very collectable.

PORTABLE WRITING EQUIPMENT

The earliest desks were nothing more than portable lapdesks, which held other essential writing paraphernalia. Inkstands of around 1770 were usually set into a portable casket, a rectangular box which contained an inkpot, a pounce pot (holding sand for sprinkling on the paper to dry the ink), a wafer box (to hold discs of sealing wax), and a drawer for the quill pens. These are rarely found complete, and if they are they fetch up to £15,000.

Letters secured with molten sealing wax were stamped with a seal, often engraved, made of metal, stone or glass. Georgian fob

Enamelled silver napkin ring; Birmingham, 1925; 1½ in (38 mm) across. The enamel decoration raises the value by about £40.
£50-£70

Silver-topped glass glue pot (left); Birmingham, 1892; 4¼ in (10.8 cm) high. It is a rarity, but of little practical use today.
£60-£80

Stamped sweetmeat dish of very thin silver, in Rococo style; Birmingham, 1910; 5 in (12.7 cm) wide. Similar pieces were made in Neoclassical style. Larger dishes are often slightly cheaper than small ones like this.
£180-£220

Miniature mirror (right) from a lady's chatelaine; Birmingham, 1910; 2¾ in (70 mm) long.
£50-£70

American stamp box; c.1900; 1⅛ in (30 mm) across. Items connected with philately are keenly collected.
£40-£70

Desktop stamp holder with glass window; Chester, 1910; 1 in (25 mm) across.
£80-£140

Silver-topped, heavy cut-glass inkwell; Birmingham, 1907; 2¼ in (57 mm) across. These are much in demand for modern offices.
£70-£120

Silver dip pen, originally from a desk set; Sheffield, 1902; 7¾ in (19.7 cm) long. The spiral-twist handle makes this an attractive item for a modern desk.
£120-£180

seals can still be found for around £50-£150, as can travelling wax-taper containers from the same period. These cylindrical, covered 'bougie boxes', as they were known, are generally made of silver and have a pierced lid which allows the coiled taper to protrude. Many have a pivoting cover to block off the hole in the lid, and also to serve as a snuffer. As bougie boxes were designed to be strictly functional they often lack decoration, but are collected for their simplicity and sturdy form. They fetch around £300-£500.

FOR SCENT AND SMELLING SALTS

Vinaigrettes are among the most commonly found silver smalls, going at prices ranging from £50 to £1000 or more. They were used from about 1770 until the late 19th century to counter the smells of bad sanitation and poor personal hygiene. These small, hinged boxes contained a sponge soaked in aromatic oil or vinegar and a pierced inner grille which held the sponge in place.

Many vinaigrettes were manufactured in London, but thousands more were made in Birmingham. Early vinaigrettes are mainly rectangular, but later 'novelty' examples can be found in the shape of a purse, book, fish, shell or flower, among others. Rectangular 'castle-top' vinaigrettes, cast or engraved with

a scene of a national monument or ancestral home, are among the most collectable. They date from around 1825 onwards, and their abundance suggests that they mark the beginning of the souvenir industry, which grew hand in hand with travel on the railways.

Buyers should inspect vinaigrettes carefully for damage, especially worn hinges, split grilles and dulled detail in the metalwork, caused by overcleaning. If the gilding inside a box appears too bright, the interior may have been regilded. Although this may be quite innocent, it could also hide repaired damage.

Small scent bottles from the 18th and 19th centuries frequently come up for sale. Many are primarily of glass (see p. 212), but others are made from porcelain, precious metals, enamel or carved semiprecious stones, and sometimes jewelled. Silver-topped, cut-glass bottles can fetch £50-£80, double-ended

bottles (which held perfume at one end and smelling salts at the other) £150-£400, and enamelled or gold-mounted bottles £400-£600. As a rule of thumb, the more fancy they are the more valuable they will be.

SNUFF AND SMOKING ITEMS

Boxes for chewing tobacco dating back to around 1680 can still be found; examples in good condition sell at auction for about £1500-£2000. But as the popularity of ready-grated tobacco – snuff – grew, snuffboxes began to replace tobacco boxes from about the 1680s. Early silver snuffboxes are mostly plain, with little decoration except for the owner's initials or crest. By the 1770s, however, new manufacturing techniques assured a

---

Enamel and gilt étui (left); c.1760; 4½ in (11.4 cm) long. Made by Bilston, this tapering oval étui shows a courting couple. Damaged examples lose half their value.
£400-£500

Late Victorian silver chatelaine clip (right); c.1870; 13 in (33 cm) long. This example has three attachments: a thimble case, a scissors case and an étui.
£150-£200

Unusual novelty trophy vinaigrette; London, 1834; 2¾ in (70 mm) high. There is a wide range of designs and prices in these small silver items.
£1500-£1800

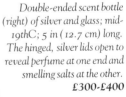

Double-ended scent bottle (right) of silver and glass; mid-19thC; 5 in (12.7 cm) long. The hinged, silver lids open to reveal perfume at one end and smelling salts at the other.
£300-£400

Oval, silver-gilt vinaigrette, shown open and closed; Birmingham, 1830; 2 in (51 mm) wide. The top is cast and the interior covered with a pierced grille.
£400-£500

plentiful supply of relatively cheap silver and gold boxes from London and Birmingham, many of which were cast or engraved with stylised flower or leaf designs.

Snuffboxes can be found in silver, gold, tortoiseshell, enamel or semiprecious stones, with silver or gold mountings. Prices vary according to materials and workmanship, the most sought-after silver snuffboxes being those cast in high relief with scenes of well-known landmarks or with hunting groups. A standard box might fetch £250, a better-quality one £500. Recently, a rare and excellent example of a castle-top snuffbox, depicting York Minster, sold for £2900.

Among the most attractive items related to smoking – which include cigarette cases, boxes, holders and lighters – are vesta cases. These small containers were designed to hold a supply of matches, and are named after the Roman goddess of the hearth, Vesta. The (non-safety) matches were struck on a serrated rasp on one edge.

Vesta cases were fashionable for a relatively short period, from about 1880 until the early 20th century, but they were made in enormous numbers in both silver and plate, and in a wide range of designs. These include plain rectangles, elaborate novelty forms such as rugby or golf balls, circular cases decorated with cast sporting scenes, and enamelled examples depicting railway tickets, playing cards and mild erotica. The price range is equally wide. Plain and engraved silver cases start as low as £20, whereas novelties fetch £300-£400. Enamelled vesta cases are the most valuable, particularly those with titillating scenes, selling for anything up to £500.

OUT AND ABOUT

At the end of the 19th century, polite society carried visiting cards. Cases to hold them were made from many materials, including tortoiseshell, mother-of-pearl, ivory and papier-mâché, but the earliest cases seem to have been of silver. Early visiting-card cases are relatively plain, but later ones have gradually more inventive decoration. Again, those with topographical scenes (some have a different view on each side) fetch most – up to £600-£800 today.

Similar cases, known as carnets de bal, held ivory leaves on which ladies made a note of partners to whom they had promised dances at a ball. Carnets and aides-mémoire – little cases for a note pad and pencil – were made and decorated in the same materials as card cases. A silver example complete with its contents may sell for between £80 and £120.

Posy holders for ladies to carry or wear were produced in large numbers in Victorian times; they held small bunches of flowers. They are often in the shape of a cornet or cornucopia and may be decorated with turquoise beads, coral or small seed pearls, or plaques of painted porcelain or enamel. Gold, silver or enamelled posy holders sell for around £500-£700, but base metal, plated or damaged examples fetch less.

Although not greatly in demand by collectors, opera glasses can make an interesting field; some of the enamelled examples are particularly attractive. The more common examples in ivory or mother-of-pearl can be found for £100-£150, whereas a prettier piece by a noted jeweller such as Cartier or Asprey might fetch £300-£400.

George II oval tobacco box; London, 1727; 3½ in (89 mm) long. Made by Edward Carnock, this box is engraved with its owner's initials.
£800-£1000

Novelty vesta cases; London, 1895 (left) and 1882; owl 2¾ in (70 mm) high. The hinged head of the owl opens to disclose the matches inside, while the square cover of the book-style case is decorated with an enamelled study of the cover of 'Punch' magazine.
£250-£300 each

Victorian parcel-gilt silver posy holder with finger ring on chain; Birmingham, 1880; 5½ in (14 cm) high. It is decorated in Aesthetic style with Japanese motifs.
£350-£400

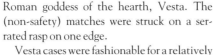

Enamelled cigarette cases; probably German, early 20thC; left-hand case 3¼ in (82 mm) wide. Erotic designs are avidly collected; damaged enamel (as on the right-hand case) reduces values considerably.
Left: £1500-£2000
Right: £700-£900

Silver card cases (clockwise from top left): Chester, 1887, 4 in (10.1 cm) high, in Aesthetic style; Birmingham, 1843, showing York Minster; possibly Scottish, c.1840, with thistles and Edinburgh Castle; Birmingham, 1838, with tartan pattern.
York Minster: £350-£450
Others: £150-£250

By appointment to the Tsar

The workshops of Peter Carl Fabergé (1846-1920) are renowned for the bejewelled Easter eggs they created for the Russian imperial family. But Fabergé also designed a wide range of objects of vertu.

CARL FABERGÉ BEGAN his career as a craftsman in his father's St Petersburg jewellery business, which he inherited in 1870. But as the firm grew, Fabergé became largely a manager, leaving manufacture to his band of highly skilled craftsmen. After being given the title 'Supplier to the Imperial Court', and making the first of the famous Easter eggs for Tsar Alexander III in 1884, Fabergé won renown that spread through Europe, culminating in an exhibition in Paris in 1900.

The First World War brought success to an end. The London branch closed in 1915, and the firm was ordered to concentrate on the manufacture of guns – though a few cigarette cases were made, in gunmetal or copper. Finally, after the October Revolution of 1917, it was taken over by a workers' cooperative. Carl Fabergé died in exile three years later.

BEAUTY AND USEFULNESS

The articles made in the Fabergé workshops fall into four main categories. Sumptuously ornamented pieces of a functional nature were created, including bell pushes, photograph frames, umbrella handles, cigarette holders and clocks, often finely enamelled and made

THE MASTER'S HAND *Carl Fabergé mainly wielded the manager's pen, not the craftsman's tools.*

with a variety of different metals such as gold, silver and platinum. Smaller items today sell at auction for about £1000-£3000, while table clocks fetch £7500-£15,000.

Hardstone ornamental figures, including animals, birds, plants and flowers, were made

in a special factory. Among others, the British royal family commissioned copies of pets and farmyard animals, and these are still in the royal collection. Human figures were carved too, but they are much rarer. While animals may fetch around £3000-£5000 at auction, human figures sell for £12,000-£15,000.

Fabergé also made a range of jewellery consisting of tiny enamelled novelty pieces, small brooches, pendants, and tiepins formed as animals, eggs and insects. All have finely executed detail. A small brooch or tiepin could today cost £2500-£3500.

But the best-known Fabergé objects are the Easter eggs made mostly for the Russian Tsar as presents for his wife and mother. They were produced every year from 1884 until 1917, many containing miniatures of the family, their palaces or pets and some with a mechanism to make them move. It is known that Fabergé made 57 such eggs, of which 46 have been identified. The rest are assumed to be lost or in private collections. When one came up for sale in New York in 1992, it fetched a record £1.8 million. However, the workshops also made plain gold or enamelled miniature eggs as a commercial product, and these sell today for anything from £1000 upwards.

Gold-mounted, enamelled Easter egg set with rubies; c.1900; 3 in (76 mm) long.
£15,000-£20,000

Guilloché design table clock of yellow enamel and silver gilt; c.1880; 4⁵⁄₈ in (11.7 cm) wide.
£10,000-£15,000

Silver and enamel desk bell push with carved hardstone lion's mask button; c.1880; 3 in (76 mm) in diameter at the base.
£800-£1000

Lily-of-the-valley flower study in jewelled gold, silver gilt and hardstone; c.1900; 4½ in (11.4 cm) tall. It sold in Geneva in November 1990 for **£51,000**

Carved bowenite rhinoceros with jewelled eyes; c.1900; 2 in (51 mm) long.
£1500-£2000

Gold cigarette case; c.1910; 4½ in (11.4 cm) wide. A map in gold, rubies and sapphires decorates the lid.
£3000-£4000

Enamel wares

From medieval crucifixes to the finest Japanese cloisonné vases, enamel has long been treasured for its deep, lustrous colours.

THE ORIGINS OF THE ART of enamelling are uncertain, but it is known to have existed as early as the 13th century BC. The technique involves applying enamel – a paste of ground glass and coloured metallic oxides – to a prepared surface most often of metal, but sometimes of porcelain or glass. The enamel may be brushed on like paint over the entire piece, or pressed into grooves or compartments. These are made by engraving the surface of the metal, a technique known as champlevé, or by fixing wires to the surface to form *cloisons* (compartments) for the cloisonné method. The piece is then fired.

EUROPEAN ENAMELS

Medieval enamellers in Europe, using the champlevé technique, worked almost exclusively for the Church producing crucifixes, vessels for the wine and host, and other ecclesiastical objects. These wares are now rarely seen outside museums.

With the invention of painted enamels in the 15th and 16th centuries, Limoges in central France emerged as Europe's major enamelling centre. Limoges ware is typically painted in thick enamels of grey, white and gold on a dark background. At auction such pieces now fetch upwards of £1000.

CHINESE ENAMELS

The earliest Chinese enamel is cloisonné from the 14th century. Some large pieces, such as incense burners 4 ft (1.2 m) high, were made in the Qing (Ching) dynasty. Some bear reign marks (see p.509), but these may be misleading; the characters *ta Ming* (great Ming) were used in Japan in the 19th century and a four-character mark, often *Kienlong*, usually indicates a 20th-century Chinese piece.

Under the influence of Jesuit missionaries in the early 18th century, the Chinese also produced flat enamels painted onto copper, commonly known as Canton enamel wares. Despite the name, the best pieces, particularly bowls and snuff bottles, are those made in the Royal workshops in Beijing (Peking). The thin copper forms were enamelled on both sides for strength, but are still easily damaged.

Chinese cloisonné enamels are still made today, although their quality has declined. Colours of modern pieces are brighter than earlier work – yellows, greens and black are typical of the 1920s and 30s – and the forms are lighter. A 7 in (17.8 cm) vase or a bowl with an incurved rim starts from around £40.

JAPANESE ENAMELS

In Japan little cloisonné was produced before the middle of the 19th century. Bowls and vases from the 1870s and 80s are of historical interest, but not technically accomplished, and their value is often as low as £150.

The 1880s and 90s saw great advances in enamelling, under Western influence. Few pieces are marked, but those that are tend to be of the highest quality. A signed, 4 in (10.1 cm) vase and cover may fetch £10,000.

Condition is vital to the price of Japanese cloisonné; a chip or scratch lowers the price to only a tenth that of an undamaged piece.

Chinese Canton enamel wine cup with mountain landscape; mid-18thC; 1¾ in (44 mm) high.
Good condition: £40-£60
With cracks: £10-£30

Chinese cloisonné vase (right) – a later copy of an 18thC original; 10 in (25.4 cm) high. The original would be worth £2000-£3000, and telling the difference is not easy.
£300-£400

Silver-gilt cloisonné and champlevé solitaire tea service; c.1880; salver 10¾ in (27.3 cm) long. This Russian service was made in Moscow. by Nemirov Kolodkin.
£4000-£5000

Japanese porcelain cloisonné vase (left); c.1870; 15 in (38.1 cm) high. The technique involved impressing wires into the body, applying enamel, then firing. There is little demand for such pieces.
£120-£180

Two silver-gilt and plique-à-jour enamel cigarette cases; late 19thC; 4 in (10.1 cm) wide. These fine examples of Russian enamel work were both made in Moscow.
£2000-£3000

Signed Japanese cloisonné vase by Ogasawara Shuzo; c.1900; 5 in (12.7 cm) high. Unsigned pieces are worth about half as much.
£2000-£3000

Collecting jewellery

It is more rewarding to buy antique jewellery that you will enjoy wearing than for investment, although there are gains to be made from timely buying.

THE VALUE OF JEWELLERY depends on the quality of the materials used to make it, its design, maker and condition, and the prevailing fashion and taste. Rare gems of the highest quality are usually a good investment because the political and physical problems involved in mining them and the scarcity of fine stones means that supply is unlikely to exceed demand. Diamonds are the exception as their supply is controlled by an international cartel to maintain prices, but demand can always be fulfilled so no dramatic rise in prices is likely.

The signature or imprint of a great jewel house such as Cartier or Tiffany adds considerably to a piece's price. Provenance can also be a significant factor – there will be considerable added value on a brooch once worn by, say, the Duchess of Windsor or Lily Langtry, especially if it is accompanied by a photograph of the original owner wearing it, and the original case. Such documentation can even be of value for historic family jewels.

Age itself does not necessarily increase value. Roman items can fetch as little as £100, while demand for the pretty, delicate jewels of the 18th century has dropped over the last few years – as have prices. Bold, high-quality Victorian jewellery and avant-garde Arts and Crafts, Art Nouveau and Art Deco pieces are increasingly sought after.

Gold, silver and precious stones have always been melted and re-formed or re-cut to suit the fashion of the day. This means that genuine period jewels in these precious materials are rare and costly. Bronze and hardstones were not considered to be worth remaking, so many

more examples exist in their original state and are relatively cheap. In the same way, jewels kept for sentimental reasons are quite plentiful.

Building a theme collection is certainly worthwhile, and interest in historical and documentary items, such as prospecting jewellery set with gold nuggets, mourning jewellery or military badge brooches, is increasing. For future collectables, look for new materials such as titanium which has been oxidised to produce a rainbow of colour, and will be linked with the 1990s, and for exclusive designer creations. Remember too that what is unfashionable today may be in great demand tomorrow.

Buying antique or secondhand pieces from a specialist retail jeweller's with an extensive stock is the easiest way to find exactly what you require. But the price you pay reflects the wide choice and back-up service that a jeweller can offer. You may pay only one-quarter or one-fifth of the price at an auction, but you may have to search a long time to find the specific style or piece you want.

LUCKY INHERITANCE *The owner of this enamel, sapphire and pearl pendant was amazed when it fetched £3850 at auction. She inherited it from a Scottish relative, and had no idea it was by the leading Aberdeen Arts and Crafts designer James Cromar Watt.*

PRIZE ITEM *This Art Nouveau bangle and ring by Fouquet, copying one designed by Alphonse Mucha for Sarah Bernhardt, fetched c. £351,000 in 1989.*

BUDGET BUY *Foiled paste shoe buckles dating from the 18thC are greatly undervalued today because they are no longer of any practical use. Beautifully worked and set in silver with gold decoration, they can sell for as little as £50 a pair.*

PROVENANCE *Sale of the Duchess of Windsor's 1949-66 Cartier 'big cats' for £2.4 million in all created such a stir that fine modern examples without provenance can fetch up to £50,000.*

Understanding jewellery

The essence of jewellery, whatever its type or age, lies in its visual appeal. Precious metals and gemstones have an intrinsic value, but style, craftsmanship and rarity can increase that value many times over.

ITEMS OF JEWELLERY may be made of an almost infinite range of materials, from precious metals and rare gems to glittering paste – glass cut to resemble gemstones – and paper-thin gilt metal. Even plastic and other modern materials that have little or no value in themselves have been fashioned into jewellery that can fetch large sums.

The essential ingredient in such recent pieces is the eye of the designer and the skill of the maker, which are virtually impossible to measure objectively. But the mainstream of precious and semiprecious jewellery is easier to assess. One gem can confidently be valued at twice the value of another; the condition of a piece may be poor, middling or pristine; it may be by a renowned master or an unknown hand; it may be made of 9, 14, 18 or 22-carat gold, or some other assayable precious metal.

The first essential is to study items in museums, shops and salerooms. Closely examine the gems and setting of an individual piece, looking at the back for stamped marks such as hallmarks (see p.479) or their foreign equivalents, design registration symbols or numbers (which can give a clue as to the earliest date the piece could have been made, but not the actual date of manufacture), and a maker's name or initials. Then try to assess whether the age, as judged by the style and materials, and the quality are compatible with the marks and apparent maker. You will find that a large amount of Victorian jewellery is not marked at all, however, and many Edwardian pieces are simply stamped '14CT'.

Factors such as damage and repairs, possible alterations and the presence of the original fitted case can be valuable signs of authenticity. Secondhand jewellery is very likely to have been altered or repaired at some time, and many small brooches or tiepin heads have been re-mounted as rings.

One notable feature of antique and early 20th-century jewellery is the care and detail with which the back was finished. Any signs of poor-quality work, such as rough edges or crude mounts, may betray alterations or a modern copy. Much Art Nouveau, Art Deco and 1940s Retro jewellery has been reproduced in recent years in the Far East.

TRIED AND TESTED *The leather aprons attached to the workbench in this 16thC engraving to catch valuable gold filings are still used by jewellers today.*

IN ITS CASE *The original case, so long as the piece fits perfectly, is a strong indication of authenticity and can double an item's value. This brooch clearly belongs in the case, but the inside shape shows that the hair comb once accompanying it is missing.*

The setting

As a general rule, the quality of the metal used for the setting – the structure of an item of jewellery – reflects the overall quality of the piece. For example, 9-carat gold (marked '9K' on an American piece, or '375' on a continental one) was used mainly for mass-produced items. Individually crafted pieces normally used 14, 18 or 22-carat gold or (since the mid-19th century) platinum, because the cost of the metal was relatively insignificant compared with that of the gemstones (see below) and labour.

Many gilt or rolled-gold pieces are stamped with what look like hallmarks, although a mark such as '18GP' in fact indicates gold plate. If you look carefully at exposed edges, you can usually see where such plating has worn away. As well as various metals which imitated gold, gilded brass and pinchbeck – a gold-coloured alloy of zinc and copper – was used in some 18th-century jewellery.

Pure 24-carat gold is generally too soft and fragile to make jewellery, though some ancient ritualistic and dowry pieces are of this quality. Just as with silver (see p.233), other metals were alloyed with the gold (in various proportions to give the various carat grades) to improve its resilience and for decorative effect. The reddish tinge of rose gold, popular in the late 19th century, for example, comes from copper, while silver gives a hint of green. Modern bright yellow gold contains both copper and silver, while white gold is an alloy with platinum or with nickel and zinc. The various types are used in combination in multicolour gold jewellery.

In many cases, the jeweller used more than one metal to craft the setting, especially when working with diamonds, which look best in a colourless mount as they can 'draw' the colour out of gold and take on a yellowish tinge. Platinum is ideal but is difficult to work, so many rings have a platinum mount with a yellow or white-gold shank; they may be marked '18CT & PLAT'. Before platinum came into use in the last century, silver was often used, but when this tarnishes it can make the jewel look very dull.

ROLLED GOLD *Worn edges (as on the petals, right) often betray a rolled gold or gilt piece. Gold content can be tested with prepared acids on a streak of gold.*

THREE-COLOUR GOLD *This bracelet is made of white, yellow and rose gold – alloys with zinc, silver and copper, and copper respectively.*

DUAL-METAL SETTING *The gold shank of this Victorian five-stone ring is topped with a silver setting for the stones.*

CLOSED AND OPEN SETTINGS

Before about the 1840s gemstones were normally set in a closed setting, surrounded by solid metal with only the top of the stone exposed. To enhance appearance and sparkle, the back of the setting was often coated in metal foil, but this was easily damaged if moisture got trapped behind the stone.

Then jewellers discovered how to cut diamonds so as to refract (bend) and reflect light without assistance from such a backing. As a result the stones could be open set – held only by metal claws or a thin rim, with the back of the stone left open – and were much more prominent. When they first appeared, such mounts were marketed as 'transparent settings', and they have remained the commonplace type used ever since.

OPEN AND CLOSED *Closed settings (as in the garnet and pearl brooch below), with the gems embedded in metal and often backed by foil, were the norm in the 18th and early 19th centuries. More modern cuts of diamond do not need such a backing, so the open setting (right) came into fashion. Such pieces are easy to clean, unlike closed settings.*

front

back

front

back

Gems and other stones

The value of precious stones may be measured in hundreds or even thousands of pounds per carat. Since there are 5 carats to the gram, or over 150 to the troy ounce, they bear far more upon the value of a piece of jewellery than does its gold content (which is worth less than £200 per ounce). Gem connoisseurs may appreciate the beauty of such stones as alexandrite (which changes from greenish to red under artificial light) or bright red tourmaline (rubellite). But the range of precious stones commonly used in jewellery is quite limited: diamonds have long been the favourite, closely followed by rubies, sapphires and emeralds.

DIAMONDS

The value of a diamond is judged by the 'four Cs' – carat weight, cut, colour and clarity. They are cut to set mathematical proportions so that by measuring the diameter and depth an approximate carat weight can be found from tables. (For example, a modern brilliant-cut diamond 6.5 mm across and 4 mm deep weighs 1 carat.) The average diamond has a very slight tinge of yellow or brown, but a water-white stone will be worth much more – as will the rare blue, red or pink-tinted diamonds or the commoner bright yellows.

Most diamonds are brilliant cut (see chart, p.484), the modern dimensions slightly rounder than those found on 19th-century examples, which had a smaller top table and broader, deeper shoulders. Older still are 18th-century pieces with flat-backed rose-cut diamonds, still commonly used in India and South America, and the occasional table-cut survivor from the 17th century and earlier.

COLOUR *Coloured diamonds are highly prized, and an unmounted, oval-cut, 3.28 carat fancy pink stone like this could fetch 40 times as much as a white gem of equivalent size, cut and quality.*

CLARITY *A diamond's clarity – the absence of blemishes, chips and scratches – is rated on a scale from flawless under ten-times magnification to piqué (heavily spotted). Black inclusions (internal spots) can be burned out by laser to improve appearance, but this leaves a minute hollow tube. The clear crystal inclusions of this stone, invisible to the naked eye, mean it is of average quality.*

BRILLIANT CUT *The round dimensions of the modern brilliant cut creates the maximum light reflection, the root of the stone's sparkle, or 'fire'. Many older gems have been re-cut in brilliant style, and historic cuts are rare.*

OLD MINE CUT *This single-stone diamond ring of 7.38 carats has been shaped with an Old Mine cut, an early form of the brilliant cut.*

CUSHION CUT *The central sapphire in this ring is cushion cut to give a rectangular shape with rounded corners. The surrounding diamonds are pavé (closely) set, so that very little of the platinum setting is visible.*

COLOURED STONES

With stones such as rubies (red), emeralds (green) and sapphires (pure blue to purple, pink, orange, gold, green and white), colour is the most important factor. Ideally it should be deep (but not dark), saturated and even, although most of these stones have some natural blemishes. The cutter normally makes the most of the stone's size and shape while keeping it symmetrical. The colour of some semi-opaque (such as opals) and opaque (such as turquoise) gems is actually shown off best with a smooth round or oval cabochon cut without any sharp edges.

Many of the less-precious stones used in cheaper jewellery come in a range of colours – amethysts (purple), aquamarines (blue-green), citrines (yellow), peridots (sage green) topaz (yellow, pink and blue) and turquoise – and can be mistaken for more valuable gems. Tourmalines range from orange, yellow, green and purple to red, the latter resembling rubies, while garnets can vary from red through orange and brown to green (often mistaken for emeralds).

Heat treatment to change or improve colour has been carried out for centuries. So long as it is not done to deceive and is permanent, such treatments are acceptable – for example, to create citrines from fired amethysts (changing purple to yellow), or to make blue topazes by heating pale yellow or near-colourless examples. Less acceptable is treating green turquoises with wax to make them blue, as they eventually revert to green, and deliberately fraudulent activities such as soaking emeralds (which are brittle and liable to damage) in oil to disguise cracks.

IMPROVING COLOUR *The high-temperature treatment of a pale blue natural sapphire crystal (left) to produce a deep blue gem (right, after cutting) is a recent development.*

CABOCHON CUT *This so-called 'black' opal is cabochon cut, with a smoothly curved surface. Opal is so brittle that it cannot be cut any other way, but in fact this shows its interplay of colours to best advantage.*

WAX-TREATED TURQUOISE *The green stone in this Victorian bracelet was impregnated with wax to make it match the brilliant blue colour of the other turquoises. But over the years it has reverted to its original colour.*

CHANGING COLOUR *Another custom that is more established is the heat treatment of a purple amethyst (left) to create a yellow citrine. The resulting colour change is permanent.*

SYNTHETICS AND IMITATIONS

There are two ways of copying gemstones. Synthetic gems are man-made reproductions which have the same chemical make-up as the natural version, while simulants look like the real thing but are made of glass, plastic or man-made stones such as cubic zirconia.

Cut-glass 'paste' may be tinted or have foil settings to add colour and aid reflection, but is much softer than gem material, so is easily scratched, and looks duller. Synthetic diamonds are uneconomic to produce in gem grades, but synthetic corundum – the mineral family encompassing rubies and sapphires – is made in quantity, including the 'fancy' sapphire colours of yellow, green, lilac and pink. These can be difficult to spot on first inspection. But an expert armed with a ten-times magnifier can usually detect the bubbles and swirls of glass simulants, the curved growth lines of synthetics and the characteristic internal structures of natural stones. Laboratory tests to measure such things as density, refractive index (the amount the material bends light) and its precise colour spectrum can also be used.

SYNTHETIC RUBY *highly magnified shows curved growth lines quite unlike those of the natural mineral.*

NATURAL RUBY *seen under a high-power microscope shows distinctive angular growth zoning and random imperfections.*

GLASS PASTE *betrays itself under the microscope by its characteristic swirls and bubbles.*

PEARLS AND OTHER ORGANIC MATERIALS

Since the late 19th century, cultured pearls have virtually replaced natural ones. They are made by inserting a small bead of mother-of-pearl into an oyster's shell so that a pearl coating grows over it. A good-quality cultured pearl looks like a natural pearl, but low-quality examples with a thin skin will show flashes of the mother-of-pearl bead under strong light, and will not last long. The most desirable pearls are a good white colour, with few blemishes. Cream, pink, yellow and grey tints also occur, as do black pearls, which are rare and very valuable. Dyed black pearls are more common, but worth much less.

Pearls are not the only organic (once living) material used in jewellery. Coral, ivory and tortoiseshell were all once popular, but realisation of the threat to species and habitats has caused a great decline in their use and in the popularity of antique examples.

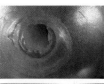

ARTIFICIAL PEARLS *Close inspection of the drill hole will show whether a pearl is an imitation (top) or cultured (bottom). The most convincing imitations are made from glass beads filled with wax and coated with fish-scale essence.*

Symbolic jewellery

Jewellery made to symbolise or commemorate a person or event rather than simply to adorn is of historical interest and is often comparatively cheap.

Posy ring; c.1680; 0.8 in (20 mm) diameter. The lettering of the inscription inside is quite simple.
£200-£300

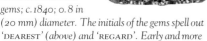

Gold rings set with diamonds and other gems; c.1840; 0.8 in (20 mm) diameter. The initials of the gems spell out 'DEAREST' (above) and 'REGARD'. Early and more complex examples may fetch six times this amount.
£150-£200 each

Locket decorated with intertwined hearts and lovers' knot; c.1780; 3 in (76 mm) long. The popularity of romantic motifs and the excellent condition of the piece are reflected in its high price.
£500-£700

Memento mori band ring in gold and enamel; c.1730; 0.8 in (20 mm) diameter. The motifs of hourglass, crossbones and skeleton are symbolic of death and the passage of time.
£1000-£1500

Gold and white enamel mourning ring; c.1810; 0.7 in (18 mm) diameter. Such rings were worn to mourn the death of children or unmarried young people.
£200-£300

Mourning rings; c.1880; black onyx insets c.½ in (13 mm) across. Enamel bands, as on the left-hand ring, represent the Holy Trinity; the inscription (ring on right) reads 'in memory of'.
Left: £200-£300; right: £80-£100

Gold mourning ring with black enamel and diamond inset, shown front (left) and back (right); c.1822; inset 0.6 in (15 mm) across. The diamonds are set in the form of a Neoclassical urn and the inscription on the back is typical.
£600-£800

Mourning ring in gold and black enamel to commemorate the death of Lord Nelson at Trafalgar; 1805 or soon after; enamel inset c.¾ in (19 mm) across.
£1200-£1500

MOST EARLY JEWELLERY – and many pieces produced right up to the 20th century – served more than merely decorative purposes, embodying some theme, device or message in its design. Such jewellery tends to be rather sombre, which keeps prices down. As a result, new collectors can start to explore at relatively low cost a field in which there is a wide range of quality and design, and often great human interest too.

LOVE TOKENS

Posy rings, engraved with amatory inscriptions and presented at weddings or betrothals, were popular from the late Middle Ages – at least among those who were rich enough to afford them. Early examples are rare, and even 17th-century examples of simple design can fetch between £200 and £800 at auction.

Gimmal rings were made as far back as the mid-16th century. The ring's shank was split lengthwise and invisibly joined so that it could be divided to reveal an engraved message or symbol on the inside face. Silver or gold examples from the 18th century without an inscription can sell for only £150-£200.

Some rings from the early 19th century copy the French custom of arranging stones to spell out a word such as 'REGARD' (ruby, emerald, garnet, amethyst, ruby, diamond) or 'DEAREST' (with sapphire and topaz for S and T). In good condition they sell at auction for about £300. More elaborate Regency period brooches and pendants can change hands for several thousand pounds.

MEMENTO MORI

Reminders of death – memento mori – were first embodied in jewellery in the mid-17th century. Pieces were made in gold and enamel, engraved and modelled with symbols of death. An enamelled ring with a skull and crossbones motif and a simple inscription such as 'in God we trust' can fetch around £1500. Grander pieces with more complex designs mounted with a skull are rare and fetch prices in the region of £3000-£4000.

Slides worn at the neck on a ribbon were made mainly in the latter half of the 17th century, and represent the transition from memento mori to mourning jewellery. They consist of a compartment enclosing a plait of woven hair under rock crystal, sometimes with an enamelled skull or skeleton motif and applied wire decoration. Although macabre, the startling imagery of such pieces fascinates many collectors, and a slide in good condition with a complex design may fetch £300-£800.

MOURNING JEWELLERY

A typical 19th-century mourning ring is a gold band (not always hallmarked) with a black enamel surround and a legend raised in gold, normally reading 'in memory of'. Engraved on the inside rim is the deceased's name, and the date and sometimes cause of death. Rings of this type are still relatively inexpensive, fetching from about £80 for a basic example, up to £500 for a more elaborate one. But prices go much higher if it is a well-known person who is commemorated.

Slightly rarer are rings in white enamel, worn when young or unmarried people died. Rings combining black and white were worn if a parent and child had died at about the same time. These fetch rather more than black enamel rings. The better-quality mourning rings of the 18th century are thinner than later versions, the shank being about ⅛ in

Necklace and pendant made from woven human hair; c.1850; c.18 in (46 cm) long unclasped. This is a complex example of the use of hair in 19thC jewellery.
£50-£60

Gold-mounted mourning pendant; 1770-80; 2 in (50 mm) long. The bereavement motifs are painted in sepia on ivory, with hair, seed pearls and wire work incorporated.
£200-£500

Victorian jet necklace and two brooches, one (top) with hair locket compartment; c.1850; necklace c.18 in (46 cm) long, brooches 1-2 in (25-50 mm) across.
Necklace: £200-£400
Brooches: £30-£50 each

Painted eye miniature mounted as a brooch; c.1820; 0.8 in (20 mm) across. The eye represents the soul and was a popular motif at the time.
£200-£300

Two hardstone fob seals; c.1770; 0.8 in (20 mm) across. The chalcedony intaglio on the top seal shows the coat of arms of the 3rd Duke of Dorset.
£200-£300 each

(3 mm) wide, with a milled border. These sell at auction for about £200-£400. Signet-style mourning rings were also popular from the Regency period. Values vary greatly but a gold and enamel example may fetch £200-£500.

Jewellery containing plaited hair of the deceased dates from the mid-17th century onwards. Rings from the 19th century may have woven hair inset around the shank, often fastened with an applied cartouche. Most mourning brooches of the late 19th century consist of a locket containing a lock or plait of hair under a thin cover of rock crystal or glass. The surround is usually Neoclassical in style, with scroll decoration against the traditional black enamel field, but some rings are decorated with pearls or diamonds. Prices vary according to the quality of the gems, but generally they sell for around £200. However, gilt-mounted examples can often be picked up at auction for as little as £50-£80.

By the 1860s jewellery made from hair was being mass-produced. It fetches low prices today – often less than £100 – owing to the modern distaste for human hair. But such pieces can make a good start to a collection.

IMAGES OF DEATH

During the latter half of the 18th century, lozenge-shaped rings, brooches and pendants were made, enclosing a sepia miniature. This depicted mourning motifs such as muses standing by a sepulchre with a willow tree in the background, or doves representing the

Holy Spirit. Decoration was added with gold wire, seed pearls and human hair, set under faceted or plain rock crystal.

A particularly popular motif was the coiled serpent with its tail in its mouth, signifying eternity. Another was the weeping eye, which was painted on ivory and often surrounded with pearls representing tears. Such pieces fetch between £200 and £400. Like other types of mourning jewellery they have survived in large numbers because they were treasured for their sentimental value.

JET JEWELLERY

Apart from hair, the most common material used for mourning jewellery in the Victorian era was jet, an extremely hard form of coal. Jet jewellery is now increasing in value, and elaborate necklaces in high Victorian taste change hands at auction for around £400. However, bar brooches can still be found for about £10 and can make a good start for the novice collector. But beware of imitations. Black glass, often misleadingly called 'French jet', can be distinguished by its cooler touch and the presence of air bubbles. Vulcanite, a type of hard rubber used to simulate jet, looks duller and may show a slightly brown tint.

HERALDIC AND MASONIC ITEMS

Signet rings, fobs and desk seals were often decorated with heraldic devices. Good 19th-century hardstone signet rings, set perhaps with agate, sardonyx or the less common lapis lazuli, are increasing in value and may now sell at auction for around £150-£400.

Armorial fob seals, worn hanging from a watch chain, were popular from the mid-17th century onwards, when many were produced in steel or gunmetal. Late 18th and early 19th-century examples are generally trumpet-shaped, set with an oval hardstone such as agate, and mounted in gold. They were gradually made heavier in design, with complex chased and engraved mounts. A standard 19th-century armorial fob may sell at auction for £300-£400, but it will make much more if the coat of arms shows a royal connection.

Large numbers of badges, watch fobs and medallions were produced for the Masonic order, largely in the early part of the 20th century. They show Masonic symbols such as the all-seeing eye, dividers and set square, skull and crossbones, and pyramid. Others may bear the coat of arms or motto of a lodge member, either engraved or in enamel. Such pieces are usually mounted in gold and silver, and sometimes jewelled. Prices are relatively low because they are common and have few collectors, but 18th-century silver examples can be worth £200-£300.

Decorative jewellery

Jewellery has been used for personal adornment, at least among the upper classes, for centuries. Styles and types have always gone in and out of vogue, leaving modern collectors with an enormous variety from which to choose.

Diamond cluster starburst spray brooch; c.1840; 2¼ in (57 mm) long. The design of this piece was inspired by the 1835 sighting of Halley's Comet.
£1000-£1200

THE VALUE OF JEWELLERY depends on several factors, ranging from the current fashions to the precious metals and gemstones used. Among the most important considerations are the quality of workmanship and the condition; desirable items in good condition are scarce and always worth more than average. Buyers should examine prospective purchases carefully for missing or damaged pieces of decoration. A maker's signature increases value, as does an inscription concerning a known person or event.

NINETEENTH-CENTURY BROOCHES

In the early 19th century, brooches were small, delicate and often rectangular, with a pastel-coloured gem or foil-backed paste at the centre surrounded by pearls or deep floral chasing. Popular designs of the period include animal forms and comet shapes inspired by the sighting of Halley's Comet in 1835. Today, large pieces of jewellery are more popular, and a typical Regency period brooch that would have sold for £200-£300 a few years ago will now realise only half that amount.

A vast number of styles were influenced by history, travel and the natural world. Pieces in the Etruscan style, for example, echo ancient Greek and Roman jewellery and are usually decorated with tiny applied beads and

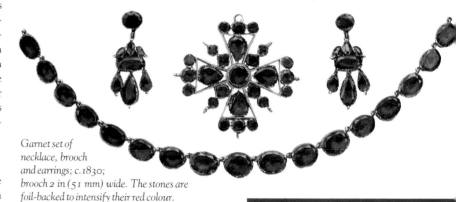

Garnet set of necklace, brooch and earrings; c.1830; brooch 2 in (51 mm) wide. The stones are foil-backed to intensify their red colour.
£2000-£2500

Gold Etruscan-style pendant; c.1860; 1½ in (38 mm) long. A dent in the raised centre lowers the value of this unusually shaped piece.
£400-£600

Edwardian diamond tiara; c.1910; 6¾ in (17.1 cm) wide. This gold and platinum example is typical of the openwork cluster-and-garland designs which succeeded the Victorian floral-and-scroll tiaras.
£5000-£7000

Gold, garnet and enamel brooch; 1860s; 2¼ in (57 mm) long. Its Oriental design with bamboo-style frame is unusual, and its condition excellent.
£2000-£3000

Gold and shell cameo brooches; c.1880; larger 2¼ in (57 mm) wide. These pieces represent two popular Victorian styles: female portraits and Classical scenes.
£600-£800; £1200-£1600

Four miniature portrait pendants; c.1840-60; largest 3 in (76 mm) long. The bottom left example depicts the young Queen Victoria.
Top left and right: £500-£800 each
Bottom left: £3000-£4000
Bottom right: £1200-£1500

LOVE DECLARED *The lady is surely feigning polite reluctance, for few can remain cool to jewellery's beauty, intricate workmanship – and value.*

wirework. Good examples are often signed by the maker and are keenly sought after. These usually fetch more than £1500.

From about 1840, naturalistic jewellery depicted birds and animals, fruits and foliage, the most fashionable being grapes and vine leaves. With the opening up of Japan to trade with Europe from the 1860s, Japanese motifs were used – for example, bamboo-shaped borders around engraved panels of storks and grasses, or fan shapes with Oriental figures, often with different-coloured gold and silver detail. Coloured gold and silver decoration applied to a matt black metal background (*shakudo*) was sought after, and many original pieces were remounted by the Victorians in European jewellery. Prices exceed £300.

Perhaps one of the most common 19th-century brooch designs is the circular or oval shape with a locket behind its central stone to house a lock of hair, a portrait miniature or a photograph. These can be found in most metals, especially gilt brass, silver or gold, and vary in price from £20 up to several hundred, depending on quality and condition.

Another Victorian favourite was the cameo, usually carved from shell or hardstone, but also produced in coral, ivory, or precious or semiprecious stones. Unusual, well-carved scenes with good detail command high prices – between £2000 and £3000 – whereas the more common profiles average around £300-£400. Gold-mounted cameos are the most sought after, while machine-carved examples fetch £100-£200.

When examining a shell cameo, hold it up to the light to spot any cracks. Joins along the raised parts may indicate a composite cameo, where the carved design has been made separately and then applied to the body. Also,

check for bubbles, which betray a moulded glass cameo. The mount should be examined as well for damage; look out for any missing decoration or bad repairs.

ANIMAL JEWELLERY

The Victorians were fond of the macabre, and many of their brooches incorporate a rabbit's foot, bird's claws, a bird's head or even an entire bird. Today such jewellery is considered distasteful and auction prices have dropped accordingly. Earrings may reach £150, but often sell for less. Some pieces are a little more acceptable, however, including sharks' teeth, tigers' claws, or a snail's operculum (the horny cover of the shell opening), which looks like a green and white pebble. These sell fairly well if mounted with plenty of decoration. Butterfly wings were also often set in silver, and change hands for £30-£300.

The most popular animal brooches, however, are gem or paste-set pieces modelled as animals – notably butterflies and birds. A novelty that is popular today depicts twin monkeys, one seated on a bar and the other hanging from the bar. Monkey brooches in paste cost £150-£200, while those with diamonds fetch at least three times this amount.

Around the 1860s, reverse crystal intaglio brooches were made which give a three-dimensional effect. The technique was used effectively on pieces depicting dogs' heads, flowers, bees and fish. Good examples are now rare, and fetch around £1000-£1500.

Towards the end of the 19th century numerous bar brooches were made. They were decorated with engraving, applied motifs, gems or paste, usually as a cluster or in a row, with a pin fitting. This style was adapted to produce novelty shapes, such as the outline of hunting horns, horseshoes, animals, birds and even children's teeth on a bar. Most examples fetch £15-£50, but £100-£300 if the design incorporates small precious stones.

BROOCHES OF THE TWENTIETH CENTURY

Platinum became a popular jewellery material in the early 1900s. The Edwardians used its pale colour to offset delicate shapes and the light hues of diamonds, pearls, peridots and aquamarines. In the early 1920s Cartier set jewellery with carved coloured gems to create a multicoloured effect often described as 'fruit salad'. These popular pieces generally sell for more than £5000 today.

The alternative but equally strong Art Deco style of the day emphasised black and white and bold abstract or geometric designs. Brooches with streamlined shapes that symbolised speed – including luxury liners,

Late 19thC brooches: (above) diamond, emerald and enamel grasshopper, 2 in (51 mm) long; (left) sapphire, diamond, ruby, pearl and garnet butterfly.
£600-£800; £400-£600

Gold and diamond bar brooch; c.1890; 1¾ in (44 mm) wide. It is decorated with a bird alighting. Bar brooches were a favourite late Victorian style.
£1200-£1500

Three painted reverse crystal intaglios; 19thC; ¾ in (19 mm) across. The set, mounted as two studs and a brooch, has a fitted case stamped Hunt & Roskell.
£1200-£1500

Egyptian Revival brooch; c.1870; 2½ in (63 mm) wide. The value of this gold, onyx and pearl piece is enhanced by its fitted case, stamped Watherston & Son, London.
£800-£1000

Gold, sapphire and ruby cowboy and lasso brooch; 1940s; 2 in (51 mm) high. It is in 'Cocktail' style, among whose popular subjects were stylised figures, often humorous.
£1500-£2000

Gold and diamond abstract cluster brooch and earstuds in twig and bead design; c.1970; brooch 2¾ in (70 mm) wide. This good modern set would be worth more if signed.
£2500-£3000

Berlin ironwork panel bracelet; c.1820; 10 in (25.4 cm) long. Pieces in sets are much sought after, especially when in their fitted case, which protects them from the danger of rust.
£600-£800

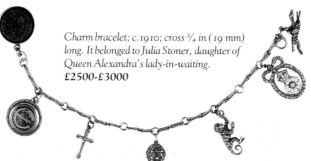

Charm bracelet; c.1910; cross ¾ in (19 mm) long. It belonged to Julia Stoner, daughter of Queen Alexandra's lady-in-waiting.
£2500-£3000

Part of gold guard chain; c.1890; 59 in (1.5 m) long. This unusually designed chain of scrolling wirework links and panels retains its near original length.
£1000-£1500

Gold, half pearl, blue enamel and cabochon gem double-headed serpent bangle; c.1880; 2¾ in (70 mm) diameter.
£700-£1000

Three Russian miniature enamel egg pendants; 1880-1910; ¾ in (19 mm) long.
£150-£200 each

Victorian gold bracelet; c.1880; 8 in (20.3 cm) long. The textured flexible links depict knots.
£2000-£2500

Florentine bracelet; c.1840; 6⅝ in (16.8 cm) long. The links of glass mosaic in gold are undamaged.
£2000-£2500

Gold, enamel and diamond snake necklace; c.1860; 15 in (38.1 cm) long. The serpent's head can be placed on the front, side or back of the neck.
£2000-£2500

planes and greyhounds – can fetch anything between £50 and £50,000 at auction today.

The 'Cocktail' or 'Retro' style, popular during the 1940s, incorporates swirls or a pleated effect, figures such as ballerinas, and stylised, often cartoon-like animals. Pieces made from a base metal can be found for as little as £5-£10, while those made from precious metals and gems fetch £300-£600.

Collectable designers from the 1950s and 60s include John Donald, Charles de Temple and David Thomas. Especially popular are pieces set with naturally formed gem crystals in textured, abstract surrounds. Many of these pieces are one-offs. Sculptural pieces from the 1970s are also sought after; among the most popular are items fashioned from solid metal, often silver or gold, with a molten metal look; they sell for £300-£600.

BRACELETS

Most other types of jewellery show the same design trends as brooches, but there are also special forms that developed outside the trends. Bracelets from the early 19th century often have a decorative clasp and either a multi-chain, cloth, woven hair (see p.269) or beadwork body. Although examples in good condition are quite hard to find, their prices are quite low – generally around £30-£100.

Chain bracelets from the mid-19th century have fairly large links, and most have one row of chain rather than several. Curb and belcher links, along with other, fancier styles, are often fastened together by a padlock-shaped clasp which is normally plain, although some are engraved. These evolved into the gate bracelet, which has three to six bars or 'gates' joined to form a flexible row varying in width. Today they sell for £200-£400.

Charm bracelets were a Victorian innovation which until a few years ago fetched little more than their bullion value – except for early or very decorative examples. However, prices have recently risen by about a half, so that for example, a bracelet with a gold value of £400 may fetch around £600 at auction.

The hinged bangle, with one hinge connecting shaped panels, also became fashionable in the Victorian era. Decorated with a wide variety of designs, bangles are extremely collectable and go for up to £3000, depending on quality. The more common mass-produced designs sell for around £400. Dents or splits are extremely difficult to repair and bring down the value. But if the damage is on

the inside and the hinge is not affected, the value will not drop by very much.

At the turn of the century the diamond, or gemline, bracelet was introduced; its flexible row of gradated or uniform-sized diamonds, other gems or pastes formed a single row around the wrist, often with a hidden clasp. Later Art Deco examples are broader, with geometric panels, and some in the 'Cocktail' style had angular panels or units making what was called a 'tank track'. Depending on the stones used, a poor-quality piece will fetch around £200, while good-quality examples command £2000-£3000.

NECKLACES

Early 19th-century necklaces are usually made of gradated pastes or gems with coloured foil backing – to improve colour or brilliance – in closed collet (continuous band) settings. Most fetch over £1000 with foil intact.

Muff and guard chains – which reached well below the waist and could thread through muff or secure other items – also date from the early 19th century. Many have been melted down, or been damaged and then shortened, so the few good examples left in their original state can sell for more than £1000. However, less impressive chains, or those of pinchbeck or gilt metal, will fetch considerably less, with Victorian examples fetching hands for an average of £300-£500.

Among the most enduring Victorian necklace styles is the snake necklace. This flexible, three-dimensional 'chain' is tapered and weighted so that the gem-set serpent's head and tail clasp can be placed at any position round the neck. Examples in their original fitted case fetch over £2000.

A fatter version called a 'gas pipe', inspired by the pipe used in some Second World War gas masks, dates from the 1940s. These have

recently come back into fashion and even modern examples average £500-£700.

In the late 19th century, Russian jewellers, especially Fabergé (see p.262), were producing egg pendants, often enamelled and set with gems. They were made as charms to add to necklaces, occasionally to bracelets, and are now keenly sought after. An average Russian egg made of silver with little decoration will sell for at least £50.

Pearl-set floral clusters were made in abundance from the early 20th century. Lightweight ones usually fetch about £150-£200, whereas the heavier necklaces of better quality go for around £400-£600. Perhaps most representative of the Edwardian era is the pearl choker made fashionable by Queen Alexandra, but rarely seen today. It had five or more rows of pearls with periodic crossbars, and was usually set with diamonds.

It was around this time that cultured pearls were perfected in Japan. They are difficult to distinguish from natural pearls except by X-ray, and as they increased in availability,

the price of natural pearls fell. Necklaces of small natural pearls now fetch £200-£300, and of larger ones £1000 or more.

Long bead necklaces became fashionable in the 1920s. Pearls were still very popular, but bright-hued beads in long strands also attracted flappers, as did shorter strands of geometric beads. With glass beads or semiprecious gemstones these now sell for about £20-£150.

RINGS AND EARRINGS

The majority of Georgian rings were dainty and multicoloured, many with a small glazed compartment behind the ring head (next to the finger) which held a treasured lock of hair or other memento (see p. 269). Similar pieces from Victorian times made a feature of the compartment. These are often called poison rings, although they too held keepsakes, not

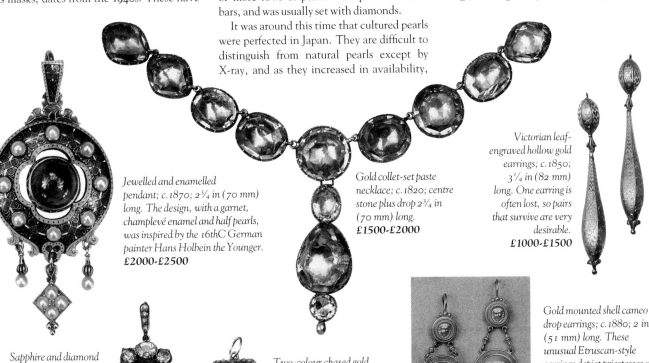

Jewelled and enamelled pendant; c.1870; 2¾ in (70 mm) long. The design, with a garnet, champlevé enamel and half pearls, was inspired by the 16thC German painter Hans Holbein the Younger.
£2000-£2500

Gold collet-set paste necklace; c.1820; centre stone plus drop 2¾ in (70 mm) long.
£1500-£2000

Victorian leaf-engraved hollow gold earrings; c.1850; 3¼ in (82 mm) long. One earring is often lost, so pairs that survive are very desirable.
£1000-£1500

Sapphire and diamond cluster pendant; c.1880; 1¾ in (44 mm) long. Unlike many, this Victorian piece uses quality stones.
£4000-£5000

Two-colour chased gold locket with diamond, ruby and turquoise; c.1825; 1 in (25 mm) long.
£500-£600

Gold mounted shell cameo drop earrings; c.1880; 2 in (51 mm) long. These unusual Etruscan-style earrings depict priestesses of Bacchus, god of wine. They still have their fitted case.
£1200-£1500

Diamond and half pearl floral panel necklace with cluster clasp and matching brooch; c.1880; brooch 1½ in (38 mm) across. The brooch can be worn on its own or attached to the centre of the necklace.
£5000-£7000

Art Deco jade, onyx and diamond drop earrings; c.1925; 3 in (76 mm) long. One piece of jade is cracked, thus reducing the value of this pair.
£1200-£1500

Sapphire and ruby cluster clip earrings; c.1980; 1¼ in (32 mm) long. They were made in Saudi Arabia for the European market.
£400-£600

Onyx and diamond 'poison' ring; c.1875; hinged cover c.⅞ in (22 mm) long. The onyx has a faceted edge and its gold frame is leaf-engraved.
£500-£700

Emerald and half-pearl ring with fern-engraved shoulders; c.1820; cluster 0.35 in (9 mm) across.
£250-£350

Gold and rose diamond hearts and lovers' knot ring with turquoise and pearl; c.1840; cluster ½ in (13 mm) across.
£400-£600

Two marquise diamond rings: (left) c.1910, oval cluster with single-stone shoulders; (right) c.1870, 15-stone pointed cluster 0.9 in (23 mm) long.
Left: £600-£800
Right: £1000-£1500

Gold and enamel stick pins representing a trout, signpost and kayak, and a yachting flag brooch; c.1900; flag ¾ in (19 mm) wide.
£250-£300; £600-£800; £150-£200; £60-£80

Gold cufflinks with the monogram of the Duke of Connaught, who presented them to Queen Victoria's son Prince Arthur; 1890; ¾ in (19 mm) long.
£300-£400

Gold and enamel yachting club stick pins and two-colour gold brooch in the form of a ski; c.1910; ski 1¾ in (44 mm) long.
Pins: £30-£40 each
Ski: £80-£100

Imitation pearl and paste necklace, yellow and white paste bangle, and floral and starfish brooches; floral brooch 2¼ in (57 mm) across. These pieces are in typical 1950s and 60s pastel colours.
Necklace: £150-£200; others: £200-£250

Floral brooch; c.1960; 2½ in (63 mm) long. This Trifari costume jewellery uses plastic and glass to imitate a gem-set original by Van Cleef & Arpels.
£300-£500

poison. On average they fetch £300-£500. A wide variety of other ring shapes were made in the 19th century, including the marquise (oval) cluster and the up-finger ring, on which most of the stones are set up and down the finger rather than across. Today, these sell for anywhere between £200 and £20,000, depending on the gems used. The Victorians also made expanding rings for women with finger joints swollen by arthritis; they are much cheaper today than modern versions.

Among the most commonly seen earrings from the beginning of the 19th century are long drops of hardstone or carved coral, made for pierced ears. These were produced well into the century, although later drops are usually a little shorter, and are lighter and easier to wear. Fringe terminals also date from the mid-19th century and have flexible spikes hanging from a panel above. Many examples were made with geometric designs that were very advanced for the time, but these are now quite rare and therefore expensive. Most gold Victorian earrings fetch around £300-£400, while silver examples sell for £100-£150.

Towards the end of the century the fashion

changed from pierced to screw fittings. These in turn gave way in the 1920s to ear clips, which remained popular until the 1960s, when piercing of ears became common again.

MEN'S JEWELLERY

Victorian men's jewels were mainly confined to useful pieces – pocket watches and chains, fob seals, buttons, signet rings, cuff links and stick (or tie) pins. In the early 20th century, larger diamond rings and bracelets, chains and medallions were fashionable for a time, and they returned to fashion during the 1960s. Now, however, many men restrict themselves to a wristwatch, cuff links and stick pin. Although these are mainly bought to wear,

they are also highly collectable. Boxed dress sets of cuff links, shirt studs and buttons in gold and mother-of-pearl fetch £150-£200. Good-quality Victorian men's gold signet rings are also popular and sell for £300-£800.

COSTUME JEWELLERY

From the 1920s, plastics and other unconventional materials such as chrome were used to create jewellery beautiful in its own right – not just an imitation of expensive gems and gold. Many firms became famous for their costume jewellery, notably Trifari, Schiaparelli, Dior, Chanel, Hobe, Eisenberg and Joseff. Such pieces are avidly collected today, and prices range from just £20-£30 up to £600-£800.

The Second World War halted the use of base metal for costume jewellery and many of the moulds were destroyed to help the war effort. American costume jewellery produced between 1942 and 1947 is therefore all made of silver, but later pieces revert to cheaper base metal. Silver jewellery of the time is more popular today as it typifies the period and can be more easily repaired. On average a good-quality brooch will fetch £300-£500.

Clocks,
Watches
& Precision
Instruments

Part of dial of English brass lantern clock; c. 1660

Understanding clocks and watches

The lure of antique timepieces lies in their combination of art and technology. Visual clues can help you to date a clock and identify its mechanics.

ECHANICAL TIMEPIECES were first made in Europe in 13th-century monasteries to call the monks to prayer. By 1380 many cities had public clocks, although domestic clocks did not appear until the late 15th century. Portable clocks became feasible when the coiled spring was devised as a source of power in the early 16th century. The first true watches date from about 1580 but were rather inaccurate before the invention of the balance wheel around 1675.

Clocks are judged on the quality of both movement and case. Rarity alone does not necessarily mean high value, but a pioneering design is desirable. Points to consider include the type of movement and its complexity (for example, if it has a striking system), style of dial and case, the maker and condition.

Wooden cases were not widely used until the introduction of the pendulum in 1658-60. French cases closely followed contemporary furniture styles, but in London they lagged by some 25-30 years (and in the provinces by even more) until the rise in influence of the great designer-furnishers such as Thomas Chippendale in the mid-18th century.

MAKING TIME *An English provincial clockmaker of the early 19thC is depicted in a contemporary print. Provincial styles lagged some years behind London.*

The movement

A clock or watch movement is composed of a 'train' of gearwheels and pinions for each function (see p. 522) – for example, the motion of the hands (the 'going' train), hour strike ('striking' train), quarter-hour strike, alarm, musical tunes and so on. The trains with their arbors (spindles) have to be held in a frame. The earliest type was the posted-frame or 'birdcage' movement. It was used for 30-hour clocks well into the 19th century, but otherwise fell out of use after 1660.

The plated movement was first developed for portable clocks in the 16th century and went on to become the most common type. Most longcase ('grandfather'), bracket and mantel clocks were made this way – as were most early watches. From the mid-18th century, some watches – especially on the Continent – were made with an individual cock (thin metal bar) to hold each wheel, rather than a solid top (back) plate. This allowed for a much slimmer mechanism.

POSTED-FRAME MOVEMENT *This type, held in a simple metal frame, was found in the earliest mechanical clocks, such as this early Gothic wall clock made of iron. After c.1580, brass was often used for the wheels and from c.1600 it was used for the frame.*

WATCH MOVEMENT *Individual cocks for each train, rather than a solid plate, allows a slimmer movement to be made.*

PLATED MOVEMENT *The parts of the train are held between two brass plates joined by pillars.*

ENGRAVED BACK PLATE *English bracket clocks often have skilfully engraved back plates. This example is in the tulip style of c.1680-95.*

DRIVES, ESCAPEMENTS AND STRIKES

Before the age of electricity, virtually all clocks were driven by either weights or coiled springs. Weight-driven clocks were designed to be set up and left in one place. Spring-driven timepieces could be moved.

An unchecked weight falls ever faster, while a coiled spring loses power as it unwinds. The escapement is the device that allows the power of the driving force to 'escape' at regular intervals. Before the introduction of the pendulum and the balance wheel – both of which have a steady rate of oscillation – escapements were rather hit-and-miss and most clocks were unreliable. (For various escapement types, see page 469.)

British spring-driven clocks of the 16th to late 19th centuries incorporated a device to compensate for the spring's decreasing force as it unwound, the fusee. This was a hallmark of the superiority of British clock-making. In German clocks, the fusee was used in the

SPRING-DRIVEN FUSEE MOVEMENT *The teeth are on the conical fusee, driven from the mainspring by a chain winding around the cone. This compensates for the spring's decreasing force as it unwinds.*

SPRING-DRIVEN GOING-BARREL MOVEMENT *This French-made carriage clock has no fusee – the first teeth are on the going barrel.*

going train, but only until the early 18th century, while in France it was used in both going and striking trains only in the 16th and early 17th centuries. After that, the spring barrel engaged directly with the train.

Electricity was used to drive clocks from the late 19th century. Except for pioneer pieces, electric clocks are rarely collected for their mechanical qualities, but Art Deco electric clocks are in demand for their stylishness.

The number of winding holes immediately indicates a clock's complexity. A single hole generally suggests that it is a timepiece with no strike, two that it is hour (or, if French, half-hour) striking, a third that there is either a quarter-strike or a chime or musical tune every three hours, and a fourth that it plays music as well as striking the quarter-hours. Clocks with 'Westminster' chimes never predate 1856-7, when the Westminster clock tower incorporating 'Big Ben' was built.

The dial

Dutch and French dials after 1660 were covered with velvet, with the chapter (hour) ring, spandrels (ornamental corner pieces) and signature plaque mounted on top. French clocks of 1700-40 often have a multi-part enamel dial – a style revived in the 19th century. From about 1725 all French dials were circular, and from 1740 most were of plain enamel – slightly convex at first, but flatter with thinner enamel from 1800. Many 19th-century French mantel and carriage clocks have a porcelain or opaque glass dial.

British clock dials from 1660 were generally square, or with an arched top from 1720. Longcase clock dials were made progressively larger in the 17th and early 18th centuries (see p.279). Most London brass dials had an applied chapter ring and spandrels, but some were flat brass, engraved and silvered. Painted dials were first advertised in Birmingham in 1772, and became common in the 1780s. Once seen as a cheap alternative to London enamelled dials, they are now believed to have been popular decorative features. They were also used in some high-grade London-made Regency and early Victorian clocks.

The cheapest 19th-century clocks, made in Germany and North America, had a dial of painted tinplate, thin pressed brass, printed card or (in 'rural' pieces) wood. A pewter chapter ring is often found on 18th-century German and some Dutch clocks.

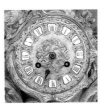

MULTI-PART ENAMEL DIAL
This 19thC French ormolu dial is set with enamel hour plaques in the style of c.1700-40.

PLAIN ENAMEL DIAL
French all-enamel clock dials appeared c.1740; Arabic numerals came after 1790.

ARCHED DIAL *The arched dial was introduced on London clocks c.1720.*

SQUARE MOUNTED-UP BRASS DIAL
Square dials were used on London longcase and bracket clocks until c.1720. This one by Thomas Moore of Ipswich dates from c.1740.

PAINTED TINPLATE *This provincial off-white painted dial imitates enamel dials made in London from c.1765 onwards. It has a moon-phase indicator and four-seasons motifs.*

FLAT SILVERED BRASS DIAL
From c.1760 to 1840, some English clocks had a dial made from a single flat sheet of engraved and silvered brass.

COLLECTING CLOCKS
Time in Your Hands

THE TRADITIONAL FIELD for serious British clock collecting encompassed only the period 1660-1720, the era of the square dial. During the 1970s this interest widened to include Georgian clocks, and in the 1980s Regency pieces. Even today, Victorian clocks are collected mainly for their 'furnishing' qualities.

Good-quality mass-produced American and continental clocks of the 19th and early 20th centuries have become collectable in the last two decades, and could still be a good area for beginners. Those of mechanical bent might be interested in uncased watch movements,

whose cases were sold for their bullion value. A collection could encompass various types of escapement and compensation mechanisms at a fraction of the cost of complete watches.

Small clocks are generally more valuable than standard-sized examples of the same type. The same applies to large pieces unless the size creates display problems. (So oversized longcase clocks are cheaper than standard pieces of the same quality, but large carriage clocks are more expensive.) Provenance is not so important as with furniture or pictures, but a good historical connection can triple the value.

MODERN COLLECTABLE
Art Deco clocks, such as this electric example, appeal for their style.

BARGAIN MASTERPIECE
An uncased Tompion watch movement can be found under £600.

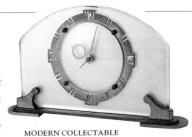

Lancashire mahogany longcase clock; c.1780; 91 in (2.31 m) high. A clock's movement is signed but the case-maker is usually anonymous; this case is by Gillows; one of the few known case-makers.
£5000-£6000

Longcase clocks

The trunk of a longcase clock is perfect for showing off cabinet-making skills, giving the owner not only a timepiece but an attractive piece of furniture.

To many people, a longcase or 'grand-father' clock immediately conjures up nostalgic images of the past. But it is also an ideal combination of mechanics and furniture. A William and Mary marquetry longcase clock can be just as good an example of cabinet-making as, say, a chest of drawers of the same period, and its value will depend on the quality of both case and movement.

LONDON AND PROVINCIAL

Longcase clocks are weight-driven and resulted from the invention of the pendulum in 1659 and, more particularly, of the anchor escapement with long pendulum in 1670.

The simplest type has a 30-hour movement (developed from the lantern clock, see p.280), a square dial and a simple flat-topped oak case. It is wound by pulling on a continuous loop of rope or chain which holds the weight and pulley.

Most longcase clocks by London makers have an eight-day plated movement, although others run for a month, three months or even, rarely, a year after winding. All these are key-wound, and the position of the winding holes on the dial and direction of winding indicate the type.

In eight-day examples, the winding holes are level with or just below IX and III o'clock, and winding is clockwise. One-month clocks have holes at VIII and IV o'clock, and are wound anticlockwise. Three-month clocks have low holes touching the inner edge of the chapter (hour) ring and are wound clockwise. Year-going clocks have holes at the base of the dial and are wound anticlockwise.

Longcase clocks were made in London until about 1810 and in the provinces until about 1845, with case design broadly following that of furniture but generally lagging some 25 years behind. Country fashions were some 10-15 years behind those of London.

Clocks by a small group of great London makers command the top prices today, from around £20,000 to over £100,000. These include Thomas Tompion, the Knibb brothers, George Graham, the Fromanteel family, William Clement, Daniel Delander, Edward

Knibb burr-walnut 8-day clock (above); c.1680; 78 in (1.98 m). It has the typical shallow domed hood and twisted columns of the period.
£80,000-£120,000

Burr-walnut clock (left); London, c.1725; 100 in (2.54 m). This has an early arched dial but predates arched trunk doors.
£5000-£8000

Oak clock; c.1790; 78 in (1.98 m). Its flat top shows provincial origins.
£600-£900

'London mahogany' clock with pagoda top; c.1780; 103 in (2.61 m).
£3000-£5000
Painted dial:
£2000-£2500

Black and gilt lacquer clock; c.1765; 94 in (2.39 m). Dark lacquer colours are much cheaper than bright ones.
£1500-£2000

Walnut and floral marquetry 8-day clock (above); London, c.1690; 86 in (2.18 m). Beware marquetry added later.
£8000-£9000

Oak and mahogany clock; 66 in (1.68 m). This small case of c.1780 is married to a movement of c.1720.
£2000-£3000

To Time other Clocks

IN THE 1720s George Graham used his deadbeat escapement and mercury pendulum to develop highly accurate longcase clocks called regulators. They were used for timing astronomical observations and for regulating other timepieces. Most regulators have a plainer case than other longcase clocks. Mid-18th-century regulators are rare, while late 18th and early 19th-century ones, as well as being fine pieces of furniture, often have refinements such as jewelling to the movement to improve accuracy even more.

Mahogany longcase regulator; London, c.1850; 77 in (1.96 m). This is by Vulliamy.
£5000-£8000

High-quality Victorian three-train quarter-chiming clock (left); mid-19thC; 84 in (2.13 m). The dial is silvered and the case pollard oak.
£3000-£4000

Dutch floral marquetry clock; c.1750; 94 in (2.39 m). The finials and bombé plinth are typical.
£5000-£6000

East, the Vulliamy family, Henry Jones and Daniel Quare. However, it is vital not to be blinded by a name: the signature on the chapter ring may have been 'stoned out' and re-engraved with a more desirable one.

Traditionally, the most sought-after clocks are the square-dialled pieces made during the 'classic' period of London clock-making, 1660-1720. These have a brass dial with a silvered-brass chapter ring and cast gilt-brass spandrels. Dials were 10 in (25.4 cm) square until 1685, 11 in (28 cm) square from 1685 to 1700 and 12 in (30.5 cm) square until around 1720. Thereafter, London dials had an arched top. But do not assume that all square-dialled clocks are early, as provincial examples with a flat-top hood were made throughout the 18th century. From the 1760s, some London clocks had a white enamelled dial and from 1780 many provincial dials were painted.

CASE STYLES

The earliest longcase clocks were architectural in style, with a pedimented hood; they generally had an ebony or ebonised pear wood veneer on oak. They stood about 6 ft (1.8 m) tall. Walnut veneer was used from the early 1670s until about 1750. An early fashion for geometrical marquetry (parquetry) was superseded by 1676, first by panels of floral marquetry, then by sinuous seaweed or arabesque marquetry. This gradually gave way from about 1710 to lacquer or japanned decoration; lacquer is rare before this, but continued until the early 19th century, especially outside London. Floral marquetry clocks generally sell today for £8000-£12,000, seaweed examples for £6000-£9000. Beware of burr-walnut clocks that were 'marquetried-up' 100 years ago. These are difficult to tell from the real thing, but are worth £2000-£3000 less.

Mahogany was first used about 1750 in London and 1760 in the provinces. A typical London mahogany longcase clock is tall and slender – around 8 ft (2.4 m) high – with a panelled plinth, and a trunk with three-quarter columns on the front corners and an arched door. The hood has a pagoda shape over it with three finials, often cut down later to suit low rooms. Mahogany clocks have been seriously collected only since the 1970s, and most fetch between £3000 and £8000.

Mahogany country clocks are generally broader and fussier than their London counterparts. Boxwood stringing, crossbanding, panels of veneer, blind frets, turned ornament and Gothic details abound. The slimmest examples command the highest prices today, with mahogany alone fetching more than oak with mahogany crossbanding (known as 'oak-and-mahogany'). Cheaper plain oak or pine clocks start at about £500.

A revival from 1875 to 1910 saw the manufacture of Sheraton-style clocks, reproduction London mahogany clocks with a musical movement or quarter-striking (the earlier longcases usually struck only the hours), and massive quarter-striking pieces with tubular chimes. The cases often have a glazed trunk and carved ornament. The Victorians loved chiming clocks, and some 18th-century movements were 'stretched' by an added third train for a quarter strike or tune.

Look out for 'marriages' of movement and case that did not originally belong together, especially in early clocks. For example, a good movement from a mediocre ebonised case may have been 'upgraded' to a walnut case, which is easily done as dials and cases were made to standard sizes. A badly married clock is worth less than the sum of its parts.

FOREIGN CLOCKS

The most common foreign longcase clocks are Dutch. French pieces are rarer and closely follow furniture styles. Dutch longcases, from about 1720 until well into the 19th century, are typified by a characteristic bombé plinth, a waisted trunk door and finials of Atlas flanked by angels. These clocks typically have elaborate striking systems and calendar indicators.

COSTUME TIME *The French Louis XV longcase clock standing by the door is almost as fancily bedecked as the young princes in this 1760s painting of George III's Queen Charlotte, by John Zoffany.*

Wall clocks

From plain Edwardian school clocks to cartel clocks mounted in elaborate ormolu, clocks to hang on the wall come in many shapes and sizes.

THE UBIQUITOUS WALL DIAL of the Victorian and Edwardian periods is familiar from countless schools, kitchens and waiting rooms. In fact, wall clocks come in many forms, the fundamental distinction being between spring-driven clocks (which mostly run for eight days) and weight-driven clocks (mostly running for 30 hours).

WEIGHT-DRIVEN CLOCKS

The earliest form of household, as distinct from public, wall clock was the Gothic chamber clock, made in Germany, Switzerland and in what is now Holland. Despite the name, these timepieces were made from around 1450 to 1650. They are very rare, but because of their bulk fetch only £5000 at auction.

A British development of the Gothic chamber clock was the lantern clock. A large bell on its top gives this timepiece its characteristic domed shape. Most London-made examples date from before 1720, although some were produced in the provinces as late as 1800. The majority run for 30 hours and have only a single, hour hand. Buying a lantern clock needs knowledge and experience, or expert advice, as many were converted to table or mantel clocks (see p.282) in the Victorian era; forged lantern clocks abound also. Prices range from £400 for an example in poor condition to more than £5000 for one in good condition by a reputable maker.

Mid-European clocks from in the 18th and 19th centuries include Black Forest wall clocks, which generally have a 30-hour movement framed in a wooden case. They are recognisable by an arched wooden dial, usually painted with bunches of flowers or country scenes, and some have a cuckoo mechanism (see p.287). They were much copied around 1800 in the eastern United States, where they are known as 'wag-on-the-wall' clocks because of their short pendulum which beats every half-second (and may hang in front of the dial).

Austrian clocks known as Vienna regulators were originally made to a very high standard during the Biedermeier period of the early 19th century. They have a high-quality movement, with small driving weights and usually no strike. Most cases are made of boxwood, ebony or birch with glazed panels, and are severe and architectural in style. These clocks are generally expensive, fetching upwards of £10,000 at auction. A second

English brass lantern clock (weights and chains not shown); c.1660; 15 in (38.1 cm) high. This is a rare example from before the 1666 Fire of London.
£2000-£2500

Vienna regulator; c.1860; 45 in (1.14 m) high. It has a simulated rosewood case and enamelled dial. The numerous German clocks of this kind are less valuable than the earlier, more severe Austrian clocks.
£500-£750

Friesland stoel clock; 18thC; 32 in (81 cm) high. This has a 30-hour posted frame movement and a verge escapement with short pendulum. The fretwork is cast lead.
£1000-£1200
20thC: £300-£500

type of Vienna regulator was mass-produced in Germany from about 1860 into the 20th century: striking and quarter-striking pieces in walnut cases abound. Many have ebonised mouldings and turned decoration, with some later examples in Art Nouveau style.

Postman alarm clocks were also made in the Black Forest in the mid to late 19th century. They have a white-painted 5 in (12.7 cm) round dial with a turned mahogany or birchwood bezel, or surround. The 30-hour

German Black Forest painted wood 30-hour wall clock; c.1820; 12¾ in (32.4 cm) high. This has a wooden movement as well as dial. Similar clocks were made in the 18th and early 19thC in the USA.
£400-£600

Regency sedan clock; c.1810; 6¼ in (15.9 cm) diameter. The brass-bound mahogany case contains a 30-hour watch movement.
£200-£250

movement is powered by a cast-iron weight.

Dutch or Friesland stoel clocks date from the 18th century. They have a painted dial, and an arched canopy, decorated with elaborate cast-lead fretwork, protrudes over the clock. Access to the brass, 30-hour verge movement with a bell at the top is through side doors. Staart clocks, which replaced the stoel type in the 19th century, have a 30-hour anchor movement. The long pendulum is housed in a boxed 'tail' below the wall bracket. The painted tin-plate dial often has a charming country or town scene. Stoel clocks fetch £800-£1200, staart clocks £500-£800.

SPRING-DRIVEN CLOCKS

The wall dial is the commonest type of British clock after the longcase, and originated in London in the 1760s. It is a spring-driven equivalent of the Act of Parliament clock (see box) and owes a debt to the French cartel clock. Early wall dials have an unglazed round

William IV wall dial; c.1830; 22 in (56 cm) high. This mahogany clock was made by Parkinson & Frodsham of London.
£500-£800

Mahogany dial clock; c.1880; 14 in (35.6 cm) diameter. The brass bezel and painted iron dial are typical features for this date.
£200-£250

French Louis XV ormolu cartel clock; c.1750; 29½ in (75 cm) high. Elaborate Rococo clocks like this were much copied in the 19thC; copies fetch £1000-£1800.
£2500-£3500

American banjo clock; c.1815; 40 in (1.01 m) high. Genuine examples fetch high prices but many late 19th and 20thC copies exist.
£20,000-£25,000

Starburst clock; 20thC; 17 in (43.2 cm) across. These clocks are common and revive an earlier French model. The carved giltwood case is Italian and the timepiece movements are usually of French origin.
£150-£200

ACT OF PARLIAMENT CLOCKS
To Avoid a Tax?

AN ACT OF PARLIAMENT passed in 1797 taxed all timepieces and – legend has it – made people hide their clocks and watches and rely on clocks in public places such as taverns and inns. The large weight-driven clocks said to result from the Act – with a dial 28 in (70 cm) across – became known as 'Act of Parliament clocks', although in reality such clocks had been made since the 1720s. The Act was repealed within a year, but the clocks continued to be made well into the 19th century. They are also known as tavern or coaching clocks. Below the dial is a trunk long enough for a one-second pendulum – 39 in (99 cm) – with a long door.

George II Act of Parliament clock by Benjamin Gray and Justin Vulliamy; London, c.1755; 48 in (1.22 m) high. The case is japanned pine.
£5000-£8000
Lesser maker:
£3000-£5000

painted wooden dial, about 15 in (38 cm) across, fixed to a movement that is housed in a wooden box. They always have a hole in the back to fit on a wall hook.

Clocks made from the late 18th century onwards have a glazed dial, the face silvered from about 1770 to 1820 and made of painted iron thereafter. Most examples dating from around 1775 have a mahogany box instead of the earlier painted pine. Georgian clocks have a wooden bezel, while Victorian and Edwardian wall dials have a turned brass one, and a half-second pendulum.

Victorian drop-dials are recognisable by their long movement box, which can extend some 12 in (30 cm) below the dial. The box has a window through which to view the pendulum. The case may be plain mahogany, or have mother-of-pearl, brass or boxwood inlay, and some are papier-mâché.

Cartel clocks were a French innovation devised in the Régence period, about 1720. These forerunners of the British wall dial are highly ornamental, many designed by leading cabinet-makers and decorated with boulle-work, ormolu or painted tin-plate. Louis XVI and Empire examples are almost always Neoclassical in style and made of ormolu, although all styles were reproduced in the 19th century. British cartel clocks made between 1760 and 1800 are carved giltwood in the Rococo style. Their silvered dials are 6 in (15.2 cm) across and have a mock pendulum and a prominent script signature.

Sedan clocks, which date from the Regency period, were often made using earlier watch movements and dials. These were rehoused in a 3 in (76 mm) circular or rectangular brass-rimmed mahogany case. The brass loop fitted at the top of the clock was for hanging the clock in a sedan chair.

American banjo clocks from the early 19th century have a glass-fronted banjo-shaped case; many are painted with patriotic subjects. Later copies sell for £3000-£4000.

Bracket clocks

Often regarded as the epitome of English clock-making, classic bracket clocks have the added surprise of beautiful engraving – at the back.

THE WALL BRACKET on which such clocks were sometimes placed gave bracket clocks their name, but they would also often have stood on a table or sideboard – as they would today. They are spring-driven pendulum clocks, most often housed in a rectangular case with a carrying handle on top. Although the earliest ones were made in Holland, they reached the peak of their development in England.

ENGLISH CLOCKS

The English bracket clock first appeared in the early 1660s and continued to be made into the 20th century. However, production declined from the mid-19th century and ceased with the disruption of the First World War. The classic period for bracket clocks is 1660-1720, when they were made with a square or rectangular dial. Thereafter the dial was usually arched at the top, except for some Regency dials which were round.

Examples from the 17th and 18th centuries have a verge escapement, 19th-century ones an anchor escapement (see p.469). However, many verge-escapement clocks were converted to anchor escapement in the 19th century. Later reconversion restores only about the value of the work – around £1500 – but a completely original verge-escapement bracket clock sells for much more.

The range of price and quality of these clocks is huge. You could pay around £1000 for a typical ebonised Victorian example or as much as £50,000 for a late 17th or early 18th-century clock by a top London maker such as Thomas Tompion. Even Regency and Victorian bracket clocks have come to be collected for the quality of the movement.

ENGRAVING

Engraved back plates are one of the glories of English 17th and 18th-century craftsmanship. The style of engraving can help to date a clock. On the first clocks – around 1660-70 – only the maker's signature was engraved on the back plate. The area engraved then spread until by about 1680 the whole plate was covered with acanthus scrolls ending in tulip flowerheads – so-called 'tulip engraving'. From around 1685 acanthus scrolls with birds,

Queen Anne clock by Daniel Quare; c.1710; 18 in (45.7 cm) high. The kingwood-veneered case has a double-basket top in repoussé gilt brass.
£10,000-£15,000

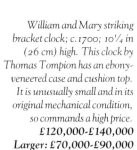

William and Mary striking bracket clock; c.1700; 10¼ in (26 cm) high. This clock by Thomas Tompion has an ebony-veneered case and cushion top. It is unusually small and in its original mechanical condition, so commands a high price.
£120,000-£140,000
Larger: £70,000-£90,000

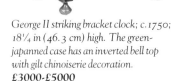

George II striking bracket clock; c.1750; 18¼ in (46.3 cm) high. The green-japanned case has an inverted bell top with gilt chinoiserie decoration.
£3000-£5000

George III quarter chiming bracket clock; c.1780; 19¼ in (49 cm) high. This clock has a mahogany bell-top case, a style that was popular c.1760-1800. An hour striking version of this clock would fetch less.
£5000-£7000

Late Regency/early Victorian mahogany-veneered chamfer-top bracket clock; 1830s; 19¼ in (49 cm) high. It has brass mounts and a painted dial.
£2000-£2500

Late Victorian/Edwardian quarter chiming bracket clock; c.1900; 21 in (53.5 cm) high. The satinwood case is mounted with gilt brass ornament.
£3000-£5000

George III satinwood table regulator in balloon case; c.1810; 14½ in (36.8 cm) high. Balloon clocks are one of the few English case styles influenced by French models. The style was revived in Edwardian times.
£6000-£7000
With conventional dial: £3000-£4000

dolphin heads and human or fantastic masks became fashionable. By 1735 these had gone, leaving only scrollwork, which became increasingly Rococo in style, in the 1740s, and included chinoiserie motifs. By 1800 engraving was sparser, and by the end of the Regency era (1830) the back plate had only a wheatear or egg-and-dart border. Most Victorian bracket clocks have no engraving.

CASE STYLES

The earliest bracket clocks, from what is known as the 'architectural' period (about 1660-73), are quite large – about 16-20 in (40-50 cm) high – and have a pediment top. But by 1675, the characteristic case style was established: a rectangular box with projecting mouldings top and bottom, a handle on top, glazed doors front and back, and rectangular panels – either glazed or with pierced frets – to the sides. Within this basic format, variations in the materials of the case and the shape of the top indicate the date.

Case materials follow the same date lines – through oak, walnut, mahogany and so on – as longcase clocks (see p.278). Few incorporate marquetry, but ebony (and later ebonising) remained popular for as long as bracket clocks were made, so that roughly one out of every two bracket clocks is black.

The clock's top from 1675 to 1720 was in the basket or caddy shape; this is cushion

moulded in wood or repoussé gilt brass. Some clocks have a double repoussé basket top, with a secondary cushion or bulbous moulded section above the first. The inverted bell top – with two contrasting curves, the lower convex, the upper concave – dates from 1720 to 1770. This style overlapped with the bell top from 1760 to 1810 – again with two contrasting curves, but with concave below convex, like a church bell. In the period 1765-1810 the arched top, and in 1815-45 the chamfered top, were very common. However, from 1780 to 1810 balloon cases were also made, and from 1810 to 1860 lancet cases. During the 19th and 20th centuries various style revivals included the arched, bell top, chamfered top, lancet and balloon case.

Victorian arched bracket clock in George III style; c.1890; 13½ in (34.3 cm) high. The case is mahogany, the dial painted.
£1000-£1500
George III example: £2000-£2500

Louis XIV pendule religieuse; c.1690; 16¾ in (42.5 cm) high. It has an ebony-veneered case and a gilt chapter ring and spandrels on the velvet covered dial. These were developed from Dutch Haagse clocks.
£4500-£5500

CONTINENTAL CLOCKS

The first Dutch pendulum clocks were the harbingers of English bracket clocks. The earliest Dutch bracket clocks (1658-70) are known as 'Haagse' clocks. They have a velvet-covered rectangular dial with brass chapter ring and spandrels. These early clocks were normally hung on the wall by the two iron loops attached to the back board.

From the early 18th century, most bracket clocks sold in Holland had a London-made movement with a Dutch-made case. Such clocks have a chapter ring with the minutes marked on lobes between the hour numerals. Some larger clocks have painted dials with automaton windmills or musicians playing in time to music. Eighteenth-century Dutch bracket clocks usually fetch around £3000 each whereas Haagse clocks sell for £5000 up to £20,000. Those featuring music and automata go for about £12,000.

The earliest French bracket clocks – 'pendules religieuses' – date from the mid-1660s and are close copies of the Dutch, with a velvet, hinged dial. French clock movements were normally put in the case from the front – the opposite of English clocks. Also, French dial doors or bezels were hinged on the left, English doors on the right.

By the early 18th century, the front mounting plate was no bigger than the chapter ring and the front door closely framed the dial. At the same time, the sides of the case began to be waisted below the dial, heralding the sinuous shape of most French Régence and Louis XV bracket clocks. During the 18th century French bracket clocks had the winding holes positioned asymmetrically, unlike those of the 19th century. Prices vary considerably, but a standard French bracket clock will sell for £1500-£2500.

French Régence scarlet boulle bracket clock; c.1730; 21 in (53.5 cm) high. The case is decorated in tortoiseshell and brass marquetry (boulle work) with cast ormolu mounts. This style of clock was much copied in the 19thC.
£2000-£2500; 19thC copy: £1000

STYLE OF THE TIME *A flounced and furbelowed lady glances at the equally dressed-up French Rococo clock on its wall bracket in Auguste Toulmouche's late 19thC painting 'Five minutes late'.*

Mantel clocks

Ranging from the frivolity of Rococo ormolu to sombre black marble, mantel clocks are often impressive but still common and affordable.

SPECIAL MANTELPIECE CLOCKS originated in France in the 1750s. They quickly became popular throughout Europe and North America, so 18th and 19th-century examples are very numerous. The idea grew to its maturity in the 1830s with the birth of the clock set: clock and matching urns, tazzas and candelabra or candlesticks.

FRENCH MANTEL CLOCKS

French mantel clocks followed styles in the other decorative arts: fanciful and generally Rococo before about 1765, then Neoclassical, and Romantic from about 1830. Most have an ormolu case – or spelter in many cheap clocks from the 1840s on – often inset with porcelain plaques. Animal and figurative clocks were always popular, the latter being among the most affordable today; they sell for £350 upwards. Rococo pieces often have porcelain figures, later examples ormolu or spelter.

Also common are 'four-glass' clocks, which look like large carriage clocks (see opposite), but with a pendulum movement. The best include a perpetual calendar dial and may fetch up to £2600. But beware of forgeries adapted from black slate clocks (see below). Only the case can distinguish these; the movement and dial are identical.

ENGLISH MANTEL CLOCKS

The best English mantel clocks come between bracket and carriage clocks in size and are of superb quality. They are wooden cased, do not have a carrying handle and do not usually strike, so are sometimes called 'library' clocks.

Cottage clocks were a response to cheap American and German imports in the 19th century. The cases are quite crude, and they use recycled 18th-century 30-hour watch movements. They fetch £150-£300.

In the late 19th century, many lantern clocks (see p.282) were either converted or reproduced with a spring fusee pendulum movement for use as mantel clocks. Both types fetch between £400 and £600 today, but only conversions have holes in the base plate for the original driving chains.

OTHER TYPES

American shelf clocks were cheap, mass-produced 30-hour clocks which from 1842 were imported into Britain in their thousands. The first were weight-driven, but from about 1850, smaller spring-driven shelf clocks were also made. These sell for £60-£90.

Victorian and Edwardian black slate or marble clocks are numerous, and this has kept prices down to £50-£80 for the simplest type, yet they are basically of good quality. Their cases use Belgian black slate (often described as 'marble') in a thin veneer on fine cement. Case styles span a wide range, and all could originally be bought in a clock set with side pieces. Cheap alternatives were made in the United States from painted or stained wood, while 'Napoleon-hat' clocks and similar types are the 1920s and 30s equivalents.

Art Deco mantel clocks – often small and angular, with the dial and movement mounted through a vertical plate – are also sought after. Whether spring-driven or electric, a stylish example will sell for around £150.

Napoleon III clock set; c.1860; 29½ in (75 cm) high. The ormolu elephant clock is signed Julien Leroy, Paris, which raises the value. The associated candelabra were not originally made for the clock.
£3000-£3500 the set

French ormolu clock with Sèvres-style porcelain mounts; c.1865; 21½ in (55 cm) high. A great variety of these clocks were made in the later 19thC.
£1500-£2000

American 'gingerbread' shelf clock; c.1860; 14 in (35.5 cm) high. These spring-driven clocks survive in their thousands. They are collected more in the USA than in Britain.
£80-£100

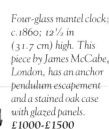

Four-glass mantel clock; c.1860; 12½ in (31.7 cm) high. This piece by James McCabe, London, has an anchor pendulum escapement and a stained oak case with glazed panels.
£1000-£1500

Art Nouveau pewter and enamel mantel clock; 1905; 7 in (17.8 cm) high. This piece for Liberty & Co has a tapering, square-section body with an enamelled dial and a shield enamelled in red, blue and green.
£1200-£1600

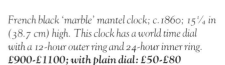

French black 'marble' mantel clock; c.1860; 15¼ in (38.7 cm) high. This clock has a world time dial with a 12-hour outer ring and 24-hour inner ring.
£900-£1100; with plain dial: £50-£80

Portable clocks

Brass carriage clocks are the most familiar type of portable clock, but the range is wide and reaches the specialist level of the marine chronometer.

TRULY PORTABLE CLOCKS must have a balance-wheel escapement, not a pendulum, so that they can continue working while being carried around. Early German spring clocks were originally portable, but many were later converted to a pendulum escapement. Before about 1580 their movements were entirely of iron, but brass replaced this over the next 20 years.

Carriage clocks were first made in France by Abraham-Louis Breguet for military use in the Napoleonic wars, but were taken up by other French makers as all-purpose travelling clocks in the 1830s. Production ceased with the First World War, but large numbers of reproductions have appeared in the past ten years.

As carriage clocks were virtually mass-produced with an eight-day movement and glass panels, they can be judged by standard criteria: French or English manufacture (the latter is usually of higher quality); movement complication, ranging from alarm to grande sonnerie with calendar (the more complex it is, the more valuable the clock); and the style and decoration of the case. When evaluating an example, you should always judge the case and the movement separately.

French carriage clocks always have a going barrel movement (see p.276). Most quality clocks carry a trademark rather than a signature. They were made in set sizes ranging from giant, 8½ in (21.6 cm) high, to the 2½ in (63 mm) subminiature. The most common size is the standard, 5½-6 in (14-15.2 cm) high. Beware clocks converted from petite to grande sonnerie striking – with too small a barrel for the striking train they stop before a full week.

English carriage clocks have a chain fusee movement and are generally larger than the standard French size – and more expensive. A signature, and often the maker's address, is usually found on both back plate and dial.

CHRONOMETERS

Marine chronometers are the ultimate portable clocks, designed to maintain accuracy in difficult conditions at sea. They were first developed in the 18th century in response to an Act of Parliament offering a £20,000 prize (over £2 million in today's money) for a robust clock accurate to within strict limits. By 1800,

see p.276

reliable chronometers were commercially viable. They were used until radar navigation systems made them obsolete.

Chronometers are suspended in gimbals, for stability, within a lidded box usually of mahogany. The Royal Navy preferred the more accurate one-day (30-hour) or two-day (56-hour) models, but modern collectors prefer the convenience of eight-day chronometers, which are rarer and much more expensive. Brass edging or banding adds value, as does a rosewood or coromandel case – which may take the auction price to £4500 for an eight-day model. Pre-1850 examples have a bowed glass over the dial.

German tabernacle table clock (left), c.1625; and crucifix table clock (right), c.1640; both 13½ in (34.3 cm) high. The tabernacle clock has dials on four sides and bells in the galleries at the top. The ball on the crucifix turns to show the hour.
Left: £3000-£6000; right: £5000-£8000

Three carriage clocks: corniche case (left), gorge case (centre) and anglaise case; 1860-90; all c.6 in (15 cm) high. All three have small knobs at the front top for activating the 'repeat' mechanism.
£250-£350; £550-£600; £450-£550

Silver French Empire carriage clock; 1823; 5 in (12.7 cm) high. This clock was made by Abraham-Louis Breguet, the first maker of true carriage clocks (1796). It is complete with the original instructions, maker's certificate and leather case.
£50,000-£80,000

French enamelled carriage clock; c.1870; 7 in (17.8 cm) high. This clock has a gilt brass anglaise case decorated with champlevé enamel. The small dial is for setting the alarm.
£2000-£2500

English carriage clock; c.1860; 8½ in (21.6 cm) high. Such clocks are typically larger and of higher quality than French carriage clocks. They are also rarer.
£3000-£5000

Eight-day marine chronometer in complete, original three-tier box; c.1875; 7 in (17.8 cm) wide. One and two-day examples sell for £1200-£2000.
£3000-£3500

Novelty clocks

Novelty clocks bear witness to the ingenuity of clock-makers over the ages and provide scope for collectors of all pockets.

Brass, gilt metal and marble French skeleton clock; c.1825; 12 in (30.5 cm) high. This model does not strike the hours, but it has the original glass and wood case. Most similar English clocks were made after 1835.
£2000-£2500
Plainer example:
£350-£1200

Austrian brass, gilt metal and wood rack clock; early 19thC; 16½ in (42 cm) high. Unlike most rack clocks it is pushed down, not up, to wind it, and travels up the rack as it unwinds.
£2200-£2600
Pull-up type: £500-£800

French mystery clock with giltwood stand; c.1860; 37½ in (95 cm) high. The dial consists of three sheets of glass. The hand is attached to the middle one, which is toothed and turned by a cog in one of the supports.
£1000-£1500

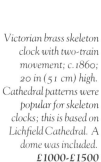

Victorian brass skeleton clock with two-train movement; c.1860; 20 in (51 cm) high. Cathedral patterns were popular for skeleton clocks; this is based on Lichfield Cathedral. A dome was included.
£1000-£1500

French mystery clock; c.1870; 14 in (35.5 cm) high. This Jacque de Fabrique novelty clock operates on the centrifugal balance (or conical pendulum) principle. The 'pendulum' is driven by the thin T-bar between it and the clock dial.
£500-£700

From homely cuckoo clocks to exquisite jewelled Cartier pieces, from clocks where all the working parts are on view to clocks that have no apparent movement and some that work by water, novelty clocks are popular with collectors today for their intriguing mechanisms and amusing forms.

SKELETON CLOCKS

A glass dome replaces the casing on a skeleton clock, and a pierced frame exposes the movement to view. Such clocks were first made in France in the late 18th century and caught on in Britain in the early 19th. Production ceased early this century, but some reproductions have been made since 1970.

The commonest, French 19th-century type is small, with A-shaped plates framing the movement, and often with an alarm or musical mechanism in the base. They are easy to find and fetch £350-£500 at auction today. British skeleton clocks have a distinctive

spring fusee movement. The best have specially made five or six-spoke wheels; four spokes indicate standard clock wheels. The frame is usually either of highly ornate scrollwork or is pierced in the form of an architectural façade, such as York Minster. Such pieces fetch £500-£2000, but an hour strike or quarter chimes add to the value – as does a platform or chronometer escapement.

A broken or cracked glass dome presents a great problem. Modern domes never seem to fit, and square-framed glass or Perspex is less attractive and needs a new rectangular base. Some modern reproduction skeleton clocks exist, but it is quite easy to distinguish their cast plates from fret-cut originals.

MYSTERY CLOCKS

With no obvious connection between the movement and the dial, or a pendulum which seems to swing of its own accord, mystery clocks live up to their name. Values depend

on the ingenuity of the 'mystery' as well as on the clock's materials and decorative appeal.

The very best glass-dial mystery clocks – in which the hands are attached to rotating glass discs – are the Art Deco creations of Cartier which fetch six figures. However, anonymous late 19th-century French glass mystery clocks can quite easily be found at prices up to £1500.

Mystery clocks with a female figure holding a free-swinging pendulum in her outstretched hand may have a cast brass or spelter case. Avoid the latter if the spelter is damaged as it is virtually impossible to repair. The movement is in the base and the large 'pendulum' is a dummy made to swing by the imperceptible turning of the figure itself. These clocks, when cast in spelter, fetch £200-£250.

A similar, more popular type has a figure – or sometimes an elephant – holding a rocking globe marked with a dial, with a pendulum hanging below. In fact the globe contains an oscillating pendulum escapement, which

Pinewood and bone cuckoo clock from the Black Forest; c.1880; 17 in (43.2 cm) high. This tabletop, spring-driven model is quite rare – most cuckoo clocks are wall-hung and driven by weights.
£300-£400

Silver-cased ticket or flick clock; 1904; 6 in (15.2 cm) high. It is very rare to find ticket clocks cased in silver; most are brass. The silver work is by S. Green & Co, Birmingham, and bears a 1904 hallmark.
£600-£700
Brass: £150-£200

French 'industrial' clock; c.1880; 9½ in (24.1 cm) high. This marble-based clock is in the form of a beam engine, surmounted by a 'beam pendulum' and flanked by cylindrical 'boilers'. This model is unusual in that the eight-day automation action of the 'machinery' is integral with the clock movement.
£1400-£1800

French novelty clocks: (left) bronze and ormolu four-dial 'Big Ben' clock; (centre) ormolu clock modelled as Nôtre Dame; (right) gilt and patinated metal, 'Eiffel Tower' clock; all 19thC; tallest 29½ in (75 cm) high.
Left and right: £1500-£2000
Centre: £2500-£3000

rocks the globe and causes the dummy pendulum to swing. Cast in spelter, these clocks range in price from £250 to £350.

'SCIENTIFIC' CLOCKS

As the name suggests, gravity clocks are driven by the power of their own weight. There are three main types: a ball descending on a chain, a canister rolling down a slope, or a canister descending a toothed rack.

Falling-ball clocks have the dial on the outside of a globe containing the movement,

and are very rare, although a few have been made in this century. Inclined-plane clocks are of late 17th-century origin but were not widely made again until the last few decades of this century. The dial is positioned on the flat front end of the canister. Rack clocks are much more common. They were originally made in the 18th century, but a number were produced in the 1920s and 30s. Early examples from the 18th and 19th centuries sell at auction for around £500-£800, while 20th-century pieces fetch around £200-£300.

Congreve clocks – invented by William Congreve in 1808 – have a ball rolling down a zigzag groove in a tilting tray that reverses at the end of each trip. The ball and tray do not drive the clock but merely regulate a spring-driven movement, which normally has separate dials for hours, minutes and seconds. A few 19th-century examples exist, and these change hands for about £20,000 if they come up for auction, but most are modern 'executive toys' selling for around £700-£1000.

'Torsion' or 400-day clocks have an ivorine or card circular dial and a disc 'pendulum' that rotates one way and then the other on a twisting metal strip. Early examples fetch around £100-£150, while modern versions can be picked up for about £50-£80. Because they only need winding once a year, they are often also known as 'anniversary' clocks.

OTHER NOVELTY CLOCKS

Cuckoo clocks originated in the Black Forest of southern Germany in about 1740. Early examples are rare, and most date from after production expanded in the 1840s and 50s. Many from that period are spring-driven table clocks, rather than wall-mounted 'Swiss chalets' driven by fir-cone weights. The latter became popular in the late 19th century and still sell in vast numbers, fetching £100-£150. The better 19th-century pieces have two birds (a cuckoo for the hours and a quail for the quarters), and fetch £400-£600.

Black Forest clock-maker figures are in the form of a standing model of a clock pedlar, with a clock slung on his back and front. The one at the back is a dummy. They are about 10 in (25 cm) high and are naturalistically painted. Early 19th-century examples are made of tôle peinte and are much more valuable – at about £1000-£1500 – than later ones with a much heavier cast-spelter case, worth £300-£500.

A wide variety of other devices have also been used in novelty clocks. Ticket clocks were the first form of digital timepiece, while 'industrial' clocks mimic machinery. Water clocks look 'olde worlde', but were made in the 1920s; they are driven by a pulley and chain attached to a float on the surface of a canister of water which gradually empties into a trough below. They sell for £150-£250.

Forward-swinging pendulum clocks have a circular dial, a stone or metal case, and an arched base with a cherub on a swing acting as the pendulum. Prices range from £250-£350 for timepieces up to £400-£600 for striking clocks, although the latter are rare.

Watches

From antique enamels to items of 20th-century power dressing and the latest trendy Swatch, among both pocket and wristwatches there are enormous variations in value.

WATCHES have progressed over the centuries from bulky and inaccurate luxury items to slim-line pieces with split-second timekeeping. Today a watch may be valuable and collectable as the prototype of later mass-produced models, for the intrinsic value of its materials, as a rarity, or as the product of a great maker or 'marque'. Curiously, women's watches generally fetch much less than equivalent men's watches.

POCKET WATCHES

Early watches, dating from before the introduction of the balance spring in about 1675, were very inaccurate but decorative. Most that survive were made in Germany or France. The earliest have an oval or octagonal case, often set with rock crystal or gems, occasionally even fashioned from a single stone. In the 1620s, painted Blois enamel cases became fashionable throughout the courts of Europe. These have sometimes been refitted with a later movement, but original pieces fetch £30,000-£50,000.

Much more likely to be seen are pair-cased watches from the 18th century. They are collected for the decorative outer case, but the important part originally was the protective inner case to keep dirt out of the balance spring escapement. The earliest examples have a metal dial, but from the late 1740s (earlier in France and Switzerland) an enamel dial was the norm. The cheapest form of case decoration was horn, either under-painted to resemble tortoiseshell or painted with a scene. Enamelled cases were more costly. Repoussé decoration is also common, the best of which is English. Poorer-quality Dutch repoussé pieces often have forged English signatures, but an arcaded (lobed), rather than plain, minute ring is a clue to Dutch origins.

Grandfather's hunter and half-hunter watches originated on the hunting field, where the unprotected glass of an open-face watch was likely to break. Hunters have a completely covered dial and must be opened

Pair-cased verge watch; c.1780; 2 in (51 mm) across. The gilt metal case of this watch is covered in under-painted horn. It was made – and is signed – by John Watson, London. **£450-£500**

Silver repoussé pair-cased verge watch; mid or late 18thC; 2 in (51 mm) across. This is a 'Dutch forgery' with false London name. Genuine London-made examples are of much better quality. **£450-£500**

Half-hunter keyless lever watch in 9-ct gold; c.1900; 1½ in (38 mm) across. The cover protects the dial, hand and glass but allows it to be read without opening. **£150-£200** **18ct: £300-£400**

Gold and enamel pair-cased verge watch, signed Grant, London; 1787; 1¾ in (44 mm) across. Top prices require mint condition. **£1500-£2000**

Triple-cased verge watch; late 18th/early 19thC; 2½ in (63 mm) across. Thousands of these watches were produced in Britain for sale in Turkey. **£500-£800**

Gold, enamel and pearl-set verge 'form' watch; Swiss, c.1820; 2½ in (63 mm) long. Novelty shapes like this are popular with collectors. **£4000-£5000**

to be read; half-hunters have a small bull's-eye glass for reading the time without opening the cover. Both were made in large numbers from the mid-19th century to the 1930s and the best have duplex or chronometer escapements.

Many hunter watches are hallmarked and can be dated accurately. However, the winding system is a further indication of date: American and Swiss manufacturers adopted button winding in about 1860, while English watches were key-wound until about 1880. Cases range from cheap gunmetal (worth around £10 today), through gilt metal ('rolled gold' or 'gold filled'), silver and 9-carat gold, up to 18-carat gold, enamelled gold and – the most valuable – jewel-studded. The dials are almost invariably of white or cream enamel. The numerous open-faced watches made in

the same period fetch about half as much as equivalent hunter and half-hunter watches.

Alongside more functional pieces, there has always been a taste for watches with an extra ingredient of decoration. These range from novelty or form watches – symbolic memento mori in the 17th century, or beetles, violins and the like in the 19th – to fantasy watches concealing erotic scenes.

Exotic watches were made for Eastern markets but are common in Britain today. Turkish market watches have Turkish numerals and a standard pair case coupled with a tortoiseshell-covered third case and often a rather crude fourth case made locally.

In the first half of the 19th century, Swiss manufacturers produced exquisitely enamelled lever and duplex watches for the Chinese

*Jacquemart watch; 19thC;
2¼ in (57 mm) across.
When it strikes, the figures
appear to hit the bells.*
£2000-£2500

*Two-colour 9-ct
gold Rolex Prince;
1929; 1½ in (38 mm)
long. Two-colour gold
is worth more than
plain. Beware copies.*
£2500-£3000

*Two 9-ct gold cushion case watches (below);
both 1930s; larger 1¼ in (32 mm) across.
The larger one is a Rolex 'Oyster' wristwatch,
with a self-sealing (screw-down) winder. The
unsigned Swiss watch on the right has a
conventional winder.*
Rolex: £800-£1000; other: £500-£600

*Gold Reverso
wristwatch; 1936;
1½ in (38 mm) long. Jaeger
Le Coultre recently restarted
production of these watches,
so modern copies abound.*
£2000-£3000

*Gentleman's platinum
wristwatch; 1935; 1¼ in
(32 mm) across. This
particular watch was sold
for a record price at
auction in 1990. It had
cost £180 in 1933 – not a
small sum then – and
turned out to be one of
only three platinum-cased
calendar, moon-phase
watches ever made by
Patek Philippe of Geneva.
The dial is silvered.*
£280,000

*Steel-cased wristwatch with calendar
and moon-phase; c.1945; 1⅓ in
(34 mm) across. Although marked
with the name of the maker Ebel,
both the dial and the movement
were probably made by Movado.*
£250-£300

*Swatch quartz wristwatch;
1985; 1¼ in (32 mm) across.
The fashionable Swiss-made
Swatch soon attained cult status,
and some models – especially
prototypes, presentation models and
limited editions – have become highly
collectable, fetching up to £20,000. Only
500 of this 'Velvet Underground' model,
wrapped in patterned stocking, were made.*
£3000-£3500

*Woman's cocktail watch;
1925-30; 2 in (51 mm)
long. This platinum and
diamond watch is by
Patek Philippe, but all
jewel-set ladies' cocktail
watches are collectable.*
£2000-£2500
**Unknown maker:
£700-£1000**

market, the back decorated with flowers or an idealised female portrait. Similar watches made for the Indian market never portray women, but have a maharajah or a hunting scene. Examples with complex striking and minute repeat may fetch £10,000 or more.

WRISTWATCHES

Ladies' bracelets set with a watch were being made by the mid-19th century, but men's wristwatches came into their own only in the First World War for use in the trenches. Their popularity was sealed by the spread of the motor car – a special model curved to fit the wrist so it could be read with both hands on the wheel is known as a 'driver' watch.

With the spread of the wristwatch came the dominance of Swiss manufacturers. Five of the 'Big Six' makers – Patek Philippe, Rolex, Jaeger Le Coultre, Vacheron & Constantin and Audemars Piguet – are Swiss. The sixth, Cartier, is French but uses Swiss movements. Secondary Swiss names – with values way below the big six – are International Watch Company (IWC), Omega and Longines.

The fashion for collecting wristwatches arose in the early 1980s as a reaction against mass-produced quartz watches. At first all 'old' wristwatches shot up in price, but those made after 1960 have now fallen from favour as they are too similar to models still in production. The metal of the case is the least reliable indicator of value, as many gold pieces are worth only bullion value. Much more important are style, maker and complexity – the most sought after being Art Deco and 'complicated' watches by the best makers.

The Rolex Prince is the watch that best epitomises the Art Deco period. It came in 9, 14 or 18-carat gold. Striped, two-colour gold models can fetch as much as £4000 in 18-carat gold. Even the numerous Art Deco watches made by lesser manufacturers or anonymous imitators can be worth hundreds of pounds.

A calendar mechanism adds significantly to the value, especially if it includes a moon-phase indicator. The best have a 'perpetual' calendar which adjusts automatically at the end of each month and allows for leap years. Other desirable watches include chronographs (precision stop watches), especially the split-second type. Extremely rare minute repeating watches sell for £10,000-£20,000, but beware of those adapted from pocket watches, worth about £1000.

Ladies' watches have not been caught up in the general collecting fervour. The one exception is small cocktail watches of the 1930s to 50s, set with precious stones. The most expensive are Cartier Art Deco models, which sell at auction for upwards of £5000.

Meteorological instruments

Barometers and thermometers still have their place in forecasting the weather, but early examples are now collectors' items too.

THE BRITISH PREOCCUPATION with the weather has led to the invention of a surprising variety of meteorological instruments over the past 200 years. Barometers and thermometers are the best known, but a wide range of others were made, especially in the 19th century. These included the barograph, which records atmospheric pressure on a revolving drum, and the anemometer, which measures wind speed. So many of these instruments were made that they are still fairly easy to find at reasonable prices, many in good working order.

MERCURY BAROMETERS

Changes in atmospheric pressure foretell weather patterns, and mercury barometers were first used to measure pressure as early as the 1660s. By the 18th century there were two main forms – the so-called stick and wheel types. Later examples often have associated instruments, most commonly a thermometer, built into the same case.

Collectors are generally interested only in instruments that still work, although there are a few specialist restorers of mechanisms. Cases can be repaired more easily. Collectability depends on date, style, materials and maker – many of the leading early barometer-makers were also makers of clocks and scientific instruments (see elsewhere in this chapter).

As barometers form part of the furniture of a room, some collectors are more interested in the appearance of the case than in the mechanism. Especially desirable are architectural cases of unusual design, such as Daniel Quare's free-standing portable pillar barometers with silver or gilt-metal mounts. These start at around £20,000 for walnut-cased models, reaching as much as £50,000 for the best ivory-cased examples.

The stick barometer is the earliest type, and consists at its simplest of a mercury-filled glass tube about 3 ft (90 cm) long, sealed at the top and mounted in a wall case, usually of mahogany. The base of the tube is open and sits in a container of mercury – the cistern. Any change in air pressure on the mercury in the cistern causes the level in the tube to rise or fall, which is measured against a scale at the upper end of the tube marked with inches and weather indications. There is often also a vernier scale for more precise readings. Many 18th-century barometers have fine marquetry cases with an ornamental architectural top

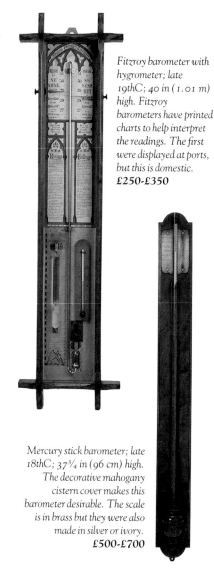

Fitzroy barometer with hygrometer; late 19thC; 40 in (1.01 m) high. Fitzroy barometers have printed charts to help interpret the readings. The first were displayed at ports, but this is domestic.
£250-£350

Mercury stick barometer; late 18thC; 37¾ in (96 cm) high. The decorative mahogany cistern cover makes this barometer desirable. The scale is in brass but they were also made in silver or ivory.
£500-£700

Angle barometer; 1770; 32¼ in (82 cm) high. Angle barometers are less common than other types, and this mahogany and brass example has particularly good engraving and well-figured mahogany.
£4000-£6000

Marine barometer; mid-19thC; 36 in (91 cm) high. This barometer is set in a gimbal mount to keep it upright no matter how the ship rolls. Such pieces are now very rare.
£1000-£1500

and shaped cistern cover. Today they fetch £800-£3000, while generally more sombre 19th-century pieces sell for £200-£800.

The wall-hung angle or 'signpost' barometer is a highly prized variant of the stick type. Its top section is bent so that the mercury moves over a greater distance for the same change in air pressure, allowing more accurate readings. Makers specialising in this type in the late 18th century include Charles Orme of Ashby de la Zouch, Leicestershire, and the London makers John Whitehurst, Watkins & Smith and Balthazar Knie. Depending on the maker, material, design and condition, values vary from £1500 to several thousand pounds.

Wheel barometers – often called 'banjo'

barometers because of their shape – are more common. Although invented as early as the mid-17th century, they only became popular in the 19th century. Changes in atmospheric pressure are shown on a dial connected to a weight and pulley system. The cases are often veneered and may incorporate other instruments such as a thermometer, hygrometer (to measure humidity) and clock. Prices today range from around £200 to £2000.

OTHER BAROMETERS AND BAROGRAPHS

Aneroid barometers work by responding to the movement of a thin, flexible metal disc covering a chamber containing a partial vacuum, and were developed in the mid-19th century. Changing pressure flexes the disc, which is connected via levers to a dial. This type of barometer was used on ships as the readings are unaffected by movement. Most aneroid barometers have a compact, wall-mounted decorative oak or mahogany case, but some are misleadingly banjo-shaped. Most fetch between £200 and £1000.

Portable or pocket aneroid barometers became popular from the 1860s onwards, and testify to Victorian skills in miniaturisation. Since air pressure varies with altitude, they could be used to calculate height on mountains or in balloons – up to about 20,000 ft (6000 m). Most were fitted into a brass watch-type case no more than 2 in (51 mm) across. Negretti & Zambra of London supplied many such pieces, some inset with a magnetic compass on the back and a tiny mercury thermometer, which today may fetch

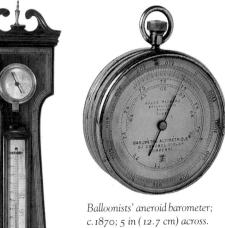

*Balloonists' aneroid barometer;
c.1870; 5 in (12.7 cm) across.
Such pieces doubled as altimeters,
but they were not very accurate.
This example is French.*
£150-£250

*Wall-mounted thermometer with
brass frame; c.1910; 10½ in
(26.7 cm) high. The white enamel
face of this thermometer is marked
for both centigrade and fahrenheit.*
£140-£220

*Sunshine recorder; 1890; base 10⅛ in (25.7 cm)
across. The recorder works by focusing the sun's
rays so they scorch its paper or cardboard cards.
Look for examples which retain their original cards.*
£500-£700

*Aneroid barometer; c.1900; 11 in
(28 cm) across. This piece has an
ebonised wood wall case, but some were
designed to look like banjo cases.
Aneroid barometers are portable and
more compact than mercury ones.*
£150-£250

*Anemometer; 1890; 7 in (17.8 cm)
high. Most portable air meters have
flat blades. This one has cups, like a
full-sized instrument.*
£150-£250
With blades: £100-£150

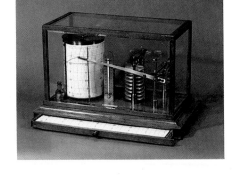

*Wheel barometer; 1840;
40¾ in (1.04 m) high. The
rosewood banjo-shaped case
also incorporates a
thermometer and a
hygrometer which raise the
value. It is signed by its
maker, A. Balla of Exeter.*
£600-£800

*Barograph; c.1910; 13 in (33 cm) long. This
oak-cased example is unusual because it has a
thermometer, but mahogany fetches more.
Condition is important as repairs are difficult.*
£250-£350

as much as £400. Other noted makers include
T. Cooke & Sons and J.H. Steward.

The barograph records changes in air
pressure as a trace on graph paper attached to
a revolving drum. The whole movement,
including its clockwork motor, is usually
mounted in a glazed case with a drawer in the
base for storing the paper. Values are affected
by quality, type of wood and accessories such
as thermometers. Good working examples
dating from 1860-1930 sell for £300-£750.

The sympiesometer is another instrument
for measuring air pressure, widely made in the
1820s and 30s and selling for around £500-
£1000 today. It has a short column of mercury
and a bulb of gas mounted in a brass or wooden

wall case; a thermometer mounted alongside
is used to correct the reading for anomalies
caused by changes in temperature.

THERMOMETERS AND ANEMOMETERS

Ever since the invention of the first accurate
thermometer in the early 18th century by
Dutchman Daniel Fahrenheit, thermometers
have been made in numerous sizes and forms.
Those from the 18th century have a scale plate
of brass and a mahogany case, while 19th-
century examples have an ivory or boxwood
plate and softwood case. Prices start at £50.

Generally more valuable are antique maximum and minimum thermometers, devised

by James Six of Colchester at the end of the
18th century to record the daily extremes of
temperature. They normally have a brass or
hardwood case, and when sold at auction
fetch between £200 and £500, the price
depending on style and date.

Anemometers are generally quite large,
with three or four revolving cups mounted on
a pole or roof to measure the strength of the
wind. A portable instrument with windmill-
like vanes and a built-in dial was devised in
the late 19th century for measuring light
currents of air in mines, flues and ventilators.
Full-size anemometers are rare today, but the
miniature versions are very collectable at an
auction price of around £100-£250.

Microscopes and telescopes

Scientists, astronomers, sailors and the general public have long employed a range of microscopes, telescopes, and other magnifying instruments as diverse as the stargazer's six-footer and pearl-encrusted opera glasses.

OPTICAL INSTRUMENTS vary hugely in sophistication and therefore in price. The earliest telescopes and microscopes dating from the 18th century or before are now difficult to find and command high prices. However, 19th and early 20th-century examples of all shapes and sizes are still very collectable, as long as they are in good condition and still in their original case.

MICROSCOPES

Microscopes used for detailed observation fall into two distinct groups: simple microscopes (commonly known as magnifying glasses),

Gould-type monocular compound microscope; c.1820; 7 in (17.8 cm) high. The case is integral to these microscopes, so they are only collectable if still together.
£350-£500

Spy glass; c.1800; 2 in (51 mm) diameter. This high quality piece made of ivory, blue enamel and brass was in fact a dress accessory, used at social functions and gatherings to see who was across the ballroom or theatre.
£150-£200

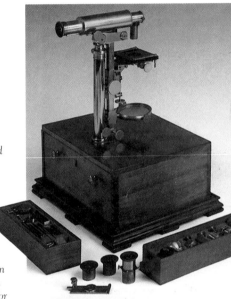

Horizontal compound microscope; c.1830; 17 in (43.2 cm) high. Horizontal microscopes are rare, and this brass and mahogany example is especially desirable, being complete with case and accessories.
£6000-£10,000

Culpeper-type compound microscope; early 19thC; 16 in (40.5 cm) high. The brass body is on its original mahogany stand.
£900-£1200; without accessories: £600-£800

German binoculars; c.1900; 10 in (25.4 cm) long. Prices depend on maker and size – larger pairs sell for more. This desirable brass and leather pair is by Zeiss.
£100-£150

Gilt metal opera glasses; early 20thC; 3 in (76 mm) wide. Decorated with blue enamelling and with mother-of-pearl extenders, this luxury pair has its original leather case stamped 'Cartier'.
£600-£700

Hand-held two-draw refracting telescope by Harris & Son; early 19thC; 18 in (45 cm) long unextended. The sliding tubes are of brass and the body tube is made of mahogany.
£250-£350

Reflecting telescope on stand; late 18thC; 27 in (68.5 cm) long. It is signed by King George III's telescope-maker, G. Adams – hence the high price.
£1000-£1500

with a single lens, and compound microscopes, which have two or more lenses.

Always check that the instrument is fully functional and optically sound, that the original lacquer on brass surfaces has not been rubbed away (a bright, shiny patina reduces the value considerably), and that all the accessories are present. Microscopes from the 19th century were typically sold in a mahogany chest which also housed tweezers, lenses and eyepieces. Without such accessories, the value can be reduced by over 70 per cent.

Simple microscopes dating from the 18th and 19th centuries are usually small enough to

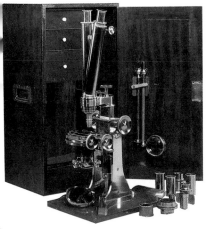

Binocular compound microscope; 1865; 20 in (51 cm) high. This piece is signed by Ross and has its original lacquer finish, case and accessories.
£2000-£2500

Monocular compound microscope; c.1840; 9 in (22.9 cm) high. This has its original mahogany case and accessories, which increase the value.
£300-£400

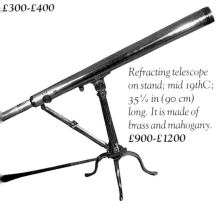

Refracting telescope on stand; mid 19thC; 35½ in (90 cm) long. It is made of brass and mahogany.
£900-£1200

fit into a pocket. Most are quite basic and made of brass (although ivory and fruitwood examples are also found), and have no means (or little means) of focusing on the image or specimen, which was held in place by a spike or pin. An 18th-century simple microscope by a maker such as Edmund Culpeper, still in its shagreen case and complete with accessories, can sell at auction for over £1000. Later examples can be cheaper, however, some fetching as little as £100. A fairly common variant is the 18th-century 'screw-barrel' microscope, especially designed for use on field trips. It has a handle at the side of the optical tube. Examples sell for £500-£1000.

COMPOUND MICROSCOPES

Compound microscopes are more complex – typically with three lenses in the wooden pasteboard or brass tube. The distance of the lower ('objective') lens from the object being examined can usually be adjusted for focusing, as can the viewing platform on which the specimen sits. Such microscopes came with several eyepieces and objective lenses.

Most early compound microscopes are based on one of two types, the Culpeper or the Cuff. Culpeper microscopes were produced from the 1720s to the early 19th century. They have an optical tube made of pasteboard or wood, which slides inside a cylindrical support sometimes covered in shagreen and supported on three legs. They came in a pyramid-shaped case with a drawer in the base for eyepieces and objectives. The Culpeper trade card of the 1730s and 40s is printed with a crossed daggers sign, and microscopes with their original card can fetch over £5000. More basic examples sell for £1000-£1500.

Cuff microscopes are completely different. The main tube is attached to a brass side pillar by a bracket, and its accurate focusing system means it is considered the earliest precision microscope, first appearing in the 1740s. Despite their greater accuracy, Cuff microscopes can be cheaper today than Culpepers, as many more were made and have survived. They fetch between £800 and £2000.

Today, some of the highest prices are commanded by instruments made between 1850 and 1900 by London makers: Andrew Ross, Powell & Lealand and Smith & Beck. These have achromatic lenses to overcome distortion. Victorian microscopes are almost always signed, and examples by any of these makers can fetch between £500 and £5000. The rarer binocular microscopes introduced in about 1862 are particularly desirable.

By the turn of the century, the market was dominated by two German manufacturers, Ernst Leitz and Carl Zeiss, who produced a

range of relatively inexpensive models for the amateur and professional. Examples can be bought today for £100-£500.

TELESCOPES

From the time of their introduction in the early 17th century, telescopes were also made along two distinct lines. The reflecting telescope uses a concave mirror to form the image, and was introduced in the mid-17th century. Examples from the 18th century sell for £500-£3000 today. Most are brass and mounted above a short column on a tripod base.

Refracting telescopes use a series of glass lenses to magnify the image and were introduced as early as 1608, although they did not become popular until the Victorian era, when achromatic lenses overcame the problem of distortion. Most have a brass, pasteboard or wooden tube, and are focused by extending or retracting the eyepiece or the whole tube.

Hand-held telescopes for use on board ship generally have a brass tube, often bound with plaited rope or mahogany, whereas military examples are more often bound in leather. Hand-held telescopes were made in very large numbers, and simple ones can be bought for less than £100. However, if they are signed by a good maker, such as Dolland, Ramsden or Adams, they can fetch as much as £500.

Large floor-standing astronomical telescopes with an equatorial mount (for alignment with the earth's axis), slow-motion, vertical and horizontal adjustment, and a mahogany tripod can be worth £1000-£2000 today with case and extra eyepieces. Smaller, less powerful instruments on a simple mount and oak tripod can be found for £600-£1000. Table-top astronomical telescopes with a 2½-3½ in (63-89 mm) diameter objective lens and brass tripod fetch £500-£1000.

OPERA GLASSES AND BINOCULARS

In the 18th and 19th centuries, opera glasses were decorative evening-wear accessories. Less powerful than a proper telescope, they were useful for viewing the action of the opera or play – and other theatregoers. Prices reflect the material used and the quality of engraving or mounting. Luxury models with semi-precious stones can fetch up to £1000, but run-of-the-mill ivory or mother-of-pearl examples go for as little as £100-£150.

Towards the end of the 19th century, binocular field glasses were introduced. They were issued in their thousands to the forces during the First and Second World Wars. Various designs, usually covered in dark leather, were made in France, Germany and Britain. So many were made that examples in good order can easily be found for under £200.

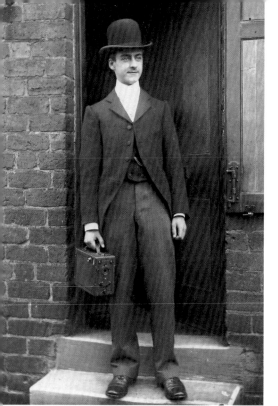

PHOTO OPPORTUNITY *At the turn of the century, technical advances in cameras moved photography out of the studio – and into the hands of amateurs.*

Cameras and optical toys

Camera collecting is an increasingly popular field, with a wide range of both upmarket and run-of-the-mill models still to be found. Optical toys are rarer, and can offer rare delight with simple moving pictures.

AFTER LOUIS DAGUERRE developed the first practicable method of photography in 1839, the taking of pictures quickly became a hobby among the well-to-do. Those who were unable to afford gadgets of their own paid the magic-lantern operator to show his story-telling images, or the studio photographer to capture their likeness on calling cards. (For photographs themselves as collectables, see page 338.)

CAMERAS

Today's collectors of cameras are spoilt for choice. Rare early 19th-century plate cameras command five-figure sums, but most early mass-produced models – made since American inventor George Eastman introduced the first Kodak in 1888 – can still be found in secondhand markets, car boot sales and local auctions for less than £50.

PLATE CAMERAS

Large plate cameras used by 19th-century portrait studios generally have a mahogany body, with brass mounts and leather bellows, mounted on a tripod stand. Such cameras in original condition can fetch from £300 up to £1000 for the most decorative models.

Portable field cameras are smaller and lighter, and were made to fold flat when not in use. A complete kit would include a leather shoulder bag with large black cloth to cloak both photographer and camera, plate holders and light oak tripod. A complete early 20th-century field camera kit sells for about £350.

Lancaster nickel-plated patent Watch-Form camera; c.1890; case 2⅛ in (54 mm) across. Disguised as a pocket watch, this concealed camera is among the most collectable. Other camera disguises included top hats, books and pistols.
£12,000-£18,000

Eastman's Box Brownie; 1901; 6½ in (16.5 cm) long. Among the simplest cameras ever produced, Box Brownies brought photography to the masses – and were even made in blue to appeal to women.
£20-£30

Biunial magic lantern; c.1880; 24 in (61 cm) high. Magic lanterns were often used by travelling showmen to present public slide shows.
£650-£850

Folding dry-plate camera; c.1920; opens to 10 in (25.4 cm) long. This portable field camera folded flat when not in use. Bands of amateur enthusiasts took such cameras on weekend field trips. One with no case or plate holder, or in a poor state, might fetch about £70.
£250-£350

Miniature Kodak folding camera; 1916; 7 in (17.8 cm) high. This model was designed to fit into a pocket. Its poor condition lowers the value.
£20-£30

The single-lens reflex plate camera, the forerunner of today's Nikons and Canons, was invented in the 1860s although it became popular only in the 1880s. Leading early 20th-century makers included Thornton-Pickard, Marion and Graflex. High-quality 'tropical' models with a teak body sell for over £1000, while less luxurious models can change hands for between £100 and £1000.

ROLL-FILM CAMERAS

Photography became far more widespread after roll film arrived in 1885. Eastman's cheap Box Brownie of 1900 was an instant success and more than 100,000 sold in a year. As a result, it and its successors can still be found for well under £50. Competitors and imitators, such as the British Ensign and German Ernemann, sell for £50-£150.

The trend towards hand-held cameras continued with the No.3 Folding Pocket Kodak, also launched in 1900. Some 500,000 were produced before it was discontinued in 1915, and it set the pattern for folding roll-film cameras over the next 50 years. Examples in good working order may sell for only £20-£50.

The twin-lens reflex camera, typified by the German-made Rolleiflex introduced in 1929, was a favourite of professionals and serious amateurs until the 1950s, and early models can change hands for £80-£150.

MINIATURE CAMERAS

The introduction in 1925 of Oscar Barnack's Leica, using 35 mm cinefilm, revolutionised camera design, and its quality is unsurpassed. A basic Leica in used condition can be bought for as little as £150, while extreme rarities can be worth over £10,000. Wartime models with Nazi insignia engraved on the top plate are particularly in demand.

Early competitors of the Leica are also collectable, including Carl Zeiss's Contax (introduced 1932) some models of which sell for £150-£200, and the Kodak Retina of 1934 (£60-£100). The rapid growth in popularity of colour photography after the Second World War was accompanied by a proliferation in 35 mm cameras, especially from Japanese manufacturers. There is already a demand for such models as the Nikon S of 1954 which, if it is in good condition, will fetch £150-£200.

Among the most eagerly collected cameras today are concealed or detective cameras made for photographing a subject secretly. The most unusual change hands for thousands of pounds, but more typical is the Houghton Ticka of 1906, which may fetch £300. It looks like a pocket watch but can take photographs when the lens-cap 'winder' is removed. The Stirn Secret or Waistcoat camera of 1886, which could be worn under a shirt with the lens sticking through a buttonhole, fetches £600-£1000 if in good condition.

OPTICAL TOYS

Long before cinema and television, the magic lantern – the earliest form of slide projector – was used to tell historic tales, travelogues and nursery stories. The hand-painted glass slides are themselves collectable at £10-£50 per set. The projectors were made between 1800 and 1930, but most found today date from about 1890-1920 and sell at auction for £200-£400. Biunial lanterns – with a pair of lenses to project two pictures at the same time – may fetch £500-£850, and triunial lanterns with three lenses as much as £1000-£1500.

A whole range of 'illusory' devices were popular in the 19th century. The Phenakistoscope and Zoetrope used a series of images turned at speed and viewed through slits to give the illusion, for example, of birds flying or horses trotting. Similarly, the Praxinoscope, invented in 1882 as a children's toy, reflected images onto a rotating cylinder of mirrors – foreshadowing the cinema. Complete with a set of image strips, Praxinoscopes today are likely to fetch between £700 and £2000, depending on condition and model.

The most commonly found 19th-century optical viewing device is the stereoscope, which has a pair of eyepieces for viewing a stereoscopic card or glass plate to create a three-dimensional image. Subjects varied from travel, theatre and works of art to battle scenes. Hand-held models can be bought for as little as £15, while more decorative table-top versions will cost between £250 and £750.

Brewster-type hand stereoscope; 1860-80; 12 in (30.5 cm) long. Presenting the viewer with a three-dimensional image, the stereoscope rapidly became an essential Victorian novelty item – even the Queen owned one. The cards are worth 50p-£5 each.
£60-£100

Praxinoscope (right); 1882; 14 in (35.5 cm) high. An illusion of movement is given by a rotating cylinder of images reflected in rectangular mirrors.
£700-£1000

Paper and card peep show of the Great Exhibition in London, 1851; 6 in (15.2 cm) wide. When extended, it shows a three-dimensional view inside the Crystal Palace.
£200-£300

Brewster patent kaleidoscope; mid-19thC; 10 in (25.4 cm) long. It has several different pattern discs to fit in the endpiece.
£1000-£1500

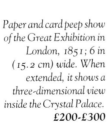

Alabaster peep egg; c.1860; 5 in (12.7 cm) high. Different scenes are viewed through the lens.
£80-£120

Phenakistoscope with case, handle and set of discs; mid-19thC; 10 in (25.4 cm) diameter. The rotating discs are viewed through a slit.
£1000-£1500

Scientific and medical instruments

Often elegant and made with great skill, precision instruments appeal to collectors for their historic importance, for their craftsmanship and ingenuity, and sometimes, too, for their macabre associations.

Transit theodolite; c.1850; 15 in (38 cm) high. Crafted mainly from brass, theodolites were used to calculate the horizontal angles and elevation.
£400-£600

French sextant; c.1850; 7½ in (19 cm) radius. Most sextants, used to measure latitude, were made in Britain, so this example is especially interesting.
£500-£700

Surveyor's level; c.1875; 14 in (36 cm) long. The spirit level on this example, unusually, is mounted below the compass, rather than above it.
£300-£400

Ship's compass; c.1850; 8½ in (21.6 cm) across. It is mounted in gimbals within the wooden case.
£250-£350

Brass ring dials; c.1700; 2½ in (63 mm) diameter. Pocket sundials were still the most commonly used timepieces in the 18thC.
£200-£400 each

North-west African brass astrolabe; c.1706; 8 in (20.3 cm) across. It is the first made by Muhammad ben Ahmad al-Battuti, one of a family of instrument-makers.
£6000-£10,000

F OR SOME 350 YEARS, the era of systematic inquiry, advances in science, medicine and technology have been dependent on precise observations, measurements and operations. Specialist apparatus was essential, and the skill and ingenuity of its maker often matched that of the user. Some great rarities of the earliest eras of scientific inquiry are worth many thousands of pounds, but there are also inexpensive items of equal fascination for the collector on a budget.

SURVEYING AND NAVIGATIONAL INSTRUMENTS

The commonest surveying instrument is the surveyor's level, which consists of a small telescope and a spirit level mounted on a tripod above a magnetic compass. Most instruments found today date from 1830-1930 and, unless unusual, sell for around £50-£250.

Theodolites are more complicated and were designed to measure both the horizontal angle between two points and their angle of elevation. Nineteenth-century examples can fetch £500-£1000 with the original case.

Until recent years, the position of a ship at sea was plotted with instruments such as a sea astrolabe, octant or sextant (all of which measured latitude), chronometer (see p.285) and ship's compass. The octant, constructed from wood, brass and occasionally ivory, measured the angle of the sun above the horizon, and came into general use after 1750. Both the octant and the more accurate sextant, which overtook the octant in the 1770s, are often found in their original mahogany case, with interchangeable telescopic eyepieces and a certificate of accuracy attached to the lid. Octants fetch around £300-£600 and sextants, which mostly date from the 19th century, sell for £400-£900.

The ship's compass indicated the direction taken by a vessel. Those found today were generally made during the 19th and 20th centuries, and fetch £100-£500. Lord Kelvin's patent binnacle compass, with compensation spheres and oil illumination for night readings, is rare and sells for £900-£1200.

POCKET SUNDIALS

Clocks and watches of the 17th and 18th centuries were notoriously inaccurate, and sundials, especially pocket ones, were the most commonly used timepieces. There are over a dozen types of sundial avidly sought by collectors today, from beautifully constructed 17th-century diptych dials made in southern Germany in gilt brass or silver (these can fetch thousands of pounds) to simple ring dials, which still go at auction for a few hundred.

Among the more complex pocket models are so-called equinoctial dials, which have a

shaped base of brass or silver inset with a magnetic compass. They are usually 2-3 in (50-75 mm) across, and fetch £300-£1000.

Many universal equinoctial ring dials – self-orientating, universal sundials – were made in the 18th century by Thomas Heath and Edmund Culpeper of London. They generally sell for £500-£1500. Butterfield dials, with an eight-sided brass or silver plate, range in price from £400 to £1000.

Diptych dials were made in large numbers in Nuremberg in the late 16th and early 17th centuries. These have two hinged plates which open out at right angles, stretching a string gnomon (which throws the shadow) taut between them; the shadow falls onto a horizontal and vertical dial. Prices range between £500 and £5000. Wooden versions with a paper dial were made in the late 18th and early 19th centuries. They are generally unsigned and change hands for £150-£250.

GLOBES AND ORRERIES

Most globes are made from a shell of plaster pasted with paper printed and hand-coloured to show segments of the earth (for a terrestrial globe) or the heavens (for a celestial one). Good condition is vital, as restoration of the plaster sphere and paper map is expensive.

A large globe mounted on a floor stand would originally have been kept in the library of a country house (see pp.41 and 127). Smaller globes about 4-12 in (10-30 cm) in diameter were mounted on a table stand. These can change hands for £2000-£10,000.

Far smaller are pocket terrestrial globes, made from pasteboard or wood with paper maps glued on. They were sold with a case composed of two hemispheres decorated on the inside with a celestial sphere showing the constellations. Eighteenth-century spheres can fetch £1500-£2500 today, while 19th-century examples sell for around £1000.

Orreries, or planetariums, are models used to demonstrate the motions of the planets in the solar system. Schoolroom models made at the turn of this century often have a cast-iron base and show only the moon and earth. They can be picked up for £300-£600. Models from the 19th century fetch £3000-£10,000.

MEDICAL INSTRUMENTS

The vast majority of old surgical instruments found today can be traced back to the time of the Napoleonic Wars (1792-1815). Knives, tourniquets, saws for the amputation of limbs,

Ivory diptych sundial; mid-17thC; folds to 3 in (76 mm) square. Many of these were produced in 17thC Nuremburg.
£1000-£1500

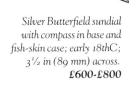

Silver Butterfield sundial with compass in base and fish-skin case; early 18thC; 3½ in (89 mm) across.
£600-£800

Terrestrial globe to fit into a coat pocket; c.1840; globe 2 in (51 mm) diameter.
£1000-£1500

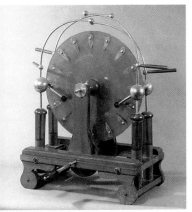

Wimshurst electrostatic generator; c.1850; 24 in (61 cm) high. This odd contraption produced static electricity, and may still be found in schoolrooms.
£800-£1200

Newton orrery; c.1850; 23 in (58 cm) across base. Orreries illustrate the movements of planets in the solar system. The planets move when the handle is turned.
£3000-£5000

bullet forceps, gunshot probes, scalpels, ligature silk and needles were just some of the rather macabre items in boxed surgeons' sets. Before 1867, when the first antiseptics were introduced, such instruments were normally of metal, with ebony handles scored with cross-hatching to give the surgeon a firm grip. After that, they were usually all metal.

Surgical sets must be complete to be collectable, as losses are almost impossible to replace. Sets dating from the first half of the 19th century range in price from £1000 to £3000, while rarities from even earlier range up to £5000. Later 19th-century sets fetch £800-£2000, while early 20th-century sets can be found for between £300 and £500.

Transportable mahogany and brass medicine chests to carry certain 'cure-all' remedies, plus implements for measuring and mixing

them, were used by physicians 200 years ago. Fairly standard chests complete with accessories can fetch £500-£1500 at auction.

The letting of blood was an all-embracing 'cure' until about 1900. A lancet was used to cut the skin and let the blood, and sets of lancets in a carrying case may be found for £50-£250. A variant is the scarificator, which made several incisions at once with the blades released by a sprung trigger. Almost all examples date from the 19th century, and can be found for £50-£150. Boxed sets of scarificators and cupping glasses – used for cupping (sucking) the skin, supposedly to draw out 'impurities' – can fetch £500-£1000.

Dental instruments fall into two distinct categories: those used for cleaning teeth, and those for removing them. Although a very few toothbrushes were available for the wealthy from the 18th century, most people used a tooth scraper or scaler with interchangeable steel blades. Most scrapers seen today were

made in the first half of the 19th century, and now sell for between £150 and £400 a set.

Instruments for pulling teeth, known as tooth keys, have a shaped handle and straight shank with a claw at the end for gripping the tooth. They sell at auction for £150-£500.

FUNCTIONAL AIDS

Between 1851 and 1917, a wide range of ear trumpets for the hard of hearing were produced by the firm of F.C. Rein & Sons of London. Made from tortoiseshell, silver plate and ivory in the form of a curling trumpet, they sell today for £100-£500. The mid-19th-century conversation tube, some 3 ft (90 cm) long, has a trumpet at one end and an earpiece at the other. Models with ivory mounts are worth £150-£500 today, but wood-mounted versions are cheaper.

Spectacle frames were originally made of leather and horn, but were later produced in silver, tortoiseshell and steel. Although a pair of 17th-century leather-framed spectacles can be worth over £5000, most 19th and early 20th-century metal-framed examples sell for less than £5 a pair. Monocles and folding lorgnettes, consisting of two metal-framed lenses on a handle were introduced in the 18th century and range in price from £50 to £250.

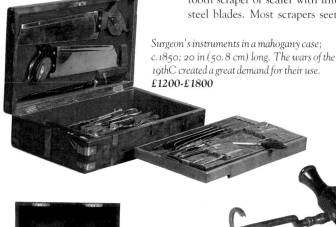

Surgeon's instruments in a mahogany case; c.1850; 20 in (50.8 cm) long. The wars of the 19thC created a great demand for their use.
£1200-£1800

Mahogany medicine chest; late 18thC; 29 in (74 cm) high. This unusually large medicine chest probably belonged to a wealthy household. It has fitted drawers, bottles labelled for everyday medicaments, weighing scales and implements.
£4000-£6000

Tooth key with ebony handle and single claw; c.1850; 5 in (12.5 cm) long. Ivory-handled examples fetch more.
£250-£350

Chinese spectacles in original case; c.1850; 2¾ in (70 mm) diameter. These brass-mounted glasses from the East are very similar to European designs produced during the 17thC.
£100-£200

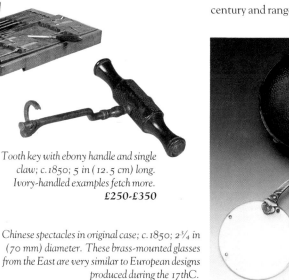

Rein & Son silver-plated ear trumpet; c.1850; 6 in (15.2 cm) long. This example is very ornate, which accounts for its high price. A less elaborate trumpet would fetch about £100.
£200-£300

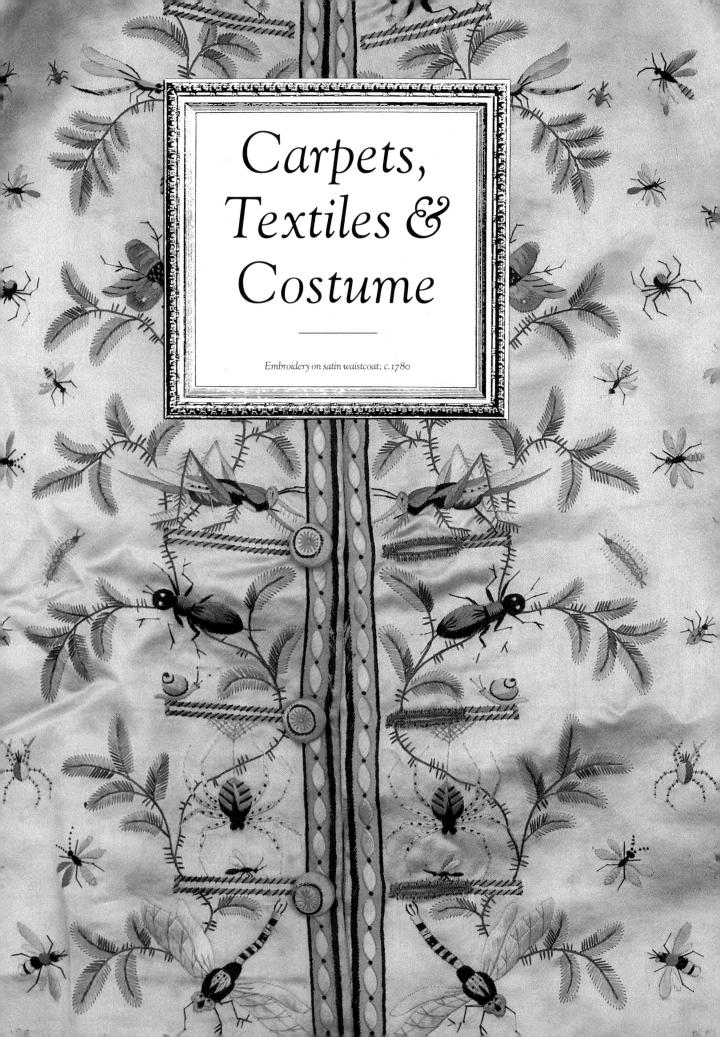

Carpets, Textiles & Costume

Embroidery on satin waistcoat; c.1780

Carpets and rugs

Despite a shady reputation, the carpet market is no more complex than that in other objects. But there are plenty of overpriced examples to avoid, and a knowledge of basic forms and styles is a definite advantage.

DEDICATED COLLECTORS of carpets believe them to represent a supreme artistic achievement, at their best combining aesthetic and technical brilliance. In practice, while some were originally intended to be works of art, most carpets were made as functional objects.

The carpets and rugs (the terms are more or less synonymous) that are most sought after by collectors are pre-20th century. Although some early 20th-century examples are also valuable, most modern carpets made in traditional designs – particularly those from India, Pakistan, Afghanistan, China and Eastern Europe – are scarcely more than expensive interior decoration, with little investment potential. The majority of collectable Eastern, or Oriental, carpets or fragments of carpets – encompassing pieces from any source between

MATERIAL WEALTH
This painting of an elderly couple by Dutch artist Elias Vonck, c.1640, depicts a rare Cairene Ottoman rug made in Cairo. Judging by its fine detail, it was probably of excellent quality, and may very well have been up to 50 years old when the work was painted.

Piled prayer rug from Melas, north-west Turkey; 19thC; 67 in (1.7 m) long. This rug is one of the greatest known examples from the desirable Melas group of Turkish village weavings. A good and more common version of the Melas prayer design could fetch around £5000, but this is a great rarity.
£20,000-£30,000

Piled carpet, western Turkey; late 20thC; 84 in (2.13 m) long. This was made under the DOBAG project, a small multi-national company set up in the early 1980s to re-introduce traditional weaving into certain villages in western Turkey. Such rugs may well become prized antiques in the future.
£500-£800

Hereke silk prayer rug, western Turkey; 1920s; 45 in (1.14 m) long. All Hereke rugs date from after 1890. This example used the 'Sultan's Head' design. Prices range from £1200 up to £50,000, depending on the quality of knotting.
£15,000-£20,000

Piled carpet in Ottoman 'court' taste from Cairo, Egypt; 16thC; 72 in (1.83 m) long. So-called 'Cairene Ottoman' carpets have survived in quite large numbers and sometimes go for comparatively modest sums, especially if they are virtually in fragments.
£40,000-£60,000

Turkey and China – date from the 18th and 19th centuries, and experts hotly debate the origins of the carpets themselves and of their designs and motifs.

WEAVING TECHNIQUES

Rugs which share idiosyncrasies of structure probably come from the same area, regardless of any differences in decoration. Technical aspects of a rug's manufacture, particularly the number of knots within a given measure (usually a square inch or 10 cm square) are considered by Middle Eastern experts to be essential aspects of a rug's quality.

WOOL AND SILK PILE

The availability and durability of wool has ensured that carpets with a wool pile are the most plentiful and diverse of all. The majority

of pile rugs woven in the East have a pile made of sheep's wool, although some older carpets use goat hair or pashmina (the wool of the Kashmir goat). Many tribal rugs from the Middle East and workshop rugs from China have large areas piled in camel hair. The extraordinary softness and lustre of so many old Chinese rugs comes from the use of wool from baby camels, and 19th-century examples can still be found at auction starting from around £2000.

Individual motifs, especially the designs found in the borders around the main decorative body (or field) of the carpet, often indicate a carpet's origin. The symbolism in Oriental carpet design is widely believed to be a melding of many influences, however, including shamanism, Chinese mythology, Buddhism, Judaism, Christianity and Islam.

Among the most desirable rugs are those with a pile made of silk. These are much more

fragile than their woollen counterparts, so very few old examples are found today. As silk has always been a luxury material, it is not normally associated with tribal weaving, although it is frequently found in the pile as small details of a design, the rest being in wool. Mixed materials are seen in many Turkoman weavings (see Tribal rugs, p. 304).

The largest-surviving group of old silk rugs are the 17th-century 'Polonaise' rugs from Esfahan in central Persia, and they still come up for sale surprisingly often. The value of such pieces depends on both the thickness of the pile and the richness of the colour.

FLAT-WEAVES

Flat-woven carpets, which have no soft pile, are popular in the West. Nowadays, Oriental flat-weaves are generally called 'kilims', although this strictly refers to the kind of flat-weaving that leaves slits in the carpet. As recently as the 1970s, collectors concentrated on pile carpets alone, and few Eastern flat-weaves were collected. Today, however, slit-tapestry kilims, sumakh weavings and all other flat-weaves are sought after.

Persian 19th-century tribal kilims go for between £500 and £50,000, depending on

Polonaise rug with silk pile, and silk and cotton foundation; Esfahan, central Persia; 17thC; 84 in (2.13 m) long. The name of these rugs stems from their display in Polish salons at 19thC Paris exhibitions; several hundred rugs have survived in various states of wear. Prices range from £30,000 to £600,000, depending on pile and colour quality.
£200,000-£300,000

Cashmere and silk rug from Kashmir; 19thC; 76 in (1.93 m) long. Persian designs such as this quickly became popular among Indian weavers.
£800

Kilim from Varamin, north-west Iran; late 19thC; 86 in (2.18 m) long. This slit-tapestry weave rug is typical of 19thC Persian tribal and village kilims.
£1500-£2000

Rug in sumakh flat-weave, from eastern Caucasus; mid-19thC; 114 in (2.89 m) long. The best examples using this famous 'dragon' design can reach four times the price of this one.
£5000

Saddle bag (khorjin) by the Shahsavan tribe, north-west Persia; 19thC. This single, detached face of the bag is worked in the sumakh flat-weave technique.
£1000-£1500

Piled carpet from Khotan, east Turkestan; 19thC; 99 in (2.51 m) long. Rugs from the oasis towns of the Tarim Basin, including Khotan, have long been underpriced and can still be found for under £5000.
£15,000-£20,000

Piled carpet; Agra, north India; late 19th or early 20thC; 152 in (3.86 m) long. Indian carpets of that period, many made in jails, have today become the most popular Oriental furnishing carpet in wealthy Western homes.
£10,000-£12,000

Chinese wool carpet; 20thC; 76 in (1.93 m) long. Popular modern Oriental carpets such as this often use traditional 18thC designs.
£250-£350

Piled carpet from the Heriz area, north-west Persia; late 19thC; 127 in (3.22 m) long. Such rugs are extremely popular and hard-wearing furnishing carpets which, at their best, can be notable works of art. Prices can go as high as £50,000.
£6000-£8000

their size and condition. Sumakh-woven bags from north-west Persia and the southern Caucasus and most 19th-century Caucasian kilims fetch between £500 and £10,000.

REGION BY REGION

The two greatest weaving cultures in history are those of Turkey and Persia (Iran). Persian makers, in particular, influenced weavers in almost every other carpet-making country. Carpets from Egypt and other important

North African weaving countries (mainly Morocco and, to a lesser extent, Algeria) are classified as Mediterranean. So too are the carpets from Spain, which have more in common with those from North Africa than with other European weavings.

Among the flat-woven carpets and best-quality Oriental-style pile rugs produced in the northern European countries are examples from Scandinavia, France, Italy and Britain. Of the many 18th and 19th-century European pile carpets on the market, those of

the highest quality can usually be attributed to Savonnerie and Aubusson in France, and Axminster and Wilton in England.

PERSIAN RUGS

It is neither cheap nor easy to create a significant collection of early Persian rugs, but there are enough good examples to make it possible. Examples from the 16th and 17th centuries (the period of the Safavid dynasty) are by far the most desirable of Persian rugs. Large fragments are expensive, but smaller ones do occasionally appear at auction.

The most extensive group of Safavid weavings found today are the red-ground, floral Esfahan rugs. (Esfahan was the capital of Persia until the present capital, Tehran, was created in the late 18th century.) These have a wool pile and a foundation of either cotton or mixed cotton and silk. Upward of 300 examples of these still exist, some very expensive mint condition rugs, others small, battered fragments starting at £400-£600.

One group of Safavid weavings with very varied designs is known as the 'vase group'. These include garden carpets, which mirror the layout of a formal Persian garden, carpets with floral lattice designs, carpets with animal designs, 'curled leaf' carpets and many others. 'Vase' carpets themselves have huge and sometimes surreal flower heads spiralling out from Chinese-inspired vases. Examples from the late 17th and early 18th centuries often

Piled carpet with the arabesque design from Garrus (Bijar), north-west Persia; late 19thC; 166 in (4.21 m) long. Arabesque carpets are among the most beautiful pieces from this date, and the best are considered by some to be great works of art.
£15,000-£20,000

Piled face of yastik, or pillow, from east Turkey; mid-19thC; c.24 in (60 cm) long. Yastiks in old and rare designs are very popular with collectors. This example still has its original flat-woven striped back.
£2000-£3000

Piled wagireh, or pattern sampler, from Bijar, north-west Persia; late 19thC; 103 in (2.61 m) long. Such samplers were sent out into the villages to show weavers alternative patterns and motifs. Prices range from £500 to over £10,000.
£8000-£12,000

Piled carpet from Esfahan, central Persia; early 17thC; 165 in (4.2 m) long. It is from one of the most extensive surviving groups of early Persian carpets. Although not exactly rarities, good examples have recently started making £100,000 or more if in good condition.
£60,000-£80,000

appear on the market, generally in poor condition, and large and often very beautiful fragments suggest that the biggest carpets must originally have been some 50 ft (15 m) in length. Even fragments are expensive, however, starting at £15,000-£20,000.

A group of Safavid carpets which share a common structure are the *jufti*-knotted rugs from east Persia. Their designs vary widely but can be very beautiful, with a distinctive palette of several rich shades of green and a vivid yellow. They appear fairly often as fragments, sometimes fetching under £4000, but good pieces go for £20,000 or more.

TURKISH AND CAUCASIAN RUGS

Turkish weavers have been producing slit tapestries (kilims), flat-weaves and piled carpets from the early 13th century. Commercial weavings from the Ushak region of west Anatolia were generally considered the finest available examples of early Turkish rugs, most

Kilim from Ushak region, west Turkey; 17th-18thC; 79 in (2.01 m) long. Fewer than ten kilims of this design have survived, but low popularity prevents price rises.
£20,000 or less

dating from the 16th century. Good early Ushak carpets may fetch over £50,000.

So-called Transylvanian rugs, probably also from the Ushak region, are still found in large numbers. 'Double niche' designs are the most common, but prayer rugs and stylised floral design rugs known as 'Smyrna' can also be found. Many Transylvanian rugs are of poor quality and are very worn. Prices range from a few thousand to tens of thousands of pounds.

Many Caucasian rugs display characteristics of Persian, Anatolian and independent

tribal weaving (see pp.304-5) in both structure and design. They reached their zenith during the 19th century, when small, thickly piled and brilliantly coloured rugs became fashionable in the West.

Rugs of the Caucasus can be divided into two distinct groups. The first are the so-called 'classical' rugs made before 1800, of which good examples come up for sale from time to time. The second group, known as Caucasian village rugs, mostly date from between 1870 and 1920. Many older Caucasian rugs fetch

extremely high prices, but far more – and especially interesting, old examples that are in poor condition – sell for between £500 and £4000. When cleaned, conserved and mounted, such beautiful, fragile old pieces make extremely handsome wall-hangings.

In general, 19th-century Caucasian rugs remain one of the main categories where a new collector with confidence and a certain amount of luck can pick up a piece of great quality for £1000 or less. These were the most popular of all Oriental weavings in the West a century ago, and large numbers were imported into Europe. Most major auctions of Oriental rugs today include several lots of these old imports, and many sell for £1000-£3000.

TRIBAL RUGS

These days, many of the pieces previously considered to be genuine tribal works of art (that is, made for local use and using designs

and colours unaffected by outside influences especially commercial ones) appear to have originated in well-organised carpet work shops. Many of the weavings of the Turkoman tribes of central Asia, for example – considered the highest achievement of tribal weaving art – were made for sale to foreigners

The great majority of tribal weavings seen today date from between 1850 and 1920. Most examples were produced by three tribal groups: the Turkomans, Iranian-based tribes and the Yuruks of Turkey. The weavers in such societies were usually women, who began learning carpet-making skills from their mothers or other female relatives as soon as they were old enough to hold and manipulate the materials and tools.

In addition to carpets, Turkoman women made a variety of bags, rugs used as tent-entrance 'doors' (*ensis*) and a range of small weavings to adorn tents or livestock. Such

Piled prayer rug; Ghiordes region, western Turkey; 18thC; 65 in (1.65 m) long. One of the best-known designs of 18thC commercial Turkish rugs, which can reach £15,000.
£3000-£5000

Piled prayer rug of the Marasali type from Shirvan area; eastern Caucasus; woven in is the date 1283 of the Muhammadan calendar (AD 1866-7); 64 in (1.62 m) long. This date is just about believable, although many dates woven into such 19thC village rugs are not.
£6000-£8000

Piled rug of the Borjalou type from the Kazak area, western Caucasus; late 19thC; 90 in (2.29 m) long. A typical example of a popular design, with vivid colours.
£5000-£10,000

Piled carpet with arabesque or Lotto pattern; Ushak region, west Turkey; 17thC; 66 in (1.68 m) long. Such 'Transylvanian'-type rugs – so called because many were found in eastern Europe – may fetch under £1000 if of poor quality and condition.
£30,000-£40,000

ems start at just a few hundred pounds, though the best will fetch thousands.

Domestic weavings known as *gabbehs*, made by many tribal groups in west Iran, are generally very coarse and heavy. Gabbehs are now collected in the West, but as a result, their quality has dropped and their prices have increased from under £100 up to £10,000 for the best 19th-century examples.

Many of the best 19th-century Yuruk rugs of Turkey (the word *yuruk* means 'nomad') have superb wool pile and a beautiful colour, often with powerful, striking designs. They still regularly appear on the market, and can sometimes be bought for £500 upwards.

RUGS OF INDIA AND CHINA

The finest north Indian rugs are those dating from the first 30 years of the 17th century, and are among the greatest examples of piled weaving ever made. They have a foundation of silk and a pile made of the wool of the Kashmir goat; their knot count can be extraordinarily high – sometimes with more than 500 knots to the square inch. Such rugs are exceptionally rare, however, and almost all

known examples are in museum collections.

Carpet-making in India seems to have been an art form imported from Safavid Persia and practised only in urban centres. Almost all Indian carpets of any age have a wool pile, although there are rare silk examples. Rug-weaving died out over most of India for more than a century before it was restarted by British government officials as a commercial venture in prisons in the mid-19th century. The resulting so-called 'jail' carpets are often

Piled rug with Karagashli design from the Kuba region, north-east Caucasus; late 19thC; 53 in (1.34 m) long. This type of design, well-known but not very popular, is typical of the region.
£3000-£4000

copies of Safavid Persian weavings, and tend to be extremely expensive today, starting from around £10,000.

Many famous weaving cities are situated in what used to be east Turkestan but is now part of western China. Strong Chinese and Mogul influences can be seen on 17th and 18th-century weavings from Yarkand, Kansu, Kashgar and Khotan. Such weavings are still available – and often extremely good value, as are 19th-century Chinese rugs and carpets with pile of soft baby camel hair.

SPANISH AND NORTH AFRICAN WEAVINGS

Spanish carpets are probably among the oldest groups of Islamic pile weavings to survive in any numbers, but almost all known complete examples from the 15th and early 16th centuries are in museums or Church institutions. Fragments occasionally come up for

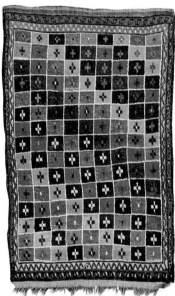

Gabbeh rug; Qashqa'i tribe, south-west Persia; 19thC; 79 in (2.01 m) long. These coarse, thick-piled domestic rugs were hardly known in the West 15 years ago. Prices start under £1000.
£8000-£10,000

Piled rug; Baluch tribe, eastern Iran; late 19th to early 20thC; 64 in (1.62 m) long. Good Baluch rugs such as this are very popular. Some exceed £10,000.
£500-£700

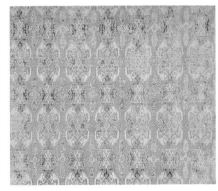

Part of a piled carpet fragment (right); Alcaraz, southern Spain; 16thC; 174 in (4.42 m) long. Early Spanish carpets are rare; this version of the Turkish arabesque is the commonest pattern.
£15,000-£20,000

Turkoman main carpet; Yomud tribe, Turkmenistan, central Asia; 19thC; 126 in (3.2 mm) long. Main carpets are the largest examples, traditionally used on special occasions. This one has the 'hooked' medallion (dyrnak gul) motif typical of Yomud rugs and occasionally found in weaving by other tribes.
6000-£8000

Needlepoint carpet (right) by the Aubusson factory, France; 1795-9; 268 in (6.8 m) long. The price of Aubusson carpets has shot up in recent years as they have become popular with interior designers. Early examples in good condition, such as this one, fetch the top prices.
£30,000-£50,000

Needlework carpet embroidered in the Persian style; Arraiolos, Portugal; 17thC; 132 in (3.35 m) long. Arraiolos carpets used a distinctive herringbone stitch. Early date, as here, and quality push prices up.
£20,000-£30,000

Flat-woven carpet; Abruzzo, Italy; 19thC; 102 in (2.59 m) long. As with most Abruzzo peasant carpets, this example is woven in two pieces, which are joined down the middle. Although quite rare, such carpets can still be found for reasonable sums.
£1500-£2000

Coarse-woven rug; Tazenakht, Morocco; 19thC; 119 in (3 m) long. Morocco is one of the few remaining sources of good old pieces. This rug, with the typical Tazenakht yellow and blue colours, has increased significantly in value since it was bought in 1992 for a few hundred pounds.
£2500-£3000

sale, but even they are extremely expensive. Within the range of more collectors are small 'loop-piled' peasant rugs from Las Alpujarras, in the far south-east of Spain. Examples from before the 19th century are now very rare, but small rugs made in the same way today and with the same designs are popular with tourists. Modern rugs should be avoided by collectors, as the materials are coarse and the colours poor, but 19th-century examples starting around £1000 are more worthwhile.

Morocco had a tradition of indigenous Berber weaving which came under Turkish influence in the 18th century. The best Moroccan rugs are from this period and use a colour range and design – usually with a central diamond medallion – based on Turkish prototypes. Some are very large – over 20 ft (6 m) long – and all are colourful. Old examples are rare, however, and late 19th and early 20th-century imitations identical in design can be distinguished by their poor,

faded purples, oranges and reds. Original 18th-century rugs are now very expensive, but later imitations sell for around £2500.

Village and tribal rugs are more affordable, particularly those from Tazenakht. These coarsely woven pieces have scattered geometric and floral motifs, predominantly in blue on yellow. They are extremely attractive, relatively inexpensive (priced from £1500 upwards) and fairly easy to find. Good examples of Moroccan tribal rugs are still being made, and 40 or 50-year-old examples can be found for reasonable sums in Morocco, Europe and North America. Western collectors have suddenly become interested in Moroccan weaving, however, so prices for worthwhile pieces may soon start climbing.

EUROPEAN CARPETS

Almost all European pile carpets which are hand-knotted use the Turkish (or symmetric) knot, and most from the 16th and early 17th

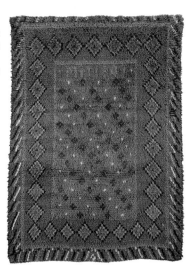

Piled rya, Finland; 1847; 70 in (1.78 m) long. These small, coarsely woven peasant rugs are most popular in Scandinavia but also have a strong international following.
£2000-£3000

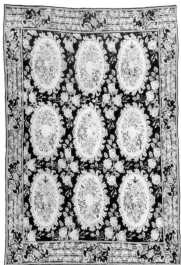

Pile carpet by Charles F.A. Voysey for A. Morton and Co, Donegal, Ireland; c.1900; 125 in (3.17 m) long. Morton's carpets in Arts and Crafts style can be bought quite cheaply unless, as here, by one of the movement's major designers.
£20,000-£30,000

Piled rug from Bessarabia, western Ukraine; late 18thC; 96 in (2.43 m) long. Piled rugs from this region are much rarer than the flat-woven kilims and they show a strong French influence.
£15,000-£20,000

Piled rug with Art Deco design; European; c.1920; 90 in (2.29 m) long. Art Deco rugs are becoming expensive, especially when, unlike this example, they are signed by a well-known designer.
£2000-£5000

centuries are copies of well-known Turkish designs. The superb 17th-century Savonnerie carpets are now very rare, but the remaining finest and earliest examples from Savonnerie and Aubusson (established in 1627 and 1743 respectively) are much collected today.

Much the same is true of English factory-made carpets, of which the earliest are from the Axminster factory, set up in 1750 by two French Huguenot refugees who had worked at the Savonnerie factory. The best Axminsters are late 18th-century examples designed by the English architect and designer Robert Adam and his contemporaries.

More recent collectable carpets include those produced in Britain between 1870 and 1930 by members of the Arts and Crafts movement and other influential designers. William Morris designed carpets for commercial firms before producing hand-knotted pieces at his Hammersmith factory. Any rug with the Morris label is now extremely expensive, as are the Donegal carpets designed by C.F.A. Voysey.

Many north European countries had a long tradition of peasant weaving, but it has died out in most. Among the most sophisticated are flat-woven Scandinavian rugs and cushions, the best known of which, *röllakans*, are from the southern Swedish province of Skåne. Some of the most beautiful are *agedynas* (cushion covers) made for the wide seat in a marriage coach, dating from the 17th, 18th and 19th centuries. Many fine examples fetch surprisingly low sums, starting at £500.

Flat-woven carpets made in eastern Europe often show the influence of Turkish weaving. Bessarabian kilims, from the province of Bessarabia in the south-west Ukraine, have become increasingly popular over the last decade. These generally have repeat floral sprays on a black or beige ground. Although quite a number of these rugs are still available, their prices can be high, starting at £1500-£2000. However, buyers should beware as they vary greatly in quality.

CARPET LITERATURE
The Last Word on Carpets

SOME COLLECTORS devote their attention solely to books and journals about carpets, a fiercely competitive field.

The first issue of the carpet magazine *Hali*, for example, appeared in 1978 at a cover price of £4, but a copy in good condition – rare, since issues have a tendency to fall apart – is now worth £500 and upwards.

Copies of large, lavish pre-1940 books, such as F.R. Martin's *Oriental Carpets Before 1800*, can now make £5000 or more, depending on condition. So too can first editions of books on Middle Eastern or Islamic art, early travel books on the area, and anthropological studies of weaving tribes.

'Hali', vol.1, no.1; spring 1978. Copies of this issue have recently sold at auction for close to £1000.

Needlework and textiles

*Embroidered pictures, samplers and everyday objects survive from as early
as the 16th century, when Mary, Queen of Scots was a noted needlewoman.*

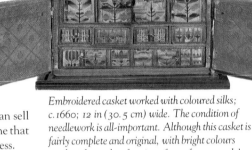

ALTHOUGH ELIZABETHAN NEEDLEWORK is rare today, a surprising number of early pieces dating from the 17th century onwards have survived. They include both so-called needle paintings, which present a picture in the form of embroidery, and also decorative household items such as bedhangings, fire screens and cushions.

Wools, silks and satins have all been in and out of fashion, stitched onto a variety of backgrounds from silk to canvas. All types of work are collectable today, although fewer pieces on silk have survived because of the more delicate nature of the fabric.

STUMPWORK AND CREWEL WORK

A type of needlework popular throughout 17th-century Britain was stumpwork. Images were built up with minute layers of buttonhole stitches to form three-dimensional 'stump' pictures. In these, figures with stumpwork robes were given padded satin faces, carved wooden hands and seed-pearl necklaces, and set among exotic or imaginary birds, beasts and landscapes.

Stumpwork panels were generally sewn on satin with untwisted floss silks, which could be separated into very fine threads. Extra

sparkle was added with coiled, silver 'purl' embroidery wire and sequins. Panels were often mounted on wooden baseboards and then made up into such objects as caskets, cabinets and mirror frames. In many cases acid from the wood has eaten into the satin ground, causing it to become brittle and cracked. Such damage severely limits the value of a piece; for example, an elaborate casket in perfect condition can sell at auction for up to £80,000, whereas one that is damaged or faded may go for £800 or less.

Loosely twisted wool yarn – crewel – was used extensively in needlework. It was the usual yarn for the numerous embroidered bedhangings made in the 17th century, whose designs often came from imported Indian textiles showing the 'tree of life'.

Many bedhangings include embroidered flowers, or other motifs, cut from earlier crewel work and used on a sturdier background. A bed curtain of this type can be bought for around £200, while a completely original piece might cost £1000-£2000.

Wool was the main embroidery material until the 1780s, especially for fire screens, chair backs, card-table covers, cushions and pictures. A typical fire screen would depict a couple in a pastoral setting, worked in tent stitch (a small, diagonal stitch). Fire screens can fetch upwards of £600, depending on the design, condition and type of mounting.

SAMPLERS

For several hundred years young girls produced samplers as needlework exercises. The older, 17th-century samplers are generally long, thin rectangles which incorporate alphabets, numbers and bands of floral and geometric embroidery. They are sometimes finished with needlepoint lace. Most 18th-century samplers are squarer, and often have a religious theme. Collectors generally prefer the more pictorial pieces, which will sell for between £100 and several thousand pounds. A map dating from the late 18th century might fetch £100-£300.

More varied 19th-century samplers can be found, ranging from pictures of the girl's house to moralistic verses. The most valuable are always those with striking or amusing subjects. These can be worth ten times as much as samplers with standard religious texts

Embroidered casket worked with coloured silks; c.1660; 12 in (30.5 cm) wide. The condition of needlework is all-important. Although this casket is fairly complete and original, with bright colours inside, it has only a fraction of a perfect example's value because the outside is faded and worn.
£600-£1000

Embroidered casket; c.1650; 10 in (25.5 cm) wide. This workbox in good, bright condition is worked in a flat, satin stitch. A casket with stumpwork and padding, used to raise parts of the design, would be worth even more.
£6000-£8000

A GENTLEWOMAN'S OCCUPATION Leisured women of the mid-18thC spent much of their time seated at an embroidery frame like this.

Stumpwork picture of King Charles I and Queen Henrietta Maria; c.1640; 21 in (53.5 cm) wide. The canopies, flowers and acorns are stumpwork, the faces satin over wood; the condition is superb.
£10,000-£15,000

English valance; c.1590; 77 in (1.96 m) wide. This short bedhanging is embroidered in wools and silks with scenes from the Book of Daniel. Such pieces are less sought after because of their awkward proportions.
£2500-£3500

Wool embroidery worked in satin stitch; c.1800; 30 in (76 cm) wide. The large moth holes in the border of this piece have halved its value.
£4000-£6000

Needlework sampler; 1840; 11⅞ in (30 cm) square. The lack of colour and pictorial interest, the religious text and the moth hole make this an inexpensive piece.
£20-£40

British silk on wool sampler; 1813; 20 in (51 cm) wide. Its muted colours and stains reduce its price. Bolder designs and personal touches from the girl who worked it give a sampler higher value.
£300-£350

or numbers and alphabets. Late 19th-century mourning samplers, stitched in memory of a member of the family, are less sought after and generally sell for £100 or less.

PICTURES ON SATIN AND SILK

The use of fine silks embroidered on satin came back into fashion in the late 18th century. Embroideries from this date have a lighter, more delicate feel to them. Some can even be mistaken for engravings at first glance, although closer inspection reveals that black and ivory silks, and even human hair, have been used to create this impression. In good condition, a piece about 18 × 12 in (46 × 30 cm) can fetch £200-£300.

Pictures combining embroidery and painting on silk were produced in quantity between 1780 and 1820, most of them with sentimental themes. Difficult parts, such as hands, faces and the sky, were painted with watercolours rather than stitched. Few of these have survived in perfect condition, as light

---

PAISLEY AND KASHMIR SHAWLS
The Pinecone Pattern

KASHMIR SHAWLS were first produced in the Kashmir region of India in the 15th century, and became popular in Europe about 1800.

Hand-woven from Tibetan mountain goat hair, Kashmirs can be dated by changes in their shape and pattern. Early pieces are plain, with a narrow border pattern woven with *buta* or *boteh* (pinecone) motifs, but by the 1850s, the curled boteh had lost its floral feel and become an abstract form. Early Kashmirs are stole-shaped, between 1830 and 1850 they are square, and after that they are almost counterpane-sized rectangles.

Machine-made European imitations of Kashmirs, far cheaper than the originals, were first produced in Paisley, Scotland (hence their name) around 1800. A vast number of good-quality shawls were soon made in a wide range of designs from centres around Britain and France.

Prices today can range from £50-£80 for a printed Paisley shawl of around 1840, to £3000-£4000 for a Kashmir shawl from the late 18th to mid-19th centuries.

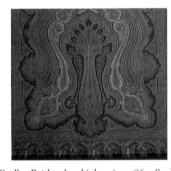

Woollen Paisley shawl (above); c.1860. Such shawls were Europe's machine-made answer to Kashmir shawls, whose front and back (below left and right) clearly show hand-weaving.
Paisley shawl: £600-£1000

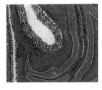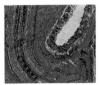

Charles II silk panel in satin stitch; c.1660; 12 in (30.5 cm) wide. This bright, unspoilt piece was made, but not used, to line a casket. The band of small panels was for the drawers.
£2500-£3500

Queen Anne embroidery in small diagonal tent stitch; c.1710; 18 in (45.7 cm) wide. Stylised clouds and animals were popular 17thC motifs, but little needlework of that century shows the sense of proportion seen here.
£1500-£2000

Berlin woolwork cat; c.1850; 6¼ in (15.9 cm) square. Looped and cut stitches make the 'fur'.
£300-£600

Needlepoint and beadwork cushion; c.1860; 17 in (43.2 cm) square. This is a relatively inexpensive flowered example of Berlin woolwork.
£100-£150

Beaded Berlin woolwork cushion; c.1850; 18 in (45.7 cm) square. It has vibrant colour, fine beadwork and a typically sentimental vignette.
£600-£1000

and temperature variations over the years have damaged the silk background. In many cases, the embroidery has remained perfect while the background has almost entirely disintegrated. Large and well-preserved examples generally sell for £400-£600.

BERLIN WOOLWORK

A revolutionary new technique for chemically dyeing wool, discovered in the 1830s, transformed the wool industry and provided a range of brightly coloured wools, dyed in Berlin, which inspired a craze for needlework. German wool manufacturers also marketed coloured design charts from which embroideries could be copied onto canvas.

Berlin woolwork was popular throughout the 19th century but reached its peak between 1850 and 1860. Fire screens, bell pulls, hats, slippers, gloves, book covers and many other items can be found decorated with the colourful Berlin wools. Beadwork, three-dimensional plushwork and glass eyes were incorporated into many pieces to add texture and interest; these can go for up to £800.

More elaborate needlework reproduced famous paintings of the day by artists such as Sir Edwin Henry Landseer. These are now among the least sought after of Berlin woolwork items, and even a large, fine piece in a good mount can fetch as little as £100-£300.

Warmth with Style

QUILTING, the art of putting together layers of material, was developed as a way of keeping warm. It originally used a simple herringbone stitch to fix one layer of material to another, with a little padding between.

Some quilted satin petticoats and cradle covers of the 18th century were decorated with appliqué work and patchwork, but quilting and patchwork reached their height in the 19th century. A European quilt was usually a random mosaic of fabric scraps made by one woman. Many American quilts were made by groups of women at 'quilting bees' and have elaborate patterns. Some of the finest American pieces are appliquéd and over-quilted 'album' quilts showing scenes

from someone's life and home. The only remotely comparable British pieces are the quilts in Welsh and Durham style.

The value of a quilt depends on its age, intricacy and condition. Elaborate American quilts easily fetch five or six-figure sums, but in Europe quilts are one of the most undervalued fields of needlework. An average 19th-century British example might fetch as little as £100-£200.

Welsh patchwork coverlet (left); c.1835; 97 in (2.46 m) long; and American album quilt; c.1840; 107½ in (2.73 m) long.
Left: £1200-£1800
Below: £100,000

Lace and linen

Lace remains one of the most underappreciated and underpriced of all antique textiles, remarkable for its delicacy and intricate workmanship.

OVER THE CENTURIES, lace has been made in four main forms: embroidered lace, which was common in the 16th century; needlepoint lace, popular in the 17th; bobbin lace, at its peak in the 18th century; and machine-made lace, including embroidered net, chemical lace and imitations of the other forms, produced in the 19th and 20th centuries.

Machine lace is identifiable by its regularity, while part of the appeal of handmade lace is the slight variations in its tension, weave and design. Collectors particularly favour early, purpose-made pieces of handmade lace – caps, engageants (cuff frills), lappets (long, ribbon-like hair adornments, often attached to lace caps) and collars – rather than simple lengths of fabric.

NEEDLEPOINT AND CUTWORK

Needlepoint lace is sewn with a needle by building up layers of tiny buttonhole stitches. It was made in many European countries, and two of the earliest forms, reticella and punto in aria, originated in Italy. The best-known French forms include point de France, point d'Argentan and point d'Alençon. The mainly floral, late 19th-century Youghal lace from Ireland, with linking hexagonal bars, is very collectable, as is point de gaze from Brussels and the floral Italian Burano lace. A collar in any of these sells for around £20-£40.

An Irish linen coverlet with cutwork and whitework (white embroidery pierced with openings where the body fabric has been cut away) averages between £60 and £100 today, or more if it has a deep, crochet-edged border. Ireland has a well-deserved reputation for producing fine linens, but even so a late 19th-century plain damask tablecloth can fetch as little as £10-£15.

NET AND BOBBIN LACE

Embroidered net, also popular in the late 19th century, was made by chain-stitching a design onto net. This tambour work was cheap, quick and effective, and today a tamboured net wedding veil usually costs £100-£150.

Bobbin lace was woven rather than sewn, made by twisting and weaving lengths of thread attached to weighted bobbins over a cushion. It is also known as pillow lace. The most famous bobbin laces were made at Honiton in Britain, Genoa and Milan in Italy, Valenciennes and Chantilly in France,

and at other centres in Malta, Spain and Belgium, including Bruges. Each centre has its own distinctive motifs and styles.

Antique bobbins are themselves collectable. They are usually made of turned bone or softwood, decorated by staining, turning, pewter inlays, brass wiring, beadwork bands, or naively engraved names or mottoes. In the auction rooms bobbin prices fluctuate, but on average a bone bobbin would fetch £8-£12, a wooden bobbin £5-£8, and a highly decorated or inscribed bobbin £10-£30; prices in antique shops are considerably higher. Any chip or break (which would cut the thread when the bobbin is used) reduces the price, and the value to collectors.

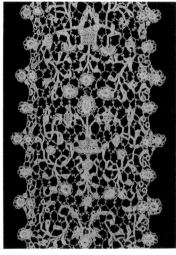

Detail of Italian point de neige lappet; c. 1690. The motif's heavy edge is created with raised cordonnets, while the 'brides' (linking bars between the motifs) are sprigged with small, snowflake-like shapes.
£100-£200 for 3 ft or 1 m

Mechlin lace flounce; c. 1760. The town of Mechlin reputedly produced the best 17thC Flemish lace, but the term also refers to a style of bobbin lace made there and elsewhere from c. 1720.
£60-£100 for 3 ft or 1 m

Brussels needlepoint appliqué collar; c. 1860; 38 in (96.5 cm) along inner rim. Needlepoint is more intricate to work than bobbin lace and therefore more highly regarded and more expensive.
£30-£50

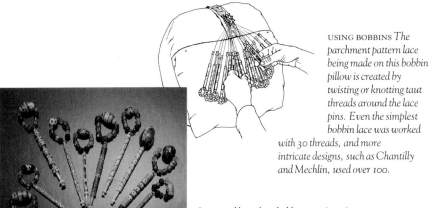

USING BOBBINS *The parchment pattern lace being made on this bobbin pillow is created by twisting or knotting taut threads around the lace pins. Even the simplest bobbin lace was worked with 30 threads, and more intricate designs, such as Chantilly and Mechlin, used over 100.*

Ivory and bone lace bobbins; c. 1850-80. Decoration varies greatly; macabre 'hanging' bobbins, inscribed with a hanged man's name and date of execution, can fetch £100 each.
Set of ten: £150-£200

Antique costume

The styles and eccentricities of earlier generations are wonderfully apparent in yesterday's fashions, providing an illuminating insight into past lives.

French or Italian brocaded silk doublet; c.1625. Men's costume of the 17thC is extremely rare: in 1989 this piece sold for a world record price of £60,000.
£60,000-£100,000

Embroidered English waistcoat; c.1780. The ivory satin is decorated with ladybirds, caterpillars and other insects.
£1000-£1500

LANGUID ELEGANCE *The attire of Warren Hastings, in his portrait by Joshua Reynolds of c.1768-9, is typical of the late 18thC.*

M OST EARLY COSTUME pieces that have survived have been kept for sentimental reasons: antique dresses, wedding veils and baby robes, carefully folded away and handed on to the next generation. There are so many of these items on the market today that they rarely fetch exceptional prices at auction.

Sometimes, however, owners come in for a pleasant surprise – even from such an unlikely source as a children's fancy-dress box. The contents of such a box made nearly £30,000 for a Gloucestershire family in the mid-1980s. The parents had let the children dress up in the clothes, thinking they were from the 1920s, but every item was 18th century.

Examples of costume from even earlier times are rare indeed – partly because when a fine gown of the 16th or 17th century was no longer needed it was unpicked so that its rich materials could be used in a new garment.

MEN'S CLOTHING

Men's clothing, apart from waistcoats, is particularly rare – and hence particularly valuable. At an auction in 1989 a French brocaded silk gentleman's bodice, or doublet, dating from the 1620s, sold for £60,000.

Waistcoats are the one item of men's clothing that have survived in some quantities, and beautifully embroidered examples from the late 18th century and early 19th can be had for £80-£150, though prices are rising.

An exceptional waistcoat can fetch £1000-£1500. Prices are rising, too, for mid-19th-century waistcoats in brocaded silk or brightly coloured and embroidered Berlin woolwork. Some buyers want them for their collection, while others plan to wear them.

WOMEN'S DRESS

Women's clothes were often altered to keep pace with fashion. This does not affect the value of a gown as long as the alteration followed soon after its creation. An 18th-century gown altered in the 18th century will keep its value. But in the late 19th and early 20th centuries there was a vogue for fancy-dress parties, and alterations done for these can reduce a gown's value to a fraction of its original worth. Sometimes they will have drastically changed the shape of a garment, or removed large sections of fabric.

Particularly rare and desirable are black 18th-century garments – not to be confused with mourning dresses of a century later. In the 19th century the accepted period of mourning was a year and a day, and due to the high infant mortality rate, many women were seldom out of black. Jet-adorned black capes of the 19th century can be found for as little as £40-£60 at auction, despite their high standard of materials and workmanship.

A brightly coloured tartan taffeta gown with separate day and evening bodices from around 1860 might cost £2000-£3000, but a

Sack-backed open robe and petticoat of yellow silk; c.1760. Brilliant colour and decoration make this an exceptional garment, despite minor alterations.
£10,000-£15,000

Fine cinnamon brocaded open robe with matching petticoat; c.1770. The decoration, of flower sprigs, is rather sparse. A denser pattern would double the robe's value.
£3000-£5000

Brocaded silk open robe; c.1750. The silk was probably made by the Spitalfields silk factories which favoured lush floral designs. Vibrant colours and bold design make this a valuable garment, despite alterations.
£4000-£6000

Printed muslin summer dress; c. 1870. Printed muslin was very popular at this time This garment, possibly of Indian fabric, is well above average in value because of its striking colours and pristine condition.
£1000-£1500

CHARLES FREDERICK WORTH

Originator of the Designer Label

AN ENGLISHMAN became the leading light of the Paris fashion world in the second half of the 19th century. Charles Frederick Worth (1825-95) was sent to Paris in 1847 at the age of 22 to learn the haberdashery trade, but his design flair and business sense took him farther than he could have dreamed.

Worth's fashion business, the House of Worth, opened in 1858 and was to influence the shape of women's dress until the end of the century. Among the many inventions now credited to Worth is the lightweight crinoline frame, which made life more comfortable for women. He is also thought to have been the first to label his dresses with his firm's name – generally on the waistband, often embossed in gold.

SIGN OF WORTH *Gowns bearing this label adorned many influential 19thC women.*

similar item in dull brown or grey could be worth as little as £100-£150, and a black late 19th-century example even less.

Christening robes and wedding dresses are both affordable and undervalued. Even 17th-century christening robes, made of plain ivory satin with a little knotted fly-braid decoration and detached sleeves, can be picked up for a few hundred pounds. Beautiful mid-19th-century christening robes, the skirts densely embroidered with flowers and ears of wheat in Ayrshire-work, sell for around £100-£150, and simpler examples are even cheaper.

WEDDING DRESSES

Similarly, wedding dresses with the most exquisite decoration can change hands at auction for under £100 – less, in fact, than a modern dress. This is partly due to the fact that most 19th-century dresses are too small to fit most present-day brides. Late 19th-century wedding dresses, composed of the most delicate Brussels bobbin lace and yards of the finest ivory satin, can fetch less than £300.

One type of 19th-century costume that is regularly bought for present-day use is loose-fitting underwear. Prices vary for waist-length petticoats and camisole bodices trimmed with delicate Valenciennes lace and ribbons, depending on the quality of workmanship and the amount of lace trimming; but camisoles usually fetch around £30-£50 and elaborate petticoats £50-£100.

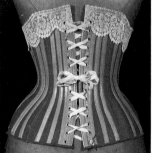

Quaker bridal outfit in dove-grey silk; c.1829. It was worn by Mary Ann Norten of Peckham Rye at the local Quaker Meeting House. Staining on the front of the gown has reduced its value considerably.
£1000-£1500

French ball gown by Charles Frederick Worth, the English designer who took Paris by storm in the 19th century; c. 1895. This gown was made for Mary Goelet, who married the 8th Duke of Roxburgh in 1903.
£5000-£8000

Fancy wool corset, with the boning covered in leather; 1883. Unusual materials and colours account for the high price of this piece.
£500-£800; plain white: £50

An Expert Examines

KERRY TAYLOR FINDS THE SUPREME PARTY DRESS

*S*O FAR AS I'M CONCERNED, *when a costume I've never seen before comes out of its bag, it's the Wow! factor that counts. Wow! it's wonderful; or oh dear, another one of those. But for me, this dress really has a top Wow! rating. There's this wonderful coloured brocade, the gorgeous silver trimming and applied streamers of ribbon work and crimson metal foil flowers running up to the waist – it's a dress for a very special occasion indeed.*

The style dates it as 18th century, but when, exactly? Well, first, it's what is called an open robe, because the skirt is open at the front to show a petticoat underneath. The bodice above closes at the front with hooks and eyes. That suggests a date after 1770.

A dress to grace the belle of the ball

Even a decade earlier, the bodice would have opened over a stomacher – a triangular panel of fabric. Another pointer is the back of the dress where, as you can see, the stripes in the fabric have been made into box pleats. Around 1750, those pleats would have fallen straight from the shoulder to the hem in a style known as the sack back. Then, in the 1770s, Paris decreed that the dress should be more fitted to the back as far as the waist, and flare out from there to the ground. And that's

what we've got here. Looking inside the bodice you can see the laces across the back which helped to keep the box pleats rigid.

Laces in the bodice's back help to fit the dress

The material itself gives another clue to the date. True, the repeat sprigged flower pattern was popular throughout the 18th century, and the figured ivory silk could as readily be from the 1760s. But the vertical gold stripes are unmistakably of the 1770s. It's all woven brocade, not embroidered as people often think. If you look at the back, you can tell by those horizontal bands of silk threading across from one pattern to the next.

Front of the pattern   Reverse of the weave

In fact, the weave is very intricate and complicated. The cloth was woven on a loom in strips 2 ft (60 cm) wide with a pattern of bold gold stripes, ivory silk flower sprigs, bouquets of blooms, ribbon swags and butterflies. There are ten separate colours altogether in the weave, including five different reds and two different greens. But what is really startling is the decoration. They used a silk gauze with a trellis stripe of silver, which is padded here and there with lambswool, gathered and sprigged with silk ribbon roses. Then there are those silver tassels, made of wire bound with pink and silver and blue thread, and the overall shimmer of scrunched-up flowers of foil.

A rich confection of metal foils decorates the dress

The reason there's so much material in the robe and petticoat is that they were worn over a pannier, a whalebone frame to push them out at each side. In addition, a young woman of the 1770s would have worn an elaborately

ressed white-
owdered wig of
antastic height
nd with equally
antastic hair
rnaments. There
vas a mass of
ewellery to catch
he eye, and this
ink lining inside
he hem to gleam
rettily as the girl
lanced. How
narvellous it all
nust have looked
by candlelight!

A hem to catch the eye

Unfortunately, the dress must have been
used for fancy dress early this century. It was
altered at the shoulders, the original silk
ruffles were removed and a Petersham
waistband was added. This lace is too regular
o be original handmade bobbin lace, but it's
quite easy to buy genuine 18th-century lace
engageants, or ruffles, to replace it. Overall,
he alterations aren't too drastic, and no
arge areas of fabric have been removed. The
dress isn't torn or stained – perspiration can
spell disaster on fine brocade like this – and it
hasn't faded. Considering this fragile textile
has survived almost intact for over 200 years
t's in surprisingly good condition.

Rough hidden stitching confirms 18thC origins

KERRY TAYLOR SUMS UP

The rarity and quality of the fantastic
decoration, combined with the glorious
striped brocade fabric, lift this dress well
above the average. Before today, I have only
ever seen gowns like this in 18th-century
Italian and Spanish paintings – never in
reality. It was probably owned by a very
young Spanish noblewoman – it's tiny across
the shoulders – to wear at court, or possibly
at her wedding. It's a difficult piece to price,
as there is nothing to compare it with. It could
easily make £10,000 to £15,000 at auction
– and possibly even twice as much as that
if, say, two museums set their hearts on it.

Twentieth-century costume

Most collections of 20th-century costume concentrate on models by the top French couturiers, but innovative and interesting examples of post-1950 design can be picked up for considerably smaller sums.

HAUTE COUTURE GOWNS – meaning literally those of 'high dressmaking' – by 20th-century designers are an increasingly popular area of collecting. They are valued not only as a sound investment, but for their artistic value and fine workmanship.

As yet, there are few areas of 20th-century costume apart from French haute couture that seem likely to increase in value. As social conditions changed after the 1950s, the gap between haute couture and the ready-to-wear lines for the mass market began to close. Many of the most distinctive and original designers, such as André Courrèges, Issey Miyake and Paco Rabanne, have worked in both fields. If you are more interested in the social and artistic history of fashion than in making a profitable investment, ready-to-wear items by such designers offer wide scope at more modest prices than couture pieces.

HAUTE COUTURE DESIGNS

International fashions for the first half of this century were dominated by a handful of Paris fashion houses, including those of Worth (see box, p.313), Paquin (founded by Mme Paquin in 1891) and Jacques Doucet. Gowns from these houses are all sought by collectors.

Paul Poiret was one of the leading designers between 1908 and 1915, having worked for both Worth and Doucet before setting up his own establishment in 1904. Poiret's designs are original and extravagantly Oriental, using flowing robes and turbans, and he is generally credited with freeing women from the corset.

Between 1907 and 1949, Mariano Fortuny produced timeless garments made from fabrics that he printed and embossed to look like ancient brocade. Fortuny's designs were much influenced by ancient Greek designs and the ideas of the Pre-Raphaelite artists of the late 19th century, as his sheath-like Delphos dresses of 1909 clearly show.

One of the best known names of the 20th-century fashion world must be that of Gabrielle ('Coco') Chanel. She was the first to use what were then humble fabrics, such as knitted jersey, for her understated chic

Utility suit of checked wool; c.1940. During the war years many such outfits, drab but elegantly tailored, were made for clothes rationing, as couturiers were forced to cut back on expensive gowns.
£60-£80

Yves Saint-Laurent mini dress; 1965. The design for this dress was taken from Dutch artist Piet Mondrian's abstract paintings, combining Saint-Laurent's humour with the strong geometrical lines so popular in the 1960s.
£1500-£2500

Christian Dior ball gown; 1955. Dior's attention to detail and brilliance of design is shown in this dress of satin and silk tulle. The size of its embroidered flower heads alters in line with the contours of the gown.
£3000-£4000

KIMONOS AND OBI
Material Tradition

*Silk Noh robe; c.1800.
The bold phoenix motif
is highly desirable.* **£8000**
*Silk obi; c.1900. It features a popular
early 20thC design.* **£50**

THE KIMONO, a loose-sleeved, straight-seamed coat, is the traditional dress of Japan, and today, examples with bold, asymmetrical designs are the most collectable. Most designs are embroidered with silk or gilt thread, but tie-dyeing, resist-dyeing and stencilling were also used. Kimonos combining several techniques command the highest prices.

Brocade robes from 19th-century and earlier Noh plays may sell for thousands of pounds; a 19th-century silk kimono with a damask ground, tie-dyed details and a bold, embroidered pattern might fetch £1000 or more; and a 1920s printed kimono as little as £50-£100.

Twentieth-century obi, or sashes, are equally undervalued, and may fetch as little as £40 at auction.

*Beaded cocktail dresses;
1920s. More wearable than
collectable, the left-hand
dress is made of
silk and beading –
haute couture but
altered. The other is
in French, mass-
produced muslin.*
Left: £80-£120
Right: £100-£200

*Christian Dior 'Bar' suit;
1947. The prototype of the
'New Look' introduced by
Dior. Few complete suits exist,
making them highly desirable.*
£10,000-£15,000

*Chanel day suit;
1968. This suit,
made of tweedy
bouclé wool fabric, is
typical of Chanel's
later designs.*
£300-£350

*Jeanne Lanvin gold lamé evening
coat; 1928-30. The body of this coat
is entirely quilted with whirling
catherine-wheel motifs. Lanvin was
known for her use of embroidered
and lavish decoration.*
£800-£1200

suits, previously almost exclusively made in silk. Her early garments (made before 1925) bear her full name – Gabrielle Chanel – while those thereafter are simply signed 'Chanel'. Chanel is credited with inventing the 'little black dress', and a black dress of hers from the 1920s and 30s is today worth over £2000.

Madeleine Vionnet was the consummate craftswoman of the 1930s, famous for her fluid, pleated dresses. She scorned shoulder and side seams and produced dresses of incredible construction.

Another original designer of the 1930s was Elsa Schiaparelli, who loved the bizarre and worked closely with the surrealist artists of the day, especially Salvador Dali. Shocking pink was Schiaparelli's trademark and was regularly incorporated into her dresses and accessories, of which her 1936 black hat, shaped like a shoe with a shocking-pink heel,

is a good example. Although much of her work was designed to surprise, she also had a rather more reserved clientele for whom she designed more conventional garments.

Jeanne Lanvin is another collectable designer whose clothes can still be found today. Her dresses are remarkable for their appliqué work, ribbon work and frivolous decoration. Then there was Madame Grès, whose Paris fashion house flourished even during the German Occupation of 1940-4. Nevertheless, she showed her disapproval of the conquerors by basing her 1941 collection on the colours of the French flag.

In the immediate postwar years, Christian Dior's 'New Look' – epitomised by his collection of the Corolle line in 1947 – shocked the world with its extravagance, but its feminine curves were vastly popular after long austerity. Dior introduced the vogue for loose-fitting

clothing, a trend which was perpetuated by Yves Saint-Laurent, Dior's assistant.

Pierre Balmain, Jacques Fath, Hubert de Givenchy, Pierre Cardin, Christobal Balenciaga and Chanel (who closed her house in 1939 but reopened in 1954) were all designing at the end of the 1950s despite the gradual decline of the couture trade. As ready-to-wear lines became increasingly popular, couture houses began to design for stores and large-scale manufacturers and also introduced their own lines of accessories – such as perfumes – to keep their businesses alive.

WHAT TO LOOK OUT FOR

Care must be taken to distinguish between gowns made at the original fashion houses and those sold in boutiques bearing the same name; boutique versions are worth a fraction of the price of haute couture. Haute couture

Callot Soeurs beaded dress; 1922. Made of tangerine chiffon and pearlised beads, dresses of this kind should be laid flat and treated with care, as heavy beading on a fine chiffon base tends to pull the fabric apart. **£2000-£3000**

Man's tweed golfing suit; c.1930. Not worth a great deal, this suit still has strong collector appeal as it is typical of its date. **£60-£100**

Chiffon dress; 1928. This cheap and cheerful dress, decorated with ribbon appliqué flowers, is attractive but not especially collectable. **£60-£100**

Mary Quant mini dress; 1967. Quant is credited by many as having invented the mini dress, and this example is made in wool and nylon jersey. **£80-£100**

gowns normally have a stamped or hand-written client number found either to one side of the main label, or on a tab behind it.

A mid-1950s Christian Dior (Paris) couture ball gown in good condition can be worth thousands of pounds, whereas a gown labelled 'Christian Dior London' would probably fetch a few hundred pounds or even less. Although the design of the boutique gown is still Dior's, and the fabric is of good quality, such pieces generally lack the hand finishing found on a couture dress. Above all, Dior himself would most certainly have played no part in actually making the dress.

Date also affects the value of a designer garment. Gowns made during the peak period of a designer's career will fetch the highest prices, and so it is preferable to possess a late 1940s or early 1950s gown labelled 'Christian Dior' rather than one from the 1960s, when Marc Bohan was the house designer. In the same way, a Madeleine Vionnet bias-cut 1930s gown is more valuable than one from the 1920s, before she reached her peak.

Take special care with early silk and satin dresses. Many silks and satins used for dressmaking in the late 19th and early 20th centuries were soaked in a compound of tin to give them a fuller, heavier feel and to make them drape and fall correctly. Unfortunately, this chemical treatment eventually caused the silk to perish and shatter. As a result, early 20th-century dresses made of silks and satins are hard to find in good condition.

READY-TO-WEAR CLOTHES

For those who cannot afford to collect named designer wear, vintage costume shops sell interesting but unnamed dresses from a few pounds upwards, although they will not hold their value in the way a designer gown does.

Another inexpensive though interesting area of collecting could be the London-based designers of the 1960s, such as Mary Quant, Ossie Clark and those who worked for Barbara Hulanicki's Biba boutique. London has never been as central to the fashion world as when Carnaby Street flourished during the 1960s, and pieces such as a Mary Quant black and white plastic 'op-art' raincoat are likely to become collector's items.

Even today there is an enormous range of designs and designers for costume collectors to choose from. Those that have attracted attention over the last 30 years include Paco Rabanne's hammered steel and plastic creations; André Courrèges' 1981 all-in-one suit of metallic jersey and spangled muslin; and clothes by influential Japanese designers of the 1980s, including Kenzo and Issey Miyake.

An Expert Examines

KERRY TAYLOR TRIES ON A FLAPPER DRESS

'IT'S NOT AT ALL GRAND – *quite humble, in fact, compared with the pannier robe of the 18th century (see p.314) – but this little dress proclaims its own period with just as much fervour. It belongs to the end of the flapper years, about 1926 to 28, when girls strove for the gamine, flat-chested look. It would be a good dress to Charleston in, for it is little more than an Art Deco tunic, festooned with cylindrical glass bugle beads. It's a merry, spirited dress, made in France, I would say. But lack of a label and – more important – lack of oversewn seams indicate that it's not haute couture. The machine-stitched beading confirms this; had the dress come from a major fashion house, each bead would have been sewn on by hand. So it was probably sold by a department store, and today is worth about £100 or a little more. But I'm sure its original owner had a lot of fun wearing it, just as a modern buyer would.'*

Just the dress for the Charleston.

Costume accessories

Accessories are a good area for new collectors, as most items are relatively inexpensive, especially those from the 19th and early 20th centuries.

Straw hat; late 17thC; 19¼ in (49 cm) wide. This wide-brimmed, straw and split-cane hat in the manner of reticella lace is probably Indo-Chinese.
£3000-£5000

T HE BEAUTY of costume accessories as a collecting field lies in the fact that most are small but exquisitely made. Shoes, bags, hats, gloves, purses and fans can all make spectacular and interesting displays and do not require much space. They can be found at auctions, markets, car boot or jumble sales, some costing only a couple of pounds.

HATS AND HAIR ACCESSORIES

Until the early years of the present century, most European women grew their hair long, pinning it up with combs and clips, and covering it when outdoors. Indeed, it was considered extremely ill-mannered in polite society to be seen outdoors without a hat until the 1960s. As a result, 19th and early 20th-century hats can still be found in considerable numbers, often at modest prices.

The earliest surviving women's hats on the market today are 17th and 18th-century embroidered caps, but these are rare and can cost thousands of pounds. So too can the wide-brimmed hats that were fashionable from the late 18th century until the early 20th; their size made them susceptible to damage and few survived in good condition.

Nineteenth-century bonnets can still be bought for less than £50, however, as can superb hats from the first half of this century. Models designed by top couturiers such as Christobal Balenciaga, Christian Dior and Elsa Schiaparelli (see pp.315-17) are sought by collectors, but even these have to be really eye-catching to make £100 or more.

One consequence of the fashion for large hats was the development of the hatpin, popular from the end of the 19th century up until the 1920s, when women began to crop their hair. Hatpins were generally sold in pairs, or sets of three or four, and range in length from about 5 to 12 in (12.5-30 cm). Their designs vary greatly, and many are topped by gold, silver, glass or semiprecious stones. Some are decorated with clusters of jewels in the shape of flowers or abstract forms while others display tiny miniature portraits of friends, family or pets. Such pins were made in large quantities and can still be picked up for a few pounds apiece.

Hair combs and clips are also very collectable, especially examples from earlier this century. Art Nouveau combs in silver and horn fetch from perhaps £50 upwards, while Edwardian combs made of tortoiseshell cost

THE FINISHING TOUCH *This late 18thC painting illustrates the striking nature of many costume accessories which are both functional and beautiful.*

Embroidered linen night cap; c.1630-50. It is thought to have been worn by Charles I at his execution in 1649.
£15,000-£20,000
£2000-£3000
without
provenance

Striped silk taffeta bonnet; c.1835-40. The high-domed crown and large brim of this rare hat would have balanced the bell-shaped dresses of the 1830s, which had exaggerated sleeves.
£400-£600

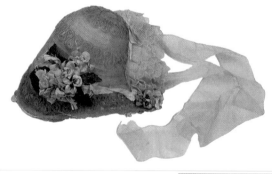

Straw bonnet; mid-19thC. This bonnet is designed to sit on the back of the head, and is trimmed with artificial silk flowers.
£100-£150

Three hats by Bes Ben; 1950s. Hats from the 1950s are an unusual and interesting field for new collectors of modest means, as these striking American hats of the period illustrate.
£60-£100 each

Pair of slap-soled shoes; c.1620. 17thC shoes of this quality are rarely seen today. Their fixed 'slap' soles prevented the wearer from sinking into mud.
£20,000-£30,000

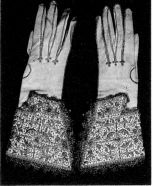

White kid gloves; early 17thC. These gauntlets bear the dense embroidery in silver thread and silver sequins common at this time.
£2000-£3000

Woman's slipper; c.1860. Morocco embroidered with gold thread. Probably made in Turkey for the European market.
£150-£250 pair

Woman's high-heeled shoe; c.1700. The silk upper is joined to the sole by a rand of white kid.
£3500-£5000 pair

Woman's mule; c.1720. This too has a white kid rand joining the sole to a silk upper.
£3000-£4000 pair

Pair of stiletto shoes; c.1955. These modern but collectable shoes bear the name of the eccentric French designer Elsa Schiaparelli.
£200-£300

BUTTONS
Practical Adornment

MOST BUTTONS collected today were made in the 19th century, when they were produced in profusion. Buttons were chosen for both their beauty and their quality of manufacture, and were used again and again, transferred from one garment to the next. Sets of buttons were made of mother-of-pearl, bone, ivory, porcelain or metal, or covered in silk, satin or leather, and were packaged in boxes, or sewn to a piece of card. Dress sets, with detachable buttons and cufflinks, were introduced in the 19th century when rigidly stiff, starched shirts were too inflexible for buttons. Uniforms are also a good source of button sets; the metal is stamped with the regimental insignia, a crest, a motto or animals and figures.

Although individual buttons or pairs from the 18th century can be found, they are quite rare and are not always easy to distinguish. Dating buttons accurately is difficult, as some styles were made over many years, while others were introduced, went out of fashion, and were then reintroduced.

Set of silver and enamel Liberty 'Cymric' buttons by Archibald Knox; c.1901.
£300-£500

---

as little as £5-£20. Hair clips made in early plastics – such as Bakelite and Erinoid – can frequently be found for just a few pounds.

GLOVES, SHOES, UMBRELLAS AND WALKING STICKS

Until the end of the 1950s, gloves were another essential part of a woman's wardrobe. They were worn outdoors and also for evening wear and cocktail parties. But although gloves enjoyed a comeback in the late 1980s, many 19th-century gloves are unwearable by contemporary women because of their tiny size. This has affected the price of antique gloves, and even today a pair of 19th-century, plain, elbow-length kid gloves in excellent condition can cost as little as £5-£10, a fraction of the cost of a new pair. Older gloves will fetch more, of course, with a good pair of beautifully

embroidered 17th-century gauntlets or 18th-century mittens fetching from £400 up to £1000 or more, depending on their quality, embroidery and condition.

Prices paid for shoes in good condition have risen tremendously over the last five years as competition between new shoe museums and dealers has intensified. Pairs of 18th-century shoes in good condition regularly sell at auction for over £1000, and 17th-century pairs can make up to £20,000. However, a pair of plain but good quality, mid to late 19th-century shoes can still cost as little as £40-£60, if they are of a fairly standard design. Some wear is acceptable and will not bring down the price. Shoes made since the 1940s are rarely collected as yet, unless they are by a top designer such as Salvatore Ferragamo or Roger Vivier. But they could well make a good

investment for someone looking to create a collection whose value will grow in the future.

Parasols and umbrellas, on the other hand, are remarkably cheap at auction at present. Early 19th-century parasols made with ribs of baleen (whalebone) and an angular, carved ivory grip can be picked up for less than £300, and carriage parasols, with folding handle and silk canopy edged with fringing, average £100 or less. Early 20th-century examples of the sturdier umbrella can be bought for as little as £5-£25. Those with a canopy in perfect condition and with an elaborate, carved ivory handle vary in price from £60 to £300.

Collectors of walking sticks look for high-quality workmanship and carving on the stick's grip, or handle. Novelty items with handles which unscrew to reveal a sword or flask are especially desirable, their prices

Selection of parasols; 19thC. The largest dates from c.1830-40, the other three from the 1850s and 60s. The rarest is the square parasol, c.1869.
£60-£300 each

Walking sticks; late 19th/early 20thC: sword stick with horn grip (top); and 'drinking core' or whisky stick (below), an advertising gimmick for Johnny Walker whisky.
Sword stick £100-£150
Whisky stick £60-£100

Elizabethan embroidered purse; c.1590-1610. The scrolled embroidery and stumpwork petals are typically late 16thC.
£1000-£1500

Selection of fans; 18th, 19th and 20thC. These range in price from £1000 for the oldest, mid-18thC chinoiserie fan (bottom left) to £100 for the early 20thC fans at the back and front right. These include two advertising fans for champagne and cigarettes. In the centre is a French painted silk gauze fan, c.1905.

Fan with Buckingham lace leaf; c.1900. The fan's wide span and mother-of-pearl sticks and guards betray its late date, even though it is based on a design of c.1760.
£100-£150

depending on the materials used, date and rarity. A carved whalebone walking stick might cost between £400 and £600, a straight forward ebonised stick with silver decoration £50-£80, and one with an unusual grip in the form of a hand or an animal head, £100.

PURSES, FANS AND HANDKERCHIEFS

Purses and bags have been used for carrying money, papers, sweetmeats and so on since the Middle Ages, but the earliest surviving drawstring purses, dating from the 16th century, are extremely rare and expensive today. Embroidered 16th and 17th-century examples are sometimes found at auction, usually fetching around £600-£2000, but the many 19th and 20th-century bags, purses and handbags can still be purchased for well under £100. Nineteenth-century misers' purses of knitted silk adorned with metal beads are usually under £40, as are stylish Art Deco bags of the 1920s and 30s or novelty-shaped bags with unusual clasps from the 1940s.

One type of accessory which has risen in value over the last few years is the fan. Lavish decoration was first applied to fans during the 18th century, when they were used by women both to keep cool and as a silent form of communication in courtship or flirtation.

The leaves of the fans were painted with all manner of decoration: romantic scenes, prayers, heroic battles, royal and patriotic portraits, political satires and slogans, songs and dance tunes, or even advertisements. The sticks and fan guards were made from a wide variety of materials – including sandalwood, mother-of-pearl, horn, tortoiseshell, ivory and occasionally plain wood – and were lavishly carved, enamelled or gilded.

Superbly painted, 18th-century fans can fetch £10,000 or more, but hand-painted examples from the 19th century are far more affordable. An example with satin or silk gauze leaves in fair condition can still be purchased for less than £100. Printed paper Art Deco fans (which were given away free by restaurants and shops in the 1920s and 30s) often carried advertisements. These are also still relatively inexpensive and could be an interesting area for new collectors.

Handkerchiefs too have been in use since the Middle Ages, although their square shape dates from the late 18th century. They were made of many materials, including printed gauze and lace-edged silk, and were variously initialled, embroidered, painted or printed with pictures, rhymes or stories. A good-quality early 20th-century handkerchief will cost from £20 to £80, while a beautiful 19th-century example can fetch up to £800.

Fine Art, Prints & Books

Detail of 'Springtime' by Helen Allingham; c.1890

Oil paintings

Portraiture and landscape are the two great traditions of oil painting in Britain. They exist today in great abundance and there are bargains around for those who search for quality.

Thomas Hudson, 'Rear Admiral Richard Tyrell'; 1748-50; 50 × 40 in (1.27 × 1.01 m). This painting is in a desirable 'untouched' and dirty state.
£5000-£7000

Follower of Thomas Lawrence, 'William, 2nd Baron Bateman'; 1830-5; 60 × 48¼ in (1.52 × 1.23 m). This uses a Lawrence design.
£8000-£12,000

Peter Lely and studio, 'Duchess of Cleveland'; c.1665, in period frame; 72½ × 57¼ in (1.84 × 1.45 m). The portrait repeats Lely's famous design of Charles II's mistress.
£12,000-£18,000

Francis Cotes, 'Lady Sarah March'; 1764; 34½ × 27½ in (87.6 × 70 cm). The combination of sitter and costume makes this a fine example of its period.
£10,000-£15,000

Martin Archer Shee, 'Earl of Albemarle'; 1818; 55¾ × 43½ in (1.42 × 1.10 m). This is a typical three-quarter-length Regency format.
£6000-£8000

THE SCOPE for confusion is endless in a field as big as oil painting, which extends from the first use of the medium during the Renaissance to the work of living artists. But the works the non-specialist is most likely to come across are British paintings predating the aesthetic revolution begun by the Impressionists – a much more restricted field.

The value of any painting will depend above all on the relative importance of the artist who painted it – as long as it accurately reflects the style or date of the artist's work, and is not a later copy. Not all artists signed their works, and signatures may have been forged or altered at a later date, so visual clues – such as the shapes of faces, composition, particular colours (reflecting both taste and pigments available at the time), brushwork and even the size and shape – may be better methods of authenticating a painting. A work that is badly damaged or heavily restored will sell for a fraction of the price of a well-preserved piece, while a famous provenance or particularly rare or charming subject matter will push up a work's value.

PORTRAITS

The more decorative a portrait, the greater its potential value. An attractive child or beautiful woman will fetch a higher price than an elderly or disagreeable subject, and glamorous and beautiful costume is more desirable than sober legal or ecclesiastical garb.

The greatest period of British portraiture stretched roughly from William Hogarth in the 1730s and 40s through to Thomas Gainsborough and Joshua Reynolds in the 1760s to 80s. Portraits of this era combine informality with elegant costume and design, and include both grand portraits and small groups, or 'conversation pieces'. Auction prices for Hogarth, Gainsborough and Reynolds can run into six or seven figures, but most works are less pricey. Paintings by Thomas Hudson of the 1740s to 50s or slightly later works by Francis Cotes, Gilbert Stuart or George Romney can be found for £3000-£10,000, while portraits by their followers go for about £400 upwards, depending on subject and condition. A dull or badly damaged Reynolds worth £10,000 could easily be outstripped by an attractive work by a minor artist.

The Romantic portraits of the Regency era used to be extremely fashionable. However, although works by Thomas Lawrence can now fetch six-figure sums, many fetch less in real terms than they did 60 years ago. Portraits of less-attractive sitters by minor hands may

All paintings are oil on canvas unless stated otherwise.

Attributed to George Gower, 'Countess of Leicester'; on panel; c.1580; 35½ × 28¾ in (90 × 73 cm). Note the magnificent costume.
£25,000-£35,000

Augustus Egg, portrait; c.1850; 13½ × 11 in (34.3 × 28 cm). The glowing colours show Pre-Raphaelite influence.
£10,000-£15,000

easily go for under £2000. Particular care must be taken to distinguish the work of major painters from that of their studios and followers, as the most popular and accessible designs, such as Lawrence's portrait of George IV, were copied and plagiarised extensively.

Portraits from the 17th century, dominated by the works of Flemish painter Anthony Van Dyck at the court of Charles I, and Peter Lely at that of Charles II, have recently risen steeply in price. Autograph works by Van Dyck – though not necessarily signed – range from £30,000 upwards, and those by Lely fetch £10,000-£60,000. The numerous examples from their studios or followers can be found for £1000-£8000. To complicate matters, Lely would often paint the face and hands, leaving drapery and background to his assistants.

Earlier Tudor and Jacobean portraiture is renowned for its fabulously elaborate costume. Most is painted on fragile oak panels, and large paintings on (continued p. 324)

PORTRAIT MINIATURES AND SILHOUETTES
Intimate Likenesses

MINIATURE PAINTING – or, as it was also known, 'the art of limning', – developed in the 16th century. Today, miniatures appeal to collectors for their small scale and intimacy, and as social records of clothing and hairstyles. Miniatures were very private possessions kept in small cabinets or worn as bracelets or lockets. They fall somewhere between old master paintings – following the stylistic trends of large-scale portraiture – and items of jewellery, often in gold or silver frames, perhaps intricately bejewelled.

Most miniatures are oval, as little as 1-3 in (25-76 mm) high, and were painted in watercolour or gouache. Early miniatures were painted on primed vellum (often backed with a playing card), but from the early 18th century most were on ivory. Enamel miniatures were also popular in the 18th century, especially on the Continent, and are relatively undervalued today. In the 19th century, larger, rectangular miniatures were popular. 'Plumbagos', drawn in graphite, are mainly of the late 17th century.

Elegant Elizabethan and Jacobean courtiers by Nicholas Hilliard and Isaac Oliver are rare in the salerooms, but there are plenty of fine 18th-century examples. Indeed, the period around 1790 is often regarded as the peak of British miniature painting with many noted practitioners, including Richard Cosway, George Engleheart and John Smart. While the best sell for over £10,000, good examples are easy to find for around £500-£2000, less-accomplished ones by unknown painters for under £200. As with all portraits, miniatures may be valued for who painted them and their artistic quality, or for whom they portray. Prices tend to be highest for children, followed by attractive female sitters and officers in colourful uniforms. Look out for signs of mould, for flaking paint and for tiny hairline cracks in the ivory.

Silhouettes were often traced with the aid of a camera obscura – an optical device throwing an image of the sitter on a screen. They became very popular in the late 18th century and were only superseded by photography in the second half of the 19th century. Silhouettes could be either cut from black paper and pasted on a white background, or painted – often on ivory, plaster or glass.

Silhouettes are generally cheaper than miniatures, starting at about £50 but rising to the high hundreds, or more, for works by noted artists such as Miers, Mrs Beetham or Augustin Edouart. The majority are head-and-shoulder profiles, sometimes with fine details such as bows and hair. You may also find full-length figures or lively family groups.

(Right) Circle of Oliver, a gentleman; c.1610. (Below right) M. Snelling, a gentleman; 1651;
£2000-£4000 each

(Top left) C. Dixon, an officer; c.1780. (Left) C.F. Zincke, a lady; enamels on metal; c.1720.
Top: £500-£700; left: £800-£1200

English School, a lady; on ivory; c.1830; 5 in (12.7 cm) high. This is in a period gesso frame.
£300-£450

Richard Cosway, a lady; c.1790. Painted on ivory, in locket with a plaited hair back.
£10,000-£12,000

English School, silhouette of a gentleman; on card; c.1820; frame 5½ in (14 cm) high.
£100-£150

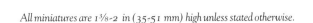

All miniatures are 1⅜-2 in (35-51 mm) high unless stated otherwise.

George Bernard O'Neil, 'Market day'; 1856; 33 × 54 in (84 × 137 cm). Such scenes from everyday life evolved from the example of Sir David Wilkie earlier in the century.
£12,000-£18,000

Francis Wheatley, 'The tender father'; 1787-8; 18½ × 14 in (47 × 35.5 cm).
£3000-£5000
Victorian copy: £400-£600

Harry Brookes, 'Too old to play'; 1888; 28 × 36 in (71 × 91 cm). Victorian genre paintings depicting children's pastimes are always very popular.
£10,000-£15,000

August Mulready, 'A penny, please?'; on panel; 1882; 15 × 11 in (38.1 × 28 cm). This work reflects the sentimentality of much late Victorian genre painting.
£3000-£5000

William Shayer, 'Rustic scene with pony'; c.1850; 13 × 11 in (33 × 28 cm). This is a typical Shayer composition. Works by his three sons fetch much less.
£4000-£6000

several panels are liable to warp and to crack at the joints. Damaged or less-imposing works can still be found for under £5000, but prices for good examples – even if the sitter is unknown – have risen to £10,000 and beyond. Their increasing rarity means that they are likely to prove a sound investment.

In contrast, the grand but rather repetitive periwigged figures painted by Sir Godfrey Kneller and his studio in the late 17th and early 18th centuries are in little demand. Even genuine works often fetch under £3000.

Similarly with Victorian portraits, the large number of sober and unimaginative works has kept prices low. Even works by famous artists can struggle to sell for a few thousand pounds, and prices for engaging 'naïve' portraits regularly exceed those for better-known painters. There are, of course, expensive exceptions – notably by the Pre-Raphaelites, by outstanding individuals like Lord Leighton and Edward Burne-Jones, and the flamboyant society portraits by John Singer Sargent at the end of the century.

GENRE PAINTING

Millais's Victorian painting 'Bubbles', used to advertise Pears soap, is on the border between portraiture and genre painting. Genre painting, which gives glimpses of everyday life, had its roots in the growth of middle-class social awareness in the late 18th century. Early pieces by painters such as George Morland and Francis Wheatley generally fetch up to £10,000. Genre painting went from strength to strength in the 19th century. David Wilkie's scenes of peasants, domestic scenes by

William Mulready and realistic paintings of modern life by William Powell Frith were all influential, and now fetch very high prices. Works by their followers can, however, be found for below £5000.

In the late Victorian period, the trend was towards sentimentality and moralising. Views of children, animals and domestic pastimes are most popular today, with the majority of works in the £300-£5000 range.

LANDSCAPES

Landscape is one of the strongest traditions in British painting, although a native school developed only in the 18th century. Its appeal is very subjective, and while J.M.W. Turner and John Constable were artists of truly international stature, the demand for most

other works depends upon their authenticity, condition and topographical interest.

British landscape paintings of the 18th century fall into two broad categories: topographical views – which include early views of country mansions and views of London and the Thames by Canaletto and his English followers – and decorative landscapes based on Classical or picturesque rules of composition. Good 18th-century topographical works are scarce; even derivative pieces now fetch £20,000-£30,000. So also do the better decorative landscapes, such as those by Irish painters William Ashford and Thomas Roberts or the influential works of Richard Wilson. Good copies can fetch £5000 or more, but poor copies of Wilson's work change hands for only a few hundred pounds.

All paintings are oil on canvas unless stated otherwise.

William James after Canaletto, 'Grand Canal, Venice'; c.1760; 15 × 25¼ in (38.1 × 64 cm). 18thC topographical views are very sought after, even if they are copies.
£15,000-£20,000

Benjamin Williams Leader, 'Moel Siabod, N. Wales'; 1859; 35¾ × 30 in (90 × 76 cm). Leader painted this scene on several occasions but this is an early and very fine example.
£15,000-£20,000

Edward Charles Williams, 'Landscape with gypsies'; c.1850-60; 20 × 28 in (51 × 71 cm). This is heavily based on Dutch 17thC landscapes.
£3000-£5000

Alfred de Breanski, 'Blea Tarn, Cumberland'; 1890s; 24 × 36 in (61 × 91 cm). Breanski was very prolific. This view epitomises the type of late 19thC decorative landscape available in large numbers today.
£7000-£10,000

BAROQUE MASTERPIECE

Rediscovered Treasure

RELIGIOUS PAINTINGS are not very popular today – at least not until an altarpiece by a leading Italian Baroque painter suddenly appears. This painting attributed to Annibale Carracci sold in 1987 for £770,000. It had been bought by the vendor's grandfather at a Somerset auction in 1930 for £5. But no one knows for where and whom it was painted nor how and when it arrived in England. But its obscurity has probably contributed to its wonderful condition; lack of restoration boosted the value.

'The Holy Family accompanied by St Lucy'; oil on panel; late 16thC; 31 × 24¾ in (79 × 63 cm).

The 19th century offers vast scope for the collector, and works by members of the Williams family illustrate the various types of landscape painting over the century. In the earlier years, Edward Williams and his son Edward Charles painted picturesque woodland scenes, whose prices today range from £1500 to £2000 for small pieces to £4000-£8000 for better or larger works. (Similar works were painted in this period by the Norwich school and the Nasmyth family.)

Later members of the Williams family, such as Sidney Richard Percy, typify the late Victorian taste for grand panoramas, with prices reaching £10,000-£20,000 for the grandest Highland vistas. Colours tend to be brighter and clearer than in early 19th-century works and the style more detailed. Similar views executed in large numbers but with great technical skill by painters such as Alfred de Breanski are also perennially popular.

SPORTING PICTURES

The British love of the turf, the chase, and animals in general has long been reflected in paintings, but the demand for sporting subjects has declined recently. Today, only 18th-century artist George Stubbs, who raised sporting painting to a level never since equalled, continues to command prices over £100,000 for even a single horse portrait.

The heyday of the sporting painter was the first half of the 19th century. Among the best were John Ferneley, Ben Marshall and John Frederick Herring, who recorded the fashionable hunts and famous racehorses of the day,

Henry Alken, Snr, 'Hunting scene'; c.1840; 9¾ × 13¾ in (24.7 × 35 cm). Alken is one of the liveliest sporting painters. Sets fetch more, works by his sons rather less.
£4000-£6000

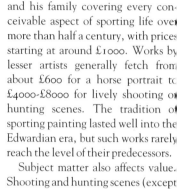

Edgar Hunt, 'The old barn'; 1929; 14 × 12 in (35.5 × 30.5 cm). Hunt's decorative farmyard scenes are very popular.
£4000-£6000; pair: £8000-£12,000

Edward Ladell, 'Still life'; c.1865-70; 18 × 14 in (45.7 × 35.5 cm). Ladell is among the best Victorian still life painters.
£6000-£8000

John Frederick Herring, Snr, 'Don Jon'; on panel; 1838; 10 × 12¼ in (25.4 × 31.1 cm). Variants with jockey or at racecourses cost more. Herring was widely copied.
£12,000-£18,000; 19thC copy: £1000-£1500

Gilbert Wright, 'The arrival of the coach'; c.1900; 10 × 13 in (25.4 × 33 cm). Wright's numerous works often look rather contrived and theatrical.
£4000-£6000

Harry Redmore, 'Shipping in an estuary'; 1864; 12 × 18 in (30.5 × 45.7 cm). Attractive marine works like this are reasonably priced and widely available.
£3000-£5000

and James Pollard, who painted coaching scenes. More plentiful and affordable are works by Henry Alken and his family covering every conceivable aspect of sporting life over more than half a century, with prices starting at around £1000. Works by lesser artists generally fetch from about £600 for a horse portrait to £4000-£8000 for lively shooting or hunting scenes. The tradition of sporting painting lasted well into the Edwardian era, but such works rarely reach the level of their predecessors.

Subject matter also affects value. Shooting and hunting scenes (except for the death of the fox) are popular, but coaching scenes, cock-fighting or bull-baiting are not. Early views of cricket – some from the 18th century – reign supreme (see p. 379), but are often forged.

STILL-LIFE PAINTING

The still-life painting tradition in Britain has never compared to the great works of 17th-century Holland. Early 18th-century paintings by Marmaduke Craddock or William Sartorius generally fetch £4000-£10,000 depending on subject and condition, flowers or fruit being more popular than dead game.

Works from the Victorian era show rather greater technical skill, although there are few well-known artists in this field. The best pieces by Edward Ladell or Charles Bale can fetch £15,000 or more, but many small fruit and flower pieces from the later part of the century go for only £1000-£1500.

MARINE PAINTING

Marine painting probably has a greater reputation and tradition in Britain than anywhere else. The first great master was the Dutchman Willem van de Velde, who worked in Britain from 1672. Even works by his studio and his early 18th-century British followers, Peter Monamy and Charles Brooking, start at around £10,000, and lesser paintings sell for several thousand pounds.

Depictions of the great naval battles of the Napoleonic Wars by such artists as Dominic Seres, Nicholas Pocock and Thomas Luny, are very popular, with prices of £30,000 or more. Ordinary shipping scenes generally sell for a few thousand pounds while, Turner apart, scenes of storm, shipwreck and disaster generally fetch only a fraction of these prices.

Shipping scenes of the mid to late 19th century generally sell for £1000 to £10,000, but provincial ship portraits may fetch less and outstanding individuals or certain schools of marine painting will fetch more.

All paintings are oil on canvas unless stated otherwise.

Drawings

Affordable works by great names are on offer to collectors who hunt out drawings, many of them made as studies for oil paintings.

Circle of Gaetano Gandolfi, study of a female head; black chalk; Italian, late 18thC; 9½ × 7¼ in (24.1 × 18.4 cm). Although the paper suffers from foxing, this is a strong and lively study.
£1500-£2500

Nicolas Lancret, lady dancing; red chalk; c.1730; 7¾ × 7 in (19.7 × 17.8 cm). French red chalk drawings are sought after and this study is for a known painting.
£4000-£6000

Salvator Rosa, two figures; ink and wash; Italian, 1640s; 3¼ × 4 in (82 × 100 mm). Drawings by this Baroque master are surprisingly cheap.
£1000-£1500

Jan van Goyen, winter scene; black chalk and grey wash; Dutch, 1631; 4¼ × 7⅓ in (10.8 × 18.6 cm). Van Goyen's charming drawings typify the Dutch interest in everyday life.
£5000-£7000

FASCINATING INSIGHTS into an artist's creative process are given by preparatory drawings, which sell for a fraction of the price of paintings by the same hand.

Old Master drawings – those by European artists of the 14th to late 18th centuries – are particularly attractive and use a wide variety of media and techniques. Rembrandt in the 17th century, for example, used pen and ink to capture informal scenes with an incredible boldness and spontaneity. His drawings are expensive, but other Dutch landscape and genre scenes can be found from £500.

Metalpoint, graphite pencil, charcoal and red, white and black chalks were also used. Red chalk drawings are particularly popular with collectors and command high prices. The superb figure drawings by the French early 18th-century artist Antoine Watteau sell for more than £50,000, but less sensitive red chalk drawings by his followers, such as Lancret and Pater, fetch much lower sums.

In the mid-18th century, pastels appealed to a taste for soft, pretty colours and were used in particular for portraits with a degree of finish akin to oil paintings. Watercolour and body colour were frequently used together

Henry Fuseli, 'Massacre of the Innocents'; pencil, brown ink and wash; 1770-8; 9¾ × 14¾ in (24.7 × 37.5 cm). This drawing came from an album bought in the 1970s, but only recently did the owner discover its importance: all the drawings were by Fuseli and it was compiled by a daughter of one of the artist's patrons.
£20,000-£30,000

with pen and ink for design and for botanical drawings (see also p. 328).

An identified hand – especially that of a major artist – will increase a drawing's value. When research demotes a work to the 'school of' a name rather than the master himself, prices tumble (as has happened recently with many 'Rembrandts'). However, the converse also applies and there are opportunities for good buys among anonymous drawings. Many artists and their followers have distinctive styles and you may be able to narrow an attribution down to a specific country, period and circle of artists.

If a drawing can be identified as a preparatory work for a known painting, this will increase its value. Subject matter is also

important: female nudes, for example, are currently more popular than religious works.

A good provenance can enhance value: many drawings passed from collector to collector – themselves often artists – and bear identifiable stamps. Damage reduces value, although some wear can be expected. When buying, always remove a drawing from a glass frame to check against reproductions. Copies made by early printing techniques are harder to spot than modern photomechanical reproductions (betrayed by a dot screen), but have a flatter quality than a drawing.

Watercolours

*A speciality of the British school in
the 18th and 19th centuries,
watercolours provide enormous
choice for the collector today.*

*Francis Towne, 'Arthur's Seat, Edinburgh';
pencil and watercolour; 1811; 6¾ × 10 in
(17.1 × 25.4 cm). The colours are similar to
the late 18thC, but Towne's way of outlining
flat areas of colour is unusual. His dramatic
mountain views attract higher prices.*
£6000-£8000

IN THE 18TH CENTURY, British artists began
to create watercolours as completed works
in their own right (rather than as studies
for oil paintings). The best exponents made
the most of watercolour's particular qualities –
its translucency and its suitability for captur-
ing atmosphere, weather and so on. Today
you can start a worthwhile collection with
only a few hundred pounds.

The 18th-century watercolourists most
often combined pen and ink drawing with
watercolour – like a colouring-in process that
evolved from the tinted drawings of the first
half of the century. The 'classic' watercolour
period, of about 1790-1840, favoured pure
watercolour applied more boldly in layers
of thin washes, with only minimal pencil
under-drawing. The only white is the
colour of the paper. Later Victorian
watercolours tend to be more brightly
coloured and heavily painted, often
with the use of opaque body colour
(gouache) or white heightening.

*J.M.W. Turner, 'Farnley Hall
from above'; watercolour;
c.1810-20; 11⅛ × 15⅝ in
(28.2 × 39.7 cm). Turner's
watercolours range from quick
sketches to highly detailed works
such as this. Farnley Hall in
Yorkshire was the home of Walter
Fawkes, one of his main patrons.*
£80,000-£100,000

LANDSCAPE AND GENRE

Landscape evolved over the 18th
century from topographical drawings
through idealised 'Picturesque' views
to the dramatic Romantic style of the
early 19th century. But topographical
drawings continued to be made, ranging from
country mansions to the new spas and the
grand town halls of industrial cities.

At the end of the 18th century and in the
first half of the 19th, artists such as John
Robert Cozens, John Sell Cotman, Thomas
Girtin, J.M.W. Turner, David Cox and Peter
De Wint – great masters of British watercolour – executed both gentle rural scenes and
wild mountain landscapes at home and
abroad. Works by Turner and Girtin may
reach six figures at auction. However, while
the best landscapes by other masters such as
Cox and De Wint fetch over £10,000, their
minor works – small views of unknown spots
or sketchbook studies – start at around £1000.

Many artists were also teachers. Watercolour painting was a polite accomplishment
for ladies and gentlemen, and almost a
requirement for those on the Grand Tour.
Good watercolours by amateurs can still be
found from around £300, with less proficient

*Mountain scene; watercolour; c.1820;
7 × 13⅜ in (17.8 × 34 cm). This is
probably by a pupil of John Varley, who is
known for his standardised compositions.*
£300-£400

*Bishop Walter John Trower, continental lake scene;
pen and ink; c.1850; 6⅞ × 10¼ in (17.5 × 26 cm).
Like much amateur work, Trower's looks attractive
but old-fashioned for its date.*
£75-£90

but sometimes charming examples or monochrome drawings selling for well below this.

In the late Victorian period, the passion for
dramatic landscapes declined in favour of
pretty cottage gardens or pastoral scenes with
cottages and children. Prices for these works
have shot up in the past few years and in many
cases they are now more expensive than early
19th-century pieces – a reversal of the situation a few years ago. The prettiest works by
Myles Birket Foster and Helen Allingham
frequently fetch more than £10,000. Watercolours by amateurs or the many members of
the Stannard family will be rather cheaper,
but are often highly sentimental.

Townscapes were also popular subjects
with artists and amateur watercolourists in the

*Helen Allingham, 'Springtime'; watercolour
and body colour; c.1890; 8½ × 10¼ in
(21.6 × 26 cm). Allingham epitomises late 19thC
taste for cottages rather than mountains and is very
popular. Sketchier examples are cheaper.*
£7000-£10,000

Albert Strange, 'Harbour View, Scarborough'; watercolour and body colour; c.1890; 15¾ × 22⅞ in (40 × 58 cm). This is a typical late 19thC marine watercolour, but cheaper than works by contemporaries such as W.L. Wyllie.
£500-£750

George Goodwin Kilburne, 'Malade imaginaire'; watercolour and body colour; c.1880; 10½ × 14½ in (26.7 × 36.8 cm). Kilburne's domestic interiors and historical scenes are common on the market today.
£1500-£2500

William Henry Hunt, still life; watercolour; c.1840-60; 9½ × 13 in (24 × 33 cm). Hunt is known for his fine stipple technique, his skill at effects such as the sheen on the plum, and for compositions with nests – hence his nickname 'Bird's-nest' Hunt.
£2000-£4000

Thomas Rowlandson, 'A Dutch academy'; ink and watercolour; 1780s/90s; 7¼ × 11 in (18.4 × 28 cm). Rowlandson is famous for bawdy social satire; here he takes on the art world.
£8000-£10,000

Myles Birket Foster, 'Vegetable market, Venice'; watercolour; c.1850-70; 22 × 18¾ in (56 × 47.6 cm). Better known for his views of an idyllic rural life, Foster here uses ever-popular Venice for a lively genre scene.
£4000-£6000

Arthur Rackham, 'Tattercoats dancing while the Gooseherd pipes'; ink and watercolour; c.1918; 10½ × 7½ in (26.7 × 19.1 cm). This is an illustration for 'English Fairy Tales'.
£6000-£8000

19th century. Many of these, particularly by artists such as Samuel Prout and William Callow, are continental scenes with the lively added touch of little figures.

Narrative and genre painting, by Francis Wheatley and other artists, was popular in the late 18th century. It became popular again – in increasingly nostalgic form – in the Victorian era, when it tended to merge with landscape.

Works by the 'Orientalists' from travels in the Middle East are now also in great demand. David Roberts, Edward Lear and others did topographical studies, while John Frederick Lewis captured the mystique of the harem. Others went even farther afield – William Daniell to India at the start of the 19th century, Alfred East to Japan at the end.

ILLUSTRATION AND CARICATURE

Little original artwork for book illustrations survives from before the late 18th century. Work for popular children's books such as the elaborate watercolours of Arthur Rackham (see p. 337) are sought after and start at around £3000, but well-done illustrations for now obscure Victorian novels are much cheaper.

Caricatures are another popular field. In the 18th and 19th centuries, Thomas Rowlandson poked fun at the upper classes and was a prolific watercolourist as well as a printmaker (see p. 334); his works appear regularly in the salerooms. Originals of illustrations for 19th-century issues of *Punch* are also collectable, as, increasingly, are those by the leading 20th-century newspaper cartoonists.

ADVICE TO BUYERS

Prices can vary enormously for works by the same artist, since they depend not only on who the artist is, but also on fashion, subject matter or location, the scale and complexity of the work, and condition. The latter is always important, as watercolour pigments – especially greens and blues – fade with exposure to bright sunlight. Other common faults to watch out for are 'foxing' – small brown spots caused by damp – and brown marks or browning of the paper from acid mounts. Both these can be improved by paper conservators, but fading cannot. It is fading that has led to the common misconception that watercolours are pale. In fact, every skilled watercolourist achieved a balance between translucency and rich colours.

Sculpture

Though a leading art form since antiquity, sculpture reached the peak of its popularity, be it of animals or heroes, only in the 19th century.

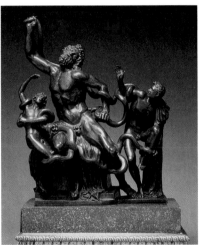

Rare bronze and marble copy of the Roman bronze of Laocoon and his sons; 18thC; 14¼ in (36.8 cm) high. Victorian copies are commoner.
£40,000-£60,000; Victorian: £3000-£4000

'The Sluggard' by Lord Leighton; 1890; 20½ in (52 cm) high. Leighton's stretching figure is one of the best known of the English New School sculptures.
£3000-£5000

Cold-painted Austrian bronzes; c.1900; tallest 11¾ in (29.8 cm) high. The temple group (left) has a sprung curtain revealing a naked girl inside.
£1100-£1400

Perseus with his winged horse, Pegasus, and the head of the vanquished Medusa; c.1880; 31½ in (80 cm) high. This model by the French sculptor Emile Picault is cast in several sizes. Prices are significantly higher for this large sized cast.
£6000-£8000

Striding lion animalier sculpture by Antoine-Louis Barye; c.1850; 8¾ in (22.2 cm) high. Values of casts vary according to the quality, patina and date of casting.
£1000-£2000

MARBLE AND BRONZE have been the most favoured media for sculpture ever since the Renaissance. Long collected by connoisseurs, sculpture reached the middle classes in the 19th century, when new demand fuelled a vast increase in bronze production. Much aped Classical models, but this period also saw the rise of naturalism. However, some of the most collectable pieces are highly stylised 1920s Art Deco figures.

BRONZE AND OTHER METALS

Bronze is a relatively inexpensive alloy – both durable and suitable for casting fine detail. Bronze sculptures are cast by the 'lost wax' process or by casting in sand, and are finished by hand. The bronze is treated to give it a particular surface finish and colour – the patina. The different patinas favoured during different periods provide a clue to a piece's date.

Other materials used for figures include cast iron and spelter. Although both are often treated to give an imitation of bronze, they are generally of lower quality and become corroded with age.

In both the 18th and 19th centuries bronzes, especially copies of Classical antiquities, were fashionable as home decorations. Often acquired on the Grand Tour, they were cast from Greek or Roman museum pieces. Typical subjects are the Venus de Milo, the Spinero or seated boy pulling a thorn from his foot, and the Discus Thrower. Most such bronzes found today date from the second half of the 19th century and can be difficult to tell apart from 17th or 18th-century bronzes worth several times as much.

Copies of famous Renaissance sculptures, such as the bronzes of Giambologna, and of 18th-century works, were also very popular in the 19th century and are still common. In addition, there were many fine sculptors producing original works in Classical style, often in large editions and various sizes. Favoured subjects included idealised figures from Classical mythology and allegorical figures in symbolic poses.

ANIMALIER BRONZES

Sculptures of animals ('animaliers') are as popular with collectors today as they were in Victorian times. Their name comes from *Les Animaliers*, a group of French sculptors who specialised in portraying animals and whose leader was Antoine-Louis Barye. His distinctive, sensitive studies are keenly sought after. Most are taken direct from nature and often

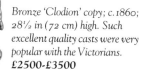

'Autumn dancer' by Ferdinand Priess; c.1925; 14 in (35.5 cm) high. Such bronze and ivory Art Deco figures are highly collectable.
£5000-£7000

Cold-painted spelter Nubian serving girl; c.1880; 57 in (1.44 m) high. Spelter can become pitted and brittle with age.
£6000-£7000

Terracotta bust by Albert Carrier Belleuse; c.1870; 29¾ in (75.5 cm) high. The fragile nature of terracotta makes restoration likely.
£3000-£5000

White marble bust of Lord Byron by Edward Hodges Baily; 1826; 29½ in (75 cm) high. Baily was an influential figure in early 19thC sculpture, producing mainly portrait busts.
£7000-£10,000

Bronze 'Clodion' copy; c.1860; 28½ in (72 cm) high. Such excellent quality casts were very popular with the Victorians.
£2500-£3500

Resin cast plaque; 20thC; 11 in (28 cm) diameter. This is a copy of an 18thC Bouchardon original.
£50-£80

painted rather than patinated finish. They are amusing and highly sought after by collectors. Values vary according to the size and subject but a small bird or dog might sell for £500 and a lifesize cockerel for as much as £2500.

Languid, slender female figures from the Art Nouveau period are very collectable. Works by sought-after artists such as the Moreau brothers (Auguste, Hippolyte and Louis), Raoul Larche and Agathon Leonard fetch £5000 up.

Even more popular are the highly decorative Art Deco sculptures of the 1920s and 30s. Mixed-media figures of bronze and ivory or bronze and marble are in particular demand and can sell for three times the price of the same model in bronze or ivory alone. Beware of modern mass-produced cold-cast bronze and plastic copies; the face and fingers tend to be rather pinched.

Members of the English New Sculpture movement of the 1880s – among them Lord Leighton, George Frampton, Alfred Drury and Alfred Stevens – also produced small works. Editions were smaller than those of continental contemporaries, so prices can be high: £15,000-£20,000 for a cast of Gilbert's 'Perseus Arming', for example.

MARBLE AND TERRACOTTA

In the 18th and 19th centuries it was fashionable to have portrait busts of the family in marble or bronze, again often executed in Rome and often in Classical style. Values depend on subject as well as artist – a bust of Byron by Edward Hodges Baily (the sculptor of Nelson's Column in Trafalgar Square) will fetch up to £10,000 today, but an unknown elderly Victorian gentleman by the same artist as little as £1000. Busts of historical figures such as Shakespeare and Newton were also popular, as were exotic blackamoors in black and coloured marble, and marble copies of famous Classical figures and groups.

Terracotta was particularly popular as a sculpture medium in the 18th century. An original 18th-century terracotta by Claude Michel Clodion of a bacchante girl might make £100,000 at auction, but a 19th-century terracotta copy might fetch only £1000. Bronze casts of Clodion's work were made in abundance during the 19th century.

Terracotta copies were always cast from a mould, but vary in quality depending on the extent of hand-finishing. Points to look for include crisp hair and fingernails. If the detail is rounded and smooth, the piece has not had a great deal of hand-modelling.

feature quite violent subjects, such as lions hunting or scenes of animal combat. Another popular animalier sculptor was Pierre-Jules Mêne, who concentrated more on domestic animals. His work was cast in large numbers.

Subject matter has an important influence on price. For instance, a superb cast by Barye of a tiger devouring an antelope could sell at auction for £3000 while a similar-sized bronze of his 'Turkish Horse' may fetch £20,000. Similarly, a Mêne study of a goat makes £300-£500, whereas his group 'Whippets at Play' sells for £1500. Collectors favour casts that are light in weight with fine detailing and a rich, dark brown patina. Handling (or 'rubbing')

over the years wears the patina, and if not too severe this can greatly enhance a piece.

Most animalier bronzes are signed with the artist's name or initials, and may also have a foundry mark. These marks are usually found on the top or side of the base, but rarely on the sculpture itself. Beware of recent poor-quality copies cast from earlier bronzes.

OTHER BRONZES

Among other popular sculptures are cold-painted Austrian bronzes dating from about 1900. Originally sold as souvenirs, they lack any great artistic merit but are high-quality castings, about 2-12 in (5-30 cm) tall, with a

Prints

Often a much cheaper alternative to paintings, prints enable the collector on a modest budget to own original works by famous artists.

PRINTMAKING DEVELOPED as a way of making multiple impressions of popular images such as holy scenes, pictures of saints and playing cards. Artists soon saw its potential for reproducing works of art, and publishers for book illustration. The earliest centres in Europe were in 15th-century Germany, the Netherlands and Italy, but there is a longer history in the East (see box, p. 335).

Traditionally, an impression is made on paper from a matrix, such as wood, copper or limestone. Each impression is an 'original', but as just one of a number of more or less identical prints, often costs less than a unique

WOODCUT *The wood is cut away leaving the design to be printed standing out in relief. The result can be very bold.*

ENGRAVING *The lines are sharply defined and even, tailing off to elegant points. Cross-hatching is used for tonal areas.*

ETCHING *Etching can produce extremely fine, delicate lines and much freer, more sketchy effects than engraving.*

AQUATINT *A network of fine lines like tiny crazy paving gives a tonal effect. Different strengths of tone allow dramatic contrasts.*

DRYPOINT *There is a characteristic smudgy look to the line, known as the 'burr' – this wears down on later impressions.*

LITHOGRAPHY *Using the repulsion between grease and water, the print has a flat, smooth quality. Here it resembles crayon.*

work. Different techniques of printmaking produce prints with distinctive individual characteristics, and with practice you can identify the processes used (see below left).

A further distinction is made between prints made by skilled craftsmen to reproduce paintings or designs originated in another medium and original works of art only ever intended to be prints. Many famous artists, such as Dürer, Rembrandt, Goya and Picasso, were also superb original printmakers.

Interest in all printmaking techniques grew in the late 19th century in France, and early this century in Britain and Germany. Muirhead Bone, Eric Gill, Paul Nash and C.R.W. Nevinson are just a few of the British artists who took up printmaking and whose works fetch from around £50 up to £1000 today.

PRINTS FROM WOOD

The earliest European prints were made from woodblocks, either as woodcuts or as wood engravings. Both techniques, known as relief

Albrecht Dürer, 'The Flight into Egypt'; woodcut; c.1503; 11¾ × 8¼ in (29.8 × 21 cm). This is an early proof; prints from the 1511 edition with text on the back fetch around £1000; later prints cost less.
£2000-£3000

Karl Schmidt-Rottluff, 'Kopf'; signed woodcut; 1913; 8 × 6 in (20.3 × 15.2 cm). The artist was a member of Die Brücke.
£1000-£2000; unsigned: £300-£500

prints, can produce very bold-looking images.

In woodcuts, the background is cut away, leaving the lines of the design standing proud to receive the ink. The resulting print can be reminiscent of a pen and ink drawing. Woodcuts from the late 15th and early 16th centuries by German artist Dürer today sell for £500-£5000 at auction. There was a woodcut revival in the early 20th century, notably by the German Expressionist group Die Brücke.

Wood engraving, invented in the 18th century, was used largely for book illustration – for example, Thomas Bewick's birds. In contrast to woodcuts, the lines of the design are engraved into the surface of the block, so that when it is printed they stand out in white against the black background.

PRINTS FROM METAL

The various techniques on copper – line engraving, stipple engraving, mezzotint engraving, etching, aquatint and drypoint – are all printed on the same type of 'intaglio' press, from the Italian *intagliare* (to engrave).

In engraving, the design is cut into the plate with a burin – a tool with a triangular cross-section – resulting in V-shaped grooves that print as sharply defined lines which tail off in an elegant point. The first copperplate engravings appeared in the second half of the 15th century. By the early 16th century, artists had recognised the advantages of

Stanley Anderson, 'The Bookseller'; engraving; c.1935; 7 × 5⅞ in (17.8 × 15 cm). Anderson and Robert Austin revived line engraving as an original medium in Britain in the 1920s.
£200-£300

MAPS
Beauty and Practicality

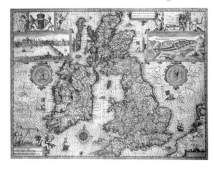

John Speed's 'carte à figure' of Britain with panoramas of London and Edinburgh; 1611; 12 × 18 in (30.5 × 45.7 cm). The plates were engraved in Holland; the colouring is later.
£1200

THE EARLIEST PRINTED MAPS, produced in Italy and Germany at the end of the 15th century, were based on those of the Egyptian geographer Ptolemy drawn some 1500 years earlier. Each successive generation of mapmakers copied or reprinted earlier plates as well as creating new up-to-date maps of their own. Mapmakers from early times incorporated topographical and allegorical details – such as town plans or regional costumes – and these *cartes à figures* reached their decorative peak in the 17th century.

Early European maps were printed in black and hand-coloured – although British atlases were uncoloured. Among the finest are maps from Holland painted by specialist map colourists. Decoration and hand-colouring disappeared in the mid-19th century.

distributing their images as prints. In Italy, Raphael, for instance, did not make his own prints but worked with engraver Marcantonio Raimondi. Engravings by Raimondi and his followers sell today for £300-£3000.

In the 19th century, steel plates came into use for reproductive engravings. As steel is virtually indestructible, vast numbers of impressions could be made for use in books. Prices for these are low, starting around £1, but the artistic quality is often poor.

The mezzotint technique was developed by engravers in the mid-17th century. It allows painterly chiaroscuro (light and dark) effects and there are no lines, only varying degrees of tone. It flourished in Britain in the 18th century and was mainly used to reproduce oil paintings. Monochrome examples sell for £100 up to £1000, coloured genre mezzotints for about twice as much.

Stipple engraving was used in the late 18th century as another way of creating continuous tone. The Italian Francesco Bartolozzi was the

Rembrandt, 'The Turbaned Soldier on Horseback'; etching; c.1632; 3¼ × 2¼ in (82 × 57 mm). This is a scarce print: unlike many Rembrandt etchings, it was not reprinted after his death.
£3000-£5000

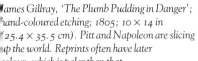

ames Gillray, 'The Plumb Pudding in Danger'; hand-coloured etching; 1805; 10 × 14 in (25.4 × 35.5 cm). Pitt and Napoleon are slicing up the world. Reprints often have later colour, which is paler than that of the early 19thC.
£200-£500

Agostino Carracci, 'Mercury and the Three Graces'; engraving after Tintoretto; 1589; 7⅞ × 10¼ in (20 × 26 cm).
£500-£1500, depending on age, condition and quality

Francisco Goya, 'Tal Para Qual' (Two of a Kind) from 'Los Caprichos'; etching with aquatint, c.1796; 7⅞ × 5⅞ in (20 × 15 cm). The tonal contrasts of aquatint are ideal for dramatic images. This is from the valuable first edition.
£1000-£1500

leading practitioner in Britain, producing portraits, genre and decorative subjects after painters such as Reynolds and Zucarelli. Monochrome examples fetch £50-£500.

The 17th century in Holland, France, Italy and even Britain (where printmaking was established later than on the Continent) was a golden age of original etching. Etching – in which the design is drawn with a fine point in an acid-resistant coating and the lines then cut into the plate with acid – gives freer lines than engraving. Some Dutch 17th-century etchings cost only £100, but those by Rembrandt range from around £1000 to over £500,000.

Except in Italy, where original etching continued, most 18th and early 19th-century European prints reproduced paintings and drawings. Caricatures were an exception; original comic engravings by artists such as Rowlandson, Gillray and the Cruikshanks (see p.48) remain, at £30-£800, still modestly priced.

Aquatint is a method of creating areas of continuous tone in an etching, similar to an ink or water-colour wash. In France and Britain, aquatint, often with an etched out-line, supplanted mezzotint and stipple in the early 19th century. Quality, hand-coloured aquatints of sporting, botanical, military or topographical subjects can fetch £500-£2000, but beware of late impressions and later lithographic facsimiles.

Although often used on the same plate as etching, drypoint is an engraving process, as the artist works directly on the copper. On the first few impressions it gives the desirable rich, velvety line, known as the 'burr'. Drypoint was used on its own by Rembrandt and his followers, and in the late 19th and early 20th centuries. Recent impressions of drypoints by French Impressionist Renoir fetch £50 or so, but the burr has gone; they are ghosts beside the few vivid prints made in his lifetime.

OTHER TECHNIQUES

In lithography, the artist does not cut into the surface of the matrix as in relief and intaglio prints, but draws with a greasy lithographic crayon on a smooth limestone block or a zinc plate. The result is a spontaneous effect close to drawing on paper. The newly invented technique was adopted by French Romantic artists in the early 19th century. It revolutionised the humorous press as it was quick, economical and permitted huge editions.

Colour lithography uses a separate stone for each colour and took off in Paris in the 1890s

Henry Alken, 'Fishing in a Punt'; hand-coloured etching with aquatint, by John Clark; 1820; 8 × 12 in (20.3 × 30.5 cm). Check the paper: early impressions are on Whatman paper watermarked with its date. **£1000-£1500**
Late impression: £100-£500

French optical print of 'Chiswick Villa'; hand-coloured etching and engraving; c.1750; 11 × 17 in (28 × 43.2 cm). This is a perspective print intended to be viewed through a 'zograscope', which reverses and magnifies the image to give a three-dimensional effect. **£100-£300**

Engraving from 'The Architectural Antiquities of Great Britain' published by John Britton; 1814; paper 10¾ × 8½ in (27.3 × 21.6 cm). This topographical plate has been broken from a book. **£10-£15**

Louis Legrand, 'Titi, ma petite chatte bien aimée'; drypoint, edition of 50; 1912; 8 × 6½ in (20.3 × 16.5 cm). French artist Legrand's subjects are usually women, but prints of cats are very collectable. **£200-£500**

or posters. But watch out for colour-printed photo-lithographic reproductions of paintings. Such 'prints' have no collector's value and can usually be detected with a magnifying glass: the image is broken into tiny dots in the same way as the illustrations in this book.

Screen printing is a stencil process which came into use in the early 20th century for advertising and packaging. It became popular with 1960s Pop Artists, such as Andy Warhol.

ADVICE TO BUYERS

The value of prints can be greatly affected by fashion, but one by a famous name will almost always be more valuable than one by a lesser or unknown artist, and a print in good condition or on good paper will be worth more than one with tears, repairs or discoloration. Early impressions, made in the artist's lifetime, will be fresher and worth more than later printings from the same plate, as a plate tends to wear and lose detail with time.

The margins of many Old Master prints were trimmed for mounting and this can detract from their value, particularly if it cuts into the image or removes lettering. Modern prints are usually preferred with margins. The artist's signature and the edition number marked in pencil in the margin were a late 19th-century innovation.

English colour stipple engraving; c.1795; 12 × 8 in (30.5 × 20.3 cm); in period frame. The colours were applied to a single plate, unlike colour lithographs which are printed from multiple stones.
£300-£500
Trimmed and unframed: £100-£120

John Raphael Smith, mezzotint after Reynolds's 'Mademoiselle Baccelli'; c.1790; 13⅞ × 9⅞ in (35.1 × 25 cm). Mezzotint is ideal for reproducing oil paintings. Condition affects value.
£100-£500

Henri de Toulouse-Lautrec, 'Le Revue blanche'; colour lithograph; 1895; 50½ × 36¾ in (128.2 × 93.3 cm). Lautrec was inspired by Japanese prints.
£14,000-£18,000
Before lettering: £20,000-£25,000

Honoré Daumier, lithograph from a series published in 'La Caricature'; 1839; 7 × 9¾ in (17.8 × 24.7 cm).
£100-£300
With text on back: £10-£20

JAPANESE WOODBLOCK PRINTS
Images of the Floating World

WHEN JAPANESE GOODS started to reach the West in the 1860s, many were wrapped in paper printed with coloured pictures of a type never seen before in Europe. The images had little sign of linear perspective, but used blocks of patterns, faces, bodies, backgrounds and foregrounds in apparent, but actually carefully considered, confusion.

The technique of monochrome woodblock printing goes back a thousand years in China and Japan; Japanese coloured prints date from the 17th century. But only in the 18th century did brightly coloured prints become popular, depicting scenes of everyday life, actors and erotica – *ukiyo-e*, 'the floating world'. The artists who painted the originals onto the block signed their name and often included a title, a number (if it was part of a series), the publisher's mark and a censor's seal.

The prints most desirable to today's collectors are those from the end of the 18th century by such artists as Kitagawa Utamaro, Toshusai Sharaku and Katsukawa Shunsei. These can fetch up to £100,000 if they are rare and in first-class condition. Desirable 19th-century prints include Katsushika Hokusai's *Thirty-six Views of Fuji* and views of Japan by Ando Hiroshige.

Toyokuni III, 'Dancers on Stage'; woodblock print from 'The 12 Months'; c.1854; 9½ × 14 in (24.1 × 35.6 cm). This impression is slightly faded and bruised.
£10-£15; if perfect: £100-£150

Books

From modern first editions to tales of discovery, the scope for the book collector is enormous. Whatever your interest or depth of pocket, there are sure to be books to fit.

Mary Eales's 'Receipts' (recipes); 1733. Condition affects value – and the condition of cookery books is often poor due to their regular use in the kitchen. **£200**

First editions of the 20thC. The Agatha Christie, published 1926, is worth around £200 despite not having its dust jacket. Dust jackets were often thrown away, hence the rarity and value of books with jackets. **£10-£1000 each**

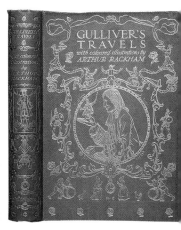

Jonathan Swift's 'Gulliver's Travels'; 20thC. The value lies in Arthur Rackham's illustrations. **£20-£80**

Beatrix Potter first editions. The date, 1908, printed at the foot of the title page indicates that this copy of 'The Tale of Jemima Puddle-Duck' is indeed a first edition. **£30-£150 each**

Charles Dickens's 'Pickwick Papers' title page; 1837. Many of Dickens's works are quite common as his books sold so well. Leather-bound editions such as this can vary greatly in price. **£30-£300**

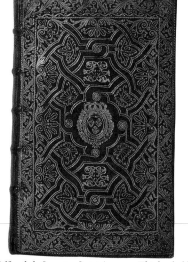

'Office de la Semaine Sainte'; 1732. This book, like so many of a religious nature, is not sought after for its subject matter and so is of little value in itself. The value lies in the elaborately tooled contemporary binding incorporating the arms of King Louis XV of France. **£1000**

W HAT MAKES a book valuable? The author, subject, date, binding, distinctive illustrations, provenance, rarity, edition, printing, usefulness – or any combination of these – are all factors in determining the value of a volume; but above all, the book and its dust jacket must be complete and in good condition.

Generally, the first edition of a book is more collectable than a later one, which is often of little or no value. First editions can be hard to identify. A date at the foot of the title page often suggests a first edition but it should not be confused with the copyright date. Later editions of a book will often bear on the title page or its reverse the words 'reprinted', or 'new', 'revised' or 'second' edition.

Among the more valuable 20th-century fiction writers to look for are Joseph Conrad, D.H. Lawrence, James Joyce, T.S. Eliot,

Evelyn Waugh (*Black Mischief*, 1932, £150 *Brideshead Revisited*, 1945, £40) and Graham Greene (a good 1932 copy of *Stamboul Train* with its dust jacket is worth about £1000, a second edition only £30; *Our Man in Havana* first edition 1958, £25).

More recent writers whose first editions are now collected include John Le Carré (*The Spy who came in from the Cold*, £150) and John Fowles (*The Collector*, £130; *The French Lieutenant's Woman*, £35). The list is endless but beware: many of the later novels by all these authors are extremely common even in first editions and fetch very little.

ILLUSTRATED FICTION

One interesting and sought-after field is illustrated books. These are usually fictional works (often children's stories, but not necessarily so) with imaginative illustrations by

Pages showing topographical plate from 'Westmorland, Cumberland, Durham and Northumberland' by Thomas Rose. Various editions were published in the 1830s with numerous engraved plates.
£200-£250

Thomas Bewick's 'History of British Birds', two volumes, 1797-1804 (left); and John Gould's 'The Birds of Australia', eight volumes, 1840-69. The latter contains 681 large hand-coloured lithographs.
Left: £50-£300
Right: £200,000 (complete)

Page from 'Kate Greenaway's Book of Games', 1889. Kate Greenaway illustrated many children's books during the last quarter of the 19thC.
£10-£75 (complete)

'Personal Narrative of a Pilgrimage to El-Medinah and Meccah' by Richard Burton; three volumes; fine first edition, 1855-6. A set in average condition might be worth only £1000.
£2000

Beatrix Potter books, can cost hundreds, even thousands of pounds for first editions. Less expensive authors include Kate Greenaway, G.A. Henty, C.S. Lewis, W.E. Johns (Biggles), Alfred Bestall (Rupert) and Enid Blyton. More recent names, such as Raymond Briggs and Roald Dahl, cost as little as £10.

TRAVEL AND TOPOGRAPHY

Although 20th century travel books are the most plentiful, many 19th-century examples can still be found. These early books can be divided broadly into 'plate' books, bought for their engraved or lithographed plates (see also p.332), and tales of travel – although the two types often overlap.

The value of a straightforward account of travel and discovery depends largely on its historical significance. Thus Gregory Blaxland's *A Journal of a Tour of Discovery across the Blue Mountains in New South Wales* (1823) – an exceedingly rare pamphlet describing the epic journey that marked the start of inland exploration in Australia – may sell at auction for over £50,000; Sir Richard Burton's *Personal Narrative of a Pilgrimage to El-Medinah and Meccah* (three volumes, 1855-6), describing his travels in disguise in Arabia, fetches £1000; while both David Livingstone's *Missionary Travels in South Africa* (1857) and Sir Henry Stanley's *How I found Livingstone* (1872) fetch about £100.

The many 20th-century travel authors worth collecting include Harry Philby (father of the spy), Sven Hedin, Aurel Stein, Captain Robert Scott, Ernest Shackleton and other Antarctic explorers. Topographical books – which relate to the history, architecture and other features of a specific town or county – can still be found in the £10-£100 range, including examples which date back as far as 1800.

NATURAL HISTORY

Plate books also have an important place in natural history, the ultimate work being John James Audubon's *Birds of America* (four volumes, 1827-38) which may fetch over £1 million at auction. Much more modest and common, but nonetheless highly popular, is the Rev F.O. Morris's *A History of British Birds* (six volumes, various editions between 1851 and 1900), which sells for around £450. The story is much the same with flower books, but these and so many other plate books are often 'broken' – that is, the plates are extracted and sold as individually framed prints.

artists such as Kay Nielsen, Arthur Rackham, Harry Clarke, Edmund Dulac, William Heath Robinson, Willy Pogany, and many others (see also p.327).

Editions in which these illustrations first appeared are the most popular; many of them were issued as limited editions of 500 or 750 copies (indicated at the beginning or end of the book), signed by the artist.

The limited signed edition of J.M. Barrie's *Peter Pan in Kensington Gardens* (1906) illustrated by Rackham is worth £850, while the ordinary unlimited, unsigned edition of the same date fetches only £150 or less. Later editions (which often have fewer plates and are smaller in size) sell for as little as £20.

Hans Christian Andersen's *Fairy Tales* have been illustrated by many artists – including Clarke, Heath Robinson, Nielsen, Rackham and Dulac – and their different

limited editions vary significantly in price, even allowing for different numbers of plates and sizes of print run. Most of these artists produced coloured illustrations, but others had their black and white illustrations, often wood-engravings, printed to a very high standard by private presses. They include Eric Gill, Blair Hughes-Stanton, John Buckland-Wright, Robert Gibbings, Agnes Miller Parker and Stephen Gooden. Much of the finest work was printed by the Golden Cockerel Press from the 1920s to 50s in limited editions. The cheapest of these start at about £50 but prices rise to £2500 for the four-volume edition of Chaucer's *Canterbury Tales* illustrated by Eric Gill (1929-31).

Classic children's books, such as Lewis Carroll's *Alice in Wonderland* illustrated by John Tenniel, A.A. Milne's Pooh books illustrated by Ernest H. Shepard, and the

Photographs

*The burgeoning of photography in the
second half of the 19th century means
that you could well find interesting
early photographs in your attic.*

KEEN COLLECTORS have been buying
photographs for about 20 years. Photographs survive in vast numbers, yet
images of great historic and aesthetic merit are
rare. The greatest 19th and 20th-century
photographers – from early figures such as
Roger Fenton and Julia Margaret Cameron
to such modern masters as Alfred Stieglitz,
Man Ray, Edward Weston,
and Irving Penn – are as
highly regarded in their
field as the greatest painters
are in theirs. So it is not
surprising that photographs
have broken the £50,000/
$100,000 barrier at auction.

Photography was inven-
ted in a number of stages,
becoming fully viable in
1839, but only widely practised from around 1850 (see
p.294). Increased commercialisation led to a
flood of photographs in the second half of
the 19th century. Few have much artistic
merit, but most are of some interest, whether as a
record of costume,
or of architecture,
famous people or his-
toric events. Many ex-
amples can be bought
for only a few pounds.

Broadly, early photo-
graphs can be divided into
so-called 'cased' images and
simple prints on paper. The
former are usually keepsake
portraits made on metal or glass and, as the
name implies, preserved in a gilt metal mount
within a leather or embossed-paper case.
Their value depends on the appeal of the
image, date, process used and the identity of
the photographer. Most sought after are early
daguerreotypes of the 1840s and 50s, made on
silvered copper plates. Prices start at around
£5 but can reach many thousands of pounds.

Most cased images are unique, being made
directly in the camera. Prints on paper were
made from a negative, so the number was not
restricted and they survive in far greater
numbers. The majority are portraits or topographical studies. 'Cartes de visite', so called

*Ambrotype portrait group; c.1870; case
4⅞ × 4 in (12.4 × 10.1 cm). Ambrotypes on
glass were the most popular cased images.*
£25-£35

*Temples near the Burning
Ghat, Benares, India, by
Samuel Bourne: albumen
print; 1860s; 9½ × 11½ in
(24 × 29.2 cm). The
Victorians loved exotic
images, above all of India.*
£300-£500

*Carte de visite
portrait of Princess Alice by
Camille Silvy; 1862; 3¾ × 2½ in
(95 × 63 mm). Silvy's work stands out among
such images and is much sought after today.*
£15-£20

*'Beach Sculpture' by John Havinden: colour
photographic print; 1937; 8 × 11 in
(20.3 × 28 cm). This early image using colour film
suggests both the Surrealist photographs of Man Ray
and the sculpture of Henry Moore.*
£1000-£1500

*Stereoscopic view; 1860s;
3⅓ × 6¾ in (8.4 × 17.1 cm). The parallel
prints give an illusion of depth when seen through a
viewer. Many examples survive. This appealing
image is by Francis Bedford.*
£20-£30

because they were the size of a calling card,
were the most popular form of 19th-century
portrait photography (see box, p.61). They
were introduced in the late 1850s and were
produced in their millions. Anonymous portraits are mostly worth little, but collectors
prize such subjects as royalty, men of letters
and theatre artists. Later came 'cabinet'
portraits, mounted on heavier card and larger-
sized at about 6½ × 4¼ in (16.5 × 10.8 cm).

The Victorians developed an enormous

appetite for photographs of places, compiling
albums of views which give an insight into the
tradition of the Grand Tour and the importance given to the British Empire. Most of
these views were taken and published by
commercial photographers. Among them was
Francis Frith, best known for his images of
Egypt and the Holy Land from the late 1850s,
but also for views of Britain and the Continent. His small prints fetch £20-£200; rarer
large ones can make over £1000. Others of
note included Francis Bedford, Samuel
Bourne (who documented the landscape,
architecture and people of India), James
Valentine and George Washington Wilson.

To be of value, a topographical photograph
must be of obvious quality, in good condition
and preferably an early view of the location.

Toys
& Dolls

Packaging of Japanese toy robot; c. 1956-60

Games and amusements

From simple building blocks to gaily painted rocking horses, battalions of tin soldiers and vintage pedal cars to spelling sets and board games, toys and games from the past are still full of enchantment.

PASSAGE OF DELIGHTS *Lowther Arcade, one of Victorian London's toy emporiums, overflows with dolls, rocking horses and other treats, in this print by Thomas Crane and Ellen Houghton.*

Boxwood and ebony chess set; late 19thC; king 3 in (76 mm) high. This 'Staunton' pattern is popular in Britain and the USA and for tournaments.
£200-£300

Snap cards; c.1910; 3½ in (89 mm) high. This set was made in Bavaria, renowned at the time for the quality of its lithographic printing in colour.
£15-£25

'The Aerial Contest'; c.1925; board 11 in (28 cm) wide. This game is, unusually, complete and in good condition.
£150-£200

ALTHOUGH GAMES like chess, draughts and mahjong have existed for thousands of years, and children's hobby horses are thought to date back to Roman times, it was only in the late 18th century that there was a great expansion of toys made specifically for children. The 19th century saw many more toys at prices the middle classes could afford, while this century has seen a growth in playthings for the under-fives.

Serious collectors demand toys that are complete, in the maker's box, in unrestored condition, but with minimal wear and tear – a tall order for something that may have been played with by generations of children.

A related area for collectors is amusement machines, which include penny-in-the-slot games, pier-head automata and fortune tellers, and pin-ball machines.

EDUCATIONAL TOYS AND BOARD GAMES

Wooden alphabet blocks covered in colour-printed paper are probably the simplest and most successful of all educational toys. Sets from the 19th century can fetch up to £150 at auction, depending on their pictures and condition. Attractive boxed spelling sets made of ivory or bone, dating from the late 18th to late 19th centuries, may reach £300.

Geographical and historical dissected puzzles date back to the 1760s (and are forerunners of the interlocking jigsaw). Most late 18th and early 19th-century games were instructional – even Snakes and Ladders originally had a moral intent. Titles ranged from the intriguing 'Before and After Marriage' to the paralysingly dull 'Chronological Tables of English History for the Instruction of Youth'. Strict households had sober 'Sunday toys' – Noah's arks and games based on the Bible or other religious texts.

The late 19th and early 20th centuries saw board games becoming less educational and more obviously fun to play. Both the colour-lithographed boxes and boards – depicting famous explorers, strange beasts, scenes from around the world, and so on – and the titles, such as 'Dangle' (a magnetic fishing game) and 'Naughty Piggiwigs', were intended to make the games appealing. Such games are now popular with collectors, especially in the United States. Prices are affected by rarity and condition, so the range is wide – £20-£500.

The games compendium containing a selection of board and card games became popular in the 19th century, mainly for adults. Common table games included dominoes, spillikins, and miniature versions of outdoor sports. They are not in much demand today and most fetch less than £100.

MODELS AND KITS

The earliest toy theatres date from the late 18th century, with printed sheets of characters and scenery from popular pantomimes and plays. Early 19th-century ones can be found in book or print shops and, as they are still being reprinted by Pollock (an original manufacturer), they fetch only £100-£300.

For would-be architects there were elaborate sets of imitation-stone building bricks. From 1880, the German firm F.D.Richter & Co made sets of various sizes, some containing over 300 bricks. They were common in Edwardian nurseries and until recently had little collectable value, but prices are now rising. The largest sets fetch up to £800, if in good condition with box and instructions.

ROCKING HORSES AND PEDAL CARS

Rocking horses reached their greatest popularity in Victorian times. The most sought after today have curved rockers rather than a flat trestle base and can fetch up to £2000. The best have well-carved features and limbs. Original paint is preferable by far to repainting even if it does show signs of wear.

By the turn of the century, the motor car already had its child-size pedal versions. Car enthusiasts pay high prices for them today – up to £20,000 for a child's racing car by Bugatti.

TOY SOLDIERS

Toy soldiers were made from the mid-18th century. Early two-dimensional cast tin soldiers from Germany have very little value today. Later soldiers are made of lead, or from the early 20th century sometimes in a composite material. They were generally sold in sets, and a complete set will always fetch more today than the same number of single soldiers.

In 1790 a Parisian firm, Lucotte, started making solid lead soldiers just over an inch (25mm) high. They have outstanding moulding and painting and are highly sought after: a complete set of 12 mounted figures in perfect condition could make £10,000. Early soldiers are marked with 'L' and 'C' on either side of a bee, those from 1825 'CBG', and those from 1875 'Mignot'. Mignot figures are of lower quality and less valuable at £300-£3000 a set.

Semi-hollow lead soldiers made from the mid-19th century in Germany, by firms such as Georg Heyde, are also collected, as are hollow cast-lead soldiers made by the British firm of William Britain (probably the most common type found in Britain). William Britain began making soldiers in 1893 and soon made zoo and farm animals as well as other models. Early soldiers made by this firm stand on a rounded base – before 1912 marked 'William Britain', after 1912 'Britain's Ltd'. After 1917 'England' was added.

Soldiers made from a mixture of sawdust, casein, kaolin and glue, date from the early 20th century. Those by O. & K. Hausser of Neustadt were marked 'Elastolin', which became a generic term for the material. Rare figures in perfect condition can fetch £300-£400.

Three toy theatres; late 19thC; central one 13½ in (34.3 cm) high. Paper theatres were popular with both children and adults and could be bought plain or coloured. The central one is by Pollock.
From left: £80-£120; £200-£250; £200-£250

Wooden Noah's ark; Germany, late 19thC; 14 in (35.6 cm) long. Prices depend on condition and number of animals.
£500-£800

'Captain Fantastic' pinball machine by Bally; 1970s; 60¾ in (1.54 m) high. Pinball machines are sought for both nostalgia value and to play.
£300-£400

Coach-built child's pedal car; c.1925; 42½ in (1.08 m) long. Fine details include opening doors, working headlamps and adjustable windscreen.
£2500-£3500

Rocking horse; c.1900; 48 in (1.22 m) long. The trestle-type was common c.1900-20 and is still relatively easy to find.
£500-£800

Group of German solid cast lead-alloy soldiers; early 20thC; 2⅓ in (60 mm) high (German No.1 size). These are unmarked.
Each figure: £20-£30

Cast-iron 'Tammany' Bank; USA, c.1890; 6 in (15.2 cm) high. Made to commemorate a bribes scandal, he drops a coin in his pocket and nods.
£100-£200

Mechanical toys

From clockwork fire engines and munching rabbits to train sets complete with level crossings, few objects bring childhood memories more vividly to life than a moving toy – or demonstrate more ingenuity by their makers.

Tin-plate van; c.1920; 7 in (17.8 cm) long. It is unusual for a toy to bear a shop's livery and often indicates it was used for promotional purposes.
£800-£1200

German tin-plate fire engine; c.1900; 7½ in (19 cm) long. In near mint condition, the toy has always been kept in its original box, which greatly boosts its value.
£1000-£1500

Märklin stationary steam engine; 1915-25; 20 in (51 cm) wide. Popular in the age before batteries, it used water and a spirit burner to make steam for powering accessories.
£800-£1200

Märklin tin-plate station; c.1904; 12 in (30.5 cm) high; figures c.1920. This small, finely detailed station is accompanied by French street lamps.
Set: £500-£800

German tin-plate saloon car; c.1930; 14 in (35.5 cm) long. Battery-operated headlamps and a uniformed driver are just two of the details that boost the value of this car.
£400-£600

French tin-plate train; c.1890; 12½ in (31.7 cm) long. This clockwork train set was designed to run on the floor, before the widespread use of tracks.
£1200-£1800

S INCE MECHANICAL TOYS were first made in the last century, the best have accurately mirrored contemporary transport – from coaches to trams, trains to spacecraft. In some cases, such as Citroën cars, the manufacturers were even the same. Most collectors tend to specialise in a particular vehicle, period, or the work of one toymaker.

LEADING MAKERS

German manufacturers were the first to make mechanically powered toys, beginning in the mid-19th century. Early toys were usually handmade of tin plate, fitted with a clockwork mechanism for winding, and hand-painted or transfer-printed. Because of the large amount of work done by hand, prices were high – the equivalent of several hundred pounds now.

Today, the most sought after 19th-century German mechanical toys are by the manufacturers Bing, Ernst Plank, Märklin, Georges Carette, S. Günthermann, Jean Schoenner

and Doll & Cie. (For trademarks see p.521.)

The introduction around 1900 of machine moulding and offset lithography (allowing colour printing straight onto metal) meant that toys could be made more cheaply and in larger quantities. French makers such as CIJ (Compagnie Industrielle des Jouets), Citroën and JEP (Jouets en Paris) started to rival German companies, and in Britain Frank Hornby (see p.346), Bassett-Lowke, Wells, Brimtoy, Lines Brothers and Chad Valley started making toys.

In the 1920s, the Japanese began copying European toys and exporting them at cheaper prices. Some of their best products were 1950s American cars. In the 1960s, Japan led the field with robots and space toys.

TOY TRAINS

Hornby model railway layouts have been popular in Britain since the 1930s. The earliest toy trains date from the 19th century,

well before Hornby started his company, and were meant to run on the floor. In the 1880s, track was introduced, and by about 1900 it was made in several different widths. In the 1930s the most widely used track was H0 or 00 ('Dublo') gauge (0.65 in; 16.5 mm), gauge 0 (1.4 in; 35 mm), gauge I (1.9 in; 48 mm) and gauge II (2.1 in; 54 mm). Value has little to do with size, however: one particular 00 gauge Märklin locomotive can sell at auction for £15,000-£18,000, while gauge I trains can be found for under £500.

Originally, toy engines were only loosely modelled on real trains. But as time passed, increasingly accurate models were brought out, until in the late 1930s models based on full-sized trains such as the *Cock o' the North*, *Coronation* and *Princess Elizabeth* appeared. Various propulsion methods were used, including steam, clockwork and electricity.

It is important to keep a locomotive and its tender together. Track *(continued p.344)*

An Expert Examines

HILARY KAY TEST DRIVES A TIN-PLATE TOY CAR

'WHATEVER VALUES *a saleroom might put on them now, all toys began as children's playthings. So for one to survive in mint condition as long as I think this one has, is something of a miracle.*

As soon as the car emerges from its box, which has been its garage for all its life, you can tell it's something special. It's not too difficult to make a guess at the date. Until really quite recently, toy vehicles always represented contemporary full-size versions that children saw every day; that was part of their appeal. Now, this looks exactly like the sort of car that was seen on the roads before the First World War – say, about 1910. Which is about the date this car was made.

The tin-plate car, still with its original maker's box

To get a more exact idea of the car's origins, you should look for a trademark. In this case, there, underneath, are the letters 'GBN', the

mark of Gebrüder Bing of Nuremberg, one of the great names in the golden age of German toymaking between 1900 and 1914. A glance at a specialist catalogue would show that this model actually dates from 1908.

It's essential to make a really close check for completeness and condition. In spite of a few scratches, the quality of the tin plate is first class and the clockwork motor is still there. It doesn't matter whether this works or not, so long as it's complete. The tyres too are important. On lesser or later toys, they would be painted, but these are rubber. True, they're flattened in patches, from the car standing overlong in one place – a pity, but at least it suggests they are original.

Flattened tyres, but a complete motor

Now, let's get down to details. Does the steering work, do the doors open? Yes, they do. Is there glass in the windows? In fact, this model never had glass, perhaps indicating that it isn't quite in the first flight of toys. Nevertheless, there's some fine work here, particularly in the accessories, like the lamp. This unscrews nicely for a closer look. There are some reproduction accessories for antique toys around, and it's difficult to tell from a quick glance if they belong. But a certain dullness in the metal of this lamp, a dustiness on the glass, says it's original.

Checking the headlamp

The scratched bumper

It is quite easy to spot retouching on the paintwork of a toy, but a complete stripping and repainting is not so readily detected. The scratches on the bumper and underside, and the fading of the varnish over the upper parts would seem to indicate that no restoration has taken place. Only analysing a chip of paint would provide final confirmation, but you can get some quick assurance by simply sniffing the toy. The aroma of fresh paint or varnish lingers for a surprisingly long time.

Sniffing to detect restored paintwork

HILARY KAY SUMS UP

What we have here is a great rarity. The car is early, it's by one of the top makers, it's in fantastic condition, and it has its original box. It would certainly make £6000-£8000 at auction. Even fairly worn and lacking its box, it would still be well into four figures. Of course, the reason for its present state is that it has always been cherished. It would have cost about two guineas new – as much as a skilled craftsman earned in a week.'

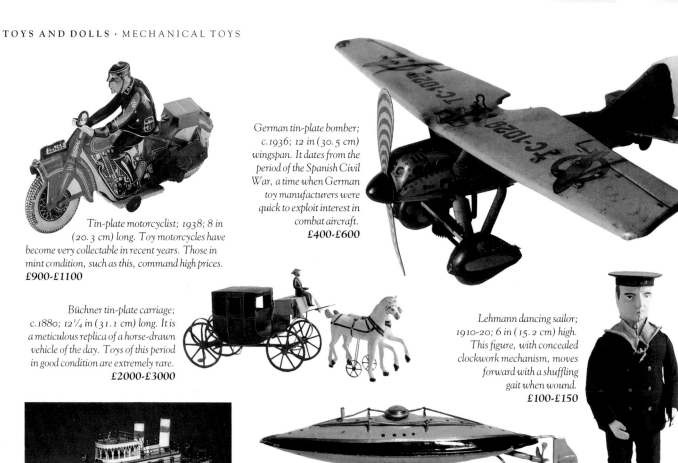

Tin-plate motorcyclist; 1938; 8 in (20.3 cm) long. Toy motorcycles have become very collectable in recent years. Those in mint condition, such as this, command high prices.
£900-£1100

German tin-plate bomber; c.1936; 12 in (30.5 cm) wingspan. It dates from the period of the Spanish Civil War, a time when German toy manufacturers were quick to exploit interest in combat aircraft.
£400-£600

Büchner tin-plate carriage; c.1880; 12¼ in (31.1 cm) long. It is a meticulous replica of a horse-drawn vehicle of the day. Toys of this period in good condition are extremely rare.
£2000-£3000

Lehmann dancing sailor; 1910-20; 6 in (15.2 cm) high. This figure, with concealed clockwork mechanism, moves forward with a shuffling gait when wound.
£100-£150

Tin-plate river boat; 1909; 19¾ in (50.2 cm) long. Made by the German toy manufacturer Märklin, and in exceptional condition, this toy represents the pinnacle of quality to many collectors.
£20,000-£30,000

German tin-plate submarine, possibly by Fleischmann; c.1915; 9 in (22.9 cm) long. Nautical toys are rarer than trains or cars, possibly because their weight sent them to watery graves.
£80-£120

Lehmann tin-plate zeppelin; c.1915; 7 in (17.8 cm) long. This is one of only two 'Shenandoah' zeppelins known to have survived.
£2000-£3000

has little value – unless it was made before 1935, or has complicated points systems or crossings. Layout accessories such as station buildings and level crossings are often as sought after as trains themselves.

CARRIAGES AND CARS

The first toy road vehicles were 19th-century clockwork carriages. These declined in popularity as trams, cars and buses became available. Dating these toys is relatively easy as they were nearly always based closely on road vehicles of the time (see p. 343).

Toy cars, in particular, reflected changing styles in detail, beginning with elegant turn-of-the-century 'vis-à-vis' (with driver and passenger facing each other) and 'tonneaux' (with a rear entrance to the passenger seats), practical 'landaulettes' (with a roof over the rear seats), later limousines and racing cars. Streamlined saloons appeared in the 1930s and American 'gas guzzlers' – Buicks, Cadillacs and Chevrolets – in the 1950s.

The most valuable types of toy car are clockwork or steam-powered models dating from 1900 to 1914, hand-painted and with hinged passenger doors, head or side lamps, and wheels with spokes and rubber tyres. In good condition they can fetch £1000 up to £20,000. Few toy cars were produced during the First World War, but lithographed vehicles dating from the 1920s are popular with collectors and cars sell for £1000. The condition of the printed decoration is important in determining value, as rust and damage can seldom be satisfactorily repaired.

BOATS, BALLOONS AND AEROPLANES

Since they were first produced in the late 19th century, water craft have been made in many designs, including river paddle boats, rowing boats, scullers, motorboats and yachts. Apart from yachts, most were initially powered by steam, but clockwork and batteries later took over. The early 20th century brought a build-up of naval power in both Europe and North America, and toy manufacturers turned to producing battleships, torpedo boats and submarines. Toy boats are scarcer than either trains or cars – possibly because they headed straight out to sea, or top-heavy designs capsized and sank. Rust would also have been a problem. As a result, models in good condition can go for very high prices.

Mechanical balloons appeared around the turn of the century and toy aeroplanes not long after. By about 1909-12, toy versions of both the Wright brothers' biplane and Louis Blériot's monoplane were being sold in toyshops. Rapid developments in aviation soon led to toys based on early passenger aircraft, flying boats, fighter planes and in the

Tin-plate scene with windmill and water pump; c.1905; 13 × 16 in (33 × 40.5 cm). Such scenes are cumbersome to display and as a result are of limited appeal to collectors.
£800-£1200

Battery-operated 'Robbie' Robot; 1956-60; 13 in (33 cm) high. Robots and space toys have become very popular in the last decade. Only those in mint condition with the original box fetch top prices.
£1700-£2000

French mechanical pig; c.1900; 10 in (25.4 cm) long. Too fragile to have been given to a child, this pig was probably intended as an adult amusement. It walks forward and grunts periodically.
£500-£800

end jets. Pre-1925 aircraft are rare collectors' pieces today. Very few were made and these were often made of fragile materials such as paper, thin wood, fabric or Celluloid which would not survive repeated heavy landings.

NOVELTY TOYS AND AUTOMATA

Some mechanical toys were not designed to be realistic, but represented amusing human or animal figures, or characters from nursery rhymes and fairy tales. Many factories made a few such novelty toys alongside other models, but two firms specialised in this area. Ernst

Musical doll; late 19thC; 19 in (48.2 cm) high. This French automaton in silks and satins has a head by Jumeau, one of the leading doll manufacturers in France.
£4500-£5500

Automaton rabbit; early 20thC; 8 in (20.3 cm) high. Rabbit automata were popular at the turn of the century. This creature emerges from its lettuce munching on a leaf.
£400-£600

Paul Lehmann, a German manufacturer, made scores of different clockwork novelty animals and figures, lithographed rather than hand-painted. Some were given amusing names – the 'Anxious Bride', for example, in which a young woman sits in a motorcycle trailer driven by a uniformed chauffeur. When wound up, the chauffeur steers an erratic course while the unhappy bride dabs her eyes with a handkerchief.

The French company Fernand Martin produced figures from Parisian life, such as chestnut roasters, waltzing couples, policemen, tipplers, waitresses and violinists. They were made from a wire armature clothed in fabric and weighed down with lead feet.

Automata are elaborate mechanical toys made for the entertainment of adults. The best were produced in France between about 1880 and 1910 by companies such as Vichy, Lambert and Roullet & Decamp.

Human automata have heads and limbs of unglazed bisque porcelain or papier-mâché – just like dolls (see p.350). Value depends on the rarity of design and manufacturer, and the variety and complexity of movements. Automata were expensive even when new, and intricate examples in good condition fetch tens of thousands of pounds at auction today. Simpler automata such as walking pigs or tigers sell for £500-£800.

'MEDIA' TOYS

Toys inspired by films, cartoons, and radio and television programmes – media toys – have been around since the 1920s. Early examples were modelled on actors such as Charlie Chaplin and Lupino Lane, and Walt Disney characters such as Mickey Mouse and Felix the Cat. A Schuco Charlie Chaplin from the 1930s could fetch as much as £800. Action films and television series from the 1960s inspired a huge range of toys, and the rarest are likely to fetch hundreds of pounds if in good condition. Toys inspired by the James Bond films are popular, as are those from programmes such as *The Man from UNCLE* and *Thunderbirds*.

Science fiction and space travel are other popular subjects for modern toymakers. Most model robots, rockets and space craft were mass-produced in Japan, and only examples in mint condition with the original box are collectable. These can sell for several hundred pounds.

Modelled in miniature

Like all small things, Dinky Toys have long proved irresistible to children. Today their appeal is as great as ever – now among adults, who pay remarkable sums for rare models in good condition.

HEN THEY WERE FIRST MADE in the 1930s, model Dinky cars cost 6d to 1s each – 2½ to 5p in present currency. Today they can fetch £1000 or more if they are undamaged. Early boxed sets can be worth as much as £5000. Even postwar rarities command similar sums.

Models that were made for only a short time are the ones most in demand today. A typical example is the Vulcan bomber, issued in 1955 in small numbers, which can fetch at least £1000. A network of collectors' clubs and associations, together with specialised dealers and regular auctions and fairs, seem likely to ensure that prices remain buoyant.

The idea of Dinky Toys grew from the Hornby O gauge model railways. A feature of these was close attention to detail, and the makers were quick to realise the need for a wide range of accessories, model buildings, miniature people and other elements to make the railway layout as realistic as possible.

As part of this range, the first group of model vehicles was issued in 1932. They were made to the same scale – 1:43 or 1/43rd – as the railway parts. This first boxed set, which included two cars, a lorry, a delivery van, a tractor and a tank, proved so popular that the range was quickly expanded. At first they were called 'Modelled Miniatures'. Early in 1934, the name was changed to 'Meccano

CHILD'S PLAY *Frank Hornby, Meccano's inventor, strongly believed in the value of constructive play.*

Miniatures', after the company's name and original product. Later the same year it was changed again and Dinky Toys were born.

By the end of 1934, there were 150 models in the Dinky Toy range, including ships and aircraft as well as a wide variety of road

vehicles. The earliest models were fairly general in style, and were simply listed as 'town sedan', 'racing car', 'tipping wagon' and so on. But within a few years identified scale models of specific vehicles were being made, and Dinky followed this pattern until the Liverpool factory closed in 1979.

The quality of casting and detailed finish were always excellent. The models have a particular period quality, and details such as styling, colours, and the slogans and advertisements carried by the commercial vehicles link them clearly to their time. This in turn is another influence on value, especially if the period is in fashion. American convertibles from the 1950s are currently prized, as are commercial vehicles from any period.

POSTWAR PRODUCTION

By 1938 about 300 models had been introduced, but the outbreak of war in 1939 slowed production. Most aircraft models then being made reappeared in camouflage finish, but production stopped in 1942 and the factory was given over to war work. The return of peace in 1945 brought Dinky Toys back to the market, and the first postwar models – a Lagonda and a Jeep – appeared in April 1946.

From then on the range expanded to include cars, commercial and farm vehicles, military vehicles and aircraft. Models made by Dinky in France were also sold in Britain, and so by the late 1970s over 1000 different Dinky Toy models had been produced.

Inevitably, Dinky had its rivals. In Britain, Corgi Toys were launched in 1956, and the Danish Tekno and French Solido ranges were also sold here. The smaller-scale Matchbox models competed from the 1950s, while in the

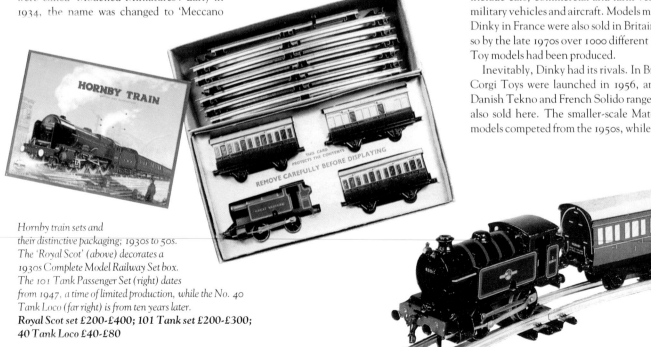

Hornby train sets and their distinctive packaging; 1930s to 50s. The 'Royal Scot' (above) decorates a 1930s Complete Model Railway Set box. The 101 Tank Passenger Set (right) dates from 1947, a time of limited production, while the No. 40 Tank Loco (far right) is from ten years later.
Royal Scot set £200-£400; 101 Tank set £200-£300; 40 Tank Loco £40-£80

American market Dinky was challenged by Tootsie and Manoil. All these ranges are now collected, along with the products of many other rivals, but there is no doubt that Dinky remains king for the serious collector.

WEAR AND TEAR

Condition is vital to the value of Dinky Toys. Models have to be in mint condition to fetch high prices, and it is even better if they are in

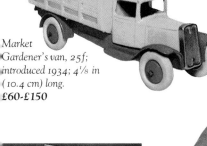

Market Gardener's van, 25f; introduced 1934; 4⅛ in (10.4 cm) long.
£60-£150

Extremely rare, mint 992 Avro Vulcan Delta Wing Bomber; 1955-6; 6 in (15.2 cm) wingspan.
c.£2000 (boxed)

Trojan delivery van advertising Oxo; 1954; 3¼ in (82 mm) long. Many commercial vehicles were modelled in the 1950s. A rare advertisement, such as Fry's Cocoa, greatly increases the value.
£200-£250

their well preserved original box. (Unless stated, values given are auction estimates for unboxed examples in near-mint condition.)

Every collector's dream is to find a shop or a warehouse with old stock that has never been sold, but most Dinky

British 40-seater Air Liner, 62 Series; 1939-42; 6⅝ in (16.8 cm) wingspan. These were regularly advertised for sale in the Meccano Magazine.
£150-£200

Chrysler 'Airflow' saloon, 30 Series Motor Vehicles; introduced 1935; 4 in (10.1 cm) long. It came in various colours. Bumpers and radiator are separately attached.
£250-£300

Boxed gift set of passenger cars; 1953. When it was first introduced, this set sold for just over £1. Today, it is worth considerably more.
£1300-£1700

33 Series Mechanical Horse and Five Assorted Trailers; introduced 1935. These were accessories for Hornby model railways.
£2500-£3000

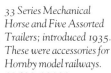

Toys are likely to have been played with regularly and are inevitably chipped and battered. Unfortunately, repainting does not increase value, so the vast majority will only be worth a few pounds. Similarly, some early examples may be in poor condition because of metal fatigue. A low-grade alloy called mazak was used to make many of the early toys, and this can crack and degenerate with age, particularly if the toy has been kept in damp conditions and fluctuating temperatures. The deterioration is irreversible.

It is becoming harder and harder to find boxed examples of mint-condition Dinky Toys at jumble and car boot sales. However, valuable discoveries are still to be made, and there is the chance that a childhood toy, carefully stored away in a hidden corner, may provide an unexpected windfall.

FRANK HORNBY

Toying with Ideas

THE SCOTTISH ENTREPRENEUR Frank Hornby (1863-1936) not only gave his name to the best known of all model railways but also invented two other toys that have since become household names: Meccano and Dinky Toys.

Hornby's first invention, while working for a Liverpool shipping company in 1901, was 'Mechanics Made Easy', quickly renamed 'Meccano'. After the First World War, with the Meccano factory firmly established in Liverpool, Hornby entered the model train market and proved himself more than equal to the lead established by German makers such as Bing and Märklin. Then in 1934, two years before his death, Dinky Toys went on the market. The models made over the next 45 years ranged from bakers' vans to space rockets, and provided a fitting memorial to one of Britain's most versatile inventors of toys.

1 Jumeau bisque doll in a wood and
   oilcloth pram
2 Fully furnished dolls' house with bisque dolls
3 English painted pine rocking horse
4 Carette limousine with clockwork motor
5 Noah's ark with animals stored inside
6 Owl clock with eyes moving at each tick
7 Hand-painted lead soldiers with box
8 Märklin train set, track and station
9 Mohair-wigged German doll in straw hat
10 German doll in lace-trimmed velvet outfit
11 Plush Steiff teddy bear with growler
12 Copeland Spode children's tea set
13 Carette four-funnel tin liner

AN EDWARDIAN
NURSERY

CHILDREN WERE TREATED as adults waiting in
the wings to enter the grown-up world until
the Victorians made a cult of family life.
Parents began to see that children had special
needs and, where money allowed, created a
separate domain for them – the nursery.
Upstairs in this nursery of about 1910, its
window safely barred and fire guarded, the
small children of a well-to-do home spent
much of their lives under the strict rule of a
nanny, and perhaps a young nursery maid.

Furnished with a few hand-me-down pieces
and a low table and chairs for the children,

this nursery had plenty of space for play. One
companion that used up excess young energy
was the trestle-mounted rocking horse,
beloved then and sought after now, when a
well-cared-for mount can fetch high prices at
auction (see p.341). The spinning top and the
drum – used only when nanny lifted it down –
allowed some lively frisking and marching
about. More decorous indoor exercise came
from parading the doll in its pram, a scaled-
down replica of an 1880s baby carriage; these
can still be found at auction for £300-£500.

FEEDING THE IMAGINATION

Quiet activities won more approval. A long-
term project created the screen, decorated
with a mass of scraps, bought in packets and
cut from cheap prints. Such an individual
piece may have a mainly sentimental value
but some go for £300-£500 in the saleroom.
The screen's decoration could inspire many a
fanciful fireside tale, as could the characters

romping along the frieze, and the inexpensive
prints bought for the walls.

Further food for young imaginations was
found in books. First editions of favourites
such as J.M. Barrie's *Peter Pan* (published
1904), Beatrix Potter's *The Tale of Peter Rabbit*
(1902) and other children's books are now
very collectable (see p.336). Not just books
but toys, too, were being produced simply to
amuse children, not to educate them.

A NEW INDUSTRY

From 1880, toy-making became a major
industry. Britain, the USA, France and other
European countries had companies that
usually made toys as a sideline to their main
business. Germany was the major force with
mainly specialist toy manufacturers.

German manufacturers Carette, Märklin,
Bing and others made toys such as the tin ship,
the train set and the limousine. These were
costly when new and, in the original box, the
car could now fetch £10,000, the train £2500
and the boat £1200. The ark, also probably
German, might contain up to 200 ring-cut
wooden animals and could now sell for £2500.

The boy's lead soldiers are typical of those
made in England by William Britain & Sons,
using their patented hollow-casting method.

Toy soldiers are keenly sought after (see p.340), and collectors will pay high prices for an Edwardian set. The wooden ball-and-cup and the wooden bricks stuck with colourful pictures were also British-made amusements.

Britain, France and Germany all produced dolls; France, and particularly the manufacturers Jumeau and Bru, had the highest reputation. Dolls dressed, as here, in children's outfits of the period can bring high prices (see p.350). The dolls' companion, newly honoured by the title of Teddy Bear, after the American President Theodore ('Teddy') Roosevelt, is a long-snouted, jointed-limb version of an all-time favourite, now commanding huge prices (see p.356). Yet his value could be matched by the dolls' house (see p.354) or perhaps by just one rare stamp in the gold-blocked album.

Dolls

Whether you collect them for their craftsmanship or beauty, their fine clothes or delicate features, the special charm of antique dolls comes from the fact that they were once the beloved companions of children of the past.

Wooden doll; c.1680; 13 in (33 cm). The value of 16th and 17thC wooden dolls has risen dramatically over the last few decades owing to their rarity. This doll's turning head makes it particularly collectable.
£71,000

NURSERY FRIENDS *Victorian girls' choice of dolls was so varied that a modern toy shop's selection seems meagre in comparison.*

MINIATURE FIGURINES have been made in various parts of the world for many thousands of years. The earliest almost always had a religious significance and were hardly dolls in the modern sense. But dolls as children's playthings can be traced back to the ancient Greeks of 3000 BC. Some examples from this period have survived because they were buried with girls who had died in childhood.

Collectors nowadays prize early dolls of all types, whether made of wood, porcelain, wax or even Celluloid. Except in the case of wooden dolls, these descriptions generally apply only to the head; the body may be of another material, such as composition – a mixture of glue and sawdust or wood pulp. However, dolls of any material that date from before the late 18th or early 19th centuries are extremely rare. (For rag and other soft dolls, see page 358.)

WOODEN DOLLS

The value of late 17th and early 18th-century wooden dolls (later called 'peg' dolls because the limbs were pegged together to allow them to move) has soared over the past few decades, thanks to their rarity. In 1974, two William and Mary wooden dolls sold at auction for £16,000, but in 1991 a single doll of similar type fetched £71,500.

Small wooden dolls of the late 18th to mid-19th centuries were often 'inhabitants' of a dolls' house (see p.354). They are usually under 8 in (20 cm) tall and are generally much cheaper than full-sized dolls. A Grödnertal peg doll (named after the region in Germany) of this small kind, complete with original costume, would fetch about £200, a larger doll £600-£800 or more.

PAPIER-MACHE AND WAX DOLLS

During the first half of the 19th century, dolls with a papier-mâché head and a kid, cloth or wooden body were produced in France and Germany. The features are less attractive than those of porcelain dolls, and the eyes painted rather than made of glass. Like early wooden dolls, they require special care to protect the delicate top layer of paint and gesso. It is possibly because of their fragility

George III wooden doll; c.1800; 15½ in (39.4 cm). Dotted eyelashes and eyebrows and heavily rouged cheeks are characteristic of wooden dolls of this period.
£500

German bisque dolls'-house dolls; c.1890; c.6 in (15 cm). This group is particularly valuable because all the dolls are in original clothes and the men have moulded moustaches and hair. They all have cloth bodies with bisque lower limbs.
£2500-£3500 the set

Papier-mâché German dolls; c.1820; 14½ in (36.8 cm) and 20 in (51 cm). Like wooden dolls, they require special attention to prevent discoloration.
Left: £800
Right: £3000

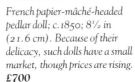

French papier-mâché-headed pedlar doll; c.1850; 8½ in (21.6 cm). Because of their delicacy, such dolls have a small market, though prices are rising.
£700

German wax over composition 'pumpkin-head' doll; c.1860; 23 in (58.5 cm). So-called because of the pumpkin-like texture of the layered wax head, such dolls are prone to cracks.
£250

Head and shoulder plate of a German bisque doll; c.1880; 6 in (15.2 cm). Ceramic dolls drop sharply in value if they have facial hairline cracks.
£1000

English waxed composition doll; c.1880; 18 in (45.7 cm). Few 19thC wax dolls have marks, which makes identification difficult.
£350

Jumeau bisque 'long face' doll (right); c.1870; 19½ in (49.5 cm). Emile Jumeau was one of the most prolific French doll manufacturers of his time, and his dolls are much sought after.
£12,000

that the market for these dolls is small, although prices have risen steadily. A papier-mâché doll in good condition with unusual moulded hairstyle and authentic clothes may now fetch £1000. Dolls from the 1840s are sometimes sold for as little as £200, but often the clothes are not contemporary or the paint on the face is slightly crazed.

The most valuable wax dolls are of the 'poured wax' type, with the head moulded from liquid wax. In contrast, 'waxed papier-mâché' and 'waxed composition' dolls are finished with a layer of wax over papier-mâché or composition. In so-called 'pumpkin-head' dolls, the wax layer extends to the hair, piled up in pumpkin-like mounds.

Some 18th-century English wax dolls can still be found, but seldom in good condition. Nineteenth-century dolls are much more common. They were made in large numbers in both England and Germany by makers such as Madame Montanari, Edwards, Pierotti, and the Meech and Marsh families. Unfortunately few dolls were stamped with their maker's mark, so identification is difficult.

Auction prices for wax dolls have fluctuated over the past few years, with the poured wax type becoming increasingly popular. Today, a poured wax doll dressed in authentic clothes can fetch £800, or over £1000 if the clothes are particularly fine. Other wax dolls have not kept up with inflation and can be found for as little as £80.

BISQUE DOLLS

The first ceramic dolls were produced in the mid-18th century, but they did not become popular until a century later when various European factories made dolls with bisque (biscuit, or unglazed porcelain) heads. Most early 19th-century bisque dolls were made in France, but few bear a maker's mark. There are some exceptions, however: dolls made by Madame Barrois often have 'EB' cut into the shoulder plate (moulded in one piece with the head); Mademoiselle Huret, who was responsible for the first articulated body, stamped her mark on her dolls and even on their dresses.

For most collectors, the rarity and price of early bisque dolls puts them out of reach: a stamped Huret doll dressed in original clothes may be worth as much as £15,000. However, among the most affordable are small François Gaultier dolls which may go for under £500.

From about the last quarter of the 19th century, bisque dolls were made in much larger quantities, in Germany as well as in France. Factories used numbered moulds and often marked the heads, making it much easier to identify makers and even individual models. (For makers' marks, see page 466.)

The most common moulds were for idealised 'dolly' faces, which were turned out in quantity; most French and German dolls from such moulds now change hands for between £300 and £500. Far more scarce are dolls from so-called 'character' moulds, which were often modelled on real children. Dolls with these heads now fetch very high prices – for example, the £91,000 paid in 1989 for a 1909 Kämmer and Reinhardt doll bearing the rare mould number 105.

Identifying character moulds means knowing something about the numbering systems of the various manufacturers. The French

Jumeau factory, for example, numbered their character moulds 201 to 225, while the next number, 226, was produced in much greater quantities by the amalgamated Société Française de Fabrication de Bébés et Jouets (SFBJ), and is worth much less.

Dolls by German firm Armand Marseille can be good value – particularly mould numbers 370, 390 and 990 – as hundreds of thousands were produced. They are priced at £100-£300 for all but the best, most elaborately dressed examples. Mould numbers 341 and 351 (known as 'My Dream Babies') are also popular with collectors, fetching £200-£400 depending on size.

In the same price range are mould numbers 300, 342 and 350 from Ernst Heubach's factory at Koppelsdorf. Both Marseille and Heubach also made character dolls, black dolls and dolls with Oriental features, all of which are now sought after by collectors, generally selling for £400 or more.

Simpler designs of pale parian bisque dolls are also good buys at £100-£160. However,

an elaborately decorated doll with china flowers or an Alice-band in its hair, or a china necklace, could be worth as much as £1000.

CHINA DOLLS

Instead of the matt finish of bisque, china dolls have a glossy glazed surface. The best have a delicately flesh-tinted face and mohair wig, or brown moulded-china hair. Makers' marks are seldom visible; many factories marked the underside of the shoulder plate.

Prices start at about £100 for German factory-made china dolls from the second half of the 19th century. These dolls have a pale face and moulded short black hair, and were produced in large quantities. At the other extreme, rarer dolls bearing the 'KPM' mark of the Königliche Porzellan Manufaktur of Berlin could fetch over £1000.

CELLULOID DOLLS

Dolls were first moulded from Celluloid – an early form of plastic – in 1863 by the American company Hyatt Brothers, but most date from

between the 1880s and the early 20th century. The head of a Celluloid doll has a lifelike flesh tint which can be difficult to distinguish from bisque. The body may be composition or Celluloid, with joints at the shoulders, neck and hips, and the hair is usually white moulded Celluloid.

Celluloid is fragile, and cracks and dents cannot be invisibly repaired. This may be the reason why prices have stayed relatively low – usually under £100. Any actual damage will make such a doll almost worthless. Marked Kämmer and Reinhardt dolls with eyes that open and close, or move from side to side ('flirty eyes'), and swivel joints are the most sought after, particularly in Germany where they can sell for up to £500.

KEWPIE AND BARBIE DOLLS

The Kewpie – a cross between a cupid and a pixie – first appeared in the drawings of the American actress-turned-illustrator Rose O'Neill. Kewpie dolls first went into production in 1913, and today an (continued p. 354)

Heubach Koppelsdorf bisque doll; c.1920; 19½ in (49.5 cm). 'Flirty eyes' that move from side to side are highly desirable, but this doll was produced in large numbers, which reduces its value.
£200-£300

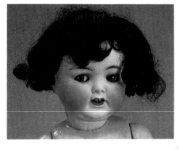

Kämmer and Reinhardt bisque 'Googly-eyed' doll; c.1910; 13 in (33 cm). 'Googly' or roguish eyes were popular during the early 20thC and almost all doll manufacturers produced dolls with these eyes.
£3500

German all-bisque 'Piano Baby' (left); c.1910; 9½ in (24 cm). Designed to sit on a piano as ornaments, 'Piano Babies' can often be found in pairs – a boy in blue, a girl in pink – or in sets of 4 to 6 naked babies in various positions.
£200

German china shoulder-head doll with mohair wig; c.1850; 22 in (56 cm). The glazed surface is shiny, the features delicate and the flesh a pale tint apart from the flushed cheeks.
£400

German bisque character doll; c.1902; 16 in (40.5 cm). Character moulds, like this number 1301, were often modelled on real-life children, and prices today depend on the rarity of the mould number.
£16,500

An Expert Examines

HILARY KAY GETS ACQUAINTED WITH
A RATHER SPECIAL BISQUE DOLL

A bisque doll 14 in (35.5 cm) tall

'IF YOU MET HER *at a toy fair, you'd certainly want to know more about this doll. Well, her head is of bisque, or unglazed porcelain, the most popular material with collectors. The next things to check are the arms, face and hands to make sure nothing is missing, and that the hands haven't faded. Little girls like to wash their dolls' hands, often to the detriment of the colour. But these are grimy, suggesting only a limited acquaintance with soapy water.*

Next, so long as the owner has no objection, you should gently pull up the wig and look at the back of the head for identification marks. Here you see the inscription 'Deposé 6EJ' – the mark, as a textbook will reveal, of Emile Jumeau, one of the best French makers.

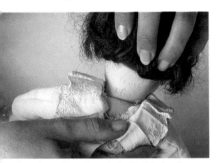

Finding the trademark on the back of the head

Even without the trademark, you can recognise the craftsmanship of the Jumeau factory from such details as the closed mouth, which collectors prefer to an open one, the

Jumeau eyes and brows

strong eyebrows and the large, lustrous eyes. Whether they are fixed, as here, or can close or move from side to side – so-called 'flirty' eyes – the eyes of Jumeau dolls are always intricately made from blown glass, and inserted from behind. Whether the eyes are mobile or not makes no difference to the value of the doll.

Trademark on the body

Much more important to the price is that all the doll's parts belong together. Any doubts, however, are allayed by finding the Jumeau mark again on the back of the body.

Try, if possible, to undress the doll. The marvellous thing about companion dolls like this is that they are always dressed like a child

Gently removing the clothes

of the same period. So the clothes you see, even the chemise, split drawers and petticoat, would have been familiar to the doll's original owner. And judging by the doll's maker and style, that was in the 1880s.

Many-jointed limbs

The bodies of bisque dolls are made of various materials. In this case, the upper limbs are of wood, but the hands, feet and trunk are made of a composition like papier-mâché. There are many joints, so the doll can be put into a variety of postures. The body is well-proportioned and, like the head, in good condition.

HILARY KAY SUMS UP

We've seen that the doll comes from one of the very best of the French makers, that the overall state is good, and that the costume is original. Dolls' clothes are not particularly valuable in themselves, but they increase the value of the toy if they were actually made for it. One last thing to do (if the wig can be removed) is to put a lance light – a small light bulb on the end of a probe – inside the head to see if there are any hairline cracks. So long as there are none, this doll would sell at auction for £3000-£5000 – a lot of money, but collectors would value this doll.'

early bisque kewpie with arms outstretched, blue wings and topknot, made by J.D. Kestner, would sell for £120-£180.

Among the biggest-selling children's toys of the last 30 years is the Barbie doll. Manufactured by Mattel Toys, the first Barbies appeared in 1959, and took their name from the designer's daughter, Barbie Millicent Roberts. Many models were produced, all with the same basic shape, but with hair, make-up and clothes to reflect a host of different themes, including air hostess, bride, teacher, chef, even astronaut.

Most collectors concentrate on Barbie dolls from before the 1970s, when the original bulbous-eyed, snub-nosed features began to change and the quality deteriorated. Later models are not popular in Britain, although in the USA they can be worth several pounds in good condition. Clothes alone, such as the 'Roman Holiday' outfit, can be worth as much as £500.

JAPANESE DOLLS

Many different kinds of doll and figurine were traditionally made in Japan, most of them for display or ritual purposes. Although Japanese dolls are currently unpopular with Western collectors, *sakura-ningyō*, or 'shelf' dolls (made purely for display on shelves), and *hina-ningyō* (dolls for special festivals) are still worthy collectables.

Sakura-ningyō are probably the most familiar to Westerners, many having been exported over the past 150 years. The favourite subjects for shelf dolls were warriors, heroes and beautiful women from the traditional *Kabuki* theatre. A mid-19th century Japanese warrior might fetch £400-£600, and dolls made for export at the turn of this century usually sell for £100-£150.

Festival dolls were handed down in families from generation to generation. The most expensive had embroidered silk costumes and delicate features, but such a pair of dolls might only reach £200-£300 at auction today.

Celluloid doll; c.1920; 4½ in (11.4 cm). Celluloid dolls were lighter than bisque, but unpopular because of their shiny finish.
£15-£20

Kewpie doll with box; 1913; 6½ in (16.5 cm). Designed by American illustrator Rose O'Neill, the kewpie doll is still in production today.
£100-£150; less without box

Barbie doll; c.1959; 11½ in (29.2 cm). The most sought-after Barbies are from the first four production runs of 1959-60.
£800-£1500 complete

Japanese festival dolls; c.1920-30; largest 13¼ in (33.6 cm). They were made to celebrate Boys' Day (May 5 each year).
£400 the set

Dolls' houses

A dolls' house reveals the past in all its intimacy and detail. From period furniture to lace curtains, almost every object has its miniature match.

ANTIQUE DOLLS' HOUSES come in all shapes and sizes, from single rooms – often with collapsible sides – to fully equipped shops for working dolls and large residences for whole families. The earliest to be made in any numbers came from Bavaria and Holland in the mid-16th century, although the remains of a possible 15th century Italian example are in a museum in Jena in Germany. Most of the early versions resembled cabinets more than houses, and were sometimes known as 'cabinet houses'. Not until the 19th century did more realistic house shapes become the norm.

Until about the 18th century most British dolls' houses were made of oak, but then cheaper woods such as lime and pine started to be used, along with other materials such as papier-mâché, tortoiseshell, glass, metal, wax and, for folding designs, paper and cardboard. Some very fine dolls' houses were made of carved bone or ivory, with decorative details so minutely worked that a magnifying glass is needed to see them.

GRAND DESIGNS

Many dolls' houses were built by cabinetmakers as a way of using up offcuts, although some were commissions from wealthy families wanting replicas of their home. Perhaps the most lavish is 'Titania's Palace', officially opened by Queen Mary in 1922. It contains painted mosaics, pictures by well-known artists and a jewelled throne for the fairy queen. In 1978 it was sold to the toy company Lego for the record price of £135,000.

Most dolls' houses on the market are late 19th or early 20th-century commercial models, which can cost as little as £300 unfurnished but several thousand pounds if fully kitted out. Furnished houses from before the 19th century are rare and expensive. Even unfurnished older houses seldom appear on the market, and when they do prices are high. In September 1991 an empty late 18th-century house on a stand sold for £13,200.

Open room designs, theatres, shops and stalls are also highly collectable. A late 19th-century, home-made wooden grocer's shop can fetch around £700, whereas a more elaborate, fully stocked butcher's shop or kitchen may go for thousands of pounds.

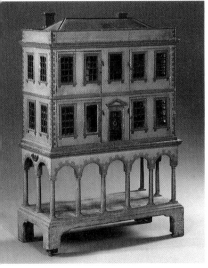

American wood and paper dolls' house; c.1890; 24 in (61 cm) high. The fretwork and frame decoration of this commercially produced house is typical for its date. It opens at the side.
£800-£1200

arge English wooden dolls' house on original rcaded stand; c.1780; 57 in (1.45 m) high. This xample is fully furnished with items of a later date. our wall sections open to reveal the interior. Such arly dolls' houses are rare.
12,000-£14,000 with furniture

DOLLS'-HOUSE FURNITURE
Mini-Masterpieces

SCALED-DOWN FURNITURE for dolls' houses can make a fascinating collection, but prices have risen in recent years – a 1½ in (38 mm) pair of 18th-century wood and ivory salt and pepper pots, for example, sold at auction in March 1987 for £1100.

Wooden dolls'-house furniture from Germany is the most common. Some, such as the 'Waltershausen' type, is printed with transfers to resemble boulle-style inlay. A typical set of sofa, table and chairs may cost as much as £750. A single tin-plate secretaire bookcase from German makers Rock & Graner can fetch as much as £500.

More affordable are Anglo-Indian bone miniature items from the late 19th century. Most pieces cost between £50 and £200. A silver tea set with maker's mark, dated 1900-10 may go at auction for £500. In November 1989 a silver chandelier fetched £2000.

Rock & Graner tinplate desk; c.1890; 5 in (12.7 cm) high. It is painted to resemble wood.
£500

French secretaire; late 19thC; 3⅓ in (85 mm) high. The fall front is decorated with marquetry.
£700

Rare 18thC Nuremberg dolls' kitchen; 18 in (45.7 cm) high. The kitchen is fitted with racks and shelves, a stove of painted 'brick', pewter hollowware, copper cauldrons, saucepans and jelly moulds, scales, a bench and a terracotta figure of a woman and a dog.
£15,500

Painted wooden grocer's shop; German; c.1890; 38½ in (98 cm) wide. The shop contains scales and weights, a money box and a chair which converts into a step ladder.
£1500-£1800

Open room house; c.1890; 54 in (1.37 m) wide. The late 19thC Rock & Graner metal furniture is painted to simulate wood and the centre rug is gros point.
£12,000-£15,000

Painted, two-storey, wooden dolls' house, possibly American; c.1880; 42½ in (1.08 m) wide. Inside there is a metal screen, a hanging lamp, a fireplace and furniture of cherry and satinwood.
£3000-£5000

Teddy bears and soft toys

Few objects provide a more intimate link with the past than an old teddy bear or a cloth doll. In good condition, however, these souvenirs of childhood can be of far more than sentimental value.

SOFT TOYS AND STUFFED ANIMALS have been popular with children for generations, but have only recently acquired value as collectables. 'Arctophiles' – as teddy bear lovers are called, after the Greek *arctos* (bear) – and other toy enthusiasts will pay thousands of pounds for the best and rarest examples. But even collectors with less to spend can find good buys.

TEDDY BEARS

Two contenders, one German and one American, have some claim to producing the first soft toy bears. The German manufacturer was Margarete Steiff, a polio victim who turned to toymaking in the 1880s as a way of gaining independence. Using material from her uncle's felt factory, she began with a elephant pincushion but was soon making fa more elaborate toys such as a mechanica dancing bear and a bear on all fours that coul be pulled along on wheels.

At the turn of the century, Steiff and he nephew started to make bears with movabl joints. The bears were stuffed with woo shavings and covered with mohair plush in range of colours, including black and silvery white. For some time the Steiff bears failed t arouse much interest, but the breakthroug came when a New York company placed a order for 3000 at the Leipzig Fair in 1903.

Meanwhile, Morris Michtom, a Russia immigrant to the United States, was making living selling sweets and toys – mostly hand made by Michtom and his wife – from a sho in Brooklyn. In 1902 the Michtoms made small bear out of furry fabric in response to newspaper story about the American presi dent, Theodore Roosevelt, who refused t shoot a bear cub on a hunting expedition Michtom called his bear 'Teddy's bear' afte

Early metal-rod-jointed Steiff bear with elephant button in left ear; German; c.1903-4; 20 in (51 cm) high. This is the second type of Steiff button – a raised elephant, used 1903-4.
£10,000; undamaged button: £500

German teddy bears; c.1910-25; largest 28 in (71 cm) high. The large ones are by Steiff, the small mechanical ones by Bing and by Schuco.
Steiff bears: black £12,000-£15,000; gold £3000-£5000; white and beige £800-£1200
Mechanical: £800-£1500

the president, and displayed it in his shop window, where it sold almost immediately.

As the Michtoms made and sold one bear after another, and it became obvious that there was a huge demand for the toys, they wrote to Roosevelt and received permission to use his name. Eventually the Michtoms' entire stock was bought by Butler Brothers, later to become the Ideal Toy Corporation, America's biggest toy manufacturer.

The Steiff bears were named *Freund Petz* ('Friend Bruin') in Germany, but they too came to be known as teddy bears after some of the imported toys were used to decorate tables at a White House reception given by Roosevelt. From then on the name stuck.

WHAT TO LOOK FOR

From 1904 onwards, teddy bears were manufactured in large numbers by German makers such as Bing, Bruin, Hermann, Schuco and Sussenguth, as well as by Steiff, and also by many American companies, among them Columbia Teddy Bear Manufacturers, Commonwealth Toy and Novelty Company, Harman Manufacturing Company, Ideal Toy Company and Knickerbocker.

British toymakers started producing bears in large numbers only in the 1920s. Names to look out for include those of Chad Valley, Chiltern, Dean's Rag Book Company, Ealon Toys, J.K. Farnell, Merrythought, Pedigree and Norah Wellings.

Before buying an old teddy bear, decide whether you want it as an investment or just for pleasure. Only bears that are in good condition with their fur intact and identifiable as being made by a well-known firm have kept or increased their value.

Steiff bears can be identified by a metal button in the left ear, from which the date of manufacture can be judged; other makes of bear may have a label or tag. Avoid unmarked teddy bears if you are looking for an investment – they can seldom be authenticated. Beware, too, of imitations: the Steiff button is now being copied by some German manufacturers. If in doubt, ask a specialist at one of the big auction houses to take a look.

Prices vary according to age, condition, maker and colour. A beige or yellow ('gold') 6½-12 in (16.5-30 cm) Steiff bear made in about 1920 and in good condition will usually fetch between £500 and £1500 at auction, but a similar, unlabelled British one only about £150-£200. Unusual colours, such as rust or cinnamon, can fetch around £2000, silver-white around £6000, and black examples will go for up to £22,000. Even a beige Steiff bear from before 1910 may be worth up to £4000. These prices depend on size.

OTHER SOFT TOYS

Many of the toymakers who produced teddy bears also made other animal toys and soft cloth dolls. Rabbits and elephants were favourite animals, followed by pigs, lions, tigers, dogs, cats and monkeys. Some had articulated joints or even a clockwork mechanism that enabled them to move or make a noise. Early rabbits (of about 1903) in good condition and clockwork tigers and lions fetch £800-£1000 at auction today, while

Collection of teddy bears from Sotheby's first specialist auction sale, held in London in October 1983. Most of the bears in this group are British-made; 1910-35; 16½-36 in (42-91 cm) high.
£110-£135 each

Silver plush Steiff teddy bear; German; c.1908; 27½ in (70 cm) high. Silver bears are more sought after than the beige ones. The button has the printed and raised Steiff 1905-50 trademark.
£6000; undamaged button: £200

Gold plush teddy bear; English; c.1935; 18⅞ in (48 cm) high. The earliest teddy bears are from Germany and the USA; most British ones date from the 1920s on.
£150-£250

clockwork elephants fetch around £500. Monkeys, dogs and cats sell for £100-£150.

Soft dolls by highly rated craftsmen can be extremely collectable. Early (1918-25) toys by the German dollmaker Käthe Kruse, with painted and varnished heads, can fetch over £1000 if in good condition.

Felt dolls by the Italian manufacturer Lenci are also sought by collectors. Those depicting famous people of the 1920s and 30s – such as Josephine Baker, Marlene Dietrich and Rudolf Valentino – and Pompadour fashion dolls and clown dolls can fetch thousands of pounds at auction. Lenci dolls with conventional faces usually sell for £300-£500.

Even for collectors on a budget, cloth dolls can be a good investment: under £100 will buy a 1920-30 long-legged, stockinette-covered French 'boudoir' doll. For £150-£300, you could buy an English velvet-covered doll by Norah Wellings, Merrythought or Chad Valley. Steiff dolls, particularly gollies, cost about the same as Steiff teddies.

RAG DOLLS

In most countries rag dolls were made in vast quantities, selling in country fairs and shops or homemade by parents for their children. In Britain, Dean's Rag Book Company started in 1903, while in France the 'Rag Bag Doll' was born in 1908. Raggedy Ann and Raggedy Andy were first made in the United States in 1915. These early painted dolls with movable arms and legs, twisted wool hair, striped socks and original clothes realise £400-£475 at American auctions, whereas in Europe they might fetch only around £100.

The most sought-after American rag dolls are those made by Izannah Walker from 1840 (but first patented 1873) and Mrs Thomas Beecher (1893-1910). A Walker doll standing 17 in (43.2 cm) high and in excellent condition, which is extremely rare to find, has been known to reach £10,000 at auction in the USA, while one in poor, flaking condition made £1600. Beecher dolls in good condition can command a price in excess of £1000 in the USA, but slightly less in Europe.

A similar American rarity is the stockinette doll by Martha Chase, who started in 1889 by hand-painting stockinette-covered heads in oil paint. A Martha Chase doll in good condition is worth £500 or more for a child model of 12 in (30.5 cm), whereas a 13 in (33 cm) adult doll can command as much as £1300.

Käthe Kruse doll; c.1928; 20 in (51 cm) high. This 'sleeping' doll is sand-filled, weighing 6 lb (2.7 kg), about the weight of a new-born baby. It is known in Germany as a 'Traumerchen' (dreaming) doll.
£3000

Boudoir doll; c.1920; 26 in (66 cm) high. Boudoir or 'salon' dolls were displayed with other possessions in the ante-room to a lady's bedroom.
£100-£150

Steiff felt doll; German; c.1913; 16⅛ in (41 cm) high. Steiff made dolls in various national costumes. The central seam down the face is characteristic.
£400

Norah Wellings sailor doll; c.1930; 8 in (20.3 cm) high. This English cloth doll is covered in velvet; the head is pressed felt, painted with an oil-based paint.
£50

Lenci felt doll; c.1927; 15¾ in (40 cm) high. Many of these Italian dolls depict famous people; they are still made.
£400

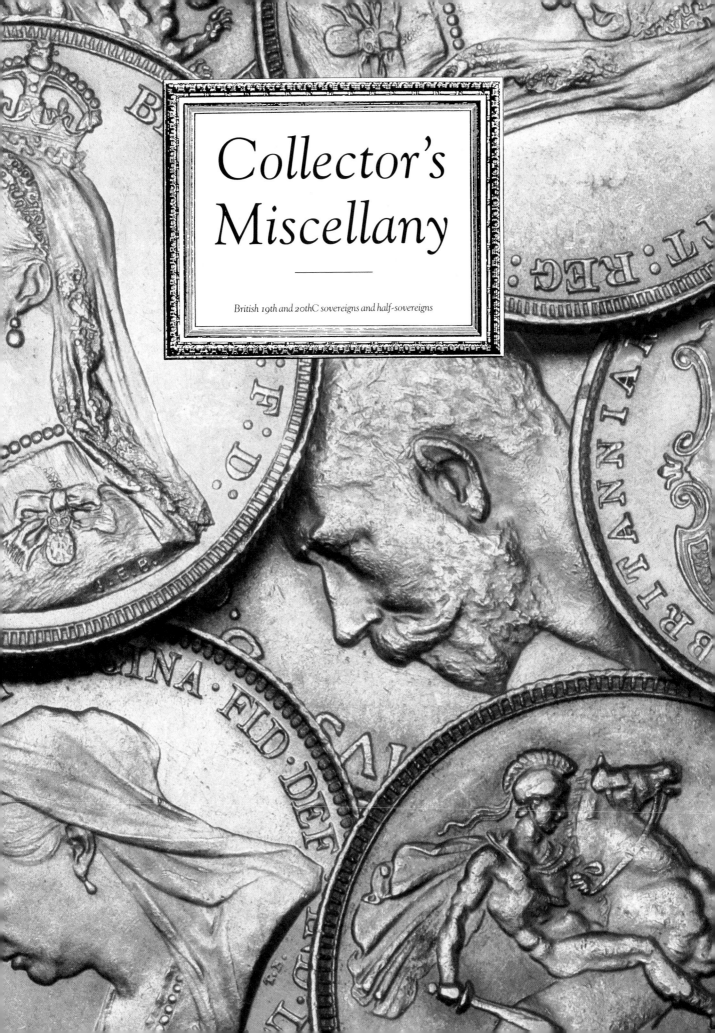

Collector's Miscellany

British 19th and 20thC sovereigns and half-sovereigns

Architectural antiques

The past 20 years have seen an increased interest in putting architectural salvage to new use, and today a number of dealers specialise in such pieces.

Cast-iron fireback dated 1588; 40 in (1.01 m) wide. This example, decorated with anchors, commemorates the English fleet's victory over the Spanish Armada.
Original: £400-£600
19th/20thC copy: £100-£200

UNTIL THE 1970s, most demolition contractors would not bother to salvage any items from the buildings they flattened. They were unaware of the value and lacked time to remove fixtures and fittings carefully. Some great bargains were found by knowledgeable individuals who dodged the bulldozers to acquire anything from an old lavatory to a complete panelled room for, at the most, a few pounds.

The spectacular rise in property prices in the 1980s encouraged house owners to invest in renovations, using original materials for both the house and the garden. Old ceramic wall and floor tiles (see p.187) for under £1 each were reinstated in kitchens and bathrooms, and York stone paving bought for £30-£40 a square yard was laid on patios.

Sadly, the rise in prices has resulted in an increase in thefts of architectural artefacts. Old empty buildings are easy prey to professional thieves who rip out doors, floors and staircases, as well as the more traditional booty of lead from roofs. Fireplaces are an especially easy target, and have even been stolen with the owners asleep upstairs.

FIREPLACES

The value of most fireplaces dropped following the slump in property prices that began in 1989, but the range is still from around £100 to an incredible £100,000 and upwards. It is worth remembering that the removal and installation of a fireplace – especially a marble one – is a skilled and expensive operation. Late Victorian black marble fireplaces, which were made in large numbers, are often not worth buying when the cost of installation is taken into account.

Fireplaces dating from the 18th century need to be examined with care, as both wood and marble examples have often been altered to fit a new location. In some cases, the marble slips – the flat panels that line the inside of the chimneypiece – have deteriorated and crumbled because of exposure to heat.

From the 16th century onwards, firebacks were used to reflect the heat into the room and to prevent damage to the brick or stonework behind the grate. Early firebacks were made by casting molten iron in a well-compressed bed of sand, in which the shape and decoration of the object were created by pressing a carved wooden board with details such as twists of

Georgian white marble chimneypiece with Siena marble slips and inlay; late 18thC; 73 in (1.85 m) wide. This Neoclassical design shows the influence of Robert Adam. Siena marble was very popular in the 18thC.
£10,000-£15,000

Edwardian white marble fireplace with cast-iron inset; c.1905; 63 in (1.6 m) wide. Grates with a cast-iron surround, as here, burned coal and small logs. The iron surround acts like a radiator.
Fireplace: £100-£200; inset: £80-£120

rope, an armorial and date. Authentic 16th to 18th-century firebacks fetch £200-£800 today, but beware: many copies have been produced over the last 100 years, and they can be difficult to spot once blackened by smoke.

BATHROOM FITTINGS

Old baths can often be picked up quite cheaply, but many require re-enamelling – an expensive job if done properly. A good Victorian roll-top bath with ball-and-claw feet can fetch £500-£800, however. Victorian brass or nickel-plated taps fetch £50-£100 today. Chromium plating, which gives a brighter finish and is more resistant to water, was introduced in the 1920s.

After the Prince of Wales almost died of typhoid in 1871 (as his father Prince Albert had done in 1861), a greater awareness of the

Puritas wash-down lavatory; late 19thC; 17 in (43.1 cm) high. It was one of many new designs to emerge from Victorian sanitary reforms.
£300-£500

Cast-iron bath with shower canopy and attachments; c.1900; 7 ft (2.1 m) long. Introduced in the 1870s, these baths have separate taps to control the water, the shower and the inside spray bars.
£3000-£5000
No canopy: £300-£500

Stained-glass divider; c.1900; 115 in (2.92 m) high. This typical turn-of-the-century hallway divider combines stained and painted glass within a painted pine frame.
£800-£1200

Architectural cornerpiece; c.1870; 24 in (61 cm) high. Carved stone gargoyles and masks removed from Victorian buildings are plentiful and quite cheap.
£80-£120

Copper cockerel weather vane; early 19thC; 35 in (89 cm) high. Weather vanes often come on the market when churches are demolished. They are cheaper in sheet iron.
£600-£1000

Wrought and sheet-iron lantern with crown; c.1840; 41 in (1.04 m) high. This grand lantern was made for Hampton Court Palace and originally had a cast-iron lamppost.
£300-£400

Bronze, gilt and enamel pub sign; early 20thC; 48 in (1.22 m) high. This well-cast sign from a Brighton pub would be sought after by railway enthusiasts.
£250-£350

Pair of English cast and wrought-iron gates; c.1860; 72 in (1.8 m) wide. These Gothic-style gates would fetch more if they were wider, to fit a drive.
£600-£1000

need for sanitary reform brought about a revolution in lavatory design. Twyfords, Shanks and Doulton all produced a wide range of sanitary ware in various colours, some decorated with relief moulding on the outside and transfer-printed patterns inside.

The use of some types of old lavatory is now illegal, but nonetheless they are still in demand, as are old seats and cistern chains. Mahogany seats sell for £80-£120, and a lavatory chain with a ceramic handle, perhaps inscribed with a motto such as 'Pull and Let Go', can be picked up for £50-£80.

DECORATIVE FEATURES

Many Victorian houses were decorated with carved wood features in a 'Jacobethan' style, copying 16th and 17th-century decorative styles. These are still sought after for their decorative sculptural qualities. Oak panelling is also in demand, especially in the linenfold pattern that was used from the 15th century onwards. Most panelling that appears on the market is Victorian but often in an earlier style. Good quality Victorian mahogany doors fetch less than £100 each; even Georgian examples are often less than £200 as they tend to be too large for modern homes. Victorian brass door handles and locks are still fairly plentiful and will cost around £50-£100 for each door. Old oak beams, taken from demolished barns and houses, sell for around £20 per cubic foot (roughly £700/m³), or more for particularly large beams.

Decorative plasterwork has been used in British homes since the 16th century. Victorian plaster ceiling roses cost about £60-£100 today, but several firms still produce plaster fittings, sometimes using original 18th and 19th-century moulds.

With the demolition or conversion of many Victorian churches and chapels, large quantities of stained glass have appeared on the market. Ecclesiastical glass is usually cheap, although Victorian and Edwardian domestic stained glass is more popular, especially the rarer, naturalistic panels of birds, animals and Pre-Raphaelite maidens.

EXTERIOR FITTINGS

Gas street lighting was introduced into Britain in 1807 and thousands of lamps were made. An original cast-iron lamppost with a sheet-iron or copper lantern will fetch £300-£500, the lantern alone £100-£150.

The simplest weather vanes were made of sheet iron or tin plate. More solid examples were constructed from two sheets of copper riveted or soldered together in three dimensions. Prices vary according to age and subject matter – British and French examples are often in the form of a cockerel.

Wrought-iron gates are also very popular, especially pairs which have an overall width of 10 ft (3 m) or more. Many 18th and 19th-century gates, which were made for carriages, are too narrow for modern driveways.

Garden statuary and ornaments

Garden statuary is still a new field for collectors, and there are bargains to be found so long as you can distinguish the genuinely old from modern copies.

Italian carved wellhead in rosso Verona marble; 19thC; 36 in (91 cm) high. Numerous copies of ancient originals were made in 19thC Italy.
£4000-£6000
Venetian original: £10,000-£15,000

Carved staddle stone (left); 30 in (76 cm) wide. These supports for tithe barns are most desirable when covered in lichen.
Set of four: £400-£600

Coade stone model of the Townley Vase; 1840; 37 in (94 cm) high. The original ancient marble vase was bought by collector Charles Townley in 1774 for £250.
£2500-£4000

Pair of composition stone lions; mid-20thC; 39 in (99 cm) high. Weathering is the principal factor in the value of a composition stone statue. A small pair 12 in (30.5 cm) high would fetch £200-£300
£3000-£5000 the pair

I**T IS ONLY** in the past few years that most people have become aware that the old statue or cast-iron bench in their garden may have some value. When selling a house, it was common practice to leave everything in the garden behind when you moved. But recent publicity about unconsidered sculptures which turned out to be worth millions has made people more cautious.

MARBLE

Vast quantities of carved marble were brought back to Britain from Italy by wealthy travellers from the late 17th century onwards. By the late 19th century a very large industry had developed in Rome, Florence, Naples, Milan and Venice to supply statues. The carvers produced a wide variety of pieces, many copying ancient Greek and Roman designs, others the Renaissance masters, and others again imitating work by 18th and 19th-century Neoclassical sculptors such as Antonio Canova and Bertel Thorwaldsen.

Perhaps the most popular are life-size copies of Classical statues, for which prices today start at a few thousand pounds and soar upwards. Religious subjects, especially 19th-century examples, have a much more limited market appeal and can often be bought at auction for only a few hundred pounds.

REAL AND IMITATION STONE

Local stone of various kinds has long been carved to make garden ornaments, but much easier to produce are those made of synthetic stone of various types. One very distinctive material is Coade stone, which was made at the Coade factory in Lambeth, London, established in the 1760s. No one has created a material to match its durability: it was non-porous to water and therefore resistant to frost damage. Coade stone was made into garden urns, statues and a wide range of architectural embellishments. Prices today range from £1000 to as much as £100,000.

Rather less durable is composition stone, a mixture of sand and cement which may contain stone or marble chips. Composition stone ornaments have been produced since the early 19th century, but the vast majority have been made in the last 50 years. Unless authentically Victorian, composition stone has little investment potential. Even modern pieces sold in garden centres can look deceptively old if encouraged to 'weather' by a coat of manure or yoghurt!

BRONZE AND IRON

Until a few years ago, cast-iron statues were looked upon as the poor relation of bronze sculpture, but in fact the two cost just about the same to produce. Although bronze is the more expensive material, cast iron is harder and has a higher melting temperature, so it is far more difficult and expensive to detail with a chisel and finish off. Cast-iron statues are prone to rust, however, and the material is brittle, so damage is more common. Statues of similar size and intricacy might still cost 50 per cent more in bronze than in cast iron.

Most 19th-century cast-iron garden furniture came from French or British foundries. French cast iron was generally more figurative than British, which is epitomised by the output of the Coalbrookdale foundry at Ironbridge, Shropshire, established in 1708. By the late 19th century, Coalbrookdale was producing a wide range of furniture as well as urns, architectural fittings and fountains, many of which are now being copied.

Modern cast-iron copies of urns and seats are sometimes immersed in sea water to accelerate rusting and give an impression of age. If the copy was cast from an original seat or urn, the foundry and registration stamps will be reproduced in the copy and are therefore no guarantee of age. As a rule, reproductions are badly finished along the casting seam marks, and do not faithfully reproduce the original domed brass nuts. It can also be difficult to date old pieces when they have been sandblasted to remove the layers of paint that have built up over time.

Wrought iron differs from cast iron in that

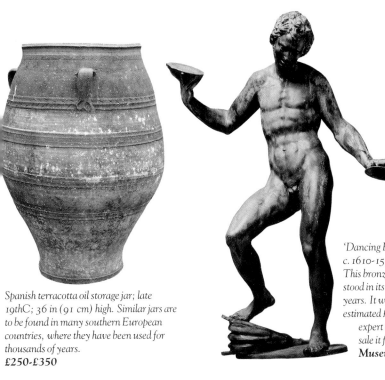

Spanish terracotta oil storage jar; late 19thC; 36 in (91 cm) high. Similar jars are to be found in many southern European countries, where they have been used for thousands of years.
£250-£350

'Dancing Faun' by Adrien de Vries; c.1610-15; 30¼ in (77 cm) high. This bronze statue, bought for £100, stood in its owners' garden for 40 years. It was to be auctioned for an estimated £1200-£1800 but an expert spotted it. In a fine art sale it fetched £6 million.
Museum piece

Coalbrookdale cast-iron seat in Lily-of-the-Valley pattern, stamped 'C.B. Dale & Co', with original bronze finish; c.1880; 61 in (1.55 m) wide. Examples with painted finish fetch £1500-£2500.
£2500-£3500

it is entirely shaped by hand and is not cast in moulds. Seats in particular were produced in a number of variations, including circular tree seats and games seats. The latter incorporated a pair of wheels at one end and a hinged footrest so that ladies watching outdoor games would not get their skirts and feet wet.

A Regency tree seat can usually be bought for £2000-£3000, a games seat for rather less. Many wrought-iron seats have been attacked by rust over the years, and have replacement feet and sometimes legs, lowering their value. The plainer designs, made of flat wrought-iron strips, were produced until the 1950s.

CAST LEAD

The tradition for lead casting was revived in the 1890s with most pieces harking back to earlier 17th and 18th-century styles. Many of the same designs are still produced by lead foundries today, and these can look considerably older than they really are, especially when certain chemicals are added to them during production. Inevitably, such pieces have little scarcity or age value, and should be bought only for their appeal; a typical pair of lead urns in a late 17th-century style, 20-24 in (51-61 cm) high, will fetch £300-£500.

Lead figures from the 18th century appear at auction from time to time, as do more recent copies. The base of such statues is one way of distinguishing original 18th-century models from late 19th and early 20th-century copies: the majority of 18th-century lead figures are fixed to a stone base, while later examples almost always have an integral lead base.

Cast-iron urn; c.1870. The design was common enough in the second half of the 19thC for urns usually 24 in (61 cm) or 30 in (76 cm) high and sold in pairs.
£600-£1000 a pair

Lead figure; early 20thC; 34 in (86 cm) high. It represents the young Bacchus, Greek god of grape-growing, wine and pleasure.
£300-£500

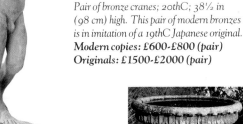

Pair of bronze cranes; 20thC; 38½ in (98 cm) high. This pair of modern bronzes is in imitation of a 19thC Japanese original.
Modern copies: £600-£800 (pair)
Originals: £1500-£2000 (pair)

Hazelwood birdbath; 20thC; 34 in (86.5 cm) high. This composition stone birdbath will be worth more once weathered.
£200

Reeded wrought-iron seat; early 19thC; 60 in (1.52 m) wide. This example was probably made by an estate or village blacksmith.
£1000-£1500

1 Decorated cast-iron weighing scales with copper pan and cast-iron weights

2 Tin-lined hastener with brass mechanism and rear 'porthole' to check on progress

3 Copper and plated dish covers

4 Bacon flake, or ladder-rack, with pulley

5 Brass trivets (pan and kettle stands)

6 Copper bain-marie

7 Elm salt box with leather-hinged lid

8 Sugar loaf and nips, mortar and pestle, and copper dredger

9 Pastry cutters and patty pans

10 Glazed earthenware flour crock

and the close-grained boxwood lemon juicer, rolling pin and pastry-cutting wheel; some wheels were of bone or walrus ivory. There is curiosity value in the sugar nips, which were used to break pieces off the tall sugar loaf. The pieces could be crushed in the mortar ready for dredging on apple pies, for example. The plentiful fresh-picked apples are evidence of the rural setting – as are the oil lamp and the candles on the mantelpiece, for by this time many houses in towns had gas lighting.

Home-cured hams are stored on the bacon flake (ladder-rack). Other meat, and provisions such as eggs, flour and milk were kept in the cool, airy larder beyond the scullery until needed. Any wasps and flies in the kitchen were lured into sweetened water in a glass trap, a pretty and useful object which would fetch £80-£100 now. Salt and bread were kept in the kitchen rather than the larder, the bread in a large earthenware crock with glazed inside, which would now fetch £200 or more.

A PLACE FOR HARD WORK

Furniture in kitchens was sparse – a couple of Windsor chairs (see p. 100) and a table. The deal table, which provided the only work surface, had to be thoroughly scrubbed every day. Although a sturdy table such as this brings a good price at auction now (see box, p. 111), it does not rival the dresser (see p. 118); smaller dressers, more convenient for modern kitchens, are most in demand.

The kitchen has few comforts except the homemade rag rug and the patchwork cushions. Neither has as much appeal to collectors as the embroidery (see p. 308) – the mistress's warning against idleness or waste. The only purely decorative items are the cook's own Staffordshire dogs on the mantel shelf. The trivets, brass candlesticks and fender, ornamental now, were for use then – and added to the cleaning chores. The never-ending chore for the kitchenmaid was dish-washing, and thankful she would be for the duckboard to lift her from the cold, often wet, flagged floor.

A collector's delight fills the open shelves of the dresser. Transfer-printed crockery was now being mass-produced in the Staffordshire potteries and elsewhere, by manufacturers such as Copeland and Ashworth. Even homely glazed stoneware jars that might once have held dry goods, drinks or pickled eggs are eagerly bought for storage or to use as vases.

Copper pans and jelly moulds also made a fine show, but were for use not ornament (see p. 366), and a trial to keep clean. Now these, and copper kettles, are snapped up to add a warm glow to clinical kitchens, while bainsmarie and large copper and cast-iron pans and roasting dishes make excellent plant holders.

11 Milk jug with bead-weighted muslin cover
12 Lemon juicer and pastry trimming wheel
13 Stacking sycamore spice tower
14 Cast-iron mincer clamped to the table
15 Ash duckboard on stone flags
16 Brass bells on springs (to tremble long enough for maids to see which room had rung)
17 Glazed stoneware jars
18 Copper jelly mould, tinned inside
19 Blue and white earthenware meat dish
20 Domed glass insect trap
21 Pine dresser with white porcelain knobs
22 Earthenware bread crock with painted tin lid

A MID-VICTORIAN KITCHEN

PEOPLE WHO LOVE THE PAST but cannot hope to buy any of its fine furniture or silver, find a good deal of pleasure and everyday history in attractive and curious goods from the kitchen.

In this country kitchen of 1870 the fire has been enclosed to harness its heat for ovens. An extra oven of a sort is the 'hastener', with its clockwork-turned vertical spit, which was moved right up to the fire for roasting meat. Ingenious but inelegant, this has not much appeal for collectors and can be picked up cheaply – as can the fire irons and the mincer.

More popular are the wood and leather bellows (which now might fetch £30-£40), and the scales (£80-£120). Scales, with brass or iron weights, were among the many goods being mass-produced in the 19th century. Others were tin baking wares, including clip-fastened fancy tins for game pies, and the battery of knives, choppers and enamelled ladles in the drawers and hanging on the wall.

More attractive – and still usable – are the stacking sycamore spice canisters, the spoons,

Domestic metalwares

Beautiful as precious metals are, they are clearly unsuited to the hard grind of everyday life. Base metals – pewter, copper, brass, iron and the like – have long been used for more down-to-earth, affordable household objects.

Iron door porter; c.1870; 12 in (30.5 cm) high. Door stops are also found in brass. This is an early example; most date from 1890-1920.
£40-£60

DINING IN STYLE *Pewter made most of the plates, chargers, drinking vessels and spoons for the tables of well-to-do 17thC families. Iron and brass were used for cooking pots and the utensils needed to tend the fire.*

Wrigglework pewter plate; c.1620; 9 in (23 cm) across. The popularity of pieces with this zigzag decoration drawn on by a gouge results in high prices.
£500-£800

'Beefeater' pewter flagon; c.1650; 12 in (30.5 cm) high. The name for these late 17thC flagons is from the shape, which is like a beefeater's (yeoman warder's) hat.
£1500-£2500

English medieval pewter flagon; 14thC; 9½ in (24.1 cm) high. This rare, eight-sided flagon was found by a man strolling beside the River Medway in Kent. He glimpsed it sticking out of the riverside silt. It was auctioned in October 1985 for £21,450.
Museum piece

PURE METALS AND THEIR ALLOYS have been fashioned into both practical and decorative objects for centuries. Hardwearing metals, including iron, pewter, copper and brass were essential for objects that got the most frequent use. Copper and brass, in particular, are back in fashion for interior furnishing – despite the polishing required to keep them looking their best.

Most pewter pieces carry a maker's 'touch' mark, and this can help in dating. Copper, brass and bronze items, on the other hand, are rarely marked, and can only be dated by the thickness of metal used, the style and the particular method of construction.

Less common base-metal alloys include spelter (zinc treated to resemble bronze) and paktong (a silvery-coloured alloy of copper, nickel and zinc), introduced from China in the 18th century. Articles in paktong are rare, and a pair of fine Georgian paktong candlesticks might fetch £1000 or more.

PEWTER

Pewter is a silver-grey alloy of tin made in Britain since Roman times. Until the 16th century it was limited to making ecclesiastical articles and items for the homes of the wealthy, while the very rich used silver and gold vessels. Over the following centuries it came to be used at every level of society, and an enormous range of objects were made in pewter between 1500 and 1800. Nearly all of them were cast in small workshops by individual craftsmen. Plates and dishes made up the vast majority of the pewter output, but spoons, mugs, tankards and candlesticks were also produced in quantity.

The pewter industry declined during the 18th century, surviving principally because of the demand for tavern drinking mugs and for items in britannia metal (see p.367). Interest in pewter itself revived around 1900 with the return of the fashion for simpler, hand-made objects that was associated especially with the Arts and Crafts movement.

Even where a small quantity of lead is included in the alloy, it is safe to eat and drink from pewter. However, such pewter must not be used for storing food and drink as the lead

William and Mary pewter candlestick; c.1690; 6 in (15.2 cm) high. It has a ball-knop stem and simple decoration on the base.
£450-£600

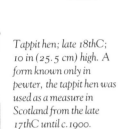

Pewter porringer with handle; 18thC; 5 in (12.7 cm) across. Stews and broths were eaten from such bowls; earlier ones were deeper.
£220-£450

Tappit hen; late 18thC; 10 in (25.5 cm) high. A form known only in pewter, the tappit hen was used as a measure in Scotland from the late 17thC until c.1900.
£275-£550

Pewter plates; 18thC; (right) 9 in (22.9 cm) across. The plain rim of this plate replaced the earlier reeded rim, and was itself succeeded by the cast lobed rim (left).
Left: £50-£80; right: £25-£40

Pewter tankards (left to right): 18thC, 5¼ in (13.3 cm) high; c.1850, 4½ in (11.4 cm) high; 1850-90, 5 in (12.7 cm) high. Body and handle shapes are often revivals and give little clue to date.
£150-£250; £20-£30; £20-£45

Lidded pewter ale or cider jug; c.1820; 6 in (15.2 cm) high. This bulbous form of jug was popular in taverns and homes from the late 18thC until the late 19thC.
£150-£250

Britannia metal teapot; c.1820; 6½ in (16.5 cm) high. Its flattened oval shape is typically Regency. Age and condition are the main influences on price.
£80-£100

a concave body from 1830. A tulip shape was popular from 1815 to 1870 and a U-shaped form peaked around 1840. Glass-bottomed mugs mostly date from Victorian times. There were hundreds of makers; the most plentiful mugs are those produced by James Yates who worked from 1860 to 1881 (but whose marks are still in use today).

All tavern mugs (but not those for domestic use) are marked with their capacity. The most common sizes are the quart to the gill (¼ pint). A variety of smaller sizes were made as spirit measures, and there are also gallon and half-gallon measures of most forms. These larger sizes are not common and were used for delivery and measuring. Depending on the type, rarity, age and condition, most 19th-century examples can be found at auction for £20-£80. Rare 18th-century mugs can fetch £100 or more, and mugs with an inscription on the body or under the foot, which are also more desirable, fetch similarly higher prices.

BRITANNIA METAL

Britannia metal was a cheaper form of pewter shaped by spinning rather than casting: thin sheets of the metal were pressed against a rotating wooden form or pattern. The seams were then soldered, and cast handles and other extras were applied.

Britannia metal tea and coffee pots were made in thousands of designs in Victorian times, mainly in Sheffield. Most pots are stamped with a maker's mark and a pattern number. Early 19th-century pots are generally simple and the most sought after, fetching £30-£80; later ones have elaborate stamped or applied decoration, and sell for £20-£50.

Many britannia metal articles were electroplated with silver after 1840, and most of these are marked EPBM (electroplated britannia metal). There is little demand for plated items, and they sell for just a few pounds.

TWENTIETH-CENTURY PEWTER

A wide range of pewter items in Art Nouveau style were commissioned by the London store Liberty's in the early 20th century. Their 'Tudric' pewter carries a pattern number, but as designs were used for over 30 years, this does not necessarily date individual items. A pint lidded tankard will sell for £150 and a vase for £75-£85. Early pieces, especially designs by Archibald Knox, can fetch £2000-£3000.

In the 1930s, there were hundreds of firms making hammered pewter wares with dimpled

can contaminate them. It is only some pewter that contains lead. Modern pewter contains none at all, but Roman pewter was made with a dangerously high lead content – in some pieces as high as 50 per cent.

The condition of pewter is crucial to its value. Minor dents and scratches do not matter, but avoid pieces with splits or holes, as pewter is hard and expensive to repair, and restored pieces do not hold their value.

PLATES, DISHES AND MUGS

Seventeenth-century pewter is now rare but more 18th-century work has survived, with plates and dishes being easiest to find. Most plentiful of all are serving dishes 16-18 in (40-46 cm) across, which usually fetch prices

between £60 and £200; larger dishes can run up to several hundred pounds. Plates, which are seldom less than 9 in (23 cm) across, can sell for £20-£40, but an inscription, coat of arms or crest will push the price up. Examples from the first 20 years of the 18th century often have a single reeded rim. This was followed by a plain-rimmed style which was used well into the next century, although between 1730 and 1780 many plates were given a lobed or wavy edge. From 1770 oval dishes were also made.

Beer consumption in public houses rose dramatically during the 19th century, and pewter mugs were turned out in quantity. They are found in several main forms. Pot-bellied, bulbous and straight-sided mugs were made throughout the century, and those with

finishes, and both tea and coffee sets are still easily found. A three-piece set of teapot, sugar bowl and milk jug usually fetches £40-£60.

BRASS, BRONZE AND COPPER

Copper, a relatively soft metal, has long been used for domestic wares both on its own and in alloys – notably bronze and brass, which are stronger than pure copper and less liable to split under heat or pressure. Bronze was mainly used for objects that were to be heated, such as cooking pots, while brass was used for decorative objects, such as candlesticks.

Birmingham became a major metalworking centre in the mid-18th century, and by the mid-19th was the world's leading brassware producer. As brass manufacture improved, bronze became less popular, but copperware continued in demand.

Care is needed to distinguish reproduction items, especially of brass, from Victorian or earlier pieces. Most 19th-century forms were made right up to the First World War, and even today there is a trade in reproductions.

CANDLESTICKS AND FIRESIDE ITEMS

Candlestick styles can be dated from the shape of the base, stem, sconce and so on, but these designs were re-used generation after generation, so dating may be tricky.

Many 18th-century candlesticks have a seamed stem, since they were cast in two parts and then soldered together. This is a good, though not sure, sign of a date before about 1780. Nearly all 18th and 19th-century candlesticks are well finished underneath, with any excess metal cleaned out. Less care was taken in finishing later sticks, which are left roughly cast. But beware: many modern candlesticks have been cleaned off to make them appear older. Genuine 18th-century candlesticks fetch from £150 to £650 a pair, depending on their style and exact age, and exceptional pairs stamped with a maker's mark fetch much more. Nineteenth-century pairs will go for between £80 and £200 and modern reproductions for as little as £20-£50.

Firedogs, or andirons, are mainly found in iron, sometimes decorated in brass, and were used for supporting either the grate or large logs directly. Examples in all shapes and sizes are collected today, and 19th-century firedogs sell for £150 or more per pair, while 18th-century examples can go for several thousand. Coal scuttles or buckets, made of both copper and brass, were

Liberty 'Tudric' pattern pewterware; 1904-10; biscuit box (below) 4½ in (11.4 cm) high. Both items were made in Arts and Crafts style and are attributed to Archibald Knox. The jug (right) has an applied enamel mount.
Box: £250-£400
Jug: £150-£200

English brass candlestick with six-sided base; c.1720; 6 in (15.2 cm) high. This example has a seamed stem which shows that the piece was cast in two parts, a good indication that it was made before 1780.
£125-£175

English lead bronze mortar; 1621; 5 in (12.7 cm) high. This decorated example is typical of the many domestic mortars used in homes for grinding spices and herbs.
£450-£700

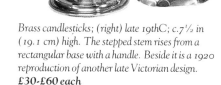

Brass candlesticks; (right) late 19thC; c.7½ in (19.1 cm) high. The stepped stem rises from a rectangular base with a handle. Beside it is a 1920 reproduction of another late Victorian design.
£30-£60 each

Lead bronze skillets: larger 1659, 7 in (17.8 cm) high; smaller c.1700, 4 in (10.1 cm) high. Skillets served as saucepans in the 16th-19thC; some are found with makers' names or inscriptions.
£250-£650 each

Victorian brass coal scuttle; 19thC; 20 in (51 cm) long. Similar scuttles are found in copper, most dating from the 19thC.
£175-£350

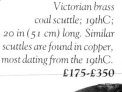

Copper warming pan; 19thC; 41 in (1.04 m). long. This is to hold hot coals; similar pans with a tap contained hot water. Later still, stoneware hot-water bottles replaced them.
£80-£150

Three copper saucepans from a set of 12; c.1870-80; largest c.14 in (35.6 cm) across. Other popular forms include examples with bowed sides and domed lids. The handles are usually iron, as here, but brass handles can also be found.
£75-£120 each

Copper kettle; 19thC; 10 in (25.4 cm) high. Kettles were also made in brass and in several sizes. They are found with wooden, glass, metal or composite handles.
£80-£150

Lipped brass preserving pan with fixed iron handle; c.1850-1900; 14 in (35.6 cm) across. Preserving pans or open saucepans had a variety of uses in the kitchen. Earlier ones have swing handles.
£100-£150

Scottish brass pint measure; c.1890; 6 in (15.2 cm) high. Sets (gill to pint) were made for measuring drinks and usually bear an excise mark to certify their capacity. Copper sets fetch less than brass.
Single: £75-£100
Set of three: £150-£200

Modern reproduction brass jardinière; 12½ in (31.7 cm) across. Victorian ones are harder to find and cost at least twice as much.
£50-£80

popular around 1700, with the growing fashion for drinking tea. They are usually made of copper, brass or a combination of the two. Those dating from the late 18th century have a flat base and handle of wood or bone, and many are bulbous in form. Later kettles may be oblong, square, round or oval, with a brass or iron handle. In general, a good brass kettle will change hands for around £100-£200, a copper example for £80-£150. Coloured glass handles were popular in the 1840s. Millions of kettles were exported from Birmingham, many of them to North Africa, and many of these are reappearing on the market, together with kettles made in the Middle East.

Apart from saucepans and kettles, the Victorians made preserving pans, fish kettles, covered roasting dishes, jelly moulds and so on – all of which are collectable today. All the copper articles to be used for cooking or serving food were originally tinned on the inside for safety, since copper dissolves in food acids and can cause poisoning. If an item is old, look for signs of this tinning, but beware if the tin is wearing thin and you want to use the article in the kitchen: it is dangerous to use and expensive to re-tin.

Until the late 19th century, most domestic brassware – including ladles, skimmers, chestnut roasters, jelly moulds and jardinières – was made for practical use. But towards the end of the Victorian era, items such as these became increasingly decorative and less functional.

As a general rule, the more robust an item is and the greater the signs of wear, the more likely it is to be an early piece. The more decorative and lightweight a piece is, the more recently it was probably made. Examples in pristine condition are almost certain to be relatively new, because all these forms are still being made today.

In the 19th century working horses were decorated with plumes and other regalia – including brass badges known as 'horse brasses'. Most examples date from 1880-1930, but hundreds of thousands of copies have been made since then which never saw the back of a horse. Genuine examples are mostly well finished on the inside and show evidence of years of polishing. Most Victorian and Edwardian badges can be bought for £20-£60 but rare badges will naturally fetch higher prices than the more common examples.

common during the 19th century, as were sets of fire tools in brass or iron and brass. Today, scuttles can fetch around £125-£300 if in good condition, while complete sets of fire tools (including poker, shovel and fire tongs) fetch between £50 and £250. As a rule of thumb, the larger the tools are the earlier and more valuable they are likely to be.

Round, long-handled warming pans that held hot embers were used to heat up beds in the 18th and 19th centuries, but were gradually replaced by copper and brass hot-water containers. The earliest examples are large, often with a brass or iron handle, and fetch £500-£1000 at auction. The smaller Victorian warming pans with a wooden handle sell for around £125-£250. Always look for

signs of wear, as a pan filled night after night with hot coals should show signs of distress.

Fenders and grates vary in value according to age and material. An 18th-century paktong grate may make more than £8000, while a 19th-century plain iron grate would fetch around £400. Fenders make from £150-£200 for 19th-century examples, while earlier or decorated pieces would fetch much more.

PANS, KETTLES AND DECORATIVE BRASSWARE

Sets of copper cooking pots with flat lids were made from the 19th century onwards. Early examples usually have brass handles riveted on both the pot and the lid, but late Victorian pans more often have cast-iron handles. A Victorian saucepan of quart size (1.14 litres) in copper or brass might make £40-£80, but early examples with brass handles and an owner's initials or crest can cost £100 or more.

Kitchen kettles are among the most sought after items today. They originally became

Treen

An astonishing range of wooden objects fall into the category called treen – small turned or carved items.

IN THE DAYS BEFORE the mass-production of ceramics, poorer homes were equipped with handmade wooden utensils, which are now eagerly sought after by treen enthusiasts. Most treen available today dates from the 19th century. Much older pieces, including wares from as early as the 16th century, are in Birmingham City Museum's treen collection of over 7000 items, the best in the world.

In the past, treen was a poor relation to furniture and works of art in the view of many collectors. Although this is no longer true and prices have risen dramatically over the past 30 years, many English pieces can still be had for as little as £25-£50. Continental treen can fetch higher prices as it was often made for the gentry and has more elaborate carving.

Welsh love spoons are often intricately carved, but the finest carving appears on items such as 17th-century ivory-inlaid wassail bowls in turned lignum vitae, an exceptionally hard wood. Few of these remain in private hands, and if one comes up for sale at auction it is likely to fetch over £10,000.

Fruitwood tea caddies are also highly collectable, especially those carved in the shape of an apple, melon, pear or gourd, good examples of which can now fetch over £2000. Small items that are far more affordable include turned fruitwood holders for perfume bottles or oil, which go for just a few pounds.

Among the most interesting treen artefacts are *trompe l'oeil* dummyboard figures. Their exact purpose is uncertain, but they may have provided the illusion of companionship for the rich and lonely, or simply acted as screens to block draughts. The figures made their first appearance in early 17th-century Europe and continued to be produced in England until the 1920s, so prices vary from as much as £10,000 a pair to £2000, depending on age.

Yew-wood salt container; late 17thC; 5⅛ in (13 cm) high. This piece has been turned on a foot-operated lathe.
£400-£600

Victorian fruitwood carpet bowls ball with weighting tube; c.1880; 3⅛ in (80 mm) across.
£20-£30

Turned hardwood jar and cover; c.1900; 9 in (22.9 cm) high.
£50-£80

Fruit bowl; early 18thC; 13 in (33 cm) across. A rich colour raises the value.
£500-£700

Snuffbox (right); c.1840; 3⅓ in (85 mm) long. This unusual box in the form of a book has a well made spine and hinge.
£120-£180

Fruitwood pepper mill (right); c.1900; 4⅓ in (11 cm) high. This is decorated to simulate 16th and 17thC jewelled ware.
£20-£30

Ebony perfume bottle holder; c.1860; 4¾ in (12.1 cm) high. Although machine turned, it shows skilful work.
£20-£40

Coquilla-nut salt pot (right); c.1800; 3 in (76 mm) high. The crack lowers the value.
£30-£50

Olive-wood, apple-shaped box and cover; c.1880; 3⅛ in (80 mm) across.
£70-£90

Victorian walnut paperweight; c.1880; 2⅓ in (59 mm) across. The wood is filled with lead and has a baize base.
£10-£20

Needle case; 19thC; 2½ in (63 mm) high. The appeal of treen is evident in this simply turned and carved everyday object.
£10-£15

Fruitwood dagger; 17thC; 6⅞ in (17.5 cm) long. A chip on the embossed handle halves its value.
£60-£90

Kitchen and home appliances

A collection of domestic equipment need not be expensive or take up much space, but it can help you re-create – literally – the flavour of the past.

Knife cleaner; c.1890; 18 in (45.7 cm) high. Cleaners with original paper labels with directions and a mock brass nameplate fetch more.
£80-£120

M IDDLE-CLASS FAMILIES a century ago depended on cooks, maids, housekeepers and butlers to keep the household running smoothly. But the number of domestic servants diminished as they went into industry or the armed services, and labour-saving devices became essential.

Such books as Mrs Beeton's *Book of Household Management* (published 1861) illustrate many collectable gadgets from copper stewpots and cast-iron teakettles to enamelled mincers and gridirons. (See also Domestic metalwares, p. 366, and Treen, opposite.)

COOKING UTENSILS AND CORKSCREWS

Choppers, peelers, graters, grinders, knives and other implements were made in their hundreds of thousands in the 19th century – usually from wrought or cast iron or sheet steel. Simple gadgets such as vegetable slicers and potato peelers can be found for as little as £5, but more elaborate designs such as a Victorian mechanical apple peeler can fetch up to £250.

Before spring-balance scales

Selection of tin openers in metal and wood; 19thC; bull's head examples 6½ in (16.5 cm) long.
£3-£20

Goodell & Co's Bonanza apple peeler (right); c.1890; 18 in (45.7 cm) long. This ingenious time-saver even took the core out of the apples it was peeling.
£100-£150

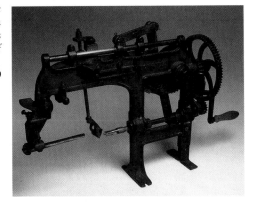

Jelly mould; c.1910; 7 in (17.8 cm) diameter. Jelly moulds were also used for making blancmange, a popular pudding.
£30-£40

came into use around the mid-19th century, kitchen scales all had a horizontal pivoted beam with balancing pans suspended from either end. Scales with their complete set of original brass weights – usually 11 pieces ranging from ⅛ oz to 2 lb – are the most sought after, with prices ranging from £5 to £500, depending on age and condition.

Jelly moulds are ideal if you want articles to use as well as display. Prices range from £10 to £15 for the plainest examples of china and earthenware to £20-£100 for late 19th and early 20th-century copper moulds. Moulds in novelty shapes are more desirable still. They were introduced in the 18th century and, after 1770, large versions were made to provide a number of helpings. Wedgwood creamware moulds appeared in the 1780s and copper moulds around 1820. By the end of the 19th century earthenware and stoneware were the most popular materials.

Many ingenious corkscrews were made between 1880 and 1920. Collectors will pay as much as £1000 for a sophisticated mechanical opener from the period, although £20-£100 is usual for more ordinary pieces. A silver or ivory handle will push up the price, particularly if in the shape of a face, animal, ship or nude figure – and so will the name of a maker, distiller or wine-shipper.

FRIDGES, COOKERS AND CLEANERS

Iceboxes were not available outside wealthy households until the 19th century. In Britain the first domestic electric refrigerator was put on the market in 1924. Early models are not highly sought after, although a 1950s refrigerator with bulbous door may fetch £50.

Gas cookers were first made commercially in 1836, followed by electric ovens in 1891. But before both of these, and well into the 20th century, many households cooked on a coal-fired range (see p. 364). Cookers are not generally considered collectable, although pre-1910 examples can fetch £100 or so.

In 1912 the first electric Hoover reached Britain, and the vacuum cleaner became a

Kenrick & Sons' patent coffee mill; c.1890; 6½ in (16.5 cm) high. Until the 20thC, coffee beans were always sold unground.
£30-£40

Selection of corkscrews; early 20thC. Basic wood, metal and bone corkscrews such as these are worth far less than those with more complicated mechanisms.
£8-£15 each

Charcoal box iron; c.1880; 8 in (20.3 cm) long. Irons that held hot embers eliminated the frequent reheating that flat irons needed.
£120-£180

Willcox & Gibbs table-top sewing machine; c.1890; 12 in (30.5 cm) long. This was one of the many wood and metal models that capitalised on the success of Singer's invention.
£100-£150

standard piece of household equipment as houses got an electricity supply. Although of little value at the moment, early 20th-century machines are worth keeping.

WASHING, IRONING AND SEWING

Scrubbing boards and wooden washing dollies (for agitating the washing in a tub) were standard equipment in every household until the introduction of hand-powered washing machines at the beginning of the 19th century (and in many homes for a long time after that). The first electric washing machine appeared on the market in 1907, but hand-operated machines lived on in many households until the 1950s. Such labour-saving devices are only of small interest to collectors.

The earliest irons, introduced in Europe in the 16th century, were 'sad' or 'flat' irons, which had to be heated on a stove. You can usually pick up later models for a few pounds. Flat irons were superseded by box irons in the 18th century. The first box irons had a metal slug which could be heated up and then placed inside the case, but later versions were adapted to take coals or embers. A decorative box iron could fetch over £100.

The first domestic sewing machine was produced by Isaac Singer in 1851. Generally, only examples from before 1890 have any value as collectables – in mint condition they may fetch several hundred pounds. (The record price paid – for a rare 1878 McQuin machine – is over £4000.)

FEEDERS AND PRAMS FOR BABIES

Until the 1850s, when glass was first used, the usual open-topped baby feeder – or pap-boat – was made from pottery (see p.202). Even though glass feeders quickly began to take over the market, Wedgwood continued to make ceramic feeders as late as 1870. Early pottery feeders are now rare, but 19th-century

Stoneware foot warmers; 19thC; c.12 in (30 cm) long. These containers held hot water and were used to warm feet both in bed and on long winter journeys.
£5-£10 each

glass versions can still be found for £5-£50

The first prams were miniature carriages built for babies of royal or aristocratic families. In ordinary homes, prams were unknown until about 1850, when pushchairs on three wheels first appeared. Thirty years later came a four-wheeled version that allowed the baby to lie down, and in 1887 a suspension system was incorporated. Only in the late 1920s did mass-production bring steel-framed prams within reach of ordinary families.

Prams from before 1800 are rare, and even a Victorian model in good condition may go for £1000 or more. Twentieth-century examples are less expensive – even novelties such as the 1908 'Kriz', which folds up into a carpet bag, will fetch no more than £200.

Ephemera

An old tobacco tin, a suitcase with its exotic labels, wartime ration coupons or cigarette cards pasted into an album – humble mementos bring back the flavour of life in the past.

Luggage labels; c. 1930. Colourful hotel labels were status symbols and vied for space on a traveller's luggage.
£1-£3

Women's magazine; 1930s. Such magazines give a picture of contemporary social life and fashions.
£1-£3

1950s comics. Since the late 19thC more than 2000 comic titles have been launched.
£1-£2 each

ONE TO KEEP *The Victorians had a passion for albums, and from the 1850s small coloured 'scraps' – such as this – were specially made for children to paste into scrapbooks.*

As INDUSTRIALISATION TOOK HOLD in Britain in the late 18th century, mass-produced goods began to pour into homes across the land. From factories came tins and bottles, boxes and jars – often beautifully decorated – for everything from bear's grease (for hair) to anchovy paste and ginger beer. From the newly mechanised presses came newspapers, magazines, advertisements, programmes, wrappers and labels. Soon even holidays were not complete without a souvenir or a postcard for those at home.

A surprising number of such items – collectively known as ephemera – have been preserved, perhaps for their sentimental value or usefulness, or simply because no one got round to throwing them away. Even things that were consigned to the bin were not necessarily lost for ever – old tips and back gardens still yield some interesting finds.

NEWSPAPERS AND MAGAZINES

Luckily for collectors, large numbers of old newspapers and magazines have survived, and most are inexpensive. Early editions of *Punch*

Exhibition guide; 1925. Such exhibitions were also sources of souvenirs made by exhibitors.
£7-£9

and *The Illustrated London News* from the late 19th century or women's magazines such as *Woman's Own* from the 1930s can be bought from market stalls for between 50p and £2. First issues always command a premium, particularly for sought-after publications such as *Vogue* and the children's comic *Beano*. Copies of the first *Beano* issued in 1938 are now worth around £600 in good condition, but other 1930s numbers cost about £25.

Old newspapers have little resale value, and even 150-year-old editions can be bought for just a few pounds. Issues from this century are generally only of value if the headline records a major event such as the sinking of the *Titanic* in 1912 (about £100) or victory over Germany in 1945 (£15). Newspapers from the Second World War are not rare, as many people saved them for historical reasons and because paper was scarce. They can be hard to distinguish from recent reprints. Most sell for only £1-£2 each at markets.

GREETINGS AND POSTCARDS

With the introduction of the Penny Post in 1840 (see p.384), a whole new industry developed devoted to cards for special occasions. Valentine cards particularly appealed to Victorian sentimentality. From 1850 to 1890 an enormous range of light-hearted and fanciful designs were produced; some had layers of paper lace and colourful paper scraps, or ingenious arrangements of strings or levers which opened out three-dimensionally.

The first Christmas card was designed in 1843 for Sir Henry Cole, but not until the late 1850s did commercial card-printing begin in earnest. Manufacturers were soon producing greetings cards for occasions including, by the turn of the century, birthdays. Cards are generally inexpensive, although the most elaborate can fetch over £100 at auction.

The first postcards were produced and sold by the Post Office in 1870, ready-printed with a halfpenny stamp which would take them anywhere in Britain. Only in 1894 were private companies allowed to produce picture postcards – opening the way for a flood of subjects and scenes. Today prices range from 10p to over £100, although many interesting examples fall within the £1-£5 bracket.

ADVERTISING MATERIAL AND PACKAGING

As mass production increased, manufacturers brought out catalogues, price lists and promotional material to inform the public about their wares. These publications provide some of the best records of changing technology and design, and of social attitudes and the lifestyles to which buyers aspired.

Competition spurred 19th-century manufacturers on to develop new and better sales techniques, most obviously in the form of posters and enamel signs. Single-colour posters (usually black type on white paper) had been plastered on walls in Britain since the 17th century, but the first giant, coloured posters on hoardings appeared only during the latter half of Queen Victoria's reign.

Posters in Art Deco style from the 1920s and 30s are particularly popular with modern collectors, especially those for London Transport, Shell and the railway companies, who commissioned the leading commercial artists of the day. The subject as well as the artist affects prices; steam engines and golfers are favourites. Top prices can be over £1000, but low-cost reproductions abound.

Manufacturers and retailers also issued a great variety of promotional gifts such as puzzles, playing cards, story books and gramophone records. Other advertisers attached their names to useful items such as pencils, rulers, spoons, bottle openers, tea strainers and even collar studs; any of these can fetch between 50p and £50 today.

Together with company records and promotional material, product packaging can tell the story of how a firm survived – or succumbed – in a competitive market, and how the

GOD BLESS AND KEEP YOU.

First World War postcards; 1914-18. An embroidered silk card (below) will fetch slightly more than the 'Song and Hymn' card on the left. **50p-£3**

Christmas card; c.1895. From 1880 to 1895 over 150,000 different Christmas cards were designed. **£1**

Early postcards; 1895-1905; $3\frac{1}{2} \times 5\frac{1}{2}$ in (8.9 × 14 cm). Picture postcards became popular towards the end of the 19thC. **£1-£5**

Enamel advertising signs; 1905-20; $18-19\frac{1}{2}$ in (45.7-49.5 cm) high. These used to hang in shops and railway stations. **Left: £200; Right: £150**

Libby's evaporated milk poster; c.1930; $17\frac{1}{2}$ in (44.4 cm) high. Posters can be found in many styles. **£40**

image of a product evolved. Only containers in good condition have any collectable value and few are worth much.

Well-known brands such as Bovril can often be traced from their launch (1886) up to the present day. The different jars, labels and slogans (such as 'Bovril prevents that sinking feeling') all contribute to a picture of the company and its customers.

Matchbox labels are probably the most popular form of packaging, but cheese and beer labels have their devotees. The choice of designs is vast, with prices from 5p to £20.

CIGARETTE CARDS

Of all promotional gimmicks, the cigarette card has been most diligently collected. It first appeared in the 1880s, initially as a way of strengthening the packet, but manufacturers soon realised its value as a marketing aid. Wills and Players began the trend in Britain by printing miniature versions of their advertisements. Once the idea caught on, the quality of the card became almost as vital a factor as the quality of the tobacco.

Cigarette cards were usually issued in series of 25 or 50, with illustrations varying from ships, cats and birds' eggs to actresses, footballers and optical illusions. Their heyday came in the 1920s, with increasingly fanciful objects inserted to entice the buyer. There were shaped cards, metallic cards, stereoscopic picture cards and even miniature gramophone-record cards. Collectors could get albums to keep their cards in, or use special mounts for framing and displaying a set. Some

Paper bookmarks; c.1900. These are often found hidden in old books.
£1-£15 each

Charity flags to pin on a lapel; 1914-18. Miniature silk flags sold for war charities were the idea of a Welsh housewife in 1914.
£1-£3 each

Cigarette cards; 1890-1905. Condition and rarity affect values.
£375-£400 per set

Coronation biscuit tins. The front two are for Edward VII (1902), that behind, 10 in (25.4 cm) high, for George V (1911).
£10-£100

Metal lapel badges; 1930s to 1950s. There are many badges for products as well as clubs. They fetch more when enamelled than in tin.
£1-£8

Miniature bottles; 1905-50; tallest 4½ in (11.4 cm). Miniatures were used to launch new brands.
£1-£10

Biscuit tins; 1890-1910; tallest 6 in (15.2 cm). Novelty shapes, such as the carriage, are the most desirable, but rusty tins are almost worthless.
£30-£250

Matchbox labels; 1900-20. Most labels are cheap; early examples on boxes are more desirable.
50p

series were even printed on silk for sewing onto cushion covers or counterpanes.

Cigarette cards died out with the outbreak of war in 1939. But since then similar cards have been issued at various times as inducements for all sorts of other products, such as biscuits, bubble gum and tea.

Over the past century, so many cards have been saved that many series are inexpensive. However, the price of a scarce set can be high. A collection of 20 Taddy's clowns from the 1920s, for example, could be worth as much as £10,000 or so. But beware of forgeries: only 15 genuine sets exist, as the company closed down while the series was still in preparation.

Individual cards can also be valuable if they are rare. The record price of US$451,000 was realised by a 1910 card with a picture of the American baseball player Honus Wagner and an advertisement for Piedmont cigarettes. Soon after it was issued Wagner asked for the card to be withdrawn, as he disapproved of smoking. Only 40 now survive, of which only two have the Piedmont advertisement.

TELEPHONE CARDS

Completely modern ephemera is seldom collected, but telephone cards are one exception. Since the cards first appeared in Britain in the 1980s, collectors have sought out special pictorial and commemorative issues, and foreign cards. The 100 unit Muirfield Golf card of 1987 is worth up to £1000 in mint condition as very few were issued, but most fetch £1-£10, or less without the packet. Only time will tell if they have any lasting value.

Phone cards are the latest worldwide collecting craze. Most are worth just over their original price if still in the packet and £1 or less without the packet. Japan has issued most designs.

Memorabilia

*Top-of-the-range mementos fetch
top-of-the-range prices, but
perseverance and an autograph book
are all you need to start a collection.*

STAR STRUCK *Film stills and autograph album pages
testify to hours spent by adoring fans at stage doors or
writing to studios – hours now valued by eager collectors.*

THE TEENAGER WHO wrote to John Lennon in the early 1960s had no idea that one day his handwritten replies would bring hundreds of pounds at auction. The photographer who snapped a young factory worker called Norma Jean Dogherty in 1945 little realised that his pictures of the future Marilyn Monroe would come to be regarded as important historical images of one of the century's most idolised women.

Most people associate memorabilia with signatures but, although these form the start of most collections, almost any kind of memento can be collected, often at little cost. Originality and provenance are of great importance. If you are unsure about the authenticity of an item consult an expert.

FILM TROPHIES

Movie enthusiasts have an enormous range of artefacts to collect, but the size of the film industry means care has to be taken. Signed photographs of screen stars are highly prized, but only those with a handwritten signature are valuable. Clear dedications and signatures of cult stars can fetch up to £500 at auction. Most prized of all are unpublished shots of cult idols, such as James Dean.

Objects associated with a particular film are much rarer and can command huge prices. The ruby slippers worn by Judy Garland in *The Wizard of Oz*, for example, went for $165,000 (£82,500), and the piano in *Casablanca* sold for $154,000 (£77,000), both in 1988 at New York auctions.

The large studios sometimes sell off film props and costumes, and not all have the same rarity and desirability. Dick van Dyke's waistcoat from *Chitty Chitty Bang Bang* might sell for £40-£80, but Janet Suzman's dress from *Nicholas and Alexandra* for £300-£400.

Cinema historians are always keen to acquire a screenplay or script, especially one annotated by a well-known director or actor. Prices reflect the importance of the script, but are usually in the hundreds. Artists' contract letters are valuable if they relate to an important star or film, starting at £500. Such material is most collectable when handwritten, dated, signed and undamaged.

Film publicity material, including premiere tickets and programmes, photographs and

*Photograph of
Laurel and Hardy,
signed in ink; 1930s. Their bowler hats
sold for £11,000 at a 1989 auction.*
£100-£150

*Poster for the film 'The Seven Year
Itch', portraying Marilyn Monroe;
1955. Posters from the last 30 years, in
good condition, are highly sought after if
the film's star has become a cult figure.*
£400-£500

*Ruby slippers from 'The Wizard of Oz';
1939. Worn by Judy Garland in the
MGM cult movie, these slippers hold
the world record price for a pair of shoes.*
£75,000-£100,000

posters, is most desirable when it relates to hugely popular films, cult stars or a particular movie genre. Today there is great interest in the graphics of low-budget science fiction and teenage thrillers which packed the drive-in cinemas of 1950s and 60s America.

Condition is particularly important with all types of mass-produced material. Posters should be without tears or holes and foyer photographs should be bright and clear, without any signs of fading.

FROM THE STAGE

As with cinema memorabilia, the greatest stage performers or productions create the greatest demand from collectors. Costumes, letters, programmes, posters, signed photographs and ballet shoes are all popular, although ballet costume and design are col-

lected as a specialist field. This stems from interest in the work of 20th-century ballet designers and choreographers, such as French fashion designer Erté, Russian artist and theatre designer Léon Bakst and his fellow-countryman, impresario Sergei Diaghilev. They were responsible for the highly original productions of the Ballets Russes from 1911.

ROCK MEMORABILIA

The first-ever auction of rock memorabilia was as recent as 1981, but specialised auction sales are now held in many countries and there is a network of specialist dealers.

Essentially the music is what makes a group famous, and it is the items directly related to the music that are the most sought after. Instruments used in memorable live performances or during recording sessions can fetch

Marie Lloyd's autographed photograph; c.1912. This tinted studio portrait of the famous music hall star is signed: 'Yours always'. Several identical portraits exist.
£30-£40

Poster for a Daly's Theatre company production in Scarborough; 1896. It is typical of its time, when Japanese taste was very influential.
£200-£300

Madonna autographed album; 1988. The cover, for 'Who's That Girl', is signed: 'Best wishes, love Madonna'.
£250-£350

Beatles dress; 1964. This rarity was autographed on the shoulder and back while worn by an usherette at the premiere of 'A Hard Day's Night'.
£2000-£3000

Jimi Hendrix self-portrait cartoon; 1966. It includes caricatures of other musicians and has five lines of song lyrics on the back.
£5000-£7000

'The Who' drum skin; c.1968. Made by Premier, Keith Moon's bass drum was used on tour in 1968, appearing at the Woodstock music festival and in many photographs of the group at the time.
£5000-£7000

Elton John's glasses; c.1973. The pop star's spectacles have yellow-tinted prescription lenses in thick novelty frames stamped with the name 'Silhouette'.
£400-£800

extremely high prices – £198,000 was recently paid at auction for the guitar Jimi Hendrix played at the Woodstock festival of 1969. Although instruments may be signed by the player, it is documentary proof of origin that counts. This can be a photograph of the owner receiving the item from the star, a letter from the player confirming former ownership of the object, or an affidavit from the owner and a witness establishing a connection.

Painted bass drums, fashionable in the 1960s and 70s, are much in demand. The combination of graphic art and the name of an important band has led to high prices when drum skins from the The Beatles, The Who and Cream have come up for sale. Costume as well as instruments can be directly associated with well-known performers and attract great interest. Michael Jackson's leather jacket and

trousers worn on stage during his *Bad* world tour in 1988 fetched £15,000 in 1990. And Madonna's gold basque, designed by fashion designer Jean Paul Gaultier and worn on her *Blonde Ambition* tour in 1990, was sold the following year for £9000.

Collectors on a more limited budget may be able to afford costumes worn for film or video performances, which are generally available for under £1000. Provenance is again vital.

Artists' own record collections are of particular interest to music historians. Apart from these, most records are classified as a separate collecting area from memorabilia. Other exceptions are acetates (trial pressings of a recording made in the recording studio) and demonstration discs. These may be slightly different recordings from known releases or, better still, previously unknown

recordings. Rarities of both kinds have been found in second-hand record shops and have fetched hundreds of pounds in the saleroom. Recorded interviews, home movies or video recordings of performers that have never been issued or broadcast are always sought after.

The most desirable signatures are those written on something connected with the music of the group, such as a concert programme or ticket, record sleeve or sheet music. But beware: many forgeries of leading group members' signatures exist. Manuscript material, song lyrics or letters giving an insight into a group's history are always popular, and thousands of pounds change hands for the most important examples.

Merchandise related to music, such as T-shirts, badges, posters and keyrings can make high prices at auction, if they are in good condition. For example, £440 was paid recently for a late 1960s teapot made in the shape of an apple – the name and symbol of The Beatles' shop, record label and company.

WELL-KNOWN FIGURES

There is an active circle of enthusiastic collectors of royal commemorative wares of all types – made of glass, wood or metal as well as ceramics (see p. 196). The most scarce of royal mementos, and by far the most valuable, are signed photographs or letters. These were usually presented by a member of the royal family to a member of the household, an estate worker or an ambassador. Some of them sell at auction for hundreds of pounds.

Letters written by well-known politicians, writers, artists, poets and other influential figures are certainly worth preserving, particularly if the text refers to a historic event or an important incident in the writer's life. Proofs and working drafts with alterations in a writer's own hand may give an insight into their mind, and new-found documents can lead to a reinterpretation of someone's character or throw new light over a particular event or controversy.

Among the most valuable and headline-grabbing of all finds, of course, are previously unknown manuscripts by great writers or composers – of which there have been recent instances. In July 1990, two music manuscripts were found in an old safe in an American theological college. They had been donated 40 years earlier by the daughter of a music collector, but had never been identified. They were found to be Mozart's working manuscripts of two of his greatest piano compositions, the K.475 Fantasia and the K.457 Sonata, both in C minor, and sold at auction for some £880,000.

One of a group of over 70 autograph letters from William Thackeray to his friend Anne Proctor; 1839–41.
£15,000-£25,000

Autographed photograph of Mikail Gorbachev; c.1990. Signatures of politicians who have made an impact on history have wide appeal.
£100-£180

One of the 28 pages of the autographed manuscript of Beethoven's Piano Sonata in E Minor, Opus 90; 1814. Most unusually, it is still privately owned.
Entire manuscript: £1.1 million

Chromolithograph of W.G. Grace; 1895; 11¾ in (29.8 cm) high. Beware of modern reproductions printed on old paper and artificially aged.
£300-£400
Reproduction: £20-£30

ITEMS TO COLLECT with a sporting connection divide readily into several main categories: historic equipment that charts the development of the sport; memorabilia associated with a sport – from souvenir pamphlets to trophies and books; paintings and prints of famous sportsmen and renowned venues; and miniature indoor versions of various sports invented by the Victorians.

Anything that belonged to a leading sportsperson will fetch a high price, especially if accompanied by some proof of provenance. Medals, trophies, statues of sporting heroes, household objects decorated to celebrate great victories, calendars, posters and books – all have been produced in their millions, and give an opportunity for collectors on a more modest budget to enter the field.

In general, sports that have been the most expensive to equip or take part in – such as golf – have become the most collectable.

GOLFING ITEMS

Golf is by far the most expensive sporting field in which to collect, partly because of its massive international following. Early equipment was expensive even when it was made in the 19th century, and is far more so now. Balls, clubs, carrying tools and learning aids

---

HISTORIC MEMORABILIA
Memories from a Momentous Past

THE ATTRACTION of an item owned by a person who changed the course of history is irresistible to some collectors. Whether the owner was a popular figure of romance or a monster makes little difference. The cap worn by Charles I (see p. 318), a ring given by Napoleon, a book inscribed by Byron or a scrap of paper scribbled on by Hitler are avidly sought by those who want to own a little piece of history.

Royalty holds a particular fascination, and combined with romance – or intimate associations – can make prices rocket. The love story of Edward VIII and Mrs Simpson ensured that the sale of Mrs Simpson's jewellery (see p. 264) fetched far above the expected prices.

Queen Victoria's fine lawn split drawers; late 19thC. This large pair of drawers has pin tucks round the leg holes and is embroidered with the Queen's monogram.
£150-£250

Sporting collectables

Hunting out old sports equipment, trophies and memorabilia can be just as much fun as the sport itself – and far less taxing. But many collectors also play.

Golf club heads (from left): Philp spoon, c.1830; Mitchell long-nosed short spoon, c.1885; Jackson of Perth putter, 1840-50. Value depends on maker, age and condition.
Left to right: £14,000, £1500, £5000

'The New Book of Golf', first edition; 1912. Golfing books from before 1900 are much rarer, but this book was published during a time of great interest in the sport, hence its value.
£100-£150

Allan Robertson feathery golf ball (left); 1840; 1¾ in (44 mm); and Marshall feathery golf ball; 1830.
Left: £7000
Right: £8000

Hardy Brothers' Cascapaedia multiplying fly reel; 1920. Named after a famed Canadian salmon-fishing river, this reel is one of a limited edition.
£6000-£8000

Stuffed trout trophy; c.1920; 36 in (91 cm) wide. Surprisingly, well-carved painted replicas of fish are more valuable than stuffed specimens; this one's naturalistic background adds extra value.
£500-£800

Silver and gold sports mementos (from top): Silver card case with golfer (c.1900), and silver golf-tee pen (c.1940). Gold and mother-of-pearl cufflinks and buttons with golfing scenes (c.1930). Silver-gilt tennis-racket brooch (c.1900).
Top: £280 and £95
Centre: £1400
Bottom: £220

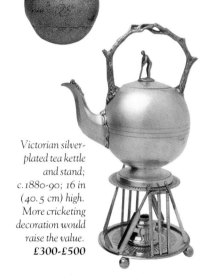

Victorian silver-plated tea kettle and stand; c.1880-90; 16 in (40.5 cm) high. More cricketing decoration would raise the value.
£300-£500

are among the most coveted items, and even rather poor-quality examples can fetch as much or more than better-quality material in the form of pictures, photographs or books. Little equipment has survived from before 1800, and when it does appear a club, say, may fetch as much as £40,000. The earliest woods and unique patent clubs dating from the late 1880s to the 1920s can fetch £100-£5000.

One of the most important milestones in golf was the introduction of the gutta-percha ball around 1848. The previous feathery balls were expensive and easily destroyed; they sell today for £1500-£13,000 each. The gutta-percha ball, superseded by the rubber-cored ball in 1902, has become a collector's item in its own right, and a hand-hammered example can sell at auction for as much as £1000.

A perennially popular subject for paintings has been Tom Morris, four times British open champion, greenkeeper and professional player at Scotland's St Andrews golf course in the 19th century. Among paintings of golfing scenes and sportsmen, the most sought after are those by the British naive painters Francis Powell Hopkins and Thomas Hodge, whose paintings fetch £1000-£10,000.

Other items sought by golfing enthusiasts include pottery and porcelain cups, ashtrays and other mementos decorated with golfing subjects. Such wares were produced by all major manufacturers between 1890 and 1935. Larger trophy pieces were sometimes given as prizes, and these can fetch up to £4000 at auction. Collectable silver objects include vesta (match) cases, hatpins, manicure sets,

brooches, charms, scorecards and walking sticks – all decorated with a golfing theme and all able to fetch significantly more than conventionally decorated equivalents.

CRICKET

The autographed cricket bat is a relatively modern idea (but one that will become collectable in the future), so photographs and scrapbooks dating from the early test matches in the late 19th century are among the most prized of cricket collectables.

Anything associated with W.G. Grace – widely considered the greatest cricketer in the history of the sport – is sought after. Prints, caricatures, paintings, photographic portraits and biographies were produced in their thousands, along with Staffordshire pottery figures which sell for £200-£400, and small parian porcelain busts for £600-£800.

Collectors also covet books and early magazines, especially copies of the fact-filled Wisden *Cricketers' Almanack* (first published in 1864), scorecards, silver-mounted commemorative cricket balls, medals and Marylebone Cricket Club (MCC) memorabilia.

Collectable silver and ceramic objects related to cricket span much the same range as those for golf, and include desk and table accessories, and trophies. Doulton made a series of ceramic character jugs, mugs, cups and vases on cricketing themes, all highly collectable and now fetching £50-£1000.

FISHING EQUIPMENT

It is angling equipment rather than other fishing collectables that is the most sought after today. Hardy Brothers of Alnwick in Northumberland have been the leading makers of reels since the last century, and their 'Perfect' range, introduced in 1891, is one of the most collected.

Other reels that are much sought after include: the earliest freshwater types; early sea-fishing reels – few of which have survived in good condition because of saltwater corrosion; and models that were produced in limited numbers, which are among the most expensive and elusive today – for example, a Cascapaedia reel which sold in 1990 for £6000. The most sought-after makers, apart from Hardy, are Farlow, Walker Bampton, Braddell & Son and Allcock.

Vintage artificial flies and fly-tying gadgets, novelty nets, hook-removing devices, rods, chairs, weighing scales, fish-carrying creels, tackle boxes, floats and lures are all collected, as are books on angling. So too are angling trophies, best known in the form of stuffed record-breaking fish in a glass case; these fetch £300-£1000. Decorative trophies that display minutely detailed carved fish can sell for as much as £1200-£1500.

FOOTBALL

Despite football's vast popularity, its memorabilia is still affordable, perhaps because there is so much of it. The cult of personality plays a large part, and collectors delight in ferreting out details of the life and scoring history of popular players.

Little vintage equipment has survived. The items easiest to find are programmes, magazines, trophies, photographs, caps and medals. Pottery figures of 'Wee McGregor', in various Scottish club colours, sell for anything from £150, depending on the club celebrated. Medals vary in value, depending on material, date and winner, from £10 up to several thousand pounds. International caps, and less frequently football jerseys, usually sell for over £100 with up to £300 paid for early caps.

RACKET SPORTS

Early rackets used for 'real' (or royal) tennis – the first racket sport – squash, badminton, ping-pong, the miniaturised Victorian game

Halifax football sugar basin; c.1902-3; 6 in (15.2 cm) across. Such wares have regional appeal, and can be worth far more in their area of origin.
£300-£500

Rugby football strip; 1900-20. Value depends upon whether the wearer was famous, and whether the strip was worn in a local, county or international match.
£100-£200

Staffordshire boxing figures; 1820; 9 in (22.9 cm) high. Famous figures in good condition, such as this, are rare.
£800-£1000

Ash and mahogany lawn-tennis racket; c.1878. The rarity of early rackets is reflected in the high price of this example.
£1400

'The Diamond Sculls 1925', painted in oil on canvas by Victor Elford; 29 × 40 in (73.5 × 101 cm). Jack Beresford, still considered the best oarsman Britain has ever produced, is shown here winning against the American champion Walter Hoover at the 1925 Henley Regatta.
£20,000-£30,000

'Gossima' and lawn tennis are all collectable. Few tennis rackets survive from the earliest days of the sport – in the last quarter of the 19th century – and those first steam-bent models were replaced by the laminated type in the 1930s. Before then, rackets tended to be lopsided and strung with heavy black gut, and those that appear on the market today sell at auction for as much as £200-£400.

As in other types of sport, a vast range of accompanying gadgets can also be collected, including racket presses, net gauges, various experimental balls and re-stringing aids. Other tennis mementos include trophies, photographs, bronzes, ceramics, books and instruction manuals. Silver inkwells, desk sets, small charms, racket-shaped jewellery and silver trophies can all be found.

Office equipment

Ingenious solutions to technical problems make primitive versions of today's high-tech office equipment fascinating objects to collect.

TELEGRAPH MACHINES, telephones and typewriters revolutionised office life in the 19th century. Today, the best and earliest machines fetch high prices at auction, but many items from early this century and simple objects, such as letter scales, inkwells and desk calendars, sell for under £100.

TELEPHONES AND TYPEWRITERS

The telegraph was the first important 19th-century business invention, in 1837. Within a few decades there were thousands of telegraph offices in Britain, yet telegraph machines are rarely seen today. Usually made of mahogany and brass, and often able to print Morse code messages on paper tape, they now sell at auction for between £100 and £500.

The telephone arrived some 40 years later, and the first London exchange opened in 1879. Some of the most elegant early wall and table telephones were made by Ericsson of Sweden from 1892. These have the handset resting on twin forks above an iron frame decorated with transfers, and now fetch £250-£500. Wall-mounted instruments with a separate hand-held earpiece cost £150-£500. Not long ago the familiar black Bakelite Neophone of 1930 was being thrown away, but today a reconditioned model can fetch £50-£200. Push-button ('A or B') coin telephones from the defunct red telephone kiosk sell for about £100, and even modern novelty telephones have become collectors' pieces.

Typewriters have a strong following among collectors. Late models are so plentiful that prices are low; much rarer are machines made in the 25 years or so after the first typewriter was patented in the United States in 1868.

Three of the most common early typewriters are the Oliver, Corona and Blickensderfer. The Oliver was patented in the United States in 1891, but production transferred to Britain under the name British Elver in 1928. The Oliver is remarkably solid. It has two banks of type bars and usually an olive-green iron frame. Pre-1900 models fetch about £100, later examples half that.

The Corona, or Standard Folding typewriter, was the first satisfactory lightweight portable, with a folding platen and roller. Patented in 1904, it was made until 1923. Early models fetch £30-£50 but later models, even in the original case, go for less.

The German Blickensderfer, with its drum-shaped type wheel, was a forerunner of the 'golf-ball' typewriter. Many models were built from 1893 to 1924, but in spite of their innovative features, they sell at auction for as little as £30-£100.

OTHER MACHINES

Calculating machines from before 1939 are all mechanically operated. The Thomas de Colmar calculator, a French model from about 1870, can fetch as much as £1500, but others may cost only a few pounds.

Before the invention of duplicating machines, copying was a laborious business. Copies were made with parallel pens or using a letter press to make an impression of the text on damp tissue paper. Stencil duplicators came into use in the 1870s, and by 1900 many large offices had a Gestetner 'Cyclostyle' or similar machine. Today they sell for up to £150.

Skeleton table telephone by Ericsson of Sweden; c.1900; c.10 in (25 cm) high. The user turned the dial at the side to call the exchange, which connected the call.
£400-£600

Oliver model 9 typewriter; 1916; c.12 in (30 cm) wide. This American machine with a down-stroke mechanism is one of 15 models produced by Oliver from 1896 to 1928.
£80-£120

British double writing machine; c.1800; c.20 in (51 cm) wide. This mahogany and brass copying machine is a very rare model patented in 1799 by Marc Isambard Brunel. It works on the parallel pen principle, with the master pen guiding a second pen.
£8000-£12,000

Mahogany and brass letter scales with weights; late 19thC; c.10 in (25 cm) wide. Letter scales first appeared c.1840. Less ornate examples fetch lower prices.
£150-£250

British perpetual calendar; 1920s; 12 in (30.5 cm) high. Desk calendars such as this one, which is built into an oak case, are still readily found in markets and junk shops.
£30-£50

Desk furniture

Writing equipment makes an interesting collection, and many attractive inkwells, pens and letter openers cost only a few pounds.

COLLECTORS HAVE VALUED inkstands, pen trays, letter openers and other items of desk furniture for a long time. Objects come in a range of materials that include glass, precious metals, papier-mâché, early plastics and leather. Collecting fountain pens, however, started in earnest only in the 1980s in the United States and spread from there to Britain and the rest of Europe.

Hundreds of thousands of fountain pens have been made and many collectors, faced with such a bewildering choice, concentrate on the pens of one maker, mechanism or period. Propelling pencils and early ball-point pens (patented in 1939 and popularised after the Second World War) are also collectable.

FOUNTAIN PENS

Early records show that English diarist Samuel Pepys owned a primitive form of fountain pen – a quill pen with an ink reservoir – back in 1663, but such pens were scarce until American inventor Louis Edson Waterman took out a patent for his leakproof fountain pen in 1884. By 1888 Waterman was offering over 50 different, guaranteed models – although most found today are from the 1920s and 30s.

The first fountain pens were made in hard, vulcanised rubber with a steel nib, but the barrel was soon being made from a wide range of materials, the most luxurious being solid gold and silver, or metal filigree over plastic. Mottled and coloured plastics were common, although tortoiseshell, steel, crocodile and

Fountain pens with precious cases: (from left) Fwan gold; c.1911; 5⅛ in (13 cm) long; £2500. Waterman gold model 552½V; c.1928; £300. De la Rue silver and lacquer; c.1915; £800. Dunhill lacquer, signed Namiki; c.1929; £1000. De la Rue Onoto with silver overlay; c.1915; £800. Waterman gold and enamel model 542½V; 1915-25; £300. Mabie-Todd gold-plated; c.1930; £80. (Bottom) Valentine Whytworth with silver overlay; c.1929; £200.

Fountain pens with standard cases: (from left) Waterman Jet Patrician; c.1930; 5½ in (14 cm) long; £250. Waterman 42; c.1915; £30. Mont Blanc 3-42G; 1950s; £30. Mabie-Todd; c.1911; £20. De la Rue Onoto; c.1915; £200. Waterman 54; 1920-30; £30. Parker Slimfold; 1950s; £3. Parker Duofold; 1950s; £5. Ford; 1935; £150. (Bottom) De la Rue Onoto; 1935; £40.

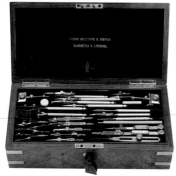

Set of Thomas Armstrong architect's drawing instruments; c.1900; walnut veneered case 12 in (30.5 cm) wide. This set is complete; its value would be lower if items were missing. £600-£900

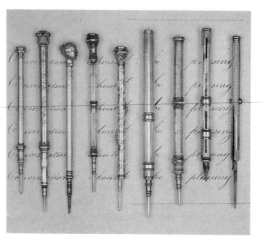

Silver and gold propelling pencils: (from left) Mordan slide action; 1830s; 3¼ in (82 mm) long; £45. Gabriel Riddle extending pencil and dip pen; 1830-50; £60. William Pearson lady's head pencil; 1852; £75. Mordan slide action; 1850-60; £55. Mordan slide action and penholder; 1860; £60. Mordan double-ended slide action and penholder; 1825; £150. Mordan extending pencil; 1840; £40. Mordan Riddle double-ended slide action and penholder; 1830; £60. Mordan pencil, pen and penknife; c.1880; £60.

*Edwardian novelty
'Briar pipe' propelling
pencil; c.1910; 1½ in (38 mm) long.
One section turns to make the whole a propelling
pencil. Similar pencils are often of gold or silver.*
£100-£150

*Wooden paper knives: (top)
c.1901; 8 in (20.3 cm) long; it has a crown and
'Edward VII' carved on it. Also three flat late-
Victorian, wide-bladed paper knives.*
£3-£5 each

*Novelty ceramic inkwell;
c.1890; 3 in (76 mm)
wide. It is printed to look
like a rugby football and
has a brass cover in the
form of a rugby cap.*
£20-£40

*Metal paperweight; 1880; 6 in (15.2 cm) long.
The handle has been cast in the form of a bar being
held aloft in a clenched hand.*
£150-£200

*Victorian electroplate silver and glass
inkstand; c.1880; 10 in (25.4 cm) wide. This
typically ornate example has a central flower
vase and stag flanked by an inkwell and a
pounce pot for powder to absorb wet ink.*
£250-£350

*Steel, brass and ebony quill cutter;
mid-19thC; 5 in (12.7 cm) long. The
case has the label of Deacons, a
Swindon goldsmith and jeweller.*
£40-£60

the Japanese designer Namiki to produce
some of the most sought-after collector's items
of today, a beautiful range of lacquer pens.
Each was hand-painted in traditional style by
Japanese artists and then coated with a
durable lacquer that was resistant to acid and
stains. They sold for £12 in the 1930s, but
today a fine example can fetch as much as
£1000 when put up for auction.

In buying an early fountain pen, condition
is important. A perished rubber sac can often
be replaced but watch out for splits in the
body, especially where there are any screw
joints, and always check that the nib has the
same name as the body of the pen and cap.
The original box is also desirable.

OTHER EQUIPMENT

Propelling pencils appeared in the early 19th
century and are still underpriced compared
with pens. Among the most notable pencils
are novelty pieces made from the end of the
19th century until the Second World War by
the silversmiths Sampson Mordan & Co of
London. These disguised, silver-cased pencils
appeared in a range of shapes including
miniature croquet mallets, spinning tops,
bugles and auctioneer's gavels. They sell for
around £200-£300. You may also come across
silver pencil holders for £5-£10; these do not
have a propelling mechanism but were made
in the late 19th century as attractive surrounds
for wooden pencils.

In the late 18th and early 19th centuries,
pocket-sized sets of drawing instruments were
supplied in a fitted shagreen-covered case.
Complete sets have become collector's items,
reaching values between £200 and £1500 if
none of the instruments is missing.

Later, larger sets of drawing equipment
were produced, which included rules, watercolours and drawing curves, all boxed in a case
up to 25 in (64 cm) long. Rules made of ivory
and brass are also collected separately.

Inkwells and pen trays have been produced
in many different designs and materials over
the past 200 years. Models made to resemble
boats, aeroplanes and cars, in silver, bronze,
ceramics and spelter can all be found. Beware,
however, of modern reproductions, especially
of brass desk sets.

Inkstands are often extremely ornate, ranging from finely worked silver or gold-plated
brass to ceramic holiday souvenirs. Many
models have two inkwells and holes or a rack
for holding pens. Victorian inkwells are often
made of cut glass with glass stoppers or brass
lids, and some travelling inkwells such as
Darkes' 'Sapphire' have an ingenious device
to prevent the ink spilling. Today the 'Sapphire' sells for £40-£80.

pigskin were also used. In the 1890s gold
superseded steel for the nib; 14 carat gold was
preferred, as it was soft enough to wear to the
writer's hand and did not scratch the paper.

The dominant makers during the 20th
century have been Waterman, Parker and
Shaeffer, all of them still in business. Parker,
in particular, has created an ideal collectors'
market by continuously developing and
changing its models, which seldom last more
than a few years at a time.

Parker launched its first pen, the 'Lucky
Curve', in 1894, and until 1921 all its pens had
a black casing. Then a radical change saw the
'Big Red', housed in oversized hard rubber. Its
success prompted the launch of pens in a
variety of colours. Today, original 'Big Reds'
sell at auction for £60-£100, plastic-cased

jade-green examples for £150-£200 and
mandarin-yellow 'Senior Duofold' pens of the
1920s for £300-£400. In general, unusual
colours will fetch more than black, which is by
far the commonest colour for early pens.

Waterman's 'Ripple' range, introduced in
1923, was made of two-tone hard rubber.
'Ripple' models and the 'Patrician' range,
launched in 1929, now sell for £30-£50 or
more. 'Patrician' pens used fashionable Art
Deco designs in plastic simulating jet, onyx,
turquoise, emerald and mother-of-pearl.

Some of the stylish 1930s pens are now
being reproduced by Parker, Waterman and
Mont Blanc for high prices, and this has also
pushed up the value of the originals.

In the early 20th century, the London pipe
specialists Alfred Dunhill joined forces with

Stamps and postal history

Even the commonest stamp can be valuable if it is still attached to the original envelope, or 'cover'; the postmark could be what makes the difference.

THE FIRST ADHESIVE postage stamp, the Penny Black, has acquired an almost mystical reputation as a rare and valuable item. Yet it is not as unusual as all that. Some 68 million Penny Blacks were printed between its issue in 1840 and its replacement by the Penny Red-Brown in 1841, and many have survived. The Twopenny Blue appeared at the same time but is generally worth three times as much today as the equivalent Penny Black, because far fewer were issued.

Many later stamps issued in limited numbers are even more desirable: the scarcer the item, the more it will be worth. And more important still can be the postmarks cancelling the stamps – an aspect of stamp collecting (or philately) which was largely ignored by early collectors and eager amateurs as they soaked stamps from their original envelopes ('covers') and stuck them into albums. (For advice on storing stamps, see page 435.)

POSTMARKS AND COVERS

Since the Middle Ages, merchants, universities and even trade guilds organised their own postal networks, often operating internationally. Letters which bear the handwritten (or 'manuscript') marks of these services are much in demand by today's collectors.

The earliest postmarks were made with a small hand stamp carved from wood, and were first used in the 17th century. By 1661 Charles II's postmaster general, Henry Bishop, had invented the first date stamp – a circle with a line across it, with a number for the date in one half and a two-letter abbreviation for the month in the other. This remained in use in cities as far afield as New York, Dublin, Edinburgh and Calcutta until 1787.

Another distinctive postmark was the triangular mark used by William Dockwra for his Penny Post, established in the London area in 1680. His service was taken over by the Post Office two years later, and similar marks were in use for over a century. Letters bearing Dockwra's original mark can be worth up to five-figure sums, but those with the more plentiful Post Office stamp are less valuable.

Postmarks bearing the name of the office of posting came into use at the end of the 17th century, although they were not common until the 1730s. Meanwhile, many postmasters wrote in the name of the place and postage charged by hand, a custom that can be deceptive for collectors. What looks like a

RAREST OF ALL *British Guiana 1 cent, 1856. This only example of the world's most valuable stamp sold for 6s (30p) in 1873, and a reputed US$1 million in 1982.*

meaningless squiggle may in fact be an unusual and valuable rate (or charge) mark.

Before 1840, postage was charged according to the number of sheets sent and the distance a letter travelled. To save on postage, letters were generally part of the same sheet as the outer wrapper, on which the address was written. These early letters are known by collectors as 'entires' (or entire letters) and are valued for their postmarks.

The importance of taking care of old envelopes – introduced after the coming of the Uniform Penny Post in 1840 – cannot be overemphasised. Even common 19th and early 20th-century stamps can be very valuable if accompanied by some rare postmark or in an unusual combination.

PICTORIALS AND SOUVENIRS

Postal stationery bearing embossed stamps was first produced in Sydney, New South Wales, in 1838. It bears the seal of the colony, and is regarded as the world's first stamped stationery. The British painter William Mulready designed the first prepaid British penny postage envelope around 1840, carrying a picture of Britannia. 'Mulreadies' soon disappeared, but a spate of caricatures eventually led to a vogue for highly decorated envelopes.

Pictorial stationery such as this can fetch high prices at auction. Both hand-drawn and printed, stamped stationery – whether postcards, envelopes, letter cards, newspaper wrappers or aerogrammes (air letter sheets) – have a strong following among collectors today. Postal souvenirs from the early days of aviation (especially pre-1910) can also fetch considerable sums and include early air mail letters and 'First Flight' commemoratives.

Modern first-day covers (FDCs) – postmarked the first day of issue of a particular stamp – are, surprisingly, of little value. Indeed, many stamps are actually commoner on FDCs than on normal envelopes. But postmarked FDCs dated between 1902 (when British stamps first came out on a particular day) and about 1950 are sought after.

Entire letter bearing a Bishop date stamp (see text) for October 10, 1739. The value of an entire depends on the letter's date, condition and content.
£20-£500

First-day Penny Black on cover; May 6, 1840. This great rarity is postmarked the very day the Penny Black was first issued. Mint Penny Blacks fetch £2750-£4500, used £150-£1600, depending on the printing plate used and the postmark colour.
£12,000-£15,000

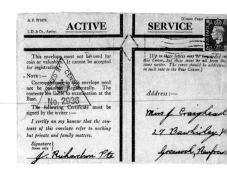

Second World War 'honour' envelope; 1943. Used by troops on active service, it was so called because the writer swore not to transmit military matters. Its value depends on both the content and postmark.
£2 upwards

First flight cover; 1930. Sent from Costa Rica to Germany on March 11, 1930, it commemorates the first air mail service on the route.
£15-£20

New South Wales 1d commemorative of 1888, marking the colony's centenary. Commemoratives are of most value in complete sets.
£3.75-£17

First World War postcard with mixed franking; 1918. Sent to Germany from the eastern front, it bears stamps and postmarks of the German Eastern Command (postmarked Riga) and Estonia (postmarked Tartu/Dorpat).
£20-£35

Paquebot cancellation; 1961. Letters posted at sea were postmarked 'Paquebot' or 'Ship Letter'. Here, a Trinidad postmark cancels a British stamp, from a letter posted on a British ship en route to the West Indies.
£1 upwards

Mulready cover (right) with additional Penny Black and Twopenny Blue; 1840. Unstamped Mulreadies are quite common, but this example with additional adhesives is very rare. The 1845 caricature (far right above) is ridiculing William Mulready's pompous drawing of Britannia.
Mulready with stamps: £5000-£6000
Unstamped: £100-£125
Caricature: £150-£250

Inverted overprint from the Panama Canal Zone. Some mistakes are so common that errors are worth less than the normal stamp. Others are rare, as here (normal value £5).
£550

Distinctive cancellations by travelling post offices (TPOs) on trains. Their value depends on their being on a complete envelope.
£1 upwards

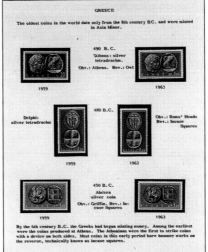

Page from a thematic album. Stamps can be collected on almost any subject – here, ancient Greek coins. Whatever its monetary value, building such a collection is more satisfying than aimlessly accumulating any stamps that come your way.

Coins and medals

Numismatics – the collection and study of coins and medals – is an accessible pursuit which can turn up interesting, and occasionally valuable, finds.

GOLDEN TOUCH *The clink of gold distracts the moneychanger's wife from her book in this masterpiece of observation painted by the Flemish artist Quentin Matsys in 1514.*

A BOX OF OLD COINS is to be found in almost every home – perhaps a piece or two handed down through the family, a few unfamiliar foreign coins from a long-forgotten trip abroad, or even Roman coppers turned up by the garden spade. Unfortunately, most of these are unlikely to be of much value, as coins were mass-produced even in ancient times, and have been saved, hoarded and collected ever since.

Historical and commemorative medals are, relatively speaking, much rarer than coins and are usually in better condition, as they are not circulated from hand to hand. Despite this, medals are generally cheaper than coins because there are fewer collectors. For military medals, see page 411.

COINS

The first coins were struck somewhere in western Asia Minor (modern Turkey) around 600 BC. They were made of electrum, a naturally occurring alloy of gold and silver, and have bold, simple designs on one side and crude punch marks on the other. Some types are known from only one or two examples. Others are quite plentiful, usually because ancient hoards of them have been discovered.

Coinage quickly evolved into a pattern of double-sided pieces of carefully weighed gold, silver and bronze, normally displaying the emblems, devices or deities of their town of issue. These Ancient Greek pieces can be particularly satisfying because of their beauty and sculptural qualities, while the starker style of Roman issues has its own appeal allied to immense historical interest.

Julius Caesar was the first living Roman whose ego was large enough for him to order his own image to be placed on a coin, in 44 BC. But he had only a short time to admire the result before being assassinated by Brutus in the same year. With astonishing audacity, Brutus promptly struck a coin designed to commemorate the deed – it showed his own gaunt portrait with two daggers, and even the date 'Ides of March' on the reverse.

WHAT THE COLLECTOR PAYS FOR

A generation ago, the rarity of a given coin was often the factor that most influenced its market value, but nowadays its condition is generally more important (see box). Invariably, a piece in 'mint' condition fetches more than a used example, and in the case of modern coins (made in the last 200 years or so) the difference can be quite staggering. A 'young head' silver crown of Queen Victoria struck in the 1840s, for example, is worth £10 or £20 in worn condition, but £500 or more in a brand new, uncirculated state.

The modern phenomenon of 'slabbing', introduced from the United States, underlines the point. It permanently seals near-perfect coins in clear plastic, each with a numerical estimate of the coin's condition by independent experts. A secondary market for

Syracusan decadrachm; c.405 BC. This silver piece is the finest known example of this coin by master-engraver Cimon. It was sold in a 1990 New York auction for US$407,000 (£210,881). **Museum piece**

Electrum third stater; Lydia, Greece; c.600-550 BC – one of the earliest coin types known. **£400-£500**

Macedonian silver tetradrachm of Alexander the Great; c.330 BC. These were struck in large numbers, this one coming from the Babylon mint. **£100-£120**

Celtic gold stater; c.AD 10-40. This coin dates from the reign of Cunobelin, ruler of the Catuvellauni tribe in Britain. **£400-£600**

Roman aureus of the Emperor Tiberius (AD 14-37). Aureus means 'gold piece'. **£1000-£1200**

Anglo-Saxon gold shilling, or 'thrymsa'; mid-7thC, unearthed in 1989. This is the best preserved of only three known examples. **£10,000-£12,000**

Bronze sestertius of Hadrian (AD 117-138). Quality pieces are occasionally unearthed. **£300-£400**

Byzantine histamenon; mid-11thC. It has a portrait of Christ on one side and the Emperor Constantine IX on the other. **£150-£200**

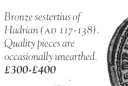

these slabbed coins has developed alongside that for conventional, unsealed coins, but prospective buyers would do well to remember that it is the coin they should be paying for.

Most collectors quickly develop a 'feel' for the condition and quality of coins once they have had a little first-hand experience in examining specimens in various grades of preservation. Old silver and copper coins sometimes appear tarnished or discoloured to the untutored eye, but they should never be cleaned without first taking the advice of an expert. An attractive old patina, which can be removed in a few seconds, will take a lifetime to reproduce.

MEDALS

The word 'medal' is rather confusing, as it has come to mean several different things. In particular, it is important to distinguish between historical medals, which normally commemorate a person, event or occasion, and war medals, normally awarded for participation in a military campaign or for deeds

'Paxs' (peace) silver penny of William the Conqueror; c.1085. This example was struck at Bristol by a moneyer by the name of Colblac.
£100-£150

Silver sixpence struck for the American colony of Massachusetts; 1652. It was recently unearthed in London, where it was perhaps lost by a 17thC traveller.
£600-£800

Spanish 8 reales; 1772. This 'piece of eight' is from the Seville mint, although similar coins were struck in Spain's American colonies, and saw circulation all over the world.
£200-£250

Charles II crown; 1666. The elephant symbol on this five-shilling piece indicates that it was made from African silver.
£1800-£2200

Heart-shaped halfpenny token; 1668. An extraordinary variety of types exist, ranging in value today from just a few pounds up to several hundreds.
£100-£200

Australian half-sovereign; 1856, struck during the Australian gold rush. It has seen plenty of use, but its date is rare.
£350-£450

George III gold 'spade' guinea, named for the shape of the shield. Brass copies were made in the 19thC.
£100-£150

American gold half-eagle; 1795. This lightly worn five-dollar piece is from the first year of issue. Early American coins still turn up in Europe occasionally.
£5000-£6000

British florin; 1849. It was nicknamed the 'godless florin' because 'dei gratia' (by the grace of God) was left off Victoria's title.
£50-£70

All the coins above (shown both sides) are approximately life-size. Values refer only to the actual specimens shown.

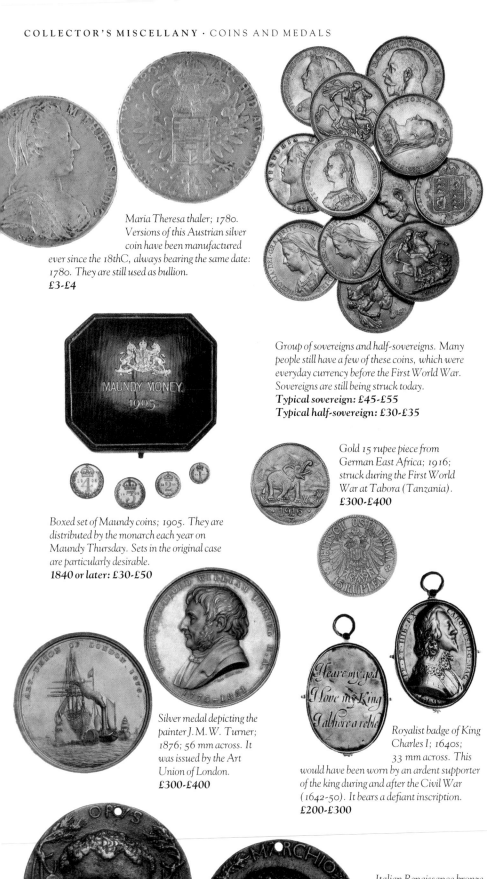

Maria Theresa thaler; 1780. Versions of this Austrian silver coin have been manufactured ever since the 18thC, always bearing the same date: 1780. They are still used as bullion.
£3-£4

Group of sovereigns and half-sovereigns. Many people still have a few of these coins, which were everyday currency before the First World War. Sovereigns are still being struck today.
Typical sovereign: £45-£55
Typical half-sovereign: £30-£35

Boxed set of Maundy coins; 1905. They are distributed by the monarch each year on Maundy Thursday. Sets in the original case are particularly desirable.
1840 or later: £30-£50

Gold 15 rupee piece from German East Africa; 1916; struck during the First World War at Tabora (Tanzania).
£300-£400

Silver medal depicting the painter J. M. W. Turner; 1876; 56 mm across. It was issued by the Art Union of London.
£300-£400

Royalist badge of King Charles I; 1640s; 33 mm across. This would have been worn by an ardent supporter of the king during and after the Civil War (1642-50). It bears a defiant inscription.
£200-£300

Italian Renaissance bronze medal by Pisanello (c.1395-1455); 67 mm across. It depicts Leonello d'Este, Marquis of Ferrara 1441-50.
£5000-£6000

All the coins above (shown both sides) are approximately life-size. Values refer only to the actual specimens shown.

of gallantry. Prize medals, such as Olympic awards, and society medals, such as Masonic jewels, fall rather uncomfortably in between the two groupings.

Although some medals were made by the Ancient Greeks and Romans, they are similar to impressive, oversized coins. The idea of the medal as an artistic medium in its own right was developed in Renaissance Italy, where prominent citizens commissioned the finest sculptors and engravers of the age to present their images on magnificent bronze portrait pieces. Rather than being forcibly struck with a die, like most coins, Renaissance medals were usually cast with their designs in high relief, and were then carefully finished by skilful hand tooling.

The boldness, beauty and sometimes humour of these 15th-century works has held an enduring appeal for collectors, with the inevitable result that myriad later copies exist. A good eye and a fair amount of experience is needed to distinguish an early medal of high quality valued at several thousand pounds from its younger brethren, some of which are virtually worthless.

In Britain, the 17th century saw a proliferation of medals varying enormously in artistic merit and quality of manufacture. Large, precious-metal examples were avidly collected by the wealthy, while smaller, cheaper versions helped to disseminate information among the populace. During and after the Civil War (1642-50), many people must have worn silver badges testifying to their Royalist allegiance as substantial numbers have survived, with typical values ranging from £100 to over £1000.

The Restoration of Charles II in 1660 heralded a 'golden age' of medal-making. Talented English and Dutch engravers – particularly, but not exclusively, Thomas Simon (1618-65) and John Roettiers (1631-1703) – vied with one another to present superb designs in sizes up to 3⅓ in (85 mm) diameter, difficult to manufacture even on modern presses. Political and satirical subjects were addressed, as were more traditional royal or historical events. Military and naval pieces were sometimes issued as rewards, and are regarded by some as the precursors of 19th-century war medals.

During the last 20-30 years, there has been a resurgence of interest in medals as an artistic medium among contemporary engravers and sculptors. Some of their best work, highly dramatic and technically innovative, may well become highly collectable in the future. Less desirable are sets of mass-marketed 'limited-edition' medallions, which generally achieve only their bullion value on resale.

Banknotes and certificates

Financial ephemera of all types makes a fascinating field for the enthusiast, and gives an insight into long-forgotten companies and financial disasters.

IT IS IRONIC that most surviving banknotes and fiscal documents are the remnants of financial failures. Of greatest interest to collectors, however, are those that do not relate to collapse – as they are much rarer.

Paper money only remains creditworthy as long as the general public has confidence in the issuing authority. In Britain this is the Bank of England, which holds a unique and unblemished record; all the printed money it has ever issued, from 1694 to the present, has remained fully redeemable at its face value – until 1914 in gold coins. Not all banknotes have been so secure, and this is even more applicable to bonds and share certificates.

The collecting of such certificates is sometimes known by the recently invented word 'scripophily'. It is particularly popular in Germany, although there are dedicated collectors in Britain, the United States and elsewhere. Other financial ephemera, such as old lottery tickets, cheques, insurance certificates, bills of exchange and postal orders, is also collected. As the market is, so far, fairly small, most material is still quite inexpensive and there are good chances of rare finds.

BANKNOTES

With the outbreak of the First World War, paper money largely supplanted gold for everyday transactions in Britain, amid general fears that the value of the gold in a sovereign could rise rapidly to more than £1. This might well have led to hoarding on a massive scale, so the August Bank Holiday of 1914 was extended to allow for gold coins to be called in and replaced with emergency £1 and 10 shilling notes issued by the Treasury. The Bank of England remained responsible for 'white fivers' and higher denominations.

The emergency Treasury notes were nicknamed 'Bradburys' after the signature they carried. The first issues were printed in great haste – and look like it – on stockpiled postage stamp paper. This proved much too flimsy for general circulation, so improved designs on proper banknote paper were prepared within a few months. The first Bradburys are now difficult to find in perfect unused condition and therefore vary widely in price from about £50 to £500, depending on their state of preservation. Later Treasury notes, issued until 1927, are visually more appealing but generally worth less. The Bank of England took charge of all banknote issues from 1928, when the majestic 'Britannia' £1 note was introduced, to be replaced eventually by the royal portrait £1 in 1960. Unusual errors, interesting serial numbers or signatures, and specimen print runs can all be desirable.

From the late 18th century up to the 1920s, privately owned British provincial banks circulated their own notes. (They are no longer authorised to do so in England and Wales, although regulations differ for Scotland and Northern Ireland.) Some of the old banking houses merged to form the clearing banks of today, but many were ruined in periodic financial crises. Indeed, the great majority of provincial banknotes bear bankruptcy stamps, and were redeemed only in part or were cancelled. Many 19th-century examples still turn up in old safes or pressed between the leaves of books. Their values

Chinese 1 kuan banknote; c. 1400; 13⅜ × 8⅞ in (34 × 22.5 cm). This is the earliest easily obtainable banknote. The paper is made from mulberry bark.
£200-£250

Ten shilling British Treasury note; August 1914; 5 in (12.7 cm) long. This first issue 'Bradbury' is printed on postage stamp paper.
£80-£120

PAPER MILLIONAIRES *By 1923, German inflation was so high that these clerks had to use laundry baskets to collect wages from a Berlin bank.*

Bank of England notes; 1930s and 40s. In the Second World War, notes over £5 were withdrawn, and the colours of £1 and 10s notes changed, to counter German forgeries.
£150-£200 the group

Cheque; 1768; 7 in (17.8 cm) long. This early cheque has a marbled counterfoil, which provided a simple but effective security device.
£15–£25

Bank of England £15 note; 1798; 7½ in (19.1 cm) long. This looks similar to the 'white fiver' of the 1950s but is far rarer. It was probably cut in half to outwit highwaymen.
£8000–£10,000

Share certificate of the Strand Bridge Company, printed on vellum; 1809; 14¾ in (37.5 cm) long. When the bridge was eventually opened in 1815, it was renamed Waterloo Bridge in honour of Wellington's victory over Napoleon.
£200–£250

Share certificate for the Channel Tubular Railway Preliminary Company; 1892; 11¾ in (29.8 cm) wide. Investors received nothing for their money but these attractive certificates
£400–£500

American Civil War bond; 1860s; 11¾ in (29.8 cm) wide. Such bonds were issued to finance the South's war effort and are still plentiful.
£20–£30

today may be as low as £10, going up to £200 or more depending on their rarity and condition.

Many old banknotes reflect past economic disasters. The most notorious was perhaps the German hyperinflation of the 1920s. Paper currency became all but worthless, and a lifetime's savings, it is said, could barely buy a loaf of bread. Not surprisingly, large numbers of notes from the catastrophe still turn up, but the vast majority are worth only a few pence, despite denominations of millions of marks.

Pre-Revolutionary Russian notes, American Civil War Confederate money of the 1860s, and assignats issued by the French revolutionary government of the 1790s are some further examples of currencies which collapsed. Although these banknotes are highly collectable, with some rare and valuable varieties to look out for, the supply of straightforward items is likely to outstrip foreseeable demand.

CERTIFICATES

Collectors of old bonds and share certificates generally stick to items which no longer have any significant equity (stock-market) value, such as the 'busted' bonds of pre-Communist Russia and China. Most of these date from 1870-1930, and can be bought for about £10 upwards. Early certificates, such as stock from the infamous South Sea Bubble crash of the 1720s, can be found from about £200.

Some certificates have real romance about them, including those of the American Express Company signed by Wells and Fargo and depicting a stagecoach, shares in the first Liverpool and Manchester Railway traversed by Stephenson's *Rocket* in 1829, or the 1870s Standard Oil Company stock signed by John D. Rockefeller. Most bonds and share certificates were prepared and printed to exacting standards. In the case of a negotiable 'bearer' bond – where the holder of the certificate was entitled to dividends without further proof of ownership – this was for security reasons. An impressive seal is sometimes found on vellum certificates dating from before 1850. Later pieces may have elaborate vignettes. The best of them can make a fine display when framed.

Occasionally, a trunk of obsolete financial documents turns up, perhaps from the archives of a Victorian businessman. When there are large numbers of identical documents, their market value temporarily falls. Experienced collectors see this as a one-off buying opportunity, while would-be investors tend to be discouraged, so the field remains very much the province of the enthusiast.

Musical instruments

Instrument makers face many demands: their creations must appeal to ear and eye, and satisfy players' technical requirements. But whether exquisite works of craftsmanship or musical curiosities, they can attract collectors.

THE HUGE VARIETY of available musical instruments can make it difficult for a collector to know where to start. A general collection is large and expensive to put together, and most people find it more rewarding to specialise in a particular type of instrument, usually one that they can play.

For pianolas and other mechanical instruments, see page 394.

BOWED INSTRUMENTS

Of all the stringed instruments played with a bow, violins are the most collectable, but their larger relatives, violas, cellos and double basses, also have enthusiasts.

Violins were first made in the 16th century, and the design perfected by craftsmen such as Antonio Stradivari, the Guarneri and Amati families from Italy, and the German maker Jacob Stainer. Most existing violins – whatever their origin – are in the style of one of these masters, so shape is little aid to identification. Labels are also misleading. Violin makers traditionally identified their instruments only with a printed paper label that was easy to forge or transfer, and even 20th-century factory-made copies often bear the facsimile of a famous signature.

Early Italian violins are rarely worth less than £20,000 – some over £500,000 – but copies, even in playing order, may be worth only £150. A rule of thumb is that the more famous the name on the label, the more suspicious you should be. Violins by lesser-known English makers of the 19th century can be bought at auction for under £1000.

Due to its immense popularity since the 17th century, the violin has not had many rivals, although an 'improved' guitar-shaped instrument was patented by Thomas Howell of Bristol and by François Chanot of Paris in the early 19th century. It was doomed to failure, but is still fun to collect and relatively inexpensive, rarely fetching more than £500.

OTHER STRING INSTRUMENTS

Guitars first appeared on the Continent during the Renaissance (14th to 16th centuries), but were not widely played until the lute fell from favour in the 18th century. Most historical examples available today date from the first half of the 19th century and vary in price from £1000-£2000 for instruments by

Violin by Antonio Stradivari; Cremona, 1707. This genuine Stradivarius is known as 'The Ex-Brustlein', after a previous owner.
£495,000

German violin probably made in the town of Markneukirchen, c.1900. Like many violins, this one bears a facsimile Stradivari label, in this case dated 1739 – two years after the master's death.
£100-£150

English ukulele banjo, c.1920. Do not trust an instrument with a George Formby signature – it will almost certainly be a facsimile.
£20-£40

Double action pedal harp by Sebastian Erard; London, c.1840; 67¾ in (1.72 m) high. Condition is an important factor in the value of a harp.
£1000-£1500

Guitar by Pons; Paris, 1823. Whereas English guitars of this date have a 'machine head' mechanism for tuning, French instruments were still using pegs.
£800-£1200

Neapolitan mandolin; c.1900. Mandolins were popular and produced in large numbers at the turn of the century. Its decoration makes this one more desirable than most.
£30-£50

VIOLIN BOWS
An Art Apart

BOW-MAKING has always been recognised as an art in itself. In fact, although the most valuable violins are all Italian, the best bows come from France. The easiest way to judge a bow's quality is to examine its mounts. Commercially made bows are usually mounted in ebony and nickel, hand-crafted bows in ebony and silver. Silver-mounted bows go for at least £300, and those by French makers such as Sartory, Viorin and Lamy over £3000. Bows by the most eminent maker of all, François Tourte, cost a great deal more – the record being £72,000. The best-known English bow-makers are James Tubbs and W.E. Hill and Sons, whose bows fetch between £700 and £4000.

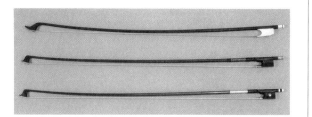

Bows (from top): ivory mounts, French, c.1770; silver and ebony mounts by Tubbs, c.1900; silver and tortoiseshell mounts by Hill, c.1950.
Top: £500; centre: £2000; bottom: £1000

leading makers François Lacôte of Paris and Louis Panormo of London, to around £500 for the work of less famous craftsmen.

Popular in 18th-century Britain was the so-called 'English guittar'. Derived from the 17th-century cittern, it looks rather like a flat-backed mandolin. Because they were so popular, English guittars are not rare and usually sell at auction for between £400 and £800, depending on condition.

The original late 18th and early 19th-century harp was as expensive and difficult to play as the modern orchestral version. Even so, it was played in many homes and considered the height of fashion when taken up by Queen Marie Antoinette of France. Many original harps are now beyond restoration, but even unrestored they can look impressive. Prices vary greatly, depending on age and condition, from under £500 to £2000 or more for a harp in playing condition.

Mandolins of the late 18th and early 19th centuries, if in good condition, can fetch up to £1000. Those from the turn of this century are common, especially in Britain where there was a vogue for them among amateur players. Most are made from cheap materials, and virtually all imported from Naples and probably worth a mere £30-£50.

KEYBOARD INSTRUMENTS

Harpsichords date back to the 15th century. Pianos first appeared in the early 1700s but did not start to replace the harpsichord until the last quarter of the century. Early grand pianos and harpsichords are very valuable indeed, with pianos seldom sold for less than £5000 and harpsichords sometimes for more than

Austrian or German zither; late 19thC; 20½ in (52 cm) long. Although always popular in Germany, zithers had only a sporadic following in Britain.
£100-£150

Two-manual harpsichord by Jacob and Abraham Kirckman; London, 1789; 94½ in (2.4 m) long. Although the Kirckmans were the leading makers of their day, players today prefer French-made instruments, which are even rarer – and dearer – than this example.
£40,000-£60,000

£100,000. Even spinets – small harpsichords – cost £15,000-£20,000.

From around 1770 until the introduction of the upright piano in about 1830, the square piano was the most popular home keyboard instrument and was produced until the middle of the 19th century. These pianos have little value now, and even 18th-century examples sometimes change hands for less than £1000.

Neither is there much demand for harmoniums, or reed organs, which were prized in many late 19th-century households. It should be possible to find a plain example for no more than £50 and an elaborately carved Victorian one for a few hundred pounds.

Concertinas were popular earlier this century, and now fetch £300-£600 in good condition with modern pitch. At present there is no market for historic piano accordions, and even unusual instruments go cheaply.

MODERN PIANOS

In the second half of the 19th century, mass production drastically reduced the price of pianos and gave them a place in the household similar to that of the television set today. Many of these instruments still survive, but few have any musical or historical value. The only exceptions, as yet, are well maintained, late 19th-century grand pianos by the great

Grand piano by John Broadwood & Co; London, c.1850, 88 in (2.23 m) long. Most late 19thC pianos now fetch very little unless in particularly good condition, as here.
£1000-£2000

English concertina by George Case; London, c.1870. Beware of leaky bellows when buying a concertina – they should stay shut even when the instrument is hung up by a thumb strap.
£300-£500

Early woodwinds (left to right): two-keyed oboe by Giovanni Panormo, Naples, c.1760; one-keyed flute by Thomas Cahusac, London, c.1770; five-keyed clarinet by Goulding & D'Almiane, London, c.1820.
Left: £2000-£3000
Centre: £500-£700
Right: £300-£500

Harmonium by Alexander Fils; Paris, c.1850; 46 in (1.16 m) wide. Most harmoniums were mass-produced in the USA and fetch about £50.
£400-£600

Great Highland Bagpipes by James Robertson; Edinburgh, c.1940. While most modern bagpipes cost just a few hundred pounds, sets by the great makers can exceed £2000.
£500-£700

makers Steinway, Bechstein and Bluthner, and those whose outstanding design or quality makes them valuable as furniture.

WOODWIND, BRASS AND PERCUSSION

For collectors starting out, woodwinds are ideal: there are few forgeries and most instruments are stamped with the maker's name.

Flutes are the most common of woodwinds, with pre-1850 examples usually made of boxwood and mounted in ivory. Early examples can be expensive – a 17th-century instrument may cost tens of thousands of pounds – but a great variety of flutes from the

early 19th-century sell for a few hundred, or less with cracks or missing keys.

Clarinets are also easy to find and the most common – English instruments with 6 to 12 keys, from the first half of the 19th century – sell for around £250-£500. Fewer amateurs played oboes and bassoons, and these instruments are relatively rare, early 19th-century examples costing £2000-£3000.

Prices of brass instruments are now rising rapidly, particularly for later types with valves. Before 1825, when the valve was invented, brass instruments could not produce a full chromatic scale, and although some specialists have always been interested

in these instruments – not least because of their unusual shapes – they are relatively inexpensive, typically around £1000-£2000.

Modern brass instruments use one of only two valve designs, but makers in the early 19th century experimented with a huge variety of devices. Instruments with valve systems that failed can be quite valuable, as few of each type were made.

The whole family of percussion instruments has been badly neglected by collectors. Early drums are rare, and tambourines only slightly more common: early 19th-century instruments, often attractively decorated, sell for about £200-£400.

Mechanical music

A tinkling musical box melody, the rolling rhythm cranked out by an organ grinder, the voice of Caruso issuing from a phonograph horn, or Elvis Presley resounding from a jukebox – all are forms of mechanical music.

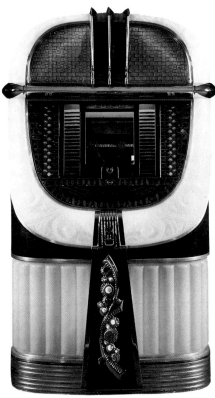

AMI Model A jukebox; USA, c.1953; 68 in (1.72 m) high. Made before the dawn of rock and roll, this 50s design was nicknamed 'The Mother of Plastic', and held forty 78 rpm records.
£2500-£3500

MACHINES TO PLAY MUSIC have been a specialist collecting field for many years. Musical boxes, phonographs and early gramophones not only illustrate the popular music but also reflect the decorative styles of their time. Even lavish jukeboxes of the 1930s to 50s are collected today.

MUSIC BOXES

The cylinder musical box movement was invented at the end of the 18th century in Switzerland and was used in novelty pocket watches and scent bottles. A clockwork mechanism turned a pin-studded cylinder to pluck the teeth of a metal comb.

The earliest mechanical music instruments in their own right date from 1810 and have the cylinder movement contained in a plain, hardwood box with the control levers and

Speaking book; France, c.1910; 12 in (30.5 cm) long. When the strings are pulled, the book makes animal noises to go with the pictures. Its value would triple if it were in perfect condition with box.
£150-£250

Manievelle musical box; c.1910; 4 in (10.1 cm) wide. These simple musical boxes were made in large numbers.
£30-£40

winding hole exposed at one end. On many rosewood or mahogany boxes of the 1830s and 40s, a hinged flap conceals the levers. The makers, all based around Geneva, included A. Bordier, Nicole Frères, Ducommon Girod and Lecoultre, whose boxes can fetch £1200-£1500 today, if in good working condition.

More sophisticated models incorporating brass bells with strikers in the form of bees or butterflies first appeared in the 1840s. Some later examples have small automata that play the bells. One attractive model even has brass Chinese figures which nod as they strike; this can sell for around £2000-£3000. By the 1870s, 'orchestral' music boxes were incorporating bells, drums, castanets, triangle, glockenspiel, zither and even small reed organs (known as *voix célestes*, or 'angel voices').

Cheaper musical novelties – from chairs and photograph albums to lavatory-paper holders – date from the late 19th-century and are popular with collectors. Most late 19th-century musical boxes   (continued p. 396)

'**A** SIGNIFICANT PART *of the value of a music box depends upon who made it. So, once you've admired the veneered and inlaid outer case, open the wooden lid and the glass inner lid and see what clues are offered. That inner lid, by the way, is a safety screen as well as a dust lid; it prevents a loosened cylinder pin flying into the face of an onlooker. There were cases of people being blinded by them before the lid was introduced in the mid-19th century.*

Opening the music box's inner safety lid

Most makers stamped their trademark or name on the base plate or on the comb that plays the music. Here they put it on both, though it's clearest on the base plate; and the

name is Nicole Frères of Geneva, one of the best makers. There's also a number, 39801. A reference book will show that this dates the box to between

Maker's name on base   *1861 and 1865.*

Maker's name on comb   *Serial number on base*

When looking at a music box, carefully check the comb, whose steel teeth make the music as they are plucked by the pins on the revolving cylinder; a rusty comb or bent pins can affect the sound disastrously. Another significant factor is the length and diameter of the cylinder. Generally, the longer and wider it is, the more notes the box can play over a greater time – which bears upon its value. In

An Expert Examines

HILARY KAY TUNES IN TO
YESTERDAY'S MUSIC-BOX MELODIES

…his box the cylinder is longer than average, …ut about 12¼ in (31 cm), and about 3⅓ in …(85 mm) wide – almost twice the usual …diameter of 2 in (50 mm). Often, this …implies that the cylinder was intended to play …overtures, or other lengthy pieces. But not in …the case of the box we have here.

…Music-making mechanism – the comb and pins

…Music boxes have a stop control, a pivoted …arm that drops into a notch in the cylinder at …the end of each tune – usually one notch per …revolution. In this instance, there are two …notches, indicating that the box plays two …tunes per revolution. At the end of each, the …cylinder clicks across to a new position – six …times in all in this case, so it can play 12 …melodies during a complete performance. …Such a 'two-per-turn' box is quite scarce.

…Beside the stop mechanism is the governor: …spinning brass vanes whose air resistance …keeps the cylinder running steadily. The …governor pivots on a garnet bearing; if this is …missing, the box will not work satisfactorily.

…Stop control mechanism and (left) governor

…Looking at the tune sheet on the inside of the …lid will tell you a good deal about the history …of the box. It lists the tunes the box plays and …their composers, together with the maker's …name again and that of the London retailer who imported the box from Switzerland. But more than that, it shows a gamme number – gamme, or gamut, meaning 'complete programme'. Here the number is 1982, which identifies this particular programme and sequence of songs; even a different order of playing would be given a different gamme number. If the number is also scratched onto one end of the cylinder – and it is – then it suggests that box and tune sheet and mechanism have always been together.

The tune sheet's chart-toppers of the 1860s

However, there's only one real way to judge the quality of a music box, and that's to play it. So, wind it gently, using the ratchet, the winding lever…Don't overwind, and do let the box wind itself down after playing – but make sure that you stop it at the end of a tune, never halfway through. Now, release the start lever, and there we are…'My Own, my Guiding Star', 'The Pilgrim of Love' and those other showstoppers of the 1860s, beautifully played, sweet and true.

Now, having played the box, let's look at the case. No sign of woodworm and, apart from some fading of the veneer and the inlay through having stood too long in strong sunlight, it's in pretty good condition.

HILARY KAY SUMS UP

We've established that the case, mechanism and tune sheet all belong to the same period, and have always been together. There's no doubt that Nicole Frères were among the very best music-box makers of their day, while the two-per-turn mechanism with its 12 tunes make this piece very collectable. I'd say that it would sell at auction for somewhere between £2500 and £3000. Even a standard Nicole Frères box, with one tune per revolution, could sell for about £1200.

Cylinder musical box; c.1900; 18½ in (47 cm) wide. This simple 'bells-in-sight' model made in Switzerland plays eight airs which are listed on the tune sheet attached to the inside of the lid.
£300-£400

Disc musical box; c.1910; 12¼ in (31.1 cm) wide. This table-top model by the German company Polyphon plays 9¾ in (24.7 cm) diameter discs, which are easy to change. The lid has a decorative lithograph inside.
£250-£350 (with discs)

Penny-in-the-slot disc musical box; Germany, c.1900; 51 in (1.29 m) high. Large machines like this were forerunners of the jukebox in bars and cafés.
£1200-£1800

Edison standard phonograph; c.1905; 9½ in (24.1 cm) wide. The cygnet horn and cylinders with this phonograph push up the value. Phonographs were soon ousted by the early 20thC gramophone.
£300-£400

Mikiphone miniature gramophone; Switzerland, 1930s; 4 in (10.1 cm) diameter. The nickel-plated case looks like a pocket watch, but inside is a complete record player with turntable, pick-up and resonator.
£300-£400

Chamber barrel organ; c.1800; 68 in (1.72 m) high. A winding handle on this domestic model operates both the cylinder and the internal bellows.
£2000-£3500

have a change/repeat lever allowing one tune to be repeated or the whole repertoire to be played. Most are Swiss but they are not always signed, and the only clue as to maker may be the style of tune sheet or a trademark.

FROM CYLINDER TO DISC

Cylinder musical boxes were usually limited to playing 6-12 tunes – and interchangeable cylinders were expensive and easily damaged. The first inexpensive machines able to play any number of separately purchased melodies were the disc musical boxes which first appeared in 1885 and soon became enormously popular. These used easily changed metal discs punched from one side.

The small table-top 'Celesta' model, with transfer-decorated softwood case, cost a mere £2 10s (£2.50) in 1898. Today, it can fetch £300-£500. Far more expensive even then was the walnut-cased 'Giant', by Polyphon, which plays 25 in (63.5 cm) discs and has room to store them. The most desirable models can sell for £10,000-£15,000 today. The discs also have some value, depending on size, manufacturer and condition.

A line from the nursery rhyme 'Mary had a little lamb' were the first words ever to be recorded and played back on a machine. They were spoken by American inventor Thomas Alva Edison, who exhibited his 'talking machine' in 1877. It played with a stylus moving against grooved tinfoil on a revolving cylinder and the sound emerged through a horn. Edison's phonograph was marketed in 1878, and after the invention of the wax cylinder in 1886 several inexpensive styles were produced. The small 'Gem' model, for example, now fetches around £200-£300.

But it was the flat disc – patented in the USA by Emile Berliner in 1887 – that established the technology that would dominate sound recording for nearly a century. A pre-1914 gramophone can fetch as much as £5000 today. Early portable models for use in the garden or on picnics sell for up to £100, while versions disguised as watches and cameras fetch £150-£200. For public concerts phonographs and gramophones with large horns were used, such as Edison's 'Opera'.

BARREL ORGANS AND PIANOLAS

Barrel organs, which were common in the 19th century, range from the portable instrument of the organ grinder to large hand-cart or horse-drawn street barrel organs.

Pianolas (automatic pianos), which played melodies using punched cards or paper rolls, were popular into the early 20th century. Sadly, pianolas are largely ignored by collectors, and most fetch only small sums.

Oriental collectables

From samurai sword fittings to bronze Buddhas, tiny netsuke to six-foot screens, priceless antiquities to modern works of art – a host of treasures bear witness to the West's enduring love affair with the arts of the Orient.

Japanese fuchi-kashira (sword mounts) made of iron decorated with tigers in gold, silver and shakudo (copper and gold); 19thC; top 1½ in (38 mm) long. These items are signed.
£400-£600

Japanese tsuba (sword guards): (left) in silver alloy showing cranes in a tree, 1850, 2¾ in (7 cm) long; (right) in iron with silver and gold warriors, 18thC.
Left: £800-£1200; right: £1500-£2000

Chinese bronze ding, or food vessel, with stylised mask decoration; Shang dynasty, c.1500 BC; 11⅜ in (29 cm) high. Such vessels were used as part of a ritual burial.
£5000-£7000

Japanese inlaid iron cabinet in the form of a temple; c.1880; 14 in (35.5 cm) high. This good-quality piece decorated in gold was made by Komai, one of the leading craftsmen of the time.
£10,000-£15,000

Pair of Japanese bronze warriors; c.1890; (left) 15 in (38.1 cm) high, (below left) 14½ in (36.8 cm). These were made by Miyao, and are inlaid with gold and mounted on gilt wood bases. Miyao is known for his lively figures and fine quality of surface finish.
£10,000-£15,000

STRANGE AS IT MAY SEEM, there is a better chance of someone stumbling on a fine piece of Japanese lacquer in their attic or an Indian religious statue in the garden shed, than of finding some British antiques. For centuries, Britain's extensive overseas trade brought rarities and art works to its shores from as far away as India and China, Burma and Thailand, Japan and Korea. Some items entered museums, but many remained in private hands, their value often unknown.

Today, there is a flourishing market for good Oriental pieces of all sorts, even modern works. High-quality carvings are among the most popular articles, as are bronzes and lacquerware. Sadly, the high prices buyers are prepared to pay means that temples in countries such as Cambodia are being stripped to satisfy Western markets.

Prices are often influenced more by demand from interior designers and decorators than from collectors, so impressive items or ones that fit a particular decorating style may fetch amounts out of all proportion to their quality.

Collectors should remember that there are costs other than the initial purchase price. Lacquer, ivory and some other Oriental materials need special care (see pp.424-35), and restoration can cost a great deal.

METAL AND STONE

Bronze religious figures, burial vessels and stone statues can all be found in Western auction rooms, many linked to Buddhism, which spread from 6th-century India across South-east Asia and into China.

The earliest metal items from China date back to the Shang dynasty (1700-1028 BC), when ritual vessels of bronze were made for burial with the dead. Bronze weapons, mirrors and harness fittings have also been found.

Such pieces have been collected in China for more than 1000 years, and Shang metalware is now widely appreciated in the West. Centuries of burial give it a rich patina in green, silver and copper tones. Far from diminishing the value, the patina greatly increases it. A depatinated piece could be worth only a few hundred pounds instead of tens of thousands.

The later Ming and Qing (Ch'ing) dynasties (AD 1368-1644 and 1644-1912) produced incense burners and braziers which often bear the Xuande reign mark (1426-35; see p.509), whatever their true date. They should have a rich, dark brown patination, and some may have been splashed with gold or inlaid with silver. Chinese bronzes are not common, however, and auction prices vary from about £200 for a late 18th-century incense burner to £10,000 for a rare Ming figure.

JAPANESE METALWARE

The Japanese did not pass through a bronze age but their ironworking skills, particularly in the manufacture of swords, have never

*Japanese bronze jardinière; c.1900; 11 in (28 cm)
wide. It has poor quality relief decoration but
original patina and was probably made for export.*
£100-£150

*Chinese ivory immortal;
late 19thC; 9½ in
(24.1 cm) high. The
carving follows the curve
of the tusk. Although it is
quite similar to 17th and
18thC examples, the
carving is more
complicated and the
newer patina appears
less warm and shiny.*
**£300-£400
17th or 18thC:
£800-£3000**

*Gilded stone Gandhara Buddha's head;
3rd-9thC; 11½ in (29.2 cm) high.
Without the gilding the price would be
much lower, around £5000-£10,000.*
£45,000-£50,000

*Tibetan gilt bronze with inset turquoise beading;
15th-16thC; 15⅜ in (39 cm) high. This seated
figure represents Vajrasattva, one of the many
deities associated with Tibetan Buddhism.*
£9000-£12,000

*Indian ivory boat; late 19thC; 10 in (25.4 cm) long. Such
carvings were made in their thousands for the souvenir and
export markets, and vary in quality.*
£200-£300

been surpassed (see p.408). Nevertheless,
bronze was used for some sword fitments, such
as the *tsuba* (sword guard), which was often
decorated with warrior figures or mythological
scenes. Tsuba are now collected as works of art
in their own right, as are *fuchi-kashira* and
menuki (sword mounts), and pieces of samurai
warriors' equipment such as the *kozuka* (the
handle of a small eating knife).

The Japanese were highly skilled at combining metals to make different colours, and
inlaying these into iron or bronze. Late
19th-century craftsmen produced much fine
work which now fetches prices ranging from
£500 to £20,000.

Bronze working received a boost with the
founding of the influential Tokyo School of
Art in 1887 (see box, p.401). Sculptors
belonging to the school produced some outstanding figures as well as functional objects
such as jardinières, *hibachi* (charcoal burners)
and vases. The high quality and decora-
tiveness has made these pieces popular, and
they tend to be expensive. Figures can go at
auction for anything between £1000 and
£10,000, and most other objects may fetch

anything from £300 to £10,000.
Many Tokyo School bronze pieces
are signed, and such names as Miyao,
who made figures, and Genryusai
Seiya, who specialised in animals, are particularly sought after. Bronzes that retain their
original finish, even if slightly changed by
years of handling, will fetch considerably
more than those that are scratched or worn.

Collectors must take great care when
buying Japanese bronzes. Some very good
copies – particularly of Tokyo School work –
are being passed off in the West as originals.

OTHER BRONZES AND SCULPTURES

Buddhas and other figures have been cast in
bronze in Thailand, Burma, Cambodia and
Java over the last 1500 years, often with only
small changes in style. Dating is difficult and
sometimes a sample has to be taken from the
core for laboratory testing. Value depends
mainly on age, surface quality and patina,
with gilded bronzes fetching top prices.

Tibetan, Nepalese and Indian bronzes
have much in common, but Indian craftsmen
favoured more contemplative poses, whereas

the Tibetan sculptors preferred dramatic postures, reflecting their more active and practical form of Buddhism. Prices vary from a few
hundred pounds to several thousand.

North Indian Gandhara stone sculptures
from the 3rd to 6th centuries occasionally
turn up in salerooms in Britain, selling for
£500 to £50,000, depending on quality,
condition and size. Even small fragments are
collected and fetch anything up to £10,000.

SMALLER CARVINGS

Wood, jade, bone and horn were all used to
fashion small figures, animals and practical
objects. Among the best known of such pieces
are Japanese netsuke.

IVORY AND JADE

The earliest Chinese ivories go back 2000
years, but most of the pieces that come onto
the market today date from the Ming dynasty

Indian ivory figure of an English lady of the Raj; carved in Delhi, c.1905; 9 in (22.9 cm) high without stand. It is rare to find a Westerner depicted so sensitively or naturalistically.
£1500-£2000

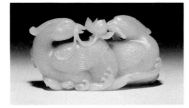

Chinese jade carving of a pair of ducks (symbolising marital fidelity); mid-18thC; 4⅝ in (11.7 cm) long. Similar carvings were often made in soapstone.
£2500-£3000

Chinese carved cinnabar lacquer box of lobed form; early 19thC; 9¾ in (24.7 cm) across. Such pieces are difficult to date, but only those from after the mid-19thC can be indented with a fingernail.
£500-£900

Japanese lacquer kodansu or box of drawers; 19thC; 4⅞ in (12.4 cm) high. This is a very fine example with black lacquer ground decorated in tones of gold, and given shibuichi (silver alloy) mounts.
£23,000; more common pieces from £80

Japanese gold lacquer table screen; late 19thC; 10 in (25.4 cm) high. The subject of ladies and samurai in spring is typical, as are the ivory inlays and small pieces of gold leaf.
£5000-£7000

Gold-lacquer Japanese shibayama aiguchi (dagger) with mother-of-pearl and ivory inlays, and silver mounts; late 19thC; 12⅝ in (32 cm) long.
£4000-£5000

or later. The immortals were favourite subjects, generally following the tusk's curve.

Copies of carvings in this style are still made today, and sometimes even artificially aged in a chimney – a trick which you may be able to detect by smell alone. Beware, too, of pieces with engraved Ming or Qing reign marks, which are almost always spurious. Genuine Ming pieces usually sell for upwards of £500.

A great number of ivory carvings were made in India in the 19th century, mainly for sale to British buyers. They typically depict subjects such as ox carts and maharajahs in palanquins or seated on elephant howdahs. The carving is usually of only mediocre quality, and prices range from £50 to £300.

Jade carvings have been made for centuries in China. Throughout the Ming and Qing dynasties, jade was used for objects such as dishes, brush pots, scroll weights and belt hooks. Prices vary greatly, depending on the quality of the work and the type of jade used.

Distinguishing jade from lookalikes such as soapstone (so called because of its slippery feel) can be difficult. One simple test is to apply a pin to the base. If a scratch is produced, the stone is not jade. Some fine soapstone carvings were made in the 18th century and are valuable in their own right, fetching £300 or more at auction.

JAPANESE NETSUKE

Although collectors today treasure the small carved toggles called netsuke (pronounced *nets'ki*) for their artistic value, the original purpose was functional. The traditional kimono had no pockets, so a small multi-tier box called an *inro* was used to hold personal belongings. The inro was hung on a cord which passed through a bead called an *ojime*, then through the netsuke which was pushed behind the *obi* (sash) to emerge at the top.

Netsuke began as twigs, but by the 17th century increasingly elaborate carvings had become popular, reaching a high point around the end of the 18th century. Various areas of Japan evolved their own schools of carving. Most of the craftsmen were peasants supplementing their income, despite modern notions that they were all famous masters.

Ivory was the most popular material, but bone, stag antler and such bizarre materials as mummified monkey's paw were also used. Whatever the material, to do its job a netsuke needs at least one hole, and usually two, to hold the cord. The holes are often cunningly concealed within the design. As in any other field, collectors are interested in famous names, but an unsigned, unidentified masterpiece is a better buy than a poorly executed signed work, however highly rated the name of the artist may be. A good piece by Kaigyoku Masatsugu could fetch £40,000, for example, but a poor work of his might sell for as little as £1000. Few early netsuke are signed, but there are exceptions and experts can often identify the style of a particular master in an unsigned work.

Subject matter is also important, with rarer subjects – centipedes and goats, for example – fetching higher prices. Because of the small size of netsuke, the tiniest chip is a serious blemish, but signs of wear are quite acceptable and a good patina also increases value. Ivory darkens naturally with age, but it can also be artificially stained.

Many netsuke show the Japanese sense of humour, particularly a love of the grotesque. Contorted faces based on professional face-pullers were a favourite subject, and at the end of the 18th century caricatures of Europeans started to appear. The earlier netsuke artists preferred to show mythological characters.

Netsuke are keenly collected today and have a strong following throughout the world – with the surprising exception of Japan, although interest is growing among collectors there too. Prices vary from a few hundred pounds up to many thousands.

LATER JAPANESE CARVINGS

As the Japanese took increasingly to Western dress in the 19th century, the demand for netsuke diminished and carvers turned instead to producing *okimono* – decorative standing figures for foreign markets. At first not much bigger than netsuke, okimono were gradually made larger, many still retaining redundant cord holes in the base.

Some ivory okimono display outstanding craftsmanship, with shibayama inlays of tortoiseshell, coral, mother-of-pearl or coconut shell. Shibayama carvings are usually sectional, with separately carved pieces joined together by pegs and fish glue. The pieces commonly come apart, but they can easily be rejoined with no loss of value. Prices range from £300 to £5000.

Other sectional carvings were made from offcuts of larger works. Although some are signed, they are usually by unskilled craftsmen and of inferior quality. Examples can be found for as little as £30.

Large numbers of group carvings in walrus (or 'morse') ivory are also available, usually representing subjects such as peasants and fishermen. Generally, these works are not of the highest quality, and fetch around £100-£300. You can distinguish walrus from elephant ivory by its granular core, although this may be disguised by crosshatching and staining on the base of the piece. Carvers also produced various functional items such as

A NETSUKE WORKSHOP *In this 1797 print by Hokusai, workers lathe-turn a kagamibuta netsuke, while a visiting traveller is offered tea.*

Japanese ivory netsuke of a Dutchman holding a crane; 18th C; 4 1/8 in (10.4 cm) high. People travelled miles to view Westerners, and netsuke would have been souvenirs. **£2000-£3000**

Japanese netsuke, ojime and inro; late 19thC; inro 3 7/8 in (98 mm) high. Inro were used to carry small items. This one has gold, ivory and mother-of-pearl decoration. The netsuke represents Ebisu, the god of food. **£2000-£2500**

Japanese ivory netsuke made in the form of a Hannya (female devil) mask, signed by Ohara Mitsuhiro; mid-19thC; 1 3/4 in (44 mm) high. The ivory has been lightly stained. **£600-£900**

Coloured ivory netsuke; c.1900; 1 3/8 in (35 mm) high. The piece is by Yatsutaka (Hoko) and depicts an actor reading from a scroll. **£1500-£2000**

Japanese ivory okimono of a basketseller and his son; c.1900; 6 in (15.2 cm) high. Any damage would greatly reduce the price. **£2500-£3500**

Three Japanese netsuke: (left) wooden boar with inlaid eyes, early 19thC; 1 3/4 in (44 mm) high; (centre) ivory sleeping boar, c.1800, with some cracks and chips; (right) modern resin netsuke. **Left: £1500-£1800; centre: £1400-£1600; right: 50p upwards**

...ases, letter openers, handles for parasols and
...nives, and games counters – all of which are
...ow keenly sought by collectors.

LACQUERWARE

Although the process of making lacquer from
...ree sap was discovered in China around 2000
...ears ago, the oldest pieces available today
...ate from the 14th century. The earliest
...apanese pieces are from two centuries later.

CHINESE LACQUER

...he range of styles of early Chinese lacquer is
...imited. In the most common types, a thick
...ayer of red or cinnabar lacquer is carved with

scenes or figures, or layers of red and black
lacquer are alternated to display coloured
stripes in the cutting. Occasionally, particularly in the Ming dynasty, black lacquer was
laid on red, and flower and leaf designs carved
through, leaving a black pattern on a red
background. Prices for Ming pieces start at
about £1000, but some Qing examples can be
found for around a few hundred pounds.

Trays and boxes are the most common
Chinese pieces, but stem cups and chests were
also made, as well as screens. Most screens
date from the early years of this century and
many are inlaid with semiprecious stones and
mother-of-pearl. An inset green stone that
looks like jade is almost always stained
soapstone. (Try the test on p. 399.) Some pieces
bear reign marks, but they are seldom reliable.
Screens go at auction for £800 up to £20,000.

LACQUER FROM JAPAN

Most Japanese lacquer is black in colour, with
naturalistic leaf and flower designs in gold
paint or inset gold leaf. Japanese craftsmen

produced, and continue to produce, hundreds
of different lacquer objects, including trays,
tea caddies and cups, and boxes. Good pieces
are expensive – boxes start at about £1000 – as
even limited damage can greatly reduce the
value of a piece. Always examine Japanese
lacquer carefully before buying, as repairs may
have to be carried out in Japan and can prove
to be very costly indeed.

In the 19th century, much lacquerware was
made for export, including table screens and
small chests of drawers called *kodansu*. The
best of these are meticulously inlaid with
mother-of-pearl, tortoiseshell and other materials. Also collectable are lacquered wood
figures of geisha, peasants, musicians and
other characters. Most of these figures fetch
around £1000 at auction.

Lacquer was also used for inro (see above,
p.399), which were used by both men and
women for carrying small items such as a
personal seal. Some lacquer artists specialised
in inro alone. Auction prices vary from about
£100 to as much as £10,000.

*Poor-quality Japanese
ivory sectional carving
of a poulterer; c.1900;
10⅝ in (27 cm) high.
This piece is made
from offcuts from
better figures.*
£250-£350

*Ivory fisherman carved
in Japan from a whole
walrus tusk; c.1900;
10 in (25.4 cm) high.
The carving is not top
quality but the figure is
decorative. Many
similar pieces survive,
the majority signed
'Tamayuki', which must
have been the name of a
factory rather than an
individual maker.*
£300-£400

*...apanese ebony vase; late 19thC; 18 in (45.7 cm)
...igh. It is carved with shi-shi (lion dogs) and inlaid
...ith ivory and amber borders.*
...5000-£8000

*Japanese ivory vase and
cover; c.1900; 5¾ in
(14.6 cm) high. Pieces
of ivory as large as this
frequently split, which
reduces the value.*
£700-£1000
If split: £100-£200

Tribal art

From the goldsmiths of Ghana and the ivory workers of old African kingdoms to the woodcarvers and weapons makers of the South Sea islands, tribal craftsmen have left a legacy of a way of life now rapidly disappearing.

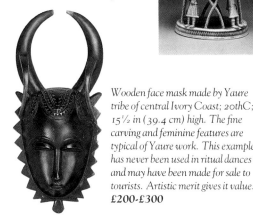

Bronze head from Benin; 16thC; 9½ in (24.1 cm) high. Heads such as this were made for the altars of 'obas' (chiefs) or as trophies after battle, but little is known about the background of this example.
£40,000-£60,000

A NY OBJECT from a tribal culture, past or present, whether used for household purposes or as part of spiritual life, is considered to be tribal art. Most of the tribal art in Britain comes from central or southern Africa, the Pacific islands, Australia or New Zealand, but native American objects also appear on the market occasionally.

Tribal art first reached Europe in the late 15th century when explorers started to bring back pieces for their patrons. Most of the objects became the property of royal and papal courts, where the first collections began.

Nineteenth-century colonial expansion brought other connections with far-off places. An 1897 British military expedition to the Benin Kingdom in West Africa found a highly developed culture with court artists expertly casting bronzes and historical plaques. Some magnificent ivory carvings were also found. Today Benin bronzes are some of the most valuable tribal art works, fetching hundreds of thousands of pounds on the rare occasions when they come on the market.

In this century tribal art has become more widely popular, partly because its influence is clearly seen in the work of artists such as Matisse and Picasso. Many missionaries and diplomats returning from abroad brought back traditional objects, further stimulating interest and feeding the European market. Since the 1950s, modern travel has opened up ever more remote places to specialists and travellers, who now bring back most of the traditional objects reaching the West.

'TOURIST' AND AUTHENTIC TRIBAL ART

Some of the pieces travellers bring home with them were genuinely made and used in tribal life before being sold, but this is increasingly unusual. With spreading Western influence, thriving local traditions and tribal cultures have declined the whole world over, and many traditional-looking handcrafts are now produced just for the tourist market. Most of this 'tourist' or 'airport' art is poorly executed and exaggeratedly exotic. Rarely, a carver may produce a piece of intrinsic artistic merit, such as the Yaure mask (see right). Otherwise, these works have no collector's value.

Experts apply strict standards of authenticity to tribal art: an object must be made by a

Bronze from Benin; late 16thC; 23 in (58.5 cm) high. This exceptionally fine casting, a trophy of the British 1897 expedition, sold for £450,000 in 1991. A similar bronze is now on display at the Museum of Mankind in London.
Museum piece

Carved ivory salt cellar from Sierra Leone; 16thC; 8 in (20.3 cm) high. It sold at auction in 1983 for £33,000.
Over £100,000

Wooden face mask made by Yaure tribe of central Ivory Coast; 20thC; 15½ in (39.4 cm) high. The fine carving and feminine features are typical of Yaure work. This example has never been used in ritual dances and may have been made for sale to tourists. Artistic merit gives it value.
£200-£300

Decorated wooden beaker from Zaire; 20thC; 4½ in (11.4 cm) high. The low price reflects this example's lack of a good patina and its late date.
£80-£120

Female Fang guardian figure from Equatorial Guinea; probably 19thC; 16 in (40.5 cm) high. Carvings such as this were placed in baskets with the bones of the dead to protect them from evil spirits.
£50,000-£60,000

master craftsman, and in the traditional manner. If intended for a ritual purpose, the correct ceremonies should have been carried out – although even experts can find this hard to establish. And the object should have been used for its intended purpose – preferably for some time – before being sold.

For amateurs without much experience, valuating a piece can be difficult. The best way to develop an eye for the real thing is to visit collections in museums and salerooms as often as possible, to become familiar with the sort of objects you are interested in.

Pay special attention to the look and feel of an object: it can reveal a great deal about age and use. For example, genuine carvings by the Fang people of equatorial west Africa (see illustration opposite) have an oily appearance and sometimes appear to 'sweat' because of the way the wood has been treated. Ivory handles on fly whisks should be smooth and shiny if they have been well used, a look which curios made for tourists will never have. A real Maori handclub will feel well balanced, but an imitation will not.

BUYING TRIBAL ART

Much tribal art was brought to Britain by people who retired here after a lifetime overseas, which gave them the opportunity to find and purchase genuine items, often for paltry sums. In the past a few collectors have also bought unrecognised valuable pieces for very little in antique shops: a sacred Hawaiian staff, for example, bought for under £100 in an English antique shop in 1990, fetched over £50,000 at auction later the same year; and

Palm-fibre cloth panel or 'shoowa' made by the Kuba tribe in Zaire; late 19thC; 80 × 23 in (203 × 59 cm). The piece consists of several rectangles sewn together. The earth colours and complex geometric designs are typical of Kuba textiles. Fine examples of similar pieces can be seen in some museums.
£1000-£1500

Decorated iron-bladed Kuba knives from Zaire; early 20thC; 16½ in (42 cm) long (above) and 13¾ in (35 cm) long (below).
£200-£300 each

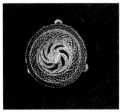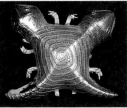

Ashanti gold weights from Ghana: (left) a filigree pendant and (right) a chameleon ring; 19thC; 1½-2 in (38-51 mm) across. The Ashanti traded in gold and used such weights to measure it. Each illustrates a proverb. Beware of modern replicas, betrayed by lightness, lack of refinement and sometimes a greenish colour.
£400-£1000 each

Ashanti wooden fertility dolls or 'akua'ba' from Ghana; 20thC; 10¼-15½ in (26-39.4 cm) high. They are given to brides to promote fertility, and most examples have decorative beadwork. Mass-produced imitations have no value.
Largest doll: £200-£250
Smaller two: £80-£120 each

Pair of wooden 'ibeji' (twin carvings) made by members of the Nigerian Yoruba tribe; late 19th or early 20thC; 9½ in (24.1 cm). Carved when twins were born, ibejis were cherished by the family. If a twin died, the ibeji was cared for as if alive.
£700-£900 the pair

Caribou-skin man's coat made by the Naskapi tribe of North America; c.1770; c.40 in (1 m) long. The garment is made from several pieces of skin sewn together with sinew, pressed flat and painted with geometric designs.
£30,000-£35,000

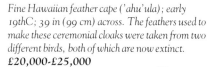

Decorated Inca vessels ('kero'); 15-16thC; 7¼-8½ in (18.4-21.6 cm) high. The three wooden beakers above are brightly painted with human and animal forms and geometric designs. The beaker on the left is carved as the head of a puma. All have some slight damage such as chips or cracks.
Top: £3000-£3500 the three
Left: £2400-£2800

Fine Hawaiian feather cape ('ahu'ula); early 19thC; 39 in (99 cm) across. The feathers used to make these ceremonial cloaks were taken from two different birds, both of which are now extinct.
£20,000-£25,000

North American 'quirt' (riding whip) handle; c.1850; 13¾ in (35 cm) long. The handle is made of antler and engraved with decorative motifs at one end. At the other is a leather wrist strap decorated with stained porcupine quillwork.
£4000-£6000

Wooden clubs from the Fiji islands; 18th-19thC; 15½-17 in (39.4-43.2 cm) long. Each has a differently carved ornamental head.
£300-£900 each

Maori greenstone pendant of an ancestor figure ('hei-tiki') from New Zealand; 19thC; 4⅓ in (11 cm) high. The stylised design is typical. The hole in the top is for hanging the pendant. It may have had inlaid eyes of shell.
£800-£1000

Carved wooden food bowls from Fiji and the Trobriand Islands; 19thC; (left) 27 in (68.5 cm) long, (right) 21 in (53.5 cm) long. These Melanesian islanders made bowls in a variety of shapes, including birds, fish and, as here, turtles.
Left: £3000-£4000; right: £500-£700

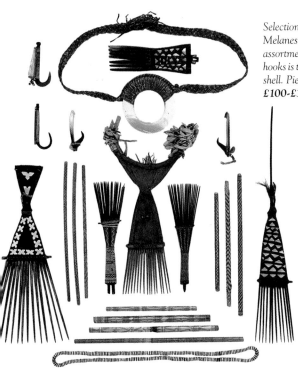

Selection of Solomon Islands artefacts from the Melanesian Mission; 19th and early 20thC. An assortment of wooden combs, sticks and fishing hooks is topped by a necklace with a central clam shell. Pieces such as these are still inexpensive.
£100-£300 each

Australian Aboriginal spear thrower ('woomera') with traditional decoration; c.1900; 22½ in (57 cm) long. By using the thrower as an extension of his arm, the hunter could reach distant quarry.
£500-£750

Wooden stopper for a gourd, made by the Batak people of Sumatra; 19thC; 6½ in (16.5 cm) high. Decorated stoppers were used on containers for magical substances. This one has a rich red patina indicating long use.
£800-£1200

a wooden Easter Island carving bought for £50 at a flea market in the United States, was sold at auction in 1990 for £175,000.

These days, bargains are rare as most of the best tribal art is in the hands of specialist dealers or collectors who know its value. Even so, buyers who are prepared to learn about the subject, and who choose carefully, can make a good investment. As with collecting of any sort, it is important to buy only pieces that appeal to you, however much – or little – you are planning to spend on your collection.

The wide range of tribal art objects – from fish-hooks to life-size statues – means that prices vary enormously. Smaller objects that are not particularly old or rare usually cost no more than a few hundred pounds. For older, rarer or exceptionally well-crafted items there is virtually no upper limit, and top prices are now comparable with those for Western art, at around £1 million or more.

WHAT TO COLLECT

Authentic objects of all sorts are highly collectable. Among the favourites are carved figures, which have ceremonial and magical functions in almost every tribal society. Masks, whether from Africa or Oceania, can be even more impressive, with wild hair and features carved to represent spirits or ancestors. Their purpose is also ceremonial, usually as part of a ritual dance.

Everyday objects provide direct contact with primitive ways of life, some now vanished for ever. Many artefacts such as bowls,

Wooden stopper from the Yuat river, New Guinea; 20 in (51 cm) long. The stopper, from a sacred flute, is in the form of an ornamental carved wooden figure with a feather and hair cap.
£15,000-£18,000

containers, spoons and combs also have artistic value in their decorative carving and ornamentation. Jewellery is less common, but beautiful pieces – often with mythological significance – were made by craftsmen as far apart as New Zealand, Brazil and Ghana. Hunting and fishing tools, weights and other utensils for making a living and for trade are equally collectable.

Woven textiles in traditional designs and colours are a good buy for collectors with a limited budget. Originally, most cloth was made from tree bark or raffia, but cotton is now more usual. Older African designs were often in earth colours, and South Sea islands fabrics rather brighter. Modern cloth from Ghana and other countries of West Africa comes in a huge variety of colours and designs, and although some types are quite valuable in Europe, African prices are still low.

Traditional weapons of all sorts, whether in wood, iron, stone or bone, are another good area for collectors. Their importance in warfare, hunting and ceremonies meant that they

were often among the most beautifully crafted and decorated of all traditional implements.

Musical instruments are different in every culture, and up to now most collectors of tribal instruments have been specialists who bought items from makers or players. Today, many examples exist in the West and most are inexpensive, often costing under £100.

TIPS FOR BEGINNERS

Because it comes from foreign cultures, tribal art is not always easy to appreciate. Experts advise new collectors to specialise in objects from just one or two regions – preferably places with which they are connected or to which they feel particularly drawn. An interesting way to start is to collect by theme, for example, maternity figures or sacred objects from a particular tribe, or jewellery, weapons or textiles from a certain region.

As well as visiting exhibitions, read as much as you can about a people before you start collecting their work: understanding the context is vital for building a good collection.

Firearms

Gunsmiths have long striven to make their works not only functional but beautiful – and that is why so many of them fetch high prices today.

THE GUNSMITH'S KEY TASK has always been to make sure that the explosive charge fires fast enough to launch the projectile before the target can strike first or move off. The oldest firearms are various forms of matchlock, fired by a slow-burning match or fuse pressed into a pinch of gunpowder to ignite, in turn, the main charge.

Matchlocks called toradors were made in northern India until early this century. The better ones, beautifully decorated and inlaid with precious metals, fetch £500-£800 at auction. The Japanese also continued to make matchlocks. These are generally of higher quality than Indian guns and have a short, heavy barrel and plain, polished stock. Early 19th-century examples fetch around £1000.

In the 16th century came the wheel-lock, which rasped a steel wheel against pyrites to make sparks – like a cigarette lighter. The wheel-lock's complexity and expense meant its popularity was short-lived, and most surviving specimens were made for the nobility.

FLINTLOCKS

The earliest firearms commonly found today are flintlocks from the 18th and early 19th centuries. These used a simple and fairly reliable mechanism: a flint striking a steel plate, or frizzen, to make the spark. Flintlocks were made in vast numbers to fire a variety of weapons from cannon to pocket pistols.

Hand guns are the most keenly collected flintlocks, but even within this group there is a bewildering range of types. So-called Queen Anne pistols, with long, screw-off barrel and curved butt, were popular throughout the 18th century and are now worth about £1500.

Simpler, but sturdily attractive, are the heavy holster pistols issued to British cavalry during the Napoleonic wars. Like most British issue firearms of the period, they usually bear the crowned 'GR' cypher of George III plus the word 'TOWER'. The ramrod is attached to swivels beneath the barrel to prevent it being lost in battle. Examples in reasonable order can fetch £500. The much rarer plain all-steel or gunmetal pistols carried by some Highland troops at this time make £600-£1000.

Officers bought their own elegantly engraved pistols from top London gunsmiths. Prices for a pair in good condition by a famous

Wheel-lock holster pistol; German, late 16thC; 24¾ in (63 cm) long. Wheel-locks rarely appear at auction. Many of the best are from Saxony, like this, with silver, gilt-brass and horn mounts engraved with foliage, sea monsters and scrolls.
£13,000-£15,000

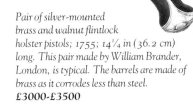

BIRDS, WATCH OUT *The gentleman in Enoch Seeman's early 18thC painting has been caught in the act of loading his long-barrelled flintlock sporting gun. A powder flask hangs from his belt.*

Brown Bess flintlock musket; 18thC; barrel 46 in (1.16 m) long. Later ones are 4 in (10.1 cm) shorter. Such guns were used for over 200 years from c.1720.
£1000-£1500

Pair of silver-mounted brass and walnut flintlock holster pistols; 1755; 14¼ in (36.2 cm) long. This pair made by William Brander, London, is typical. The barrels are made of brass as it corrodes less than steel.
£3000-£3500

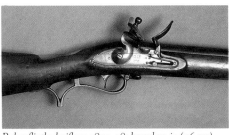

Baker flintlock rifle; c.1800-38; barrel 30 in (76 cm) long. This was the first issue British rifle. The butt had a brass-covered hollow for tools.
£1200-£1500

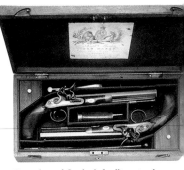

Pair of cased flintlock duelling pistols; 1815; 15 in (38.1 cm) long. These pistols are by Joseph Manton, a leading London maker. The fitted case still has its accessories and trade label. Beware of sets falsely put together as pairs.
£5000-£6000

gunsmith and complete with fitted case and accessories, such as bullet mould and powder flask, start at around £1000.

But the pinnacle of the gunsmith's art was the duelling pistol – long-barrelled, light and perfectly balanced. In mint condition, good London-made cased pairs sell for upwards of £5000. But beware of cased sets assembled from odd parts, with the pistols perhaps refinished and inscribed with a false name.

Long flintlock guns are in less demand from collectors but may still have a romantic history. For example, a Brown Bess – the British infantryman's nickname for the land musket, his principal weapon for more than 100 years – might have seen action at Waterloo. It is worth looking for the stamped regimental number and checking on that unit's history. A Brown Bess looks formidable with its 42-46 in (1.06-1.16 m) smooth-bore

barrel topped by a 17 in (43.2 cm) bayonet. Such guns can make as much as £1500 today.

Towards the end of the Napoleonic wars, the Baker rifle was developed. The weighty 30 in (76 cm) barrel has seven grooves of rifling inside and was accurate at five times the distance of a smooth-bore musket – up to 250 yds (230 m). With its added interest as a specialist's weapon, the Baker rifle generally sells for more than the Brown Bess.

Some of the finest flintlocks were sporting guns. Early ones had a very long, single barrel, but by the late 18th century double-barrelled guns were coming into favour. These are often beautifully engraved and carry the maker's name on the rib between the barrels. Prices vary but good examples fetch £3500 or more.

Among other desirable flintlock guns of the period are the shorter carbines, carried by certain cavalry regiments, and that attractive

curiosity, the blunderbuss. This has a wide or flared barrel intended to spread the shot. It was popular with gamekeepers and householders, and also with mail-coach guards for protection against highwaymen. Blunderbusses are often engraved 'For His Majesty's Mail Coach', or with quips such as 'Fly or Die', and most fetch around £600-£1000 today.

PERCUSSION WEAPONS

A major new development came in the early years of the 19th century: the percussion cap. This was much like the cap used today in toy pistols, except that the small explosion fired the main charge. It eventually came to be used in most types of gun, and flintlocks could be quite easily converted to use it. Today, unconverted flintlock pistols are worth half as much again as their converted equivalents.

Nevertheless, high-quality percussion guns can fetch prices just as high as flintlocks. A good cased pair of percussion duelling pistols, complete with fittings, will sell for upwards of £6000, and percussion sporting guns can also make high sums at auction.

During the 1840s, the race began to produce a reliable multi-shot hand gun. So-called pepperbox revolvers with four to six barrels are keenly collected, as are the familiar Wild West revolvers made by the American firms of Colt, Remington and others. But by the late 1850s, the modern metal-cased, breech-loading cartridge was in full production, and later firearms are tightly controlled by law.

Flintlock blunderbuss; Flemish, c.1800; 23⅜ in (59.5 cm) long. The muzzle is flared and a spring-loaded bayonet attached to the barrel provides protection when reloading.
£800-£1000

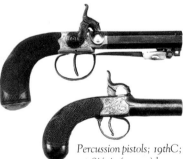

Percussion pistols; 19thC; top 8¼ in (21 cm) long. Small pistols were used for personal defence. Top is a Birmingham-made belt pistol, still in good condition; bottom is a pocket pistol.
Top: £450-£500; bottom: £150-£180

Percussion target pistols; c.1850; case 18 in (45.7 cm) long. This is a typical pair of continental mid-19thC target pistols probably made in Liège. The fluted ebony butts are characteristic.
£2500-£3000 the set

Double-barrelled percussion sporting rifle; 1864; barrels 30 in (76 cm) long. This example is by J. Purdey of London – one of the most sought-after names and still in business today.
£5000-£6000

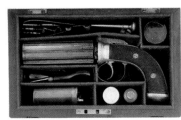

Self-cocking bar-hammer percussion pepperbox revolver in case; c.1845; case 11½ in (29.2 cm) long. Such guns were popular before the advent of true revolvers.
£800-£1000

GUN LAW AND SAFETY
Never in Fun

IN BRITISH LAW, anyone who buys, sells or owns a working reproduction of an antique gun, or an antique that fires self-contained cartridges or bullets, is subject to strict controls. You must hold an appropriate firearms or shotgun certificate and be able to show that the weapon has been proof-tested. A gun can be deactivated by a gunsmith, but this destroys all but its decorative value.

Always make sure old flintlock and percussion weapons are unloaded, for dry gunpowder can remain explosive for a very long time. Push a piece of dowelling down the barrel, mark it at the muzzle, then lay it alongside. If there is a difference in length, the gun may still contain a charge; take it to a gunsmith to have the charge drawn.

Swords, daggers and bayonets

Man's long quest for the perfect means of cutting or stabbing his enemy has produced highly crafted tools of great interest and occasional beauty.

THE SWORD has changed little in principle since the days of the Vikings and Normans, though its variations are numerous. Between the mighty two-handed claymore of the Highland clans and the elegant rapier is an array of edged weapons, each suited to a particular method of fighting.

In Britain it is illegal to buy or sell certain types of weapon less than 100 years old (which may be hard to prove), including swordsticks, push daggers, butterfly knives, blowpipes and most Far Eastern martial arts weapons.

SWORDS

Swords pre-dating the 17th century are rare outside museums. The earliest examples to turn up regularly today are Cromwellian broadswords, which fetch upwards of £500 at auction. The smallswords worn by late 17th and early 18th-century gentlemen as part of formal wear are far more plentiful. Finely made examples with a hilt of filigree steel, silver or occasionally gold, can be worth £600 in good condition. Later versions – still worn by diplomats and courtiers – start at £100.

But most plentiful of all are weapons from the end of the 18th and beginning of the 19th centuries – the years of the Napoleonic wars. Swords were still the main cavalry weapon and were issued in two main types: the long, weighty broadsword of the heavy cavalry, and the curved, slashing sabre of the light regiments. Though made in great numbers, well-preserved examples command good prices – up to £300 for a 1796-pattern sabre with its original scabbard or around £150 for a humble Royal Navy boarding cutlass.

Officers' swords of the period bear a royal, regimental or naval cypher on the hilt and may be inscribed with a record of the owner's deeds. These are highly collectable: Lloyds Patriotic Fund naval swords, for example, can sell for as much as £20,000.

Swords of the past 150 years – identified by the royal cypher – are also worth looking for, particularly those with a famous maker's name, such as H. Wilkinson, etched on the blade. Most sought after are those from obscure units or the short reign of Edward VIII. All these regulation swords, and their continental and American counterparts, are rising in value, especially if accompanied by the original scabbard and swordknot – the leather or gilt-embroidered loop and tassel tied around the hilt. In recent years, hundreds

'Mameluke'-style officer's sword (below); London, early 19thC; blade 31¼ in (79.5 cm). Napoleon's defeat of the Mamelukes made these popular.
£700-£1000

Infantry officer's sword; 1796 pattern; blade 32 in (81 cm). These are quite common but here the blade and scabbard are in near-perfect condition. Plain examples or ones in average condition fetch less.
£600-£800

Japanese daisho; smaller 19 in (48.2 cm). This comprises a small late 16thC wakizashi blade, a larger 19thC katana blade and lacquer scabbards.
£5000-£7000

Chiselled steel hilted smallsword with gold decoration (above); Spanish or Portuguese, mid-18thC; blade 39 in (99 cm). These were fashion accessories.
£1400-£1600

Silver-mounted kukri, 2nd King Edward VII's Own Gurkha Rifles; early 20thC; blade 13¾ in (34.9 cm). This is a presentation version of an old Gurkha weapon.
£250-£350

Bowie knife; probably Sheffield, mid-19thC; 12 in (30.5 cm). Good early American-made examples can fetch ten times as much.
£200-£300

Silver-mounted Highland dirk with knife and fork en-suite; hallmarked 1914; blade 11½ in (29.2 cm). These daggers are highly collectable.
£350-£500

Left-hand dagger; German, c.1610; 19¾ in (50.2 cm). It was used in duelling with a rapier in the right hand.
£3000-£4000

Plug bayonet; late 17thC; 7 in (17.8 cm). Blades on some examples are stamped with the maker's mark.
£500-£700

of copies from India and the Far East have come onto the market, so be wary of 'bargains' and buy from a reputable source.

The apogee of the swordsmith's art is seen in the blades made by Japanese masters. Folded and forged many times before being given their razor edge, their style has remained unchanged for centuries, so it takes an expert eye to assess the subtle differences that determine value. The value of late 19th-century pieces is about £200; machine-made blades of the 1920s onwards fetch less. But an ancient blade re-dressed as a Second World War weapon can fetch six figures.

DAGGERS

Daggers have been used as personal weapons since the Stone Age. The wavy-bladed Malay kris and the Gurkha kukri – good specimens of which can sell for £200 and £100 respectively – make a colourful start to a collection.

Western weapons include the daggers used in the left hand with rapiers in 16th-century duels – most now museum pieces. Easier to find are the dirks of the Scottish Highlands, with bog-oak hilt, semi-precious stone set in the top and miniature knife and fork in the scabbard. Late 19th-century military examples with a well-etched blade and silver mounts in a fitted case, with an accompanying skean-dhu knife to tuck in the top of the sock, are worth around £1000. Ivory-gripped, gold-cyphered naval midshipmen's dirks of the time of Nelson can fetch £300-£500.

Hunting knives are also highly collectable. The most famous type is probably the Bowie knife. The enormous, clipped-back blade was probably invented by the American Colonel Jim Bowie in the early 19th century, and was quickly adopted by frontiersmen. The cutlers of Sheffield cashed in on the demand, and exported thousands to the USA, often engraved with patriotic American slogans. Good examples command £500 or more.

Lesser fry include the trench and fighting knives of the two World Wars, and the Nazi ceremonial daggers that were issued to everyone from serving officers to the Hitler Youth and stationmasters. You will see plenty of them at antique fairs for £35 up to £200. But beware: many are reproductions.

BAYONETS

Bayonets were used by some European armies as early as the 1680s. The earliest are plug bayonets which plug into the gun muzzle, but the socket bayonet which fits over the muzzle was soon developed. Today bayonets range in price from around £2 to £250, but always make sure the bayonet still has its appropriate scabbard and frog (belt loop).

Armour

Few collectors can acquire a complete suit of armour, but helmets and other parts may be more affordable.

A FULL SUIT of European armour, as worn at Agincourt or a tournament of the medieval or Tudor eras, is unlikely to surface today, as most are in museums. If you were to find such a thing, it would probably be a 19th-century copy. Nonetheless, copies are decorative and well made, and some fetch as much as £1500 at auction.

There is always a chance of a piece of plate armour turning out to be the real thing – a funerary helmet, for example. These close helmets, of the visored type that enclose the head, were carried at funerals of people of standing long after similar helmets had ceased to be worn on the battlefield. They are decorated with a carved crest (or a tall spike that once carried a crest), and now sell for £500 or more.

The earliest battle helmets likely to be found belong to the period when firearms had already made full armour obsolete. They might be pieces such as the late 16th-century morions with raised combs, as seen in pictures of the Spanish Armada. These fetch up to £2500. The wide-brimmed steel helmets worn by pikemen in the Civil Wars and the lobster-tailed, three-bar visored helmets of Cromwell's New Model Army cavalrymen are more plentiful, and sell for about £500 each if not over-restored. A Cromwellian cavalryman's breastplate with authentic armourer's test-mark – a ball-shaped indentation – will generally fetch £800 upwards.

FROM OTHER CONTINENTS

Indian and Persian armour of the 18th and 19th centuries is also collectable. Persian inlaid helmets, for instance, complete with chain-mail neck guard and sliding nose-bar, fetch up to £1000. Chain-mail shirts, barely altered since the Crusades and worn by the Mahdi's cavalry against Gordon at Khartoum, Sudan, in the 1880s, sell for around £300.

The vogue for Japanese armour gets more intense by the year. Generally, it is composed of small, lacquered metal plates laced together to make large, flexible sections. Most pieces on the market are 19th century and prices for full suits start at around £1500.

Close helmet; early 16thC with later gorget plate to protect the neck; 10½ in (26.7 cm) high. This is the type of helmet carried at funerals and is probably English.
£7000-£9000

Comb morion; German, 1572; 30¾ in (78.1 cm) high. This helmet has finely executed etching, but repairs have been made to the brim.
£4500-£5000

Lobster-tailed pot helmet with a ribbed skull and adjustable nasal bar in the front; mid-17thC. This example may have been produced in Germany.
£350-£400

Japanese suit of armour in medieval style; c.1860. Japan evolved a distinctive style of armour with small plates laced together. The helmet comprises a metal skull piece with plates to protect the neck. Such armour is highly collectable.
£8000-£12,000

Miscellaneous militaria

The impedimenta of war – from uniforms, kit and badges to the soldier's small personal possessions – give collectors a fascinating glimpse of the individual's side of soldiering.

Guidon of the 10th (Prince of Wales' Own Royal) Light Dragoons; early 19thC; 5¼ in (13.3 cm) wide. Guidons are small pennants carried as a regimental standard. Early examples such as this are rare in good condition.
£4000-£4500

Captain's full dress uniform, King's Own Royal Regiment of Norfolk (Imperial) Yeomanry; early 20thC. Edward VII is said to have helped with the design of this uniform.
£3000-£4000

Victorian shoulder belt plates: (from left) Royal Monmouth Regiment, 25th Punjab Infantry and 35th Sikh Infantry; 19thC; largest 3½ in (8.9 cm) high. Indian regiments are popular.
£180-£240; £350-£450; £200-£300

Officer's shako, Yorkshire Hussars; c.1830-56; with plumes, 20 in (51 cm) high. This form, adopted in 1830, was replaced by the busby in 1856.
£2500-£3000

Rope-tensioned side drum, 1st Battalion Coldstream Guards; after 1918; 16½ in (42 cm) high. This was made by George Potter & Co and bears the insignia of a famous regiment.
£400-£450

UNIFORMS, BADGES AND INSIGNIA have been part and parcel of warring since the earliest times – distinguishing friend from foe, leader from the led, cavalry or artillery from other specialists, or members of one regiment or crew from another. All served to single out the individual while emphasising attachment to a special group.

INSIGNIA GALORE

Most plentiful are the flotsam and jetsam of the Second World War. Material from Nazi Germany is particularly varied, since practically everyone was mobilised into one service or another, each – military or civilian – with its distinctive insignia. Most such material is quite cheap, except for the insignia of certain Waffen-SS units or of sought-after Allied units such as the SAS. However, so many replicas have been made for films that even genuine articles fall under suspicion, helping to depress prices.

Old uniforms can have considerable value. A late 18th-century scarlet levée coat of the London and Westminster Light Horse Volunteers, for example, sells for around £2500. Elaborate 19th-century ceremonial armour is also collected. A Prussian Garde du Corps officer's helmet of the 1870s complete with its crowned eagle crest is worth about £3500.

Most enthusiasts find it easier to house small, striking items such as the metal plates that were worn on the shoulder crossbelt. Early examples bear only the regimental insignia and number; later ones show battle honours as well; those for officers have gilt and enamel decoration. They were abolished for most regiments in 1855, and generally make £100-£400. When dating such items, remember that most British army regimental names are relatively new, and until 1881 many regiments were known only by number.

Other attractive items include the cavalry officer's sabretache, in use until the turn of the century, and the shoulder pouch with belt – both embroidered with the regimental badge. A sabretache from a famous regiment may be worth £1000 or more in good condition. In the 18th and early 19th centuries, officers wore on the chest a gilded, crescent-shaped gorget engraved with the Royal Arms, which now sells for about £150. Gorgets were revived by the Nazis for standard bearers, military police and guard units; these can fetch £250.

HATS AND HELMETS

Military headgear is always appealing to collectors, and went through some curious changes (see also armour, p.409). In 1800, all infantry ranks wore the shako, a tall, leather cylinder with a small peak – except for the bonneted Highlanders, top-hatted Marines and the Grenadiers, who continued to wear their traditional bearskins. (An 18th-century bearskin may fetch £2500.)

Various other forms of shako followed from 1812 to 1869. Ten years later the blue cloth spiked helmet (still worn in modified form by the British police) arrived, and before the

Officer's dress sabretache of the 6th (Inniskilling) Dragoons; c.1830; 12 in (30.5 cm) high. Cavalry officers slung these pouches from the waist. This is in good condition for its date.
£1000-£1400

Trench art; 1914-18. Such pieces were adapted from shell cases, bullets and scrap metal using tools from military workshops and repair shops near the front. Quality, complexity and prices vary greatly.
Biplane: £100-£150
Others: £15-£80

Officer's parade cuirass, Prussian Garde du Corps, with star of the High Order of the Black Eagle; c.1912. Armour had largely gone from battle by the 18thC, but ceremonial armour is worn to this day.
£3500-£5000

First World War gift boxes; 1914-18; 5 in (12.7 cm) wide. Queen Mary's gift boxes to the troops were often kept as souvenirs by their recipients. They are worth most with unopened packets.
£80-£100
Empty tin: £10-£20

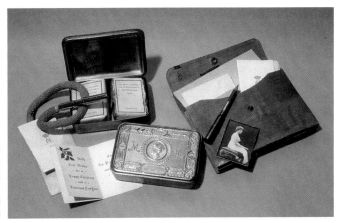

19th century was out certain British units were wearing forms of topi or the slouch hat.

The 1817 Household Cavalry helmet with Grecian pattern and large bearskin is particularly rare and may fetch as much as £6000.

PERSONAL EFFECTS

Of humble origins but sometimes quite valuable today are the small mementos of war, such as the soldier's 'housewife' – a canvas hold-all that contained his 'eating irons', shaving gear and sewing tackle. These hardly changed from Victorian times to the Second World War, and are all the more personal for bearing the owner's name and number.

Paybooks, soldier's record and proficiency books, discharge papers and passes – especially from the last century or earlier – all find a ready market, as do diaries and letters (particularly if describing a famous engagement). Many collectors seek souvenirs and 'trench art', such as inkwells made from cannonballs and pipes carved with the regimental crest by soldiers in the Crimea. The First World War produced a wealth of objects made out of cartridge and shell cases, from cigarette lighters to dinner gongs. Then there are small oddities like the tins of tobacco presented to the men in the trenches by Princess Mary at Christmas 1914, which can make £100 if still unopened, £25 or less if incomplete.

MEDALS AND DECORATIONS
For Valour and Service

FEW WORKS OF ART are more strongly linked to their original owner than medals. Most pre-1939 British awards have the recipient's name, rank, number and unit or ship engraved on the back. With detective work you can find out about the recipient, how the award was won – and if it is genuine.

Those generating the greatest excitement are bravery awards, from the Victoria Cross (VC) downwards. Few VCs come up at auction; when they do they fetch upwards of £10,000, depending on the recipient's fame. Lesser gallantry medals, such as the Military Cross and Distinguished Service Order, tend to reach prices in the hundreds, and more for a particularly interesting act. Bravery awards are worth more if accompanied by campaign medals or personal effects such as diaries. Campaign medals alone – given for

having been on active service during a particular period – are sometimes also of interest. One given to a unit in the thick of the Battle of Waterloo in 1815 may fetch £400, one for a reserve regiment only £120.

After Waterloo, most campaign medals have bars marking the battles that the wearer took part in. Those for famous battles are the most sought after, but also the most reproduced. Few 20th-century campaign medals have much value and Second World War examples do not even bear the recipient's name. However, the 1982 South Atlantic Medal now sells for about £70, and the recent Gulf Medal may eventually be valuable.

Foreign medals and decorations tend to be comparatively cheap. A French Legion of Honour costs around £25, and a Second World War German Iron Cross 2nd Class from £15.

Group of RAF gallantry medals (left) including DSO and DFC; 1939-45. Queen's South Africa medal (right); 1899-1902. This went to a 14-year-old in the Mafeking Cadet Corps.
Left: £18,000-£19,000 the set
Right: £450-£500

Nautical collectables

Many of the most ardent collectors of 'nauticalia' – items relating to ships and the sea – are themselves boat owners, but the decorative carvings of scrimshaw work can be appreciated without any nautical knowledge.

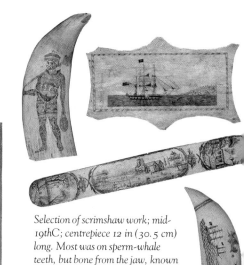

W IDELY DIFFERENT KINDS of antiques are included among nautical items: precision instruments, ceramics and fine art among them. Chronometers and navigational instruments (see pp. 285 and 296), 'Rodney's Sailor' Toby jugs, ships' fittings, paintings and, above all, sailors' craftwork provide their own glimpses of life at sea.

SAILORWORK AND SCRIMSHAW

Much of the best nautical craftwork was created by 19th-century seamen on whaling trips, which could last for up to five years and involve many idle hours. Whaling sailors developed their own handicrafts, among the best known of which are scrimshaw (carvings in ivory, wood and so on) and woolwork portraits of ships. Some sailors also brought back shell-work souvenirs – 'sailors' valentines' – from foreign ports.

Most scrimshaw was made from the teeth of sperm whales, which were generally engraved with scenes of life at sea, portraits of those left at home, or views of contemporary events. At auction today, they fetch anything from £200 to £12,000, depending on the quality of work and subject matter. Whaling scenes are the most keenly sought.

Collectors need to beware, however, as large numbers of replica scrimshawed whale teeth are being made from injection-moulded resin. This can usually be identified by its rather greasy surface and warm feel when compared with a real whale's tooth. The pieces are also often over-decorated and dated, unlike most originals. Modern reproductions on real teeth also exist. These can usually be identified from the whiteness of the ivory and the style of decoration, which is too finely worked and too modern in appearance. Technical mistakes and anachronisms in whaling scenes may also be a giveaway.

Sailors' valentines made of shells and often with heart motifs or mottoes such as 'forget me not' are usually mounted in an octagonal case. They were not made by sailors themselves but were bought in the West Indies, and some bear the name 'Barbados'. These valentines can now fetch up to £800.

Many model ships in bottles and three-dimensional shipping scenes, or dioramas, were made by sailors and fishermen in the late 19th and early 20th centuries. Ships in bottles generally fetch between £100 and £300,

Cruise poster by H. K. Rooke; 1927; 41 × 26 in (104 × 66 cm). Posters from the heyday of sea travel in the first half of this century are much collected. This example is from the Peninsular & Oriental Steam Navigation Co, or P & O.
£100-£150

Selection of scrimshaw work; mid-19thC; centrepiece 12 in (30.5 cm) long. Most was on sperm-whale teeth, but bone from the jaw, known as panbone (top right), whalebone and walrus tusks were also used.
Teeth: £200-£1000
Panbone: £500-£2000

Woolwork picture; 1860s; 22 in (56 cm) wide. Sewn woolwork portraits of ships are fairly common. Most of them are naive in style and use strong colours. This example is in a maple frame.
£400-£600

Ship in bottle in decorative fretwork stand; c.1890; 14 in (35.5 cm) long. Most ships in bottles are fairly crudely constructed. They were erected inside the bottle by pulling on threads attached to the rigging.
£250-£350

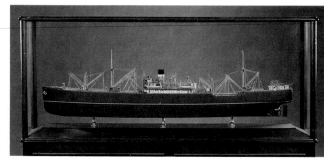

Scottish shipbuilder's model; 1920s; 60 in (1.52 m) long. This is a full-block model of the cargo ship 'City of Lille'. Detailed models such as this are usually mounted in a glass case.
£5000-£7000

depending on their size and intricacy. Complex shipping dioramas sell for as much as £1000, or smaller ones for £150-£200.

SHIP MODELS AND FITTINGS

Shipbuilders' models are much more detailed and precise. They were used from the 17th century onwards to show the internal construction of the hull, and the stern and bow decoration, to prospective buyers. Apart from their intrinsic beauty, such models give a fascinating insight into how ships were built in the 17th and 18th centuries.

Nineteenth-century dockyard models are normally made from laminated wood and are often half-block models. These show one side of the hull only, to indicate its shape to the builders, and they have little deck detail or decoration. Rare 17th-century ship models will sell for £50,000, or even more, whereas simpler, half-block models for commercial vessels will generally go for between £300 and £500.

Pond yacht; c.1900; 48 in (1.2 m) long. Detailed wooden yachts with linen sails such as this were once a common sight on ponds in parks.
£400-£600

In quite a different class are the highly detailed scale models often presented to the owner of an important vessel when it was launched. They are generally mounted in a glass case and bear a plaque giving the details of the shipyard and marine engine maker. The value of such a piece depends on its size and quality, and on the type of vessel. An average-sized 6-10 ft (1.8-3 m) model can fetch between £5000 and £25,000 at auction. A half-block version with full deck details will usually reach £2000-£5000.

There is always a demand for ships' equipment, and larger pieces – such as ships' wheels and binnacle compasses – are sought after as interior decoration for homes and restaurants, as are brass portholes (£50-£100 at auction) and bells. Painted sea chests sell at about £300-£500, but many replicas exist.

Ship's wheel on stand; c.1910; 51 in (1.37 m) high. This example is made of mahogany and brass, but others are in teak.
£600-£900

One of a pair of navigational masthead lamps; c.1900; 15 in (38.1 cm) high. These brass lamps have ebony handles. Their white light shone forward and aft.
Pair: £800-£1000

Chadburn bridge telegraph; c.1920; 46 in (1.16 m) high. Brass telegraphs such as this were used for passing orders from a ship's bridge to its engine room.
£800-£1200

Ship's bell; c.1900; 12 in (30.5 cm) high. Brass bells such as this are popular with collectors. One bearing a ship's name – especially if it is renowned – would fetch more.
£300-£400

Railway collectables

Relics of past journeys, such as locomotive nameplates, old signal arms, timetables and even luggage labels, have a new value as collectors' items.

'Lockheed Hudson' brass on steel nameplate still in place; 1941; 72 in (1.8 m) across. Locomotive nameplates, especially those of the Great Western Railway, fetch high prices. **£8500-£9500 (nameplate alone)**

Great Western Railway guard's lamp; pre-1923; 6 in (15.2 cm) across. **£90-£140**

Poster and information board with cast-iron signs; early 20thC; board c.40 in (1 m) high. The caution sign was originally from an engine cab. **Caution sign: £100 Other signs: £20-£40 each**

Railway poster; c.1930; 50 in (1.27 m) wide. Many such posters were produced but they are rare in mint condition. **£400-£600**

Timetables; 1879-1919; largest 9½ in (24.1 cm) high. On the left is a working staff timetable; the paperback timetables were for the public and cost just a few pence. **Hardback: £60-£80 Paperback: £20-£30**

T HE HAUNTING WHISTLE of the steam engine is a thing of the past but the romance of railways lingers, not only in old locomotives maintained and run by enthusiasts, but in the incredible amount of railway paraphernalia that is collected.

Collecting railwayana (as these relics are commonly called) began in earnest only as electric and diesel engines began to displace steam some 40 years ago. Today, almost anything from a station or train may interest a collector. There were more than 100 railway companies before 1923 – each with its own coat of arms or device to be seen on rolling stock, and often on crockery, cutlery and fittings – so the choice of material is vast. In 1923 the companies were grouped into the 'big four' (Great Western; London, Midland and Scottish; London and North Eastern; and Southern), which survived until 1948.

Railway collectables sell at specialist auctions (advertised in railway magazines), major auction houses and 'swap meets' for enthusiasts. And near London's Euston Station is a Collectors' Corner sponsored by British Rail.

HARDWARE AND PRINTED MATTER

Brass engine nameplates from well-known locomotives are the most highly prized railwayana: some can command five-figure sums. Below this level, fittings can range in price from a few pounds to three or even four-figure sums for the rarest items. A cast-iron smoke-box number plate might fetch £150-£400, a gleaming brass signal-box clock £150-£300. Steam cab fittings such as pressure gauges and regulator handles are mostly still on engines preserved in museums or tourist railways, but oil-lit headlamps can be found for around £30.

Pre-1948 postcards of stations and engines reveal much about the old company liveries – both of the staff uniforms and the rolling stock. You can pay around £5 for cards in good condition, and about the same for a genuine button from a uniform or a long-gone special excursion ticket. Pre-1923 buttons are now scarce and may be replicas.

Most printed material costs under £100, but value depends on rarity, interest and on condition. It ranges from colourful posters, some by well-known artists, to paper hand-bills that advertise day trips. Even accident reports and timetables – including working timetables that tell the 'inside' story of freight as well as passenger trains – can make intriguing reading. Railway Clearing House maps, which show by district all the railway lines of the pre-1923 companies, start at £175, but luggage labels, even from before 1923, are among the cheapest items at less than £1.

Motor and flying accessories

Interest in automobilia and aeronautica – as collectables relating to cars and aircraft are called – has grown tremendously over the past 15-20 years, with collectors focusing on early equipment and accessories.

As the spiralling prices reached by old motor vehicles have put them out of reach of all but the rich, many collectors have turned to more affordable works of art and accessories for period cars and aircraft. These range from picnic trunks, radiator mascots and old car horns to RAF 'scramble' bells, propellers and flying jackets.

MOTORING COLLECTABLES

From their introduction in the 1890s, car radiator mascots were made both as trademarks for specific makes of car, and as bonnet accessories for motor enthusiasts. One of the best known is the Flying Lady emblem of the Rolls-Royce from 1911. The original, called 'Spirit of Ecstasy', was sculpted by Charles Sykes. Early nickel-plated examples made for the Silver Ghost of 1911 onwards can fetch £500 and more. Cheaper vintage-period mascots include the Rover's Viking, the Vulcan's smith and anvil, the Riley's ski lady, and the Armstrong Siddeley's sphinx. Buyers should beware of modern reproductions, however.

Mascot designs from the 1920s in the form of human figures, birds of prey and other animals can all be found, including figures of Bruce Bairnsfather's First World War cartoon soldier 'Old Bill', complete with tin hat and walrus moustache. They now change hands for £150-£300. Among the most collectable mascots are high-quality humorous castings, such as John Hassall's comic policemen and aviators, and fantasy pieces. In good condition, these can fetch up to £750.

A series of elegant, clear and coloured glass mascots were produced in the late 1920s and 30s by the French master of moulded glass, René Lalique (see p.227). All Lalique's work

is highly collectable, and mascots still in good condition or with special features (such as an illuminated base and coloured filters for night-time motoring), reach auction prices from £300 up to well over £25,000 for rare models such as the fox and green-tinted frog.

Much more affordable are car manufacturers' and motoring organisations' name badges, designed to be clipped to the radiator grille or a badge bar. Pre-1950 badges and plaques are very collectable; prices range from just a few pounds up to as much as £300.

Among the pieces of original equipment most popular with collectors are early motoring horns and headlamps. Singularly exotic is the Boa Constrictor horn, first made in about 1910; such horns are now worth £400-£1000. Smaller, less ornate brass horns fetch under £100. Again beware modern replicas.

Among the most collectable car headlamps are the large acetylene models of Edwardian

days. A pair of such lamps can fetch £1000 or more at auction, whereas 1920s Lucas 'King of the Road' oil headlamps usually make £200-£400 and a pair of more humble oil lamps from an early Model T Ford under £200.

Many of the high-class tourers and limousines made between 1910 and 1935 had a luxurious interior, with matching fittings and motoring luggage. Interior side 'companions' held such items as toilet and smoking accessories, a mirror, a clock, a cocktail cabinet and a speaking tube for talking to the chauffeur. Today such side companions will sell for £500-£800 if in good condition, while leather motoring luggage made by the French manufacturer Louis Vuitton can make £200-£1000 per item. Wicker or leather-bound picnic sets

Pair of acetylene headlamps; 1910; 10 in (25.4 cm) across. Brass lamps such as these burned acetylene gas, produced by water and calcium carbide in a small generator mounted on the running board.
£1500-£2000 the pair

Car mascots; 1920s and 30s; 5¾-6 in (14.6-15.2 cm) high. This female figure, Lejeune Indian snail racer and golf caddy are among the hundreds of mascot designs produced during the two decades.
Indian: £800-£1200; others £300-£700

Zeppelin lithograph; c.1910; 12 in (30.5 cm) high. This early lithographic print by French artist Ernest Montaut was hand finished in watercolour, as were all his prints.
£100-£150

Enamel motoring badges; 1930-60; 3-4 in (76 -101 mm). Most badges were nickel or chrome-plated brass, and many were enamelled.
£100-£150 the set

Combined motoring picnic set and footrest; c.1910; 24 in (61 cm) wide. Made of plated metal, wood and enamel by the British firm Finnigan, this case is fitted with four place settings.
£1000-£1500

Michelin 'Mr Bibendum' advertising figure (right); 1930s; 24 in (61 cm) high. More often called the Michelin man, this well-known figure is made of plaster.
£100-£200

Shellmex glass petrol pump globe; 1950s; 20 in (51 cm) high. These advertising pump globes are very collectable today.
£100-£140

Enamel motoring advertising signs; 1930-60. Signs such as these could be seen at garages all around the country up to 30 years ago. They are very collectable, especially those in good condition.
£80-£120 the set

Irvin flying jacket; 1939-45. Leather jackets lined with sheepskin were widely used by Second World War flying crews.
£150-£200

Aircraft propeller; c.1940; c.84 in (2.13 m) across. This two-bladed propeller is made of laminated wood.
£400-£600; 4-bladed: £1000-£1500

fitted with six or eight place settings range from £200-£300 for 1930s examples up to £5000 for the best Edwardian sets.

Paintings, prints, posters and even old photographs of cars and other forms of transport are collected today, especially the lithographic prints of cars, speedboats, aircraft and airships produced by French artist Ernest Montaut between 1900 and 1909. Every print is titled and examples can still be found for around £200-£500 each. Modern reproductions cost less than £40.

FLYING COLLECTABLES

The field of aeronautica is not as large as that of automobilia, and is generally restricted to mementos of the early years of aviation, souvenirs from the Second World War and flying kit. Brooches, pen and ink trays, pocket watches, ceramics and prints were all produced from around the first decade of this century to celebrate the invention of the aircraft, and model aircraft in bronze, porcelain or silver are particularly desirable.

There is a wealth of relics from the Second World War, such as aircraft instruments, joy sticks, flying helmets and seats. Among the most eagerly sought pieces are sheepskin flying jackets which can be bought for £100-£300; RAF station 'scramble' bells fetching £500-£800; sector clocks which go for between £800 and £2000 and aircraft propellers, which can sell for anything from £200 to £1000 depending on their age, condition and type.

By Pedal Power

IN THE PAST TEN YEARS collectors have shown much interest in bicycles and tricycles made from the mid-19th to early 20th centuries. The distinctive Penny Farthing is probably the most popular model and may fetch more than £1000 in good condition, while the earlier but less attractive 'boneshakers' change hands for £500-£1000. As they are made largely of wood, it is important to check if any parts are rotten or have been replaced. The more comfortable 'sit-up-and-beg' bicycles made from 1910 until the 1940s may still be usable and can be picked up for as little as £50-£150.

Accessories are also eagerly sought by collectors, and many of the collectables of the motoring enthusiast have their equivalent in bicycliana. However, prices tend to be much lower than for automobilia.

Michaux vélocipède; 1868; 54 in (1.37 cm) long. This French bicycle has wooden-spoked wheels.
£600-£1000

Hercules Bicycles advertising poster; 1950s; 12 in (30.5 cm) high.
£15-£20

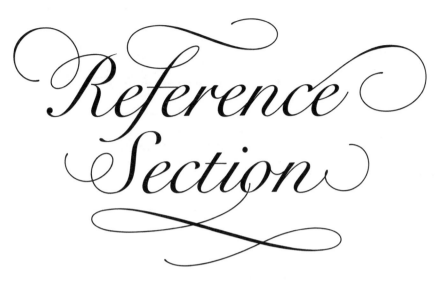

Reference Section

BUYING AND SELLING ANTIQUES

Tips and tactics on where and how to buy
and sell antiques and collectables, whether at
markets, shops or auctions.

418-423

CARING FOR ANTIQUES

Guidelines on the care and display, handling,
cleaning and restoration of treasured materials and
objects, to ensure that antiques and collectables
maintain their value and condition.

424-435

A-Z OF ANTIQUES

A glossary of key people, places, methods,
materials, terms and objects to help you find your
way in the world of antiques and collectables.

436-529

PERIODS AND STYLES CHART
530

INDEX
530-541

ACKNOWLEDGMENTS
542-544

Buying and selling antiques

Britain is the richest country in the world in which to hunt for or inherit antiques because of its long, eventful history of invasion, conquest, trade and invention – there are more antiques per square foot in Britain than anywhere else in the world.

THE PROBLEM for the would-be collector is where and how to begin. Few seasoned buyers of antiques buy haphazardly; they collect along set lines, accumulating objects that relate to one another. They constantly weed out and upgrade their collections, ending up with a few great objects rather than many mediocre ones, with the added bonus that these will appreciate at a much greater rate than inferior pieces. You may prefer a more casual approach, but putting order into your buying of antiques does enable you to build up knowledge and experience in a certain area.

BUYING ANTIQUES

The golden rule is to go for what you like and not just what you believe would make a good investment. Only research and experience will give you the confidence to tell whether an antique is genuine and reasonably priced. Once you have decided what you are looking for, spend time getting a feel for the subject and for the prices being asked. Visit museums, stately home collections, antique markets and shops – look in reproduction shops too, to check on what is being mass-produced.

Whether you are buying at auction, from a high street dealer or from a market stall, don't worry unduly about paying too much for an item. If you could find a modern equivalent it would probably cost more and be less well made than a genuine, solid antique piece. There are no fixed prices in the world of antiques; if you want an item enough it is worth whatever you are prepared to pay.

Never rush into buying anything. If you think you have spotted the 'buy-of-a-lifetime', the chances are that it's a dud. Certainly never be rushed by an eager seller. Think it over. Will the piece fit into your home? Will you still like it in a year's time? Can you afford to insure it adequately?

WHERE TO BUY

The outlets from which to buy range from car boot sales through to the Bond Street galleries. The former are not necessarily the cheapest nor the latter the most expensive. Nor are provincial sales, antique markets or shops always cheaper than London outlets. A specialist country dealer may well charge more than a London shop. Antique fairs can be among the most expensive locations – but you may be able to find some bargains if you have built up some specialist knowledge. Always remember you are dealing with hardened professionals who, whatever the location, are concerned with covering their overheads and making a profit.

One advantage of established retail outlets is that they may let you take an item such as a painting or piece of furniture on a sale or return basis, so that you can see how it looks in your home. You may have to lodge a post-dated cheque with the dealer, but there is no commitment to buy at the end of the day. However, be sure to check who is responsible for the insurance.

If an antique shop or individual dealer is a member of a trade association such as the British Antique Dealers' Association (BADA) or the London and Provincial Antique Dealers' Association (LAPADA), you will have a greater degree of protection in the event of dissatisfaction.

LOOK OUT FOR MISFITS

You can learn to take advantage of certain quirks of venue. 'Bottom-end' venues such as junk shops, general market stalls and car boot sales are not necessarily the only places to pick up bargains. An average-quality piece set among low quality goods may look better than it is, and a non-specialist seller, ignorant of a piece's real value, is just as likely to charge too much as too little. On the other hand you could find an average piece that lowers the tone of a smart specialist shop and is therefore priced cheaply for a quick sale. Look out for items that don't fit their surroundings: a bronze figure in a furniture shop, for example, or a silver toast rack on a jewellery stall.

Never admit to 'just browsing'. This will immediately brand you as easy prey and may weaken your bargaining position. It is better to specify some area of interest such as oak furniture or silver smalls.

Ask the seller to tell you as much as possible about the piece you are interested in, including age and condition, and whether any restoration work has been carried out. Generalisations or any sign of evasion should ring warning bells of reproductions, forgeries and under-cover restoration.

Look for a price ticket. The price marked is rarely the price you need to pay. Questions such as 'What's your best price' or 'What can you do on this' mark you down as someone to be taken seriously, and will almost invariably result in a discount.

ASK FOR DISCOUNTS

Many tickets have a code beneath the marked price which indicates a trade discount. For example, T5 or T20 will mean a discount of £5 or £20. Deduct this sum and ask the seller if he can do better. However, don't pose as 'trade'; you could lose the legal protection you have as a private buyer. Having obtained the 'best' price, a hesitation and then 'what about cash', may produce a further discount.

For large items, most dealers will, if asked, deliver free within their area as they will have built delivery costs into their price.

Always get a receipt that lists age, material and any damage or restoration as well as value. A receipt for a painting should include full attribution and note of signature and date. Should a problem arise you will get your money back. Without a receipt you will not. At fairs, car boot sales and markets you are less likely to get a receipt, and it is a case of *caveat emptor* – 'let the buyer beware'.

OTHER SOURCES

Buying from a private advertisement may yield a good piece for a low price, as no overheads are involved and the seller might be keen to get rid of an item or to raise money. But you are completely reliant on your own judgment and have no protection in law if you are sold a forgery. Bear in mind that anything worthwhile in the classified advertisements columns is likely to have been spotted by dealers, and that an advertisement stating 'no dealers' may have been inserted by a dealer who is trying to offload a bad buy.

Valuable items bought abroad should be declared at the British Customs control and the receipt produced. No UK duty or Value Added Tax (VAT) is payable on any item

REPRODUCTIONS, FAKES AND FORGERIES

Is it Genuine?

REPRODUCTIONS have been made in every century, and have a legitimate place in the retail market, as long as they are sold as such. A trader can place a forgery among genuine antiques and commit no offence. But if he tells you that a fake or reproduction piece is genuine, he has broken the Trade Descriptions Act. If he claims ignorance, and you buy an article on the assumption that it is genuine and it turns out not to be so, you are unlikely to get your money back.

The definition of an antique is an article that is over 100 years old. So if you buy an object in good faith from an 'antique' shop, and it turns out to be less than 100 years old, you could have cause for complaint. However, 'antique' in common parlance is now synonymous with 'secondhand' and you are unlikely to win a court case. Major auction houses give a five-year guarantee against selling a forgery.

Damage or restoration to a piece can have a dramatic effect on its value. If in doubt seek advice from an independent expert or restorer before buying.

Persuading a trader to take an item back for any other reason than clear-cut misrepresentation is difficult, if not impossible. If you have the opportunity to examine a piece thoroughly before buying, you will have little comeback if you subsequently discover it to be a fake, a forgery, or damaged.

BUYING IN A SHOP *Don't be afraid to touch things in an antique shop. If you plan to spend good money on a piece, examine it closely. Then, if you like what you see, ask the seller for details of its origin, age and condition.*

over 100 years old. Tax on more recent items varies according to the class of object. However, getting it out of the country of origin might involve some negotiation. Most countries have laws governing the export of works of art. These vary considerably, so check with the appropriate embassy before leaving Britain if you intend to buy abroad.

BUYING AT AUCTIONS

It is not true that a careless movement of hand or head will land you with a valuable piece you cannot possibly afford or want. But you do need to familiarise yourself with auction procedures before you go to one. It is worth attending several as an observer, noting how the auctioneer operates and how regular buyers attract attention. Because auction sales cut out the dealer and his mark-up, they

are places to pick up a bargain. But never be tempted to buy anything unless you have viewed it carefully beforehand and set yourself a price limit. Following the items for sale (or 'lots') and comparing the prices paid with the auction house estimates is another way of gaining knowledge and confidence.

THE CATALOGUE

Most auctioneers provide a catalogue of items in advance of the sale, available from the auction house. Descriptions of an individual item can vary from a few words to a ten-page description and provenance with colour pictures, according to the importance of the piece and the expertise of the cataloguer. The condition may not be given, or in minor or country sales there may be the abbreviation a/f ('as found' or 'all faults'). This means there is something wrong with the piece, that you as buyer accept it in the condition in which it is

sold, and there is no comeback. There should be a glossary of terms in the front of the catalogue but if not, or if you want further clarification, ask the auctioneers.

Many auction houses now give **estimates**, which are usually in the form of a price range which the auctioneer expects the lot to make. The **reserve**, which must not be above the lower estimate figure, is the minimum price at which the seller is prepared to sell; it is confidential information and is neither quoted in the catalogue nor disclosed to buyers. Double-check just before the sale whether estimates have been revised since the publication of the catalogue. The auctioneer may be able to give some idea of the level of interest in the lot, although he should not say what bids he has received.

All catalogues should include **Conditions of Sale**, which you should read carefully as they indicate your rights and list charges payable. The Conditions of Sale serve as a disclaimer against a wrongful description or attribution made by the auction house. In theory the auction house is protected if it labels a table 'late Georgian' and you later discover it to be an Edwardian copy. You as buyer must satisfy yourself that the piece is as described. To get money back on a wrong attribution could be long and costly legally.

VIEWING

All lots are on view before the sale, either a few hours beforehand at a small country auction, or for about two weeks at a major auction house. This is when to check whether the piece has been restored, and that it is of the period, condition and attribution described in the catalogue. Make a note in your catalogue of any damage. Some major auction houses will, on request, give you a detailed condition report. If you subsequently discover other faults not listed on this, you will have grounds for a claim against them. Also note how much you are prepared to pay. Don't increase this figure later; time and distance can distort judgment.

An auctioneer may decide to sell the contents of a house in situ rather than move them to the auction rooms. Such a sale at a stately home invariably attracts great publicity and crowds of bidders keen for souvenirs, and although items are likely to have a clear pedigree or 'provenance', prices often soar to high levels. Viewing is usually dependent on the purchase of a catalogue which will admit two.

Saleroom notices may be displayed, giving the latest information on lots that have been withdrawn, or 'A' lots which have been added since the catalogue was printed. Notices on individual lots give additional information which could affect your decision to buy.

THE SALE

At most major London auctions and country house sales, you register your name and address when you enter the saleroom, and are issued with a 'paddle' with a number. You can use this to bid, but its main purpose is to be held up when your bid has been accepted so that the auctioneer can record your number. Alternatively, on acceptance in some major sales, a runner brings you a card to complete, while at minor sales you call out your name.

Arrive early if you want a seat, although standing at the front will give you a useful view of the bidders, auctioneer and items as they are sold. It also enables you to establish the auctioneer's individual style, and the jumps, or **increments**, by which he raises the bids (usually between 5 and 10 per cent). The

auctioneer has total control of the sale and can make such changes as he thinks fit, including withdrawing or re-offering lots. The latter can happen if the auctioneer has made a mistake or if two people think they have bought a lot, but such cases are rare.

Do not start the bidding or come in as the first opposition. Wait until bidding has stopped then raise your hand. This will deflate the apparently successful buyer. The auctioneer calls your bid: 'New place, £230.' He turns to the underbidder: 'Against you now at £230 . . .', at which point, with luck, the underbidder will retire. The auctioneer will probably say 'Selling then, at £230 . . . at £230. All done at £230?' and bring down his hammer to signal the end of the bidding.

You can offer up a bid which is less than the established increments. For example, if your bidding limit is £500 and another bidder ends up at that sum, you either give up or go one bid higher. If this means going to £550 – more than you want to pay – it is acceptable to increase your bid by a lower increment, say, to £520. The auctioneer decides whether or not to accept your bid. If he accepts, he offers the same low increment to the underbidder. However, if the underbidder accepts and you then revert to 10 per cent increments, you clearly misled the auctioneer and will not be offered the same chance again.

Bid discreetly. Once you've attracted the auctioneer's attention a nod, wink or raised finger is enough to indicate your next bid. Under British law a successful bid is made at auction by the auctioneer writing down the hammer price and the purchaser's name or number, not by bringing down the hammer. This forms an unbreakable contract between seller and buyer, not between buyer and auctioneer. However, if you do default on payment, the auctioneer will pursue you for the debt plus any costs he may incur, including interest. He could also resell the lot and sue you for any losses. Once your bid has been accepted you become liable for the price plus any other charges (see below), and for the lot itself. If the lot were damaged by the auction house staff before you had taken possession of the piece, it would still be your risk, although it is unlikely that any reputable house would enforce this, and you could claim compensation on the grounds of negligence on the part of the auction house staff.

PAYING AND COLLECTING

Payment will be accepted in cash or by cheque. In the former case you can take away your buy immediately. Cheques will need to be cleared unless you are known to the auctioneer or have an arrangement with him. Very few auction houses accept any form of credit card. Usually lots need to be cleared within a certain number of days of the sale and there may be charges for overdue payment or storage on lots not promptly removed.

BUYING AT AUCTION *The saleroom can be intimidating until you know what's going on. In this typical saleroom scene, the auctioneer, hammer in hand, is centre stage facing the buyers. On his right sits his clerk, who records the sale details, and on his left a porter, who holds up small items for buyers to see. On the extreme right, telephone in hand, sits the clerk who takes telephone bids. One buyer displays his 'paddle' which identifies him as a bidder.*

If a lot fails to reach its reserve (see p.419), it is left unsold, or 'b/i' (bought in) – that is, it is still the property of the owner. You can approach the auctioneer after the sale and ask whether a particular lot was sold. If not, you can make an offer for it either at the unsold price, above or below it. The auctioneer will probably not tell you the reserve price, but may give you some clues. Even if your offer is well below the reserve the owner may prefer to accept it rather than have no sale at all.

If you cannot attend the auction or are unwilling to bid, you can instruct someone else to bid for you. A reputable auctioneer will buy for you as cheaply as possible and not take you up to your top bid. He will neither charge for the service nor expect a tip. However, this course might be risky with a dishonest auctioneer who might be tempted to take the bidding above what was dictated by the reserve or other bids in order to earn himself a higher commission. It may be safer to leave a bid with a sales clerk or the senior porter, in which case a tip of say 5 or 10 per cent would be appropriate if the bid is successful. Alternatively, you could ask a dealer to bid for you; a usual charge for this would be 5-10 per cent of hammer price – which is far less than

the 50-100 per cent mark-up which would apply in the dealer's shop.

The **hammer price** is the last bid called out by the auctioneer as he brings down his gavel, but this is not the price the successful bidder pays. Most auction houses charge a **buyer's premium**, usually 10-15 per cent of the hammer price, plus VAT on the premium element only. VAT is rarely payable on the hammer price too; if it is, this will be stated in the catalogue, or on a saleroom notice.

SELLING ANTIQUES

Whatever your reasons are for selling an item you naturally want the best price you can get. The price you sell at depends on fluctuating tastes and fashions as much as on the basic rules of supply and demand.

Insurance valuations are not appropriate indicators of market value, as they are way above auction prices. Better to do some research in antique retail outlets. You could try obtaining competitive quotes from a number of dealers, but a wise dealer will always ask what price you have in mind rather than committing himself to a figure first. Alternatively, you can take a piece into a

major auction house – whether or not you are intending to sell through them – for a free assessment and auction estimate.

Some auction houses run 'discovery days' around the country, to which the public can take pieces for examination; there may be a small charge as they are often in aid of charity. BBC television's *Antiques Roadshow* does a similar job, but be prepared for long queues. Watch out for events which purport to give advice but may actually be a means of buying cheaply from the unsuspecting.

SELLING TIPS AND TACTICS

Once you have established the price at which you are prepared to sell, you can offer the item to a trusted dealer, perhaps the one from whom you bought the piece in the first place. He may haggle over the price, but aim for 50-70 per cent of the estimated retail value.

Selling through a classified advertisement in a newspaper is risky. Thieves may answer the advert, and come round to assess whether your place is worth robbing. Equally risky is to sell to **'knockers'** – casual callers who knock at your door or drop a card through your letterbox, asking for any junk or offering house clearance services. Knockers' usual

BUYING IN MARKETS *Market traders are notoriously 'here today and gone tomorrow', so you need to be even more cautious dealing with them than when buying in a shop. On the other hand you have a better chance of picking up a bargain – provided that you know what you are looking for.*

trick is to offer inflated prices for a few worthless items and then, having softened you up, try to talk you into parting with a valuable piece for next to nothing. Never let such casual callers into your house, let alone sell anything to them. You should inform the police immediately.

If disposing of house contents after a death, there may be some valuable pieces involved, so contact the local representative of a major London auction house. There may be no charge for this visit, and there may be something in the house that needs the international exposure of the London market. For the rest of the contents, the representative should be able to recommend a reputable local auctioneer, who will take what he can handle, and call in a house clearance firm for the remainder.

SELLING THROUGH AUCTIONS

Selling through an auction house takes time, possibly two to four months from delivery of the goods to when they go on sale. However, if the piece is desirable, competitive bidding will usually result in a better price than selling through any other source, especially if the sale focuses on a specialist area. The auctioneer's

income is directly related to the value of the goods he sells, so it is in his interest – as well as yours – to sell for as high a price as possible.

The competition generated by the international following at London auctions will almost certainly mean that you will get a higher price there than in the provinces. A particularly rare item might also benefit from the greater research resources, greater publicity and competition, and international contacts of a major London house.

CHOOSING AN AUCTION HOUSE

If you are selling a large item, a set or a collection, get an auction house expert to appraise it at your home. Otherwise you can take a smaller piece in to an auction house and get on-the-spot advice from a specialist on estimated selling price, reserve price, commission and other charges.

You can seek a competitive quote from a second auction house but don't be tempted by the highest figure; this may be a bid to win the business, and could be downgraded at the time of the sale. Base your choice on the reputation of the auction house and the specialist department you are dealing with, and on your judgment of the expert himself. Ask for back catalogues and the corresponding price lists to see how estimates

and actual selling prices have compared. Blank lot numbers indicate unsold lots, giving an idea of the reliability of the auction house.

Your goods are left with the auction house and you are given a receipt recording agreed details and a **property number**, which should be quoted on any subsequent correspondence. You will be sent a catalogue before the sale along with confirmation of the reserve – the lowest price at which you are prepared to sell. If the bidding does not reach the reserve, the piece remains yours; you need to check when consigning the lot whether you are still liable for a charge. If the auctioneer suggested the reserve figure, you should not have to pay a charge, but if you went for a higher reserve, up to 5 per cent may be payable.

If the goods are to be delivered by a carrier, make sure that you, the carrier and the auction house each has an identical copy of the inventory of items. The auction house checks that everything has arrived safely. Insurance during transit will normally be part of the carriage cost, but check to make sure that this is the case.

Illustrations in a colourful catalogue may seem expensive but if the auction house suggests it, take their advice. As a rough guide, paying a maximum of ten per cent of the reserve is sensible. At this level, your costs will be covered if the illustration generates just one extra bid. The illustration charge is usually payable whether or not the lot sells. Make sure you know what the cost will be before you sign the contract.

If the lot is unsold, it is termed 'bought-in'. It remains yours and can either be collected (when charges, if any, are paid) or re-offered in a future sale with a lower reserve. Re-offered lots tend to be recognised by buyers and usually fetch less than the previous unsold price. For this reason, it is important that reserves should be realistic in the first sale, protecting the lot from selling too cheaply, but ensuring that it sells.

AUCTION COSTS

As vendor, you pay the auctioneer's commission fee, which varies between 10 and 20 per cent of the hammer price. This rate may vary from department to department in the auction house, and there may be a minimum charge payable per lot. While your property is with the auction house it is covered by their insurance (unless you request otherwise) for a charge of around 1 per cent of the hammer price. If the lot does not sell first time and is subsequently re-offered and sold, commission is only paid once.

OWNING ANTIQUES

Keep an up-to-date register of every purchase, not only for your own interest, but as reference for a restorer if a piece is damaged, and for the police and the insurance company in case of theft. A loose-leaf file is best as it enables easy re-arrangement. Note where,

when and from whom you bought each piece and the cost. If bought from an auction, keep the catalogue or cut out the entry and stick it on the file card. Keep all receipts, including any for restoration work. Every piece should have a clear, black and white photograph (which is easier than colour for the police to reproduce and circulate in the event of theft). Descriptions relating to the item from reference books, similar pieces in museums, exhibitions or other collections, and comments from collectors and experts are also useful additions. Make a note, too, of any insurance revaluation.

SECURITY

By far the greatest proportion of art theft is not by specialised, up-market burglars, but by the common thief who will lift a family treasure along with the television. Breaking through the obstacles presented by locks and alarm systems takes time and generates noise, neither of which a thief can risk. Exterior lights which come on automatically with an infra-red beam are a further deterrent, but at the very least fit the best deadlocks on all exterior doors, and window locks on all windows. Local police stations often have a crime prevention officer who will visit your home to advise on security measures.

If you are burgled, give the police your record files and inform your insurance company immediately. Police and insurance companies work closely together, and will circulate descriptions and photographs. Commercial operations such as the Art Loss Register run up-to-date lists of stolen works of art worth over £1000 for circulation to the trade. Dealers and collectors wishing to ensure that their potential purchases are not stolen property, can check against the Register's database for a fee of £10.

INSURANCE

If you want to be sure of recovering the value of stolen goods, up-to-date insurance cover is a must, but it can be expensive. If you are under-insured, the company will not pay out the full amount, discounting by the under-evaluation. The insurance figure is effectively what you would have to pay to replace the piece on the retail market – about double the auction price, and in the case of jewellery, about five times the auction price. Many insurance companies insist upon specific security measures for valuable items, and will not accept your claim if you fail to take such precautions. It is worth briefing a professional broker to find an insurance company that is geared to the needs of collectors. He should not only obtain the most sympathetic

premiums, but also arrange for special cover at auctions and in transit, for example.

Before completing the insurance forms, get a written valuation from a reputable auction house or a specialist dealer. (The insurance company is more likely to accept such a valuation without question in the event of a claim.) A non-specialist valuer may undervalue goods through ignorance, resulting in low compensation if they are stolen, or overvalue them to get a higher valuation fee, which will also result in inflated insurance premiums.

Valuation charges are about 1½ per cent of the estimated value of the piece plus expenses, and 1 per cent for subsequent revaluation without a visit. The valuer should also be able to advise on how often your policy should be updated. Works of art do not appreciate at a fixed rate, but tend to lurch up and down. Lodge a copy of the valuation and insurance policy with a bank or solicitor.

One way of reducing the risk of theft is to lodge items such as jewellery, which you may want to use only occasionally, in the bank. Charges for storage and withdrawal vary, and you can arrange insurance cover only for the times you take the piece out of the bank. It is unlikely to be stolen or fire damaged in the bank but both are possible and it must be your decision whether it is insured or not. Check whether the storage environment is suitable for the type of item you are lodging. There are also specialist depositories with controlled conditions and security. Fees are payable according to the amount of space taken.

Caring for antiques

Carelessness, ignorance and neglect are the main causes of damage to antiques and collectables; value and craftsmanship can be ruined by over-zealous cleaning or misguided treatment.

THE IDEAL CONDITIONS for preserving fragile and precious objects are not necessarily the most comfortable for people to live in. But it is possible to strike a balance, and the care and preservation of antiques is often simply a matter of common sense, good housekeeping, and understanding how different materials can be affected by heat, light, humidity and pollution.

Organic materials, for instance – those made from once-living matter, such as paper, leather and wood – are more sensitive to their environment than stone, ceramics, metals and glass. Objects made from a variety of different materials need to be treated with the most vulnerable material in mind.

LIGHT

All light ultimately destroys organic materials; it fades colours, breaks down fibres and alters the chemical make-up. The most harmful component in light is the ultraviolet (UV) wavelengths. UV-free lights and UV filters for fluorescent tubes are available from specialist lighting suppliers. Other barriers against ultra-violet, such as self-adhesive film or spray-on varnish, can be applied to windows which are not leaded, of stained glass or prone to condensation. If you are having double glazing installed, you could consider glass which excludes UV rays.

Long exposure to weak light is as damaging as strong light for a shorter period. Where strong daylight streams in through windows during the day, ensure that there are no vulnerable items in its path. Blinds and net curtains have a filtering effect on strong daylight, and curtains can be drawn when a room is not in use during the day. Infrared rays from ordinary, incandescent bulbs radiate dehydrating heat, and are harmful if allowed to spotlight a work of art or build up in the enclosed space of a display cabinet. It may be better to light a display from outside the cabinet rather than within it. Fibre-optic lamps with adjustable levels of light and cool beams are available, but are very expensive.

TEMPERATURE AND HUMIDITY

Temperature and humidity together or individually can cause materials to expand or contract. Organic materials readily absorb moisture in a damp environment and so expand, and release moisture in a dry atmosphere and so contract. Such movements can lead to wood warping, splitting and cracking. In a damp atmosphere, too, tarnishing and corrosion of metals is more rapid. The ideal 'museum' level of relative humidity for antiques is around 55 per cent, which is a perfectly acceptable level for living in, although a centrally heated home may be on the dry side at 40-45 per cent. You can check humidity levels with humidity indicator cards or strips or with a simple hygrometer, available from garden shops. Humidifying and dehumidifying devices range from simple gadgets which clip onto radiators to expensive, freestanding electric models. Beware, however, as warmth combined with over 60-65 per cent humidity provides ideal conditions for mould spoors to germinate and for wood to warp.

An atmosphere that fluctuates between extremes of temperature and humidity is most damaging of all. A piece of furniture, for example, which has been in a cold, damp house for generations, will have adjusted to its environment. But if it were suddenly to be moved to a warm, centrally heated room, it would warp and crack, and veneered surfaces might peel away from the carcass. So aim for as constant a temperature as possible. The central heating, for example, could be kept

---

MATERIALS FOR CLEANING AND RENOVATING ANTIQUES

YOU WILL FIND the following items useful in the care of antiques. For specialist suppliers, refer to an antiques dealer, conservator or advertisements in antiques magazines.

microcrystalline wax – fine, colourless wax, such as Renaissance wax, which gives a protective coating to furniture, metals and materials such as jade and marble.

non-ionic detergent – an effective alternative to mild washing-up liquid; the non-ionic quality reduces water's surface tension, allowing deeper penetration into the surface to be cleaned.

brushes – of different size and softness for cleaning awkward spots: shaving brush or make-up 'blusher' brush; 2-3in (50-75mm) decorator's paintbrush; artist's paintbrushes – squirrel hair and hogshair types; baby's hairbrush (for silver); banister brush; shoe brush.

acid-free tissue (for wrapping), albums, envelopes and mounting card.

white blotting paper (for spot-testing colour fastness).

well-washed white linen or cotton cloth (for wrapping and dusting); unfrayed, lint-free dusters; metal and jewellers' polishing cloths; chamois leathers.

cotton wool and cotton-wool buds.

orange, satay or cocktail sticks.

methylated spirits; white spirit; pure alcohol; de-ionised water.

long-term metal polishes; silver dip; chrome polish.

light penetrating oil.

adhesives – epoxy resin for glass and china; water-soluble glues for wood and textiles.

on low at night and not set too high during waking hours. Keep rooms well aired and vulnerable items away from condensation, steam, direct heat from radiators or lights, or chilly walls against the outside of the house.

POLLUTION

Car exhaust fumes, factory emissions and burning fossil fuels produce a greasy film of fine dust, and gases which combine with moisture to form acids in the atmosphere. These can slowly eat away at vulnerable materials such as textiles. Destructive substances within the house include acetic acid in the form of vinegar and vapours from freshly painted rooms. Formaldehyde is given off by some composite woods like chipboard and acts as a corrosive itself or causes destructive reactions in other materials. Air conditioning and glass or Perspex-fronted display cabinets provide protection but are not usually necessary. General awareness of the problems should suffice: ventilate rooms well if they have been filled with smoke from cigarettes, open fires or candles, and if you live in a town keep sensitive, unprotected articles away from open windows.

VERMIN AND INSECTS

Rats, mice, woodworm and other beetles, moths, silverfish, thrips and thunderflies are among the creatures that invade northern European homes. Commercial insecticides and pest repellents may be effective, but may also damage the piece you are trying to protect. Preventative measures such as regular close inspection – every year for books and textiles, twice a year for furniture – is the best defence, so that a problem is identified before too much damage is done. If any pieces are infested, isolate them from other furniture to halt the spread of insect larvae, and seek expert advice. See also *Dealing with Woodworm*, p.426, and *Textiles*, p.432.

RESTORATION

Few of us can afford to take every damaged object to a conservator (conservation expert). But with antiques, never leap recklessly into home repair; you could damage a piece irretrievably and destroy its value. A home repair is unlikely to be the 'invisible mend' a specialist could achieve, and you may find that your handiwork needs to be undone, in a far more involved and expensive professional repair, later on. If you do make a temporary repair, be certain of the type of material you are dealing with and its vulnerabilities, and make sure that the repair is reversible – by using a water-soluble glue, for example.

Some antiques are worth more unrepaired than repaired, even if the work is done by a professional. If in doubt, consult the conservation department of a major auction house or museum before any repair or major restoration. Take a clear photograph of any valuable object when you first acquire it; if it is subsequently broken, this could provide useful reference for the conservator.

A recommendation – from a friend, a trusted dealer, a local or national museum, or the conservation department of a major auction house – is the best starting point for finding a reliable restorer. The Museums and Galleries Commission, the United Kingdom Institute for Conservation, and conservation training institutions such as the Courtauld are also useful sources. Look for a specialist conservator or a large workshop that employs specialists. Ask what materials and methods are going to be used for the job – if it is suggested that a veneer is to be glued with epoxy resin rather than reversible animal glue, find another conservator. The cost of restoration depends mainly on how long the repair will take, plus cost of materials and Value Added Tax. It bears no relation to the value of a piece; as a paper conservator commented, 'whether a print is worth £20 or £10,000, we treat it in the same way and charge the same rate'.

Get a written estimate of the cost and completion date. Check whether delivery is included in the price. When the piece is handed over to the conservator, get a receipt, and check who is responsible for insurance during restoration. On completion, ask for the details of restoration to be included on the receipt. Keep this as a record (see p.423).

Furniture

Antique furniture is rarely kept solely for display purposes, but certain precautions are necessary if it is to withstand daily wear and tear.

TREAT YOUR ANTIQUE FURNITURE with respect for its original purpose. The surface of an old desk, for example, was not designed to withstand the pressure of a ballpoint pen. Tilting back on a chair, opening a drawer by only one of two handles, dragging furniture rather than lifting it, all put unnecessary strain on the structure. Before lifting furniture, empty any contents and remove detachable parts for carrying separately. Take hold of the lowest part of the main frame – not, for example, the top surface of a table – and pick up chairs under the seat.

SURFACE CONSIDERATIONS

A surface patina, even if it is marked and damaged, contributes to the character, authenticity and value of a piece of furniture and the aim should be to preserve it. If restoration is necessary, the original finish should be matched as closely as possible. French polishing or the tough synthetic varnishes of the 20th century should never, for example, be used to replace wax or shellac.

Oil or beeswax polishes are the most common finishes on 16th and 17th-century furniture, and on oak and country furniture to the 19th century; they are more resistant to minor bruises and spills than varnish or lacquer. Resin and shellac varnishes came to be used on fine furniture from the end of the 17th century. Like lacquered and japanned finishes, these are spirit-based, and so can be marked by other solvents such as alcohol, as well as by heat, damp and abrasives. French polishing, introduced in the early 1820s, is a method of applying shellac that achieved a high-gloss finish with less effort but is less durable and prone to chip. Newly applied French polish is particularly vulnerable; it can take up to six months to harden completely.

Other finishes include graining and ebonising, in which a surface is stained to resemble an exotic wood; this effect will wear away with too much rubbing.

Veneered furniture is particularly vulnerable to dry or damp conditions, or if water or polish seeps beneath the surface skin, causing the veneer to buckle, lift or split. Inlaid finishes such as marquetry and boulle are even more sensitive as the various materials used react to heat and humidity at different rates, resulting in uneven stress over the surface as a whole.

DUSTING AND CLEANING

Frequent dusting is important, especially on a waxed surface which is soft and absorbs dirt, and especially before cleaning or polishing, as particles of dust are abrasive. Use a clean, dry duster with no frayed edges (which could catch) for most jobs, but for any surface that has begun to lift or crack, use a soft-bristled brush (also handy for crevices). Check that no grit is lodged in the brush, and cover sharp edges with masking tape. Feather dusters are to be avoided as the feathers break and the spines could scratch a delicate surface.

Spot-test an inconspicuous part of a piece of furniture before trying any cleaning medium. No fluids should be used to clean porous materials such as mother-of-pearl or ivory, or damaged lacquered, painted or veneered surfaces. A sound waxed or lacquer surface can be cleaned with a soft, damp cloth (add a tablespoonful of non-ionic detergent to a washing-up bowl of warm water). Wipe the surface with a clean cloth rinsed and wrung out in clear water and dry immediately with absorbent paper. Never use detergent on bare, unpolished or damaged wood surfaces where it might penetrate and stain.

If spillages are dealt with immediately, they are unlikely to harm a sound wax or lacquered surface. Candlewax may lift off easily in a slab when cold, or can be warmed with a hot-water bottle wrapped in a clean cloth and then scraped off with a fingernail or orange stick. Deeply engrained stains should be left for an expert to deal with, or left to contribute to the character of the piece. You can try treating the whitish marks left by the damp base of a glass, for example, by wiping with a little metal polish, if the surface finish is not delicate and as long as it is wiped clean with a damp cloth and dried immediately.

WAXING

All sealed wooden surfaces can be waxed to bring out the colour and grain of the wood and to provide protection against staining. But overwaxing will actually cause dullness. Furniture that has been waxed and polished over the years should only need buffing with a soft chamois leather or duster, and a waxing maybe once every few months.

Some solvents used in furniture polishes, especially the spray-on types, may leave a whitish bloom on some surfaces or gradually dissolve lacquered finishes. They should not be used on any lacquered surface and only sparingly on wax. A microcrystalline wax is the best medium for giving light, protective and burnishable coating to most surfaces, including ebonised wood, lacquer and French polish. Apply the wax over an area about 1 ft (30 cm) square at a time, burnishing with a soft, clean cloth as it dries. Use a soft-bristled brush for carved surfaces, leaving no surplus polish in the crevices.

FURNITURE MOUNTS

Brass mounts, such as handles and other fittings, do not need to be ultra-bright on antique furniture; light burnishing as you dust should be adequate, or buff with a long-term silver cloth. Metal cleaners should not be used as they can harm the wood around them.

The gold finish on ormolu is very delicate and should never be polished, even with a dry cloth, and especially not with cleaning fluid. Even fingerprints, which are acidic, can damage gilding. In time the brass or bronze base corrodes, giving the finish a spotty, then black, appearance. The mounts can be lacquered (see *Metalware*, opposite) but even this will fail in time. Other than dusting ormolu gently and regularly with a soft brush there is little else to do; never have it regilded if you want to retain the value.

CARING FOR GILDED SURFACES

Water-based gilding remains water soluble and should only ever be dusted, whereas oil gilding may be cleaned by gently dabbing with barely moistened cotton wool. Water gilding is applied over layers of gesso and a yellow or dark red size, and may be burnished to a high shine, although some areas may be left matt. Oil gilding is sometimes applied directly onto wood and has a matt finish.

Chips in a gilded surface can be filled with a fine surface filler and disguised with yellow ochre watercolour paint. Avoid using 'gold' metallic paint for areas of any size, as it clashes with the true gilding. A professional gilder's aim is to match the original techniques and materials, and to retain as much of the original surface and patina as possible.

DEALING WITH WOODWORM

Adult furniture and pinhole beetles lay eggs in crevices in wood. The eggs hatch into larvae (woodworm) which eat into the wood, leaving tunnels some 1 mm in diameter, before they emerge as beetles and fly away, usually between May and August. Active infestation is revealed by freshly bored holes and deposits of sawdust, or 'frass'.

Check – and treat – any new purchase before you take it into the home, and check all wooden objects twice a year for infestation – especially bare and softwood surfaces such as the inside of drawers or backboards. Upholstered or particularly delicate furniture should be professionally fumigated, but on other items, a good quality, clear, low-odour woodworm fluid can be applied at home.

The most effective time for treatment is late spring or early summer. Remove any detachable upholstered parts and only treat the unfinished surfaces of the wood – solvent in the fluid will damage waxed, polished, varnished, lacquered or painted surfaces. Carefully paint on the insecticide. Injecting insecticide, using a hypodermic syringe and

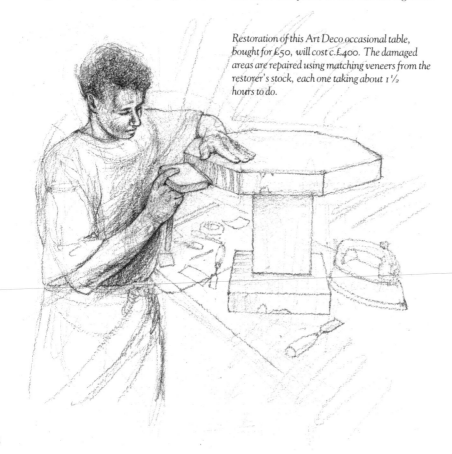

Restoration of this Art Deco occasional table, bought for £50, will cost c.£400. The damaged areas are repaired using matching veneers from the restorer's stock, each one taking about 1 ½ hours to do.

needle to reach deep into the holes, should be left to an expert. Following treatment, fill the holes with soft wax to blend in with the surrounding wood.

RESTORATION

Unlike many other antiques, which may be devalued by restoration, a piece of furniture which has been sympathetically and honestly restored into usable condition, using traditional methods and materials, can be worth more than a damaged item. If you do make minor repairs yourself, only ever use water-soluble wood glue.

Almost all furniture made before the mid-20th century depends on well-jointed solid timber for strength, so weaknesses in joints, pivots, moving parts, or on load-bearing surfaces, or signs of rot or woodworm, must be fixed before the piece is used again. A restorer can reinforce or replace rotten or wormed timber with sound wood, saturate it with resin or fill it with a mixture of animal glue and sawdust. Sticking doors or drawers may be eased by a touch of candle wax, but if they are misshapen, they need to be trimmed by an expert. Chipped or lifted veneer should

be professionally repaired as soon as possible, but exposed edges can be temporarily protected with masking tape and detached pieces kept in a plastic bag.

If stripping is necessary and will not remove a valuable patina, it should be done by a furniture conservator. Acid stripping swells and rots wood fibres.

Dry, cracked leather on desk-tops (and bookbindings) can be revitalised with a lanolin and beeswax preparation such as Connolly's Hide Food. Spot-test the dressing on an inconspicuous area; if it leaves no stain, then apply it sparingly with a soft cloth. Let the dressing absorb (about 24 hours) before gently buffing with a clean duster.

UPHOLSTERY

Upholstered furniture must be vacuumed regularly to guard against a build-up of dust and pests, if necessary using a net of fine-meshed stocking over the nozzle of the vacuum cleaner to prevent any loose pieces being irretrievably sucked off.

Fine, old upholstery fabric should be reserved for display only, although a loose

Gold leaf is so delicate that it must be transferred from the gilder's tray to the receiving surface with a soft-haired brush.

cover can offer some protection. However, on some seat furniture, upholstery can be rewebbed or restuffed, or the fabric replaced with a sympathetic alternative, without detracting from the value of the piece – but seek expert advice first. Do make sure that newly re-upholstered drop-in seats are returned to the correct chair, and that any new covering is not so tightly fitting that it strains the leg joints.

Metalware

Individual metals react at different rates and in different ways to natural conditions, and their care, handling and restoration varies accordingly.

DESPITE THEIR APPARENT TOUGHNESS, metals can be scratched, dented or fractured, or may corrode. If metals are combined with other materials, as in jewellery or furniture, care must be adapted to the weaker material. If possible, detach the metal parts and clean them separately. (See also *Sculpture and statuary*, p.428.)

GENERAL CLEANING

Cover the working surface with a soft cloth, and wear cotton gloves, as fingerprints can leave deposits which cause tarnishing. Before cleaning, check for loose parts or splits in the metal. Proprietary metal polishes should be used as little as possible as they actually remove a small amount of metal. Regular dusting with a soft cloth, and a soft-bristled brush for awkward crevices, reduces the need for major cleaning. For grime or light tarnish, metals apart from bronze and iron can be washed in warm water with a little mild liquid detergent, but only immerse objects if they are all-metal, with no weaker materials;

cotton buds are useful for cleaning small areas. Rinse the articles and dry thoroughly with absorbent paper. Never put precious metal objects in a dishwasher as the salts and detergents may pit and stain the surface.

For heavier-duty cleaning on silver, brass and copper only, you can use long-term metal polishes which have an in-built tarnish inhibitor that reduces the need for frequent cleaning. First of all, use a soft brush to remove dust and dirt which could scratch the surface if rubbed in; do not be tempted to dislodge stubborn stains from any metal with wire wool or an abrasive cloth, which could scratch the surface. Apply the cleaner with a cloth or soft brush in a gentle circular movement. Rinse and dry the item at once with an absorbent paper towel, and remove polish from crevices with a dry, soft brush.

Silver, copper and brass can be sealed against corrosion with lacquer, but this not only deprives an object of a sometimes desirable patina, but the lacquer is easily scratched and marked by fingerprints, and can

soon look patchy. A light coating of microcrystalline wax applied after cleaning is an effective and less radical barrier. Lacquer is worth considering for display items with intricate decoration which would wear away with too much cleaning.

SILVER

To reduce tarnishing on silver that is not on display, wrap it in acid-free tissue or undyed cotton or linen. Sulphurous foods such as egg and Brussels sprouts cause tarnishing, so the sooner table silver is washed after contact with them, the better.

Tarnishing is not actually harmful to silver, but over-zealous cleaning is, and with a plated object, for example, will expose the base metal core. Metal polishes should be avoided on pieces that are worn, on clocks or watches (where they could seep into the mechanism) or on niello work. Silver or jewellers' cloths and silver dip (which can be wiped on large objects with cotton wool swabs) or foam, are the least abrasive cleaners. Limit the number of items treated per jar of dip, as particles of silver from cleaned objects can give items dipped subsequently an unsightly deposit that is difficult to remove.

Silver which contains a large proportion of copper may corrode if it has been in a damp

It will cost c. £250 to repair this Edwardian candlestick, one of a pair worth c. £130. Candles allowed to burn too low caused the pitch loading to expand, splitting the outer casing of silver. The restorer realigns the metal on a raising stake and will then repair the splits with a hard silver solder.

atmosphere, causing a green crystalline deposit. This verdigris may be wiped off plated silver with methylated spirits, but if it appears on solid silver it should be chemically treated by a metal conservator.

Worn electroplate can be resilvered, either professionally or using a proprietary replating agent. The attractions of a bright new surface,

however, must be balanced against the possibilities that finish and colour may not be true to the original and the sharpness of any engraved decoration may be dulled. The process may well devalue an antique piece, particularly in the case of Old Sheffield plate.

GOLD

Establish whether a gold object is solid or plated, silver gilt, or ormolu (see *Furniture mounts*, p.426), for gold is soft, and the thinner the layer, the more easily it will be rubbed away. Gold also scratches easily, but does not tarnish unless it has high silver content (as in some 9-ct gold). Light dusting should be enough, but gold objects can be washed as long as no weaker materials such as porous gemstones are present (see *Jewellery*, opposite).

COPPER AND BRASS

The patina which forms naturally on brass and copper is a sought-after and valuable asset on some antique pieces (brass carriage clocks, for example), and such pieces should never be cleaned with metal polishes. Copper tarnishes to brown and corrodes to a relatively stable green patina; brass eventually acquires a matt, greenish-brown surface. Both metals scratch easily. Regular, light burnishing with a soft cloth or chamois should be adequate, or use a long-term silver cloth for light tarnishing (see also *Furniture mounts*, p.426). For heavier stains, long-term brass and copper cleaners or impregnated wadding can be used.

PEWTER

Pewter is easily dented and scratched. Old pewter has a high lead content which reacts and corrodes more quickly in acid conditions, so avoid keeping the metal in oak furniture,

which is particularly acid, and always wrap in acid-free materials for long-term storage.

Whether pewter should be allowed to develop a matt, tarnished surface or polished to a silvery finish is debatable. A dull gleam induced by regular, light buffing with a dry cloth is a good compromise. If the surface is heavily stained or very dull, try gently wiping it with a rag impregnated with linseed oil and talcum powder; remove this mixture using cotton-wool swabs moistened with methylated spirits, and then wash, rinse and dry thoroughly. If warty spots or powdery corrosion appear (caused by lead reacting with acids in the atmosphere), pewter should be treated by a metal conservator.

IRON AND STEEL

If exposed to damp, iron and steel rust rapidly, and will then pit, flake and eventually disintegrate completely. Cast iron and wrought iron can be given a barrier coating of paint or graphite, but overpainting the original finish may reduce value. A microcrystalline wax or light penetrating oil are also suitable for steel. Bear in mind that direct heat cracks paint, so iron grates and firebacks in use should be black leaded.

Before cleaning iron or steel, make sure the metal is absolutely dry. If the object is tough enough, remove loose rust and paint with wire wool or a wire brush followed by a commercial rust remover or wire wool soaked in paraffin. Wipe clean and dry thoroughly, then coat with a rust inhibitor.

Remove minor rust spots with a mild abrasive cloth and a few drops of a light penetrating oil, or gently scrape them off with a scalpel. Methylated spirits or white spirit are also useful cleaning agents. Severe rusting needs professional treatment, such as sandblasting or chemical stripping to restore the surface to good metal which can then be given a protective coating.

For *Bronze and spelter*, see p.429.

Sculpture and statuary

Maintaining the surface or patina of sculptures and statues of stone, bronze, spelter or lead, whether kept indoors or outside, is a top priority.

PRUDENT SITING OF OUTDOOR SCULPTURE in a sheltered position is the first step to practical conservation. Water dripping from a tree will stain a statue placed beneath, and mould, algae and lichen form more readily on objects exposed to northerly

weather. In extreme cold, stonework can split or shatter, as moisture absorbed by the stone expands on freezing. Removing soil from urns and troughs will lessen the danger of frost damage, but it is not practical to wrap an object against frost as moisture becomes

trapped. Outdoor pieces can be raised above ground level on plinths with built-in, damp-proof membranes, and should be kept clear of plants such as ivy, and of fallen leaves, both of which can stain and also secrete weak acids that may pit the surface. Cover all items before spraying garden chemicals.

STONE AND MARBLE

Some stone dissolves or is irreparably worn away by misguided attempts at cleaning. Limestone, sandstone and Coade stone form a weathered surface crust, which if removed will expose a vulnerable, crumbly surface beneath. If the surface is smooth and hard you can lightly hose it with water, easing loosened dirt with a soft-bristled brush. Algae and lichen do little harm, and in most cases add to a statue's value, but can be removed, if the surface is sound, by brushing with a solution of a teaspoon of dichlorophen (available from a garden shop) to a pint (570 ml) of water.

Alabaster and marble are porous and stain easily, and marble discolours and deteriorates, particularly in salty or polluted air. Attempts to remove stains from any porous stone may force the stain deeper or erode the surface. Alabaster and soapstone are very soft, easily scratched and broken, and gradually dissolve in water, so should be dusted regularly to prevent build-up of dirt. However, a sound surface can be wiped (not rubbed) gently with cotton wool barely moistened in a mixture of ½ pint (285 ml) each of white spirit and distilled water and one teaspoon of mild or non-ionic detergent. Rinse each section as you go with cotton wool dampened with distilled water. The solution is also suitable for cleaning hardstones such as polished granite, onyx, blue john, jade and agate.

To liven up and protect a cleaned surface of any of the above materials, apply a light coat of microcrystalline wax with a soft-bristled brush and buff gently with a clean white cloth. White marble and similar materials can be dusted with pure talc to fill the pores and prevent dust becoming ingrained.

Plaster is very porous and water-soluble, and should only ever be regularly and gently dusted with a soft-bristled brush.

Major repairs to, or restoration of, stonework should be done by a specialist, who will use a special resin compound mixed with ground-up stone to match the object. If you want to try mending a minor break yourself, use a quick-setting epoxy resin adhesive.

BRONZE, SPELTER AND LEAD

The desirable, dark or greenish-brown patina that forms on bronze must be preserved, so do not use metal polish or solvent on any bronze, or even water on indoor bronzes; dusting should suffice. A dull patina can be revived by a very light coating of microcrystalline wax. Test an inconspicuous area first to make sure the patina is stable – an artificially induced or painted one may not be. Apply the wax with a soft-bristled brush and burnish gently with a soft cloth. Archaeological bronzes or items which have been exposed to salty air may develop 'bronze disease' – small, powdery, green spots on the surface. You can wax a small area immediately, but anything more serious should be taken to a conservator for specialist treatment.

Spelter is softer and more brittle than bronze, and is prone to corrosion about which little can be done. Figures are often thinly cast and fragile, so do hold them at the most solid part. Painted or gilded figures should not be allowed to get wet, but dusted lightly with a soft-haired artist's brush. Unpainted spelter can be waxed as for bronze, above.

Lead is heavy and very soft, easily dented and scratched, and poisonous – so always wash your hands after handling. Corrosion appears as a white, powdery coating. Dust indoor lead regularly. A sound surface can be

The iron 'skeleton' of this early 19thC cupid corroded and expanded, splitting the lead 'skin'. The restorer dismembers the figure to flush out the old material with a high pressure jet and inserts stainless-steel dowels.

cleaned with a soft-bristled brush or cotton wool moistened in water with a few drops of non-ionic detergent. Rinse and dry well immediately. Microcrystalline wax helps to prevent further deterioration: apply one or two coats (leaving an hour between coats) and buff gently with a soft cloth.

Jewellery and gemstones

Because we wear jewellery as we move around, it is at great risk from accidental damage or loss unless special care is taken.

FRAGILE GEMSTONES or crystal beads shatter if hit against a hard surface. A soft, 18-carat gold ring wears paper-thin if it is worn constantly, especially if it lies next to another ring of harder metal.

It is asking for trouble – in the form of damage or loss – if you wear jewellery while doing domestic work. A diamond will not be harmed by immersion in hot water, but it could split in two if knocked hard. Emeralds, sapphires, aquamarines and opals may well shatter on exposure to even hand-hot water.

The colour of stones such as topaz and turquoise changes with prolonged exposure to strong light; opals chip and crack very easily when exposed to heat; and pearls may loose their lustre and yellow or darken if they get too dry. Ivory is particularly prone to cracking in heat, sunlight or a dry atmosphere, or if it gets wet. Costume jewellery is often made of base metals such as brass and copper which may corrode, and simulated stones which may gradually fade over time.

To guard against loss, regularly check that chain links, fastenings and settings are secure. Constant opening and closing weakens a clasp, and sharp edges on beads fray the thread on which they are strung. If a pearl necklace is worn a great deal – the lustre is said to improve as pearls absorb natural oils from the skin – it should be checked about every six months, and professionally restrung if necessary, with strong, purpose-made necklace thread, knotted between each pearl both to prevent the beads rubbing against each other and to guard against all the pearls scattering if the string breaks. Pin heavy brooches into material that is sturdy enough to take their weight (if necessary, into the strap of an undergarment), and consider having safety chains fitted.

Apply hairspray and perfume *before* you put on your jewellery. These substances usually contain alcohol or chemicals which act as solvents or chemical reagents on certain materials, including plated gold, mother-of-pearl, amber, jet, coral and on porous gemstones such as turquoise, opals and pearls.

STORAGE

Avoid mixing different types of jewellery in one box. Many materials used in jewellery, ranging from precious stones, glass and jade to shell cameo, ivory and enamel, may become chipped if they are kept jumbled up with other, harder materials. A hard, sharply cut stone like a diamond will scratch gold, silver and softer stones.

Necklaces and strings of beads can be hung or wound around a roll of acid-free paper to prevent tangling. Otherwise, keep each item of jewellery in its own box, or wrap it separately in clean, acid-free tissue or soft, pure cotton or linen cloth.

CLEANING

Knowing the materials in a piece of jewellery is vital before any cleaning process is undertaken, so check with a jeweller who works with antique pieces. Ancient jewellery should be cleaned professionally as age and the softer metal used make it very fragile.

Porous stones like opals and pearls should never be immersed in water as they lose their natural lustre. These and most other items,

including most metal jewellery, can be gently buffed with a soft jeweller's cloth (available from a jewellers'), or wiped gently with a very slightly dampened chamois leather. Remember that plated and rolled gold will wear if rubbed too much, and on no account should the matt-finish gold found on some 19th-century jewellery be polished. (See also *Metalware*, p.427.)

If a strung necklace or bracelet gets wet the thread will shrink and eventually rot. As long as the beads are water-resistant, they can be cleaned individually with slightly dampened cotton-wool buds. Enamel is very delicate and should only be dusted gently or blown clean. Ivory, too, should only be cleaned with a dry, soft-bristled brush as it absorbs water and stains; for ingrained dirt go to an expert.

Stones in a closed setting should not be allowed to get wet as water may lodge behind the stones and trigger corrosion, or weaken any adhesive. Clean instead with a cotton-wool bud dipped in clear pure alcohol, then rinse and dry with cotton buds.

If you are confident that a piece can be safely immersed in water, do not risk losing it for ever by washing it over an open sink or plughole. Instead put some lukewarm water with a few drops of mild or non-ionic detergent in a small bowl. Place this on a tray with raised edges and covered with a towel or cloth. Immerse the item in the water and very gently ease out the dirt with a soft-bristled brush, or a wooden cocktail stick for

Before the setter can set stones into an item of jewellery, the mount must be held stable in a bed of plaster of Paris.

stubborn grime in small areas. Rinse the jewellery in a separate bowl of clear water and allow it to dry naturally on a piece of absorbent kitchen paper. Cameos, jet, gold and silver items can all be cleaned in this way.

RESTORATION

Jewellery repairs should be carried out by a reputable jeweller who is used to working with antiques, and should be combined with an overall check of settings and clasps. If you want to glue an item of jewellery yourself – a hard gemstone, for example – remove any old adhesive first and remember that the repair is unlikely to be easily reversible.

Ceramics and glass

Accidental breakage is probably the highest risk factor for ceramics and glass objects, but can be minimised by careful handling and cleaning.

CERAMIC AND GLASS objects are not affected by bright light or normal household fluctuations of humidity and temperature. The adhesives used on restored pieces, however, will be discoloured or weakened by strong light or water.

Make sure your hands are clean and dry before handling glass and unglazed china as greasy fingerprints can leave indelible marks.

Wearing cotton gloves while handling china and glass is not recommended as grip is reduced. Pick up an item by the soundest part – never the handle – support the base, and watch out for loose parts such as lids, and weaknesses caused by restoration and cracks.

A cabinet or shelf for displaying china or glass must be stable, so that vibrations from normal household movement will not cause

the pieces to 'walk'. Felt or chamois-leather pads can be cut to fit beneath the base of an item to protect the shelf or table beneath. Put plants or cut flowers in a separate container within a treasured vase, with a protective pad between, to guard against water stains.

Only sound, uncracked plates should be wall-hung. Use acrylic or plastic-coated fittings (available from most good china shops), which can be adjusted to fit the plate.

CLEANING

Use an artist's paintbrush to remove dirt and dust from any incised or delicate relief decoration before washing. Most glass and lazed ceramics can be washed in warm water with a little non-ionic or mild household detergent added. Never put fine glass, including modern lead glass, pottery or antique ceramics in a dishwasher.

Before washing fragile objects, place a cushioning material such as towels or foam rubber in the base of the washing basin and over the taps. Wash and rinse items one at a time and put them to drain for a few moments on a towel. Dry immediately.

Glazed, low-fired earthenwares such as delftware, faience and maiolica may have an unglazed foot-rim, or cracks or chips which expose the porous surface beneath the glaze. Don't immerse these items – it is safer to wipe them with cotton wool moistened in the detergent water. Other items requiring special care – assuming they are objects of antique value and kept for display only – and which it is advisable simply to dust regularly, are:

● crizzled glass, on which a network of fine surface cracks has formed, a condition that is aggravated by moisture;

● any unglazed, low-fired pottery – water, together with any impurities in it, will be absorbed into the porous body;

● objects with metal or ormolu fittings, or which are mended with iron rivets;

● items with gold leaf or delicate overglaze decoration which might flake easily;

● ancient or excavated glass or ceramic glazes with a flaking iridescence; no attempt should be made to scrape or clean the surface.

REMOVING STAINS

You may be able to shift 'tidemarks' from glass, such as wine stains in a decanter, with a solution of denture cleaner and warm water, or with acetic acid (or vinegar). Leave either in the glass for 24 hours, then rinse, drain and dry thoroughly. Methylated spirits or pure alcohol can be tried for alcohol-based perfume bottle stains; change the alcohol every hour or so until the stain has gone.

Ammonia or an ordinary household bleach which contains chlorine will remove stains on most glass, as long as there is no gilding or other fragile decoration. On ceramics, however, this is unsuitable as it may aggravate the stain or cause permanent discoloration. Instead, and only on a soft or hard-paste porcelain surface with no gilt or lustre decoration, obtain 20-volume hydrogen peroxide from a chemist and add a few drops of ammonia. Wear rubber gloves. Dampen strips of cotton wool in the solution, then lay them over the stain or crack and leave for about an hour. Do not let the strips dry onto the surface – the object can be placed in a plastic bag to retain the moisture. You may

need to renew the 'dressings' several times.

Most enamel-painted decoration on ceramics (see *Overglaze colours*, p. 153) comes to no harm using this technique, but do not use it on pale blue or greenish-blue 19th-century enamels, as they may disappear.

CHANDELIERS

Before dismantling a cut-glass chandelier for a major clean, photograph the piece intact, and work out a system of identifying the lustres so that you know where to put them back. Turn off any electrical connection and do not let water seep into the hollow branches of the chandelier. Wash the lustres in a detergent solution, checking that the metal hooks are sound, rinse thoroughly and dry immediately to prevent corrosion of the metal. Polish with a soft, lint-free cloth.

MIRRORS AND WINDOW GLASS

Never use commercial glass cleaners for mirrors, stained or leaded glass, as the chemicals in them can act as a solvent on glass that is stained with a coloured varnish, on a gilt or varnished frame, and on lead or putty. Remove as much dirt as possible from indoor glass with a soft chamois leather. For more stubborn stains wipe with a cloth moistened in warm water with a few drops of methylated spirits and some mild household detergent, then rinse with clean water using a well-wrung-out chamois leather. Protect the frame

with a piece of thin card. Where grime has built up on stained or leaded window glass, brush it off gently with a clean soft-bristled brush and, as long as the surface is stable, clean with cotton wool just dampened with the same solution used for mirrors.

RESTORATION

If a breakage occurs, wrap each broken piece in acid-free tissue, and collect even the smallest shards. Resist any temptation to try to fit the pieces together yourself, as you could damage the crisply snapped edges.

Glass can rarely be mended invisibly, unless a break is at a convenient join between cup and stem, for example. However, synthetic resins with a refractive index similar to that of glass are now available, and cracks and holes can be filled. Chips can sometimes be ground out with minimal loss of value. A conservator may also be able to re-create missing pieces such as a decanter stopper or the blue-glass liner of a salt.

Ceramics can be so skilfully repaired with modern adhesives, and then repainted or glazed, that the original damage is almost undetectable (see p. 164). But the restored area may discolour in time, especially if it is exposed to water, and some glazes – lustre glazes especially – can never be faithfully reproduced. The problem with attempting any repair yourself is that the adhesives which are strong enough to be effective, such as Loctite or Superglue, are not easily reversible, and a more complicated and expensive professional repair may be needed at a later date.

Before retouching this bone china bird, the restorer degreased the broken edges with acetone (which evaporates rapidly and can be used on any piece that has been fired at a high temperature). She used a two-part epoxy resin glue to bond the broken pieces.

Timepieces, precision instruments and mechanical toys

Delicate instruments require delicate treatment – all too often these objects suffer from thoughtless display and over-enthusiastic handling.

CLOCKS, SCIENTIFIC INSTRUMENTS, musical boxes and automata are likely to be harmed if subjected to direct sunlight, extremes of temperature or damp. A common, but one of the worst, places for a clock is over a working fireplace. Dust may clog sliding or moving parts of scientific instruments and mechanical items, so keep these in a box or display cabinet when they are not in use. Movement can affect the working of mechanisms too; longcase clocks and wall-hung instruments, for example, should be screwed to a wall or onto a solid wooden wall bracket or mount.

Before moving a mechanical object, check that there are no detachable parts; do not rely on handles, but hold the object with both hands under its base. Secure the pendulum of a spring clock by the clip or screw clamp found on many English bracket and mantel clocks; otherwise, remove the pendulum and use folded paper to wedge the ticking 'crutch piece' firm. On a longcase or other weight-driven clock, remove weights and pendulum, and 'take down' the clock by separating case, hood and movement. If a mechanism is set in motion while being moved, let it run down completely.

Mercury barometers should be moved with special care, and kept upright in transit; if the mercury moves suddenly its weight could shatter the glass tube. On a stick barometer, turn the little key square at the base until the column of mercury reaches the top of the tube. Wheel (banjo) barometers must be 'corked' by a specialist before being moved.

WINDING

With longcase clocks, if you go away for longer than the next due winding, stop the clock to avoid damage to the escapement when it winds down. It should be impossible to over-wind a mechanism; simply turn the key firmly to the point of resistance. Always use the correct key for the item, and make sure it is not warped, rusty, worn or split. To adjust the minute hand of a clock, gently turn the hands clockwise (never anti-clockwise) with your fingertips. If the hands jam, move the minute hand back a fraction but never back past the hour. If this does not free them, leave the job to a clockmaker.

CLEANING

A photographer's soft-bristled brush with built-in puffer is ideal for dusting lenses and delicate or intricate surfaces; less fragile surfaces can be wiped with a soft, dry, lint-free cloth. Avoid metal polishes which may seep into the movement or destroy a valuable patina such as that of a brass carriage clock (see *Metalware*, p.428). For stubborn marks on a glass face, use cotton wool just dampened in a mild detergent solution or methylated spirits. Rinse with damp cotton wool and buff

The needle on this aneroid barometer had jammed against the dial; the cost of repair, cleaning and resetting was c.£70. To reset a barometer yourself, phone the local weather centre for the mean barometric pressure for your locality and altitude, and, within an hour, adjust by turning the screw in the back of the case.

gently dry with a chamois leather. Major cleaning of parts, especially if dismantling is involved, should be left to a specialist. Even oiling the mechanism of a valuable object can be risky if you don't know where to apply it, and too much or too thick an oil attracts abrasive grime and clogs the mechanism.

RESTORATION

If a mechanism stops, forcing it to go may aggravate the damage; repair should be left to a specialist. Even if they are in good working order, clocks and watches with delicate mechanisms should be checked and serviced every five years, and those with larger, stronger mechanisms every decade.

Textiles and costume

The delicate fibres and the dyes of antique textiles and costumes make them particularly sensitive to changing atmospheric conditions.

ANTIQUE TEXTILES need special protection as they are easily torn and absorb stains and smells. So keep them out of reach of children and pets, and away from smoke, food and drink. In a dry atmosphere, textiles can become brittle; in damp they rot with mildew and mould, and an overdose of light breaks down fibres, fades colours and causes discoloration. Many textiles incorporate materials of different strengths, such as beads or fine embroidery, which must be taken into consideration in cleaning and display. Handle antique textiles as little as possible to avoid damaging delicate fibres, and check them regularly for early signs of damage, mould or insect infestation.

Samplers and embroidered pictures are sometimes found mounted on stretchers like oil paintings, but this strains both fabric and stitches. Instead, any small, flat textile can be framed and mounted on a fabric-covered, acid-free board with a window mount to prevent the textile coming into direct contact with the glass (see p.434). Never use drawing pins or staples to secure textiles as they tear the fibres and may corrode and stain the fabric. Stainless steel pins can be useful, however, to support heavy folds which otherwise might sag and tear on a costume that is displayed on a stand (padded stands can be made to measure).

Every so often, give an antique costume or textile a rest from display – a conservator will advise how often. Choose a dark, dry place, and remove any pins. Always wrap in acid-free materials, never coloured tissue or newspaper as both are highly acidic. Store coloured and white fabrics separately just in case dyes run. When packing, avoid sharp folds – use tissue if necessary to support the inside of any creases – as they strain the fabric.

Lay flat textiles horizontally or rolled around a roll of card or tissue, and interleave with more tissue or linen. To prepare three-dimensional textiles (such as garments) for storage, loosely fill out the shape with crunched-up tissue or a padding of cotton or linen and an inert stuffing material. Place a final layer of tissue over the items and put them in a container lined with acid-free material. Large costumes can be hung on a padded wooden hanger (never wire as it might corrode and stain the fabric) and protected from dust by a cotton or calico bag. Check that the garment hangs well – that the shoulder of the hanger is not too long and distorts the fall of the sleeves, for example.

Mothballs may help deter pests and mould, but they should neither come into contact with the fabric, nor take the place of regular checking. As long as they have not begun to attack the fabric, insect larvae or mould can be brushed off gently. Do this outside on a fine day, away from other textiles when the fabric is dry and well aired. Serious infestation should be dealt with by a conservator.

CLEANING AND REPAIR

There is a high risk of irreparably damaging and devaluing an important or delicate antique fabric by inexpert cleaning or repair. Before attempting any spot removal, or wet or dry cleaning of an antique textile, check with an expert as it may need to receive special treatment from a conservator.

Every time a textile is cleaned, it gets a little weaker; it is therefore wise to tolerate a certain level of dirt. Never iron dirty textiles as heat seals dust into the fabric, fixes stains and may cause fading. If the fabric is sound and has no loose bits like beads or tassels, dust can be removed by gentle vacuuming. If necessary, cover the nozzle with a fine-mesh net or stocking and secure with an elastic band. Feathers, sequins and elaborately decorated fabrics can be dusted with a soft brush or blown with a hair dryer set on cool.

A textile conservator is able to restore torn areas almost invisibly, matching dyes, threads and tension, and can strengthen weak fabrics by 'couching' onto a backing with very fine thread and stitching. Conservators generally avoid using glue, as it is rarely reversible and may stain or destroy the texture of the textile. However, to fix something that was glued originally, a water-based adhesive such as Tenaxatex may be used.

CHECKING COLOUR FASTNESS

ALWAYS SPOT TEST antique textiles for colour fastness before using any liquid to remove a mark. First place white blotting paper beneath the item. Soak a small piece of cotton wool in water mixed with the cleaning agent you are to use. Place it on an inconspicuous area of the textile and watch for any reaction. If any trace of colour appears on the cotton wool or blotting paper, quickly dry the area with a medium hot hair dryer and do not wash the item. Test each colour in the same way.

Carpets, rugs and tapestries

If they are kept free of dust and placed where they will not get heavy wear, many antique carpets and rugs can be used normally.

WHETHER HUNG against a wall or in use on the floor, carpets and rugs should be against a flat, clean, dry surface. Floor carpets need an underlay – with a slightly tacky surface to reduce slip – cut to fit their size exactly. Never nail or glue the carpet to anything. On stone or tile floors lay moisture-proof paper beneath the underlay. Place antique floor carpets wisely – they are likely to get least wear in a bedroom; placed before a fire, they risk being scorched, or under a dining table they may be stained by food or drink or damaged by movement of chairs. Rubber pads or wooden cups, available from a good furniture store, will relieve the localised pressure of furniture feet. Move carpets around occasionally so that wear is not always concentrated on the same area.

DISPLAY

Delicate or rare pieces should only be wall-hung, lengthways so that the weight is taken by the warp. Small pieces can be mounted by a specialist framer onto a linen backing and fitted into a wooden stretcher, and then box-mounted with a Perspex window for further protection. For larger textiles, stitch wide Velcro tape along the top on the reverse side (taking care to sew between the carpet threads, not through them), and staple the receiving Velcro strip to a wooden batten fixed to the wall. Heavy textiles may need additional support tapes running vertically down the back to help spread the weight. Dyes fade in intense light from bright sunshine or spotlights. Use cool-beam, fibre-optic, or low-wattage incandescent lights for any highlighting effect, and draw curtains when a room is not in use during the day.

CLEANING

Dust should never be allowed to build up in carpets as it has a sandpaper effect on the fibres. Major cleaning beyond dust removal should be kept to a minimum and done by a conservator. Proprietary carpet cleaners should never be used on antique pieces, as they can have a clogging effect. If a carpet is tough enough to be in use, it will benefit from regular vacuuming. Go in the direction of the pile, and vacuum the back and the floor beneath about every 6 months.

For a fragile or wall-hung piece, it may be sufficient to shake out loose dirt regularly, or to use a low-suction setting or fitting on the vacuum cleaner and fix a fine-meshed net or stocking over the nozzle with an elastic band. Clean both back and front every 6 months – if possible do this during the summer months when moths are breeding.

Treat accidental spills immediately: soak up surplus liquid with a plain white paper towel or a clean, colourfast tea towel. Sprinkle table salt liberally over the stain to draw out remaining moisture, and vacuum when dry. A good dousing in soda water which is then soaked up with clean towels is effective for urine and other light stains. Soak old stains with a solution of two tablespoons of salt to a pint of water – but beware: salt can have a bleaching effect. A carpet made after around 1870 may contain synthetic aniline dyes, which were of variable fastness when first introduced, so do a spot test (see above).

Wax can be gently lifted off with a fingernail and the remainder absorbed into white blotting paper pressed on with a lukewarm iron. Remove chewing gum by pressing with ice cubes in a plastic bag to chill and harden it, then try easing it off gently with your fingernail. If any of the above methods do not work easily, a stain should be left until it can be treated by a conservator.

STORAGE

For long-term storage choose a cool, dark, dry, well-ventilated place. Folding causes creases and uneven wear, so roll the rug, right side out, around an acid-free cardboard or inert plastic tube (a plastic drainpipe is ideal) of as wide a diameter as practicable. Roll in the direction of the pile, from the top of the carpet – the pile moves smoothly away from the top like a cat's fur when stroked in the right direction – or, with a tapestry-weave, in the direction of the warp. Smooth out as you roll and interleave with acid-free tissue. Finally, tie a dustproof sheet around the roll and store it horizontally – never vertically, as this distributes the weight unevenly.

RESTORATION

Fraying, holes, burns or other damage to antique carpets or tapestries must be repaired by a specialist. Expert repairs involve exact matching of dyes, threads and knots, and possibly inserting a patch or reinforcing the warp and weft.

Paintings, drawings and printed items

How and where a picture is hung is crucial to keeping it in good condition. Photographs, books and stamps, too, benefit from proper care.

HANG A PICTURE SECURELY, in a spot that is neither damp, nor above a fire or radiator, nor too bright. Make sure air circulates around it by letting it lean away from the wall at the top. If a picture is to hang on an exterior wall, glue corks to the lower corners of the frame for extra insulation.

Use metal picture wire and one or two steel or brass picture hooks depending on the size and weight of the piece. Heavy, glazed pictures may also need to be supported at the base on brackets fixed to the wall. Screw eyehooks into the frame, never into the stretcher or backboard. With a heavy picture, put a pair of hooks on each side, fastening the wire to the lower pair and running free through the upper pair. Then, if one hook gives way, the painting will still be supported.

FRAMING

Whether you learn to mount and frame pictures yourself or go to an expert, it is important to understand how framing and mounting help to conserve a work of art. **Oil paintings** must be set in a frame deep enough to accommodate the painting on its stretcher. The frame can be lined with velvet ribbon or inert foam-rubber strips to protect the edges of the painting. If the rebate is too deep, it can be padded out with cork or balsa-wood strips. If it is too shallow, the frame can be built up with strips of wood.

Mirror plates or brass plates screwed into the frame and overlapping the stretcher hold picture and stretcher firmly in place.

As oil paintings are coated with varnish, they do not need to be glazed.

Works of art on paper must be mounted on acid-free board. Check whether an existing mount is acidic by looking at the bevelled edges of the 'window'; if there is a brown stain around the line of the window, the board is likely to be made from poor quality wood pulp and should be replaced. The mount separates the glass from the picture; this not only prevents the work from being rubbed and from sticking to the glass but also provides a thin layer of air, which deters mould.

The frame must be deep enough and strong enough to hold the backing board, mounting board and glass (see illustration, opposite). The backing board helps keep dust and insects out – especially if it is sealed with gummed paper tape around the edges – and secures the picture firmly in its frame. As it is likely to be made of wood or hardboard and acidic, it should not touch the back of the picture and can also be coated with polyurethane varnish or covered with acid-free paper.

Paintings on paper do not have a protective layer of varnish, and so need to be glazed. Glass also keeps out insects such as silverfish, thunderbugs or thrips, which not only feed on the paper, but may die and leave stains.

Acrylic (Perspex) sheeting is lighter and less fragile than glass but scratches easily and attracts dust more readily. 'Clip-frames', cuts of glass and (acidic) hardboard clipped together, are not dust and insect-proof and are unsuitable for long-term mounting.

LIGHTING

Most pigments used for works of art on paper are extremely sensitive to light and fade dramatically; for this reason, precious items should never be photocopied. Oil paints are less likely to fade but will dry and crack with heat from direct light. Beware of 'purpose-made' picture lamps; the bulbs are usually ordinary incandescent lights which will overheat the area they illuminate. Even cool beam lamps should not be left on for long.

STORAGE

Store framed pictures in a cool, dark, clean, dry place. Remove hooks or any projections that may harm the frames or pictures. Stand the pictures on wooden blocks to raise them above floor level and place acid-free board between each. Ensure the largest, heaviest pieces take the weight at the back and place a weight in front of the stack. Cover the lot with a clean sheet – never polythene as this encourages mould. Unframed works of art on paper should be stored in an acid-free box or folder. Place acid-free tissue between each work and store horizontally. Sulphur vapour from certain substances, including some plastic folders, causes paper to discolour.

CLEANING

Beyond removing surface dust with a soft squirrel brush, or dusting the case of a miniature, the cleaning of pictures, whether of oils or on paper, is a job for the professional. See also *Mirrors*, p.431.

CONSERVATION OF OIL PAINTINGS

Conservation work of any sort should be left to a professional. For instance, go to a restorer at the first signs of paint lifting off or flaking,

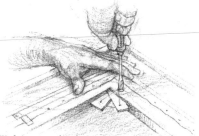

Wedges inserted in the stretcher are adjusted to give the right degree of tension to the canvas.

The mount for a work of art on paper is like a six-sided box (the four sides of the frame, the glass and the backing board) which creates a micro-environment. The print is attached to the backing board with Japanese tissue paper and starch glue (see box). A paper conservator might charge around £40 for mending a tear, cleaning and flattening a smallish print in fair condition.

for once it starts, deterioration can be rapid. Remove the painting from the wall and lay it face up, so that the paint does not fall off. The varnished surface on oil paintings often yellows with time and may need to be removed (without dissolving the paint layers beneath) and renewed. A whitish bloom on the surface of an oil painting, brought on by a damp atmosphere, can be treated. Bitumen, which was used in some 19th-century oils, can form deep cracks with age. These are difficult to treat beyond a little filling and retouching to make the problem less obtrusive.

CONSERVATION OF WORKS OF ART ON PAPER

For most works of art on paper – including watercolours, drawings, prints, photographs and books – there are common conservation problems associated with the paper rather than with the printing or painting process.

The more acidic a paper is the quicker it deteriorates – turning brown and crumbly in light, or in damp conditions developing mould or little brown spots known as 'foxing'.

Overall discoloration is usually due to a low-grade paper which becomes increasingly acidic with age. The problem is aggravated if the paper is in contact with acidic materials such as cheap mounting board, so displaying or storing pictures, stamps or books in acid-free materials is an absolute priority.

The light-sensitive silver salts in photographs are particularly vulnerable to chemicals. Photographs should ideally be displayed in albums with highly alkaline paper and mounted on corner mounts or stamp hinges, or in closed frames or transparent, acid-free polyester or polythene envelopes.

Stains and foxing of watercolours can sometimes be professionally removed by a skilled washing process. The carbon printing ink used for books and most European prints is quite stable, and can also be washed by a conservator without harming its density.

BOOKS

Display books on a shelf that has been painted or varnished, and ideally lined with acid-free card. Don't forget that strong light will fade the spines. If the shelves are within a cabinet, make sure there is adequate ventilation.

Book-ends should be as large as the books they confine so that pressure is spread equally over the surface. Volumes should never be packed too tightly on a shelf. To remove a book, reach over the top of it and ease it out from the back of the shelf, or part it from the volumes either side and grasp it by the sides.

Boards that have fallen off the sides of books can be temporarily held in place by tying cotton or crepe bandage around the book from top to bottom, which will not be visible when the book is on the shelf with other volumes. Rebinding may devalue a rare book. A skilful craftsman can ease off an old spine, rejoint the original boards and reattach the original spine. But even this process, known as 'rebacked with spine laid on' may reduce the value. If broken bindings are repaired or renewed, the original pieces should be kept safely as documentary evidence. For leather treatment, see p.427.

STAMPS

Only remove a stamp from its envelope or card if you are sure its post mark is of no value. Never steam, but 'float' stamps off in lukewarm water and then dry between layers of white blotting paper. Any mounting material that actually touches the stamps must be acid-free. Chemically inert PVC sleeves are useful for mounting complete envelopes or cards, but make sure they do not seal completely as condensation may form. Loose-leaf albums combined with transparent photo-mount corners are ideal, with stamps displayed on one side of each leaf only so that facing pages do not rub or catch.

Never use adhesive tape or the gum of the stamp itself to fix it to a surface, but gummed stamp hinges with the minimum amount of moisture at the top of the stamp. You should be able to peel the stamp off again without damaging it. Hinges should not be used for mint stamps, as this could reduce their value. Use Hawid plastic mounting strips instead.

A-Z of antiques

Words in **bold type** *within an entry in this glossary denote significant or alternative terms, or alternative spellings. Words in* SMALL CAPITALS *refer to another entry which might further enhance your understanding of the subject. Pottery and silver marks appearing in the text are selected examples and are not necessarily the only ones used by that particular maker.*

A

Aalto, Alvar (1898-1976) Finnish architect and furniture designer whose work during the 1920s and 30s had an enormous impact on 20thC design. Although mass-produced, Aalto's furniture is highly original, distinguished by clean, simple lines and curves, and the innovative use of materials such as moulded plywood and tubular steel.

abacus See COLUMN.

Abbotsford style Term introduced in the late 19thC for imitation Jacobean, Stuart, Tudor and Gothic furniture made in the 1820s and 30s. It was named after Abbotsford, the Scottish home of the 18th-19thC poet and novelist Sir Walter Scott, which was furnished in this style.

abrash Term for the faint banding of colour shades usually found in vegetable-dyed Oriental carpets made by nomadic tribes. This is due to slight variations in shade of different batches of wool that were dyed at different times. Abrash is most obvious over a large, plain field of uniform colour. Unfortunately, unscrupulous modern weavers often fake an abrash to try to make a rug look older.

acacia Very durable, whitish-yellow wood with brown veining, also known as robinia. Acacia was used as a veneer in the late 17th and early 18th centuries, as a decorative crossbanding on 18th and early 19thC country furniture, and occasionally for chairs and small cabinet work such as boxes in the ARTS AND CRAFTS MOVEMENT of the late 19thC.

acanthus See DECORATIVE MOTIFS.

accordion pleat A series of narrow, machine-made, overlapping pleats, often used on lightweight fabrics for soft furnishings.

achromatic lens An 18thC development combining FLINT GLASS and crown glass to remove distorting colour fringes from the image. It was patented by Englishman John Dollond in 1758 and used in telescopes and microscopes.

acid etching See ENGRAVING.

acid gilding See GILDING.

acid polishing A chemical process which restores a polished surface to glass after it has been cut. The glass is dipped in an acid solution which removes a fine surface layer.

acorn flagon Pewter vessel about 12in (30 cm) high, with its base in the shape of an acorn cup, and a domed, acorn-like lid capped by a FINIAL. It was used for serving wine or ale in Yorkshire in the first half of the 18thC, and is also known as a **York flagon.**

Act of Parliament clock See TAVERN CLOCK.

Adam, Robert (1728-92) NEOCLASSICAL architect and interior designer. See p.36.

adjustment marks File marks found on many pre-19thC coins which have been 'adjusted' (filed down) to the correct weight. It was a worldwide practice which occurred from ancient times until the early 19thC, when new manufacturing techniques made it possible to cut blanks from consistently rolled metal sheets. Excess metal was filed off overweight blanks before the coins were struck to ensure that they were of consistent weight. Sometimes blanks were made deliberately overweight to avoid the more expensive remelting process necessary for underweight coins.

adlerglas See HUMPEN.

adze Long-handled axe with the blade at right angles to the shaft, used in furniture-making, for heavy trimming and shaping. The slightly hollowed-out seats of WINDSOR CHAIRS, for example, were shaped with an adze with a curved cutting edge.

Æ Common abbreviation for bronze and copper from the Latin *aes,* found in coin catalogues and also seen as **æ.**

aerography Late 19thC technique of applying colours to ceramics through a stencil with an airbrush or atomiser. It resulted in a gradual transition of colours and soft-edged, slightly grained images, and was often used to 'dress up' cheap pottery and porcelain.

Aesthetic movement Decorative arts movement with a Japanese influence, which flourished in Britain from *c.*1870 – a precursor to ART NOUVEAU. The movement was recognised in the USA but not in France or elsewhere in Europe. It overlapped with the ARTS AND CRAFTS MOVEMENT although it had already begun to decline by the late 1880s. See p.64.

affenkapelle A set of porcelain monkey musicians – the term is German for 'monkey band'. The sets, each one comprising some 20 figures, were introduced by MEISSEN in Germany during the mid-18thC, and were reproduced there and at many other European factories in the 19thC. See also SINGERIE.

agate Fine-grained quartz used as a semiprecious stone in CAMEO and INTAGLIO work and in jewellery such as signet rings and brooches, particularly during the 19thC. When polished, agate reveals variegated tones of soft browns and oranges, blues, greys or greens, often with irregular milky bands.

agate ware Staffordshire pottery resembling the veinings and colouring of natural agate. It was produced in the 18thC by firms such as WEDGWOOD and WHIELDON. There were two types: **solid agate,** made from kneading together two or three differently coloured clays to give a marbled effect all the way through the body; and **surface agate,** in which a plain earthenware body was applied with a 'joggled' liquid clay SLIP of mixed agate-like colours to give a surface-only finish. See p.174.

aide-mémoire Slim, decorated case fitted with a pencil and note pad, usually measuring about $3\frac{1}{2} \times 2\frac{1}{4} \times \frac{1}{4}$ in (90 × 55 × 5 mm). The ivory leaves of 18thC aides-mémoire, or **tablettes,** continued until the early 20thC, although some have been replaced with paper. The cases were decorated in materials such as gold, silver, ivory, enamel and tortoiseshell. See also CARNET DE BAL.

AIDE-MÉMOIRE *in a leather cover set with engraved silver plaque; 1844.*

aigrette Hair or hat ornament, usually of gold or silver, made in the shape of a feather or as a holder for a feather. Aigrettes were fashionable in the 17th and 18th centuries and from the late 19th to early 20thC.

air-beading Circular or tear-shaped bubbles of air incorporated into glassware for decorative effect. The molten glass is pricked with a metal point, and glass drawn over the hole. A **tear** is formed when the glass is drawn into shape.

air twist See TWIST.

Akerman, John (*fl.*1719-55) London glass merchant who introduced CUT GLASS to Britain *c.*1719.

alabaster A dense, finely grained, marble-like mineral, a form of gypsum. It is normally white, yellow or red in colour, and translucent when thinly cut. Alabaster is easy to carve and became particularly fashionable for pedestals, vases and clock cases in the late 18thC and again *c.*1890.

albarello Cylindrical, slightly waisted ceramic drug pot, with a groove around the neck for securing a parchment cover. Albarelli originated in 12thC Persia, but ornamental MAIOLICA versions were made in Spain and Italy in the 15th and 16th centuries, with a revival in the 19thC, and in Dutch and English DELFTWARE from the second half of the 16thC.

ALBARELLO *Italian maiolica dating from the mid-16thC; 11 in (28 cm) high.*

albert Single or double metal chain with a bar for securing in a buttonhole at one end, and a swivel attachment to hold a pocket watch at the other. A Birmingham jeweller presented Queen Victoria's consort, Prince Albert, with one of these in 1845, and so the name was coined.

album quilt Personalised patchwork quilt, its design being of particular significance to the recipient. A typical design might have names and dates stitched into some of the patches. The quilts were fashionable in the USA in the mid-19thC. See p.310.

alburnum See SAPWOOD.

alder Durable wood native to northern Europe which polishes to a flesh-coloured, knotty finish. It is an easy wood to turn, and was used in the 18th and 19th centuries for country furniture, and occasionally for the turned members of Windsor chairs.

ale glass Stemmed glass dating from the 18thC used for drinking ale, which was more potent than today's beer. The glasses are similar to wine glasses but with a slimmer, more elongated bowl. From 1740, some examples were engraved with hops or ears of barley, or enamelled. 19thC ale glasses are similar in shape to champagne flutes. Short-stemmed versions are known as **dwarf** or **short** ales. See box p.475.

Alençon lace Venetian lace-makers established the Alençon lace factory in north-west France in 1675. Production declined in the 18thC but flourished again under Napoleon and the Second Empire. **Point d'Alençon** refers to needlepoint LACE with distinctive *modes* (fillings) between the basic mesh, made both at Alençon and elsewhere.

alentours Wide tapestry with a central picture surrounded by a border simulating gilded wood, in turn bordered by rich ornament such as *trompe l'oeil* figures and flowers. Alentours tapestry was first introduced in 1714 at the GOBELINS tapestry factory in France.

ale warmer Copper or brass cup with a long wooden or iron handle used for warming ale over an open fire. Early 18thC examples were shaped like a large boot or shoe; cone-shaped cups ('donkey's ears') were introduced in the late 18thC. Both styles were widely produced in the 19thC, and modern reproductions abound.

alexandrite A green or greenish-brown gemstone which glints varying shades of red under artificial light. The gem was discovered in the Ural mountains, Russia, in 1830, on the birthday of Tsar Alexander II. A synthetic form of CORUNDUM exhibits similar colour changes and is sold in the Middle East as alexandrite, but is of little value.

alexandrite glass Transparent ART GLASS with colour gradations of citron-yellow through to rose and blue produced by successive reheating of individual parts of the glass. The process was patented by Thomas WEBB & Sons, a Stourbridge glasshouse, in 1886. In a later version, designs were cut through an outer shell of rose and blue glass to reveal a clear yellow base beneath.

Alloa Glassworks Scottish glass factory established in 1750. It specialised mainly in dark green bottles which were roughly stipple engraved with commemorative events, names and dates. The most common dates found are from 1830 to about 1850.

all over A carpet design based on a pattern or motif that is repeated all over the main area or field of the piece, stopping at the borders.

alloy A metal such as bronze, pewter or brass formed by melting together two or more elements such as copper, zinc and tin. Metals are normally used in the form of alloys to make them more durable and easier to work; STERLING STANDARD silver, for example, contains a proportion of copper or some other base metal.

aluminium Very light, silver-coloured metal discovered in 1827. From the 1850s it was occasionally used for figurines and plaques, and sometimes combined with gold for bracelets. Aluminium was back in fashion from the early 1920s onwards for ART DECO cocktail equipment, cigarette collectables such as ashtrays, and useful household articles such as jelly moulds and teapots.

amalgam Any of various ALLOYS in which mercury is combined with another metal, for example, tin, silver or gold.

amatory jewellery Brooches, rings and other jewellery with amorous motifs or inscriptions designed to be given as love tokens. Examples of amatory jewellery include posy rings, which are plain rings with messages inscribed on the inside and were very fashionable in the 16th and 17th centuries, 16thC betrothal rings with a heart-shaped mount set with a miniature portrait, and jewellery made of, or set with, locks of hair. There was a surge of demand for love brooches in late Victorian times. See p.268.

amber Soft, fossilised resin from a prehistoric variety of pine tree, ranging in colour from pale yellow and honey to reddish-brown, brown, red and almost black.

Sea amber mainly occurs along the southern shores of the Baltic Sea, especially near Lithuania, although it is also found on the coasts of eastern England and the Netherlands; **pit amber** is mined in Burma, Sicily, Romania, Poland and Mexico. Amber was popular in Celtic Britain, and again in the Victorian era.

The best-quality amber is clear, and rare specimens contain embedded insects (although these can be introduced artificially). Amber has been imitated in plastic and glass.

Amberina Type of ART GLASS, shading from golden-amber at the bottom to deep red at the top, developed by Joseph Locke at the New England Glass Co, in 1883. Amberina was widely manufactured in the USA and was also made in a PRESSED-GLASS form in north-east England.

amboyna Durable mottled reddish-brown wood with a tight grain from the East Indies. It is a variety of PADOUK, and was used by cabinet-makers, mainly for its highly decorative effect, in VENEERS, INLAID DECORATION and BANDING in the 18th and 19th centuries.

ambulante General term for a light, portable 'occasional' table used during the second half of the 18thC in France. It might apply to a work table or bedside table, for example, that had no fixed position but was moved around as required.

amen glass Rare British wine glass with a DRAWN STEM, produced c.1745, the bowl engraved with a Jacobite hymn ending with the word 'amen'.

American Colonial style All-embracing term for North American furniture and architectural style dating from the early 17thC pioneer settlements to the establishment of federal government in 1789.

American Federal style Furniture of the early years of American independence (1789-1830) generally adorned with patriotic or military symbols such as the eagle.

amethyst Semiprecious, pale mauve to deep purple form of QUARTZ. Amethysts turn golden-yellow with HEAT TREATMENT to form CITRINE.

amorini Italian term often used for the winged cupids which were popular ornamental subjects during the RENAISSANCE and after.

They were a particular feature of the CRESTING and front STRETCHERS of chairs, cabinet stands and tables, and on ceramics 1660-80.

AMORINO *carved in wood, from a 17thC Spanish altar frieze.*

amphora Two-handled jar with a rounded body and narrow neck. Amphorae were used in ancient Greece, Rome and China for storing wine and oil. They re-emerged in an ornamental guise in 18thC Europe, particularly in NEOCLASSICAL silverware and as a decorative motif – on ANTWERP lace, for example.

AMPHORA *of the type used in ancient Greece for storing wine and oil.*

ampulla A two-handled container used for wine or water in ancient Rome, and since as a decorative vessel; a small version of an amphora.

Anatolia Major area of Turkey that is part of the Asian continent, as opposed to Thrace, which is on the European mainland, often referred to in the context of carpets.

andirons The precursors to fire grates, consisting of a pair of metal fire irons placed at either side of an open hearth to support burning logs. In the late 17th and early 18th centuries, coal-burning stoves largely replaced andirons except in country areas. With the grates of the 19thC, a shortened form of andirons made a comeback as purely decorative features or to support long-handled FIRE IRONS. Andirons are also known as **firedogs**, as 16thC examples (now rare) were often cast in the shape of seated hounds. Versions with many feet are called **firecats**, because if dropped they always land, catlike, on their feet. See p.368.

ANDIRONS *made of cast iron for an inglenook fireplace; mid-19thC; 24 in (61 cm) long.*

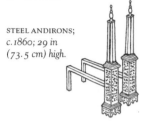

STEEL ANDIRONS; *c.1860; 29 in (73.5 cm) high.*

anemometer Instrument for measuring wind force. See p.291.

aneroid barometer A barometer introduced to the domestic market, c.1850, which uses disc-like, flexible metal bellows containing a partial vacuum, instead of a column of mercury, to measure changes in air pressure. The term aneroid is derived from a Greek word meaning 'liquid-free'. As the air pressure changes, the movement of the bellows is enlarged by being linked to a pointer set against a dial. See pp.290-1.

angel HAMMERED gold coin current 15th-17thC which depicts St Michael spearing a dragon. Angels were first issued in Britain in the 1460s to replace the NOBLE, with a face value of a third of a pound (6s 8d or 33⅓p). Later angels were revalued at up to 11s (55p), and were sometimes pierced for use as TOUCHPIECES.

Angell, Joseph, II (*c.*1816-91) British silversmith who exhibited at the 1851 Great Exhibition (see p.57). His claret jugs, table centrepieces, tea and coffee sets are elaborate in style with ornately chased relief work, Rococo scrolls and **JA** ENAMELLED decoration.

angle barometer Barometer in which the upper part of the mercury tube is nearly horizontal. In this form, the visible movement of the mercury is spread over a longer scale than in a STICK BAROMETER, and readings are clearer. Angle barometers, also known as **signpost** or **diagonal barometers**, were introduced in the early 18thC. See p.290.

angle chair See CORNER CHAIR.

Anglo-Indian furniture Furniture made on the Indian subcontinent, from the mid-18thC onwards, to European designs and often inlaid with ivory. Most of the work was for colonial administrators and their families, although aristocratic Indians were also commissioning it by the early 19thC. Production continued until the end of the 19thC.

Angoulême sprig Porcelain decoration used at a Paris factory owned by Louis, Duke of Angoulême in the 18th and 19th centuries. It was a feature of CHANTILLY porcelain in the 18thC, and copied at DERBY, WORCESTER and LOWESTOFT in the 18th and 19th centuries. It is also known as a **barbeau** (French for 'cornflower').

an hua Chinese for 'secret decoration'. The description refers to a delicate design incised or scored on a porcelain body before glazing and only visible when the finished piece is held against the light. It occurs rarely in the MING DYNASTY from the early 15thC and QING DYNASTY porcelain of the Yongzheng emperor's reign (1723-35).

aniline dyes Chemical dyes for carpets and other fabrics, introduced c.1870. They tended to run or fade and were replaced by colour-fast CHROME DYES in the early 20thC.

animal furniture Late Victorian craze for articles made from or fashioned around birds and animals fresh from the taxidermist. Examples included hollowed-out elephant feet used as liqueur stands, lamp bases of stuffed birds, and tiger-skin chairs, complete with paws and head, or supported on giraffe or zebra legs.

Animaliers, Les 19thC French sculptors of small, lifelike models of wild and domestic birds and animals, usually in bronze. See p.330.

animal interlace A decorative ornament or motif often seen in CELTIC STYLE work representing intertwined elongated and stylised animal forms.

annealing Process of strengthening glass or metal objects during manufacture by a controlled and gradual reheating and cooling. This avoids the build-up of internal stress that could lead to cracking.

annulet 1 In architecture and cabinet-making, a flat, narrow band encircling a COLUMN. 2 In heraldry, a small circle or ring in coats of arms.

anthemion Stylised honeysuckle motif. See DECORATIVE MOTIFS.

antimacassar Piece of loose material draped over an upholstered chair back to protect it from stains from the user's head. The term comes from macassar oil, a common hair dressing for men in the 19thC. Victorian antimacassars were commonly of white crochet; they were preceded in the 18thC by silk versions that guarded against the powdered wigs and greasy make-up of the Georgians.

antimagnetic watch Watch in which mechanism is made of materials that are unaffected by magnetic fields (which cause inaccuracies). Gold and palladium, for example, were used in CHRONOMETERS from the late 18thC, and palladium alloys and nickel steel have been used since then.

antimony Metallic element with hardening properties, used in a range of alloys, including pewter.

antique Object valued for its age, workmanship, beauty or rarity. Generally only objects that are more than 100 years old.

Antwerp Centre of tapestry, lace-making and pottery in the Netherlands (since 1832, Belgium). The **Antwerp tapestry** industry reached its peak in the 17thC, with designs reminiscent of the paintings of Rubens. **Antwerp pottery** produced TIN-GLAZED EARTHENWARE in the 16thC and work inspired by Italian MAIOLICA in the latter part of the century. Its importance declined with the establishment of DELFT.

Ao See KUTANI

aogai Japanese mother-of-pearl decoration introduced c.1620 on lacquered articles. The use of the blue-green inside of the abalone (*aogai* in Japanese) was introduced to Japan from China, where it was used during the late Ming dynasty (1368-1644). In the 18thC, the Japanese Somada school originated a type of mosaic work using fine slivers of aogai, a style that was extensively copied throughout the 19thC.

Apostelhumpen See HUMPEN.

apostle spoons Spoons traditionally made in sets of 13, the handles topped with figures of Christ and his 12 apostles. The figures are identified by different emblems held in the right hand. Usually in silver, but sometimes in pewter or brass, the earliest known part of a set dates from c.1460. The spoons were made throughout Europe,

and were popular, either singly or in sets, as christening presents in the 16th and 17th centuries. In 19thC Britain, coffee spoons, usually all depicting the same apostle, were mass-produced. See p.258.

apple Very hard, reddish-brown fruitwood with an irregular grain. Like other fruitwoods, it is particularly suited to TURNING. It has mostly been used for the legs, stretchers and spindles of country-made chairs and tables, especially in the 17th and 18th centuries, and by 20thC artist-craftsmen. From the 17thC, applewood was often stained black (ebonised) or gilded and used for applied carvings, INLAID DECORATION and picture frames.

applied decoration Surface ornament made, modelled or carved and then fixed to the body of an item.

apron Lower front edge of a piece of furniture, beneath the surface of a table, or seat of a CHAIR, for example.

aquamarine Blue to green variety of the gemstone BERYL. Greenish aquamarines were fashionable in the 19thC, but since the 1920s sky-blue stones have been popular, produced mainly by HEAT TREATMENT.

aquatint PRINT made by an etching process invented in the 1760s that enables several tones of varying intensity to be produced. Tiny particles of resin are dusted onto the metal printing plate and fused on by heat. Areas not to be printed are coated with a special varnish. The plate is exposed to acid which bites into the exposed metal, producing tonal areas like those of an ink or wash drawing when printed. See p.332.

Æ Abbreviation of the Latin word *argentum* (silver), used in coin catalogues; it is also seen as **ar** or **AR**.

arabesque Interwoven, symmetrical patterns of branches, tendrils and scrolls. It is a familiar motif in Islamic and HISPANO-MORESQUE designs, and throughout Europe c.1760-90. See DECORATIVE MOTIFS.

arbalest See CROSSBOW.

arbor A shaft, axle or spindle carrying a wheel and PINION in a clock, watch or music-box mechanism. See TRAIN.

Arcadian Stoke-on-Trent pottery producing CRESTED WARE in the 19th and 20th centuries including militaria and animals, particularly black cats in various poses.

arcading Decoration composed of a series of rounded arches often found on furniture backs and panels of the late 16th and 17th centuries.

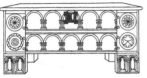

ARCADING *on a medieval walnut chest. The two rows of Romanesque arches are incised into the wood.*

architect's table 18thC table used by artists, architects and draughtsmen, the top of which tilts on a ratchet to make a drawing board. See pp.122-3.

architectural style General term for furniture and clock cases, bearing architectural features, for example, COLUMNS and PEDIMENTS.

architrave Term describing the moulded frame around doorways, windows and panelling in furniture.

argand lamp Oil lamp invented in Geneva *c.*1782 and widely made in the USA and Europe. From 1810 argand lamps were fitted with an adjustable burner.

ARGAND LAMP *made of Sheffield plate with plain glass shades; c.1790; 27 in (68.5 cm) high. The oil for burning is gravity-fed from the vase-shaped reservoir.*

argentan See NICKEL SILVER.

argentan lace A form of French needlepoint lace, typically showing flowers on a hexagonal background and first made in the late 17thC.

Argyle A late 18thC gravy container, also spelt **argyll**, usually of silver or Sheffield plate and said to have been designed by the Duke of Argyll. Gravy in an inner vessel is kept warm by hot water in an outer cavity. See p.158.

ARGYLE *The opening to the outer cavity is on the handle; 4¹/₂ in (11.4 cm) high.*

Ariel glass Type of ART GLASS developed in Sweden *c.*1936. It contains trapped bubbles or channels of air. Patterns are sandblasted into a glass core, which is then encased in another layer of glass, thus trapping channels of air where the pattern has been cut away.

Arita Japanese ceramics centre from the early 17thC, the home of IMARI and KAKIEMON porcelain.

ark A chest (made by an arkwright) typically made of oak, with a canted lid. Arks were used for storing flour or meal, especially in the north of England, until the 19thC.

ARK *held together with wedges and pegs – no iron was used as it would taint the flour; 38 in (96.5 cm) high.*

armada chest An iron-bound strongbox for storing valuables in the 16th and 17th centuries, often with a large, complicated lock on the underside of the lid. Some were for the use of officers at sea, and would have been bolted to the deck of the owner's cabin. Usually of German make, the chests could be anything from a few inches to 6ft (1.8 m) long. The name itself was a fanciful Victorian invention recalling chests imagined to be used by the Spanish Armada.

ARMADA CHEST *with strengthening iron straps and a lid stay; mid-17thC; 30 in (76 cm) long. The spike gives extra leverage on the key.*

armchair Any single chair with arms, as distinct from a SIDE CHAIR or a CORNER CHAIR. See p.101.

armet Medieval helmet enclosing the head and with a pivoted visor.

armillary sphere A scientific globe used for teaching astronomy and cosmography from *c.*1500 onwards. 16thC examples show the movements of the planets in the solar system, and were often made in pairs; one showed the Ptolemaic (Earth-centred) universe, the other the Copernican (Sun-centred) universe.

armoire French name for a large, plain cupboard or PRESS, from the 16thC onwards. An armoire usually has two doors, and sometimes one or two shelves inside. The German version of an armoire is known as a **kas**. See p.140.

armorial The term used to describe a coat of arms. Armorial is also used to describe designs in which heraldic motifs are prominent. CHINESE EXPORT PORCELAIN dinner services decorated with family crests or armorials were commissioned by the European aristocracy in the 17th and 18th centuries, and are known as **armorial porcelain**.

Arnold, John (1736-99) British clock and watchmaker, noted for his work on pocket and marine CHRONOMETERS and precision watches.

Arnold made highly accurate REGULATOR clocks for the Royal Observatory at Greenwich. From 1787, Arnold was in partnership with his son John (*d.*1843), who continued the business after his father's death. The firm was subsequently run by Edward Dent (1830-40), and three years later by Charles Frodsham, a leading marine chronometer-maker.

Arras French 13th-16thC TAPESTRY centre from which the word 'arras' – used generally for a high-quality wall-hanging or tapestry – is derived. Arras porcelain factory produced noted tableware, 1770-90, and Arras lace, pure white and gold, was sought after in the 17th to 19th centuries.

Art Deco Style affecting all forms of design from the mid-1920s to the 30s. The name comes from the French *arts décoratifs* (decorative arts), following the Paris EXPOSITION DES ARTS DÉCORATIFS in 1925. See pp.71-74.

Art furniture Part of the eclectic, mid to late 19thC British and US AESTHETIC MOVEMENT. Art furniture rejected earlier Victorian opulence and comfort in favour of simpler shapes showing Japanese influence. The movement's name, first coined by designer Charles EASTLAKE, was taken from that of the Art Furniture Company, which manufactured pieces by architect William GODWIN.

Early pieces were often made from black woods such as black walnut, but satinwood and mahogany were later used. Turned legs and supports and minimal decoration (usually shallow

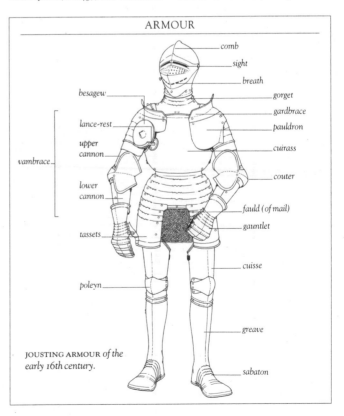

ARMOUR

comb
sight
breath
gorget
gardbrace
pauldron
cuirass
couter
fauld (of mail)
gauntlet
cuisse
greave
sabaton

besagew
lance-rest
upper cannon
vambrace
lower cannon
tassets
poleyn

JOUSTING ARMOUR *of the early 16th century.*

carving of incised lines heightened with gilding) were typical. Designers who influenced or were associated with the movement include Bruce TALBERT, Charles VOYSEY, Robert EDIS, Charles Eastlake, William BURGES and Christopher DRESSER.

art glass A general term for late 19th and early 20thC glassware produced principally for decorative effect, and including AGATE, ALEXANDRITE and TORTOISESHELL GLASS. See p.221.

Art Nouveau Decorative arts style distinguished by curves and flowing lines, asymmetry and flower and leaf motifs, prevalent from the 1880s to the First World War. See p.70.

Arts and Crafts movement The work of British artist-craftsmen in the late 19th and early 20th centuries who rejected machine-made goods in favour of those made by hand. The rather purist attitudes of its followers and the high cost of their products led to the decline of the movement in Britain after 1900. Its influence was apparent in the USA until the First World War, and also in continental Europe, especially Scandinavia and Austria. See p.64.

ash A tough, springy, whitish-grey wood native to Britain. Readily available and inexpensive, the solid wood was much used in making country furniture in the 18th and 19th centuries. As a veneer, it is found on some Georgian furniture, and ash BURRS are sometimes seen in CABINET work. Ash is still traditionally used for BENTWOOD chairs.

Ashbee, Charles Robert (1863-1942) British architect, designer and writer who became a leading light in the ARTS AND CRAFTS MOVEMENT. He designed furniture – a lighter version of the movement's country style – and ART NOUVEAU-style silver and metal ware. He founded a school of arts and handicrafts in London which later moved to the Cotswolds. Ashbee later recognised the inevitable role and advantages of machinery in 20thC arts and crafts, but his early work played a significant part in breaking away from Victorian traditions. See p.64.

asmalyk Rectangular, five-sided or seven-sided weavings made by Turkoman nomads and designed to hang on camels' flanks.

asparagus tongs Scissor-action or pressure-grip 18thC tongs, often of ornamented silver or SHEFFIELD PLATE, for serving asparagus. They are also known as **chop tongs** as they could be used for serving meat. Usually, the

lower jaw is serrated and has an upturned end, and a clip holds the jaws together when not in use. **Asparagus eaters**, like small sugar tongs, were introduced in the 20thC.

aspidistra stand Three or four-legged wooden, wickerwork or ceramic plant stand for holding a flowerpot. The stands were fashionable in the late 19thC, when aspidistras were popular plants; they are sometimes known as JARDINIÈRE stands.

Asprey London retail company, founded in 1781, producing and dealing in gold and silver, jewellery and other luxury items. It was particularly known for elaborate vanity cases containing bottles and mirrors mounted in chased silver and gold. The firm, based in New Bond Street, is still run by the family.

assay 1 The testing of metals for purity of gold or silver content, carried out by an assay office or an institution such as a guild, according to standards set by government. In Britain there are currently four active assay offices: London, Birmingham, Sheffield and Edinburgh, each with its own distinctive hallmark.
2 The term is also used to describe a sample piece of work by a craftsman on registration with a guild. See HALLMARK; STERLING STANDARD.

Astbury ware Lead-glazed earthenware made by John Astbury (1686-1743) and his contemporaries c.1730-70, in Staffordshire, and later Yorkshire. Relief decoration was SPRIGGED onto a red or brown body, then covered with thick honey-brown, green or yellow GLAZES. Models of horses and riders, figure jugs of sailors and musicians, and useful wares were produced. Astbury is also credited with the addition of ground flint and white Devonshire clay to Staffordshire earthenware, which improved its colour and plasticity.
Thomas WHIELDON was an apprentice of Astbury's. **Astbury-Whieldon ware** is Astbury-style pottery with Whieldon's coloured lead glazes. Typical articles have relief decoration in clays that contrast with the main body, and lead glazes stained with metallic oxides. See p.175.

astragal Small, semicircular beading or MOULDING used on the glazing bars of glass-cabinet doors.

astrolabe A circular instrument with a movable arm for calculating the altitude of the sun and plotting the position of the stars, for astronomical and navigational purposes. Astrolabes were used from the 2nd century, and

although obsolete in Europe by the 18thC, forgeries continued to be made in the Middle East. See p.296.

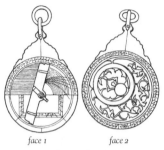

ASTROLABE *showing both faces; Islamic; late 18thC; 2½ in (63 mm) across.*

astronomical dial Clock or watch dial that shows the movement of the sun, moon, planets and stars as well as telling the time.

athénienne A multipurpose lidded urn, set on a highly ornamented, three-legged stand. Invented by the Frenchman J.H. Eberts in 1773, it could be used as a plant or washstand, perfume burner or candelabra.

atlas 1 Any volume or book of tables, charts, maps or plates that systematically illustrates a subject.
2 The singular of **atlantes**, male figures used as columns in architecture or furniture (see CARYATID).

atmos clock A clock in which the movement is wound by changes in atmospheric pressure. The clock was devised by J.E. Reutter in 1928 and manufactured by the Swiss firm of Jaeger-le-Coultre.

Aubusson Town in central France famous for its carpets and fabrics since the 16thC. Aubusson tapestry-woven carpets in LOUIS XVI and EMPIRE styles were widely used in the late 18th and 19th centuries. Aubusson tapestries with scenes from the fables of La Fontaine and contemporary prints were popular in the 18thC. Interest was revived this century with designs from artists such as Raoul Dufy and Graham Sutherland. See p.306.

Ault Pottery British art pottery founded by William Ault at Swadlincote, Derbyshire, in 1887. It produced ornamental earthenware, sometimes with AVENTURINE glazes, including articles designed by Christopher DRESSER.

aumbry A simple cupboard dating from medieval times. Originally the aumbry, **ambry** or **almery** consisted of a recessed shelved area in a wall enclosed by wooden doors, and later developed into a freestanding

cupboard for storing food, with pierced ventilation holes in the doors, which was used until the 16thC.

Ʌ Abbreviation for the Latin *aurum* (gold), commonly used in coin catalogues; it is sometimes seen as **av** and **AV**.

automata Mechanical figures of varying sizes animated by clockwork, and later by battery, and in the 18th and 19th centuries produced mainly by clock-makers. Automata were created for display and for adults. They were often elaborately dressed and capable of detailed movements such as drinking or smoking, or depicted an animated scene with birds or figures. In the late 19thC, automata were largely replaced by mass-produced, mechanical toys aimed at the children's market. See p.345.

autoperipatetikos Smooth-moving walking doll patented in the USA and Europe in 1862. It has brass leg casings shaped like boots and the walking movement is made by a rotating curved bar concealed within the legs or appearing beneath the feet.
The name is derived from the Greek for 'self-propelling'.

aventurine 1 Translucent glass containing metallic specks. The name comes from *avventurina*, Italian for the brown quartz (also known as 'goldstone') that the first form of the glass resembled. This 'gold aventurine', developed in the early 17thC, owed its appearance to copper oxide used in its manufacture. The addition of chromium in the 1860s led to **green aventurine**, while chrome and tin combined led to **pink aventurine**. Other processes for producing these colours were subsequently developed in France and the USA.
2 A term also used to describe a LACQUER or GLAZE of the same speckled appearance as aventurine glass. It may be applied to wood or pottery. See also NASHIJI.
3 The name sometimes given to the minute clippings of gold wire sprinkled over furniture in the process of JAPANNING.

Axminster carpets 1 Hand-knotted carpets made for the luxury market in the 18th and 19th centuries at the Axminster Carpet Factory in Devon. The factory, founded in 1750 by two French HUGUENOT refugees from the SAVONNERIE FACTORY, was merged with WILTON Carpet Factory in 1835.
2 Mechanically woven, double-wefted carpets made at the Wilton factory following its takeover of Axminster, and copied at KIDDERMINSTER. See also MOORFIELDS, FULHAM, CHENILLE.

Ayrshire work Type of CUTWORK embroidery on white muslin which hails from the Scottish county of Ayrshire. The work was most widely used during the mid-19thC for christening robes, women's collars, cuffs and caps. See p.313.

B

Baccarat Leading French glassworks founded in 1764. Its first products were SODA GLASS tableware and window glass. From 1816 it began to produce high-quality lead crystal and decorative glassware. It is especially noted for its MILLEFIORI paperweights and SULPHIDES, which became popular in the mid-19thC and remain highly collectable to this day.

Bacchus, George, & Sons Birmingham glassworks founded in the early 19thC that produced some of the first PRESSED GLASS in Britain. Its high-quality CASED GLASS wares were shown at the Great Exhibition of 1851. The works also specialised in CUT, ENGRAVED and coloured tableware, and paperweights.

bachelor's chest A low, compact chest of drawers made during the first half of the 18thC, with a top that folds out to form a table. A **bachelor's table** has compartments for dressing and shaving equipment and surfaces for playing cards or writing.

BACHELOR'S CHEST; c.1725; 29 in (73.5 cm) high. The top is supported by the pull-out lopers.

back board The wooden backing to an item of CASE FURNITURE or a framed mirror. Good-quality 18th and early 19thC furniture usually has panelled back boards. From the late 19thC, PLYWOOD became more common.

back plate Hindmost member of the pair of metal plates which holds the mechanism of a clock in place, sometimes engraved with decorative motifs and/or the maker's name.

back screen An article, usually of woven cane, which was clipped to the back of a dining chair to shield its user against the heat of a fire, introduced in the early 19thC.

backstaff Navigational instrument with rods supporting two scaled arcs, invented by Englishman John Davis in 1594. It was the precursor of the 18thC OCTANT. The observer stood with back to the sun and aligned one scale on the horizon, the other on the shadow cast by its sighting piece. The two scale readings added together gave the sun's height and thus the latitude could be calculated.

backstamp Term used by commercial potteries for the mark printed on the underside of their wares.

backstool An early form of armless chair introduced in the late 16thC. It is a three or four-legged stool with a back extending from the rear legs. At the time, the word 'chair' only applied to seats with arms, and it was not until the early 18thC that the backstool became known as a **single** or a SIDE CHAIR. See pp.17, 96.

bacon cupboard A type of SETTLE, made up of a long bench with a panelled cupboard doubling as a backrest, and often drawers set beneath the seat. It was a familiar item of farmhouse furniture from the Middle Ages to the 19thC.

BADA British Antique Dealers' Association, an organisation of antique shops and individual dealers, formed to maintain standards within the trade.

BADA LOGO The 16thC Italian goldsmith and sculptor Benvenuto Cellini.

baff The Farsi word for 'knot' in the context of carpets. **Armeni-baff** are knotted by Armenians; **bibi-baff** are, strictly speaking, very finely woven rugs knotted by a *bibi* (princess) of the Bakhtiari nomads of central Persia, but came to be used to describe any finely knotted Bakhtiari rug.

baguette See JEWEL CUTTING.

bail handle A simple, curved metal handle, as in a semicircular drawer pull, or the handle of a kettle.

Baillie Scott, Mackay Hugh (1865-1945) British architect of international repute, who also designed plainly shaped furniture decorated with colourful INLAID work and metalwork, in the style of the ARTS AND CRAFTS MOVEMENT.

Bain, Alexander (c.1811-77) Scottish clock-maker and scientist who patented the first ELECTRIC CLOCK in 1840.

baize Loose-woven, woollen material, usually dyed green or red and used from the 17thC to describe a flannel-like cloth produced in the eastern counties of England. It was used for covering card and billiard tables, and for lining drawers.

Bakelite A durable, opaque, easily dyed PLASTIC patented by Leo Baekland in 1907. It is a 'thermosetting' plastic – the ingredients heated under pressure in a mould, resulting in a very hard, heat-resistant material. Bakelite was used for cheap ART DECO jewellery – in the form of imitation amber or jet buckles, for example – ornaments and numerous other articles, from ashtrays to radio cabinets. See p.76.

balance A wheel in a clock or watch that regulates the action of the ESCAPEMENT mechanism and thus of the timepiece itself. Its effect was erratic before the invention c.1675 of the **balance spring**. This uses a spiral hairspring to make the movement of the balance wheel more regular and ISOCHRONOUS; it was as significant a development in the field of portable clocks and watches as the PENDULUM was for standing clocks. However, the elasticity of the spring is very susceptible to heat and cold, making a spring balance less accurate than a pendulum. The problem was overcome by the development of various forms of compensation balance from the mid-18thC, especially in association with the development of CHRONOMETERS.

baldric Sword belt, usually of leather, which is worn over the shoulder and diagonally across the chest.

ball clock See GRAVITY CLOCK.

ball foot See FEET.

balloon clock See BRACKET CLOCK.

ball turning A series of turned wooden spheres of equal size used as ornamentation on the legs and horizontal STRETCHERS of chair and table legs, mid-17th to early 18th centuries. See TURNING.

Baillie Scott, Mackay Hugh (1865-1945) British architect of international repute, who also designed plainly shaped furniture decorated with colourful INLAID work and metalwork, in the style of the ARTS AND CRAFTS MOVEMENT.

baluster A turned column or post, usually one of many supporting a rail to form a **balustrade**. The shape is seen in table legs and chair backs, drinking-glass stems and silverware.

BALUSTER shapes like these originated in architecture but have been adapted to many different materials.

bamboo furniture Furniture made either from, or in imitation of, bamboo. It was popular during the vogue for CHINOISERIE in the late 18th and early 19th centuries, usually crafted in strong woods such as beech and then turned, carved and painted to imitate real bamboo.

A late Victorian craze for genuine bamboo furniture resulted in an abundance of rather fragile tables, bookcases, chairs, WHATNOTS and pot stands; in the USA at the same time, sturdier simulated forms were fashionable.

banding A decorative, INLAID or VENEER strip, in contrasting wood or sometimes metal. Banding may by used as a border on a door panel, table top or drawer front. **Straight banding** is cut along the grain of the wood; **cross banding** is cut across the grain; **feather banding** or **herringbone banding** is formed of two narrow pieces of veneer laid at an angle to each other to give a chevron effect.

Very fine banding is known as **stringing** or **line inlay**.

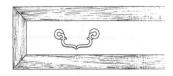

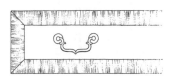

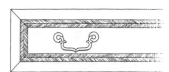

BANDING (top) straight banding; (centre) cross banding; (bottom) herringbone or feather banding.

banjo barometer See WHEEL BAROMETER.

banjo clock Pendulum WALL CLOCK resembling an upturned banjo, introduced by the Willard family of clock-makers in Boston, USA. Many reproductions were made in the late 19th to mid-20th centuries. See also GIRANDOLE. See p.281.

Bank of England dollar Silver coin struck for a few years at the beginning of the 19thC. Circulating examples, also known as **bank tokens**, were all dated 1804, inscribed with the word 'dollar' beneath an image of Britannia on the reverse, and had a face value of 5s (25p). The 3s and 1s 6d denominations were struck in 1811. The entire coinage was made obsolete in 1816.

Banko ware Pottery made by, or in the style of, Japanese 18thC potter Numanami Shigenaga. The wares are typically decorated with human figures, monkeys or other animals picked out in enamels or glazes with touches of UNDERGLAZE blue. The style was revived in the 19thC. Most common are enamelled grey stoneware teawares, often in the form of a lotus or other flower. See p.176.

Banko seal

banner screen See POLE SCREEN.

bantam work See LACQUER.

bar back See CHAIR.

barbeau See ANGOULEME SPRIG.

barber's bowl Shaving dish, usually ceramic but also silver or other metal, used by barbers in the 17th, 18th and 19th centuries. A semicircular section cut out of the rim fitted beneath a client's chin. This could also be placed around an arm and used as a **bleeding bowl** for blood-letting (surgery being one of the barber's major functions until the 19thC). See p.203.

BARBER'S BOWL *of creamware; c.1775-80; 12 in (30.5 cm) across.*

Barcelona chair See MIES VAN DER ROHE, Ludwig.

barefaced tenon See JOINING.

bargello Embroidery design in which the colours, usually worked in pointed or flame-shaped patterns, graduate through their various shades. It is also known as **flame stitch**, **Florentine stitch** and **Hungarian stitch**.

barge ware A dark brown, glazed EARTHENWARE with white clay relief patterns, produced in Derbyshire, c.1860-1910. Motifs of birds and flowers were tinted green, blue and pink. Practical containers such as large teapots (with a miniature teapot FINIAL), jugs and chamber pots were the main lines. It was sold at Measham, Leicestershire, on the banks of the Ashby-de-la-Zouch canal, and is also known as **bargee** or **Measham ware**.

bargueño See VARGUEÑO.

barion cut See JEWEL CUTTING.

barley-sugar twist See TURNING.

Barnack, Oscar (1879-1936) German microscope designer and inventor of the Leica camera, launched in 1925 by German company, Leitz. The Leica was the first miniature precision camera of its kind. See p.295.

barograph A type of ANEROID BAROMETER that records air pressure, introduced in the 18thC. The aneroid mechanism moves a pen against a slowly turning drum on which graph paper is mounted. See p.291.

barometer Instrument for registering atmospheric pressure and forecasting weather conditions, first made in the late 17thC. See ANEROID, ANGLE, FITZROY, STICK and WHEEL BAROMETERS, and also p.290.

baroque pearls Pearls of irregular shape that were widely used in BAROQUE and RENAISSANCE jewellery of the 15th to 17th centuries. The pearls were often decorated with gemstones or enamelling to take the form of mythological figures.

Baroque style An extravagant and heavily ornate style born from the architecture of 17thC Italy. For the first time, sculptors played a crucial role in the design of furniture, ceramics, ivory and silver, joining forces with gilders and earning recognition as craftsmen in their own right rather than as the employees of joiners and CABINET-MAKERS. Their influence was evident in elaborate, rather architectural furniture and in the abundance of cupids, cornucopias,

and other such decoration set in symmetrical, curvaceous designs.

The style dominated the decorative arts throughout Europe in the late 17th and early 18th centuries, and in a less elaborate form in the USA during the first half of the 18thC. It paved the way for the lighter, more frivolous and colourful Rococo style. See p.22.

barrel A hollow, cylindrical metal box or drum in a clock or watch that contains the driving or going spring and is connected to the first wheel in the TRAIN. The casing has, from c.1580-1600, almost universally been of brass. A **going barrel** has the first wheel of the train mounted on the same ARBOR, thus dispensing with the two-part FUSEE. It was used for the striking trains of 17thC German Renaissance clocks and for both going and striking trains of French spring-driven clocks from c.1680, as it gives adequate timekeeping for most domestic purposes.

Barr, Flight & Barr See WORCESTER.

Bartoluzzi, Francesco (1727-1815) Pioneer of the process of stipple ENGRAVING and owner of a large print works in London in the 18thC. He produced society portraits and domestic and rural scenes. See p.176.

Barum ware Earthenware pottery made in Barnstaple, North Devon, and popular from c.1879 until the early 20thC. Specialities include simple jugs and vases with representations of birds, flowers, marine life or dragons painted in SLIP in soft colours, and sometimes with outlines incised. See p.171.

basal rim See FOOT-RIM.

basaltes ware A very hard and fine-grained black STONEWARE made by a number of Staffordshire potters and improved by WEDGWOOD c.1768. It found a ready market as a relatively cheap medium for reproducing, in ceramic form, the Classical bronzes and cameos which were popular in the late 18thC. Products included vases (some examples are bronze-glazed), large busts, medallions and domestic pots. See p.168.

bas d'armoire French term for a low 18thC chest with double doors enclosing cupboards and drawers.

base metals The term for all non-precious metals including copper, lead, iron and tin, and their alloys such as brass, pewter, bronze and nickel silver.

basin stand See WASHSTAND.

basket glass Glass container in the shape of a basket, for sweets or fruit. OPENWORK sides, attached to a moulded base, are made from pieces or threads of glass pincered together.

Baskerville, John (1706-75) Although best known as a typographer, Baskerville was also a key manufacturer of JAPANNED metalware. He was based in Birmingham and is credited with introducing polychrome painting on japanned bases.

basket-top clock A BRACKET CLOCK with either a REPOUSSÉ metal dome or a cushion-moulded (flat-topped with curved edges) wood dome. See p.282.

basketwork A generic term for chairs and other furniture made of wicker, cane, or woven, coarse sea grass. **Wickerwork** furniture, in which the basket weave is worked around a frame of stiff rods, was popular in Victorian times for use both indoors and outside, and ranged from round-seated single chairs to lounge chairs with foot-rest extensions. See also LLOYD LOOM.

bas relief See RELIEF.

basse-taille See ENAMELLING.

bassine-cased watch Shallow, circular pocket watch dating from the mid-17thC, with a rounded cover and back which curves gently into the central band. The case is often finely decorated with ENAMEL.

bassinet A hooded wickerwork basket used as a cradle, and later used to describe late 19thC baby carriages with a hooded basketwork body.

Batavian ware Early 18thC CHINESE EXPORT PORCELAIN named after the Dutch East India Company trading station at Batavia (now Jakarta), Java. It is typically in the form of tea services decorated with blue and white, often fan-shaped panels, and with a coffee-brown glaze on the outer side of bowls and saucers. Copies of the style made at MEISSEN in Germany and LEEDS, England, were also known as Batavian and Kapuziner ware.

Bateman family London family of silversmiths producing domestic silverware in the 18th and 19th centuries. Hester Bateman (1708-94), the best-known member, was trained by her husband John, and on his death carried on the business with her sons. A vast amount of domestic silver marked by its grace of line and simplicity of decoration was produced with her mark, including tableware, snuffboxes, seals and wine labels. Hester retired in 1790, and her sons Peter and Jonathan, and Jonathan's wife, Ann carried on the firm. The change in management was marked by substituting a thread decoration for Hester's beading. Ann Bateman's son William took the business – and the style of Bateman silver – into the Victorian era.

Bath metal An inexpensive bronze-like alloy used by some independent 18thC coiners (as opposed to the Royal Mint) and from the late 18thC for small boxes and buttons.

batik Distinctively patterned and dyed fabric from the East Indies, brought to Europe by the Dutch in the 16thC. In the batik process, melted wax is applied to parts of the design not intended to take colour, and the cloth is then dyed. This is repeated as necessary for other colours, the wax being washed out with hot water after each dyeing. Some batik is also hand-painted. The process was used in 16th and 17thC Europe for dyeing expensive fabrics such as velvet, but the bold batik colours and patterns were printed on cotton and dyed by other processes from the 19thC.

bat-printing See TRANSFER-PRINTING.

Battersea ENAMEL factory based in Battersea, London, specialising in items such as snuffboxes, plaques, wine labels, and watch and toothpick cases. Early porcelain boxes made at CHELSEA had Battersea enamel lids. Designs were often transfer-printed onto a white enamel ground, then painted in delicate colours. The factory, run by John Brooks, pioneer of the TRANSFER-PRINTING process, only lasted three years (1753-6) but its influence lived on in enamelware produced in South Staffordshire and Birmingham.

Bauhaus A German school of design founded in Weimar in 1919 by Walter Gropius, an architect-designer. The Bauhaus aimed to produce prototype designs for everyday, mass-produced items. It explored the manufacturing processes and new materials of the 'machine age' such as stainless steel and plastics, and coordinated the skills of architects, engineers, painters, sculptors and designers. The school was closed by the Nazis in 1933, but revived in the German city of Ulm after the war, and inspired industrial design in the mid-20thC. See p.72.

baywood See MAHOGANY.

bead moulding See MOULDINGS.

beadwork A form of embroidering textiles using small, coloured glass beads with, or instead of, needlework. Beadwork was a popular covering for small boxes and mirror frames in late 16th and 17th-century Europe, particularly in Britain, and in the 19thC for chair covers, purses, pictures and other objects. See p.310.

beaker Drinking cup without handles or stem, and usually with a foot rim. Early beakers were made in wood, glass and pottery, although from the 11thC there were silver, silver-gilt and gold examples. British beakers are usually more plainly decorated than their continental counterparts. In the 18thC, glasses generally replaced beakers for table use. See p.247.

SILVER BEAKER; *late 17thC; 8 in (20.3 cm) high.*

bearskin Tall, military black fur hat, originally made from bear skin. It has been worn by British guardsmen since the 18thC, and is now part of their ceremonial dress.

Beauvais Centre for weaving in northern France. The Beauvais Tapestry Factory was founded in 1664, and ultimately amalgamated with GOBELINS in 1940. Typical Beauvais tapestries – in the form of wall-hangings, carpets and furniture covers – have COMMEDIA DELL'ARTE scenes or extracts from contemporary paintings, framed by heavily festooned drapes; Classical and CHINOISERIE motifs are also seen. They are brilliantly coloured, often with a dominant yellow ground known as 'Spanish tobacco'. From 1725, imitation Beauvais tapestries were made in Berlin. The 19thC brought specialisation in furniture covers.

Becker, Carl (*d.* 1830) Notorious German forger of ancient Greek coins, who operated in the early 19thC. Fortunately for modern collectors, his extensive repertoire of copies was exposed and published after his death.

bedstead The framework of a bed, which raises mattress and bedding material above floor level. Bedsteads

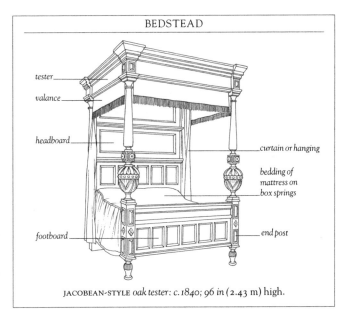

BEDSTEAD

tester
valance
headboard
curtain or hanging
bedding of mattress on box springs
footboard
end post

JACOBEAN-STYLE *oak tester: c.1840; 96 in (2.43 m) high.*

only became widespread in Europe from the early 17thC. Monument-like bedsteads with elaborately carved wooden canopies were made during the RENAISSANCE, the canopies designed to provide privacy, protection from draughts, dirt and insects. The emphasis shifted from woodwork to fabric hangings in the mid-17thC, and a host of different bed styles were introduced over the next century. 19thC bed designs tended to be more functional. See pp.138-9.

beech A pale, smooth and straight-grained wood, one of the most inexpensive hardwoods available. Beech was often stained and used as a substitute for walnut in country furniture, especially chairs, of the 17th and 18th centuries. It is also seen gilded or painted. Although subject to woodworm, beech has the advantage of taking close nailing without splitting. See p.100.

Behrens, Peter (1868-1940) German illustrator, architect, craftsman and designer of industrial and domestic fittings. Behrens's early furniture, ceramics, jewellery and glass designs were in ART NOUVEAU style, but by 1898 he was designing simple, stream-lined household objects for commercial production. He was a founder member of the DEUTSCHER WERKBUND, 1907, a group of German artists and manufacturers. LE CORBUSIER, Walter Gropius and Ludwig MIES VAN DER ROHE all worked under Behrens c.1910.

Beilby, William and **Mary** A brother and sister team of glass enamellers in the late 18thC. They decorated wine glasses and decanters with colourful

heraldic designs or rustic scenes with romantic ruins and creepers, usually in white enamel. See pp.213-14.

bellarmine Bulbous brown STONEWARE jug with a bearded head in low relief on the narrow neck, and frequently with relief coats of arms on the body. Bellarmines originated in 16thC Germany, the bearded head said to be that of Cardinal Roberto Bellarmino, a leader of the Counter Reformation much hated by German Protestants. Many bellarmines were exported to Britain (where they were also known as **greybeards**), and copied particularly at John DWIGHT's Fulham pottery in London. Reproductions were made in Germany until the late 19thC. See p.170.

Belleek A ceramics factory in County Fermanagh, Northern Ireland, founded in 1857. Its speciality was a delicate PARIAN porcelain. Wares are wholly or partly treated with a clear or pearlised, and sometimes iridescent, glaze. Belleek table and ornamental items are often decorated with or in the shape of shells and other marine life. Porcelain strips woven into baskets and perforated designs are also typical.

1863-91

belle époque French for 'fine period', generally used to describe an elaborate and sumptuous decorative arts style which was prevalent in Europe from the end of the 19thC up until World War I.

bell-metal A tough bronze alloy used for bells and occasionally for cooking utensils such as skillets.

Belter, John (1804-63) German-born US cabinet-maker, after whom **Belter furniture** (carved and upholstered bentwood suites) was named. Belter's revived Rococo style was very popular and he displaced cabinet-maker Duncan PHYFE as New York's leading craftsman. He patented a plywood process using rosewood which was then ornately carved.

BELTER SOFA of 'parlor furniture' type; c.1855; 78 in (1.98 m) long.

Benares brassware Indian-style brassware, including trays and table tops. The genuine articles were made in India, but imitations were produced in Birmingham from the late 19thC, and sometimes exported to India and imported back again to suggest authenticity.

bends The curved runners or rockers of a ROCKING CHAIR located between the back and front feet.

Benson, William (1854-1924) British architect and leading furniture and metalwork designer in the ARTS AND CRAFTS MOVEMENT.
Unlike the more purist members of the movement, Benson was not dismissive of mass-production methods, and his factory at Hammersmith, London, produced commercial domestic objects such as chandeliers, 1883-1923.

bent-limb doll Doll with limbs that are in one curved piece rather than jointed. The bent-limb style is normally reserved for baby dolls and was first introduced on COMPOSITION dolls in 1910, and on vinyl models from the late 1930s. See DOLLS.

bentwood Lightweight solid or laminated timber, usually birch, soaked in hot water or steamed to make it pliable so that it is easily worked into curves.
The technique was originally used for 18thC WINDSOR CHAIRS, but a distinctive style of bentwood furniture really became established in the mid-19thC with the work of the Austrian furniture-maker Michael THONET.
Thonet bentwood is strong, light, graceful and made from solid timber; it was soon seen in homes, cafés and hotels throughout Europe.
In the 20thC, designers such as Alvar AALTO, Marcel BREUER and others, widened the range of the bentwood styles, usually by using laminated timber. See p.99.

BENTWOOD CHAIR with woven cane seat, made by Thonet; c.1850.

Bérain, Jean (1637-1711) French draughtsman, engraver and designer, and one of the originators of the LOUIS XIV style. Bérain worked as court designer from 1674, and his published symmetrical designs influenced ornamentation on contemporary furniture, carpets and silverware. Mid-18thC Moustiers FAIENCE was very often decorated in a so-called **style Bérainesque**.

bergère French name for a deep, tub-shaped, upholstered armchair of the early 19thC, with continuous top and arm rails and a slightly concave back. Some versions are caned between the arms and seat and have a loose seat cushion. See p.103.

REGENCY BERGÈRE with sabre legs and leather upholstery.

Berlin German ceramics centre with FAIENCE factories from 1678, a minor porcelain factory founded 1751, and a factory established 1763 which was known mainly for the production of dinner services and figures in restrained Rococo style. In the 19thC this factory produced BLANKS which were sent to outside decorators for painting.

1763-70

KPM
1832-70

Berlin iron jewellery Early 19thC cast-iron jewellery made principally in Germany. People were given Berlin iron in exchange for their precious jewellery to boost the Prussian State gold reserves. Items such as brooches, necklaces and crosses in CLASSICAL or GOTHIC-style designs were typically crafted in delicate OPENWORK patterns and lacquered black. Production continued in Germany and Paris until the end of the 19thC.

Berlin woolwork Home-worked embroidery popular in the 19thC in Europe and the USA, using wool which was originally dyed in Berlin. German wool manufacturers marketed the wools by providing coloured pattern charts that could be easily transferred onto canvas. See p.310.

beryl A mineral that forms several varieties of gemstones, notably EMERALD and AQUAMARINE. The stone in its purest form is colourless, but impurities cause pale-coloured varieties of gems, including yellow, pink and green beryl.

bevel General term for any edge cut at an angle to a flat surface.

bezel 1 Metal rim or band set around the edge or inside the shutting edge of a container. 2 Rim or setting edge of a ring that holds the stone or ornament, often loosely applied to the whole setting. 3 Metal rim holding the glass of a watch or clock face.

bi Flat jade disc, also spelt **pi**, with a hole in the centre. It symbolised heaven and was used ritualistically in China until the end of the reign of the last emperor in 1912.

bianco-sopra-bianco Italian for 'white-on-white', referring to TIN-GLAZED EARTHENWARE with white-painted decoration introduced by the Italians on MAIOLICA in the 16thC. It is seen in mid to late 18thC Lambeth and Bristol DELFTWARE and Chinese and English porcelain. See p.154.

Bible box 17thC box, usually of oak, with a hinged lid. Bible boxes were designed to hold the family Bible or other books or writing materials. Some, designed to double as a lectern, have a sloping lid.

bidri Indian metalwork – copper, lead and tin alloy, blackened with a mixture of sal ammoniac and saltpetre, and INLAID with silver or brass. Bidri ware such as spice boxes and the bases for hookah pipes was imported from India in the 19thC.

Biedermeier A restrained NEOCLASSICAL decorative arts style originating in Germany in the early 19thC, which was most evident in furniture design. See p.142.

Biemann, Dominik (1800-57) Prominent BOHEMIAN glass engraver. He specialised in portraits but also engraved hunting scenes, landscapes and Old Master paintings. His work appears on glasses, beakers and medallions, usually signed with various spellings of his name (Bieman, Biman or Bimann).

biggin Late 18th and 19thC style of British coffee pot in silver or SHEFFIELD PLATE. The design is attributed to the London silversmith George Biggin (d.1803). The pots have a cylindrical or barrel-shaped body and a short spout with built-in filter for ground coffee; the handle is usually of hardwood, such as ebony, or ivory. Biggins were either warmed on a stand over a spirit lamp or placed on a fire hob. See p.251.

billet 1 A Romanesque (pre-GOTHIC) ornamental motif or moulding using alternating blocks or cylinders. 2 The THUMBPIECE on tankards and flagons.

Billies and Charlies 19thC forgeries of medieval amulets, pilgrim badges, figures and seals. Many were cast by William Smith and Charles Eaton of London – hence the name. The men claimed to have found the objects in the Thames' riverbed. The forgeries were often made in poor-quality pewter with relief decoration.

Billingsley, William See DERBY; SWANSEA.

Bilston enamels Articles of jewellery and OBJECTS OF VERTU made in Bilston and other parts of Staffordshire in the 18th and early 19th centuries. Most enamelled objects made in Britain at this time, including boxes, scent bottles and candlesticks, came from the Bilston area. Some incorporated small ENAMEL plaques, others were coated in white enamel and then painted with motifs of landscapes, flowers and birds. See p.260.

birch A native timber of northern Europe, creamy in colour, tinged with pink or yellow, and with a fine, even, wavy grain. It has been used mainly as a solid wood for chairs and country furniture, especially in the 18thC, and is seen in BIEDERMEIER furniture. Selected pieces were occasionally used as a cheap substitute for SATINWOOD. In the 19thC cheap birch furniture was mass-produced, and after the invention of the rotary cutting lathe in 1890, it was common as a veneer and for PLYWOOD.

birdcage The wooden hinged mechanism which is found on some 18thC TRIPOD TABLES. It is fixed at the op of the pedestal and enables the able surface to swivel, tilt, fold or be xed horizontally. See p.114.

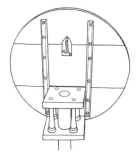

BIRDCAGE *mechanism on a tripod table; .1740. A brass catch locks the movable op into place when in use.*

ird's-eye maple See MAPLE.

iscuit Fired but unglazed ceramics. Biscuit PORCELAIN has a crisp, dry appearance that was used for statuettes and reproductions of Classical sculptures, initially by SÈVRES from 1753, and later by DERBY and porcelain factories throughout Europe. **Biscuit-firing** is the term for the first firing prior to glazing. See BISQUE and PARIAN.

iscuit barrel Barrel-shaped biscuit container dating from near the end of the 19thC. Some examples have a matching tray to catch falling crumbs. Biscuit barrels were made in various materials including electroplated silver, solid silver or ceramics, and often in glass with metal mounts.

iscuit warmer Late 19thC silver stand for serving and keeping warm biscuits at the table. The warmers, also known as **folding biscuit boxes,** consist of a stand with a central column with either a handle or finial and two or more bowls which open out horizontally and close vertically onto the column.

isque Term for the unglazed, matt-surface BISCUIT porcelain that was the most popular material for dolls' heads from the mid-19thC to the 1930s, and revived 1960-80. Flesh colour and features are painted on after an initial firing, then fired again at a low temperature to fix the colours. The term **all-bisque** refers to a doll with head, limbs and body made of bisque.

izarre silk A FIGURED silk cloth fashionable for dresses in Europe c.1695-1720. Designs were inspired by Oriental textiles, typically with tropical foliage, flora and jagged lines, woven in gold or silver thread. The cloth was produced in Britain at the SPITALFIELDS SILK FACTORIES.

blackamoor See GUÉRIDON.

black basaltes See BASALTES WARE.

blacking A rust-resisting treatment applied to guns or armour, using either chemicals or paint.

black jack British tankard-shaped leather jug, popular until the 18thC. It was lined with pitch to make it watertight, and often had a metal rim.

blanc-de-Chine 18thC French term for porcelain made in Fujien province in south-eastern China from the 17thC (late MING dynasty) to the present. Unpainted wares, including small, finely modelled figures, large sculptured models of deities and other wares often with relief decoration were exported to Europe. The ware was copied by nearly all early European porcelain factories including ST CLOUD, MENNECY, Bow and CHELSEA during the 18thC. See p.166.

blank 1 A prepared piece of metal ready for striking into a coin, also known as a **flan**, or, particularly in the USA, as a **planchet. 2** A cartridge with a charge of powder but no bullet. **3** Undecorated glass or ceramic item (also called **in-the-white** in ceramics) that is passed to an outside decorator or factory for painting or printing.

bleeding bowl See BARBER'S BOWL; PORRINGER.

bleu persan See NEVERS.

blind Earl See DECORATIVE MOTIFS.

blind fret See FRETWORK.

blind tracery Typical GOTHIC decoration carved in relief on a solid background, often found on furniture.

blockfront An American 18thC CASE FURNITURE design in which the centre section is a flattened concave curve flanked by outer sections of flattened convex curves.

bloom Dull, matt surface on old glassware. This may be caused by too much alkali in the glass, by the presence of sulphurous smoke during reheating, or by the wearing away of decoration such as gilding.

blue and white The most widely used and longest-lasting decorative ceramic colour scheme, in which cobalt blue is an UNDERGLAZE colour.

Cobalt blue retains its true colour over a wide range of firing temperatures, from low-fired earthenwares to the most highly fired porcelains. See p.161.

blue cloth helmet Cloth-covered helmet with a top spike worn by the British army from 1879 and still worn by some military bands.

blue dash Simple blue on white decoration comprising oblique, regularly spaced, cobalt-blue dashes. The decoration is found on the rim of 17th-18thC London and Bristol delftware CHARGERS. See p.186.

blueing The heat treatment of iron or steel which forms a thin surface layer of blue oxide. This retards rusting, and was also used to decorate armour.

blue john A type of crystalline fluorspar with bands of yellow, purple, blue and white, mined in Derbyshire. It was popular in the late 18th and late 19th centuries, when it was used for OBJECTS OF VERTU, candlesticks and candelabra.

blunderbuss A shoulder gun with a flared muzzle for scattering shot widely, increasing the probability of a hit without taking aim. In the 18thC it was commonly used as a house or coach defensive weapon.

boarded construction See JOINING.

board-ended stool The dining seat of the 14th, 15th and 16th centuries. Instead of legs, the stools were supported on boards which were vertical or inclined inwards towards the seat and held firm by horizontal APRON pieces.

bobbin See LACE, TURNING.

bob pendulum A short, light-weighted PENDULUM which swings through a wide arc, and is associated with a verge ESCAPEMENT. It can be either pear or lens-shaped.

bocage A French term meaning 'thicket', used to describe ceramic foliage or flowers that provide a background for a central subject. Bocage is typical of Rococo style, often framing figures in a canopy or arbour, and was particularly popular from the 1750s to the 1770s.

body Mix of materials that forms the basic structure of an article, as in the paste of PORCELAIN.

body colour See GOUACHE.

Bohemia Region of what was later Czechoslovakia, renowned for its elaborately engraved glass. The earliest wares, dating from the 14thC, were made of **Waldglas** (forest glass) – a crude, mould-blown product which used wood ash as a source of potash for

the FLUX. Finer, Venetian techniques were introduced in the 16thC and wheel ENGRAVING was common.

The development of LIME GLASS a century later provided a better medium for decoration and led to facet CUTTING and elaborate engraving. One of the most noted engravers was Ludwig Moser who specialised in portrait work. Although independent artists produced much of the finest work under the patronage of German princes, factories such as those at Haida (now Novy Bor) and Karlsbad (now Karlovy-Vary) also produced fine-quality ware from the mid-19th to early 20th centuries, including CASED GLASS and FLASHED GLASS in brilliant colours. See p.229.

bois clair See RESTAURATION STYLE.

bois durci Mid-19thC EBONY substitute, made from sawdust and animal blood or other water-soluble protein. The mixture coagulated on heating and could be die-stamped into decorative mouldings for furniture, medallions and trays.

boiserie French term for 17th and 18thC wooden wall panelling ornately decorated with carving. Boiseries were often painted white with the ornamentation highlighted in gold or bright colours, and might also incorporate paintings.

bole Red or yellow, fine ochre clay used as a ground by gilders prior to applying gold leaf (see GILDING).

bolection moulding A furniture moulding used where two surfaces of differing levels meet.

bombard A large jug made of sewn leather and lined with pitch or resin to make it watertight; used from medieval times to the 18thC.

bombé Literally translated from the French as 'bulging', a term used for a swelling shape seen originally on chests of drawers and commodes of the Louis XIV period. The outward swell or curve towards the base of a piece was a popular feature during the Rococo period. See p.140.

bonbonnière Small container for sweets popular in the 18thC. Also known as **comfit** and **sweetmeat boxes,** they were crafted in a variety of materials, particularly silver and porcelain, and often in novelty shapes such as a shoe or a head.

bone ash Calcium phospate from burned and ground animal bones, which was used as a fusing and stabilising agent in soft-paste

PORCELAIN, particularly in 18thC English factories, in BONE CHINA, and as a whitening agent in CREAMWARE.

bone china A modified hard-paste PORCELAIN containing up to 50 per cent bone ash. Its introduction by SPODE in 1794 was an important step in the development of European ceramics; by the early 19thC, most British porcelain factories were making bone china, and the recipe is still used today. Bone china is tougher and cheaper to make than soft-paste porcelain, and slightly softer but again cheaper to mass-produce than hard-paste porcelain. See p.150.

bone lace See lace.

bonheur-du-jour A lady's elegant, slender-legged writing table often fitted with toilet accessories. Shelves and pigeonholes, sometimes enclosed by a TAMBOUR or CYLINDER FALL, are set at the back of the table surface. There may be a cupboard or shelves above for ornaments. Bonheurs-du-jour were introduced in France in the 1760s and soon afterwards produced in Britain. See pp.122-3.

bore Inner surface of a gun barrel. The diameter of the bore is the **calibre**.

Boreman, Zachariah See DERBY.

borne Circular, upholstered Victorian OTTOMAN-type sofa, sometimes known as a **conversation seat**, which has three or four seat divisions and a central cone providing a backrest. See p.105.

Boston rocker See ROCKING CHAIRS.

boteh One of the most common motifs used on Oriental weavings, and the inspiration for the European PAISLEY pattern. See p.309.

geometric Caucasian boteh   *mother and child boteh, southern Persia (Iran)*

paisley boteh   *English floral shawl boteh*

BOTEH *are thought to represent curving leaves or palm fronds.*

Böttger, Johann (1682-1719) German alchemist and inventor of European hard-paste PORCELAIN. Böttger also pioneered a very hard RED STONEWARE (1709), a glazed, white porcelain (1709) and **Böttger lustre**, a pale purple lustre glaze made with gold (c.1715). In 1710 he was appointed director of the newly formed MEISSEN porcelain factory. See p.173.

bottle stand See COASTER.

bottle ticket A small plaque, also known as a **bottle label** or **wine label**, for hanging around the neck of a wine bottle or decanter, which bears the name of the contents.
   Bottle tickets were first made in silver in the 1730s, and later in enamel on copper, SHEFFIELD PLATE, porcelain or glass. Some bottle tickets carry the name, initials or family crest of the owner. See pp.248-9.

boudoir doll Elaborately and fashionably dressed, long-limbed doll designed as an ornament for an adult's bedroom, rather than as a child's toy. The dolls were popular c.1915-30, but continued to be made in the 1940s. Most have cloth bodies, although there are also COMPOSITION, wax and ceramic examples. See p.358.

bough-pot See FLOWER-BRICK.

boulle A MARQUETRY technique, also known as **buhl work**, using metal (usually brass) and tortoiseshell in reverse patterns, sometimes combined with other materials and often set in an ebony VENEER. It was a popular technique in France from the late 17thC through to the 19thC, and in Britain from 1815.
   The term is associated with the French cabinet-maker and ÉBÉNISTE **André Boulle** (1642-1732) of the LOUIS XIV period in France. He specialised in elegant, highly ornamented furniture – mainly for the nobility. He also produced cases for LONGCASE CLOCKS and barometers, gilt-bronze chandeliers, candelabra and ANDIRONS. See p.93.

Boulton, Matthew (1728-1809) Inventor, entrepreneur and leading metalware manufacturer. His factory at Soho, Birmingham produced not only furniture mounts, buckles, buttons, snuffboxes and sword hilts, 1759-66, but also, as a private mint, struck Britain's first copper pennies in 1797. Boulton established the Birmingham assay office in 1773 and his factory, using the designs of Robert Adam and a host of local craftsmen, greatly contributed to the city's successful silver industry. From the 1760s he specialised in SHEFFIELD

PLATE, becoming Britain's primary producer. ORMOLU objects, such as vases, candlesticks and clock cases, and mounts for ornaments and ceramic pieces were also produced. Much of Boulton's later work was staff-designed for mass production. See pp.39, 44, 243.   **MB**

bourdalou Oval-shaped receptacle for urine, designed for use by women when travelling. Bourdaloues, also known as **coach pots** or **slippers**, date from c.1710 and were generally made of porcelain or pottery, occasionally of silver, japanned metal or glass. They look rather like large sauceboats, but the front lip curves inwards rather than out. See p.203.

Bow With CHELSEA, one of the first soft-paste PORCELAIN producers in Britain. It was the largest of the 18thC English porcelain factories, and made a broader range of products for a wider market than Chelsea.
   Bow was founded in the East End of London by Irish painter Thomas Frye in 1744. Soft-paste porcelain was produced by 1748, introducing the use of BONE ASH. The body is tougher than that produced at Chelsea, but has a 'lumpy', bluish tinge to the glaze and an orange TRANSLUCENCY when held to the light.
   Until the late 1750s, the bulk of Bow's output imitated Oriental porcelain. For a time it was the largest producer of BLUE AND WHITE porcelain in Europe, and also made BLANC-DE-CHINE wares. Figures were a feature too, and often of native British design. They are less finely modelled and more thickly glazed than those made at Chelsea and often unpainted.
   Some table and decorative ware followed a modified Rococo style and contemporary fashions in silverware, with applied shells and seaweed on table centrepieces and scrolled bases for figures, for example. From the late 1750s, Bow decorations were inspired by MEISSEN, SÈVRES and WORCESTER, but with lower-quality results. Some 30 years after its foundation, Bow was bought by DERBY following a period of decline. Few Bow wares carry a mark, although the device of a dagger and anchor painted in dark iron red is occasionally found on flatwares and figures. See pp.158, 172, 175.

bowenite See SERPENTINE.

bow-front A curving, convex front on a chest of drawers, commode, cabinet or sideboard, also known as **swell front**.

bowie knife A knife with a broad curved-back blade, named after James Bowie (1796-1836), a Kentuckian

colonel. It was popular in the USA but most were manufactured in Britain. See pp.408-9.

box bedstead Bed enclosed on three sides by framed panelling, on the fourth side by curtains or sliding panels, and above by a flat TESTER. Box bedsteads were seen in poor households in Scotland and the north of England and Wales up to the mid-19thC.

boxlock A FLINTLOCK or percussion firearm with the firing mechanism mounted centrally on the stock.

box stool A 17thC JOINED oak stool with a box beneath a hinged seat.

boxwood A very close-grained, yellow HARDWOOD native to Europe. It was especially popular for stringing (see BANDING) in the late 18th and early 19th centuries. It was also ideal for blocks for wood ENGRAVINGS and for moulds. The undulating figure of the wood from its roots and branches made box a popular material for INLAID WORK and MARQUETRY in the 16th and 17th centuries.

bracket clock A general term for a spring-driven clock, usually wooden-cased, with a vertical dial on the front face and generally with a PENDULUM-controlled ESCAPEMENT. The movement, or mechanism, is contained between two vertical plates. The term originates from the fact that although most clocks of this type stood on pieces of furniture, some were furnished with a supporting wall bracket. In the 17th and 18th centuries, they were called **spring clocks**. See box and pp.282-3.

bracket foot See FEET.

braganza foot See FEET.

Brandt, Edgar (1880-1960) The most renowned French metalworker of the ART DECO period, and designer of furniture, screens and decorative panels. He used a combination of metals, such as iron, brass and copper, and is also known for his wrought-iron work, often with a hammered finish. Brandt formed a company in New York called Ferrobrandt.

brandy bowl Shallow, oval bowl with two opposing handles, used both for tasting and for drinking brandy. Brandy bowls were made in Holland in the 17th and 18th centuries and revived in the 19thC; in the early 18thC, versions made in New York were exported to Britain. See p.249.

brandy saucepan See PIPKIN.

BRACKET CLOCK

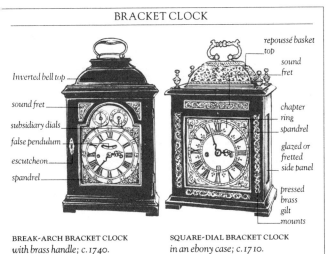

Inverted bell top

sound fret

subsidiary dials

false pendulum

escutcheon

spandrel

repoussé basket top

sound fret

chapter ring

spandrel

glazed or fretted side panel

pressed brass gilt mounts

BREAK-ARCH BRACKET CLOCK
with brass handle; c.1740.

SQUARE-DIAL BRACKET CLOCK
in an ebony case; c.1710.

brass A strong, yellow alloy of copper and zinc; a higher level of zinc produces a yellower metal. Brass is malleable and easy to work. It has been worked in Britain from the Middle Ages. Large-scale production came c.1700, with better-quality metal from c.1720. Some small brass ornaments and mounts for clocks were silvered. In the 19thC, thin sheet brass was introduced and designs were stamped out under presses to produce ornaments, inkstands, letter racks and door furniture. See p.366.

breakfast can See COFFEE CAN.

breakfast table A small, light, four-legged table with two extendible hinged flaps. The custom of entertaining friends to a late breakfast died out towards the end of the 18thC, and the term became more generally applied to lighter and smaller versions of dining tables for use in the breakfast room. See p.108.

breakfront Term used to describe a piece of furniture with part of its front projecting. Breakfront bookcases, sideboards, wardrobes and clothes presses were popular in the 18th and 19th centuries. See p.140.

BREAKFRONT *library bookcase with a broken pediment; mid-18thC.*

breech The closed end of a barrel, where the charge or cartridge is placed. Breech-loading weapons were easier to load than muzzle-loading ones. Although they were used from the 15thC, it was not until the 19thC that they were perfected.

Breguet, Abraham-Louis (1747-1823) Swiss-born watchmaker working in Paris from c.1762. He specialised in **subscription** or **souscription watches** which were made to order for clients or subscribers, and self-winding watches. In 1795, Breguet invented an escapement mechanism called the **tourbillon** which reduced errors caused by the changing position of a watch as it was carried around. He also developed **montres à tact** which have knobs set at each hour for telling the time by touch in the dark.

Breguet's watch cases are often very thin, with gold or silver dials. He signed his pieces 'Breguet à Paris' until 1791, when he developed a hidden signature to discourage forgeries. He went into partnership with his son Louis-Antoine c.1807.

breloque Small ornament worn on a watch chain or CHATELAINE. It was typically made of gold or enamel and often in the form of a tiny statuette. Porcelain breloques were made at CHELSEA and DERBY in the 18thC.

Bretby Art Pottery Derbyshire earthenware pottery, established 1883. Bretby made pieces to the designs of Christopher DRESSER.

Breuer, Marcel (1902-81) Hungarian-born furniture designer and architect, specialising in interiors. Breuer trained at the BAUHAUS school of design. His furniture was easily mass-produced and he was largely

responsible for introducing chrome into ordinary households for the first time. Many of Breuer's designs were produced by the THONET brothers' furniture factory in Vienna. Breuer left Germany for Britain in 1935 and two years later settled in the USA.

brides See LACE.

bright-cut engraving Method of engraving metal articles especially ADAM-style silverware, developed in late 18thC Birmingham. The engraving instrument, or graver, has a double edge which removes slivers of metal and burnishes the cut surface to produce a smooth, polished, FACETED decoration. See p.235.

brilliance Radiant brightness of a diamond or other transparent gemstone, enhanced by the skilled arrangement of FACETS. A stone's brilliance is enhanced if the facets cause a greater deflection of light entering a stone and a minimal loss of light through the stone's base.

brilliant cut See JEWEL CUTTING.

brin See FAN.

briolette See JEWEL CUTTING.

Briot, Nicholas (c.1579-1646) French DIE-sinker who produced machine-made coins of very high quality for Charles I in the 1630s.

brisé fan See FAN.

bristle doll See PIANO DOLL.

Bristol 1 A centre for British glass-making from the mid-17th to 19th centuries. Bristol glass-making was established c.1651; in the 18thC opaque white glass resembling porcelain and often decorated in similar style was important, but the city became best known for its 'Bristol' blue glass made in the late 18thC, most notably by Lazarus and Isaac Jacobs. It was used to make DECANTERS, finger bowls, patch boxes and liners for silver casters, and other wares, which were often gilded. Blue glass was produced at many other factories in Britain and firm attribution is usually impossible. The city's glass-makers were also noted for their high-quality cutting, engraving and enamelling. See also NAILSEA. **2** An important ceramics centre for the production of TIN-GLAZED EARTHENWARE in the 17th and 18th centuries. This initially followed the style of Italian MAIOLICA, and later of DELFTWARE. In 1750 a soft-paste PORCELAIN formula containing SOAPSTONE was pioneered at a Bristol

factory founded by Benjamin Lund. A limited range of BLUE AND WHITE domestic ware was produced. This soapstone formula was perfected by WORCESTER, which took over Lund's company in 1752.

In 1770, William COOKWORTHY, the chemist who made Britain's first hard-paste porcelain, transferred his PLYMOUTH factory to Bristol. The Bristol factory closed in 1781, the patent rights transferring to NEWHALL in Staffordshire.

britannia metal A type of PEWTER containing no lead but a high proportion of tin, and shaped by a process known as SPINNING. This formed objects around a pattern (or model) on a power-driven wheel, which produced thinner wares than the earlier cast pewter. Britannia metal was made extensively in Sheffield, London and Birmingham.

From the second half of the 19thC it was often used as the base metal in ELECTROPLATING instead of copper or nickel silver and marked 'EPBM' (electroplated britannia metal). This is softer than electroplated nickel silver (EPNS) and melts easily, so is difficult to repair. See p.367.

Britannia standard The compulsory standard for silverware in Britain 1697-1720. The proportion of pure silver (95.8 per cent) to base metal is higher than that for STERLING STANDARD silver (92.5 per cent).

It was introduced as a deterrent against the practice of melting down sterling silver coinage to make domestic silverware. After 1720, the production of Britannia silver was optional. See HALLMARKS.

broad Gold £1 coin struck in 1656 which was circulated for only a short period. Broads usually bear a portrait of Oliver Cromwell.

broadloom See LOOMS.

broadsword A cutting sword with a flat, wide, double-edged blade.

brocade Finely woven textile with coloured threads added to form a raised pattern on the upper surface of the material, making a richly figured cloth. (The word brocade derives from the Latin *brocare* meaning 'to figure'.) Originally the ground patterns of flowers and scrolls were in gold or silver, and the fabric was known as **cloth of gold**; coloured silk threads came later, and today, cotton and man-made fibres are used. Brocade can be made in various weights for dressmaking or furnishings. **Brocantine** is a brocade with a raised pattern that imitates embroidery.

Brocard, Philippe-Joseph (1867-90) French glass-maker who revived 13th-century Syrian techniques of enamelling in brilliant colours. Early works copied Islamic lamps and tableware, but later output was original – mainly MOULDED GLASSWARE decorated with more subdued ENAMEL colours.

brocatelle 1 Imitation BROCADE made of cotton or coarse silk, with a raised pattern in the warp and a flat weft background. The term is often used to refer to any cloth with a raised pattern. **2** A variegated marble which was used to make table tops in the 18thC, also known as *brocatello*.

brockage A mis-struck coin, on which the design appears normally on one side, but with the same design in INTAGLIO or INCUSE form on the other. It is caused by a previously struck coin failing to eject from the pair of DIES.

Brocot, Achille (1817-78) French clock-maker who devised the **Brocot suspension** which enabled time-keeping to be regulated by altering the length of the PENDULUM suspension spring by a key turned in the dial. He also introduced a JEWELLED deadbeat ESCAPEMENT, sometimes called a visible escapement as it was often mounted in the middle of the dial.

broderie anglaise Mid-19thC CUTWORK embroidery, usually of linen or cotton, made in Britain and parts of Europe from the late 18thC. Floral patterns are formed by embroidering around holes cut in the fabric in buttonhole stitch.

Brogden, John (fl. 1842-85) London based jeweller who specialised in antique and archaeological styles. Typical Brogden pieces incorporate Classical motifs and reliefs inspired by the Etruscan, Assyrian and Egyptian civilisations and pieces mounted with the claws of tigers or vultures.

bronchit Matt black decoration painted on glass. The technique, also known as **bronzite**, was developed c.1910 in Vienna. The motifs – flowers, figures, animals and geometrical shapes – anticipated ART DECO style.

bronze Hard alloy of copper and tin which develops a brown or green surface patina with age. Bronze has been used for various utensils requiring strength and durability, such as buckets, cooking pots and lamps, as well as for weapons, statues, ornaments and furniture. Bronze is usually shaped by CASTING and then chiselled to add sharp detail. See p.368.

bronzes d'ameublement French term used to describe small gilt-bronze fittings, including clock-cases, fire-dogs, lamps and lighting appliances.

Brown Bess The nickname for the FLINTLOCK musket used by the British army 1720-1840. See p.407.

browning The process of artificially oxidising the metal parts of a firearm to produce a dull brown lustre finish and a guard against rusting.

brown stoneware See SALT-GLAZED STONEWARE.

Brücke, Die Group of artists founded Dresden, Germany, 1905. Although it broke up in 1913, the group's Expressionist style had a considerable impact on public taste, reviving, for example, an interest in WOODCUTS and other graphic arts. See p.332.

brushing slide A sliding shelf between the top drawer and the top surface of a chest of drawers or above the middle drawer of a TALLBOY. Its function was to provide a pull-out surface on which clothes could be laid out for brushing prior to wearing.

BRUSHING SLIDE *on an 18thC chest.*

Brussels carpets See MOQUETTE.

Brussels tapestry The most technically refined tapestry in Europe from the 15th to 17th centuries – when the GOBELINS factory in Paris became the main production centre. Brussels tapestry hangings were prized for detailed, realistic compositions, perfection of technique and colour and fine materials. They continued to be produced to a lesser degree throughout the 18thC.

budai Buddhistic figure signifying long life, prosperity and happiness. It is also spelt **butai** and **putai**, and in Japanese as **hotei**. The figure is depicted either alone or with children tugging at his ear lobes, pot belly or the sack of treasures by his side.

CHINESE BUDAI *made of carved bamboo; mid-17thC; 5¼ in (13.3 cm) high.*

buffet See COURT CUPBOARD.

buhl work See BOULLE.

Bulle clock The commonest form of electric battery clock, patented in 1922 by the Frenchman Maurice Favre-Bulle. Bulle clocks were marketed from 1924 in Britain by the British Horo-Electric Company until 1939. They are mounted on a circular base covered by a glass dome which contains the clock with its battery, electromagnet and hollow PENDULUM.

bullet teapot Early 18thC silver or ceramic teapot with a spherical or polygonal, bullet-shaped body, and usually a flat lid. The design was revived in the 19thC.

bullion 1 Gold or silver in the form of bars or ingots; the meltdown value of an object based on its actual metal content. **2** Silver wire twisted into threads and used to decorate church vestments and military uniforms; also known as **bullion lace**.

bull's eye 1 See LENTICLE. **2** The bubble-shaped glass in the cover of a half-HUNTER CASED watch.

bureau A chest of drawers with a desk area above. It is enclosed by a sloping flap which opens, supported by pull-out LOPERS, to reveal a writing surface. At the back of this are recessed pigeonholes and small drawers. Bureaux were introduced during the 17thC and over the next 200 years adopted various forms, including the **bureau bookcase**, topped by bookshelves with glazed or panelled doors and the **bureau cabinet** with panelled doors above. See pp.128-31.

bureau bed Bed that can be folded away into a bureau-like CARCASS with dummy drawers. In the 18th and 19th centuries, various bed disguises were popular in households where space was at a premium, including library PRESS beds, piano beds – complete with dummy pedals – and table beds.

bureau-plat French term for a flat-topped writing desk with a FRIEZE containing drawers. See p.123.

Burges, William (1827-81) British architect and designer in 19thC GOTHIC REVIVAL style. Burges's interpretation of 13thC furniture style resulted in square, solid pieces covered with surface decoration including paintings. See p.63.

burgonet Light metal helmet, with peak, neck guard and hinged cheek flaps, used mainly by light-horsemen in the 16th and 17th centuries.

Burmese glass An opaque ART GLASS shading from yellow at the bottom to pink at the top, developed by the Mount Washington Company of Massachusetts in 1885. The colours came from mixing uranium or gold oxides with the molten glass. From 1886 Thomas WEBB & Sons produced 'Queen's Burmese Glass' in Britain, after a tea set bought by Queen Victoria from the US manufacturer.

burr 1 Knotty whorls in the grain of wood where there were dense, fibrous swellings on the trunk or roots of a tree, which were used in decorative VENEERS. See PARQUETRY. **2** See DRYPOINT.

busby A military fur hat with a bag hanging from one side, often with a plume. It was worn originally by 18thC Hungarian hussars, but other European hussar regiments adopted it.

Bustelli, Franz Anton (1723-63) Swiss-born porcelain modeller. He was chief modeller at the NYMPHENBURG Porcelain Factory 1754-63. His COMMEDIA DELL'ARTE characters were unsurpassed in their sense of movement and grace.

butler's tray Portable tray, usually rectangular, with handholds at each end and mounted either on legs or a folding stand. Butler's trays were used from the early 18thC for serving drinks and removing glasses. They are also known as **standing trays**. See p.145.

BUTLER'S TRAY *of mahogany with stand; late 18thC; 30 in (76 cm) long.*

buttoned upholstery Padded upholstery with a buttoned, quilted effect introduced in the second half of the 18thC. Strong thread is pulled through the covering material and stuffing to the framework or webbing and hidden on the outside by buttons.

buttons Buttons first became widespread in Europe in the 17thC. British buttons from c.1700 were moulded or stamped in metal with hand-painted enamel and porcelain examples later in the century. In the 19thC buttons were mass-produced in a variety of materials. See p.319.

button-wound watch See KEYLESS WATCH.

C

cabaret A small tray, usually of porcelain, with matching set of cups, sugar bowl, milk jug and tea or coffee pot. A breakfast cabaret is known as a **déjeuner**, a set for two a **tête-à-tête**, and a set for one person as **solitaire**.

cabinet A piece of furniture incorporating both drawer and cupboard space designed for the storage or display of small objects, especially precious ones.

The word 'cabinet' – to the end of the 16thC exclusively and to a lesser extent to the early 19thC – referred to a small room in which precious articles and works of art were displayed. Towards the end of the 17thC it was applied to furniture. Their popularity during the Louis XIV and British RESTORATION period and their elaborately VENEERED surfaces promoted the specialised new skill of **cabinet-making**. Although cabinet-making is particularly associated with Queen Anne and Georgian furniture, the term is now used generally to apply to all CASE FURNITURE. See pp.132-4.

cabinet-ware Porcelain – usually cups, saucers and plates – which was made for display rather than for practical use. Typical examples include early soft-paste PORCELAIN made at CHELSEA in the 1740s which is not resistant to hot water but displays a high standard of decoration.

cabochon See JEWEL CUTTING.

cabriole A curvaceous profile seen in furniture, supposedly inspired by the shape of a wild goat's hind legs. It is usually associated with the shape of legs on chairs and tables, in the form of a shallow 'S' curve, with a broad hip and knee or shoulder tapering to a slim concave leg below. The cabriole leg was so popular that the late 17th to mid-18thC is sometimes known as the **Cabriole Leg Period**. See p.91.

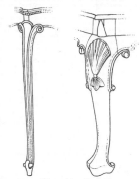

CABRIOLE; *'French' style (left), c.1770; English (right), c.1730.*

cache-pot Ornamental container for a pot holding a growing plant, usually without a drainage hole. The name is derived from the French *cacher* (to hide). See JARDINIÈRES and p.200.

cachou box A 19thC gold or silver box to hold cachous – pills for sweetening the breath. The boxes, which were made in Britain, are very small – 1-2 in (25-50 mm) in length – with a hinged lid, and sometimes a ring attached for hanging from a CHATELAINE. The boxes are usually decorated with CHASING or ENAMELLING. They remained popular until c.1910.

cadogan Lidless, peach-shaped teapot which is held upside down to be filled at the base. A tube leading up from the base ensures the contents do not spill when it is upright. A Chinese wine pot, brought to Britain by the Hon Mrs Cadogan, is said to have inspired the first examples produced at ROCKINGHAM in the late 18thC. MEISSEN in Germany, COPELAND, DAVENPORT and other Staffordshire potteries soon followed suit.

CADOGAN TEAPOT; *c.1810; 5½ in (14 cm) high. The cutaway section shows the internal tube from the base.*

Cafe, John (*fl.*1740-57) A London-based silversmith who is best known for his candlesticks and snuffer trays. John was succeeded by his brother William, who continued the prolific production of candlesticks until 1772.

cage cup A cast or blown, thick-walled glass BLANK carved in relief and then undercut, leaving the decoration in the form of a net or cage still attached to the main body of the vessel. This form of cup was also known as a **diatreta**, taking its name from the *diatretarii*, the Roman glass decorators who originated it.

cagework Term for decorative, PIERCED or CHASED silver mount that encloses an inner, plain section of an object. The cagework technique probably originated in Germany, but was used in Britain extensively on late 17thC tankards, beakers and two-handled cups. A **cagework box** is a

snuffbox comprising plaques of various materials, such as agate or ivory, set in a pierced metal frame.

caillouté Porcelain decoration, of a lacy network of oval and circle outlines, usually painted in gold. The word is French for 'pebbled'. The design was introduced at SÈVRES in the mid-18thC, notably set against a rich dark blue background, and is also seen on WORCESTER, DERBY and SWANSEA ware. See DECORATIVE MOTIFS.

cairngorm Yellowish-brown to smoky yellow variety of QUARTZ. It is the most important stone in Scottish jewellery. The stones were originally found in the Cairngorm mountains, and have been much simulated in glass (detectable by gas bubbles), and are now usually imitated by applying HEAT TREATMENT TO Brazilian AMETHYSTS.

calamander See EBONY and p.91.

Calcite glass Creamy-white ART GLASS developed c.1915 by Frederick CARDER in the USA. Its translucency, achieved by adding bone ash to the molten glass, made it particularly suitable for lampshades. It was also used in conjunction with AURENE glass, to make CAMEO GLASS.

calendar clock Clock with separate indications on the main dial, or with extra dials for the phases of the moon, the day, month and, more rarely, the year. Calendar information appeared on public clocks from the 14thC, and on domestic clocks from the 16thC.

calibre See BORE.

calico Plain-weave cotton cloth originally imported from Calicut, a port in south-west India, during the 17th and 18th centuries and later manufactured in Britain. It was used, with painted or printed patterns, for soft furnishings especially during the 18th and 19th centuries.

calotype The world's first negative-positive technique of photography, pioneered by British scientist William Henry Fox Talbot (1800-77) in 1841. The process allowed an infinite number of prints on paper to be made from a single paper negative. The calotype eventually superseded the DAGUERREOTYPE.

cameo Gemstone, hardstone or shell cut to reveal a design in relief. Cameos were originally made from gemstones with different coloured layers to provide a contrasting background. They were widespread in the Roman era and revived during the Italian RENAISSANCE and NEOCLASSICAL

period. Shell cameos were carved with Classical-style portraits and mythological scenes, in Naples and Rome in the 19thC and exported to Britain to be used as seals and jewellery. They remained fashionable throughout the 19thC.

cameo glass Glassware made up of two or more layers of glass in contrasting colours (see CASED GLASS) in which part of the outer surface is carved by hand or etched away with acid to leave a cameo-effect design in relief. Acid-resistant paint is applied to the design area on the white outer casing; when the glass is dipped into an acid solution, the treated design area remains intact while the exposed area around it is etched away to reveal the coloured glass beneath. See SULPHIDES and p.222.

camera obscura A dark box with a small opening or lens through which the image of an object is projected and focused onto a facing surface. The device was used particularly by 17th to 19thC artists to produce accurate paintings and drawings.

CAMERA OBSCURA *A portable box type; c.1840; 6 in (15.2 cm) high.*

campaign furniture 18th and 19thC portable furniture, including washstands, writing chests, chests of drawers, beds and chairs, primarily for military use. The furniture is usually of mahogany or teak, with brass fittings and removable feet. Chests would be made in halves and other pieces to unscrew so that they could be stacked flat for travelling. See p.137.

campana Inverted bell-shape seen in ceramics and metalware since Classical times and particularly popular in the early 19thC.

CAMPANA-SHAPED *vase of Italian black marble; c.1910; 29½ in (75 cm) high.*

canapé French term for a settee used from the late 17thC. It is upholstered with some of the wooden structure, such as the top rail or apron, left exposed. See p.106.

cancellation mark The means of marking ceramic products that are substandard or part of a discontinued range, by painting or scratching one or two strokes over the original factory mark. MEISSEN, for example, had a range of cancellation marks to denote whether a piece was to be sold IN-THE-WHITE, unglazed, or rejected.

candelabrum Branched form of a candlestick, often made as a pair (candelabra) and used in Europe since the Middle Ages. See pp.254-5.

candle slide Small wooden support for a candlestick, occasionally found on 18thC desks, tables and bureau cabinets, which slides into a built-in recess when not in use.

candle-stand See TORCHÈRE.

candlestick Utensil for holding a single candle, used in Europe from the 10thC or earlier. See pp.254-5.

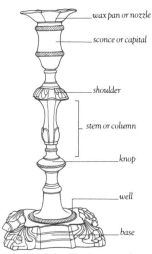

wax pan or nozzle

sconce or capital

shoulder

stem or column

knop

well

base

CANDLESTICK *English silver example with Rococo influences; mid-18thC; 10 in (25.4 cm) high.*

cane 1 The woven fibrous strips from the stems of a group of palms known as **rattans**, which are used in furniture. Canework came to Europe from China via the Dutch East India Company trade in the 17thC. It was popular in Europe in the second half of the 17th, and again from the end of the 18thC. The Chinese wove the outer fibres of the trees into very fine-meshed, silk-like, opaque panels. The Europeans used wider strips of cane, resulting in a light, straw-coloured, open mesh, usually with octagonal holes. Cane is

a reasonably cheap material, strong yet light in weight and elastic. In the 19thC the coarser strips of the rattan palms were used in the production of BASKETWORK furniture.
2 A stick of glass, sometimes multicoloured, made by arranging coloured lengths or rods of glass in a bundle, melting then MARVERING (rolling) them in clear glass to form a cane. The cane is then reheated and drawn out until it is ⅛ -½ in (3-13 mm) in diameter. When cool, the cane can be sliced into thin crosswise sections to form the MILLEFIORE effect commonly seen in paperweights and MOSAIC GLASS. Canes can also be combined with TWISTS in drinking-glass stems.

caneware Cream to light brown fine STONEWARE developed by Josiah WEDGWOOD from the 1770s, sometimes decorated with bright blue, green and red enamel colours. Caneware vessels were moulded to simulate lengths of bamboo lashed together. See p.160.

canted An obliquely angled, chamfered or bevelled edge.

canteen Set of domestic tableware or cutlery in a fitted wooden case with a hinged lid and often with two or three drawers. There are usually 6 to 12 place settings. The first canteens were portable cases carrying the eating implements of 17thC travellers and military officers. See pp.240-1.

canterbury A **music canterbury**, originally designed in the late 18thC, is a wooden stand divided by rails into

MUSIC CANTERBURY; *c.1825; 19 in (48.2 cm) wide.*

SUPPER CANTERBURY; *c.1810; 27 in (68.5 cm) high.*

sections for storing sheet music. Some examples have a drawer or drawers fitted underneath the top rails. A **supper canterbury** is a low wooden trolley used in the 18thC for cutlery and plates – similar to a deep partitioned tray on legs. See pp.124-5.

cantilever chair A chair made using the cantilever principle, in which the load is supported only at one end. Mart STAM's 1920s tubular-steel prototype combined strength and lightness, but its shape was so new – the seat appeared to be floating in midair – that the public were afraid to sit on it. More commercially successful examples were produced a few years later by designers Ludwig MIES VAN DER ROHE and Marcel BREUER.

CANTILEVER CHAIR *of tubular steel and leather, designed by Mart Stam; 1926.*

Canton 1 CHINESE EXPORT PORCELAIN decorated in Canton (Guangzhou). In Europe, Canton generally applies to 19thC Chinese porcelain decorated with panels of flowers and scenes with figures on a gilt and green scrolled ground.
2 Canton's enamelling workshops also produced enamel-painted copper known as **Canton enamel**. The Chinese acquired enamelling techniques from Europe in the 18thC and developed their own distinctive products, almost entirely for export, decorated particularly in FAMILLE-ROSE and famille-verte colours. See p.263.
3 In the USA, the term is used to describe porcelain decorated with UNDERGLAZE-blue landscapes similar to the British WILLOW PATTERN, which was exported from the Chinese port, late 18th and early 19th centuries.

capacity marks Marks, also known as **standard** or **excise** marks, found on measures used in public markets and taverns for the sale of both dry and wet goods, such as grain, wine or ale. Originally there were many different local standards, but these were standardised in England in 1826. Scotland retained its own system into the 19thC. See p.369.

cap-and-ball See PERCUSSION LOCK.

capital See COLUMN.

capstan table See DRUM TABLE.

carat 1 Unit for measuring the weight of gemstones, including diamonds and pearls. It was standardised in 1914 as one-fifth of a gram (200 mg), equivalent to 3.086 grains. **2** Measure of the fineness of GOLD, based on 24 units. A 22 carat gold piece is an alloy of 22 parts pure gold and 2 parts another metal, such as silver.

carbine A firearm similar to a MUSKET or RIFLE but usually with a shorter barrel and firing range and commonly carried by cavalry. See p.407.

carboy Large bottle used for storing liquids such as acids or for display purposes in pharmacies. The body of the vessel is often bulbous with a long, narrow neck and matching stopper. Carboys were usually made of clear glass in order to show the colour of the liquid inside.

carbuncle See GARNET.

carcass The main body of a piece of case furniture, before doors, drawers or shelves are added, and onto which veneers are laid.

Carder, Frederick (1864-1963) British glass designer who (1880-1903) worked for STEVENS & WILLIAMS. He moved to the USA, where he co-founded the STEUBEN GLASSWORKS. Here, inspired by the ART NOUVEAU movement, he experimented with coloured glass, various finishes and the LOST-WAX process.

Cardew, Michael (1901-82) A key figure in 20thC British art pottery, who trained with Bernard LEACH at St Ives in the 1920s. He left to start his own pottery at Winchcombe, Gloucestershire, where he made everyday items such as bowls and cider jugs, in SLIP-decorated, lead-glazed earthenware. Unlike Leach, his work followed English rather than Japanese pottery traditions. A period in West Africa from 1942 marked a change to stoneware, African motifs and deep blue and green glazes highlighted by orange-brown brushwork decoration. See p.184.

card table A semicircular or rectangular folding table, used for card playing, introduced in the 17thC. Typical features include a green baize surface, a small drawer and sometimes wells to contain counters. A variation of the late 19thC is the **envelope table**, which has four hinged triangular pieces that open out to form a square, lined playing surface, often decorated with MARQUETRY. See pp.115-17.

CARPET KNOTS

THE TURKISH KNOT, *also known as the Ghiordes or symmetrical knot; used on nearly all Turkish, Caucasian and British carpets, and by most Turkoman tribal groups.*

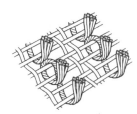

THE PERSIAN KNOT, *also known as the senneh or asymmetric knot; used on most Persian, central Asian, Indian and Chinese carpets. It produces more knots per square inch and more detailed pattern definition than the Turkish knot.*

THE SPANISH KNOT, *used on Spanish carpets, is looped around single alternate warps, making horizontal and vertical lines slightly rough, and the diagonals smooth.*

THE JUFTI KNOT *covers four warp threads making a coarser weave; found on 17thC Persian rugs and 19th and 20thC rugs from eastern Iran.*

---

carillon A series of bells rung either mechanically or manually. Mechanical carillons have been used in domestic and public clocks since the 14thC to strike the hours or play tunes, as in MUSICAL CLOCKS.

Carlton House desk A writing table with a low superstructure and drawers at the back and sides of the writing space. The name derives from the original design made for the Prince of Wales's bedroom at his London residence, Carlton House. See p.123.

Carlton Ware Earthenware and porcelain produced from c.1890 at Carlton Works, Staffordshire, which traded as Wiltshaw & Robinson. The pottery is known in particular for producing ART DECO ornamental ware such as porcelain vases with enamelled and gilded decoration and LUSTRE wall masks, vases and plaques painted in delicate pastel shades. The pottery also produced CRESTED WARE, coffee sets and cruets. See p.178.

carnet de bal Ivory leaves in a decorative case on which the names of dancing partners were inscribed in pencil in the 18th and 19th centuries. **Tablettes** are similar, but the leaves can be removed from the case.

carnival glass Cheap PRESSED GLASS with a highly iridescent finish, produced mainly in the USA c.1908-

1924. It is so called because it was said to have been used as prizes at carnivals and fairs. See p.228.

Carolean Style of furniture made during the reign of the British king Charles I (1625-49). The term is sometimes misleadingly used for **Restoration style**, dating from Charles II's restoration to the throne in 1660.

Carr, Alwyn Charles Elison See RAMSDEN, OMAR.

carriage clock The first truly portable type of clock produced in large numbers, developed from COACH WATCHES and small portable table clocks. They have a spring-BALANCE escapement, a glazed rectangular brass case, and a carrying handle. Heights range from 3 in (76 mm) to 8½ in (21 cm). Carriage clocks were introduced by French clock-maker Abraham-Louis BREGUET c.1796. Over 90 per cent of them were produced in France, particularly during the height of their fashion, 1850-1914. The limited numbers made in Britain are generally larger and of higher quality than standard French versions, and have chain-FUSEE movements, while the French clocks have spring going-BARRELS. See p.285.

carte à figure Map incorporating decorative and informative details such as an ornamental border with

town views or inset pictures of local traditional costume. The style was at its height in the 17thC. See p.333.

carte-de-visite Portrait photograph, usually full length, but occasionally head and shoulders, mounted on a small card with the photographer's credit on the reverse. The idea was patented by French photographer Adolphe-Eugène Disdéri in 1854. He used a special camera containing a number of lenses; several poses could be achieved on a single negative. Cartes-de-visite were mass-produced during the mid-19thC. See p.338.

cartel clock Spring-driven wall clock set in an ornate, ROCOCO or NEOCLASSICAL-style frame or case, and produced in France, Germany, Austria and Italy c.1735-1900. Giltwood versions were also made in Britain c.1750-1800, often with a false PENDULUM in the dial. See p.281.

Carter, Stabler & Adams See POOLE POTTERY.

Cartier French jewellery firm founded in Paris in 1847. Cartier at first specialised in enamelled gold set with gemstones, but is perhaps best known for its ART DECO jewellery and watches. Cartier introduced the first wristwatch in 1904 – of the round-cornered square design still seen today.

carton See COMPOSITION.

cartonnier A piece of furniture fitted with compartments to hold papers, either freestanding with a cupboard below and clock on top, or an accessory for placing on a desk.

cartoon The full-scale, preparatory design – either drawn or painted – for a tapestry, painting or mosaic. A small sketch, which is enlarged to make a cartoon, is known as a **petit patron**.

cartouche A decorative detail or object suggestive of a sheet of paper with scrolled edges. In ceramics or silverware, it may take the form of an oval or shield with a decorative feature or inscription, and a scrolled frame, and in furniture a tablet shape with curled edges. Cartouche borders are seen on old maps and prints.

carver An elbow chair – a chair with arms within a set of armless or single dining chairs.

carving The skill of the woodcarver in furniture-making, as opposed to that of the carpenter, CABINET-MAKER or joiner. The craft gained greater status from the late 17thC until the later part of the 18thC; it became

highly specialised particularly for cabinet stands, candelabra, mirror frames and console tables, which might then be gilded.

caryatids Sculptured female forms, taken from Classical Greek style, widely used as ornamental supports on furniture and chimneypieces from the late 16thC onwards. The 19thC male equivalents are known as **atlantes**.

CARYATID *with a cushion on her head, from a French side cabinet; 1865; 14 in (35.5 cm) high.*

cased glass Glassware consisting of two or more layers in different colours. The outer casing is blown first into a cup shape. A second layer is blown into it and the two are then reheated so that they fuse together. The process is repeated if further casings are required. The outer layer can then be engraved or cut to reveal the contrasting layer beneath. See CAMEO GLASS and p.212.

case furniture Term for pieces of furniture which are intended to contain something – cupboards, cabinets, chests, bookcases and clothes presses, for example.

cassolette 1 Glass or ceramic vase, usually one of a pair, with a reversible lid. The inverted lid serves as a candle holder. 2 Ornate, late 18thC PASTILLE BURNER like a small brazier on a stand (see ATHÉNIENNE), and made of bronze or gilt metal.

Castellani, Fortunato Pio (1793-1865) Italian antique dealer, goldsmith and jeweller based in Rome. From the early 1820s he imitated Etruscan and Roman jewellery and reproduced the ancient technique of making granulated gold. He also produced jewellery with FILIGREE decoration and miniature mosaic work. His sons carried on the family business and their work became popular in Britain, where it has been frequently copied. The Castellani mark is a monogram of interlaced Cs.

caster Container with a perforated lid used for sprinkling condiments such as sugar, pepper and nutmeg, usually in silver or pewter. Matched sets are known as CRUET sets. See p.245.

casting Process of forming metal, glass or ceramic objects by pouring the molten material into a mould and letting it cool and harden. Metal items may be **sand cast** in which a mould shape is pressed into densely packed quartz and sand contained in an iron frame. See also LOST WAX and p.233.

cast iron Impure form of iron which has been cast and moulded. It has been used since the Middle Ages, but most extensively from the 18thC particularly in the Victorian era. Cast iron is brittle, but cheaper than **wrought iron**.

Castleford ware Fine white STONEWARE with a slight translucency, made at Castleford near Leeds c.1800-20. It has a smooth texture similar to that of PARIAN WARE with low relief decoration. The most common articles made were jugs and teapots, often with distinctive blue enamel trimmings. See p.171.

cat See PLATE-WARMER.

cat's eye General term for several varieties of gemstones which when viewed in a certain direction and light display a streak, likened to a cat's eye. The effect is a result of a fibrous inclusion, such as asbestos, naturally occurring within the gem, and is enhanced by a smooth cabochon cut (see JEWEL CUTTING).

caudle cup Small, covered, one or two-handled cup with a saucer used for caudle, a spiced gruel of eggs, bread or oatmeal, and wine or ale. Usually intended for invalids or nursing mothers, the cups were made of silver or pottery, principally in the late 17th and early 18th centuries.

Caughley Shropshire pottery probably founded c.1750, and best known for its soft-paste PORCELAIN, called **Salopian ware**, produced from 1772. Caughley was noted for the excellence of its potting techniques rather than for the originality of its design. It openly imitated the shapes and designs of articles produced at WORCESTER, 40 miles (64 km) away, sometimes even reproducing Worcester's crescent mark.

In the late 1780s and 90s, much of Caughley's output was decorated in bright enamels with some impressive gilding by the Worcester OUTSIDE DECORATOR Robert CHAMBERLAIN. Dainty, CHANTILLY-style floral decoration is typical, together with Oriental-style blue and white tableware. The pottery closed c.1812, business being transferred to COALPORT. See p.163.

cauliflower ware CREAMWARE pottery introduced by Josiah WEDGWOOD and Thomas WHIELDON in the 1750s. Teaware, lidded bowls, tureens and punch pots were made in the form of a cauliflower. The idea later extended to melons, pineapples and maize and was copied at other potteries and in porcelain at CHELSEA and WORCESTER. Reproductions were made during the mid-19thC but are of inferior quality in modelling, glazing and colours.

cauling A means of flattening a VENEER onto a CARCASS and removing excess glue. The caul, a heated piece of wood, is clamped over the surface. The heat melts the glue coating on the carcass enabling the veneer to stick; the clamps are tightened, squeezing out any excess glue.

cavetto See MOULDINGS.

cedar Light reddish-brown aromatic timber from North America and the West Indies. Because of its aroma and insect-repellent qualities it was often used from the 18thC by cabinet-makers for the linings of drawers, boxes and chests, and for trays in clothes presses. See p.155.

celadon A European term for Chinese STONEWARE, initially developed during the SONG DYNASTY, with a translucent green glaze, and generally applied to any similar green-glaze. The shade varies according to the iron-oxide content. The word 'celadon' possibly comes from a character of that name in a 17thC French romance by Honoré d'Urfé, who wore a green coat. See p.166.

cellaret An all-embracing term introduced in the 18thC, for wine coolers and WINE CISTERNS. It is also used for trays or compartments fitted into a drawer or sideboard, for holding bottles of wine and spirits.

CELLARET or wine cooler, with brass mounts; 1770; 28 in (71 cm) high.

Cellini jug Heavy, ornate jug, moulded with masks, STRAPWORK and CARYATIDS. The style is typical of that employed by the Renaissance goldsmith and sculptor Benvenuto Cellini. See p.247.

Celluloid See PLASTIC.

Celtic style The decorative style of the Celts, a people who were originally from the western half of central Europe and then spread into Spain, Italy and the British Isles c.250 BC. Celtic motifs, with their curvaceous line patterns and stylised animal and human forms, were absorbed into English and Irish art, and were revived at the end of the 19thC by ART NOUVEAU artists, and particularly the GLASGOW SCHOOL.

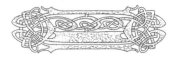

CELTIC INTERLACING on an early 20thC silver brooch from Liberty's Cymric range.

centrepiece See EPERGNE.

centrifugal casting See LOST WAX.

ceramics Clay-based products which are hardened by firing. The term, from the Greek *keramos* (clay), embraces all pottery including EARTHENWARE, STONEWARE PORCELAIN and BONE CHINA. See p.149.

chafing dish Vessel of silver or other metal, used for heating food and warming plates over a charcoal brazier or spirit lamp on the dinner table or sideboard. The dish rests on a stand supported by legs, which afford space for a heating device. Chafing dishes were used extensively from the 16thC. The term is sometimes used to refer to the brazier itself.

CHAFING DISH; silver with ebony handle; c.1815; 15 in (38.1 cm) long.

chair See boxes, p.453.

chaise longue French term for an upholstered or cushioned chair with a whole or part back, and a long seat.

CHAISE LONGUE with scroll back, serpentine rail and cabriole legs; c.1860.

Chamberlain See WORCESTER.

Chambers, Sir William (1726-96) NEOCLASSICAL architect and furniture designer, and, with Robert Adam, joint architect to King George III. Chambers was the first British architect to visit China, and as a consequence his CHINOISERIE work had a more authentic feel to it than much of that popular in the mid-18thC.

chamberstick Holder for a single candle with the sconce set into a saucer with a carrying handle attached, designed for bedroom use. Chambersticks were made from the 17thC and often had a SNUFFER attached. See pp.254-5.

chamfered Edge that is planed or cut at an angle, usually applied to stone and woodwork.

champagne glass It is uncertain whether special glasses were reserved for drinking champagne during the 17th and early 18th centuries. From the 1770s until the mid-19thC, FLUTE glasses were favoured – a trend that has returned today, because the narrow mouth retains the bubbles for longer. From c.1830, a wide shallow bowl of 4-6 fl oz (115-175 ml) capacity was popular. See p.475.

champagne tap A tap for dispensing champagne from a bottle without removing the cork. Similar in shape and size to a corkscrew, it consists of a pointed tube with a spout and a spigot on one end. With the spigot closed, the champagne retains its bubbles. The taps were made, usually in electroplated silver, from the late 19thC. See p.248.

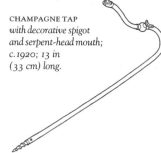

CHAMPAGNE TAP with decorative spigot and serpent-head mouth; c.1920; 13 in (33 cm) long.

champlevé See ENAMEL.

Chang ware Range of ART POTTERY developed by the DOULTON factory during the early 20thC. Typical Chang ware has a thick, glutinous glaze in shades of red and grey. The glaze, applied in layers, has a pronounced CRACKLE.

The name 'Chang ware' is intended to reflect the Chinese inspiration.

CHAIR BACKS

balloon; c.1840 bar; c.1825 comb; c.1770 ladder; c.1770

lattice; c.1780 hoop; c.1780 lyre; c.1770 panel; c.1605

ribbon; c.1755 shield; c.1775 stick; c.1790 wheel; c.1775

PARTS OF CHAIRS

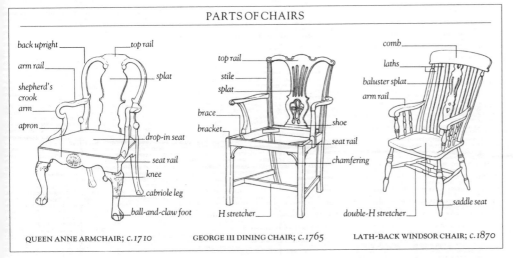

back upright, top rail, arm rail, splat, shepherd's crook arm, apron, drop-in seat, seat rail, knee, cabriole leg, ball-and-claw foot

QUEEN ANNE ARMCHAIR; c.1710

top rail, stile, splat, brace, bracket, shoe, seat rail, chamfering, H stretcher

GEORGE III DINING CHAIR; c.1765

comb, laths, baluster splat, arm rail, saddle seat, double-H stretcher

LATH-BACK WINDSOR CHAIR; c.1870

Chantilly A soft-paste PORCELAIN factory on the Prince de Condé's estate near Paris, c.1725-89. Early Chantilly porcelain has a distinctive white tin GLAZE and often KAKIEMON-style decoration. After 1740, a lead glaze was used and decoration was mainly naturalistic, featuring birds and flowers, including the **Chantilly sprig** – a cornflower with two leaves, and two sprays of forget-me-not flowers. The Chantilly lacemaking industry began in the late 17thC. It is particularly famed for its delicate handmade BOBBIN lace of the 19thC. This is usually a black silk lace with the pattern outlined in a thicker strand of silk.

1725

chapter ring Ring on the DIAL of a clock marked with the time divisions.

character doll Term used from c.1890 for a doll with a distinctive, naturalistic expression, or with features modelled on those of a real child or famous person. A **portrait doll** is a French-made character doll and was popular from the 1850s.

char dish Flat-bottomed pot used from the 17th to 19th centuries for serving potted char (a relative of the trout) and often decorated on the outside with painted fish. The pots are about 1 in (25 mm) deep and 6-10 in (15-25 cm) across, and found in DELFTWARE and CREAMWARE.

charger Large circular or oval plate used for serving meat or for hanging as a wall decoration. The word is probably derived from the French *charger*, 'to fill'. See pp.186-7.

chasing Any method of decorating silver and other metalware in which the metal is repositioned, rather than removed by chiselling or carving. EMBOSSING and REPOUSSÉ are both forms of chasing. Bold, high-relief patterns are embossed; finer detail is added by the repoussé technique.

Flat-chasing is also worked from the front using hammers and punches, resulting in very shallow, low-relief patterns similar in effect to ENGRAVING. See p.235.

chatelaine Ornamental clasp or chain with a hook from which items such as keys, watches, seals and trinkets were hung. Chatelaines were worn at the waist, mainly by women, from the 17thC; they became less fashionable from c.1830, but made a comeback c.1890-1910. They were made in various metals and often ornamented with enamelling, beading and tassels. See p.259.

Chawner, Henry (1764-1851) London silversmith who worked with his brother, William, and was known as a spoon-maker. He was the son of a silversmith, Thomas Chawner, and in 1796 established a partnership with the EMES family, producing fine-quality silverware. **HC**

Chelsea With Bow, one of the earliest PORCELAIN factories in Britain, founded mid to late 1740s. Chelsea was the only 18thC English factory producing exclusively for the luxury porcelain market. Minor offshoots, including the so-called 'Girl in a Swing' workshop, an elusive establishment named after its most famous figure subject, obscure the early years of production. However, the following periods, named after the factory marks used at the time, are generally agreed.

Incised triangle period (1744-9) Little survives, but the ware was lighter and more translucent than that of Bow, with a glassy finish.

Raised anchor period (1749-52) Tableware reflects the silver fashions of the day, and there is also a strong MEISSEN influence in decoration, shapes and figure modelling. Oriental styles were adopted, particularly those

453

of Japanese KAKEIMON porcelain. From the 1750s, the trinkets known as TOYS became a Chelsea speciality.

Red anchor period (1752-8). The porcelain became a more consistent creamy-white. Although Meissen themes such as COMMEDIA DELL'ARTE figures are apparent, the factory developed its own distinctive style and reached its peak in artistic design. Botanical painting and tureens modelled in the form of birds were outstanding features.

Gold anchor period (1758-69) SÈVRES was the dominant source of inspiration, resulting in brightly painted and lavishly gilded tableware with rich ground colours and scenes based on the work of the French artist Antoine Watteau. The introduction of BONE ASH into the paste produced a lighter, more opaque body and enabled more complex shapes to be produced, as in elaborate Rococo vases.

In 1770, the Chelsea factory was sold to DERBY, although production did not cease until 1784. The products of the two factories merged stylistically into what became known as **Chelsea-Derby ware**. See pp.158, 175.

chenille 1 A soft, tufted cord of silk, cotton or woollen yarn used in embroidery or for fringing fabrics. 2 Any fabric made of chenille cord and, more generally, any of various imitation velvets produced from the 19thC. These include **Chenille Axminsters**, which are large, velvet-like carpets made using a two-loom weaving process at the AXMINSTER carpet factory.

chequerwork A form of decoration on furniture in which alternating squares or rectangles of contrasting colours or textures imitate the pattern of a chess or chequerboard. Chequerwork was used extensively as an INLAID DECORATION in the 16th and 17th centuries.

cherry The most popular fruitwood for furniture-making as it is hard and even-textured, with a superficial resemblance to mahogany, and polishes to a good finish. The cut wood of the British species varies in colour from pinkish-yellow to red-brown. Cherry was used particularly on the TURNED members of country-made chairs and tables in the 17th and 18th centuries, and by artist-craftsmen at the end of the 19th and in the early 20th century.

chesterfield Victorian design of well-padded, over-stuffed sofa, often buttoned, and with back and arms of the same height. See p.107.

chestnut Horse chestnut is a native European species which produces a pale yellowish wood sometimes with a hint of pink. It has a close, even grain and has been used over the centuries for drawer linings, TURNED work, carving and INLAID DECORATION, but it lacks durability. **Sweet chestnut** is light reddish-brown, sometimes used as a substitute for oak in panelling, but rarely seen in CASE FURNITURE.

chest of drawers Storage chest fitted with drawers which began to supersede the panelled chest or coffer in the 17thC. See COMMODE, TALLBOY and also pp.135-7.

cheval mirror Long, floor-standing, framed mirror held between two uprights so that the angle can be adjusted. Cheval mirrors were made from c.1750 and are also known as **horse dressing glasses** (*cheval* is French for horse). See p.144.

CHEVAL MIRROR; 75½ in (1.92 m) high.

cheveret Small 18thC English writing desk, with slender, tapering legs and a set of small drawers and pigeonholes on top. It is sometimes known as a **lady's cabinet**.

chiffonier French term for a tall chest of drawers, made in Britain from the 1750s. The term came to include small sideboards or side cabinets with a cupboard below, BUFFETS and side tables. See p.133.

chimera Decorative motif, seen in the 18th and 19th centuries, which originated in Classical mythology. It combines the features of a winged goat or lion with a serpent's tail.

CHIMERA *Figure used as a table support.*

china Unspecific (and therefore to be discouraged) term for ceramics. See BONE CHINA.

china cabinet A glass-fronted display cabinet for porcelain or CABINET-WARE, introduced in the late 17thC when it was fashionable to collect CHINESE EXPORT PORCELAIN.

china clay A white clay virtually free of impurities such as iron, also known as kaolin. It is used in ceramics for its qualities of strength and whiteness, and is an essential ingredient of PORCELAIN. The Chinese refer to the porcelain formula metaphorically as 'bones and flesh', CHINA STONE being the bone, china clay the flesh.

china stone Feldspathic rock, also known as **china rock**, which is the essential fusing agent in hard-paste PORCELAIN. When fired at a high temperature, the pulverised rock melts to a glassy paste (vitrifies) and binds with CHINA CLAY to give true porcelain its special strength and impermeability. It is also combined with lime and potash in a glaze that can be fused onto a permeable EARTHENWARE body in a single firing to make it waterproof. The Chinese equivalent of china stone is **petuntse**.

china table See TEA TABLE.

Chinese export porcelain Chinese porcelain products imported into Europe from the 16thC, and reaching a peak in the 17th and 18th centuries. Technically superior to European ceramics until the 18thC, Chinese porcelain was in great demand, and had a profound influence on European manufacturers who tried to capture its quality and decorative effects. The holds of East India trading vessels, especially from Holland and Britain, might be filled with flint for use in Chinese porcelain manufacture on the outward journey, and with china on the way back. The china was stacked beneath the principal cargoes of tea and silk (which had to be stored above the waterline), providing valuable ballast on the return journey. Most of the wares were of fairly ordinary quality, but there was a thriving private 'super cargo' trade in higher quality porcelain often specially commissioned by the Western aristocracy. See pp.155-7.

Chinese reign marks See REIGN MARKS.

Ch'ing dynasty See QING.

chinkin-bori Japanese LACQUER technique, which originated in China. Stylised geometrical or floral diaper (see DECORATIVE MOTIFS) patterns are engraved into a lacquer base and then filled with gold powder, foil, or coloured lacquers.

chinoiserie Chinese-style ornamentation in the 17th and 18th centuries. Characteristics of the style include pagoda shapes, FRETWORK, motifs of mandarin figures, birds and river scenes, dragon FINIALS and carved feet. From c.1690, such decoration was applied to LACQUERED furniture, engraved on silverware and painted on ceramics, especially Dutch DELFT. Chinoiserie was back in fashion during the Rococo period of the mid-18thC. See p.48.

chintz Cotton furnishing fabric in plain dyes or with printed patterns, and from the 1850s with a highly glazed finish. The word is from the Hindu *chīnt* (variegated) and at first applied to painted or printed CALICOES imported from India in the 17thC.

chip carving Medieval and 16thC wood decoration made by chipping out a pattern with a gouge or chisel. The pattern is usually contained within a circle, or roundel. See p.91.

Chippendale, Thomas (1718-79) Leading British cabinet-maker whose work was extremely influential during the early Georgian period and much imitated later. See p.33.

chocolate pot Covered vessel for preparing and serving hot chocolate, used since the second half of the 17thC. The silver chocolate pot has a hinged or detachable flap or finial in the lid though which a **molinet**, or rod, can be inserted to stir up the chocolate sediment. Molinets are usually made of wood with a knop or terminal in silver or ivory. A ceramic chocolate pot may be indistinguishable from a coffee pot. See pp.174, 251.

CHOCOLATE POT *with stirring rod; silver; c.1710; 9½ in (24.1 cm) high.*

chop tongs See ASPARAGUS TONGS.

choreutoscope An optical toy introduced in 1866 consisting of a lantern with a window and shutter. Various different images in glass slides (see MAGIC LANTERN) are passed across the window. Each image is viewed for a fraction of a second before the shutter falls and the next image is projected, giving the illusion of movement.

CHOREUTOSCOPE *Turning the handle pulls the strip of slides back and forth past the window, creating the illusion of a dancing skeleton.*

chota-peg Miniature jug used for individual servings of alcohol, dating from British colonial India at the end of the 19thC. *Chota* is the Hindi word for 'small measure'.

Christofle, Charles (1805-63) Founder of L'Orfèvrerie Christofle, a large firm of goldsmiths, silversmiths and jewellers, established in Paris, 1829. In 1842, Christofle obtained the sole rights to produce ELECTROPLATED wares in France from the British silversmiths, ELKINGTON. The firm also produced furniture and bronze furniture MOUNTS.

chrome dyes Chemical, colour-fast dyes for carpets and other fabrics, introduced in the early 20thC. Although they lack the subtlety and variety of natural vegetable and insect dyes, it can be difficult to distinguish between them.

chromium A very bright and hard, silvery metal used in the production of stainless steel and as a decorative, corrosion-resistant plating material. Although discovered in 1798, its decorative potential was not realised until it began to be commercially available in 1925. MODERN MOVEMENT designers such as LE CORBUSIER and BREUER used chromium plate on the tubular-steel furniture that had such an impact on 1930s design.

chronograph A precision stopwatch that has the facility to zero the seconds hand before restarting it. A **split-seconds chronograph** has two stop seconds hands, one above the other, each of which can be stopped independently.

chronometer A portable timepiece of great accuracy. In Britain the term is used specifically for one with a detent ESCAPEMENT, and in Switzerland for one with a lever escapement, which meets an official rating of timekeeping.

Chronometers were originally developed in the 18thC for use at sea so that a ship's longitudinal position

could be calculated accurately. Unlike pendulum-driven clocks, which are accurate only if stationary, chronometers aimed to be reliable even when subjected to temperature changes and the movement of a ship. The standard Greenwich mean time on the chronometer was compared with the ship's local time gauged by the position of the sun or the stars.

Mapping survey chronometers are set in a box; marine chronometers are usually in a drum-shaped case pivoted in gimbals (two rings at right angles to each other) in a wooden box with a glass lid. Pocket CHRONOMETERS were used both at sea and as pocket watches on land. All chronometers have a seconds hand; some show fractions of seconds. Most surviving examples are from the 19th and early 20th centuries. See p.285.

chronoscope A watch, also known as a **wandering-hour watch**, introduced c.1675, on which the hour is displayed through a semicircular arc in the dial. The numeral, carried on a rotating disc, takes one hour to move around the semicircle and then disappears from view behind a decorated cover, to be replaced by the next hour at the other end. The scale for the minutes appears along the edge of the semicircle. Chronoscopes generally stopped being produced c.1730, but there are some 20thC revivals.

CHRONOSCOPE *pocket watch; c.1690; 2⅛ in (54 mm) across.*

chryselephantine sculpture The term for Ancient Greek wooden statues overlaid with gold and ivory, which in the 20thC refers to cast-bronze figures with ivory flesh parts, popular 1910-30.

Cipriani, Giovani Battista (1727-85) Florentine engraver, painter and draughtsman, and founder-member of the Royal Academy of Arts in London (1768). Cipriani moved to Britain in 1753, and his greatest contribution to late 18thC NEOCLASSICAL style lay in his paintings of nymphs and figures, some on satinwood furniture.

circumferentor An early 17thC surveying instrument with a central compass surrounded by a brass circle

marked with degrees, over which arch several sights to guide the eye. From 1758, English surveyors used it with a THEODOLITE allowing them to measure both horizontal bearings and elevation at one time.

ciré French for 'waxed', referring to a hard, glossy finish given to fabrics, especially ribbons.

cire perdue See LOST WAX.

cistern barometer Barometer containing a straight glass tube, closed at the top end and with the bottom end immersed in a small chamber, or cistern, containing the mercury. The cistern cover is often decorated with bronze mounts and wooden carvings. See SIPHON barometer.

citrine A variety of quartz, usually pale yellow although occasionally red-brown to red-orange. The main source of citrine is Brazil. It is often confused with yellow TOPAZ.

clair de lune French for 'moonlight', used to describe a porcelain GLAZE of milky lavender-blue. The effect was achieved by adding a touch of cobalt blue to a feldspathic glaze, and is most commonly seen on 18thC Chinese porcelain, sometimes combined with a CRACKLE of black or brownish-red. It was also used at MEISSEN without the crackle effect.

claret jug 19thC wine jug, generally with a glass body held in decorative silver or silver-gilt mounts. A claret jug usually has a hinged lid with a THUMBPIECE which is often decorated with a figure. See p.247.

Classical See NEOCLASSICAL.

claymore Strictly, a two-handed Scottish sword introduced in the 16thC; the word is from the Gaelic *claidheam-mor* (great sword). Since the 18thC the term has also referred to a Scottish sword with a basket HILT.

clepsydra See WATER CLOCK.

Clichy Firm of glass-makers founded c.1837. It specialised in MILLEFIORI, producing fine and highly collectable paperweights, inkstands, vases and other domestic objects. See p.229.

Cliff, Clarice (1899-1972) Staffordshire pottery decorator famed for her distinctive, brightly coloured designs for A.J. WILKINSON at its Newport Pottery. Cliff set up her own studio at Newport in 1927 and launched the hand-painted 'Bizarre' range the following year. She occasionally used designs by

contemporary artists such as Paul Nash and Laura Knight on her pottery. By the end of her career, Cliff had produced around 2000 patterns and 500 new shapes. See pp.178, 183.

clipping The illegal practice of shearing metal from the edge of a precious-metal coin for profit – a universal practice dating from ancient times. Clipping was relatively easy to do with HAMMERED coins, although it could be detected with careful and consistent weighing. The penalties were severe for those who were caught; sentences of death or limb amputation have been recorded. Clipping was largely stopped with the introduction of machine-made coins in Britain from 1662.

clobbering The technique of overpainting an already existing design on ceramics. The Dutch, in particular, used clobbering to embellish Chinese BLUE AND WHITE export and MEISSEN porcelain during the 18th and 19th centuries. See p.166.

CLOCK AND WATCH KEYS

clock keys

c.2½ in (63 mm) long

1 *hand-finished key for bracket clock; c.1680-1720;* **2** *crank-handle key for longcase and regulator clocks; c.1700-1840;* **3** *carriage clock double key; 1860-1920.*

watch keys

c.¾ in (19 mm) long

1 *enamelled key; c.1765;* **2** *crank key; c.1735.*

clock hands Pointers on the dial of a clock which indicate the time. They are found in brass, silver and other metals, sometimes decorated with enamel. Early clocks have single hour hands in sturdy, arrowhead or spear shapes. The first PENDULUM clocks of the mid-17thC have hand-fretted, filed and chased hands; at this time, too, minute hands became a standard feature. As the size of LONGCASE CLOCKS increased at the beginning of the 18thC, the hands became bigger and bolder. From *c*.1790, clock hands were stamped out by machine to create ornate scrolls and curves. 19th and 20thC clock hands are much plainer and the minute hand is closer in size to that of the hour hand.

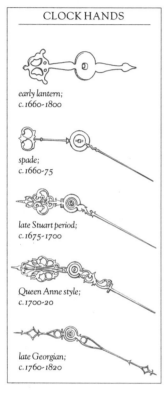

CLOCK HANDS

early lantern;
c.1660-1800

spade;
c.1660-75

late Stuart period;
c.1675-1700

Queen Anne style;
c.1700-20

late Georgian;
c.1760-1820

clockwatch Any watch which strikes the hour and sometimes quarter hours automatically as the hands go round.

cloisonné See ENAMELLING.

close helmet Helmet protecting head and neck dating from the 15thC.

close-plating The method of coating iron or other base metals with a film of silver that preceded SHEFFIELD PLATE. It was used from early times – for plating knife handles, for example – and in the 18thC for small objects such as buttons and buckles. The objects were dipped in molten tin; silver foil was pressed over the surface, and the metals fused with a hot soldering iron.

close stool Lidded stool which conceals a pewter or earthenware chamber pot or similar vessel beneath the seat. The alternative terms of **night** and **necessary** stools were replaced in the 19thC by what the Victorians called a **night commode**.

cloth of gold See BROCADE.

club foot See FEET.

Clutha glass ART GLASS developed by J. Couper & Sons of Glasgow *c*.1885, and mostly designed by Christopher DRESSER. Its name is thought to come from the Gaelic word for the River Clyde. It is usually green, yellow or amber (occasionally turquoise or black), with numerous air bubbles, irregular cloudy streaks and flecks of AVENTURINE.

Cluthra glass Cloudy, bubbly ART GLASS developed in the USA by the British designer Frederick CARDER. The effect was created by adding saltpetre (potassium nitrate) to the molten glass; the chemical reacts with the heat to form the large, random bubbles. Cluthra glass is CASED with an outer layer of heavy, clear glass.

coaching clock See TAVERN CLOCK.

coach pot See BOURDALOU.

coach watch Large, portable timepiece in the form of a 4-6 in (10-15 cm) diameter pocket watch. Such watches, often with an elaborately decorated case, were used in coaches during the 18thC. Many have hour or hour and quarter-hour striking mechanisms. See also CLOCKWATCH, SEDAN WATCH.

Coade stone Clay-based artificial stone invented by Mrs Eleanor Coade at her London factory *c*.1769. It resembles natural limestone, but is more durable. Coade stone was much used for garden statuary until the mid-19thC. See p.201.

Coalbrookdale 1 Shropshire iron foundry established 1708, which produced decorative and utilitarian cast iron ranging from ornamental vases to stoves and seats.
2 See COALPORT.

Coalport Porcelain factory established on the banks of the River Severn in Shropshire, 1795, which absorbed the nearby CAUGHLEY factory four years later.
A form of BONE CHINA was produced at Coalport from 1798 but only achieved the soft white translucency and smooth surface for which the ware is now celebrated after 1810. A hard, clear, and highly lustrous lead GLAZE, introduced 1820, further improved quality and enhanced the bright ENAMEL colours used. A maroon ground, introduced the following year, became one of Coalport's trademarks.
Until this time, output had concentrated on simply decorated tableware, although there were Oriental-style designs too, including the WILLOW PATTERN, and the much

imitated Indian tree pattern which was first used at Coalport. From the 1820s, however, decoration became more opulent and lavishly gilded. The next decade saw an increase in range and even more elaborate designs. Masses of finely modelled, flower-encrusted vases, candlesticks, baskets, clock cases and jugs were made up to 1840. Up to 1815, pieces were marked (if at all) 'Coalbrookdale', 'CD' or 'C. Dale' after the neighbouring town. Ornamental vases made in the 1890s often incorporate small landscape panels (signed by the artist) within JEWELLED line borders. These cabinet pieces competed strongly against WORCESTER and DERBY porcelain of the same period.

coal-tar dyes See ANILINE DYES.

coaster Circular stand, usually of silver, SHEFFIELD PLATE and/or wood, within a raised rim or gallery, for port or other wine bottles or glasses. Coasters were used in Britain from the 1760s. The name is derived from the after-dinner custom of rolling back the tablecloth and coasting, or sliding, the port from person to person on a smooth-bottomed stand. Double coasters on wheels are known as **wine trolleys**. See pp.248-9.

cock beading Prominent wooden BEAD MOULDING commonly used to edge British walnut and mahogany drawer-fronts, *c*.1730-1800.

coffee can Cylindrical porcelain coffee cup, about 2½ in (60 mm) wide and high. Larger versions are called **breakfast cans**. See pp.173-4.

coffee pot Covered vessel, generally of silver or ceramic, for serving coffee, used in Britain since the mid-17thC, when coffee was first imported. The spout is normally directly opposite the handle, although sometimes at right angles to it, and is higher on the body than would be the case on a teapot, to avoid the coffee sediment escaping. See pp.173, 252-3.

coffered Panelled construction in which the panels are thinner than the depth of the framework. See JOINING.

coin glass Drinking glass or jug with one or more coins enclosed in the KNOP or FOOT. Although examples exist from the early 18thC, the date on the coin rarely signifies the year the glass itself was manufactured. Such pieces were made to commemorate special occasions like a coronation.

cold painting Decoration, also known as **cold pigments**, on ceramics painted in oil or lacquer-based colours

that, unlike enamels, are not fused onto the surface by FIRING. Even when coated with varnish, the colours are prone to flaking and wear. Cold pigments were used on some Meissen RED STONEWARE and Berlin FAIENCE, but few examples survive. See also HIGH-TEMPERATURE COLOURS.

Cole, Sir Henry (1808-82) British designer of ceramics and household objects, who designed an award-winning tea service for MINTON, 1846, under the pseudonym Felix Summerly. His firm, Summerly's Art Manufacturers, operated 1847-50 designing household wares, with an emphasis on good industrial design. Cole also assisted in the organisation of the Great Exhibition, held in London in 1851.

collar Ring applied to the stem of a wine glass to disguise a join, used when a glass was made in separate pieces and fused together. It is frequently seen where a bowl or foot joins a stem, but may also be seen around large KNOPS.

column Vertical support, circular in cross-section. In their pioneering **orders of architecture** (see box opposite), the ancient Greeks introduced three distinct styles – Doric, Ionic and Corinthian – and the Romans later added the Tuscan and Composite orders. All of these orders are seen reproduced in furniture, furnishings and decorative objects. See also PEDIMENT.

combed decoration 1 A decorative effect on ceramics achieved by scratching or incising the clay while still moist with a comb-like instrument. The incised areas are flooded with a translucent GLAZE. This technique is seen particularly on Chinese CELADON wares of the northern SONG DYNASTY.
2 Pattern on ceramics achieved by coating the body with a liquid clay SLIP and creating either wavy or zigzagged lines or a **feathered** effect with a metal brush or comb. The technique was developed by John DWIGHT, John ASTBURY and Thomas WHIELDON, and is commonly found on 17th and 18thC Staffordshire slipware.
3 A glass-making technique in which threads of opaque glass are applied to the body, flattened into the still-molten surface by MARVERING, and then combed to create a feathered icing effect.

comfit box See BONBONNIÈRE.

commedia dell'arte Italian comic theatre genre featuring characters such as Punchinello (or Punch),

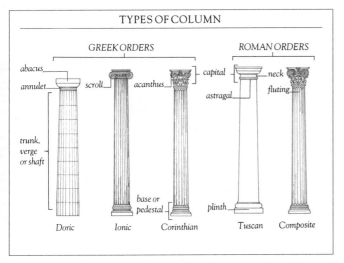

TYPES OF COLUMN

GREEK ORDERS

abacus
annulet
scroll
acanthus
trunk, verge or shaft
base or pedestal

Doric   Ionic   Corinthian

ROMAN ORDERS

capital
astragal
neck
fluting
plinth

Tuscan   Composite

Harlequin and Columbine. It developed in the 16thC but was a source of inspiration in every area of the decorative arts during the 18thC. See MEISSEN. See box below.

commemoratives Objects inscribed or decorated to commemorate an event or a person. See pp.196-8, 384-5.

commode In the late 17th and early 18th centuries, the French name for a low chest of drawers. The word gradually came to describe any low cupboard or chest which was of a decorative French pattern.

The **commode chair**, with a hinged seat enclosing a chamber pot, was introduced in the mid-Georgian period, and known by the Victorians as a **night commode**. See pp.135-7.

Compagnie des Arts Francais See SÜE & MARE.

compass card Freely rotating circular card in a navigational or surveying compass that is marked with the points of the compass. It has a compass needle mounted beneath so that it swings to point to magnetic north.

compendium 1 A container for a set of games or objects, as in a 19thC **writing compendium**. This is a shallow, ornate box for holding writing materials when travelling, which opens out to provide a writing surface.

2 A multifuctional or combination scientific or navigational instrument, such as a portable SUNDIAL combined with a wind vane.

complication A watchmaker's term for pocket watches that not only tell the time, but incorporate extra features such as automatically changing calendars, stopwatch or REPEATER mechanisms.

comport Ornamental glass or ceramic stand dating from the 18thC, with a shallow dished top and sturdy stem.

COMPORT *of pressed glass; c.1900; 2²⁄₃ in (68 mm) high.*

They are 5-18 in (12.5-46 cm) tall, and were designed to hold sweetmeats, fruit, cakes or bread. See TAZZA.

composition or **compo** Plaster-like material made from whiting (chalk), resin and size or glue, and used to make relief mouldings on furniture. Compo can be pressed into moulds when wet, and is hard enough to be carved when dry. It was widely used in Britain in the second half of the 18thC. A version of compo based on wood-pulp materials mixed with ingredients such as eggs, crushed bones or bread was used for dolls' bodies c.1820-1940. **Carton** is a cheap form of this used for dolls' bodies in the 1920s and 30s.

Comyns, William Founder of a London silversmiths which produces hand-made dressing-table services, photograph frames and other items from 1848. See pp.257-8.

concertina action The folding frame of a type of CARD TABLE popular in the mid-18thC. The hinged sides straighten as the backlegs are pulled out, and fold back concertina fashion.

confidante Double or triple-seated chair set in a curving S-shaped framework, designed so that two or more people can converse more easily than if they were sitting side by side. A mechanical version with swivelling seats is known as a **sociable seat**. Confidantes were popular in Victorian and Edwardian times. See p.107.

CONFIDANTE *An early Victorian three-seater version.*

console table Type of side table supported by one or more legs at the front, and fixed to the wall with brackets at the back. See p.120.

conversation seat See BORNE.

Cookworthy, William (1705-80) The first producer of true PORCELAIN in Britain. The discovery of CHINA CLAY and CHINA ROCK deposits in Cornwall led to Cookworthy's successful formula in 1768 at his PLYMOUTH factory. Cookworthy was probably also involved in the development of soft-paste porcelain incorporating SOAPSTONE used at BRISTOL and WORCESTER.

Cooper, Susie (b.1903) British pottery designer and painter. She studied at the Burslem School of Art in Staffordshire and set up her own company in 1929. Her designs are Modernist but appealed to a wide but fashion-conscious market. In 1966 Cooper became senior designer at the WEDGWOOD factory. See pp.178-9, 195.

Copeland See SPODE.

Copenhagen Danish porcelain factory noted since the late 18thC for animal and human figures and smoky underglaze-blue decoration. Copenhagen first produced soft-paste PORCELAIN, 1759-65. Hard-paste porcelain was first produced in 1774 by a firm that in 1779 became The Royal Danish Porcelain Factory (sometimes referred to as the **Royal Copenhagen Porcelain Manufactory**). Porcelain figures were produced from c.1780.

The company declined in the early 19thC but revived when it was taken over by the Alumina Faience Manufactory in 1882. Architect Arnold Krog, appointed artistic director in 1885, introduced a revolutionary new glazing technique which washed the whole of a piece of porcelain with colour as opposed to the previous style of painting small areas, and the earlier formal style of figure-modelling was replaced by more naturalistic forms.

In the early 20thC came ART NOUVEAU-style designs, and from the 1920s STONEWARE models with glazes that were Chinese-inspired. *c.1775 on*

Coper, Hans (1920-81) German studio potter who settled in Britain in 1939 and shared a studio with fellow potter Lucie RIE. Coper identified strongly with the Modern movement, producing roughly textured sculptural pieces. See p.185.

COMMEDIA DELL'ARTE FIGURES

Lalage and Harlequin   *Lucinda and Pierrot*   *Julia and Pantalone*

NYMPHENBERG FIGURES *modelled by Franz Anton Bustelli; porcelain; c.1760; c.5 in (12.7 cm) high.*

Copland, Henry (1720-53) Engraver and designer of the early Georgian period. Copland was an early exponent of the Rococo style in England as seen in *A New Book of Ornaments*, a much-copied pattern book he compiled with Matthias LOCK, published 1752. He and Lock worked together on several other publications, including Thomas CHIPPENDALE's *The Gentleman and Cabinet Maker's Director*.

copper Comparatively soft, reddish metal which is used both in its own right and as an alloy in BRONZE, BRASS, fine PEWTER and PINCHBECK. It is also used to impart strength to silver and gold. Gilded copper was a substitute for gold in the Middle Ages in domestic and church pieces. From *c.*1742, copper was fused with silver to make SHEFFIELD PLATE. Pure copper can be coated with tin to prevent corrosion. See pp.368-9.

coquillage Shell ornamentation found in Rococo-style designs.

coral A hard, organic substance, formed from the skeletons of marine polyps and used for personal adornment since Egyptian times. The variety chosen for jewellery is solid, without visible indentations, and varies in colour from pinkish-white to red. Coral jewellery became popular in Britain in the mid-19thC when it was imported from Naples and Genoa.

Coralene Trade name for a type of glass decoration developed in the USA. Coral-like forms were painted on glass in ENAMEL and small glass beads were fused onto them. The technique was used for both figurative and natural designs, and was also popular in Britain and Europe.

cordial glass Small-bowled drinking glass with a long, thickish stem and 1-1½ fl oz (30-40 ml) capacity. It was used for drinking cordials – potent, concentrated tipples taken after tea – in the 18thC, and is also known as a **liqueur glass**. See box, p.475.

cordonnet See LACE.

core Shape made of clay or mud and straw around which glass was moulded. The technique, dating from 1500 BC, died out when blowing was introduced but was revived in the late 19thC for making MOSAIC GLASS.

cornelian A red variety of the quartz gemstone chalcedony, which is used in jewellery, especially in signet rings and beads, and for SEALS. The gems range from medium, slightly cloudy red to clear, deep red.

corner chair Chair introduced in the early 18thC with a single front leg, and low back and top rail. This type of chair is also known as an **angle** or **writing chair**. See p.96.

corner cupboard Freestanding or hanging cupboard built on a right angle to fit into a corner. Movable types on stands were made during the 18thC, some with glazed doors for the display of china or ornaments. The French version, called an **encoignure**, is normally enclosed by doors with shelves above. See p.134.

cornice The decorative projection or moulding above a frieze in architecture or topping a piece of furniture such as a bookcase, cabinet or the TESTER of a bedstead.

Corning Glassworks Major US glass factory founded 1868 and still in operation. It developed the heat-resistant glass known as Pyrex (1908). In 1918 the company acquired the STEUBEN GLASSWORKS, renowned for its ART GLASS, and the British designer Frederick CARDER became director of the whole operation.

coromandel See EBONY.

corridor carpet See RUNNERS.

corundum Extremely hard mineral, of which the sapphire and the ruby are varieties. Ruby is the red variety of corundum; pink, yellow, blue and green corundums are classed as sapphires. The rarest and most valuable rubies – flawless and deep in colour with strong fluorescence or FIRE – are second only in value to very fine emeralds and pink, blue and green diamonds. The traditional source of blood-red rubies was Burma, but light red stones have been mined in Sri Lanka (Ceylon). The ruby is often confused with a less-precious gemstone, the **red spinel.**

The most prestigious sapphires, ranging in colour from clear cornflower to deep blue are the 'Kashmir blue' sapphires, imported to Europe from India since 1862.

Corundums can be artificially produced, but under a microscope reveal curved striation and gas bubbles which do not occur in the natural stone. See p.267.

costrel See PILGRIM BOTTLE.

costume jewellery Articles of jewellery made from base metals, PINCHBECK or silver and set with imitation gems, such as PASTE. Some quality examples are made for leading couturiers, such as Chanel and Christian Dior.

cosy corner An upholstered and cushioned seat made to fit the corner of a room, popular in Britain in the late 19thC. The term was also applied to a comfortably furnished corner.

Cotswold school English late 19th to early 20thC furniture-designer and craftsman's association in the Gloucestershire Cotswolds. It was set up in 1894 by Sydney and Ernest Barnsley and Ernest GIMSON, who were also connected with the ARTS AND CRAFTS MOVEMENT. The designs made use of traditional methods and untreated English woods. Dutch cabinet-maker Peter Waals was one of the foremost designers.

cottage clock Small, inexpensive wood MANTEL CLOCK produced in Britain in the 19thC. The clocks are fitted with a watch movement which goes for only one day after each winding. Cottage clocks, like SEDAN CLOCKS, provided a means of recycling 18thC pocket-watch movements as these were too fat for the slim-cased pocket watches of the time. See p.284.

couch A 17thC development of the DAY BED with a long, upholstered seat and a back and headrest at one end. In the 18th and early 19th centuries, the term became more or less synonymous with settee.

couched work Embroidery in which a thread is laid along the fabric and then held in place by over-stitching.

counter box Small, circular container made of silver, wood or ivory, used for storing gaming counters. They date from the 17thC. Fine silver examples contain thin, silver counters; others contain ones made of iron or mother-of-pearl.

countermark A mark, also known as a **counterstamp**, struck onto an existing coin or the cut part of a coin some time after it was initially struck. An ancient practice, still in use today, carried out usually as an emergency measure to revalue the currency or to validate a foreign piece for use in another country.

COUNTERMARK *of George III on a 1785 Spanish-American 8 reales piece circulated in Britain, January-June 1804.*

country furniture General term for furniture made by provincial craftsmen using local and indigenous woods such as oak, elm, ash and fruitwoods. Durability and function were of greater importance than aesthetic design and comfort. Country furniture is typically individual in design. See p.100.

Courtauld II, Augustine (*c.*1685-1751) The most prolific and probably most skilled member of the Courtauld family of silversmiths. He was of French extraction but based in London, producing conservative and plain QUEEN ANNE-style domestic silverware. His son Samuel Courtauld I (1720-65) made elaborate Rococo-style wares, and following his death, his wife Louisa continued the business in partnership with George Cowles (1768-78).

court cupboard A cupboard, the forerunner of the SIDEBOARD, dating from the 16thC. It consists of two open shelves, sometimes with a small central cupboard in the upper tier. Court cupboards were popular again in the GOTHIC REVIVAL of the early 19thC. See p.119.

courting chair See LOVE SEAT.

court sword See DRESS SWORD.

cow creamer Cream jug of silver or ceramics in the form of a cow, particularly popular in the second half of the 18thC. See p.174.

Cowles, George See COURTAULD, Augustine.

cracked ice Chinese porcelain ground in varying intensities of blue, irregularly crossed with dark lines to create a cracked-ice effect. It was introduced in the 17thC, and little copied in Europe, apart from some rare examples in Bristol DELFTWARE and WORCESTER porcelain. See p.162.

crackle A network of fine lines on a ceramics glaze caused when the rates of contraction of body and glaze are sufficiently different to cause a tension between the two. The effect can be deliberately produced to create a matrix of hairline cracks. These are sometimes enhanced with an iron-oxide stain, a technique perfected in SONG DYNASTY wares.

Over time, perhaps centuries after a piece was fired, the tension between body and glaze coupled with, for example, a change in temperature, may result in a fine network of cracks known as **crazing**.

crackled glass See ICE GLASS.

cranberry glass Cheap, pinkish-red glass developed in Britain during the late 19th and early 20th centuries. It became popular in Britain and the USA for drinking glasses and later for bowls and vases with TRAILED or ENAMEL decoration. See p.225.

crazing See CRACKLE.

cream pail See PIGGIN.

creamware A refined, cream-coloured, lead-glazed EARTHENWARE which ousted DELFTWARE from its dominant position and threatened many continental porcelain manufacturers, including MEISSEN. Creamware was lightweight, durable and inexpensive. It represented a key British contribution to ceramics development and was exported and copied throughout Europe. The creamware paste incorporates white Devon clay and ground burnt flints, and can be fired to a slightly higher temperature and level of vitrification than ordinary earthenware. It was developed in Staffordshire potteries c.1740 and was improved by Josiah WEDGWOOD who marketed it as **Queen's Ware** in 1765.

At first, small motifs were added as decoration, but later examples were enamelled or TRANSFER-PRINTED. Colour could be introduced during glazing – as in Wedgwood's CAULIFLOWER WARE – and powdered metallic oxides were sometimes dusted on before firing for different finishes.

Around 1780, to compete with CHINESE EXPORT PORCELAIN, the basic yellowish creamware glaze was replaced by a bluish one, which came to be known as **pearlware**, although the paste itself remained the same. Pearlware continued into the 19thC and was ideal for blue-printed designs as produced by SPODE and DAVENPORT. See p.168.

credence table Small table often designed to fit into a niche, and used in church in the 19thC for placing the Sacrament vessels on. The name now also refers to late 16th and early 17thC

CREDENCE TABLE of oak with gate-leg opening on wooden hinges; c.1620; 32 in (81 cm) high.

tables with a hinged top which, when closed, have a semicircular or three-sided surface.

credenza Italian word for a sideboard now often used to describe a type of low Victorian cabinet, sometimes with rounded ends and glazed or solid panel doors. See pp.133-4.

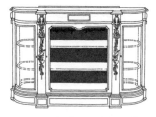

CREDENZA of walnut; with typical bowed glazed ends and central door; 1860; 43 in (1.09 cm) high.

Creil A factory whose name has become synonymous with TRANSFER-PRINTED earthenware in France, although subsequently much was made elsewhere. Creil was founded in 1795, and became the first French pottery to produce CREAMWARE to imitate and compete with the mass of inexpensive tablewares exported from British factories such as WEDGWOOD. Designs, transfer-printed in black, sepia or reddish-brown are of buildings, people, landscapes, hunting scenes and, in the late 19thC, of satirical subjects. Creil twice joined forces – 1818-25 and 1840-95 – with the nearby creamware factory at Montereau, and although Creil closed in 1895, Montereau continued using its name until 1955.

L.M & Cᵉ
1841 on

crested ware Ceramic ornaments bearing the crests or arms of the town in which they were to be sold, generally as souvenirs. The Staffordshire potter William Goss popularised crested ware in the late 19thC. See p.199.

cresting Carved or moulded ornament on the top rail of a chair, or at the top of a cabinet or mirror frame.

cretonne Strong, plain-weave material with a slightly ridged appearance, named after Creton, Normandy, where it was first made. It rivalled CHINTZ as an upholstery fabric in the late 19thC and was also popular in the 1920s and 30s.

crewel-work Embroidery worked with a fine, loosely twisted woollen (or **worsted**) yarn on a canvas or linen background, popular in the late 17thC, and in early Georgian and Victorian times. See p.308.

Crich ware Brown STONEWARE produced at Crich, Derbyshire, during the second half of the 18thC. See CROUCH WARE.

cricket table Small, simple, three-legged, portable table that continued to be made into the 19thC. The tables were common in taverns as they could be used on an uneven floor.

CRICKET TABLE Oak; c.1780; 21 in (53.5 cm) diameter.

cristallo A Venetian SODA GLASS developed in the 15thC in which the soda element comes from the ashes of barilla, a saltwater marsh plant. This, together with the decolorising agent manganese oxide, produces a colourless glass that resembles rock CRYSTAL. Its fragility means that it can only take surface decoration such as ENAMELLING, TRAILING and GILDING, as opposed to cutting. See p.207.

crizzling Fine network of cracks in glass caused by excess alkali in the ingredients. This problem was largely overcome by George RAVENSCROFT in 1676 when he added lead oxide to the METAL. See p.207.

Cromwellian Term used to describe furniture made during the Commonwealth (1649-60). Severe and rigid forms and the lack of ornamentation reflect the Puritan austerity of the times. A **Cromwellian stool** is a BACKSTOOL dating from Oliver Cromwell's mid-17thC Puritan England, with straight back and seat upholstered in leather and studded with brass-headed nails.

Cromwellian clock See LANTERN CLOCK.

crossbow A bow mounted horizontally on a wooden tiller and with the cord drawn back by hand or,

in later examples, by a mechanical device. The powerful crossbow fired short arrows known as **quarrels**. These weapons were popular with hunters and target shooters. The crossbow is also known as an **arbalest**.

cross-hatching See HATCHING.

crouch ware Brown, salt-glazed, 17th-18thC STONEWARE made at Burslem, Staffordshire, from local clays and sand. The origin of the name is unknown. It may be derived from the French cruche (pitcher), or alternatively crouch ware may have been made from crouch-clay, found near Crich in Derbyshire. It is not the same as CRICH WARE, however.

crown Large British coin of silver or smaller coin of gold, traditionally with a face value of 5s (25p).

Crowns were first struck in 1551, and are still made from time to time as commemorative pieces. The most recent issue, for Queen Elizabeth the Queen Mother's 90th birthday in 1990, was revalued by the Royal Mint at £5, although it is still confusingly called a crown. See p.387.

crown glass A clear optical SODA GLASS with low light refraction.

cruet Small, stoppered bottle shaped like a decanter, originally used for holding water and wine at the altar, but subsequently used for condiments such as oil and vinegar at the table. Early examples dating from the 16thC were made of earthenware or pewter. In the 18thC glass examples became more widespread, and bottles were kept together in a frame which usually had a carrying handle.

Cruet sets, as these came to be known, frequently consisted of five or more bottles or CASTERS. Small cruet sets may consist of only two or three containers – for salt, pepper and mustard. See p.245.

crystal 1 Natural crystalline quartz also known as **rock crystal**, which is usually colourless and transparent. Carved crystal was highly prized during the RENAISSANCE period. In the 19th and 20th centuries it was used for cameos and seals and was also

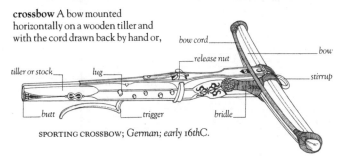

SPORTING CROSSBOW; German; early 16thC.

polished or faceted for jewellery.
2 Heavy, colourless, transparent lead glass made in imitation of hardstone and quartz carvings from the East. It is heavily cut, engraved and then polished to its original glossy surface. See LEAD CRYSTAL and p.207.

crystallo-ceramie See SULPHIDES.

Cubism Early 20thC movement in painting, led by artists Pablo PICASSO and Georges Braque, that combined lines, shapes and geometric patterns to emphasise the structure of objects from several viewpoints at once. It greatly influenced the ceramics, wallpapers and textiles of the ART DECO movement.

cuckoo clock Clock with a striking mechanism that activates the appearance of a wooden cuckoo from behind trap doors. The birdcall is mimicked by two small organ pipes. The clocks originated c.1740 in the Black Forest in Germany, although few examples survive from before 1840. Swiss examples were not made before the late 19thC.

cuirass See ARMOUR.

cuisse See ARMOUR.

cullet Broken or imperfect glass which is set aside to be returned to the furnace to make a fresh batch of molten glass. It usually constitutes about a tenth of the batch.

cup and cover Carved decoration shaped like a bowled cup with a domed lid, found on some bulbous turned furniture legs and bedposts in the 16th and 17th centuries. See pp.19, 21.

curl Decorative feather-like FIGURE on some woods achieved by cutting the wood at a certain angle and valued for VENEERS.

curtain piece See FRIEZE.

cut-card work Decorative technique in silverware, in which shapes and patterns are cut from a flat sheet of metal and soldered flat onto the body of an article to create a design in sharp relief. It was particularly popular on French and British silver of the late 17th and early 18th centuries.
    The technique was adapted to furniture by gluing a FRETWORK design onto a background of the same or contrasting wood as an alternative to solid carving. See p.236.

cut glass Glass which is decorated by cutting patterns into the surface with a rotating wheel. The technique has been known since the 8thC BC, but

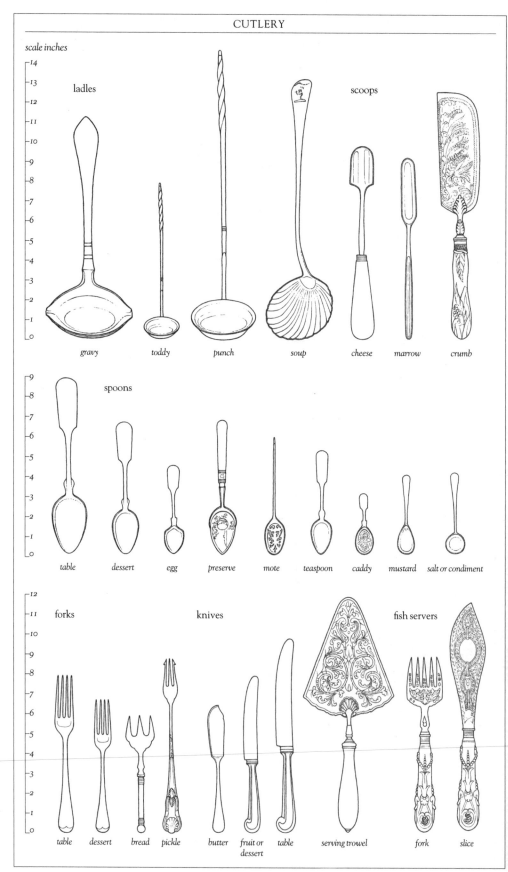

CUTLERY

scale inches

ladles   scoops

gravy   toddy   punch   soup   cheese   marrow   crumb

spoons

table   dessert   egg   preserve   mote   teaspoon   caddy   mustard   salt or condiment

forks   knives   fish servers

table   dessert   bread   pickle   butter   fruit or dessert   table   serving trowel   fork   slice

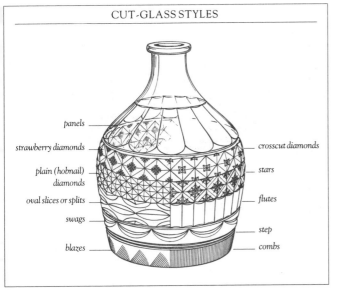
D

d Pre-decimalisation abbreviation for PENNY.

dagger Short, pointed, bladed weapon usually double-edged for thrusting, parrying and stabbing.

daguerreotype The first practicable photographic process, invented by the French painter and theatrical designer Jacques Louis Daguerre (1789-1851) in 1839. It produced a positive image, formed of tiny globules of mercury, on a silver-coated copper plate. The daguerreotype could only be reproduced by being rephotographed, and exposures took up to 30 minutes. It was eventually superseded by the CALOTYPE process. See p.338.

daisho The term for a matching pair of Japanese samurai swords or sword and dagger, popular from the 15thC, made up of the words *dai* (long) and *sho* (short).

damascening Process of setting fine pieces of contrasting metals into a metal body, such as the blade of a sword or a casket, for decoration. The technique was originally developed in Damascus in the Near East and was adopted in Europe in the 17thC. Gold, silver or copper wires were inserted into fine grooves cut into an iron, brass or bronze body and then hammered into the surface. European craftsmen tended to apply the decorative metal superficially on a crosshatched or 'toothed' surface which easily became worn away. This method was known as 'counterfeit' or 'false' damascening.

damask A reversible fabric used for table linen, curtains and upholstery. Damask was originally woven in silk and later in linen, wool and man-made fibres. Its characteristic appearance is due to the upper and lower surfaces of the same weave forming the pattern and tonal variation. Damask with silver, gold or coloured metallic threads running through it is known as **damassin.**

Most damask, coloured red or plum, was imported from Italy until the late 17thC, when production began in Britain. Red and blue damask was popular for window curtains and upholstery throughout the Georgian period. The Dutch pioneered linen damask for luxury tablecloths and napkins in the 15thC, but from the 17thC, Germany and Ireland became increasingly important centres.

darned netting See FILET.

Daum Glass factory run by brothers Auguste (1853-1909) and Antonin (1864-1930) Daum in 1875 in Nancy, France, and known for ART NOUVEAU and ART DECO vases and mushroom-shaped lamps. See p.223.

davenport A small desk, usually with a sloping writing surface and four drawers set sideways into the case beneath. The first record of the design is of a desk made for a Captain Davenport, probably for use at sea, in the late 18thC. There are many variations of the basic style. See p.122.

Davenport Porcelain and earthenware factory founded by John Davenport at Longport, Staffordshire, in 1794. BONE CHINA was introduced c.1800, and the tea services which often closely imitated DERBY in decoration. Ornamental articles, however, were more individual to Davenport, featuring both monochrome and multicoloured landscapes and skilfully painted flowers and fruits.
Production declined from the 1870s and the factory closed in 1887.

c.1820

---

was not practised in Britain until LEAD CRYSTAL was developed in the 18thC. See box above and pp.209, 220.

cutlass A short sword with a wide, flat blade, the term first appearing in the 16thC.

cutlery Implements for eating and serving food. Only spoons and knives were used until 1660, when Charles II returned from exile in France with the idea of setting a table with a full set of cutlery. See box below and pp.240-1.

cut money Coins cut into pieces, officially or otherwise, to provide small change. This was a particularly common practice in parts of the British Empire in the late 18th and early 19th centuries.

cut steel See FACETED STEEL.

cutwork A lace-like form of decorating linen in which shapes are cut out of the material and filled in

with geometric, buttonhole-stitched designs. It is of 15thC Italian origin and was used extensively in the 16th and 17th centuries and was revived in the 19thC. See DRESDEN WORK, AYRSHIRE WORK and p.311.

cylinder fall A curved lid that rolls or slides beneath the top surface of a desk or bureau when opened. It can be rigid, or slatted as with a TAMBOUR. The style was popular in the late 18thC and again c.1890-1910.

cyma Term for a moulding with a partly concave and partly convex curve in profile. See MOULDINGS.

cypress Hard, durable, reddish, close-grained timber of southern Europe. Like cedar, it has long-lasting aromatic qualities which keep moths and insects at bay, and is resistant to worm. Cypress was considered a rare, exotic wood in medieval Europe and has been widely used for chests and boxes in Britain from the 16thC.

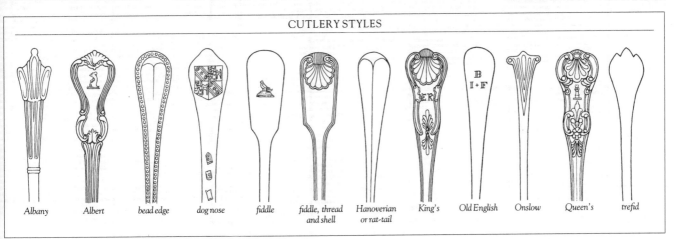

day bed A term known from the 16thC for an upholstered couch or sofa with a sloped backrest at one or both ends used for reclining on during the day. See p.107.

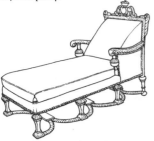

DAY BED *with gilded walnut frame and velvet upholstery, dating from the late 17thC; 5 ft (1.52 m) long.*

deaccession The sale of an item or items that were originally donated to an institution such as a museum or gallery in order to raise funds.

deal Pine and other soft coniferous woods used for the CARCASS of furniture or for cheap country furniture. The name is from the Dutch *deel* (part of), as the wood for a carcass is sawn into sections.

decanter Glass bottle with matching STOPPER used for serving wine at the table, and for spirits. See box below.

Deck, Joseph-Théodore (1823-91) French ceramics artist noted for his brightly coloured earthenware and naturalistic motifs inspired by

Japanese, Chinese, Turkish and Egyptian art. In 1861 he introduced his **bleu de Deck** – a turquoise glaze. During the 1870s Deck produced JAPONAISERIE-style plates and vases, and in the 1880s worked in porcelain using FLAMBÉ glazes. In 1887 Deck became administrator at SÈVRES.

decorative motifs See opposite.

Décorchement, François (1880-1971) French glass artist who produced ART NOUVEAU and ART DECO decorative wares and was a leading exponent of translucent PÂTE DE VERRE glass.

déjeuner See CABARET.

de Lamerie, Paul (1688-1751) Dutch silversmith who became the leading London silversmith of his time, and who, in 1716, was appointed goldsmith to King George I. De Lamerie's early work from 1713 includes domestic silverware in QUEEN ANNE and HUGUENOT styles. In the 1730s, he launched a more flamboyant Rococo style, especially in large CAST and EMBOSSED pieces. In the 1740s he returned to more restrained decoration. His work includes FLATWARE, wrought silver items and wine cisterns. See p.245.

Delft The centre for TIN-GLAZED EARTHENWARE in Holland from the mid-16th to mid-18th centuries, which profoundly influenced the

course of European ceramics. Delft potters and decorators finally established the move away from Italian MAIOLICA styles and colours towards the BLUE AND WHITE colour schemes and decorative techniques of CHINESE EXPORT PORCELAIN. Factories elsewhere in Europe followed suit.

By the mid-17thC, Delft was making vases, plaques, tiles for wall panels, house and shop signs, and table services. The addition of a lead glaze, known as KWAART, enhanced the brilliance of the colours and gave a glossier finish closer to that of Chinese porcelain than achieved on English delftware. In the 17thC enamel colours brought IMARI-style decoration and the FAMILLE-verte palette. **Delft noir** used polychrome colours on a black ground. **Delft doré**, a Japanese-style decoration in red, blue and gold, was introduced in the 1720s.

Gradually, an individual Dutch style emerged, incorporating landscapes based on the paintings of contemporary Dutch artists, and Oriental designs were adapted to vases and ornamental ware in typically European shapes. The rise of MEISSEN and SÈVRES, and the emergence of English CREAMWARE, contributed to Delft's decline by the end of the 18thC. The industry was revived in 1876, producing blue and white wares, LUSTREWARE and a product known as 'New Delftware'. See pp.186-7.

delftware The name given to British TIN-GLAZED EARTHENWARE. Following the Dutch lead, British MAIOLICA in

the Italian style was introduced in the mid to late 16thC, principally at Southwark and Lambeth in London. But it was the emulation of the DELFT approach to Oriental styles, with Dutch-style landscapes, and from 1690, the use of a second, lead or KWAART glaze, that characterised delftware. Barrel mugs, jugs, wine bottles, CHARGERS and bowls were typical products. The body of English delftware was softer, the finish less glossy, and the products less refined than their Dutch counterparts.

Most delftware was decorated in blue and white, although HIGH-TEMPERATURE COLOURS broadened the palette in the early 18thC, especially at the BRISTOL potteries. LIVERPOOL and DUBLIN were also major producers, with a substantial output of TRANSFER-PRINTED tiles from 1750. Delftware production declined with the development of the more refined CREAMWARE towards the end of the 18thC. See pp.154-5.

della Robbia The original della Robbia family were 15thC Florentine potters and sculptors, producing MAIOLICA ware. Their work, notably that of Luca della Robbia, inspired artist-potter Harold Rathbone to found the **Della Robbia Company** of Birkenhead in 1894 which produced tiles, plaques, bottles and vases in ARTS AND CRAFTS style using SGRAFFITO techniques under a coloured transparent lead glaze. See p.184.

de Morgan, William (1839-1917) Leading British ceramics designer whose work was inspired by William MORRIS, with whom he set up a pottery at Merton Abbey, London. De Morgan's most characteristic work includes his early tiles and pottery with LUSTRE decoration and ceramics influenced by HISPANO-MORESQUE colours and designs. He also ran a studio pottery in Fulham, London, from 1888 to 1907. See pp.186-7.   *1882 on*

Dent, Edward (1790-1853) Clock-maker noted for his pocket watches, marine CHRONOMETERS and the construction of the 'Big Ben' clock in London (which was completed by his stepson, Frederick). Dent was in partnership with John ARNOLD 1830-40 and then worked on his own.

dentil See DECORATIVE MOTIFS.

Derby A city renowned for its porcelain. Derby's first factory making soft-paste PORCELAIN was founded *c.* 1750, and concentrated mainly on figures, vases   (continued p.464)

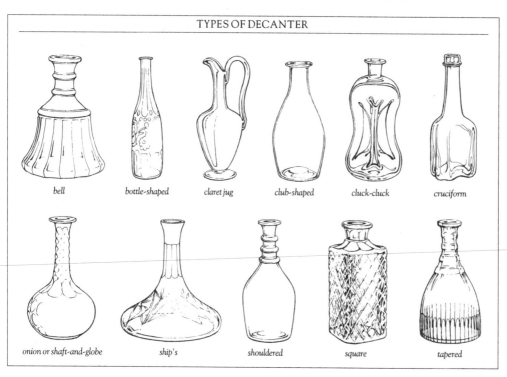

TYPES OF DECANTER

bell   *bottle-shaped*   *claret jug*   *club-shaped*   *cluck-cluck*   *cruciform*

onion or shaft-and-globe   *ship's*   *shouldered*   *square*   *tapered*

DECORATIVE MOTIFS

acanthus   anthemion or honeysuckle   arabesque   aster   Angoulême sprig   auricular   beading

bellflower   C-scroll   caillouté   cartouche   Chantilly sprig   cloud band   cornucopia or horn of plenty

dentil   diaper   dragon   egg and dart or egg and tongue

espagnolette   foliate scroll   fond or faux bois   fleur-de-lis   fluting   gadrooning

Greek key or Greek fret   grotesque   guilloche   husk

interlocking T   lambrequin   linenfold   lotus   lozenge   lunette

'onion'   osier   pagoda   palmette

patera   potato flower   quatrefoil   reeding   running Vitruvian scroll

S-scroll   scale   shell   shu (long life)   strapwork

draped swag   floral swag   trophies of war   vine leaf   whorl   yin-yan

SOME COMMON MOTIFS, *which in various forms may be incorporated into designs on ceramics, furniture, metalware or textiles.*

and CABINET-WARE. Derby figures can be identified by three unglazed patches on the base, and earlier glazed figures often have a DRY EDGE. Early examples were some of the finest ever modelled in Britain. In the 1770s Derby pioneered the use of unglazed BISCUIT models in Britain.

William Duesbury, initially an outside decorator for the factory, took over as director in 1756, producing articles quite openly in imitation of MEISSEN porcelain. Characteristic Derby ware of the period includes ink sets, potpourri vases and salts decorated with landscape scenes set with tiny figures.

Duesbury acquired the CHELSEA porcelain factory in 1770 – the products were known as **Chelsea-Derby** until the factory's closure in 1784 – and Bow in 1775. The product range broadened dramatically, and a stronger china body incorporating bone ash was introduced. SÈVRES took over from Meissen as the main source of inspiration, with NEOCLASSICAL decoration and rich ground colours of claret and turquoise. In the 1770s, too, the 'Japan' patterns inspired by IMARI porcelain, which became strongly identified with Derby for the next two centuries, were introduced. Most memorable of all is the work by artists such as Thomas Steele, Zachariah Boreman, William 'Quaker' PEGG and William Billingsley, whose work included exquisitely painted flowers, fruit and Derbyshire landscapes.

BONE CHINA replaced soft-paste porcelain in the early 19thC, but from 1811 the emphasis shifted to inexpensive products, and quality declined. The factory closed in 1848. Crown Derby Porcelain Co. was set up in 1876 and produced decorated and gilded bone china. See pp.157-60.

c.1782-1825

derringer Small pocket PERCUSSION-LOCK pistol invented by US gunsmith Henry Deringer (1786-1868).

Design registration System introduced 1842 enabling British craftsmen and designers to take out patents on their original designs. Registered designs are marked with a symbol or number – a diamond-shaped mark was used 1842-83 and thereafter the letters RD followed by up to six digits were used.

The marks are not a guide to the date of manufacture as they relate only to the design, which might continue for many years. See box right.

dessert service A set of crockery, usually porcelain, for eating and serving desserts, comprising fruit comport(s), sweet sauce and sugar tureens, and dessert plates. The fashion for having a special service separate from the dinner service began in the second half of the 18thC – sometimes to the point of setting a separate table for dessert – but had died out by the end of the 19thC.

De Stijl Radical early 20thC Dutch design group of artists and architects, founded by architect Theo van Doesburg, 1917. The group had a lasting influence on 20thC design, partly through its connection with the German BAUHAUS school, where van Doesburg lectured, and also through the success of abstract painter Piet Mondrian (1872-1944). Mondrian's paintings, using blocks of primary colour and straight lines, epitomised the group's aim of producing revolutionary art. The angular, sculptural, painted-wood 'Red Blue' chair of architect-designer Gerrit RIETVELD, who joined De Stijl in 1918, sums up the group's challenge of the accepted early 20thC design principles of simplicity, fitness for purpose and logical construction.

detent See ESCAPEMENT.

deutsche Blumen Literally translated as 'German flowers' – referring to painted floral decoration which was widely used at porcelain and FAIENCE factories throughout Europe. The style was introduced at VIENNA in the 1720s but perfected at MEISSEN c.1740 and later used at WORCESTER, Bow and CHELSEA. The lifelike flowers, based on contemporary botanical illustrations, appear as single blooms or in loose bunches, and replaced the more stylised INDIANISCHE BLUMEN. A version that incorporated a shadowing effect is known as **ombrierte Blumen** (shadowed flowers).

Deutscher Werkbund Group of German businessmen, artists, craftsmen and industrialists who, 1907-34, were influential in setting high standards in industrial design.

dhurri A FLAT-WEAVE floor covering made in India, typically from pastel-coloured cotton. It is the Indian equivalent of the Persian (Iranian) and Turkish KILIM, although these are usually made of wool.

The majority of dhurries were made in Indian jails, and began to be exported cheaply and in quantity to the West from the 19thC. However, pre-20thC examples are now quite rare and valuable. See INDIAN JAIL CARPETS and p.305.

diagonal barometer See ANGLE BAROMETER.

dial The 'face' of a clock or watch on which the time, calendar or astronomical information is registered. The term can refer to the whole face or to the individual discs or rings, such as the calendar dial, on which the periods of time are inscribed. Dials first appeared c.1350. Previously, hours were recorded by a single strike of a bell. A **dial plate** is the metal plate in a clock or watch which is attached to the front plate of the MOVEMENT, and to which the metal CHAPTER RING or enamel dial is fixed.

diamond Considered the most valuable precious stone. Diamond is the hardest known naturally occurring substance, and refracts (bends) light and disperses colour very strongly. These qualities give the stones great BRILLIANCE and FIRE especially since the 17thC when diamond cutting was developed and improved. The value of a diamond depends on size, colour and the number of flaws. Completely colourless stones are rare; most diamonds are slightly tinged with yellow or brown. Rare red, blue and green shades are known as **fancy diamonds** or **fancies**. A diamond's colour and clarity can be altered by HEAT TREATMENT. See p.266.

diamond-point See ENGRAVING.

diaper See DECORATIVE MOTIFS.

diatreta vase See CAGE CUP.

die Any of various devices used for cutting out, forming or stamping a material. In coins, for example, the designs on each of the two sides of the BLANK are struck simultaneously by a pair of dies or punches, either by hand or machine; usually the more complicated obverse die, or **pile**, is fixed on a solid base, while the reverse die, or **trussel**, moves up and down.

dimity White cotton, simple TABBY-weave fabric sometimes patterned, used for bed and window curtains from the late 17th to early 19th centuries and as a dress material in the early 19thC. It was imported from India before production started in Lancashire in the 18thC.

ding ware With YINGQING, the earliest Chinese porcelain wares, dating from the SONG DYNASTY (960-1279). Dishes are the most common, but some bottles, ewers and vases have been excavated from burial grounds. Many forgeries have been produced in Hong Kong and Taiwan.

diplomatic sword See DRESS SWORD.

Directoire style French decorative furniture style which peaked during the Directoire government (1795-9). The style was a simplified and austere version of the LOUIS XVI style. Minimal decoration was used, and Republican symbols – such as the cap of liberty and the fasces (a bundle of rods bound around an axe) – appear frequently on furniture, FAIENCE and textiles. The Directoire style merged into the EMPIRE period.

dirk 1 A long single-edged knife, traditionally used by Scottish Highlanders and still worn by officers

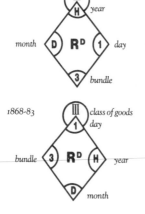

REGISTRY OF DESIGN MARKS

1842-67 · class of goods · year · month · day · bundle

1868-83 · class of goods · day · bundle · year · month

DATE AND LETTER CODES			
A	1845, 1871	N	1864
B	1858	O	1862
C	1844, 1870	P	1851, 1877
D	1852, 1878	Q	1866
E	1855, 1881	R	1861
F	1847, 1873	S	1849, 1875
G	1863	T	1867
H	1843, 1869	U	1848, 1874
I	1846, 1872	V	1850, 1876
J	1854, 1880	W	1865
K	1857, 1883	X	1842, 1868
L	1856, 1882	Y	1853, 1879
M	1859	Z	1860
A	December	H	April
B	October	I	July
C	January	K	November
D	September	M	June
E	May	R	August
G	February	W	March

THE REGISTRY OF DESIGN MARKS *used 1842-83: (top) example for September 1, 1843; (bottom) example for September 1, 1869.*

TYPES OF DOLL

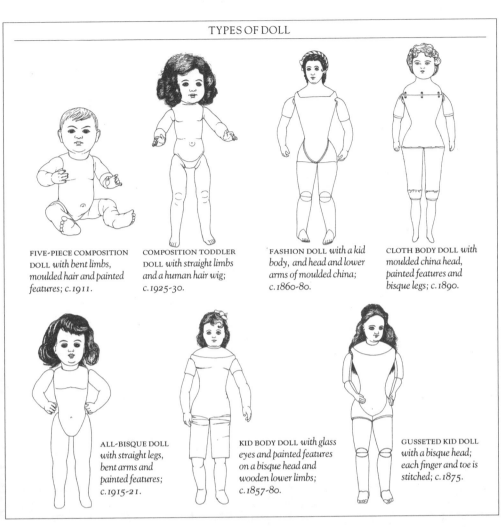

FIVE-PIECE COMPOSITION DOLL *with bent limbs, moulded hair and painted features; c.1911.*

COMPOSITION TODDLER DOLL *with straight limbs and a human hair wig; c.1925-30.*

FASHION DOLL *with a kid body, and head and lower arms of moulded china; c.1860-80.*

CLOTH BODY DOLL *with moulded china head, painted features and bisque legs; c.1890.*

ALL-BISQUE DOLL *with straight legs, bent arms and painted features; c.1915-21.*

KID BODY DOLL *with glass eyes and painted features on a bisque head and wooden lower limbs; c.1857-80.*

GUSSETED KID DOLL *with a bisque head; each finger and toe is stitched; c.1875.*

JOINING DOLLS

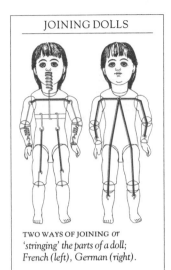

TWO WAYS OF JOINING *or 'stringing' the parts of a doll; French (left), German (right).*

---

of Scottish regiments of the British army. **2** A short dagger with either a straight or curved blade, carried by naval officers in the late 18th and early 19th centuries.

dish ring Hollow, waisted cylindrical ring of pierced, chased or fretwork silver used to support hot dishes and to protect the surface of tables and sideboards. Dish rings were made from the early 18thC and are erroneously known as **potato rings**. See p.244.

dispensary Medicine cupboard about 9-13in (23-33 cm) high with shelves and racks on the inside of the doors.

distressed Trade term for a work of art, normally a piece of furniture in obvious need of repair. The term is also used to describe a wood surface which has become rough and uneven through age, or which has been made to appear older than it is.

divan A long couch or sofa without back or arms and often set against a wall. The word 'divan' is Turkish, and

both the divan and the OTTOMAN seat (from which the divan developed) are based on Turkish state furniture.

Dixon, James, & Sons Sheffield firm of silversmiths, established in 1806, which became the leading maker and exporter of BRITANNIA METAL and ELECTROPLATED wares to the USA in the mid-19thC. **J·D&S**

dog of Fo Stylised Chinese Buddhist lion (*Fo* means Buddha), in Chinese mythology one of a facing pair of

BUDDHIST LIONS *of porcelain; 16½ in (42 cm) high. The female has a cub at her feet; c.1660-1720.*

temple guardians. They are found as modelled figures in painted decoration on porcelain. The Japanese version is called **shi-shi**.

doily 18thC term for a fringed napkin, named after a London linen mercer by the name of Doily. From the 19thC the term was applied to the circles of decorative cotton or linen placed on serving plates beneath cakes and sandwiches.

doll marks Marks found on some dolls identifying maker's name, batch or style number, size or diameter of head, trademark and sometimes the number of components used to make the doll (see box, p.466). Such marks are normally only found on dolls made by the most famous and established manufacturers. See box, p.464.

Where the marks appear on the body varies according to maker and type of doll. Marks on BISQUE dolls, for example, are usually found on the back of the head. In addition, official registration or patent marks may appear, as follows:

Déposé or **Deponiert** – patent application registered, France and Germany, late 19thC;
Breveté or **Bté** – French for patented;
SGDG (*sans garantie du Gouvernement*) – without government guarantee, from 1850;
DRGM (*Deutsches Reichsgebrauchsmuster*) – German, patent registered, from 1909;
Ges Gesch (*Gesetzlich Geschutzt*) – German, patent registered, from the end of the 19thC;
PAT and **PATd** – patented, Britain and USA, from the end of the 19thC.

dome Blown glass cylinder, one end of which is domed, while the base is trimmed straight to allow it to stand upright. Domes were used in Victorian times to protect collections of stuffed birds or animals, arrangements of wax fruit and other displays, and as protective covers for AUTOMATA and SKELETON CLOCKS.

door furniture Collective term for all door fittings, including door-knockers, handles and knobs, door-stops, hinges, letterboxes, finger plates and decorative emblems or ESCUTCHEONS.

Door furniture tended to be purely functional until the late 18thC when, in accordance with the rise of the interior design concept, ornate Rococo and Neoclassical examples earned their place as ornamental accessories. See HINGE.

doorstop See DUMP and p.366.

double-cloth carpets See INGRAIN CARPETS.

doubloon Loosely applied nickname for Spanish or Spanish-American 16th-19thC gold coins, in particular the *dobla escudo*.

DOLL MARKS OF LEADING MANUFACTURERS

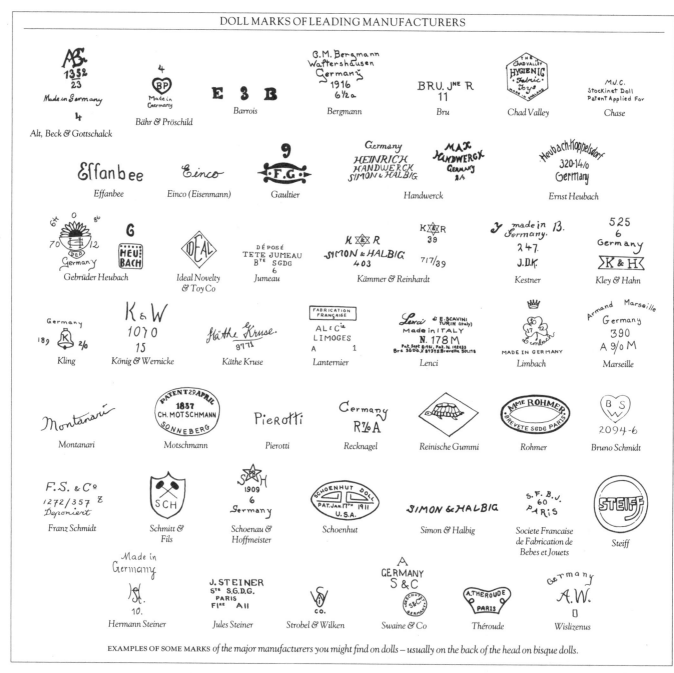

EXAMPLES OF SOME MARKS *of the major manufacturers you might find on dolls – usually on the back of the head on bisque dolls.*

doucai A Chinese palette outlined in underglaze blue, the design then glazed and enamelled by filling parts or all of the pattern with translucent FAMILLE-VERTE colours; formerly spelt **tou-ts'ai**. See WUCAI and SANCAI.

Doulton Ceramics factory founded by John Doulton (1793-1873) in Lambeth, south London, 1818. The factory's success in the first half of the 19thC was based on its STONEWARE chemical and sanitary products. In the 1860s, a close association with students from the Lambeth School of Art led to the development of

Doulton studio art wares. Artists included Arthur, Hannah and Florence Barlow, John Broad, Mark Marshall, Frank Butler and George Tinworth. In 1872 Doulton launched **Lambeth faience** (UNDERGLAZE-painted earthenware). Later came **silicon ware** (a vitrified, unglazed stoneware), and **marquetry ware,** made of marbled clays in chequerwork patterns. In 1882 Doulton launched a high-quality PORCELAIN range at its Burslem factory and from 1900 was known for its tile panels and

1902 on

porcelain figures, particularly its ART DECO examples. See p.184.

Dovecot Studios See EDINBURGH TAPESTRY COMPANY.

dovetail See JOINING.

dram glass Short-stemmed, small-bowled glass with a heavy foot, used for drinking spirits. Types of **dram glasses** known as **firing glasses** were made in Britain from 1740 until the 19thC. They were used for toasts and hammered on a table to make a noise like gunfire. See box, p.475.

draw-leaf table Extendible table with the top divided into three leaves, known from the 16thC. The two outer leaves slide beneath the central one when the table is shortened. See p.108.

DRAW-LEAF TABLE *with one leaf half extended; c.1900; 6 ft (1.83 m) long (when closed).*

drawn stem A drinking-glass stem that is drawn out as an extension of the bowl when the molten glass is being blown, as opposed to one that is shaped separately and then attached.

drawn thread work A type of embroidered fabric in which some of the threads are drawn out to form geometrical or other patterns in relief. It was introduced in the 15thC or possibly earlier.

Dresden MEISSEN-style ceramics produced by various factories in the Dresden area of south-eastern Germany in the 19thC. Until the 1970s the term 'Dresden' referred to the Meissen factory itself.
   Crown Dresden is porcelain produced by OUTSIDE DECORATOR Helena Wolfsohn, in Dresden in the 1870s. Wolfsohn originally used the Meissen royal factory mark on her products, in particular the **AR** (Augustus Rex) mark. Following a lawsuit brought by Meissen, she adopted a crown with 'D' scripted beneath. Her work was typically decorated with pastoral scenes (which were inspired by the French artist Antoine Watteau) interspersed with panels of flowers.

Dresden work A form of CUTWORK embroidery on muslin developed in Dresden in eastern Germany during the 18thC. It was used mainly for aprons and handkerchiefs in the mid-18thC. Dresden work was a cheap alternative to BOBBIN LACE and was copied in various countries, including Britain in the 1750s.

dresser A long table, sometimes in the style of a sideboard with cupboard, drawers or open storage space below, and/or open shelves tiered or stepped above. From medieval times, a dresser, or **dressing board**, was where food was garnished or 'dressed' before it was served.
   Welsh dresser is a term dating from the late 19thC, used to describe a freestanding dresser with cupboard and drawers, and shelves above. Welsh dressers were made from the late 17thC in Wales, Lancashire and elsewhere. See p.119.

Dresser, Christopher (1834-1904) British decorative-arts writer and designer whose distinctive style anticipated the concept of the MODERN MOVEMENT. Dresser advocated the importance of design linked with function. He began his career as a botanist, but turned to the study of the arts and published *Principles of Design*; he was art director of the LINTHORPE POTTERY 1879-81. Dresser's designs, often influenced by

Japanese style, were applied to carpets, glassware, furniture, pottery and textiles. He designed simple, geometric silverware for ELKINGTON, James DIXON and Hukin and Heath. See pp.184, 247.

dressing table A term introduced in the 17thC for a small table with drawers designed to be used for grooming and dressing. In the 18thC, designs incorporated compartments and drawers for a wide range of toilet accessories, and mirrors became standard for the first time. See p.141.

dress sword A sword worn as part of a uniform or regalia and not for use as a weapon, also known as a **court** or **diplomatic sword**.

drop-front See FALL-FRONT.

drop-leaf table A development of the GATELEG table, with one or two leaves which open out, supported on hinged legs, arms or brackets, to extend the surface area. See p.109.

drop seat Detached padded seat designed to fit into a rebate on a chair frame, introduced in the late 17th to early 18th centuries.

drum clock 1 Early TABLE CLOCK with a drum-shaped case often of gilt brass and especially popular in the 16thC. 2 Late 18th or 19thC French clock movement fitted into a brass, drum-shaped case.

drum table Large circular table made from the late 18thC through the 19thC, with drawers set into a deep FRIEZE, and supported on a central pedestal or tripod. A variant used for dining, and with a shallower, expandable top is the **capstan table**; other variants are referred to as **library** or **writing tables** according to their purpose. **Rent tables**, with four drawers for each quarter year or seven weekday drawers and a till set into the table top, were used for rent collection until the early 19thC. See p.122.

drum teapot Silver, flat-bottomed, cylindrical teapot with a straight spout, flat lid and single handle of wood, popular 1760s-90s.

DRUM TEAPOT *with chain connecting lid to handle; silver; late 18thC.*

dry-edge figures SLIP-cast porcelain figures made at DERBY, 1750-5. They are so called because they have an unglazed, dry edge around the base.

drypoint A printmaking technique in which a drypoint needle is used to score the design directly into the metal plate. Unlike the true ENGRAVING process, the metal is not actually dug out and removed, but is thrown to the sides of the grooves, creating slight ridges known as **burrs**. These hold some ink which transfers to the final print giving it distinctive smudgy lines. See p.332.

ducat Any of various former European gold coins which used the ducat standard set in the 13thC. A gold ducat consistently weighs 3.5 g of .986 fine gold.

duchesse A French term for a day bed with a curved back. A **duchesse brisée** is a version made in two or three parts – including a foot end with a low, curved back and sometimes a stool in the middle to extend the length.

DUCHESSE BRISÉE
comprising chair and footstool; c.1780.

duelling pistols FLINTLOCK or PERCUSSION pistols dating from the 18thC, usually in pairs. See p.406.

Duesbury, William See DERBY.

Dufrêne, Maurice (1876-1955) French designer of furniture, metalwork, carpets and glass in ART DECO and MODERNIST styles who specialised in lavish, custom-built pieces and interiors.

dumbwaiter A mobile stand with two or more tiers of circular trays around a central column on a tripod

DUMBWAITER;
c.1770; 42 in (1.06 m) high.

base with castors. Dumbwaiters were designed to be placed near a dining table for self-service, and introduced in Britain in the 1720s. See p.145.

dummy board Cut-out image of a human figure, such as a pedlar, maid or footman, or animal such as a cat, in painted wood. They were possibly used as fire screens in late 17thC Britain, but by the mid-18thC were purely ornamental. Reproductions were made in the mid-19thC and in the 1920s and 30s.

dump 1 Heavy glass doorstop, also known as a **door porter**, made of scrap molten glass which would otherwise have been dumped. Bottle factories often made doorstops as a sideline. 2 See HOLEY DOLLAR.

duplex See ESCAPEMENT.

Dux See ROYAL DUX.

Dwight, John (c.1637-1703) Pioneering London potter who produced the first identified British STONEWARE in the 1670s. By the beginning of the 18thC, he had developed a greyish (or **mouse-coloured**) SALT-GLAZED STONEWARE and introduced the first fine RED STONEWARE to Britain. Dwight's influence spread quickly to Staffordshire with the ELERS brothers who had worked with him.

E

Eames, Charles (1907-78) US architect and furniture designer, who, with his colleague Eero SAARINEN, explored the potential of new materials such as plywood, aluminium and steel. He developed his knowledge of plywood moulding during the Second World War, later using the technique to create furniture – chairs, tables, screens and storage units – that were fluid, light and strong. See p.81.

earthenware Product made from clay that is only fired to the point at which the particles form a single mass but do not vitrify into a glassy, impermeable substance. The resulting body is porous, and a glaze is needed to make it waterproof. Because of the low firing temperatures, glazed earthenware can take a wide range of metal oxides as colouring agents, and is often brightly decorated. See p.149.

East India Companies Trading companies from the West who opened up trade with the countries of the Far

East, including India and China, from the 15thC onwards. The Portuguese were the first Europeans to start the long-distance trade, soon followed by the British, French and Dutch, and then the USA. The British company, set up in 1601 to trade for spices, flourished for more than 200 years importing and exporting furniture, carpets, silk, embroidery and porcelain. See p.167.

Eastlake, Charles (1836-1906) Architect and furniture designer associated with the ART FURNITURE MOVEMENT, c.1870-90. See p.63.

Eastman, George (1854-1942) An American dry-plate camera manufacturer who in 1888 introduced the Kodak camera – the first camera designed to use a flexible roll film. The film was a roll of paper coated with a light-sensitive emulsion.

ébéniste French cabinet-maker who specialised in VENEERING, a technique known in ancient civilisations but revived in early 17thC Europe. The word 'ébéniste' was coined as much of the 17thC French furniture used an ebony veneer.

ebonite See VULCANITE.

ebony A very close-textured hardwood which is black in colour. Ebony is unusually resistant to decay. It is, however, brittle, and from the 17thC in Britain was most commonly thinly cut as a VENEER, and used for BANDING and INLAID DECORATION. Other woods such as fruitwoods, were stained black, or **ebonised**, to imitate ebony and are much more common than the real thing. **Coromandel** is similar in colour and weight, but mottled grey or brown or striped with black and yellow. **Calamander** is a light brown ebony, mottled and striped with black, which was popular for Regency veneers and banding.

écuelle The French term for a late 17th and 18thC lidded bowl with two handles made in silver, pewter or ceramics. It was generally used for serving soup. In English, the term most commonly used is PORRINGER, although silver versions are sometimes known as **equelles**. See p.155.

Edinburgh Tapestry Company Non-profit-making workshop established 1912. Until 1940, the company produced large, commissioned tapestry scenes; after 1946, smaller, coarser-weave panels designed by contemporary artists were more typical. The company was also known as the **Dovecot Studios** or **Dovecot Tapestries**.

Edis, Robert ARTS AND CRAFTS MOVEMENT furniture designer and author of the influential publication *The Decoration and Furniture of Town Houses*, in 1881. See pp.64, 68.

Edo period (1615-1867) Prosperous period in Japanese history when the arts flourished and Edo (now Tokyo) became the new capital city.

Egermann, Friedrich See LITHYALIN GLASS.

egg and dart See DECORATIVE MOTIFS.

eggshell porcelain An extremely delicate Chinese porcelain from the early 18thC, later produced by the Irish BELLEEK porcelain factory and the Japanese KUTANI factories in the late 19th and early 20th centuries. See p.176.

Egyptian blackware A fine black STONEWARE, produced in Staffordshire from c.1710, which could be polished to a shine. Wedgwood's BASALTES WARE is a more refined version.

Egyptian taste Interest in Egyptian architecture, symbols and hieroglyphics, initially prompted by Napoleon's invasion of Egypt in 1797, and which were incorporated into the work of NEOCLASSICAL designers and architects as decorative motifs. The early 19thC furniture designs of English designer and collector Thomas HOPE helped introduce Egyptian taste to Britain. See p.177.

elbow chair See CARVER.

electric clock A clock that is driven by electricity, first produced in Britain by Alexander BAIN in the 1840s.

The clocks fall into three main categories: **free pendulum clocks**, in which the pendulum receives an electric impulse to maintain momentum; clocks with automatic rewinding powered by a small electric motor; and **synchronous clocks**, regulated by the alternating current of mains electricity.

electrogilding See GILDING.

electroplating The method of plating metal by an electrolytic process. The best known electroplated articles are those of silver and CHROMIUM. The former replaced the SHEFFIELD PLATE process in the mid-19thC. The process was first patented in Sheffield in 1840. NICKEL SILVER was soon found to be the most successful base for electroplating; it may be marked EPNS (electroplated nickel silver). Copper and BRITANNIA METAL (EPBM) were also used. Unlike Sheffield plate, the

silver deposited in the electroplating process is free of all impurities, and the end products tend to be a colder, less mellow metallic colour. See p.237.

electrotyping A refinement of the electroplating process in which silver-plated articles are reproduced from moulds. A mould is used as one of the electrodes in an electroplating vat, and by electrolysis is lined – more thickly than in straightforward electroplating – with the silver. The mould is then freed to leave a hollow shell in the shape of the finished article. Introduced in 1843, electrotyping was expensive but accurate, good for making exact copies of complex metalwork and prompting a mid-19thC interest in naturalistic decoration on silverware. See p.237.

Elers, David and **John** (fl.1686-1700) Dutch brothers trained as silversmiths, who came to Britain c.1688 and made a significant impact on the development of British ceramics. They worked with John DWIGHT at his Fulham potteries in London (1690-3) and then moved to Staffordshire to set up their own business. The combination of the Dwight influence and the Elers' own expertise helped to establish Staffordshire's unique place in history as an important international ceramics centre.

The Elers specialised in fine RED STONEWARE decorated with relief patterns in white, which was much imitated by other factories.

Elkington Birmingham-based metalworking firm, whose proprietor George Elkington (1801-65) patented the first silver ELECTROPLATING process in 1840. From then on, the firm concentrated on electroplating and electrotyping, leasing out the patent to other silversmiths, and on producing tableware and presentation pieces by Christopher DRESSER and other designers.

Ellicot, John (1706-72) Master clock-maker to King George III, who developed a form of compensated PENDULUM and improved the cylinder ESCAPEMENT. His father and his son, both called John, were also notable clock-makers in their own right.

elm English elm is a hard and flexible wood, light golden-brown in colour and with a coarse, irregular grain. It has a tendency to warp and is prone to worm. The timber was often used in country furniture.

The wych elm or Scotch elm is harder than the English variety, with a straighter, finer grain and it takes a good polish.

Eltonware Pottery produced from 1881 by English art potter Sir Edmund Elton (1846-1940) at his family home in Somerset. Elton, a follower of the AESTHETIC MOVEMENT, was influenced by Far Eastern, South American and European art. Decorative Eltonware vases, jugs and bowls use various coloured slips and lustre, lead, metallic or monochrome glazes.

embossing The means of producing a relief design, on metal or leather for example, by hammering on the reverse side of the material. Objects such as pots and tankards are embossed with a long-handled, dome-headed snarling-iron.

On silverware, embossing is used for the basic, large-scale relief shapes in a design, and finer detail is added by REPOUSSÉ and flat-CHASING techniques. See p.235.

emerald One of the rarest and most valuable precious stones, depending on highly variable quality. Emeralds range in colour from pale to dark green, the most valuable being dark green with BRILLIANCE and clarity. Flawless stones are extremely rare.

Emes, Rebeccah (fl.1808-29) London-based silversmith who worked in partnership with her brother-in-law, William Emes. Following his death in 1808, she formed a partnership with her business manager, Edward Barnard, and went on to produce numerous items including tea and coffee services, EPERGNES and tankards.

Empire style Furniture and furnishings style popular in France c.1804-30 and in the USA c.1810-30 and beyond. See p.45.

enamel A smooth, glassy, protective or decorative medium that can be fused onto a metal, glass or ceramic surface by firing. **Enamel colours** are made out of powdered glass and pigmented metallic oxides such as gold, copper and manganese suspended in an oily medium. This can be painted onto glass or ceramic objects, and during firing, the oily medium burns away and the others fuse together.

In **enamelware**, coloured enamel pastes are applied to a metal body by various techniques and then fired. In **basse-taille** (low relief) **enamelling**, a design is carved on the body and the whole area is covered with one or more layers of translucent enamels. In **champlevé enamelling**, the ground is cut away and the hollows filled with the enamel paste, leaving the raised areas free. In **cloisonné enamelling**, fine metal wire is fixed onto the body and the resulting network of *cloisons* (compartments) filled with enamel paste. See pp.153, 209, 263.

encoignure See CORNER CUPBOARD.

end-of-the-day glass See FRIGGERS.

engine-turning Engraved decoration on metal and other materials, of circles, waves or narrow grooves, produced on a lathe. See p.236.

engobe See SLIP.

engraving 1 Method of decorating by cutting fine lines or dots into a glass, metal or other hard surface.

In **acid engraving** or **acid etching**, the subject to be decorated is coated with an acid-resistant wax, varnish or gum, and the design incised through this with a fine steel point. Alternatively, areas to remain in relief are coated with the acid-resistant substance, leaving the background exposed. The object is immersed in acid which 'eats away' the exposed areas. Depth and texture are achieved by adjusting the time of exposure to the acid. The process was used to decorate late 15thC armour, and from the 16thC, mainly developed as a printing process. See CAMEO GLASS.

Diamond-point engraving involves using a diamond point to scratch a design on a glass surface. The technique was developed in 16thC Venice, but gradually spread throughout Europe. It is seen mainly on CRISTALLO and FLINT GLASS – often for calligraphy.

Stipple engraving was developed in 17thC Holland. A diamond-pointed tool is tapped against the surface, resulting in dots of varying density. The patterns thus created show great subtleties of light and shade.

Wheel engraving is believed to date from c.1500 BC, but the technique flourished in Europe from the 16thC. The surface to be decorated is held over a treadle-operated rotating wheel fitted with an abrasive disc and a pattern is ground into the surface. The method can create shallow **surface engraving**, or deeper CAMEO and INTAGLIO effects. See p.209.
2 A PRINT made from an inked steel or copper plate into which a design has been cut. See also AQUATINT, MEZZOTINT. See p.332.

ensi Small squarish rugs woven by several of the nomadic Turkoman tribes of central Asia to cover the tent entrance. Many have a cruciform design and are wrongly referred to as **hatchli** (cross) rugs.

entablature See COLUMN.

entrée dish Shallow silver or SHEFFIELD PLATE serving dish with or without a cover, made in Britain from c.1760. See pp.242-3.

envelope table See CARD TABLE.

epaulette Military shoulder strap often fringed with gold braid.

EPBM See ELECTROPLATING.

epergne An elaborate stand, usually of silver or glass, for the centre of the dining table with branching arms supporting removable receptacles, such as fruit or sweetmeat dishes and condiment holders. Epergnes came to Britain from France c.1715; the name is from the French *épargner* (to save), the idea being that dinner guests were saved the trouble of passing dishes. See pp.225, 246.

EPNS See ELECTROPLATING.

equation dial See MEAN TIME; QUARE, DANIEL.

Erinoid Type of plastic designed to imitate tortoiseshell and used to make fashion accessories such as hair clips in the early 1900s.

escapement Part of the mechanism in a clock or watch that controls the driving force (either a weight or a spring) and allows it to 'escape' at regular intervals. This counteracts the tendencies of both an unchecked weight to accelerate and a spring to weaken on unwinding. See also BROCOT and REMONTOIRE.

The **verge escapement** was introduced with the first mechanical clocks. It was originally used with an oscillating bar or **foliot** with weights at either end, and after the introduction of portable clocks and watches c.1520, with a BALANCE wheel.

The **anchor** or **recoil escapement**, invented c.1670, operates in association with a PENDULUM; it replaced the verge escapement in LONGCASE clocks some 15 years after their introduction, but was not used in BRACKET CLOCKS until c.1800. The motion of a seconds hand linked to an anchor escapement is characterised by a very slight backward movement (or recoil) after each forward movement.

The **deadbeat escapement**, in use by 1715, was also for pendulum clocks. It evolved from the anchor escapement, but the seconds hand stops dead after each forward motion.

The **lever escapement**, an adaptation of the deadbeat invented in 1754, is used with a balance wheel. From c.1820 it was used increasingly for watches and CARRIAGE CLOCKS.

The **duplex escapement**, also for balance-wheel mechanisms, has either two escape wheels or, more often, a single escape wheel with two sets of teeth. It was perfected c.1750 and used for high-grade watches and carriage clocks 1750-1850.

The **detent** or **chronometer escapement** is used with a balance wheel, and incorporates a detent, or locking device, of either spring or pivoted form, which alternately locks and unlocks the escape wheel. Developed from the mid-18thC and widely used in the 19thC, it proved one of the most accurate escapements of all. See box below.

écritoire A term used for early BUREAUX, generally referring to small, portable writing desks. The standard form made from the 16thC onwards consisted of a group of small drawers enclosed by a fold-down front which doubled as a writing surface.

The term also refers to an 18th and 19th century Continental writing desk with a FALL-FRONT, enclosing a fitted interior, either with cupboards or drawers below. See p.131.

escutcheon 1 A term for a carved shield on a pediment. **2** Any protective metal plate on furniture, particularly a keyhole plate. **3** A small metal nameplate on a clock face or a firearm, for example.

estampille Maker's mark – name, initials or monogram – stamped on French furniture particularly during the second half of the 18thC. The mark was struck with an iron stamp and appears in INTAGLIO.

étagère See WHATNOT.

etching See ENGRAVING.

Etruscan style A late 18thC offshoot of NEOCLASSICISM introduced by architect-designer Robert Adam, c.1774. Many of Adam's designs were ostensibly based on the architecture, art and ornament of the ancient Italian country of Etruria (now Tuscany and Umbria). The use of boldly contrasting black, white and terracotta was typical of his interiors but the colour scheme was in fact taken from Greek pottery.

étui A small container made of porcelain, metals, tortoiseshell, gemstones or other materials. Often delicately ornamented, étuis were popular from the early 17thC for

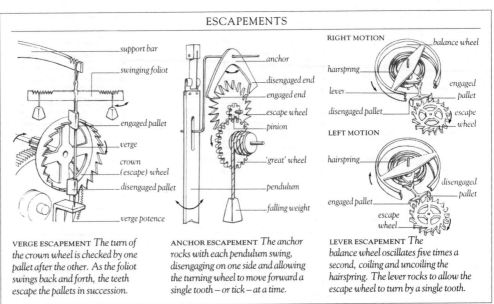

ESCAPEMENTS

VERGE ESCAPEMENT *The turn of the crown wheel is checked by one pallet after the other. As the foliot swings back and forth, the teeth escape the pallets in succession.*

ANCHOR ESCAPEMENT *The anchor rocks with each pendulum swing, disengaging on one side and allowing the turning wheel to move forward a single tooth – or tick – at a time.*

LEVER ESCAPEMENT *The balance wheel oscillates five times a second, coiling and uncoiling the hairspring. The lever rocks to allow the escape wheel to turn by a single tooth.*

carrying small items for example sewing implements, a slim pencil or knife. See p.259.

ewer Large serving jug made of precious or base metals or ceramics. **Ewer-and-basin** sets were used for hand-washing at the dining table, but less common after the arrival of table forks in the late 16thC.

excise marks See CAPACITY MARKS.

exergue The area sometimes left free below the design on a circular coin, often used for the date, artist's initials or a small design feature.

Exeter carpets Woollen carpets made in Exeter, Devon, in the mid-18thC using Turkish knot (see CARPET KNOTS). Exeter carpets were among the earliest to be made in Britain, their elaborate designs based on SAVONNERIE patterns, with ROCOCO scrolls, floral motifs and foliage.

Exposition Internationale des Arts Décoratifs et Industriels Modernes An exhibition held in Paris, 1925, which played a major role in establishing ART DECO style. It was a French-dominated showcase for all fields of the decorative arts. See p.71.

F

Fabergé, Peter Carl (1846-1920) Russian designer and manager of the Fabergé workshops which produced meticulously crafted OBJECTS OF VERTU and jewellery. See p.262.

faceted steel Decorative steel studs cut with facets which were fashionable in the 18th and 19th centuries and used for buttons, belts, sword hilts and jewellery. Woodstock, near Oxford, and Matthew BOULTON's factory in Birmingham were the main centres of production.

facets 1 Small, flat surfaces ground onto cut gemstones. Some cuts enhance colour at the expense of brilliance. See JEWEL CUTTING. 2 Angular, light-reflecting surfaces in BRIGHT-CUT ENGRAVING.

façon de Venise High-quality, late 16th and 17thC glass made in the VENETIAN STYLE, mainly in Britain, Germany and the Netherlands.

faience The name given to the French TIN-GLAZED EARTHENWARE which developed from Italian MAIOLICA. The term is also used for tin-glazed earthenware products from

Germany and Scandinavia; the British equivalent of faience is DELFTWARE, the Dutch DELFT.

Faience was first produced in any quantity in France from the late 16thC, mainly by Italians (the term derives from the Italian town of Faenza). Early designs were Italian style; from the 17thC they emulated Chinese porcelain, and in the 18thC, MEISSEN. High quality, extravagantly decorated faience was made for the aristocracy early in the 18thC, but by the end of the century the development of CREAMWARE for everyday use, and PORCELAIN for finer products, significantly reduced the production of faience wares in Europe.

A tin-glazed earthenware designed for everyday use was known as **faience blanche**. It was produced in the 17th and 18th centuries, first in Italy then throughout most of mainland Europe.

Faience fine is the French version of the British creamware produced from the 1760s. It was introduced in 1768 in France and is usually **lead glazed** rather than tin glazed. See pp.160, 165.

fairings Cheap porcelain groups of human or animal figures made for sale or as prizes in fairgrounds 1860-1914. They were often lighthearted or comic in theme, with innuendo captions beneath. The fairings, made c.1860-90 in Germany and Austria for the British market, were produced in moulds and had solid bases. From 1890 to c.1914, hollow imitations were being mass-produced. See p.204.

fairyland lustre LUSTREWARE decorated with fairyland scenes by Daisy Makeig Jones, registered by the WEDGWOOD factory in 1915 and marketed throughout the 1920s and into the 30s. See p.187.

fake A genuine object altered in some way, not necessarily to deceive. See also FORGERY and p.419.

fall-front The hinged lid on a desk, BUREAU or SECRETAIRE that folds down to form a writing surface, often supported by pull-out LOPERS. It is also known as **drop front**.

famille-rose, famille-verte Commonly used French terms for 'families', or palettes of enamel colours used on Chinese porcelain. Famille-verte, introduced in the mid-17thC, dominated by green (and also containing yellow, aubergine, black and blue), was largely replaced by famille-rose c.1720. **Famille-noire** is famille-verte with the background filled in black, and **famille-jaune** is similar but with a yellow ground. The last two are often painted onto an unglazed BISCUIT body. See pp.166-7.

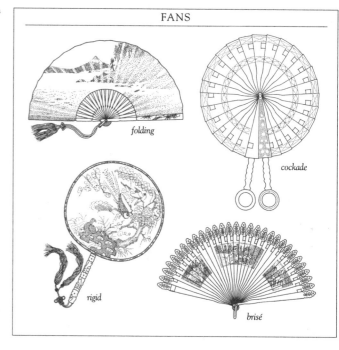

FANS

folding

cockade

rigid

brisé

fan An essential accessory for women, especially in 18thC Europe, used to create a breeze and to communicate modesty, coyness or discreet flirting.

The **rigid fans** of the ancient civilisations and Renaissance Europe have a long handle topped by a leaf of parchment, fabric or feathers within a rigid frame. **Folding fans** originated in China and came to Europe with the Portuguese in the 15thC. Ribs of bone or similar material are covered with a pleated, semicircular leaf of paper, silk or lace. **Brisé fans** are made entirely of overlapping ribs of ivory, mother-of-pearl or bone with a ribbon threaded through the upper ends. (*Brisé* is French for 'folding'.)

A **cockade fan** can be pleated or brisé but opens out into a complete circle. See box above.

farmer's watch Type of pocket watch mass-produced in Britain in the first half of the 19thC, the dial often decorated with a painted rural scene. Large versions are sometimes referred to as **turnip watches**.

farthing A quarter of an old British PENNY (0.104p). It was issued in silver in the 13thC, in copper from 1672 and in bronze 1860-1956. Farthings ceased to be legal tender in 1961.

fauld See ARMOUR.

faux bois French term for a secondary wood such as beech painted to simulate an exotic wood such as rosewood; an effect used in the early 19thC. See DECORATIVE MOTIFS.

faux-montre An 18th or early 19thC pill or patch box in the form of a dummy watch, hence the French term meaning 'false watch'. Some are made of BILSTON ENAMEL.

Favrile glass Trade name for a type of iridescent ART GLASS developed by the US designer Louis Comfort TIFFANY c.1892. It was made in a variety of colours, the oil-on-water effect created by spraying the hot glass with metallic salts, or by applying acid or metallic lustres to a cooled surface. It was mainly used for vases. See p.219.

feather-edge Engraved or BRIGHT-CUT patterns of fine, slanting lines that decorate the edge of silverware. Feather-edging was used on FLATWARE c.1760-90 and on the handles of silver CUTLERY from the late 18thC onwards.

feet See boxes, pp.471, 477.

feldspar porcelain A tough form of BONE CHINA which contains pure feldspar in place of Cornish CHINA STONE, which is only part feldspar. The first successful feldspar body was produced at COALPORT, but SPODE was the first to name the body and mark pieces 'feldspar porcelain' c.1820. The idea was soon taken up by other Staffordshire potters.

fender A low screen or rail of cast iron, copper, brass or steel designed to stop coals rolling out of the hearth. Fenders were introduced in the late 17thC when raised baskets or grates lifted the fire off the ground. They may be movable pieces or a continuation of the fixed fire surround. A **fender curb** is a shallow version used on a broad, deep hearth. **Club fenders** or **seat curbs** are combined fender and padded seat connected by metal bars.

festival dolls English term for *hina-ningyo* – extravagantly dressed Japanese dolls made for doll festivals at which Japanese boys and girls were ceremoniously initiated into traditional customs. The dolls were traditionally handed down from generation to generation. See p.354.

festoon See DECORATIVE MOTIFS.

fielded panel A flat, raised panel in a wall or a piece of furniture with bevelled edges.

figure 1 The markings, grain or pattern on a piece of wood. 2 A **figured** textile is one with a pattern of figures or naturalistic subjects as opposed to one that is plain or striped. 3 Human or animal form. See pp.190-5.

filet Netting with a pattern or design embroidered into it to create a LACE effect, popular 16th to early 17thC and late 19th to early 20thC. It is also known as **lacis** or **darned netting**.

filigrana See LATTICINO.

filigree Lace-like decoration made with fine gold or silver wire. It was widely used in Europe from the late 17thC on jewellery and for OPENWORK panels set in boxes, baskets and cups. Birmingham was a manufacturing centre in the 18th and early 19th centuries but thereafter much filigree came from Malta, India and China.

fillet 1 A small ledge supporting a shelf. 2 A small, narrow band found on architectural features in furniture, such as on a fluted COLUMN. 3 A leatherworking wheel tool used in bookbinding to make straight or parallel straight lines. The term can also refer to the line itself.

finial See KNOP.

firangi An Indian sword with a straight, strengthened blade for use with both hands. The blade was often imported from Europe, hence the name *firangi*, or 'foreigner'.

fire The bright flashes of coloured light displayed by a gemstone resulting from its high refractive index and strong dispersion of light. The fire of a stone is improved by FACETING. There is more fire in a correctly faceted diamond than in any other natural colourless gemstone – emeralds and rubies have BRILLIANCE, not fire.

fireback Cast-iron panel at the back of a fireplace to retain and radiate heat, to protect the adjacent wall and for decoration. Firebacks are also sometimes known as **fireplates, iron chimneys** and **reredos**. See p.360.

firedogs See ANDIRONS.

fire gilding See GILDING.

fire irons Collective name for a matching set of tools for stoking and cleaning a domestic fire, including tongs, poker, shovel, brush, sometimes a fork, and before the use of coal, a hook for handling logs. 18thC fire irons were usually of polished iron or steel and tended to be larger than later versions. Twisted handles were popular in the 1790s. In the 19thC, fire irons were mainly made in brass.

firelock See FLINTLOCK and WHEEL-LOCK.

fire polishing Technique applied to PRESSED GLASS to give it greater brilliance. Moulded objects are heated at the mouth of the furnace to remove the dullness sometimes imparted from the trace elements in the iron mould.

firescreen See POLE SCREEN.

firing The process of baking ceramics in a kiln. An initial or BISCUIT firing causes a chemical change to take place in the clay paste, binding the particles to form a hard, rock-like body. Firing

temperatures vary for different ceramics: up to 800°C (1450°F) for EARTHENWARE; 1200-1450°C (2200-2650°F) for STONEWARE; 1100-1200°C (2000-2200°F) for soft-paste PORCELAIN; and over 1400°C (2550°F) for hard-paste porcelain. Subsequent firings may fuse the GLAZE or ENAMEL colours onto the body. See pp.149-50.

firing glass See DRAM GLASS.

Fisher, Alexander (1864-1936) British sculptor, painter and silversmith who specialised in ENAMELLING. He invented a widely copied technique that created an illusion of depth in translucent enamel by using a foil background. Much of his silverwork features CELTIC motifs.

fish pattern See HERATI PATTERN.

Fitzhugh pattern CHINESE EXPORT PORCELAIN with a trellis border in underglaze blue or overglaze iron red, and inner flower clusters, thought to be named after a family who commissioned the design. It was copied by various English factories.

Fitzroy barometer A cheap, serviceable mercury STICK BAROMETER which was mass-produced from c.1870. It includes printed paper weather-forecasting charts based on 'Fitzroy's Rules' which were introduced on earlier marine barometers designed by Admiral Robert Fitzroy.

Fitzroy barometers were made in variously styled cases, and typically also included a thermometer, and a storm gauge. See p.290.

flagons Large vessels for serving wine or beer, like large-scale TANKARDS, which were made throughout Europe, generally in pairs. Flagons have a flat bottom, slightly tapering sides and a handle and thumbpiece, often with a hinged lid. They were rare before the 17thC and usually made of ornate silver, to hold Communion wine. Towards the end of the 17thC their use increased in taverns and households. See p.366.

flambé The French for 'flamed', referring to a lustrous, rich crimson-red ceramics glaze with flashes of brilliant blue. The effect was produced by FIRING a copper glaze in a reducing atmosphere – one that removes oxygen from the glaze. The technique was used on Chinese porcelain of the late 17th and 18th centuries, and rediscovered and widely applied in Europe in the late 19thC. See also SANG-DE-BOEUF.

flame stitch See BARGELLO.

flan See BLANK.

flange neck Doll's neck with a ridged base used to secure a bisque, china or composition head to a cloth body.

flashed glass Glass objects dipped into molten glass to give them a fine outer layer, thinner than on CASED GLASS, which is often in a contrasting colour. The flashing may be cut or ground away in a pattern to expose the layer underneath. See p.208.

flask Stoppered glass, ceramic or silver container for holding liquids, often alcohol. Those for table use generally have a bulbous body and a short neck. Small flasks for carrying on the person tend to be flattened ovoids in shape, and also called **pocket bottles** or **spirit flasks**. See box, p.472.

flatbacks Pottery figures designed to be viewed from the front only, with flat, unmodelled and undecorated backs. They were intended as decorations for cottage mantelpieces and produced mainly in the 19thC by STAFFORDSHIRE POTTERIES. The figures were easily reproduced in moulds, decorated in UNDERGLAZE blue, and embellished over the glaze with bright enamel colours. Later models have a more limited colour range, some in black and white with gilding. Late 20thC reproductions made from the original moulds abound. See p.194.

flatware In silverware, the term strictly refers to articles of tableware made from a flat sheet without a cutting edge, such as spoons, forks, sifters and slicers, although in modern usage the term also includes knives.

The term also refers to other objects of flattened form, such as plates, saucers, shallow dishes and salvers, as opposed to cups, bowls and tureens (HOLLOW-WARE).

flat-weave Generic term for any form of carpet or rug with a flat, tapestry-like weave with no pile, including the KILIM and SUMAKH. See pp.301-2.

Flaxman, John (1755-1826) British NEOCLASSICAL sculptor and artist who designed and modelled for WEDGWOOD, producing friezes and portrait medallions, from 1775. In the late 18thC he worked mainly as a marble sculptor and also produced models for silver for Paul STORR.

flecked glassware Type of glass decorated with random coloured specks. The technique, originally developed by the Romans in the 1stC AD, involves rolling a GATHER of molten glass over broken chips of glass

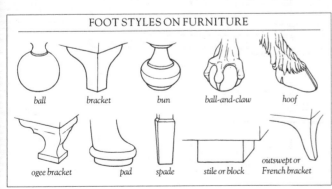

FOOT STYLES ON FURNITURE

ball *bracket* *bun* *ball-and-claw* *hoof*

ogee bracket *pad* *spade* *stile or block* *outswept or French bracket*

FLASKS

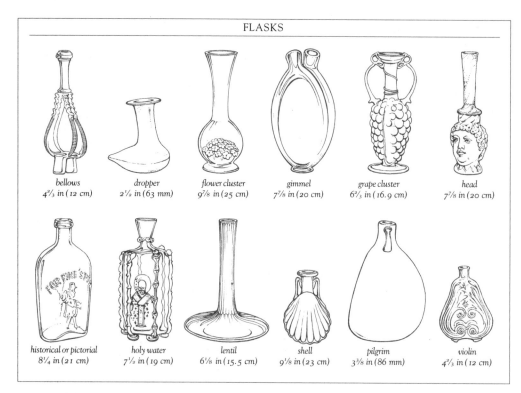

bellows
4²/₃ in (12 cm)

dropper
2½ in (63 mm)

flower cluster
9⅞ in (25 cm)

gimmel
7⅞ in (20 cm)

grape cluster
6²/₃ in (16.9 cm)

head
7⅞ in (20 cm)

historical or pictorial
8¼ in (21 cm)

holy water
7½ in (19 cm)

lentil
6⅛ in (15.5 cm)

shell
9⅛ in (23 cm)

pilgrim
3⅜ in (86 mm)

violin
4²/₃ in (12 cm)

on a MARVER, and then blowing it. Flecked ware is often called NAILSEA glass, but it was also made at many other factories. Flecked glass was used to make jugs, flasks and novelty items such as ROLLING PINS.

FLECKED GLASS *oil flask; c.AD 80-90;*
3⅝ in (92 mm) high.

Flemish lace See LACE.

Flight & Barr See WORCESTER.

flint glass See LEAD CRYSTAL.

flintlock Type of ignition mechanism on a firearm used from the early 17thC until the early 19thC. Sparks were generated by friction between a piece of flint and a steel plate, the **frizzen**. Below the frizzen is a pan set next to a touch-hole in the breech. The sparks ignited powder in the pan and, via the touch-hole, fired the main charge in the breech. See pp.406-7.

flock Paper or cloth used as wall covering, with a stencilled design picked out in glued-on powdered wool

to give a contrasting velvety texture. Flock was first used in France and Britain in the early 17thC and was very fashionable in the 18thC.

Florentine mosaic See PIETRA DURA.

Florentine stitch See BARGELLO.

florin Originally, a gold coin issued in Florence in the 13thC. In Britain, a silver florin – face value 2s (10p) – was first issued in 1849. The word 'florin' no longer appeared on these coins after 1936, although the denomination still exists in the form of the modern 10p piece.

flow blue Term used to describe the fuzzy and blurred cobalt-blue transfer prints on Staffordshire earthenware of the 1860s to 90s.

flower-brick Brick-shaped container with holes pierced in the top for cut flower stems. DELFTWARE versions were popular in the 18thC. Larger, semicircular vessels with separate flower-holders are called **bough-pots**.

flower table Table or stand specifically designed for holding plants or cut flowers. Some have inset, wire-covered trays which were filled with wet sand to hold cut flowers.

flute Tall, stemmed drinking glass for wine with a slender bowl which flares out or narrows at the rim. Flute glasses were particularly popular 1773-1850. See also RATAFIA.

fluting Semicircular parallel grooves which run vertically up a COLUMN.

flux A substance added to a glass or ceramic BODY that lowers the temperature at which the fusion or melting of base materials takes place during firing or smelting. Potash, bone-ash, borax, lime and soda are common flux materials.

fly braid A decoration of knots and bunches of floss SILK – popular on 18thC dresses and christening gowns.

fly leaf and bracket Parts of a drop-leaf extending table: the fly or drop leaf of which is supported by a hinged fly bracket or rail.

fob chain 18thC term describing the chain used to secure a small pocket watch. The term originated from the fob pocket (in the waistband of men's breeches), and the word fob came to refer to any small ornament attached to a fob chain, such as a **fob seal**.

In the late 19thC, ladies' ornamental watches suspended from a brooch on a short chain or strap were known as **fob watches**. The watch face was sometimes displayed upside-down so it could be read easily by the wearer.

Foley China Works Staffordshire pottery founded 1860 and initially operated by Wileman & Co. The pottery was known for its simple, bold designs and brightly coloured decoration. The firm was renamed Shelley Potteries in 1925 and from the 1930s became a leading producer of ART DECO china, and children's

FLINTLOCK PISTOL

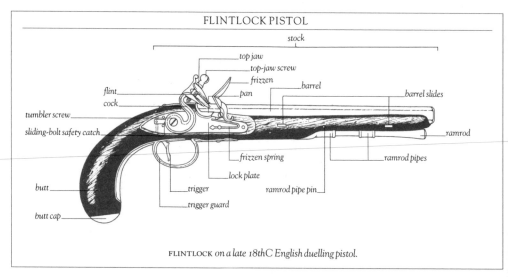

stock
top jaw
top-jaw screw
frizzen
flint
pan
barrel
barrel slides
cock
tumbler screw
sliding-bolt safety catch
ramrod
frizzen spring
ramrod pipes
butt
lock plate
ramrod pipe pin
trigger
trigger guard
butt cap

FLINTLOCK *on a late 18thC English duelling pistol.*

crockery. Tea sets and dinner services are notable for their distinctive shapes, and floral, geometric and banded patterns – many by leading British artists such as Vanessa Bell, Duncan Grant, Laura KNIGHT and Graham Sutherland. The inverted cone-shaped cups and sharp triangular handles of the 'Mode' range and the square plates of 'Vogue' are typical.

foliated A cabinet-making term referring to leaf-shaped ornament.

folio stand See PORTFOLIO TABLE.

Follot, Paul (1877-1941) French interior decorator and early ART DECO designer of furniture, textiles, carpets and metalwork. His furniture is finely made with expensive materials such as ivory and SHAGREEN. Early examples showed an ART NOUVEAU influence in their curving lines, and c.1929 came a more geometric, Art Deco style.

Fontaine & Percier French architect-designer team who were mainly responsible for establishing the EMPIRE STYLE of the late 18th and early 19th centuries. Pierre-François-Léonard Fontaine (1762-1853) and Charles Percier (1764-1838) were employed by the Emperor Napoleon to provide an interior-design style that reflected his life and empire. They designed furniture, silverware, textiles and were the first to coin the term 'interior decoration'.

foot See boxes, pp.471,477.

foot-rim Slightly projecting rim on the base of an object, also called a **foot-ring** or **basal rim**.

foot-warmer Portable container of hot coals or water, used throughout northern Europe to keep feet warm. Most foot-warmers consist of an inner container made of stoneware or metal with a perforated outer case of wood, wrought iron, copper or brass, and were sometimes wrapped in carpet.

forgery A deliberate attempt at deception. See also FAKE.

forks See CUTLERY.

form watch Watch made in the form of another object. Early examples of the 17thC were intended as a *memento mori* (reminder of death), often in the form of a cross or a skull. 19thC revivals included stringed instruments, shells and flower heads.

Fouquet, Alphonse (1828-1911) French jewellery designer who specialised in enamelling and was inspired by RENAISSANCE designs.

Many of his designs are carved onto precious stones. His son Georges (1862-1957) joined the firm in 1881 and took it over in 1895, designing pieces in ART NOUVEAU style.

foxing Brownish-yellow spots or stains, or other discoloration on paper, a form of fungal growth caused by damp. See pp.327,435.

Franck, Kaj (1911-89) Finnish designer who did much to bring modern Scandinavian design to international status during the 1950s and 60s. He was an independent designer of lighting, furniture and textiles, noted for his disciplined FUNCTIONALISM, and was artistic director of Finland's leading ceramics factory Arabia, 1946-78.

Frankenthal German porcelain factory founded 1755 which produced a type of hard-paste PORCELAIN with a glaze able to absorb enamel colours. Frankenthal produced tablewares in the style of MEISSEN and SÈVRES. Figures and statuettes in various styles including COMMEDIA DELL'ARTE and CHINOISERIE were a speciality. The factory closed in 1799.

free-blowing Glass-making process in which the glass is shaped in its molten state by blowing air through a blowing iron without the use of a mould. See p.208.

freedom box See SEAL.

free pendulum clock See ELECTRIC CLOCK.

French jet See JET.

French polish Form of lacquer used on furniture consisting of shellac dissolved in a solvent giving a harder, shinier finish than beeswax. It was introduced late 18thC and became popular in the early 19thC. See p.93.

fretwork 1 Geometric, trellis-like pattern of intersecting vertical and horizontal lines repeated to form a continuous band.
2 The technique of cutting thin pieces of wood with a fine-bladed saw (fret saw) to form shapes or patterns. The fretwork pattern might be left **open**, as on table GALLERIES, or **blind**, in which the fretwork is carved upon or applied to a solid surface and cannot be seen through. It is sometimes seen backed by fabric such as pleated silk, as on a decorative panel on a door or a cupboard. See CUT-CARD WORK.

frieze 1 An ornamented, horizontal band of painted or sculptured decoration. **2** The horizontal band

beneath the CORNICE of a bookcase or cabinet. A convex horizontal band beneath a cornice is known as a **cushion frieze**. A **frieze rail** is the horizontal length of wood beneath the top of a table or desk stand, and is also known as a **curtain piece**. See box, p.500. **3** See COLUMN.

friggers Unique novelty glassware items such as bells, pipes or toys made by glass-makers, not for use, but to demonstrate their skills. See p.230.

frit 1 Powdered glass which is melted, allowed to solidify and then re-ground and used as a fusible substance in the manufacture of soft-paste PORCELAIN. **2** The ingredients that are mixed and fired to make glass.

frizzen See FLINTLOCK.

Fromanteel family Large Flemish family of clock-makers working in London in the 17th and early 18th centuries. In 1658-9 John Fromanteel visited Holland to learn the art of PENDULUM clock-making. The family proceeded to make the first pendulum clocks for the London market c.1659.

frosted glass See ICE GLASS.

frosted silver Decorative effect on silverware produced by acid treatment. All commercial silver contains a proportion of copper. If the article is heated and dipped into a suitable acid, the copper component is eaten away, leaving a textured surface. This process was used to decorate silver articles in the 19thC, especially as a background for highly polished decoration on silver or silver gilt.

frozen Charlotte A doll cast or modelled as a single complete piece. Frozen Charlottes were usually made of glazed porcelain and were also

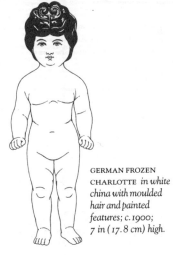

GERMAN FROZEN CHARLOTTE *in white china with moulded hair and painted features; c.1900; 7 in (17.8 cm) high.*

known as **solid chinas**. They were produced from the mid-19thC to c.1910. Some have a flesh-coloured china face and neck and a white china body. CELLULOID versions appeared from the early 20thC.

fubako Long, rectangular Japanese LACQUER box designed for carrying letters or messages.

FUBAKO *decorated with floral medallions and gilt-metal handles; c.1920; 15¾ in (40 cm) long.*

fuchi See KODOGU.

fuddling cup A vessel often with three or more small cups and interlinked handles. It was offered in jest as a challenge to drink from one cup without spilling the contents of the others. Fuddling cups were made in TIN-GLAZED EARTHENWARE, especially in the West Country, in the 17th and 18th centuries.

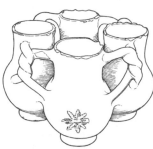

FUDDLING CUP *of tin-glazed earthenware; late 18thC; 3½ in (89 mm) high.*

Fulham Carpet Manufactory The London site where the first large, Turkish-knotted woollen CARPETS were made in Britain. It was founded in 1750 by a Frenchman, Pierre Parisot, with the expertise of two SAVONNERIE weavers. The high prices charged for the carpets forced the factory's closure in 1755, but the techniques were adopted by Thomas Whitty, founder of the AXMINSTER Carpet Manufactory.

Fulham pottery See DE MORGAN, William.

fuller Groove in a blade of a sword or dagger designed to strengthen and lighten the blade. See SWORD.

fumed oak The result of exposing new pieces of oak to ammonia solution to give them an appearance of age. The wood turns grey before fading to yellow-brown. The technique was popular in the 1930s and 40s and was used by the British designer Sir Ambrose HEAL.

Functionalism Austere, early 20thC design movement based on the premise that 'form follows function'. The movement's ideas were best expressed in the book *Ornament and Crime* (1908), by architect Adolf Loos (1870-1933). Functionalism's impact on industrial design was particularly effected through the BAUHAUS school.

Fürstenburg Small Bavarian PORCELAIN factory founded 1747 which produced hard-paste porcelain from 1753. Early wares include Rococo-style vases and tableware in rich colours and gold, painted with landscapes, birds or figures. From 1770 the factory was influenced by BERLIN and SÈVRES and produced busts, statues and painted wall plaques with ornamental Rococo frames. From c.1790 Fürstenburg followed the NEOCLASSICAL style and later the EMPIRE style products of Sèvres.

19thC

fused plate See SHEFFIELD PLATE.

fusee Coned-shaped device in clocks to even out the decreasing force of a going spring on unwinding. The device was invented c.1500, used to the late 17thC in continental clocks and to c.1750 in continental watches. In Britain its use in clocks and watches continued until c.1880-1900. See also BARREL and TRAIN.

fusil A lightweight MUSKET with a FLINTLOCK mechanism used in the 17th and 18th centuries.

fustian The name for various textiles woven in a similar way to velvet with a short piled surface. They include a coarse material of cotton and flax used for bed-hangings and clothes in medieval Europe, a wool fabric made using the same weaving technique in the 14thC, and from the 16th to 19th centuries, coarse TWILLED cotton cloth, velveteen and corduroy.

G

gabbeh Term for heavy, coarsely woven domestic rugs from west Iran. Gabbehs are typically woven in thick wool and brightly coloured to a bold design. See p.305.

gadrooning Continuous convex curves or reeding on metalwork, but also imitated on furniture and ceramics. Gadroon borders are made

up of interlocking, repeated comma-like bosses, the resulting effect being of a circle in motion. On European TIN-GLAZED EARTHENWARE painted gadroon borders, known as **false gadrooning**, simulate a three-dimensional effect.

Gainsborough chair 20thC term for an open-sided armchair with upholstered seat, back and arm pads, and concave arm supports. See p.101.

GAINSBOROUGH ARMCHAIR *Named after the artist Thomas Gainsborough, who probably seated his models in similar chairs; c.1760.*

Gallé, Emile (1846-1904) French designer and maker of glass, ceramics and furniture, who was particularly influential in the ART NOUVEAU movement and founded the NANCY SCHOOL in the late 19thC.

He founded a glass factory at Nancy, north-east France, in 1867 (closed 1931) and produced much ART GLASS. Among the many techniques he developed were the surface decorations MARQUETERIE SUR VERRE and verreries parlantes.

From the mid-1880s Gallé also designed and made furniture. He drew loosely on 18thC styles, but added carving or marquetry decoration. In the 1890s he experimented with PORCELAIN and STONEWARE. See p.222.

gallery A raised border or miniature railing of wood or metal used as an ornamental surround to the top of a table, tray, shelf or cabinet.

BRASS GALLERY *on an early 19thC sideboard. Curtains were sometimes hung from the rails to act as splashbacks.*

SPINDLE GALLERY *on a tray-top tripod table; c.1765.*

galloon Braid, lace or ribbon woven from silver, gold or silk threads, used for trimming upholstery, uniforms and sometimes dresses.

Gandhara Province in Pakistan from which came stone carvings combining Indian and Mediterranean influences. Early examples date from the 2nd and 3rd centuries and depict Buddha in Graeco-Roman costume. Later examples, usually heads, are made of STUCCO or TERRACOTTA. The sculpture was much collected in Victorian times. Most common items seen today are reliefs, Buddha figures and miniature stupas (shrines).

gaozu See STEM CUP.

garden carpet A Persian carpet design which reflects the layout of a formal garden or *Chahar Bagh* (four gardens), which is specifically mentioned in the Koran as a feature of Paradise. The earliest surviving examples date from the first half of the 17thC. See p.302.

garnet Family of minerals including six varieties of similar red gemstone, namely: pyrope (rhodolite), almandine, grossular, andradite (demantoid), spessartite, and uvarovite. The most common garnets used for jewellery are the very dark red **pyrope** or **Bohemian** stones, which are usually rose-cut (see JEWEL CUTTING) or, on bead necklaces, naturally faceted, and almandine garnets which are usually cut en cabochon (and known as **carbuncles**) or emerald-cut.

garniture Matching set of three, five or seven ornaments, usually vases, for decorative display. A **garniture de cheminée** is a set for the mantelpiece. The ornaments were originally – at the end of the 17thC – Japanese or CHINESE EXPORT PORCELAIN, or Dutch DELFT copies, comprising an odd number of baluster vases and covers with an even number of intervening 'beaker' vases of cylindrical or waisted form. Silver versions were made in small numbers in Europe, and in the late 18thC the term was also used to describe clock and candlestick sets. Dressing-table sets are known as **garnitures de toilette**; a set for a side table as a **garniture de table**.

gasolier Decorative gas lighting piece made in the latter half of 19thC of brass or other metal. It resembles a chandelier, with branches holding burners emanating from a central shaft, but is hollow to allow gas to be piped through.

gate-leg table A type of drop-leaf table with a structure hinged like a gate beneath that pivots out to support the leaves. The gate-leg was introduced in the late 16thC and in common use up until the end of the 18thC. See p.108.

GATE-LEG TABLE *on bobbin-turned legs; late 17thC; 49 in (1.25 m) wide with leaves open.*

gather Blob of molten glass that is collected from the furnace on the end of a blowpipe in order to be blown into shape. See p.208.

gauffering 1 Term describing the impressed decoration on gilded edges of book bindings, applied with heated finishing tools. 2 The term **gauffered** describes the relief pattern on any textile other than velvet. Velvet decorated in this way is described as **stamped velvet**.

genre painting Style of painting linked with the ideals and 'sensibility' of the Victorian middle classes, in which domestic scenes with a moral, sentimental, historical or literary theme were popular. See p.324.

Georgian style British 18thC style characterised by the proportions and ornaments of CLASSICAL architecture, applied universally to buildings, furniture and decorative art forms. Passing styles within the period, including Chinese and GOTHIC, were also accommodated.

The Georgian era is divided into two main periods: the early Georgian period, 1720-60, under the reign of George I up to 1727 and George II thereafter, and the late Georgian period, 1760-1800, under the reign of George III. The term 'Georgian style' also sometimes includes the REGENCY period to 1830.

German silver See NICKEL SILVER.

gesso A form of plaster which can be carved and gilded or painted for use as a decorating medium on furniture. Gesso (pronounced *jesso*) is a dense mix of powdered chalk and size which hardens on drying. It is built up in layers onto a surface or over a wire framework, or cast into a mould. The material was often used in place of wood for detailed relief work on chairs, mirror frames and PIER tables from the mid-18thC and increasingly in the 19thC.

Gibbons, Grinling (1648-1721) Dutch-born sculptor who moved to Britain at 19 and became renowned for his carved decorations in wood, marble and stone. His craft was applied to chimney pieces, picture and mirror frames, panelling, tables and cabinet stands. He was appointed master carver in wood to King Charles II, a position he held until the reign of George I. He was commissioned by Sir Christopher Wren to carry out work in St Paul's Cathedral and Hampton Court Palace. See p.24.

gilding The coating of glass, ceramics, metals, wood and other materials with a layer of gold.
Gold leaf can be pressed on a sized or GESSO surface, or mixed with lacquer and painted on, but both methods are prone to wear. A more durable but matt surface is produced by mixing ground gold leaf with linseed oil, gum arabic and mastic, and then drying at a gentle heat.
Water gilding and **oil gilding** are the processes used for furniture and decorative objects. In furniture they are applied to a GESSO surface. Water gilding is so called because the gold leaf is floated on water on the receiving surface. With oil gilding, adhesion is from a sticky tape incorporating linseed oil. This produces a more durable, but matt surface. Water gilding can be burnished but is prone to flake and is water soluble. See p.426.
Acid gilding is a process used on ceramics to give contrasting matt and polished gilt surfaces. Acid is used to etch out parts of the glazed design, leaving the rest of the surface slightly raised. When the body is gilded and polished, the acid-treated areas are left matt. The technique was introduced by MINTON'S in the late 19thC, and later copied by other firms.
Size gilding was the earliest method of gilding TIN-GLAZED EARTHENWARE. Linseed oil was applied to the object and gold leaf stuck onto it. As this gilding was not fired, little of it survives today.
Honey gilding, in which the ground leaf is mixed with honey and brushed on and fired onto ceramics or glass at a low temperature, was the main

method of gilding ceramics in Europe in the 18thC. It could be laid on thickly and was hard enough to be tooled or CHASED.
Mercury or **fire gilding** is a process used to apply a gilt finish to metal, ceramics and glass. Ground gold was amalgamated with mercury, and painted onto the object which was then subjected to a low-temperature firing, the mercury vaporised, leaving a thin film of gold. It was then burnished to a brilliant state. It is more durable, easier to apply and fix than honey gilding.
Matt gilding is a variation of mercury gilding, much used on bronze figures and ornaments in Paris by designers such as Pierre Gouthière, from the end of the 18thC.
In the 19thC **electrogilding**, in which a thin gold coat is applied by ELECTROPLATING, replaced fire gilding, which gave off toxic fumes.
Liquid gold is a solution of powdered gold leaf and oils containing sulphur. Used on MEISSEN porcelain by 1730, and in Britain from the mid-18thC, it produces a film of metal with a similar effect to that of LUSTREWARE.

Giles, James (1718-80) British outside decorator who was responsible for some of the finest decoration on WORCESTER and CHELSEA porcelain. His London studio also decorated opaque white, green and blue glassware with NEOCLASSICAL designs similar to those found on Giles's work for Worcester.

Gillows The most successful firm of British 18thC furniture-makers outside London, founded in Lancaster by Robert Gillow (1704-72), a joiner. The company was later renowned for its elegant, well-made, solid but simple pieces in GEORGIAN and REGENCY styles, and also for its clock cases. The company appears to be the first British firm to stamp its furniture. The stamped mark 'Gillows' or 'Gillows Lancaster' can usually be seen on the top of drawer fronts. The firm continued to flourish, changing its name to Waring & Gillow Ltd in the early years of the 20thC. See p.142.

giltwood Any wood that is gilded, whether with gold paint or gold leaf.

gimmal A flask made of tinted or transparent glass or stoneware from the 17thC. The flask, designed to hold oil and vinegar, has an interior division to make two separate containers each with its own spout.

gimmal ring Mid-15th to 18thC wedding or engagement ring consisting of two or three interlocking hoops which fit together to form one

hoop. The setting also splits and joins again to form an ornament, such as a heart or clasped hands. See p.268.

Gimson, Ernest (1864-1919) Artist-craftsman and designer, working with furniture, embroidery, metal and plaster. His furniture is traditional with turned legs and rails, spindle backs and rush seats, and was greatly influenced by William MORRIS. He was involved early on in the ARTS AND CRAFTS MOVEMENT. See p.64.

girandole 1 An ornate candle-holder, or sconce, often heavily carved and gilded and in the 18thC often backed by a mirror.
2 An elaborate US made clock, resembling a BANJO CLOCK, designed c.1818 with gilded decorations, including scrolls, festoons and birds.
3 In jewellery, pearl or gem drops suspended in groups of three or more from an earring, pendant or brooch.

gisarme See POLEARMS.

glacé Upholsterer's term for cloth with a highly lustrous surface finish.

glaive See POLEARMS.

Glasgow School Group of designers and architects centred around the Glasgow School of Art in the late 19thC. Hallmarks of the group's austere version of ART NOUVEAU

include stylised floral motifs, CELTIC ornament, painted or inlaid stained glass and applied metalwork ornament on furniture which generally followed straight or gently curved lines. Their work was exhibited widely in Europe, and influenced early European industrial designers, especially in Germany and Austria.

glass Hard, transparent or translucent substance made from the fusion of silica, such as sand or flint, and an alkali, such as potash or soda. When heated to about 1100°C (2000°F) the ingredients fuse together and become molten. In this state the METAL, as it is technically called, can be shaped by blowing, casting, moulding or pressing. Glass can be coloured by adding metallic oxides to the FRIT. See p.207.

glasses, drinking The shape, size and decoration of drinking glasses, particularly British ones, often indicate their date as well as purpose. See box below and pp.476-7.

Glastonbury chair 19thC term for a type of folding chair dating from the late 16thC, said to be based on one used by the Abbot of Glastonbury, and reproduced in the 19thC.

glaze In ceramics, a vitreous (glass-like) coating which gives a decorative and impervious finish. Glazes can be

TYPES OF DRINKING GLASS

toasting *wine* *ale* *ratafia*
goblet
cordial *dram* *toastmaster's* *rummer* *champagne*

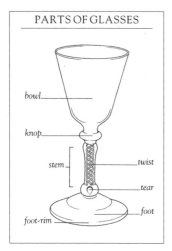

PARTS OF GLASSES

bowl

knop

stem — *twist*

— tear

— foot

foot-rim

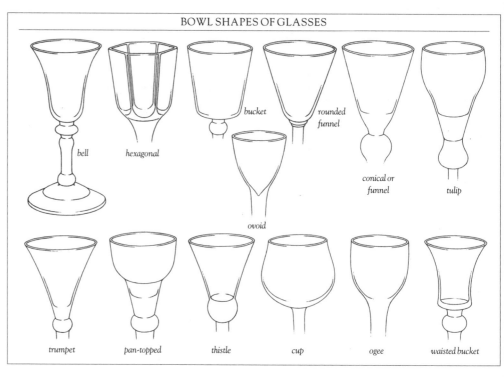

BOWL SHAPES OF GLASSES

bell *hexagonal* *bucket* *rounded funnel*

ovoid *conical or funnel* *tulip*

trumpet *pan-topped* *thistle* *cup* *ogee* *waisted bucket*

matt or glossy, soft or hard, smooth or textured, of varying opacity and colour. They are composed of a glass-forming ingredient (usually silica), a FLUX (to reduce the melting point of the silica), and alumina to help fix the glaze to the clay body. Glazing takes place either before firing (known as **green** or **raw-glazing**), or after the first, BISCUIT firing when the body has been hardened off.

Lead glaze was perhaps the earliest manufactured glaze, known from 1700 BC, and using ground lead or lead oxide as the flux agent. The lead lent greater translucency and depth of colour to the glaze. It was used on EARTHENWARE and soft-paste PORCELAIN in Europe until substituted in the 19thC by less toxic flux materials such as borax. See SALT-GLAZED STONEWARE, TIN-GLAZED EARTHENWARE.

A **smear glaze** can be a deliberate, very light glaze applied to the marble-like PARIAN WARE, for example, or an unintentional coating of leftover glaze from a previous firing. See p.151.

globe Sphere showing a map of the world (**terrestrial globe**) or of the heavens (**celestial globe**), that is usually mounted on an axis and can be turned. See p.127.

gnomon The projecting arm of a SUNDIAL, also known as the **style**. It casts a shadow, the tip of which points to markings round the rim of the dial that show the time. For accurate reading, the angle of the gnomon must be related to the latitude in which the sundial is set.

Gobelins TAPESTRY works established in 1662 in Paris and still in operation today. Gobelins produced tapestries and carpets in traditional, Classical styles taken from designs, or cartoons, by eminent painters, such as Raffaello Raphaël. In the mid to late

19thC, Gobelins produced tapestry portraits for royalty and panels for Parisian theatres. The quality of the work declined with the introduction of chemical, ANILINE DYES in the late 19thC and the use of these was suspended in the early 20thC. Gustave Geoffroi, director 1919-25, set a new policy of commissioning cartoons from 20thC artists, such as Jean Weber, and of using improved synthetic dyes.

goblet Drinking vessel usually with a large bowl on a stem and foot.

Godwin, Edward William (1833-86) British architect, designer and member of the 19thC AESTHETIC MOVEMENT. His light, graceful ART FURNITURE was often made from ebonised wood, showed Japanese influence in its simple lines, and was easily mass-produced. *Art Furniture*, a catalogue of his designs, was influential, especially in the USA.

gold The most versatile precious metal of all. It is more ductile than any other metal, with the capacity of being drawn out into a fine wire, and so malleable that it can be beaten into a leaf 4 millionths of an inch (a 10 thousandth of a millimetre) thick. Gold is resistant to corrosion, and to the action of solvents. Pure, 24 CARAT gold is too soft and heavy to work on its own, and so it is usually alloyed with other metals such as copper. In 14 carat gold, 14 parts of gold are mixed with 10 parts of other metal;

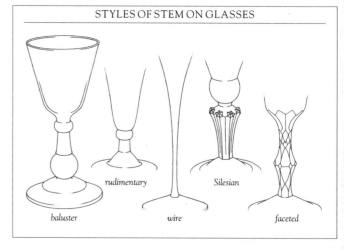

STYLES OF STEM ON GLASSES

baluster *rudimentary* *Silesian* *faceted*

wire

the finest alloys are 18 and 22 carat. The colour of the gold varies according to the type and quantity of metal used in the alloy. Copper lends a reddish tinge, silver a hint of pale green; a combination of copper and silver results in a brighter yellow than pure gold. 18 carat white gold is an alloy of 25 per cent platinum and 75 per cent pure gold. See p.265.

gorget See ARMOUR.

Goss, William (1833-1906) Staffordshire potter renowned for his CRESTED WARE and porcelain ornaments. Goss's Falcon Pottery was founded in 1858 to produce dressing-table ornaments and jewellery such as brooches and pendants, in PARIAN

porcelain. He began marketing parian figures, and the crested wares which became popular holiday souvenirs, in the 1890s. See p.199.

W.H. GOSS
1862 on

Gothic Revival The original Gothic style flourished from the 11th to 15th centuries. Its essential characteristics of soaring, slender lines, pointed or ogee arches, and TRACERY contrast with the low, rectangular emphasis of the early 16thC RENAISSANCE style which followed. Gothic style was reworked at various times but particularly c.1750-70 and 1800-75.

The interiors and furnishings of writer Horace Walpole's house at **Strawberry Hill**, Twickenham, London, epitomised 18thC Gothic,

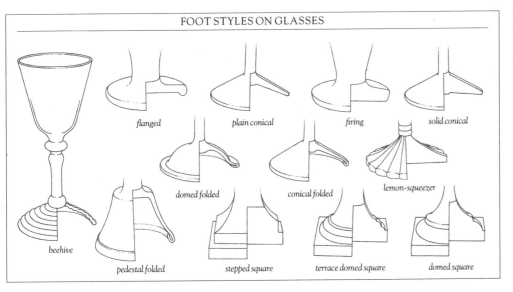

FOOT STYLES ON GLASSES

flanged   *plain conical*   *firing*   *solid conical*

domed folded   *conical folded*   *lemon-squeezer*

beehive

pedestal folded   *stepped square*   *terrace domed square*   *domed square*

and from 1760 Gothic-style tracery appeared on work by Thomas CHIPPENDALE and others.

The 19thC Gothic Revival started with poorly executed and over-elaborate Gothic motifs on European furniture and metalwork, dubbed by the Victorians as ABBOTSFORD STYLE and known as **Troubadour style** in France and **Dantesque** in Italy. British architect Augustus PUGIN reacted against this excess in the 1830s, with more authentic methods of construction and decoration.

Later furniture designers who followed his lead include William BURGES, William MORRIS, Bruce TALBERT, and Charles EASTLAKE.

gouache Water-soluble artist's paint in which the colour pigments are mixed with a chalky white medium and gum to produce an opaque paint (as opposed to the translucency of WATERCOLOUR paint).

Gouache was widely used for MINIATURES as well as for larger paintings – sometimes in conjunction with watercolours.

gouge carving Carved decoration consisting of shallow depressions scooped out with a gouge. It is found mainly on late 16th and 17th-century British oak furniture. See p.90.

Goupy, Marcel (1886-1980) French ART NOUVEAU and ART DECO artist and designer of glass and ceramics who designed for various factories such as ST LOUIS. His work includes glassware decorated with stylised flowers in ENAMEL colours, and both earthenware and porcelain table services decorated with birds and stylised flowers.

goût Grec See LOUIS XVI style.

gout stool A footstool introduced in the late 18thC, designed to ease the discomfort of gout sufferers.

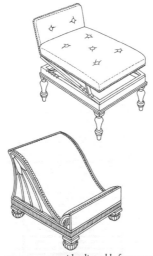

GOUT STOOLS *with adjustable frame and buttoned upholstery (top); c.1800; 19 in (48.2 cm) long; and carved mahogany with padded seat (bottom); c.1820; 14 in (35.5 cm) long.*

Graal glass See ORREFORS.

Graham, George (1673-1751) 18thC clock and watch-maker who brought an unprecedented high degree of accuracy to LONGCASE clocks. He made few clocks, but many watches. His introduction of the deadbeat ESCAPEMENT in 1715 replaced the less accurate anchor escapement, and his mercury PENDULUM in 1726 helped control the pendulum's vulnerability to heat and cold. He also developed the cylinder escapement for watches, which led to slimmer-cased designs. Graham married the niece of clock-maker Thomas TOMPION, and was in

partnership with him in London, continuing the serial numbers initiated by Tompion. See p.279.

graining 1 The patterned edge markings on a coin, also known as **milling**. The practice of graining or edge-lettering (as seen on the modern £1 coin) was usual in Britain from 1622 to guard against CLIPPING. **2** The decorative, painted imitation of wood grain or marble onto furniture. Graining was acceptable in the 18th and 19th centuries but was associated with cheap, low-grade furniture during the late Victorian period.

gramophone A type of mechanical music player patented in the USA by Emile Berliner in 1887, using flat discs rather than the cylinders of Edison's PHONOGRAPH. Early 20thC models used a large, trumpet-shaped horn to amplify the sound, and by the 1920s gramophones were housed in a case.

grandfather chair High-backed, open armchair, dating from c.1850.

grandfather clock See LONGCASE CLOCK.

grand feu colours See HIGH-TEMPERATURE COLOURS.

Grand Rapids furniture Inexpensive, mass-produced furniture of ART NOUVEAU, RENAISSANCE Revival and other styles made at Grand Rapids, Michigan, USA, c.1850-1930 and exported to Europe.

Grand Tour European tour made by young, wealthy 18thC men, following completion of a formal education. The aim was to absorb the culture, history and contemporary art of the great European cities. See p.30.

gravity clock Clock powered by the falling of its own weight. A type which is suspended on a chain is known as a **ball clock**, a **rack clock** is one mounted on a toothed rack. An **inclined plane clock** has its movement encased in a canister which rolls down a slope marked with the days of the week.

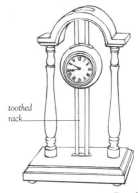

toothed rack

RACK-TYPE GRAVITY CLOCK; *French; c.1875; 18 in (45.7 cm) high. The weight of the mechanism drives the gear train over the teeth on the left-hand brass rod.*

Gray, Eileen (1878-1976) Irish architect and furniture designer who became the best European LACQUER artist of the period. Gray made decorative ceramics, including domestic earthenware, as well as wood, lacquer and modernist tubular steel furniture, characterised by plain, linear forms.

Greatbach, William (1735-1813) English potter who made transfer-printed cream-coloured wares and fruit-shaped tablewares, glazed by Josiah WEDGWOOD for whom he worked 1788-1807.

Great Exhibition An international Exhibition of the Works of Industry of All Nations, to give its full title – held in 1851 at the original Crystal Palace in Hyde Park, London. See p.56.

greave See ARMOUR.

greybeard See BELLARMINE.

griffin Mythological creature with an eagle's head and wings and a lion's body, used as a decorative motif during the RENAISSANCE period.

GRIFFIN *A detail from an oak court cupboard support; c.1670.*

grille 1 Brass latticework used as panels in the doors of CABINET furniture, often replacing glass during the late 18th and early 19th centuries. **2** See VINAIGRETTE.

grisaille, en A painting technique used on ceramics and glass using shades of grey and black to imitate either sculpted stone relief, or engravings as on Chinese JESUIT WARE c.1720-50.

groat British silver coin with a face value of 4d (1.66p). Its name derives from the word 'great', because of the coin's size compared with the smaller PENNY. Groats were mainly used 1350-1560, but were issued before and after these dates.

    The Britannia groat, for example, was issued in the 19thC. This was the same size as the silver 3d but thicker and displayed the face of Britannia.

groove-and-tongue Carved decoration found on items of furniture like concave fluting partially filled with a convex moulding.

Gropius, Walter See BAUHAUS.

gros point A large cross stitch usually in wool on a canvas ground. *Point* is French for 'needle stitch'.

grotesque Extravagant DECORATIVE MOTIF in which figures of humans, mythological beasts, birds, animals and sphinxes are used at the whim of the artist. The design elements are loosely linked by motifs such as intertwining scrolls, STRAPWORK or foliage.

    Grotesque decoration was used in virtually every medium of the decorative arts – carved, INLAID or painted on furniture; ENGRAVED, CHASED or modelled on silver; woven into BEAUVAIS tapestries; and painted on MAIOLICA. It was particularly popular during the RENAISSANCE and Rococo periods, as well as later in the eclectic high Victorian period and in Germany at the same time. The word stems from the Italian *grotte*, the subterranean ruins where ancient Roman motifs of this type were discovered during the Renaissance.

Groult, André (1884-1967) French interior decorator and designer of ART DECO furniture. Groult's furniture features curved lines, harmonising colours and fine materials.

ground Base or background colour.

guard chain A long chain, usually of gold, and originally one from which a watch and various other objects were suspended. Guard chains were popular in Britain from the early 19thC until the early 20thC. See p.272.

guéridon Stand for holding a candelabrum or torch, a tray or a basket. Some early guéridons were in the form of a black human figure – now known as **blackamoors** – and were imported to Britain from Holland, Italy and France in the latter half of the 17thC. The term has come to be commonly used for small occasional tables associated with the LOUIS XV and LOUIS XVI periods, with a FRIEZE drawer and platform.

GUÉRIDON in the form of a blackamoor on removable base; c.1880; 5½ ft (1.68 m) high.

GUÉRIDON with caryatid-topped inswept legs; c.1850; 31½ in (80 cm) high.

guilloche A continuous pattern of interlacing circles derived from Greek and Roman architecture and used to decorate plain or moulded surfaces on furniture. See DECORATIVE MOTIFS.

guinea A British gold coin first struck under Charles II in 1663 and so called because some of the bullion gold used to make the first pieces was imported from Guinea by the Africa Company. The PROVENANCE MARK of an elephant or elephant and castle was the Africa Company symbol, and is found on some of the coins. After some fluctuation, the value of the coin settled at 21 shillings (£1.05). The last golden guinea was struck in 1813, but the term denoted 21 shillings until the introduction of decimal currency. Guineas with a pointed shield on the reverse side, issued 1787-99, are often known as **spade guineas**. See p.387.

guls The dominant repeating motif on weavings of the nomadic Turkoman tribes of central Asia. Gul designs vary greatly, but are usually based on an octagon shape containing stylised flowers – *gul* is the Farsi word for 'flower'. The motifs are thought by some writers to be tribal emblems, and therefore provide a clue to a carpet's origin. See box below.

Gumley, John (1691-1727) Cabinet-maker and manufacturer of mirrors and chandeliers. Gumley was appointed royal cabinet-maker to King George I in 1715.

gunmetal Strong alloy of copper and tin developed in the 19thC to make guns and also cast to make domestic HOLLOW-WARE, candlesticks and furniture ornaments.

gun money A large, base metal coinage supposedly made from melted-down cannons. It was issued in Ireland by King James II following his exile from England in 1688.

gutta percha Rubbery material made from the resin of an East Indian tree, used in the late 19thC for furniture decorations, dolls and golf balls.

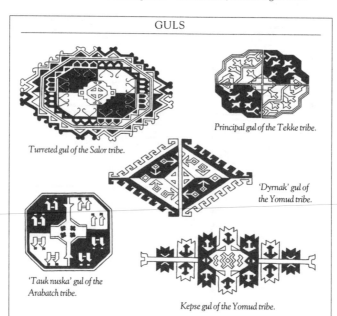

GULS

Turreted gul of the Salor tribe.

Principal gul of the Tekke tribe.

'Dyrnak' gul of the Yomud tribe.

'Tauk nuska' gul of the Arabatch tribe.

Kepse gul of the Yomud tribe.

H

Hafner ware See TILES.

Haig, Thomas (c. 1727-1803) Cabinet-maker, upholsterer and business partner of Thomas CHIPPENDALE. After Chippendale's death in 1779, Haig continued in partnership with Chippendale's son Thomas until 1796.

halberd See POLEARMS.

half-hunter See HUNTER-CASED WATCH.

halfpenny See PENNY.

half-tester Bed with a canopy or TESTER, supported by the headboard or posts, that covers a quarter to a third of the bed area. Half-testers were used in late medieval times and revived in the 17th, 18th and 19th centuries.

hall chair Hard-seated single chair designed for the entrance hall, dating from the early 18thC. See p.95.

Hallett, William (c. 1707-81) Early Georgian cabinet-maker. He became a business partner in the cabinet-making firm VILE & COBB in 1752.

hallmarks The official marks of an ASSAY office or guild stamped on articles with a precious metal content. The term applies more loosely to the complete set of marks found on an article of SILVER, PLATINUM or GOLD, including the date mark and the maker's mark. Various hallmarking systems exist throughout Europe. In Britain, the term 'hallmark' literally means the mark of the Goldsmith's Hall, the original assaying office established in London in 1300.

    All but the smallest articles of STERLING SILVER, gold and platinum should be hallmarked, providing a guarantee of the quality of the metal, identifying the assaying office, date checked, and the sponsor or maker – whoever was responsible for sending it to the assay office. This includes any item over ½ oz (15.5g) apart from those whose appearance would be ruined by a hallmark, such as items of jewellery. If an article is added to or its use is changed it must be resubmitted to the assay office.

    The **King's Mark**, or **Leopard's Head** was introduced 1300 as a guarantee of quality. When the Lion Passant took over this role in the 16thC, the Leopard's Head became the **town mark** of the London assay office. Other assay offices had their own official stamps or **town marks**. The (continued p.480)

UNDERSTANDING HALLMARKS

TO INTERPRET HALLMARKS accurately you need to refer to one of the standard reference works such as *English Silver Hall Marks* edited by Judith Banister, *Discovering Hall Marks on English Silver* by John Bly, or *Jackson's Gold and Silver Marks* edited by Ian Pickford. These tabulate the cycles of date marks for each of the main assay offices.

A TYPICAL SET *of silver hallmarks*

From left to right: leopard's head, town mark for London; date mark for 1801-2; sponsor's mark of Paul Storr; lion passant sterling silver mark; King George III duty mark.

TOWN MARKS

THE MARKS ILLUSTRATED below were used for the specific dates given. They are typical examples; there were many variations in the shape and size of the cartouches and in the finer details of the design.

LONDON
Operating 1300-present.

 1720-4   1856-95

Leopard, uncrowned from 1820.

BIRMINGHAM
Operating 1773-present.

 1900-25 Anchor

CHESTER
Operating 1570-1962.

 1726-60   1809-23

Three wheatsheaves and a sword, used in addition to leopard's head.

DUBLIN
Operating 1638-present.

 1741-6

Harp and crown, from 1730 used in conjunction with the figure of Hibernia.

EDINBURGH
Operating 1552-present.

1759-80
1806-9

Triple-towered castle, used in conjunction with thistle 1759-1974 and subsequently with lion rampant.

EXETER
1701-1883

 1857-83

Early marks from civic and ecclesiastical records – Roman letter X, crowned or uncrowned – in 16th and 17th centuries. From 1701 a triple-towered castle.

GLASGOW
Operating 1681-1964.

 1763-84

The city arms – an oak tree with a bird on top, a bell and a salmon – sometimes with a signet ring in its mouth.

NEWCASTLE
Operating 1701-1884.

 1717-21

Three castles, used in conjunction with London assay marks from 1702.

NORWICH
Operating 1565-1706.

1636-7

The city arms – a castle on a lion rampant, and/or crowned rose.

SHEFFIELD
Operating 1773-present.

Crown, replaced in 1975 by a rose.

YORK
Operating c. 1560-1859.

 1608-13   1839-59

Split fleur-de-lis and leopard's head to 1697, in conjunction with London assay marks from 1701.

DATE MARKS

EACH ASSAY OFFICE operates its own cycle of date letters and determines the typeface and style of cartouche used, so in a given year, as 1795-6 (right), for example, there is considerable variation.

London   Birmingham   Chester   Dublin

Edinburgh   Newcastle   Sheffield   York

SPONSOR'S MARKS

THE SPONSOR'S mark identifies the craftsman or workshop responsible for forwarding the article for assay. It is not compulsory, but is usually included. Some sponsor's marks are illustrated with the entries for silversmiths in this glossary.

 Paul de Lamerie

 Mappin & Webb

STANDARD MARKS

STANDARD HALLMARKS on gold are generally as for sterling silver, accompanied by the carat unit. Sometimes the town mark doubles as a standard mark, as with Dublin's crowned harp; most English assay offices use variations of the lion passant.

LION PASSANT MARKS

London

1544-5 1680-97 1796-1821 1821-36

Britannia standard with lion's head erased, compulsory silver standard 1697-1720; voluntary thereafter.

Birmingham   Chester

1773-98 1950-92   1730-62 1901-26

Newcastle   Sheffield   York

1725-8 1787-91   1918-68 1836-59

Complete set of London hallmarks for 18-carat gold, 1876.

IMPORTED GOLD AND SILVER

Although standard, town, duty or sponsor's marks sometimes appear on foreign silver, they are inconsistent and unreliable. From 1842, all sterling standard foreign silver imported into Britain had to be stamped with the letter F or, later, with the import marks of the individual assay offices.

 London, Birmingham, Sheffield 1867-1904

London   Birmingham

1904-6   1906-1950   from 1904

Edinburgh   Sheffield

1904 on   1904-6   1906 on

DUTY MARKS

THE SOVEREIGN'S HEAD or duty mark was compulsory 1784-1890 to denote duty paid. The marks do not correspond exactly with the reigns as there was some delay before a new stamp was made after a sovereign's death. The jubilee and coronation marks were optional.

 1784-6 George III   1786-1821 George III   1821-34 George IV   1834-7 William IV

   1837-1890 Victoria   1934-6 George V jubilee mark   1952-4 Elizabeth II coronation mark

heraldic symbol of the **Lion Passant**, introduced 1544, replaced the Leopard's Head as the national hallmark of sterling silver.

The **date mark** or **assay letter** was introduced 1478. Its purpose is to identify the assay warden by the date the article was assayed. As the warden changed annually, a different letter of the alphabet was stamped on. Once all letters in an alphabetical cycle were used up, a new cycle was started in a different typeface and/or with a different frame. Individual assay offices have different cycles.

The **Maker's** or **Sponsor's Mark**, introduced 1363, identifies the silversmith, originally by means of a symbol suggestive of his name, his products or location. From the 17thC, initials or the first two letters of the craftsman's name were more common.

The **Duty Mark** or **Sovereign's Head** occurs on silverware 1784-1890, when a new silver tax was imposed; the head of the reigning monarch denotes duty paid. The hallmark of BRITANNIA STANDARD silver applied to all silver produced 1697-1720.

The **Lion's Head Erased** appears on Britannia standard silver; on London silver it replaced the Leopard's Head, but was used as well as the town mark by other assay offices. See box, p.479.

hall stand Stand for hats, coats and umbrellas introduced in the early 19thC. Some are very ornate, especially those made wholly or partly in CAST IRON. In the 1860s, BENTWOOD versions became popular and were common in hotels, restaurants and offices.

hammered 1 Usual method of hand-striking a coin design onto BLANK metal using a pair of DIES. This method was used until the mid-17thC. **2** Metal articles shaped by hand, a process used since ancient times. The metal is gently hammered into shape over a wooden block or leather pad. See PLANISHING, RAISING and p.234. **3** See MARTELÉ.

Hampelmann See JUMPING JACK.

Hancock, Robert (1731-1817) Staffordshire-born engraver whose work was the principal source of TRANSFER-PRINTED designs on Bow, WORCESTER and CAUGHLEY porcelain, and probably also on BATTERSEA enamels.

hands See CLOCK HANDS.

hand cooler A small, round or egg-shaped piece of glass, crystal or stone, such as marble or agate, used from the 18th to late 19th centuries to keep the hands cool. Most were about 1½-2 in

(40-50 mm) across, some made into miniature paperweights, and others intricately carved by glass houses such as BACCARAT and CLICHY.

hand warmer Portable container for hot metal, coals or charcoal which was used to keep the hands warm. Most examples have an outer case of pierced metalwork, such as copper or brass, surrounding the inner container and heat source.

hanger Short general-purpose sword used by huntsmen, horsemen and sailors in the 17th and 18th centuries.

Harache, Pierre I (*fl.* 1682-98) HUGUENOT silversmith who, together with his son, Pierre II (*fl.* 1698-1717), specialised in silver figurative ornaments, decorated with CHASING, EMBOSSING, GADROONING, PIERCED and CUT-CARD WORK. Their marks, styles and designs are very similar to one another.

hard metal See BRITANNIA METAL.

hard-paste See PORCELAIN.

hardstone Gemstone whose colour and formation makes it suitable for carving objects such as urns and also for use in decorative techniques such as INLAID DECORATION, mosaic and CAMEO. Typical examples include agate, lapis lazuli and malachite.

hardwood A botanical term for wood taken from a broad-leaved tree. Hardwoods are generally harder than SOFTWOODS, although not necessarily stronger, and include some of the finest furniture timbers such as mahogany, oak and walnut.

hare's furglaze See TEMMOKU.

harewood Sycamore or maple wood which is stained with iron oxide to give a green or silvery finish, and also known as **silverwood**. It was used from the 17thC and especially popular in the second half of the 18thC. The San Domingo SATINWOOD, a bright yellow wood that turns grey when it has seasoned, is also known as harewood.

harlequin set A set of objects such as cups and saucers of a common style, but each piece decorated differently. The term is also applied to originally unrelated objects – of furniture, for example – which have been 'matched up' to make a set.

harlequin table A form of PEMBROKE TABLE with a small box-like structure concealed in the central body which springs open to reveal a nest of drawers and compartments.

Harrison, John (1693-1776) A Lincolnshire-born carpenter who became an innovative clock-maker. Most clock-makers used metal for mechanical parts of a clock, trying different methods of lubrication to make them more reliable and smooth-running. Harrison was unique in questioning the basic material, and his early clocks have wooden wheels made of the naturally oily LIGNUM VITAE. He also made the first CHRONOMETER, in a bid to win a reward offered by Parliament in 1714 for a timekeeper accurate enough to be used for navigation at sea, and was finally granted the £20,000 prize in 1773 thanks to the support of King George III. In 1728 Harrison introduced the first gridiron PENDULUM with built-in temperature compensation.

hatchli rugs See ENSI.

Haviland See LIMOGES.

haystack A conical 19thC measure used in Irish taverns with a stepped neck, and usually of pewter; English versions are slightly different in form and of brass or copper. They are also known as **haycocks** or **harvesters**.

Heal, Sir Ambrose (1872-1959) Artist-craftsman and furniture-maker and designer. He joined Heal & Son, the London-based family furniture-making business, in 1893 and designed all of its furniture from 1896 to the 1930s. Early pieces show the influence of the prevalent ARTS AND CRAFTS MOVEMENT, and his range of stylish but durable furniture at reasonable prices had a considerable influence on furniture design in the early part of the 20thC. Towards the end of his working life (*c.*1939), Heal experimented with new materials, including steel and aluminium.

heartwood The hard inner core and oldest part of a tree. It is denser and darker than the outer layers of SAPWOOD, and does not contain living cells; as the tree grows, the area of heartwood increases.

heat treatment Process of changing or eliminating the colour of a natural or synthetic gemstone by controlled heating. See p.267.

Hennell family Silver craftsmen working in a London-based family business, established by David Hennell in 1735. Over 30 personal silver marks were registered by the family until the last son, Samuel, died in 1837. A second Hennell firm was established in 1809 by David's grandson, Robert (*b.*1769) which operated until 1887.

Hepplewhite, George (*d.*1786) British NEOCLASSICAL cabinet-maker whose pattern book *The Cabinet-Maker and Upholsterer's Guide* illustrated prevailing fashions in a way that was easily interpreted by ordinary cabinet-makers. See p.39.

herati pattern Common floral motif used on Oriental carpets, and said to originate in the region of Herat, Iran. Typically it consists of a stylised floral rosette arranged in two-way or four-way symmetry, enclosed within a diamond shape. The motif is also known as the *mahi* or **fish** pattern in the carpet trade because of its resemblance to fishes, or more recently, as the **in-and-out** pattern.

FOUR-WAY HERATI PATTERN *from a Persian carpet; late 19thC. The pattern repeats over the entire field of the carpet.*

hibachi Japanese term for a charcoal burner, usually of bronze or cast iron, and used for warming rooms.

high-temperature colours Certain metal oxide pigments that can withstand the high firing temperatures used to fuse them onto an unglazed ceramic body. They are used as UNDERGLAZE colours painted onto the BISCUIT body of porcelain, or painted onto the raw glaze (known as **inglaze**) of TIN-GLAZED EARTHENWARE before the glaze firing. Colours include green from copper, purple from manganese, yellow from antimony and blue from cobalt and are also known as **grand feu colours**. See p.152.

hilt The hand grip of a sword or dagger. Until the 15thC, swords usually had a straight hilt with a **crossguard** and **pommel**. Later hilts are more elaborate, in terms of both protection and decoration. See box, p.481, and SWORD.

hinge Folding metal joint which allows doors and lids to open and shut; it can be decorative as well as functional. Before the 16thC, **pin hinges** were used on boarded and panelled furniture (see JOINING): a loose pin or barrel acts as a pivot which is pushed through corresponding holes in the two parts to be joined. The **wire hinge**, consisting of two interlocking loops of wire, was introduced in the 16thC, and is often seen on 17thC coffers.

From the beginning of the 18thC, hinges tend to be concealed. A **butt hinge** is sunk into the edge of the surface so that only a narrow line of metal is visible externally. And in a **blind hinge**, the pivoting pin and tube are set within the hinge plate so that they are flush with the surface. The join can be further disguised by a **rule joint** – a hinged joint used on screens or the fold-down leaves of tables so that there is no gap in the outer surface when the leaves are down.

On lidded metal and ceramic objects, a **book hinge** with a rounded back like the spine of a book may be seen, sometimes with the ends of the pin concealed by ornamental caps, and **box hinge** is found on some stoneware jugs with silver or pewter lids and mouth rims.

hipped Cabinet-making term for a CABRIOLE LEG which extends to or rises above the level of the seat as opposed to ending at the base of the seat rail, and which is often ornately carved from the knee upwards.

Hirado ware Sparsely painted blue and white porcelain made at the Mikawachi kilns for the lords of Hirado, an island near ARITA, Japan. Most pieces are likely to be 19thC, although production may have been as early as the late 17thC.

Hispano-Moresque ware Spanish TIN-GLAZED EARTHENWARE that used techniques and designs brought by the Moorish invaders in the 8thC. The most notable wares are decorated with LUSTRE introduced from the 13thC and used especially at Malaga, and in the Valencia area in the 15thC. The

ware inspired the development of Italian MAIOLICA and was arguably the first pottery of any artistic value to be produced in Europe since the ancient civilisations. See p.165.

Höchst German ceramics factory operating 1746-96. It began making FAIENCE useful wares, painted in enamel colours, then produced hard-paste PORCELAIN from 1750, concentrating on Rococo-style tablewares and statuettes, notably by Johann Peter Melchior (1742-1825).

c.1763

Hoffmann, Josef (1870-1956) See WIENER WERKSTÄTTE.

Hogarth, William (1697-1764) British painter, caricaturist and silver engraver who depicted the social classes of Georgian times in works such as *A Rake's Progress* and *Marriage à la Mode*.

Holbein carpets Family of Turkish carpets incorporating various octagonal motifs, named after the German painter Hans Holbein the Younger, who depicted such carpets in his paintings. The designs actually date from the second half of the 15thC, predating Holbein's paintings by nearly a century. The term embraces small-pattern Holbeins with rows of alternating lozenges and octagons, originating in the Ushak region of western Anatolia, and large-pattern Holbeins with two or three large octagons, woven in Turkey.

holey dollar Australia's famous first coin – a Spanish PIECE OF EIGHT with the centre cut out and COUNTER-MARKED, and a face value of 5 shillings (25p). Holey dollars were issued in

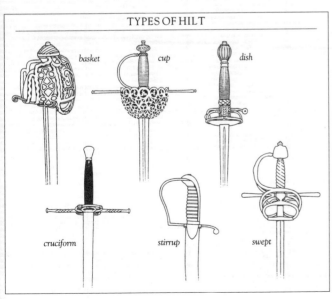
obverse *reverse*

AUSTRALIAN HOLEY DOLLAR *showing the countermarks 'New South Wales', 'Five shillings' and the date '1813'.*

New South Wales in 1813 and withdrawn 1829. The pieces cut from the centres formed coins in their own right known as **dumps** and with a face value of 1s 3d (6.25p).

Holland, Henry (1745-1806) Late Georgian architect and furniture designer whose work anticipated that of French EMPIRE STYLE. See p.42.

hollow-ware Term for gold, silver, pewter and ceramics ware that is hollow, such as bowls and drinking vessels – as opposed to FLATWARE.

holly Hard, white wood with a close grain and fine texture, often stained a different colour. Holly was used for small pieces of INLAID DECORATION in solid oak and walnut in the 16th and early 17th centuries and for MARQUETRY from the late 17th to late 18th centuries.

honey gilding See GILDING.

hood 1 Removable part of a clock which hides the mechanism and surrounds the dial. **2** Semi-circular top of a mirror frame or a cabinet.

Hooke, Dr Robert See TOMPION, Thomas.

Hope, Thomas (1769-1831) Dutch-born author-traveller, collector, furniture designer and patron of the arts. He moved to England in 1795 with a huge collection of antique vases and sculpture. His *Household Furniture and Interior Decoration*, published 1807, became a 'bible' for Regency style containing designs for solid pieces of furniture, based on Classical lines and decorated with symbolic motifs taken from Ancient Greek and Egyptian architecture. See p.42.

Höroldt, J.G. See MEISSEN.

horse-brass Flat or slightly curved brass plate with PIERCED, ENGRAVED or STAMPED decoration designed to ward off evil, advertise the trade of the horse's owner or to bring good luck. Horse-brasses were familiar harness trappings in Britain in the 19thC; examples before 1860 are rare,

although similar badges were used in the Middle Ages. Most examples seen today are reproductions.

horse dressing glass See CHEVAL MIRROR.

horsehair Coarse stuffing from the mane and tail of horses used to upholster seat furniture from the mid-18thC, and widely used throughout the 19thC.

horseshoe table Table introduced in the 18thC which is shaped like a segment of a ring, sometimes with rounded flaps at either end for extending the surface area. There is often a central pivoted device to move bottles to any point of the radius.

Horta, Victor (1861-1947) Belgian ART NOUVEAU architect, teacher and designer. His interiors and furniture are characterised by sinuous lines and contrasting areas of space, and by the use of wrought iron, curved metalwork and INLAID DECORATION. They were much copied throughout Europe.

hotei See BUDAI.

Huguenots Protestant refugees from France, known for their highly skilled craftsmanship and who influenced decorative arts in Europe from the end of the 17thC. In 1685, Louis XIV of France revoked the Edict of Nantes, which had allowed French Protestants religious freedom of worship. As a consequence, Britain and other European countries received a flood of Huguenots fleeing persecution. Many of these were cabinet-makers, tapestry and cloth weavers or silversmiths, and their work was of the highest quality. They introduced several new CABINET-MAKING techniques, including MARQUETRY, VENEERING, JAPANNING and GESSO work.

Many of the finest silks from the major 18thC SPITALFIELDS SILK FACTORIES in London were the work of Huguenot designer James Leman. Particularly influential was the silverwork produced by Huguenot craftsmen such as David WILLAUME. It is generally solid, decorated with CUT-CARD WORK, STRAPWORK, intricate ENGRAVING and the application of cast ornaments in human and animal form. The distinctive Huguenot styles gradually merged with native styles from around 1725.

The refugees also brought with them several new vessels, including the soup tureen and the ÉCUELLE.

humpen Large German 17th-18thC drinking vessels. Glass examples were almost cylindrical in shape, often lidded and decorated with ENAMEL.

TYPES OF HILT

basket *cup* *dish*

cruciform *stirrup* *swept*

Reichsadlerhumpen, or **adlerglas,** carry the double eagle of the Holy Roman Empire, with the armorial bearings of 56 imperial families on its wings. **Kurfürstenhumpen** are painted with pictures of the Holy Roman Emperor and his Electors, and others, called **Apostelhumpen,** with religious scenes.

Hungarian stitch See BARGELLO.

hunter-cased watch Pocket watch with a hinged metal cover over the dial. These were first used, from *c.* 1840, in the hunting field, as the unprotected glass of an OPEN-FACED WATCH in a rider's waistcoat pocket was liable to be knocked and broken. A **half-hunter** case has an opening cut in the centre of the lid with an additional CHAPTER RING engraved around it to allow the hands to be read without exposing the full dial.

Huygens, Christian See PENDULUM.

Hyalith Opaque scarlet or black BOHEMIAN glass, often with gilding, developed in the early 19thC, probably in imitation of Wedgwood's ROSSO ANTICO and BASALTES WARE. It was used mainly for ornaments.

hyacinth See ZIRCON.

I

ice glass ART GLASS with a frosted outer surface that resembles cracked ice. It is made by rolling a partly blown glass object over powdered glass, and then reheating it and blowing it into shape, or by plunging white-hot glass into cold water so that it becomes veined with tiny cracks. Ice glass, also known as **frosted glass, crackled glass** and **verre craquelé,** was made in 16thC Venice and revived by British glass-maker Apsley PELLATT *c.* 1840.

ichiraku See NETSUKE.

Imari Distinctively decorated Japanese porcelain made at ARITA from the late 17thC and shipped from the port of Imari. The panelled decoration, dominated by UNDERGLAZE blue, iron-red enamel and gilding, with occasional additions of black, green, aubergine and yellow enamels, was based on local textiles. The designs, also known as **Japan patterns,** were copied in Europe throughout the 18thC. In the 19thC Imari-inspired patterns were imitated at DERBY and SPODE. See pp.167, 181.

imbricated ornament Carved fish-scale decoration found on furniture.

impasto 1 White or coloured liquid clay SLIP applied thickly to a ceramic body and then worked so that it is slightly raised from the body before glazing. **2** The term also applies to the thickness of paint in oil painting.

in-and-out pattern See HERATI PATTERN.

Ince & Mayhew (*fl.* 1759-1802) English cabinet-makers William Ince and John Mayhew worked together from 1759 onwards. Their early ornate work in Rococo style later developed along more restrained NEOCLASSICAL lines. The partners published *The Universal System of Household Furniture,* which contained over 300 designs similar to those of Thomas CHIPPENDALE. Ince and Mayhew also built furniture based on designs by Robert Adam.

incised decoration Decoration that is cut or carved into the surface with a sharp metal point.

inclined plane clock See GRAVITY CLOCK.

incuse A design impressed into the surface of a coin to create an INTAGLIO effect rather than a relief design.

indianische Blumen German for 'Indian flowers' – a term for painted floral decoration on ceramics inspired by Oriental and more specifically KAKIEMON, originals. The designs were introduced at MEISSEN in the 1720s, and imitated by other European factories including CHELSEA. From the 1740s indianische Blumen were superseded by DEUTSCHE BLUMEN (German flowers).

Indian jail carpets Large, heavily woven pile carpets produced in northern-Indian jail workshops in the 19thC. The industry thrived in response to growing Western demand after examples were shown at the Great Exhibition in London in 1851. The designs were based on earlier Persian styles. Flat-weave DHURRIES were also woven in Indian jails – in far larger quantities than the pile rugs, as they were easier to make. See p.305.

inglaze See HIGH-TEMPERATURE COLOURS.

ingrain carpets British FLAT-WEAVE carpets that are reversible, having the same pattern appearing in a different colour on either side. They are also known as **double-cloth carpets,** and have been woven since *c.* 1824 at many factories, particularly KIDDERMINSTER, but developed mainly in the USA from 1850.

inkstand Container for writing implements, including inkpot, POUNCE box, sealing wax, hand bell and quill pens, in use from the 16thC onwards. The implements either fit into a box or rest on a matching tray. **Standish** is the common term for pre-18thC silver inkstands.

inlaid decoration Technique used on solid wood furniture, in which details of coloured woods, ivory, metal or mother-of-pearl are set into cut-out recesses some ⅛ in (3 mm) deep. First used in 15thC Italy, the technique reached France, Holland, Germany and Britain the following century, and was popular on Elizabethan and early Stuart oak and walnut furniture. Designs were fairly simple – geometric, or using flower and vase motifs. As VENEER and MARQUETRY techniques were perfected, inlaying died out. See p.90.

inro Small container designed to hang from the belt, worn by Japanese men from the 14thC. The original purpose was to hold a SEAL – the word is literally translated as 'seal basket' – but inro were later used for other personal effects such as medicine or tobacco, and by the 18thC had become purely decorative. Inro are usually of LACQUER on wood, typically 3-5 in (7.5-12.5 cm) long, shallow and oval, and made up of several close-fitting compartments. See NETSUKE and pp.399-400.

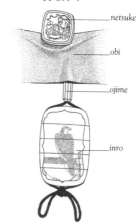

INRO hung from the obi (sash), secured by a netsuke (toggle) and ojime (slip-bead); late 19thC.

intaglio Decorative technique (or object made by the technique) of incising a figure or design into the surface of hardstones (as in SEALS) and glass (see ENGRAVING, wheel) especially, and also ceramics and metalwork. Intaglio is the opposite of CAMEO work, in that the design, not the background, is cut away to give an image in relief.

intarsia An Italian term for pictorial MARQUETRY or INLAID DECORATION found on 15th and 16thC Italian panelling and furniture. Various woods, tortoiseshell, metals and ivory were chosen for colour and texture to create a realistic architectural perspective, or a symmetrical still-life group of objects such as musical or precision instruments.

interior painting Decorative technique which involves painting a watercolour picture on the inside of a bottle using an angled brush inserted through the neck. It was particularly popular for decorating SNUFF BOTTLES.

in-the-white See BLANK.

investment casting See LOST WAX.

Iribe, Paul (1883-1935) French caricaturist and designer of jewellery, furniture, textiles and other interior furnishings. Iribe began working in a flowing ART NOUVEAU style, but his later, simpler forms influenced the ART DECO movement. He is noted for well-upholstered furniture with fine carving or inlaid woodwork. In the early 1900s Iribe worked with French fashion designer Paul Poiret and from 1914 for American film director Cecil B. De Mille. In 1930 he went to Paris and made jewellery for Coco Chanel.

iridescent glass Glassware that appears to be rainbow-coloured when viewed from certain angles and in certain lights. Ancient glass which has been buried often develops a natural iridescence due to attack by minerals in the soil. The same effect has been created artificially by treating glassware with metallic oxides.

Irish glass Heavy, ornate LEAD CRYSTAL, produced from *c.* 1780 in Belfast, Cork, Dublin and Waterford following the removal of a ban on exporting glass from Ireland and to avoid the high taxes payable in England. English factories at STOURBRIDGE, Sunderland and St Helens have recently been identified as the source of much of the glass previously described as Irish.

iron chimney See FIREBACK.

ironstone china See STONE CHINA.

Islamic style Ornamental style applied throughout the decorative arts both in Middle-Eastern Islamic countries, North Africa and Spain. It is in abstract style – often colourful, symmetrical patterns with inscriptions or kufic script – because the Koran forbids the representation of Allah, the human form and animals.

In 15thC Spain following the Moorish (Islamic) occupation, Islamic style was combined with Christian GOTHIC in the **Mudéjar** style.

Isnik pottery Coarse-bodied Turkish earthenware, either coated with a white SLIP or TIN GLAZED, decorated with bright, HIGH-TEMPERATURE COLOURS under a glassy quartz glaze. Bright blue, green, turquoise and an IMPASTO red were typical, and blue and white Chinese-inspired wares were also made. Production centred on Isnik (ancient Nicaea), 60 miles (95 km) south-east of Istanbul, from the 15thC onwards. Quality declined in the 17thC, but the style was copied in Europe from the late 19thC.

isochronous motion A clock-making term meaning equally beating, that is, each beat occupying an equal period of time. A PENDULUM is naturally isochronous, while a BALANCE wheel only becomes so when linked with a balance spring.

istoriato TIN-GLAZED EARTHENWARE, particularly Italian MAIOLICA, with a scene from a historical, mythological or biblical story. Literally translated as 'with a story in it', istoriato was introduced in the early 16thC. It represented a move from the production of purely practical wares to articles designed for display.

ivory Hard, dentine tissue from the tusks of elephants and other mammals. From the earliest times ivory was used in China for carvings and in Japan for NETSUKE figures, as a base for miniature paintings and for decoration. In the West, ivory has been used for ornaments, jewellery and furniture. Its use declined in the 15thC but interest was revived in the 18thC, especially in the Victorian era. See MORSE IVORY and pp.398-401.

ivory glass Cream-coloured glass wheel-engraved or moulded to look like carved ivory. THE ENGRAVING was treated with a coloured stain to highlight details of the design, and some pieces were then decorated with GILDING or ENAMELLING. The technique was applied to various ornamental wares, some in Oriental styles, and was a speciality of Thomas WEBB & Sons in the late 19thC.

Ivrene Ivory-coloured, slightly iridescent ART GLASS developed by the designer Frederick CARDER during the 1920s. The colour was created by adding the minerals feldspar and cryolite to molten glass, and the iridescence was achieved by spraying the finished object with tin chloride and then reheating it.

J

Jackfield ware Ceramics imitation of Japanese LACQUER ware initially produced at Jackfield in Shropshire from c.1750. It is also known as **japanned ware** and is covered in a glossy black glaze with gilded decoration. It was also produced by ASTBURY, WHIELDON and WEDGWOOD.

Jacobean period Reign of James I in England, 1603-25. See pp.16-21.

Jacob, Georges (1739-1814) French master MENUISIER whose work spanned the LOUIS XVI and EMPIRE periods. His early ROCOCO work soon gave way to a Neoclassical LOUIS XVI style, and by the early 1780s he was one of the leading chair-makers in Paris. After the Revolution, he worked for the designers FONTAINE and Percier before forming Jacob-Desmalter & Cie in 1803 with his second son, François.

Jacobite glass Wine glasses, tumblers and decanters used for loyal toasts to James II and his descendants, Roman Catholic Pretenders to the British throne. Production began in 1688 and the objects were engraved with mottoes, portraits and symbols of the Jacobite cause, supposedly including a thistle, an oak leaf, a caterpillar and a carnation, and a six, seven or eight-petalled rose which represented the British crown.

The cause was lost in 1770 and production of the glassware ceased a few years later. Since then all Jacobite glassware has been widely faked especially in the late 19thC.

Jacquard loom See LOOMS.

Jacquet-Droz Firm of watch and AUTOMATA makers. The partnership between Pierre Jacquet-Droz and his son, Henri-Louis, was set up in Geneva, Switzerland, in 1787. The firm was known for its exquisitely decorated enamelled and automata watches in the first half of the 19thC. They also created life-like automata of human figures drawing and painting.

jade General term for the minerals nephrite and jadeite. Nephrite, from Turkestan, Siberia and the Far East, is hard and translucent, and 'rings' when struck. It ranges in colour from white (the highly prized 'mutton-fat jade') to various shades of brown and green ('spinach jade'), and has a greasy look when polished. Jadeite is rarer, harder and more easily fractured. It is dark green, emerald or variegated white with emerald, or green and lavender;

the translucent emerald green 'imperial' or 'true' jade is the most precious form of jadeite.

Both minerals are too hard to be carved with cutting tools and instead are shaped by abrasives. Nephrite figures and ritualistic implements have been sculpted by the Chinese from Neolithic times, but the 18thC was a particularly prolific period. At this time too, they began to work in jadeite, but mainly for items of jewellery. Real jade remains unmarked when scratched with a steel tip. See pp.398-9.

jambiyah A curved dagger with a double-edged blade. It is a traditional Arab weapon but found in various forms from North Africa to Iran and from East Africa to western India. The jambiyah was often contained in an ornamental scabbard and tucked through a belt at the front of the body.

japanning British term for imitation Oriental LACQUER introduced in the latter half of the 17thC. Metal or wooden surfaces are coated with several layers of various gums such as SHELLAC, as distinct from the resin of the Oriental lacquer tree which is used in true lacquer.

High quality japanning is done with spirit-based varnishes which have a transparency that almost matches the finish of genuine lacquer. It can usually be distinguished from true lacquer by the Westernised designs and greater range of ground colours including black, dark green, and the British speciality of sealing-wax red.

The initial spate of japanned cabinets, mirror frames and boxes at the end of the 17th and early 18th centuries was followed by a fashion for japanned LONGCASE clocks 1720-70. Then there was a lull until the 19thC, when the Victorians revived the craft, especially in the form of japanned PAPIER-MÂCHÉ. See PONTYPOOL WARE, BILSTON ENAMELS, JACKFIELD WARE and p.93.

japonaiserie European decoration copied from imported Japanese PORCELAIN and LACQUER. In the late 18thC, **Japan patterns** (see IMARI) appeared on British ceramics at WORCESTER and DERBY. This fashion declined in the 1820s, but in the 1860s a craze for Japanese style swept every area of design.

jardinière A term used for the ornamental container for a plant pot. Heavily moulded and glazed MAJOLICA jardinières, usually on a stand, were a feature of Victorian drawing rooms, and ornately wrought-iron versions combining table or stand with inset pot were also popular. See pp.200-1.

jargon See ZIRCON.

jasperware A smooth, matt-finish fine STONEWARE introduced by Josiah WEDGWOOD in 1774. Jasperware was much imitated in its time, and is still produced today. It is unglazed, similar in texture to BISCUIT porcelain, and colours include tones of green, lavender, yellow or black as well as the famous 'Wedgwood blue', with relief designs in NEOCLASSICAL style applied in white. The paste itself was stained with metal oxides such as cobalt to produce **'solid jasper'**, but after 1777, a coloured surface wash was applied to a white base resulting in **jasper dip**.

Jasperware can be burnished to a glossy finish – which is sometimes seen on cups and bowls. It is mainly seen unpolished, however, in the form of vases, plaques, cameos and other ornaments. See p.168.

Jazz Modern style See ART DECO.

Jeanneret, Charles Edward See LE CORBUSIER.

jelly glass One or two-handled 18thC glass, usually with a long vase-shaped bowl and short stem, for serving a single portion of jelly or similar type of sweet dessert.

Jennens & Bettridge English manufacturers of PAPIER-MÂCHÉ furniture and works of art, 1816-64. They patented a form of INLAID DECORATION in papier-mâché using coloured glass, ivory, mother-of-pearl, tortoiseshell and gemstones. See p.51.

Jensen, Gerreit (fl.1680-1715) Anglo-Dutch cabinet-maker, whose rich Dutch version of LOUIS XIV style influenced WILLIAM AND MARY furniture. Jensen's furniture was noted for its metal inlay MARQUETRY that was similar to BOULLE work.

Jesuit ware Chinese porcelain of the mid-18thC often decorated en grisaille with Christian subjects meticulously copied from European engravings. The term is misleading, however, as many of the subjects were erotic and not always aimed at the Jesuit market.

jet Black, glossy, fossilised wood – a very hard form of coal – that is carved and highly polished to make jewellery and ornaments. Jet has been used for decoration since the Bronze Age. It was mined extensively on the Yorkshire coast near Whitby and widely exported c.1805-75. It was popular for buttons and MOURNING JEWELLERY in Victorian times. Spanish jet is softer and cheaper than the British form, and **French jet** is the term used for glass imitations. See p.269.

JEWEL CUTS

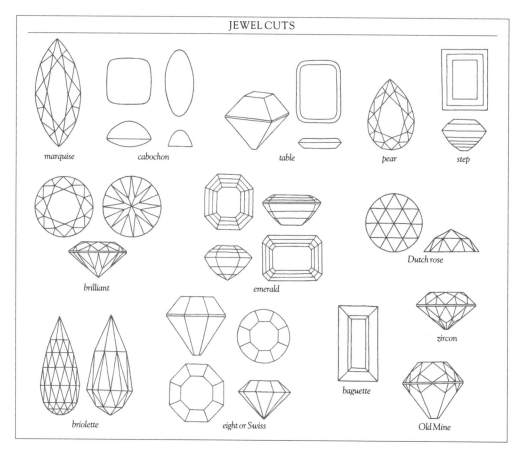

marquise

cabochon

table

pear

step

brilliant

emerald

Dutch rose

zircon

briolette

eight or Swiss

baguette

Old Mine

jewel cutting Process of shaping a gemstone to give it symmetry, and enhance its brilliance, beauty and value. The resulting shapes are either in smooth cabochon form or with many FACETS. Diamond and precious-stone cutting is said to have begun in Belgium in 1475. See box above.

jewelled decoration Ceramics decoration like brightly coloured gems, created by fusing drops of coloured enamel over gold and silver foil. The technique was employed at SÈVRES c. 1778-86, and used in the mid-19thC at WORCESTER, COALPORT and MINTON porcelain factories, though not always on a foil ground.

jewelling Term that refers to the use of hard gemstones (usually synthetic rubies or diamonds) as bearings in watches or clocks to reduce the wear (and hence deterioration in timekeeping) caused by the pivots of cog spindles in their pivot holes. Jewelling was first patented in London in 1704, and was a jealously guarded secret among British makers well into the 18thC. As a result it is not generally found in continental watches until the 19thC.

jewel setting 1 The mount in which a gemstone is set in a ring, pendant,

brooch or other item of jewellery. **2** The style in which a gemstone is secured in a finger ring. In a **closed setting** the underneath of the stone is enclosed and may be backed with coloured foil to enhance its colour. In an **open setting** the underneath of the stone is exposed. In the 19thC several variations of the open setting were introduced and largely superseded the closed setting.

Joel, Betty (1896-1985) British furniture designer who, with her husband David, designed simple, functional furniture for wide domestic use in the 1920s – often in teak or oak, but also in exotic woods such as Indian laurel and silverwood. Pieces have the date of manufacture, the name 'Joel' and the name of the craftsman on a card fixed behind glass.

Johnson, Thomas (1714-78) British furniture-maker, designer, carver and gilder in Rococo style. He published several pattern books of elegant display pieces, such as mirror frames, candlesticks and side tables.

joined stool 16th-17thC, four-legged oak stool with pegged joints, TURNED legs and a deep APRON. See p.94.

joined table See REFECTORY TABLE.

joining Technique of fitting pieces of wood together to the standard required in furniture-making. The words **joined** or **joint** indicate that a piece has been constructed using **mortise-and-tenon** or **dovetail** joints, rather than pegged with wooden dowels or iron pins at the angles, as in **boarded construction**. See pp.91-92.

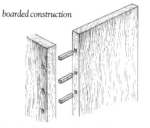

boarded construction

In the 16thC came **panelled construction** – panels held in grooves cut into vertical timbers called **stiles** (at the corners) and **muntins**, and horizontal timbers, or **rails**.

panelled construction

By the end of the 15thC the **mortise-and-tenon joint** was in general use in furniture construction. Two sections of wood are joined at an angle by means of a projecting **tenon**, which fits into a cut-out section of corresponding shape and size called a **mortise**. A tenon ridged on one side only is known as a **barefaced tenon**, whereas a **barefaced tongue** refers to a join where the protruding 'tongue' of wood fits flush on one side of the join.

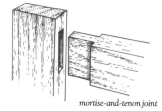

mortise-and-tenon joint

Two pieces of wood can be joined at an angle by means of wedges or dovetail-shaped projections in one piece fitting into corresponding cut-out sections in the other. This is known as a **dovetail joint**. A **through-dovetail** shows through the front of the piece of furniture, resulting in a slightly uneven surface for veneering.

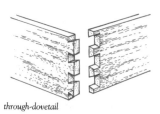

through-dovetail

A refinement of the through-dovetail is the **stopped** or **lapped dovetail** in which the jointed wood does not show on the outer surface of the furniture.

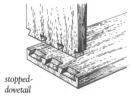

stopped-dovetail

Jones, Inigo (1573-1652) Leading CLASSICAL architect of the Jacobean period. Many of his buildings are the earliest in British architecture to adopt Classical themes, and his ideas had considerable impact on the work of later designers such as William KENT and Robert Adam. See p.20.

Jones, Owen (1809-74) British designer, architect and writer who influenced Victorian decorative styles and the ART NOUVEAU movement. Following visits to the Middle East and Spain, Owen popularised the mathematical structure and stylised natural forms of ISLAMIC and HISPANO-MORESQUE styles in his book *The Alhambra*, and world design in *Grammar of Ornament*.

Jones' influence extended to Christopher DRESSER and Frank Lloyd WRIGHT. See p.61.

jufti knot See CARPET KNOTS.

Jugendstil Name of the German ART NOUVEAU movement, which peaked 1896-1900. It is named after a Munich magazine called *Die Jugend* (Youth). The style incorporated languid, stylised flowers and figures in its early stages, and later showed a more geometrical tendency inspired by British designer Charles Rennie MACKINTOSH.

jumping jack Wooden or cardboard doll, known as a **pantin** in France, and **Hampelmann** in Germany, with a length of string hanging between the legs which is connected to each loosely jointed arm and leg. When the string is pulled the limbs jerk upwards and outwards. Jumping jacks have been made from the late 17thC.

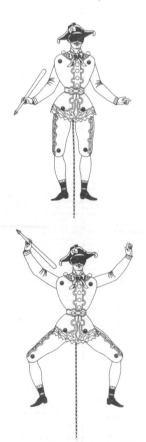

CARDBOARD JUMPING JACK *in 18thC harlequin costume. The limbs are loosely pinned to the body and move when the string is pulled; 8 in (20.3 cm) high.*

K

kagamibuta See NETSUKE.

Kaga ware See KUTANI.

Kakiemon The name given to a distinctive palette of colours used initially on Japanese porcelain c.1660, comprising turquoise, dark blue, yellow, iron-red, black and occasionally brown. The name is that of the potter credited with the palette's invention, Kakiemon I, although the palette is more likely to have evolved gradually. It was copied at the early European porcelain factories during the first half of the 18thC, especially at MEISSEN, CHANTILLY, CHELSEA and BOW. Only BLUE AND WHITE wares with no evidence of Kakiemon enamels have been unearthed at the known Kakiemon kiln site near ARITA, suggesting that the enamelling was done elsewhere. See p.167.

kakihan Script mark of a Japanese artist (equivalent to the British monogram), which is used to identify Japanese metalwork, NETSUKE, ceramics and LACQUER.

kaleidoscope Optical toy consisting of a tube containing mirrors and pieces of coloured glass or paper, popular during the 19thC. Changing patterns appear when the tube is rotated.

KALEIDOSCOPE *on wooden stand; English; late 19thC; 13 in (33 cm) long.*

Kandler, Charles Frederick (*fl.*1727-73) London silversmith, regarded as second only to Paul DE LAMERIE. Kandler made some highly decorated pieces such as wine coolers, tea kettles and tableware, in Rococo style; they typically had handles cast in the form of birds. Later, NEOCLASSICAL designs were simpler.

Kändler, Johann Joachim (1706-75) German porcelain modeller responsible for the eminence of the MEISSEN factory where he was chief modeller 1733-75. Kändler established the porcelain figure – both human and

animal – as an art form and influenced figures produced at other German factories from the 18thC until the 20thC. His work was imitated throughout Europe. See pp.191-2.

kaolin See CHINA CLAY.

kard Indo-Persian straight-bladed, single-edged knife, rather like a kitchen knife. It was carried in a wide scabbard covering much of the hilt.

kashira See KODOGU.

katar Pointed, double-edged Indian dagger with an H-shaped hilt which was gripped on the crossbar and used with a forward-thrusting action.

Kauffmann, Angelica (1741-1807) Swiss-born painter. Kauffmann lived in England (1766-81) before moving to Italy with her husband, artist Antonio ZUCCHI. Her work included wall, ceiling and furniture designs for architect Robert Adam.

kenares See RUNNERS.

kendi Globular ceramic or metal drinking vessel with a breast-shaped spout, made in the Far East. Chinese porcelain kendi were exported to the Middle East from the 15thC.

KENDI *in blue and white porcelain; c.1660-85; 8½ in (21.6 cm) high.*

Kent, William (1684-1748) Painter, architect, designer and landscape gardener. Kent's buildings were inspired by the austere, Classical lines of PALLADIAN STYLE architecture, which he had studied in Italy 1709-19, and influenced also by Inigo JONES. Kent's house interiors, however, had a more ornate, BAROQUE style and richly carved, ARCHITECTURAL-STYLE furniture, which formed part of a unified scheme. Kent was an acknowledged authority on taste in his own lifetime, and had a great influence on contemporary style. See p.30.

Kerr & Binns See WORCESTER.

keyless watch Watch which is wound by means of an attached key, a ribbed knob or button, rather than by

a separate key. The keyless, or **button-wound** watch was first patented 1820 and much modified and improved during the 19thC, but not generally adopted in Britain until after 1880.

kick Indentation in the base of glass objects, designed to increase stability.

Kidderminster Key centre for carpet-making from the late 17thC. The Worcestershire factories initially produced FLAT-WEAVE carpets, which were largely superseded in 1749 by hard-wearing MOQUETTE carpets.

The town was the first British carpet centre to use the Jacquard LOOM in the early 19thC, and the industry continued to expand throughout the 19th and 20th centuries.

kilim 1 A FLAT-WEAVE rug. Technically, the word as used in the East refers only to 'slit-tapestry' weavings, so called because the weft is discontinued with each change of colour, creating slits. The word kilim is of Persian (Iranian) origin, but the rugs are mainly associated with Anatolia in central Turkey, although they are also made in the Caucasus – where they are known as *palas* – and elsewhere. Kilims are noted for bright, almost garish, colours and bold designs, often incorporating stylised animals and birds.
2 Kilim can also refer to the flat, woven fringe used to finish off the edges of a PILE carpet. See pp.301-2.

kindjahl A double-edged sword or dagger of south-east Europe and Iran. The hilt tapers inwards from the shoulder to form the handgrip then broadens out again to provide a handstop; there is no crossguard.

king's pattern See CUTLERY.

kingwood See ROSEWOOD.

kinji Japanese term meaning 'ground gold', used for highly polished gold LACQUER on furniture and other decorative objects. Powdered gold is painted or sprinkled onto a lacquered base and then covered with several layers of clear lacquer.

kiseru See TABAKO-IRE.

Klint, Kaare (1888-1954) Danish architect, furniture designer and academic who was largely responsible for the Europe-wide popularity of Scandinavian furniture in the 1920s and 30s. His furniture designs made effective use of natural materials such as unvarnished wood and undyed leather and textiles. They were simple, highly practical and geared to the principles of ergonomics.

klismos A Classical chair style from ancient Greece with a shallow, concave backrest and slightly splayed legs. It was said to be the first chair which provided a comfortable, relaxed sitting position. The style was revived in Europe during the late 18th and early 19th centuries.

KLISMOS CHAIR *with U-shaped back and sabre legs; c.1820.*

kneehole A recess or opening to provide leg space, introduced to desks, dressing tables and bureaux in the late 17thC. The **kneehole desk**, introduced in the 18thC, is a desk made in one section with a central recessed cupboard below the FRIEZE drawer and three drawers either side. See p.121.

knives See CUTLERY.

knock-down furniture Term (often abbreviated to KD) used from the late 19thC for furniture that is readily dismantled or folded.

Knole sofa Upholstered sofa which transforms into a DAY BED when the arms are lowered on an iron ratchet. The Knole sofa dates from the early 17thC, named after an example at Knole, Kent, and was much copied in Victorian times. See p.107.

knop Decorative knob of various shapes, and seen, for example, as part of the stem of a drinking glass or as a TURNED feature in furniture. When the knop forms an endpiece, as on a spoon handle, lid or chairback, it is known as a **finial**. See box below.

Knox, Archibald See TUDRIC.

knuckle joint Interlocking joint of wood used as a hinge on the brackets of drop-leaf tables. See p.109.

knurling A decorative edging seen particularly on late 19thC gold and silver. It is an irregular version of GADROONING with grooves cut at varying intervals to create an effect similar to oblong bead moulding.

kobako Small, shallow Japanese LACQUER box, sometimes with a tray, for storing incense, and similar in style, shape and decoration to a KOGO.

KOBAKO *The three-in-one box (left) fits into the container (right), and stands on the tray; 4½ in (11.4 cm) across.*

kodansu Japanese for 'small box-chest', describing a small LACQUER cabinet containing a nest of drawers enclosed by a door for holding personal accessories. It often has engraved silver mounts.

KODANSU *with lockable door; 19thC; 4⅛ in (10.4 cm) high.*

kodogu Japanese term for the metalwork and metal mountings on a sword. Kodogu includes the **tsuba** (sword guard), **fuchi** and **kashira** (terminals at the top and bottom of the hilt), **menuki** (hilt ornaments), **kogai** (skewer), **mekugi** (rivet securing the blade of a sword) and **kogatana** (utility knife). The **kozuka** is the long, flat handle of the kogatana and sometimes refers to the knife itself.

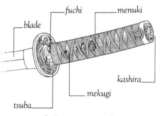

fuchi menuki
blade
kashira
mekugi
tsuba

KODOGU *of a Japanese sword.*

KOZUKA *made of copper and decorated with gilt-tasselled gourds; 18thC; 3⅞ in (98 mm) long.*

kogo Shallow, lidded, miniature Japanese box for storing incense (*kogo* means 'incense box'). Kogo are normally of wood covered with LACQUER, but sometimes of ceramic or metal, and are of various shapes. They are usually highly decorated. Kogo first appeared in the 12thC for use at incense and tea ceremonies. Peak production was in the 19thC, when many were exported to the West.

kokeshi Traditional wooden Japanese folk doll with a cylindrical body, round head and painted features. Dating from the 17thC, kokeshi are thought originally to have been mementos from healing springs, or to have played a role as protective totem figures in local folklore. See p.354.

KOKESHI *of traditional 'ninepin' shape; late 17thC; 10 in (25.4 cm) high.*

kraak porselein Dutch term for blue and white CHINESE EXPORT PORCELAIN of the late 16th and early 17th centuries usually decorated in UNDERGLAZE blue. Kraak was later extensively imitated at the DELFT potteries. The term comes from the Portuguese carracks, ships carrying cargoes of Oriental china, which were captured by the Dutch. See pp.188-9.

kris A traditional dagger of Malaya and the East Indies. The blade is usually rough and either straight or SERPENTINE, widening at the hilt; the grip is straight or acutely angled.

Krog, Arnold See COPENHAGEN.

kufic script Ancient Arabic writing, often used in a stylised form.

kukri The traditional knife of Nepal, with a curved, broad blade. Those that were carried by Gurkha troops have a black leather scabbard containing two implements; one for use as a small knife, the other a sharpening steel. See pp.408-9.

Kurfürstenhumpen See HUMPEN.

kurk The name used in the carpet trade for the finest wool available for weaving carpets. It is shorn from the underbelly of sheep and is used to make extremely soft and fine carpets. The word is Armenian for 'wool'. It is most commonly used in the context of 19th and 20thC rugs from Kashan, a major weaving centre in Iran.

Kutani Various wares made in the region of Kutani, Japan, from the 17th to the early 20th centuries (see p.176). They include the following:
1 Thin EGGSHELL porcelain tea and coffee services which were painted predominantly in shades of grey and gold, and sometimes marked 'Kutani'. LITHOPHANES are occasionally incorporated into the base of the cups. The quality can be good, but this is rare. More common are items mass-produced in the 20thC, which tend to have TRANSFER-PRINTED outlines filled in with sloppy painting.
2 A relatively heavy PORCELAIN

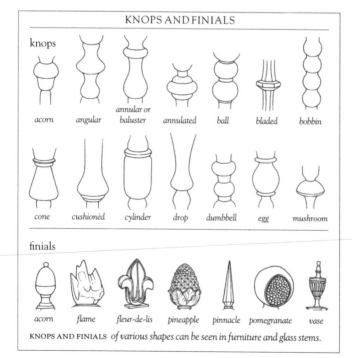

KNOPS AND FINIALS

knops

acorn angular annular or baluster annulated ball bladed bobbin

cone cushioned cylinder drop dumbbell egg mushroom

finials

acorn flame fleur-de-lis pineapple pinnacle pomegranate vase

KNOPS AND FINIALS *of various shapes can be seen in furniture and glass stems.*

decorated predominantly in iron-red ENAMEL with detailing in black, greys and gilding, occasionally with other colours. It is seen on large dishes, pairs of vases and figures of the MEIJI period (1868-1912).

3 Oatmeal-coloured EARTHENWARE, sometimes called **Kaga ware**, covered in brocade and panel designs, often carrying the Kutani mark. Wares, made from c.1860, include steep-sided dishes, incense burners with figure or shi-shi (Buddhist lion) handles and finials.

4 **Ao** (green) or **Ko** (old) Kutani are mainly dishes with a porcelain or straw-coloured STONEWARE body, the inner surface painted with asymmetrical brocade or geometric panels outlined in black and filled in with a palette of thick but translucent enamel colours. Deep green is most common; smoky yellow, aubergine, blue and occasionally dark iron-red are also seen. The undersides are often completely green with a black wavy line. Some pieces date from the 17thC, but most found in Europe date from the 19thC.

kwaart A second, lead glaze added to TIN-GLAZED EARTHENWARE after decoration and firing. It was introduced on DELFT ware in the 17thC, to enhance the brightness of the colours and give a smooth, glassy finish. The idea was taken up by the British, at BRISTOL for example, during the early 18thC, but with less striking results.

Kyoto Centre of Japanese ceramic production 1615-1868, noted particularly for enamelled and gilt pottery initiated by the 17thC potter Ninsei. Much SATSUMA ware of the MEIJI period (1868-1912) was made or enamelled in Kyoto.

L

laburnum Hard, dense yellowish wood with variegated brown streaks. It was a popular choice for INLAID and VENEERED decoration, especially OYSTERING after the Restoration, and at the end of the 18thC for crossbanding.

lac burgauté French term for Oriental LACQUER work with mother-of-pearl INLAID DECORATION.

lacca contrafatta Italian term for cheap, imitation LACQUER, used on furniture in Italy, especially Venice, since the 18thC. Paper scraps or cut-out prints are stuck to the surface and covered in layers of varnish.

lace Delicate, openwork fabric of silk, cotton or other thread used mainly as a trimming or accessory to clothing. Designs generally take the form of central motifs made up of numerous threads, several of which may be collected at the edge with a whipping stitch to create a ridged effect known as a **cordonnet**. The elements are joined either by slender threads known as **brides** or by a fine mesh, known as the **reseau**. Any additional decorative motifs used to replace the reseau are known as **modes**.

Lace developed from an embroidery technique known as DRAWN THREAD WORK. Two distinct types evolved in Italy and Flanders (an area now mainly in Belgium) during the 16thC. In **bobbin lace** (also known as **pillow** or **bone lace**), threads attached to bobbins are intertwined to form the pattern. **Needlepoint lace** is sewn with a needle and a single thread, using embroidery buttonhole stitches.

The various forms of needlepoint are often named after their supposed town or country of origin, such as **point de Venise**. However, **point d'Angleterre** is not, as the name suggests, English needlepoint, but a very fine pillow lace made in Flanders, notably Brussels, during the 17thC. **Flemish** and **Belgian** lace are often interchangeable terms although strictly speaking Flemish should be restricted to 18thC laces and Belgian to 19thC ones.

Machine-made lace was a product of the Industrial Revolution. The net was machine-made and later hand-embroidered. The first machine-made net appeared around 1764.

Chemical lace is an imitation lace produced in Germany and Switzerland in the 1880s. It is in fact a machine-embroidered technique identified by the soft, fuzzy texture of the design.

lace glass See LATTICINO.

lacewood See PLANE.

lacework A very fine OPENWORK technique for decorating PORCELAIN developed in the 18thC, probably at MEISSEN. A mesh-like gauze is dipped into liquid clay. When fired, the gauze burns away, leaving a hard skeleton behind. The technique was used on porcelain figures by many European factories from the 19thC onwards.

lacis See FILET.

Lacloche Parisian firm of manufacturing and retail jewellers established by the four Lacloche brothers, 1897. The brothers originally made luxurious, Oriental-style enamelled jewellery, and in the 1920s adopted the ART DECO style.

lacquer A hard, glossy, natural resin made from the sap of the Chinese lacquer tree. The sap is applied in thin layers – sometimes as many as 100 – to a base material, normally wood or fabric. Each layer is dried and polished before the next is applied. Eventually a thick, smooth surface is built up which can be dusted with gold or silver flecks or worked in relief. Colours, usually black and red, can be added to the opaque or transparent lacquer.

Differently coloured layers were sometimes applied and topped by a black surface, so that various decorative effects could be produced by cutting through the stratified colours. This was known as **guri incised lacquer**, or **coromandel lacquer** or **bantam work**.

In Japan a technique known as **shibayama** was produced by adhering pieces of mother-of-pearl, ivory and stones to a surface – rather like INLAID DECORATION – and then surrounding with lacquer. See JAPANNING.

ladies' chair Small easy chair, with buttoned upholstery, introduced in the mid-19thC and often paired with a larger **gentleman's chair**. The seat is deep and low, and the back inclined and high. There are both low-armed and armless versions.

lady doll A BISQUE doll designed to look like an adult woman in face, figure and dress.

lady's cabinet See CHEVERET.

Lalique, René (1860-1945) Innovative French designer and maker of jewellery and glassware. See p.227.

Lambeth faience See DOULTON.

lambrequin A design based on a pendent drapery effect. The word originally described a scarf worn across a knight's helmet which was stylised in heraldic designs as the mantel around a coat of arms.

In the latter part of the 17thC, the French applied the term to swagged or festooned drapery. The theme was adapted by furniture-makers and carved on picture and mirror frames.

Around 1700, a lambrequin border pattern was developed for ceramics decoration at ROUEN in France, and was much used over the next 50 years. **Style rayonnant** is a variation in which the lambrequin motif radiates from a central point. A similar motif is seen on mid-17th to mid-18thC English silver cups. See DECORATIVE MOTIFS.

lampwork Glass shaped by heating it over a small flame. The technique is used to make small figures and ornaments. See p.208.

lance A spear designed to be carried by mounted soldiers. Although superseded by the sword and firearms from the 17thC, the lance was re-introduced by the French cavalry who adopted it from the Polish lancers during the Napoleonic Wars, and in Britain in 1816.

Langlois, Peter (fl.1759-81) French cabinet-maker based in London c.1760-70 and an exponent of LOUIS XV and LOUIS XVI styles. His commodes are noted for their fine MARQUETRY decoration and gilt-bronze mounts, and a number of Adam-style CARD TABLES and PIER TABLES are attributed to him.

Lannuier, Charles-Honoré (1779-1819) French-born cabinet-maker who from 1805 was the leading furniture-maker in New York, USA. His work shows a delicate interpretation of the French DIRECTOIRE style, featuring Classical forms and motifs.

lantern clock Simple brass clock introduced in Britain in the 1620s, and the most common type of domestic clock throughout the 17thC. Its distinguishing features include a POSTED-FRAME construction containing the movement, side panels that can be opened, and a bell on top surrounded by a fretwork gallery. True lantern clocks – or **Cromwellian clocks**, as they were also called – are weight-driven wall clocks which were sometimes mounted on oak brackets.

The first examples were controlled by a BALANCE wheel and verge ESCAPEMENT; by the 1660s, they were fitted with a verge and BOB PENDULUM, and later by a long pendulum with an anchor escapement. A revival of demand for the clocks in the second half of the 19thC produced spring-driven versions, or earlier examples were fitted with spring-driven movements within the original posted frame. See p.280.

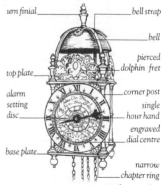

BRASS LANTERN CLOCK; c.1670; 15 in (38.1 cm) high.

LAPADA London and Provincial Antique Dealers' Association, an organisation of antique shops and individual dealers formed to maintain standards in the trade.

LAPADA *members can display this logo.*

lapis lazuli Semiprecious, opaque blue gemstone containing golden flecks of pyrite ('fool's gold').

lapping Method of finishing edges on metal ware by soldering thin strips of metal over them. It was used particularly for concealing the copper visible on the edges of SHEFFIELD PLATE objects. See p.239.

larch Yellowish to reddish-brown timber used for the carcass work of CASE FURNITURE in the late 18thC. It is fairly hard and durable, but has a tendency to warp.

latticino Term used to describe glass decorated with a pattern of white, or sometimes coloured, threads of glass. Latticino is from the Italian for 'milk'. The technique is also known as **filigrana** (thread-grained). It was developed in 16thC Venice and has been used to produce three main effects on glass: **vetro a retorti**, which has twists embedded in clear glass; **vetro a reticello**, which has a fine network of crossed threads; and **vetro a fili**, which has a spiral or helix pattern.

Laub und Bandelwerk German for 'foliage and scrollwork', a BAROQUE-style framing motif similar to STRAPWORK, common in early 18thC.

lava glass Dark blue lustre ART GLASS developed by the US designer Louis C. TIFFANY in the late 19thC. It has iridescent gold streaks – supposed to resemble flows of lava – and was originally called **volcanic glass**.

laver Large vessel of brass, bronze or other metal with one or two spouts, used to hold water for washing hands or feet. Earliest lavers, or **lavabo**, date from the 14thC and continued in use until c. 1800.

lazy Susan A revolving stand placed in the centre of a dining table and used to hold condiments.

Leach, Bernard (1887-1979) Founder of the 20thC art pottery movement (see p.184). Leach went to Japan to study graphics but was instead captivated by the pottery tradition. He returned to Britain to found the St Ives pottery in Cornwall. His own work is greatly influenced by Korean and Japanese forms and glazes.

lead crystal Glass containing a high proportion – 25-30 per cent – of lead oxide. Lead glass refracts (bends) the light more than non-lead glass, thus giving extra brilliance. It can be blown more thickly than SODA GLASS and is therefore more suitable for cutting and ENGRAVING.

The original but incorrect name for English lead crystal is **flint glass**. The misnomer came about when George RAVENSCROFT, a British manufacturer trying to produce a substitute for Venetian CRISTALLO, used finely ground flints and potash instead of the traditional Venetian sources of silica and soda. These new ingredients led to the formation of fine cracks – CRIZZLING – which was remedied by replacing a proportion of the potash with lead oxide. See p.207.

lead glaze See GLAZE.

leather-encased watch A pocket watch enclosed in a leather strap for the wrist. It was a popular conversion when wristwatches first became fashionable after the First World War.

Le Corbusier (1887-1965) Swiss-born architect whose real name was Charles Edward Jeanneret. Many of his furniture designs of the 1920s were for the leading European furniture-makers THONET, and were exhibited in his building for the EXPOSITION INTERNATIONALE in Paris in 1925, the Pavilion de L'Esprit. Le Corbusier's vision of a world where technology and fine design combined to create the ideal living environment was highly influential, although his theories were often misapplied.

Leeds pottery With WEDGWOOD, a leading British producer of CREAMWARE from the late 18thC. Leeds creamware was widely exported throughout Europe. It is light in weight, and PIERCED DECORATION was a speciality. A common Leeds feature is a handle formed of two intertwined strips ending in a relief motif of flowers, leaves or berries. Most was undecorated, but some black TRANSFER-PRINTING and blue-printed or painted and enamelled ware exists.

Leeds pottery also produced fine-grained AGATE, PEARL, LUSTRE and TORTOISESHELL wares, some fine STONEWARE and small figures similar to those of Staffordshire potter Ralph WOOD. Few genuine products carry factory marks, but other factories copied Leeds ware – often using a Leeds mark – in the late 19th and early 20th centuries.

legend The lettering on a COIN, including the monarch's titles and sometimes a motto.

Legrain, Pierre (1889-1929) Eminent Parisian furniture designer, interior decorator and bookbinder who contributed significantly to ART DECO style. Most of his furniture was designed in the 1920s. It reflected African and CUBIST influences and was often incorporated from luxury materials such as ebony, silver, sharkskin and LACQUER.

Lehmann, Kaspar (1565-1622) German engraver of glass and precious stones, who did much to perfect the technique of wheel ENGRAVING. He was given the monopoly on glass engraving throughout the Habsburg Empire. He worked mainly on fragile CRISTALLO glass and trained a number of people who later became eminent engravers, including Johannes Hess and Caspar Schindler.

lenticle Glass panel in the door of a LONGCASE CLOCK, through which the pendulum may be seen. It is sometimes known as a **bull's eye**.

Lethaby, William (1857-1931) British architect and designer of furniture, metalwork and ceramics who influenced the ARTS AND CRAFTS MOVEMENT. He was principal of London's Central School of Arts and Crafts 1896-1911, and Professor of Design at London's Royal College of Art 1900-18. His furniture was mainly rustic and unvarnished, and often decorated with floral MARQUETRY. He also designed pottery for WEDGWOOD.

letterwood See SNAKEWOOD.

Liberty British retail firm established in 1875 by Arthur Lasenby Liberty (1843-1917). The company specialised in imported Moorish, Eastern and Egyptian furniture for resale in Europe, commissioned Art Nouveau designs in fabrics, pottery, silver (see CYMRIC) and pewter (see TUDRIC), and had a major influence on style in the late 19th and early 20th centuries. See p.70.

library steps Steps for reaching high bookshelves, which came into general use in the libraries of private households in the mid-18thC. Some library steps folded or converted into stools with padded seats or even elbow chairs and were called **metamorphic chairs**. See p.127.

lignum vitae Extremely hard, oily, dense, dark brown wood from the West Indies – one of the earliest woods to be imported to Britain before 1650. The wood was made into drinking bowls, pestles and mortars, and similar items; the 18thC clockmaker John HARRISON even used it for the wheels in his early clocks because of its natural lubrication. Lignum vitae was used for oyster PARQUETRY on late 17thC furniture, and in the 18thC for small areas of VENEER.

lime Soft, fine-grained, creamy-white European wood. Lime proved a great success with woodcarvers as it cuts well with or across the grain. The master carver Grinling GIBBONS and his school used it extensively.

Limehouse Porcelain factory in the East End of London. In its brief period of operation, c.1745-8, it became the first British factory to produce BLUE AND WHITE soft-paste PORCELAIN, and possibly the first to add SOAPSTONE successfully to the formula for whiteness and plasticity. Teapots and sauceboats, many echoing the silver shapes of the day, and shell-shaped dishes were the main lines.

limning An archaic expression derived from the old English word for illuminating (as in manuscripts), and which is now coming back into use to describe the technique of MINIATURE painting. See p.323.

Limoges A major centre for European ENAMEL work production since the 12thC, and French ceramic production since the late 18thC. Several families of potters established factories in this city in Limousin, central France, in the 18th and 19th centuries, including the Franco-American Haviland family. Most production was of domestic wares, often finely TRANSFER-PRINTED (in outline or in total) botanical designs.

Limoges enamel ware is painted on copper predominantly in white, blue and gold on a dark blue or black ground. The enamelling industry declined in the 18thC, but was revived c.1820-50 by craftsmen such as Julian Robillard. See p.263.

linen Durable textile made from the fibre of the flax plant, which is bleached to improve whiteness and texture. Among the best quality is 15th-18thC Dutch linen from Haarlem. Linen production declined in the 18thC as the yarn broke easily on a power loom. When the problem was overcome in the late 19thC, cotton had taken over the market.

line inlay See BANDING.

linen-fold Style of woodcarving, especially on panelling, to resemble hanging folds of fabric. See DECORATIVE MOTIFS.

linen press 1 Device for pressing linen, known in various forms from medieval times to the 18thC. It basically consists of two flat boards which can be pressed tightly together (with the linen between) by means of a spiral screw. **2** A term for a cupboard for the storage of linen, normally with sliding trays enclosed by doors with drawers below.

linen smoother Glass object used for pressing linen in the 18thC. The vertical handle projecting from the middle of the heavy, circular base is often ribbed to give a better grip. In Britain, linen smoothers were also known as **slickers**, **slick stones** or **smoothing irons**.

LINEN SMOOTHER; *18thC; 5½ in (14 cm) high.*

liner Glass container, often blue, that fits snugly inside metal objects such as sugar basins and salt cellars. The glass lining prevents the contents corroding the metal and perhaps being contaminated by it. Blue glass also helps to show off any PIERCED DECORATION on the metal container.

Linnell, John (1729-96) Furniture designer and cabinet-maker. Linnell's early CHINOISERIE pieces included Rococo-style beds and sofas. His later furniture was designed to fit the interiors of houses by architects Robert Adam and Henry HOLLAND, among others, and became increasingly influenced by the NEOCLASSICAL style.

Linthorpe British STUDIO POTTERY, 1879-89, near Middlesbrough, Yorkshire, with Christopher DRESSER as art director for the first three years. The pottery produced decorative wares, including teapots, distinguished by simple lines, thick richly coloured glazes often with Japanese or Peruvian influences. Later wares used SLIPS and SGRAFFITO as decorative techniques.

lion of Fo See DOG OF FO.

liqueur glass See CORDIAL GLASS.

liquid gold See GILDING.

lit-en-bâteau French for 'boat-shaped bed' – an EMPIRE-style bed with curving head and footboards, often forming S-shaped scrolls.

LIT-EN-BATEAU; *Empire style; c.1800.*

lithography A printing process in which an image is drawn on a stone or metal surface with a greasy crayon. When water and then ink are poured over the surface the crayonned areas repel the water but retain the ink. These areas transfer to paper, metal, and other surfaces when printed under pressure. See p.332.

lithophanes Thin, translucent PORCELAIN panels or plaques that on being held to the light reveal a picture or design with a three-dimensional effect. Lithophanes were usually made of unglazed, BISCUIT porcelain, and were set into lampshades and lanterns, hung in windows or moulded into the base of mugs. A wax master of the design was modelled from which a plaster mould was made as a cast for the porcelain paste. Subjects were typically on religious themes or based on paintings. The process was invented in France in 1827 and taken up on a large scale at MEISSEN and BERLIN 1830-50, and also at MINTON, BELLEEK and WORCESTER.

Lithyalin glass An opaque or translucent marbled glass with a surface resembling polished gemstones in a wide range of colours. It was first made by the Bohemian glass artist Friedrich Egermann in 1829, and was copied by other Bohemian and French manufacturers, sometimes with ENGRAVED, cut or painted decoration.

Liverpool Centre for ceramics from 1710 producing TIN-GLAZED EARTHENWARE. Specialities of the period were blue-painted punchbowls, and tiles TRANSFER-PRINTED in black or red with contemporary subjects and characters. From the 1780s, CREAMWARE was the main output, decorated in cobalt blue, ENAMEL colours, or with blue or black transfer-printed designs.

A number of porcelain factories sprang up in Liverpool, such as Gilbody (1754-61), Chaffers (1754-65), Philip Christian (est.

1765) and, in the final decades of the 18thC, Pennington. The history of Liverpool porcelain is still incomplete; fluctuations in the make-up of the porcelain paste and cross-fertilisation of designs between the factories, make identification very difficult without chemical analysis.

livery bed 16th and 17thC term for a servant's bed. Until the last decades of the 19thC, this would be simply a straw-stuffed mattress lying on a wooden pallet.

livery cupboard 15th to 17thC cupboard. It was used for storing food and drink and sometimes rested upon a stand known as a **livery board**, which doubled as a bench.

LIVERY CUPBOARD *made in oak; early 17thC; 53 in (1.34 m) high.*

Lloyd Loom Patent name for a tough material woven from wires covered in machine-twisted paper so as to resemble wicker. It was popular in the 1920s and 30s, for linen baskets, chairs and small tables. See p.104.

loading A filler such as pitch or resin used to add density and weight to a hollow article made from a thin sheet of metal such as a silver candlestick.

lobing Rounded decoration which projects horizontally, as on the rim of a plate or dish, or vertically as on the cover of a tureen.

Lobmeyr Glassworks in Vienna, Austria, that achieved an international reputation from 1864 under the leadership of Ludwig Lobmeyr. The company produced fine cut and engraved glass and iridescent ART NOUVEAU glass until c.1900.

lock See FLINTLOCK, SNAPHAUNCE, MATCHLOCK, PERCUSSION LOCK.

Lock, Matthias (fl.1740-69) Master carver and Rococo-style furniture designer. Lock published several influential books of his designs, and his carving featured natural themes

and Rococo shells and scrolls. He is believed to have been employed by Thomas CHIPPENDALE.

long arm A long-barrelled shoulder gun. See box, p.490.

longcase clock Tall, narrow, floorstanding clock, also known as a **grandfather clock**. The case protected the PENDULUM, and was introduced soon after its invention in 1657. The clocks were produced from the 18thC until c.1820 in London, c.1845 in the provinces, and revived c.1880-1910. See pp.278-9.

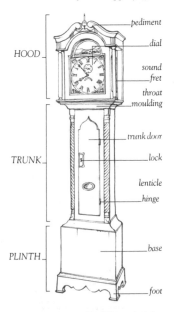

LONGCASE CLOCK; *English provincial; c.1790; 78 in (1.98 m) high.*

long Eliza Attenuated figure of a Chinese woman seen as a decoration on 18thC Chinese porcelain, some Dutch and English DELFTWARE, and on WORCESTER porcelain of the 1760s. The name comes from the Dutch *Lange Leizen.*

long table See REFECTORY TABLE.

Longton Hall Probably one of the first Staffordshire producers of soft-paste PORCELAIN. In its decade of operation (1750-60), distinctive wares included dishes, sauceboats and tureens moulded in the form of overlapping leaves, and what came to be known as 'Snowmen' figures – because of their poorly defined features and unpainted but thickly glazed bodies. Although many later figures were based on MEISSEN designs, some were original and notable for their exuberance of form and fresh colours (such as a vivid yellow-green) based on those used for SALT-GLAZED STONEWARE.

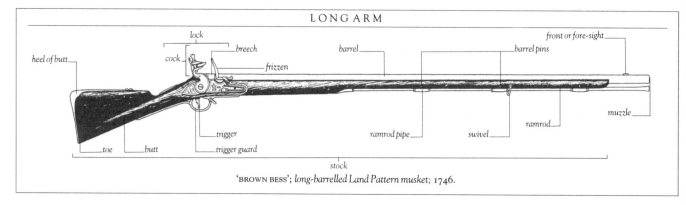

LONG ARM

heel of butt · lock · cock · breech · frizzen · barrel · front or fore-sight · barrel pins · muzzle · ramrod · swivel · ramrod pipe · trigger · trigger guard · toe · butt · stock

'BROWN BESS'; long-barrelled Land Pattern musket; 1746.

looms Devices for producing textiles by interweaving thread or yarn. Different looms provide distinctive weaves which can sometimes provide a clue to origin.

There are four basic types of loom used for Oriental carpets:

The **horizontal** or **flat loom** is easily transportable and used by nomadic tribes of central Asia, producing small, narrow rugs of uneven shape and width.

The **fixed vertical**, **upright** or **village loom** is a permanent fixture and used by village and town weavers. It produces carpets of a similar length to the loom itself – around 9 ft (2.7 m) – and more regular in shape than those produced on a horizontal loom.

The **Tabriz vertical loom**, invented by the craftsmen of Tabriz and used throughout central and north-west Iran, produces carpets twice the length of their width.

Carpets produced on the **roller beam** or **Kerman type** of vertical loom are up to 40ft (12m) in length.

In Europe, early hand looms could only weave cotton and fine woollens. Then, with the invention of Edmund Cartwright's steam-powered loom in 1786, the textile-weaving industry was mechanised, resulting in increased production and a wider range of fabrics, soft furnishings and carpets.

The **Jacquard loom** was introduced at the beginning of the 19thC. Invented by Frenchman Joseph-Marie Jacquard (1752-1834), it used punched cards to control the weaving of the pattern by guiding hooks to lift the appropriate warp threads. Not only could this loom weave very complicated patterns, but only one person was needed to operate it. Previously, an assistant had to manually lift groups of warp threads in the long, slow job of setting the pattern. The Jacquard loom was first used in Britain at KIDDERMINSTER. It was not until 1850 that the first power looms for carpets were in operation in Britain. The power-driven **wide power loom** was first developed for chenille AXMINSTER carpets in 1869, and

capable of weaving carpets 9-12 ft (2.7-3.7 m) wide. **Broadloom** carpets were introduced after the First World War, and are woven on looms over 12 ft (3.7 m) wide.

Loos, Adolf (1870-1933) Austrian Modernist architect who was an early practitioner of FUNCTIONALISM and industrial design that emphasised practicality and minimal decoration. After working briefly with the architect Frank Lloyd WRIGHT in the USA, Loos settled in Vienna where he produced several documents, including *Ornament und Verbrechen* (Ornament and Crime), denouncing the use of ornament. He designed simple furniture in strong, vigorous shapes, and glassware for the Viennese firm J. & L. Lobmeyr.

loo table 19thC oval tilt-top table supported on a central pillar, designed for an early 19thC card game called lanterloo, or 'loo'. See pp.112-13.

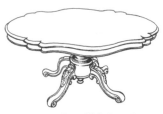

LOO TABLE *with moulded edge and apron; c. 1860; 60 in (1.52 m) across.*

lopers Sliding wooden rails that support the desk panel of a bureau or the leaf of an open folding table.

lost wax Method of casting metal or glass objects, used since ancient times, which achieves greater definition than straightforward mould-casting methods. It is also known by its French name of *cire perdue*. A plaster cast is made of the original model that is to be reproduced. When set, this plaster mould is separated into several pieces and the original model removed. The inside of the mould is coated with wax to the required

thickness of the finished article. For hollow objects, the central cavity of the mould is filled with clay and the mould is reassembled. The whole lot is heated to melt the wax so that it drains, or is 'lost', through holes in the mould. The space left by the wax is then filled with the molten material. When cool, the mould is separated and the clay core removed leaving a replica in the new material.

Most lost-wax processes use flexible rubber moulds which can be easily removed and reused, and **investment casting** in which metal is forced into the mould centrifugally.

Lotto carpets Carpets with a distinctive geometrical pattern of alternating rows of octagons and crosses made up of stylised foliage. Motifs are invariably in yellow with blue details on a red ground. They are named after the 16thC Italian painter Lorenzo Lotto who in fact depicted a far wider range of designs in his paintings. 'Lotto' carpets were made throughout the 16th, 17th and 18th centuries; most are thought to come from the Ushak region of western ANATOLIA. Later examples tend to be coarser in style.

LOTTO CARPET *A detail showing the classic geometrical arabesque design.*

Loudon, John Claudius
(1783-1843) Landscape gardener, architect and author, best known for his comprehensive *Encyclopaedia of Cottage, Farm, and Villa Architecture and Furniture*, published 1833. It was used as a pattern book by builders and furniture-makers throughout the Victorian period.

Louis Phillipe style An extravagant style prevalent in France during the reign of King Louis Phillipe (1830-48). It featured flamboyant curves and heavy ornamentation including enamel plaques, bronze mounts and MARQUETRY. The style followed on from the EMPIRE STYLE of Napoleonic times.

Louis XIV style The style inspired by the Court of the 'Sun King', Louis XIV (reigned 1643-1715) and his palace at Versailles, which made France the leading influence in European decorative arts. It coincided with the PURITAN, RESTORATION, WILLIAM AND MARY and QUEEN ANNE periods in Britain.

Louis XIV style was opulent BAROQUE modified by Classical lines, and marked by flamboyant craftsmanship. Cabinet-making was notable for fine veneers and intricate marquetry, with lavish expenditure on materials such as PIETRE DURE, exotic woods, tortoiseshell, LACQUER work and even precious metals.

In ceramics, it was the time of radiating LAMBREQUIN designs at ROUEN potteries and CHINOISERIE vases at NEVERS. The king encouraged industries such as these with generous financial incentives.

Louis XIV style spread throughout Europe, aided by a flourishing export trade, and the dispersal, to Britain, Holland and Germany in particular, of skilled French HUGUENOT craftsmen after 1685. See p.28.

Louis XV style The height of the frivolous excesses of ROCOCO style in France, roughly covering the period 1720-50, although the king continued to reign until 1774.

Although the style had a less wide-ranging impact on fashions elsewhere in Europe, it is notable for some of the finest GOBELINS tapestries, delicately painted CHANTILLY and MARSEILLES faience and SÈVRES porcelain, and the high-legged commode with SERPENTINE front and ORMOLU ornament. See p.36.

Louis XVI style A French style which coincided with the late Georgian period in Britain. Its main characteristic – a Classical reaction against the fussiness of Rococo style – actually predated King Louis XVI's accession to the throne in 1774 by 20 years. The Classical influence gave the style its contemporary 1760s name of *goût Grec* (Greek taste). See p.36.

love seat Small settee or wide armchair popular from the late 17thC in Europe. Love seats were just wide enough to seat two people in intimate proximity. Love seats are also known as **courting chairs** and the French version as **marquise chairs**.

loving cup See TYG.

lowboy Term for a small, elegant side or dressing table of the late 17th and early 18th centuries, usually with two deep drawers flanking a short central drawer. See p.141.

Lowestoft A Suffolk pottery operating *c*.1757-1802, and making soft-paste PORCELAIN, mostly for the local market. Its output included commemorative souvenirs, tablewares decorated with the words 'A Trifle from Lowestoft' and naive Chinese-influenced landscapes.

In the 1770s, an anonymous painter produced memorable tulip designs, often featuring a fully blown bloom.

'Lowestoft' was also a misleading name given to what is now described as CHINESE EXPORT PORCELAIN, possibly because the Chinese wares were unloaded at the port.

lunette Derived from the French word *lune* (moon), applied to a semicircular decoration either carved or INLAID on furniture or incorporated into a textile design. See DECORATIVE MOTIFS.

lustre 1 Glass or crystal drop, either smooth or FACETED, used to decorate light fittings, as on a chandelier, and ornamental glasswares. **2** Vase with crystal drops hanging from the rim, 19thC English style. See p.218.

lustreware Pottery with an iridescent or metallic finish. A metal oxide is dusted or painted on the glaze and fired in a reduced atmosphere, converting the oxide back to metal. Gold, silver, copper and metallic pink, purple and dark red are the most common pigments. Lustre finishes are a characteristic technique of HISPANO-MORESQUE WARE, and of some Italian MAIOLICA. In the 18thC MEISSEN used a lustre technique developed by Böttger and known as *Böttger lustre* or *Perlmutter* (mother-of-

pearl). Towards the end of the 19thC, they were adopted by British studio potters such as Bernard MOORE and at William DE MORGAN's Fulham factory. See p.165.

lutestring A glossed silk fabric with a ribbed pattern, used from the 14th to 16th centuries. It applied specifically in the 17thC to a form of TAFFETA which was stretched and then coated with a glossy gum. Lutestring or **lustring** was used in the 17th and 18th centuries particularly as a dress fabric and for bed and window curtains.

Lynn glasses 18thC drinking glasses, tumblers and decanters attributed to glass houses in King's Lynn, Norfolk. The vessels are decorated with horizontal ribbing.

M

machine knotting Mechanical carpet-making technique for reproducing hand-knots, usually Turkish, invented in Britain *c*.1900. Later machines were able to produce a wider variety of knots and patterns in more varied colours. Belgium is particularly well known for machine-knotted carpets in a variety of Oriental patterns.

Macintyre, James, & Co Staffordshire pottery at Burslem from *c*.1847 which mainly produced utility ceramics. The company opened an ART POTTERY studio in 1897, for a time under the direction of William MOORCROFT before he set up independently; this closed in 1913.

Mackintosh, Charles Rennie (1869-1928) Scottish architect, designer and leading ART NOUVEAU figure. Mackintosh's best-known building was the new Glasgow School of Art (1897), where he himself had been trained and which became the focal point for a group of revolutionary designers – the GLASGOW SCHOOL – around the turn of the century. Mackintosh's interior schemes were

CHARLES RENNIE MACKINTOSH's *ladder-back chair designed for the Willow Tearooms, Glasgow; c.1903.*

often sparse, and his furniture combined straight and gently curving lines to create pieces that were more sculptural than functional. His work was far more influential on the Continent, especially Austria and Germany, than in Britain. He devoted his later life to watercolour painting.

Mackmurdo, Arthur (1851-1942) Architect, designer of textiles, wallpapers and furniture, and a pioneer of the ART NOUVEAU decorative style in Britain. He founded the Century Guild (1882), which aimed to put glass-blowing, pottery, woodcarving and other decorative crafts on a par with painting and sculpture. Mackmurdo's lasting contribution to 19thC design was his swirling decorative motif (often seen on his chair backs), later widely adopted by Art Nouveau artists. He also had a considerable influence on the architect-designer Charles Voysey. See p.67.

ARTHUR MACKMURDO's *floral motifs on this 1880s dining chair epitomise Art Nouveau style.*

magic lantern A simple image projector using hand-painted or photographic glass SLIDES. The images were initially lit by natural light, candles, oil or gas. Then came limelight (lime glows brilliantly when hot) or paraffin lamps, some of which were later converted to use electricity. The magic lantern was especially popular during Victorian and Edwardian times and used at public shows and as a form of home entertainment. See pp.294-5.

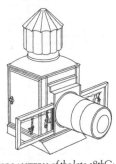

MAGIC LANTERN *of the late 18thC; 15 in (38.1 cm) high.*

magnetic compass A navigational device for finding the earth's magnetic north. It has been used in Europe from the 13thC to the present day.

magot French name for a chinoiserie figure – usually a Chinese Buddha – which was produced in the 18thC by many European porcelain factories including MEISSEN and CHANTILLY.

During the 19thC the word was also used in a derogatory manner to describe CHINESE EXPORT PORCELAIN. Magots are also known as **pagods**.

mahogany Strong and durable, close-grained hardwood native to central and northern South America and the West Indies. Mahogany varies in colour from red to dark brown and is sometimes spotted.

The wood was first imported in quantity to Europe in the early 18thC. Because of the great girth and height of the tree, the timber was available in lengths and widths previously unknown to European craftsmen, enabling them to use a single cut of wood for a table-top or the front of a large piece of furniture.

Mahogany furniture became a British speciality in the mid-18thC, and was used by all major cabinet-makers, but spread later to France and, with the French EMPIRE STYLE, to the rest of Europe. In the 1800s African mahogany, which is lighter in weight, began to be used. See pp.90-91.

maine gauche Dagger used in the left hand to parry an opponent's blade while using a RAPIER. It was popular in Europe in the 16th and 17th centuries.

maiolica TIN-GLAZED EARTHENWARE produced in Italy from the 13thC, although the term 'maiolica' was not coined until the 14thC. It originally applied to HISPANO-MORESQUE LUSTREWARE imported to Italy from Spain via the island of Majorca – from which the word is thought to be derived. Maiolica production reached its peak during the 16thC at centres such as Faenza and Florence, and led directly to the development of FAIENCE in France. See p.165.

majolica 19thC British and US lead-glazed earthenware which echoed the strong colours, rich relief work and thick glazes of 16thC Italian MAIOLICA, especially that produced by the DELLA ROBBIA family in Florence, Italy, in the 16thC. Majolica was introduced in Britain by MINTON, using a cane-coloured body to set off the thick, coloured glazes. WEDGWOOD followed suit, reviving its 18thC green-glazed ware with leaves moulded in relief, and using a white earthenware body and translucent glaze. The finest exponent of all, however, was probably George Jones, also of Staffordshire.

The popularity of majolica spread to Sweden, throughout Europe and North America in the late 19thC, often drawing design ideas from the Far East. See p.165.

Majorelle, Louis (1859-1926) French ART NOUVEAU and ART DECO furniture-maker and metalwork designer who was a key figure in the NANCY SCHOOL, and in 1925 served on the jury of the Paris EXPOSITION INTERNATIONALE DES ARTS DÉCORATIFS. His studio, Maison Majorelle, operated from the late 1890s until the Second World War. Majorelle's early furniture exhibits flowing, sculptural forms and fine proportions; later pieces follow the more geometric lines of Art Deco. He also produced elaborate metal mounts for DAUM glassware and lamps.

malachite Bright green stone with bandings and circular markings in dark and pale green. It is found mainly in Russia, and used for table tops, veneers, vases and INLAID DECORATION, and in jewellery, either carved or cabochon cut. The Russian jeweller FABERGÉ used the stone extensively. See JEWEL CUTTING.

mameluke hilt See SHAMSHIR.

mandarin palette A combination of ENAMEL colours including a distinctive purplish-red and pink, and gold – a variant of the FAMILLE-rose palette – used on CHINESE EXPORT PORCELAIN in the late 18th and early 19th centuries. Typical panel scenes of families out-of-doors, sometimes alternating with panels of flowers, are set against a densely celled or trellised ground and often framed in underglaze blue. The palette was imitated on some English porcelain and STONE CHINA.

mandau Borneo head-hunter's sword. The blade is often decorated and the hilt is carved from bone or horn, sometimes in the shape of an animal's head. The scabbard is made of two pieces of wood bound together with thongs.

mantel clock A general term for any spring-driven clock specifically designed to be placed on a mantelpiece, generally smaller and shallower than a BRACKET CLOCK, and without a carrying handle. See p.284.

maple The field maple, one of the first North American woods to be exported to Europe for use in the furniture trade. It is whitish in colour with veins and wavy darker lines running

through, polishes to a fine finish and is excellent for TURNING.

The American sugar or hard maple is distinguished by highly decorative markings known by the apt names of 'bird's-eye', 'fiddleback', 'blister' and 'curly', which are caused by buds that failed to break through the bark.

Bird's-eye maple, in particular, was popular for VENEERS in the early 19thC Regency period and for Victorian and Edwardian bedroom suites.

marbled glass Streaked glass with the appearance of marble. It was made in Venice from the 15th to 17th centuries and involved combining two or more colours of molten glass. See AGATE GLASS and ONYX GLASS.

marbling The process of decorating a surface to resemble marble, practised in Europe from the 13thC. It was used particularly on woodwork and furniture from the early 17thC and on table and COMMODE tops in the 18thC. The late Victorian ARTS AND CRAFTS MOVEMENT disapproved of such imitation of an authentic material, but marbling made a comeback in early 20thC furnishing and decoration.

marcasite Originally common crystallised iron pyrites (iron sulphide), and later a misnomer for pyrite or white iron pyrites (iron disulphide). True marcasite is almost white, resembling pale bronze. The substitute pyrite was popular in Europe from the 18thC. Marcasite is usually set in silver or pewter and rose cut (see JEWEL CUTTING) or mounted in a pavé setting to increase its sparkle.

Maria Theresa thaler A large Austrian silver coin always dated 1780 and bearing the head of Empress Maria Theresa, also known as an **MT dollar** (the word 'dollar' comes from thaler). The coin is still being struck today to the original design, and persists as a standard bullion-style currency in some parts of the world, including the Middle East. See p.388.

MARIA THERESA THALER *showing the arms of the Holy Roman Empire; 1780.*

Marinot, Maurice (1882-1960) French painter and leading ART DECO glass-maker, mainly active 1911-37. Many of his pieces feature deliberate

inclusions in the glass, such as bubbles or chemical specks, and his early work (pre-1922) is often decorated with brightly coloured ENAMEL flowers or figures. His output was limited and most has been lost, but his influence was considerable both in Europe and the United States.

Marot, Daniel (1663-1752) French-born architect and designer. Marot worked in Holland and England as architect to William of Orange. He was probably the first designer in Britain to create complete room interiors (furniture, hangings, upholstery and fittings), some 70 years before the Adam brothers. His BAROQUE designs influenced furniture designers such as William KENT.

marotte See POUPARD.

marqueterie sur verre Style of decorative glassware (literally translated as 'marquetry on glass') developed by the French designer Emile GALLÉ. Pieces of hot glass, often shaped like flowers, were smoothed into a glass object of contrasting colour by MARVERING when the glass was still molten.

marquetry Decorative VENEER on furniture which is made up of shaped pieces of wood, or other materials such as ivory, metals and mother-of-pearl, arranged in a pattern of contrasting colours. Floral designs and SEAWEED MARQUETRY are often seen, as are geometric patterns (see PARQUETRY). Marquetry largely replaced INLAID DECORATION in the early 17thC, firstly in Germany and the Low Countries; it was taken up by the French ÉBÉNISTES, and in Britain from c.1675. The NEOCLASSICAL period in Britain brought a resurgence of interest in the technique during the 1760s. See also BOULLE and p.93.

marquetry ware See DOULTON.

marquise See LOVE SEAT.

Marseilles potteries Group of prominent 18thC FAIENCE factories in southern France noted for their informal, brightly coloured enamel-decorated wares, featuring scenes from nature incorporating flowers, fish and seascapes, produced before 1770.

Some of the finest work was from the factory run by Veuve Perrin. ⟨VP⟩ 1753

martelé French for 'hammered' and used to describe the uneven surface given to metal, especially copper and silver, by HAMMERING, as a form of ART NOUVEAU decoration. The term also applies to the FACETED GLASS, which resembles hammered metal, invented by the DAUM brothers.

Martha Gunn See TOBY JUG.

marvering Process of rolling molten glass on a marble or smooth iron table to shape it and to add decorative effects as in ICED GLASS or LATTICINO. The surface is known as a **marver**, from the Italian word for marble.

maser Wide, flat-bottomed shallow bowl made of TURNED wood, usually maple, or sometimes walnut or beech, used from the 13th to 15th centuries.

matchlock The earliest gun-firing mechanism, developed in the early 15thC, in which the powder charge was ignited by a glowing wick (or 'match') soaked in nitre and dilute alcohol, and held in an S-shaped pivot called a **serpentine**. When the trigger was pressed, the serpentine moved forwards and applied the match to the powder in a pan so igniting the main charge. The mechanism was used in the Orient long after it had been discarded in Europe. See box below.

match vase See SPILL VASE.

matryushka Traditional wooden Russian peasant dolls of varying sizes that fit inside each other. Matryushka means 'little mother'.

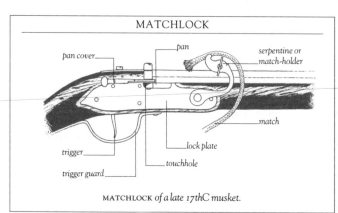

MATCHLOCK

MATCHLOCK *of a late 17thC musket.*

matt gilding See GILDING.

matting Method of giving a textured, matt appearance to a silver or other metal surface, either by using acid or by punching closely spaced dots with a punch or similar tool. The process dates from the 16thC and was widely used in the 17th and 18th centuries for decorating vessels. In the 19thC, matting commonly served as a background for CAST or CHASED ornament, and relief design and matted gold was especially popular in 19thC jewellery. It is also known as **bloomed gold**.

Maundy money See p.388.

Mayhew, John See INCE & MAYHEW.

mazarine 1 Dish liner, usually of silver with decorative pierced patterns, to fit in a fish or meat dish so that the juices can strain. 2 Rich, deep blue ceramic colour, characteristic of SÈVRES porcelain. The colour was imitated at WORCESTER, and also at CHELSEA from c.1755, particularly during the **red anchor period**.

CERAMIC MAZARINE *and dish; c.1780; 17½ in (44.4 cm) across.*

mean time The standard form of time measurement shown on most clocks, representing the average (or 'mean') of the differing daily rate of solar time. **Solar time** is time measured by the course of the sun as on a SUNDIAL; it is inconstant, differing slightly from day to day. **Sidereal time** is time as measured by the motion of the stars. The sidereal day is four minutes longer than a solar day, and there is one day less than in a solar year.

The **equation of time** indicates the difference (either fast or slow) between solar and mean time, which agree only on four days in each year – April 16, June 14, September 1 and December 25. An **equation dial** on a clock or watch shows the interrelation between mean time and solar time, either by two sets of hands or on a subsidiary calendrical dial.

Measham ware See BARGE WARE.

medallion Thin, oval or circular tablet, used as a decorative motif – in Oriental carpets, for example – inset into a panel of furniture, embedded in glass for display purposes, decorated

with painted or relief motifs on ceramics, or, in terms of jewellery, worn as a pendant or brooch.

MEDALLIONS *of porcelain and marble are mounted in the panels of a Neoclassical cabinet; c.1865.*

MEDALLION *Engraved glass portrait; c.1835; 5½ in (14 cm) high.*

Medici Porcelain factory founded by the Grand Duke Francesco I de' Medici; the first producer of soft-paste PORCELAIN (c.1575-87).

meerschaum A white, soft, porous mineral suitable for carving, taken from the German word for 'sea foam'. It was exported from Turkey and the Black Sea to Vienna, Budapest and Paris in the 18th and 19th centuries where it was made into pipes, cigarette holders and ash bowls. Peak production was c.1870-1900. It is also known as **sepiolite**.

Meiji period Japanese period (1868-1912) during which art was affected by increased contact with the West, including industrialisation, European techniques and the export of Japanese wares worldwide.

meiping Chinese vase form, with a narrow neck and broad, bulbous shoulders. The vases were designed to hold a single stem of cherry blossom.

MEIPING VASE *of stoneware; 12thC; 15½ in (39.4 cm) high.*

Meissen The first true PORCELAIN producer in Europe, some 12 miles (19 km) from DRESDEN, in what is now the south-eastern part of Germany. The man responsible was Johann BÖTTGER, Meissen's first director in 1710, who discovered the secret of making white hard-paste porcelain c.1708 – over 800 years after the Chinese. Superb modelling and painting were characteristic of Meissen porcelain, and for the next 50 years its products were unsurpassed, widely exported and much imitated.

Initially the factory made fine RED STONEWARE, with relief and engraved designs influenced by BAROQUE metalwork. The first true porcelain, put on the market in 1713, was similar in style, in the form of teaware, statuettes and Chinese BLANC-DE-CHINE-style figures.

From 1720, the yellowish tinge of the early porcelain had given way to a brilliant white. This was the era of the painter-decorators, led by J.G. Höroldt, who improved ENAMEL colours and specialised in fantastic CHINOISERIE designs. From the 1730s, exquisitely detailed harbour and military scenes were reproduced on a wide range of ware.

In the 1730s, the sculptors, with J.J. KÄNDLER at their head, became dominant, producing a range of COMMEDIA DELL'ARTE characters, animals and birds, dinner services richly decorated in relief, and sculptural vases and tablewares. Rococo style was perfectly in tune with the delicacy of Meissen porcelain. The more restrained NEOCLASSICAL style dominated from the 1760s, but standards started to decline due to economic pressures and as the French factory at SÈVRES began to make its mark. Throughout the 19thC, Meissen quality remained unchanged and there were few innovations, although the late 1890s and early 1900s saw the start of a more inventive approach in the ART NOUVEAU manner. Copies of 18thC figures were made but lack the detail of the originals. See pp.157-9.

X
XX
1725-63

mekugi See KODOGU.

Melchior, Johann See HÖCHST.

memento mori See MOURNING JEWELLERY and p.268.

Mennecy French soft-paste PORCELAIN and FAIENCE factory founded in Paris, 1734. It was moved to Mennecy 1748, then to Bourg-La-Reine 1773, and was closed in 1806. Typical porcelain products included tea services, small vases, knife handles and novelties such as snuffboxes and

walking-stick heads in a muted Rococo style. Porcelain production is thought to have ceased c.1780, and CREAMWARE was produced instead.

menuisier A French joiner who specialised in making small (*menus*) objects in plain or carved woods, as distinct from an ÉBÉNISTE who specialised in VENEERED work. The distinction was in force from the mid-17thC until the French Revolution of 1789, after which time the guilds were disbanded.

menuki See KODOGU.

mercury gilding See GILDING.

Merton Abbey English ARTS AND CRAFTS factory in South London founded by William MORRIS in 1881 and in operation until 1940. It produced carpets, printed textiles, stained glass and wallpaper. William DE MORGAN and the artist Edward Burne-Jones were linked with the factory.

Mestrelle, Eloye (*d.*1578) French coin-maker who introduced the first mechanical coining techniques to Britain c.1560. Ousted from the Royal Mint by fellow workers who feared that the improved production methods might cost them their jobs, Mestrelle turned to forgery, for which he was eventually hanged.

metal A glass-making term for the fused ingredients, in either molten or solid form, from which glass is made.

metal head dolls Dolls with metal heads on kid, cloth, COMPOSITION, wooden or metal bodies, dated from the mid-19thC. The head was stamped out of sheet metal, such as brass, copper, zinc, lead, pewter or tin. The majority of metal heads were made in Germany c.1861 until the 1930s and exported to Britain, France and the USA during the early 1900s.

metamorphic chair See LIBRARY STEPS.

metropolitan slipware Lead glazed red earthenware, decorated with white trailed SLIP, and used to make chamber pots, bowls, mugs and jugs, in London c.1630-1730.

mezzotint A type of print first popular in the 18thC, which is distinguished by effects of light and shade produced by tonal rather than line ENGRAVING.

The entire surface of the copper plate is roughened with a tool called a rocker, and then areas are scraped or burnished to produce different textures that are more or less receptive to ink; rough areas retain the ink and form the shaded parts of the design, while the smooth, polished sections remain ink-free. See p.333.

microscope Scientific instrument used for magnification, especially of objects too minute to see clearly with the naked eye. Early single-lens microscopes were little different from magnifying glasses, but in 1590 Dutchmen Hans and Zacharias Jannsen invented the **compound microscope**, which had a lens at each end of an adjustable tube. The image was blurred at high magnification, and development was slow until the invention of the ACHROMATIC lens about 200 years later. See pp.292-3.

Mies van der Rohe, Ludwig (1886-1969) German architect and designer working in the early 20thC Modernist style. He produced simple, stylish furniture from the 1920s onwards, experimenting with CHROMIUM-plated steel to create, among other chair designs, his **Barcelona chair** of 1929 which is still in production today. He was director of the German BAUHAUS school of design from 1930, and emigrated to the USA in 1938. See p.78.

MIES VAN DER ROHE'S *Barcelona chair with leather upholstery and chromed steel frame.*

mihrab A motif based on the shape of a prayer niche in a mosque, commonly a dominant part of the pattern on Oriental PRAYER RUGS. Although the mihrab is primarily associated with Islam, it actually predates Moslem carpets and was probably an ancient symbol which was simply adopted by the Islamic world.

millefiori Italian for 'thousand flowers' – a decorative glass-making technique. The 'flowers' are made from transverse slices of coloured glass CANES, which are embedded in a clear glass body when it is still in a molten state. Although the technique was used in early Egyptian and Roman MOSAIC GLASS, the name millefiori was not applied until the 16thC when it was revived in Venice.

It has since been applied to vases, bowls, door knobs and paperweights some of the best producers being BACCARAT, BACCHUS, CLICHY, ST LOUIS and TIFFANY. See p.229.

milling See GRAINING.

minaudière See VAN CLEEF & ARPELS.

Ming dynasty The penultimate of the great Chinese dynasties, 1368-1644. The period saw a diversification and consolidation of already established PORCELAIN techniques including the perfection of BLUE AND WHITE wares. ENAMEL colours were introduced in the late 15thC and Ming porcelain was traded with the West from the 16thC. The trade grew rapidly, so that by the end of the period, exports of ceramics, textiles, LACQUER and other works of art were thriving. The dynasty fell to the invading Manchus who founded the QING DYNASTY.

miniatures The term on its own usually refers to miniature paintings up to a few inches across. Miniature **portraits** were developed from illuminated manuscript work and were popular from the 16thC onwards. They are usually in WATERCOLOUR or GOUACHE; early examples are on VELLUM and from the 18thC on ivory.

Oil miniatures are rare, generally dating from the 16th and 17th centuries and of Dutch or Flemish origin. **Enamel on metal** miniatures, popular in the 18th and 19th centuries, were often found on OBJECTS OF VERTU (see PLUMBAGO and p.323).

Miniature furniture was produced in the 18thC both as proof of a cabinet-maker's skill (they were sometimes required as final proof of an apprentice's readiness for entry into the trade, and were known as **apprentice pieces**) or as advertisements, to be placed in a shop front to attract attention.

Miniature ceramics popular in the late 18th and 19th centuries, especially in Britain, include domestic tea and coffee services, made for some dolls' houses.

Miniature books under 3 × 2 in (75 × 50 mm) were produced from c.1773, including calendars, Bibles, church notes and tide tables.

mintmark A small letter or symbol on a coin that denotes its place and sometimes its period of origin. On British HAMMERED coins, a change of mintmark normally occurred following a TRIAL OF THE PYX.

Minton One of Britain's leading ceramics factories during the Victorian era. It was founded by Thomas Minton at Stoke-on-Trent in 1793 and throughout its history has often led the way in adapting fashions to the field of ceramics, resulting in a huge range of styles. Minton were just behind SPODE in the production of BONE CHINA c. 1800, although none was produced 1816-24.

In 1850 Minton introduced the richly coloured and heavily glazed MAJOLICA, but the most ambitious and notable contribution to ceramics history was the intricate and expensive PÂTE-SUR-PÂTE decoration applied to Classically shaped vases. Minton shares with Copeland (see SPODE) the claim for being first to produce the fine, white porcelain known as PARIAN in the 1840s.

A distinctive turquoise blue enamel (inspired by SÈVRES' *bleu céleste*) is a special feature of Minton, seen at its most striking in the 'cloisonné' range of wares imitating Chinese cloisonné ENAMELLING on metal, much of which was designed by Christopher DRESSER. The factory has continued to produce high-quality porcelain throughout the 20thC.

c.1873 on

miquelet lock An early form of the FLINTLOCK mechanism, also known as a Mediterranean or **Spanish flintlock**, in use from the first half of the 17thC to the 19thC. See box above.

mirror painting Painted decoration applied to glass, especially MIRRORS and SNUFF BOTTLES. The technique is also known as **reverse painting** because the foreground details are painted first and the background details last.

mitre-cutting A CUT-GLASS technique using a V-edged wheel to make a sharp groove.

mixed cut A combination of two different cutting styles on a gemstone. See JEWEL CUTTING.

mixed franking A combination of two or more postage stamps from different countries appearing on the same envelope. Before international traffic of mail was regulated in 1874, an envelope might acquire an extra stamp for each country it passed through to cover the next leg of postage. See p.385.

mocha ware Pottery decorated with moss or fern-like designs. It is named after mocha stone, a form of quartz with branch-like markings. A drop of pigment, said to be composed of tobacco juice, stale urine and turpentine, grew chemically on a

---

MIHRAB

MIHRAB *Two examples of the many variations found on prayer rugs.*

MIQUELET LOCK

MIQUELET LOCK *on an early 17thC Spanish pistol.*

SLIP-coated body while it was still slightly moist achieving the feathered effect. Mocha ware was produced for the lower end of the domestic market, especially in the form of mugs and jugs, from the 1780s and throughout the 19thC.

modeller In the ceramics industry, the sculptor or workman responsible for the creation of a 'master' figure, group or any three-dimensional form. The master model is then cast so that moulds can be made and the original figure copied repeatedly for commercial production.

Modern movement Loosely used term for work by early 20thC designers and architects, which attempted to create a new approach to design suitable for a technological world. Modernism was embraced by international designers experimenting with new materials and techniques, including Walter GROPIUS, Marcel BREUER, LE CORBUSIER and Ludwig MIES VAN DER ROHE. See pp.71-77.

modes See LACE.

mohair Material originally made from pure spun goats' hair, and later from a mix of spun wool, cotton and silk, used for upholstery and hangings in the 17th and 18th centuries.

Mohair was also used to make dolls' wigs in the 19thC.

moiré Finely ribbed furnishing fabric, usually silk or silk mixture, that has a lustrous finish with a watered or wavy figure. The word is a French adaptation of MOHAIR, from which the fabric was first made. **Moreen** or **morine** is the now obsolete English version of moiré, which referred to a strong woollen material sometimes mixed with cotton and used for bed and window curtains in the 18thC.

molinet See CHOCOLATE POT.

monopodium A decorative support used on tables and chairs, consisting of the head and one leg of an animal, usually a lion.

The monopodium was first seen in Roman furniture, and was revived by late 18thC NEOCLASSICAL designers such as Thomas HOPE.

monteith Large silver or sometimes ceramic bowl with a notched or scalloped rim which appeared in late 17thC Britain and Europe. It was initially used to cool wine glasses, which were suspended over ice or in iced water from notches around the rim. Later examples often have a detachable rim, allowing the bowl also to be used for serving punch.

Montereau See CREIL.

montre à tact See BREGUET.

moons Translucent spots, sometimes also known as stars, in some French and British soft-paste PORCELAIN caused by bubbles in the paste, seen when a piece is held up to the light.

moonstone Colourless gemstone with a blue sheen from the feldspar family, found mainly in Sri Lanka. Moonstones were very sought after in the late 19thC and were popular with ARTS AND CRAFTS jewellers.

moon vase See PILGRIM BOTTLE.

Moorcroft, William (1872-1946) Staffordshire artist-potter known for his distinctively coloured and decorated tableware. Plant forms inspired his motifs throughout his life.

Moorcroft worked for James MACINTYRE & Co from 1898. Backed by the LIBERTY family, he established his own factory at Cobridge, Staffordshire in 1913.

Moorcroft's early pieces were ART NOUVEAU style in a palette of blues, greens and yellows. From the early 20thC he experimented with different finishes, including LUSTRE, vivid FLAMBÉ glazes and from the 1930s, matt glazes combined with simple forms and dramatic colouring. See p.184.

Moore, Bernard (1850-1935) Staffordshire artist-potter whose successful experimentation with Chinese FLAMBÉ and SANG-DE-BOEUF glazes became a characteristic of his work. He produced simply shaped decorative ware such as vases in porcelain and earthenware forms, much of it decorated by ceramics artists such as Hilda Beardmore.

Moore, James (c. 1670-1726) Royal cabinet-maker at the time of King George I and in partnership with John GUMLEY from 1714. Moore supplied quality carved and gilt GESSO furniture to many aristocratic houses.

Moorfield carpets Hand-knotted carpets made by Thomas Moore in Moorfields, London, in the mid-18thC. Moore was the main competitor of Thomas Whitty, founder of the AXMINSTER Carpet Manufactory, and produced high-quality pieces in NEOCLASSICAL style, many for the architect Robert Adam.

moquette Sturdy carpeting and upholstery textile woven in a similar manner to VELVET – on narrow looms, using coarse wool and LINEN. The production of moquette carpets, also known as BRUSSELS carpets, occurred

from the 16th to the 18th centuries in Britain at KIDDERMINSTER, WILTON, Norwich and Bradford.

moreen See MOIRÉ.

morion A crested 16th-17thC metal helmet with the brim upcurving at front and rear. See p.409.

Morocco leather Fine-grained, elastic, soft but firm leather used by bookbinders, upholsterers and furniture-makers. It was originally goatskin, produced by the Moors in Spain and Morocco; later, sheepskin was also used. Morocco leather became a popular bookbinding material in Europe from the 16thC, and by the 18thC was also used for the production of furniture.

Morris, William (1834-1896) Artist-craftsman, designer, social reformer, writer and the main inspiration behind the ARTS AND CRAFTS movement. See pp.62-63, 67.

morse ivory Walrus tooth, which was carved into small decorative and religious pieces in northern Europe. It has a slightly different texture from elephant IVORY, is harder to carve and liable to crack. See SCRIMSHAW.

mortar Flat bottomed bowl used in Europe from the 11thC for pounding pharmaceuticals or foods. Mortars are usually made from a hard material such as marble, stone or bronze, and are used with a pounding utensil of the same material called a **pestle**.

mortise and tenon See JOINING.

mosaic glass Coloured glass made since ancient times and popular in the late 19thC. Pieces of glass are fused together, the colours remaining separate, then stretched into a long CANE which is sliced crosswise or diagonally. The slices are then arranged on a core of the desired shape, covered with an outer mould to hold everything in place and heated until their edges fuse together. Alternatively, mosaic glass is arranged in flat plaques for use as hung decoration, or reheated and blown or shaped into various objects, including MILLEFIORI and jewellery. See p.208.

Moser, Koloman (1868-1918) See VIENNA SECESSION, WIENER WERKSTÄTTE.

mother-of-pearl The smooth, iridescent lining of the shell of certain molluscs, including pearl, oyster, abalone, nautilus and river mussel. The iridescence fades on exposure to sunlight over time. Mother-of-pearl,

also known as **nacre**, is used in jewellery and was popular for INLAID DECORATION and MARQUETRY mainly in the 17thC, and in the 19thC on papier-mâché furniture.

Mother-of-pearl Satin-glass See PEARL SATIN-GLASS.

Motschmann doll One of the earliest types of doll with a degree of articulation in the limbs, made by German doll-maker Charles Motschmann in the 1850s. The upper arms and legs and torso are made of cloth, and the head, upper chest, pelvis and lower arms and legs are of non-flexible material such as COMPOSITION. A press squeaker was often inserted into the cloth midriff. Although his name has become a generic term for such dolls, Motschmann was neither the first nor the only manufacturer to make them.

MOTSCHMANN DOLL *with cloth joints, painted face and china body and limbs; c.1857; 12 in (30.5 cm) high. The dolls often have inset glass eyes.*

moulded glass Glassware made by blowing or pressing molten glass into a mould; produced in antiquity, and commercially since the 1830s.

mouldings Any shaped ornament or projection cast in plaster or carved in wood or stone and applied to furniture, furnishings or to frame wall panels. Most mouldings are based on architectural features, especially those used c. 1720-1850, which were mainly taken from Classical Roman and Greek architecture. Non-architectural mouldings include the bead and quirk, bead and flush, and bead and butt, all of which were invented by joiners, often to disguise joints. See box, p.496.

mounts Term for all metal parts found on furniture, whether part of the construction – applied to prevent wear – or performing some function, such as a hinge or keyhole. Mounts can also be purely ornamental as in the

DETAILS OF MOULDINGS

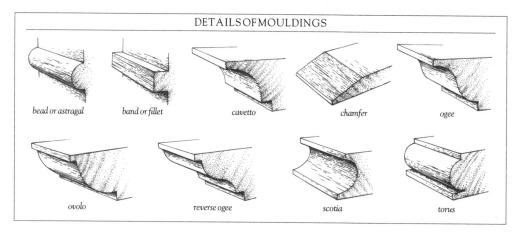

bead or astragal   *band or fillet*   *cavetto*   *chamfer*   *ogee*

ovolo   *reverse ogee*   *scotia*   *torus*

ORMOLU or bronze decoration on 18thC French and British furniture.

The term also embraces silver or other metal parts applied to glass and ceramic objects, such as handles and spouts on jugs and decanters.

mourning jewellery Articles of jewellery worn in memory of the deceased. Money was often allocated in the will of the deceased for spending on memorial jewellery. From the late 18thC onwards, brooches, pendants and particularly rings were typically set with gemstones and decorated with sentimental motifs, including weeping willows, broken columns or a lock of hair from the dead person. Mourning jewellery in JET, or glass imitations of jet, reached its height of popularity after the death of Prince Albert, Queen Victoria's consort, in 1861.

Similar items of jewellery with motifs such as skulls, skeletons or coffins were intended as a reminder of mortality. These are known as **memento mori**, literally meaning 'remember you must die', and were common during the 16th and 17th centuries. See p.268-9.

moustache cup Mid-19thC cup with a small guard added to the rim to prevent the user's moustache getting wet. Alternatively a **moustache mount** could be clipped onto the rim of a cup.

MOUSTACHE CUP *with a lip for protecting a gentleman's waxed moustache; saucer 7½ in (19.1 cm) wide.*

moustache spoons Spoons with a moustache guard, made in silver and ELECTROPLATE for left or right-handed use and patented in the USA in 1875.

Moustiers potteries Group of leading FAIENCE factories in southern France, operational from the 17thC. The best work was produced *c.*1710-40, using motifs based on the designs of leading LOUIS XIV-style draughtsman Jean BÉRAIN in an UNDERGLAZE blue on a white base. The designs made extensive use of GROTESQUE and ARABESQUE patterns.

movement The complete mechanism of a clock or watch, automaton or musical box, also known as the **works**. The movement can be weight, spring or electrically driven. See TRAIN.

Mucha, Alphonse (1860-1939) Czech-born artist, illustrator and designer of textiles, furniture and jewellery, known particularly for his ART NOUVEAU posters of the French actress Sarah Bernhardt. He lived in Paris, where he collaborated on designs with French jeweller Georges FOUQUET, before moving to New York in 1904 where he worked with Louis Comfort TIFFANY. See p.264.

Mudéjar style See ISLAMIC STYLE.

Mudge, Thomas (1715-94) Innovative clock and watchmaker, who was apprenticed to George GRAHAM. Mudge invented the lever ESCAPEMENT *c.*1754 – the forerunner of the escapements found in modern mechanical watches and travelling clocks. From *c.*1770 he worked mainly on marine CHRONOMETERS.

muff chain A long chain worn around the neck with fasteners at each end to be joined when threaded through a lady's fur muff.

muffineer 1 Round dish with domed cover used for serving hot muffins. **2** Small caster first used late 18thC for sprinkling muffins with cinnamon or salt. Examples are usually of silver, sometimes with a porcelain body, and have finer holes than a sugar caster.

muffle kiln See PETIT FEU.

mug Term used from the mid-17thC for a drinking cup with a single handle and rim without a lip. Mugs are generally smaller than TANKARDS and usually lidless. They are found in silver, pewter, glass or ceramics and were used for beer, wine or ale; small silver mugs were made for children.

mulberry A hard, heavy, golden to reddish-brown timber with dark streaks. Mulberry was used as a VENEER and for small articles such as boxes, during the Queen Anne period at the beginning of the 18thC.

mule A coin that has been mistakenly struck on one side with a design intended for another coin, resulting in a 'hybrid' of two types that were never meant to be together.

mule chest 17thC, mainly English, forerunner of the chest of drawers. It consists of a main, box-like storage area with a hinged lid, and with two drawers, side by side, beneath.

mull Late 18th and early 19th-century Scottish ornamental snuffbox, often with a decorated lid. Mulls were generally made of horn, ivory, shell or similar material with silver or pewter mounts, although some examples are made entirely of metal. A large type of mull was intended for passing around the dinner table. Some of these are made from a complete ram's head, and may have various utensils attached such as a spoon, a rake and a spike for mixing the snuff, and a hare's foot for wiping the upper lip.

muntin See JOINING.

Murray, Keith (1893-1981) New Zealand-born architect and designer of silver, glass and ceramics. In the 1930s Murray designed simple tableware and decorative items, including engraved LEAD CRYSTAL for glass-makers STEVENS & WILLIAMS, plain but elegant ceramics for WEDGWOOD and silverware for Mappin & Webb. From 1938 he worked solely as an architect.

musical clock Clock incorporating or linked to a musical movement which plays periodically or on the operation of a cord or lever. The tune is played on bells or a toothed comb. See CARILLON.

Musical watches were made in the late 18th and 19th centuries mainly in Switzerland, but also in Britain. The tune is played via a pinned, rotating disc or cylinder on a nest of bells or on a toothed comb.

music plates Late 17thC Dutch dessert plates decorated with the words and music of a song to be sung at the meal's end. They were made in DELFTWARE in the late 17thC, were reproduced at MOUSTIERS, NEVERS and ROUEN, and extensively copied during the 19thC.

musket Long-barrelled shoulder gun with a smooth BORE, loaded through the muzzle, used from the late 16th to late 19th centuries.

muzzle The forward, discharging end of the barrel of a firearm.

mystery clock A clock, usually in a novelty or ornate form, in which there is no visible connection between the clock mechanism and the dial. A common type has a standing figure holding an apparently free-swinging pendulum. The clocks were fashionable in Britain and France in the 19thC and during the ART DECO period, especially those made by CARTIER, *c.*1920. See pp.286-7.

N

Nabeshima Japanese porcelain made at Okawachi, 5 miles (8 km) north of ARITA. Nabeshima is the name of a Japanese prince who founded the kilns at the end of the 17thC.

The porcelain was made as presentation ware for the local nobility and was of significantly higher quality than most of that exported to Western markets. Nabeshima was characterised by sophisticated decoration and limited shapes, particularly in the first half of the 18thC. Much of the decoration was outlined in UNDERGLAZE blue and filled with overglaze enamels. Thick CELADON glazes, often combined with BLUE AND WHITE or ENAMELLED designs, were also used. Little

Nabeshima reached Europe before the late 19thC. The style has continued right up to the present day.

nacre See MOTHER-OF-PEARL.

nails Hand-made nails were used particularly from Roman times for fixing hinges and locks before the advent of SCREWS. They were also used concurrently with wooden dowels, for JOINING planks before the introduction of mortise and tenon joints, although they are seen on COUNTRY FURNITURE made well into the 18thC. Machine-made nails were made from the early 19thC.

Nailsea Glasshouse Bristol glassworks operating 1788-1873. It produced CROWN and sheet glass, bottles, household ware and flasks. The household wares were made in a pale green glass with no decoration. The flecked and festooned glassware, including jugs, carafes, rolling pins and flasks, which is often called Nailsea glass was almost certainly made elsewhere.

namas Also known as **namazlyk**. See PRAYER RUG.

Nancy School Late 19thC French ART NOUVEAU design group with a philosophy of combining art with nature, founded by French designer Emile GALLÉ. Members of the school included the sculptor, painter and designer Victor Prouvé (1858-1943), glass artists Auguste and Antonin DAUM, and metalworker and cabinet-maker Louis MAJORELLE.

Nanking ware Traditional though misleading name given to blue and white CHINESE EXPORT PORCELAIN made at Jingdezhen. The wares were shipped to Europe via the city of Nanking (Nanjing) during the 18th and early 19th centuries. They were usually decorated with Chinese landscapes and buildings, and sometimes with European-influenced borders. See p.161.

nashiji Japanese LACQUER technique developed in the early 19thC. Flecks of gold, silver, copper or metal alloys were evenly sprinkled between layers of clear or coloured lacquer, creating a speckled appearance similar to that of AVENTURINE glass. (*Nashiji* is Japanese for 'pear-skin ground'.)

Nash, John (1752-1835) Architect whose building style epitomised Regency taste. See p.45.

Naturalistic style Term generally used to describe a British furniture style fashionable c.1840-65. It was

characterised by flowing curves and leaves and flowers elaborately carved in deep relief – as well as luxurious, informal, deep-cushioned chairs.

nautilus cup Drinking cup made from the snail-like nautilus seashell, with silver or silver-gilt MOUNTS. The cups were made in the 16th and 17th centuries, primarily in Italy, Germany, Austria and the Netherlands, although some British examples do survive. They were intended for display rather than use. The mounts are usually decorated with figures and shapes associated with the sea, such as mermaids.

Navajo rugs Rugs woven by the Navajo Indians in the south-west USA from the late 19thC. Early abstract designs were replaced by pictorial rugs in the early 20thC, but the 1930s saw a revival of traditional designs and the use of vegetable dyes.

NAVAJO RUG; *80 in (2.03 m) long. Traditional colours are white, black, tan and grey.*

necessaire Small case made of wood covered in leather or SHAGREEN, or sometimes silver or enamel, designed to carry travel necessities, such as toiletries or sewing equipment. Necessaires were particularly popular in the 18thC and were also made in the 19thC. See p.257.

necessary stool See CLOSE STOOL.

needle painting Silk and satin embroidered pictures painted with watercolour in parts and produced in quantity during the late 18th and early 19th centuries. See p.308.

needlepoint See LACE.

nef Medieval table ornament in the shape of a fully rigged ship, usually made of silver set with precious stones or ENAMELLED. It was used to hold a nobleman's or guest of honour's wine, eating utensils, or as a ceremonial salt container. The nef was much copied in silver during the 19thC.

Nelme, Anthony (d.1722) London silversmith who made articles such as candlesticks, teapots and

PILGRIM BOTTLES, marked 'AN' or 'Ne'. His son Francis carried on the business.

Neoclassical style Style based on the decorative forms of ancient Greece and Rome which dominated design in architecture, furniture and ornamentation in late 18thC Europe. The architect Inigo Jones (see p.20) used Classical themes in the early 17thC, inspired by the work of Italian RENAISSANCE architect Andrea Palladio (see PALLADIAN). In the mid-18thC the true Neoclassical period emerged in France – following the excavation of Pompeii – and proceeded to spread throughout Europe. In Britain architect-designer Robert Adam was the main proponent. See p.36.

netsuke Ornamental Japanese toggle worn at the waist above the OBI or sash. A cord passed through holes in the base from which was hung an INRO or a pouch. Netsuke were made from the 17thC in a wide variety of materials, but became redundant when the Japanese adopted Western dress in the 1870s. Most take the form of figures, animals or plants but there are some variations: **Manju** (rice cake) resembles a bun – either solid or pierced. **Ichiraku** is made from woven or braided metal, rattan palm or bamboo, forming a basketwork box or gourd. **Kagamibuta** is a shallow bowl with a decorated metal lid. **Sashi netsuke** are rod-shaped, up to 5 in (12.5 cm) long, typically depicting an insect or animal perched on a twig or branch. See pp.399-400.

netted glassware See RETICULATED.

Nevers A leading French centre for making FAIENCE from the 16thC. The first pottery was founded by three Italian brothers and produced wares in the Italian MAIOLICA tradition. French styles with Chinese decoration date from the 17thC, with predominant colours of flat yellow, white, red and blue. In the late 17thC the potteries were famous for **bleu persan** ware, with Persian-inspired designs in light colours on a dark blue background.
By the 18thC Nevers wares had been overtaken in popularity by those of ROUEN and MOUSTIERS. In the late 18thC, before a number of potteries closed, they were the main suppliers of **faience patriotique** – wares decorated with inscriptions and symbols of the French Revolution.

Newcastle glassware Tyneside has been a major centre of glass-making since the 17thC, when a number of French and Italian craftsmen settled there, many of them skilled

enamellers and engravers. Local manufacturers made large quantities of window glass, tablewares and ornaments, sometimes sending the products to Holland for decorating. During the 19thC Newcastle also produced PRESSED GLASS.

New Sculpture movement British movement c.1880-1910, concerned with naturalistic modelling, often in bronze, using the accurate LOST-WAX casting process. See pp.330-1.

nickel silver A white alloy of nickel, copper and zinc commonly used as the base metal for ELECTROPLATING. The result is called electroplated nickel silver (EPNS). Being a similar colour to silver, worn areas are less obvious than when copper is the base metal. Nickel silver was also marketed as **German silver** and **argentan**.

niello Decorative technique on metal, often silver; an engraved design is filled with a black compound of sulphur and powdered copper, silver or lead and is fixed by heating. See p.236.

nien hao See REIGN MARKS.

night clock A clock with PIERCED hour numerals and minute divisions which are illuminated when an oil lamp is placed behind the dial. Night clocks originated c.1670, and are most common in Italy. A few were made in Britain before 1700. The clocks tended to catch fire and became obsolete after REPEATER mechanisms were invented in the late 17thC. See also PROJECTION CLOCK.

night commode See CLOSE STOOL.

noble The standard gold coin of medieval England, showing the king in a ship. Its face value was originally 6s 8d (33.33p) – one-third of £1. The noble was struck in large quantities from 1350. In 1464 it was redesigned as a **rose noble**, or **ryal** and revalued at 10s (50p). The coin remained in circulation throughout the 15th and early 16th centuries.

nocturnal A 16th and 17thC circular navigating instrument for use at night. The number of hours before or after midnight was measured by the difference between two pointers – one set to the date and hour on the instrument scale, the other directed at the pole star. Nocturnals are found in wood or brass; metal ones often have 'teeth' on the scale so the hours could be counted in the dark.

Noke, Charles (1858-1941) British ceramic artist and modeller at DOULTON and art director 1914-36. In the late 19thC he introduced two types of earthenware – **Holbein ware**, decorated with portraits, and **Rembrandt ware**, decorated with coloured SLIP. See p.183.

Northwood, John (1836-1902) English glass-maker who specialised in CAMEO GLASS. From the age of 12 he worked for a number of glass-making firms in and around STOURBRIDGE, Worcestershire, eventually founding his own company. He won a £1000 prize for his copy of the PORTLAND VASE, a 1stC Roman urn in cameo glass. See p.222.

Nottingham lace LACE with a machine-made net ground and embroidered white decoration, often in two thicknesses of thread, made from the mid-19thC.

nulling See KNURLING.

Nuremberg Bavarian city that was a centre for German 16th-18thC metal, ceramic and glass industries. The metal industry was noted for clocks, watches and scientific instruments, particularly weights, and for pewter with moulded bas-relief decoration. The city gave its name to the **Nuremberg egg**, a 16thC watch with a spring-driven movement which hung from a cord at the belt.

Ceramic production in the 16thC centred mainly on Hafnerware stoves and TILES, and in the 18thC a wide range of TIN-GLAZED EARTHENWARE. Glasswork included 17thC HUMPEN – brightly coloured enamelled drinking vessels – and *Schäpergläser*, glasses decorated in black ENAMEL which were named after their original designer, Johann Schäper (1621-70).

nursing chair Mid-19thC term for a single chair used for breast-feeding infants, with a seat only 13-15 in (33-38 cm) above the ground.

Nymphenburg Porcelain factory founded outside Munich in 1747, which moved to Nymphenburg, Bavaria in 1761. Hard-paste PORCELAIN was made from the beginning, but from 1757 its quality improved and it was used to make Rococo figures, including those modelled by Franz BUSTELLI.

The Nymphenburg factory also produced VEILLEUSES and tableware and specialised in the production of cane handles and small boxes. During the late 18th and early 19th centuries Nymphenburg mainly produced busts, reliefs and Classical figures, and tableware in SÈVRES Empire style. Early 20thC products include ART NOUVEAU tableware and figures.

O

oak Pale, hard and heavy timber that darkens to a rich brown with age and polishing. It was the main furniture-making wood during medieval times up until about c.1660 – a period sometimes referred to as the Age of Oak. Oak furniture tends to be solid, heavy and simple in design. From the 1660s, the timber was mainly used for provincial furniture and for CARCASS work and drawer linings, but was again popular in the ARTS AND CRAFTS MOVEMENT of the late 19thC. See p.89.

obelisk A tall, four-sided shaft, usually monolithic and tapering, rising to a pyramidal point.

obi Wide sash or waistband used to hold a kimono in place, part of Japanese national dress. See INRO.

objects of vertu English term, roughly translated as 'precious objects', for small luxury articles in gold, silver or porcelain and often decorated with precious and semiprecious stones, ENAMEL and LACQUER. Objects of vertu, such as SEALS, snuffboxes, BONBONNIÈRES and ÉTUIS, were popular 17th to 19th centuries. See pp.256-62.

obsidian Natural glass produced by volcanic action. It is usually black or black-banded, and can be cut and polished and used as a gemstone.

obverse The side of a coin or medal upon which the principal minting authority is recorded, usually (but not invariably) the 'head' side. The opposite side of the coin, the 'tail', is known as the **reverse**.

occasional table Small, portable table which can be moved about easily to suit the occasion.

octant Navigational instrument which measures the angle of the sun above the horizon. It was invented by John Hadley in 1731, but was superseded by the more accurate SEXTANT in the late 18thC. See p.296.

ogee Double curve shape used to describe an onion-shaped arch of 'S'-shaped MOULDING and reproduced in many decorative forms.

ogee clock See SHELF CLOCK.

oil gilding See GILDING.

oil painting A picture painted with coloured pigments ground in an oil such as linseed and applied onto a

prepared surface such as canvas or wood. The finished painting is usually coated with varnish which tends to discolour with age. See p.322.

ojime A slip bead securing the cord on a Japanese NETSUKE. See INRO.

okimono Japanese sculptured figures usually made of ivory but also of bone or wood. They were made as ornaments for the home during the Meiji (1816-1912) and Taisho (1912-26) periods, and exported to Europe and the USA.

Old French Early Victorian revival of Louis XV Rococo style. See p.50.

olive Yellow-green, fine-grained timber with a wavy, mottled grain. It was introduced to Britain from Spain and Italy in the second half of the 17thC and used mainly for its decorative quality, particularly in ornamental VENEERS.

ombrierte Blumen See DEUTSCHE BLUMEN.

Omega workshops London workshops founded in 1913 by Roger Fry (1866-1934) to encourage young artists and improve standards of decorative design – aiming to relate modern art to daily life and bring out the creative pleasure of the artist. Designs were simple and decorated in bright colours, the most successful products being textiles and pottery. Simple panelled furniture, often flimsy, was bought ready-made from manufacturers and painted in the distinctive style.

Fry belonged to the Bloomsbury Group of writers and artists, members of which, including painters Duncan Grant (1885-1978) and Vanessa Bell (1879-1961), were also involved in the project. Although the workshops closed in 1919, they heralded a new approach to British 20thC design.

omnium See WHATNOT.

on-glaze See OVERGLAZE.

onion pattern Porcelain decoration first used on 18thC MEISSEN tableware and popular at many other potteries. It was derived from a Chinese design that included stylised peaches, leaves and flowers, which were mistaken for onions. See DECORATIVE MOTIFS.

Onslow pattern Scroll pattern used mostly on the handles of mid-18thC serving spoons and ladles. It was named after Sir Arthur Onslow (1691-1768), six times Speaker of the House of Commons. See CUTLERY.

opalescent glass 1 A specific type of iridescent glass developed by the British glass-maker Frederick CARDER for the STEUBEN GLASSWORKS in the USA. Its appearance, similar to that of a natural opal, was created by cooling the glass object with compressed air and then reheating it. The glass was produced in pink, blue, yellow and green.
2 American ART GLASS which has a raised design in opalescent white glass against a coloured background. The technique was developed in the late 19thC, and produced in Britain on art glass and PRESSED GLASS. See p.226.

opal glass Translucent white glass developed in 17thC Venice and later made throughout Europe. It was particularly popular in Britain during the 19thC for cheap ornamental wares. TRANSLUCENCY was achieved by adding BONE ASH to the molten glass. When held up to the light, the glass shows slight reddish tones.

open-faced watch Pocket watch with a glazed dial exposed to view and backed by a single metal case, dating from c.1830 into the 20thC.

openwork General term for the decorative technique of cutting variously shaped holes through the body of a piece of silver, furniture or ceramics to form a pattern. See PIERCED DECORATION, LACEWORK and RETICULATED.

OPENWORK *ceramic basket; c.1770.*

order of architecture See COLUMN.

organzine See SILK.

ormolu Mercury-GILDED bronze used for figures and decorative MOUNTS on clocks and furniture. The word is from the French *or moulu*, 'ground gold'. Highly toxic fumes emanating from the mercury made this process dangerous and it was superseded by ELECTROPLATING in the mid-19thC.

Orrefors Swedish glass factory founded 1898. In the 1920s, the factory was known for its innovative engraved glassware, including **Graal** glass, a form of CAMEO GLASS. In the 1930s, designer Sven Palmqvist developed **ravenna** and **kraka** – heavy glass with inlaid colours.

orrery Small clockwork or hand-cranked model of the planetary system – a popular astronomical demonstrational apparatus or educational demonstrator during the 18th and 19th centuries. An orrery might complement an ASTROLABE or a pair of celestial and terrestrial globes in a library or schoolroom. See p.297.

osier pattern Raised basketwork ceramics pattern in sections between radial ribs, first used as an edging on 18thC MEISSEN porcelain.

ottoman A low upholstered seat without arms and with or without a back (also known as a **Turkey sofa**), which was designed to seat several people. The idea was introduced to Britain from Turkey (the Ottoman Empire until 1922) in the late 18thC. The **ottoman footstool**, introduced in the early 19thC, was used as a fireside seat. A **box ottoman** has a hinged seat which lifts to reveal storage space below. See BORNE, DIVAN.

Ottoman carpets Oriental carpets woven in workshops anywhere in the Ottoman Empire from the mid-16th to the late 17th century, as opposed to indigenous Turkish weavings of the same period. See p.300.

outside decorator Ceramics decorator who worked independently of a factory on bought-in blanks. In Germany the decorators were known as **Hausmaler** and were responsible for some of the best decoration in the first half of the 18thC.

Dutch enamellers decorated MEISSEN, Chinese and Japanese porcelain and Staffordshire CREAMWARE, and there were several independent studios in Britain from c.1750 to the early 1800s.

over and under Two-barrelled gun with one barrel above the other.

overglaze A term used in ceramics for the method or order of painted or TRANSFER-PRINTED decoration applied on the glaze rather than beneath it (UNDERGLAZE). Overglaze ENAMEL colours are mixed with a FLUX such as potash or lime which enables them to fuse onto the glaze when the article is fired again – at a lower temperature firing than for underglaze HIGH-TEMPERATURE COLOURS. See p.153.

overlay glass See CASED GLASS.

overstuffing Upholstery in which the padding is carried over the chair-frame edges. Overstuffing was commonly used on early 18thC chairs.

ovolo See MOULDINGS.

oxidised silver Silver in which the surface is heated to give it a dark coating of silver sulphide. This enhances the shadows on decorated areas. See also PATINA.

oystering A decorative form of VENEERING using slices of wood cut in vertical cross-section from the branches of small trees, such as laburnum and walnut, to create a pattern of repetitive whorls on furniture. The technique originated in Holland. It was popular in Britain for drawer fronts, and for cabinet and bureau doors from the late 17th to early 18th centuries. See p.92.

P

padouk Hard, heavy wood, varying from golden-brown to crimson in colour with a darker figuring. It was imported to Britain from the Andaman Islands in the Bay of Bengal and from Burma from the 18thC, and used for decorative woodwork such as FRETWORK, and occasionally for chairs. AMBOYNA is a variety of padouk from the East Indies.

pagod See MAGOT.

pair-cased watch Pocket watch with a glass-fronted inner case containing the movement, and fitting into an outer case of metal. Such watches were very widespread in Britain from c.1670 to 1830.

paisley pattern A cone or almond-shaped motif which originated in 17thC India, and is derived from the Oriental BOTEH. The name comes from Paisley, a Scottish cotton centre where shawls decorated with the motif were made in the 19thC. See p.309.

paktong Chinese for 'white copper' – the name given to a silvery-coloured alloy of COPPER, ZINC and NICKEL. It was made in China from ancient times for money, hinges on furniture, domestic items and – because of its ringing quality – for bells and gongs. Although its export from China was illegal, some reached Britain in the 18thC; a similar alloy was made in Britain which led to the development of NICKEL SILVER.

Palissy, Bernard (c.1510-90) French Renaissance potter whose distinctive designs in multicoloured, lead-glazed earthenware were extensively imitated in the latter 19thC. Busy natural history themes are most characteristic of Palissy's style – dishes and plates with reptiles, shells, fish and animals moulded in high relief on a pond-like ground, and blues, greens, browns and yellows as the predominant colours. See p.186.

Palladian style Classical architectural style inspired by the 16thC Venetian architect Andrea Palladio, which influenced later furniture and interior decor styles throughout Europe. The style was brought to Britain by architect Inigo Jones (see p.20).

Grand-scale architectural designs were translated into furniture and interiors by 18thC architect-designers such as William KENT. Typical features are PEDIMENTS and COLUMNS, and Classical motifs combined with BAROQUE decoration, such as marbling and gilding. See p.30.

palmette See DECORATIVE MOTIFS.

Palmqvist, Sven See ORREFORS.

pandora Early 19thC French doll used to model dresses and hair styles.

panel Flat surface set within a grooved framework as used in furniture or to cover a wall. It may sit proud of or flush with the frame. For **panelled construction** see JOINING and p.89.

pannikin See PIPKIN.

pantin See JUMPING JACK.

Pantin, Simon (d.1728) London-based HUGUENOT silversmith who produced dinner pieces for the aristocracy and much domestic silverware in Queen Anne style with traces of ornate Huguenot decoration.

pap-boat Small, boat-shaped, silver or ceramic vessel used for feeding infants and invalids in the 18th and 19th centuries. See p.202.

paperweights Small, heavy, decorative objects, usually of glass, but also of bronze or semiprecious stone, used to stop papers blowing away. The earliest glass paperweights were made in Italy and BOHEMIA c.1843, but the most ornate and valuable examples were made in France at BACCARAT, CLICHY and ST LOUIS. From 1848 they were produced at many British glassworks, the best being made by BACCHUS. See MILLEFIORI and p.229.

papier-mâché Material made of a mixture of pulped paper, glue, chalk and sometimes sand, which is moulded, then baked and decorated to make ornaments and lightweight furniture. It was first used in Europe in France during the 17thC – the term is French for pulped paper – and was developed and patented in Britain by Birmingham furniture-maker Henry Clay from 1772, and further developed in the early 19thC by the Birmingham firm of JENNERS & BETTERIDGE. Clay produced small items such as tea trays and panels for tea caddies, as well as larger pieces of furniture.

The papier mâché surface is ideal for painting or JAPANNING and can also be inlaid with materials such as mother-of-pearl. See pp.51, 112, 350-1.

parcel gilt Term used to describe silverware or furniture, parts of which are gilded, such as areas of carved or moulded decoration.

parian Fine-grained, hard-paste white PORCELAIN with marble-like appearance. The name comes from Paros, an Aegean island where Greek and Roman marble was mined. **Parian ware** was developed in Britain at either COPELAND or MINTON in the 1840s. It is usually unglazed and uncoloured and was used to make dolls' heads and SLIP-CAST to make busts and figures. See p.194.

Parisienne French fashion doll of the mid to late 19thC. Parisiennes are elegantly dressed, often with a wardrobe of clothing and exquisitely made miniature accessories.

parquetry A form of MARQUETRY with a balanced, geometric pattern. The designs rely on the contrasting grains or colours of different woods. Oyster parquetry consists of small branches cut transversely to produce circles or ovals reminiscent of oyster shells, which are laid in rows. Parquetry was used by British cabinet-makers from c.1660, and was particularly fashionable in 18thC France and Italy. See p.93.

partisan See POLEARMS.

partners' desk Large flat-topped desk at which two people can work facing each other, made from the mid-18thC. The desk has drawers and cupboards on each side and stands on two pedestals. See p.121.

partridge wood Hard, dense, straight-grained wood from South America. Its name comes from the brown and red, feather-like pattern of its markings. 17thC cabinet-makers used the timber for PARQUETRY and INLAID DECORATION; in the late 18thC it was used sparingly as a VENEER.

parure Matching set of jewellery, usually including a necklace, brooch, bracelet and earrings. Parures were first worn in the 16thC and came into vogue again in the 19thC.

pashmina Literally 'little wool', used in the context of Oriental carpets for cashmere – the wool of the Kashmir goat – in some 16th and 17thC Indian weavings. See p.305.

paste 1 Cut glass used to simulate gemstones in COSTUME JEWELLERY. Paste is usually colourless but may be tinted by a foil backing. **Strass** is a particularly fine-quality paste made with LEAD CRYSTAL. Paste is lighter in weight and more easily scratched than a true gemstone. See p.267.
2 The term used for the unfired mixture of clays and other substances used to make a ceramic body.

pastel A drawing or sketch executed in crayons made of ground colour pigments, chalk, water and gum. A fixative is necessary to seal the powdery pastel colours to the base material, which is usually paper.

pastille burner Vessel for the burning of pastilles – tablets of aromatic infusions bound in gum arabic. The burners have been known since Elizabethan times and were usually of silver until the 19thC. In the 1830s and 40s, pottery and porcelain burners, often in the form of model buildings, were popular; the aromatic fumes escaped through chimneys and windows. See CASSOLETTE.

patchbox 1 Storage compartment in a RIFLE butt for small cloth or leather patches used to wrap around the bullet to ensure its tight fit in the barrel, common on US and continental rifles of the 18th and 19th centuries.
2 Small OBJECT OF VERTU – a box for holding the patches used in the 18thC to disguise spots on the skin.

patch marks Discoloured circles on the unglazed base of a porcelain figure where balls or pads of clay were placed during the firing to prevent dribbles of running glaze from cementing the figure to the kiln floor. Patch marks typically occur (in threes or fours) upon DERBY figures.

pate The circular piece of cork, card or COMPOSITION which covers the hole in the crown of a doll's head and to which the wig is usually fixed.

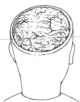

CORK PATE *on a French bisque doll;
c.1860. The wig is glued or pinned to the
pate or glued onto the outside of the head.*

pâte de verre Literally 'glass paste', a substance made from powdered glass, often coloured, mixed with water and a FLUX to help the ingredients to fuse. The paste was applied to a mould in successive layers and fired, then sometimes carved when cool. The technique was perfected in France during the 19thC, the translucent glass being ideal for ornaments.

Patek Philippe Swiss watchmaking company, established as a partnership between Polish watchmaker Antoine Patek and Frenchman Adrien Philippe c.1844. In the late 19thC the partnership replaced Abraham-Louis BREGUET as the most prestigious continental maker. Patek Philippe is known particularly for its ART DECO designs of the 1930s, but also pioneered the first stem KEYLESS-winding watch in the 1840s, and the first perpetual calendar wristwatch in 1925. See p.289.

patent furniture 19th and 20th-century furniture with mechanical devices that adjust or transform the size or function of the piece – such as adjustable chairs and expanding tables. The furniture was often, but not invariably, made under official patents in Britain and the USA.

patera Small circular or oval ornament in low relief, usually resembling a flower or acanthus leaves. See DECORATIVE MOTIFS.

pâte-sur-pâte Literally translated as 'paste on paste' – the process of building up layers of porcelain SLIP to give a translucent, three-dimensional effect in low relief. The operation involves painting a thin wash of slip onto a coloured but unfired piece of porcelain. Subsequent layers, sometimes in different colours, are added when the earlier layers are dry, gradually – sometimes over weeks or months – building up a design in varying thicknesses and intensities. The design can then be sharpened by engraving and the piece fired. The technique was developed at SÈVRES c.1850-75 and perfected by MINTON from 1870. See p.183.

patina The surface colour and finish built up by age, wear and polishing. A patina on wood furniture shows depth and grain and helps indicate its age. A patina on metals such as bronze or copper results naturally from oxidisation or can be artificially induced by chemical treatment.

pattern A sample coin made to evaluate its design.

pauldron See ARMOUR.

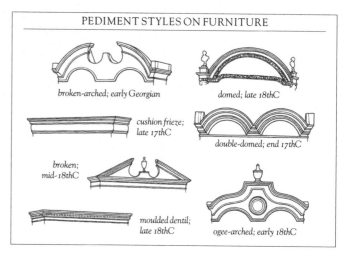

PEDIMENT STYLES ON FURNITURE

broken-arched; early Georgian

domed; late 18thC

*cushion frieze;
late 17thC*

double-domed; end 17thC

*broken;
mid-18thC*

*moulded dentil;
late 18thC*

ogee-arched; early 18thC

pavé The French word for 'paved', referring to a jewellery setting in which gemstones, typically in groups of seven, are set very close together like paving stones to hide the backing metal. The technique was popular in the late 18th and 19th centuries.

pear Pink to yellowish-white timber used in country furniture and often stained black (ebonised), as it takes a stain well. In the late 17th and early 18th centuries, pearwood was widely used for picture and mirror frames and cabinet stands.

pearl Pearls form when foreign particles are covered by organic tissue, called nacre, or MOTHER-OF-PEARL, in the shells of certain molluscs. A **wild** or **true pearl** occurs naturally, whereas a **cultured pearl** forms around an artificially implanted particle.
  Pearls vary in colour according to the habitat of the mollusc, ranging from shades of pink to black. They are often named after the mollusc in which they were formed, as in clam or mussel pearls; the finest are Oriental pearls from the pearl oyster.
  Pearls are classified according to their shape and lustre – the most valuable being spherical and drop-shaped specimens with a satin-like lustre. Other valued pearls include the irregularly shaped BAROQUE PEARLS, tiny **seed pearls**, and **blister pearls** which grow attached to the interior of the shell. See p.267.

Pearline glass Translucent, usually blue, PRESSED GLASS developed in Britain in 1889. It is seen mainly in ornamental wares and has raised opalescent decoration.

pearl satin-glass Type of ART GLASS with trapped-air decoration developed in both France and the USA in the late 19thC. The glass has a pearly appearance and was sometimes decorated with acid ENGRAVING. It went under several names, including **verre de soie, mother-of-pearl satin-glass** and **pearl ware**. A British version made by Thomas WEBB & SONS and STEVENS & WILLIAMS c.1880 is known as **quilted-cushion glass**. The molten glass was blown into a diamond-patterned mould. When cool the patterned glass was covered with a thin layer of clear glass to create an air space around each diamond. Finally the object was given a satin finish by treating it with hydrofluoric acid.

pearlware See CREAMWARE.

Pêche, Dagobert See WIENER WERKSTÄTTE.

pedestal A solid, moulded or carved support variously adapted to form stands for urns, sculptured figures, lamps and furniture.

pediment The triangular or curved gable surmounting the façade of a Classical-style building which has been much adapted in furniture design, especially in cabinets, bookcases and LONGCASE clocks of the 18thC. See box above.

pedometer Instrument for measuring walking distances used in the 19thC. The watch-like device was strapped to the leg and a weighted arm on a ratchet clicked up each step.

peep-show Optical toy popular in Victorian times. It is based on the CAMERA OBSCURA, usually in the form of a box containing a pictorial scene which is magnified by a small lens and viewed through an eyepiece when held up to the light. Peep-shows could be large enough to be used by travelling showmen and viewed by four of their customers at a time, or small enough to be condensed into a **peep-egg**. See p.295.

Pegg, William 'Quaker' (1775-1851) Porcelain painter responsible for some of the most lavishly decorated DERBY ware of the early 19thC. Large gilded urns, DESSERT SERVICES and tureens with richly coloured botanical designs – of parrot tulip flowers, for example, and often incorporating fruit, vegetables and insects – were typical of his output. He was employed at Derby 1796-1800 and 1813-17; his work is unsigned.

peg tankard 16thC tankard with a vertical row of pegs or studs inside to measure the contents. Peg tankards are found in silver, silver-gilt or base metal. A few replicas were made at York in the 18thC.

peg wooden doll Small wooden doll of the 18th to late 19th centuries, with limbs pegged together at the joints for articulation. See p.350.

PEG WOODEN DOLL *from the Grödnertal; c.1830; 11 in (28 cm) high.*

Peking enamel Finely painted ENAMEL on copper made for Imperial use, akin to CANTON enamel but of far higher quality.

Pellatt, Apsley (1791-1863) English glass-maker based in Southwark, south London, who in 1819 introduced the French process of embedding ceramic medallions in clear glass (SULPHIDES). In 1831 and 1845 Pellatt patented methods of producing PRESSED GLASS, and in 1850 he revived the early Venetian process of making ICE GLASS. During his career Pellatt published a number of books about glass-making. See p.212.

Pembroke table Small, light table said to have been introduced by the Countess of Pembroke (1737-1831) in the second half of the 18thC, with two drop leaves and one or more drawers set beneath the centre section. Pembroke tables were used as ladies' breakfast or writing tables. They were

often reproduced in the SHERATON STYLE during the late Victorian and Edwardian periods. See SOFA TABLE, HARLEQUIN TABLE and pp.116-17.

pendulum A rod with a heavy metal weight, or bob, attached to the end, which swings under the influence of gravity and has a naturally ISOCHRONOUS MOTION or beat. In a clock, the pendulum is linked to an ESCAPEMENT mechanism, in order to regulate the action of the going TRAIN. The going train, in turn, gives an impulse to the pendulum on each swing, so maintaining its movement. The pendulum's potential was first

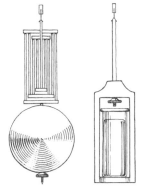

TEMPERATURE COMPENSATING PENDULUMS *Gridiron pendulum (left) and mercury pendulum (right).*

recognised by Italian astronomer Galileo Galilei in the 16thC, supposedly as he watched a chandelier swinging in Pisa Cathedral. Only in 1657, however, was it successfully applied to regulate a clock by the Dutchman Christian Huygens. The first British clock-maker to make pendulum clocks was John FROMANTEEL c.1659.

The regulating capacity of the pendulum provided a breakthrough in accurate timekeeping. However, simple pendulums were also vulnerable to temperature changes; they shorten and beat more quickly when cold and lengthen and beat more slowly when warm. An effective solution was provided by the incorporation of various **temperature compensation** devices. The two most common forms, both introduced in the 1720s, are George GRAHAM's mercury pendulum and John HARRISON's gridiron pendulum with the rod composed of alternating brass and steel. Both work on the counterbalancing effect of the differing rates of expansion of different metals in opposing directions. At the beginning of the 20thC, Charles Edouard Guillaume introduced the nickel-steel 'Invar' pendulum which was not affected by temperature at all.

penny Originally a standard silver coin used in medieval England which was derived from the Roman *denarius* – hence the pre-decimalisation abbreviation 'd'. Early pennies were sometimes cut in half or quarters to make **halfpennies** and **fourthlings**, or FARTHINGS, although these later became round coins in their own right. The first copper pennies were minted in 1797. See p.389.

penwork A late 18th to early 19th-century style of decoration on furniture, boxes, fans and other wooden objects. Black ink was used on pale wood such as pine or satinwood, and flowers, scrolls, arabesques or designs drawn on with a fine quill pen, and then protected by varnishing. CHINOISERIE penwork patterns are common on REGENCY furniture.

pepperbox An early form of revolver which has a barrel block with several chambers. Both FLINTLOCK and PERCUSSION pepperboxes were made in the 18th and 19th centuries.

Percier, Charles (1764-1838), and **Fontaine, Pierre-François-Léonard** (1762-1853) French architects, interior decorators and designers of furniture, silverware and textiles. They were leading architects to Napoleon I from the turn of the century until 1814 and largely responsible for creating the Classical EMPIRE style. Their elegant furniture designs were regularly constructed by cabinet-maker Georges JACOB from 1791.

percussion lock A type of gun mechanism introduced in the early 19thC. A small amount of explosive powder enclosed in a metal cap fits over a nipple in the breech and is detonated by being struck by the hammer when the trigger is pressed. This sends a burst of flame into the powder charge, which explodes and propels the bullet from the barrel. An alternative name for a percussion-lock weapon is **cap and ball**. See p.407.

Pergolesi, Michelangelo (d.1801) Italian-born engraver, decorative artist and designer. He lived in Britain for the last quarter of the 18thC, working with architect Robert Adam.

peridot A gem ranging in colour from dark green to yellow-green. Peridots are usually faceted or polished and sometimes confused with emeralds and green CORUNDUMS. See p.267.

period Belonging to a particular time. A 'Sheraton period' table, for example, dates from Sheraton's time, whereas a 'Sheraton style' table is a later piece made in Sheraton style. For main periods, see p.530.

Perrin, Veuve See MARSEILLES.

Persian knot See CARPET KNOTS.

perspective glass A small hand-held telescope which was made for popular use during the 17thC.

pestle See MORTAR.

petit feu Low-temperature firing of ceramics in a muffle kiln – a small, inner kiln, rather like an enclosed box within a main kiln – which enables ENAMEL colours to be fixed onto glazed pottery or porcelain.

petit patron See CARTOON.

petit point A very fine, small, diagonal embroidery stitch usually on a canvas ground.

petuntse See CHINA STONE.

pew group Staffordshire SALT-GLAZED STONEWARE or glazed earthenware group of two or three figures, sometimes playing musical instruments, seated on a church pew or high-backed bench. Pew groups were produced in the 18thC and reproduced in the 19th and 20th centuries. See STAFFORDSHIRE POTTERIES and p.193.

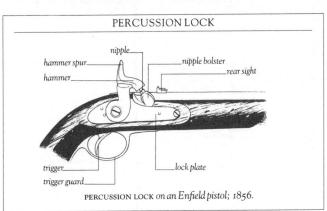

PERCUSSION LOCK

nipple
hammer spur
hammer
nipple bolster
rear sight
trigger
lock plate
trigger guard

PERCUSSION LOCK *on an Enfield pistol; 1856.*

PEWTER STANDARD MARKS

Henry VIII

William III

George IV

William IV

Imperial mark

Victorian mark after 1879

PEWTER STANDARD MARKS *Although many different standard marks were used throughout the country, they can help to date many pieces.*

pewter Alloy made from tin, with hardening agents such as lead, copper and more rarely antimony, added. New pewter is silvery in colour, becoming grey as it oxidises, and eventually turning almost black. Quality pewter contains mainly tin and little lead. English pieces made before the 17thC show little decoration. Lower grades of pewter were used for tavern ware and spoons.

Before 1503, English pewter was marked with a guild mark (a hammer or crowned hammer, and later a rose or crowned rose) but thereafter the London Guild required individual maker's marks.

Early examples are simple initials, but from *c.*1600 these were placed in a circle (often beaded). 17thC marks are often pictorial, while 18thC examples are larger and more complex. Over 6000 marks have been recorded on English pewter. Elsewhere in Europe, marking systems included a town mark, a maker's mark and a quality mark. See p.366.

phenakistoscope A 19thC optical toy, also known as a **magic disc** or **fantascope**. Illustrated circular cards are fixed onto a disc with slits at intervals around its circumference. A handle is fixed to the centre of the disc, and the disc is spun. The user looks through the slits at a mirror where the image is reflected and appears to be moving. See p.295.

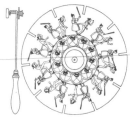

PHENAKISTOSCOPE; *1833; 9 in (23 cm) diameter. The handle is fixed to the centre of the viewing disc.*

phonograph Early machine for recording and reproducing sound, using a wax cylinder. It was invented 1878 by Thomas Edison in the USA. See GRAMOPHONE and p.306.

Phyfe, Duncan (1768-1854) Leading US cabinet-maker. His furniture was beautifully made from the finest woods, usually based on designs from the pattern books of British cabinet-makers Thomas SHERATON and Thomas HOPE.

piano dolls Miniature painted wooden dolls made in Germany *c.*1800-1940, designed to 'dance' on a piano or similar instrument. The dolls actually stand on supports of wire or bristle, between which the 'real' legs are suspended, the feet not quite coming into contact with the surface. When the piano is played, the vibrations cause the figures to move as if dancing. They are also known as **spinet dolls, bristle dolls** and **harpsichord dolls**.

Piano babies are all-BISQUE dolls made in Germany from *c.*1910 and designed to sit or lie on a piano.

TRADITIONAL PIANO DOLLS; *German; c.*1860; 1½ in (38 mm) high.

Picasso, Pablo (1881-1973) Spanish-born artist whose highly individual style greatly influenced 20thC European art and ceramics. Picasso

began his prolific ceramic work in 1947 in the Madoura pottery at Vallauris in southern France. Many of the artist's hand-modelled and hand-painted originals were replicated at the pottery and sold in limited editions. See p.185.

pickelhaube A spiked helmet worn by German troops, introduced in the early 19thC and copied elsewhere.

pickled furniture Wooden furniture that has been stripped of paint using a coating of lime to reveal the plaster base coat beneath, resulting in a pale, white-veined finish. The process, used in the 20thC, is usually applied to furniture made of light-coloured woods such as ash or pine.

picture-back A type of teaspoon mass-produced from sheet metal from 1740 to the end of the century, with fancy motifs stamped on the underside of the bowl. The spoons are Old English or Hanoverian in style (see CUTLERY) and motifs ranged from Rococo shells to flowers, birds, or politically inspired symbols of Liberty or Empire. See p.241.

picture clock A framed picture in which a working clock face is incorporated – into a church tower or town hall for example. Some examples are linked to a musical movement or chime. Picture clocks were popular in the 19thC, and were mainly produced in continental Europe.

A **picture-frame clock** is an Austrian or French BEIDERMEIER wall clock, dating from the second quarter of the 19thC. The enamel dial has a gilt surround set within a gilt border like a picture frame.

pieces of eight Large silver coins struck throughout the Spanish Empire from the 15thC with a face value of eight *reales*, the standard Spanish unit of currency of the time. Together with the gold DOUBLOON, they featured importantly in international trade and pirate treasure. See p.387.

reverse   *obverse*

'PIECE OF EIGHT' *minted in Lima, Peru; 1755. This is a 'pillar type'; later examples have portraits.*

piecrust A scalloped decorative rim reminiscent of the crimped edges of a pie, which was popular on furniture

and silverware (when it is known as a **Chippendale rim**) in the mid-18thC, and much reproduced in the 19thC.

PIECRUST TOP *on a tripod tea table of the late 19thC; 28 in (71 cm) high.*

piéfort A coin deliberately struck on an unusually thick BLANK, often as a collector's or commemorative piece rather than for general circulation.

pier The section of wall between two windows, a site often put to decorative use in interior design. Tall, slim **pier glasses** (also known as **trumeau mirrors**) were popular features from the late 17thC. They are mirrors, often ornately framed, designed to be fixed to a pier and complemented by a small, freestanding **pier table** or a COMMODE beneath. See p.143.

pierced decoration Intricate decoration made by cutting shapes through a solid surface such as metal, wood or ceramics to form a pattern. In ceramics, the clay body is pierced or **reticulated** before firing. Pierced decoration known as **devil's work** was practised in China by the 16thC, and is a feature of some late 18thC British CREAMWARE. It was revived in a very intricate form by the Royal WORCESTER factory in the 1880s, notably by George Owen. See p.152.

Piercing on silver is done by hand with a fine saw or, since the 19thC, by die-stamping (see p.235). It can be practical as in sugar casters or potpourris, as well as decorative as in an outer casing for a cup or jug. See OPENWORK, FRETWORK, LACEWORK and RETICULATED.

pietra dura Italian for 'hard stone', which has come to apply specifically to a 'jigsaw' of semiprecious stones and different coloured marbles used to create a patterned surface.

Pietra dura is built up piece by piece, each sliver of stone intricately cut and then glued edge to edge with the next, and laid on a backing stone such as slate. It can take days for a fine wire-bladed bow saw to cut through some harder stones such as jasper and agate. The finished surface is highly polished and used to decorate cabinets and table tops. Pietra dura is also known as **Florentine mosaic**. See p.113.

piggin A small, glass, silver or ceramic bucket-shaped container, 2-4 in (50-100 mm) high, used as a dipper for transferring milk or cream from a larger container in the 18thC, and also known as a **cream pail**.

PIGGIN *or cream pail of stoneware with engine-turned decoration; c.1700; 2½ in (63 mm) high.*

pilaster A flattened – rectangular in section – Classical COLUMN topped by a moulded or sculptured capital. Pilasters appear on chests, cupboards and chimneypieces of the 16th and 17th centuries, on CABINET-WORK throughout the 18th and early 19th centuries, and in the form of the tapering **pilaster leg** in furniture.

pile 1 Raised, upper surface of carpeting or other textile such as VELVET, also known as the **nap**, and made either by teasing or combing a woven surface, or by shearing looped ends that are woven or 'knotted' into a fabric. See also FLAT-WEAVE. **2** The obverse DIE in coin-making.

pilgrim bottle A flattened, spherical or pear-shaped vessel with loops on either side of the neck to which a chain is attached so that it could be hung from a belt. The ceramic pilgrim-bottle shape was known in ancient China as well as in medieval Europe. In both cases the form reflects original leather and metal shapes with no foot-rim, which were designed to sling from a saddle. The bottles are also known as **costrels**, and Chinese versions as **moon flasks**. Decorative pilgrim's bottles have been made since the 16thC, including elaborate embossed silver examples and similarly shaped scent bottles in the 18thC. See FLASKS.

Pilkington's Royal Lancastrian
Pottery, established near Manchester in 1892 by the Pilkington family, who also owned coal mines and glass-houses. The pottery initially manufactured tiles and, later, other ceramics, developing an innovative, hard, transparent glaze and LUSTRE

finishes. Large-scale production began in 1903, and from 1913 the wares were known as **Royal Lancastrian**. The pottery closed in 1957.

pillar-and-claw table See TRIPOD TABLE.

pillar carpet Chinese carpet without a border made from c.mid-18thC to fit around a pillar or column, giving a continuous pattern.

CHINESE PILLAR CARPET *When wrapped around a pillar vertically the dragon's body appears to be continuous.*

pillow lace See LACE.

pinchbeck Alloy of zinc and copper that resembles gold, and often used as a misnomer for ROLLED GOLD. It was invented by Christopher Pinchbeck, a watch and clock-maker, in London c.1720. It was used for many inexpensive items, such as watch-cases, snuffboxes, seals and clasps, but was superseded by gilded metal, rolled gold and 9 carat gold.

pine General term for a family of coniferous softwoods widely used in furniture-making. The wood is coloured straw to pale red-brown and often prominently grained. It was highly valued in the 16thC, particularly because of the wide planks which could be produced from it. The timber's smooth surface later led to its use as a base for GILDING. Its wide planks also made pine seem suitable for the carcasses of VENEERED furniture – and it was cheaper than oak – but, as a softer wood, in time it tends to warp. During the 19thC, pine was widely used to produce cheap furniture which was often painted.

pinholes See MOONS.

pinion Small cog in clock mechanism which transmits the driving force to the next wheel in the TRAIN.

pipe stopper An instrument with a flattened, circular end, and often an ornate handle, for compressing burning tobacco into a pipe bowl. Pipe stoppers were popular in the 19thC and were made in a variety of

materials, especially copper, brass, and hand-carved wood and ivory. The handles often feature a grotesque bird or animal, or a human caricature.

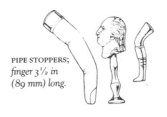

PIPE STOPPERS; *finger 3½ in (89 mm) long.*

pipkin Small, silver saucepan with a bellied, pear-shaped or cylindrical body, used since the 17thC for warming beverages.

The pipkin usually has a long, straight handle at right angles to a pouring lip or spout, and was occasionally accompanied by a spirit burner and stand. Large examples may have hinged covers. Most surviving pipkins are from the 18thC. **Brandy saucepans** are small versions for warming brandy.

piqué 1 INLAID DECORATION of fragments of gold and silver in tortoiseshell or ivory boxes, fans, buttons and jewellery. Piqué was introduced in Italy in the mid-17thC. In Britain, Matthew BOULTON mechanised the technique during the 1760s. It was revived by ART DECO craftsmen in the 1920s.

Piqué point is composed of tiny points of metal; **piqué clouté** has larger points arranged in a pattern; **piqué posé** has flakes of gold or silver; in **piqué d'or** minute gold figures and ornaments are set into tortoiseshell. **2** A **piqué diamond** is a flawed stone, containing inclusions which appear as spots sometimes visible to the naked eye. See p.265.

pistol Small, hand-held firearm, introduced in the 16thC.

Pistrucci, Benedetto (1784-1855) Italian gem engraver who produced superb coin designs for the British Royal Mint in the early 19thC. His St George and the dragon design is still used on modern SOVEREIGNS.

planchet See BLANK.

plane A white, close-grained and tough timber often used by late 18th and early 19thC cabinet-makers as a substitute for beech, especially for the production of painted chairs and the underframing of CARD TABLES and PEMBROKE TABLES.

planishing Process of toughening, smoothing and polishing metal by HAMMERING it with a broad, smooth-

faced hammer. Planishing removes marks made by any previous shaping of the piece and ensures uniform thickness of the metal. See p.234.

plaque Ceramic panel with RELIEF or painted decoration for walls or furniture. A **tableau** is a large, painted porcelain plaque with an integral frame. See p.187.

plastic A man-made substance which can be moulded under heat and pressure and which hardens on cooling. The first usable plastic – Celluloid – was developed in the USA c.1863, and used for making dolls' heads and bodies and also in both the USA and in Europe for various objects such as combs and cutlery handles, but it was brittle and highly inflammable. Celluloid is plant fibre treated with alcohol which is combined with other ingredients and compressed hydraulically, then moulded into shape by steam or hot air.

The first completely synthetic and relatively efficient plastic was BAKELITE, patented 1907. PVC, polystyrene, acrylic and nylon were adapted to textiles and a wide range of useful wares from the 1930s. In 1942, Earl Tupper introduced cheap plastic domestic ware in the USA, but not until the 1960s were plastics widely used for furniture.

plate A term for articles made of gold or silver for ceremonial use – particularly in church – or for domestic purposes. Not to be confused with silver or gold-plated wares such as SHEFFIELD PLATE and ELECTROPLATE.

plate armour Overlapping metal plates, usually hand-beaten and joined by rivets or leather straps, worn as protection against weapons.

plateau Oval or circular plate or stand made of silver with a reflective glass or mirror surface, which was used as a platform for an EPERGNE, candelabrum or other elaborate table-centre decoration in the late 18th and 19th centuries. See p.246.

plate bucket A straight-sided, metal-hooped wooden pail, sometimes with a lining of metal, and about 1-1½ ft (30-45 cm) deep. The buckets were

PLATE BUCKET; *c.1760; 14 in (35.5 cm) diameter. The slot in the side eases removal of plates.*

used for carrying dirty plates from the dining room and have a vertical slot to allow easy removal of the contents. Sometimes the slot was later blocked up so that the pail could be used as a wastepaper basket.

plate camera A camera which records an image on a light-sensitive plate of glass. See p.294.

plate-warmer Metal or wooden stand for holding plates before an open fire, used in the 18th and 19th centuries. Plate-warmers vary in shape but often form a tripod. One type, known as a **cat**, comprises three crossed rods.

platinum Valuable, rare and untarnishable, silvery-white metal – harder, stronger and with a higher melting point than gold. Platinum was first used to make jewellery in South America from the 15thC, both in its pure form and mixed with gold. It only appeared in Europe as a decorative medium in the mid-19thC when the oxy-hydrogen blowpipe made it possible to melt the metal for crafting. It is often used in settings for diamonds or other stones, either pure or in the form of an alloy, usually with iridium. To be hallmarked, the metal must be at least 95 per cent platinum.

plique-à-jour A technique similar to cloisonné ENAMELLING that produces a translucent stained-glass effect. Wire is soldered onto a metal base, or former, to form cells which are then filled with translucent enamel colours. After firing, the base is dissolved away to leave a coloured, glass-like shell. Until the 19thC, the method was used mainly in Russia and Scandinavia, for ornamental tableware, but in the late 19thC it became popular with French and British jewellers, especially those working in ART NOUVEAU style. The Japanese developed a similar technique for vases and bowls c.1900 using molten glass instead of enamels. See p.263.

plum Hard, heavy, yellow to brown fruitwood used for the TURNED work on 16th and 17thC COUNTRY FURNITURE and INLAID DECORATION.

plumbago A type of MINIATURE popular in the late 17thC which was drawn in plumbago, or graphite – the soft, steel-grey to black form of carbon used in lead pencils. Plumbagos are usually larger than other portrait miniatures – around 4-6 in (10-15 cm) high as opposed to 2-3 in (50-75 mm).

plush Fabric similar to VELVET but coarser and with a longer pile, sometimes called 'poor man's velvet'. Hard-wearing wool plush has been used for upholstery since at least the 18thC, but in the 19thC was especially popular for table coverings and curtains. High-grade plush was woven from silk, cotton or a combination of both. In the 20thC plush was used for teddy-bear fur. See p.357.

Plymouth The Devon town where, in 1768, Britain's first hard-paste PORCELAIN was made under pottery owner William COOKWORTHY. Production was moved to BRISTOL two years later.

2

1768-70

plywood Wood composite made of at least three layers, or plies, of wood VENEER glued together under pressure. The grain of each sheet is laid at right angles to that of the layers above and beneath to increase strength and prevent warping.

Plywood was used in 18thC furniture-making, but its potential was only fully explored by BEIDERMEIER craftsmen and the Vienna furniture-makers THONET in the 19thC for making BENTWOOD furniture. During the 1920s and 30s plywood became a 'natural look' alternative or addition to tubular steel, and was used by designers such as Alvar AALTO, Gerrit RIETVELD and Marcel BREUER.

pocket bottle See FLASK.

pocket watch General term for a portable timekeeper carried in the pocket, first made in the mid to late 16thC. Earlier watches had been worn hanging on a chain around the neck. Pocket watches were replaced by wristwatches from the 1920s. See also HUNTER-CASED WATCH and p.288.

pointillé Technique for decorating leather with impressed gold dots used in bookbinding from the 17thC.

point de Venise, point d'Angleterre See LACE.

poker work Means of decorating woodwork, using a hot tool to burn patterns into a surface, practised since at least the early 17thC in Italy. It was particularly popular during the Victorian period in Britain and during the ARTS AND CRAFTS MOVEMENT which encouraged home crafts. It also appears on COTTAGE-STYLE furniture of the early 20thC.

polearms Long-staffed weapons with a blade used for cutting or thrusting. They include the earliest spears and pikes, the half-moon-bladed **gisarme** used until the 1500s, the **partisan**, with its long, tapered blade, used from the mid-14thC, the **halberd**, **glaive** and **poleaxe** or **ravensbill**. Polearms became redundant on the battlefield with the advent of gunpowder, but many survived as parade arms and emblems of rank. The **spontoon**, for example, was carried by British Royal Artillery sergeants until 1845, the boarding pike still used by navies until the early 20thC, and a 19thC fashion for ceremonial polearms resulted in a new wave of manufacture.

Halberds and partisans are still carried today by the Yeoman Wardens of the Tower of London, and the Swiss Guards of the Vatican.

pole screen A small adjustable screen mounted on a pole designed to shield a lady's face from the heat of the fire. Another type of adjustable pole screen is the **banner screen**, with a panel of needlework or painted wood hanging from a horizontal bar which can be raised or lowered on a vertical pole of wood or metal.

A **writing firescreen** combines writing table and firescreen. Some are in the form of a slim writing desk with a drop front above a cupboard, and supported on raised feet so that the furniture piece itself formed the screen; a gap at floor level allowed heat to reach the writer's feet. A simpler version is a table fitted with a sliding screen of pleated silk at the back. Both types were introduced during the late 18thC. See p.144.

poleyn See ARMOUR.

pomander Small, spherical or apple-shaped container with a pierced lid used to carry aromatic herbs. Pomanders were originally worn around the neck or wrist as a means of guarding against odours, and have been known by this name since the 16thC. See also VINAIGRETTE.

pommel See SWORD.

Pomona glass Frosted ART GLASS developed in 1885 in the USA. Clear glass was blown into a mould and when the object cooled the surface was acid-ENGRAVED to create the frosted appearance. The surface was then stained amber or rose and decorated with painted fruits and flowers. Pomona glass is mainly seen in the form of decorative tablewares.

Pompeiian See ETRUSCAN STYLE.

Ponti, Gio (1891-1979) Italian designer-architect and founder of the Italian architecture and design magazine *Domus* (1927).

Ponti designed furniture, notably his 'Superleggera chair' which became a familiar sight in Italian restaurants. The designer is also known for his ART DECO-style ceramics and silverware, and light domestic goods ranging from door handles to coffee machines and cutlery and bathroom fittings.

GIO PONTI's *Superleggera chair with rush seat; 1957. The design was inspired by an Italian fisherman's chair.*

pontil mark Circular mark on the bottom of a glass object left by the pontil, the iron rod to which the glass is attached for the final stages of shaping. On early glassware the mark was left rough, or pushed upwards to make a KICK, but this was also done on forgeries. A pontil mark or **punty**, is no proof a piece was handmade, as it is seen on some PRESSED GLASS.

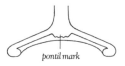

pontil mark

THE PONTIL MARK *shows where the molten glass was attached to a rod-like carrying iron during shaping.*

Pontypool ware 18thC tin-plated ironware with a JAPANNED finish. The objects, which include trays, vases and boxes, are richly decorated with flowers or country scenes and gilding. Thomas Allgood and his sons produced the ware at Pontypool, South Wales, using a coal-based varnish and applying it in many coats with firing between each – a long process that made the products expensive. Similar but lower-quality items made in Birmingham and elsewhere are often wrongly called Pontypool ware.

Poole Pottery ART POTTERY studio in Poole, Dorset, producing hand-decorated earthenware and stoneware, established 1921. It was founded by potters John and Truda Adams, designer Harold Stabler and ornamental pottery manufacturer Owen Carter of the Dorset tile company Carter & Co. The pottery produced bold, simple-shaped vases, jugs and candlesticks, decorated with lively colours and a characteristic matt glaze developed by Carter. From 1963 the company traded as Poole Pottery.

poplar A hardwood produced by a genus of trees native to Britain. It is creamy-white to yellow or grey in colour with a close grain. It is liable to shrinkage and unsuitable for CABINET-WORK, but is seen in late 16th and early 17thC INLAID DECORATION and in some late 17thC MARQUETRY.

poplin Plain style of woven fabric, used for soft furnishings, in which the WEFT passes in turn under and over the WARP, as in darning. However, the wefts are fewer and thicker than the warps, giving the fabric a ribbed finish. Any type or mix of yarn – wool, silk, cotton, for example – can be woven in this way, but the original had silk warp and wool weft and was made at Avignon in France, for a time the seat of popes (1377-1408), hence its original name *papeline* (papal).

porcelain True or hard-paste porcelain is a white, translucent material, non-porous, strong and heat-resistant. The secret of its manufacture lies in the essential ingredients of CHINA CLAY and CHINA STONE particles which fuse at high temperatures, binding the clay into an impermeable paste. See p.150.

Hard-paste porcelain was produced in China from about the 8thC, but not achieved in the West until the 18thC as the ingredients were unknown. MEISSEN was the first European factory to succeed, c.1708, and by the middle of the century Austrian, Italian and other German factories were also in production, using German clay.

The first British hard-paste porcelain was made at PLYMOUTH in 1768, following the discovery of Cornish china clay. True porcelain cannot be marked easily with a file; its glaze is thin, and enamelled colours can be felt slightly above the surface.

Soft-paste or **imitation porcelain** attempted to reproduce the quality and appearance of the true porcelain made in China without access to the same ingredients. It is a mixture of white clay and other ingredients, such as ground bones, flint, glass, SOAPSTONE and china stone. Unlike true porcelain, the surface can be marked with a file, the glaze is coarser, less glittering, and sometimes uneven, and the enamelled colours sink into the surface, sometimes completely. Soft-paste porcelain was first made in Europe for the MEDICI family in 16thC Italy. In the early 18thC it was produced by SÈVRES and other French factories and, c.1745, by CHELSEA and Bow in Britain.

BONE CHINA, a variation of hard-paste which contains bone ash, was introduced in 1794 and used for tea and coffee services and other tableware. See p.157.

porringer Small bowl or cup with or without a lid and a single or pair of tab (or flat) handles, set horizontally. The term is derived from 'pottager', a vessel for pottage or stew.

Porringers were made throughout the 17th and 18th centuries, in silver, pewter and DELFTWARE, and revived in the late 19thC. The Americans use the term to describe a shallow, one-handled BLEEDING BOWL. See BARBER'S BOWL.

PORRINGER; *silver 18thC; 6½ in (16.5 cm) diameter.*

porter's chair Hooded armchair with high back and wings and leather upholstery, for the porter or page boy to sit in. The chairs were popular in the GEORGIAN period.

PORTER'S CHAIR *with leather upholstery; 65 in (1.65 m) high. The cupboard under the seat is a common feature.*

portfolio table or **stand** Item of drawing room or library furniture designed for the display of artwork. The 18thC version was simply a small easel, like a bookrest, that stood on a table. In the 19thC, when Victorian homes had pretensions to artistic taste, a **folio stand** was a familiar sight; it is a small table with an adjustable top; a stand with two slatted panels hinged on one side forming a 'V' which could be opened on a ratchet to take more folios; or incorporated into a music CANTERBURY.

Portland Vase Blue and white CAMEO GLASS vase dating from about the 1stC Roman Empire, once owned by the Duchess of Portland, and now in the British Museum. WEDGWOOD made copies in JASPERWARE. The best glass replica was made by John NORTHWOOD in 1876. See p.222.

portrait doll See CHARACTER DOLL.

posset pot Two-handled, 17th to early 18th-century cup used for holding posset – a hot, spicy milk drink curdled with ale or wine. Posset pots were usually lidded, and spouted versions were made in order to draw off the liquid from below, avoiding the floating ingredients. Posset gave way to punch in the second half of the 18thC. The pots are found in SLIP-WARE and DELFTWARE, and in ornamental glass and silver.

posted-frame movement A clock movement, also known as a **birdcage movement**, which is held in a cage formed by four corner posts as opposed to one held by front and back plates. It was universally used in the earliest mechanical clocks, and usually in non-portable clocks to c.1650, in LANTERN CLOCKS to c.1800 and in TURRET CLOCKS to c.1850.

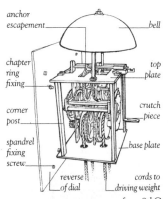

anchor escapement — bell

chapter ring fixing — top plate

corner post — crutch piece

spandrel fixing screw — base plate

reverse of dial — cords to driving weight

POSTED-FRAME MOVEMENT *of an 18thC provincial English longcase clock.*

Post-Modernism 1970s and 80s reaction against the rationalism and functionalism of MODERNISM. It is either of two trends: one which reverts to more traditional, formal, even Classical approaches; the other seeks to go beyond art, form and meaning altogether, and favours works which are anarchic, outrageous or transitory. Post-modernism is closely identified with radical Italian design groups, including **Archizoom, Studio Alchymia** and **Memphis**.

potato ring See DISH RING.

potichomania The 19thC fashion for decorating glass so that it resembles porcelain. Prints were glued to the inside of glass vases which were then overglazed in white.

pot lids Decorative lids, originally for shallow, circular pots containing bear's grease (used as a men's hair dressing), toothpastes, potted savoury pastes or relishes. They were a speciality of F. & R. Pratt, a Staffordshire pottery (see PRATTWARE) 1846-80, and were typically decorated with TRANSFER-PRINTED landscapes, portraits, buildings or reproduction paintings. The bases are usually plain and have no bearing on the value of the lid, the scarcity of the print being the major factor.

potpourri A mixture of flower petals and spices, or their essences, used for scenting the air. Potpourri containers were popular from the mid-18thC and made in silver or pottery.

pottery 1 General term covering items made from any ceramic material, that is, anything made of clay. **2** Specific term referring only to items made from either EARTHENWARE or STONEWARE. See p.149.

pottery marks Identification marks on ceramics, which may include details such as pattern name, initials or symbols of manufacturer and craftsmen, and dates of manufacture or establishment of factory. They are usually found on the underside of the piece, but are occasionally incorporated into the decoration itself. Pottery marks are not reliable indicators of origin as forgery has been rife, especially during the 18thC. See Chinese REIGN MARKS.

pouffe Term introduced in Victorian times for a low, upholstered OTTOMAN or a large, solidly stuffed, frameless footrest that is also large enough to be used as a seat.

pounce 1 The process of making a design on the reverse side of silver or other metal to make a pattern of small relief dots; see EMBOSSING. The result is referred to as **pouncework**. **2** A fine powder which was rubbed into parchment to slightly roughen it for writing and make it receptive to ink. Pounce was also used before the invention of blotting paper in the 18thC to dry the ink. It was sprinkled from a small **pounce pot** or **pounce box** which had a perforated cover.

Pounce was also sprinkled through a perforated paper pattern to reproduce a design on fabric or ceramic which was placed beneath.

POUNCE POT *from a silver inkstand; 1738; 2¼ in (57 mm) high.*

pound 1 British currency with a face value of 20s (100p), first struck in the form of gold coins in the reign of Queen Elizabeth I. Silver pounds appeared during the Civil War (1640s); the first £1 banknotes were issued as an emergency measure by the Bank of England between 1797 and 1826 but were not commonly seen until the introduction of the Treasury £1 note in 1914. The present £1 coins were issued in 1983. **2** Unit of weight. See TROY WEIGHT.

poupard Small carved wooden doll, made throughout Europe from the late 17thC. Simple versions are carved in one piece, and represent a baby in swaddling clothes. Later dolls have separately made limbs attached to a turned body and head, and are often found in family, farm, village or Noah's ark groups. Poupards with a musical movement, triggered when the doll is twirled, are also called **marottes**.

POUPARD; *c.1910;*
13 in (33 cm) high.

powder-blue Cobalt-blue ground colour applied to ceramics in powdered form, prior to glazing. In China the blue powder was blown on through a bamboo tube with a piece of silk over the end to diffuse the powder. This insufflation technique was copied at MEISSEN in the first half of the 18thC, at Bow, WORCESTER, LOWESTOFT and CAUGHLEY in Britain, and at SÈVRES in France (where it was known as **bleu soufflé**). WEDGWOOD imitated the effect on BONE CHINA by stippling the freshly painted surface with a fine-grained sponge.

powder-decorated glass British ART GLASS developed by John Davenport in 1806. The process involved applying a paste of powdered glass to an object and scraping a design into it with a pointed tool. The design, often inspired by sport or heraldry, was then fused onto the glass.

Powolny, Michael (1871-1954) Austrian potter, a founder in 1905 of the Wiener Keramik (Vienna Ceramic) workshop which was closely linked with the VIENNA SECESSION and WIENER WERKSTÄTTE. Powolny made figures with simple lines and a cubist style of decoration, mainly in black on white. His later pieces include stoneware animal figures with rich coloured glazes.

Prattware CREAMWARE or pearlware ceramic body decorated in a distinctive group of inglaze colours associated with, but not limited to, the Staffordshire family of Pratt, c.1789-1820. The glazes in green, yellow, black, ochre and blue, are seen on many commemorative wares of the Napoleonic Wars. See p.198.

praxinoscope Optical toy popular in Victorian times, which consists of a cylindrical or polygonal box, open at the top, with a series of pictures arranged along the inside. Mirrors inside the box reflect the images of the pictures. When the box is rotated the reflections blend together giving an illusion of movement. See p.295.

prayer rug Term applied to any Oriental rug with a MIHRAB – the stylised representation of the Mecca-facing prayer niche inside a mosque – as the prominent motif. The rugs were often used as wall-hangings. See SAF.

precious stone Term limited to diamonds, emeralds, rubies and sapphires; pearls are also usually included. Other gemstones are generally termed semiprecious. The value of precious stones depends on rarity, size and quality, and on workmanship, such as FACETING.

precision clock Timepiece for accurate timekeeping rather than decoration, such as a REGULATOR or marine CHRONOMETER. Those with finely cut wheels and pinions to reduce friction were made from the second quarter of the 18thC.

Pre-Raphaelites Group of artists who set up the Pre-Raphaelite Brotherhood in order to evoke the style and spirit of Italian painting prior to Raphael. The society, which included Dante Gabriel Rossetti, Holman Hunt, John Everett Millais and others, was short-lived (1848-52) but had a lasting influence.

press Tall cupboard used for storing linen and clothes, typically with two doors enclosing shelves, mounted on a base containing drawers. It was a familiar household item from the 17th to the 19th centuries. See p.139.

press bed See BUREAU BED.

pressed glass Glassware made by pressing molten glass into a patterned iron mould. The technique was in widespread use from the mid-1820s in the USA and from the 1830s in Europe, and speeded up the mass manufacture of household wares. It was often used to make cheap reproductions of CUT GLASS but can be distinguished by the lack of sharp edges. See p.226.

press-moulding A means of creating ceramic shapes, mainly figures, using plaster moulds. Clay or PORCELAIN paste is pressed by hand into a mould, left to harden and shrink and then freed. The technique was already in use in China during the Tang Dynasty (618-906), for making animal and human figures for furnishing tombs.

During the early 18thC the method was used in Europe to make the small relief ornamentation which was applied, or SPRIGGED, onto the main body with a liquid clay SLIP before firing. Dishes with ridged or incised decoration were made by pressing the clay onto convex moulds with the patterns cut into them, and parts of figures could be press-moulded and later joined together with slip.

pricking Decoration formed by pinprick marks forming initials, dates or other inscriptions on metalware. It was less skilled and cheaper than engraving, and practised mainly in the 16th and 17th centuries.

prie-dieu 1 A low-seated, upholstered chair with a high, straight back, popular in Victorian times, also known as a **praying chair**. The chairs, used for both praying and sitting, were well-suited for women's voluminous skirts of the period. See p.105. **2** Desk with a low platform on which to kneel in prayer and a shelf on which to put devotional books, in use from medieval times. See p.105.

princewood See ROSEWOOD.

print A design or picture transferred from an engraved plate, woodblock, lithographic stone, or other medium. In printing processes such as etching, line ENGRAVING, AQUATINT and MEZZOTINT, the design to be printed is cut into a ground such as a metal plate; when ink is applied it collects in the cut parts. In relief processes the ground is cut away around the area to be printed leaving a raised surface, as in a WOODCUT. In a lithographic process the ink is held on a flat, water-repellant surface. See p.332.

printie See CUT GLASS.

press bed See BUREAU BED.

prismatic cutting CUT GLASS pattern, developed in the 19thC and made using a disc with a V-shaped edge to cut close-set horizontal, or vertical, grooves. The resulting sharp ridges act as prisms, twinkling in the light.

projection clock Early 19thC development of the NIGHT CLOCK produced in Britain and on the Continent. A lantern, housed inside a bronze or tin-plate clock case, threw an image of the clock dial and hands onto the facing wall.

proof A coin carefully struck from specially prepared DIES on a pre-polished BLANK, resulting in a coin of superior quality and finish.

proof marks Stamped marks indicating that a gun barrel has been tested and found to be safe. See RIFLE.

provenance mark A mark denoting the origin of the metal from which a coin is made. It may be lettering, such as 'EIC', on a coin struck from gold imported by the East India Company, or a symbol, such as the Prince of Wales's feathers on a coin struck from Welsh silver. See GUINEA.

prunt Decorative blob of glass, applied to a glass object, either randomly or in patterns. Prunts featured on Italian, German and British glassware from the 16th to 19th centuries. They may be pointed or globular, raspberry-shaped or impressed with a lion's head.

PRUNTS *on an early 16thC German vessel; 3⅓ in (84 mm) high.*

psyche See CHEVAL MIRROR.

puff box Covered container deep enough to hold face powder and a powder puff, often part of a lady's dressing-table set or toilet service.

Puff boxes are usually round in shape and made of silver, glass and porcelain; some examples have a hinged lid fitted with a mirror. They date from mid-19thC.

Pugin, Augustus (1812-52) English architect, designer and leading figure of the early Victorian revival of 14thC GOTHIC style. See p.54.

Puiforcat, Jean (1897-1945) French silversmith who exhibited at the 1925 Paris EXPOSITION DES ARTS DÉCORATIFS. His early ART DECO-style pieces are streamlined with geometrical decoration, but his work after the 1920s, such as tea services and soup tureens, is functional, almost without ornament and with a smooth, hand-produced finish.

pump pot See SELF-POURING TEAPOT.

punched work Style of decoration on metalware, common in the 16th and 17th centuries and popular again in the 19thC. It is made by tapping a blunt-ended punch into the surface and making several indentations in rows or clusters. See p.235.

punch glass In the 19thC, a stemless, cup-shaped glass with a handle, for drinking punch and sometimes part of a set with a punchbowl.

punch pot Silver or ceramic pot, like an oversized teapot, usually with a globular curved spout and handle. The pots were made in the mid-18thC for brewing and serving punch. Some rest on a stand. See p.249.

punty See PONTIL.

purdonium Box-shaped coal scuttle, often of JAPANNED wood or metal, named after the Mr Purdon who either devised it, or was the first person to have one, in the mid-19thC. The coal is held in an inner box (which is removed for filling). A small shovel is held in a slot on the back of the box. Some purdoniums have padded tops.

PURDONIUM *of walnut with brass detail; c.1880; 11½ in (29.2 cm) wide.*

Puritan style Plain, utilitarian, yet often elegant style, also called **Commonwealth** or **Cromwellian**, prevailing in England after the execution of Charles I and the abolition of the monarchy in 1649.

Luxury and ornament were avoided in furniture, tableware and dress. Furniture in typical Puritan style was straight-lined with decoration limited to minimal TURNING or

carving on the legs. The style was abandoned with the restoration of Charles II in 1660. See p.21.

purl Coiled, gold or silver coloured wire often tinted in shades of blue or green, used to form foliage on 17thC embroidered pictures. The hollow wire was coiled by winding it tightly around a thin rod, then cut into short pieces. These were then sewn in place like beads.

purpleheart Tropical hardwood from Central and South America which is naturally brown and is a purplish colour when freshly cut. It has an open grain and smooth texture and was used mainly for VENEER BANDING and INLAID DECORATION in the 18thC.

putai See BUDAI.

putto A nude boy, cherub or winged boy's head portrayed in garden statuary, sculpture, painting and ornamentation from the 15thC.

puzzle jug Jug with several spouts and holes pierced in its neck, designed to make both pouring and drinking without spillage virtually impossible. The liquid is drunk by sucking a nozzle connected to a hidden tube. Puzzle jugs were popular throughout Europe from the 17th to 19th centuries, and made in EARTHENWARE and STONEWARE. See p.204.

PUZZLE JUG; *delftware; c.1730; 9½ in (24.1 cm) high.*

Pyrex Trade name of a type of glass that withstands heat-shock, first made in 1912 to prevent railway workers' lanterns from shattering when the lamps were lit in cold conditions, and today identified as a future collectable. The glass, toughened by its high borax content, was developed in the USA by the CORNING GLASS WORKS.

pyrope See GARNET.

Pyx, Trial of the Periodical monitoring of the weight and purity of coins and coinage metal. From early times the coins for sampling have been stored in a sealed box called the 'pyx', a practice which continues today.

qingbai See YINGQING.

Qing dynasty The last of the Chinese dynasties, sometimes spelt **Ch'ing**, which replaced the MING DYNASTY in 1644, although it was not consolidated until the 1680s during the reign of the Emperor Kangxi (1662-1722). It ended in 1912. During the Qing dynasty, FAMILLE-verte and famille-rose palettes were established, porcelain production reached its height of delicacy and Ming BLUE AND WHITE wares were copied. Trade with the West peaked towards the end of the 18thC, but exported blue and white deteriorated in quality, although some fine pieces were made, even in the 19thC. Cloisonné ENAMELS, bronzes, textiles and furniture were all exports via the port of CANTON. See REIGN MARKS.

quadrant Instrument used in navigation for measuring altitude, made up of a quarter-circle of wood or metal marked with a graded scale of angles. From the late 16thC quadrants made of brass, or brass and mahogany, with a pivoted radius, or index arm, came into use.

QUADRANT *with plumb line and bob and stamped with a 90 degree scale; English; brass; mid-17thC; 4 in (10 cm) radius.*

quaich 17th, 18th and 19th-century Scottish drinking vessel, usually made of silver in the form of a shallow bowl with two flat handles. Medieval examples were often made from wooden staves, and some silver vessels were decorated to simulate this effect. Small quaiches were for individual use; larger, ornate varieties were passed around at ceremonies, as with the TYG. See p.247.

Quare, Daniel (1647-1724) English clock-maker whose clocks, watches and barometers contributed to London's rise to supremacy in horology in the late 17th and early 18th centuries. His watches were among the earliest to be fitted with REPEATER mechanisms. Quare was also notable for making LONGCASE CLOCKS,

usually of long duration between windings, and fitted with unusual extras such as a secondary, **equation dial** set into the case which showed the relationship between MEAN TIME and solar time, and BRACKET CLOCKS.

quarrels See CROSSBOW.

quartering Type of VENEERING using four pieces of wood with the same grain pattern to form a surface; each quarter has a pattern that is a mirror image of the one alongside. See p.92.

quartetto tables Set of four small tables, slightly decreasing in size from one table to the next, so that they can be fitted into each other to form a **nest** or used separately. See p.112.

quartz The most common of stones, used for decoration since the Classical period. When free from impurities, it is a colourless rock crystal; other forms most commonly used as gemstones since the 19thC include the AMETHYST in all shades of violet, the CAIRNGORM in yellow and brown, and the yellow CITRINE which is often wrongly referred to as TOPAZ.

The physical properties of quartz are such that when an electric current is passed through a precision-cut piece of quartz it pulsates regularly. This is used in clocks and watches in place of mechanical ESCAPEMENTS to regulate the driving force of an electric battery, resulting in much greater accuracy. The first quartz clock movement was invented by W. A. Morrison of the Bell Laboratories in 1929.

Quartz glass Trade name for crackled-effect ART GLASS developed by the English designer Frederick CARDER for the STEUBEN GLASSWORKS in the USA. A GATHER of molten glass was dipped into cold water, which created a fine network of cracks on the outer surface. The glass was then reheated to fuse the cracks and rolled over powdered glass. The whole was then covered in clear coloured glass. Sometimes the outer surface was treated with acid to give a satin finish.

Queen Anne style Early 18thC British design style that developed principally during the reign of Queen Anne (1702-14). In the late 19thC, a version known as **Queen Anne Revival** emerged in architecture and reproduction furniture. See p.25.

Queen's Ware See CREAMWARE.

quilling TRAILED glass decoration consisting of closely spaced FESTOONS, often used at NAILSEA GLASSHOUSE near Bristol and at ALLOA GLASSWORKS in Scotland.

R

Race, Ernest (1913-64) English textile and furniture designer, whose work combined the traditional with the modern and was internationally acclaimed. He is probably best known for his comfortable and ingenious chairs, such as the 'BA' chair (1947) of cast aluminium. See p.79.

rack clock See GRAVITY CLOCK.

radiogram A combined wireless set and GRAMOPHONE with a single inbuilt loudspeaker, popular in Britain 1930-1960.

raising Technique of making metal HOLLOW-WARE. A flat disc of metal is hammered over an anvil-like stake to gradually raise the sides to the required shape and depth. See p.234.

raku Porous-bodied Japanese pottery coated with a thick lead GLAZE, in colours ranging from dark brown and light red to straw, green and cream. The ware was first made in the 16thC, and being closely associated with the TEA CEREMONY, is still used in Japan today. See p.176.

Ramsden, Omar (1873-1939) Sheffield-born silversmith, associated with the ARTS AND CRAFTS MOVEMENT. Ramsden specialised in the design of silver and gold presentation and ceremonial pieces, including plates, wine cups and MASERS. In 1898, he established a London workshop with silversmith Alwyn Charles Elison Carr, who executed Ramsden's designs. They produced handmade, Arts and Crafts and CELTIC-style objects in silver and other metals such as pewter and wrought iron. Carr left the workshop in 1918 and Ramsden continued producing ART DECO silver.

range tables Sets of identical small tables that can be fitted together to form one large table, made in the late 18th and early 19th centuries.

Raphael ware See ISTORIATO.

rapier A SWORD with a long, narrow, stiff blade designed for thrusting rather than cutting, often with an elaborate HILT and bar or cup to protect the hand. The weapon was popular in the 16th and 17th centuries.

ratafia glass A speciality glass used for drinking ratafia, an almond and fruit liqueur popular from the mid to late 18thC. It is flute shaped and sometimes known as a **flute cordial**.

rate mark A mark on postage stamps indicating the rate of postage to be recovered from the recipient; a device used before the introduction of the fixed rate penny postage in 1840.

rattan See CANEWORK.

ravensbill See POLEARMS.

Ravenscroft, George (1618-81) British glass-maker who in 1673 was employed by the London Glass-Sellers' Company to produce a 'home-grown' rival to Venetian CRISTALLO. Initially his new flint glass was subject to CRIZZLING, but by 1676 he claimed he had overcome this, and was allowed to impress his products with his own seal in the shape of a raven's head. Although the problem was far from resolved – all known sealed pieces have since deteriorated – and Ravenscroft is no longer credited with the invention of LEAD CRYSTAL, he did produce some of the finest vessel-glass of the time. See p.207.

Ravilious, Eric (1903-42) English engraver, ceramics decorator and designer of glassware and furniture. His best-known designs were for WEDGWOOD POTTERY, 1936-9.

raw glazing See GLAZE.

reading chair Chair fitted with a small, adjustable surface on which to rest a book. The bookrest on 18thC examples was attached to the top rail on the back of the chair, and the occupant sat astride the seat, facing backwards. Mid-19thC reading chairs had swivel bookrests and candle brackets fitted to the arms. There are also small tables with adaptations for reading, such as a hinged top that can be angled. A late Victorian version has revolving book trays on a supporting pillar. See p.102.

recoil escapement See ESCAPEMENT.

red spinel See CORUNDUM.

red stoneware Unglazed fine STONEWARE made by adding ground burnt flint to the clay paste for extra hardness. It was produced in the 17thC in YIXING, China, and in the early 18thC by Böttger of MEISSEN in experiments to make porcelain. It was widely used in Staffordshire potteries during the 18thC for vases, teapots and ornaments. Decoration included SPRIGGING in white or black SLIP. A later refinement was WEDGWOOD's ROSSO ANTICO in the 1760s. See p.150.

reeding The converse of FLUTING – a relief decoration of parallel, convex ribs, or reeds. See DECORATIVE MOTIFS.

refectory table The modern term for the predominant table design of the 15th to 17th centuries. Also known as **joined** or **long tables**, they are usually of oak and the top is joined to a fixed frame. Sturdy legs at the corners are linked by STRETCHERS which doubled as footrests to avoid contact with cold stone floors. Refectory tables were common kitchen and farmhouse furniture until the 19thC. See pp.108-9.

regard jewellery 19thC rings and brooches set with gemstones whose initial letter spells out a word. For example 'regard' – Ruby, Emerald, Garnet, Amethyst, Ruby, Diamond. This acrostic theme was also used for personalised jewellery in which the wearer's name was spelt out.

Régence style French style covering the regency of Philippe d'Orléans (1715-23), although evident c.1710-30 – the beginnings of the early GEORGIAN period in Britain. It was lighter and less formal than the preceding LOUIS XIV style, and marked the beginnings of Rococo taste in France.

Regency style General term for several furniture and decorative styles found in Britain c.1800-30. It was named after the Prince Regent (later George IV), who ruled for his father 1811-20, although it was established before and continued for a decade or so after this period. See pp.42-48.

regulator A weight-driven PENDULUM clock with the emphasis on accuracy of timekeeping rather than on ornament. Regulators are usually in the form of a LONGCASE clock, with a temperature compensation facility for the pendulum, a deadbeat ESCAPEMENT, and no striking mechanism. **Workshop regulators** were made by the clock-maker for his own use, to set other clocks by. **Table regulators** are spring-driven with a deadbeat escapement and a **regulator dial** – one with minutes marked on the edge of the main dial and two smaller, separate dials for hours and seconds. See VIENNA REGULATOR and p.279.

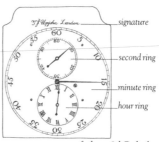

REGULATOR DIAL *of a late 18thC clock; 10 in (25.4 cm) wide.*

Reichsadlerhumpen See HUMPEN.

reign marks Marks in seal or script form on Chinese porcelain, giving the name of the emperor and usually the dynasty. Gradually, it became commonplace to mark a piece not with the current ruler's name, but with an earlier emperor's **nien hao**, or mark. This was sometimes out of respect to a previous period, sometimes to avoid punishment for the prohibited use of the reigning monarch's name on wares not intended for his own use. As a result, 'imitations' far outnumber genuine reign marks. See box opposite.

relief Decoration that projects out from the surrounding surface. The terms **bas**, **medium** and **high relief** refer to the depth of the decoration.

remontoire Any driving force, such as a weight or spring, in a clock or watch that is automatically rewound at regular intervals by the mainspring of the MOVEMENT. This rewinding facility results in a more regular driving force than could be provided by the mainspring itself; it has a similar function to the FUSEE but is more effective. A **remontoire** or **constant force escapement** incorporates a remontoire device to ensure constant force between the escape wheel and the BALANCE.

Renaissance Revival of Classical ideals in European art and literature from the late 14th to early 17th centuries. See p.14.

rent table See DRUM TABLE.

repairer Craftsman responsible for joining the separately cast or moulded parts of a ceramics figure into a complete piece.

repeater A clock or watch with a striking mechanism activated at will, which tells the user the time without his actually having to look at the timepiece. Repeating devices were introduced by British clock-makers in the 1680s and are still being made today. The mechanism is activated by a cord or lever to sound (or 'repeat') the last hour, quarter hour and subsequent minutes, and more rarely the last five minutes.

repoussé A form of CHASING on silver and other metals to provide intricate patterns and to sharpen detail. The technique involves first EMBOSSING (pushing out) the general shapes from the reverse of the piece to create a three-dimensional effect on the outer surface. The *repoussé* (pushed back) element comes in when the finer

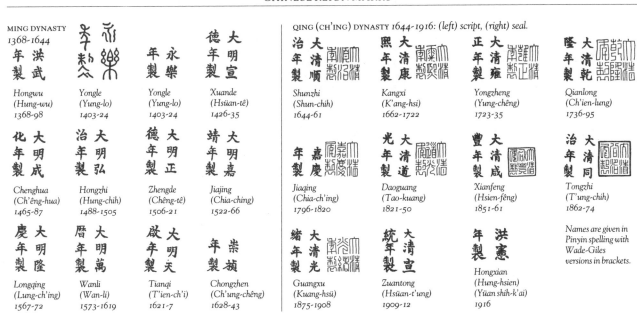

CHINESE REIGN MARKS

MING DYNASTY
1368-1644

Hongwu
(Hung-wu)
1368-98

Yongle
(Yung-lo)
1403-24

Yongle
(Yung-lo)
1403-24

Xuande
(Hsüan-tê)
1426-35

Chenghua
(Ch'êng-hua)
1465-87

Hongzhi
(Hung-chih)
1488-1505

Zhengde
(Chêng-tê)
1506-21

Jiajing
(Chia-ching)
1522-66

Longqing
(Lung-ch'ing)
1567-72

Wanli
(Wan-li)
1573-1619

Tianqi
(T'ien-ch'i)
1621-7

Chongzhen
(Ch'ung-chêng)
1628-43

QING (CH'ING) DYNASTY 1644-1916: (left) script, (right) seal.

Shunzhi
(Shun-chih)
1644-61

Kangxi
(K'ang-hsi)
1662-1722

Yongzheng
(Yung-chêng)
1723-35

Qianlong
(Ch'ien-lung)
1736-95

Jiaqing
(Chia-ch'ing)
1796-1820

Daoguang
(Tao-kuang)
1821-50

Xianfeng
(Hsien-fêng)
1851-61

Tongzhi
(T'ung-chih)
1862-74

Guangxu
(Kuang-hsü)
1875-1908

Zuantong
(Hsüan-t'ung)
1909-12

Hongxian
(Hung-hsien)
(Yüan shih-k'ai)
1916

Names are given in Pinyin spelling with Wade-Giles versions in brackets.

REIGN MARKS *of six characters read (from top right down)* 1 'great', 2 *dynasty*, 3 *Emperor's first name;* (top left down) 4 *Emperor's reign name*, 5-6 *period made.*

---

decorative details are added by selective pushing back of these raised surfaces from the front. The article is laid on – or if hollow, filled with – a firm yet yielding base of pitch and the design POUNCED or hammered in, using a wide variety of punches and other specialist tools to give different effects. Repoussé was used widely on late 16th and 17thC silver, and revived in the 19thC in Britain and elsewhere in Europe. See p.235.

reproduction An honest re-creation of an earlier object, as opposed to a dishonest FORGERY.

reredos See FIREBACK.

reseau See LACE.

reserve 1 An area on a piece of pottery or porcelain that is left free of – or 'reserved' from – ground colour ready for a painted decoration in ENAMEL colours. The slight ridge where the ground ends might be concealed by a painted line, which also frames the design. The term also refers to an area on textiles that is left free of colour or pattern (see BATIK). **2** Minimum price a seller at auction is prepared to accept. See p.419.

resist lustre Metallic decoration, often in silver, applied to glazed pearlware (see CREAMWARE) and other ceramics in Britain from c.1810-30. The design is painted or stencilled in wax, or some other material resistant to the lustre, and then fired.

Restauration style An adaptation of the French EMPIRE style from the time of the post-Revolution restoration to the throne of the French monarchy, 1815-30. Decorative wares became more brightly coloured and **bois clair** furniture, made of light-coloured woods (also known as **style duchesse de Berry**), was fashionable.

Restoration style Furniture style linked with Charles II's reign, from the time of his restoration to the British throne (1660) until his death in 1685, or sometimes to the end of the 17thC. See p.26.

reticello glass See LATTICINO.

reticulated Pierced, interlaced or interwoven to form a net or web-like pattern. In glassware this is achieved by: engraving or cutting; by the LATTICINO technique; undercutting an OPENWORK net (see CAGE-WORK); pincering strands of glass to form a basket-weave effect; or by covering glass with, or blowing it into, a wire netting (**netted glassware**). In ceramics and silver, see PIERCED DECORATION.

reverse See OBVERSE.

reverse painting See MIRROR PAINTING.

revolver Firearm with a turning cylinder that holds several cartridges. Although some examples were produced earlier, the weapon only became common from the mid-19thC.

revolving chair Chair with a swivel seat. Revolving chairs existed as early as the 16thC, and adjustable-height music stools were introduced in the late 18thC. A revolving comb-back WINDSOR CHAIR was developed in the 1770s, and in the mid-19thC in the USA a successful prototype with an adjustable back set the pattern for the next century. British versions were at first designed principally for invalids, but by the end of the 19thC had become desirable office furniture.

rhinestone 1 A colourless quartz much used by 19thC jewellers. **2** Term often used c.1900 for multicoloured glass stones. **3** Modern term for any coloured glass PASTE.

rhodium A hard, durable silvery-white metallic element which is used to form high-temperature alloys with PLATINUM or plated onto other metals. Many Victorian silver or gold brooches have been 'modernised' – and ruined – by rhodium plating to make them look like platinum.

ricasso See SWORD.

rice-grain Decoration used on Oriental porcelain from the 12thC, but particularly found in 18thC and modern Chinese wares. The effect of see-through 'grains' is created by making holes in the body of the pot before glazing and firing. Sometimes grains of rice were pressed into the vessel walls. On firing, these burned off, and the glaze flooded the holes.

Richardsons Glass-makers based at Wordsley near STOURBRIDGE 1829-1930. By the 1840s, the firm was an important producer of CASED, TRANSFER-PRINTED, and CUT GLASS, and in the 1860s pioneered new ENGRAVING machines for complex patterns. They were one of the first firms to produce CAMEO GLASS successfully in the 1870s. The firm was finally taken over by THOMAS WEBB & SONS in 1930.

Ridgway, Job (1759-1813) English potter who worked at SWANSEA and LEEDS potteries before establishing a factory at Hanley, Staffordshire, in 1794 with his brother George (c.1758-1823). The factory relocated to Shelton in 1802 and produced STONE CHINA and PORCELAIN. His sons, John (1785-1860) and William (1788-1864), continued running the factory upon his death and produced BONE CHINA tableware, garden statuary and BLUE AND WHITE ware.

Rie, Lucie (b.1902) Austrian-born art potter (see p.184) who moved to Britain in 1939 and was influenced by Bernard LEACH. Rie's elegant and functional STONEWARE and PORCELAIN, often conical or trumpet-shaped in form, are covered in either a very plain GLAZE, or in a bubbly thick glaze of almost volcanic appearance, heightened by the use of iron oxides. The thick glazes are not unlike those of Hans COPER, with whom she shared a studio for many years. See p.185.

Riesener, Jean-Henri (1734-1806) Among the best known and most versatile of all French furniture-makers. German-born Riesener was appointed ÉBÉNISTE to Louis XVI in 1774. He used gilt-bronze MOUNTS and MARQUETRY extensively as decoration. Riesener continued working through the French Revolution, removing all royal emblems from pieces of furniture, until 1801.

Rietveld, Gerrit (1888-1964) Dutch architect-designer, the son of a joiner, who abandoned traditional methods of joinery in his furniture designs. His furniture is characteristic of the DE STIJL group, the Dutch artists' association which he joined in 1919, resulting in pieces that are starkly geometric in line, rather like abstract sculptures. Natural wood surfaces are invariably painted in primary colours, the construction is deliberately left exposed, and sections are screwed together rather than joined. Following the worldwide economic depression of the 1930s, Rietveld designed inexpensive furniture typified by his crate chair, using simply cut sections of packing-case wood.

rifle A firearm developed from the 15thC with a barrel which has spiral grooves cut into the bore – the rifling. This causes the bullet to spin, resulting in greater stability of flight and accuracy. See p.406.

rocking chair Chair resting on curved runners (known as bends) connected to the front and back feet. Rocking chairs were introduced in the USA and Britain in the 1760s, but it was the Americans, whose attitudes and tastes were more relaxed than those of the Georgians and Victorians, who led rocking-chair fashions over the next century. See box below.

Rockingham A Yorkshire pottery and porcelain factory on the estate of the Marquis of Rockingham, 1745-1842. It produced earthenware similar to that at LEEDS and some with a treacle-like glaze, including the lidless CADOGAN teapot. From 1826, Rockingham made fine-quality BONE CHINA tea and DESSERT SERVICES, vases, and well-modelled animals and figures. During the 1830s, extravagant floral decoration appeared particularly on ornamental ware.

1830 on

Rococo European decorative style, a development of BAROQUE, in the 1730s. Rococo is characterised by curving, asymmetrical motifs based on rock, shell, floral, leaf and other natural shapes. Chinese and Indian motifs are also common. Delicate carving emphasises the curving lines of furniture, and frames are swirling and elegant. The name 'Rococo' is derived from the French words *rocaille* (rockwork) and *coquillage* (shellwork). The style reached its peak in Britain *c*.1740s and 50s, and was revived again in Britain and the USA in the early to mid-19thC. See p.34.

rod Thin stick of glass of a single colour. It is made by rolling a small GATHER of molten glass on a MARVER and then stretching it to the desired thinness. Rods may be moulded to give different shapes in cross-section (stars, hexagons, etc) but they are generally used in cylindrical form. Rods may be arranged in a pattern and fused together to make CANES, cross-sections of which are used in MILLEFIORI and MOSAIC objects.

Roentgen, David (1743-1807) German furniture-maker of the 18thC who specialised in sumptuous pieces,

the earliest decorated with pictorial MARQUETRY. He also used many mechanical devices in his furniture, such as built-in clocks and concealed drawers. Roentgen supplied furniture to both the French and Russian royal families, but was ruined by the French Revolution of 1789-99.

Rolex Watch company founded in London in 1905 by Swiss watchmaker Hans Wilsdorf (*c*.1881-1960). The company moved to Geneva in 1920. Rolex launched the 'Oyster' range of watches in 1926, and the 'Prince' range in the 1930s. See p.289.

rolled gold A form of gold plating in which very thin sheets of gold – of any CARAT value – are fused at a high temperature to a base metal such as copper and then rolled to form a sheet of the required thickness, maintaining a uniform layer of gold throughout. Rolled-gold wire is made by enclosing a base-metal core within a rolled-gold tube and drawing out to the required degree of fineness. The process was introduced in the early 19thC, and applied to ÉTUIS and inexpensive jewellery. See p.265.

rolled paper work A late 18th and early 19th-century decorative technique which used tightly rolled strips of paper or card glued onto boxes, tea caddies and other small objects to form patterns.

Rollos, Philip (*fl*.1697-1721) London-based HUGUENOT silversmith who produced very large, ornate silverware incorporating much CUT-CARD work, GADROONING and CAST figurative decoration from 1705. He was commissioned by British royalty, and made pieces for the general market.

Römer A German wide-bowled, green-tinted drinking glass with a thick hollow stem often decorated with PRUNTS, atop a coiled foot. It was developed in the late 15th to early 16th centuries, but reached the height of its popularity from the late 17thC to *c*.1825 and was widely copied throughout Europe. It was the glass from which the British RUMMER eventually evolved.

rose cut See JEWEL CUTTING.

rose medallion See CANTON.

Rosenthal German manufacturer of porcelain tablewares, founded 1879 and still one of Germany's largest porcelain producers. See p.188.

rosewood Heavy, durable tropical hardwood, very dark brown with a rippled grain of near-black running

through. The name comes from the fragrance released when the wood is cut. Rosewood was used for INLAID DECORATION in the 17thC, and as a veneer from the 18thC, but usually for small panels and for decorative BANDING. It was little used for the main body of a piece of furniture until the early 19thC. See p.91.

A related species first imported to Britain from Brazil in the late 17thC is **kingwood** or **princewood**. It is rich deep brown but with purplish tones that give it the alternative name of **violet wood**. Kingwood was used as a veneer, for PARQUETRY and cross-banding, and was particularly popular in France. See TULIPWOOD.

rosso antico 1 A type of red marble. **2** Red STONEWARE made from *c*. 1770 at the WEDGWOOD factory. See p.168.

Rouen One of the first French centres, during the 16thC, for the production of TIN-GLAZED EARTHENWARE in the Italian MAIOLICA tradition. This evolved into French FAIENCE, for which Rouen was the most influential centre by the close of the 17thC. Distinctive decorative styles were developed, including the formal, embroidery-like LAMBREQUIN (see DECORATIVE MOTIFS), borders and *style rayonnant*. Tableware, ewers and other vessels at this time reflect the shapes found in silverware; they are BLUE AND WHITE, but the occasional touch of red was also used during the early 18thC.

By the 1720s, the full range of HIGH TEMPERATURE COLOURS was used for Chinese-style designs in FAMILLE-VERTE colours, and from 1740 Rococo-style garlands and shells framing pastoral scenes were dominant. Enamel colours were introduced in the 1770s in a bid to imitate porcelain decoration, but by the end of the century the industry was in decline due to competition from English CREAMWARE.

Royal Dux Bohemian porcelain factory founded 1860 in Dux (now Duchov,) noted for its JUGENDSTIL decorative ware, much of which was exported to the USA. Typical of Dux ware are figures of water nymphs on shells, **Amphora ware** – vases often with handles in the form of sinuous female figures – busts, wall plaques and tiles.

1860

Rozenburg Pottery and porcelain factory founded 1883 near The Hague, Holland. The most notable early products are a kind of updated DELFT-style – blue and white ware with abstract decoration. The introduction of a fine EGGSHELL

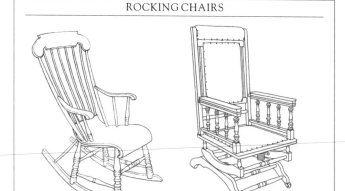

ROCKING CHAIRS

BOSTON ROCKING CHAIR *with rolled arms and seat in careful proportion to the bends; c.1830.*

SWING OR PLATFORM ROCKER; *c.1900. This chair rocks on a fixed base to which it is attached by springs.*

earthenware in 1889 set the Rozenburg factory apart from its contemporaries.

Shapes of Rozenburg pieces are distinctive too, with attenuated AMPHORA-like vases and clean, simple lines moving from curved to flat planes. Decoration was inspired by Javanese BATIK designs; it included flowers, birds and foliage and was executed in fresh OVERGLAZE colours.

ruby See CORUNDUM.

ruby glass Glass containing copper oxide, or occasionally gold oxide, to give a rich, brilliant red colour, much used for decorative vases and jugs. The technique for its manufacture was invented in the 17thC and is still used today. See p.220.

rug In Britain and other parts of Europe, a piece of carpet that is small enough to hang on a wall, or that measures up to 6 ft (1.8 m) long; anything larger than this is classified as a carpet. In practice the terms are almost interchangeable.

Ruhlmann, Emile-Jacques (1879-1933) French cabinet-maker and interior decorator of the ART DECO era, who also designed porcelain, fabrics and wallpapers. His pre-1925 furniture was based on NEOCLASSICAL forms. Later work was influenced by CUBIST art, and in the 1930s featured tubular steel and plastics.

rule joint See HINGE.

rummer Large-bowled, shortish-stemmed drinking glass for long drinks such as beer and cider. See pp.213-14.

Rundell, Phillip (1743-1827) Founder of Rundell, Bridge & Rundell, the most successful English firm of silver and goldsmiths in the first half of the 19thC. The firm became goldsmiths to King George III and produced a wide range of silverware for the aristocracy.

runners A term for long, narrow Oriental carpets made for export to the West from the 19thC. Those made in Persia (Iran) are known as **kenares**.

Ruskin pottery Art pottery founded 1898 by William Howson Taylor (1876-1935) at Smethwick, near Birmingham. The pottery specialised in making Chinese-style vases decorated with FLAMBÉ, mottled or monochrome glazes. Taylor also experimented with HIGH-TEMPERATURE and LUSTRE glazes to

achieve a variety of colours, textures and patterns across a wide range of products including useful wares, candlesticks, hat pins, buttons and cuff links. The pottery remained active until 1935.

Russell, Sir Gordon (1892-1980) Influential 20thC furniture designer and manufacturer linked with the British MODERN movement. His Russell Workshops in Broadway, Worcestershire, produced both his own machine-made furniture based on traditional English designs (such as ladder-back rush-seated CHAIRS) in yew and oak, and designs by other designers such as Alvar AALTO and the THONET brothers. See p.142.

Russia leather Leather treated with an oil distilled from birch bark to make it particularly hard-wearing. It was used for upholstery in the late 17thC and throughout the 18thC in Britain and the USA.

rustic furniture Furniture, particularly chairs, with framework or parts in the form of tree branches popular in the mid-18thC. Actual branches – of yew or fruitwood, for example – were cut and stripped of bark to form table or chair legs, or the texture and form of branches was imitated in elaborate carving. In the 19thC, versions were made in cast iron, STONEWARE and TERRACOTTA, as well as wood (see p.201). The term also refers to furniture made by amateurs for use in farmhouses and farm cottages.

ryal See NOBLE.

S

Saarinen, Eero (1910-61) Finnish-born US architect and designer. Saarinen worked with fellow architect Charles EAMES and explored the use of plastics in furniture, producing the first moulded plastic chairs. His *Tulip* chairs and tables of 1957 used moulded glass fibre with aluminium supports in the base for extra strength. See p.78.

sabaton See ARMOUR.

Sabino, Marius-Ernest (1878-1961) French glass-maker of the ART DECO period, especially 1923-39. Sabino's work imitated many of the glassblowing techniques and decorative motifs of his contemporary René LALIQUE.

sabre Curved 18th-19thC cavalry sword with a single cutting edge, designed for slashing.

sabre leg Early 19th-century curved chair leg which resembles the line of a sabre blade, most closely identified with the REGENCY period.

From 1815 a sabre leg was sometimes referred to as a **Waterloo leg** after the Battle of Waterloo.

sabretache A decorated flat pouch suspended from the belt of cavalry officers and worn until the early 20thC. See pp.410-11.

saddle seat Solid wooden seat with two slight depressions separated by a central ridge, commonly seen on Windsor chairs (see p.100). It is also a term for a wide, U-shaped seat.

saddle stool Three-legged, solid wood stool with saddle-shaped seat.

saf The name given to Oriental rugs with designs of multiple prayer niches, or MIHRABS. Examples, often fragmentary, are known from the 16thC. The mihrabs on many safs are small and close together suggesting they were not used as prayer rugs but as decorative wall-hangings.

sagger A fireclay vessel used to hold and protect objects during firing.

St Cloud Ceramics factory near Paris founded in 1664 to produce FAIENCE. Later, in the early 18thC, a separate concern was established producing cream-coloured soft-paste PORCELAIN with a thick glaze.

The factory's peak period was 1725-50. Early pieces were moulded after the Chinese style with prunus boughs or decorated in UNDERGLAZE blue. KAKIEMON-style decoration was characteristic after 1730, and many pieces were mounted in silver. The factory closed in 1766.

1722 on

St Louis French glassworks founded in the Münzthal, Lorraine, in 1767. At first it imitated English LEAD CRYSTAL, but c.1839 it began to produce original, fine-quality tablewares, elegant ornamental wares made of OPALESCENT and other coloured glass, LATTICINO and paperweights. The factory is still in operation and has revived the production of SULPHIDES.

St Ives pottery See LEACH, Bernard.

Salopian ware See CAUGHLEY.

salt General term for any container used for table salt, ranging from the large, ceremonial **standing salt** of the 14th to 16th centuries to the more common **salt cellar** (a shallow, open bowl) and **salt caster** (similarly shaped

to a sugar caster but smaller). Salt cellars are often gilded or have a glass liner to prevent corrosion by damp salt. A **trencher salt**, most popular 1640-1750, has no feet and rests flat on the table. See pp.160, 244.

salt-glazed stoneware STONEWARE with a thin, clear glaze with a slightly pitted texture, produced by throwing salt into the kiln during firing.

There are two basic types. **Salt-glazed coarse stoneware** was developed along the Rhine at Westerwald, Germany, for bottles (see BELLARMINE) and tankards, and adapted by British potters such as John DWIGHT of Fulham in the late 17thC. Although the clay is grey, a wash of iron oxide matures it to a brown surface colour, hence its alternative name of **brown stoneware**. **Tigerware** is a mottled version.

Salt-glazed fine white stoneware, incorporating a finer-grained white clay, was introduced in STAFFORDSHIRE POTTERIES c.1720 as a substitute for Chinese porcelain. It is typically decorated with STAMPED or SPRIGGED motifs, sometimes with incised or moulded patterns, and from c.1745 with more intricate decoration, sometimes painted in ENAMELS. It was superseded by CREAMWARE. See p.150.

salver Plate or tray, usually of silver or silver-gilt, used for the formal offering of food, drink, letters or visiting cards. Large, heavy, oblong or oval silver salvers evolved into what we know as trays in the 18thC. Small, flat salvers are known as *waiters*. Glass salvers, popular in Britain from the 18thC, usually have a central stem like a TAZZA. See pp.224, 243.

Sam Browne An officer's belt designed to support a holster and sword. It has crossed belts and was named after General Sir Samuel Browne, VC, a one-armed British officer who is said to have designed it.

sampler An embroidered panel of fabric sewn as a reference for, or as a demonstration of, a range of different stitches. By the 18thC most samplers were sewn by children, following patterns out of books. They typically incorporate letters, numbers, a short poem or motto, the name and age of the child and the date. See p.308.

Samson, Emile (1837-1913) Founder of one of France's best-known 19thC reproduction porcelain and earthenware factories, 1845. The firm initially specialised in providing replacements for 18thC SÈVRES, MEISSEN, CHELSEA and DERBY figures and Chinese services. Gradually copies of wares from all the well-known European factories were produced. Such pieces usually carried Samson's own mark based on the appropriate original, but this was often removed by people wishing to pass on the pieces as genuine.

sancai Chinese term meaning 'three colour', used to describe an effect created on ceramics by using three mineral colours in a GLAZE, usually yellow, green and brown (sometimes dubbed 'egg-and-spinach').

sandblasting Process used for creating matt surface finishes on glass, invented in the USA in 1870. A design area is masked off and the object is subjected to a high-pressure jet of sand or powdered iron to leave the exposed area with a rough, greyish finish. See p.209.

sand glass Instrument for measuring time, consisting of two bulbous glass chambers connected by a narrow channel. The whole is often mounted within a wooden frame for stability. Upending the device allows a quantity of sand to trickle from one chamber to the other taking an exact period of time, usually one hour.

Sand glasses, which preceded clocks and watches, were manufactured from the 16thC, but they were not made in Britain until c.1610.

sand-moulding Technique of shaping glass or metal objects where the design to be cast is formed in a mould containing fine casting sand and other ingredients.

sang-de-boeuf French for 'ox blood', used to describe a startling plum-red ceramics GLAZE. In areas where the glaze lies thickly on the ceramic body, such as near the base of a vase, it forms dark patches like coagulated ox blood. The effect is achieved by firing a copper glaze in a reducing atmosphere (one rich in carbon monoxide) and was developed in the late 17th and 18th centuries in China simultaneously with FLAMBÉ glazes. European potters imitated the technique in the 19thC.

sapphire See CORUNDUM.

sapwood Newly formed, soft whitish wood of a tree between the outer skin of bark and the central core of HEARTWOOD, also known as **alburnum**.

satin Cloth made of SILK threads or other material, made shiny by being passed through heavy rollers. Satin is used for dresses, coats, curtains and sometimes upholstery. The reverse, duller side of the fabric is known as **sateen**. Where satin and sateen are combined to form a pattern, the fabric

is known as a DAMASK. **Satinet** is an imitation satin mixed with cotton or rayon, usually used for dress fabrics.

satinwood Smooth, fine-grained yellowish wood, popular for furniture from the late 18thC. West Indian satinwood became fashionable c.1770, and the paler East Indian variety in the early 19thC. Both were used for VENEERS, decorative panelling, and INLAID DECORATION. In addition, the pale colour made satinwood an ideal surface for painted decoration. See also HAREWOOD and p.91.

satsu bako See TEA CEREMONY.

Satsuma Western name for type of Japanese earthenware exported throughout and since the MEIJI period (1868-1912). It is named after the Satsuma provinces, but was made in many parts of Japan, notably in KYOTO. Satsuma ware is a fine-grained, cream-coloured pottery covered in a clear to yellowy GLAZE usually with a very fine CRACKLE. The decoration, sometimes done at a second workshop, varies from mass-produced broad designs to exquisite miniature scenes finely enamelled and gilded. Japanese sources suggest the Satsuma tradition dates from the 17thC, but firm identification of any pieces earlier than the 19thC is difficult. Some of the finest pieces were made c.1900. See p.167.

savonarola See X-CHAIR.

Savonnerie Parisian carpet workshop established 1627 in a former soap factory – the name comes from the French *savon* (soap). Oriental carpet-making techniques were employed with Turkish-knotted wool or silk (see CARPET KNOTS). The factory made large carpets with Classical motifs, landscapes and mythological subjects, and their patterns were widely copied throughout Europe ('savonnerie' generally refers to all European carpets of similar design). Lighter, Rococo-style floral designs were used from the early 18thC. The Savonnerie factory closed in 1825 and the business transferred to the nearby GOBELINS premises. See p.307.

saw-cutting See FRETWORK.

scagliola Mock marble or imitation PIETRA DURA made from plaster of Paris or clear crystals of gypsum (selenite), various pigments and chips of marble. It was produced in ancient Rome but revived in 16thC Italy, and imported to Britain for interior architectural features such as columns and wall panels in the 18thC. Scagliola was also used for the tops of

tables and commodes, and increasingly, from the 1790s, when Britain produced its own, for dwarf columns and pedestals.

scale pattern See DECORATIVE MOTIFS.

scarificator A 17thC medical instrument, consisting of a number of blades released by a sprung trigger, which was used for letting blood. The blades made several incisions on the skin at once, and from c.1800 were also used for preparing the skin for vaccination. See p.298.

schwarzlot Form of German glass and ceramics decoration in black, late 17th and early 18th centuries. The landscapes, figures and flowers are often fleshed out with iron-red and sometimes GILDING.

Scottish glassware Scotland has been involved in glass-making since the early 17thC. The first glassworks was founded at Wemyss, near Glasgow, in 1610, but the industry became centred in Leith, Edinburgh, from 1628. At first only green bottles were produced; in fact, from c.1664 it was illegal for the Scots to buy bottles from anywhere else. But by the end of the century Leith wares included drinking glasses and novelties known as FRIGGERS.

Other centres of glass-making were established at ALLOA, Prestonpans and Perth. Since the 1860s Edinburgh has become well known for its fine LEAD CRYSTAL.

scratch blue A SGRAFFITO technique on white SALT-GLAZED STONEWARE with the decoration incised into the surface and filled with blue (or brown) pigment prior to firing.

The technique was produced mainly by STAFFORDSHIRE POTTERIES c.1724-76 and revived in the late 19thC by artists such as Hannah Barlow at DOULTON.

scratch carving Simple decoration on 16th and 17thC furniture. Designs consist of single lines carved into the surface of the wood. See p.90.

screws Metal screws with tapering, threaded bodies and slotted heads were first used during the early decades of the 18thC.

Early threading was hand-filed; lathe-turned screws date from the second half of the 18thC, and sharp-pointed, machine-made screws from the mid-19thC.

scrimshaw work Small carvings in horn, bone, whale tooth, walrus tusk, ivory, shells or wood, engraved using a

knife and needle, made by sailors on long voyages. Scrimshaw work dates from the 17thC. See pp.412-13.

scutcheon See ESCUTCHEON.

seal Engraved stamp for impressing a design or monogram onto sealing wax or for printing it on paper. Used since ancient times, ornamental seals returned to fashion in the 16thC when they were worn by men on a neck chain or CHATELAINE, in the 17thC on watch chains, and during the early 18thC Regency period suspended from small FOBS at the waist.

Small seals are also found set into finger rings, and at the other end of the scale set in large, sculpted mounts with heavily ornamented handles.

Various materials were used for the seal matrix and its setting, including various gemstones. Glass seals, mounted in gold, silver, brass or steel, were popular from c.1740. See p.256.

SEAL An *Edwardian desk seal*; 3 in (76 mm) long.

A **seal box** is a small, usually round, silver or gold container similar to a snuffbox, and used to hold the official seal for important documents.

They are often engraved on the lid with the crest of a city or institution such as a university. Prominent citizens given the freedom of a city were often presented with a seal box known as a **freedom box**.

seat curb See FENDER.

seaweed marquetry Flowing marquetry style popular on WILLIAM & MARY furniture from the 17th and early 18th centuries. The effect was achieved by setting a light wood such as holly or box against a contrasting dark walnut ground in seaweed-like patterns. See p.93.

secretaire Chest of drawers with a desk area concealed behind a false drawer-front. Instead of the angled fold-down BUREAU, the top 'drawer' pulls out and the front drops down to form a writing surface and reveals recessed pigeonhole compartments and small drawers behind. Secretaires were introduced during the late 17th to early 18th centuries. See p.131.

sedan chair Portable enclosed chair for one person, used by the upper classes in Britain and France during the 16th, 17th and 18th centuries. The chair was fixed on poles on either side and carried by two men. A person could be carried from one house to another without setting foot outside. When not in use, sedans were kept in the entrance hall of large houses.

sedan clock Small, portable, early 19thC timepiece, sometimes used in a sedan chair. It has a brass-bound, rectangular or circular, turned mahogany or TOLEWARE case with an enamel watch dial. Sedan clocks provided one way of recycling 18thC watch movements which were too thick for the slim-cased pocket watches then in vogue. See p.280.

Seddon, George (1727-1801) Cabinet-maker and founder of one of the best-known firms of British furniture-makers which was a rival of the Lancaster-based GILLOWS. It employed hundreds of craftsmen during its heyday in the 1780s.

self-pouring teapot Teapot whose lid is a cylinder with a vent-hole in the finial. When the lid is raised to its full height, the vent is stopped with the finger so that when pushed down the cylinder displaces the liquid through a downward-pointing spout.

In the USA self-pouring teapots are known as **pump pots**. The pots were made during the later 19thC in pottery, BRITANNIA METAL and ELECTROPLATED silver.

SELF-POURING TEAPOT *of britannia metal; 1885. Pushing the lid down forces tea to pour through the spout and into a cup placed below.*

semainier French boxes, cupboards and chests of drawers with seven compartments, one for each day of the week. The nearest British equivalent was the WELLINGTON CHEST, made in the mid-19thC.

semiprecious stone Term used to refer to all gemstones except PRECIOUS STONES. Gemmologists and jewellers consider the description too general and refer to stones by individual names. The term does not apply to synthetic gemstones, glass and PASTE

or to organic substances used in jewellery, such as amber, coral, jet and tortoiseshell. See p.267.

Senneh knot See CARPET KNOTS.

sepiolite See MEERSCHAUM.

serpentine 1 Descriptive term for an undulating profile, especially in furniture. **Serpentine fronts**, with a convex curve in the centre flanked by slightly concave sides, were seen on Rococo chests of drawers, cabinets and sideboards in the 18thC. From the late 17thC, some chairs had curving **serpentine stretchers**.
2 Mineral which ranges in colour from various shades of brown to shades of green, and is often mottled in appearance. The green varieties are the most valuable and sometimes resemble nephrite JADE. Serpentine is used for carving CAMEOS and INTAGLIOS as well as in architecture as a decorative stone. **Bowenite** is a harder variety of serpentine and cream, grey or pale green in colour.
3 See MATCHLOCK.

Seto Japanese ceramics centre, in production from the 9thC. It is best known for its 19thC vases and useful wares decorated with paintings of birds, fish and landscapes, mostly in UNDERGLAZE blue.

settee Upholstered seat with back and arms for two or more. See p.106.

settle Long wooden bench with arms and a panelled back which was designed to seat two or more people. A high-backed settle – sometimes with storage space beneath the seat or a cupboard in the back – was a familiar sight on either side of the hearth in farmhouse kitchens and inns from the 16th to 19th centuries. A **settle table** is a wooden settle with a hinged back that folds over to rest on the arms and form a table. See p.105.

Sèvres French national porcelain factory and a leading influence on European ceramics fashions c.1760-1815. Soft-paste PORCELAIN was manufactured exclusively from c.1740 until the discovery of local CHINA CLAY deposits enabled true porcelain to be produced from 1768.

From the 1750s, Sèvres acquired and maintained its lead in French ceramics, largely due to royal patronage. Louis XV granted the factory a monopoly to produce porcelain in the MEISSEN style, 1745-66, and even after this was relaxed, no other French company was allowed to produce porcelain with coloured ground or gilding. In the 1750s the factory introduced striking

enamel grounds of rich, dark royal blue, pea-green, sky-blue (*bleu céleste*), rose-pink and yellow, enriched with gold and enclosing panels or medallions of superbly painted landscapes, figures or flowers. Figures were also successful, mostly left white, but above all, from the 1750s, figures and groups in unglazed BISCUIT porcelain.

From the swirling effects of ROCOCO style, forms moved towards the more restrained NEOCLASSICAL style in the 1770s. The toughness of true porcelain meant that a broader palette of HIGH-TEMPERATURE COLOURS could be used; gilding was applied even more freely at this time, and JEWELLED DECORATION was introduced.

With the French Revolution, Sèvres lost the benefits of its royal patronage, but by 1800 revived with the backing of Napoleon – huge urns, vases, plaques and dinner services were made for him. This was EMPIRE style – much copied by many other factories. New ranges were introduced in the ART NOUVEAU and ART DECO periods. See pp.157, 159.

sewing table See WORK TABLE.

sextant Navigational instrument using mirror reflections to measure the sun's altitude, developed from the OCTANT in 1757 by Captain John Campbell. It was not in common use until the mid-19thC and was made until modern times when periscopic types were used on aircraft. See p.296.

sgraffito Technique of creating a design on a pottery surface by scratching or scoring through an unfired SLIP coating to expose the darker body beneath. In 16thC sgraffito ware from the Bologna area of Italy, for example, designs were incised in the white slip coating to reveal a red clay ground. The technique has been much used throughout Europe since medieval times, particularly on country pottery from south-west Britain – it was a feature of Barnstaple pottery throughout the 18th and 19th centuries – and was often inscribed to commemorate special events such as harvests and christenings. See SCRATCH BLUE and p.152.

shagreen 1 Highly polished skin of sharks and sting rays, used from the 17thC for covering knife cases, hip flasks and other small items.
2 Untanned leather, originally made in Persia (Iran), with a coarse, granular finish and usually dyed green.

Shaker furniture Furniture made by the Shakers, a puritanical community in the USA founded by emigrants

from Britain in 1774. The Shaker men made articles notable for their simplicity of construction and appearance, economy of design and material, yet high quality of craftsmanship. The styles remained unchanged until the late 19thC when output and quality declined as the communities decreased in number.

SHAKER *armchair and side table made of cherrywood; c.1815.*

shako A style of military headdress. The name is used for a variety of caps, the most common feature being a tall, cylindrical crown and a small peak. British soldiers wore shakos for much of the 19thC. See p.410.

shamshir A SABRE originating in India and Persia (Iran), with a long, slender curved blade designed for making slashing cuts. A common type of shamshir has a **mameluke hilt**, with a crossguard terminating in acorn-like finials and a pommel curving over at right angles to the grip.

Sheffield plate Thin layer of SILVER fused to a sheet of copper. Also known as **'Old Sheffield'** and **fused plate**, the process of fusing the precious and base metals together by heating and rolling was invented by Thomas Bolsover in Sheffield in the 1740s. In the 1760s, the introduction of double-plating (which coated both sides of the copper sheet) made Sheffield plate a more convincing, lower cost alternative to objects made of solid STERLING silver. Wire made by a similar process widened the scope of design to include OPENWORK and wirework articles.

The difficulty of concealing the copper at the edges, and of the proneness of the silver coating to wear, to some extent limited the range of products to luxury hollow-ware salvers, cruets, bread or cake baskets. Sometimes, part of an article, such as the stand of a tureen, would be made in Sheffield plate, the main body in sterling silver. The introduction of ELECTROPLATING from 1840 made Sheffield plate obsolete by 1880. Sheffield plate is usually unmarked except for the maker's name in some cases. See p.233.

shelf clock A type of cheap clock developed in the USA in the 19thC which is slim enough to stand on a narrow shelf. The clocks are often in a plain rectangular case, with a glass door. A variation, produced in bulk 1822-1914 and exported to Britain, is the **ogee** (or **OG**) **clock**, made in various sizes, with curved OGEE-shaped moulding on the frame. See p.284.

SHELF CLOCK *with an ogee-moulded frame; 1840; 15¾ in (40 cm) high.*

shelf dolls English term for *sakura-ningyo* – Japanese dolls designed as ornaments for a shelf. They are based on legendary Japanese heroes and heroines and have been exported to the West from c.1900. See p.354.

shellac 1 Varnish made from the secretions of a scale insect on trees in India and the Middle East. It was used by European craftsmen to imitate Oriental LACQUER. Shellac, dissolved in alcohol, is also used in FRENCH POLISHING on furniture. See p.425. **2** Early form of plastic, invented 1868 and used to make gramophone records and moulded ornaments.

Shelley potteries See FOLEY CHINA WORKS.

Sheraton, Thomas (1751-1806) British cabinet-maker whose *Cabinet-Maker's and Upholsterer's Drawing Book* encapsulated the elegant, NEOCLASSICAL furniture style named after him. See p.30.

shibayama See LACQUER.

shilling A British coin of ancient origin, but since its revival in 1550, a silver piece with a face value of 12 old pence, and after decimalisation replaced by the 5p piece. Shilling is abbreviated to 's'.

shi-shi See DOG OF FO.

shot glass 1 Glass container 1-3 in (25-76 mm) tall that was filled with lead shot in which to clean and support quill pens. **2** A US term for a small tumbler for a single measure – or 'shot' – of whiskey.

sideboard Dining-room furniture piece, developed, as it is known today, in the last quarter of the 18thC. Sideboards were designed for the storage and display of tableware and for serving food, and usually have a central drawer flanked by cupboards or drawers. See pp.118-19.

side cabinet See CHIFFONIER.

side chair Simple chair without arms, also known as a **single, upright** or **small chair**. See p.95.

sidereal time See MEAN TIME.

side table General term for any easily movable table designed to stand against a wall, or in a dining room as an additional table for food, plates and dishes, and sometimes referred to as a **serving table**. See p.120.

signpost barometer See ANGLE BAROMETER.

sileh rugs See SUMAKH.

silhouette Outline of a figure, either painted or cut out of paper and mounted on card, popular from mid-18thC to c.1880, and revived in the 1920s. See p.323.

silicon ware See DOULTON.

silk The fine, lustrous, supple fibre produced by certain insect larvae and spiders, especially the silkworm. Silk cloth was produced c.700 BC by the Chinese and remained a closely guarded secret until the 6thC AD, when it spread to France, Spain, Italy and Sicily. The main silk production centres today are southern Europe, Japan, India and northern China. The best-quality silk is **net silk** which is very slightly twisted, and reflects light especially well. The waste from net silk is **spun silk**. Silk which has yet to be spun and woven is **raw silk**, of which there are a number of varieties such as **floss silk** (for fine embroidery), **organzine** (for the warp of quality silk fabrics) and **tram** (for the weft of quality silk fabrics).

silk-screen printing A printing process based on the stencilling principle, in which a stretched screen of silk or other fine fabric is coated with ink-resistant substance in the design areas to be left blank. Coloured ink is forced through the uncoated areas onto the printing surface. Layers of different colours can be applied using different stencils.

silver Precious metal which is lighter and slightly less malleable than gold, but unlike gold is prone to tarnishing due to chemical reaction with pollutants in the air. Silver products are made from an alloy of pure silver and a small proportion of a base metal such as copper to improve strength and durability. The proportion of pure silver varies according to standards set by different countries. See BRITANNIA STANDARD, HALLMARKS, STERLING STANDARD and p.233.

silver-electroplated glass British glass, also known as **silver-deposit glass**, produced c.1890-1920. A design was painted in a FLUX, placed in a silver solution and subjected to an electric current, which fixed the silver to the painted surface.

silver gilt Silver plated with a thin layer of gold. See p.234.

Silveria glass Silvery ART GLASS made by enclosing silver foil between two layers of clear glass. The technique was developed by John NORTHWOOD II, c.1900, and was made at STEVENS & WILLIAMS.

silvering 1 The silver version of gilding in which a thin film of silver is applied to a surface using silver leaf. The technique was introduced in the latter part of the 17thC and used on elaborately carved cabinet stands and tables. When LACQUERED or varnished, the silver takes on a yellowish tinge, and was sometimes used as a cheap alternative to gilding. **2** The film of tin foil and mercury, silver or other reflective material applied to glass in a mirror.

silver table See TEA TABLE.

silverwood See HAREWOOD.

singerie Monkeys dressed up in human clothing, popular as a decorative theme in the 18thC. It is found in most forms of art and although it was not much used after 1800, it was revived in the 19thC after the publication of Darwin's *On the Origin of Species*. See AFFENKAPELLE.

single chair See SIDE CHAIR.

siphon barometer Barometer that has a J-shaped glass tube containing mercury. The WHEEL BAROMETER was developed using a siphon tube.

size gilding See GILDING.

skean dhu Gaelic for 'black knife' – a Scottish Highlander's DIRK that was held in the sock against the leg when not in use.

skeleton clock Clock with its workings exposed in an open framework, usually housed under a glass dome and mounted on a wooden or marble base. Skeleton clocks were made in France from c.1750, and became popular in Britain in the Victorian era from c.1840.

SKELETON CLOCK *in a glass dome; c.1870; 15½ in (39.4 cm) high.*

slag glass See LAVA GLASS.

slick stone See LINEN SMOOTHER.

slider See COASTER.

slip Liquid clay used as a finish or as a decorating medium on pottery, or as a medium for casting hollow-ware and particularly figures. Slip, or **engobe**, is also used to join the various parts of an object figure or group of figures that have been cast in separate moulds.

A decorative slip can either be used as a dip or poured over an article of pottery to coat it, or made into a stiffer mixture and piped or **slip-trailed** (also known as **tube-lining**) on the surface of the body. The process precedes firing. Mixed clays are used or metal oxides added to achieve different colours and effects. Pottery decorated with slip is known as **slipware**. See also SGRAFFITO and p.152.

Slip-casting is a forming process in which the liquid clay is poured into a porous plaster mould which absorbs much of the moisture, leaving a layer of clay to harden on the mould walls. Surplus slip is poured out, the mould removed, and the resulting clay shell fired. See p.151.

A **slip glaze** or **Albany slip** contains a high proportion of clay and produces a greenish or brownish finish. It was used at Albany, near New York, and on SALT-GLAZED STONEWARE from the 19thC onwards.

slipper See BOURDALOU.

smallsword Lightweight and elegant, short SWORD which dates from the late 17th and 18th centuries.

smalt A blue pigment produced by grinding a coloured glass mixture containing cobalt oxide to a fine powder. It was used in the manufacture of BRISTOL blue glass and in POWDER-BLUE ground in ceramics.

smear glaze See GLAZE.

Smith, George (c.1786-1826) REGENCY furniture-maker, upholsterer and designer. Smith popularised the circular dining table and the OTTOMAN sofa in Britain and published several books of his designs. His furniture was much influenced in the early years by collector and Egyptologist Thomas HOPE, and Smith also used GOTHIC and Chinese motifs widely. His later work became increasingly heavy and over-decorated, a foretaste of Victorian furniture. See p.43.

snakewood Deep, bright red tropical hardwood with irregular dark markings resembling those of a snake or hieroglyphic characters – hence its names – snakewood and **letterwood**. Snakewood is difficult to work because of its hardness but is seen as an INLAID DECORATION on 17thC furniture and occasionally in late 18th and early 19thC VENEERS.

snaphaunce A form of ignition similar to the FLINTLOCK using flint and steel. See box below.

snap table A table with a top that snaps or folds down vertically over the supporting pillar, as in 18thC TRIPOD TABLES. See BIRDCAGE.

snuff bottles Small bottles, 2-6 in (5-15 cm) high, used for holding snuff. Most were produced in China from the 18thC and were made from a variety of materials, including glass, ivory, porcelain, agate and jade. The bottles are usually round or oval in shape, with a spoon attached to the inside of the stopper and are often richly carved or ENAMELLED. Glass

bottles sometimes have INTERIOR PAINTING. Large numbers of Chinese snuff bottles were exported to the West from the mid-19thC onwards.

snuffer Implement used to trim or cut candle wicks. See p.255.

soapstone A form of magnesium silicate, or talc, used in its solid white, red, greyish or greenish form for carved ornaments, particularly in China. In the mid-18thC, particularly in Britain, powdered soapstone, or **steatite**, was sometimes used as a binding agent in soft-paste PORCELAIN paste. It provides good resistance to sudden temperature changes, improved whiteness and plasticity.

sociable seat See CONFIDANTE.

soda glass Glass made with soda (sodium carbonate) rather than potash (see BOHEMIA) as the FLUX agent. The soda was originally derived from marine plants (see CRISTALLO), but later produced chemically. In its molten state, soda glass is easier to manipulate than potash glass, but in its finished form it is light and fragile, and cannot be CUT.

In Britain, soda glass was superseded in the 17thC by LEAD CRYSTAL, which was stronger and more RESONANT, but continued to be made until the early 19thC on the Continent, and is still used for some Venetian-style glass today. See p.207.

sofa Any movable seat on which to recline, now virtually interchangeable with SETTEE. The word is derived from the Ottoman *sopha* (the dais on which the Grand Vizier received guests). See pp.106-7.

sofa table A development of the PEMBROKE TABLE although narrower and longer, made from the late 18th to mid-19th centuries. There are usually two shallow drawers at the front and normally flaps at both ends supported

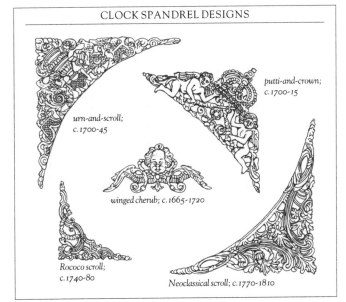

CLOCK SPANDREL DESIGNS

urn-and-scroll; c.1700-45

putti-and-crown; c.1700-15

winged cherub; c.1665-1720

Rococo scroll; c.1740-80

Neoclassical scroll; c.1770-1810

by FLY brackets. Early examples have end supports whereas later tables stand on pedestals. Sofa tables were designed to complement the length, line and height of a sofa, and were typically used by women for writing, drawing or reading. See p.117.

soft-paste porcelain See PORCELAIN.

softwood Timber from cone-bearing trees which is generally softer than HARDWOOD and therefore easier to work. Softwoods include PINE, CEDAR, spruce and YEW.

solid china See FROZEN CHARLOTTE.

solid jasper See JASPERWARE.

solitaire See CABARET.

Song dynasty Chinese dynasty, sometimes spelt **Sung**, of great ceramic development, AD 960-1279. Porcelain was improved and it is the most likely period of the invention of UNDERGLAZE blue. STONEWARES were given highly sophisticated GLAZES in a wide range of colours and the practice of patronage of ceramics was established. The first Song dynasty wares reached Europe at the end of the 19thC and became a source of inspiration for STUDIO POTTERS in France and Britain.

Sonneberg Town in southern Germany famed for doll-making. Early dolls of turned wood were produced from before 1700; from 1807, mass-production techniques resulted in the large-scale manufacture of PAPIER-MÂCHÉ heads. The peak production period, however, started c.1850, from when Sonneberg dolls in BISQUE,

COMPOSITION, wood, wax and china were produced and exported throughout the world.

souscription watch See BREGUET.

sovereign A British gold coin first issued by King Henry VII in 1489 and revived in 1817 with a fixed value of £1. Gold sovereigns are still made today, mainly for trading in the bullion market. See p.388.

soy frame Late 18thC British bottle stand, similar to a CRUET, usually made in silver or SHEFFIELD PLATE.

spandrel The corner space between an arch or circle and a rectangle. Originally an architectural term for the space between one arch and the next in ARCADING, it is used in the context of carpet and textile patterns. On a clock dial, spandrels refer to the ornamentation in the four corner spaces between the CHAPTER RING and the DIAL plate. See box above.

Spanish flintlock See MIQUELET.

Spanish knot See CARPET KNOTS.

spatterware See SPONGED WARE.

spelter Zinc alloy, often containing lead, used as a substitute for bronze. Spelter was much used in the 19thC for cheap, cast articles such as candlesticks and clock cases. It was popular as an inexpensive medium for ART NOUVEAU applied ornament and ART DECO figures. See p.429.

spider-leg table Gate-leg table with particularly slender, turned legs, and with more or less standard dimensions

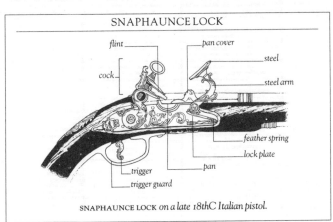

SNAPHAUNCE LOCK

flint

pan cover

steel

cock

steel arm

feather spring

lock plate

trigger

pan

trigger guard

SNAPHAUNCE LOCK *on a late 18thC Italian pistol.*

of around 28 in (71 cm) high, with a 36 × 30 in (91 × 76 cm) surface. The tables were produced both in Britain and the USA during the second half of the 18thC.

SPIDER-LEG TABLE; c.1790; (open) 31½ in (80 cm) long.

spill vase Single or pair of cylindrical vases or a wall-hanging vase, designed to hold spills or matches for lighting candles and pipes. Some examples have a rectangular holder for a matchbox. They were made in porcelain, pottery or brass from the late 19thC. Spill vases are also known as **paper cases, match vases** or **match stands**. See p.183.

spindle A slender, TURNED rod based on the shape of a spinning-wheel spindle, which is often seen on the upright members or horizontal stretchers of a CHAIR.

spinet doll See PIANO DOLL.

spinning 1 Metalworking technique used since Egyptian times to form hollow containers from sheet metal by pressing the metal against a rotating wooden core on a lathe (see p.234). **2** Technique used to turn wool, cotton and flax into thread suitable for weaving using a spinning wheel, first seen in the 14thC.

Spitalfields silk factories Centre of silk weaving in London from the late 17thC, at its peak during the 18thC. Many early designs were French-influenced, brought over by HUGUENOT weavers. In the early 18thC velvets, DAMASKS and silk BROCADE were produced for dressmaking. In the 1770s the industry fell into irreversible decline when patterned materials went out of fashion. See also BIZARRE SILK.

spittoon Open or conical-topped container made of metal or ceramics used for spitting into. Some are small for hand-held use, others are larger and rest on the floor.

splat The vertical member of a CHAIR back, rising from the seat to the top rail. See box, p.453.

Spode Staffordshire ceramics factory founded by Josiah Spode in 1770. Early production included CREAMWARE, pearlware and blue-printed earthenware. Spode perfected the BONE CHINA formula, and in the 19thC was noted for its REGENCY-STYLE ornamental ware and useful wares with bat-printed designs (see TRANSFER-PRINTING). William Copeland became a partner in 1833, and sole proprietor in 1847, when PARIAN porcelain figures were introduced. Finely crafted table services and vases continued to be made into the 20thC.

sponged ware Inexpensive pottery with mottled colour effects applied by a sponge. It was produced and exported in quantity by Staffordshire potteries in the 1820s, and was popular for the next three decades. In the USA it is known as **spatterware**.

spontoon See POLEARMS.

spoons See CUTLERY and pp.240-1.

sprigging The addition of separately made relief ornamentation onto a ceramic body, cemented in place with SLIP. The clays used for sprigging may be in a contrasting colour to that of the body, but need to be of similar consistency for the pieces to adhere successfully during firing. Sprigging was developed by Thomas WHIELDON in the early 18thC, then taken up by other Staffordshire potters, notably on Wedgwood JASPERWARE. See p.152.

Sprimont, Nicholas (c.1716-71) Flemish-born HUGUENOT silversmith and porcelain manufacturer who was based in London and specialised in Rococo pieces decorated with human figures, dolphins, shells, crabs and various other natural motifs. See CHELSEA.

spring-driven clocks See BALANCE, BARREL, FUSEE, TRAIN.

spur marks Light indentations or pimples in a ceramic glaze found on the base or rim of some plates, dishes and figures. They – and the similar **stilt marks** – are made by cones or pegs used to support the body in the kiln or to prevent stacked wares from sticking to each other. The marks can aid identification; they are characteristic, for example, of CHELSEA and ARITA porcelain. See PATCH MARKS.

squab A flat, loose cushion, as opposed to fitted upholstery, usually tied to the frame of an armchair with corner tapes and used from the 17thC. Squab stools have a raised rim to hold a cushion in place.

Staffordshire potteries The largest concentration of ceramics factories in Britain since the 17thC. At the heart of 'The Potteries' are the so-called 'five towns' (in fact six) of Stoke-on-Trent: Burslem, Hanley, Stoke, Tunstall, Longton and Fenton. The availability of a variety of local clays and coal for fuel provided the essential foundations for the industry to develop.

From the mid-18thC, the early pioneering techniques and wares of Staffordshire potters such as Thomas WHIELDON, John ASTBURY, the ELERS brothers and, above all Josiah WEDGWOOD, had a profound influence on European ceramics, and an expanding international export trade was established.

Almost every stage of British ceramics development can be traced in the Staffordshire potteries, from SLIP-ware and other lead-glazed earthenware to SALT-GLAZED and fine STONEWARE, CREAMWARE and BONE CHINA, embracing both utility and luxury markets.

Linked particularly with Staffordshire are the many animal and human figures produced in the 19thC. These were made in moulds by the thousand, often depicting notorious or famous contemporary figures, sometimes marking significant events such as coronations, murders, expeditions or wars. See FLATBACKS.

stained glass Glass coloured with metallic oxides, or by FLASHING. Since the 11thC it has been used for making windows, often in churches. The early technique was to cut the glass into pieces to fit the design, paint faces and draperies with black or grey ENAMEL, and then fix the pieces into a lead framework, hence the term 'leaded light'. By the 16thC larger panels of glass were being used and the design was painted on in coloured enamels.

Stained glass began to appear in houses from the 14thC. Medieval styles and techniques were widely imitated until the late 19th and 20th centuries, when designers such as Sir Edward Burne-Jones and William MORRIS in Britain and John La Farge and Louis TIFFANY in the USA experimented with new applications and designs.

stainless steel Strong, corrosion-resistant steel containing chromium and nickel, invented in Britain 1913. It became a popular material for cutlery after 1945, when Scandinavian designs in the material were first seen.

Staite Murray, William (1881-1962) British engineer, painter and STUDIO POTTER whose best work is seen in large, simply decorated vases, influenced by the Japanese potter Shoji Hamada, and by his contact with potter Bernard LEACH.

Stam, Mart (1899-1986) Dutch architect and furniture designer who worked with the BAUHAUS design school in Germany and created the first chair using the CANTILEVER principle in 1924. See p.72.

stamped velvet See GAUFFERED.

stamping 1 Impressing a design or mark into a ceramic or metal body with a stamp. See DIE-STAMPING. **2** The process of pressing low-relief ornamentation made separately in an INTAGLIO mould onto a ceramic body, fixing it with a liquid clay SLIP and firing. See also SPRIGGING.

standing cup Large, ceremonial drinking vessel, used in Britain and other parts of Europe from the Middle Ages to the 17thC and later copied for display. They were made of silver, silver-gilt, copper-gilt, or pewter, and consisted of a covered bowl resting on a KNOPPED stem, supported by a spreading foot. Very elaborate examples incorporated real coconut shells, sea shells and ostrich eggs.

standing tray See BUTLER'S TRAY.

standish See INKSTAND.

stater Ancient Greek coinage of gold or silver. See p.386.

steatite See SOAPSTONE.

stem See GLASSES, DRINKING.

stem cup Chinese drinking vessel with a wide shallow bowl and a stem widening at the base, also known as a **gaozu**. Most stem cups are of porcelain and became popular in the MING period, but earlier examples exist.

STEM CUP; Chinese porcelain; 16thC; 5½ in (14 cm) diameter.

stencilling A simple method of decoration in which a design or lettering cut from card or other material is used as a template for reproducing a pattern onto a surface placed below. Stencils were used from the 17th to the 19th centuries to decorate walls and were popular during the ARTS AND CRAFTS MOVEMENT as a furniture decoration.

step cut See JEWEL CUTTING.

stereoscope A 19thC instrument for viewing two drawings or photographs of the same object, pictured at slightly different angles, to produce a single, three-dimensional image. It was invented by British scientist Charles Wheatstone in 1838. See p.295.

STEREOSCOPE *to stand on a table; c.1880; 15¾ in (40 cm) high. Other versions were hand-held.*

sterling standard The proportion of pure silver to base metal set for British sterling silver. From 1300, apart from the period 1697-1720, when the BRITANNIA STANDARD was enforced, the legal standard has been 92.5 per cent pure silver, the remainder being one or more base metals such as copper, to lend strength and workability. See HALLMARKS.

Steuben Glassworks Leading US glass factory founded by English designer Frederick CARDER in 1903. It was taken over by the CORNING GLASSWORKS in 1918, but continued to produce vast quantities of ART GLASS. From the mid-1930s the factory specialised in LEAD CRYSTAL, ornamental wares including commissioned designs from various artists and sculptors such as Jean Cocteau, Salvador Dali, Eric Gill and Graham Sutherland.

Stevengraphs Trade name for English silk pictures made by Thomas Stevens of Coventry on a Jacquard LOOM, 1879-1938. They are approximately 2½ × 6 in (6 × 15 cm) and followed themes such as horse races, transport and portraits of famous people.

Stevens & Williams Family firm of glass-makers based at Brierley Hill near STOURBRIDGE, established in the 17thC. In the 19thC, the firm was one of the top three factories in the

Stourbridge area, alongside RICHARDSONS and Thomas WEBB. Products included CAMEO, LEAD CRYSTAL, ENGRAVED and many coloured glasses. In the 20thC, the firm changed its name to 'Royal Brierley' after receiving a royal warrant in King George V's reign, and has become known for its commemorative glassware.

stick barometer The simplest and earliest type of BAROMETER, invented in the 17thC. It consists of a mercury-filled glass tube set within a long, narrow wall case. The mercury level is read directly against a simple vertical scale. See p.290.

Stickley, Gustav (1857-1942) New York furniture designer who made solid, plain furniture in the style of the ARTS AND CRAFTS MOVEMENT, later known as **Mission furniture**.

stickwork See TUNBRIDGE WARE.

stile See JOINING.

stilt marks See SPUR MARKS.

stipple engraving See ENGRAVING.

stirrup cup Drinking cup, frequently in the shape of an animal's head, used for the final drink before setting off on a hunt. The cups, common from the mid-18thC, have neither handle nor foot, and were made in pottery and porcelain, silver and glass. See p.248.

STIRRUP CUP *of silver; 1806; 4½ in (11.4 cm) long.*

stockinette Elastic, machine-knitted, silk or fine cotton fabric used 1860-80 and 1920-40 as a material for dolls' bodies. It is also seen, though rarely, stretched over the head of a PAPIER-MÂCHÉ doll.

stomacher 1 A decorative, often elaborately embroidered or jewelled, triangular panel of material inserted into a bodice on a woman's dress and worn over the chest and ending in a point over the stomach. Stomachers were a feature of women's dresses from the late 15th to late 18th centuries. **2** Large, triangular brooch worn from the 18thC on the centre of a woman's dress bodice. Some were made in sections to be worn as a sequence of two or three brooches. Stomachers,

also known as *devant le corsage* or **corsage brooches**, were especially popular in the Edwardian period.

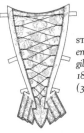

STOMACHER *of silk embroidered with gilt threads; early 18thC; 14 in (35.5 cm) long.*

stone china An extremely hard, white clay body used for heavy-duty table services, which was developed in the early 1800s at various Staffordshire potteries. The body is opaque and covered in a glaze with an often blue-grey tinge, and the design is painted over a blue, black or puce printed outline. Popular styles include those derived from Chinese FAMILLE-ROSE export services or anglicised versions of IMARI porcelain patterns.
   'Ironstone china' was a term patented in 1813 by Charles Mason, possibly in a bid to corner the market and to mislead competitors. Analysis suggests that the slag iron purported to be part of its make-up, is not actually present. While Mason's (later Ashworth's) was the main producer of 'ironstone', other Staffordshire factories followed suit. See p.155.

stoneware One of the three fundamental ceramic bodies, the others being EARTHENWARE and PORCELAIN. Stoneware is a very hard, dense material made from a clay fired to a point at which the individual grains of clay fuse together, rendering the finished product impervious to liquid. The manufacture of stoneware was first introduced to Britain from Germany in the late 17thC. See RED STONEWARE, SALT-GLAZED STONEWARE and p.150.

stool The most basic and oldest form of single-person seating, consisting of a seating platform with no back, and three or four legs. See pp.94-95.

stopped dovetail See JOINING.

stopper Glass, ceramic or metal piece that fits in the neck of a bottle or DECANTER. Stoppers were frequently decorated to match the container. See box right.

Storr, Paul (1771-1844) The most eminent English silversmith of the 19thC, working in London and noted for his NEOCLASSICAL and ROCOCO silverware which he made on a grand scale. He supplied some of his work to royalty and nobility, and worked for

RUNDELL, Bridge & Rundell, the Crown goldsmiths, for a time. In 1822, he established his own firm, Storr & Mortimer. See p.232.

Stourbridge glasshouses Glass-making centre in Worcestershire. Glass factories were established there in the early 17thC by a group of HUGUENOT glass-makers. It was the most important 19thC English producer of fine table and decorative glass, including coloured, LEAD CRYSTAL, engraved and CAMEO GLASS. See Thomas WEBB & SONS, STEVENS & WILLIAMS, RICHARDSONS.

strapwork Decorative motif incorporating interlacing bands or ribbon-like straps. It was popularised by illustrators and engravers in 16thC Flanders, and was a feature of Elizabethan style. Strapwork designs are seen in wrought-iron work, carved in low-relief on furniture, STAMPED, CAST or ENGRAVED on silver, and painted on ceramics. The German version, LAUB UND BANDELWERK, is seen on early MEISSEN porcelain. See DECORATIVE MOTIFS.

Strawberry Hill Gothic See GOTHIC REVIVAL.

straw marquetry Decoration using short coloured lengths of straw to form marquetry pictures or patterns and applied to items such as furniture, boxes and mirrors. It was popular from the 17th to 19th centuries, particularly in France.

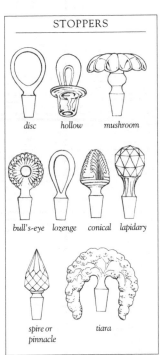

STOPPERS

disc   *hollow*   *mushroom*

bull's-eye   *lozenge*   *conical*   *lapidary*

spire or pinnacle   *tiara*

stretcher The horizontal bar or rail that connects and supports the legs of chairs, stools, cabinets and tables. Stretchers are found in a variety of styles on the lower part of the leg on 16th and 17thC furniture. By the early 18thC they were used only on a limited basis, and by the end of the century they were considered unfashionable. See CHAIR.

striking systems The blows struck on bells, or gongs of coiled wire, to sound periods of time on a clock. **Hour striking** sounds the number of hours at each hour, whereas a **passing strike** sounds one blow at each hour. A **half-hour** or **French strike** is hour striking with an additional single blow at each half-hour. **Quarter striking** is also hour striking with the addition at each quarter-hour of either a double blow on a smaller bell or six or eight blows on a nest of bells. The term **chiming** indicates a quarter strike on a nest of bells and should not be used to refer to the hour strike.

A **grande sonnerie** strikes the hours and the quarters at every hour and quarter-hour; and a **petite sonnerie** strikes the hours only on the hour and successive quarter-hours by single, double or triple 'ting-tang' on two bells. A **Dutch strike** counts out the hour both at the hour on one bell and at the previous half-hour on a differently toned bell.

stringing See BANDING.

strut clock Small, slim, bedroom or travelling clock, with an easel-like strut behind, or sometimes with a swivel strut at the base. The clock was introduced c.1845 by Thomas Cole (1800-64) and was produced by various clock-makers to c.1880.

stucco An Italian term for a slow-setting plaster composed of gypsum, sand and marble powder. It is used for sculptures and relief decorations on walls and ceilings.

studio pottery Ceramics made or decorated by independent artist-craftsmen. See pp.184-5.

stumpwork Type of needlework in which layers of buttonhole stitching and sewn-on decorations such as seed pearls create three-dimensional 'stump' pictures. See p.308.

style See GNOMON.

style rayonnant See LAMBREQUIN.

sucket fork or **spoon** Combined spoon and fork, the two-pronged fork being at the tip of the spoon handle. It was used mainly to eat succade –

preserved fruit, either in syrup or candied. Most surviving examples are of 17th-18thC.

Süe & Mare French furniture-making company operational 1919-28, officially known as the **Compagnie des Arts Français**, but better known by the surnames of its two founders, Louis Süe and André Mare. Its high-quality ART DECO furniture made of luxurious materials was usually commissioned, and the company also designed interiors and decorative objects.

sugar box A box with a lid used for holding and serving sugar. Some examples have two compartments for different types of sugar as well as room for a spoon. Sugar boxes are found in silver or porcelain. See p.253.

sugar nips Early type of sugar tongs like a pair of scissors but with arms instead of blades. Sugar nips were introduced in the mid-18thC for breaking pieces off sugar loaves.

sulphides White ceramic CAMEOS and MEDALLIONS embedded in clear glass, a technique believed to have been first patented in 1818 by Pierre-Honoré Boudon de Saint-Amans. A thin layer of air under the glass gives them a silvery appearance. Sulphides are seen set in paperweights, in the base of goblets, perfume bottles and tumblers, and were widely produced in the early 19thC. Fine examples were made by BACCARAT, CLICHY and Apsley PELLATT. See p.212.

sumakh A FLAT-WEAVE technique used in Oriental rug-making, with a complicated, almost embroidery-like weave. The sumakh or soumak technique is widespread in the Caucasus, seen in the similar **verneh** and **sileh** rugs of the southern Caucasus, and also in the wearings of the nomadic Turkoman tribes in eastern ANATOLIA, Iran and other parts of central Asia. See p.301.

Summerly's Art Manufactures See COLE, Henry.

Sunderland ware Domestic pottery such as chamberpots, jugs and plaques made in large quantities in Sunderland, England, c.1800-50. It is decorated with black TRANSFER-PRINTED designs of sailing boats, bridges, emblems and inscriptions, some hand-coloured and framed with splashes of purple-pink LUSTRE.

sundial Device for telling the time by the sun. The dial has a central protruding arm known as a GNOMON, and as the sun rises the shadow cast by the gnomon indicates the time on

markings round the edge of the dial. A pocket sundial known as the **Butterfield dial** – invented by Michael Butterfield (fl.1670-1724) and made of silver or brass with an octagonal base and adjustable bird gnomon – was widely copied up to the late 18thC.

Both pocket and fixed sundials were widely used from the 15th until the mid-19th centuries, after which accurate pocket watches and the introduction of standard time made them obsolete. See p.297.

Sung See SONG.

Sutherland table A mid-Victorian, drop-leaf table with a central section that is unusually narrow compared with the broad leaves, and a GATE-LEG construction beneath. See p.117.

suzuribako Japanese LACQUER box used for writing materials (*suzuribako* means 'ink-stone box') dating from the 13thC onwards.

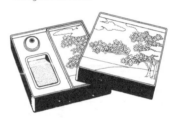

SUZURIBAKO; *late 17thC; 8½ in (21cm) long. This example incorporates a water pot and an inkstone.*

swag See DECORATIVE MOTIFS.

swaging The process of shaping the edge of a piece of silver FLATWARE or other metal using a tool called a **swage block** which consists of compatible blocks – one with the edging design in relief and the other with the design recessed. The metal edge is pressed between the blocks to mould the metal. The process is still used today to make hand-forged spoons.

Swansea The most important pottery and porcelain centre in South Wales in the late 18th and early 19th centuries. The Cambrian Factory, producing CREAMWARE, EARTHENWARE and BASALTES, was active from c.1767. But it was for the finely modelled and decorated, high-quality soft-paste PORCELAIN produced from 1814, with the help of William Billingsley from Nantgarw, that Swansea became famed. From 1822 the factory produced only earthen-ware and finally closed in 1870.

sweetmeats Dry sweetmeats such as chocolates, nuts and dried or candied fruits, were popular from the 17th to early 19th centuries, and various

containers – in silver, glass and ceramics – were made to hold them (see BONBONNIÈRE). Porcelain sweetmeat figures carrying a bowl were made as part of DESSERT SERVICES notably at MEISSEN and CHELSEA.

A **sweetmeat dish** is one dish with several compartments. A **sweetmeat set** is made up of separate containers, usually sections of a circle, which when placed together form a composite piece. These were popular in the late 18th to early 19th centuries. Tall-stemmed **sweetmeat glasses** were used in Britain in the late 17th and early 18th centuries for 'wet' sweetmeats such as jellies and custards. They are more usually known as JELLY GLASSES. See also EPERGNE and p.224.

swell front See BOW FRONT.

swing glass See CHEVAL MIRROR.

sword General term for any weapon with a handle and a long blade used for cutting and thrusting. It encompasses the lightweight RAPIER, the two-handed CLAYMORE, and the curved-bladed SABRE. Swords carried by foot soldiers are shorter than those for mounted soldiers. Simple crossguards gradually gave way to knuckle-guards for greater hand protection in late 15thC Europe. Rapiers, and their direct descendants, the small swords, were carried for personal protection or as part of court dress, rather than in a military context, from the 16th to

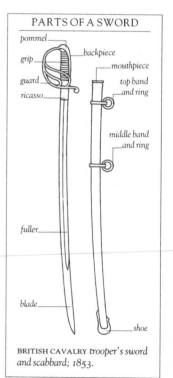

PARTS OF A SWORD

pommel
grip
backpiece
guard
mouthpiece
ricasso
top band and ring

fuller
middle band and ring

blade
shoe

BRITISH CAVALRY *trooper's sword and scabbard; 1853.*

18th centuries. Swords were still standard sidearms for some armed forces in Europe into the early 20thC, but apart from their continuing role as part of a dress uniform, they were replaced by bayonets from the 18thC.

sycamore Hard, milky-white, European wood, related to the North American MAPLE. It has a fine, even grain and natural lustre. Solid sycamore furniture was made in medieval times, and from the late 17thC the wood was used in floral MARQUETRY on walnut furniture, sometimes stained green or grey to make HAREWOOD, and for VENEERS. Because it has no taste, sycamore was much used for domestic ware.

syllabub glass Wide-bowled, stemmed, 18thC glass used to serve syllabub, a creamy dessert. See p.224.

sympiesometer Type of barometer used for measuring air pressure, comprising a short column of mercury and a bulb of gas, mounted in a brass or wooden wall case. It was widely made in the 1820s and 30s.

synchronous clock See ELECTRIC CLOCK.

synthetic gem A man-made gem with the same chemical composition as a natural gem, as opposed to an **imitation** which only looks like the natural stone. See p.267.

T

tabako-ire Japanese tobacco pouch which was hung from a kurawa (ashtray) NETSUKE. A **tabako-bon** is a tobacco cabinet, also known as a **tabako-dansu**, which has drawers for tobacco, a metal or china container for charcoal, and hooks for hanging a **kiseru** (pipe). 19thC examples are often decorated with LACQUER. A **kiseru-zutsu** is a pipe holder.

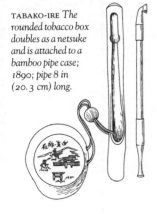

TABAKO-IRE *The rounded tobacco box doubles as a netsuke and is attached to a bamboo pipe case; 1890; pipe 8 in (20.3 cm) long.*

tabby 1 17thC term for SILK taffeta with a changeable surface finish like shot silk. **2** A basic weave in which the warp thread is woven alternately over and under each weft thread.

tabernacle clock A German clock of the RENAISSANCE period in the form of a turreted tower, often with a dial on each of the four vertical sides, and with a balustraded gallery top containing hour and quarter-hour bells. Most German town guilds in the 16th and 17th centuries required an apprentice to make a tabernacle clock, with many additional astronomical and calendar dials, as a **masterpiece clock** before qualifying as a master clock-maker. See p.285.

tableau See PLAQUE.

table clock Specifically, a spring-driven clock set within a flat-based case of metal or wood. The dial is either on the upper or front surface, sometimes with subsidiary dials on the sides and back. Table clocks were first made in France and Germany in the 16thC. British BRACKET CLOCKS and MANTEL CLOCKS fall into the table clock category. See DRUM CLOCK.

table cut See JEWEL CUTTING.

tablette See AIDE-MÉMOIRE.

taffeta Fine TABBY-weave silk fabric used in Britain since the 14thC, and especially from the 16th to 19th centuries, for cushion covers, counterpanes and curtains. From the 17thC, taffeta was stretched and a gum-like substance applied to give a glossy, watered finish.

Talbert, Bruce (1838-81) Architect and furniture, metalwork and wallpaper designer. Talbert's furniture is simple and functional – a reaction against the overly elaborate GOTHIC REVIVAL. It is bulky but practical and well-proportioned, and decorated with panels of lighter wood, tiles, Gothic tracery or shallow carving. Talbert published an influential pattern book in 1867.

talking doll In the early 19thC, dolls that could say 'mama' or 'papa' were developed in Germany by Johannes Mälzel of Regensburg (the sound was produced by a bellows when the limbs were moved), and in Britain by Anthony Bazzoni of London.
 Some talking dolls dating from the late 19thC contained phonographic wax cylinders.

tallboy High chest comprising one chest on top of another, with seven or more full-width drawers and a top pair

of half-width drawers. The top chest is generally slighlty narrower than the lower one. Tallboys, also known as **chests-on-chests**, were introduced in the early 18thC and derived from the **chest-on-stand** – a chest of drawers on a stand like a LOWBOY. See p.135.

tambour 1 A flexible shutter used for roll-top desk lids and sliding doors for cupboards. Tambour covers are made from narrow slats of wood glued to a canvas or linen backing, and were developed in France in the 18thC. **2** A pair of wooden hoops that form a frame to hold embroidery while it is being worked on. The resulting design, stitched in a continuous line of cross-stitches, is known as **tambour work** and was used to decorate white muslin dresses and accessories, especially 1780-1850. See p.121.

TAMBOUR TOP *on a 'bureau à cylindre' in Louis XV period; c.1730.*

tang Long shank on sword blade to which the hilt is fitted.

tankard Drinking vessel with handle for beer, ale or cider. The earliest surviving tankards from the 16th and 17th centuries retained the same basic form – straight, tapering sides with S-shaped handle, rectangular THUMBPIECE and a hinged lid – until lidded tankards went out of use in the 18thC. Open tankards or MUGS were used from the 19thC. See pp.172, 247.

tantalus Decorative stand, case or box for cut-glass DECANTERS, fashionable from the mid-19thC until the Edwardian period in Britain. It is usually for two or three decanters, but can be for up to six. The decanters can only be removed by raising or lowering the overhead handle or bar which locks them in place.

TANTALUS *of mahogany and silver; c.1900; 15 in (38.1 cm) long.*

tapestry Handwoven fabric in which a design or picture is worked in during manufacture using the weft (crosswise) threads, although the term is loosely used for any woven wall-hanging or upholstery. Tapestries are usually woven with wool, silk or both, and take the name of the factory that produced them, such as GOBELIN.

tapestry-weave See KILIM.

targe Light Scottish circular shield made of wood and leather with central boss, used 16th to 18th centuries.

tastevin Small, shallow bowl or cup for wine-tasting. The French version has a single ring handle and is often attached to a chain or ribbon worn around the neck. The 17thC British version has two scroll handles.

TASTEVIN *of silver; French; c.1789.*

tavern clock Georgian wall timepiece with a weight-driven movement, which was developed c.1720 and made into the early 19thC. The large dial is unglazed and the trunk below it houses the weights and a seconds-beating PENDULUM. The clocks were also known as **Act of Parliament clocks**, after a 1797-8 Act which taxed clocks and timepieces. This supposedly resulted in private owners putting away their clocks and relying on public clocks. The Act was soon repealed, following a petition from clock-makers. See p.281.

tazza Italian for 'cup', originally the name of a shallow drinking vessel used in 16th and 17thC Italy. It later came to refer to other shallow or virtually flat dishes raised on a central stem also known as COMPORTS.

TAZZA *of glass; 6 in (15.2 cm) high.*

tea bowl Small, tapering circular cup without a handle and sometimes with a saucer, for drinking tea. The first European examples were based on the Chinese tea bowl and made in silver from the late 17thC and in ceramics and glass during the 18thC. See p.175.

tea caddy Box or casket with a hinged lid and lock used for storing tea leaves. Caddy is derived from the Malay *kati*, a unit of weight for tea. When tea was first introduced to Britain in the 17thC it was stored in porcelain jars, also known as caddies, which were imported from China. Tea was very expensive in the 18thC and kept in lockable silver or wooden caskets, originally known as **tea chests**. By the end of the century the name had changed to caddy. See pp.252-3.

tea ceremony wares Pottery such as bowls, water jars, tea caddies (**natsume**), charcoal burners (**hibachi**), incense boxes (**kogo** and **kobako**), utensil box (**satsubako**) used for the traditional Buddhist tea ceremony. In Japan the ceremony is known as *cha no yu* (hot water for tea). Much Japanese tea ceremony ware, such as RAKU ware, is rough, irregularly shaped earthenware, in keeping with the simple origins of the ritual. See p.176.

tea-dust glaze Greenish-brown GLAZE popular on Chinese 18thC porcelain. Known as *cha ye mo*, it was achieved by blowing green glaze powder through a fine gauze onto a brown glaze before firing.

teak One of the hardest, strongest and most durable furniture timbers of all. True teak is from India and Burma, but other similar woods are wrongly called teak. It is usually golden-brown in colour and darkens with age to medium and deep brown, sometimes with dark markings. It is slightly oily and smells leathery. It is so hard that cabinet-makers often charged a higher price to cover the costs of the extra work involved and the repair of blunted tools. Teak was used sparingly in the 18th and 19th centuries for table tops, chairs, chests, and CAMPAIGN FURNITURE.

tea kettle Large vessel resembling a teapot made for holding hot water, produced in ceramics, silver and SHEFFIELD PLATE from the early 18thC and ELECTROPLATE from the mid-19thC. The kettles usually had a matching tripod stand and spirit lamp. The tea kettle was superseded by the tea urn c.1760, but was revived in the 19thC. See pp.250-1.

teapot Covered vessel, generally of silver or ceramics, used for infusing and serving tea, and made in several different styles and sizes. Tea was first imported to Britain in the second half of the 17thC. Teapots are generally shorter and rounder than COFFEE or CHOCOLATE pots, and the spout, which is always opposite the handle, is positioned nearer the bottom of the

pot. PUNCHPOTS closely resemble teapots although they are usually much larger. See pp.177-8, 250.

teapoy 1 Small tripod table which was introduced in the early 19thC. From the 1820s, the table top was replaced by a wooden box which was used to store tea. **2** Large, earthenware or porcelain TEA CADDY.

tear See AIR-BEADING.

tea table Small, lightweight, easily moved table. TRIPOD TABLES were replaced by four-legged examples with a galleried or tray top towards the end of the 18thC, and these were also known as **silver tables** or **china tables**. Some versions have a fold-over top – rather like a CARD TABLE without the refinements for games.

TEA TABLE *with fold-over top; c.1765; 30 in (76 cm) high.*

SILVER TABLE *with pierced gallery; c.1750; 28 in (72 cm) high.*

tea urn Large, pear-shaped, lozenge-shaped or spherical hot-water urn with two handles, a domed cover with finial and a spigot and tap. Some examples have a red-hot iron inserted into a central tube in the body of the urn, others are heated by a spirit lamp.

Tea urns were made in silver, ELECTROPLATE, copper, JAPANNED metal or porcelain, largely replacing the tea kettle from the 1770s to mid-19thC in Britain and Europe. See pp.250-1.

telescope Instrument for magnifying distant objects, invented in the early 17thC, and consisting of telescopic wooden or metal tubes containing lenses. See pp.292-3.

temmoku glaze Black or dark brown GLAZE found on Chinese 10th-13thC (SONG dynasty) STONEWARE. The ware was also made in Japan for use in the tea ceremony. The glaze, when streaky, is known as a **hare's fur glaze**.

tempera Painting medium consisting of powdered colour pigments, egg yolk or egg white and water; used for panel painting until the 15thC when it was superseded by oil paint.

tenon See JOINING.

tent stitch Small diagonal stitch that spans one mesh of canvas or other material, worked in horizontal or diagonal rows.

term Short for **terminal figure**, a half statue or bust on a pillar or pedestal.

TERM *One of a pair, with an Ionic capital top; c.1730; 56 in (1.42 m) high.*

terracotta The name, translated from the Italian as 'baked earth' for a low-fired unglazed earthenware. The clay used is often rich in iron and therefore fires brick-red.

A vogue for Classical Greek style c.1860-80 prompted British factories to produce terracotta wares, including WEDGWOOD, MINTON, DOULTON and Torquay Potteries. Terracotta has been used for a wide range of wares – from figures, plaques, candlesticks and vases to garden urns and flowerpots.

Terracotta can be made with a slightly glossy surface and is suitable for painted decoration without any need for subsequent glazing and firing. The body is usually left unglazed, but some practical pieces such as jugs are glazed on the inside in order to make them waterproof.

tester A wooden canopy over a bedstead, chair or pulpit. The tester is supported on four posts, or on two posts and a back panel or headboard. See BEDSTEAD and p.138.

testoon British silver portrait coin issued by kings Henry VII and Henry VIII, with a face value of 12d (5p), later known as the SHILLING c.1550.

tête-a-tête See CABARET.

thaumatrope 1 Optical toy, developed in the late 1820s, consisting of a card or disc with two different figures drawn on each side. When it is rotated the two figures appear to combine into one.
2 Cylinder bearing a series of figures on the inside and a series of slits on the outside. The figures are viewed through the slits and when the cylinder is rotated appear to be moving. The effect is similar to that produced by a ZOETROPE.

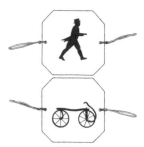

THAUMATROPE *When spun the man appears to be riding the hobbyhorse; c.1880; 2½ in (63 mm) wide.*

Thebes stool Wooden stool with a thonged leather or wooden seat based on an Egyptian design and introduced by LIBERTY in 1884. See p.94.

theodolite Surveying instrument for measuring vertical and horizontal angles, invented in 1571 by a British mathematician, Thomas Digges, but developed by engineer Jesse Ramsden c.1790. It incorporates a small telescope which moves horizontally and vertically, and often a magnifying lens and spirit level. See p.296.

Thonet Brothers Austrian furniture-makers established Vienna, 1842, which specialised in BENTWOOD furniture, perfected by its founder Michael Thonet (1796-1871). Furniture was exported to the USA and Europe, especially after mass-production techniques were introduced in 1859.

By 1871 Thonet Brothers was the largest furniture-making firm in the world. The company changed its name to Thonet-Mundus in 1923, producing tubular steel chairs designed by Marcel BREUER, Ludwig MIES VAN DER ROHE and LE CORBUSIER among others.

threading 1 Threads of molten glass used to decorate glassware, similar to, and often referred to as TRAILING. Threads or trails of glass are applied onto the glass body when it is still in its molten state, and can then either be left raised on the surface or rolled into the glass body. From 1876 threading was usually carried out by

machine and generally known as threading, while the term trailing tends to be reserved for the hand-applied decoration. See p.208.
2. In silver, narrow lines engraved around the border of an object, and also known as a **thread edge**.

thumbpiece Metal knob or lever, also known as a **billet**, on the lid hinge of a vessel, allowing it to be opened with the thumb while holding the handle with the fingers.

THUMBPIECE *on the hinged cover of a silver beer jug; 1709.*

thuya Soft, close-grained, reddish-brown wood with a mottled figuring, imported from Africa and the USA and sometimes seen in VENEERS and INLAID DECORATION.

Tiffany & Co Leading American jewellery firm founded 1837 in New York by goldsmith Charles Tiffany (1812-1902). The firm gained an international reputation for jewellery, especially diamonds, watches, gems and silverware. It introduced the STERLING STANDARD to the USA in 1850, which was later legalised for American sterling silverware. In 1886, Charles Tiffany designed the **Tiffany setting** with curved prongs to secure a solitaire diamond to a finger ring.
Charles's son, **Louis Comfort Tiffany** (1848-1933), founded an interior design company in New York in 1879 which later became Tiffany Studios. In 1880 he patented FAVRILE GLASS and for the next 20 years produced art, mosaic and stained glass pieces as well as ART NOUVEAU vases, bowls and lamps with glass shades. From 1902 he concentrated on jewellery, and also produced pottery and designed furniture, wallpapers and fabrics in ART NOUVEAU style. The studios closed in 1932, but Tiffany & Co still operates. See p.219.

tigerware See SALT-GLAZED STONEWARE.

tigerwood See ZEBRAWOOD.

tiles Decorated ceramic slabs for roof, wall or floor decoration. MAIOLICA tiles of 15thC Italy were designed for flooring, but their bright colours inspired Spanish and Portuguese

pictorial wall tiles. The Dutch produced monochrome blue and white or manganese purple and white wall tiles which were exported throughout Europe from the 17th to 19th centuries. Key centres for decorative tiles in Britain were BRISTOL, LAMBETH and LIVERPOOL from the late 17thC, and in France, ROUEN, NEVERS and Lisieux.
In Germany and other parts of central Europe, tiles with incised or relief designs, covered with a green, yellow or brown lead GLAZE were made by the *Hafner* (stove-makers).
Demand for decorative tiles fell in the early 19thC, but revived in the mid-century. The British output came from Staffordshire potteries, particularly MINTON. The medieval technique of making **encaustic tiles**, in which tiles are inlaid with clays of contrasting colours and fixed with heat, was also revived. At the end of the century glazed tiles were made in ARTS AND CRAFTS, AESTHETIC and ART NOUVEAU styles. See p.187.

till Locking compartments for keeping money, fitted into a medieval chest or casket – the forerunner of the drawer in a chest of drawers.

timepiece Any timekeeping device, generally used to indicate one that does not strike the hours or quarters.

tin Soft, brittle, silvery-white metal usually combined with other metals to make alloys such as BRONZE and PEWTER. Tin is also used to line other metals in a process known as **tin-plating**. This gives a rust-resistant finish or a protective covering to the interiors of brass or copper vessels.

tinder-box Wooden or metal box used from the 15th to 19th centuries for keeping tinder for fire-making. The box may be pocket-sized or larger for household use, and also contained a flint and steel for making sparks and sometimes brimstone matches for transferring the flame. Some 16thC boxes have a WHEEL-LOCK mechanism for producing sparks.

tin-glazed earthenware
Earthenware coated in an opaque white-ground glaze. The addition of tin oxide to a basic lead GLAZE resulted in an impermeable, more refined, white surface than previously achieved in the West. Tin glazes were used almost exclusively on earthenware, but were occasionally used by porcelain-makers to whiten a cream body, such as at CHANTILLY c.1730 and CHELSEA c.1745.
Tin-glazed earthenware was first made during the Mesopotamian civilisation, c.1000 BC, but did not

reach western Europe until the 8thC, when Moorish invaders introduced the techniques to Spain (see HISPANO-MORESQUE WARE). From the 13thC Italians began to develop their own style of tin-glazed earthenware which became known as MAIOLICA; the French followed suit with their version, FAIENCE, the Germanic countries with **fayence**, and the Dutch and British produced DELFTWARE.
Colours for decorating tin-glazed earthenware were at first limited to HIGH-TEMPERATURE COLOURS. From the 18thC, ENAMEL decoration was sometimes added after the tin glaze had been fired, and a second, lead glaze or KWAART was applied to give a brighter finish. See p.165.

tin toy trademarks Initials or trademarks used by the most important makers of mechanical toys from the late 19thC. Some companies such as Bing, Carette and Günthermann, changed their marks from time to time, making accurate dating possible. Trademarks were applied in a variety of ways: stencilled or rubber-stamped on the body; applied as a transfer, a printed tin-plate lozenge or embossed brass plate; or impressed directly onto the body of the toy. See box below.

toaster Long-handled toasting fork for holding bread, muffins or other food over an open fire from the 16thC. The toaster became increasingly popular from c.1720, and sometimes had a telescopic facility or a fitting for resting the fork on the bars of a grate or fender. See p.241.

toasting glass Tall, slender-bowled wine glass with a very slim stem used for drinking a toast, and made in Britain c.1725-1800. Its capacity is 2-4 fl oz (50-115 ml). A **toastmaster's glass** dating from c.1725-50, is similar

but has a thickened base and sides allowing a capacity of only ½-¾ fl oz (15-20 ml), to ensure that the toastmaster remains coherent. See GLASSES, DRINKING.

Toby jug Earthenware jug shaped like a figure, usually a seated stout man in 18thC dress wearing a three-cornered hat. Recognisable Toby jugs were first made c.1760 at Burslem, Staffordshire by Ralph WOOD. Some female versions are known as MARTHA GUNN. See p.172.

toddy Stronger form of punch; drinking vessels for toddy are usually smaller than those for punch, and date from the late 18th to mid-19th centuries. A **toddy lifter** was used to transfer the punch from bowl to glass. Shaped like a miniature decanter with a slim neck, a bulbous body and a hole at either end, it operates on a siphon principle. A quantity of punch is drawn into the lifter by immersing the bulbous end into the punch, and closing the thumb over the neck hole. When the thumb is released, the liquid pours out. See p.249.

Toftware Late 17thC decorative SLIP-ware dishes made in Staffordshire by Thomas Toft (d.1689) and others. The designs are executed in a naive style in brown and white slip.

toile 1 Basic dress pattern made of muslin. 2 Linen cloth, or in the late 19thC, a fabric of silk and linen. 3 The pattern of a piece of bobbin lace. 4 **Toile du Jouy** is a printed cotton fabric made in France in the late 18thC, usually printed with romantic, figurative scenes in either red or blue on an ivory ground.

Tokyo School of Art Japanese group of artists founded 1887 by Ishikawa Komei. The school was influenced by

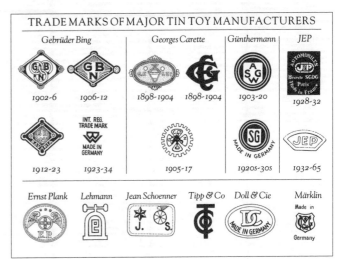

TRADE MARKS OF MAJOR TIN TOY MANUFACTURERS

Gebrüder Bing		Georges Carette		Günthermann	JEP
1902-6	*1906-12*	*1898-1904*	*1898-1904*	*1903-20*	*1928-32*
1912-23	*1923-34*	*1905-17*		*1920s-30s*	*1932-65*

Ernst Plank	Lehmann	Jean Schoenner	Tipp & Co	Doll & Cie	Märklin

Western art and art schools while retaining the traditional skills of Japanese craftsmanship. See p.401.

toleware Name from the French *tôle peinte* ('painted tin') for small objects of hand-painted tin-plate such as boxes, trays and coffee mills. The technique originated in France *c.*1740. Toleware was mass-produced from the 1760s into the 19thC in Birmingham and elsewhere in Britain.

Tompion, Thomas (1638-1713) British clock and watch-maker who gained international recognition for his outstanding mechanical skills and craftsmanship. He was established in business by 1671, and was the first clock-maker to employ a system of serial numbers to identify timepieces. His system was continued by his successor in the business, George GRAHAM. From 1674 Tompion worked with the British scientist Robert Hooke on various timekeeping improvements, including the BALANCE spring, which helped to give the English a technical lead in watchmaking. See p.278.

tooling Work or ornamentation done with tools; especially stamped or gilded designs on books or leather.

topaz Precious gemstone, ranging in colour from white through to sherry-brown and blue. Orange-red varieties are the rarest and most highly prized. Pink or 'rose' topaz is the result of HEAT TREATMENT applied to yellow topaz. Topaz is hard and polishes well, but it is highly susceptible to cleavage or splitting. It is usually cut as ovals or oblongs and is often confused with the abundant and less valuable **citrine**.

top-plate The watchmaking equivalent of the back plate in a clock, so-called because a watch movement is assembled face down.

torchère Portable stand for a candle, also known as a **candle-stand**. Torchères, can be in the form of standards to place on the floor or, especially from the mid-18thC, small enough to be set on a dressing or writing table.

TORCHÈRE *on scrolled tripod stand; c.1690; 37 in (94 cm) high.*

tortoiseshell Dark brown, mottled shell of certain species of sea turtle which can be moulded by heating, and thickened or enlarged by joining pieces together under pressure. It was especially popular for INLAID DECORATION on English and French furniture in the 17th, 18th and early 19th centuries (see BOULLE), and for jewellery inlaid with PIQUÉ work in Britain in the 1860s.

tortoiseshell glass Mottled brown ART GLASS developed in Europe and the USA *c.*1880. It is made by rolling a GATHER of clear molten glass over broken pieces of brown glass, adding a yellowish-brown stain.

touch mark See PEWTER.

touchpiece A PIERCED coin hung from the neck of a supplicant at a touching ceremony. A piece touched by the monarch was thought to be a guard against disease.

tourbillon See BREGUET.

Tournai The leading porcelain factory of the Low Countries, from its foundation in 1751 to the end of the 18thC. It produced soft-paste PORCELAIN tableware very much in the style of French porcelain of the time, particularly that of SÈVRES. Exotic birds, naturalistic flowers and pink monochrome landscapes are characteristic themes. Some of the figures made, particularly those left 'in-the-white', are similar to DERBY figures. In the 1790s, the factory merged with the nearby St Armand-des-Eaux which made reproductions of 18thC porcelain while Tournai made household wares, until the mid-19thC.

c.1756-81

toys 18thC English term for small ornamental objects and novelties crafted in materials such as porcelain, silver or gold, ivory or tortoiseshell. miniature ornaments, seals, scent bottles, decorative knife handles, thimbles and pomanders, for example, would be typical gifts bought from the 18thC 'toyman'. See p.260.

tracery Architectural term dating from the 17thC and used to refer to the carved, ornamental stone OPENWORK which decorates the top of a Gothic window. It is also found on vaulted ceilings, doors and panels. Tracery was used extensively during the first half of the 19thC on the backs of chairs and hall seats.

trader's token An unofficial coin issued by an individual or company to supply a local need for small change.

trailing See THREADING.

train In clocks and watches, the series of wheels and driving pinions linking the source of power (a weight or a spring) to the hands, the strike or other end-function. A clock or watch may have a single 'going train', or may also have a STRIKING, musical or alarm train. See box below.

transfer-printing A method of printing onto solid objects such as ceramics and glassware which made the mass production of designs possible for the first time. Invented in Britain in the mid-18thC, it was not used widely in continental Europe until the 19thC. The process involves taking a tissue print from a copper-plate ENGRAVING, and transferring this to the receiving object. In ceramics this can be either over or under the GLAZE. Designs were initially monochrome, sometimes coloured in later. Multicoloured transfer-printing did not become established until the 1840s.

A form of transfer-printing called **bat-printing** was used in Staffordshire in the early 19thC. The designs were transferred to the glazed earthenware by means of a flexible sheet – or bat – of glue or gelatine. See p.153.

Transitional Chinese porcelain, mostly BLUE AND WHITE, produced in the Transitional Period (*c.*1620-80) covering the last two decades of the MING dynasty and the beginning of the QING dynasty. Imperial orders disappeared with the internal warfare following the fall of the Ming dynasty and were only partly replaced by orders from the scholar-gentry class. This move is reflected in the proliferation of wares for the writing table such as cylindrical brush pots and in painted decoration depicting more expansive landscapes and everyday rather than imperial scenes. Exports to the West were limited and were mainly of KRAAK PORSELEIN.

translucency The term for the degree to which a substance such as porcelain or glass allows light to pass though it (thickness permitting) and the quality or colour of that light on passing out of the body. See p.149.

treasure trove Hidden or buried money, or precious objects whose owner is unknown. See p.423.

treen Derived from an old word for 'wooden', the term refers to small domestic articles made of TURNED or carved wood, such as bowls, platters and spoons. See p.370.

tremblant An item of jewellery such as a brooch, AIGRETTE or pendant with an ornament – a flower or bee, for example – on a coiled spring which trembles when the wearer moves.

trembleuse Silver or ceramic cup and saucer, fashionable in the 18thC, with a central raised ring in the saucer to hold the cup firm.

TREMBLEUSE *of Viennese porcelain with pierced ring wall; c.1725-30.*

GOING TRAIN OF A PENDULUM CLOCK

movement pillar

suspension spring

crutch-piece pin

pinion

arbor

back plate

pendulum rod

pendulum bob

escapement incorporating escape wheel and pallets

hour hand

front plate

fusee

spring barrel

trencher salt See SALT.

trestle table The earliest form of dining table, consisting of planks of wood held together by cross-bearers on the under-surface, and initially rested, unfixed, over two or more folding supports, or trestles. In the 16thC trestles were fixed to the table top. Trestle tables were reintroduced as part of the early Victorian GOTHIC REVIVAL. See p.108.

trial An experimental coin, banknote or stamp, possibly of unfinished design, and often struck or printed on a material different to that intended for circulation.

tricoteuse Term used to describe a small, 19thC French work table with a rail bordering the edge. The term is from *tricoteur* 'knitter'.

tripod table Small-topped table supported on a slender pillar and a tripod of outward-facing feet. These were popular OCCASIONAL TABLES and for serving desserts and tea in the 18thC Georgian period. Some versions have a top that snaps or folds down vertically over the supporting pillar. See BIRDCAGE and p.112.

trivet Wrought-iron stand with three or four legs on which to place pots or kettles taken from the fire.

trompe l'oeil Decoration on a flat surface that appears three-dimensional. The term is French for 'deceive the eye'.

troy weight Traditional weight system used by goldsmiths, silversmiths and jewellers from 1526. The name comes from the town of Troyes, France, and was probably brought to Britain by Henry V, *c.*1420. The basic unit is the troy ounce (oz), divided into 20 pennyweights (dwt); 12 troy ounces make one troy pound (lb). A troy ounce is about 10 per cent heavier than an ordinary (avoirdupois) ounce. In some auction catalogues weights are quoted in troy ounces and decimal fractions. Troy weight is still used but metric grams are now taking over. See box above.

trumeau mirror See PIER.

trumpeter clock A clock similar in design and appearance to the CUCKOO CLOCK, but with a model military bugler sounding a trumpet on the hour or quarter hour. The trumpet sound is operated by bellows. Another variant on the theme is a clock with mechanically played drums.

trussel See DIE.

TROY WEIGHT CONVERSION CHART

TROY	AVOIRDUPOIS*	METRIC
1 dwt	24 gr (¹⁄₁₆ oz)	1.56 g
5 dwt	96 gr (¼ oz)	7.78 g
18¼ dwt*	1 oz	28.35 g
1 oz (20 dwt)	1¹⁄₁₀ oz	31.1 g
2 oz	2⅕ oz	62.21 g
3 oz	3⅓ oz	93.31 g
4 oz	4⅜ oz	124.41 g
5 oz	5½ oz	155.52 g
10 oz	11 oz	311.04 g
12 oz (1 lb)	13 oz	373.24 g
14 oz 11⅔ dwt*	16 oz (1 lb)	453.59 g
20 oz	22 oz	622.07 g
50 oz	55 oz	1.5552 kg
100 oz	110 oz	3.1104 kg
*Approximate		

tsuba The metal hand guard on a Japanese sword or dagger, often finely decorated. See KODOGU and p.397.

tube lining See SLIP.

tubular steel furniture Furniture with a tubular steel framework, generally chromium plated. The earliest tubular steel chair was designed by the Hungarian Marcel BREUER in 1925 and made by the THONET Brothers of Vienna.

Tudric Trade name for table and decorative ware of PEWTER marketed by the London retail store LIBERTY during the early 20thC to accompany its CYMRIC silver range. Many of the Celtic-inspired ART NOUVEAU designs were created by Archibald Knox (1864-1933). See p.368.

tulipwood Hard, heavy wood, yellowish-brown with a pinkish tinge, from Central and South America. It was used for decorative VENEERS and BANDING during the 18th and early 19th centuries, especially on 18thC French furniture. See ROSEWOOD.

tulwar The most common type of Indian sword, usually single-edged and often curved. The hilt is entirely metal with a flat disc-like pommel.

tumbler Flat-based drinking glass with neither stem, foot nor handle. Tumblers are variously shaped and sized, but unlike BEAKERS never have a flared mouth. In the 17thC, heavy metal tumblers with curved sides were designed to tumble back to an upright position if set down awkwardly.

Tunbridge ware Articles such as trays, table tops, tea caddies, picture frames and games boards, decorated with a low-cost, mass-produced MARQUETRY developed at Tunbridge

Wells, Kent, in the mid-17thC. Rectangular-section rods of various woods were glued together then cut across in thin slices to produce a multi-coloured veneer. A similar technique was used in the 19thC for small **stickwork** articles, such as egg cups, turned on a lathe. See p.146.

tureen Circular or oval, deep, covered bowl of porcelain, pottery, silver or silver plate, made from the early 18thC for serving soup, sauce, vegetables or stew. **Sauce tureens** are smaller, plainer versions.

Turkish knot See CARPET KNOTS.

Turkish style An exotic furnishing style developed in mid-19thC Britain for the comfort of smokers. It drew inspiration from Middle Eastern themes probably because Turkey was associated with fine tobacco. The

characteristic elements include fretted and arcaded woodwork; small four, six or eight-legged JAPANNED tables inlaid with mother-of-pearl; upholstered chairs incorporating a panel of Oriental carpet; pierced brass incense burners and lamps.

At first, the style was confined to the smoking room, but in the 1880s, as smoking became more widely tolerated, the **Turkish corner** became a popular feature in the drawing room. It centred on a high-backed corner divan seat with an Eastern-style canopy and frame.

Turkoman (or **Turkman**) Generic name for nomadic tribesmen from central Asia known for their fine weaving. Turkoman carpets have a woollen pile and usually a red and black colour scheme. See pp.304-5.

turning The shaping of wood and other materials such as metal and ivory on a lathe. The material is clamped onto the lathe and rotated, or turned, at an even rate while the craftsman shapes it by cutting or filing, so producing a symmetrically carved object. Wood turning has been a principal decorative effect on furniture since medieval times and developed particularly during the late 16th and 17th centuries.

Different woods are more or less suited to turning but the introduction of high-speed, power-driven lathes in the 19thC enabled virtually any wood to be turned in a greater variety of shapes, and with a more uniform and symmetrical result than that achieved by the hand or foot-operated lathe. See box below and p.89.

turnip watch See FARMER'S WATCH.

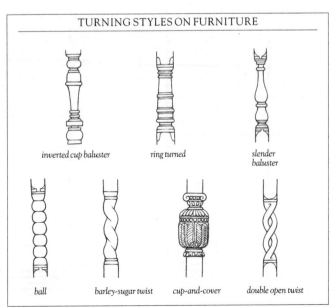

TURNING STYLES ON FURNITURE

inverted cup baluster   *ring turned*   *slender baluster*

ball   *barley-sugar twist*   *cup-and-cover*   *double open twist*

526

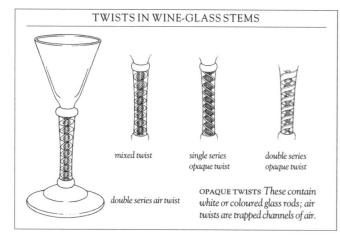

TWISTS IN WINE-GLASS STEMS

mixed twist

single series opaque twist

double series opaque twist

double series air twist

OPAQUE TWISTS *These contain white or coloured glass rods; air twists are trapped channels of air.*

turquoise Blue-green gemstone widely used, cut en cabochon (see JEWEL CUTTING), in 19thC jewellery. Turquoise probably takes its name from the French for Turkey, from where it first reached Europe. The bluer the colour the more prized the gem – the best-quality stones come from north-east Iran. See p.267.

turret clock A clock with its dial on the outside wall of a building and its movement inside.

twill Fabric in which the weave forms diagonal, herringbone or diamond lines. The weft passes over two or more, and under one or more warps.

twist Form of decoration in the stem of a drinking GLASS, popular in the second half of the 18thC and revived in the 19thC. White or coloured glass RODS are trapped in the glass while it is still in a molten state and then twisted. An **air twist** is a twisted air channel in the stem. See box above.

tyg Two or three-handled drinking vessel, also known as a **loving cup**, usually large and of ceramic or silver, for passing from guest to guest at the end of a banquet. The term is loosely used for any two-handled cup. Earthenware tygs with SLIP decoration and sometimes initials or dates as part of the design, were common in the 17th and 18th centuries. See p.197.

U

undercut Ornamental carving cut so deeply that the decoration not only stands out from the body of the material but in parts stands free of it.

underframing The support structure under, for example, a seat, table top, dresser or other cabinet.

underglaze Design or colours applied, cut or incised into a ceramic body before glazing and firing. See HIGH-TEMPERATURE COLOURS, p.152.

unite A British 17thC gold £1 coin. Handsome **triple-unites** were struck by King Charles I at Shrewsbury and Oxford mints in the 1640s.

upholsterer's chair Single chair with fabric-covered back and seat. The chairs were hired out in the 17thC to private households by upholsterers.

upright 1 Frame of a CHAIR back in one piece with the back legs. 2 Any vertical support on furniture.

urn stand A small table on which to stand a TEA URN, often with a pull-out slide for a teapot. The stands were introduced in the mid-18thC.

URN STAND *with a pull-out slide and serpentine gallery; c.1780; 14½ in (36.8 cm) wide.*

Utility scheme British scheme introduced during the Second World War which enforced manufacturers to produce standardised designs to reduce wastage of raw materials. An official Design Panel hoped to encourage plain, durable but modern designs. Utility furniture tended to be rather drab, but its influence continued throughout the 1950s. Utility ceramics were also produced – simple pieces in white or cream. See p.179.

Utility logo

V

Val-Saint-Lambert, Cristalleries du The principal glass factory in Belgium, founded on the site of a monastery near Liège in 1825. At first it produced English-style glassware, but later manufactured its own designs of ART GLASS in ART NOUVEAU and ART DECO styles.

vambrace See ARMOUR.

Van Cleef & Arpels Firm of jewellers founded in Paris, 1906, noted for a style of setting stones without the metal holds showing (known as **invisibly set**). The firm also introduced the **minaudière** for women – a decorative metal box with sections for such items as make-up, comb, money and cigarettes.

van de Velde, Henri (1863-1957) Belgian designer and architect, an influential practitioner and teacher of ART NOUVEAU style, and a founder of the design group DEUTSCHER WERKBUND. He designed simple but elegant, sparsely decorated furniture, with parallel curves earlier and elongated angular shapes later, as well as porcelain for MEISSEN, jewellery, and metalwork.

vandyke rim Scalloped border on glassware or ceramics, named after the pointed lace collars seen in portraits of the English court by the Flemish artist Sir Anthony Van Dyck (1599-1641).

VANDYKE RIM *on a drinking glass of the mid-19thC.*

vargueño 19thC term for a Spanish 16th to 17th-century drop-front desk resting on a chest or trestle stand and with elaborate INLAID DECORATION.

varnish Transparent, oil or spirit-based liquid giving a hard, clear surface layer. Expensive furniture may have ten or more layers of resin dissolved in spirit, each coat being dried and polished before the next application. Cheaper furniture may have only two or three coats, with no polishing in between. Varnishing was used from the late 17thC while FRENCH POLISHING appeared about 1820. Today, varnish has been largely superseded by polyurethane lacquer and cellulose finishes. Oil-based varnish is used for pictures. See p.425.

vase carpets Term for Persian carpets made using a triple weft technique. In each set of three wefts, the outer threads were of wool and pulled taut, and the middle one was of silk or cotton and slack. This altered the overall tension of the weave and resulted in a more durable fabric. It was used for a wide range of different designs, including those with a vase or vases within the field pattern and GARDEN carpets. See pp.302-3.

'Vaseline' glass Yellow-green glass, wrongly said to have an oily sheen. Uranium oxide gives the colour. The glass was first made in the 19thC in Germany by Joseph Riedel, who called it **Annagrün** and **Annagelb**. It quickly became popular for low-cost vases and other decorative items. See p.225.

Vauxhall Porcelain works operating 1751-64, the fourth main London factory of the period after CHELSEA, Bow and Limehouse. A SOAPSTONE soft-paste PORCELAIN formula was used for products ranging from tea wares, candlesticks and snuffboxes to chamber pots and flowerpots. Decoration was mainly Chinese-style blue and white, often similar to DELFTWARE produced at nearby LAMBETH, but there were also some high-quality hand-painted designs, and – a Vauxhall speciality – outlines TRANSFER-PRINTED in two or three colours and then overpainted with ENAMEL colours.

veilleuse French for 'night light', and used in the 18th and 19th centuries for a device to keep broth or a drink warm on the bedside table. The flame from a small oil lamp or candle, placed in the cylindrical base, heated a covered cup or a teapot set on top of a cylinder.

vellum Fine parchment made from calf, lamb or kid skin used for the pages and binding of early books.

velvet A costly, dense-pile fabric originally of cotton or linen with a silk PILE. It is woven with two warps (two sets of lengthwise threads), the second warp being looped and cut with wire to form the pile. In **figured velvet**, the design is formed by leaving some areas of the pile uncut. In **pile-on-pile velvet**, the length of the pile is varied, or some areas are left free of pile.
Velvet was first imported into Britain from Italy in the 14thC. Then in the late 17thC it was used as an upholstery fabric on furniture for the well-to-do. By the early 18thC velvet was being produced at SPITALFIELDS SILK FACTORIES. In the 20thC most velvet has been woven from man-made yarn or a mixture of natural and man-made fibres.

veneer A thin layer of decorative wood, or sometimes TORTOISESHELL or ivory, glued over a wooden body or CARCASS. Veneering was practised in ancient Egypt, Greece and the Roman Empire, and rediscovered in the early 17thC. The craft came to Britain from Holland a few decades later, and by the 18thC French and British cabinet-makers had raised it to a fine art. They cut woods such as walnut, satinwood and rosewood to make fullest possible use of grain and colour. The thickness of a veneer depends on the quality of the wood and how it is cut; generally 18thC hand-sawn veneers are $\frac{1}{16}$ in (1.6 mm) thick; 19thC circular saw veneers, $\frac{1}{32}$ in (0.8 mm) thick, and the veneers produced by the machine-powered tools of the late 19thC are thinner still. See BURR and p.91.

Venetian glass Venice has been an influential centre of glass production since c. AD 450, although the glass-houses moved from the city itself to the nearby island of Murano c.1290. Early wares were opaque, including beakers and beads, but with the development of clear CRISTALLO in the 15thC, Venetian glass came to dominate the European market. Elegant wine glasses with elaborate surface decoration (**façon de Venise**) were particularly popular, and were widely copied throughout Europe.

Venetian glass-makers led the field in making vividly coloured glassware, and played an important part in developing MILLEFIORI and LATTICINO techniques. When LEAD CRYSTAL, with its greater strength and clarity, began to be developed in Britain in the late 17thC, the Venetian glass industry went into decline, but was revived in the late 19thC.

Venini, Paolo (1895-1959) Foremost modern Italian designer of glass, with his own factory at Murano from 1925. His designs combine rich colour and texture with simple lines, and sometimes incorporating techniques such as MILLEFIORI and LATTICINO. A celebrated design was a free-form bowl resembling the folds of a cupped handkerchief.

verdigris A green powdery deposit which develops on copper, brass or bronze after long periods of exposure to air. Unlike the gradual oxidisation process that forms a desirable PATINA, verdigris is dreaded by coin and medal collectors in particular, as it is very difficult to treat on small objects.

verge escapement See ESCAPEMENT.

vermiculé Patterned with a mass of little worm-like lines; a decoration developed for SÈVRES c.1750.

verneh A distinctive type of strong, FLAT-WEAVE rug originating in the southern Caucasus. See SUMAKH.

vernier scale A short, sliding scale attached to the main scale on some instruments and barometers in the 19th and 20th centuries to make minute readings possible. The scale was invented 1631 by French mathematician Paul Vernier.

VERNIER SCALE *from a cistern barometer; c.1820. The movable secondary scale permits more accurate readings to one-hundredth of an inch.*

vernis martin A decorative technique which reproduced the effect of Chinese LACQUER. Patented by Frenchman Guillaume Martin (after whom it was named) and his brothers in the 18thC, it was the French and Swiss version of JAPANNING. The lustrous, translucent finish used up to 30 coats of coloured, monochrome or gold-dusted varnish. Vernis martin was used to decorate OBJECTS OF VERTU, ÉTUIS and furniture.

verre craquelé See ICE GLASS.

Verre de Soie See PEARL SATIN-GLASS

verre églomisé Glass with gilded decoration that is not fired onto the surface but protected by varnish or metal foil. The gilt surface could be engraved with a fine needle point. The technique dates from ancient Rome, was revived in the Middle Ages, and again in the 18thC by Paris art dealer Jean-Baptiste Glomy, after whom the process is now named.

Verzelini, Jacopo (1522-1616) Venetian glass-maker who came to Britain in 1571 and was granted a 21-year monopoly in 1574 to make glass in the Venetian style.

vesta case Case or box for 'vestas' – the friction matches of wax or wood that preceded the safety match. The cases were produced from the second

VESTA CASES *of metal; c.1900; 2-3 in (51-76 mm) long.*

half of the 19thC usually in silver and other metals, but also in a variety of materials such as PORCELAIN and PAPIER-MÂCHÉ. Pocket-sized and larger table versions were made later, often in novelty shapes. See p.261.

vetro a fili reticello See LATTICINO.

Victorian era Queen Victoria's reign (1837-1901) during which taste was much influenced by the rising middle classes. See pp.49-69.

Vienna Innovative porcelain factory founded 1719 which produced hard-paste PORCELAIN soon after MEISSEN. Early pieces are high BAROQUE with painted CHINOISERIE, flower or landscape decoration. In 1744 the factory was taken over by the state and produced Meissen-style ROCOCO figures and tableware. In the late 18thC Vienna produced simple, NEOCLASSICAL pieces with GILDING and landscapes and portraits painted in panels on a brilliantly coloured ground, and Classical figures in BISCUIT porcelain. The factory began to decline from the late 1820s, finally closing in 1864.

Throughout the 19thC the Vienna shield mark was much used by other factories and decorating workshops copying the Vienna style, hence the widespread use of inverted commas – 'Vienna' – to denote the origin of such pieces in cataloguing.

c.1750-1820

Vienna regulator Originally a highly accurate, weight-driven and PENDULUM-regulated wall clock, like a small, elegant LONGCASE CLOCK, with a glass-panelled case. The clocks were first made in Vienna from the early 19thC, but c.1860 versions of much inferior quality were mass-produced in Germany for the European and US markets. The Viennese examples, made during the BIEDERMEIER period (1815-45), commonly have restrained rectilinear cases with PEDIMENTED tops; later German types are fussier in style, with a profusion of turned ornament. See p.280.

Vienna Secession A group of artists and designers who, influenced by the rectilinear, vertical designs of Scottish architect-designer Charles Rennie MACKINTOSH and the GLASGOW SCHOOL, broke away from the artistic establishment in Vienna. Two leading figures, Josef Hoffmann and Kolomon Moser, went on to establish the WIENER WERKSTÄTTE.

vignette 1 Decoration of vine leaves and bunches of grapes, used in medieval carvings and fashionable

again for friezes on furniture in NEOCLASSICAL style. 2 Picture or decoration (on porcelain, for example) whose edges fade into the surround instead of having a sharply defined border.

Vile & Cobb (1751-64) Cabinet-making partnership between William Vile (c.1700-67) and John Cobb (c.1715-78). Their furniture was noted for its consistently excellent workmanship, although it was overshadowed by Thomas CHIPPENDALE's output.

Vile, the senior partner in the firm, was in 1761 appointed cabinet-maker to the royal household by King George III, for whom he produced some of the finest English furniture in Rococo style, using rare woods and delicate MARQUETRY decoration.

vinaigrette Small, gilt-lined metal box designed to hold a sponge soaked in spiced vinegar or aromatic oil, and held in place by a grille. The aroma was inhaled when the hinged lid was raised, to fend off foul smells or to revive swooning ladies. Vinaigrettes became popular and fashionable items from the late 18thC until the end of the 19thC. See pp.212, 260.

violet wood See ROSEWOOD.

vitrine A display cabinet with glass doors or lid and often glazed sides as well, in which small items of interest such as coins or fossils were kept. Vitrines were introduced in the second half of the 18thC and reproduced later in the 19thC. Towards the end of the 19thC the **vitrine table**, with a lined display compartment and glass top and sides, was introduced. See p.133.

Vitruvian scroll See DECORATIVE MOTIFS.

voider An early form of tray, used for clearing scraps from the dining table in the 17thC, that evolved into the BUTLER'S TRAY. See p.145.

volcanic glass See LAVA GLASS.

volute A decorative coil – as for example on ornamental handles on pottery and at the ends of the horizontal comb-piece topping some WINDSOR CHAIR backs. It was copied from the coils near the top of an Ionic COLUMN in Classical architecture.

voyeuse Low-seated chair for sitting astride with the elbows resting on the padded top of the back – while watching card games for example. It was first made in France in the mid-18thC. A similar chair for ladies to kneel on (since they could not sit astride with modesty) is called a **voyeuse à genoux**.

VOYEUSE *of giltwood, with lyre back and padded top rail; c.1785.*

Voysey, C.F.A. (1857-1941) British architect and designer who believed in functional design, and was associated with the ART FURNITURE movement. He was also influenced by the purist ideas of William MORRIS and the ARTS AND CRAFTS MOVEMENT. His best furniture was produced 1895-1910, and he designed wallpapers and fabrics. Voysey influenced both ART NOUVEAU style and the development of industrial design. See pp.67-69.

vulcanite Hard, black material made by heating rubber with sulphur and used to simulate JET in jewellery and for some early fountain pens. It is also known as **ebonite**. See p.269.

Vulliamy family Three generations of a clock-making family of Swiss origin working in London c. 1750-1854. Justin (c. 1730-90), Benjamin (1747-1811) and Benjamin Lewis (1780-1854) made LONGCASE, BRACKET, MANTEL and CARRIAGE CLOCKS. Benjamin Lewis had the unfortunate tendency to replace the original movements of clocks sent in for repair with his own new movements. See p.279.

W

Waals, Peter See COTSWOLD SCHOOL.

Wackerle, Josef (1880-1959) German porcelain modeller who broke away from the convention of imitating 18thC figures and produced statuettes of sporting girls and figures in contemporary dress. He was artistic director of the NYMPHENBURG porcelain factory 1906-9, and later produced some models in modern dress for the BERLIN porcelain factory.

Wagner, Otto (1841-1918) Viennese architect and furniture designer, a pioneer of FUNCTIONALISM with his

conviction that 'nothing that is not practical can be beautiful'. His work influenced other key designers such as Josef Hoffmann and Adolf Loos, and from 1899 he was a member of the VIENNA SECESSION. Wagner's furniture is distinguished by its lack of ornamentation, functional quality and combined use of metal and wood. Some of his BENTWOOD designs were produced by the THONET brothers.

wainscot Wood panelling or a piece of furniture with much panelled work. The term was used in medieval times to describe oak timber suitable for wagon (wain) construction, and later for straight-grained oak suitable for panelling. A **wainscot bed** is one with solid panels at its head and/or foot; a **wainscot chair** is a panel-backed chair.

waiter See SALVER.

Waldglas See BOHEMIA.

wall clock A general term for a weight or spring-driven clock intended for wall-mounting, including the CARTEL CLOCK, LANTERN CLOCK, GIRANDOLE, TAVERN CLOCK and REGULATOR.
 A **hooded wall clock** has a hood that can be lifted off from the wall-mounted movement. A **wall dial** is a Georgian, Victorian or Edwardian spring-driven timepiece with a circular dial in a wooden surround. Some versions have a short box extension with a glazed aperture through which the motion of the PENDULUM can be seen. See p.280.

wall pocket Pottery or glass vase for hanging on the wall to hold flowers, popular in the 18th and 19th centuries. It is most often in the shape of a flat-backed **cornucopia**.

walnut A close-grained hardwood, light golden-brown to dark greyish-brown in colour with dark streaks and often with a rich grain pattern. Walnut took the place of oak as the most favoured wood for furniture-making c. 1660 until the introduction of mahogany in the 1720s. The European species was used for high-quality solid furniture in Tudor England, and for the finest Italian, German and French furniture of the 16th and 17th centuries.
 European walnut became scarce after 1709 following severe weather in France, but the darker American walnut was used throughout most of the 18thC. See p.90.

Walter, Alméric (1859-1942) French ART NOUVEAU and ART DECO glass-maker. He specialised in thick, opaque PATE-DE-VERRE pieces, such as

sculptural ornaments, ashtrays and small dishes in greens, yellows and turquoise, often decorated with naturalistic forms such as insects, small reptiles and sprays of berries.

Waltham Watch Company The first of several American watch companies to mass-produce cheaper watches for the general public. The company was established in the mid-19thC, and together with the Swiss industry initiated the decline of the more conservative and exclusive British watch trade.

Walton, George (1867-1933) Scottish architect and designer of metalware, textiles, furniture and glassware. He was a member of the GLASGOW SCHOOL, which established the British version of ART NOUVEAU style, and his polished iron and copper candlesticks and chandeliers are typical of this genre. His furniture designs, some for the retail business LIBERTY and some for High Wycombe manufacturers, echoed 18thC forms with their emphasis on high backs and strong vertical lines.

wandering-hour watch See CHRONOSCOPE.

wardian case A glass-sided case like a miniature greenhouse for growing display plants such as ferns or tropical species indoors. The name comes from Victorian naturalist Nathaniel Ward, who transported botanical specimens from his travels in this way. Domed wardian cases mounted on stands were popular in Victorian parlours.

wardrobe Term used from the early 19thC for a large, freestanding cupboard with hanging space for clothes. In the 18thC, clothes were stored in PRESSES. See p.140.

warming pan Round, lidded container made of copper or brass, with long wooden, iron or brass handle. The pan held hot coals or charcoal – or later water – and were used to warm beds. It became popular in the 16thC but was replaced in the 19thC by metal or STONEWARE hot-water bottles. Most later examples were purely decorative. See p.368.

washstand A three or four-legged stand for holding a washbasin, a common item of furniture in the USA and Europe from the 18thC. Larger, heavier models with a marble or tiled top, drawers, and a cupboard for a chamber pot beneath were popular in the 19thC. See p.142.

watchman's clock See TELL-TALE CLOCK.

watch paper A disc of paper with the name of the watch-maker or repairer decoratively printed on it, used in Britain from the 18thC. The papers are usually placed at the back of an open-face watch case or in the back of the outer PAIR-CASE.

watch stand Small stand of wood, ceramics, brass or other metal designed to hold a pocket watch at night or for standing on a table so that it can serve as a miniature clock.

WATCH STANDS; *brass (left); 7¾ in (19.7 cm) high; and Staffordshire pottery (right); 11 in (28 cm) high.*

water clock Clock run by the regular flow of water from one container to another, based on the **clepsydra**, an ancient timekeeping device, and revived in the 18th and 19th centuries. Many copies of these revivals, with false signatures and dates, were made in the 1920s and 30s.

watercolour Water-soluble pigments mixed with a preparation of gum and dissolved in water before being transferred to paper. Watercolour is translucent, whereas GOUACHE is opaque. See pp.328-9.

Waterford Irish glass was produced at Waterford from 1729. Flint glass was superseded by the fine-quality LEAD CRYSTAL for which the town is best known in 1783. From then until it closed in 1851 the factory produced various tablewares, including bowls, glasses and decanters. The bluish tinge often said to distinguish Waterford glass is a myth. A new factory opened in 1951 producing traditional Waterford styles.

water gilding See GILDING.

Waterloo leg See SABRE LEG.

wax doll Doll with head, and sometimes limbs, made wholly or partly of bleached beeswax, popular c.1750-1930s. Solid wax may be carved into shape or liquid wax poured into a mould. Eyes are either painted on or small black beads stuck on with a drop of wax. **Waxed-composition** refers to a wax coating over a COMPOSITION base; colour can be applied to the base itself prior to the wax coating, or directly onto the wax. See p.351.

waywiser Large, wheeled device for measuring distances on the ground. Waywisers were used by the Post Office to measure postal routes prior to 1840, as the charge for sending letters was based on distance. As the device was pushed along, the distance was recorded on a brass dial situated beneath the handle.

WAYWISER; *late 18thC; wheel 31½ in (80 cm) diameter. The dial measures in yards, poles, furlongs and miles.*

Webb, Philip (1831-1915) British architect and furniture designer, closely linked with William MORRIS. Webb designed jewellery, glass, metalwork and embroidery for Morris's decorative arts firm (see p.63), but concentrated mainly on the design of solid oak furniture. He disliked veneers but sometimes adopted stained or painted surface finishes, or an applied GESSO or lacquered leather feature. Webb's designs were highly influential in the ARTS AND CRAFTS MOVEMENT with its ideals of handcraftsmanship.

Webb, Thomas, & Sons Family firm of glass-makers based around STOURBRIDGE, Worcestershire, since the early 1830s. From its founding the firm has made a variety of household wares, but in the 19thC it was especially noted for engraving and fine CAMEO GLASS, and from 1886 it also made BURMESE GLASS. The company closed in 1991.

Wedgwood, Josiah (1730-95) Staffordshire potter and factory owner whose innovations revolutionised the British ceramics industry. See p.168.

Wedgwood pottery The pottery founded in 1759 at Burslem, Staffordshire, by Josiah Wedgwood that gave Britain, and Staffordshire in particular, its special place in the history of world ceramics.

The factory was a pioneer of new products such as those modelled by William GREATBACH, and coloured with lead glazes developed by Wedgwood during his partnership with the Staffordshire potter Thomas WHIELDON. Then came CREAMWARE – the Wedgwood version was known as **Queen's Ware** in honour of Queen

Charlotte, the firm's patron – which rivalled porcelain throughout Europe in the 1760s and 70s and competed with the endless supplies of CHINESE EXPORT PORCELAIN.

Other landmarks included a fine RED STONEWARE such as ROSSO ANTICO, the black BASALTES and the JASPERWARE that came to be the company's best-known product. By the mid-18thC the products ranged from brooches and snuffboxes to statuettes, plaques and tablewares. They were widely copied and exported all over Europe and the USA.

The successes of the 18thC maintained styles for some time into the 19thC, and emphasis shifted from handcrafted pottery to production of BONE CHINA, still produced, and MAJOLICA. In the 20thC a genuine attempt to escape from the 18thC cliché was made by the input of designers such as Keith MURRAY, C.F.A.VOYSEY and Eric RAVILIOUS.

Wellington chest Early 19thC British chest of drawers with six to twelve shallow drawers for storing coins or other small articles. A hinged flap overlaps the drawers on one side and is fitted with a lock.

Welsh dresser See DRESSER.

Wemyss ware Cheerfully decorated pottery produced at the Fife pottery near Kircaldy in Scotland, 1880-1930, and imitated elsewhere. It is distinguished by brightly coloured UNDERGLAZE motifs of flowers, fruit, berries and birds. A wide variety of products were made including table ware, especially jam pots; useful ware such as jugs and washbasins; and novelty products such as doorstopper pigs. Wemyss is pronounced 'weemz'.

whatnot A lightweight, compact stand with three or more shelves on which to put knick-knacks, books or ornaments. Whatnots appeared towards the end of the 18thC, and continued as drawing-room features throughout the Victorian era. In Victorian times a whatnot was known as an **omnium** and the French equivalent is an **étagère**. See pp.124-5.

CORNER WHATNOT; *c.1860; 56 in (1.42 m) high.*

RECTANGULAR WHATNOT; *c.1850; 40 in (1.01 m) high.*

wheel barometer A mercury BAROMETER in which the mercury tube is concealed in the back of the case and the reading is taken from a dial like a clock face. As the mercury rises and falls with air pressure changes, a weighted cord, connected by a pulley to a float resting on the surface of the mercury, causes the pointer wheel to move. The British scientist Robert Hooke is credited with its invention in the mid-17thC, but few were made until the mid-19thC. See pp.290-1.

wheel engraving See ENGRAVING.

wheel lock A firearm ignition system developed in the early 16thC. A metal wheel with a roughened edge was rotated by a spring mechanism. A piece of pyrites, gripped by the doghead, was pressed against it. When the trigger was pressed the wheel rotated against the pyrites, generating sparks which ignited the gunpowder. The wheel lock made it possible for loaded weapons to be carried safely as the doghead could be pulled clear of the pan containing the gunpowder. See box below and p.406.

wheel of life See ZOETROPE.

Whieldon, Thomas (1719-95) Influential master potter at Fenton Low, Staffordshire, c.1740-80. The modellers Aaron WOOD and William

GREATBATCH, and Josiah SPODE (who was to found his own great factory), were among Whieldon's apprentices, and Josiah WEDGWOOD was his partner, 1754-8.

Whieldon mainly produced SALT-GLAZED STONEWARE and CREAMWARE in the form of tea services and knife and fork handles, but it was his use of coloured lead GLAZES, in the days before ENAMEL colours, that characterised his output. Early examples, in the 1750s, were limited to shades of olive-green, grey, brown and slate blue, with yellow and orange being introduced later.

During the partnership with Wedgwood, mottled glazes included marbled, agate, and notably tortoiseshell effects, and the green and yellow glazes that were to lead to CAULIFLOWER WARE were developed.

white gold An alloy of gold with either platinum or with zinc and nickel. White gold was a popular setting for diamonds in the late 19thC. It is similar in colour to PLATINUM; the two metals can only be distinguished by an acid test.

white metal 1 A soft, base metal alloy, often abbreviated to 'WM', which was used for inexpensive commemorative medals, especially in the 19thC. When preserved 'as new', the material looks attractive but it is susceptible to wear and corrosion. **2** Trade term sometimes used to describe silver which is below the STERLING STANDARD and cannot by law carry a British hallmark.

whitework Any CUTWORK embroidery in white thread on a white or natural ground, such as AYRSHIRE WORK and BRODERIE ANGLAISE.

wickerwork See BASKETWORK.

Wiener Werkstätte Austrian association of artists and craftsmen founded in Vienna in 1903 by the

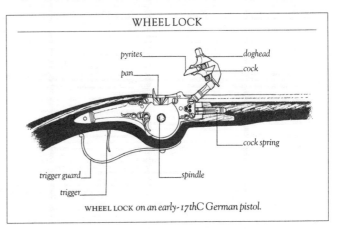

WHEEL LOCK

pyrites
pan
doghead
cock
cock spring
trigger guard
spindle
trigger

WHEEL LOCK *on an early-17thC German pistol.*

designers Josef Hoffmann and Koloman Moser. Textiles, wallpapers, ceramics, metalwork and furniture were produced with an emphasis on handmade articles and FUNCTIONALISM – in which the design reflected the object's purpose.

Early products showed some of the rectilinear version of ART NOUVEAU style which was pioneered by Charles Rennie MACKINTOSH and the GLASGOW SCHOOL. Hoffmann's geometric patterns anticipated the ART DECO style of the 1920s. Furniture, carpet and ceramics were often strikingly simple, some of Moser's furniture displaying a clean-lined, modern treatment of Oriental and Egyptian designs.

Following the First World War came freer styles typified by the ornate silverware and naturalistic themes of Dagobert Pêche. Pêche also worked in furniture, ceramics, glass, textiles and wallpapers. The workshop closed in 1932, unable to compete commercially with industrial production.

wig block A head-shaped piece of wood on a stand to hold a wig, or a smaller rounded top on a longer-stemmed **wig stand**.

WIG BLOCKS *of blue and white faience (left), late 17thC; and yew (right), mid-18thC; both 12 in (30.5 cm) high.*

Wilkinson, A.J. Staffordshire pottery at Newport which employed art potter Clarice CLIFF and other leading artists of the 1930s. From 1929 the pottery mass-produced Cliff's designs alone.

Willaume, David, I (1658-1741) HUGUENOT silversmith who worked in London using many techniques and designs which were far advanced. His pieces are individualistic – a large teapot decorated with three rows of CUT-CARD work is typical and ranged from salvers and cutlery to elaborate tableware. His son **David Willaume II** (1693-1761) took over the business in 1716. For a time the two silversmiths were thought to be one and the same.

William and Mary style British decorative arts style linked with the reign of King William III and Queen Mary (1689-1702). See pp.22-29.

willow Strong yet soft, white to pinkish, flecked wood. Because of its long fibres, it was used for the dowels in early JOINED construction. The young shoots have long been used for WICKERWORK. In the 17th and 18th centuries it was sometimes dyed black to imitate EBONY.

willow pattern A Chinese-influenced pattern, based on a Chinese legend but designed in Britain, which was widely TRANSFER-PRINTED on pottery and porcelain tableware in UNDERGLAZE blue. It was first engraved by Thomas MINTON for the CAUGHLEY pottery in Shropshire c.1780, and much imitated, even by the Chinese. See p.163.

Wilton carpets Early carpets produced in Wilton, Wiltshire, from the late 17thC, were INGRAIN carpets, made using a FLAT-WEAVE technique with a bulky texture.

In 1740, narrow Brussels looms were set up by two former SAVONNERIE weavers to produce MOQUETTE carpets in competition with KIDDERMINSTER manufacturers. In 1769, Blackmore & Son combined the Wilton and AXMINSTER businesses. The Wilton industry increased in the 1840s, making luxury hand-knotted as well as machine-made carpets.

Windsor chair Term applied to a chair with a solid wooden seat with sockets into which turned legs and back and arm spindles are fitted. The term has been in use since c.1724, but its origin is uncertain, as this type of chair was not confined to Windsor, Berkshire, but made in many provincial areas. A variety of timbers was used, sometimes all in the same chair, such as beech for the turned members (legs and spindles), elm or sometimes yew for the seat, and ash, elm and some fruitwoods for the BENTWOOD parts. Yew examples are the most desirable today. High Wycombe, Buckinghamshire, was a leading centre of Windsor chair production by the early 19thC. See p.100.

wine cistern A container for holding several bottles of wine, also known as **wine fountain**. They were made of marble or various metals and woods, but in the 18thC were often mahogany bound in brass, lined with lead and were watertight, in order to hold ice.

A **wine cooler** holds a single bottle in ice, and is usually made of ceramics, or in SHEFFIELD PLATE or electroplated SILVER. See pp.146, 248-9.

wine funnel A funnel sometimes with a curved spout and a sieve for separating sediment, used for decanting red wine from the 17th to 19th centuries. The funnels are found in silver, porcelain, pewter or silver plate. Late 18th and

early 19th-century examples are smaller and plainer than those made after the 1820s. See p.248.

wine table 1 Semicircular table sometimes with a pivoted arm and coaster fitted to the inside curve which could be swung across to pass wine to fellow drinkers. Wine tables were used for after-dinner drinks around the hearth from the late 18th to early 19th centuries, hence the alternative names of **social** or **fireside tables**.
2 A small table with a galleried top to hold decanters and clean glasses, and notches cut out of the rim where dirty glasses can be hung by the foot.

HORSESHOE WINE TABLE; c.1810; 65½ in (1.66 m) long. The coasters are hinged to a pivoted brass rod.

WINE TABLE *with platform top, birdcage tilting mechanism, and notched edge for glasses; late 18thC; 32 in (81 cm) high.*

wine trolley See COASTER.

wine waiter Table on castors with partitioned top for holding wine bottles, used in the 18thC to circulate wine during a meal. Some wine waiters incorporate a cupboard.

wing chair Upholstered chair with wings extending either from the upper part, or from the whole length of the

WING CHAIR *in Chippendale style with leather upholstery; c.1770.*

back in order to protect the occupant's head from draughts. Wing chairs were first introduced during the latter part of the 17thC.

Woodall, Thomas and **George** Two of the most important late 19th and early 20th-century British cameo glass carvers, trained by John NORTHWOOD and then employed by Thomas WEBB & SONS of Stourbridge. Their joint works are rarely signed 'T & G Woodall' and are in Victorian Classical style, although George in particular had a talent for figure compositions. His early work was hand-carved, while later pieces were worked with an engraver's wheel. In the late 19thC, the brothers headed a team of up to 70 craftsmen producing inkwells, candlesticks, door panels, scent bottles, plaques and vases.

woodcut A PRINT formed from a design carved in relief on the plank surface of a woodblock. The background is cut away leaving the design raised, and it is this which receives the ink. The inked design prints and the background remains free of ink. In a WOOD ENGRAVING, the design is cut into the endgrain surface so that the background is in relief and takes the ink, and the engraved design shows white on the finished print. See p.332.

Wood, Ralph (1715-72) One of a famous family of STAFFORDSHIRE potters to whom many Staffordshire figures, often of provincial characters, and flatwares are attributed – although sometimes on rather slim documentary evidence. Many TOBY JUGS and rustic groups with in-glaze colour are attributed to Wood and his son, also Ralph (1748-95). See p.172.

Wood, Samuel (c.1704-94) Prolific London-based silversmith, a specialist in CRUETS and CASTERS.

Worcester The longest-lived British 18thC porcelain factory, continuing to this day (as the Royal Worcester Porcelain Company).

The factory was founded in 1751, and the takeover of Benjamin Lund's BRISTOL factory the following year gave it a head start in the manufacture of soft-paste PORCELAIN. The factory's output was concentrated on domestic ware until 1760. This was usually painted or printed in dark UNDERGLAZE blue, decorated in Oriental fashion, and in shapes inspired by the silverware of the period and by Rococo style.

The use of SOAPSTONE in the porcelain paste produced a body which was resistant to hot water, and put Worcester ahead of its competitors in the manufacture of tea and coffee services in particular. However, the new paste proved to be less suitable for the production of ceramic figures.

In 1763, the factory made a definite move towards the luxury market, and wares imitating MEISSEN, SÈVRES and Japanese designs were produced. These were often finished by outside decorators such as James GILES.

A new period began in 1783 under the Flight family and, from 1793, under the Flight and Barr families, with an improved soft-paste formula. Products ranged from simply decorated teawares to elaborate REGENCY vases, and ornaments decorated in rich enamels and gilding by first-class artists such as Thomas Baxter and Samuel Astles.

BONE CHINA was introduced in 1800 but only achieved pure TRANSLUCENCY and whiteness from 1820. Some decoration was done by Robert Chamberlain's rival Worcester factory. The resulting ware, together with Chamberlain's own bone china produced since 1791, became known as 'Chamberlain's Worcester'. The two companies merged in 1840.

New management in 1852 changed the factory's name to **Kerr & Binns**, and from 1862 it became the **Royal Worcester Porcelain Company**.

Victorian Worcester is often richly gilded and painted in enamels – flushed colours against an apricot ground. Specialities included JAPONAISERIE in the 1870s and 80s, figures, including children, modelled by James Hadley (1837-1903), PARIAN WARE ornaments and elaborate RENAISSANCE-style vases. High-quality painted decoration, often signed by the artist, was frequent at the end of the 19th and early 20th centuries. See p.164.

1783-92

work table A small table with a bag or box suspended beneath the top in which to store articles related to the use of the table – such as needlework or chess pieces. Work tables date from the early 19thC, and were popular in the Victorian era. See p.115.

wreathing Spiral ridges of slightly increased thickness on the inside of some HOLLOW-WARE, shaped, on the wheel, by the potter's fingers.

wrigglework Zigzag pattern used on British pewter and silverware in the 17th and 18th centuries. An engraving tool was pushed over the surface at a 45° angle, while rocking or turning the object. See p.366.

Wright, Frank Lloyd (1867-1959) US architect and designer whose work had a widespread impact on 20thC decorative arts. Wright designed his buildings to fit in with their environment, with complementary interior furnishings and fittings. Although he was closely connected

with the American ARTS AND CRAFTS MOVEMENT, he did not reject mechanical methods, and much of his work has a machine-made look which was to inspire the Dutch furniture designer Gerrit RIETVELD.

Wright explored the potential of new materials such as painted and TUBULAR STEEL and his work was dominated by an emphasis on the angular; long narrow slats were a recurring feature in his furniture.

writing chair See CORNER CHAIR.

Wrotham ware Slipware produced by a group of potteries in Kent c.1612-1712. The coarse reddish body of the pieces was coated with white clay SLIP, decorated with slip-trailed swirls or STAMPED motifs and then covered with a yellowish lead GLAZE. Candlesticks were a speciality and TYGS and other vessels survive, some with the name of potters such as Nicholas Hubble, John Green and George Richardson inscribed.

wrought iron Ironwork that is drawn and worked into elaborate shapes on an anvil while hot. It is not as hard or brittle as **cast iron** and is used for objects such as grilles, screens, garden furniture, candle-holders and ANDIRONS. Wrought iron has been made since ancient times.

In the late 19thC, William MORRIS, a central figure in the ARTS AND CRAFTS MOVEMENT, encouraged the use of decorative wrought ironwork in Britain, a pattern echoed throughout Europe. One of the finest exponents was the French designer and metalworker Edgar BRANDT.

wrythening Spiral or diagonal ridges, fluting or REEDING especially fashionable on 17th-19thC glass. It is also found on furniture, pewter and silver – the top of a **wrythen-top spoon** is a spirally fluted oval.

wucai The Chinese term for a porcelain palette consisting of five colours (wu is the Chinese word for five). The design is not outlined in UNDERGLAZE blue (as in DOUCAI). Wucai was formerly spelt **wu-ts'ai**.

Wyon family A family of gifted and prolific coin and medal engravers who dominated British DIE engraving during most of the 19thC. Thomas Wyon (1792-1817) was an engraver at the Royal Mint 1811-15 and designed the Waterloo medal of 1815. His brother William (1795-1851) was the chief coin engraver at the Royal Mint from 1828 until his death, and his work included the early portrait of Queen Victoria that appeared on the 1840 Penny Black postage stamp.

X, Y, Z

X-chair Medieval-style chair with X-shaped framework. Variations on the X-frame theme were adopted in 15thC Italy for folding wooden chairs, in 18thC Britain by SHERATON, and for strip-metal chairs in the mid-19thC. An X-chair is sometimes called a **savonarola**.

yao Chinese word for 'ware'.

yataghan A SWORD which has a blade with a double curve and large curled grips on the hilt. It was popular in the Balkans and in the Near East during the 19thC.

yew Although a softwood, the timber of this native British species is very dense and strong. The wood is golden-brown in tone, close-grained and polishes to a fine finish; and as the trunks tend to twist, the wood is often beautifully FIGURED. Yew has been a popular medium for the framework of country-made furniture since the 16thC, and from the 17th for turned drawer knobs and spindles; in the following century the sticks, bows and legs of the best quality WINDSOR CHAIRS were of yew. Yew, particularly the whorled and knotted BURR wood, has also been used as a VENEER, and was favoured by 20thC artist-craftsmen such as Ernest GIMSON and Sir Gordon RUSSELL.

yingqing With DING WARE, one of the earliest Chinese PORCELAIN wares, dating from the SONG DYNASTY (960-1279). *Yingqing* (misty-blue) refers to the translucent blue glaze, formerly known as **qingbai**. The wares – mainly bowls – survive today having been dug up from burial grounds, but have also been reproduced in Hong Kong and Taiwan. See p.166.

Yixing Chinese potteries specialising in RED STONEWARE. Products, particularly teapots, were exported to Europe in the 17thC, and inspired similar ware produced at Meissen, and by the ELERS brothers in England from the late 17thC. See p.166.

York flagon See ACORN FLAGON.

zebrawood A decorative, reddish-brown wood barred with dark stripes, also known as **tigerwood**. It is a hard, heavy, Brazilian timber, most commonly seen in BANDING and INLAID DECORATION.

In the late 18thC and throughout the 19thC, zebrawood was sometimes used as a VENEER for complete surfaces of bureaux, desks and tables.

zinc Bluish-white metallic element. It is used to form various alloys such as brass, bronze and nickel silver. Zinc was not produced commercially in Britain until the 18thC. See SPELTER.

zircon Gemstone which ranges in colour through yellow, red and orange to green. Colourless, golden-brown and sky-blue versions are produced by HEAT TREATMENT. Most of the mineral suitable for gemstones comes from the Far East and Sri Lanka. Yellow and brown shades of zircon were often termed **hyacinth**, and transparent or colourless types are sometimes known as **jargons** or **jargoons**. Colourless zircons are sometimes used as substitutes for DIAMONDS, but are not as hard or brilliant.

zoetrope Optical toy popular in Victorian times. It consists of a revolving cylinder which is open at the top and has a series of pictures arranged along the inner surface. The pictures are viewed through slits around the edge of the cylinder and appear to be moving when the box is rotated rapidly.

The zoetrope was developed in the 1830s and is also known as a **zootrope** or **wheel of life**. See p.295.

ZOETROPE *made of tin plate; c. 1870; 16½ in (42 cm) high. The picture strips are interchangeable.*

Zucchi, Antonio Pietro (1726-91) Italian painter and designer of furniture and household fittings. He travelled with architect Robert ADAM in Italy and, on coming to England in 1766, did a great deal of work with him on house interiors. Zucchi was the second husband of painter Angelica KAUFFMANN.

Zwischengoldglas Glass vessel decorated with engraving and gold or silver leaf, and then sheathed with another layer of glass to enclose the design. The name literally means 'gold between glass'. This technique dates from c.300 BC, but most surviving examples were made in Bohemia between 1730 and 1755. It is seen mainly on beakers or goblets decorated with hunting, heraldic or religious images. See p.209.

PERIODS AND STYLES

MAJOR PERIODS (see The Story of Style)	BRITISH RULERS since 1485	PREVAILING STYLES OF THE TIME	FRENCH PERIODS
1066-1550 MEDIEVAL AND EARLY TUDOR pages 12-15		pre-1500 Gothic	
	1485-1509 Henry VII		
	1509-1547 Henry VIII	c. 1500-1630 Renaissance	
	1547-1553 Edward VI		
1550-1660 ELIZABETHAN AND JACOBEAN pages 16-21	1553-1558 Mary I		
	1558-1603 Elizabeth I		
	1603-1625 James I		1610-1643 Louis XIII
	1625-1649 Charles I		
	1649-1660 Commonwealth	c. 1630-1720 Baroque Puritan	1643-1715 Louis XIV
1660-1720 RESTORATION AND QUEEN ANNE pages 22-29	1660-1685 Charles II		
	1685-1688 James II		
	1689-1702 William & Mary Mary d. 1694		
	1702-1714 Anne		
	1714-1727 George I		1715-1723 Régence
1720-1760 EARLY GEORGIAN pages 30-35	1727-1760 George II		1723-1774 Louis XV
		c. 1730s-50s Rococo Gothic Chinoiserie	
1760-1800 LATE GEORGIAN pages 36-41	1760-1811 George III d. 1820	c. 1760s-1820 Neoclassical Empire	1774-1793 Louis XVI
			1793-1799 Directoire
			1799-1815 Empire
1800-1830 REGENCY pages 42-48	1811-1820 Prince Regent then 1820-1830 George IV		1815-1830 Restauration
1830-1850 WILLIAM IV AND EARLY VICTORIAN pages 49-54	1830-1837 William IV		1830-1848 Louis Philippe
	1837-1901 Victoria	Revivalism Rococo Revival Gothic Revival Old French Japonaiserie Classic Revival	
1850-1870 MID-VICTORIAN pages 55-61			1848-1870 Second Empire
1870-1914 LATE VICTORIAN AND EDWARDIAN pages 62-70		c. 1860s-80s Arts & Crafts Aesthetic movement Queen Anne Revival	1871-1940 Third Republic
	1901-1910 Edward VII	c. 1890-1910s Art Nouveau Liberty style	
	1910-1936 George V		
1914-1940 BETWEEN THE WARS pages 71-77		c. 1920s-30s Art Deco	
	1936 Edward VIII		
1940-1970 POSTWAR YEARS pages 78-82	1936-1952 George VI	Modern movement Scandinavian style	1945-1958 Fourth Republic 1958- Fifth Republic
	1952- Elizabeth II		

For Chinese reigns 1368-1916, see page 509.

530

Index

Page references in *italics* refer to illustrations. In general, no entry is included where the only reference would be to an identical headword in the A-Z of antiques (pp. 436-529).

A

F

Acknowledgments

Illustrations are identified by their position on the page: t top, c centre, b bottom, l left, r right, and combinations such as cl centre left; occasionally for clarity a brief description is given instead. Illustrations credited 'V & A' are reproduced by courtesy of the trustees of the Victoria and Albert Museum, London. Those credited 'Brit Lib' are reproduced by permission of the Board of the British Library. Illustrations credited 'Millers' are reproduced by permission from 'Miller's Antiques Price Guide' and 'Miller's Collectables Price Guide'. 'Christie's' indicates Christie's Colour Library; 'Mallett' indicates Mallett, New Bond St, London W1; 'Nat Trust', The National Trust; 'Bridgeman', The Bridgeman Art Library; and 'Phillips', Phillips the Fine Art Auctioneers. Credits in italics denote Reader's Digest copyright. A credit following an oblique stroke indicates the owner of the photograph or the object, and that before the stroke the supplier of the photograph. Artists of original paintings and drawings for this book are credited on page 5. The publishers thank Paul Reeves, Kensington Church St, London W8, for supplying the electric lamp depicted on page 65, and Max Factor Ltd for supplying the lipstick depicted on page 73.

In the *A-Z of antiques*, doll marks are reproduced by permission from 'The Collector's Encyclopaedia of Dolls' by D.E. and E. Coleman, publ. Robert Hale. Silver marks are reproduced by permission from 'Jackson's Silver and Gold Marks' edited by Ian Pickford, publ. Antique Collector's Club, Woodbridge, Suffolk, 1989. Chinese reign marks are reproduced by permission from 'A Handbook of Chinese Art' by Margaret Medley, publ. Bell & Hyman, an imprint of Harper Collins Ltd. Pewter marks are reproduced by permission of Peter Hornsby. Tin-plate toy marks were redrawn from 'The Art of the Tin Toy' by David Pressland, publ. New Cavendish Books.

cover *Vernon Morgan*. 1-7 *Clive Streeter*. 10-11 *Ken Adlard*. 12 t Brit Lib Ms Add 42130 f 181v; b The Burrell Collection. 13 l Brit Lib Ms Add 42130 f 182; r Michael Holford. 14 tl English Life Publications Ltd; bl The Ancient Art & Architecture Collection; br Bridgeman/Private collection. 15 tr Brit Lib Ms Roy 14e1 f 3. 16 bl Christie's. 16-17 By courtesy of Sherborne Castle Estates. 18 tl V & A. 20 tl Birmingham Museums & Art Gallery/A. J. Hendry; r Angelo Hornak. 21 tl *Michael Crockett*/Carpenter's Company. 22 t Birmingham Museums & Art Gallery. 23 cr ET Archive; bl Christie's. 24 t Nat Trust (photographer Mark Fiennes); r Nat Trust. 25 l Christie's; tr Tate Gallery. 28 b Angelo Hornak/V & A; t Bridgeman/Stapleton Collection. 30 Christie's. 31 Laroon, 'A Musical Tea Party' (detail), Royal Collection, St James's Palace/©HM the Queen. 32 Albright-Knox Art Gallery, Buffalo, New York, Gift of Seymour H. Knox. 33 tr from 'The Chippendale Director'. 36 bl Christie's. 36-37 Bridgeman/Stapleton Collection. 37 br Sotheby's. 38 John Bethell/Nat Trust; bc Bridgeman/Stapleton Collection; tr Sotheby's. 39 bc from 'Cabinet-Maker and Upholsterer's Drawing-Book'. 40 bl Sotheby's. 42-43 ET Archive. 43 cr ET Archive/National Maritime Museum. 44 t Yale Center for British Art/Paul Mellon Collection. 45 cl Edifice/Lewis; r Hubert Josse. 48 cl Permission of the Trustees of the British Museum; br Hugh Palmer, from 'Jane Austen's Town & Country Style' by Susan Watkins. 49 t Fine Art Photographs/Courtesy Mr & Mrs R. Holmes.

50 tl ET Archive; c Christie's. 51 tr Bridgeman/Stapleton Collection. 52 cl Sotheby's. 54 tr Salisbury & South Wiltshire Museum; bl A.F. Kersting; bc Christie's. 55 t Christie's. 56 c ET Archive; br V & A. 57 tr ET Archive; cr Museum of London. 60 t V & A; cl Sotheby's. 61 c Antony Mason. 62 t Fine Art Photographs. 63 ET Archive. 64 bl Angelo Hornak. 66 tl Angelo Hornak; cr Bridgeman/Mallett & Son (Antiques) Ltd. 67 t Nat Trust. 70 cr Christie's; bl London Transport Museum; tl York Castle Museum. 71 British Film Institute. 72 bl Christie's. 74 tr Museum of London/Bush family; cl Lee Curtis; c The Advertising Archives. 75 cr Country Life. 76 bl Christie's. 78 bl The Hulton Picture Company. 78-79 Elizabeth Whiting. 79 tr Elizabeth Whiting; b Peter Newark's Pictures. 80 tr Arcaid; cl Georg Jensen. 81 Arcaid. 84-85 *Ken Adlard*. 87 Sotheby's. 88 tr, bc Christie's; bl Sotheby's; br *Andrew Stewart*/Art Furniture, Camden. 89 tr Ann Ronan at Image Select; cl, br Christie's; c, cr Sotheby's; (*cradle*) The Trustees and Guardians of Shakespeare's Birthplace; bc William Stokes Antiques. 90 tr, bc, br Christie's; tc, c, cr Sotheby's. 91 (*dovetails*) John Bly; rest Sotheby's. 92 Sotheby's. 93 (*seaweed marquetry*) Christie's; (*ormolu mounts*) By kind permission of the Earl of Harewood; rest Sotheby's. 94 tc, cr Sotheby's; tr, c, br Christie's; bl Fine Art Photographs. 95 tl, cl Christie's; tr National Gallery of Ireland; cr Millers/Christie's New York; br *Michael Crockett*/M.S.M., The Furniture Cave, Chelsea. 96 tl, c, bc Sotheby's; cl, bl Christie's; cr Phillips. 97 *Laurie Evans* (*except tr*). 98 tc Christie's; c Millers/Bearnes, Torquay; rest Sotheby's. 99 tl, tr Christie's; tc *Andrew Stewart*/Art Furniture, Camden; cl Millers/Christie's; cr Sotheby's; bl Phillips.

100 (*box*) *Laurie Evans*; cl *Mike Mirecki*/Linda Helm, Islington; c Christie's; bl Ipswich Museum & Galleries; bc Peter Greenhalf Photography. 101 tl New Leaf Books Ltd; tc, cr Sotheby's; tr Millers/Christie's; c Christie's. 102 (*Victorian chair*) Peter Greenhalf Photography/Furnace Mill, Lamberhurst; cl Bridgeman/Stapleton Collection; br Christie's; rest Sotheby's. 103 cl Sotheby's; c Phillips; cr *Stuart Chorley*/The Old Cinema, Chiswick; bl, br Christie's. 104 (*Lloyd Loom label*) Private collection; (*Howard chair & detail*) *Stuart Chorley*/Piers von Westenholz, London SW1; tc, cr Peter Greenhalf Photography/Pamela Lynch, Wilton; tr *Andrew Stuart*/Art Furniture, Camden; cl Millers/Christie's; c Christie's; br Sotheby's. 105 cr *Roy Farthing*/Richard Glass, Whaley Bridge; bl Peter Greenhalf Photography/Pamela Lynch, Wilton; bc Christie's; br Phillips. 106 tl Fine Art Photographs; tr Millers/Christie's New York; c, cr Christie's; bc Phillips; br *Stuart Chorley*/The Old Cinema, Chiswick. 107 tl Christie's; tc Phillips; cl Peter Greenhalf Photography/Furnace Mill, Lamberhurst; c *Michael Crockett*/Anthony Outred, The Furniture Cave, Chelsea; bc Sotheby's. 108 tl Bridgeman/Stapleton Collection; tc, cl Christie's; cr *Andrew Stewart*/Denzil Grant, Bury St Edmunds; bl Peter Greenhalf Photography; br *Stuart Chorley*/Jazzy Art Deco, Camden. 109 bl Christie's; rest *Laurie Evans*. 110 tc *Mike Mirecki*/Linda Helm, Islington; bl Millers/Christie's; cr, br Sotheby's. 111 c Sotheby's; bl Millers/Christie's; tl *Stuart Chorley*/The Dining Room Shop, Barnes; tc, cl, detail *Stuart Chorley*/The Old Cinema, Chiswick; bc *Stuart Chorley*/Aberdeen House Antiques, Ealing. 112 cl Phillips; br Millers/Sworders, Bishop's Stortford; rest Sotheby's. 113 bl Christie's; cl, bc Sotheby's; br Bridgeman/Stapleton Collection. 114 *Laurie Evans* (*except tl*). 115 tl Sotheby's; tr Millers; cl *Christopher Fransella*/Bushwood Antiques, Islington; c Mallett; br Millers/Woolley and Wallis, Salisbury. 116 tl Sotheby's; cl Mallett; bc *Stuart Chorley*/The Old Cinema, Chiswick; cr *Christopher Fransella*/Bushwood Antiques, Islington. 117 tl Sotheby's; tc Millers; tr Christie's; cl Mallett; c *Stuart Chorley*/The Old Cinema, Chiswick; cr Millers/Christie's. 118 cl By kind permission of the Earl of Harewood; cr Phillips; bl Mallett; bc Millers/Sotheby's; br *Andrew Stewart*/M.S.M., The Furniture Cave, Chelsea. 119 cl Phillips; cr Neptune Antiques, Long Melford; bl Christie's; br Millers/Paul Hopwell Antiques, West Haddon. 120 tl Millers/Christie's; tr Mallett; bc Sotheby's; c, br Christie's. 121 tr V & A; cl, cr Sotheby's; c, bl Mallett; bc New Leaf Books Ltd. 122 tl, bc Sotheby's; cl, bl Christie's; br Millers/Christie's. 123 c Mallett; bl Christie's; bc *Roy Farthing*/Pat & Terry Gasson, Surrey; rest Sotheby's. 124 tl *Stuart Chorley*/The Old Cinema, Chiswick; tc Peter Greenhalf Photography; cl Sotheby's; c *Roy Farthing*/Carling & Sinclair, Long Melford; cr Phillips; b Fine Art Photographs. 125 c Master and Fellows, Magdalene College, Cambridge; bc Christie's; br *Stuart Chorley*/Adams Antiques, Camden. 126 tl Millers/Christie's; tc, bl *Stuart Chorley*/The Old Cinema, Chiswick; cl Christie's; br Sotheby's. 127 c, bl Phillips; bc Christie's; br Millers/Christie's New York. 128 tl, tc, cl Mallett; tr Sotheby's; cr Phillips; bl Brit Lib Ms Harley 4380 f 1. 129 tl, cr, tr Christie's; c Millers/Christie's; bl *Stuart Chorley*/The Old Cinema, Chiswick. 130 *Ian O'Leary* (*except tl*). 131 l *Ian O'Leary*; r Sotheby's. 132 tr, bl Christie's; cr Sotheby's; br Bonhams. 133 tl, tc, bl Sotheby's; cl, c Phillips; bc Christie's. 134 tl Christie's; tc *Peter Jones*; bc Peter Greenhalf Photography; br Phillips. 135 tc Christie's; cr, bc Sotheby's. 136 cr (*1930s tallboy*) *Stuart Chorley*/The Old Cinema, Chiswick; tl Fine Art Photographs; tc, cr Christie's; tr Sotheby's; br Mallett. 137 tl *Jon Sparks*/Leighton Hall, Carnforth, Lancs; tc *Mike Mirecki*/Linda Helm, Islington; tr Bridgeman/Stapleton Collection; cl Millers; c Millers/Christie's; cr *Christopher Fransella*/Bushwood Antiques, Islington; br Sotheby's. 138 tl, c, br Christie's; tr Bridgeman/Stapleton Collection; cl, cr Sotheby's; bl *Stuart Chorley*/Dreams, London NW1; bc *Christopher Fransella*/Bushwood Antiques, Islington. 139 c *Stuart Chorley*/Bushwood Antiques, Islington; cr *Michael Crockett*/J.W. Weatherall, The Furniture Cave, Chelsea; bc Millers/Christie's. 140 tc Millers; tr Mallett; c *Michael Crockett*/J.W. Weatherall, The Furniture Caves, Chelsea; cr Sotheby's; bc Phillips. 141 cl *Roy Farthing*/Pat & Terry Gasson, Surrey; c Millers; bl Millers/Christie's New York; cr, bc, br Sotheby's. 142 cl *Ian O'Leary*/Rupert Cavendish Antiques, Chelsea; c, br *Stuart Chorley*/The Old Cinema, Chiswick; cr, bl Christie's. 143 tr, c, cr Christie's; bl Bridgeman/Stapleton Collection; bc Sotheby's; b *Stuart Chorley*/The Old Cinema, Chiswick. 144 tr, c *Stuart Chorley*/The Old Cinema, Chiswick; cl Phillips; cr *Stuart Chorley*/ Effi Rer, Glass Restoration, London, NW1; bc *Stuart Chorley*/The Clock Gallery, Ealing; br *Roy Farthing*/Christina Chance Antiques, Chester. 145 tl *Andrew Stewart*/Art Furniture, Camden; tr *Roy Farthing*/Coombe House Antiques, Lewes; cl, c Sotheby's; bl *Roy Farthing*/Granville Antiques, Petworth; bc, br Peter Greenhalf Photography. 146 tl Phillips; tc, cl, bc Sotheby's; cr *John Vigurs*/Tunbridge Wells Museum; bl Phillips. 147 Sotheby's. 148 tr (*Hans Coper dish*) Christie's; rest Sotheby's. 149 tr Bill Steltzer; rest Sotheby's.

150 (*Chelsea*) Millers; bcBridgeman/Stapleton Collection; rest Sotheby's. 151 (*portrait figure*) Lars Tharp; (*solid-moulded figure*) Millers; (*faulty glaze*) *Martin Cameron*; rest Sotheby's. 152 (*sgraffito*) Christie's; bl, br *Martin Cameron*; rest Sotheby's. 153 (*famille-rose, combined decoration*) Sotheby's; rest *Martin Cameron*. 154 tr Christie's; b Bridgeman/Stapleton Collection. 155 tl Christie's; tc Robert Copeland, Stoke-on-Trent; rest Sotheby's. 156 Sotheby's. 157 cr Christie's; rest Sotheby's. 158 c, tr *Chris Halton*/John Sandon; cr, bc Sotheby's; br Millers/Christie's. 159 bc *Chris Halton*/John Sandon; rest Sotheby's. 160 tc By courtesy of the Wedgwood Museum Trustees, Barlaston, Staffs; bc *Ian O'Leary*/Valerie Howard Antiques; rest Sotheby's. 161 tr Bridgeman/Christopher Wood Gallery, London; c Lars Tharp; bc Christie's; rest Sotheby's. 162, 163 Sotheby's. 164 *Ian O'Leary* (*except tl*). 165 tc Millers/Christie's; tr, c Christie's; cr, bl Sotheby's; br Phillips. 166 (*celadon dish*), br Sotheby's; tc Bridgeman/Stapleton Collection; cl Millers; c, cr, bl Lars Tharp. 167 bl *Chris Halton*/Private collection; rest Sotheby's. 168 tc By courtesy of the Wedgwood Museum Trustees, Barlaston, Staffs; bc Christie's; rest Sotheby's. 169 c Christie's; tr, cr Phillips; bl Sotheby's br Millers/Christie's. 170 tc, c Sotheby's; tr, bc Christie's; cr Jonathan Horne Antiques Ltd, London W8; br Millers. 171 tl Millers/Christie's; tc, bl Phillips; cl A. & J. Speelman, London W1; bc Sotheby's. 172 tc Phillips; rest Sotheby's. 173 tr Sotheby's; cr, br Christie's. 174 tl Sotheby's; bl Angelo Hornak; bc Albert Amor Ltd; rest Christie's. 175 tl, c Albert Amor Ltd; cl Christie's; bl, bc Sotheby's. 176 c Christie's; rest Sotheby's. 177 (*creamware*) ET Archive; (*Kakiemon, saltglaze, Chelsea, Staffs creamware, Meissen*) Christie's; (*Worcester*) Albert Amor Ltd; (*c. 1880 Staffs*) *Martin Cameron*/Sotheby's; (*Chinese*) Millers; rest Sotheby's. 178 tc ET Archive; cl, c Christie's; bl Millers/Christie's New York; bc *Stuart Chorley*/Private collection; br Millers/Church Street Antiques, Godalming. 179 t, tl, bl Sotheby's; cl Sotheby's/Mr & Mrs Klitgaard; c *Stuart Chorley*/David Mark & Richard Chamberlain, The Antique Centre, London W8. 180 cl Christie's; cr, b Millers/Christie's; rest Phillips. 181 cl Millers/Christie's; c *Chris Halton*/John Sandon; tl, tc, bc Phillips. 182 cr *Stuart Chorley*/Barnes Antiques, Putney; rest Phillips. 183 tr *Chris Halton*; cr, bl, br Phillips; bc Sotheby's. 184 tl, tr Sotheby's; c, cr Phillips. 185 br Lee Miller Archives; rest Sotheby's. 186 Sotheby's. 187 cl Millers; c, bl Sotheby's; bc Bonhams. 188 tl *Laurie Evans*/Whites Stall, Alfie's, London NW8; (*Poole Pottery*) Sotheby's; (*Royal Worcester*) Phillips; cl Sotheby's; bl Rosenthal Studio House Ltd, London; rest *Martin Cameron*. 189 *Martin Cameron* (*except tl*). 190 tc Millers; c Millers/Christie's; tl, bc, bl Sotheby's. 191 cl Millers/Christie's; c, bl Sotheby's. 192 tl Millers; tc, cl, bl Millers/Christie's; tr, cr, bc Sotheby's; br Millers/Christie's New York. 193 tl Millers/Christie's; (*hawk*) Christie's; tr Lars Tharp; rest Sotheby's. 194 tl Millers/Christie's; tc, tr Christie's; rest Sotheby's. 195 bl Christie's; rest *Martin Cameron*. 196 Bonhams. 197 tc *Glynn Clarkson*/Sotheby's; tr, c, bl Bonhams; cr *Stuart Chorley*/Britannia, Gray's Antique Market, London W1; br Lars Tharp. 198 t Gordon Park Publicity Ltd, Manchester; c Rob Gee, Flea Market, Islington; cr *John Lawrence*/Cobwebs, Southampton; br Lars Tharp. 199 cl Peter Greenhalf; rest Sotheby's.

200 tc, cr Sotheby's; tr, bc Phillips; c By Courtesy of the Wedgwood Museum Trustees, Barlaston, Staffs. 201 tl Millers;(*Minton seat*) Sotheby's; (*Chinese export*), tc, bl Phillips; (*gnome and furniture*) *Chris Halton*. 202 tr ET Archive; c Millers/Sotheby's; cr *Chris Halton*/John Sandon; br Sotheby's; b Phillips. 203 (*spittoons*) Christie's; (*chamber pot*) *Chris Halton*/ohn Sandon; (*barber's bowl*), tr, c Phillips; (*Minton wash set*), bc, *Chris Halton*/Henry Sandon; br *Chris Halton*/John Murray Collection. 204 tl, tc, c Sotheby's; tr Fitzwilliam Museum; cr Millers/Breck Antiques, Nottingham. 205 Sotheby's. 206 (*fake glass*) Sotheby's; tc, bc Broadfield House Glass Museum, Dudley; bl Phillips. 207 tc, c Sotheby's; tr The Mansell Collection; (*flint glass*), cr Broadfield House Glass Museum, Dudley; br Christie's. 208 tc Christie's; cr, bc Sotheby's; rest Broadfield House Glass Museum, Dudley. 209 tc Sotheby's; tr, cr *Laurie Evans*; (*sand-blasting, electrogilding*), c Broadfield House Glass Museum, Dudley; bc, br Christie's. 210 t Christie's; rest Broadfield House Glass Museum, Dudley. 211 cl, b Broadfield House Glass Museum, Dudley; rest *Laurie Evans*. 212 tl, cr, bl Sotheby's; tr Christie's; cl Broadfield House Glass Museum, Dudley; c Andrew Stewart/Gallerie Moderne, London; br Robert Opie. 213 (*twisted stem glasses*) Phillips; (*ruby goblet*) Sotheby's; tl, cr, bc Broadfield House Glass Museum, Dudley; tr Millers/Christie's. 214 bl 'The Silber & Fleming Glass & China Book'; rest Broadfield House Glass Museum, Dudley. 215 *Laurie*

Evans(except tl). 216 *c, bl, bc* Museum of London; *cr* Broadfield House Glass Museum, Dudley; *br* Sotheby's. 217 *br* Delomosne and Son Ltd, North Wraxham, Wilts; *rest* Christie's. 218 *tl* Sotheby's; *cr* Christie's; *rest* Peter Greenhalf Photography. 219 *tc* Alistair Duncan; *cl* Haworth Art Gallery; *c* Christie's; *rest* Sotheby's. 220 Sotheby's. 221 *tl* Sotheby's; *bl* Angelo Hornak; *rest* Broadfield House Glass Museum, Dudley. 222 *tl* Michael Holford; *(baccarat vase)*, *tc, tr* Broadfield House Glass Museum, Dudley; *c* Sotheby's; *(Webb bowl) Stuart Chorley*/Barnes Antiques, Putney. 223 *tc* Philippe Garner; *c* Phillips; *rest* Sotheby's. 224 *(sweetmeat dish)* Sotheby's; *tr* Broadfield House Glass Museum, Dudley; *bl* Bridgeman/Roy Miles Fine Paintings, London; *cr, br* Peter Greenhalf Photography. 225 *cl* Broadfield House Glass Museum, Dudley; *rest* Peter Greenhalf Photography. 226 Broadfield House Glass Museum, Dudley.
227 *(Je Reviens)* Andrew Stewart/Gallerie Moderne, London; *t* Andrew Stewart/Collection of Mr & Mrs Utt; *cl, bc* Sotheby's; *cr, br* Christie's. 228 Broadfield House Glass Museum, Dudley. 229 *Ken Adlard*/Sotheby's. 230 *c* Sotheby's; *cr* Angelo Hornak; *rest* Broadfield House Glass Museum, Dudley. 231 Sotheby's. 232 *tr, br* Christie's; *bl Clive Streeter*; *(silver tankards)* Phillips. 233 *c* Ann Ronan at Image Select; *cr* Sotheby's. 234 Sotheby's.
235 *tr, c, cr* Christie's; *bc, br* Sotheby's. 236 *(silver teapot)*, *tr Clive Streeter*; *(engine turned)*, *br* Sotheby's; *rest* Christie's. 237 *tr* Christie's; *c Clive Streeter*; *bc, br* Sotheby's. 238 *Clive Streeter (except tl)*. 239 *Clive Streeter*. 240 *tc, cr* Sotheby's; *tr* Christie's; *c Roy Farthing*/Jane Pollock, Penrith; *br Stuart Chorley*/Goldsmith & Perris, Alfie's Antique Market, London.
241 *tl, cl, c* Christie's; *tc Stuart Chorley*/Private collection; *bl Roy Farthing*/Mary Cook Antiques, Kensington Church St, London W8. 242 *cr, br* Christie's; *tr, bl* Bridgeman. 243 *(entree dish)*, *cl, c* Sotheby's; *rest* Christie's. 244 *cl, cr* Christie's; *rest* Sotheby's. 245 *(cauldron salts)* Phillips; *bl* Sotheby's; *rest* Christie's. 246 *c, bl* Sotheby's; *rest* Christie's. 247 *c* Sotheby's; *rest* Christie's. 248 *tr, c* Sotheby's; *rest* Christie's. 249 *tl* Millers; *bl* Sotheby's; *rest* Christie's.
250 *(Old Sheffield teapot)* C.J. Vander, London EC1; *bl* ET Archive/V & A; *rest* Christie's. 251 *bl, bc* Christie's; *br* Sotheby's. 252 *cl* C.J. Vander, London EC1; *rest* Christie's. 253 *cl* Sotheby's; *rest* Christie's. 254 *cr* Sotheby's; *tr, br* Christie's. 255 *cl Stuart Chorley*/Sitch & Co Ltd, London W1; *bl*, Sotheby's; *rest* Christie's. 256 *bl* ET Archive; *tr, bc* Christie's; *(two seals)* Sotheby's. 257 *(necessaire)* Hancocks & Co, London W1; *rest* Christie's. 258, 259 *Theo Bergestrom*. 260 *(silver chatelaine) Michael Crockett*/The Thimble Society, Gray's Antiques Market, London W1; *c* Sotheby's; *rest* Christie's. 261 Christie's. 262 *t* Bridgeman/Stapleton Collection; *rest* Christie's. 263 *tr* Sotheby's/David Battie; *cl* Christie's; *rest* Sotheby's. 264 *tr, br* Sotheby's; *bl, bc* Christie's. 265 *tr* The Mansell Collection; *rest* Christie's. 266 *(garnet brooch) A. & C. Cooper*/N. Bloom & Son, London W1; *c* Ken Scarratt; *rest* Christie's. 267 *(wax treated)*, *tc* Christie's; *rest* Ken Scarratt. 268 *(back of gold ring)* Sotheby's; *rest* Christie's.
269 *bl* Sotheby's; *rest* Christie's. 270 *bl* Mary Evans Picture Library/Christie's; *rest* Christie's. 271-3 Christie's. 274 *(poison ring, open)*, *tl A. & C. Cooper*/N. Bloom & Son, London W1; *rest* Christie's. 275 Sotheby's. 276 *tr* Ann Ronan at Image Select; *br Stuart Chorley*/Richmond Clocks, Richmond, Surrey; *rest* Sotheby's. 277 *(flat silvered dial)* Christie's; *(plain enamel dial)* Sotheby's; *(Art Deco) Stuart Chorley*/Jenny Mortimer; *tr, c, cr* Derek Roberts Antiques; *rest* Sotheby's. 278 *(lacquer longcase) Roy Farthing*/David & Sarah Pullen, Bexhill-on-Sea; *(London mahogany; oak and mahogany)* Sotheby's; *(oak flat-top)* Derek Roberts Antiques; *rest* Christie's. 279 *tl* Sotheby's; *(Dutch longcase)*, *bl Stuart Chorley*/Richmond Clocks, Richmond, Surrey; *bc* Royal Collection, St James's Palace/©HM the Queen.
280 *tc, tr* Sotheby's; *c Roy Farthing*/David & Sarah Pullen, Bexhill-on-Sea; *cr Stuart Chorley*/Patrick Capon, Islington; *bc* Derek Roberts Antiques. 281 *tl Roy Farthing*/Gerard Campbell, Lechlade; *tc, bl* Sotheby's; *cl Stuart Chorley*/Clock Gallery, Ealing; *c* Stuart Chorley/Richmond Clocks, Richmond, Surrey; *cr* Christie's. 282 *tc, tr* Christie's; *c* Millers/Christie's; *cr Jeff Wilkinson*/ Strike One Islington Ltd; *bc, br* Peter Greenhalf Photography; *b* Sotheby's. 283 *bc* Fine Art Photographs/Galerie Berko; *rest* Sotheby's. 284 *cl, c* Christie's; *cr Stuart Chorley*/City Clocks London, Finsbury Park; *rest* Sotheby's. 285 *c* Sotheby's; *br* Derek Roberts Antiques; *rest* Christie's. 286 *tl* Sotheby's; *tr, cl* Derek Roberts Antiques; *c* Christie's; *cr Stuart Chorley*/ The Clock Gallery, Ealing. 287 *tl Stuart Chorley*/The Clock Gallery, Ealing; *cl* Sotheby's; *tc, c* Christie's. 288 *(underpainted horn) Michael Crockett*/J. Waxman, The Connoisseur, Gray's in the Mews, London W1; *tr* Phillips; *c* Christie's; *cr, bc* Sotheby's; *rest Michael Crockett*/Donald Lambert. 289 *bl* Christie's; *rest* Sotheby's. 290 *tc* Millers/Christie's; *tr Christopher Fransella*/Arthur Middleton, Covent Garden; *cl Stuart Chorley*/Barometer Fair, Bury Place, London; *c* Sotheby's. 291 *tl Stuart Chorley*/Barometer Fair, Bury Place, London; *cl* Sotheby's; *rest Christopher Fransella*/Arthur Middleton, Covent Garden. 292 *(opera glasses)*, *tc, br* Sotheby's; *tl, cl, c Christopher Fransella*/Arthur Middleton, Covent Garden; *cr* Millers/Christie's; *bl Stuart Chorley*/Howard Antiques, Chelsea Antiques Market. 293 *tl* Sotheby's; *cl, bl Christopher Fransella*/Arthur Middleton, Covent Garden. 294 *tl* The Science Museum, London; *c* Robert Opie; *cl, cr, bc* Sotheby's; *br Andrew Stewart*/Donna Thynne. 295 *cl, c* Robert Opie; *(praxinoscope)*, *bc Glynn Clarkson*/Mike Smith Collection, Nutley, East Sussex; *br, bl Glynn Clarkson*/Mike Smith–Janet Hill Collection, Nutley, East Sussex.
296 *tc, cl Christopher Fransella*/Arthur Middleton, Covent Garden; *tl, tr* Sotheby's; *c Stuart Chorley*/Principia Antiques, Marlborough, Wilts; *cr* Millers/Christie's New York.
297 *(Butterfield sundial)* Millers/Christie's; *tl* Nat Trust (photographer Roy Fox); *cl, c, bc* Sotheby's; *bl Christopher Fransella*/ Arthur Middleton, Covent Garden.
298 *cl, c Christopher Fransella*/Arthur Middleton, Covent Garden; *rest* Sotheby's. 299 Christie's.
300, 301 Ian Bennett. 302 *cl* David El Kelaty; *rest* Ian Bennett. 303-7 Ian Bennett.
308 *tr* Phillips; *cr, bl* Christie's; *br* Sotheby's. 309 *(sampler)* Close Antiques, Alresford, Hants; *(tiger)* Sotheby's; *tr* Bridgeman/Stapleton Collection; *rest* The Antique Textile Company, Portland Rd, London. 310 *(needlepoint cushion)* Millers/Christopher Matthews, Harrogate; *cr* Sotheby's/Hilary Kay; *rest* Sotheby's. 311 *(Brussels needlepoint)* Lunn Antiques, London SW6; *tr* The Antique Textile Company, Portland Rd, London; *cr, br* Courtesy of Luton Museum Service; *bc* Sotheby's. 312 *tr* National Portrait Gallery, London; *br* Sotheby's; *rest* Christie's. 313 *cr* Spink & Son Ltd; *bc* V & A; *br* Christie's; *rest* Sotheby's. 314 *Ian O'Leary (except tr)*. 315 *tl, cl Ian O'Leary*; *cr* Millers; *bc, br* Sotheby's. 316 *tr* V & A; *rest* Sotheby's. 317 *tl* Sotheby's; *tc* Millers; *cl* Millers/Academy Costumes Ltd, London SE1; *c* V & A; *bc Ian O'Leary*. 318 *(night cap)*, *tc* Christie's; *tr* Phillips; *cr Roy Farthing*/Angels, London WC2; *bc* Peter Greenhalf Photography; *br* Sotheby's. 319 *(central slipper, shoe, mule)*, *tl* Christie's; *tc, cl* Sotheby's; *cr* The Button Queen, London W1. 320 *(walking sticks)* Michael German, Kensington, London W8; *tc* Sotheby's; *cl* Millers/Christie's; *bl* Courtesy of Luton Museum Service; *bc* Christie's.
321 Christie's. 322 *tc* Sotheby's; *c* Sotheby's/Courtesy of Meissner Fine Art; *rest* Christie's. 323 *tl* Sotheby's; *cl* Bridgeman/Forbes Magazine Collection, New York; *(miniatures bl, br) Michael Crockett*/Alma Antiques, Camden Passage, London; *(other miniatures)* Christie's. 324 *tr* Christie's; *rest* Sotheby's. 325 *tl, br* Phillips; *cl* Sotheby's; *tr, bl* Christie's. 326 *tl, bl* Sotheby's; *tc, bc* Christie's; *cl, c* Phillips. 327 *br* Christie's; *rest* Sotheby's. 328 *c, cr* Bridgeman/ Stapleton Collection; *rest* Christie's. 329 *tl* Bridgeman/Stapleton Collection; *rest* Christie's. 330 Sotheby's. 331 *(terracotta bust) Michael Crockett*/Natasha Edwards; *tl* Christie's; *rest* Sotheby's. 332 Bridgeman/Stapleton Collection. 333 *tl* Jonathan Potter, London W1; *rest* Bridgeman/Stapleton Collection. 334 *tc, br* Bridgeman/Stapleton Collection; *c, bc* Sotheby's/David Battie. 335 *cl* Phillips; *c, bl* Bridgeman/Stapleton Collection; *bc* Christie's; *br* Sotheby's. 336 *tr* Bridgeman/Stapleton Collection; *rest Michael Crockett*/Sotheby's. 337 *tc* Bridgeman/Stapleton Collection; *c* Christie's; *rest Michael Crockett*/Sotheby's. 338 Courtesy Philippe Garner. 339 Sotheby's. 340 *tl* Bridgeman/Antony Crane Collection; *c* Robert Opie; *tr, cr* Sotheby's. 341 *(Noah's ark)*, *br* Robert Opie; *tc, tr, c* Sotheby's; *cr* Peter Greenhalf Photography; *bc* Phillips. 342 *(tin-plate train)*, *cl* Robert Opie; *tl* Christie's; *tr, c, cr Stuart Chorley*/Pierce Carlson, Gray's in the Mews, London W1. 343 *Clive Streeter (except tr)*. 344 *tl* Millers/Mint & Boxed, Edgware, Middlesex; *tr, c, bc* Robert Opie; *cl* Sotheby's; *rest Stuart Chorley*/Pierce Carlson, Gray's in the Mews, London W1. 345 *cl, bl* Sotheby's; *rest* Christie's. 346 *tc* Robert Opie; *rest* New Cavendish Books, 'The Hornby Gauge 0 System' by Chris & Julie Graebe. 347 *(boxed gift set)* Phillips; *rest* New Cavendish Books, 'Dinky Toys & Modelled Miniatures' by Mike & Sue Richardson.
350 *tl* Bridgeman; *tr* Christie's; *cr, b* Sotheby's. 351 *cr* Christie's; *rest* Sotheby's. 352 Sotheby's. 353 *Clive Streeter (except tr)*. 354 *bl* V & A; *rest* Robert Opie. 355 *br* Christie's; *rest* Sotheby's. 356 *b* Phillips; *rest* Sotheby's. 357 Sotheby's. 358 *tc, bc* V & A; *c, br* Sotheby's; *cr* Peter Greenhalf Photography/Mechanical Music and Doll Collection, Chichester. 359 Sotheby's.
360 *tc, tr* Sotheby's; *rest* Sotheby's/Drummonds of Bramley, Surrey. 361 *tc* Sotheby's/Drummonds of Bramley, Surrey; *cl, c* Sotheby's; *rest Stuart Chorley*/London Architectural Salvage Company, London EC2. 362 Sotheby's. 363 *(lead figure) Michael Crockett*/T. Crowther & Son, Fulham; *cr Stuart Chorley*/London Architectural Salvage Company, London EC2; *br* Haddonstone Ltd; *rest* Sotheby's. 366 *tl, cr* Sotheby's; *tr* Peter Greenhalf Photography/Wenderton Antiques, Kent; *cl, c* Peter Hornsby. 367 *bl Stuart Chorley*/Jack Casimir, London W11; *rest* Peter Hornsby. 368 *cr, br* Peter Greenhalf Photography; *rest* Peter Hornsby.
369 *tc, cl* Peter Greenhalf Photography; *rest Stuart Chorley*/Jack Casimir, London W11. 370 *Laurie Evans* (with thanks to M. & D. Seligmann, London W8, for supplying fruit bowl & salt container). 371 *br* Robert Opie; *rest* Peter Greenhalf Photography. 372 Peter Greenhalf Photography. 373-5 Robert Opie. 376 *tc, cr* Phillips; *tr, c* Christie's. 377 *(Beatles dress)* Christie's; *tc* V & A; *tr* Phillips; *rest* Sotheby's. 378 *tl* Phillips; *tr* The Mansell Collection; *cl* T. Vennett-Smith, Gotham, Nottingham; *bl, bc* Sotheby's. 379 *(golf balls)*, *tl, tr*, Sotheby's; *tc Michael Crockett*/Sean Arnold, Gray's Antiques Market, London W1; *cl* Manfred Schotten Antiques, Burford, Oxon; *c* Peter Greenhalf Photography/Manfred Schotten Antiques, Burford, Oxon; *cr* Peter Greenhalf Photography. 380 *tc, tr* Sports Design International; *c Stuart Chorley*/MS Antiques, Alfie's, London NW8; *cr, bc* Manfred Schotten Antiques, Burford, Oxon. 381 *tr* Peter Greenhalf Photography; *c* Bonhams; *cr, br* Sotheby's; *bc Christopher Fransella*/Arthur Middleton, Covent Garden. 382 *bl* Sotheby's; *rest* Bonhams. 383 *(paper knives)*, *tc*, Peter Greenhalf Photography; *tl Stuart Chorley*/Jasmin Cameron, Antiquarius, London SW3; *cl* Sotheby's; *c Stuart Chorley*/Mr Poole, Cornelissen & Son, London WC1; *(metal paper-weight) Stuart Chorley*/Donna Thynne. 384 *cr* Christie's; *rest* James A. Mackay. 385 *c* Christie's; *rest* James A. Mackay. 386 *tl* ET Archive; *rest* Sotheby's. 387 Sotheby's. 388 *tc* Christie's; *rest* Sotheby's. 389 *bl* Popperfoto; *rest* Sotheby's. 390-3 Sotheby's. 394 *tl, tc* Sotheby's; *c* Peter Greenhalf Photography/Mechanical Music & Doll Collection, Chichester; *rest Clive Streeter*. 395 *Clive Streeter (except tr)*. 396 *tl, tc* Sotheby's; *c* Robert Opie; *cl, bc* Peter Greenhalf Photography; *bl* Peter Greenhalf Photography/The Mechanical Music & Doll Collection, Chichester. 397-9 Sotheby's.
400 *tl* Photograph © 1992, The Art Institute of Chicago, Katsushika Hokusai, Japanese, 1760-1849, 'A Wood Turner at Work', from the book 'Sandara Kasume', woodblock print, 1797, 31.6 × 22cm, Clarence Buckingham Collection, 1925.3205; *rest* Sotheby's. 401 Sotheby's. 402 *tr* Millers/Christie's; *bc* Christie's; *rest* Sotheby's. 403 Sotheby's.
404 *cr* Bonhams; *bl, br* Sotheby's; *rest* Christie's. 405 *tl, c* Christie's; *tr, cr* Sotheby's. 406 *bc* ET Archive; *rest* Christie's. 407 *cl, bl* Christie's; *tc, c, bc* Sotheby's. 408 *tc* Millers/Wallis & Wallis, Lewes; *tr* Millers/Christie's; *(silver kukri)*, *tl, c, bl* Christie's; *bc* Sotheby's; *(bowie knife)*, *br* ET Archive. 409 *cr* Wallis & Wallis, Lewes; *rest* Christie's. 410 *tc* Wallis & Wallis, Lewes; *rest* Christie's. 411 *tr, cr* ET Archive; *bc* Phillips; *rest* Christie's. 412 *tc* P & O Art Collection; *tr, br* Sotheby's; *rest Stuart Chorley*/Langfords, London SW10. 413 *c, bl* Sotheby's; *cr* Christie's; *rest Stuart Chorley*/Langfords, London SW10. 414 Railfotos. 415 *br Stuart Chorley*/Sotheby's; *rest* Sotheby's. 416 *cr* Sotheby's; *bc David Edwards Photography*/The National Cycle Museum, Lincoln; *c, br* Peter Greenhalf Photography; *rest Stuart Chorley*/Sotheby's.

The publishers acknowledge their indebtedness to the following books, which were consulted for reference during the preparation of *Treasures in Your Home*.

The American Heritage History of American Antiques from the Revolution to the Civil War (American Heritage Publishing); *Antique Barometers* by E. Banfield (Wayland Publications); *The Antique Furniture Trail* by V.J. Taylor (David & Charles); *Antique Oriental Rugs and Carpets* by P. Bamborough (Blandford Press); *The Antiques Care & Repair Handbook* by Albert Jackson & David Day (Dorling Kindersley); *The Antiques Directory: Furniture* by Judith & Martin Miller (Mitchell Beazley); *Antiques Roadshow* edited by M. Devine (BBC Books); *The Antiques Roadshow Collection, 1991 & 1992* (Eaglemoss Publications; partwork); *Antiques Roadshow: Experts on Objects* edited by C. Lewis (BBC Books); *Antique Weapons for Pleasure and Investment* by R. Akehurst (John Gifford); *Antiquitäten Porzellan* by A. Bangert (Wilhelm Heyne Verlag, Munich); *Architectural Antiques* by Alan Robertson (Unwin Hyman); *The Architecture of Britain* by Doreen Yarwood (B.T. Batsford); *Arms and Armour* by V. Norman (Weidenfeld & Nicolson); *Arms and Armour in Britain* by A. Borg (HMSO); *Art Deco Furniture* by Alistair Duncan (Thames & Hudson); *Art Deco Source Book* by Patricia Bayer (Phaidon); *The Arthur Negus Guide to British Glass* by John Brooks (Hamlyn); *The Arthur Negus Guide to British Silver* by Brand Inglis (Hamlyn); *Art Nouveau and Art Deco Silver* by A. Krekel-Aalberse (Thames & Hudson); *The Art of the Tin Toy* by David Pressland (New Cavendish Books); *Arts and Crafts Carpets* by Malcolm Haslam (David Black Oriental Carpets); *The Arts and Crafts Movement* by Steven Adams (Apple Press); *The Arts & Crafts Movement* by Elizabeth Cumming and Wendy Kaplan (Thames & Hudson); *Authentic Decor* by Peter Thornton (Weidenfeld & Nicolson).

Barometers by A. McConnell (Shire Publications); *Blue & White Transfer Ware 1780* by A.W. Coysh (David & Charles); *The Book of Sheffield Plate* by S.B. Wyler (Bonanza Books, New York); *British and Continental Arms and Armour* by C. H. Ashdown (Dover Publications); *British Design Since 1880* by Fiona MacCarthy (Lund Humphries); *British Furniture 1880-1915* by Pauline Agius (Antique Collectors' Guide; Baron Publishing); *The British Kitchen* by D. Yarwood (B.T. Batsford); *Buying Antique Furniture* by Rachel Feild (Macdonald).

Chats on Old Sheffield Plate by A. Hayden (EP Publishing); *Clocks and Watches* by A. Smith (The Connoisseur); *Clocks and Watches* by H. Tait (British Museum Publications); *Clocks and Watches: The Collection of the Worshipful Company of Clockmakers* by C. Clutton & G. Daniels (Sotheby Parke Bernet Publications); *Clocks: An Owner's Handbook* by R. Good (British Museum Publications); *Clocks in Colour* by A. Nicholls (Blandford Press); *Coins of England and the United Kingdom* edited by Peter Seaby & P. Frank Purvey (Seaby Publications Ltd); *Coins: Pleasures and Treasures* by J. Porteous (Weidenfeld & Nicolson); *Collecting Antique Firearms* by Dr. M. Kelvin (Stanley Paul); *Collecting Dolls* by N. Earnshaw (Collins); *Collecting for Tomorrow: Spoons* by G. Belden and M. Snodin (Pitman); *Collecting Small Silverware* by Stephen Helliwell (Phaidon/Christie's); *The Collector's Book of Dolls* by B. Gerwat-Clark (Apple Press);

ACKNOWLEDGMENTS

The Collector's Encyclopedia of Dolls, vols 1 & 2, by Dorothy, Elizabeth and Evelyn Colman (Robert Hale); *The Collector's Encyclopedia of Toys and Dolls* edited by Lydia Darbyshire (New Burlington Books); *The Collector's Encyclopaedia – Victoriana to Art Deco* (Collins; Studio Editions); *Collins Encyclopedia of Antiques* (Collins); *The Complete Encyclopedia of Antiques* edited by L.G.G. Ramsey (The Connoisseur); *The Complete Victorian House Book* by Robin Guild (Sidgwick & Jackson); *A Concise History of Costume* by James Laver (Thames & Hudson); *A Concise History of Interior Decoration* by George Savage (Thames & Hudson); *The Connoisseur Period Guides – Tudor; Stuart; Early Georgian; Late Georgian; Regency;* and *Early Victorian* edited by Ralph Edwards and L. G. G. Ramsey (The Connoisseur); *The Conran Directory of Design* by S. Bayley (Conran Octopus); *Contemporary Decorative Arts* by Philippa Garner (Apple Press); *Country House Floors 1660-1850* by Christopher Gilbert, James Lomax and Anthony Wells-Cole (Leeds City Art Galleries); *The Country Life Antiques Handbook* edited by T. Hughes (Hamlyn); *The Country Life Book of Watches* by T.P. Camerer Cuss (Country Life).

Decanters and Glasses by T. Hughes (Country Life Books); *Decorative Art 1880-1980* by Dan Klein and Margaret Bishop (Phaidon-Christie's); *Decorative Art: The Studio Yearbook of Furnishing and Decoration, vols 46 & 48*, by R. Holme and K. Frost (The Studio Publications); *Decorative Tiles Throughout the Ages* by Hans Van Lemmen (Bracken Books); *The Decorative Twenties* by Martin Battersby (Herbert Press); *Derby Porcelain* by F. Barrett and A. Thorpe (Faber and Faber); *Design and Decoration in the Home* by N. Carrington (B.T. Batsford); *Dictionary of Country Furniture* by M. Fildee (The Connoisseur); *A Dictionary of English Costume 900-1900* by C. & P. Cunnington & C. Beard (A. & C. Black); *The Dictionary of English Furniture* by Ralph Edwards (Antique Collectors' Club; 3 vols); *Dictionary of 19th Century Antiques* by George Savage (Barrie & Jenkins); *The Dictionary of World Pottery and Porcelain: From Prehistoric Times to the Present* by L.A. Boger (A. & C. Black); *Dinky Toys & Modelled Miniatures* by Mike and Sue Richardson (New Cavendish Books); *Directory of Gold & Silversmiths* by J. Culme (Antique Collectors' Club); *Discovering English Furniture* by John Bly (Shire Publications); *Discovering Hall Marks on English Silver* by John Bly (Shire Publications); *The Doulton Figure Collectors Handbook* by Kevin Pearson (Kevin Francis Publishing Ltd).

Edwardian Interiors: Inside the Homes of the Poor, the Average & the Wealthy by Alastair Service (Barrie & Jenkins); *The Elements of Style: An Encyclopaedia of Domestic and Architectural Details* by Stephen Calloway (Mitchell Beazley); *Encyclopedia of Antiques* by Arthur Negus (Hamlyn); *The Encyclopedia of Collectibles* (Time-Life Books; 16 vols); *The Encyclopedia of Toys* by C.E. King (Quarto); *Encyclopedic Dictionary of Numismatics* by R.G. Doty (Robert Hale); *English and American Textiles* by Mary Schoeser and Celia Rufey (Thames & Hudson); *English and Irish Glass* by G. Willis (Guinness Superlatives); *English Bottles and Decanters 1650-1900* by D.C. Davis (Charles Letts); *English Chairs* (Victoria & Albert Museum/HMSO); *English China* by Geoffrey Godden (Barrie & Jenkins); *English Costume* by Doreen Yarwood (B.T. Batsford); *The English Country House* by Olive Cook (Thames & Hudson); *The English Country House: A Grand Tour* by Gervase Jackson-Stops and James Pipkin (National Trust; Weidenfeld & Nicolson); *The English Country House and its Furnishings* by Michael Wilson (B.T. Batsford); *English Decoration in the Eighteenth Century* by John Fowler and John Cornforth (Barrie & Jenkins); *English Delftware* by F.H. Garner and M. Archer (Faber and Faber); *English Domestic Brass 1680-1810 and the History of its Origins* by Rupert Gentle and Rachel Feild (Elek Books); *English Domestic Clocks* by H. Cescinsky & M.R. Webster (Hamlyn); *English Furniture AD 43-1950* by E. T. Joy (B.T. Batsford); *English Furniture Styles 1500-1830* by Ralph Fastnedge (Penguin); *English Glass for the Collector 1660-1860* by G. Bernard Hughes (Lutterworth Press); *The English Home* by Doreen Yarwood (B.T. Batsford); *English House Clocks* by A. Bird (David & Charles); *English Interior Decoration 1500-1830* by Margaret Jourdain (B.T. Batsford); *English Interiors 1790-1848: The Quest for Comfort* by John Cornforth (Barrie & Jenkins); *English Lantern Clocks* by W.F.J. Hana (Blandford Press); *English Papier Mâché of the Georgian and Victorian Periods* by Shirley Spaulding De Voe (Barrie & Jenkins); *English Silver Spoons* by M. Snodin (Charles Letts); *English Windsor Chairs* by Ivan Sparkes (Shire Publications); *European and American Carpets and Rugs* by Cornelia Bateman Faraday (Antique Collectors' Club).

Fabergé – 1846-1920 by A. Kenneth Snowman (Debrett's/Victoria and Albert Museum); *Fans* by H. Alexander (B.T. Batsford); *Fashion Thru Fashion Plates 1771-1970* by Doris Langley Moore (Ward Lock); *The Fashionable Fire Place 1660-1840* by Christopher Gilbert and Anthony Wells-Cole (Leeds City Art Galleries); *Fifties Source Book* by Christopher Pearce (Quarto); *The Fine Art of Fashion: An Illustrated History* by Julian Robinson (Bay Books); *Firearms: A Collector's Guide 1326-1900* by J. Durík, M. Mudra, M. Sáda (Hamlyn); *Firegrates and Kitchen Ranges* by David Eveleigh (Shire Publications); *Flintlock Guns and Rifles* by Fred Wilkinson (Arms and Armour Press); *The Flintlock: Its Origins and Development* by T. Lenk (The Holland Press); *Flintlock Pistols* by Fred Wilkinson (Arms and Armour Press); *A Fortune in Your Attic* by Tony Curtis (Lyle Publications); *Furniture: A Concise History* by E. Lucie-Smith (Thames & Hudson); *Furniture in Colour* by Lanto Synge (Blandford Press); *Furniture of Temple Newsam House and Lotherton Hall* by Christopher Gilbert (National Art Collections Fund and Leeds Art Collections Fund).

Gas Lighting by D. Gledhill (Shire Publications); *Gimson and the Barnsleys* by Mary Greensted (Alan Sutton Publishing); *Glass* by George Savage (Weidenfeld & Nicolson); *Glass Through the Ages* by E. Barrington Haynes (Penguin); *Going for a Song: English Furniture* by Arthur Negus and Max Robertson (BBC); *The Golden Age of Toys* by J. Remise (Edita, Lausanne); *The Golden Age of Venetian Glass* by H. Tait (British Museum Publications); *The Goldsmith's and Silversmith's Handbook* by S. Abbey (Technical Press); *The Goldsmiths and Silversmiths of England* by C. Lever (Hutchinson); *The Grandfather Clock* by E.L. Edwardes (John Sherratt & Sons); *The Guardian Book of Antiques 1700-1830* by Donald Wintersgill (Collins); *Guide to the Bethnal Green Museum of Childhood* (Victoria and Albert Museum); *Gun Collecting* by G. Boothroyd (The Sportsman's Press); *Guns Through the Ages* by G. Boothroyd (Sterling Publishing Co, NY).

Hallmarks (Assay Offices of Great Britain; leaflet); *Handbook to Hall Marks on Gold and Silver of Great Britain and Ireland* by W. Chaffer (William Reeves Booksellers); *Heirloom: An Introduction to Collecting Antiques* edited by John Bly (Boxtree); *Historic Paper Hangings* by Anthony Wells-Cole (Leeds City Art Galleries); *A History of Costume in the West* by Francois Boucher (Thames & Hudson); *The History of English Interiors* by Alan and Ann Gore (Phaidon); *A History of English Wallpaper* by A.V. Sugden (J.L. Edmonson, 1926); *The History of Furniture* (Macdonald); *The History of Interior Decoration* by Charles McCorquodale (Phaidon); *A History of Pottery* by Emmanuel Cooper (Longman); *The History of Silver* edited by Claude Blair (Macdonald Orbis); *History of the English House* by Nathaniel Lloyd (The Architectural Press); *Home in the Twenties and Thirties* by Mary and Neville Ward (Ian Allan); *The Hornby Gauge 0 System* by Chris and Julie Graebe (New Cavendish Books); *Household Treasures* by M. Miller (Guinness Publishing).

An Illustrated Dictionary of Ceramics by G. Savage & H. Newman (Thames & Hudson); *An Illustrated Dictionary of Glass* by H. Newman (Thames & Hudson); *An Illustrated Dictionary of Jewelry* by H. Newman (Thames & Hudson); *An Illustrated Dictionary of Silverware* by H. Newman (Thames & Hudson); *An Illustrated Guide to Eighteenth-Century English Drinking Glasses* by L.M. Bickerton (Barrie & Jenkins); *The Illustrated History of Antiques* edited by Huon Mallalieu (Running Press); *An Illustrated History of Interior Decoration* by Mario Praz (Thames & Hudson); *In the Deco Style* by Dan Klein, Nancy McClelland and Malcolm Haslam (Thames & Hudson); *Interiors* by Margaret and Alexander Potter (John Murray); *Introduction to the Decorative Arts* edited by A. O'Neill (Quintet Books); *Irons in the Fire: A History of Cooking Equipment* by Rachel Feild (The Crowood Press); *Is It Genuine? How to Collect Antiques with Confidence* edited by John Bly (Mitchell Beazley); *Islamic Rugs* by K.H. Turkhan (Arthur Barker); *Jackson's Silver & Gold Marks of England, Scotland & Ireland* edited by Ian Pickford (Antique Collectors' Club); *Jane Austen's Town and Country Style* by Susan Watkins (Thames & Hudson); *Kitchen Antiques* by Mary Norwak (Praeger); *Kitchenware* by J. Marshall (Pitman); *Lalique Glass* by N. M. Dawes (Viking).

The Letts Guide to Collecting Dolls by Kerry Taylor (Charles Letts); *The Letts Guide to Collecting 20th-Century Toys* by J. Opie (Charles Letts); *Life in the English Country House* by Mark Girouard (Penguin); *Looking after Antiques* by A. Plowden & F. Halahan (Pan Books); *The Lyle Official Antiques Reviews 1990-2* by Tony Curtis (Lyle Publications); *Magic Lanterns* by D. Greenacre (Shire Publications); *Marks of London Goldsmiths and Silversmiths c. 1697-1837* by J.P. Fallon (David & Charles); *Masterpieces of Glass* (Trustees of The British Museum); *Mechanical Toys* by C. Bartholomew (Hamlyn); *Meyer's Handbook of Ornament* by F. Meyer (Omega Books); *Miller's Antiques Checklists: Art Deco and Furniture* (Mitchell Beazley); *Miller's Guides to Antiques 1985-92* (MJM Publications/Miller's Publications); *Miller's Pocket Dictionary of Antiques* by Judith & Martin Miller (Mitchell Beazley); *Miller's Understanding Antiques* by Judith and Martin Miller (Mitchell Beazley); *Modern English Furniture* by J.C. Rogers (Country Life); *The Movies Begin* by P. Spehr (Newark Museum, NJ, USA).

Nailsea Glass by K. Vincent (David & Charles); *The National Trust Book of English Domestic Silver 1500-1900* by T. Schroder (Viking); *The National Trust Book of English Furniture* by Geoffrey Beard (Penguin); *The National Trust Book of Furnishing Textiles* by Pamela Clabburn (Penguin); *The Needleworker's Dictionary* by P. Clabburn (Macmillan); *The New Look: Design in the Fifties* by L. Jackson (Thames & Hudson/Manchester City Art Gallery); *News of the World Better Homes Book* edited by R. Smithells (News of the World Publications); *Nineteenth-Century Decoration: The Art of the Interior* by Charlotte Gere (Weidenfeld & Nicolson); *Nineteenth-Century English Furniture* by Elizabeth Aslin (Faber & Faber).

Old Cooking Utensils by David Eveleigh (Shire Publications); *Optical Amusements: Magic Lanterns and Other Transforming Images* by Richard Balzer; *Optical Toys* by B. Harley (Shire Publications); *The Opulent Eye: Late Victorian & Edwardian Taste in Interior Design* by Nicholas Cooper (The Architectural Press); *Oriental Antiques in Colour* by M. Ridley (Blandford); *Oriental Carpets* by G. Curatola (Souvenir Press); *Oriental Carpets and Rugs* by Ian Bennett (Hamlyn); *Oriental Rugs* by Majid Amini (Macdonald); *Oriental Rugs and Carpets* by F. Formenton (Hamlyn).

The Penguin Dictionary of Decorative Arts by J. Fleming and H. Honour (Viking); *Period Details* by Judith and Martin Miller (Mitchell Beazley); *Persian and other Oriental Carpets for Today* by N. Fokker (George Allen & Unwin); *Phaidon Guide to Antique Weapons and Armour* by R. Wilkinson-Latham (Phaidon); *Phillips Collectors Guides: Royal Memorabilia* by Peter Johnson and *Tin Toys* by Nigel Mynheer (Boxtree); *The Price Guide to Antique Silver* by Peter Waldron (Antique Collectors' Club); *Price Guide to Victorian, Edwardian and 1920's Furniture* by John Andrews (Antique Collectors' Guide; Baron Publishing); *The Price Guide to Victorian Furniture* by John Andrews (Antique Collectors' Club); *Rare Carpets* (Orbis Books); *Restoring Furniture* by K. Davis and T. Henvey (Orbis); *The Romantic Interior: The British Collector at Home 1750-1850* by Clive Wainwright (Yale University Press); *Rugs and Carpets of the Orient* by K. Larson (Frederick Warne); *Rugs and Carpets of the World* edited by Ian Bennett (New Burlington Books); *Rugs to Riches: An Insider's Guide to Oriental Rugs* by C. Bosly (Unwin Hyman).

Seventeenth-Century Interior Decoration in England, France & Holland by Peter Thornton (Yale University Press); *Shawls* by P. Clabburn (Shire Publications); *A Short Dictionary of Furniture* by J. Gloag (George Allen & Unwin); *A Short History of English Furniture* (Victoria & Albert Museum/HMSO); *Silver Flatware: English, Irish and Scottish 1660-1980* by Ian Pickford (Baron Publishing); *Silver Studio of Design* by Mark Turner & Lesley Hoskins (Michael Joseph); *Smoking Antiques* by A. & C. Scott (Shire Publications); *Sotheby's Caring for Antiques* edited by Mette Tang Simpson & Michael Huntley (Conran Octopus); *Sotheby's Concise Encyclopedia of Furniture* edited by Christopher Payne (Conran Octopus); *Sotheby's Concise Encyclopedia of Glass* edited by D. Battie & S. Cottle (Conran Octopus); *Sotheby's Concise Encyclopedia of Porcelain* edited by David Battie (Conran Octopus); *The Style of the Century 1900-1980* by Bevis Hillier (The Herbert Press); *Swords in Colour* by R. Wilkinson-Latham (Blandford Press).

Teapots and Coffeepots by Philip Miller (Midas); *Techniques of the World's Great Masters of Pottery & Ceramics* edited by Hugo Morley-Fletcher (Quarto); *Times Past* (Marshall Cavendish; partwork); *Towards Post-Modernism: Designs Since 1851* by Michael Collins (British Museum); *Traditional Style* by Stephen Calloway & Stephen Jones (Pyramid Books); *Treasures of the Tower: Crossbows* by G. Wilson (HMSO); *Twentieth-Century Decoration: The Domestic Interior from 1900 to the Present Day* by Stephen Calloway (Weidenfeld & Nicolson).

Understanding Dolls by C. Goodfellow (Antique Collectors' Club); *Victorian and Edwardian Furniture and Interiors* by Jeremy Cooper (Thames & Hudson); *The Victorian and Edwardian Home* by Jenni Calder (B.T. Batsford); *The Victorian Catalogue of Household Goods* edited by A. Smith (Studio Editions); *The Victorian Farmer* by David Eveleigh (Shire Publications); *Victorian Furniture* by S. Jervis (Ward Lock); *The Victorian House Catalogue* edited by A. Smith (Sidgwick & Jackson); *Victorian Interior Design* by Joanna Banham, Sally Macdonald and Julia Porter (Cassell); *Victorian Table Glass and Ornaments* by Barbara Morris (Barrie & Jenkins); *Victorian Things* by Asa Briggs (B.T. Batsford); *Victorian Tiles* by Hans van Lemmen (Shire Publications); *The Visual History of Costume* by Aileen Ribeiro and Valerie Cumming (B.T. Batsford); *A Visual History of Costume: The Seventeenth Century* by Valerie Cumming (B.T. Batsford); *Wallpaper* by Clare Taylor (Shire Publications).

Wallpapers: A History and Illustrated Catalogue of the Collection of the Victoria & Albert Museum by Charles C. Oman and Jean Hamilton (Sotheby Publications); *Wallpapers, 17th Century to the Present Day* by Joanna Banham (Studio Editions); *William de Morgan Tiles* by J. Catleugh (Trefoil); *The Woodworker's Handbook* by The London College of Furniture (Pelham Books); *World Ceramics* edited by R.J. Charleston (Hamlyn); *World Coin Encyclopedia* by E. Junge (Barrie & Jenkins); *World Furniture* edited by H. Hayward (Hamlyn).

TYPESETTING Apex Computersetting, London, England
SEPARATIONS Colourscan Overseas Co Pte Ltd, Singapore
PAPER Les Papeteries de Condat, Neuilly, France
PRINTING Maury Imprimeur SA, Malesherbes, France
BINDING Reliures Brun SA, Malesherbes, France

40-331-1